COP 1

NOV 1 9 '74   REF. SERV.

A11701 578044

D1443595

The Encyclopedia of

TENNIS

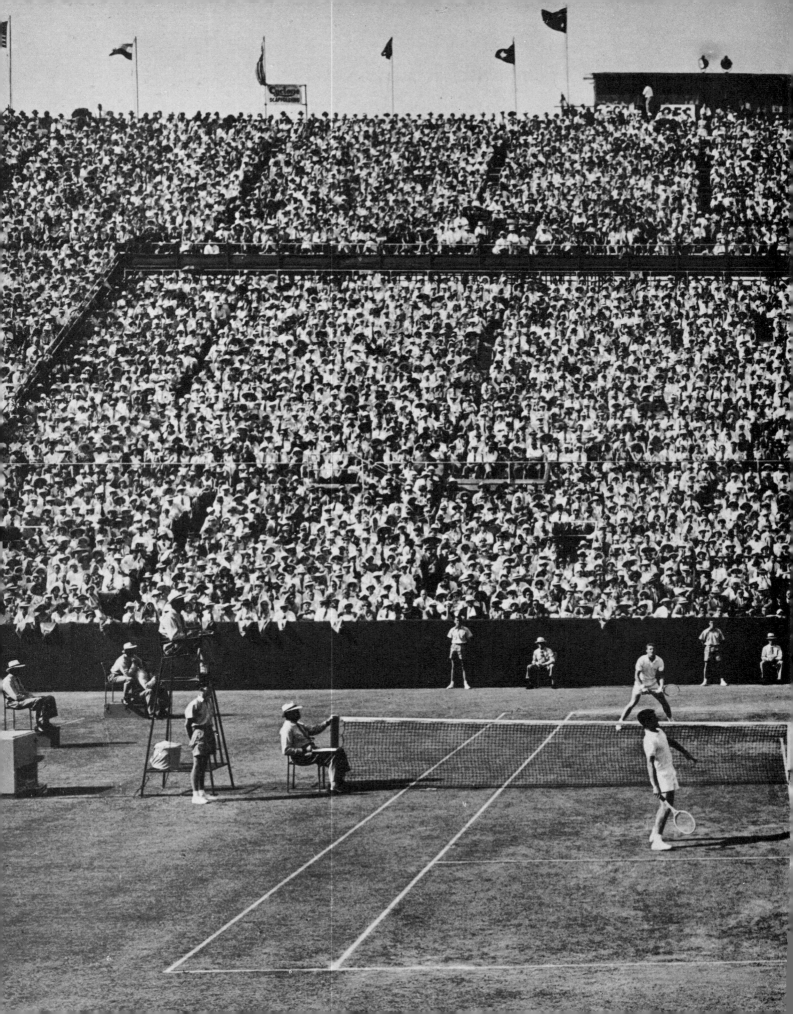

The Encyclopedia of

TENNIS

Edited by Max Robertson
Advisory Editor Jack Kramer

A Studio Book
The Viking Press
New York

Copyright © 1974 by Rainbird Reference
Books Limited

All rights reserved

Published in 1974 by The Viking Press, Inc.
625 Madison Avenue, New York, N.Y. 10022

SBN 670-29408-X

Library of Congress catalog card number:
73-10776

This book was designed and produced by
Rainbird Reference Books Limited
Marble Arch House, 44 Edgware Road,
London W2, England
House Editor: Perry Morley
Designer: Jonathan Gill-Skelton
Records Research: Vicki Robinson

Text filmset and color plates printed by
Jolly & Barber Ltd, Rugby, England
Text printed by Butler & Tanner Limited,
Frome, Somerset, England
Bound in Great Britain

Contents

Color Plates

Contributors

The Rt Hon. The Lord Aberdare. President, Tennis and Rackets Assn. Authority on real tennis; author, *The Story of Tennis* (1959) and the article on Tennis in the *Encyclopedia Britannica* (1973). Amateur Real Tennis champion four times and MCC Gold Prizewinner five times.

[JB]   John Barrett. Davis Cup player for Great Britain 1956-7 and non-playing Davis Cup captain 1959-62; particularly well-known for his views on junior training. Lawn tennis correspondent, *Financial Times;* Tennis Consultant to Slazengers Ltd.

[ABe]   Alain Bernard. Winner of the Criterium de France 1929; ranked in first series after 1929 season. Professional journalist since 1930; contributor to *Le Figaro, Jour-Echo de Paris, Tennis et Golf, France-Soir, Tennis de France,* etc,; winner of the gold medal of the Association des Journalistes Sportifs.

[AB]   Antonin Bolardt. International Secretary of the Czechoslovak Tennis Association. Captain of the Czechoslovak Davis Cup and King's Cup teams.

C. H. T. Brown. Director, En-tout-cas Limited, internationally famous builder of hard tennis courts.

[LB]   Lucy Bullard. Italian Tennis Federation.

Arthur Cole. One of the best known British tennis photographers. Production Director of *Tennis World* magazine.

[BC]   Bud Collins. American sporting journalist, well known for his graphic writing in the *Boston Globe* and as a television commentator on tennis. Author, with Rod Laver, *The Education of a Tennis Player.* Winner, with Janet Hopps, of the 1961 US National Indoor Mixed Doubles title.

[ECC]   E. C. Condon. Secretary, past Vice-President and past Executive Director, Canadian LTA; past President, Ontario LTA.

[DC]   Dennis Cunnington. British sporting journalist. Lawn tennis correspondent, Press Association.

Allison Danzig. Highly regarded American sporting journalist; on the staff of the *New York Times* 1923-68, reporting on lawn tennis, football, rowing, real tennis, rackets, and squash rackets; author of many books including *The Racket Game, Elements of Lawn Tennis;* co-editor, *The Fireside Book of Tennis.* Elected to the US National Lawn Tennis Hall of Fame and to the Rowing Hall of Fame, 1968. Former president, Lawn Tennis Writers' Association of America.

[MD]   M. Dessart. Secretary-General and Treasurer, Fédération Royale Belge de Lawn-Tennis. Has played lawn tennis for 44 years; champion, Belgian veterans' doubles 1972-3.

[LD]   Louis Duffus. South African journalist; sports editor, the *Daily News* (Durban) and the *Star* (Johannesburg) for 14 years; he was the first special correspondent to cover South African Davis Cup matches. Author of six books including one on South Africa in the Davis Cup. Presented with award for services by the S. African Lawn Tennis Union in 1970.

[MdP]   Margaret duPont. Wimbledon champion 1947, US Champion 1948-50, French champion 1946 and 1949; ranked world no 1 in 1947-50. Vice-President, Southwestern Tennis Association; writes weekly column for *El Paso Herald-Post.* Co-owner, with Margaret Varner Bloss (former world Badminton champion), of racing stable.

[KME]   K. M. Ernest. Hon. Secretary, Penarth Lawn Tennis Club for 23 years. Past Assistant Hon. Secretary and Hon. Secretary, now Hon. Life President, Welsh LTA.

Captain Mike Gibson. Official Wimbledon referee since 1963, succeeding his father-in-law, Col. W. J. Legg. He has also refereed at Forest Hills and in South Africa.

[DG]   David Gray. British sporting journalist; sports editor, the *Guardian* 1961-6, lawn tennis correspondent since 1956.

Gladys Heldman. American journalist. Editor, *World Tennis* magazine and initiator of the World Tennis prize-money circuit for women.

[OvdH]   O. van der Heul. Executive Secretary, Royal Netherlands LTA.

[SH]   Sten Heyman, Chairman of the Board of the AB Svenska Idrottshallar, builders and administrators of sports halls. Secretary, Swedish LTA 1956-69; chairman of its Technical Committee since 1970.

Harry Hopman, C.B.E. Australian Davis Cup player 1928, 1930, 1932, playing captain 1938-9 (captain of the first Australian, as distinct from Australasian, team to win the Davis Cup), non-playing captain 1950-59; captain of 16 winning years altogether. As a tactician and trainer his record is unrivalled. President LTA of Victoria 1964-9; Australian selector 1962-9. Now president, Port Washington Tennis Academy, Long Island, N.Y. Author, *Aces and Places* (1957), *Better Tennis for Boys and Girls* (1972).

[RKK]   R. K. Khanna. Vice-President, International Lawn Tennis Federation (the first Asian to be elected to this office); member of its Committee of Management since 1967. Hon. Secretary, All India LTA and Asian Lawn Tennis Federation. Captain of the first Indian team to reach the Davis Cup Challenge Round (1966).

Jack Kramer. US no 1 in 1946-7; his Wimbledon victory in 1947 was the most decisive since the abolition of the Challenge Round. He then became a playing professional and was later the leading impresario of the professional game. A well known television commentator on tennis.

[AL]   A. Lăzărescu. General Secretary, Rumanian Lawn Tennis Federation since 1966. Assistant lecturer, Sports Department of the Physical Education and Sports Institute (ISEFS) of Bucharest, 1959-66; since 1966 press officer of the same Institute.

Roy McKelvie. Editorial director, *Tennis World* magazine. Tennis journalist of 40 years' experience, having been on the staffs of the *Guardian, Star, Daily Mail* and *Sunday Express.* Co-author, with Jaroslav Drobný, *Champion in Exile.*

Dan Maskell, O.B.E. Known for his television commentaries on Wimbledon, which he has covered for the BBC since 1951. Tennis professional all his life, playing and teaching; won British Professional title 16 times. First permanent Coach to the All England Lawn Tennis and Croquet Club, 1929-39, 1946-55; LTA Training Manager 1953-73.

Anthony J. Mottram. Britain's no 1 player 1946-55 and Davis Cup stalwart 1947-55. National Coach since 1970. Author, *Quick Ways to Better Tennis, Modern Lawn Tennis* (with Joy Mottram), *Improve Your Tennis* and *Play Better Tennis.*

[GM]   Geoff Mullis. Assistant General Manager, Commercial Union Assurance Company, with special responsibility for Commercial Union's tennis interests worldwide.

[JO]   John Oakley. British sporting journalist; sports editor, *Dagenham Post* at 17; later on staff of *Nottingham Evening Post, Yorkshire Evening News* and Press Association, London. Joined *London Evening News* in 1960; now lawn tennis and football correspondent. A keen sportsman, he plays table tennis, lawn tennis, golf and squash.

[YO]   Yoshiro Ohta. Member of Japanese Davis Cup team 1927-30. Executive Director, Japanese LTA; professor of Japan Women's Physical Education University.

[GPdO]   Guillermo Perez de Olaguer. Editor and publisher of *Tenis Español.*

Fred Perry. Leading British player before World War II; the only man to win Wimbledon three times running (1934-6) since the abolition of the Challenge Round (1922); he also won the US Championships three times (1933-4, 1936). Television and radio commentator.

[AQ]   Adrian Quist. Davis Cup stalwart for Australia between 1933 and 1948; one of the greatest doubles players of all time, winning the Wimbledon men's doubles with Jack

Crawford in 1935 and again 15 years later with John Bromwich. He won the Australian doubles ten times running (1936–40, 1946–50), an all-time record for a major championship.

[BR] Basil Reay, O.B.E. General Secretary, International Lawn Tennis Federation and the Davis Cup since August 1973 (previously Hon. Secretary, 1948–73); Secretary (British) Lawn Tennis Association, 1948–73.

[MR] Max Robertson. British radio sporting commentator, known particularly for his BBC radio commentaries on Wimbledon, which he has covered every year since World War II. Also BBC television commentator (11 Olympic Games, summer and winter) and programme presenter.

[FES] F. E. Storer, Editor, *Tennis U.S.A.*

[LT] Lance Tingay. Highly respected British sporting journalist. Lawn Tennis correspondent since 1952 of the *Daily Telegraph*, which began its tradition of good tennis correspondents with A. Wallis Myers.

Ted Tinling. Leading designer of active sportswear, associated primarily with tennis. As playing captain of Sussex for many years, he competed several times at Wimbledon, Through his association with the Riviera, where he first became interested in the organization of tennis tournaments, he became a close friend of Suzanne Lenglen and, in 1937, made his first tennis dress for her last world tour as a professional. For ten successive years (1952–1961) he dressed a Wimbledon singles winner – a record. In 1973 the five major championships (Australian, French, Italian, Wimbledon and the US Open) were won by players wearing his dresses.

[TT] Tom Todd. Has been researching the early history of lawn tennis for the last 25 years; helped to organize the centenary celebrations of Major Harry Gem's first game in Leamington in 1872. Co-founder of the Veterans' Lawn Tennis Club of Great Britain; a keen but indifferent player for nearly 60 years.

[JDV] J. D. Vickerman. An Auckland delegate on the Council of the New Zealand LTA for over 25 years and a member of the Management Committee for 12 years. Manager of the 1967 Linton and Wilson Cup teams. In his national administration he has concentrated on activities to develop the game in the community through coaching and particularly in promotion and publicity.

Peter Wilson. British sporting journalist, known for his lively but authoritative writing in the *Daily Mirror*. He has seen every Wimbledon final, except two, since 1929. Apart from lawn tennis, which has been a lifelong interest, his *forte* is boxing.

Acknowledgments and Notes on Illustrations

The publishers are indebted to the following for permission to quote from their publications: The Lawn Tennis Association for the Rules of Lawn Tennis on pages 95–106; the passages by Mrs D. Lambert Chambers on pages 151–2, which originally appeared in *The LTA Book of the Game*, edited by Max Robertson, and published for the LTA by Max Parrish & Co. Ltd, 1957; and for the tables of received odds and owed odds on page 259; Syndication International for the passages by Peter Wilson on pages 160, 161 and 163 which originally appeared in the *Daily Mirror*; the *Daily Telegraph* for the passage on page 170 by H. S. Scrivener, which originally appeared in the *Morning Post*, and the reports on page 189 from the *Daily Telegraph*; the BBC Reference and Registry Services for the extracts from letters and memos on pages 185 and 188; Ed J. Burrow & Co. Ltd for the passages on pages 139–40, which originally appeared in René Lacoste, *Lacoste on Tennis*, published for the Dunlop Sports Co. 1928. The quoted passages on pages 152 and 155 originally appeared in F. R. Burrow, *The Centre Court and Others*, published by Eyre & Spottiswoode (Publishers) Ltd in 1937. Those on pages 155 and 156 originally appeared in W. T. Tilden, *My Story*, published by Hellman, Williams & Co., 1938. Those on pages 344–5 originally appeared in *American Lawn Tennis* magazine, 15 August 1923.

The producers of this book wish to express their grateful thanks to the staff of *Tennis World Magazine*, the US National Lawn Tennis Hall of Fame and Tennis Museum, Inc., and to Mr A. J. Mottram for technical advice, to all contributors and many others who suggested sources of information and illustrations, and also all those who are indicated by the following list of illustrations, especially the governing bodies and staffs of the libraries and museums and the individual owners of photographs. Every effort has been made to trace the primary sources of illustrations; in one or two cases where it has not been possible, the producers wish to apologize if the acknowledgment proves to be inadequate; in no case is such inadequacy intentional and if any owner of copyright who has remained untraced will communicate with the producers a reasonable fee will be paid and the required acknowledgment made in future editions of the book.

Colour Illustrations
Page 41 ILTF/CU Masters' Tournament, Barcelona.
    Photo: Tennis World Magazine

42–3 Detail from *The Story of David and Bathsheba, 16th-century painting in the collection of the Marylebone Cricket Club. Photo: Derrick Witty*
44 Forest Hills. *Photo: Tennis World Magazine*
85 Arthur Ashe. *Photo: Colorsport*
86 Maria Bueno. *Photo: Gerry Cranham*
103 Davis Cup. *Photo: Tennis World Magazine*
104 Margaret Court. *Photo: Tennis World Magazine*
153 Evonne Goolagong. *Photo: Tennis World Magazine*
154 Pancho Gonzalez. *Photo: Gerry Cranham*
171 Chris Evert. *Photo: Gerry Cranham*
172 Roy Emerson. *Photo: Sportsworld*
205 Françoise Durr. *Photo: Gerry Cranham*
206 Lew Hoad. *Photo: Gerry Cranham*
223 Ann Jones. *Photo: Gerry Cranham*
224 Billie Jean King. *Photo: Gerry Cranham*
273 Rod Laver. *Photo: E. D. Lacey*
274 Jan Kodeš. *Photo: E. D. Lacey*
291 John Newcombe. *Photo: E. D. Lacey*
292 Ilie Năstase. *Photo: Colorsport*
333 Ken Rosewall. *Photo: Colorsport*
334–5 Wimbledon men's doubles. *Photo: Gerry Cranham*
336 Stan Smith. *Photo: Sportsworld*

Drawings
The drawings throughout the book are by Brian Watson. The aerial view of Wimbledon on page 177 is based on one by Nigel Holmes that appeared in the *Radio Times* dated 24 June 1971.

Monochrome Photographs
Title page Record Davis Cup crowd at White City, Sydney, 1954. *Photo: Australian Information Service*

Page 13 Plate from Walter Wingfield, *The Game of Sphairistike or Lawn Tennis*, 5th edition, 1876. *Photo: British Museum*
15 Plate from Jan Amos Komensky (Comenius), *Orbis Sensalium Pictus*, facsimile of 1658 edition. (The first edition, in Hungarian, was published in 1654.) *Photo: British Museum*
16 Plan of court for *jeu de paume* at the Louvre, 1555, from Antonio Scaino, *Trattato del giuco della palla*, facsimile of 1591 edition. *Photo: British Museum*

Acknowledgments and Notes on Illustrations

17 Title page of Charles Hulpeau, *Le Jeu Royal de la Paulme*, 1632, reproduced in Julian Marshall, *Annals of Tennis*, 1878. *Photo: British Museum*

18 a. *Le Serment du Jeu de Paume*, painting by Jacques Louis David *Photo: The Mansell Collection* b. Tennis court at Windsor, from John Norden, *Description of the Honor of Windesor*, 1607, reproduced in J. M. Heathcote *Tennis*, 1890. *Photo: British Museum*

19 a. Artist's conception of 16th-century tennis at Windsor. *Illustrated London News. Photo: London Electrotype Agency* b. James, Duke of York, reproduced in Julian Marshall, *Annals of Tennis*, 1878. *Photo: British Museum*

20 *The Tennis Player*, painting by Arthur Devis. *Photo: The Mansell Collection*

21 a. 18th-century tennis. *Photo: The Mansell Collection* b. Henry Leaf Cup. *Photo: Sport and General, courtesy Tennis World Magazine*

22 a. Title page from Walter Wingfield, *The Game of Sphairistike or Lawn Tennis*, 5th edition, 1876. *Photo: British Museum* b. Patent granted to Walter Wingfield for his game of tennis, 1874. *Reproduced by courtesy of the Controller of Her Majesty's Stationery Office and the National Reference Library of Science and Invention. Photo: John R. Freeman Ltd*

23 Print published for the centenary celebrations of the Leamington Lawn Tennis Club. *Courtesy Tom Todd. Photo: David Rudkin*

24 Sketch made at the Championship Lawn Tennis Match, Wimbledon. *Illustrated London News*, 26 July 1879. *Photo: London Electrotype Agency*

25 Match between Lawford and W. Renshaw. *The Graphic*, 1881. *Photo: London Electrotype Agency*

26 a. Mixed doubles in Bermuda, 1893. *Photo: Bermuda News Bureau* b. Passenger list of the S.S. Canima, 2 Feb. 1874. *Courtesy of the US National Archives*

27 Early lawn tennis in England. *Photo: Tennis World Magazine*

29 a. Club de Dinard. From E. de Nauteuil, *La Paume et le Lawn-Tennis*, 1898. b. St Moritz. From A. Wallis Myers, *Lawn Tennis At Home and Abroad*, 1903. *Photos: British Museum*

30 a. Särö. From A. Wallis Myers, *Lawn Tennis At Home and Abroad*, 1903. *Photo: British Museum*

b. Mrs Atkins and A. W. Gore. *Photo: Scottish LTA*

31 R. Lycett and R. W. Heath. *Photo: Topix*

33 Wimbledon Centre Court, 1925. From A. Wallis Myers, *Fifty Years of Wimbledon*, 1926. *Photo: David Rudkin*

34 a. J. Borotra, 1933. *Photo: Topix* b. H. Cochet and J. Brugnon. *Photo: London Electrotype Agency*

35 a. R. Lacoste. *Photo: Presse Sports* b. The Duke of York (later King George VI), 1926. *Photo: Radio Times Hulton Picture Library*

36 a. J. D. Budge and G. von Cramm, 1937. *Photo: Topix* b. King Gustaf V of Sweden and Prince Chichibu, 1926. *Photo: Radio Times Hulton Picture Library*

37 Italy *v.* India in the Davis Cup Inter-Zone Final, 1952. *Photo: Australian Information Service: John Tanner*

38 L. Hoad/K. Rosewall *v.* M. Rose/R. Hartwig, 1953. *Photo: Tennis World Magazine*

39 E. V. Seixas and M. A. Trabert. *Photo: Tennis World Magazine*

40 L. Brough and M. Connolly, 1952. *Photo: Topix*

46 J. Drobný. *Photo: Tennis World Magazine*

47 Prospect Park, Brooklyn, N.Y., 1886. *Photo: Museum of the City of New York*

48 Staten Island Cricket Club, 1880. *Photo: Staten Island Historical Society*

49 H. Ward and D. Davis. From A. Wallis Myers, *Fifty Years of Wimbledon*, 1926. *Photo: David Rudkin*

50 a. M. Sutton. From D. K. L. Chambers, *Lawn Tennis for Ladies*, 1910. b. M. E. McLoughlin. From J. P. Paret, *Methods and Players of Lawn Tennis*, 1915. *Photos: British Museum*

51 The Sutton sisters. From A. Wallis Myers, *The Complete Lawn Tennis Player*, 1908. *Photo: British Museum*

52 a. J. A. Kramer, 1933. *Photo: Associated Press Ltd, courtesy Tennis World Magazine* b. F. Perry *v.* H. E. Vines, 1937. *Photo: United Press International*

54 Tom Brown, 1946. *Photo: Central Press Photos Ltd, courtesy Tennis World Magazine*

55 R. Riggs *v.* J. A. Kramer, 1947. *Photo: United Press International*

57 A. Gibson, 1957. *Photo Sport and General, courtesy London Electrotype Agency*

58 a. Pennsylvania Championships, 1965. b. Rock Creek Park, Washington, D.C. *Photos: Ed Fernberger*

59 a. Davis Cup Challenge Round, 1970. *Photo: Ed Fernberger* b. US Davis Cup team, 1971. *Photo: Russ Adams Productions*

60 L. E. Stoefen. *Photo: Topix*

61 W. T. Tilden. *Photo: Topix*

62 F. Perry. *Photo: Keystone Press Agency Ltd, courtesy Tennis World Magazine*

63 G. Moran. *Photo: Topix*

64 a. K. Rosewall. b. L. Hoad. *Photos: Australian Information Service*

65 a. R. A. Gonzalez. *Photo: E. D. Lacey* b. Longwood, Boston, 1971. *Photo: Ed Fernberger*

66 The Spectrum, Philadelphia, 1971. *Photo: Ed Fernberger*

68 K. Fageros. *Photo: Central Press Photos Ltd., courtesy Tennis World Magazine*

69 B. J. King. *Photo: E. D. Lacey*

71 F. Durr, 1972. *Photo: Ed Fernberger, courtesy World Tennis Magazine*

73 a. O. K. Davidson. b. J. Clifton. *Photos: Syndication International*

75 M. Cox. *Photo: Tennis World Magazine*

76 M. C. Riessen. *Photo: Tennis World Magazine*

77 J. Heldman. *Photo: Tennis World Magazine*

78 A. Stone. *Photo: Tennis World Magazine*

80 WCT semi-final, Dallas, 1973. *Photo: World Championship Tennis*

82 A. Gimeno. *Photo: Tennis World Magazine*

83 a. A. Mayer. b. A. Metreveli. *Photos: E. D. Lacey*

89 Wimbledon semi-final, 1890. *Illustrated Sporting and Dramatic News*, 12 July 1890. *Photo: London Electrotype Agency*

91 I. Năstase. *Photo: Topix*

92 Wimbledon, 1973. *Photo: E. D. Lacey*

110 K. Susman, V. Suková and Col Legg. *Photo: Tennis World Magazine*

112 a. Captain M. Gibson and R. Casals. *Photo: Syndication International* b. B. C. Evelegh. From A. Wallis Myers, *Fifty Years of Wimbledon*, 1926. *Photo: David Rudkin*

115 Marking out a court in Hungary, 1909. *Photo: Pál Szöke*

116 Wimbledon Centre Court. *Photo: Tennis World Magazine*

118 Tennisquick Court. *Photo: Norman Lay, courtesy En-tout-cas Ltd*

119 Racket making. *Photo: Dunlop Ltd*

120 Ball manufacture. *Photo: Dunlop Ltd*

121 a. Racket stringing. b. Ball moulding. *Photos: Dunlop Ltd*

123 a. M. D. Whitman. *Photo US National Tennis Hall of Fame* b. H. Ward. From A. Wallis Myers, *The Complete Lawn Tennis Player*, 1908. *Photo: British Museum*

125 H. L. Doherty. From G. W.

Beldam and P. A. Vaile, *Great Lawn Tennis Players*, 1905. *Photo: British Museum*

126 G. Brown. *Photo: Topix*

127 a, b, c, d. Forehand drive (C. Mottram). *Photos: Tennis World Magazine*

129 a, b, c, d. Backhand drive (E. Goolagong). *Photos: Tennis World Magazine*

130-1 a, b, c, d, e, f. Service (V. Wade). *Photos: Tennis World Magazine*

132 a, b, c. Forehand volley (S. Smith). *Photos: Tennis World Magazine*

133 a, b, c. Backhand volley (L. Hoad). *Photos: Tennis World Magazine* d, e, f, g. Smash (J. D. Newcombe). *Photos: Tennis World Magazine*

135 John Barrett with five 'Barrett Boys'. *Photo: Evening Post, Port Elizabeth, South Africa*

136 Davis Cup, 1965. *Photo: Australian Information Service: J. Fitzpatrick*

140 R. Lacoste and J. Borotra. From A. Wallis Myers, *Fifty Years of Wimbledon*, 1926. *Photo: Tennis World Magazine*

142 E. Goolagong. *Photo: E. D. Lacey*

143 V. McGrath. *Photo: Topix*

145 F. Perry. *Photo: Topix*

146 R. Laver. *Photo: Alfred Eisenstaedt*

147 A. Mortimer. *Photo: Syndication International*

149 L. Bergelin. *Photo: Keystone Press Agency Ltd, courtesy S. Heyman*

150 J. A. Kramer. *Photo: Topix*

151 S. Lenglen. *Photo: Sport and General*

152 D. Lambert Chambers. From A. Wallis Myers, *Fifty Years of Wimbledon*, 1926. *Photo: David Rudkin*

155 H. Cochet and W. T. Tilden. *Photo: Topix*

156 a. H. E. Vines. *Photo: Sport and General* b. J. Crawford. *Photo: Topix*

157 H. Wills and H. Jacobs. *Photo: Topix*

158 a. J. Drobný. *Photo: Topix* b. J. E. Patty. *Photo: Tennis World Magazine*

159 M. Connolly and D. Hart. *Photo: Topix*

160 a. C. Pasarell. *Photo: Tennis World Magazine* b. R. A. Gonzalez. *Photo: Central Press Photos Ltd, courtesy Tennis World Magazine*

161 M. Court. *Photo: Tennis World Magazine*

162 B. J. King. *Photo: Topix*

163 a. K. Rosewall. *Photo: Alfred Eisenstaedt* b. C. Richey. *Photo: E. D. Lacey*

164 C. Evert. *Photo: Topix* b. E. Goolagong. *Photo: Tennis World Magazine* c. S. Smith. *Photo: Topix*

165 I. Năstase. *Photo: Topix*

167 W. T. Tilden and R. Lacoste. *Photo: Topix*

168 J. D. Budge. *Photo: Keystone Press Agency Ltd, courtesy Tennis World Magazine*

169 R. Laver. *Photo: Sport and General, courtesy Tennis World Magazine*

174 a. S. Lenglen. *Photo: Topix*
b. H. Wills Moody. *Photo: Topix*

175 a. L. Brough. *Photo: Central Press Photos Ltd, courtesy Tennis World Magazine*
b. M. Court. *Photo: Sport and General, courtesy Tennis World Magazine*

176 Sketch of Wimbledon. *Illustrated Sporting and Dramatic News, 20 July 1878. Photo: London Electrotype Agency*

180 a. Cartoon from *Daily Mirror, 7 July 1934. Photo: Syndication International*
b. Wimbledon, 1935. *Photo: Topix*

181 Cameramen. *Photo: Tennis World Magazine*

182 P. Lotz. *Photo: Tennis World Magazine*

183 I. Năstase. *Photo: Tennis World Magazine*

184 a. Max Robertson. b. John Snagge. *BBC copyright photographs*

185 Gerald A. Cock. *BBC copyright photograph*

186 a. S. de Lotbinière. b. Freddie Grisewood. *BBC copyright photographs*

187 Bert Kingdon. *Courtesy Bert Kingdon*

189 a. Dan Maskell. *BBC copyright photograph*
b. Jack Kramer. *Photo: Alfred Eisenstaedt*

190 Cartoon from *London Evening News, 14 June 1946. Reproduced by permission of Associated Newspapers Group Ltd; photo: British Museum*

191 a. Billy Knight. b. Peter Dimmock. *BBC copyright photographs*

192 a. Bryan Cowgill. b. A. P. Wilkinson. *BBC copyright photographs*

193 BBC Television camera overlooking No 1 Court. *BBC copyright photographs*

195 a. M. J. Anderson. *Photo: Tennis World Magazine*
b. A. M. Arias. *Photo: Central Press Photos Ltd, courtesy Tennis World Magazine*

196 a. J. Asbóth. b. A. Ashe. *Photos: Tennis World Magazine*
c. H. W. Austin. *Photo: Sport and General, courtesy Tennis World Magazine*

197 Davis Cup 1907 Challenge Round. From A. Wallis Myers, *Fifty Years of Wimbledon, 1926. Photo: David Rudkin*

198 a. J. Crawford and A. K. Quist. *Illustrated London News 13 July 1935. Photo: London Electrotype Agency*
b. F. Sedgman. *Photo: Press Association Ltd; courtesy Tennis World Magazine*

199 A. K. Quist and J. E. Bromwich. *Photo: Herald, Sydney*

200 a. Australian ladies' team, 1925. From A. Wallis Myers, *Fifty Years of Wimbledon, 1926. Photo: David Rudkin*
b. E. Goolagong and Vic Edwards. *Photo: Australian Information Service: J. Fitzpatrick*

201 a. Lew Hoad and Ken Rosewall. *Photo: Central Press Photos Ltd, courtesy Tennis World Magazine*
b. L. Ayala. *Photo: Tennis World Magazine*

202 W. Baddeley. From A. Wallis Myers, *Fifty Years of Wimbledon, 1926. Photo: David Rudkin*

204 P. Betz. *Photo: Central Press Photos Ltd, courtesy Tennis World Magazine*

207 a. N. Bolton. b. J. Borotra. *Photos: Topix*

208 S. Bloomer Brasher. *Photo: Keystone Press Agency Ltd, courtesy Tennis World Magazine*

211 British Hard Court Championships, 1937. *Photo: Kodak Museum*

212 a. J. E. Bromwich. *Photo: Sport and General; courtesy Tennis World Magazine*
b. A. L. Brough. *Photo: Tennis World Magazine*

213 Maria Bueno. *Photo: Central Press Photos Ltd, courtesy Tennis World Magazine*

214 Toronto tournament, 1881. *Canadian Illustrated News, 3 Sept. 1881. Photo: Public Archives of Canada; courtesy E. C. Condon*

216 R. Casals. *Photo: Tennis World Magazine*

217 Mrs D. Lambert Chambers. *Illustrated Sporting and Dramatic News, 21 May 1910. Photo: London Electrotype Agency*

218 M. Connolly. *Photo: Topix*

219 a. J. Connors. *Photo: Topix*
b. M. Court. *Photo: E. D. Lacey*
c. G. von Cramm. *Photo: London Express News and Feature Service*

220 a. Bohemian tennis players, 1898 *Photo: Czechoslovak LTA*
b. V. Černik. *Photo: Associated Press, courtesy Tennis World Magazine*

221 a. V. Suková. *Photo: Tennis World Magazine*
b. K. Koželuh and family. *Photo: Czechoslovak LTA*

222 Paddle tennis. *Photo: Czechoslovak LTA*

225 a. O. K. Davidson. b. S. Davidson. *Photos: Tennis World Magazine*

226 Davis Cup. 1902. *Photo: Jean Kertesz, courtesy Pál Szöke*

227 a. Davis Cup, 1913. From A. Wallis Myers, *Fifty Years of Wimbledon, 1926. Photo: David Rudkin*
b. F. Perry/G. P. Hughes v. J. Borotra/J. Brugnon. *Photo: Topix*

228 Budapest, 1938. *Photo: Pál Szöke*

229 Melbourne, 1947. *Photo: Australian Information Service: Eric Wadsworth*

230 Davis Cup, 1952. *Photo: Australian Information Service: W. Brindle*

231 Davis Cup doubles semi-final, European Zone A, at Edgbaston, 13 June 1969. *Photo: Press Association Ltd*

232 a. The Davis Cup. *Photo: Russ Adams Productions*
b. Max Decugis in Budapest, 1908. *Photo: Pál Szöke*

233 a. The Dewar Cup. *Photo: John Dewar & Sons Ltd*
b. Lottie Dod in 1887. From A. Wallis Myers, *Fifty Years of Wimbledon, 1926. Photo: David Rudkin*
c. The Doherty brothers. From *R. F. & H. L. Doherty on Lawn Tennis, 1903. Photo: David Rudkin*

234 a. J. Drobný. *Photo: Topix*
b. C. Drysdale. *Photo: Tennis World Magazine*
c. Dubler Cup. *Photo: Foto Duijts; courtesy L. Dubler*

235 a. M. duPont. *Photo: Syndication International*
b. F. Durr. *Photo: Tennis World Magazine*

237 a. R. Emerson. *Photo: Tennis World Magazine*
b. C. Evert. *Photo: Ed Fernberger*

238 a. R. Falkenburg. *Photo: Syndication International*
b. *Punch* cartoon, 10 Oct. 1874. *Photo reproduced by permission of Punch*
c. Budapest fashion plates. *Photo: Pál Szöke*

239 a. M. Watson. From A. Wallis Myers, *Fifty Years of Wimbledon, 1926. Photo: David Rudkin*
b. C. Sterry. *Illustrated Sporting and Dramatic News, 21 May 1910. Photo: London Electrotype Agency*
c. D. Lambert Chambers. *Photo: Sport and General*
d. M. Sutton. From A. Wallis Myers, *Fifty Years of Wimbledon, 1926. Photo: David Rudkin*
e. S. Lenglen. *Photo: Radio Times Hulton Picture Library*

240 a. H. Wills. From A. Wallis Myers, *Fifty Years of Wimbledon, 1926. Photo: David Rudkin*
b. G. Moran. *Photo: Associated Press Ltd*
c. H. Jacobs and D. Round. *Photo: United Press International*
d. B. J. King. *Photo: Topix*

241 T. Tinling and Virginia Slims girls. *Photo: Tennis World Magazine*

b. B. J. King. *Photo: United Press International*

242 Federation Cup. *Photo: Africamera*

244 a. A. Gobert. *Illustrated Sporting and Dramatic News, 29 June 1912. Photo: London Electrotype Agency*
b. S. Mathieu. *Photo: Topix*

245 S. Lenglen and H. Wills. *Photo: Kodak Museum*

246 The Four Musketeers. *Photo: Tennis de France*

247 B. Destremau. *Photo: Topix*

248 M. Bernard. *Photo: Tennis de France*

249 1972 French Championships. *Photo: Tennis World Magazine*

250 N. Fraser. *Photo: Australian Information Service*

251 S. Fry. *Photo: Central Press Photos Ltd, courtesy Tennis World Magazine*

253 H. Henkel. *Photo: Keystone Press Agency Ltd, courtesy Tennis World Magazine*

254 A. Gibson. *Photo: Central Press Photos Ltd, courtesy Tennis World Magazine*

255 E. Goolagong. *Photo: E. D. Lacey*

256 Green Shield. *Photo: The Green Shield Trading Stamp Co. Ltd*

257 a, b, c. Grips. *Photos: Tennis World Magazine*

258 a. E. Hansell etc. *Photo: US National Tennis Hall of Fame*
b. D. Hard. *Photo: Tennis World Magazine*

259 D. Hart. *Photo: Tennis World Magazine*

260 a. R. Hewitt. *Photo: Tennis World Magazine*
b. B. Hillyard. From A. Wallis Myers, *Fifty Years of Wimbledon, 1926. Photo: David Rudkin*

262 Hungarian stamps. *Photo: David Rudkin*

264 P. Lall. *Photo: Tennis World Magazine*

266 M. Langrishe. From J. J. Treacy, *Fitzwilliam's First Fifty, 1927. Photo: Tennis World Magazine*

268 N. Pietrangeli. *Photo: Sport and General, courtesy Tennis World Magazine*

269 Italian Championships. *Photo: Tennis World Magazine*

270 a. A. Panatta. *Photo: Tennis World Magazine*
b. H. Jacobs. *Photo: Syndication International*

271 C. Janes. *Photo: Tennis World Magazine*

272 Softball tennis championships. *Photo: E. Kawatei*

275 a. Japanese National Championships. *Photo: E. Kawatei*
b. A. Jones. *Photo: Tennis World Magazine*

277 B. J. King. *Photo: Tennis World Magazine*

278 a. J. Kodeš. *Photo: E. D. Lacey*
b. J. Kramer. *Photo: Associated*

Press Ltd, courtesy Tennis World Magazine

279 R. Laver. *Photo: Tennis World Magazine*

281 a. London Grass Court Championships. *Photo: Sport and General*
b. T. Long. *Photo: Central Press Photos Ltd, courtesy Tennis World Magazine*

282 a. C. McKinley. *Photo: Topix*
b. F. McMillan. *Photo: Director of Information, South African Embassy*

283 D. McNeill. *Photo: Associated Press Ltd*

285 Statuette marked 'R. J. Morris sculp. 1884'. *Photo: Derrick Witty, courtesy Max Robertson*

286 a. H. Wills Moody. *Photo: Topix*
b. A. J. Mottram. *Photo: Tennis World Magazine*

287 I. Năstase. *Photo: Tennis World Magazine*

289 J. Newcombe. *Photo: Topix*

294 a. A. Wilding. *Photo: Pál Szöke*
b. Northern Lawn Tennis Championships. From A. Wallis Myers, *The Complete Lawn Tennis Player*, 1908. *Photo: British Museum*

295 a. T. Okker. *Photo: Alfred Eisenstaedt*
b. A. Olmedo. *Photo: Tennis World Magazine*

298 D. Pails. *Photo: Central Press Photos Ltd*

299 C. Pasarell. *Photo: Tennis World Magazine*

300 G. Patterson. *Photo: Topix*

301 John Player cigarette cards. *Photo: courtesy John Player & Sons*

302 a. The Queen's Club. From *The Queen's Club*, 1897. *Photo: David Rudkin; courtesy The Queen's Club*
b. J. Jedrzejowska. *Photo: Topix*

303 A. Quist. *Photo: Tennis World Magazine*

305 W. and E. Renshaw. From A. Wallis Myers, *Fifty Years of Wimbledon*, 1926. *Photo: David Rudkin*

306 a. N. Richey. *Photo: Syndication International*
b. R. Riggs. *Photo: Topix*

308 a. M. Rose. b. K. Rosewall. *Photos: Tennis World Magazine*

309 Royal Albert Hall. *Photo: Rothmans of Pall Mall Ltd: Martin Koretz*

311 E. Ryan. From Max Decugis, *Tennis, Hockey, Paumes, etc.*, 1913. *Photo: British Museum*

312 Scoresheet. *Photo: courtesy Umpires' Association of Great Britain*

313 a. F. E. Schroeder. *Photo: Syndication International*
b. Miss L. H. Paterson. *Photo: Scottish LTA*

315 a, b. Scottish Championships. *Photos: Scottish LTA*

317 S. Smith. *Photo: Tennis World Magazine*

318 I. Vermaak. *Photo: Central Press Photos Ltd, courtesy Tennis World Magazine*

319 E. Sturgess. *Photo: Barretts Photo Press Ltd, courtesy L. Duffus*

320 S. Price. *Photo: Tennis World Magazine*

321 M. Orantes and M. Santana. *Photo: Australian Information Service: J. Crowther*

322 Sphairistiké. *Photo: John R. Freeman Ltd, courtesy B. Reay*

324 F. Stolle. *Photo: Tennis World Magazine*

325 K. Susman. *Photo: Press Association Ltd, courtesy Tennis World Magazine*

326 S. Fick. *Photo: G. Riebicke, Berlin; courtesy S. Heyman*

327 L. Payot. *Photo: Topix*

328 R. Taylor. *Photo: E. D. Lacey*

329 a. W. T. Tilden. *Photo: Syndication International*
b. P. Todd. *Photo: Topix*

330 M. A. Trabert. *Photo: Tennis World Magazine*

339 US Indoor Championships. *Photo: Ed Fernberger*

340 O. Morozova. *Photo: Tennis World Magazine*

341 a. Virginia Slims. *Photo: Rocky Weldon, courtesy World Tennis Magazine*
b. H. E. Vines. *Photo: Keystone Press Agency Ltd*

342 V. Wade. *Photo: Fotosports International*

343 Newport. *Photo: Tennis World Magazine*

345 Wightman Cup team 1949. *Photo: Keystone Press Agency Ltd, courtesy Tennis World Magazine*

346 a. W. Shaw and V. Wade. *Photo: E. D. Lacey*
b. P. Bartkowicz. *Photo: Ed Fernberger*

347 Wimbledon. *Illustrated Sporting and Dramatic News*, 14 July 1877. *Photo: London Electrotype Agency*

348 J. T. Hartley. *Illustrated London News*, 24 July 1880. *Photo: London Electrotype Agency*

349 Wimbledon, 1923. From A. Wallis Myers. *Fifty Years of Wimbledon*, 1926. *Photo: David Rudkin*

350 a. Wimbledon, 1953. *Photo: Tennis World Magazine*
b. Trophy. *Photo: A. C. Cooper Ltd; by permission of the All England Lawn Tennis and Croquet Club*

351 a. Outside courts. *Photo: Tennis World Magazine*
b. Trophy. *Photo: A. C. Cooper Ltd; by permission of the All England Lawn Tennis and Croquet Club*

352 Wimbledon, 1949. *Photo: Syndication International*

353 Pony roller. *Photo: Topix*

355 Wimbledon, 1972. *Photo: Tennis World Magazine*

Editor's Preface

That this book was long overdue became quickly apparent to any contributor trying to write authentic material for it. Facts, unequivocal facts, about the early history of lawn tennis have to be dredged from waters so muddied and so full of hidden snags that only a Pilate could steer an unquestioning course.

A simple fact like the date of birth of Mrs Lambert Chambers has been falsely perpetuated by reference after reference as 1872 – only to be discovered on application to the Registrar of Births, as having been in truth 3 September 1878. Nor are the actual origins of the game by any means certain. Areas of doubt lie between the beginnings at Lansdowne House, Leamington, Nantclwyd Hall, Bermuda, Nahant and other early mentions of lawn tennis or forms of it. I must admit to some dalliance with PELOTA and at least one other GERMAIN to the issue, but in the main I have been faithful to thee, SPHAIRISTIKÉ, in my fashion!

So wholly aware of imperfection, the producers and I would be most grateful to any reader for proof of omission or commission. Apposite information will readily be used to correct any future edition of this work, if favour and demand should warrant one. If any organization or company feels slighted, omission of information represents, in many instances, not our intention but our inability to extract details from its officials. More than welcome, too, would be any historic photographs (and there must be many fading in family albums) of sufficient interest and clarity to reproduce in a new volume.

With this disclaimer given, may I say that I truly believe this book to be as complete and authoritative as was possible in the time and space available. I have been fortunate indeed in the contributors who have rallied for the game – all well known to the international tennis public and most of them champions of their various spheres. By no means all are professional writers but their standard of performance would befit any 'OPEN' forum. I am grateful to them, for their time is precious.

That this work has been fashioned and tempered at all has been almost entirely due to the absolute dedication and professionalism of its house editor, Perry Morley. A host of other people have generously helped to a greater or less degree. I cannot here refer to them all but to the following our debt is considerable: Mr Basil Reay and Miss Shirley Woodhead of the ILTF, the staff of the United States Lawn Tennis Association and of many other national LTAs, Major A. D. Mills, Mrs E. Stopke and the staff of the All England Lawn Tennis and Croquet Club; Mr R. F. Chatham of the Lawn Tennis Umpires' Association of Great Britain; Mr A. J. Mottram, Mr John Barrett, Mr Geoff Mullis (Queen's Messenger Extraordinary), Mr Léon Dubler, Dr Irving Bricker, Sir Terence Langrishe, Mr M. W. Renshaw, the staff of World Championship Tennis, Mrs R. H. Haire and the staff of the US National Lawn Tennis Hall of Fame and Tennis Museum, Inc (Newport, Rhode Island), the BBC and the staff of its Archives Library at Caversham, the Manor House Hotel, Leamington Spa, Leamington Spa Public Library, Mr Patrick Hickman Robertson, Mr Arthur Cole, Mr Michael Cole, and Mr Tom Todd, St Peter Port, Guernsey.

History and development, alas, do not stand still – least of all at the moment in tennis. As we go to press the situation is not (as we had hoped lucky timing would make it) 'open' and shut, but even more open with the conflict between ATP and the ILTF as yet unresolved and the growing threat of WTT driving in another wedge of dissension.

But the first hundred years we have tried to capture in essence at least. And now for the testing. Have you a query about the history of one hundred years of the game or the exploits of its finest exponents? If so we hope we are now able to answer it.

Max Robertson
London, 1973

How To Use This Book

As a work of reference this book is divided into three sections:

Part 1 contains general articles on the history and development of lawn tennis, playing the game, and reporting the Wimbledon Championships.

Part 2, arranged in a single, alphabetical sequence, includes articles on activities in all the tennis-playing countries in the world whose governing bodies are affiliated to the International Lawn Tennis Federation; associations, sponsors and manufacturers; terms used in scoring, play and equipment; and brief career details of great players. We have included those who won the singles of any of the 'Big Four' championships, recognizing that we may sometimes have been less than fair to players who, because of distance or contemporary competition with the greatest (e.g. Tilden or Lenglen), did not reach the top of the 'Big Four' or did not compete in them when they were at their peak. We have concentrated on the greatest players of all time rather than on the most recent. To them we have added several in the top flight today and a few who look likely to be there very shortly.

Part 3 contains detailed records of the Wimbledon, US, Australian and French Championships, the ILTF Grand Prix, the World Championship of Tennis, Records of All Time, and the Davis, Federation and Wightman Cups.

Where it is thought that the reader may gain from reading other entries, these are indicated within articles by small capitals (All England Championships see WIMBLEDON) and where the reference is from Part 1 to Part 2 or *vice versa* this is made clear.

For consistency, English spellings have been adopted for technical terms. Place names are given as currently used in the country concerned, except for a few cities (Munich, Prague etc.) where the English spelling is more widely known. All personal names are spelled as the owner would himself, complete with accents. For names transliterated from the Cyrillic and Arabic scripts the most widely used forms have been adopted.

A note on the abbreviations used in the entries on players in Part 2 will be found on page 194.

PART 1

History and Development

The Origins of Lawn Tennis
The Rt Hon. The Lord Aberdare

Before 1870 there was only one game called 'Tennis'. This was the ancient game known originally to the French as '*Jeu de Paume*' and now called Real Tennis in Great Britain, Royal Tennis in Australia and Court Tennis in the United States to distinguish it from its more popular modern descendant, Lawn Tennis. The terminology of the two games alone is sufficient evidence of their close relationship, but they also share other features which confirm it. The ball is struck back and forth over a net by means of a racket strung with gut; the ball may only bounce once; two services are allowed; and, most significantly of all, lawn tennis has adopted the strange system of scoring by 15s from its ancient ancestor.

Why then after many centuries of real tennis did lawn tennis suddenly develop in the 1870s? The simple answer is that only then had man learned to make a rubber ball that would bounce on grass. Real tennis is played indoors on a floor of flagstones or more recently of concrete. On several occasions efforts were made to translate this magnificent game into the open, but all failed for want of a suitable ball. The real tennis ball was once stuffed with hair. Claudio in Shakespeare's *Much Ado About Nothing* says in reply to Don Pedro 'No; but the barber's man hath been seen with him; and the old ornament of his cheek hath already stuffed tennis balls'. Later the present real tennis ball was developed, made up of pieces of cloth tightly bound together with string and covered with flannel. The ball is hard and bounces well on a stone or concrete floor, but it is useless on grass.

The nearest to success were a group of people in 1767 who played a game they called 'field tennis' at the Red House in Battersea Fields near Ranelagh. No details of the game itself are known except that 'the field, which was of 16 acres in extent, was kept in as high order and smooth as a bowling green'. According to William Hickey, the game seems to have been preceded by a mighty meal and interspersed with 'draughts of cool tankard, and other pleasant beverages'. So popular did the game become that in 1793 the *Sporting Magazine* reported that 'Field Tennis threatens ere long to bowl out cricket'. But no more was heard of it thereafter.

There has been much speculation as to why the game ever came to be called tennis. There can be no doubt that it was originally a French game. The earliest known references to it occur in French ecclesiastical manuscripts in the 12th and 13th centuries and several parts of the court bear French names – *dedans, grille, tambour, bandeau*, for example. Yet in France it was always known as *jeu de paume*, 'the game of the palm'; and it continues to be so called even today, many centuries after the racket was first brought into use. Many ingenious solutions have been propounded, none of them convincing. The most likely is based on the supposition that before serving, the French players called out '*tenez!*' rather like the rackets marker calling out 'play!'. The evidence for this theory is that in a Latin poem of 1641, written by a Frenchman and dedicated to Cardinal Richelieu, the tennis players call out '*accipe*' or '*excipe*' before serving and it is reasonable to suppose that this might be a Latin translation of '*tenez*'. At any rate this was the explanation preferred by Dr Samuel Johnson in his famous *Dictionary*.

The method of scoring by 15s is medieval in origin – and, of course, 40 is only an abbreviation of the original 45. The whole game was worth 60 points and divided into four equal stages worth 15 points each. The number 60 had a special significance in olden days: there were 60 degrees in the segment of a circle, 60 minutes in an hour, 60 seconds in a minute. Deuce is simply a corruption of the French *à deux*, indicating that one player had to win two consecutive points for the game.

The word 'love', meaning no score, has also led to some fanciful speculation about its origin. It has even been suggested that it is a corruption of the French *l'œuf*, representing a round or nought like the duck's egg in cricket. But the French can hardly be described as cricket fans, tennis is a much older game and there is no evidence that they ever used such an expression. It is more likely that the word 'love' came to be

Right This picture of two ball games in a 1658 edition of a children's encyclopedia is accompanied by an explanatory verse, a translation of which is here reproduced from Julian Marshall's *Annals of Tennis* (1878) with the original Latin for the words identifying numbered items in the picture:

In a *Tennis-Court (Sphaeristerio)*[1]
They play
with a *ball (Pila)*[2]
which one throweth
and other taketh
and sendeth back
with a *Racket (Reticulo)*[3];
and that is the sport
of noblemen
to stir their body.
A *winde-ball (Follis)*[4]
being filled with air
by means of a *Ventil*
is tossed to and fro
with the *fist (Pugno)*[5]
in the open air.

equated with nothing in such phrases as 'a labour of love' and 'neither for love nor money'.

The use of the word 'service' to mark the opening stroke of each point is almost certainly derived from the fact that in early days the ball was set in motion by a servant. Henry VIII (1509-47) certainly employed a servant for this purpose, and in those days there was clearly no intention of winning a point by service; it was just a convenient way of starting a rally and best performed by a lackey.

Such are the interesting similarities of the two games of tennis. Apart from the open nature of the lawn tennis court as opposed to the walled real tennis court, the most striking difference between the two games lies in the use of the 'chase' in real tennis. This is not an easy concept to explain, but it is of very real benefit in giving some additional advantage to skill over brute force.

The system of chases requires a 'marker'; he is usually a professional and stands at one end of the net. His task, as well as acting as umpire and keeping the score, is to 'mark' the chases, i.e. to decide the point at which the ball strikes the floor on its second bounce. In lawn tennis, when a ball bounces twice, it is 'dead' and the player on that side of the net loses the point. Not so in real tennis; it makes a chase at the point of its second bounce – or, incidentally, if it enters one of the 'galleries', netted openings down one side of the court.

To establish the chase made, the floor of the court is marked by lines parallel to the back wall at intervals of one yard with a shorter line indicating the half-yard mark. These are numbered 1 to 6 from the back wall and the marker uses them to describe the chase, e.g. Chase 1 yard or Chase 3. The lower the number, i.e. the nearer the back wall that the ball bounces on its second bounce, the better the chase.

When a chase is made, neither player scores a point. The chase is put into cold storage until either a second chase is made or one player reaches 40. The players then change ends and play for the chase or chases. To win the point, the other player now has to make a better chase than the one made by his opponent. This means that he has to make each ball that he strikes in the course of the rally bounce at its second bounce nearer the back wall than his opponent's original chase. Hence the typically undercut stroke used by real tennis players, which brings the ball down sharply when it strikes the back wall.

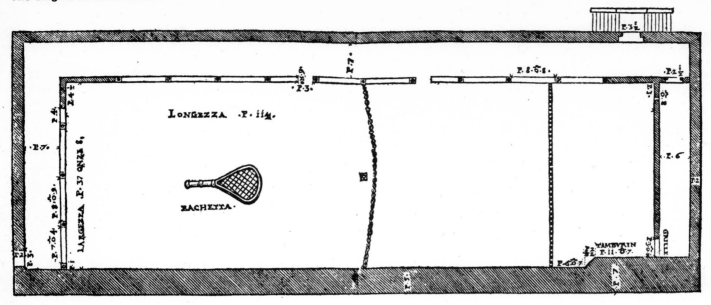

Clearly the chase is one feature of real tennis that it was impossible to carry forward into lawn tennis, but it still remains a dominant feature of real tennis as played today.

The history of the ancient game of tennis is woven into the social fabric of medieval Europe. It seems likely that the strange shape of the court is due to the fact that it was originally played in a cloister. Just as an Eton Fives court is modelled on the layout of the Eton Chapel steps where the game first developed, so it seems likely that the game of tennis began in a cloister. The sloping roof round three sides of the court, the pillars supporting it, the hatch (grille) in one corner – all suggest a cloister. The fact that the earliest mention of the game occurs in ecclesiastical manuscripts lends added weight to this theory.

The 12th century saw its earliest development. Ecclesiastical students in particular were keen on it, but bishops and archbishops took part also. In the early days the ball was struck with the palm of the hand (hence *jeu de paume*) and it was not until later that first a glove and then a racket was developed. The early racket was a very primitive instrument with a wooden head and it was probably not until the early 16th century that a racket strung with gut came into general use.

Tennis first became a royal game in the reign of King Louis X of France (1314-16), who is said to have died of a chill contracted by drinking a beaker of cold water immediately after an energetic game of tennis. In those early days much betting took place on the outcome of a match. A Treasury account of 1355 records the purchase of Brussels cloth for King Jean II (1350-64) to settle his tennis debts, and in the reign of his son, Charles V (1364-80), also a very keen player despite a swollen right hand, there is a story that the Duke of Burgundy twice pledged his doublet for a tennis debt – the first man ever perhaps to 'lose his shirt' at the game.

The first known woman to play tennis is mentioned in 1427, when 'there came to Paris a woman called Margot, young, from 28 to 30 years old, who was of the country of Hainault and who played better at hand-ball than any man had seen and played very strongly both forehanded and backhanded, very cunningly, very cleverly, as any man could, and there were few men whom she did not beat, except the very best players'.

Louis XI (1461-83) took a keen interest in the game and in 1480 standardized the ball by ordering that it must be 'stuffed with good hide and wool wadding and not containing sand, ground chalk, metal shavings, lime, bran, sawdust, ash, moss, powder or earth'. His son, Charles VIII (1483-98), was the second French king to lose his life as a result of tennis, when he struck his head on the lintel of the door leading to the court and subsequently died. His cousin, who succeeded him as Louis XII (1498-1515), was a

Above Antonio Scaino's *Trattato del Giuoco della Palla* (1555) contains this plan of Henri II's tennis court at the Louvre.

fervent supporter who enjoyed many games with his subjects in his home town of Orléans, where at that time there were some 40 courts.

The golden age of tennis in France was in the 16th century. François I (1515-47) set the example, which was followed with enthusiasm by his courtiers and by humbler folk all over France. He built courts wherever he went, including a covered court at the Louvre and an open court at Fontainebleau; he even included a tennis court on board his 2,000-ton four-masted man-of-war, *La Grande Françoise,* built to outclass King Henry VIII of England's *Great Harry.*

His successor, Henri II (1547-59), certainly one of the foremost players of his day, built a second court at the Louvre. A diagram of this court is contained in the first known book on tennis, *Trattato del Giuoco della Palla,* written in 1555 by an Italian priest, Antonio Scaino da Salo. It is astonishing how closely the design of this old court at the Louvre corresponds to that of a modern court.

King Charles IX (1560-74) was brought up to play tennis and is shown in a contemporary picture holding a small racket at the age of two. He continued to play, mainly at the Louvre, and in 1571 granted a constitution to the newly formed Corporation of Tennis Professionals. This established three grades of professional – apprentice, associate and master – and gave them important rights in respect of the management of courts as well as the manufacture of balls and rackets. One of these professionals, Forbet, wrote the first known rules of the game in 1592, later published in 1599.

His successor, Henri III (1574-89), was no outstanding player, but Henri IV (1589-1610), formerly Henri of Navarre, played with tremendous enthusiasm wherever he went, and built several new courts, including a new covered court at Fontainebleau. Evidence of the popularity of tennis at this time comes from a report of the Papal Legate after a visit to Paris in 1596 that there were 250 well-appointed courts in the city and that the game gave employment to 7,000 people.

Louis XIII (1610-43) and Louis XIV (1643-1715) both played tennis, but it seems that its popularity had passed its peak, for in 1657 the Dutch Ambassador reported that the number of courts in Paris was 114, less than half the number in 1596. By 1783 the number had dwindled to 13, and a few years later the French Revolution put a temporary stop to the game. But not before a tennis court had achieved immortal historical fame – the court at Versailles, scene of the famous tennis-court oath, when the Third Estate, locked out of the normal meeting place of the States-General by order of the King, met on 20 June 1789 and vowed not to disband until France had a constitution. This historic event was recorded in paint by Jacques Louis David and the court is today a museum dedicated to the Revolution.

In the meantime tennis had spread all over Europe. In England, earliest mention of the game occurs in statutes forbidding it and encouraging the practice of more warlike sports such as archery. But such restraints did not apply to the King himself and it seems likely that Henry V (1413-22) was at least familiar with the game when he received a gift of tennis balls from the French Dauphin. Shakespeare made the King reply:

> When we have matched our rackets to these balls,
> We will, in France, by God's grace, play a set,
> Shall strike his father's crown into the hazard.
> Tell him, he hath made a match with such a wrangler,
> That all the courts of France will be disturbed
> With chases.

Tennis seems to have been played even earlier in Scotland, perhaps because of the close ties that existed with France.

As in France it was the 16th century that saw the establishment of tennis as the game of kings. Henry VII (1485-1509) played frequently in courts at Woodstock, Windsor, Wycombe, Westminster and Sheen.

Henry VIII (1509-47) was a very keen player and an excellent description of him as a young man was given by the Venetian Ambassador, Sebastian Giustiniani, in 1519.

Above Charles Hulpeau's *Le Jeu Royal de la Paulme* (1632), of which this is the title page, contains the earliest extant set of rules for the game of tennis. These indoor tennis courts were often used for other forms of entertainment, notably the performance of operas. Note the short handle of the 17th-century racket.

Right The scene of the tennis-court oath at Versailles, painted by Jacques Louis David
Below The tennis court built for Charles II at Windsor Castle was in the moat below the Round Tower.

His Majesty is 29 years old and extremely handsome; nature could not have done more for him; he is much handsomer than any other sovereign in Christendom; a great deal handsomer than the King of France; very fair, and his whole frame admirably proportioned. On hearing that François I wore a beard he allowed his to grow, and as it is reddish, he has now got a beard which looks like gold. He is extremely fond of tennis, at which game it is the prettiest thing in the world to see him play, his fair skin glowing through a shirt of the finest texture.

At his Palace of Whitehall, which he wrested from Cardinal Wolsey, he had four tennis courts, two covered and two open, the larger open court known as 'The Brake'. The foundations of the smaller covered court can still be seen from Cockpit Passage within the Cabinet Office. He naturally included a tennis court in St James's Palace, built for Anne Boleyn, and on dispossessing Cardinal Wolsey of Hampton Court Palace he built a new court there about 1530. This famous court is still in use, although very largely restored at the same time as the rest of the palace in the reign of William and Mary, whose monogram is painted on the wall by the net. Much of the ancient brickwork still survives, however.

About the same time in Scotland King James IV (1488-1513) built an open court at his Palace of Falkland which is also still in use. This is a unique court and the only surviving example of a French type of court known as *jeu quarré*, as opposed to *jeu à dedans*. It has no dedans, but instead two winning openings known as *le trou* and *la lune*.

Queen Elizabeth I was no player of tennis, but was certainly an interested spectator and planned a new court at Windsor Castle, although this was never completed. The interest of the Tudor monarchs in tennis was carried on by their Stuart successors. James I (1603-25), in his *Basilicon Doron*, written in 1598, recommended the game by its Scottish name 'the cache' to his eldest son, Prince Henry and repaired the Brake court at Whitehall for his benefit. Unfortunately Prince Henry died in 1612, but his younger brother, later Charles I, was an equally enthusiastic player, even on occasion playing at 6 a.m. in the court at St James's Palace. Records show that at this period there were 14 tennis courts in London, all of them now disappeared, but in some cases leaving street names such as Racquet Court or Tennis Court behind them. A number of other courts were in play outside London, and even a few in Ireland. A new court was built about 1635 in James Street off the Haymarket. This was destined to become one of

Right An artist's conception of an earlier (16th-century) game at Windsor
Below James, Duke of York (later James II), as shown in *The True Effigies of our Most Illustrious Soveraigne Lord King Charles, Queene Mary, with the rest of the Royall Progenie* (1641)

THE HIGH BORNE PRINCE IAMES DVKE OF YORKE
borne October 2 the 13. 1633.

the best-known London courts and remained in use until 1866. Its outer walls can still be seen in the present Orange Street.

Undeterred by the Civil War, Charles I (1625-49) continued to play tennis whenever he could. He played at Oxford with Prince Rupert and in 1643 obtained special consent from Parliament to have material for a tennis suit sent from London to Oxford. But Oliver Cromwell's victory put a temporary stop to tennis playing in England and available courts were put to other uses, for storage or the quartering of troops.

Charles I, however, had imparted a love of the game to his two sons, later Charles II and James II. A print of 1641 shows the latter at the age of 8 in the Brake court at Whitehall. Both continued to play tennis while in exile in France, and on the restoration of the monarchy the game resumed its royal status in England. Charles II (1660-85) played regularly at Whitehall and at Hampton Court and in 1662 set in hand the construction of a splendid new covered court at Whitehall, partly on the site of the Brake court. Samuel Pepys in his diaries makes note of the construction of this court and writes of the King's play. He admired his prowess on occasion, but deplored the flattery heaped upon him.

Charles II also built a new court at Windsor, which survived until 1782. An Italian writer makes mention of six courts in London at this period, of which two were destroyed in the Great Fire of 1666. Other evidence points to the existence of six courts in Cambridge, seemingly all open courts, and four in Oxford, all covered courts.

The succession of the Hanoverian kings, however, brought a rapid decline in the popularity of tennis. Some courts were closed, others put to different use, as theatres or other places of public entertainment. There was a short flicker of revived interest when Frederick, Prince of Wales, son of George II (1727-60), took up the game, but his untimely death, ascribed by some to a blow from a tennis ball, marked the end of Hanoverian patronage.

But tennis was by no means confined to France and Britain; in its heyday in the 16th century it was popular all over the continent of Europe. It was known in Spain from early days and was played by Henry I, King of Castile (1214-17), who, like Louis X of France, is said to have died from drinking cold water immediately after an energetic game of tennis in 1217. Later Philip I of Castile (1504-06) was a very keen player. On his way from the Netherlands in 1506 to claim his throne, his ship was driven by storm to land at Weymouth and he was entertained as a guest at Windsor by Henry VII. Here,

Right In this French painting of an 18th-century tennis player, note the longer racket handle and slightly offset head – much nearer today's version of the real tennis racket than those shown on page 17.

it is recorded, he played tennis with the Marquis of Dorset, 'but the Kyng of Casteele played with the Rackete and gave the Lord Marques XV'. It seems that the Marquis of Dorset played with his hand, but it should be remembered that in those early days the racket was a very primitive instrument. Philip III (1598-1621) was an ardent player, as were Philip V (1700-24; 1724-46) and Louis I (1724). Charles III (1759-88) also took an interest and created the office of Judge of Ball Games and Rackets. A game of tennis shown in a Flemish painting of the 16th century can be seen on pages 42-3.

In Italy tennis courts existed in Florence, Mantua, Venice, Rome, Milan and Turin. In the Low Countries there were courts at Antwerp, Brussels and elsewhere. Switzerland had several courts including those at Neuchâtel, Geneva, Basle and Berne. In Sweden, King Eric XIV (1560-68) built a court in Stockholm. There were a great many courts also in central Europe – in the German states and the Austro-Hungarian Empire. They are known to have existed at Augsburg, Salzburg, Linz, Strasbourg (2), Leipzig (2), Munich, Nuremberg, Mannheim, Frankfurt, Nördlingen, Weimar, Giessen, Stuttgart, Jena, Regensburg, Dresden, Auersberg, Tübingen and several at Cologne.

In Prague there were four courts in the mid-16th century, one of them much played in by the Emperor Rudolf II (1576-1612). Berlin boasted a large and well-built court and Vienna at one time had four courts, one of which at the Auersberg Palace remained in use into the early 20th century. There was certainly one court in Russia at St Petersburg (now Leningrad), which existed until 1866.

Above Contrast the modern-looking net in this 18th-century game of tennis with the fringed rope shown on page 17. There was still considerable variation in the size and shape of rackets.
Below A 20th-century game of real tennis: Lord Aberdare (near side of net) playing R. A. McNeil in the 1963 Henry Leaf Cup at the Queen's Club, London. Lord Aberdare was the winner, 6–0, 6–3. He also won the Amateur Real Tennis title four times.

By the middle of the 17th century tennis had also spread to the New World and was known in New York.

The old game of tennis gave birth to another great game – rackets – in England in the mid-18th century. Certain gentlemen imprisoned for debt in the Fleet and King's Bench prisons whiled away the weary hours by hitting balls up against the massive prison walls with their tennis rackets. A simple but exciting game was developed and soon spread outside the prisons.

Originally the single front wall was used, as in the original prisons and as used for pelota in southern France and Spain; this form of rackets was known as the Open Court game. But it was in time superseded by the present Close Court game with front, back and two side walls. The popularity of the game was finally established when it was taken up by the public schools and the Universities of Oxford and Cambridge.

Rackets in turn led to the invention of squash rackets, first played at Harrow School in the 1880s. The development of a rubber ball allowed a game similar in nature to the original rackets to be played more cheaply in a smaller court with a lighter racket.

By the end of the 18th century it looked as if tennis were dead. The French Revolution and the Napoleonic wars had finished it in France and most of Europe; in England it had lost its royal leadership. But a significant revival took place in the 19th century in England under the stimulus of Victorian prosperity. Courts were built at many famous country houses, including some still in use today at Hatfield House, Petworth House, Canford Manor, Holyport Grange, Hardwick House, Moreton Morrell, Seacourt and in Scotland at South Bar, Troon.

Three new courts were built at Cambridge, of which one is still in use, while Oxford by contrast was reduced to one opposite Merton College. The first University match took place at the old court in James Street, Haymarket, in 1859. There was even a revival of royal interest in tennis when the Prince of Wales, later King Edward VII, played at Oxford in 1859.

A court was built at Lord's Cricket Ground in 1839 and was renovated in 1866 when the James Street court was closed. The University match was transferred to Lord's and the Marylebone Cricket Club became the headquarters of the game. It was for this reason that in the early days of lawn tennis the MCC was invited to codify the rules of the new game (see THE BIRTH AND SPREAD OF LAWN TENNIS).

Other clubs providing tennis for their members came into existence. In London, the Prince's Club and the Queen's Club; in Manchester, the Tennis and Racquet Club; and others in Leamington and Brighton.

This revival of interest soon spread to other English-speaking countries. In 1874 Mr T. Smith-Travers opened a court in Hobart, Tasmania, and his example was followed in 1882 in Melbourne, where a court was built at 345 Exhibition Street. Both these Australian courts are still in use.

In 1876 two American amateurs, Mr Hollis Hunnewell and Mr Nathaniel Thayer, took an English professional, Ted Hunt, from Oxford to the United States and built a court in Buckingham Street, Boston. The 12-year-old boy, Thomas Pettitt, engaged by Hunt to sweep out the court, later became the first American world champion.

In 1888 a second court was built in Boston and in 1890 New York acquired its first court at the Racquet Court Club. When this club moved in 1918 to its present site on Park Avenue, two new courts were built which remain in use today. Other American courts which remain in play were built at Tuxedo Park, Philadelphia, Greentree, Long Island, and Aiken, S. Carolina.

In France very few courts remained in use, although two new ones were built at the Tuileries and a great French professional, J. Edmond Barre, held the world championship from 1829 to 1862. Today two courts remain in use, in Paris and Bordeaux.

This magnificent old game is still regularly played by a small band of enthusiasts. Its lusty infant, lawn tennis, grows ever more popular but the older game retains its charm, and its unique feature, the chase, gives some encouragement to the older, less agile player. It remains under royal patronage in Britain as the present Prince of Wales played it enthusiastically at Cambridge.

The Birth and Spread of Lawn Tennis, 1860-1914
Lance Tingay

Two men merit recognition as the founders of lawn tennis, Major Harry Gem, solicitor and Clerk to the Birmingham Magistrates, and Major Walter Clopton Wingfield, member of the Honourable Corps of Gentlemen-at-Arms at the court of Queen Victoria.

In 1858 Major Gem and Mr J. B. Perera marked out a lawn in Edgbaston as a tennis court. Most of the adjuncts of the venerable game of real tennis, the penthouse, dedans, sidewalls, tambour and so on, necessarily had to be discarded but in the first instance the chase markings across the court were retained. For 12 years the game thrived on Edgbaston turf until 1870 when a move was made to Leamington. The Leamington Lawn Tennis Club, the first, so far as is known, to be devoted *exclusively* to lawn tennis, was founded in 1872 with Major Gem as president.

Major Gem and his friends were not unique in adapting tennis as a lawn game. It was played out of doors in Elizabethan times. But the prime honour as founder of lawn tennis has for long been accorded to Major Wingfield, whose bust adorns the entrance hall of the Lawn Tennis Association headquarters in London, and probably rightly so.

The first record of Major Wingfield playing his version of lawn tennis was at Lansdowne House in London in 1869 with a net 2 ft high. In February 1874 he applied for a patent of his 'New and Improved Court for Playing the Ancient Game of Tennis' and the next month he issued the first edition of his booklet on 'Sphairistike'. The use of this Greek word, meaning ball game, was possible only in an age when all gentlemen were presumed to have acquaintance with the classics. It was soon contracted to 'Sticky' and that in turn abandoned by the use of the alternative description 'Lawn Tennis'. The patent received provisional protection for three years but was not taken further.

The sets of Major Wingfield's game sold at 5 guineas and comprised balls, four rackets and the netting which made up the court. It achieved popularity and seems to have been commercially successful. A notion of its success can be gleaned from the fifth edition of the major's booklet in 1875. There he proudly records the names of distinguished personages who had already bought the game. The list included 11 princes and princesses, seven dukes, 14 marquises, three marchionesses, 54 earls, six countesses, 105 viscounts, 41 barons, 44 ladies, 44 honourables, five right honourables and 55 baronets and knights – quite a large segment of Debrett and the Almanach de Gotha.

The court was hourglass-shaped, wider at the baseline than at the net. The major emphasized 'the whole science of the game for out of doors depends on the court being smaller at the net than at the base'. Its length was 60 ft (18·29 m), 18 ft (5·49 m) shorter than today. It was 21 ft (6·40 m) wide at the net, 30 ft (9·14 m) at the baseline, compared with 27 ft (8·23 m), the standard width of a singles court today.

Service was from one side only. The server stood in a lozenge-shaped box in the middle and delivered the ball to a service court between the service line and baseline on the other side. The height of the net was 4 ft 8 in (1·42 m) at posts directly on the sidelines and, according to contemporary illustrations, was intended to be at the same height in the centre.

It was not long before lawn tennis began to replace croquet as a summer pastime. Other manufacturers produced imitations. Within a few months the game had grown into a lusty baby in need of discipline, for there were about as many codes of rules as there were players. There was then, of course, no Lawn Tennis Association, no All England Lawn Tennis Club (it was founded in 1869 but for croquet only) to legislate.

It fell to the Marylebone Cricket Club to intervene in its capacity as the governing authority of rackets and tennis, with which the new game was intimately connected. In November 1874 the MCC secretary suggested that the tennis committee should adjudicate on the rules of lawn tennis. No one, not even the Leamington Club, then two years old, seems to have dissented.

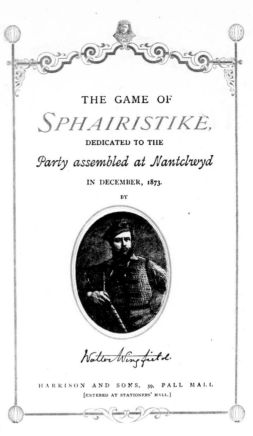

Major Walter Clopton Wingfield seen *above*, on the title page of his book, took out a patent (*below*) for his game of lawn tennis in February 1874.

Above Before Major Wingfield was granted his patent, however, a game of lawn tennis was being played by Major Harry Gem, the President and founder of the Leamington Club, the first purely lawn-tennis club in the world. The picture, from a sketch made by Harry Gem himself, shows Gem, on the left near the net, with his friend Jean-Baptiste Perera, playing against Dr Wellesley Tomkins, near the net, and Dr Frederic Haynes, both of the Warneford Hospital. This was the first game played when the club was inaugurated in the summer of 1872 on the lawns of the Manor House Hotel.

All interested parties were invited to a public meeting in March 1875. A sub-committee was appointed, comprising the Hon. Spencer Ponsonby Fane, the Hon. E. Chandos Leigh, the Hon. C. G. Lyttleton, W. Hart Dyke Esq. and J. M. Heathcote Esq. On 25 May they issued the first official code.

It was more than half way to modern lawn tennis. A tribute to the influence of Major Wingfield's game was the retention of the hourglass-shaped court, 78 ft (23·77 m) long (which it still is), 30 ft (9·14 m) wide at the base, 24 ft (7·31 m) in the middle (the mean of which, 27 ft (8·23 m), is the present dimension). The net was a formidable obstacle, 5 ft (1·52 m) at the sides, 4 ft (1·22 m) in the centre. The service court extended 26 ft (7·92 m) from the net and delivery had to be made with one foot outside the baseline as in the rules of Mr J. H. Hales. His further suggestion that the ball bounce twice within the court for the sake of women, whose dress prevented their running back and forth, was rejected.

Points (15 up for a game with deuce at 14 all), were scored only by the server, who kept 'hand in' until he lost a rally. Faults, as in rackets, could be taken and two deliveries were allowed. Methods of handicapping were also laid down and to this end the posts were 7 ft (2·13 m) high. A player thus handicapped was required to play the ball above a cord stretched across at this height.

No one appears to have objected to these rules. Major Wingfield accepted them cordially. Yet they were short-lived, possibly because the committee, in their wisdom, were at pains not to insist on their being strictly followed. The new code declared that the dimensions of the court could be altered in accordance with either the state of the turf or the capabilities of the players. Thus stood lawn tennis in 1875 but elsewhere in London that year events took place which had a momentous influence on its development. From a pastime it was transformed into a sport.

The All England Croquet Club, founded in 1869, had failed to thrive. Its four acres next to the London and South Western Railway line near Worple Road, Wimbledon, required a rent of £50 rising to £100 a year and payment of this and other expenses proved bothersome.

Accordingly, when in 1875 Mr Henry Jones, one of the club's founders, suggested lawn tennis as an added attraction, the idea was approved. The new game prospered, so much so that by 1877 the name was changed to the All England Croquet and Lawn Tennis Club and players of the original game were ousted from the committee.

The Prince's Club, in Hans Place, Knightsbridge, also took up lawn tennis about the same time. From there had come proposals to lower the height of the net to 3 ft (0·91 m). It was not obvious in those years that the All England Club had more importance than Prince's, where a handicap doubles tournament was a popular feature. Prince's, however, departed from the history of lawn tennis; until its demise in World War II it found greater fame in the world of tennis and rackets.

In 1877 the finances of the All England Club had again deteriorated. The pony roller was in need of repair and the funds were not forthcoming. Mr Henry Jones proposed a lawn-tennis tournament for all comers. Mr J. H. Walsh, editor of *The Field*, liked the idea and persuaded his proprietors to support it. *The Field* came in with a silver challenge cup worth 25 guineas. The first Wimbledon Championship was born.

That first meeting, from Monday 9 July to Thursday 12 July, with the final scheduled for Monday 16 July so that the Friday and Saturday would be free for all to attend the Eton and Harrow cricket match at Lords, would have been noteworthy as the starting point of its many famous successors. It was more significant than that. It was, so far as can be ascertained, the first open (open, that is, in the old sense of all-

Below Spectators at Wimbledon in 1879, the year that Canon J. T. Hartley defeated V. 'St Leger' Gould. Both made history. Hartley, who had to return to Yorkshire for Sunday duties between his semi-final and final on the Monday, was the only clergyman to reach a Wimbledon final. Gould was the only Wimbledon finalist to be convicted for murder. He was tried in Monte Carlo and sent to Devil's Island in 1908, where he died in September 1909.

Spectators

comers – professionals being barred as a matter of course in those days) lawn-tennis tournament in the world. And the rules then framed became, without major alteration, the rules everywhere.

If no one dissented from the MCC rules of 1875 no one minded departing from them either. Indeed in 1876 the indefatigable Mr Jones publicly advocated tennis instead of rackets scoring. A variety of rules hardly mattered with a purely social game but a cup worth 25 guineas demanded that prospective competitors be told exactly what they were in for.

The rules committee of the inaugural Wimbledon Championship comprised Mr Jones, Mr C. G. Heathcote and Mr Julian Marshall. The code they adopted then was substantially the code as it is today, the most basic point being the adoption of a rectangular court 78 by 27 ft (23·77 by 8·23 m) and scoring as in tennis. Some details have changed. The first Wimbledon tournament had a net 5 ft (1·52 m) high at the posts, 3 ft 3 in (0·99 m) at the centre. As in the MCC code the service line was 26 ft (7·92 m) from the net – now the distance is 21 ft (6·40 m). What is now a let on service was considered good but, as now, two deliveries were allowed and a fault could not be taken.

The size and weight of the ball have changed. In 1877 the requirements were a diameter of $2\frac{1}{4}$–$2\frac{5}{8}$ in (57–67 mm), a weight of $1\frac{1}{4}$–$1\frac{1}{2}$ oz (35–43 g). Six games up comprised a set with no advantage games being played.

Only a men's singles championship was held. The first men's doubles championship was staged in Scotland in 1878. The Irish were the first to give women a blessing and the Irish women's singles championship, first held in 1879, is the oldest in the world.

Below The fifth round of the All-Comers' Match at Wimbledon in 1881. W. Renshaw beat Lawford 1-6, 6-3, 6-2, 5-6, 6-3, and went on to defeat the holder, J. T. Hartley, 6-0, 6-2, 6-1. Note the abacus scoreboard.

The first Wimbledon winner, from an entry of 22, was Spencer W. Gore, an Old Harrovian of 27. His name will endure as the first lawn-tennis champion and it would be pleasant to be able to picture him as a wholehearted enthusiast for the game he graces. He was nothing of the sort. In 1890 he wrote:

> . . . it is its want of variety that will prevent lawn tennis in its present form from taking rank among our great games. . . . That anyone who has really played well at cricket, tennis, or even rackets, will ever seriously give his attention to lawn tennis, beyond showing himself a promising player, is extremely doubtful: for in all probability the monotony of the game as compared with the others would choke him off before he had time to excel in it.

So much for Mr Gore. The enthusiasm of the 1878 winner, P. F. Hadow, was not much greater. He was a planter on leave from Ceylon and took up the game for the first time that summer. Having won Wimbledon he went back to Ceylon and never again even saw a first-class game until he was persuaded to turn up at the silver-jubilee celebrations in 1926.

Before Wimbledon's start in 1877 the game had begun to spread across the world, carried by British enthusiasts and, despite the record books, there is gratification for British national pride that the first 'Champion of America' was an Englishman, O. E. Woodhouse.

The game came to the United States via Bermuda. By early 1874 the British garrison there was playing a form of lawn tennis with imported equipment. Mary Ewing Outerbridge played in January, grew keen and when she returned to New York she carried a set of this equipment with her. Her brother, A. Emilius Outerbridge, helped her erect a court in the grounds of the Staten Island Cricket and Baseball Club.

A court was also laid down at the home of William Appleton at Nahant, a suburb of Boston, in August 1874. Dr James Dwight and F. R. Sears, elder brother of Richard Sears, played there, to the astonishment of local inhabitants who, hearing of the new British game, watched it under the impression it was cricket. For the next few years lawn tennis was played sporadically in New England with balls and equipment differing from one place to another. A club tournament was held at Nahant in August 1876.

The first open meeting was staged at the Staten Island Club in September 1880. It was advertised and a letter was received from O. E. Woodhouse in Chicago saying he was a member of the West Middlesex Club in England and could he please take part. Woodhouse was no novice. Only two months before he had beaten both William and Ernest Renshaw at Wimbledon, each by three sets to one, before losing to H. F. Lawford in the All Comers' final. He is believed to have been the originator of the smash.

Above Mixed doubles (*left*) at Cleremont, Bermuda, then the home of Sir Brownlow and Lady Grey. This tennis court was the first in the western hemisphere and must surely, as the Bermudian authorities claim, have been in use not later than the end of 1873. Authorities differ on the source of the Bermudian equipment, for Major Wingfield did not officially apply for his patent until 23 February 1874 (see page 22). But lawn tennis was clearly in the air and possibly Major Wingfield saw a threat to the commercial possibilities of his game and was therefore spurred to take out a patent for the hour-glass court. It was certainly as a visitor to Bermuda that Mary Ewing Outerbridge learned the game, no later than January 1874, for she returned to New York, arriving on 2 February 1874 on the S.S. *Canima*, whose passenger list is reproduced *above*, and her brother, A. Emilius Outerbridge, who was in the shipping business in New York City, helped her erect a court at the Staten Island Cricket and Baseball Club in the spring of 1874.

Above An early family game of lawn tennis in England

The event for which Woodhouse entered was the Championship of America. His début was sensational. He served overhead, a method not before seen in the United States, and though James Rankine held this phenomenal performer to a close match in the opening round all further opposition crumbled until the final. There Woodhouse was hard pressed by the Canadian J. F. Hellmuth. At the end the score to Woodhouse was 15-11, 14-15, 15-9, 10-15, two all in games but a winning margin for the Englishman by 54 points to 50.

This was one year before the first official championship of the United States, at Newport, Rhode Island, in 1881. This followed the formation of the United States (National) Lawn Tennis Association some months before, predating its British counterpart by some seven years. Whether because of Woodhouse or not the US Championships between 1881 and 1885 were restricted to American citizens. When Richard Sears, who dominated the US meeting every year to 1887, won in 1881 he played another Englishman, J. J. Cairnes, for a special trophy. Cairnes, about whom nothing appears to be known, was the winner.

The first task of the USLTA, the doyen of all national associations, was to standardize the rules. They adopted those of the All England Club *in toto*.

Australia took readily to lawn tennis and it quickly put out its roots as an organized sport there. The oldest of the state championships, those of Victoria, were first held in 1880. New South Wales followed in 1885, Queensland in 1890, South Australia in 1890, Tasmania in 1893 and Western Australia in 1895. The first Australian national championships had to wait for the creation of Australia as a nation in 1905. The first lawn-tennis club in New Zealand is believed to have been formed as early as 1875. The first national championships were staged 11 years later in 1886.

By the early 1880s the game had spread round the world. It was played in Panama in 1878. In 1881 there was a tournament in Durban. The South African championships as such go back to 1891. A French writer affirms that in 1881 a tournament was staged on the summit of Mount Olympus. When grass was not available courts were constructed on varying surfaces, gravel, concrete, asphalt, clay, sand and brick dust. A basalt court built in Australia in 1881 was declared entirely satisfactory.

British players introduced the game to France, in particular to the resorts, to Dinard, Le Touquet and the Riviera. The first club in France was the Decimal Club, founded in Paris in 1877. The Racing Club, founded in 1882, organized the first international championship in France in 1889. The French national championships were instituted in 1891 but confined until 1925 to French citizens. The championships of Germany began in 1893.

As a pastime one of the social delights of lawn tennis was the ability of men and women to play together. As an organized sport it put women into a less important role not only because of the basic disparity of standard between the sexes but also because of the restriction of women's clothing. The overhead service did not become a commonplace among women until after World War I.

The Irish pioneered championship lawn tennis for women in 1879, staging both a singles and mixed event, though not a women's doubles. Wimbledon brought women in for the first time in 1884, though it was not until the turn of the century or thereabouts that the event can be said to have flourished. There were 13 entrants for the women's singles in 1884, 16 the following year but entries grew fewer until there were only four in 1890.

There was perhaps more militancy by women in lawn tennis in the United States. The USLTA was asked in 1888 to authorize a women's championship. It responded frostily that it had no power to do so. This fear of acting *ultra vires* vanished within the next 12 months. Its protecting wing was extended to women and the championships given to the Philadelphia Cricket Club.

This was no more than the recognition of a *fait accompli*. The club organized the first women's championship in 1887. No one would underestimate the pioneers of women's lawn tennis. Not until 1902 was the women's singles in the US Nationals reduced from the best of five sets to the best of three. At Wimbledon women played the best of three from the start, though in other British tournaments in the 1880s best-of-five-set matches were quite often played.

The first recorded international match took place in 1883 when the American brothers C. M. and J. S. Clark got the consent of the American doubles champions, James Dwight and Richard Sears, with whom they were on fairly level terms, to act as a representative national side. At Wimbledon on 18 and 23 July they played against the famous British twins, William and Ernest Renshaw.

British superiority, first shown by Woodhouse in 1880, was vindicated. The Renshaws won the first match 6-4, 8-6, 3-6, 6-1, the second by 6-3, 6-2, 6-3, better in strokes and strategy. The Renshaws played two up or two back, the Clark brothers one up and one back but they immediately adopted the British tactics on their return.

Dwight and Sears were the first Americans to play in the Wimbledon Championships. They did so in 1884. Five years later in 1889 E. G. Meers, one of the top ten men in Britain, was the first Englishman to play in the official American championship meeting. There was an increasing interchange of players thereafter and the national rivalry in due course led to the inauguration of the DAVIS CUP competition in 1900 (see PART 2).

Belgium began its national championships in 1895, Switzerland in 1898. A championship of Europe, staged at different venues in different countries, was started in 1899 and continued until after World War I. Portugal inaugurated its championships in 1900, encouraged no doubt by King Carlos II who was famous as a zealot for lawn tennis. When the first of the modern Olympics were held in Athens in 1896 lawn tennis was one of the sports and it held its place until 1924 (see OLYMPIC GAMES, PART 2).

By 1913 lawn tennis was so international in its character that its administrative imperfections were apparent. On the one hand there was the USLTA, the senior national organization founded in 1881. The (British) LTA was formed in 1888, taking over the administration of the British game from the All England Club and its joint committee with other clubs. But, evidently more by accident than design, the (British) LTA found itself in charge of most of the game round the world, the United States excepted.

No fewer than 24 nations were represented on the (British) LTA by 1913, sometimes as national associations as such and sometimes by clubs in foreign countries that lacked associations of their own. A representative from the Ealing Lawn Tennis Club in a London suburb could at the annual general meeting of the LTA expect to find himself with a representative from the Moscow LTC on one side and one from the Athens LTC on the other.

The International Lawn Tennis Federation was founded after a meeting in Paris on 26 October 1912. The first president was Mr R. J. McNair, then chairman of the British

Above, right Mixed doubles at the Club de Dinard, a resort where lawn tennis was popular in its early days
Below, right The 1899 Swiss Championships at St Moritz

Above The Crown Prince of Sweden (later King Gustaf V), on the far side of the net, playing in a mixed double at Särö
Right Mrs Atkins (Miss H. Jackson), Scottish Ladies' Singles Champion 1890-2, and A. W. Gore, Scottish Men's Singles Champion 1892-3, playing at Dyvours, Edinburgh, in 1892. Gore was an outstanding baseliner who competed at Wimbledon every year from 1888 to 1927, winning the singles title three times, 1901, 1908-9.

LTA. Its first annual general meeting was held in March 1913 and the founder members, numbering 12, were Australasia, Austria, Belgium, the British Isles, Denmark, France, Germany, Holland, Russia, South Africa, Sweden and Switzerland (see ADMINISTRATION OF THE WORLD GAME).

The absence of the United States was notable, the more so since the original idea of the Federation was mooted by an American, Douane Williams, in 1911. He did so, though, as secretary of the Swiss national association. The United States did not join until after World War I.

Not only the creation of a world governing body reflected the international character of lawn tennis by 1914. By then, an Australian, Norman Brookes, and a New Zealander, Anthony Wilding, had made themselves Wimbledon singles champions, an American, May Sutton (1905 and 1907), was twice holder of the women's singles title. Frenchmen, Max Decugis and A. H. Gobert, had taken the Wimbledon doubles. An Englishman, Laurie Doherty, had (1903) won in the United States. An Irishman, J. C. Parke, had (1912) taken the Australian title. There were English, Irish, American and French names on the roll of German champions.

The first international seeds were sown long before. In 1858 when Major Gem marked out his court in Edgbaston he did so with Mr Perera, who was Portuguese.

The Growth of the Game, 1919-1939
Lance Tingay

World War I had small effect on the growth of lawn tennis. Most of the leading championships were in full swing in 1919 and it is noteworthy that the Paris peace conference was the occasion of an inter-Allies tournament at St Cloud. Even defeated Germany resumed its championships in 1920, a year when the number of tournaments in England and Wales was 111. In 1913 there had been 78.

Only in Russia did the game die. There had been international championships in St Petersburg in the immediate pre-war years and, indeed, the last women's singles champion of Imperial Russia (1914) was the American Elizabeth Ryan. Even in the worst hardships of the post-revolutionary period there was enough personal enthusiasm to stage an unofficial championship in Georgia, violin strings being used to replace the worn-out gut of old rackets. Vladimir Landau, who later settled in Monte Carlo, was the sole Russian champion of the period between the world wars, for the communist régime did not favour a game that had aristocratic rather than proletarian echoes. Only after World War II did the USSR bring back lawn tennis to Russian soil.

The most striking example of the quick revival of the game was the success of the Wimbledon Championships in 1919. Inevitably in a sport so individualistic there had been a cult of personality. This, immediately before World War I, was typified by the popularity of the New Zealander Tony Wilding, who did not survive the conflict. In the decade covering the turn of the century there had been the Doherty brothers, Laurie and Reggie. Before that there were the Renshaw twins, Willie and Ernest, who laid the foundation of the technique of the modern game. All combined high skill with richness of personality.

Right R. Lycett and R. W. Heath playing F. M. B. Fisher and M. J. G. Ritchie in the fifth round of the 1919 Wimbledon Championships. Lycett and Heath won 12-10, 8-6, 6-3, but were defeated by R. V. Thomas and P. O'Hara Wood in the final.

But no player had combined such high skill and so rich a personality as the French-woman Suzanne Lenglen, whose promise as a prodigious 15-year-old in 1914 had had to wait for its fulfilment. She began her unique seven-year spell of invincibility by winning Wimbledon against the defence of the old champion Dorothea Lambert Chambers in one of the most dramatic and exciting finals ever staged in the world's premier tournament (see CENTRE COURT CLASSICS).

The unmatched skill and magnetic appeal of Mlle Lenglen was the key factor in transforming lawn tennis from a participant into a spectator sport. The All England Club, still on its original site in Worple Road, had not stands enough to hold the crowds. The old garden-party had gone for good.

The following year another personality added to what for Wimbledon had become an embarrassment of riches. This was the American William Tatem Tilden, who won Wimbledon in 1920 and successfully defended in 1921. All-time ranking lists are inevitably a matter of opinion rather than proof but few such rolls have been compiled without Tilden joining Mlle Lenglen as the best players of any period.

The All England Club had clearly outgrown itself. In 1922 it moved to a new site in Church Road, Wimbledon, financed mainly by an issue of £50 debentures which paid no dividend but entitled the holder to seats behind the Royal Box on the Centre Court for each day of the Championships. The new ground had as its focal point stands which accommodated about 11,000 spectators with further capacity for 3,000 standing. Ambitious as it seemed at the time it proved to be an underestimate. Wimbledon's Court One, almost as famous as the Centre Court it adjoins, was originally laid as a hard court for use in events other than the Championships.

Wimbledon modernized itself in other ways. With the change of ground the old Challenge Round system of playing the singles events was abolished, the holder being required to play through. Apart from the DAVIS CUP (which did not abandon the Challenge Round until 1972) this link with a 19th-century conception of sport had lingered at Wimbledon long after it had died elsewhere.

Not only at Wimbledon did increasing crowds reflect the growth of popular interest. The West Side Club at Forest Hills, New York, opened its Stadium Court in 1923, its capacity, about 17,000, being more than the Centre Court at Wimbledon. A few years later the French followed suit. The vast concrete arena of the Stade Roland Garros at Auteuil, on the south-west edge of Paris, was opened to stage the French defence of the Davis Cup in 1928.

If Tilden and Mlle Lenglen were the catalysts by which lawn tennis transformed itself they also marked the beginnings of another aspect of the sport inseparable from its popularity, the eroding of strict amateur standards. Before 1914 shining-white amateurism was not sullied. What benefits the Dohertys, for instance, got from the game comprised no more than invitation to the best house parties, a special tea tent reserved for them. Around 1910 the (British) LTA seriously considered suspending a player who, hard up and hungry, had exchanged prize vouchers for food. A few years before, a party of leading British players met with criticism for accepting the hospitality of the King of Portugal.

It seems certain that both Tilden and Mlle Lenglen benefited financially by their appeal and prowess. But discretion was great and, indeed, throughout the inter-war period lip service to the ideals of amateurism was universal, even if by the 1930s there was growing cynicism as to how some leading players maintained themselves without visible means of support. The floodgates were not to open until the post-1946 era. The division between amateurs and professionals remained sharp.

Mlle Lenglen became a professional in 1926 and Tilden some years later. Their change of status transformed the professional game, bringing in a race of professional players as distinct from coaches. It was an accelerating process. Of the Wimbledon champions between 1919 and 1930 only Tilden and Henri Cochet became professionals. Between 1931 and 1939 four champions, Ellsworth Vines, Fred Perry, Don Budge and Bobby Riggs changed their status.

Some of the paths along which lawn tennis in the early 1920s developed proved to

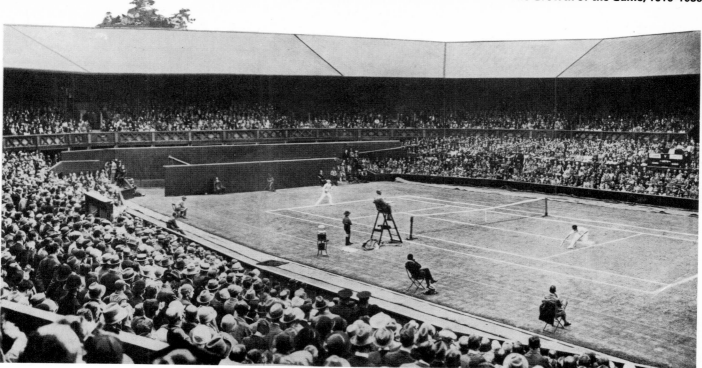

Above The Centre Court at the New Wimbledon. In this final (1925), René Lacoste (left) reversed the 1924 result by defeating Jean Borotra (with the beret) 6-3, 6-3, 4-6, 8-6. This photograph aptly illustrates Borotra's love of the forecourt.

be blind alleys. The most notable was the series of world championships sanctioned by the ILTF on its formation in 1913. Three such titles were awarded, for grass, for hard courts and for covered courts.

The World's Hard Court Championships were first staged in 1912 in Paris, switching for just one year to Brussels in 1922. The World's Grass Court Championships was the title awarded to Wimbledon, starting in 1913. Apart from the grandiose title the only change it meant was the inauguration of women's doubles and mixed doubles events which had not hitherto been consistently held.

The World's Covered Court Championships changed their venue from year to year. Stockholm had them in 1913, Paris in 1919. Queen's Club staged the event in 1920, not as a new event but as an added title to the London Covered Court meeting. They were in Copenhagen in 1921, at St Moritz in 1922 and at Barcelona in 1923.

It became obvious that high-sounding titles are not in themselves enough to create tournaments. Wimbledon, of course, was Wimbledon and the added title meant little. Only the Hard Court tournament justified itself and it is noteworthy that Mlle Lenglen won the women's singles four times out of its seven years, including 1914. But the Covered Court event never rose above European status.

The demise of the World Championships after 1923 was, however, brought about by the attitude of the United States. In lawn tennis as in politics in those days it was rather isolationist and in any case jealous of the reputation of the American Championship *vis-à-vis* their counterparts elsewhere. It had remained outside the ILTF on its formation. The abandonment of the title of World Championships was the tacit *quid pro quo* for the United States joining the international governing body.

Lawn tennis featured as one of the sports in the OLYMPIC GAMES (see PART 2) from 1896. Whether the Games themselves benefited much by the inclusion is hard to assess. The prestige of lawn tennis in the Olympics fell short of that created elsewhere. By 1924 there was dispute between the ILTF and the International Olympic Committee over the definition of amateurism. Lawn tennis ceased to be an Olympic sport thereafter.

Another resounding title in the inter-war period was the Championship of Europe. Men's singles and doubles were the events, the singles first being staged at Bad Homburg in Germany in 1899. The tournament was peripatetic. Belgium, France, Holland,

Above Jean Borotra, the 'Bounding Basque'
Right Henri Cochet (playing the shot) and
Jacques (Toto) Brugnon in a men's doubles
final at Wimbledon

Sweden and Ireland all held it in one year or another. Dublin held it in 1907, New-castle in 1909, Scarborough in 1913. Its fading echoes were heard where it began, in Bad Homburg and as late as 1930 and 1932.

The oddest of the fine-sounding titles occupies little space in the records. This was the All England Married Couples Championship played, apparently, for just the one year at Nottingham in 1923. The winners were Mr and Mrs F. T. Walker.

Women's lawn tennis obtained recognition of its growing popularity with the institution in 1923 of the WIGHTMAN CUP (see PART 2), the trophy donated by Hazel Wightman, winner of many US national championships. Like the Davis Cup it originated as a team contest between Great Britain and the United States. Unlike the Davis Cup it never grew beyond this restriction, though in the first instance it was visualized as at least a three-part contest with France participating. Staged annually in alternate countries, it was first held as the inaugural match for the new West Side Club stadium at Forest Hills. In both the period under review and later the contest pinpointed the superiority of American women's standards over the British. Between the wars Great Britain won the Wightman Cup only four times, in 1924, 1925, 1928 and 1930. As a spur and fulfilment of ambition for women players of both nationalities it proved invaluable.

A major impetus was given to the game round the world when France, after knocking on the door with increasing loudness for some years, won the Davis Cup in 1927. Hitherto only Great Britain, the United States and Australia had been victors. It was the first success for a hard-court as distinct from a grass-court nation. Here again the cult of personality stirred the popular imagination for the Davis Cup triumph represented the peak of success for the four Frenchmen inevitably known as the Four Musketeers, Jacques Brugnon, Henri Cochet, Jean Borotra and René Lacoste, all quite different in technique and style of play; Lacoste was the last great player to be a baseliner pure and simple.

Participation in the Davis Cup had in any case been rising steadily, from five nations in 1919 to 26 in 1927. In 1928 the figure rose to 33, which proved to be the peak of the inter-war period.

A booming game in France was reflected when in 1925 the French Championships were thrown open as an international championship for all comers. Hitherto it had been restricted to French nationals and there had been little incentive to make it open while Paris staged the World's Hard Court Championships. In effect, if not in name, the French meeting became the world hard-court championship, a status

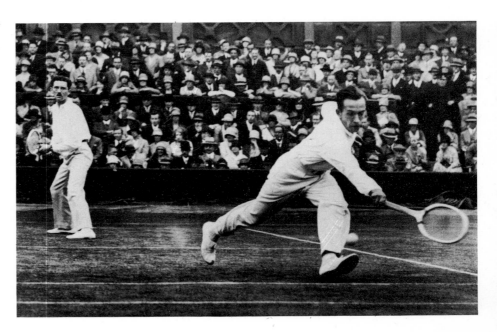

Above René Lacoste
Below The Duke of York (later King George VI) playing in the 1926 Wimbledon Championships. His partner in the men's doubles was Wing Commander Louis Greig (later Sir Louis Greig and Chairman of the All England Club, 1934-53); they were defeated in the first round.

maintained over the years. For the first three years the event was staged at its old venue, the Racing Club at St Cloud, but it moved to the Stade Roland Garros at Auteuil in 1928.

The high status of the French Championships was reflected in its winners. While one or the other of the musketeers, Lacoste, Cochet or Borotra, carried off the men's singles up to 1932 (and they did the same at Wimbledon from 1924 to 1929) an Australian, Jack Crawford, an Englishman, Fred Perry, two Germans, Gottfried von Cramm and Henner Henkel, and two Americans, Don Budge and Donald McNeill, did so afterwards.

On the French Riviera the game escalated. It had become a major lawn-tennis centre at the turn of the century, mainly because of British players. After 1919 the Riviera tournament season, extending over the first three months of the year, became increasingly international. Mlle Lenglen, born in Compiègne in the north of France, made her home in Nice. Its Avenue Suzanne Lenglen commemorates that fact. The year 1926 perhaps marked the peak of high international competition, for that was when Mlle Lenglen played her only match against the up-and-coming young American Helen Wills, a clash that brought worldwide interest. The season on the Riviera was bustling and crowded. In 1926, for instance, there were three tournaments staged in Monte Carlo and three in Nice. Cannes had as many as seven at five different clubs.

What was to become an important tournament, the Italian Championships, began in Milan in 1930. Tilden was the first winner. Political events obtruded here more than elsewhere, for the onset of the war between Italy and Abyssinia brought its cessation after 1935.

The rising standards of the game around the world were reflected in the growing diversity of nationality recorded in the lists of the world's top ten players from year to year. Japan got a rating in 1920 with Z. Shimizu, Spain with Manuel Alonso in 1921. Jean Washer was the first Belgian to get such status, in 1923. Jan Koželuh appeared for Czechoslovakia in 1927, Baron U. L. de'Morpurgo for Italy in 1928. The first South American was a woman, Anita Lizana of Chile, in 1938.

Scandinavia and Sweden in particular had royal enthusiasm to feed lawn tennis. One of the most diligent Riviera competitors was Mr G., the pseudonym of King Gustaf V of Sweden, whose favourite event was a mixed doubles with a good partner, often Mlle Lenglen. His trophies fill a glass showcase at the leading club in Stockholm. Two important events were initiated by Sweden in 1936. Both, not surprisingly in view of the restricted outdoor season, were indoor fixtures. The first, the SCANDINAVIAN (covered-court) CHAMPIONSHIPS (see PART 2) were shared between all four countries, moving from year to year between Stockholm, Copenhagen, Oslo and Helsinki. The second was the King of Sweden's Cup, normally known as the KING'S CUP (see PART 2) and the equivalent on covered courts to the Davis Cup. It has necessarily had mainly a European interest but is open to challenge from any nation.

The ILTF, numbering 12 associations at its formation in 1913, had 33 nations represented when it met in 1935. In that year the number of clubs affiliated to the British LTA exceeded 2,500 for the first time. In Britain the major growth of the game had been on hard courts. The BRITISH HARD COURT CHAMPIONSHIPS (see PART 2) were inaugurated at Torquay in 1924, moving to Bournemouth in 1927.

By the 1930s four championships had become well defined as the outstanding tournaments, those of Wimbledon, the United States, France and Australia, all on grass except for France. The first man to win the singles in all of the four was the Briton Fred Perry, a feat achieved when, having been US champion in 1933 and 1934, Australian and Wimbledon champion in 1934 also, he won the French title in 1935.

The GRAND SLAM (see PART 2), the winning of all these titles in the one year, was first achieved by the American Donald Budge in 1938. The feat was more than an outstanding sporting achievement. It symbolized lawn tennis as a world game. The singles last eight at Wimbledon can be taken as representative of the aristocrats of the game. In that year, among both men and women, there were Americans, Czechs, Yugoslavs, Britons, Germans, Swiss, French and Poles.

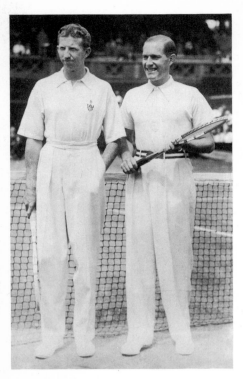

Lawn tennis was a faster game in 1939 than in 1919. The stitchless ball came into use about 1924, making for rather more pace and reducing the effect of spin. Around 1931 the pressure inside the ball was increased, again making for more speed of shot.

Experiments with new types of rackets did not get far. A British player, F. W. Donnisthorpe, built himself a racket of enormous size in the 1920s, claiming an enhanced quality of volleying. It remained a freak. Entirely metal rackets, both frame and strings, were made. They too had scant success.

Basically the game did not much change in technique. There were fine volleyers, fine half-volleyers, stupendous smashers before 1914 and the Californian Maurice McLoughlin exploited a cannonball service. But the emphasis changed to more and more play from the net. Lacoste was the last great champion to play entirely from the back on the theory that the groundstroke could always beat the volley. His fellow French musketeer, Borotra, was the apostle of the serve-volley technique to a degree not seen before. But he and all other players assumed that such tactics were impossible to sustain over a long match without respite, because of the physical demands.

The greater transformation was in women's technique. For a woman to serve overhead in 1919 was, if not a novelty, not all that common. By 1939 no first-class player did anything else. Mlle Lenglen had amazed spectators by her acrobatic exploits and her ability to volley and smash. But the heart of her skill was in her superb control from the ground. So it was with her successor as the world's outstanding woman player, the American Helen Wills Moody.

The first woman to adopt the masculine technique of the ruthless serve-volley aggression was the American Alice Marble, the triple champion at Wimbledon in 1939. Except that less muscle power meant less speed and less weight of shot she did all that a man could do. It was her example that set the pattern for the women's game after World War II.

Above Donald Budge (left) and Gottfried von Cramm (right) in 1937, the year that Budge beat von Cramm 6-3, 6-4, 6-2 to win the Wimbledon singles title
Below King Gustaf V of Sweden ('Mr G'), second from the left, and Prince Chichibu, second son of the Emperor of Japan (third from left) at Nice in 1926

Postwar Development, 1946–1967
Lance Tingay

After the end of World War II the capacity of lawn tennis to pick itself up where it left off in 1939 varied from nation to nation. The least affected was the United States where the national championships had continued without a break. The heat of wartime passion was reflected at the first postwar meeting of the ILTF in 1946, when Bulgaria, Finland, Germany, Hungary, Italy, Japan, Libya, Rumania and Thailand were expelled. In the same year Jean Borotra was refused entry to the Wimbledon Championships because he had been Minister of Sport under the Vichy government of France, although in fact he had been subsequently imprisoned by the Nazi authorities. Public opinion soon came round to the view that the decision had been over-hasty. The cohesive forces of lawn tennis as a world game soon made themselves felt. Finland, Hungary, Italy and Rumania were readmitted to the Federation as early as 1947. Germany and Japan came back in 1950 and entered the Davis Cup again in 1951.

The Davis Cup provides a barometer for measuring the growth of the international game. In 1946, 21 nations played. In 1963 there were 49. By 1939 the number of nations that had taken part was 41. By 1967 the number was 62. Not the least significant newcomer was the USSR in 1962. The USSR came into the ILTF in 1956, though it was not strictly a newcomer since Imperial Russia had been a founder member, and the first participation of Russian players overseas was at the Wimbledon Championships in 1959.

In the immediate postwar years the standard of performance was set by American players, with Australians not far behind. Apart from 1946 every men's singles champion at Wimbledon up to 1952 was American. The US women's standard was unrivalled, so much so that from 1946 to 1955 only one non-American became a singles semi-finalist at that meeting which, without obvious effort, resumed its status as the premier individual tournament of the game.

The nations that crowded into the Davis Cup competition did so well aware that their teams would be outclassed long before they arrived in any of the later rounds, for the diversity of standards inevitably broadened. There were four occasions before 1939 when a Davis Cup rubber was resolved by a score of 6-0, 6-0, 6-0. Between 1955 and 1967 eight rubbers came to an end with a similarly devastating whitewash.

Below In the first 1952 Davis Cup Inter-Zone Final at Brisbane, Italy beat India by 3 matches to 2. Italy (G. Cucelli, nearer the net, and M. del Bello) are on the far side of the net, in play against India, S. Misra (left) and N. Kumar.

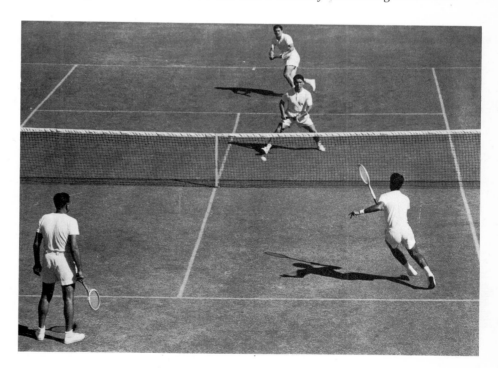

In the 1950s and 1960s tennis was booming in Australia. Lew Hoad and Ken Rosewall played Mervyn Rose and Rex Hartwig in the 1953 Wimbledon doubles final. Hoad, left, and Rosewall (far side of the net) defeated the left-handed Rose and Hartwig 6-4, 7-5, 4-6, 7-5.

The challenge round of the Davis Cup became the preserve of the United States and Australia. This stranglehold was not broken until 1960 when Italy came through to challenge Australia, albeit with scant success. Between 1946 and 1959 the Davis Cup, at the top level, was exclusively an Australian–American contest.

Australia stopped American domination by winning the Davis Cup in 1950. The Australian Frank Sedgman won the Wimbledon singles in 1952. These successes reflected rising Australian standards. These in turn reflected a booming Australian game, not only in the number of highly skilled participants but in spectator interest. The peak year, perhaps, for public interest in the game was 1954 when the Challenge Round of the Davis Cup at the White City, Sydney, brought a capacity crowd (25,568) for each of the three days.

From this sporting climate emerged some of the finest players the game has known, Lew Hoad, Ken Rosewall and later Rod Laver. Towards the end of the period under review Australian enthusiasm began to fall off somewhat, though this was not until the Australian women's game had risen to heights not before achieved, led by Margaret Smith (Court), who won major titles in numbers earlier reckoned impossible.

The influence of Australia on the game at large can hardly be overestimated. There was a new approach to the acquisition of high skill under the direction of Harry Hopman, for many years the Australian Davis Cup Captain and training manager. His insistence on the most rigorous training methods, work in the gymnasium, long road runs and the like was obviously successful. He transformed the top lawn-tennis player from a talented hitter of a ball to a finely tuned athlete able to extend his physical capacity to limits not before achieved.

Lawn tennis cannot be measured in the same way as athletics; there are no barriers to be passed comparable to the four-minute mile. But before 1939 the assumption was that it was physically impossible to sustain the demands of serve-and-volley tactics for the duration of a five-set match. By the time Roy Emerson won his first Wimbledon singles title in 1964 they were taken for granted by every male player who presumed to be of world-class standard.

Right Vic Seixas (left) and Tony Trabert, who lost to Rex Hartwig and Mervyn Rose in 1954. The winners' score was 6-4, 6-4, 3-6, 6-4.

Increasing specialization at lawn tennis demanded by higher standards inevitably brought growing professionalism. The technical status of all Australian Davis Cup sides, for instance, between 1946 and 1967 was amateur. But no player could have sustained his place at that level of the game without adopting a professional approach and making it a full-time activity.

For many years, until 1968 in fact, the traditional amateur-professional distinction was maintained in lawn tennis. In the early postwar years the division worked happily enough, just as it did before 1939. The status of the leading playing professional was clear-cut. After developing skill and fame in the amateur events he signed a contract with a professional promoter, getting the security of a guarantee. Madison Square Garden in New York became the leading venue for notable professional matches and tournaments in the United States. The Empire Pool and Sports Arena at Wembley was its equivalent in London.

In the ten years 1946 to 1955 there were 17 men who won the singles titles of France, Wimbledon and the United States. Of these outstanding players ten maintained their amateur status and the remainder left the discipline of the ILTF-controlled game for professional security. They were Yvon Petra, Jack Kramer, Frank Sedgman, Ricardo Gonzalez, Frank Parker, Ken Rosewall and Tony Trabert.

The amateur game, though the loss was regretted, thrived exceedingly nonetheless. There was no diminution. On the contrary, the enthusiasm of the smaller nations was made evident by the expanding Davis Cup and elsewhere by the growing repute of national championships. The German meeting in Hamburg, for instance, was resumed in 1948 and by 1960 had grown to high international status. So, too, with the Italian meeting which resumed in Rome in 1950. The South African Championships were also built into an event of world importance.

Another striking aspect of postwar development was the growth of the junior game, generally by positive effort on the part of national associations anxious to improve its playing standards at the adult level. By 1958, for instance, it could be held as a re-markable feat that the American Earl Buchholz achieved the Grand Slam of junior

Above Maureen Connolly (right) after defeating Louise Brough (left) 7-5, 6-3, to win her first Wimbledon title in 1952. She retained it in 1953 and 1954, a unique record of winning all three Wimbledons at which she competed.

Colour plates
Open Tennis. A general view of the 1972 Commercial Union Masters Tournament in Barcelona. In this semi-final, Ilie Năstase defeated Jimmy Connors, 6-1, 6-3, 6-2.
Overleaf **The Origins of Lawn Tennis.** Tennis on an outdoor court forms one of the pastimes at the king's court in this 16th-century representation of the Biblical story of David and Bathsheba. Note the black walls of the court, against which the white ball shows up well.

championships, for he took the junior titles of Australia, France and the United States and won Junior Wimbledon.

The emphasis on junior development was worldwide but stressed most in Great Britain, probably because the financial resources of its national association were better than most countries. The BRITISH JUNIOR CHAMPIONSHIPS (see PART 2) began in a humble way in Ventnor, Isle of Wight, as far back as 1908. In 1909 the entry for the girls' singles was four. In the late 1950s the interest in the exploits of Christine Truman was such as to merit nationwide television coverage.

Junior interest spilled over to international level. With French initiative the GALEA CUP competition (see PART 2) was founded in 1950. A similar competition for girls, the ANNIE SOISBAULT CUP (see PART 2) was started in 1965.

In the women's game it was many years before the very high standard of the leading Americans met with serious challenge from elsewhere. Pauline Betz, Margaret Osborne, Louise Brough and Doris Hart had virtually unchallenged supremacy until the advent of an even finer American player, Maureen Connolly. In 1953 she emulated the 1938 feat of Don Budge by winning the Grand Slam. Her virtual invincibility was founded on groundstroke, not volley, skill.

Miss Connolly had to retire in 1954 after breaking a leg and she died tragically early (1969). She was almost certainly one of the greatest women players of all time, ranking alongside Suzanne Lenglen and Helen Wills Moody. In the context of the world game, though, she emphasized American superiority. Between 1946 and 1958 the American and Wimbledon women's singles championship rolls contain none but American names.

In 1958 an 18-year-old Brazilian, Maria Bueno, ventured overseas for the first time and won the Italian championship in Rome. Her subsequent career made women players round the world realize that they were not barred from top success by not being American. Apart from her achievements – Wimbledon champion in 1959, 1960 and 1964, US champion in 1959, 1963, 1964, and 1966 – she had personality and magnetic appeal to make the women's events rival those of the men whenever she appeared. Her grace and style, her imperious demeanour, were in the line of Mlle Lenglen, though she never approached that French player's invincibility on the court.

In 1961 the Australian Margaret Smith began her uniquely successful career. Her rivalry with Miss Bueno – and she had much the better of it – provided a *motif* for world lawn tennis for the next decade and raised interest in the women's game to something approaching the level of the men's.

In 1963 the women's game received a recognition it probably had long deserved. To mark the 50th anniversary of the founding of the ILTF, the FEDERATION CUP (see PART 2) was founded, the equivalent for women of the Davis Cup for men. The first competition, at the Queen's Club just before the Wimbledon Championships and coincidental with the London title meeting, was not particularly successful. Later ones were and the Federation Cup became a major event of the international calendar.

With the start of the Federation Cup there were fears in both the United States and Great Britain that the prestige of the Wightman Cup would diminish. This did not prove to be the case. In both countries Wightman Cup rather than Federation Cup status remained the ambition of every keen player.

In financial terms the Federation Cup was unlikely to be, and was not, self-sustaining. In this it differed from the Davis Cup, where each tie between nations is staged as an event on its own and where the finances are organized to make prosperous ties support those that are not. Sponsorship soon became a prerequisite for the promotion of the competition, with working practice lagging behind the original rules laid down.

If finance became a factor in the Federation Cup it did no more than follow the postwar pattern of the game. The term 'shamateurism' first came into use some time in the inter-war period. The problems of enforcing a code of amateurism bedevilled the administration of the game from 1946 onwards to an increasing degree. The widening popularity of the game, its ever-rising standards of play, its sustained growth into all parts of the world made for the difficulties.

DAVID·CVI·RA[?]
SABIA·[?]V[?]I·I[?]
COR·S[?]G·V[?]II·I[?]
AB·HOSTIBVS
OCCIDEDVM·IN
PRÆLIV·MI[?]·[?]
ANNO·15[?]·[?]

It was still possible in 1949 for the Californian Ted Schroeder to come over to Wimbledon and win at his first and only attempt, to come from nowhere to represent the United States in the Davis Cup and generally to achieve great success like an amateur genius of old. Schroeder was in any case a genius of improvisation so far as his match winning was concerned.

For most the top standards in the game demanded full-time specialization and the adoption of lawn tennis as a full-time career. Old-time amateurism was increasingly eroded. Between 1946 and 1967 the amateur administrators tried in vain to create rules of amateurism that were realistic, mainly by restricting the time in a year when expenses could be given to amateur players.

In the meantime while 'expenses' given to leading players became larger and larger, so much so that the term universally came to mean payment by another name, the owedly professional game added increasingly to its recruits. Lew Hoad, Ken Rosewall and Rod Laver were among the distinguished players who opted for the richer rewards and greater security of a promoter's contract. Rosewall became a professional after winning the American singles in 1956, Hoad some months later in 1957 after winning Wimbledon for the second time. Laver changed his status after the most spectacular career in the history of the game in 1962, when he not only won the GRAND SLAM (see PART 2) but took the Italian and German titles as well.

By 1960, if not before, two aspects of lawn tennis were crying for reform. The tradition of the old-established tournaments, Wimbledon, the US National, the French Championships meeting and the like, demanded that the best players, irrespective of status, should compete in them. At the same time the absurdity of the definition 'amateur', a pure technicality implying no more than the acceptance of the discipline of the ILTF, became manifest.

The reform, when it did come, was from pressure by what had long been regarded as the mainspring of conservatism, the All England Club and the British LTA. As early as 1960 Great Britain, with support from France, Australia and the United States, proposed at the annual meeting of the ILTF that the leading championships should be 'open' to professionals. The proposal failed to meet the necessary two-thirds majority by five votes.

In 1964 the All England Club urged the LTA to make Wimbledon open despite ILTF rules. A motion to this effect was defeated only with difficulty at the Annual Meeting of the British governing body that year.

Within the ILTF opposition to reform tended to harden rather than relax. The change when it did come was brought about by an overt revolution by one of its oldest and most respected members, Great Britain. The catalyst which forced a one-time conservative association to act in defiance of a constitution it had played a leading part in creating was a complaint by the Austrian authorities in the summer of 1967. They asked the British LTA to discipline the leading British player, Roger Taylor, for not fulfilling the terms of a contract they alleged he had made with them. This for many leading British LTA members was the last straw, being asked to sit in judgment on an amateur player who had, supposedly, torn up one contract for payment in favour of one with better terms.

In due time the leading LTA members decided that the only realistic course was to recognize the *de facto* situation of professionalism by abolishing all distinction between amateurs and professionals. A motion to this effect was approved at the annual LTA meeting in December in defiance of the rules of the world's governing body. Inevitably the power of the international authority proved no stronger than that of one of its most important members. A few months later, early in 1968, ILTF rules were amended so as to allow all member nations freedom to adopt any code they liked. Thus ended after 90 years (if 1877 be taken as the starting point) the amateur-professional distinction in lawn tennis. In turn it raised problems of its own but at least the shadow of moral obloquy had been lifted.

The major aspect of the growth in the game after 1946 was in its international character. The ease and speed of air travel meant that leading exponents had the whole

Colour Plate
The United States Story. A general view of Forest Hills, New York

Right Jaroslav Drobný, an outstanding hard-court player. His prime success at Wimbledon came in 1954 when he beat Ken Rosewall 13-11, 4-6, 6-2, 9-7.

world as their parish. Budge Patty (Wimbledon champion in 1950 and French champion the same year) and Jaroslav Drobný (Wimbledon champion 1954, French champion 1951, 1952) were outstanding examples. It meant a lawn tennis season extending over virtually the whole year.

The division between amateurs and professionals at the top level became increasingly unsatisfactory in the number of outstanding players who, because of their status, were barred from the leading championships. A striking example was the American Ricardo (Pancho) Gonzalez, who became a professional after winning the US championship for the second year in 1949 before developing his highest skill. There can be no doubt that his calibre as a player merited his ranking among the finest performers of all time but his rare skill was displayed mainly in exhibition matches or in professional events lacking the tradition and prestige of the established 'amateur' tournaments.

The base of the amateur game broadened. In the 1930s the four most important tournaments were the championships of Wimbledon, the United States, Australia and France, all but the last being grass-court events. By the late 1960s the championships of Italy, Germany and South Africa, all hard-court tournaments, had risen in status at least to that of Australia. The importance of the Riviera circuit of tournaments declined and South African and Caribbean tournaments attracted players at its expense.

Grass as a surface maintained its importance mainly because the Wimbledon and US Championships (until 1972) continued to be played on it; most nations, Australia apart, played on a variety of hard courts both in and out of doors. A pressureless ball came into use in the late 1960s but without meeting wide acceptance outside Scandinavia. To some degree metal rackets began to replace wood when it was found possible to overcome the former difficulty of stringing them with natural gut.

By 1967 membership of the ILTF was 85 and lawn tennis ranked as one of the most international of all sports.

The United States Story
Allison Danzig

After World War I lawn tennis in the United States became a major sport, commanding the interest of the public and the attention of the press on a national scale.

The two tennis players generally ranked as the United States' best of all time rose to world ascendancy – William T. Tilden II and Helen Wills. Their exploits on the court, along with the temperamental Tilden's flair for the dramatic and for getting into hot water with the USLTA, put the game in the headlines as seldom before and contributed to its spread in popular appeal around the world.

Through the 1870s (see THE BIRTH AND SPREAD OF LAWN TENNIS) lawn tennis had been confined to the northeastern section of the United States, though the New Orleans Lawn Tennis Club, founded in 1876, claims to be the oldest lawn tennis club in the country. The first tournament of which there is any record – a closed handicap event in which games of 15 points were played as in rackets – was held at Nahant, Mass., in August 1876 and the first open tournament was held at Staten Island in 1880 when an Englishman, O. E. Woodhouse, won it to become unofficially the first Champion of America. There were no established rules of play. The scoring, height of the net, distance of the service line from the net, and the size of the ball varied from place to place.

Chiefly to correct this situation, the United States National Lawn Tennis Association (the 'National' was dropped in 1920) was organized in 1881 at the Fifth Avenue Hotel in New York City, with 34 clubs represented, and the first official championship was conducted that year at the newly built Newport Casino in Rhode Island, the summer watering place of society's '400'. New England, particularly Boston and its environs, was the cradle of the American game even though the first court was put down 200 miles to the south on Staten Island, N.Y. Besides Nahant and Newport, there were the Longwood Cricket Club in Brookline, Mass., where the first Davis Cup matches were

Below Lawn tennis in Prospect Park, Brooklyn, New York, in 1886

held in 1900; Harvard University in Cambridge, Mass., which had courts in 1878, held the first inter-scholastic championship in 1891 and produced the perennial national champions: Dr James Dwight of Boston, president of the USNLTA for 21 years and the first American to play at Wimbledon (1884) and Richard D. Sears of Boston, winner of the championship at Newport from the start in 1881 to 1887.

In these early years lawn tennis was almost exclusively the pastime of the wealthy who could afford the luxury of a private court or were members of a club that converted part of its carefully cultured cricket turf for the new game. By the early 1880s the game was being played in Pennsylvania at the Philadelphia Cricket Club, the venue of the women's championship in 1887; the University of Pennsylvania; the Merion Cricket Club; the Tennis Club of Germantown; and also in Manchester, Mass., Providence, R.I.; in New Jersey at the Orange Lawn Tennis Club, St George's Cricket Club in Hoboken, Newark, Jersey City, Montclair, Plainfield, Short Hills and Englewood; in Connecticut at the Hartford Golf Club, where the first Intercollegiate Championship was held in 1883; the New Haven Lawn Tennis Club and Yale University; in New York State at the Meadow Club, Southampton, New York (City) Tennis Club, Newburgh and Flushing, and in Pittsburgh, Pa.

As early as 1880 the Cincinnati Tennis Club in Ohio was founded (playing on the indoor courts of the city Music Hall), the oldest lawn tennis club west of the Alleghenies and scene of one of the oldest tournaments, the Tri-State Championships. Later in the 1880s the game spread to Chicago in the Middle West and to Atlanta, Ga., in the South; before the 1890s it was being played in the Far West. The Southern Championships were first held in 1886 in New Orleans, La. A year later the Scarlet Ribbon Club of Chicago was authorized by the USNLTA to conduct a tournament for the Championship of the Western States. That same year tennis was being played at the Olympic Tennis Club in Seattle, Wash., four months before Washington entered the Union. In 1896, at the time of the Klondike gold strike, the club became the Seattle Tennis Club.

Above The Staten Island Cricket Club courts in 1880, six years after the Outerbridges (see page 26) first played there. By this time the net was 3 ft 3 in (0·99 m) high, 3 inches (8 cm) higher at the centre than it is today. This photograph points clearly to the rule then in force (changed in 1885) that the server should have one foot on the line when serving.

Right Two leading Eastern players of the early days, Holcombe Ward (left) and Dwight Davis (right), president of the USNLTA and founder of the Davis Cup in 1900. Ward and Davis were doubles partners in the first Davis Cup match, at Longwood, near Boston, where they beat E. D. Black and H. Roper Barrett (British Isles) 6-4, 6-4, 6-4. America won the contest by 3 matches to 0 (one was not played and one was not finished).

Samuel Hardy, famous as a player, Davis Cup captain and editor, was one of the pioneers of Californian lawn tennis with his brother Sumner Hardy. He related that in the late 1880s an itinerant Englishman appeared in his father's California home and introduced the new game to him and his six brothers on the family croquet lawn. A few years earlier, in 1884, the California LTA was organized in San Francisco. In 1889 it was allotted the Pacific Coast sectional championship by the USNLTA and lawn tennis had 'officially crossed the continent'. The championship was played at Del Monte in Northern California. The Southern California Tennis Association championships had started in 1887.

In the 1890s lawn tennis clubs were being organized across the United States – in Nebraska, Minnesota, North Dakota, on the Pacific Coast and in the South, as well as in the East. More and more people of moderate means were playing and the game was taken up by Army and Navy officers. In 1895 there were 106 member clubs in the USNLTA, representing all sections of the country. Tournament tennis was confined largely to college players and others from families of considerable wealth. Professionalism was unknown except for a few teachers. Expense payments were unheard of. The championships were won by collegians, chiefly from Harvard, with Yale, Cornell and Columbia also represented; they were interested in the parties and good times rather than financial gain, even though the Newport Casino was now admitting the public and charging admission to the championships, putting up a portable grandstand obtained from a circus in 1892.

The most skilled players were almost entirely Easterners and the only tournaments of consequence except on the Atlantic seaboard were in Chicago, Minneapolis, Minn., and San Francisco, though Samuel and Sumner Hardy and George Whitney and his brother Robert were establishing reputations in California. Seldom did an Eastern player of rank compete in the Middle West until the National Clay Court Championships began there in 1910. Most Western players found the expense of going East prohibitive, and also they were at a disadvantage on the grass courts of the East, virtually unknown in the West. The award of the National Doubles Championship to Chicago in 1893, held in connection with the World's Fair, was made to boost interest in the game and gave the West the opportunity to see leading players of the country.

In 1899 occurred an event of marked significance in promoting interest in the game in the Far West and ultimately throughout the country and around the world. A group of leading Eastern players from Harvard, including Dwight F. Davis, Malcolm Whitman, Holcombe Ward and Beals Wright and in the charge of George Wright, went to Monterey, Calif., by invitation to engage in an official match with a team from the California Association, Samuel and Sumner Hardy and Robert and George Whitney. So great was the interest in the match that others were arranged in Oregon, Washington and Victoria, British Columbia. The enthusiasm shown at these matches so impressed Davis that he conceived the idea of putting up a cup for international competition between the United States and Great Britain. On his return to Boston he conferred with James Dwight, president of the USNLTA and the 'Father of Lawn Tennis in America', who was keenly in favour, and this led to the start of the DAVIS CUP (see PART 2) competition in 1900 between teams from the British Isles and the United States.

So great was the stimulus of the Davis Cup matches that, whereas in 1900, because of the Spanish-American war and the rise of interest in golf, there were only 44 member clubs in the USNLTA, in 1908 there were 115, and State Championship tournaments were held in all but three States. The Southwest was coming into the picture with one of the game's most honoured figures, Dr Daniel A. Penick of the University of Texas. President Theodore Roosevelt's 'Tennis cabinet', a group of friends with whom he rode, walked and played tennis on the White House courts, helped to make the country tennis-conscious.

With the turn of the century two women players arose in California whose fame was to become international: May Sutton (Mrs Thomas Bundy) and Hazel Hotchkiss (Mrs George Wightman). May Sutton won the US Championship in 1904 at the age of 16, the youngest ever to do so. In 1905 she went back to England, where she had been born, and became the first player from the United States to win the Wimbledon Championship, repeating her success in 1907. Hazel Hotchkiss, daughter of a covered-wagon California pioneer, took up tennis on the one asphalt court in Berkeley at the University of California and developed a mannish-style volleying game that won her the US championship in 1909–11 and 1919. She met George Wightman (later president of the USLTA) on one of her trips East and they were married in 1912. She won 43 national titles but is most famous for the trophy she put up, the WIGHTMAN CUP (see PART 2), inspired by a letter from Suzanne Lenglen of France after her victory in 1919.

In 1909 Maurice McLoughlin came East with Melville Long. Known as the 'California Comet' and 'Red Mac', McLoughlin awakened the American public to the fact that lawn tennis was not a tea party but a red-blooded sport. His match with Norman Brookes of Australia in the 1914 Davis Cup Challenge Round before a vast crowd on the

Below, left May Sutton won the US women's singles titles at the age of 16 and was the first overseas player to win at Wimbledon (1905) when she was 17. She won Wimbledon again in 1907.

Below, right Maurice ('Red Mac') McLoughlin won the US men's singles title in 1913-14. He was the first men's champion from west of the Mississippi and was the first to develop the cannonball service.

new grounds of the West Side Tennis Club in Forest Hills, N.Y., with its record-breaking set of 17-15, received national attention and the game gained stature and won new followers. The financial success of the Challenge Round was a factor in the success of the fight, led by Julian Myrick, Holcombe Ward, Karl Behr and Raymond Little, to move the men's championships from Newport to Forest Hills, a suburb of New York City, in 1915. This was a big step in making the game accessible to the masses. McLoughlin, the first champion from west of the Mississippi, learned tennis on the asphalt public courts of Golden Gate Park in San Francisco; this was another indication of the trend the game was taking.

For the first time now, the treasury of the USNLTA was bulging. At the 1916 annual meeting cash assets were reported as $35,000 and there was a big increase in membership. With its new-found affluence the association created the office of field secretary to handle the many details of the growing organization and assist the officers and committee. Before the United States entered World War I in 1917, the USNLTA started the junior and boys' championships (and the girls' in 1918), the beginning of a program of development of young players that was to be a factor in the supremacy of its men and women for most of the 1920s, late 1930s and 1940s.

To revert to the 1920s and the boom in lawn tennis after World War I, Paul B. Williams, field secretary of the USLTA (no longer the USNLTA), wrote in the 1921 *Guide*:

1920 was the greatest season in the history of American tennis. From Portland, Maine, to Los Angeles and from Palm Beach to Portland, Oregon, led the trail of the rackets criss-crossing through a maze of sectional, state, city and county championships, intersectional matches and a host of lesser tournaments in which many thousands of players took part. It was an All-American season. Without the stimulus of foreign players or of matches with other nations played here, the game advanced tremendously. . .Tennis is spreading so rapidly that there is hardly a town of any size in the United States without some sort of a club.

The ascendancy of the United States as the holder of the Davis Cup 1920–6 and the celebrity of Tilden and Helen Wills, and also of William Johnston, Vincent Richards and Dick Williams, contributed to the great rise in public interest. The world's foremost players, both men and women, were coming to the United States to compete in the national championships and also in such grass-court invitation fixtures as Seabright, Newport and Southampton. The building of the Forest Hills stadium of the

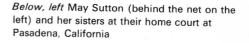

Below, left May Sutton (behind the net on the left) and her sisters at their home court at Pasadena, California

West Side Tennis Club, the largest lawn tennis arena in the world next to Wimbledon, and its opening in 1923 with the first international match for the Wightman Cup, added to the game's stature. That year the USLTA became a member of the ILTF. Up to then, Julian Myrick had led in opposing affiliation because the Federation had awarded to Great Britain perpetually the holding of the world championship on grass.

During Mr Myrick's administration, in 1920, the USLTA changed its constitution to authorize sectional associations. Formerly authority had been exercised on a club basis, each affiliated club having one vote regardless of the number of its members. The West and the Far West were ahead of the East in organizing. The Western and California sections took advantage of their new powers in 1920; the Pacific Northwest and Missouri Associations followed suit in 1921; the New York LTA, the Eastern LTA and the New England LTA were formed a little later and the Southern LTA was virtually recognized as a member in sharing in the distribution of USLTA funds. Today there are 17 sectional associations: the Eastern, New England, Middle States, Middle Atlantic, Southern, Florida, Western, Northwestern, Missouri Valley, Texas, Southwestern, Intermountain, Southern California, Northern California, Pacific Northwest, Hawaii and Puerto Rico. They embrace nearly 2,800 member clubs and 53 district associations.

The East's grip on the administration of lawn tennis began to relax in the 1920s just as it was to be broken on the courts with the success of champions from California who followed McLoughlin, Johnston and Mrs Wightman – Doeg, Vines, Budge, Riggs, Hunt, Kramer, Schroeder, Gonzalez, Larsen; Wills, Jacobs, Marble, Betz, Brough, Osborne, Connolly. In 1923 Dwight F. Davis of St Louis was elected president, the first non-Easterner to be so honoured. In 1928 the annual meeting was held in the Middle West (Chicago) for the first time. It had been confined to New York City until Philadelphia was picked in 1927.

But the eastern United States continued to be the staging area of the major events in the 1920s and 1930s. Except for the Pacific Southwest Championships at the prestigious Los Angeles Tennis Club, the Pacific Coast Championships in Berkeley, the National Clay Court Championships in the Middle West and the River Oaks Invitation in Houston, Tex. (see separate entries in PART 2), the most important tournaments, attracting the largest crowds, were held on turf in metropolitan New York, Philadelphia and Boston and a few other communities on the Atlantic seaboard.

Despite the depression in the late 1920s and 1930s there was no marked falling off in attendance, with so many exciting and glamorous players on view – Tilden, Johnston, Helen Wills, Vines, Budge, Riggs, Lacoste, Cochet, Borotra, Brugnon, Perry, Austin, von Cramm, Crawford, Bromwich, Quist, Alonso, Norton, Shimizu and Kumagai. The strong interest in the game in the 1930s was reflected in the attendance figures for both amateur and professional play. The biggest crowd at Forest Hills since the Tilden–

Above Jack Kramer (aged 16) at the 1933 Los Angeles City Championships. He was to win the US Championships in 1946-7, Wimbledon in 1947, and become one of the best-known professionals in the game.
Below Fred Perry (right), in his professional début, defeated Ellsworth Vines at Madison Square Garden in 1937. A record crowd paid a record price for tickets.

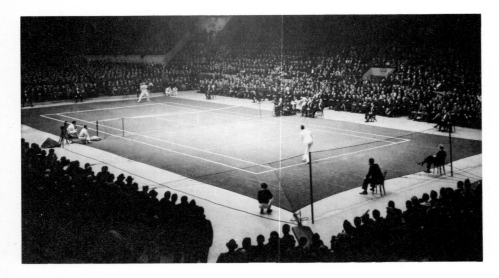

Lacoste final of 1927 (over 13,000) saw John Doeg defeat Frank Shields in the 1930 final. In 1937 there were 14,000 present on successive days for the first time as von Cramm defeated Riggs in the semi-finals and lost to Budge in the final. A record gallery of 16,000 saw Tilden beat Vines at Madison Square Garden in New York on Vines' pro début there in 1934. Topping these were the 17,630 who paid $58,119.50 to see Perry, in his professional début, defeat Vines at the Garden in 1937. Tickets sold at a record price of $9.90.

Much of the finances and energies of the USLTA was being directed toward making tennis the 'game of a lifetime' for more and more people and providing the wherewithal for boys and girls who lacked the means to pay for the equipment, instruction and court rental fees.

The national championships for juniors and boys were started in 1916 at Forest Hills, N.Y. The girls' championships started in 1918 in Philadelphia. There were 50 tournaments for juniors in 1918. In 1919 it was decided to have a national ranking for juniors, boys and girls. Activity was greatly increased in 1920 with the establishment of a nationwide system of centres of play. Schools, colleges and clubs held preliminary tournaments which qualified for championships of cities designated as centres. Winners of these championships were eligible to compete for national titles. The championships (juniors and boys) moved to Boston in 1921 and in 1924 to Chicago's South Side Tennis Club turf with an upsurge in the entry. In 1925, 20 states from all sections were represented. Even during the Depression the entry continued to rise.

As early as 1917 the USNLTA created a division called the National Recreation Municipal Federation and in 1927 sponsored the first National Public Parks Tennis Association, with headquarters in St Louis, Mo. Before this the National Public Parks championship had been held in 1923. By 1928, 24 cities were represented in the championships at Cleveland, Ohio, and in 1929 activity on public parks courts had increased so much that 3,500,000 permits were reported issued. San Francisco was among the busiest centres of public parks tennis: in 1921 a tournament was held there in which more than 1,000 boys and girls entered. Cincinnati, Ohio, was a leader in the 1930s. Between 1932 and 1946, 120 municipal courts were built, 26 with lights for night play and with free instruction for beginners. About the same time the New England sectional association, under the leadership of Joseph W. Thurston of Hartford, Conn., who was later chairman of the committee running the public parks program for the whole country, was attracting national attention. In 1935 the national championships drew players from over 80 cities.

The tennis clinic gave invaluable aid to the Junior Development program. Starting in 1927, it was the brainchild of Dr William P. Jacobs, president of Presbyterian College of Clinton, S.C., who had long felt that tennis in the South was not on a par with that in the East and West.

In 1935 the USLTA started a new plan of systematic training and development for young players to bridge the gap between junior and adult competition: the Junior Davis Cup program, which grew out of an idea suggested by Captain James H. Bishop of Culver Military Academy, was started by the USLTA. In 1938 the Junior Wightman Cup program, a similar program for girls, was instituted. The first chairman was Alrick H. Man, Jr, later Davis Cup team captain.

In their administration of the affairs of the USLTA the officers and committee were faced with taxing problems over amateurism, but this was not until some 40 years after the association's formation. In 1882 the question had come up and it was voted that 'none but amateurs shall be allowed to enter for any match played by the association'. For 25 years or more, with few players needing financial aid, the issue of amateurism was of negligible concern. In 1912 the amateur status of players working for sporting goods concerns was questioned, but they were permitted to do this so long as they handled sporting goods in general and not just tennis merchandise. A move to stop paying players travelling and entertainment expenses was defeated in 1912 and again in 1914. In 1917 players were ordered not to allow their names to be used in tennis advertising nor to receive pay for articles published under their names which they did not write. It was manufacturers' policy to use the names of the most prominent players on their rackets, though they were not paid. In 1920 the USLTA took steps to stop this.

It was in the 1920s that amateurism became a vexing problem, especially concerning players writing for publications for pay. Tilden and Richards were particularly involved in controversy over their journalistic efforts, and Julian S. Myrick, the 'power behind the throne' after his term as president ended in 1923, was the object of their wrath. In 1924 with controversy raging, the amateur rule was interpreted to forbid players to write current reports on tournaments in which they were competing and receive substantial compensation for them. The next year a new 'player-writer' rule was adopted, upholding the interpretation on current daily reports, though permitting all other journalistic activity. The problem, however, was far from solved. In 1926 Richards, after repeatedly defeating Tilden to merit the number one spot in the rankings (which omitted him completely), left the amateur ranks and joined Suzanne Lenglen, Mary K. Browne, Howard Kinsey and others in signing professional contracts to tour under the management of C. C. Pyle (see THE START OF THE PRO GAME). But Tilden remained and his bickerings with the USLTA continued until in 1928 he was removed from the Davis Cup team, of which he was captain, charged with violating the rule he had helped to write, by his daily reports on the Wimbledon Championships. He was barred from playing against Italy, but the French were so indignant when he was also banned from the Challenge Round in their new Roland Garros stadium that the US ambassador, Myron T. Herrick, interceded and he was restored to the team. On his return home he was barred from competing in the 1928 National championships. After winning the US Championship for the seventh time in 1929, he announced he was forfeiting his amateur status to make films on tennis for pay. He then took up a career as a professional player and showed remarkable durability in his 40s in defeating or extending players 15–20 years younger.

The USLTA Amateur Rule Committee in 1931 urged the curbing of expense payments to players by clubs. The next year 14 prominent players signed a petition addressed to the Seabright Lawn Tennis and Cricket Club requesting more liberal expense allowances to assure them of room and meals for the duration of its invitation tournament. They were barred from playing there again. In 1935 the USLTA supported the 'eight-weeks' rule of the ILTF, begun by European countries and designed to prevent amateurs receiving living expenses throughout the year. This was superseded by the 12-weeks rule in 1941.

During World War II lawn tennis events did not stop in the United States as they did in Europe, though activities were restricted and were co-ordinated with the war effort. When hostilities ended the USLTA was ready to move into high gear under Holcombe Ward, who had served as president since 1937. He was one of the ablest leaders the organization has had, a man of strict integrity and the highest principles. He was inflexible in enforcing amateur regulations. It was during his administration, in 1942, that the United States Board of Tax Appeals recognized the USLTA as an amateur sports governing body (the oldest in the country) engaged in educational and public welfare work and so exempt from federal income tax.

There was an upsurge in interest in lawn tennis after World War II, although not as great as that in the 1920s. From the resumption of full-scale operations in 1946, when the Wimbledon, French and Australian Championships were renewed, along with the Davis Cup and Wightman Cup matches, attendance at lawn tennis venues rose. For the first time since 1937, Forest Hills in 1946 was jammed and the gates were closed on successive days, with thousands turned away. A new name, Tom Brown, brought on the stampede. With the scorching velocity of stroke of Ellsworth Vines he beat Frank Parker and Gardnar Mulloy, but lost to Jack Kramer in the Championship final. Kramer, with Ted Schroeder, introduced what was hailed as a new style of offensive tennis in December 1946 and crushed Australia in the Davis Cup challenge round. In 1947 there were back-to-back jams again at Forest Hills to see Parker defeat John Bromwich in the semi-finals and take the first two sets from Kramer before

Below Tom Brown was Jack Kramer's partner in the 1946 men's doubles at Wimbledon. They beat Geoff Brown and Dinny Pails 6-4, 6-4, 6-2 to win the Championship.

Left Bobby Riggs (left) playing Jack Kramer (right) in the opening contest of a professional tour which Kramer won by 69-20 in matches. This opener, at Madison Square Garden, New York, in 1947, drew a crowd of over 15,000 in spite of 24 inches of snow.

bowing. When, a few months later, Kramer made his professional début at the Garden in New York against Bobby Riggs, 15,114 of the 16,052 who had purchased tickets costing $55,730.50, fought their way there through a raging storm that deposited 24 inches of snow on the city. Sheer lunacy, it was called.

The Junior Development program was high on president Ward's priority list. In his last year in office, in 1947, there were 121 chairmen of local committees working on the program. Ninety juniors and 64 boys qualified for the national championships at Kalamazoo College and 72 girls for the championships at the Philadelphia Cricket Club. There were 221 tennis centres designated to hold tournaments. Activity in the Junior Davis Cup program increased so much at the end of the war that in 1947 there were 65 official squads – twice the number in 1946. In 1947 Robert Piatt of Louisville, Ky., led in the organization of the conspicuously successful Junior Davis Cup and Junior Wightman Cup programs there. He was to serve as vice chairman of the Junior Davis Cup Committee of the USLTA under Tom Price of Cincinnati. Jack Kramer, Pancho Gonzalez, Donald Budge, Bill Talbert, Jack Bushman, Bob Malaga, John Powless and John Hendrix have been among the heads and coaches of the Junior Davis Cup team, and Marion Wood Huey of Miami, Fla., and Pat Yeomans of California have been among those who have furnished conspicuous leadership for the Junior Wightman Cup program.

In connection with Junior Development, the USLTA organized the School Tennis Development Committee. On the committee were headmasters, principals and tennis directors from 50 prominent schools of the East, South and West. Percy Rogers of Phillips Exeter Academy was the 1943 chairman and that year 4,500 schools were reported to have teams.

In 1951 the National Tennis Educational Foundation, a non-profit-making organization, was set up by Lawrence A. Baker of New York (president of the USLTA in 1948-50), to develop interest in tennis, particularly among juniors. Many sectional foundations and lawn tennis patrons' associations were also formed to promote junior tennis development and provide instruction and equipment in clinics. One of the most famous of these is the Eastern Tennis Patrons' Association, in which Alastair Martin, Daniel Johnson, Dwight F. Davis, Jr, Robert Kerdasha, Leslie FitzGibbon and Eugene Scott have played leading roles. Another is the Youth Tennis Foundation of Southern California, in which the late Perry T. Jones was prominent. He was also president of the Southern California Tennis Association, director for many years of the PACIFIC SOUTH-WEST CHAMPIONSHIPS (see PART 2), and was Davis Cup captain in 1958-9.

In 1958 Los Angeles was designated as the best centre for junior development by the USLTA. Under Jones a program was sponsored by the Foundation and the Southern California Tennis Association to bring lawn tennis to public parks and high schools.

With 280 high schools under their jurisdiction, 200,000 boys and girls took part. The Foundation's clinics had previously attracted 100,000 students. Other cities honoured next to Los Angeles in the junior development competition were Chattanooga, Tenn.; Houston, Tex.; Louisville, Ky.; Rochester, N.Y.; Salt Lake City, Utah; Springfield, Ohio; Wilmington, Del.; Baldwin, N.Y.; Baton Rouge, La.; Charleston, West Va.; Grand Rapids, Mich.; Hinsdale, Ill.; Modesto, Calif.; Muskegon, Mich.; Phoenix, Ariz.; Providence, R.I.; Bakersfield, Calif.; Belton, S.C.; Cambridge, Md.; Cincinnati, Ohio; Fort Lauderdale, Fla.; La Jolla, Calif.; St Louis, Mo.; Seattle, Wash.; Suffolk, Va.; and Upper Ridgewood, N.J.

The San Diego Patrons' Association in California was organized in 1950 and conducted competitions in advanced, intermediate and beginners' classifications in age groups of 12, 14, 16, and 18 years for boys and girls. Fifteen years earlier Harper Ink had started a tournament for San Diego's school pupils. Maureen Connolly and Karen Hantze, later internationally famous, won it six times each. William Kellogg of La Jolla, a prominent figure in the USLTA, which he has often represented at the meetings of the ILTF, sponsored the Albert Hernandez Junior Memorial Tournament for boys 16 and under in San Diego. The Kentucky Patrons' Foundation was organized in 1952 with Robert Piatt a leading figure. By 1959 its tournament had become the strongest combined boys' and girls' event in the country, with 250 entries from 25 states and Hawaii and Mexico.

The Philadelphia Tennis Patrons' Association was organized in 1953, with William J. Clothier and Richard Sorlien among the leaders. Working with the Philadelphia Department of Recreation, it gives instruction to hundreds of youngsters daily in playgrounds and parks. The Junior Development program in the Philadelphia area has received considerable financial support from the professional international indoor championships at the Spectrum, directed by Edward and Marilyn Fernberger. Most of the $47,000 profit from the 1972 tournament was given to the junior program.

The National Tennis Educational Foundation's coffers swelled during the administration of president Barnes. In 1964, the record sum of $29,256.60 was contributed to its work by 659 friends of tennis. In 1972, under the leadership of Alastair B. Martin, who headed the USLTA in 1969 and 1970, and Daniel Johnson, the NTEF entered into a relationship with the Boy Scouts of America designed to bring 4,600,000 boy scouts and 3,100,000 girl scouts into the tennis program.

One of the ablest directors of the Junior Tennis Development Committee of the USLTA was the late Martin L. Tressel of Pittsburgh, chairman (1957-60) and president of the USLTA (1965-6). Its program included clinics for players of all levels, provided by district associations, clubs and parks, staffed by local professionals and amateur players; workshops for teachers and coaches to demonstrate and develop techniques for teaching tennis; and little leagues. The American Association for Health, Physical Education and Recreation, a division of the National Educational Association, and the Junior Development Committee of the USLTA jointly ran a national program for teaching tennis to physical education teachers in elementary and high schools, and the University of California at Berkeley agreed to allow college credit for those attending these tennis schools. This was an important step in introducing tennis into the school system across the country.

Tennis Workshop, a manual for students and a lesson guide for teachers by Eve Kraft, with a foreword by John Conroy, and based on many years of work in the Junior Development program at Princeton, offered a new approach to group tennis teaching.

A film, 'Tennis for Everyone', produced in California by Perry T. Jones, was made available by the USLTA in 1963 to sectional and district associations and clubs.

Tennis workshops and schools for teachers have been held in recent years at many universities and other institutions.

More and more free tennis instruction has been offered at public parks, courts and in municipal centres, particularly in Texas and California. Recently commercial sponsors – Coca Cola, Uni-Royal and Philip Morris – have provided funds for the National Junior Tennis League 'inner-city' program for teaching the game to boys and girls who ordinarily would not have an opportunity to play. Sheridan Snyder of New York started the movement in 1969 in the public parks, after establishing a reputation as director of the Nassau Bowl tournament at the Nassau Country Club in Glen Cove, L.I. In 1971 Harry Hopman, famous Australian Davis Cup captain, was co-ordinator of a 10-week program conducted on New York City playstreets. More than 20 cities have such an inner-city program staffed and financed by volunteers.

The USLTA has concentrated more and more on spreading the gospel of tennis as the game of a lifetime. In 1958 it began to register all tournament players at a fee of $3 for adults and $1 for juniors, part of which goes to the sectional associations, to be used for the junior program.

In 1967 the USLTA, under the leadership of president Robert J. Kelleher, entered into an agreement with the Licensing Corporation of America, granting it, for a stipulated royalty return, exclusive licensing rights to products, services and programs bearing the USLTA endorsement, and netting the association $150,000 in 1967-9. Deciding to do its own negotiating for royalties from endorsements, the USLTA did not renew the contract and raised about the same amount in 1970, 1971 and 1972. The association engaged an executive director, Robert Malaga of Cleveland, in 1967. Its annual gross income has increased to approximately $500,000.

Part of this increase has come from the rise in tournament attendance and receipts since the start of open tennis and from sanction fees of six per cent of the prize money offered in each event. These fees came to about $100,000 in 1972. The attendance record at Forest Hills for the US Amateur Championships was 90,000 in 1965. In 1970, 122,990 saw the open championships there. In 1972 a new record of 130,000 was set in spite of the fact that many of the top players were eliminated early. They included Evonne Goolagong of Australia, 1971 Wimbledon champion (in the third round), Ken Rosewall and Rod Laver of Australia (in the second and fourth rounds, respectively) John Newcombe of Australia (in the third round), Tom Okker of the Netherlands (in the third), Jan Kodeš of Czechoslovakia (in the second). On the final two days records were set with 14,683 and then 14,696. Although Chris Evert, the 16-year-old sensation of the previous year, had been eliminated in the semi-finals, 14,683 turned out to see Billie Jean King retain her title with a 6-3, 7-5 victory over unseeded Kerry Melville of Australia, who had eliminated Miss Evert. The next day the record was broken again when Ilie Năstase of Rumania, seeded fourth, became the first player from Eastern Europe to win the championship. He defeated the sixth-seeded Arthur Ashe 3-6, 6-3, 6-7, 6-4, 6-3, after Ashe seemed to have victory surely in his grasp at 3-1 and 30-0 in his favour in the fourth set.

Ashe won the first US Open Championship in 1968 as an amateur, to general astonishment, and he also won the US amateur title, the first male Negro to do so, as well as the first player of the United States to win since Tony Trabert in 1955. In 1963 he had become the first Negro to represent the United States in the Davis Cup. The trail had been blazed for Ashe by Althea Gibson, who became the first to win the US and Wimbledon titles in 1957 and also the first to play in the Wightman Cup. She was champion again at both Wimbledon and Forest Hills in 1958.

In 1972 Năstase led Rumania against the United States in Bucharest in the first DAVIS CUP (see PART 2) championship round played in continental Europe since the French lost to Great Britain in Paris in 1933. Twice before Năstase had led his country against the United States in the Challenge Round, in 1969 in Cleveland and in 1971 in Charlotte, N.C. The first time the United States won, 5-0; the second time it narrowly came through, 3-2 in the last Challenge Round (discarded in 1972). The victory was the fourth in succession for the United States, the first time it had held the cup so long since it defeated Australia in 1946-9. Australia, under the command of Harry Hopman, dominated the international team competition (1950-67), but the loss of its top three players to the professional ranks, when open tennis started, left it virtually defenceless. The United States not only found itself displaced as the top tennis power by a nation of 11,000,000 people during those years but plumbed depths of adversity in the 1960s such as it never before had experienced.

Below Althea Gibson, the first Negro to win the US and Wimbledon titles (both in 1957) and also the first to play in the Wightman Cup. She won again at Wimbledon and at Forest Hills in 1958.

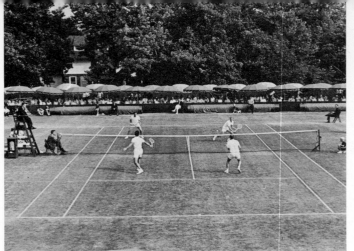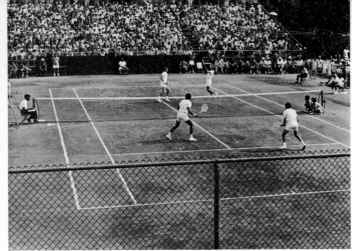

In 1966 for the eighth time since 1956 there was an all-Australian final in the US Championship, both players, Fred Stolle and John Newcombe, being unseeded. That year a professional tournament was held for the first time on the lawns of the Newport Casino – a round-robin competition using the VASSS method of scoring (see PART 2). Two years before, the US professional championship had been held for the first time on the Longwood Cricket Club turf.

The tennis schedule and calendar have changed drastically since open tournaments were sanctioned in 1968. Clubs which had held major fixtures, some for 50 years or more, had to give them up or be satisfied with a minor event because they could not put up the prize money to attract top-ranking players. Other clubs, without tennis tradition and largely unknown, have been awarded top attractions.

Even before 1968 many of the blue-ribbon grass-court fixtures had been given up by Eastern clubs. Among them were the Seabright Lawn Tennis and Cricket Club, the Agawam Hunt Club, Westchester Country Club, Nassau Country Club and the Maidstone Club. Newport, cradle of the US championships and the shrine of the National Lawn Tennis Hall of Fame, gave up the men's invitation amateur tournament it had held from 1915 on and conducted a women's professional tournament in 1971. The Longwood Cricket Club gave up the national doubles conglomerate to confine itself to the US professional championship outside the jurisdiction of the USLTA. The Meadow Club of Southampton, where the world's best competed for many years, now holds an amateur tournament without prize money, and the Germantown Cricket Club, scene of Davis Cup Challenge Round matches and the national Championships, no longer is a major venue. Since 1965, apart from the US (Open) CHAMPIONSHIPS at Forest Hills (see colour plate, page 44), the leading US title matches have included the US National Indoor, Salisbury, Md.; the Thunderbird, Phoenix, Ariz.; the Caribe Hilton, San Juan, P.R.; the Masters, St Petersburg, Fla.; RIVER OAKS, Houston, Tex.; the US NATIONAL HARD COURT, Sacramento, Calif.; the US NATIONAL CLAY COURTS at various venues in the Middle West; the Pennsylvania (Grass), Philadelphia; the EASTERN (Grass), South Orange, N.J.; the NEWPORT Casino, Newport, R.I.; the PACIFIC COAST, Berkeley, Calif.; the PACIFIC SOUTHWEST (Open), Los Angeles, Calif.; the Macon Indoor, Macon, Ga.; and the Jacksonville Invitation at Jacksonville, Fla.

Until 1964 the Davis Cup Challenge Round had never been played in the United States except in the East and always on grass. That year and again in 1969-70 it was held in Cleveland and in 1971 in Charlotte, N.C. The Wightman Cup too had been played on the Atlantic seaboard until in 1957 it went to the Edgeworth Club in Sewickley, Pa. Since then the venue has been Sewickley again (1959), the Cycle and Saddle Club of Chicago (1961), the Cleveland Skating Club (1963) and the Harold T. Clark Stadium in Cleveland (1965, 1967, 1969 and 1971).

The East's complete predominance has been ended not only in the award of the major attractions but also in the officers elected to conduct the affairs of the Association. It was not until 1923 that a non-Easterner, Dwight F. Davis of St Louis, was elected president and another 10 years passed before a second, Harry Knox of Chicago, took charge. But since then the picture has completely changed. Victor Denny of Seattle,

Above, left The Merion Cricket Ground in 1965, when Roy Emerson (far left) and Fred Stolle defeated Vic Seixas (near left) and Billy Lenoir 6-2, 6-1, 6-1 in the Pennsylvania Lawn Tennis Championships
Above, right Rock Creek Park, Washington, D.C. in 1971, when Tom Okker (right) and Marty Riessen (left), on the near side of the net, defeated Bob Carmichael (left) and Ray Ruffels (right) to win the men's doubles in the Washington Star International

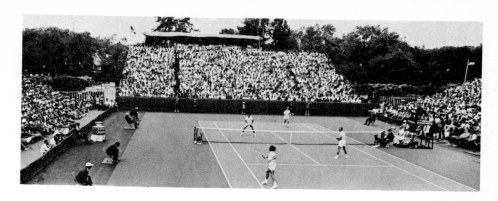

Right The men's double in the Davis Cup Challenge Round, Cleveland, 30 August 1970. Bob Lutz (left) and Stan Smith (United States), on the near side of the net, defeated Christian Kuhnke (left) and Wilhelm Bungert (West Germany), 6-3, 7-5, 6-4. The overall score was 5-0 to the United States, the third win in a row. *Below* The United States held the Cup in 1971, when the last Challenge Round in the competition was played in Charlotte, North Carolina. The team members, seen here after their 3-2 victory against Rumania were (left to right) Erik Van Dillen, Stan Smith, non-playing captain Ed Turville and Frank Froehling. The United States won again in 1972, when the Final Round was played in Bucharest (see colour plate, page 103).

George E. Barnes of Chicago, Edward A. Turville of St Petersburg, Fla., Robert J. Kelleher of Beverly Hills, Calif., and Robert B. Colwell of Seattle, Wash., have each served two terms since 1958.

The number of people involved in the administration of the Association's affairs has vastly increased. There are innumerable committees for various championships and rankings, including juniors, boys and girls in all the age groups. Approximately 700 officers and committee members are involved in the organizational and promotional work of the USLTA. All of them serve on a voluntary basis except for the Executive Director and his headquarters staff.

For years the Amateur Rule Committee was one of the most important and its decisions and actions in restricting and disciplining the players, principally on expense payments, made headlines in the press. The eight-weeks rule, the 18-tournament rule, the 150-day limitation on foreign travel and the limitation of eight tournaments abroad were among the most publicized restrictions. In 1963 William Kellogg presented a resolution to the ILTF Committee of Management, calling on it to enforce the amateur rules governing allowable expenses. In 1968 the USLTA offered an amendment to the ILTF constitution, providing for substantial self-determination by each member nation in establishing amateur rules for its nationals, and threatened to resign if the amendment failed. Since the sanctioning of open tournaments players of various categories were permitted to accept prize money and payments for endorsements, and amateurism is no longer an issue of any consequence. See PLAYING STATUS (PART 2) and ADMINISTRATION OF THE WORLD GAME (PART 1).

The open tournament was an issue in the 1930s and then was forgotten until 1957 when a special committee appointed by president Renville McMann recommended in favour of an open but the USLTA tabled it. In December 1959 a special committee of the ILTF proposed the holding of eight major open tournaments as an experiment in 1961. At the Paris meeting in July 1960 the United States voted, with Britain, France and Australia, in favour of the proposal but it was beaten by a few votes. In 1961 and 1962 the USLTA annual meeting decided to support the principle of self-determination, permitting each nation to hold an experimental open if it so chose. In 1963, despite the objections of Turville, George Barnes, Victor Denny, Kellogg and four of the five officers, the USLTA reversed its policy and took a position solidly against open tournaments in any form anywhere in the world and against home rule. In 1968 when the die was cast and the British, on 14 December 1967, had thrown down the gauntlet in revolt against the ILTF and decided to conduct Wimbledon as an open event, the USLTA, in annual session in February, supported the British in adopting a resolution to amend the Federation rules to 'provide for substantial self-determination by member national associations as to whether an open tennis tournament or tournaments shall be held in the country of the member association'.

The revolution was on, and in 1970 manifested itself in the first major change in scoring in more than three quarters of a century: the introduction with the permission of the ILTF of the 'sudden death' 9-point tie-break in the US Open Championships as an experiment (see TIE-BREAK, PART 2).

The Start of the Pro Game
Fred Perry

Professional tennis really began in 1926 thanks to the foresight of an American industrialist C. C. ('Cash and Carry') Pyle. A keen follower of sport in all forms, he realized that people were prepared to spend money in search of amusement. Deeply involved in extravaganzas such as six-day bicycle racing, dance marathons and roller-skating derbys, he saw the possibilities of a nationwide professional tennis tour. He knew he needed famous names. He scooped the best. Amateur tennis officials gasped when he signed the fabulous Suzanne Lenglen for a sum in the region of $75,000. He had robbed women's tennis of its greatest name and biggest crowdpuller. He persuaded Mary K. Browne, the biggest draw in American women's tennis, to follow suit. A touch of spice was added by the acquisition of Vincent Richards, Howard Kinsey and Harvey Snodgrass – all big names in American tennis. To make sure that Suzanne Lenglen was happy, he raided France and signed Paul Feret. After opening in Madison Square Garden to a gate of some $40,000, Pyle was on his way across the country. When it was over, he had pocketed close to $83,000 from the promotion. The players had made money, the public were satisfied and Pyle had proved his point.

Pyle soon tired of his new toy. Vincent Richards took the reins and promptly swooped into Central Europe to sign Karel Koželuh, a Czechoslovak professional reputed to be the greatest player in Europe, although he had never taken part in the main championships. He had played with Suzanne Lenglen on her short European tour and was tailormade for professional tennis. Despite the formation of a Professional Tennis Association in the United States and a series of exhibition matches there, it was soon evident that new blood would be needed to keep public interest. People just would not support matches involving the same players. Ramon Najuch of Germany, Paul and Edmund Burke of France and Emmet Pare of the United States filled the gap to a degree, but gross gates of the tours declined at an alarming rate. Professional tennis suffered from continued sniping by amateur tennis officials. It needed a shot in the arm.

The great William T. 'Big Bill' Tilden provided it. His running battles with the USLTA (see THE UNITED STATES STORY) were legendary. A controversial figure, Tilden was perhaps the greatest player the world has ever seen. He brought life and drama to the game as well as brilliant tennis. There was a touch of the theatrical in his make-up – he had once tried his hand at acting with disastrous results – and he could pull in the crowds. In 1931, he toured America with a series against Karel Koželuh, made a second trip with Vincent Richards in 1932, and a third in 1933 when he brought the German Champion Hans Nüsslein all the way from Europe. Yet gates continued to decline. By this time, Tilden had taken over the promotion of tours together with Bill O'Brien. To these two must go the credit for establishing the basis and foundation for the future of the professional game. They enticed Ellsworth Vines into the fold in 1934. A huge crowd of some 14,000 witnessed the opening at Madison Square Garden and the subsequent tour was most successful. New names were added from time to time, for example, George Lott and Lester Stoefen. The pattern had been established: a professional tour throughout the United States to find a professional champion, then a move to sign the top amateur player into the ranks two years later. However, promoters were running into problems. Once the tour started, expenses were high and constant, regardless of the number of cities visited. Difficulties arose in trying to find suitable venues within reasonable striking distance and more or less on the same travel routes. Tours took place during the winter months, but there were far too few indoor facilities for their needs. Larger ones had to be reserved well in advance to avoid clashes with basketball and ice hockey – two of the most popular sporting events in the United States. University and high-school gymnasia were pressed into service, but conditions were bad and crowd facilities far too small. Air travel was non-existent. Touring meant tedious rail travel or strength-sapping trips by car over hundreds of miles between cities.

Below Lester Stoefen, signed up by Tilden in the 1930s

Professional tournaments were scarce. Few clubs would risk the wrath of the USLTA by permitting the professionals to use their courts during the tennis season with the amateur circuit in full swing. Detractors were quick to knock this lack of *bona fide* tournaments, classing the tours as exhibitions and demonstrations. Amateurs – champions in their own right – who had joined the professionals were no longer welcome at amateur events or at tennis clubs affiliated to national LTAs. The confrontation was absolute. Amateurs were not permitted to play against professionals except in official matches. Needless to say, permission was seldom given. Tilden and

Below, left The great William T. ('Big Bill') Tilden in 1927. He toured the United States professionally in the 1930s and then became a promoter.

Vines continued their tours for three years, together with Cochet and another Frenchman, Martin Plaa. European jaunts became more frequent. Tournaments in Paris and Southport were sandwiched between exhibitions in various cities but the liaison between the official bodies and the professionals never progressed with the times.

In 1935 came the 'All-American' tour of Tilden, Vines, Lott and Stoefen, doubles experts extraordinary – but doubles was not what the public wanted. The returns dwindled from over $250,000 to just over $175,000. Bill O'Brien wanted an international flavour again, particularly as he had the Vines image to work with.

Fred Perry cast his lot with them in 1936. Vines and Perry opened in Madison Square Garden in January 1937 under the promotion of a New York syndicate headed by two former tennis greats, Frank Hunter, a Davis Cup player and partner of Tilden in doubles, and Howard Voschell. A gate of over $50,000 on that opening night set the seal on a tour that grossed well over $400,000 by the end of April. Americans wanted to see the Britisher get clobbered.

It was Perry's turn to feel the wrath of officialdom. The proposed pro tour in England during the summer of 1937 almost died on the vine when it was announced that no tennis club affiliated to the Lawn Tennis Association would be permitted to stage the Perry *v*. Vines matches. Had it not been for the help of an old friend of Perry's, the late Bernard Sunley, they would have been in trouble. He rescued them by building a portable wooden tennis court and transported it to wherever they played outdoors – usually football grounds instead of tennis clubs. Their only indoor matches were staged in Edinburgh and Wembley. The three-night stint there set the pattern and Wembley became the professional tennis centre in Britain. The official body ignored them completely. In fact, Perry was asked to tender his resignation from all the clubs of which he was a member – honorary or not – on the grounds that the membership was open only to amateur players. Needless to say, those restrictions have since been lifted for all rebels who deserted the amateur fold.

A second American tour was not as successful and it became increasingly obvious that new blood was needed every two years. Vines and Perry toured through South America in the summer of 1938 and discovered an untapped source of interest for the future. The next man in was Donald Budge, a Grand Slam winner and great performer. With Jack Harris managing the promotion, Perry and Vines undertook the 1939 tour in two stages: the first a series of matches between Vines and Budge, the second between Budge and Perry. Thus they hoped to play all the larger cities twice and avoid the smaller arenas for the first year. Although 70 matches were played in all, the gross take of just over $250,000 fell far short of the 1937 tour. The prospect of war in Europe was too much to combat. Newspaper publicity – a vital requirement for all sporting tours – was scarce and the public was hardly in the mood to patronize tennis matches. The professional game faced a crisis at a time when plans had been scheduled for the expansion of tours to various countries. Cochet had been to Russia, Vines to Japan, and to many countries in South and Central America with Perry. All such trips had to be cancelled. There could be no national or international amateur championships and the lifeblood of the professional game – incoming amateur champions – was cut off except for those from the United States. The high cost of promoting and staging a professional tour was not worth the risk. Meanwhile amateur associations had become more liberal in their treatment of their stars, allowing them more latitude in expenses and permissions to travel abroad. Amateurs were beginning to feel free.

But the vision of 'Cash and Carry' Pyle had not been wild. His point had been proved. The public were prepared to pay for their sporting interests and entertainment. He was right when he said that professional tennis could and should be classed as theatre. Already tension between amateur officials and professionals had been eased. Professional tournaments and a championship had been established in the United States. Pyle might well have been the pioneer, but to Bill Tilden and Vincent Richards must go a great deal of the credit for the growth of the game under difficult circumstances. Vines, Cochet, Hunter, Budge and many others played their part in the all-important formative years.

Above Fred Perry. After winning the Big Four Championships (though not in the same year) he became a professional, touring North and South America in the late 1930s.

The Postwar Pro Game
Bud Collins

Great hopes for the professional game after World War II did not fully materialize until late 1967 when Dave Dixon of New Orleans convinced Lamar Hunt of Dallas, Texas, a man of several sporting ventures, to become his partner in World Championship Tennis, a promotional firm. Until then, significant financial backing was absent although a few promoters, notably Jack Kramer, had experienced some success, principally with nomadic one-night stands.

The Dixon-Hunt alliance in WCT, along with George MacCall's National Tennis League, embracing 14 of the world's foremost players, was influential in speeding Wimbledon and LTA insistence on the adoption of open competition by the ILTF in 1968. Before 1967, the amateur game had lost personnel to the pros one or two at a time, the defections sporadic. Abruptly, when 1968 began it was announced that WCT and NTL had skimmed the cream: John Newcombe, Tony Roche, Cliff Drysdale, Nikki Pilić, Roger Taylor to the former, Roy Emerson to the latter. Never before had there been such a momentous professional harvest at one time. Along with these, WCT included established pros Butch Buchholz, Dennis Ralston and Pierre Barthès, completing a group Dixon labelled the Handsome Eight. NTL's standbys were Rod Laver, Ken Rosewall, Pancho Gonzalez, Fred Stolle and Andrés Gimeno. MacCall also signed four women, Billie Jean Moffit King, Rosie Casals, Ann Haydon Jones, and Françoise Durr, to tour with his male troupe. Later, in 1970, the NTL men were to be absorbed by WCT; the women became free agents, eventually affiliated with, and were mainstays of, the Virginia Slims pro tour at the end of 1970 (see THE WOMEN'S PRO GAME).

Between 1926, when competitive professional tennis was launched by C. C. Pyle (see THE START OF THE PRO GAME), and 1968, the custom was for a promoter to sign a contract with an amateur, guaranteeing the amateur a set figure or a portion of the gate receipts for a tour of the United States and perhaps other countries. The matches, usually staged in indoor arenas, were generally regarded as exhibitions, and had little impact on the sporting scene. While the pros may frequently have been the best players in the game, traditionally amateur fixtures, such as Wimbledon, the US Championships at Forest Hills, and the Davis Cup, continued to carry the most prestige. Though usually well compensated, the small band of pros tended to be forgotten publicly when they abandoned amateurism.

Immediately after World War II, however, some of the tours did command considerable public interest. American Jack Harris, promoter of prewar tours with such players as Ellsworth Vines v. Don Budge and Fred Perry v. Budge, contracted Bobby Riggs to play a tour against Budge in 1946-7. Riggs, the 1939 Wimbledon champion just out of military service, was to oppose the acknowledged pro champion, Budge. It was a relatively short tour, Riggs winning 23 matches to 21.

That led Harris to sign the top amateur, Jack Kramer, to challenge Riggs in 1947-8. He also signed Pancho Segura (Ecuador), and Dinny Pails (Australia), to play a companion match on the nightly odyssey. This tour was extremely well received, and the opener (Riggs v. Kramer) at Madison Square Garden in New York drew 15,114 people – one of the largest tennis crowds ever – despite the fact that New York was paralysed by a raging blizzard. Kramer won that tour by 69-20 in matches and became the pro king. He made $85,000, Riggs $50,000.

In 1949 Harris withdrew from promotion and Riggs got his baptism as a promoter, staging the next tour by enticing Pancho Gonzalez into a series against Kramer. This was the longest head-to-head tour, extending from October 1949 to May 1950, Kramer emphasizing his dominance, 96-27. Both he and Gonzalez made $72,000. Frank Parker was also involved, having signed to face Segura.

In 1950-1 the glamour girl of the game, Gussie Moran, was contracted by Riggs to tour against Pauline Betz while Kramer opposed Segura. Betz was far superior, in strokes if not wardrobe, but the women had little appeal professionally. Pauline and Jack were big winners of an unsuccessful tour.

Below Gertrude ('Gorgeous Gussie') Moran. She was contracted by Bobby Riggs to tour against Pauline Betz in 1950-1.

Above Ken Rosewall (*left*) and Lew Hoad (*right*) were two of the greatest amateurs who joined up with Jack Kramer to challenge the professional champion Pancho Gonzalez.

Kramer decided to assume a dual role as promoter and player in 1952 when he persuaded Frank Sedgman to leave amateurism following the Davis Cup. Another Australian, Ken McGregor, came along to face Segura. Although he lost in 1953 to Kramer, 54-41, Sedgman made $102,000, the first to exceed $100,000. That was Kramer's last tour as a principal, an arthritic back causing him to retire except for occasional appearances. He continued as promoter and put together a 1954 round-robin tour of Gonzalez, Segura, Sedgman and Don Budge, with others filling in from time to time. For the first time a tour loser (Gonzalez) was invited back as a principal, and he demonstrated his coming of age by winning the tour. He was to remain on top for nearly a decade, and, remarkably, a player to reckon with into the 1970s.

A string of amateur champions joined up to challenge Gonzalez – unsuccessfully: Tony Trabert (1956), 27-74; Ken Rosewall (1957), 26-50; Lew Hoad (1958), 36-51; Ashley Cooper, Mal Anderson and Hoad in a round-robin tour (1959); Alex Olmedo, Rosewall and Segura (1960); Andrés Gimeno, Olmedo, Buchholz, Barry MacKay, Hoad, Sedgman, Trabert, Cooper (1961).

Althea Gibson, Wimbledon champion of 1957 and 1958, after her US championship at Forest Hills in 1958, became one of the rare women to try touring as a pro. She and Karol Fageros, another American, signed with the Harlem Globetrotters basketball team to play a match before each of the games during the winter of 1958-9. Miss Fageros could not extend Miss Gibson, who won almost all the matches. It was a short-lived pro career for both women.

By 1962, when Gonzalez had (temporarily) retired, and Kramer had withdrawn from being a full-time promoter, the pro game was in danger of fading altogether. Rosewall, not a colourful player, was preeminent, and none of the best amateurs wished to commit himself to an uncertain pro career. The amateur game was at the height of its own special lucrativeness in under-the-table payments, and the pros were desperate for new blood. For the first time since World War II, there was no tour in the United States, the financial backbone of any season. Rosewall and Hoad were considering retirement, but they made one last effort to lure the 1962 Grand Slammer, Rod Laver, to join them. With a personal guarantee of $125,000 for one year, Rosewall and Hoad convinced fellow Australian Laver to begin in 1963 a career that would become the most remunerative of any professional tennis player. Laver has said, 'I don't know whether Hoad and Rosewall could have made good their offer if the tour had been a bust, and I doubt that I'd have held them to it. But their sincerity impressed me, as well as their belief that if we could just keep it going some day pro tennis would thrive as a significant sport.'

Laver was beaten badly by both Hoad and Rosewall in the early stages of 1963, the customary initiation of the new boy. But soon it became apparent that he would assume leadership before long, and his portion of the receipts exceeded the guarantee.

The significant year for pro tennis was 1964 when the New England Merchants National Bank of Boston assumed sponsorship of the US Pro Championships. One-night matches were no longer profitable in the United States, and there was no plan for an American tour until the Merchants Bank and the Longwood Cricket Club decided to bring the defunct championship from the West Side Tennis Club at Forest Hills, where it had gone bankrupt in 1963, to Boston. Edward Hickey, an officer of the bank, and John Bottomley, president of Longwood, enlisted Jack Kramer's aid. This show of interest enabled the pros to secure several other sponsors for a short summer tournament circuit with about $80,000 in total prize money.

Although the pros had played infrequent tournaments, and had hoped to play more, they were seldom strong enough in personnel or financial backing to stage a week-long traditional event. Anchored by the $10,000 event in Boston a circuit of sorts began; still, the going was rough until the advent of open tennis in 1968. But at last, in 1964, the pro emphasis shifted from roving one-night stands to conventional tournaments.

London and Paris were host to annual professional tournaments, but the US Professional championship is the oldest event, beginning in 1927 on a vacant lot in New York called the Notlek Tennis Club and missing only the war year of 1944. Until moving to Boston in 1964 the event was shaky, and in 1963 the players were not paid, except for Pancho Gonzalez, the only one with enough drawing power to demand a guarantee in advance. A field of eight was all that could be mustered for the 1963 championship.

In 1965 the scoring reformer, James Van Alen, welcomed the first professional invasion of the Newport (Rhode Island) Casino, where the US Championships had begun in 1881. He put up $10,000 prize money on condition that the players used his radical VASSS (VAN ALEN STREAMLINED SCORING SYSTEM, see PART 2) round-robin medal-play format. The players were paid $5 per point. It was at Newport that the pros first played Van Alen's tie-break, eventually refined to 9-point 'sudden death' and adopted by the US Open and most American tournaments in 1970 (see SCORING and

Above Pancho Gonzalez, perhaps the greatest player never to have won Wimbledon, was top professional for nearly a decade from 1954. He was still a player to reckon with in the 1970s.

Below, right Longwood Cricket Club Stadium, Boston, seen here in 1971, has been the home since 1964 of the United States Professional Championships.

TIE-BREAK, PART 2). Even Wimbledon instituted a form of tie-break in 1971, a victory for Van Alen's reforms that few had expected. In fact Van Alen was able to use the pros as public guinea pigs for his innovations only because they were in no position to resist, on behalf of tradition, anyone willing to finance a tournament. As pressure grew within British tennis circles for open play, Wimbledon tested the atmosphere by presenting an eight-man pro tournament late in the summer of 1967, which Laver won from Rosewall. This was the pros' first appearance on the hallowed turf, and they were well received. It was at that time that both George MacCall and Dave Dixon made moves to enter pro tennis as promoters. Both sought the same leading players, and MacCall secured most of them for his National Tennis League: Laver, Rosewall, Gonzalez, Gimeno, Stolle and Emerson. Rebuffed, Dixon gained permission from his wealthy partner, Lamar Hunt, to go high in signing the leading amateurs: Newcombe, Roche, Drysdale, Pilić, Taylor. To these he added established pros Ralston, Barthès, and Buchholz and began an ambitious tour with VASSS scoring as World Championship Tennis.

Now that practically all the bright players had defected from amateurism, the pressure was greater than ever on the ILTF to accept open tennis, which they did (see OPEN TENNIS).

Neither the NTL nor WCT tours did well at first. WCT lost heavily, and early in 1968 Hunt and his nephew, Al Hill, Jr, bought out Dixon's interest and set about re-organizing it. The reorganization was begun under Bob Briner and continued under his successor Mike Davies.

From the beginning of open tennis, at the British Hard Court Championships in April 1968, WCT and NTL – and then WCT, which swallowed NTL – coexisted uneasily with the ILTF. An essential difference was that the promoters insisted on payment by each tournament of a management fee (exclusive of prize money) for the service of delivering the promoter's players. There were other differences leading to the mutual agreement at Wimbledon of 1971 to part company, thus closing down open tennis from 1 January 1972. Peace between WCT and the ILTF was re-established in spring 1972, but not in time to prevent a closed Wimbledon limited to amateurs and independent pros. However, the peace did enable the USLTA to operate the US Open as usual.

In 1970 WCT demonstrated their preference for going it alone in purely professional tennis by announcing a $1 million World Championship of Tennis scheme for 32

Below, right The Spectrum, Philadelphia, home of the United States Professional Indoor Championships. The 1973 tournament was watched by 60,000 spectators.

players: 20 $50,000 events from which the top eight finishers would emerge for a $100,000 tournament leading to a $50,000 first prize.

In November 1971 the first World Championship of Tennis was completed in Dallas, home base of WCT, with Ken Rosewall overcoming Rod Laver, 6-4, 1-6, 7-6, 7-6, for $50,000, the largest prize in tennis up to that time. 'I never thought I'd see the day', said Rosewall, who had considered retiring during the lean days of a decade before and had experienced several seasons when he earned less than on that November afternoon. 'When we started playing $10,000 tournaments in 1964 that seemed like a million dollars to us – and now $50,000 for a winner!'

To coordinate with television desires in the US, the 1972 World Championship of Tennis was concluded in May. The last 10 tournaments of the 1971 season were counted as the first 10 of the 1972 season; then 10 more were played in the winter of 1972, most of them televised, marking the first time that tennis had ever been televised on a regular series basis by a commercial network in the US.

Once more Rosewall, aged 37, won the championship and $50,000 from Laver in a 3-hour-34-minute match that excited millions of televiewers across America. Throughout 1972 the WCT tournaments were well attended and publicized and Rosewall's 4-6, 6-0, 6-3, 6-7, 7-6 victory over Laver in the grand final seemed to establish the pro game once and for all with the American public who had been unaware of pro tennis only a few years before.

Shortly after the WCT-ILTF peace was made, half-way through 1972, the Association of Tennis Professionals came into being, an organization of professionals set up to watch over their own welfare, concerned with conditions, prize money, tournament qualifications, retirement schemes etc. Jack Kramer was made its director in September. Many such organizations had arisen and failed since World War II, notably the International Tennis Players Association in 1960 under Kramer. However, for the first time this union, ATP, with more than 60 charter members, contained nearly every top player and seemed a force to reckon with. One of its goals was to ensure that all players would be eligible for the Davis Cup, and that the Cup schedule would be shortened so that it would be feasible for all to take part. In 1961 the pros' answer to the Davis Cup had been the Kramer Cup with four teams aligned according to continents: Australia, Europe, North America and South America. The competition lasted two years, Australia beating North America in 1961 and South America in 1962. The World Cup was put into competition in 1970 as a prize-money team event between the US and Australia, and seemed likely to continue. Australia was victor in 1970 (5-2), 1972 (6-1) and 1973 (5-2) while the US won in 1971 (4-3). In 1972 $30,000 was at stake and $20,000 went to the winning Australians. The location, Hartford, Connecticut, was contracted to play host at least until 1977.

Considerably more spectacular than the ascendancy of the men's pro game was that of the women's, which was virtually non-existent until NTL signed King, Casals, Durr and Jones in 1968, just before the start of open tennis. Those four women did poorly as gate attractions for NTL, but when their contracts were up in 1970 they were instrumental, with Gladys Heldman, the American publisher of *World Tennis* magazine, in founding a separate prize-money circuit for women. Largely through the backing of Virginia Slims cigarettes, and because of the women's militancy in opposing low prize money compared with the money paid to men in the traditional tournaments, the circuit became viable. Other sponsors were enlisted and women's prize money rose from less than $40,000 total to about $600,000 in the United States alone by 1972, the United States being the base of operations. On their own, playing numerous cities off the usual tennis track, the women did handsomely in publicity and prize money. Billie Jean King earned a record (for women) $117,000 in prize money in 1971, winning 19 of 30 tournaments, and $119,000 in 1972. (See THE WOMEN'S PRO GAME.)

Oddly enough the biggest money tournament for women at the close of the 1972 season in Boca Raton, Fla., was won by an amateur, 17-year-old Chris Evert, who was obliged to decline the $25,000 first prize, highest ever for a woman. Runner-up Kerry Melville collected $15,000.

The Women's Pro Game
Gladys M. Heldman

Women's professional tennis from 1947 until September 1971 consisted of sporadic exhibitions between two (or at most four) girls who played at clubs or sparsely filled arenas in one-night stands. In the spring of 1947 Pauline Betz (Wimbledon champion 1946) and Sarah Palfrey Cooke, both US National Champions, turned professional and offered their services at a minimum guarantee of $250 for a weekday ($500 for a Saturday, Sunday or holiday), to be split between the two of them and their manager, Elwood Cooke. Their tour was not financially successful. Another attempt was made in 1950-51 when Bobby Riggs signed Gussie Moran and Pauline Betz to play a series of pro exhibitions along with the men.

In the autumn of 1958 Althea Gibson, twice Wimbledon Champion and US National Champion, turned professional with Karol Fageros ('The Golden Goddess'), and the two girls joined up with the Harlem Globetrotters to play one-night stands as openers before the basketball games. The promoter got the lion's share of the proceeds, and at the end of the season both girls ended up wiser but not much richer. Between then and the end of 1967 women's professional tennis virtually ceased to exist (see THE POSTWAR PRO GAME).

At the end of 1967, men's pro promoter George MacCall signed four leading women players to join up with his top eight men. The players were all-time great Billie Jean King, former Wimbledon Champion Ann Jones of Great Britain, French No. 1 Françoise Durr and promising 19-year-old Rosie Casals. Each of the girls received a guarantee and they played under MacCall with reasonably good success for two years. At that time, a woman tennis player who could make $25,000 a year was considered to have done handsomely.

The contract between the four girls and George MacCall ended in 1970, and they began to play as independent pros under ILTF and USLTA auspices. Prize money in both American and European tournaments was very small, and only at Wimbledon or Forest Hills could the winner make as much as $3,000 or even $4,000. Many of the British tournaments offered only £300 for the entire women's field, and the top American events other than Forest Hills had prize money varying between $1,000 and $4,000. The leading women players occasionally made disgruntled statements to the press about the disparity in the prize money between men and women, but this was not effective in raising prize-money standards.

The crisis came in August 1970 when the women players discovered, to their great dismay, that Jack Kramer was offering $50,000 in prize money for the men's event at the Pacific Southwest Championships but only $7,500 for the women. The girls were expected to travel at their own expense from New York to California to play in this event, but if the top 15 or 20 women in the world undertook the gamble, only eight of them (the quarter-finalists) would be eligible for any prize money at all. It was in August that Billie Jean King and Rosie Casals approached Gladys Heldman to organize a boycott by the women players against the Pacific Southwest if the prize money were not raised. After several conversations with Jack Kramer in which he was adamant about not increasing the money, Mrs Heldman suggested to a meeting of some 20 girls, held in their locker room at the West Side Tennis Club in Forest Hills, that women players should not be asked to boycott the Pacific Southwest since many of them lived in Southern California or were not in the top class and would therefore want to compete, but that she would arrange a $7,500 tournament for the top eight women players the same week in Houston and would apply for a USLTA sanction. These proposals were accepted and reported back to Jack Kramer, who indicated that he would not protest.

Houston applied for a sanction and the Houston Racquet Club erected bleachers, sold tickets and got ready for the big event. Three days before the tournament was to start, the club and the eight players involved were telephoned by the head of the USLTA Schedule and Sanctioning Committee and told that no sanction would be

Above Karol Fageros ('The Golden Goddess'). She played an unsuccessful season of one-night matches with Althea Gibson before basketball games in the late 1950s.

given and that both the club and the players would be suspended if the event was held. Some of the girls were already in Houston and others were on their way. *World Tennis* was in constant touch with the USLTA to get a sanction but was told that the only way would be to make the event an 'amateur' tournament, with money being given 'under the table'.

One hour before the tournament was to start, a group of those involved including Jim Hight, President of the Texas Tennis Association, two representatives from Philip Morris Inc., parent company of Virginia Slims (who had agreed to put up a large portion of the prize money), the eight women players and Gladys Heldman, met in the clubhouse to decide what should be done. The girls unanimously refused to play for money 'under the table' but, in order to protect the club from suspension, they voted to sign for $1.00 as contract pros to Mrs Heldman for a period of one week. When the meeting was over the girls announced their decision to the press. They were now contract pros for $1.00.

Within a few days each girl had received a telegram from the President of the USLTA informing her that she was suspended and no longer eligible for the Wightman Cup, Federation Cup or for a National Ranking. These eight women players were Billie Jean King, Rosie Casals, Nancy Richey Gunter, Peaches Bartkowicz, Val Ziegenfuss, Kristy Pigeon, Judy Dalton and Kerry Melville. Within an hour Mrs Heldman's daughter Julie, who had been unable to play because of a bad arm, had also signed for $1.00.

This was the beginning of the *World Tennis* (WT) Women's Pro Tour and the Virginia Slims Prize Money Circuit. Within a few weeks Mrs Heldman was able to set up a series of contract pro tournaments for the 1971-2 winter and spring season and to sign up another 10 girls, among them Ann Jones, Françoise Durr, Karen Krantzcke and Mary Ann Eisel. The women's rebellion caught fire but no one was really sure if the public would come out to watch. To their great surprise and delight, the public adored the women and enjoyed the slower pace, greater variation and top consistency of the women's matches as compared with the men's. In 1969-70, total prize money for the women's pro circuit in the United States between the months of October and May had been $2,000; during the same period the following year, the women were able to play for prize money of $200,000. In the group were eight of the world's first ten and nine of the US first ten. Overseas officials did not feel that these girls were really 'contract pros' and strongly urged American officials to lift their suspension. A newly elected group of USLTA officials did so, and in February 1971 the girls were again eligible for all official teams and for a ranking.

In the spring and summer of 1971, there was a great deal of friction between the USLTA and the WT Women's Pro Tour. Traditional tournaments such as those at Merion, Pa., and Orange, N.J., were offering prize money to the women of $2,500; WT had competing tournaments in which minimum prize money was $20,000 and at Houston the prize money was $40,000. These Virginia Slims tournaments were open to all tournament players, but as late as April they still could not get a USLTA sanction. Eventually a compromise was reached, but the situation was uneasy and unhealthy, and it was felt that the women would again be suspended at the September USLTA meeting.

During the 1971 US Open at Forest Hills, the USLTA issued an ultimatum to the WT Women's Pro Tour. There could be no more minimum prize-money standards, the women's pro tour must not conflict with any traditional event, there could no longer be preliminary or qualifying rounds, the women's pro tour would have to pay a sanction fee of 6 per cent of advertised prize money to the USLTA and Mrs Heldman would have to resign. The ultimatum was turned down by the players and Virginia Slims, and it looked as though the 19 girls would once again be contract pros. When the news leaked out, another 10 top players approached Mrs Heldman to join the group and the tour had 29 pros. The Chairman of the Board of Philip Morris Inc., Joseph F. Cullman III, held a press conference at Forest Hills in which he announced that his company would no longer sponsor the television of the US Open Championships if

Below Billie Jean King. She was one of the top four women to sign up with George MacCall in 1967, before becoming an independent pro in 1970. In 1971 she became the first woman to earn more than $100,000 in the game. By 1973 she had broken Louise Brough's post-World-War-II record with five Wimbledon wins before signing with WTT.

the WT women pros as well as the men contract pros (WCT) were barred. When one reporter asked what he would do with the television money of $250,000, he said he would put it into the Virginia Slims Prize Money Circuit. A few days later the USLTA voted not to bar the women pros.

The 1972 WT Women's Pro Tour had far more prize money than the previous year (some $500,000) and a total of 55 players. The tour opened in San Francisco in January but not exactly with the USLTA blessing. In 1971 the sanction fee for each Virginia Slims tournament was $480; the USLTA wished to raise this fee to 6 per cent of the advertised prize money in 1972. The women and the tournaments baulked. When San Francisco refused to pay more than $480, every participant in the tournament was notified that if she played, she would automatically be suspended. All but one of the women played, and three days later the USLTA lifted the suspension.

It was obvious that these continual fights were not helping the game. There was need for a contract to satisfy both groups, and former US Davis Cup Captain Donald Dell offered his services as negotiator. Helping him, to the women's total surprise, was Jack Kramer. Negotiations began in the first week in February, and after five days of proposals and counter-proposals, a contract satisfactory to both the USLTA and the WT Women's Pro Tour was signed. The Women's Pro Tour was guaranteed autonomy under the USLTA umbrella, and signing this agreement were Bob Colwell (President of the USLTA) and Gladys Heldman.

Sadly, the agreement lasted only a few short months. While the contract was still in effect, the USLTA urged various top women players not to compete on the Virginia Slims Circuit, and the President of the USLTA said that the Women's Pro Tour rules, which were incorporated in the contract, were no longer acceptable. There was an additional dispute over the International Grand Prix rules, which penalized the Virginia Slims tournaments and those who played in them.

In September 1972 the USLTA announced that it was going into the professional promoting business and would organize its own USLTA Women's Pro Tour. It stated that it would hold 22 tournaments with prize money of over $600,000 in 1973. The number of tournaments dwindled to eight and the amount of prize money to $220,000. The Virginia Slims Circuit for 1973 was also announced, with a minimum of 18 tournaments and prize money of $700,000. As it turned out, the Virginia Slims Circuit included 20 tournaments and had prize money of more than $800,000. The women now split into two groups – the USLTA group with Chris Evert and Evonne Goolagong as the stars, and the Virginia Slims group with Billie Jean King, Margaret Court, Kerry Melville, Rosie Casals, Nancy Gunter and Françoise Durr as the headliners. The USLTA, for so many years a purely amateur association which would not even allow a pro to compete in their tournaments, entered the professional promotion business on a full scale in order to combat the WT Women's Pro Tour (the Virginia Slims Circuit).

The Women's Pro Tour developed its own organization, the Women's International Tennis Federation (WITF). During approximately 20 weeks of 1973 the girls agreed to play in WT tournaments; during the rest of the year they were free to play wherever and whenever they wanted. Virginia Slims was the largest individual sponsor; at least 10 of the tournaments were sponsored by other companies. In return, the players agreed to give at least one clinic per person each tournament week and to make at least one other appearance or do one interview as well. The tournament promoter paid $1,000 sanction fee to WITF. This money was used to help qualifiers who made little or no prize money to travel from one tournament to another. The promoter did not pay any travel expenses of players nor appearance money or guarantees. The women played for prize money only and they took their chances.

As a result of the women's organization, Billie Jean King made over $100,000 in prize money in 1971 and again in 1972. Margaret Court earned over $75,000 in the first four months of 1973, with Rosie Casals not far behind with $60,000.

On 1 May 1973 an agreement was reached to end the 'war' between the WITF players and the USLTA-ILTF group. The USLTA-ILTF officials agreed to rescind the bar on the participation of WITF players in the French Championships, Wimbledon and all other international events. In return, the girls agreed not to hold their own circuit in 1974 and to play a USLTA-sponsored circuit instead. The 60-odd members of WITF lost their independence, but spectators would now be able to see all the women players in competition against each other. Virginia Slims would be permitted to sponsor individual tournaments but the 'Virginia Slims Circuit' would be replaced by the 'USLTA Circuit'. The players had proved that women's tennis could attract large crowds and be financially profitable.

In the summer of 1973, US Open chairman Billy Talbert made the astonishing announcement that the prize money at Forest Hills would be the same for the women as for the men. He had found a sponsor, Ban Deodorant, to contribute the additional $55,000. Then World Team Tennis, an American association of tennis franchise owners, presented their new formula to the players. They hoped to entice 48 men and 48 women into playing league matches in May, June and July 1974, and they indicated that they would put $6,000,000 into the game during one year. Salaries for men and women were to be approximately equal, and the first players to sign were John Newcombe and Billie Jean King, the latter at $100,000 per year for five years. Other women who soon followed were Margaret Court, Evonne Goolagong and Linda Tuero. Men included Owen Davidson, Clark Graebner and John Alexander.

The ILTF, through its generous sponsor Commercial Union, decided to fight World Team Tennis by putting more money into the ILTF tournaments in May, June and July. It was expected that 12 ILTF tournaments in these months would have additional prize money of $100,000 each.

And so the pro game for men and women gets richer and richer as the various powers battle over the men and women pros, waging their war with ever-increasing money incentives.

Below, left Françoise Durr at the Washington Virginia Slims tournament in 1972

Open Tennis
John Barrett

Open tennis became a reality on Monday, 22 April 1968, when the Australian left-hander, Owen Davidson, who was then employed as the British National Coach, defeated one of his pupils, John Clifton, 6-2, 6-3, 4-6, 8-6, on the Clubhouse court at the West Hants Club, Bournemouth, in the opening match of the Hard Court Championships of Great Britain. After years of hypocrisy and increasingly flagrant breaches of the unworkable amateur rules the game had at last become honest, but not by unanimous approval of all the tennis-playing countries in the world and not in the way that Britain had envisaged when the revolt was proposed at the LTA's Annual Meeting in December 1967.

An extraordinary general meeting of the ILTF summoned at Sweden's request met in Paris on 30 March 1968 to consider Great Britain's announcement that it would defy ILTF rules and hold open tournaments in Britain in 1968. To the tennis world this would mean an open Wimbledon, something which the All England Lawn Tennis Club had worked for since 1959 when the members at an extraordinary general meeting had called upon the LTA to stage an open championship. Since that time the AELTC had steadfastly refused to act without the support of the LTA. The change had to be constitutional.

After much debate in Paris a compromise was reached whereby the notion of amateurism was retained and national associations were allowed self-determination in deciding the status of their players, except where relations with professionals were concerned. Players would be divided into four categories. Three catered for those who acknowledged the authority of their national associations: registered players (those registered with their own national associations, who could receive money for playing and could play in the Davis Cup; teaching professionals, who received money but were ineligible for Davis Cup play; amateurs, who received no money. The fourth category was for contract professionals, players who did not acknowledge the authority of their national associations. The first three categories could play in all tournaments but the contract men could play only in the limited number of open tournaments agreed for 1968.

The British had wanted to end all categories to make everyone a 'player'. Long experience had taught them that rules beyond which players must not step were unenforceable.

This Paris compromise sowed the seeds of future discord. To understand the troubled events of the years since 1968 it is necessary to analyse the motives of the various groups whose actions shaped them.

The ILTF is the body that nominally governs the game throughout the world. Founded in 1913 with 12 voting countries represented, in 1973 it had 99 member nations, 64 with voting rights and 35 associate members without votes. Its chief functions are to arrange the international calendar, administer the Grand Prix competition and preside over the rules of the game. Any major rule change requires a two-thirds majority of votes cast. The number of votes each nation possesses is determined by seniority so the four major nations that have won the Davis Cup (Australia, France, Great Britain and the United States) have 12 votes each, giving them a strong though not a controlling voice in the Federation's affairs. The ILTF's business is conducted through an annual meeting held during the second week in July and various special committees. The Management Committee has a certain degree of executive power but not enough to take the quick decisions that are becoming increasingly necessary in a fast-changing world game. An Emergency Committee was created in 1972 to overcome this problem.

The President of the ILTF is now elected for a two-year term and there are two Hon. Secretaries; one, Basil Reay, who until August 1973 was also the Secretary of the British LTA, has held the office since 1948. The system has its drawbacks. The President has a limited time in which he can exert significant influence on the course of

Above The first Open tennis match took place on 22 April 1968 at the Hard Court Championships of Great Britain, when Owen Davidson *(left)* defeated his pupil John Clifton *(right)* at Bournemouth.

world events. Unless he is a man of outstanding ability he depends too heavily upon the permanent official who thus himself exerts a considerable influence. At the 1973 Annual Meeting the retiring President, Danish lawyer Allan Heyman, was re-elected for a third year.

This system worked satisfactorily for the leisured world of amateur tennis for which it was invented in 1913. The delegates to the ILTF were and still are those elder statesmen of each nation who had risen to the top of an often oligarchical system. Rarely were they themselves past players of the highest international class, so that they seldom understood fully the problems which faced the top-level game and its players. In the graceful days of garden-party tennis between the two world wars, when only a handful of leading players could make a living from the game through illegal payments, this may not have been a serious shortcoming. But as the game became increasingly professional, in fact if not in name through the 1950s and '60s, the administrators became further and further divorced from the realities. The gulf between the rulers and the international tournament players inevitably widened and widened.

Various half-hearted attempts were made to alter the unworkable and outmoded amateur rules which for lack of a policing system were unenforceable. So farcical was the system and so deeprooted the hypocrisy that those very delegates who held their hands on their hearts at ILTF meetings and swore that their nations at least were not making illegal payments, would return home and pay players at their own tournaments out of sheer expediency.

The ILTF was perpetually short of money. Each member nation paid an annual subscription and nations could be expelled for failing to meet their dues. In 1972 subscriptions were doubled in order to establish a permanent, paid secretariat, the lack of which had rendered the ILTF incapable of quick, unified action on vital issues in the past. The Grand Prix, which began in 1970, provided a heaven-sent opportunity to increase income through a levy on each tournament admitted to the competition. The Davis Cup has been the greatest unifying force among the member nations, but paradoxically it is administered not by the ILTF but by the Davis Cup Nations' Committee. Although there is much overlapping of membership and despite a clear case for centralizing control, the latter committee jealously guards its independence and authority.

After 1945 Davis Cup matches were also the main source of income for many of the individual nations, a factor which assumed importance as the competition became devalued after the introduction of open tennis. Certainly for Australia and the United States the competition has been something of an annual bonanza since the war.

Some nations, such as the Eastern European bloc and France, Italy and Spain, were supported financially by their governments; for Britain the profits from Wimbledon, some £50,000 annually, financed its entire game.

Because of its unique position as the world's top event, Wimbledon has always exerted an important influence on affairs. Herman David, Chairman of a shrewd and knowledgeable committee at the All England Club since 1958, has seen clearly the needs of the modern game. Behind the scenes, impatient of the ineptitude of the ILTF, he has constantly urged the LTA to action and he publicly described the pre-open days of shamateurism as a 'living lie'. After the 1967 defeat of a British proposal to introduce a limited number of open tournaments by a majority of 56 at the ILTF meeting in Luxembourg, he said, 'It seems we have come to the end of the road constitutionally and that the only way to make the game honest is by unconstitutional action – but any unconstitutional step must be taken by the LTA.'

To the players there has never been another tournament like Wimbledon, not merely for its unrivalled organization, charming setting, perfect playing conditions and frenzied public support, but also in the unique worldwide reputation it achieves for its champions. This is something that the professional game had always lacked. Before 1968 the small group of touring professionals, which included 13 men who had won the Wimbledon or US singles titles, played excellent tennis in relative obscurity.

It was with the idea of displaying the undoubted skills of the then amateur leaders to a new and wider public that Dave Dixon persuaded the Texan oil millionaire Lamar Hunt to found WORLD CHAMPIONSHIP TENNIS INC. (see PART 2) with Hunt's nephew Al Hill, Jr, in 1967. He succeeded in signing up eight leading players who began their professional playing careers in January 1968 in Sydney. Although the start in Australia was a success the early experiences in the United States were disastrous. The ideas were too revolutionary and Dixon did not understand that tennis had to be promoted in traditional tennis centres. After six weeks Dixon decided to withdraw; his share of WCT was bought out by Hunt, who gave executive control to Bob Briner and brought in Michael Davies, who had long experience of both amateur and professional tennis as a player.

WCT's quite open intention was to make money – for itself and its players. The contracts signed in 1967 offered large guarantees for a stated number of weeks' play and the players' air fares were also paid. To cover these guarantees WCT had to recover sizeable sums. They staged events of their own, mostly in the United States, and competed in the few open events of 1968. At those tournaments WCT tried to obtain either a corporation fee or a share in the profits of the meeting – as they did in the 1968 French Championships. Both these methods of recompense were later declared illegal by the ILTF.

A second professional group, the National Tennis League, began in 1967. Run by George MacCall, a Californian lawyer who had formerly been the US Davis Cup Captain, the NTL took over the large guarantees of the professional group originally run by Jack Kramer but which in 1965 had formed its own association, the International Professional Tennis Players Association, to run its affairs. NTL's arrival spelled the end of the IPTPA and added to the suspicions of the ILTF that the game was slipping out of its control.

A successful 8-man pro tournament at Wimbledon in August 1967, won by Rod Laver from Ken Rosewall, just a month after John Newcombe had beaten the German Wilhelm Bungert in a one-sided final at the Championships, had whetted the British appetite for open tennis. It is significant that the LTA had sanctioned the tournament on an affiliated ground. In the past the control of the stadia had been one of the strongest weapons used against the pros and it was one used again in 1972 when war was declared on the promoters.

This was the climate in which the British LTA held its annual meeting in December 1967. Inspired by a rousing speech from the retiring chairman, Derek Penman, and despite the threat of expulsion from the ILTF, the meeting overwhelmingly voted to remove the distinction between amateurs and pros in Britain. The inevitable result would be open tournaments in 1968. The LTA said that furthermore it was prepared to go it alone rather than continue with the existing state of deception.

The ILTF countered with a threat to suspend the LTA's membership from 22 April

1968. At the end of January Derek Hardwick, the new chairman, and Derek Penman were sent to visit Australia, New Zealand and the United States to explain the reasons behind the LTA's actions and to enlist support. The special general meeting called by Sweden in Paris showed that their persuasiveness was spectacularly successful. The delegates saw the danger of breaking up the ILTF.

The first year of open tennis passed in a mixture of nostalgia and high excitement as familiar names from the past brought history to life on the courts and some revered reputations toppled. Britain's Mark Cox became the first 'player' to beat a professional—his first victim was the proud king of pro tennis in the 1950s, Pancho Gonzalez, and he added the scalp of double Wimbledon champion Roy Emerson for good measure before losing to Rod Laver in the semi-finals. The ageless Ken Rosewall, at 33, won that first open tournament, the British Hard Court Championships, from Laver and went on to a spectacular four-set victory against Laver in the final of the French Open, his second

Below Mark Cox was the first 'player' to defeat a professional, when he beat Pancho Gonzalez at Bournemouth in 1968.

title there after a gap of 15 years. Laver reinstated himself in most people's eyes with a commanding display in the Wimbledon final against Tony Roche, his third title since 1961, but the season ended on a note of surprise in the United States when Arthur Ashe, still technically an amateur, won the US Open by beating Emerson, Cliff Drysdale and Clark Graebner to reach the final where he out lasted Tom Okker, the Dutch professional, in five rugged sets. But he could not accept the prize money, which went to his delighted opponent. The total prize money at this first major open in the United States was $100,000. Altogether 17 opens were held in eight different countries. Open tennis had surely arrived.

In the euphoria many thought that the problems were over. The ILTF believed that the promoters would conveniently disappear as open tournaments rewarded the players with prize money honestly earned. They could not believe that professional tournaments would succeed; they were now unnecessary.

They did not realize that changes were taking place in the game. The promoters had started to involve a new public who keenly supported indoor tennis played mostly in the evenings. These events were richly sponsored, run by local committees and well promoted as a new arm of show business. This was not new; Kramer had organized such events in the 1950s but now the United States was entering a period of boom; there were many fine new indoor arenas, like the mighty Spectrum Stadium in Philadelphia which could hold 13,000 spectators round two courts. Money was pouring into the game from commercial sponsors; prize money was soaring; more players were available and they were known to be the best in the world thanks to open tennis. Most significantly, American television was starting to realize the potential of tennis as a game with popular appeal. At last the promoters could see the prospect of future profits which, without open tennis, it would have been difficult if not impossible to achieve.

The 1969 season opened in an atmosphere of uneasy alliance. Many ILTF delegates were still convinced that pro tennis would die through excessive overheads on guarantees and travel expenses and lack of demand for professional-only events. The promoters were seen as parasites feeding off the fat of amateur tennis and burrowing beneath the skin of a fast-expanding game in the United States to set up new professional events bringing profit to both promoters and players, but no income for the game's development. The corporation fees asked at amateur-run events and open events too were seen almost as protection money. However, in principle nothing prevented the existing amateur bodies from promoting the pro side of the game themselves. What they lacked was leadership.

Certainly the early expenses of the promoters were high. WCT had added more players to their list, including Tom Okker, Marty Riessen and Ray Moore, and admitted a loss of undisclosed proportions in 1968. It was probably considerably larger then the $150,000 reported as NTL's 1968 deficit. George MacCall had added Billie Jean King, Rosemary Casals, Ann Jones and Françoise Durr to his troupe in 1968, an expensive experiment which lasted only two years. Small exhibition tours were a failure, but these same four girls became the cornerstones of a highly successful women's tour which began in September 1970 (see THE WOMEN'S PRO GAME).

Despite the running war the pros played in all the principal tennis events of 1969. Sensibly, the two groups worked together in providing players for the open tournaments but the tournament organizers were worried that they might eventually be held to ransom. Laver scored a unique second Grand Slam, Ann Jones won her Wimbledon title and then caused consternation in the United States by withdrawing from the US Championships after being seeded no. 1. At the same tournament, where the prize money had risen to $125,000, Laver and Roche withdrew from the men's doubles to attend a pro tournament when rain forced the Championships into a third week. The pull of contracts against tradition was increasing.

At the national level the most notable event was a second French Revolution: a young team of forward-thinking administrators led by the former French Champion, Marcel Bernard, and including Philippe Chatrier, Robert Abdesselam, Pierre Darmon

Above Marty Riessen, signed up by WCT in 1969

and Benny Berthet, ousted the old guard and paved the way for bold innovation and imaginative leadership which included the formation of a paid national squad with John Newcombe as their coach.

In the ILTF too the old guard disappeared. Giorgio de'Stefani, President of the Italian Federation, retired from the Management Committee as did his supporters Jean Borotra of France and Dr Heinrich Kleinschroth of Germany. During his steadfast opposition to open tennis de'Stefani had endured an embarrassing exposure in the world's press of the payments made by the Italian Federation to their Davis Cup player of the early 1960s, Orlando Sirola. The new President was the former Australian test cricketer Ben Barnett.

The July meeting issued a statement attempting to define more clearly the area of authority wielded by the Federation over players. Its first principle, 'The ILTF will legislate for Amateurs, Players and Touring Professionals' was hardly likely to impress Messrs Hunt and MacCall. Before the meeting the big four (Australia, France, Great Britain and the United States) had made it known that they were ready to quit the Federation and deal directly with the promoters unless the natural spread of open tournaments was allowed. Their obvious seriousness resulted in plans to extend the calendar in 1970 and a calendar committee was formed. At last the ILTF was beginning to realize that the scheduling of tournaments to dovetail with events organized by the professional promoters instead of conflicting with them really mattered. The professionals have always complained that the calendar is organized too late. Today, despite attempts to speed decisions, this criticism is still made.

The Davis Cup Competition enjoyed a second year of mediocrity and was doomed to a third as the Davis Cup nations voted by 21 to 19 to continue to exclude the pros in 1970. Thus the players who were winning the major championships, with the exception of Arthur Ashe and his American team mates, were absent from Davis Cup play and the event suffered, as did the incomes of many of the competing nations. Ashe's continued independence on the advice of his manager, the shrewd Washington lawyer Donald Dell, irritated the promoters, who resented their intrusion as a bargaining force with tournament organizers. At one stage they even tried to have Dell's players banned but without success.

Early in 1969 plans were being made by some of the leading players to resurrect the Players Association; it came into being as the International Tennis Players Association under John Newcombe's chairmanship. The players felt the need to establish their own positions among the power blocs that were growing around them, but they were ahead of their time. The ITPA did not survive for more than 18 months because the interests of all the players did not yet coincide. Some were under contract to one of the two professional groups, some felt a strong allegiance to their national associations; others, like Ashe, stood in between and cherished their independence. Nor was the game yet prosperous enough to support more than 20-30 players at the highest level, so the lesser men were sometimes suspicious of the motives of their leaders.

At the end of 1969 the ILTF announced plans for an experimental Grand Prix competition in 1970 (see ILTF GRAND PRIX, PART 2). The brainchild of Jack Kramer, the competition would link together the leading tournaments of the season by awarding points to the players for the round they reached. At the season's end the leaders on points would be awarded prizes from a large bonus pool to be accumulated by levies from each of the tournaments, based on their prize money as well as a contribution from the original sponsor, Pepsi-Cola. The clear intention of the Grand Prix was to make it attractive for players to resist the promoters' blandishments. Strict financial controls were introduced. There would be no guarantees. Players could play only for prize money and WCT was urged to restructure its contracts so that a percentage of a player's prize money could be retained by the company. This was resisted by WCT, who continued to press for lump sum appearance money at open tournaments to cover its outgoings in guarantees and administrative overheads.

The promoters' answer to the new threats was swift. On 1 February 1970 Mark Cox and Graham Stilwell, who had taken Great Britain to the Inter-Zone final of the Davis

Above Julie Heldman (Gladys Heldman's daughter) was one of the first nine players to sign with her mother's Virginia Slims circuit in 1970.

Cup in 1969, were signed by WCT for about £10,000 per year for three and four years respectively. Ismail el Shafei, Egypt's only player of note, went with them. Owen Davidson and Bill Bowrey became the seventh and eighth Australians in the group and Torben Ulrich was signed up from Denmark. By April there were 24 contract men, 18 with WCT and six with the ailing NTL; a merger was expected.

In February the £10,000 Rothmans International became a closed WCT event, instead of one of the Opens that WCT had been granted in return for its players' participation at the major open championships. The fact that a £500 sanction fee would have been paid to the ILTF if the tournament had been open may have contributed to the decision. The Italian Championships in Rome in May lost its Grand Prix status and became a WCT event when it transpired that guarantees had been paid, an action prohibited by the new Grand Prix rules.

The financial failure of the French Covered Court Championships the previous November, another Open which had been given to WCT, fostered a distrust of the French in WCT minds and when in May none of the pros played in the $100,000 French Open due, they said, to travel weariness resulting from a punishing schedule, the mistrust became double-sided.

By now Michael Davies was in executive control of an enlarged WCT, which had absorbed NTL in May, and later in the year, when the dates for the 1971 Grand Prix were being discussed, he was coopted to the calendar committee. This was the first voice the pro game had ever had on an ILTF Committee.

Davies, like Hunt, believed in the future of a pro game independent of the ILTF, but the stakes were getting high. WCT's contract guarantees for 1970 were about $360,000 and air travel plus executive expenses accounted for another $500,000. Even Wimbledon's enlarged prize money of $100,000 (£41,650) was too low for a two-week event, Davies argued, 'the players simply cannot make their guarantees. Some are at $2,000 per week for up to 35 weeks in the year', he said. And whose fault is that, asked the ILTF with some justification. It was not its duty to contribute to the profits of a private company or to enrich still further players who were already well paid at the expense of the development of the game at large. The official attitude was summed up at the Wimbledon meeting of tournament organizers called to explain the rules of the Grand Prix competition. 'The Grand Prix' said a prominent official, 'was designed to kill off the promoters'. WCT had suspected as much all along.

Ashe had now become an important piece in the game and WCT was desperate to have him and the other members of the US team, but Dell turned down an offer of $1 million for a five-year contract. He was prepared to wait for the right moment.

It was not long coming. The richest tournament in the world, the $176,000 US Open at Forest Hills had hardly begun when WCT dropped its bombshell. In 1971, it announced, there would be a $1 million circuit of 20 tournaments for the World Championship of Tennis. Thirty-two players, to be selected by a panel of international tennis writers, would be invited to take part and there would be a final tournament in Dallas, televised nationally, for the eight leaders on points—with a world record first prize of $50,000. The effect on ILTF officials, gathered in New York to announce the enlarged 1971 Grand Prix, could hardly have been more profound. Davies had made no mention of his plans to his colleagues on the calendar committee and for that he was never forgiven.

The $1½ million Grand Prix was duly announced immediately afterwards and open warfare seemed inevitable. The 32 players nominated by the press did not hesitate long. They were being guaranteed a minimum of $600 per week for 20 weeks and the chance of winning a fortune. As John Alexander, Dick Crealy and Allan Stone signed, any hopes of an Australian Davis Cup revival were dashed for good and the disappearance of Frew McMillan and Bob Maud added to South Africa's already troubled existence. But these signings were overshadowed when WCT played its trump card. After long negotiations Dell was at last satisfied that the right moment had arrived and WCT duly announced the signing of Ashe, Bob Lutz and Charlie Pasarell. Now only Cliff Richey, Clark Graebner and Stan Smith were left independent in the United States.

Below Allan Stone joined WCT in 1970.

To add to the confusion there was a revolt by some of the leading women in September. As a protest at the low prize money for women at the Pacific Southwest Tournament in Los Angeles, Gladys Heldman, the owner of *World Tennis* magazine, signed up some players on a token $1 contract and with the aid of Philip Morris Inc. she was soon able to announce the Virginia Slims circuit with prize money of $150,000 for the winter tour and a nucleus of nine players who included Billie Jean King, Rosie Casals, Nancy Gunter, her daughter Julie Heldman, all Americans, and the two Australians Kerry Melville and Judy Dalton. Before the tour began in January 1971 nine more had joined including Britain's Ann Jones, the Wimbledon Champion, and Françoise Durr of France. (See THE WOMEN'S PRO GAME.)

The USLTA at first suspended the players but in February, recognizing that if you can't beat them you join them, removed the suspension in return for sanction fees of $480 from each tournament. Mrs Heldman, unlike WCT, was not in business to make profits so she did not have to ask for corporation fees or executive expenses. Everything went into prize money. During the year the tour flourished; by September 60 players had joined the group and the girls had prospered as never before. Mrs King had won an astounding $117,000, Miss Casals $70,000 and Miss Durr $50,000 – figures that put these three girls into the combined top-ten list that included the men.

Led by the United States the game was fast changing its character. More than $1 million in prize money had been played for in 1970 and there were no signs that the pace would slacken. As the year drew to a close the deadlock between the ILTF and WCT over the scheduling of tournaments in 1971 and the conditions under which the contract pros might play in open events showed no signs of being broken. The two sides were not even talking. A total estrangement had resulted from the way in which WCT had announced their own competition.

Despite the urgings of the world's press the ILTF president, Ben Barnett, was showing no initiative in reopening talks. The USLTA was in a real dilemma. Having tasted success with open tennis for three years at Forest Hills it knew that the sponsor and the television company would not continue with support in 1971 without the pros. This argued for a settlement. On the other hand they were losing their best players to WCT without the guarantee of their participation in Open events and this suggested they should attack.

While the ILTF Management Committee was meeting during the Embassy Championships in London in November, secret informal talks were taking place, also in London, between Michael Davies, Derek Penman, chairman of the LTA, and Derek Hardwick, the ILTF's chief spokesman on the Grand Prix. The meetings were held under the astute chairmanship of Teddy Tinling, who had been closely associated with tennis all his life as a player, referee and fashion designer. He was also a close friend of Davies and the one man he might listen to. After many days and several nights of discussion a formula was reached that, it was hoped, might end the deadlock. On 14 November, just in time to prevent the USLTA from banning all professionals in 1971, a statement was issued jointly by the LTA and WCT saying that it was in the best interests of the world game that they should cooperate to produce a single, unified circuit. They also recommended that the ILTF should appoint Hardwick as their sole spokesman in dealing with the pros.

Predictably there was an angry retort from Ben Barnett, who was annoyed that the British had talked privately with WCT without consulting the ILTF. He rejected the idea that Hardwick should speak for the ILTF and said that they would prefer to speak directly to Hunt and not to Davies.

This episode illustrates graphically the complications which have constantly arisen through the interplay of the various personalities involved. The British found it difficult to bring themselves to negotiate with a man who had once been one of their less than favourite sons. For their part Hunt and Davies, as forthright businessmen, found it maddening and frustrating to face the amorphous fog of the ILTF which spoke with many voices – if it could be persuaded to speak at all in time to get things done.

On 23 November it was reported that Alastair Martin, president of the USLTA, had signed a private contract with Hunt for the participation of WCT players at Forest Hills, and at the end of November an ILTF negotiating team, consisting of Robert Abdesselam (France), Robert Colwell (United States) and Hardwick (Great Britain), finally went to WCT headquarters in Dallas, itself a significant acknowledgment of the growing strength of that organization. By 8 December there was a communiqué stating that 'The ILTF and WCT will work together towards the development and spectator appeal of the game throughout the world'. An agreement in principle had been reached for the participation of the WCT men at Wimbledon, Forest Hills, and the French Open in 1971.

It was an uneasy truce. Even as the new year arrived with hope for a brighter future, Wayne Reid, president of the Australian LTA, was talking of freezing Hunt out of world tennis by putting players under contract to their national associations and making it unappealing for them to sign except for astronomical sums. Already this was being done in France, Germany, Italy and Spain, and the British were discussing it. As the 1971 season began an extended and ambitious WCT program gathered momentum with tournaments in the United States, South Africa, Italy and Iran. The success of the Italian Championships in Rome, where local players were included in the draw of an Open tournament that was nevertheless one of the 20 World Championship of Tennis tournaments, astonished and delighted Italian officials, who had their best gate and highest profit ever. To the ILTF it spelled danger. Control even of its very own national championships might slip from its grasp unless it remained constantly vigilant.

The event that really destroyed ILTF confidence in the good intentions of WCT was the almost total boycott of the French Championships by the contract professionals. After five months of almost constant travel and play, few of the WCT men had the stomach to face two hard weeks of five-set matches on clay with pressureless balls which would inevitably mean long, punishing rallies. Despite Hunt's personal appeal to his players to compete (the contracts made direction impossible) and despite WCT promises to the ILTF, only Ashe of the leading group appeared and the French were snubbed for the second year running. The talks that followed in London, with the object of creating a linked circuit for 1972, opened in a mood of resentment and suspicion. Failure became certain as both sides refused to budge from entrenched positions.

WCT claimed that certain *negotiating* points had been listed as its *demands* in a document circulated by the Management Committee to its members. At a disastrous press conference held at the end of Wimbledon feeling ran high. Herman Davis said: 'We have been asked to increase our payment from £10,000 to £20,000 for the appearance of the WCT players at Wimbledon next year. They also want to negotiate our television arrangement and wish to select the make of ball we use. It is out of the question. I deplore the fact that there are two governing bodies in tennis. Wimbledon stands firmly behind the ILTF.'

The calmest man in the room was Hunt, who claimed that WCT were prepared to cooperate on a 'cost only' basis at all the major events in 1972. Significantly he could not put a figure on it. He did not explain that the TV and ball provisions related to arrangements that had already been agreed for the American part of their own tour. The ILTF claimed that to accede to WCT demands would milk the game of $400,000.

There seemed no solution to the immediate problems and it was no surprise when the ILTF meeting in Stresa two weeks later voted overwhelmingly to ban all contract professionals from all events and grounds controlled by member nations from 1 January 1972. After four years of open tennis, during which the game had boomed as never before in its history, the prospect loomed of a return to the dark ages of split worlds.

In October the new ILTF President, Allan Heyman, a Danish lawyer practising in London, announced plans for an enlarged Grand Prix in 1972 'to save the leading independents from the clutches of WCT'. There seemed little likelihood of a settlement with the professionals and he went on to say, 'I do not see that WCT can play any positive part in tennis'.

Above The 1973 World Championship of Tennis semi-final in Dallas between Rod Laver (far end) and Stan Smith, who went on to win his first WCT final against Arthur Ashe, 6-3, 6-3, 4-6, 6-4

On 9 November an interview with Hunt was published in which a figure of £4,580 was quoted as his price for the participation of his players at Wimbledon. It seemed that an olive branch was being proffered but the ILTF chose to ignore anything but a direct approach to itself. Derek Hardwick put it plainly. 'If he has a proposition to make why has he not written to the ILTF? I have always believed WCT would be prepared to play at Wimbledon for nothing. The argument has always been over a united world circuit and not over participation in two or three tournaments.'

Heyman had always made it clear that he would be happy to talk directly with Hunt to discuss any plan for peace. Again there was reluctance to become involved with Davies. On 17 November Heyman played a masterly card. He announced that the Commercial Union Assurance Company would replace Pepsi-Cola as sponsors of the Grand Prix with a donation of £100,000 for 1972 and a similar sum for 1973. Fears that a shortage of star players would deter sponsors were thus spectacularly dispelled. However, a damper was put on the announcement with the news from the United States that Stan Smith had agreed to join the professionals when he came out of the army the following autumn.

Nine days later WCT staged its World Championship of Tennis final in Dallas before 8,200 excited spectators in the Municipal Auditorium and before millions more throughout the nation who watched a gripping match on television. Ken Rosewall's epic four-set defeat of Rod Laver did a tremendous amount to maintain WCT as a real force in the game and to confirm that tennis was a viable television sport in the United States. Hunt's dream of a 'successful competition in professional sport that is, at the same time, an artistic success' had come true. The final seal of success followed shortly afterwards when WCT announced that eight of its finals in 1972, including the Dallas play-offs in May (it had restructured its year to start in June and end in May) would be televised nationally. At last WCT was on a sound financial footing.

The 1971 season was a curious one. On the courts Evonne Goolagong won her Wimbledon title and another fresh-faced teenager, Chris Evert, burst upon the scene spectacularly at Forest Hills, where she reached the semi-final at her first attempt. Jan Kodeš won his second French title and surprised everyone — and himself — by reaching the final at Forest Hills, where he lost to Stan Smith. Billie Jean King passed the $100,000 mark in prize money and the United States won the last Challenge Round of the Davis Cup against Rumania. By a curious coincidence Ken Rosewall, who had won the first Open tournament in Bournemouth in 1968, also won the last, the Australian Championships of 1972, which began in the last days of 1971 and brought the curtain down on four glorious but troubled years of Open tennis.

The next year opened with a sense of frustration that the administrators had not found a formula to bring peace and prosperity to a game that was so obviously ripe for future expansion. A glimmer of hope appeared in the United States in February when Gladys Heldman, the leader of the women's liberation movement in tennis, was appointed by the USLTA as co-ordinator of women's tennis in the United States and director of the women's tour. With power over scheduling, and a reasonable figure for sanction fees proposed, it seemed that Mrs Heldman might bring peace at last to women's tennis. Her winter tour in 1972 had expanded to $302,000 in prize money, which was not too far short of the men's total of $400,000 for the US Indoor Circuit. She was proving her point that the women could succeed on their own. (See THE WOMEN'S PRO GAME.)

Behind the scenes Heyman was bringing his keen legal brain to bear on the conflict facing the men's game. With valuable help from Donald Dell, who acted as an intermediary with Hunt, and assistance from Kramer (whose knowledge of the professional game's history was unrivalled), he began to discuss secretly with Hunt a formula that would give each party what it wanted.

After a meeting in Copenhagen on 17 April between Hunt and the Management Committee, The Agreement was announced, to begin in 1973 and to last for eight years. Effectively it divided the year into two periods. The first four months would be allocated to WCT events, the remaining months to the ILTF and the Grand Prix events.

WCT would stage 22 tournaments in two groups of 11 each with 32 players and it would hold four special events. The ILTF agreed not to schedule any events during the WCT period with prize money in excess of $20,000. WCT undertook not to renew any contracts as they expired so that eventually all players would become independent and WCT would be merely promoting tournaments – albeit important ones. This made sense for it had always worried the players as well as the ILTF that any company should own a large slice of the game's assets through its player contracts. Sadly The Agreement was reached too late to secure the entries of the WCT men in the French Championships or Wimbledon, though a special dispensation was made for Forest Hills where, surprisingly, the contract professionals were eclipsed as Ilie Năstase won his first major title from Arthur Ashe.

In May WCT staged a second final in Dallas where Rosewall and Laver played another epic match, won again by an exhausted Rosewall in five thrilling sets. Significantly, 21 million people saw the match on American television. Tennis had truly arrived on the US sporting scene.

During the year the independent professionals made the most of the absence of the WCT men. Andrés Gimeno won the French title, his first major crown, and Stan Smith improved upon his 1971 loss in the Wimbledon final to beat Năstase for the title in the match of the year.

Perhaps the most important happening of 1972 was the formation during Forest Hills in September of the Association of Tennis Professionals, a 50-strong players' union which contained all but a handful of the world's leading players, both ex-WCT men and independents. Jack Kramer agreed to become its Executive Director and Cliff Drysdale was elected President. With the ending of contracts and the rapid escalation of prize money the time was ripe for such a body to appear. The players, learning from professional golf, decided to take a hand in their own destiny. If there were any doubt of their sincerity or earnestness it was dispelled by the knowledge that the players had each paid $400 as an annual subscription. Kramer saw the body as 'the greatest potential force for good in the game' but there were anxious frowns on some ILTF faces. Having contained the ambitions of WCT they were worried that the control of the top-level game might yet slip from their grasp.

Above Andrés Gimeno was French champion in 1972, when he was an independent professional.

Otherwise it was a lean year for the men and the women saved the show. Billie Jean King stamped her class on affairs by winning in France, at Wimbledon and at Forest Hills, and she announced that unless Wimbledon prize money was increased considerably in 1973 she would not defend her title.

Meanwhile Mrs Heldman had lost some of her original support, especially within the USLTA. It was no surprise when in September she resigned from the USLTA and announced about a month later the formation of the Women's International Lawn Tennis Federation which did not recognize the USLTA's authority. With some sixty girls she embarked upon a third Virginia Slims circuit despite the ILTF threat to ban the girls from competing in events controlled by it.

With commendable speed the USLTA created from scratch a women's tour of eight tournaments organized by Edy McGoldrick, the Wightman Cup captain, so that there were two separate women's circuits running side by side at the start of 1973. By early May, Chris Evert ($41,000), Evonne Goolagong ($23,000) and Virginia Wade ($22,650) were the leading money winners of the USLTA circuit, and Margaret Court ($75,000), Rosemary Casals ($59,550), Kerry Melville ($34,075) and Billie Jean King ($25,100) headed the Virginia Slims circuit begun the previous autumn.

Because of their attitude the Virginia Slims girls were told, in a letter sent on 15 April by the ILTF, that they were ineligible for prize money from the 1973 Commercial Union Grand Prix. The letter also gave them until 30 April to sign a form stating that they recognized the authority of their national associations, or be suspended. But a compromise was soon found.

On 27 April the USLTA president, Walter Elcock, announced the terms of an agreement with the chairman of Philip Morris, Joseph Cullman III. The remaining Virginia Slims tournaments were to be sanctioned and all women players would be eligible

Above Without many of the best players, the 1973 Wimbledon brought some surprises. Unseeded Alex Mayer *(left)* defeated no. 1 seed Ilie Năstase in the quarter-finals of the men's singles. Alex Metreveli *(right)* was beaten by Jan Kodeš in the final.

for all national championships. The newly formed women's Professional Tennis Players Association which, in effect, consisted of the Virginia Slims girls, ratified the decision three days later. All the girls signed the ILTF form. By 19 June plans had been agreed to merge the two rival circuits into one: from September 1973 all Virginia Slims tournaments would be sanctioned by the USLTA and all women professionals would be able to enter them.

If the women's game was sailing into calmer waters, the men's game was not. 1973 had started peacefully enough with the two WCT circuits occupying the centre of the stage and the US Indoor Circuit providing a platform on which to display the skills of Jimmy Connors ($37,700) and Ilie Năstase ($20,125). But trouble was soon to follow.

Even while the world focused its attention on the WCT Dallas finals in May, when Stan Smith won his first World Championship from Arthur Ashe, there were disquieting rumblings about a new form of tennis competition that, if successful, would revolutionize the whole existing framework of international tennis. World Team Tennis, the brainchild of Dennis Murphy, who had helped to launch the American Basketball Association and the World (Ice) Hockey Association, envisaged a three-month season of league matches between 16 American cities, beginning in May 1974. Each team would need three men and three women, engaged on lucrative contracts: a total of 96 players would not be available to compete in the European tournaments during that period.

Jack Kramer and the Board of ATP were steadfastly opposed to the concept of World Team Tennis, believing that it would not be in the long-term interests of the players or the game to destroy a major part of the Grand Prix circuit.

Close cooperation between ATP and the ILTF might have prevented large-scale defections to WTT, but, as the delegates of both groups were packing their bags for talks during the French Championships in mid-May, a bombshell suddenly exploded.

The 'Pilić Affair' will be remembered as the first trial of strength between the players and the administrators. When the Yugoslav Federation suspended their leading player for not playing in the Davis Cup tie against New Zealand, the Board of ATP threatened to withdraw all its 70 or so players from the French Championships if Pilić were not allowed to play there. To solve the immediate problem Allan Heyman agreed to an appeal hearing of the case by the Emergency Committee of the ILTF (something not allowed for in the ILTF rules). The hearing was held towards the end of the tournament in the presence of Kramer, Donald Dell (attorney to ATP), the Yugoslav Davis Cup captain and Pilić himself.

Although the three-month suspension was reduced to one month (which included the first week of Wimbledon), the ATP delegates were not satisfied. They argued that since all their members acknowledged the authority of ATP, not that of their national associations, Pilić could not be disciplined by the Yugoslav Federation.

To add to the confusion, the Italians defied the ILTF ban and allowed Pilić to play in Rome. To ATP it appeared that the ILTF might be using the Pilić Affair to break up the Association by including Wimbledon in the period of suspension. As a last resort, to give the ILTF a way of saving face, ATP even brought an injunction in the English High Court, seeking to restrain the ILTF and the All England Club from refusing Pilić's entry. Mr Justice Forbes, while not deciding upon Pilić's innocence or guilt as to whether or not he said he would play for Yugoslavia, found that the ILTF had acted within its rules and that Pilić had received natural justice. The injunction was refused.

Despite the court's decision, the ATP directors felt unable to recommend that their members should appear at Wimbledon without Pilić, because this would destroy the purpose for which ATP had been founded – to support its members against unfair treatment.

To the administrators' astonishment, and in the face of persistent press criticism, 79 members did withdraw from Wimbledon before the postponed draw on Friday 22 June. Only Năstase, Ray Keldie and, after much soul-searching, Roger Taylor, remained. Predictably, the public attended in almost record numbers to rave over Taylor and the teenage Swede, Björn Borg. The tournament was won by Jan Kodeš of Czechoslovakia from Alex Metreveli of the USSR. A threat of support for the men from Billie Jean King, president of the new Women's International Tennis Association, did not materialize. She defended her title and won again to beat Louise Brough's postwar record of Wimbledon singles titles.

Attempts to reopen negotiations foundered on the bitterness that had been aroused and, although meetings were held towards the end of the tournament, agreement could not be reached on the composition of a proposed World Professional Tennis Council to govern the money game. At the Annual Meeting of the ILTF in Warsaw in July no heed was given to the players' request that they should be considered as Independent Professionals. The delegates readily approved a motion to give them wide powers to suspend any players who entered into contracts with new promoters – their only defence against possible WTT encroachments.

Shortly before the US Open in August, Năstase, for his part in the Wimbledon drama, was fined $5,000 by the ATP Disciplinary Committee and debarred from any ATP-organized tournaments for a year. During Forest Hills Taylor received the same treatment; Keldie's fine was lower because it was considered that his role had been less important.

Despite a rising tide of support for WTT, whose generous franchise holders lavishly entertained prospective candidates for their teams, the ATP Board once more declared themselves unanimously against the league concept. WTT's Commissioner, former US Davis Cup captain George MacCall, indulged in a marathon talk-in with anyone who would listen in an effort to silence his opponents. However, even suggestions that WTT players would be released for the major European championships and Davis Cup matches in 1974 failed to impress either the ATP or the ILTF, which were talking again of a World Professional Council.

Colour plate Arthur Ashe won the first US Open Championship in 1968.

Administration of the World Game
Basil Reay

Colour plate Maria Bueno, of peerless grace and timing, was a national heroine in Brazil after her Wimbledon triumphs in 1959 and 1960. She won again in 1964 and also won the US singles in 1959, 1963-4 and 1966.

Although lawn tennis as it is known today was first played in England 100 years ago and the US Lawn Tennis Association, the British LTA, and many others were established before the end of the 19th century, there was no international organization until 1913. Until then it was generally but unofficially recognized that the British LTA was the parent body and had the unofficial right to make the rules of the game.

In about 1910 the Hungarian LTA proposed that there should be a central controlling body and the same idea also came forward from Dublin. Nothing was done, however, until July 1912 when the British and French representatives at a Davis Cup tie between the British Isles and France talked at Folkestone. As a result of these talks members of several national associations, representing Australasia, Austria, the British Isles, Belgium, France, Spain and Switzerland, met in Paris in October that year and agreed to do all possible to establish an international organization to control the game. On 1 March 1913 the following associations were represented at the inaugural meeting of the International Lawn Tennis Federation in Paris: Australasia, Austria, Belgium, British Isles, Denmark, France, Germany, Holland, Russia, South Africa, Sweden, Switzerland; the United States was informally represented without a vote.

At first there was some doubt as to whether Britain and the United States would cooperate. It was essential that they should do so as England was the home of the game and the Davis Cup competition was first played in the United States. The British delegates voted for the establishment of the ILTF and have continued since to give it every support; but the United States remained outside for ten years. After World War I the ILTF was in a very weak position with few members and no money. Germany and its allies were excluded for a time and without the United States the ILTF was regarded as basically a European organization.

However, between 1921 and 1923 important decisions were taken, in particular, the ILTF was given the right to frame the rules of the game – and as a compliment to Great Britain it was agreed that they should be 'for ever in the English language'. To please the Americans, the title 'world championships' was abolished, although Wimbledon has continued to be regarded as the premier tournament and has the most coveted title. In place of a world championship a special category, ILTF OFFICIAL CHAMPIONSHIPS (see PART 2) was created. Finally the United States applied for membership in 1924 and was accepted. The ILTF was at last a world body, firmly established; by 1939 there were 59 nations affiliated. This was the calm period in its history when the administration of the game was quite straightforward.

Lawn tennis is administered by national Lawn Tennis Associations in an ever-increasing number of countries. The method of organization varies according to the size of the country and development of the game, but the LTAs all have the same object, to foster and control the game and to encourage as many people as possible to play.

The way the LTA of Great Britain is run can be taken as an example as it is basically the same as many others. The LTA governs the game in England, Scotland and Wales (but not Northern Ireland which, as far as tennis is concerned, joins with the Republic, the two being jointly controlled by the Irish LTA). At the bottom of the pyramid there are the clubs and schools which provide the facilities for play. These clubs send representatives to the county associations (in other countries these may be regional, provincial, or state bodies), which have committees to organize competitions, select teams and coach players; in turn the county associations are affiliated to the national body, to which they send delegates. The LTA has a council whose detailed work is divided among committees which meet regularly and are responsible for such activities as the training of coaches who will teach young players, the development of coaching centres, and the training of young players who show promise. The LTA, with the help of the schools' associations, encourages the development of the game in all types of schools and runs school team competitions. It also organizes tournaments and championships, both senior and junior (because without tournament play no one can make progress) and selects teams for national and international competitions, culminating in the DAVIS and FEDERATION CUPS (see PART 2). There are many other activities. For example, the LTA of Great Britain helps its 3,000 clubs with loans for providing courts, purchasing grounds and erecting clubhouses.

The whole organization is amateur but the administration in Great Britain and many other countries is carried out by a paid secretary and staff from a central office.

The cost of financing these activities varies from country to country. In Britain most of the game's income comes from the Wimbledon Championships. Most national LTAs are helped by government grants, Olympic funds, and, in some cases, football pools. Practically everywhere there is some revenue from tournament fees and from a national annual levy on club members which varies from a nominal 15p per player in Britain to several dollars per player in the United States. Until the coming of open tennis, tournaments were allowed to pay only very modest expenses to competitors; now that substantial prize money can be paid and advertising is allowed most of this prize money comes from television and sponsorship. So tournaments able to find rich sponsors pay the biggest prizes.

However, in spite of all these changes, national LTAs have control over their players and tournaments, even if they do not always exercise it. In turn the national LTAs are governed by the ILTF. With a world game there must be international administration, otherwise there would be chaos.

The management of the ILTF is, in theory, very simple. Each LTA sends two or three delegates to an Annual General Meeting where every alternate year a President and Committee of Management of 11 members are elected. This Committee, which operates on behalf of the nations between the annual meetings, is chaired by the President. It has a representative from each country that has won the Davis Cup three times: Australia, France, Great Britain and the United States. There are occasional murmurs from the not-so-favoured countries that these 'big four' have too much power; in any case, two of them have not won the Davis Cup for 30 years! The other seven members of the Committee include 'at least one from Asia, one from South America, and at least two from Europe'. Europe predominates because tennis is played in more European countries than in any other area, a fact very clearly shown in the Davis Cup, which regularly attracts 32 entries in the European Zones, but only about ten in the Eastern and ten in the American.

The President, a member of the Committee of Management, is now elected by the annual meeting every two years, but may not serve for two periods in succession. It may seem that he would come from one of the great powers but this is not so – the best-known President, Charles Barde, came from Switzerland. The Committee of Management, the heart of the ILTF, meets two or three times a year but subcommittees meet frequently to arrange such matters as the international calendar. Each member serves as an individual and does not have to account to his national LTA. The members are unpaid but receive an expense allowance. The Committee puts proposals to the annual meetings and acts on their instructions in accordance with the ILTF Rules. There have been occasions when the Committee has had to make immediate decisions and seek approval later. For example, in March 1972 it came to an agreement with a professional promoter (WORLD CHAMPIONSHIP TENNIS, see PART 2) that required ratification by the next General Meeting. Its decisions are often reached by a bare majority; with the members' different backgrounds and varying personal opinions and loyalties there is not always complete agreement. For example, in the years when many people pressed for Open tournaments (see OPEN TENNIS) there was a very distinct division in the Committee, usually with the majority against the change.

Until 1973 the work of the ILTF was carried on by the Honorary Secretaries who, with an Honorary Treasurer, were elected each year by the annual meeting. They were unpaid but their expenses were met. According to the Rules one had to be well versed in English, the other in French; in the first 60 years of the ILTF there were only two English and four French Secretaries. When the ILTF was founded it was agreed that

Above The semi-final between H. S. Barlow and E. W. Lewis in 1890. Barlow defeated Lewis 7-5, 5-7, 6-3, 6-2 and was in turn beaten by W. J. Hamilton in the All-Comers' final. There was no international organization for the game at this time: the ILTF was not founded until 1913.

the official language should be French with an official English translation. In fact, and certainly in the last 30 years, the effective centre of administration has been in London. The credit should be given to the British LTA, which encouraged its leading administrators, Anthony Sabelli and then Basil Reay, to give so much to the international body and made no charge to the ILTF for the many expenses incurred. The Honorary Treasurer is also based in London, where the accounts have been kept for the past 30 years. In 1973 the first paid General Secretary was appointed.

Since the first years of the ILTF it has always been recognized that the more mature tennis countries should have more votes. In fact in 1913 it was agreed that Great Britain, the founders, should have six votes as against five from the others. At the time of the 'open' crisis (see OPEN TENNIS) when the 1968 Extraordinary General Meeting was held in Paris, the allocation was as follows:

Australia, France, Great Britain, United States of America, 12 votes each; Canada, Czechoslovakia, Italy, New Zealand, South Africa, 9 votes each; Austria, Belgium, Denmark, German Federal Republic, Japan, Netherlands, Poland, Switzerland, USSR, 7 votes each; Argentina, Finland, Greece, Hungary, India, Ireland, Norway, Pakistan, Spain, Sweden, United Arab Republic, Yugoslavia, 5 votes each; Brazil, Bulgaria, Ceylon (now Sri Lanka), Chile, China, Colombia, Cuba, Ecuador, Iran, Israel, Mexico, Monaco, Peru, Philippines, Portugal, Rumania, Turkey, Uruguay, Venezuela, 3 votes each; Algeria, Bolivia, Burma, German Democratic Republic, Indonesia, Jamaica, Korea, Lebanon, Luxembourg, Malaysia, Morocco, Sudan, Thailand, Trinidad and Tobago, Tunis, Viet Nam, 1 vote each.

Voting powers have been the cause of many bitter arguments and much bad feeling although the distribution of votes is legal and has been approved by the General Meetings. In recent years delegates from Eastern Europe have proposed 'one country one vote' as in the United Nations. They claim it is a matter of simple arithmetic ('one association equals one vote') – but do 2,000,000 American players equal 100 players from a new nation? It seems obvious that Australia (12 votes) with more tennis courts per head of the population than any other country and a fantastic record of achievement, is entitled to more votes than Monaco (three votes) with one club; but the critics ask why Austria has nine votes and Argentina only six. They have a point. The general feeling is that the voting power should be more flexible, varying with the development of the game in each country. In 1968 the committee tried to make modifications in the regrading and nearly succeeded, but was foiled by a handful of delegates who did not wish their LTAs to lose some of the voting power that they had had for years. A committee, reporting in July 1973, did not support the idea of one nation one vote but favoured a reduced scale of one to six votes. No decision was taken.

The committee based its calculations on reports received from the various countries but national figures given have been described as 'misleading' – in one case an association said it had 30 clubs in one town, but when players visited the town in question they found only three. It is impossible to know exactly how many people play tennis in any country. Although, for example, the British LTA has accurate details of clubs, tournaments and results in international events it does not know how many people play, because there are so many players in non-affiliated clubs, public parks, etc.

One important fact remains – decisions can only be taken by the required majority of votes, usually two-thirds (but four-fifths in very important matters at the Annual Meetings).

The ILTF differs further from the United Nations in that a country failing to pay its subscription for three successive years is expelled. No country can send a representative to a meeting unless it has paid its subscription for that year.

During World War II the ILTF was dormant. In the immediate postwar years the whole climate of the administration changed. Many contentious matters were discussed and voted on although some decisions were reached only after long and often acrimonious debate. Yet, in spite of the many differences in outlook and background, the atmosphere has been remarkably friendly. Among the matters discussed and decided on, not of course to the satisfaction of all concerned, were affiliation, amateurism and professionalism, the Grand Prix and sponsorship.

Rule 2 of the ILTF Rules makes it clear that there can only be one affiliation from each country. In 1950 an application for re-affiliation was received from Germany – from West Germany, where the old association, the Deutscher Lawn Tennis Bund, had been reformed and, in fact, had never ceased to function. Germany was one of the original ILTF countries and had a wonderful record at all levels of the game. There was, however, the question of East Germany. The re-affiliation of West Germany was approved by 114 votes to 7 but 28 countries abstained. East Germany remained outside the Federation although there were pious hopes that the players could move from West to East and *vice versa* and the German team might include East Germans. It did not work and eventually East Germany was affiliated as a separate country.

China first affiliated to the ILTF in 1938. When the Republic of China (Taiwan) was admitted in 1970, the People's Republic of China (Peking) withdrew in protest, stating that the ILTF were lackeys of American imperialism and that there was only one China (see TAIWAN, PART 2).

Then there was the case of South Africa, where lawn tennis is governed by the South African Lawn Tennis Union, an all-white organization which had done a great deal for the game and produced fine players. Unfortunately, due to restrictions of its own government, it was unable to allow non-white players to join its clubs or play in its tournaments. This caused bitter feelings, not only in South Africa but throughout the world. Matters came to a head in 1961 when the South African Sports Association, a non-racial body, appealed to the ILTF for help and said that, as it was not represented by the national body, it wanted direct affiliation to the ILTF so that all South African players would be recognized. The application could not be approved because of the rule that there could be only one affiliation per country. Pressure was put on the ILTF by various political organizations and it was proposed several times by the East European nations that the all-white governing body should be dis-affiliated. By a substantial majority on each occasion this proposal was turned down. However, although South Africa remained inside the ILTF, strong action was taken by the non-white players and political organizations through the Davis Cup competition, from which South Africa was excluded in 1970 and 1971, and through the Federation Cup. As a result of all this, dramatic changes were made in South Africa. In 1969, during a visit by the ILTF's Honorary Secretary, Basil Reay, the leading non-white organization, with 16,000 members, was admitted to membership of the South African Lawn Tennis Union. In 1972 South Africa was allowed to stage the Federation Cup on condition that all players, whatever their religion, colour or politics, could take part. The South Africans happily cooperated and non-white players appeared on South African courts in the Federation Cup. In the South African Championships the same year non-white South African players took part for the first time – a breakthrough for the ILTF.

The greatest problem the ILTF has had to face is that of 'amateurism'. As early as 1882 the USLTA ruled that 'none but amateurs shall be allowed to enter for any match played by this association'. For many years it was agreed by all associations that they were administering an amateur game.

There were suspicions that some players were not true amateurs. In 1910 the Olympic Council asked the British LTA to define an amateur lawn-tennis player. That same year some amateurs were suspended by the LTA because they exchanged tournament prizes for 'consumable goods'. The trouble had started because it was generally considered that it was wrong for anyone to make money from playing: an amateur was a gentleman, a professional was an artisan. By 1933 it had become obvious that the rules on amateurism were being broken so an ILTF committee was set up, reporting in 1934 to a specially convened meeting of the ILTF nations. The minutes of the discussion covered 50 pages and decisions were taken on such subjects as travelling and hotel expenses, matches between professionals and amateurs, and the maximum period during which an amateur could claim expenses.

Right Ilie Năstase of Rumania, an 'amateur' in 1972, when he was runner-up at Wimbledon and won Forest Hills

None of this prevented continued infringements of the rules, but the ILTF vainly hoped that the national LTAs and players would obey the rules now that they had been liberalized. Everyone realized that players just could not be expected to play in tournaments throughout the world and reach world class unless they were allowed to receive some expenses and so the eight-week rule (allowing a player to have limited expenses for eight weeks) was evolved. This did not work either. The ILTF office had to check tournament reports and announce to all concerned when each player had had his allocation. This was impossible and the rule was broken everywhere – if not openly, at least 'under the table'. Year after year complaints were made about the way players and tournaments disregarded the rules.

In 1958 everyone knew that the rules were too vague and to some extent unenforceable. The general opinion, firmly held, was that amateurism must be retained but that, while the rules should change with the times, amateur players should not earn their living from the game. There should be a limit on the period during which a player could have expenses, and there should be a daily allowance which could only be exceeded with ILTF permission. The maximum allowed in any country was £5 per day but the administrators knew that the better players received far more; a new word 'shamateur' came into use. It was also decided that a player could have living expenses for 150 days in the year. Realizing that this was exceeded very often, the ILTF allowed 210 days, fully aware that 365 days would soon follow.

At the Annual General Meeting in 1960 a fresh idea came forward that there should be a new category of authorized players who would, with some limitations, be allowed to receive more than bare expenses. This was not voted on but left over for discussion.

Then came a really startling proposal: 'that as an experiment the eight ILTF official championships and a maximum of five others should stage an "open" tournament in 1961'.

By this time a small group of players under contract to Jack Kramer had openly turned professional and were playing in their own restricted exhibition matches and tournaments (see THE POSTWAR PRO GAME). This new proposal would have allowed them and other leading professionals to play in the top tournaments with amateurs. There was immediately strong opposition. The Swiss delegate, one of the founders of the ILTF, said 'the influence of the Kramer professional circus is waning' and that no change should be made. The Irish delegate shouted that it was stupid to invite the 'Kramer circus' to play in the leading tournaments; it would give them a 'blood transfusion'. After a long debate the motion was lost; although 134 votes were cast in favour and 75 against it did not have the necessary two-thirds majority.

For the next ten years, the scene was one of deep division and constant struggle, unprecedented in the hitherto harmonious proceedings of the ILTF. On one side was the pressure group of countries which were losing their best players to the contract

Above The 1973 Wimbledon opened uneasily, after 79 of the members of the Association of Tennis Professionals had withdrawn. The ILTF had one of its most fraught years, while Wimbledon, without most of the best players, still drew record crowds.

professionals and which felt that it was out of date in the modern world of sport to distinguish between 'classes' of players. This group, in particular the British and some others, constantly attempted to press for the relaxation and liberalization of the rules excluding non-amateurs from ILTF tournaments. On the other side were those who had always been amateurs and passionately believed that to maintain the principle of amateurism was one of the fundamental objectives of the ILTF; those who could not afford professionals for their tournaments (most small countries); and those (e.g. East Europeans) who were simply not interested in professionals at all, since they were not allowed to pay players in their tournaments. This anti-professional group did not see why they should 'bend' the rules to accommodate a handful of players and considered that without the stimulus of playing in ILTF events the professionals would soon be unable to continue. However, in the face of unremitting attack from the pressure group, the 'amateurs' were forced into a series of rearguard positions, ending in capitulation.

In 1962 Britain said the only answer was to delete the words 'amateur' and 'professional' from the rules and allow national LTAs to make any rules they liked for their own and visiting players. An American delegate said this would 'sound the death knell of amateur tennis'. A French delegate said this was a bad idea as it would enable the players 'to make personal gain'. An Australian said the abolition of amateurism would ruin the Davis Cup. A number of people felt it was an invitation to chaos. Ninety-five votes were cast in favour, 133 against. Again there was no two-thirds majority. At the same meeting it was proposed that there should be a few 'experimental' open tournaments, but before any decision could be taken the meeting had to decide if a bare majority or a two-thirds majority was required. Some said it would mean that the rules were being changed. A distinguished legal expert from Finland said that any resolution which would cause a change in the rules 'or a like effect' needed a two-thirds majority. Eventually it was decided that a two-thirds majority was needed. The motion was lost when 120 voted in favour and 102 against; a bare majority would have carried the day.

In 1963 the question came up again when it was admitted that any attempt to limit the period for expenses simply led to cheating and hypocrisy. In 1967 the British, Australian and US LTAs again asked for open tournaments as they wanted to see the best players, professional and amateur, on courts together. The Bulgarian delegate, speaking in opposition, said open tournaments would prevent the inclusion of lawn tennis in the Olympic Games and harm small nations. The Australians, who had supported the idea of open tournaments, were taken aback when the President said he had received a letter from Australia giving six reasons why it should be opposed. The Australians quickly replied that they had reconsidered the matter and that there 'should be an experiment'.

After the meeting of July 1967 the British LTA decided that drastic steps would have to be taken. In the autumn private meetings were held with the French, Americans, and Australians, and with promises of their support the LTA went ahead at its own annual meeting in London in December 1967 and passed the following resolution in defiance of the ILTF:

> That all reference to amateurs and professionals be deleted from the Rules of the Lawn Tennis Association and that the Association itself should legislate only for players and take local autonomy to make such rules as they may require regarding the status of their own players and visitors when playing in this country.

On 8 January 1968 all other countries were told what had happened and the President of the ILTF announced that his committee had empowered him to suspend the LTA from 22 April. This caused great concern among the tennis nations. There was certainly some sympathy with the British stand but practically all countries were against the abolition of the distinction between amateurs and professionals. The USLTA went so far as to threaten to withdraw from the ILTF if open tennis was not approved. The Australian LTA supported the British demand for open tournaments and also said that there should be one class of players, but it insisted on working legally and was not in favour of direct action.

To save the LTA, its friends, in particular Sweden and the United States, called for an Emergency ILTF Meeting on 30 March 1968. Delegates from 47 countries, without one dissentient, decided that each country could determine the status of its players and approved the principle of open tournaments. The meeting did decide, however, that the notion of amateurism must remain – they flatly refused to end the distinction between amateurs and professionals. The British LTA had achieved its main object, although it was conceded that touring or contract professionals (those who did not accept the authority of national associations) could only play with the others in a limited number of open tournaments declared 'open to all' by the ILTF. That year 17 open tournaments were approved (see OPEN TENNIS).

After the famous 1968 decision, players could earn large prizes and it was found that an increasing number of them signed contracts with promoters. This caused concern among the 'amateur-minded' officials who saw that many players were no longer free to play in their own national tournaments or the Davis Cup, and two plans were evolved to prevent this drift to the promoters. Some LTAs signed contracts with their players in return for their services. Then the ILTF decided to organize a series of Grand Prix tournaments for which it found a generous sponsor. The idea was to give players some inducement not to sign with a promoter.

In 1970 and 1971 the ILTF GRAND PRIX (see PART 2) was sponsored by Pepsi-Cola. A number of tournaments were selected for inclusion in the competition, provided they paid the ILTF a small fee and paid 10 per cent of their advertised prize money into a pool, to which was added the sponsor's contribution. This pool was distributed among the leading players at the end of the year. In 1972 a new sponsor, the Commercial Union Assurance Company, came along with an even larger contribution, nearly £250,000.

The ILTF tournaments were not short of money, particularly in the United States, where sponsors poured money into tournament promotion. In Britain too sponsors, who were allowed to advertise at tournaments and indirectly on television, provided most of the prize money which could be paid to the players. To save the game the ILTF not only encouraged the payment of large prizes but allowed the advertisements which had previously been so strictly forbidden. Fortunately, some LTAs were able to direct the sponsorship to other activities and established training schemes with the sponsors' contributions. (See SPONSORSHIP, PART 2.)

Admittedly the ILTF helped to establish tournaments where large prizes were paid, but it did not neglect other aspects since it spent part of its modest income on the Amateur Championships of Europe and Asia. It was obvious that most countries could not find the substantial prize money needed for Grand Prix tournaments. They relied on smaller events and the Davis Cup to keep the game alive and the ILTF had to think of them first.

From 1968 to 1971 the ILTF approved a worldwide series of open tournaments and administered them as Grand Prix competitions, charging the organizers a small fee to help to defray the expense of work which had increased considerably in the London office. In the summer of 1971, however, World Championship Tennis (WCT), the leading promoters with over 30 contract professionals including most of the best players in the world, announced that it could not allow its players to compete in the three important Championships at Wimbledon, Forest Hills and Paris, unless certain requests were met by the ILTF. These suggestions, which caused an uproar, were that WCT should receive substantial payments (£20,000 in the case of Wimbledon) in addition to the already generous prize money for the players. WCT also suggested that it should select the ball for each event and charge the manufacturer a fee, and that it should also receive a proportion of the television fees. The ILTF Committee flatly refused to agree, taking the view that this would hand over control of the game to WCT. At the Annual General Meeting in Stresa, Italy, on 7 July 1971 it was unanimously decided that from that day touring professionals under contract to WCT could not play in any event authorized by a national LTA, nor could WCT hold any of its tournaments on the courts of national LTAs. The ILTF took a very firm stand but made it clear that it would always be prepared to talk with the promoters as its aim was the establishment of a unified circuit of tournaments. At the Stresa meeting the ILTF was more united than ever. It was clear that WCT had obliged the ILTF to abandon the idea of open tennis for which so many had fought so hard and so long; but it was hoped that this was only temporary.

In March 1972 WCT, realizing that there was a poor future for contract pros playing on their own, made tentative approaches to the ILTF. Its 1971 proposals were forgotten and a compromise was soon reached. At the ILTF Annual General Meeting in Helsinki, Finland, on 12 July 1972, peace was made when it was decided, with only one dissentient, that the contract pros could play with the others in ILTF tournaments. Furthermore, WCT was to be allowed to arrange its own series of tournaments – open to all – for a limited period each year, the WCT and ILTF tournaments to be based on a unified circuit.

In its first 60 years, the ILTF has grown from a very small European organization to a world body governing tennis in nearly 100 countries. Obviously the whole spirit of the game has changed: while amateurism is preserved for the many millions of those who play with no thought of financial reward, the leading tournaments are now 'big business'. Because of the constantly changing situation it has become increasingly difficult for part-time staff to deal with the many urgent matters and therefore a permanent ILTF office has been established in London.

Presidents of the ILTF

H. O. Behrens	Germany
H. Wallet	France
C. Barde	Switzerland
P. de Borman	Belgium
E. R. Clarke	South Africa
A. E. M. Taylor	Great Britain
J. M. Flavelle	Australia
M. Rances	France
L. J. Carruthers	USA
G. Uzielli	Italy
P. Gillou	France
J. E. Griffith	Great Britain
R. B. Kingman	USA
R. H. Youdale	Australia
D. Croll	Netherlands
G. de'Stefani	Italy
J. Borotra	France
R. N. Watt	Canada
P. da Silva Costa	Brazil
B. A. Barnett	Australia
A. Heyman	Denmark

Playing the Game

The Rules and their Interpretation
Captain Mike Gibson

Rules of Lawn Tennis

(Approved by the International Lawn Tennis Federation 12 July 1972, when Rule 3 was amended)

Reproduced by courtesy of The Lawn Tennis Association
Barons Court, West Kensington, London, W14 9EG

The Singles Game

1   The Court shall be a rectangle, 78 ft (23·77 m) long and 27 ft (8·23 m) wide. It shall be divided across the middle by a net, suspended from a cord or metal cable of a maximum diameter of $\frac{1}{3}$rd of an inch (·8 cm), the ends of which shall be attached to, or pass over, the tops of two posts, 3 ft 6 in (1·07 m) high, the centre of which shall be 3 ft (0·91 m) outside the Court on each side. The height of the net shall be 3 ft (0·914 m) at the centre, where it shall be held down taut by a strap not more than 2 in (5 cm) wide. There shall be a band covering the cord or metal cable and the top of the net for not less than 2 in (5 cm) nor more than $2\frac{1}{2}$ in (6·3 cm) in depth on each side. The lines bounding the ends and sides of the Court shall respectively be called the Baselines and the Sidelines. On each side of the net, at a distance of 21 ft (6·40 m) from it and parallel with it, shall be drawn the Service lines. The space on each side of the net between the service line and the sidelines shall be divided into two equal parts called the service courts by the centre service line, which must be 2 in (5 cm) in width, drawn half-way between, and parallel with, the sidelines. Each baseline shall be bisected by an imaginary continuation of the centre service line to a line 4 in (10 cm) in length and 2 in (5 cm) in width called the centre mark drawn inside the Court, at right angles to and in contact with such baselines. All other lines shall be not less than 1 in (2·5 cm) nor more than 2 in (5 cm), in width, except the baseline, which may be 4 in (10 cm) in width, and all measurements shall be made to the outside of the lines.

NOTE   In the case of the International Lawn Tennis Championship (Davis Cup) or other Official Championships of the International Federation, there shall be a space behind each base line of not less than 21 ft (6·4 m), and at the sides of not less than 12 ft (3·66 m).

2   The permanent fixtures of the Court shall include not only the net, posts, cord or metal cable, strap and band, but also, where there are any such, the back and side stops, the stands, fixed or movable seats and chairs round the Court, and their occupants, all other fixtures around and above the Court, and the Umpire, Net-cord Judge, Foot-fault Judge, Linesmen and Ballboys when in their respective places.

NOTE   For the purpose of this Rule, the word 'Umpire' comprehends the Umpire, the persons entitled to a seat on the Court, and all those persons designated to assist the Umpire in the conduct of a match.

3   The ball shall have a uniform outer surface and shall be white or yellow in colour. If there are any seams they shall be stitchless. The ball shall be more than two and a half inches (6·35 cm) and less than two and five-eighths inches (6·67 cm) in diameter, and more than two ounces (56·7 grams) and less than two and one-sixteenth ounces (58·5 grams) in weight. The ball shall have a bound of more than 53 inches (135 cm) and less than 58 inches (147 cm) when dropped 100 inches (254 cm) upon a concrete base. The ball shall have a forward deformation of more than ·220 of an inch (·56 cm) and less than ·290 of an inch (·74 cm) and a return deformation of more than ·350 of an inch (·89 cm) and less than ·425 of an inch (1·08 cm) at 18 lb (8·165 kg) load. The two deformation figures shall be the averages of three individual readings along three axes of the ball and no two individual readings shall differ by more than ·030 of an inch (·08 cm) in each case. All tests for bound, size and deformation shall be made in accordance with the Regulations in the Appendix hereto.

4   The players shall stand on opposite sides of the net; the player who first delivers the ball shall be called the Server, and the other the Receiver.

5   The choice of sides and the right to be Server or Receiver in the first game shall be decided by toss. The player winning the toss may choose or require his opponent to choose:

a   The right to be Server or Receiver, in which case the other player shall choose the side; or

b   The side, in which case the other player shall choose the right to be Server or Receiver.

6   The service shall be delivered in the following manner. Immediately before commencing to serve, the Server shall stand with both feet at rest behind (i.e. further from the net than) the baseline, and within the imaginary continuations of the centre mark and sideline. The Server shall then project the ball by hand into the air in any direction and before it hits the ground strike it with his racket, and the delivery shall be deemed to have been completed at the moment of the impact of the racket and the ball. A player with the use of only one arm may utilize his racket for the projection.

7   The Server shall throughout the delivery of the service:

a   Not change his position by walking or running.

b   Not touch, with either foot, any area other than that behind the baseline within the imaginary extension of the centre mark and sideline.

NOTE   The following interpretation of Rule 7 was approved by the International Federation on 9th July, 1958:

   7   *a*   The Server shall not, by slight movements of the feet which do not materially affect the location originally taken up by him, be deemed 'to change his position by walking or running'.
   b   The word 'foot' means the extremity of the leg below the ankle.

8   *a*   In delivering the service, the Server shall stand alternately behind the right and left Courts beginning from the right in every game. If service from a wrong half of the Court occurs and is undetected, all play resulting from such wrong service or services shall stand, but the inaccuracy of station shall be corrected immediately it is discovered.

b   The ball served shall pass over the net and hit the ground within the Service Court which is diagonally opposite, or upon any line bounding such Court, before the Receiver returns it.

9   The Service is a fault:

a   If the Server commit any breach of Rules 6, 7 or 8;

b   If he miss the ball in attempting to strike it;

c   If the ball served touch a permanent fixture (other than the net, strap or band) before it hits the ground.

10   After a fault (if it be the first fault) the Server shall serve again from behind the same half of the Court from which he served that fault, unless the service was from the wrong half, when, in accordance with Rule 8, the Server shall be entitled to one service only from behind the other half. A fault may not be claimed after the next service has been delivered.

11   The Server shall not serve until the Receiver is ready. If the latter attempt to return the service, he shall be deemed ready. If, however, the Receiver signify that he is not ready, he may not claim a fault because the ball does not hit the ground within the limits fixed for the service.

12   In all cases where a let has to be called under the rules, or to provide for an interruption to play, it shall have the following interpretations:

a   When called solely in respect of a service that one service only shall be replayed.

b   When called under any other circumstance, the point shall be replayed.

13   The service is a let:

a   If the ball served touch the net, strap or band, and is otherwise good, or, after touching the net, strap or band, touch the Receiver or anything which he wears or carries before hitting the ground.

b   If a service or a fault be delivered when the Receiver is not ready (see Rule 11).

In case of a let, that particular service shall not count, and the Server shall serve again, but a service let does not annul a previous fault.

14   At the end of the first game the Receiver shall become Server, and the Server Receiver; and so on alternately in all the subsequent games of a match. If a player serve out of turn, the player who ought to have served shall serve as soon as the mistake is discovered, but all points scored before such discovery shall be reckoned. If a game shall have been completed before such discovery, the order of service remains as altered. A fault served before such discovery shall not be reckoned.

15   A ball is in play from the moment at which it is delivered in service. Unless a fault or a let be called it remains in play until the point is decided.

16   The Server wins the point:
  a   If the ball served, not being a let under Rule 13, touch the Receiver or anything which he wears or carries, before it hits the ground;
  b   If the Receiver otherwise loses the point as provided by Rule 18.

17   The Receiver wins the point:
  a   If the Server serve two consecutive faults;
  b   If the Server otherwise lose the point as provided by Rule 18.

18   A player loses the point if:
  a   He fail, before the ball in play has hit the ground twice consecutively, to return it directly over the net (except as provided in Rule 22 *a* or *c*); or
  b   He return the ball in play so that it hits the ground, a permanent fixture, or other object, outside any of the lines which bound his opponent's Court (except as provided in Rule 22 *a* and *c*); or
  c   He volley the ball and fail to make a good return even when standing outside the Court; or
  d   He touch or strike the ball in play with his racket more than once in making a stroke; or
  e   He or his racket (in his hand or otherwise) or anything which he wears or carries touch the net, posts, cord or metal cable, strap or band, or the ground within his opponent's Court at any time while the ball is in play; or
  f   He volley the ball before it has passed the net; or
  g   The ball in play touch him or anything that he wears or carries, except his racket in his hand or hands; or
  h   He throws his racket at and hits the ball.

19   If a player commits any act either deliberate or involuntary which, in the opinion of the Umpire, hinders his opponent in making a stroke, the Umpire shall in the first case award the point to the opponent, and in the second case order the point to be replayed.

20   A ball falling on a line is regarded as falling in the Court bounded by that line.

21   If the ball in play touch a permanent fixture (other than the net, posts, cord or metal cable, strap or band) after it has hit the ground, the player who struck it wins the point; if before it hits the ground his opponent wins the point.

22   It is a good return:
  a   If the ball touch the net, posts, cord or metal cable, strap or band, provided that it passes over any of them and hits the ground within the Court; or
  b   If the ball, served or returned, hit the ground within the proper Court and rebound or be blown back over the net, and the player whose turn it is to strike reach over the net and play the ball, provided that neither he nor any part of his clothes or racket touch the net, posts, cord or metal cable, strap or band or the ground within his opponent's Court, and that the stroke be otherwise good; or
  c   If the ball be returned outside the post, either above or below the level of the top of the net, even though it touch the post, provided that it hits the ground within

the proper Court; or

d If a player's racket pass over the net after he has returned the ball, provided the ball pass the net before being played and be properly returned; or

e If a player succeeds in returning the ball, served or in play, which strikes a ball lying in the Court.

NOTE to Rule 22   In a singles match, if, for the sake of convenience, a doubles Court be equipped with singles posts for the purpose of a singles game, then the doubles posts and those portions of the net, cord or metal cable and band outside such singles posts shall at all times be permanent fixtures, and are not regarded as posts or parts of the net of a singles game.

A return that passes under the net cord between the singles and adjacent doubles post without touching either net cord, net or doubles post and falls within the area of play, is a good return.

23   In case a player is hindered in making a stroke by anything not within his control, except a permanent fixture of the Court, or except as provided for in Rule 19, a let shall be called.

24   If a player wins his first point, the score is called 15 for that player; on winning his second point, the score is called 30 for that player; on winning his third point, the score is called 40 for that player, and the fourth point won by a player is scored game for that player except as below:

If both players have won three points, the score is called deuce; and the next point won by a player is scored advantage for that player. If the same player win the next point, he wins the game; if the other player wins the next point the score is again called deuce; and so on, until a player wins the two points immediately following the score at deuce, when the game is scored for that player.

25   A player (or players) who first wins six games wins a set; except that he must win by a margin of two games over his opponent and where necessary a set shall be extended until this margin be achieved.

26   The players shall change sides at the end of the first, third and every subsequent alternate game of each set, and at the end of each set unless the total number of games in such set be even, in which case the change is not made until the end of the first game of the next set.

27   The maximum number of sets in a match shall be 5, or, where women take part, 3.

28   Except where otherwise stated, every reference in these Rules to the masculine includes the feminine gender.

29   In matches where an Umpire is appointed, his decision shall be final; but where a Referee is appointed, an appeal shall lie to him from the decision of an Umpire on a question of law, and in all such cases the decision of the Referee shall be final.

In matches where assistants to the Umpire are appointed (linesmen, net-cord judges, foot-fault judges) their decisions shall be final on questions of fact. When such an assistant is unable to give a decision he shall indicate this immediately to the Umpire who shall give a decision. When an Umpire is unable to give a decision on a question of fact he shall order the point to be replayed.

In Davis Cup matches only, the decision of an assistant to the Umpire, or of the Umpire if the assistant is unable to make a decision, can be changed by the Referee, who may also authorize the Umpire to change the decision of an assistant or order a point to be replayed.

The Referee, in his discretion, may at any time postpone a match on account of darkness or the condition of the ground or the weather. In any case of postponement the previous score and previous occupancy of Courts shall hold good, unless the Referee and the players unanimously agree otherwise.

30   Play shall be continuous from the first service till the match be concluded; provided that after the third set, or when women take part, the second set, either player is entitled to a rest, which shall not exceed 10 minutes, or in countries situated between Latitude 15 degrees North and Latitude 15 degrees South, 45 minutes and

provided further that when necessitated by circumstances not within the control of the players, the Umpire may suspend play for such a period as he may consider necessary. If play be suspended and be not resumed until a later day the rest may be taken only after the third set (or when women take part the second set) of play on such later day, completion of an unfinished set being counted as one set. These provisions shall be strictly construed, and play shall never be suspended, delayed or interfered with for the purpose of enabling a player to recover his strength or his wind, or to receive instruction or advice. The Umpire shall be the sole judge of such suspension, delay or interference, and after giving due warning he may disqualify the offender.

NOTES *a* Any Nation is at liberty to modify the first provision in Rule 30 or omit it from its regulations governing tournaments, matches or competitions held in its own country, other than the International Lawn Tennis Championships (Davis Cup and Federation Cup).

b When changing sides a maximum of one minute shall elapse from the cessation of the previous game to the time players are ready to begin the next game.

The Doubles Game

31 The above Rules shall apply to the Doubles Game except as below.

32 For the Doubles Game, the Court shall be 36 feet (10·97 m) in width, i.e. 4½ feet (1·37 m) wider on each side than the Court for the Singles Game, and those portions of the singles sidelines which lie between the two service lines shall be called the service sidelines. In other respects, the Court shall be similar to that described in Rule 1, but the portions of the singles sidelines between the baseline and service line on each side of the net may be omitted if desired.

33 The order of serving shall be decided at the beginning of each set as follows:
The pair who have to serve in the first game of each set shall decide which partner shall do so and the opposing pair shall decide similarly for the second game. The partner of the player who served in the first game shall serve in the third; the partner of the player who served in the second game shall serve in the fourth, and so on in the same order in all the subsequent games of a set.

34 The order of receiving the service shall be decided at the beginning of each set as follows:
The pair who have to receive the service in the first game shall decide which partner shall receive the first service, and that partner shall continue to receive the first service in every odd game throughout that set. The opposing pair shall likewise decide which partner shall receive the first service in the second game and that partner shall continue to receive the first service in every even game throughout that set. Partners shall receive the service alternately throughout each game.

35 If a partner serve out of his turn, the partner who ought to have served shall serve as soon as the mistake is discovered, but all points scored, and any faults served before such discovery, shall be reckoned. If a game shall have been completed before such discovery, the order of service remains as altered.

36 If during a game the order of receiving the service is changed by the receivers it shall remain as altered until the end of the game in which the mistake is discovered, but the partners shall resume their original order of receiving in the next game of that set in which they are receivers of the service.

37 The service is a fault as provided for by Rule 9, or if the ball touch the Server's partner or anything which he wears or carries; but if the ball served touch the partner of the Receiver, or anything which he wears or carries, not being a let under Rule 13 *a* before it hits the ground, the Server wins the point.

38 The ball shall be struck alternately by one or other player of the opposing pairs, and if a player touches the ball in play with his racket in contravention of this Rule, his opponents win the point.

Appendix   Regulations for Making Tests Specified in Rule 3.

i   Unless otherwise specified all tests shall be made at a temperature of approximately 68° Fahrenheit (20° Centigrade) and a relative humidity of approximately 60 per cent. All balls should be removed from their container and kept at the recognised temperature and humidity for 24 hours prior to testing, and shall be at that temperature and humidity when the test is commenced.

ii   Unless otherwise specified the limits are for a test conducted in an atmospheric pressure resulting in a barometric reading of approximately 30 inches (76 cm).

iii   Other standards may be fixed for localities where the average temperature, humidity or average barometric pressure at which the game is being played differ materially from 68° Fahrenheit (20° Centigrade), 60 per cent and 30 inches (76 cm) respectively.

   Applications for such adjusted standards may be made by any National Association to the International Lawn Tennis Federation and if approved shall be adopted for such localities.

iv   In all tests for diameter a ring gauge shall be used consisting of a metal plate, preferably non-corrosive of a uniform thickness of one-eighth of an inch (·32 cm) in which there are two circular openings 2·575 inches (6·54 cm) and 2·700 inches (6·86 cm) in diameter respectively. The inner surface of the gauge shall have a convex profile with a radius of one-sixteenth of an inch (·16 cm). The ball shall not drop through the smaller opening by its own weight and shall drop through the larger opening by its own weight.

v   In all tests for deformation conducted under Rule 3, the machine designed by Percy Herbert Stevens and patented in Great Britain under Patent No. 230250, together with the subsequent additions and improvements thereto, including the modifications required to take return deformations shall be employed or such other machine which is approved by a National Association and gives equivalent readings to the Stevens machine.

vi   Procedure for carrying out tests:

   a   Pre-compression. Before any ball is tested it shall be steadily compressed by approximately one inch (2·54 cm), on each of three diameters at right angles to one another in succession; this process to be carried out three times (nine compressions in all). All tests to be completed within two hours of pre-compression.

   b   Bound test (as in Rule 3). Measurements are to be taken from the concrete base to the bottom of the ball.

   c   Size test (as in paragraph iv above).

   d   Weight test (as in Rule 3).

   e   Deformation test. The ball is placed in position on the modified Stevens machine so that neither platen of the machine is in contact with the cover seam. The contact weight is applied, the pointer and the mark brought level, and the dials set to zero. The test weight equivalent to 18 lb (8·165 kg) is placed on the beam and pressure applied by turning the wheel at a uniform speed so that five seconds elapse from the instant the beam leaves its seat until the pointer is brought level with the mark. When turning ceases the reading is recorded (forward deformation). The wheel is turned again until figure ten is reached on the wheel scale (one inch (2·54 cm) deformation). The wheel is then rotated in the opposite direction at a uniform speed (thus releasing pressure) until the beam pointer again coincides with the mark. After waiting ten seconds the pointer is adjusted to the mark if necessary. The reading is then recorded (return deformation). This procedure is repeated on each ball across the two diameters at right angles to the initial position and to each other.

Suggestions On How To Mark Out A Court

The following procedure is for the usual combined Doubles and Singles Court. (See note below for a Court for one purpose only.)

First select the position of the net; a straight line 42 feet (12·8 m) long. Mark the centre (X on the diagram) and, measuring from there in each direction, mark:

   at 13 ft 6 in (4·11 m) the points a, b, where the net crosses the inner sidelines,

   at 16 ft 6 in (5·03 m) the positions of the singles posts (n, n),

   at 18 ft 0 in (5·49 m) the points A, B, where the net crosses the outer sidelines,

   at 21 ft 0 in (6·40 m) the positions of the net posts (N, N), being the ends of the original 42 ft 0 in (12·8 m) line.

Insert pegs at A and B and attach to them the respective ends of two measuring tapes. On one, which will measure the diagonal of the half-court, take a length of 53 ft 1 in (16·18 m) and on the other (to measure the sideline) a length of 39 ft 0 in (11·89 m). Pull both taut so that at these distances they meet at a point C, which is one corner of the Court. Reverse the measurements to find the other corner D. As a check on this operation it is advisable at this stage to verify the length of the line CD which, being the baseline, should be found to be 36 ft 0 in (10·97 m); and at the same time its centre J can be marked, and also the ends of the inner sidelines (c, d), 4 ft 6 in (1·37 m) from C and D.

The centre line and service line are now marked by means of the points F, H, G, which are measured 21 ft 0 in (6·40 m) from the net down the lines bc, XJ, ad, respectively.

Identical procedure the other side of the net completes the Court.

Notes: (i) If a Singles Court only is required, no lines are necessary outside the points a, b, c, d, but the Court can be measured out as above. Alternatively, the corners of the

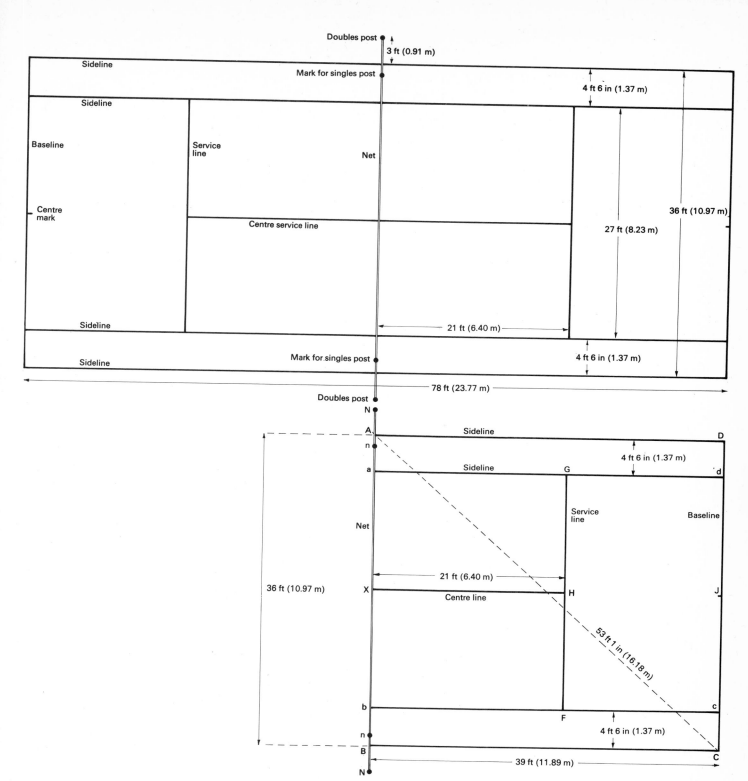

Doubles post

3 ft (0.91 m)

Sideline

Mark for singles post

4 ft 6 in (1.37 m)

Sideline

Baseline

Service line

Net

36 ft (10.97 m)

27 ft (8.23 m)

Centre mark

Centre service line

Sideline

21 ft (6.40 m)

Sideline

Mark for singles post

4 ft 6 in (1.37 m)

78 ft (23.77 m)

Doubles post

N

A

Sideline

D

n

4 ft 6 in (1.37 m)

a

Sideline

G

d

Service line

Baseline

Net

21 ft (6.40 m)

36 ft (10.97 m)

X

H

J

Centre line

53 ft 1 in (16.18 m)

b

c

F

4 ft 6 in (1.37 m)

n

B

C

39 ft (11.89 m)

N

Above Plan of the courts (see Rules 1 and 32)
Right How to mark out a court (see text for instructions)

baseline (c, d) can be found if preferred by pegging the two tapes at a and b instead of at A and B, and by then using lengths of 47 ft 5 in (14·46 m) and 39 ft 0 in (11·89 m) The net posts will be at n, n, and a 33 ft 0 in (10 m) singles net should be used.

(ii) When a combined Doubles and Singles Court is to be used for singles and it is not intended to move the net posts and use a 33 ft 0 in (10 m) net, the ordinary 42 ft 0 in (12·8 m) doubles net must be stayed up at the points n, n, 3 ft 0 in (0·91 m) outside the singles sidelines, by means of 3 ft 6 in (1·07 m) singles posts. To assist in the placing of these singles posts it is desirable that the points n, n, should each be shown with a white dot when the court is marked.

Cases and Decisions

Addenda to the Rules of Lawn Tennis (Approved by the International Lawn Tennis Federation)

Rule 4   Case 1   Does a player, attempting a stroke, lose the point if he crosses an imaginary line in the extension of the net,

    a   before striking the ball,

    b   after striking the ball?

Decision   He does not lose the point in either case by crossing the imaginary line and provided he does not enter the lines bounding his opponent's Court (Rule 18*e*). In regard to hindrance, his opponent may ask for the decision of the Umpire under Rules 19 and 23.

Case 2   The Server claims that the Receiver must stand within the lines bounding his Court. Is this necessary?

Decision   No. The Receiver may stand wherever he pleases on his own side of the net.

Rule 6   Case 1   May the Server in a singles game take his stand behind the portion of the baseline between the sidelines of the Singles Court and the Doubles Court?

Decision   No.

Case 2   If a player, when serving, throws up two or more balls instead of one, does he lose that service?

Decision   No. A let should be called, but if the Umpire regards the action as deliberate he may take action under Rule 19.

Rule 9   Case 1   After throwing a ball up preparatory to serving, the Server decides not to strike at it and catches it instead. Is it a fault?

Decision   No.

Case 2   In serving in a singles game played on a Doubles Court with doubles and singles net posts, the ball hits a singles post and then hits the ground within the lines of the correct Service Court. Is this a fault or a let?

Decision   In serving it is a fault, because the singles post, the doubles post, and that portion of the net, or band between them are permanent fixtures. (Rules 2 and 9, and note to Rule 22.)

Rule 10   Case 1   A player serves from a wrong Court. He loses the point and then claims it was a fault because of his wrong station.

Decision   The point stands as played and the next service should be from the correct station according to the score.

Case 2   The point score being 15 all, the Server, by mistake, serves from the left-hand Court. He wins the point. He then serves again from the right-hand Court, delivering a fault. The mistake in station is then discovered. Is he entitled to the previous point? From which Court should he next serve?

Decision   The previous point stands. The next service should be from the left-hand Court, the score being 30/15, and the Server has served one fault.

Rule 12   Case 1   A service is interrupted by some cause outside those defined in Rule 13. Should the service only be replayed?

Decision   No, the whole point must be replayed.

Case 2   If a ball in play becomes broken, should a let be called?

Decision   Yes.

Rule 18   Case 1   In delivering a first service which falls outside the proper Court, the Server's racket slips out of his hand and flies into the net. Does he lose the point?

Decision   If his racket touches the net while the ball is in play, the Server loses the point (Rule 18*e*).

Case 2   In serving, the racket flies from the Server's hand and touches the net before the ball has touched the ground. Is this a fault, or does the player lose the point?

Decision   The Server loses the point because his racket touches the net while the ball is in play (Rule 18*e*).

Colour plate **Davis Cup.** In the first Final Round (the Challenge Round having been abolished) in 1972, the United States defeated Rumania 3-2 in Bucharest, in probably the most bitterly fought tie in the Cup's history. Here Stan Smith (USA) is seen playing against Ion Ţiriac (Rumania), whom he defeated 4-6, 6-2, 6-4, 2-6, 6-0.

Colour plate **Great Players of All Time.**
Margaret Court, Australia's greatest woman
player, has won every singles and doubles title
of every important championship. She was a
Grand Slam Winner in singles in 1970 and
took the Grand Slam of mixed doubles with
Ken Fletcher in 1963. She is considered by
many to be the greatest woman athlete the
game has known.

Case 3   A and B are playing against C and D; A is serving to D. C touches the net before the ball touches the ground. A fault is then called because the service falls outside the Service Court. Do C and D lose the point?

Decision   The call 'fault' is an erroneous one. C and D had already lost the point before 'fault' could be called, because C touched the net while the ball was in play (Rule 18*e*).

Case 4   May a player jump over the net into his opponent's Court while the ball is in play and not suffer penalty?

Decision   No; he loses the point (Rule 18*e*).

Case 5   A cuts the ball just over the net, and it returns to A's side. B, unable to reach the ball, throws his racket and hits the ball. Both racket and ball fall over the net on A's Court. A returns the ball outside of B's Court. Does B win or lose the point?

Decision   B loses the point (Rule 18*e* and *h*).

Case 6   A player standing outside the service Court is struck by a service ball before it has touched the ground. Does he win or lose the point?

Decision   The player struck loses the point (Rule 18*g*), except as provided under Rule 13*a*.

Case 7   A player standing outside the Court volleys the ball or catches it in his hand and claims the point because the ball was certainly going out of Court.

Decision   In no circumstance can he claim the point:
1   If he catches the ball he loses the point under Rule 18*g*.
2   If he volleys it and makes a bad return he loses the point under Rule 18*c*.
3   If he volleys it and makes a good return, the rally continues.

Rule 19   *Case 1*   Is a player liable to a penalty if in making a stroke he touches his opponent?

Decision   No, unless the Umpire deems it necessary to take action under Rule 19.

Case 2   When a ball bounds back over the net, the player concerned may reach over the net in order to play the ball. What is the ruling if the player is hindered from doing this by his opponent?

Decision   In accordance with Rule 19, the Umpire may either award the point to the player hindered, or order the point to be replayed. (See also Rule 23.)

Rule 21   *Case 1*   A return hits the Umpire or his chair or stand. The player claims that the ball was going into Court.

Decision   He loses the point.

Rule 22   *Case 1*   A ball going out of Court hits a net post and falls within the lines of the opponent's Court. Is the stroke good?

Decision   If a service; no, under Rule 9*c*. If other than a service; yes, under Rule 22*a*.

Case 2   Is it a good return if a player returns the ball holding his racket in both hands?

Decision   Yes.

Case 3   The service, or ball in play, strikes a ball lying in the Court. Is the point won or lost thereby?

Decision   No. Play must continue. If it is not clear to the Umpire that the right ball is returned a let should be called.

Case 4   May a player use more than one racket at any time during play?

Decision   No; the whole implication of the Rules is singular.

Case 5   May a player request that a ball or balls lying in his opponent's Court be removed?

Decision   Yes, but not while a ball is in play.

Rule 23   *Case 1*   A spectator gets into the way of a player, who fails to return the ball. May the player then claim a let?

Decision   Yes, if in the Umpire's opinion he was obstructed by circumstances beyond his control, but not if due to permanent fixtures of the Court or the arrangements of the ground.

Case 2   A player is interfered with as in Case No. 1, and the Umpire calls a let. The Server had previously served a fault. Has he the right to two services?

Decision   Yes; as the ball is in play, the point, not merely the stroke, must be replayed as the Rule provides.

Case 3   May a player claim a let under Rule 23 because he thought his opponent was being hindered, and consequently did not expect the ball to be returned?

Decision   No.

Case 4   Is a stroke good when a ball in play hits another ball in the air?

Decision   A let should be called unless the other ball is in the air by the act of one of the players, in which case the Umpire will decide under Rule 19.

Case 5   If an Umpire or other judge erroneously calls 'fault' or 'out', and then corrects himself, which of the calls shall prevail?

Decision   A let must be called unless, in the opinion of the Umpire, neither player is hindered in his game, in which case the corrected call shall prevail.

Case 6   If the first ball served – a fault – rebounds, interfering with the Receiver at the time of the second service, may the Receiver claim a let?

Decision   Yes. But if he had an opportunity to remove the ball from the Court and negligently failed to do so, he may not claim a let.

Case 7   Is it a good stroke if the ball touches a stationary or moving object on the Court?

Decision   It is a good stroke unless the stationary object came into Court after the ball was put into play in which case a let must be called. If the ball in play strikes an object moving along or above the surface of the Court a let must be called.

Case 8   What is the ruling if the first service is a fault, the second service correct, and it becomes necessary to call a let either under the provision of Rule 23 or if the Umpire is unable to decide the point?

Decision   The fault shall be annulled and the whole point replayed.

Rule 30   *Case* 1   A player's clothing, footwear, or equipment becomes out of adjustment in such a way that it is impossible or undesirable for him to play on. May play be suspended while the maladjustment is rectified?

Decision   If this occurs in circumstances not within the control of the player, of which circumstances the Umpire is the sole judge, a suspension may be allowed.

Case 2   If, owing to an accident, a player is unable to continue immediately, is there any limit to the time during which play may be suspended?

Decision   No allowance may be made for natural loss of physical condition. Consideration may be given by the Umpire for accidental loss of physical ability or condition.

Case 3   During a doubles game, may one of the partners leave the Court while the ball is in play?

Decision   Yes, so long as the Umpire is satisfied that play is continuous within the meaning of the Rules, and that there is no conflict with Rules 33 and 34.

Rule 33   *Case* 1   In doubles, one player does not appear in time to play, and his partner claims to be allowed to play single-handed against the opposing players. May he do so?

Decision   No.

Rule 34   *Case* 1   Is it allowable in doubles for the Server's partner to stand in a position that obstructs the view of the Receiver?

Decision   Yes. The Server's partner may take any position on his side of the net in or out of the Court that he wishes.

History of the Rules

The modern game of lawn tennis is usually considered to date from February 1874, when Major Walter Clopton Wingfield patented his new game, 'Sphairistike'. A month after this, a set of rules was published under Major Wingfield's authorization.

The court was 60 ft (18·29 m) long, 30 ft (9·14 m) wide at the baseline, and 21 ft (6·40 m) at the net posts, which were 7 ft (2·13 m) high, and supported a net 4 ft 8 in (1·42 m) high at the centre. One side of the court was designated the 'serving court', and had a lozenge-shaped 'service crease' in the middle of it, where the server was required to stand while putting the ball into play. The other, or 'receiving' court, was divided at approximately half way by a line parallel to the baseline, and by a perpendicular line running between these two. Thus the area into which the server was required to project the ball was almost the exact opposite of what it is today.

Despite the publication of Major Wingfield's rules, innumerable variations appeared as the game increased in popularity. Eventually, it became apparent that some standardization was needed, and the Marylebone Cricket Club was asked to provide a set of rules. This step was more logical than it might seem, for the MCC was then the governing body of tennis and rackets, as well as of cricket.

Early in 1875 a public meeting was convened to discuss the new rules, and in May the MCC rules were published. The court was still hourglass-shaped, but now 78 ft (23·77 m) long (as at present), 30 ft (9·14 m) wide at the base, and 24 ft (7·31 m) at the net. The net posts were 7 ft (2·13 m) high, but now supported a net 5 ft (1·52 m) high at the posts and 4 ft (1·22 m) high at the centre. The service line was placed at 26 ft (7·92 m) from the net, and the centre line was now between the service line and the net (as we know it).

Scoring was as in rackets; the first player to reach 15 points won the game, except when the score reached 14-all, which was now called *deuce*. The principle of 'hand-in' and 'hand-out' was retained (only the player who was 'hand-in' could serve and win points).

The server was now required to stand with one foot behind (i.e. farther from the net than) the baseline. A second service was allowed if the first failed to go in the proper court after clearing the net; if the ball went into the net the server lost the point.

The size of the ball was laid down as $2\frac{1}{4}$ in (5·71 cm) in diameter and $1\frac{1}{2}$ oz (42·5 g) in weight, but there was tremendous disparity between individual balls, due to the crudity of manufacture.

Improvement though these rules were, they were still not the authoritative code which the game needed. At the end of the section dealing with court dimensions was a provision that they 'may be modified as circumstances may render expedient'.

In 1877, the All England Croquet and Lawn Tennis Club proposed to hold the first Lawn Tennis Championship. It was obvious to the Committee that the existing rules were inadequate for the purposes of a championship, and a subcommittee of three, Henry Jones, C. G. Heathcote, and Julian Marshall, was appointed to formulate a firm code of rules.

The court became a rectangle of the same dimensions as today (78 ft by 27 ft, 23·77 m by 8·23 m). The net posts were placed 3 ft (0·91 m) outside the sidelines and were now 4 ft 9 in (1·45 m) high with the net 3 ft 3 in (0·99 m) at the centre. The service line was placed 26 ft (7·92 m) from the net. Real tennis scoring was adopted in its entirety. A second service was allowed if the first was a fault, irrespective of how the first was committed. The first player to win 6 games won the set, and it is interesting to recall that when the score reached 5 games all, 'sudden death' (i.e. only one more game) was played. The size of the ball and the weight were confirmed, but specifications as to hardness and bounce were not introduced until the 1920s.

The remaining rules were much as they are today, with some minor modifications, and it says much for the gentlemen concerned that the rules they produced have proved to be so clear and precise.

By 1878 it had become evident that the server in the 11th game of any set had an undue advantage over his opponent, and the principle of the advantage set was introduced in the 1878 Championships. The necessity for this did not arise until the Challenge Round, when P. F. Hadow beat the holder, S. W. Gore, by the amazing score of 9-7 in the final set.

In 1880, the service line was moved to 21 ft (6·40 m) from the net, and the net posts were lowered to 4 ft (1·22 m); they came down to 3 ft 6 in (1·07 m) in 1882. The idea of a service 'let' (a ball which touches the net and is otherwise good) was introduced; previously this had been deemed a good service. In addition, players were forbidden to touch the net or volley the ball before it had crossed the net.

The rule about correcting a mistake when a player served out of turn was introduced in 1886. In the following year H. M. Goodman of Edgbaston, Birmingham, wrote to *The Field* Lawn Tennis Calendar advocating a change in the scoring system: points from 1 to 100, with players changing ends every 10 points (compare with VASSS, PART 2).

The end of the beginning came in 1888, with the formation of the Lawn Tennis Association (this was not the first of its kind; it was preceded by the United States Lawn Tennis Association, formed in 1881). At this time the copyright of the rules was held by Mr H. Cox of *The Field*, who had received it from the original three authors. He paid a royalty to the All England Club of a penny for each copy sold. The new Association arranged for this copyright to be passed to them, because they felt it was wrong that one man should hold it.

Since then various small changes have taken place, but the only two of any great consequence have been those made in the foot-fault rule and in the introduction of the tie-break.

Interpretation of the Rules

The present rules, coupled with the explanatory 'Cases and Decisions' are extremely simple to understand. Nonetheless, a few still cause confusion among players and spectators alike, and are worth closer study.

Rule 5 – Choice of sides, service, etc. The writer has known an ex-Wimbledon Champion to win the toss and say 'I'll receive from that end'; the opponent accepted this and was about to walk to the other end. In fact, of course, the person who wins the toss cannot have two bites at the cherry. He may only choose the side, choose to serve or receive, or make the opponent choose. Only when the opponent is given the first choice does the winner of the toss have the right to the second choice.

Rules 12a and 13 – Service lets. Players, especially, are often in a quandary as to whether one or two more services are allowed when play is interrupted after the first service has been a fault. Two more services (i.e. the whole point is replayed) in all cases except when the second ball being served has touched the net and is otherwise good (13a), or when the receiver was not ready, be the service good or a fault (13b). The cat running onto the court during a rally, the linesman's call which should not have been made and which distracted a player, the collapse of the umpire's chair all call for two more services.

Rule 19 – Matters that hinder opponents. This rule covers simple cases, but when a player, by his behaviour, continues to hinder his opponent deliberately, then most nations have regulations that lay down the action the umpire should take.

Rule 22c – Ball returned outside the net post and below the level of the net. This occurs perhaps once or twice in a season. If the ball is otherwise good (i.e. falls within the proper court, this is a good return. But if it hits the umpire, his chair, the net-cord judge, or any other 'permanent' fixture (other than the net, net post strap or band), it is not a good return even though is should fall in the proper court.

Rule 22e – Ball lying on the court. Players are allowed to request opponents to remove a ball lying on the court before starting to play a point. If, during a rally, the ball in play should strike a loose ball on the court, and that loose ball could have been removed before the point began, play must continue, no matter who wins the point. Only if it is not certain that the ball returned was the correct one can the point be re-played. This applies to any other object on the court which could have been removed before the point began (Rule 23, case 7).

Rules 35 and 36 – Serving and receiving service out of order. In every instance except for receiving service out of order in doubles, a mistake is rectified as soon as it is discovered, and all points (and games) played, stand. If the wrong partner receives service in doubles, then the altered order stands for that game, but the original order is resumed next time. However, all points stand.

Evolution of the Foot-fault Rule

There has always been a rule laying down where the server must stand to deliver the ball. In Major Wingfield's rules the server was required to stand in the 'service crease', but there was no penalty if the server stepped out of it.

The MCC rules required the server to keep one foot behind the baseline until the ball was struck, and the service was to be deemed a fault if he failed to do so. This rule remained in force until 1885, when it was decided that a service was not to be con-sidered 'a fault if the server's foot, which is beyond the baseline do not touch the ground when the service is made' (see photograph on page 48).

The following year the rule was changed again; the server was now required to have his front foot on the line when the ball was struck. It was not until 1903 that the server had to keep both feet behind the line until striking the ball.

The rule then remained unchanged until 1958, except for a minor clarification in 1954, which explained that the provision that the server 'shall not change his position by walking or running' did not apply to 'slight movements of the feet which do not materially affect the server's original position'. In 1958 the restriction against having both feet off the ground at the time of hitting the ball was finally dropped, thereby giving the present-day rule.

The Tie-Break

At the original Wimbledon Championships in 1877, the first player to win six games won the set. This meant that at five games all only one more game was played (and the set was won by six games to five). The next year the modern idea of having to hold a clear lead of two games to win an 'advantage set' was introduced, and stood until only recently.

With the rise in the overall standard of tournament players, the improvements in equipment, and the pressure of the modern ball, matches began to get longer and longer, and marathon sets of 12-10 and over became more frequent. The increase in spectator interest in lawn tennis and the greater coverage given by television inevit-ably led to a demand for some means of reducing the length of matches.

For many years James Van Alen of Newport, Rhode Island, worked on this idea and produced a series of suggestions, the Van Alen Scoring System (VASS) and the Van Alen Streamlined Scoring System (VASSS). These included playing a 31-point set, and, in normal scoring, tie-break games. His systems were played at the occasional tournament, as an experiment, but did not catch on at that time. But in 1970 the USLTA announced that it would be using a 'tie-break' in the Championships at Forest Hills that year. The ILTF agreed to the experiment, and, although not the Van Alen system, the tie-break had arrived.

At the present time there are two main tie-breaks being played, with minor varia-tions on each of them. The ILTF has authorized nations to experiment. The main systems are the 9-point 'sudden death' and the 12-point. These come into operation at any time when the game score is level, as decided by the user nation, but generally at either six games all or eight games all, either in every set or in all bar the final set (third in a best-of-three set match, fifth in a best-of-five).

'Sudden death' – the 9-point system – has tremendous drama, but dispenses with the principle of having to be two points ahead to win a game. The player due to serve (A) serves the first two points, his opponent (B) the next two, and they change ends. A serves two more points. The first to win five points wins the game and set. If this point has not been reached, B has two more serves. Should the score now stand at 4 points each, B serves a third point – the sudden death. One variation allows the receiver to choose in which court he will receive the final serve, another allows the server the choice. At Forest Hills in 1970 a men's doubles match was lost on the ninth point of the final set tie-break by a double fault!

The 12-point tie-break comes in many more variations but all have the same basis. The game is the best of 12 points, i.e. the first to win seven points. But, should the score reach six points all, then the game continues until one player has a clear lead of two points. The major variations are in the order of service and the change of ends. In one system player A serves one point, B then serves two points, A two points, and so on until a player wins the game. The alternative is that each player serves two points in turn until the score reaches six points each, when they start to serve single points. Ends may be changed after every four or six points. This tie-break may also produce terrific tension and has the advantage that a player must lose at least one point on his own service before he loses the game. No tie-break can be absolutely fair, but the 12-point seems to have more to recommend it than any other in use.

Below The 1962 finalists, Vera Suková *(left)*, runner-up, and Karen Susman *(right)*, champion, with Colonel W. J. Legg, O.B.E., referee 1951-1962. In the background is umpire Harry Targett, apparently a Czech supporter.

Refereeing and Umpiring
Captain Mike Gibson

The management of the playing side of lawn-tennis tournaments is in the hands of a referee. He is, of course, responsible to the committee running the event. He may well be called upon to assist in the selection of players if the entry is over-subscribed, in the seeding of the events and in conducting the draw. It therefore helps if he has a thorough knowledge of the standard of the players who will enter that tournament.

His main duties can be summarized under four headings: (a) to finish the event on time; (b) to entertain the public; (c) to look after the interests of the players; (d) to administer the rules. The emphasis on (b) or (c) will depend on the type of tournament – whether it be a major international event or a family 'fun' event.

The first duty of the referee is to count the number of matches to be played. In any event the number of matches is one fewer than the number of entries. He must add up the total of finals and semi-finals (for his last few days). He then divides by the number of further days, and that gives the number of matches which must be played each day. This will show how many courts and how many hours of play will be required each day. Some allowance is usually made for bad weather.

Next he has to consider the spectators and the players. In a major tournament he will have to entertain the public with good, interesting matches for six or seven hours each day. To find such matches requires a certain amount of planning ahead and an ability to guess who the winners of the previous matches will be. By looking at the draw for each event, he can see who is likely to come through to the later stages. These players are very important to him, and their matches must be arranged so that they do not suddenly get an overload late in the tournament. He can also see which matches will be of the greatest spectator interest. The task now is to juggle these two factors to ensure that the best matches are ready to be played on the days and at the times wanted. This is work which must be done in advance, and then adapted when the upsets start or weather interferes.

Nothing that has been said above, though, should detract from the basic fact that a tournament is for all the players who compete, and they must all be looked after as much as possible. The lesser players of today may be the stars of tomorrow, and deserve consideration.

As a result of the tie-break, the length of matches no longer has as much effect on the referee's schedule as it used to do, but bad weather and the state of the courts can cause havoc. The referee is the final arbiter on whether play should continue or not, and this is one of the most difficult decisions he ever has to make. It is easy to say that the state of the match, the players involved or the difficulties the referee is having with his schedule should not affect his decision, but of course they do. If the light is failing or drizzle beginning it is highly unlikely that a match will finish satisfactorily, so it is fairer to call it off. Some tournaments allow for play both in daylight and under floodlights. If a match is going to run through from one to the other, the lights should be switched on at a suitable moment before the daylight fades, in order to let the players get used to the artificial light. Finally, the referee has the last word on the rules of the game and, therefore, must know them backwards. The only way to ensure this is by constant revision.

With the money and prestige now involved in lawn tennis, the standards of behaviour on court have tended to slip. Although this is true of only a small minority of players it does mean that nowadays the referee is more likely to be called in to settle disputes than in the past. It must be remembered, though, that the umpire is in control of the match and that the referee cannot usurp his powers. A player may not appeal to the referee on any question of fact, but only on a point of law on which he disagrees with the umpire's ruling, or when the umpire declares himself unable to decide. The referee may remove an umpire if he believes it is in the best interests of the match, but he must inform the committee of his action.

It can be seen that the referee is very much a 'back-room' man. Most of his work

Above, left Rosie Casals fails to ace non-smoking referee Captain Mike Gibson (who succeeded his father-in-law, Colonel W. J. Legg). She is being told to change her Slims line. Wimbledon court etiquette would have been even stricter in the time of B. C. Evelegh *(right),* Wimbledon referee, 1890-1906.

takes place behind the scenes, and a great deal of it before the tournament actually starts or outside the hours of play. During playing time he keeps track of the results, assessing how they affect his future plans and adjusting where necessary.

It cannot be stressed enough that without players there would be no tournament, and they do deserve every consideration. The order of play for the following day should be produced in good time for the players to check it before they leave the ground. In this way they can plan their day, and the spectators will know what is in store for them. The best tournaments are those in which everyone knows what is expected of him, and this also means that the referee has time to plan in peace.

The umpire is as old as the game. There were umpires and linesmen at the very first championship at Wimbledon in 1877.

One of the weaknesses of lawn tennis is that so many umpires and linesmen are required. In the early days it was considered that an umpire and seven linesmen were sufficient for a major competition. The seven consisted of two baselinesmen, two sidelinesmen, two service-linesmen and one centre-service-linesman. All those on lines running the length of the court looked after the whole court (i.e. through the net to the far end). Today, no important match (for example, Davis Cup, Wimbledon, or Forest Hills centre court), would have fewer than the full complement of umpire and twelve assistants. Each of the linesmen on a longitudinal line covers only his half of the court, up to the net, and a foot-fault judge and net-cord judge have been added. In no other game in the world are there a maximum of four players and thirteen 'on court' officials!

Of course this is the extreme. Most tennis matches are played without an umpire at all and a considerable number of championship matches have either a single umpire, or possibly an umpire and three or four linesmen at the most. Why therefore this disparity? The reason, of course, is that some matches are watched by the critical eyes of 15,000 spectators and millions more in front of their television sets. The importance of the occasion, the hundreds of thousands of 'would-be linesmen' and the dreadful eye of the television camera (plus the 'play back') make it essential that every line is covered. Of course mistakes can still be made but the fact that a linesman is covering every line often saves a match from becoming a shouting contest between the umpire and the spectators.

An umpire (linesmen are included here) needs three main qualities. He must be fully conversant with the rules, he must have confidence in himself and he must have tremendous powers of concentration. The rules of lawn tennis are not as complicated as those of many other sports, but still cover a considerable number of pages. They are not difficult to learn, but constant revision is needed. An umpire should, in the writer's opinion, re-read the rules every three or four weeks, and especially just before he officiates at a major championship. To pull out his rule book in the heart of a match and look up a knotty point just isn't on!

Confidence, so they say, is born of knowledge and this is particularly true of tennis. To the players concerned, the result of their match is of the utmost importance, be it a lowly club affair or the final of Wimbledon. Whether there are 15 spectators or 15,000, the match will proceed smoothly if the umpire has confidence in himself, because the players will have confidence in *him*. A good voice, projected so that everyone can hear is a great help. A firm tone, but not patronizing or bullying, is essential. The ability to know when to chivvy or reprimand a player can make or mar any match.

Thirdly concentration is essential. 99 per cent of all the mistakes made by umpires occur because for that moment the official forgot to concentrate. In modern times, the ball can travel at over 100 mph. If, in the split second when the ball hits the ground close to the line, the linesman has just remembered that he forgot to lock his car door, the chance of an error in calling is immediately present. Concentration is one of the main qualities required by an umpire or linesman. It becomes even more important when a match stretches out to over three hours on a hot summer afternoon.

An umpire, acting by himself, is responsible for the complete match, i.e. calling all the lines, foot faults, net cords and the scoring. He also has the last word on any question of fact. When he is assisted by linesmen, the linesman is entirely responsible for cases of doubt (e.g. should the linesman be unsighted or unsure) the umpire can, at the linesman's request, give a ruling, or order a let to be played. There are occasions when an umpire is certain that a bad call has been made. He can attempt to persuade the caller to reverse his decision but he must never bring undue pressure to bear, otherwise the linesman loses his confidence and the players theirs in him.

The calling of 'foot fault' always raises tempers. The rule, as it stands, means that a fault must be called if the player (a) touches the line, or the court within the line before he hits the ball, (b) crosses the imaginary extension of the centre service line before he hits the ball, or (c) materially changes his position. If a player commits one of these offences, he has served a fault just as certainly as if he had hit the ball into the net, or outside the correct service court. An umpire, acting alone, can very easily see if a player steps on the baseline, or into court, in the act of serving and must call 'fault'. A baselinesman can obviously cover all three offences and if in his opinion the player contravenes one of them must call him. A fault is a fault whether it be obvious (such as hitting a ball into the net) or not, and the server who foot-faults has no right to be warned.

Most major tennis nations have an Umpires' Association. Members are dedicated to the game but are not necessarily ex-players. In fact very few players of top class go on to umpire when their playing days are over (possibly they realize what a thankless task it is!). In addition, younger men find it difficult to give up the time that the game demands. A football match lasts about 1½ hours, a day's tennis perhaps 12 hours! However, it is not always the young who are the best umpires. Be that as it may, every association needs new blood and anyone with a knowledge of the game who is keen to enter the ranks of the umpires will find a welcome at his national association. The address of the secretary can always be found from the headquarters of the LTA of the country concerned.

At present almost all the umpires in the world are amateurs. The age-old cry is that they will be better if they are paid. Until this is tried it is impossible to say if it is true. However, it is difficult to see how a major championship could afford professional umpires and linesmen in the near future. Wimbledon uses 180 officials in the first week and over 100 in the second. The mind boggles at the cost! Most people are happy to give of their best for a lunch and tea, a small daily allowance and the chance to acquire a few Centre Court seats. Their best is a very good best.

It is most invidious to single out particular people because the writer has not had the opportunity of watching the game in every country in the world. Two umpires, however, should be mentioned. The first is a formidable, suntanned, bald Frenchman called Gil de Kermadec who can control a partisan crowd of 14,000 at Roland Garros with a magnificent 'sh. . .' over the microphone, while operating the electric scoreboard at the same time. The second is a globetrotter called Bertie Bowron who some years ago completed the 'Grand Slam' by umpiring at the four major Championships of Australia, France, Britain, and the United States in the same year. In addition he is fluent in English, French, Italian and many other languages. These two people and the many thousands of others less well-known help to make this wonderful game run smoothly.

Court Surfaces
C. H. T. Brown

Lawn tennis, like other games originating in England, began as a game to be played on grass – on the lawns that were so much a feature of Victorian England. The growth in the popularity of the game during the last two decades of the 19th century was very rapid and before long it had spread to many other parts of the world.

Since few climates in the world can equal that of the British Isles for the culture of fine turf, alternative surfaces had to be found. In hot and dry climates grass was dispensed with altogether and even in Britain the limitations of grass were soon recognized. By 1900 a variety of 'hard' surfaces was already in use. These were usually waterbound materials such as burned pit shale (blaes), sand and ash. Tarmac courts had also appeared, reducing the requirement for maintenance. In South Africa an ideal material had been discovered in the giant termite ant heaps abundant in that country. They are made from a mixture of sand and clay masticated by the insects to bind it into a solid structure. It was discovered that, when crushed to an appropriate size, this ant-heap material could be rolled into a hard, smooth surface giving excellent playing conditions for tennis.

In 1909 the late Commander Hillyard, R.N., for many years the Secretary of the All England Club and at that time Captain of the English Tennis Team, toured South Africa and played on these courts for the first time. On his return he described them to a friend who was a brickmaker in Leicestershire, where Commander Hillyard lived. The brickmaker, Claude Brown, immediately began crushing and blending burned clays in his brickyard. The first court constructed from these was laid at Commander Hillyard's home and was an immediate success. It was the beginning of an era in tennis-court construction because Brown soon gave up brick production altogether, founded the En-tout-cas Company and devoted all his energies to the production of the first successful proprietary hard court.

The 1920s were years when tennis enjoyed immense popularity and many thousands of courts were constructed both in the United Kingdom and throughout the world. The need for maintenance and the susceptibility to adverse weather conditions of both grass and clay surfaces were recognized from the beginning and there was continual experimentation with alternative materials, but they were slow to be accepted. It was not until the early 1930s that the 'non-maintenance' courts, usually bitumen-bound, began to be laid in any numbers. Unfortunately the playing conditions were often inferior and they were unpopular with good-class players. Their life, too, was somewhat limited.

After World War II the cost of labour rose sharply. The building of grass and clay courts dwindled rapidly and non-maintenance surfaces were laid in huge numbers. The type of construction in various parts of the world increasingly reflected the materials locally available, the price that the court could command and, most important of all, the climate and the length of the tennis season. In temperate climates such as in the United Kingdom, porous draining surfaces were and still are considered essential. Elsewhere, however, and especially in North America and in tropical and subtropical areas, impervious, smooth surfaces were almost universally adopted. These impervious surfaces are usually concrete or bitumen macadam with coloured sealing coats applied to the surface. They continue to be best-sellers to this day.

A major innovation was a porous concrete surface, which first appeared in numbers in the mid-1950s to meet the need for an entirely maintenance-free court combining porosity with first-class playing qualities. Complicated construction techniques delayed its introduction, but, fully developed as it is now, it is undoubtedly the outstanding hard-court surface for temperate climates.

What of the future? The inexpensive bitumen-bound courts, whether pervious or sealed with coloured finishes, will obviously be used for a long time. Porous concrete is likely to continue to provide a pervious, long-lasting, high-quality tennis surface, especially in rainy climates. Today is, however, the age of synthetic substances and

Above Marking out a court in Hungary in 1909

especially of plastics. These materials have come to be regarded as the universal panacea for all manufacturing and constructional problems. Moreover, they are produced and their uses developed and exploited by immensely powerful commercial companies, which invariably look to the leisure field for new outlets for their products. A wide variety of new surfacing materials has been tried for tennis, ranging from woven and needled carpets to exceedingly complex and expensive resinous and plastic pavements. It is interesting to note, however, that it is usually the materials, not the ideas, that are new: rubber sheeting was tried for tennis courts in the mid-1920s as were various resinous materials (unsuccessfully). These new synthetic surfaces show promise of valuable development to come. Already they have solved specialized problems, such as the need for portable surfaces for prestige events. It is more likely, however, that it is with the next generation of synthetics that real progress will be made.

The main factors to be considered when contemplating the installation of a court are size, orientation and location, levels, drainage and surround fencing.

Since 1877 the size of a doubles court has been 78 ft × 36 ft (23·77 m × 10·97 m). Courts constructed today are usually for doubles. These dimensions are for the play lines themselves: the court area is substantially larger to allow ample room for movement outside the play lines. For championship tennis an overall size of 120 ft × 60 ft (36·59 m × 18·29 m) is recommended, but this can be regarded as an absolute maximum; 114 ft × 56 ft (34·76 m × 17·07 m) is adequate for good club play and is the minimum size recommended by the LTA. 110 ft × 54 ft (33·54 m × 16·46 m) is adequate for private, domestic courts. Smaller areas increasingly restrict play. If two or more courts are constructed alongside each other without dividing fences some saving can be made.

Tennis courts should be so orientated that the sun inconveniences the players as little as possible. The best orientation will depend on the geographical location of the court and the time of the day and the time of the year that play is most likely to take place. In the United Kingdom an orientation of NNW/SSE is regarded as the best, but even this is not ideal if autumn and winter play is likely and, with the introduction of better hard courts, out-of-season tennis is becoming increasingly popular.

Tennis courts should ideally be level; it is standard practice to lay them to falls to improve the shedding of water from the surface and substructure and sometimes to minimize site levelling. A fall of 6-9 in (15-23 cm) in the length of a court or 4 in (10 cm) across a court is ample and will not be noticed by the players.

Adequate provision must be made to dispose of water from both the surface and the substructure. Usually a perimeter drain incorporating a pipe and porous back filling is adequate, but, in very bad conditions, it may be necessary to carry spur drains under the court itself. On good sites the thickness of the foundation layer is usually sufficient to dispose of surface water percolating through the court itself. If the surface is impervious it must be laid to falls to shed the water.

Surround fencing is not essential to the game, but it is convenient to have the balls retained on the court area. In the United Kingdom a height of 9 ft (3 m) is considered adequate and 12 ft (4 m) ample. In many parts of the world, however, 12 ft (4 m) is regarded as a minimum and the specifications vary widely. The netting is usually fixed to steel uprights either of angle, T or tube section. The most popular netting is chain-link steel wire netting, usually plastic-covered to improve its life and appearance. For grass courts a temporary surround of steel uprights and cross rods with woven textile netting is often used. It is simply erected by driving it into the turf and draping the netting on the horizontal top rod, like a curtain. It can be removed when not in use.

A wide variety of factors are involved in deciding upon a surface. The quality of play given by a particular surface includes such factors as speed and height of bounce and the type of foothold. In the past a fast, relatively low bounce has always been considered most desirable and championship courts have usually reflected this preference. The factors affecting speed and height of bounce are complex and not fully understood, but it appears that a fast bounce results from surfaces that allow the ball to skid along the surface as it bounces. Surfaces that grip the ball result in a

Above The Wimbledon Centre Court is surfaced with probably the world's most carefully tended grass. The lines are always in the same places, which means that the same areas are worn down by the end of the Championships. The baselines have to be resown almost every year.

slower, higher bounce. Finely mown grass, sands and clays and concrete surfaces allow varying degrees of skid.

Porous concrete and some of the newer synthetic surfaces give a medium-fast game without unduly favouring the power player. The accuracy with which they can be laid, and the texture of their surfaces, give truer bounces and better foothold than clay courts. It is held by some that the very fast championship surfaces have for too long favoured the power player, at the expense of the touch player and the enjoyment of the spectators.

Foothold is also a somewhat controversial subject. That the foothold must be adequate is obvious: falls are distracting and dangerous. On clay courts some players have evolved a game that involves a great deal of rather exaggerated sliding about. It seems, however, that most players can quickly adapt to and eventually prefer a surface that gives a firmer foothold. Certainly the ability to react quickly is greatly improved and so, probably, are overall skills on a surface allowing much less movement of the feet.

Where rain is frequent or evaporation rates are slow it is very important that the surface gives good foothold when damp. Some smooth surfaces must be allowed to dry completely before play is possible. Surfaces vary very considerably in the speed with which they are fit for play after rain or winter snows and frost. Grass is notoriously bad in this respect, whereas porous concrete is comparatively unaffected by rain or frost. Tennis has probably come to be regarded as a summer game only because of the lack, until recently, of surfaces fit for play during the winter months. The popularity of covered courts in areas with severe winters and the advent of porous concrete for more temperate climates are making tennis an all-year-round game.

A grass court, if properly constructed, can last indefinitely so long as the maintenance is adequate. Clay courts, subject again to maintenance and regular top dressing, will last a lifetime. This cannot be said of many of the 'non-maintenance' surfaces. In particular, those bound with bitumen have a much more limited length of life before resurfacing or reconstruction is necessary. The bitumen becomes brittle and breaks down as a result of weathering and mechanical wear until disintegration of the surface begins to occur. Virtually all synthetic and plastic surfaces become brittle and their colours fade with exposure to sunshine (ultra-violet light in particular), although improved plasticizers which delay ageing are always being developed. Unfortunately, the longer the life of the plastic, the more expensive it tends to be. Concrete courts, pervious or impervious, seem to last almost indefinitely if properly constructed. Renewal of surface colouring may be necessary.

Surfaces vary widely in their requirements. Grass and clay require regular maintenance, which in fact must be carried out almost daily if a first-class surface is to be preserved. Maintenance, and especially the labour involved, have become so costly that non-maintenance surfaces have supplanted grass and clay except at clubs and stadia where the necessary ground staff can be provided.

Grass is the traditional surface for lawn tennis and has achieved the ultimate in perfection at the Centre Court, Wimbledon. Its disadvantages, however, are clearly indicated by the fact that grass accounts for fewer than 1 per cent of all new tennis courts constructed. The cost of maintaining a grass court in first-class condition can be very high, mainly because of the cost of skilled labour. Even if funds are available, groundsmen with the necessary skills and experience are becoming exceedingly scarce. When a first-class surface is obtained it is very vulnerable to adverse weather conditions and quickly becomes worn. In the United Kingdom grass courts are only really available for play for about four months and then require major renovation for the following season.

Construction techniques and the types of grasses used vary widely in different parts of the world. In the United Kingdom, various seed mixtures are recommended, but the fastest surfaces are usually obtained with the fine species of grass such as *Festuca* and *Agrostis*. An appropriate mixture is 50% Chewing's Fescue, 20% Crested Dogs Tail, 30% New Zealand Brown Top. Where harder wearing qualities are required, these can be achieved somewhat at the expense of the fineness of the turf by adding smooth-stalk meadow grass, e.g. 40% Chewing's Fescue and 10% New Zealand Brown Top.

The growth of fine grasses is encouraged by soil with a neutral or slightly acid pH. Coarser grasses and weeds tend to flourish more as the alkalinity rises. Weeds should be controlled with appropriate selective weedkillers. Clover is to be avoided as it wears away quickly and can be slippery.

To give the best playing conditions grass courts should be dry and mown very closely. A 'grassy' surface will be slower and, if damp, give a poor foothold.

There is an almost infinite variety of 'clay' courts in play in the world today. The materials used are always indigenous, either natural or semi-manufactured, hence this variation. Clay is usually, but by no means always, an ingredient. The term 'clay' court is used generically to describe the type of court that is basically constructed of loose material bound together into a firm, smooth surface by watering and rolling. Although the construction of the court and, in particular, the selection, preparation and mixing of the material for the final playing surface are very important, the frequency and skill with which the court is subsequently maintained is even more significant. It is usually only at larger clubs and wealthier venues that this type of court can be prepared to perfection, hence clay's rapid decline in popularity for all but tournament play.

Natural unburned clay is frequently used, especially in the United States, but has to be mixed with sand, cinders, etc. to improve its drainage and reduce stickiness when wet. In Europe, clay is normally used in its burned form, e.g. crushed brick, crushed roofing tile, crushed burned pit shale or mixtures of two or more of these materials. In Africa and other parts of the world laterite (a naturally occurring mixture of clays and silica sand) of appropriate texture and grading can make a first-class tennis surface. The ant heaps mentioned above are also still extensively used.

The quality of the game played on clay courts varies as much as the surfaces. Generally the game will be slower than on grass and will favour the touch player rather than the player who relies on a fast power game. The courts themselves are susceptible to variations in the weather and can be put out of action relatively quickly by rain and take some time to recover. They are put completely out of use by frost, which puffs up the surface and makes it soft and sticky.

Bitumen is very cheap and readily available everywhere in the world. A large majority of the 'non-maintenance' courts in use in the world today is constructed with bitumen. Its only real drawback is that it has a relatively limited length of life before, as a result of weathering and oxidization, it begins to lose its flexibility and strength. It also tends to soften and become sticky in very hot weather and to become brittle and fragile in very cold conditions. With bitumen tennis courts, the need to re-surface or reconstruct after a period of years, depending upon the type of construction, must be accepted. Fortunately the materials and techniques used are relatively so cheap as to make this acceptable.

Bitumen courts fall into two main categories: pervious and impervious. In temperate climates, or where rainfall is regular and evaporation rates slow, pervious bitumen courts are either preferred or considered essential. The very smooth painted impervious bitumen courts laid to falls to shed the water may stay damp and therefore be slippery for too long.

Above Laying a Tennisquick court

Techniques for constructing pervious bitumen courts vary widely. There is usually a porous foundation layer of clinker, hard core, crushed stone, etc., and a bitumen-bound wearing course. Crushed, graded stone or gravel is used for the wearing course. The grading of the stone and the quantity of bitumen used, together with the amount of rolling, controls the degree of porosity achieved. The finished surface can either be left the natural black or painted an appropriate colour, taking care not to reduce the porosity of the surface. Alternatively, a fine, coloured grit can be applied to the finished macadam surface. This not only improves the appearance, but also has a tendency to improve the speed of the bounce, which is normally rather high and slow on this type of court.

Impervious bitumen surfaces are preferred where porosity and rapid drying are not so important. In this case a foundation layer will also be used, but the playing surface will be a dense bitumen macadam which is entirely sealed and impervious to the passage of water. Because of this it is essential to lay this type of court with a cross fall to shed surface water, and a high degree of accuracy must be achieved in laying the final surface to avoid puddles. This kind of construction can be cheaper and, when finished with a proprietary tennis court colouring and sealing compound, will give a faster and better game. But unless elaborate precautions are taken, these courts can be very susceptible to damage by frost.

Smooth concrete courts have enjoyed a limited success for many years, being particularly popular in the United States and Australia. They are entirely maintenance free and, because the surface is so smooth, give a fast, low bounce. They can be painted to improve their otherwise drab appearance. If they are not to crack and deteriorate, they must be carefully and expensively constructed, using steel reinforcing and expansion joints. Being totally impervious and relatively non-absorbent, they are too slippery to be successful in damp, temperate climates. They also tend to be unpopular on the grounds that they are hard on the feet, although this is probably one of those objections which are more imaginary than real.

The full potential of concrete was not realized until the advent of the porous concrete court, pioneered under the name Tennisquick in the mid-1950s in Europe. The principle of 'no fines' porous concrete (in which the stone aggregate used has had all the fine particles removed, resulting in a honeycomb texture) has been known for a very long time. How to construct it so that it presented a smooth, even, attractive surface which was instantly porous and yet unaffected by frost and heat expansion took many years of painstaking development. The snags have clearly been overcome and the oldest courts in Europe, now more than 20 years old, show no significant signs of deterioration. The great breakthrough represented by these courts is the fact that they offer a completely non-maintenance surface for temperate climates which, for the first time, provides playing conditions of the very highest standard. Rainwater passes instantly through the surface so that play can start again immediately the rain has stopped. Because no water is held in the surface it is unaffected by frost. It gives excellent foothold even when damp.

Courts constructed with new synthetic materials are constantly being developed. They come in bewildering variety as more and more new materials are discovered and launched by the companies that manufacture them. None can really be said to have 'caught on' as an outdoor surface. Almost always they are impervious surfaces more suited to climates where hot, dry weather can be expected throughout the tennis season. Plastic surfaces in particular, though giving excellent foothold when dry, can be impossibly slippery when damp. They are also very expensive. Traditional construction methods use materials that are intrinsically very cheap. The new synthetic surfaces have so far been many times more expensive, without necessarily offering advantages of sufficient significance to merit this extra cost. However, the necessity for better playing conditions, better appearance, greater length of life and, possibly more important than all of these, an increasing scarcity of skilled labour for court construction, will almost certainly lead to the gradual adoption of these new synthetic materials.

The Development of Playing Equipment
Tony Mottram

Above In the production of modern wooden rackets, 'bends' wide enough for three rackets are made by laying continuous strips of wood ('laminations') covered in special adhesive around a mould. The wedges and leatheroid inserts are then hammered into place and a pressure of several tons is applied to press the frame into shape. After this the dried 'bends' are sawn into three rackets.

Although there is nothing in the rules of lawn tennis governing the size or shape of a racket it seems remarkable that over the years the general specifications of rackets have shown comparatively little change. They have altered of course in methods of construction and in the use of modern materials, but throughout the 100 years of lawn tennis as it is played today, the rackets used have been 25-27 in (63·5-68·6 cm) long and within a weight range of 12½-16½ oz (354·4-467·8 g).

Experience has shown that these limited specifications provide the best performance for adults. A much bigger racket is unwieldy and slow-moving. Some freaks have been tried, e.g. the huge racket used by F. W. Donnisthorpe (see page 36). Too small a racket does not give the player a satisfactory purchase on the ball at impact. It is the ball with its standardized diameter and weight that has always been a principal factor governing racket design.

Until the recent trend of experiments with metal frames, virtually all rackets were made of wood. Early models look crude alongside some of today's productions. They were not so strong, nor did they need to be, since the power game as now practised had not yet arrived and the ball was softer than it is today, a higher compression being introduced into the Rules in the early 1930s. Leather grips were not at first in vogue and cricket's influence could be seen in the way that some racket handles were wrapped with twine. In general though the wooden handles of rackets were fluted for extra gripping power. Their shape varied considerably. Some were square, others slightly oblong as they tend to be today, and some took rounded forms. A handle end shaped like a fishtail was quite the latest thing during the early 1920s. One of the rackets of this time also incorporated a quaint scoring device—a small pointer on the end of the handle, turned after each point as a means of keeping the score.

The advent of the power game with its cannonball serving and harder hitting in the 1930s began to influence racket design. Greater speed was also encouraged by changes in the Rules to provide for a harder ball. All this meant greater strains and stresses on rackets and to withstand them laminated frame construction soon superseded one-piece frames. Racket shafts began to take on slimmer lines. Square edges were rounded. The streamlining process had begun.

Until the 1930s it was the vogue for tennis rackets to be produced with their natural timber finish. But it was not long before painted rackets began to attract a widening public. Leather grips quickly superseded plain wood handles. There were also experiments about this time with the shape of the racket head. This had always tended to be slightly bulbous at the top and the Australians exaggerated this shape by giving an almost flat top to some of their rackets. Jack Crawford, the Wimbledon winner in 1933, was one of its most notable users. Then just before World War II rackets began to be more symmetrical in shape, probably due to the introduction of machine stringing with the more uniform tension it imposed around the racket head.

The heart of a tennis racket is in the strings, which play a vital part in a racket's performance. They influence speed and control and their resilience, or lack of it, governs the player's 'feel' or 'touch'.

Virtually all the early rackets were gut strung with a heavier gauge of string than today's. When laminated frames began to appear it was found that stringing tensions could be raised. This had the effect of shrinking the 'sweet spot' – that area on the racket face, just below the centre, from which the ball reacts sweetly for the player. As a result thinner strings of 18 gauge were produced. These gave the player a marvellous feeling of power because of their high resilience. But during the postwar period, when playing techniques came under closer scrutiny than previously, it was found that this gauge was too lively for most tournament players. The trend in strokeplay at this time was to develop fast footwork from which slow strokes could be made with shoulder weight behind them. For this method of hitting, which survives today in part, an over-lively string was found to be disadvantageous. The ball came off the string too quickly, preventing the player from developing the full degree of touch in the follow-through for which his strokeplay was designed. A slightly thicker string – known in the trade as 'easy 17 gauge' – was found to be the answer. This type of stringing is at present used by nearly all tournament players the world over.

Originally strings were of gut. Today synthetic strings, a comparatively modern innovation, fill a pressing need in the game because best gut is expensive, accounting for approximately half the cost of a new racket. But when you buy gut you are buying performance, not necessarily durability. For most juniors and many club players, durability in a string is more important than the string's high performance, much of which is wasted on players of limited skill. Synthetic strings are available in differently woven forms: their cost generally varies according to the degree of resilience they provide. The multi-strand type are more expensive and more resilient than those with a mono-filament. One great advantage of synthetic strings is that they are impervious to moisture, unlike gut which quickly softens and snaps if left exposed to damp. This makes synthetic strings ideal for juniors or club players who play throughout all seasons of the year.

Modern development in frame design is now concentrated on the construction of metal rackets. These can be made thinner in section than wooden frames, which means that the racket can travel faster through the air. The advantage is therefore most marked in serving and smashing where the fastest possible racket head speed is desirable. There may be an advantage too for the volleyer in fast exchanges at the net, but it is debatable whether metal rackets help to make groundshots more effective. There is a contrary theory that a wooden frame is better, since its greater air resistance holds the racket head back to minimize the tendency to 'slap' at the ball which usually leads to a loss of control. At any rate, it is interesting to note that only five years or so after metal frames made their general début in international tennis, about as many players were returning to wood as were being converted to metal.

Metal rackets were in use more than 40 years ago. These, however, had wire stringing which, lacking much resilience, gave them an immediate disadvantage in top-class play. Today manufacturers appreciate that metal frames must be linked with gut strings, not quite so easy as it might appear, since attaching the stringing to the frame creates a problem.

Fibreglass is another new material used for making rackets. There are also rackets that can be assembled from three main components – head, shaft and grip. This could be a boon to players: if a string breaks the player need only slip a new head into the existing shaft.

Weights of rackets, their balance, and shapes and sizes of grips follow the changes in tennis technique. The light rackets of 13½-14 oz (372·7-396·9 g) popular in the 1920s and early 1930s gradually gave way to heavier models just before World War II when the American Donald Budge won the world's first Grand Slam with a 16-oz (435·6 g) racket, with which he struck the ball a formidable blow.

For some years after 1946, rackets used in international tennis ranged in weight, 13-14¾ oz (368·5-404·0 g) for men and 12½-13¾ oz (354·4-379·8 g) for women. Today, with the emphasis moving more and more on to speed of foot and serve-and-volley tactics, slightly lighter rackets are becoming popular again.

Grip sizes depend largely on the size of a player's hand. As a general rule a large hand can more easily accommodate a 5-in (12·7-cm) grip than a small hand which might best be suited to one with a circumference of 4½ in (11·4 cm). The most suitable shape of grip is usually governed by the player's manner of holding the racket. Most players seem to prefer grips of slightly oblong shape but a more pronounced platform is often preferred by players who place the thumb across the back of the handle for their backhand drive. The balance of a racket is a matter of individual preference. The writer does not think there is anything to be gained by having an excess of weight either in the head or the handle. Rackets that balance around their mid-point are more in favour with most players.

The tension of the stringing, however, does lend itself to quite widely differing

Below In the manufacture of a modern tennis ball, Melton cloth blanks are wrapped around a rubber core.

Above, left After a racket frame has been tested to ensure that there are no flaws, holes are drilled by 32 automatic drills and the frame is painted by electrostatic deposition. Trimmings are added before the final lacquering. The last stage is stringing, seen here.

Above, right Balls covered with Melton cloth are moulded in this press. Every ball is then weighed, tested for compression, and dropped through an electronic bounce machine before being graded and packed.

views. Players who hit the ball extremely hard generally prefer their rackets to be strung very tightly. Those whose games depend more on touch and control prefer a slightly lower tension which allows the ball to sink further into the strings. Stringing tension readings can be misleading because different machines use different scale loading. Today virtually all stringing is done on machines that clamp the racket head into position to eliminate any distortion of the frame – a weakness of hand-stringing methods.

Tennis balls have shown few changes over the past 20 years. Unlike the freedom that exists in racket design, the weight, size, bounce, and compression of balls are all bound by regulations. Only those balls passing the most stringent random tests receive the stamp of acceptance by national associations. There have been alterations in the material for covering tennis balls. This is now made from a mixture of wool and nylon that does not impair playing qualities but provides a longer life (see BALL, PART 2).

One innovation in ball manufacturing that has come since the mid-1960s has been the pressureless ball. Unlike the normal tennis ball, which carries an internal pressure to keep it hard, the pressureless ball acquires its hardness solely from the way its core is constructed. Its advantage comes from uniform playing qualities no matter how long it may have been in the shop before purchase. The pressure in the normal ball gradually drops after manufacture. Tournament players, however, prefer the playing qualities of the normal ball. It is more responsive to the racket strings than the pressureless type which feels harsh and heavy.

Developments in clothing and shoes have also played a part in meeting the greater demands of athleticism in modern tennis. The long white flannels which could still be seen at Wimbledon after World War II are garments of another era. Today's champion attires himself in smartly cut but comfortably fitting shorts and shirts with short sleeves. He uses shoes specially made for the game with sole patterns carefully designed to suit the local court surface. (See FOOTWEAR, PART 2.)

Women's tennis, however, has developed not only as a highly athletic art, but as a stage for the presentation of a wide range of shorts, tops, skirts and dresses (see FASHION, PART 2). The commercial aspects of tennis on colour television has also put the 'predominantly white' etiquette of the game under considerable pressure.

The Development of Technique and Strokeplay
Tony Mottram

It is just 100 years ago that lawn tennis as it is known today was evolved on the lawns of England's stately homes. A more energetic outdoor pursuit than croquet was being sought by middle-aged men of private means and plenty of leisure. Lawn tennis not only suited their inclinations but in those late Victorian times fitted itself perfectly to the emerging athletic emancipation of women. Croquet and the lawns on which the new game was first played both influenced early techniques. The ball kept low on grass and the most effective return was seen by the first players to be with the vertical croquet swing. This allowed the ball to be dug up with slice – a stroke copied from real tennis and rackets, both much older games and from which lawn tennis was derived.

From its garden-pastime beginning, lawn tennis expanded rapidly into clubs. Interest also spread abroad as international competition followed. The Renshaw brothers, Ernest and William, who led Great Britain for an 8-year period from 1881, were largely responsible for the early development of the basics of modern technique. Until they arrived on the scene, S. W. Gore, P. F. Hadow and J. T. Hartley, who won at Wimbledon from the first Championship there in 1877, brought to the tennis court their rackets technique – a game at which all three excelled. The Renshaws, however, saw effective lawn tennis methods as being more than a crude assortment of strokes borrowed from existing games, and their zeal and enthusiasm took the new game into the first stage towards becoming a vigorous, skilful, and competitive art.

It must be remembered that before 1880 the height of the net at the posts was 4 ft 9 in (1·45 m). This limited the speed of baseline driving and encouraged long rallies with careful returns. The game became a test of patience and endurance.

The first sign of ingenuity in breaking the *impasse* came with the introduction of volleying. In his quaint little book, *Lawn Tennis* (1889), H. W. W. Wilberforce recalls:

> I well remember playing in a club match in the country where one of the players threw down his racket and refused to go on playing against a low fellow who insisted on volleying his best stroke, a heavily cut [real] tennis stroke, which had up to then been regarded by his fellow club-men as unreturnable.

It was the Renshaws who developed volleying in competitive tennis as an effective tactic to challenge the hitherto supreme baseline play of such men as Lawford and Lubbock. Although the net had been lowered in 1880 it still stood at 4 ft (1·22 m) at the posts. This limited the speed and angle of passing shots and allowed the Renshaws to play from just behind the service line – an ineffective position today – from where they were able to dominate the 'rests', as rallies were then called.

A balance between the two opposing styles of play was struck with the further lowering of the net to 3 ft 6 in (1·07 m) at the posts in 1883. William Renshaw continued to dominate only because he saw that volleying could not succeed unless backed up by skill with drives.

A transitional period of technical and tactical development followed. For instance Ernest Renshaw used the lob as the basis of his success. Others were experimenting with volleying from a daring position, much closer to the net than ever before. At the same time different stroke techniques were evolving all over the world as lawn tennis spread to surfaces other than grass. In continental Europe lawns suitable for tennis have always been difficult to grow, and the first hard courts were built of local materials. One of the first was at the Hôtel Beau Site in Cannes during the early 1890s and it was so perfectly constructed (from clay excavated from the Esterel Mountains of the Côte d'Azur) that its surface became famous with leading players who all wished to play on *terre battue*.

By the turn of the century not only were the clay courts of France and the ant-heap surfaces of South Africa well known and well liked, but covered hard courts were being built in Britain and many European countries (see COURT SURFACES). Scandinavia

Above Malcolm D. Whitman *(left)* was the
exponent of the 'reverse twist' service at the
turn of the century. It curved and twisted the
opposite way to Holcombe Ward's 'American
twist' service *(right)*.

was a pioneer area of indoor play and wood courts began to make their appearance at
this time.

Britain was also experimenting. It is recorded for example that the Renshaws developed their play on asphalt – a type of court that at £300 a time was as expensive as
concrete. Courts were also constructed of shale, brick dust, ash and ground slate and
were much cheaper at around £120. Some of them, however, were dirty and dusty to
play on. Wilberforce records that 'fine particles of cinder, getting into the player's
shoes, drive him to distraction'.

North of the Border the climate demanded porous hard-court construction. The
blaes courts of Scotland were made from a mixture of burned clay and coal ash in
plentiful supply at the pits.

The different surfaces produced a variety of playing conditions which influenced
local players' technique – as indeed they can and do today. Britain's grass courts and
the clay courts of continental Europe gave the ball a low bounce that encouraged the
use of an open racket face and an open grip. The English grip, as it became known, was
widely copied throughout Europe and was subsequently called the Continental grip,
as it still is today. It allowed both the forehand and backhand strokes to be made without change. (See GRIPS, PART 2.)

In the United States too, a one-grip method was being tried. Although grass-court
tennis was flourishing in the East, the cement courts of California brought their own
difficulties. The ball's higher bounce off cement could not easily be handled with an
open grip. A much more closed grip was needed that allowed the racket face to come
over the ball. Placing the hand at the back of the handle allowed the player to hit the
high-bounding ball with great power.

This Western grip created its own problem in backhand play. A considerable
change of grip was needed. The solution was seen to be in keeping the Western grip
for both drives and simply using the same face of the racket for both.

The method did not last long. It was vulnerable to shots played straight at the
player to crowd him. Players also began to learn how to keep the ball low even on
cement, and then the inborn weakness of the Western grip with its closed racket face
was immediately exposed.

American influence on technique can be traced back to the beginning of Davis Cup
play in 1900. When the first matches were held at the Longwood Cricket Club just
outside Boston, Mass., Reggie and Laurie Doherty were not available to play for
Britain and their places were taken by Arthur Gore, Herbert Roper Barrett and Ernest
Black.

The American team of Dwight Davis (who had donated the Cup), Malcolm Whitman
and Holcombe Ward mesmerized the British players by their serving. Davis had the
fastest service of that time and Ward was a particularly fine exponent of a new type
of service called the 'American Twist'. He could curve the flight of the ball and vary the
angle of its kick off the ground in a most disconcerting fashion. Whitman for his part

had perfected a reverse twist service which curved and kicked the opposite way to Ward's. This variation of serving style nonplussed the British team. (See DAVIS CUP, PART 2.)

The United States won this inaugural contest without losing a match. Gore, Barrett and Black returned home the wiser, to recount their experiences.

Until then, the service had been regarded more as a stroke with which to put the ball into play than one that could be used to win points. Early serving had all been underhand with the feet astride the baseline. When overhead serving developed the Rules were altered and the front foot had to be kept in contact with the baseline. Later on both feet were required to be kept clear of the line; subsequently there were further restrictions on the movement of the server's feet as the technique of volleying behind the service began to develop.

The ball's cover and also its internal pressure have greatly influenced serving technique. Until about 1927 the ball available in Britain had a stitched seam. This sometimes produced an uneven profile, quite apart from seam weaknesses. The ball was softer too before the late 1930s when its internal pressure was raised to speed up the game. Until then it was possible to elongate the ball with a heavily spun service which could be made to react with a vicious kick off the ground.

Increasing the ball's pressure accentuated the need to hit it hard. Certainly there had been fast servers like Maurice McLoughlin of California, who served with venomous speed and accuracy when he was at his peak just before World War I, and Bill Tilden, who bestrode world tennis in the 1920s. It is unlikely, however, that with a softer ball they could have generated the same speed as Bob Falkenburg, who cannonball-served his way to win Wimbledon in 1948. Falkenburg's overhead stroke was a mighty blow and his power in this department was never more clearly displayed than when he struck a smash on the Centre Court at Wimbledon with such force that the ball bounced into the Royal Box.

The softer ball used before World War II affected other sides of lawn tennis besides the service. Because the ball was difficult to put away for winners, a slower, more careful tempo of play was encouraged. Volleying had certainly arrived as an established technique, but it was seen to be chiefly of value for finishing off openings created by preliminary sparring from the baseline. Films made at this time more accurately portray the game's evolving technique than the growing number of books that were being written about it.

These films show the relatively slow speed of the rallies compared with modern play. Control over the ball comes only while the racket strings are in contact with it. Players of this era could hold the softer ball on the racket face for longer than today's stars. As a result groundstrokes exerted a much stronger initiative than they do today. Precise length and the accuracy of passing shots and lobs were outstanding characteristics of matchplay in the two decades between the world wars. Woe betide aggressive net-rushers who failed to prepare their volleying sorties with sufficient thought and care.

It is interesting also to compare photographs of Wimbledon taken 40 years ago and today. These reveal the way the game's technique has advanced during that time. In the older ones all the players were in the backcourt. In present-day examples, one of the players is inevitably either in the forecourt or on his way there.

To see the evolution of drives it is necessary to return to the early 1900s. The technique of slicing down on the ball, borrowed from rackets and real tennis, soon gave way to a new method of bringing the racket face up on the ball to impart topspin. Greater speed, with a bigger safety margin, could be obtained in this way. H. F. Lawford was one of the pioneers of this method of forehand drive. It was soon to develop into one of the game's orthodox strokes and – in a more refined form – it is still one of the orthodox strokes today.

Backhand problems were the common weakness of many of the early players. Photographs in some of the first instructional books show a 'straight bat' style with the player's head over the ball and the racket braced with the thumb extended along

the back of the handle. It must have been exceedingly difficult to play low balls with this method and especially when they were wide of the racket.

The development of backhand play seems to have lagged behind progress in serving, volleying and forehand driving in the years before World War I. Early instructional books provide hints in a general sense but little in the way of precise methods. The lack of strong 'two-winged' players was mentioned by Wilberforce and the pictures of the leading players of that time in backhand drive action show how handicapped they must have been with their upright stance, dropped racket head and position close to the ball.

One of the first players of note to emerge as a fine exponent of the backhand drive was Laurie Doherty, Wimbledon champion 1902-6. Progressive technique could be seen in his method. His grip placed the thumb across the handle for support instead of in the hitherto more popular position along the handle. As a result, he was able to play his stroke with the racket in a more horizontal position. He could strike the ball from a wider sideways position, from where both greater power and control could be produced. Most backhand strokes of this period, however, were produced with slice. The topspin shot was not considered to be either suitable or effective from this side of the body.

It was under the enormous influence of Bill Tilden of the United States that lawn tennis began to develop along more precise and sophisticated lines. Tilden himself, with a reliable and accurate sliced backhand, developed a topspin return through determination and assiduous practice. In a world where lawn-tennis courts were springing up in their hundreds in every country, Tilden acquired an international reputation of being the game's leader in technical knowledge and in his ability both to demonstrate and impart it to others. He gave a tremendous impetus to the development of tennis technique as an exact science. 'A tennis ball does nothing without reason' he once said.

Women's tennis also gathered momentum during this period through the example of Suzanne Lenglen and the blaze of publicity that always surrounded her exploits. This remarkable Frenchwoman brought the grace of ballet dancing to the centre courts of the world and she was in the forefront of changing fashions of tennis attire (see FASHION, PART 2). The speeding up of the game demanded something less cumbersome and restricting than the crinolines, voluminous dresses and large hats of its early years. Suzanne Lenglen not only dared to show her ankles but she astonished spectators by wearing dresses which revealed her calves! Her stroke technique, recorded on film, may seem old-fashioned by today's standards, but her fine athleticism and superb control engendered tremendous interest and enthusiasm throughout the world in women's tennis.

Quickening influences on the game also affected men's dress, although it was not

Above, left Laurie Doherty, Wimbledon champion 1902-6. His backhand grip placed the thumb across the handle for support (the more usual grip today) instead of along the handle, allowing him greater power and control than had been seen hitherto.

until the late 1930s that the inhibiting effect of traditional tennis attire for men and women was cast aside. Shorts for men rapidly ousted long white flannels. Short-sleeved shirts replaced the cricket variety with rolled up sleeves. Women's dresses became shorter. Skirts were introduced and finally shorts. The game was apparently poised to leap into a new era of speed and competitive athleticism.

Almost on the eve of war at the 1939 Wimbledon a clear indication of the future trend in women's play was given by the American, Alice Marble. Tall, strong, fit and fast, and dressed in the shortest shorts that had been seen at Wimbledon, this athletic Californian showed that the serve-and-volley style of play need not be restricted to men. Miss Marble served aces almost at will. Her second service was a viciously spinning variety of the American Twist. She moved straight in behind it and volleyed and smashed like a man. Suddenly it seemed that technique in women's tennis had taken giant strides forward.

For nearly seven years the game was forced to mark time. When international play was resumed in 1946 it was immediately apparent that Alice Marble's example had been well copied. A group of American players, among them Pauline Betz, Margaret Osborne and Louise Brough, used their serving and volleying to storm through the baseline play of their nearest rivals. The long-held belief that women could never become volleyers was killed for all time.

Meanwhile on the men's side, the idea of playing with two hands was undergoing a reappraisal. It had been seen between the wars, one of the first exponents of this method being the Australian, Vivian McGrath. The principle was that a double-handed grip would provide such an increased purchase on the ball that control over the forehand or backhand drives would be improved considerably. The method had its own weakness in restricting a player's reach. But the ball could certainly be hit extremely hard under full control when it was not too wide. In the first few years of postwar play after 1946 a young and dynamic Australian called Geoff Brown demonstrated the technique to the full. Not only did he hit his double-handed forehand drive with tremendous pace, but in doubles he aimed his shots frequently straight at one of his opponents at the net, bringing to tennis the earlier and controversial body-line theory of cricket.

Brown was good enough to reach Wimbledon finals with this method. So was another Australian, John Bromwich. Both Brown and Bromwich had two-handed forehand strokes and played the drive on the other wing with their left hands, thereby eliminating the backhand. But whereas Brown was all power, Bromwich was the master of touch. Another double-hander of the immediate postwar period, the stout-hearted Pancho Segura from Ecuador, played his backhand in the orthodox fashion. In fact double-handed players seem destined to adorn the game in the future. The advantages and disadvantages of the style seem well balanced.

A factor in more recent years that has put the game's technique under closer inspection than ever before has been the emergence of professional play. The lucrative careers opened to the most successful players put the entire development and training of talented young players under a microscope. Their coaching now begins at the ages of five or six, and more and more opportunities for play and practice are available for the best ones. The key to success as a professional player is now seen to be an early and disciplined start along precise lines, so that full mastery of advanced and sophisticated stroke-play and technique is achieved before full physical maturity. In this way a modern champion's effective playing life can be stretched to span almost 20 years.

Physical condition and sound methods are vital for top players' success since speed of shot and mobility play such a large part. However, a relatively new field is now being explored – that of mental conditioning, depth of concentration and allied factors – to help the emerging young star to achieve the right state of mind.

The differing methods of players throughout the hundred years of the game's history have all helped lawn tennis to progress. It is as well to remember, though, that physical technique apart, the most successful exponents in each decade have all been blessed with a God-given asset – a sound *temperament*.

Above Geoff Brown, Wimbledon finalist 1946, was the exponent of a tremendous double-handed forehand drive.

The Basic Teaching of Tennis

Tony Mottram

Although certain inherited qualities of character such as courage and temperament are vital factors for success in the competitive side of the game, sound *technique* can be acquired by coaching and practice.

As in other forms of teaching, successful coaching requires experienced instructors who are able to communicate their knowledge. Coaching has steadily grown in importance over the past 50 years. The earliest coaches nearly all came from an apprenticeship as ballboys. Later, as 'markers', they became human ball-throwing machines, directing a stream of returns to their clients' requirements. The game was still young then and they had little experience on which to draw. Tennis was a social pastime and, if it was a status symbol to play, there was little status in being a professional coach.

Between the two world wars the game developed rapidly and more and more tournaments made their appearance. Coaching also began to develop but, because of the seasonal nature of the game, most of its coaches were part-timers. Retired officers from the services found the atmosphere congenial. Many of them lacked competitive experience but they brought a greater sense of importance, through their rank, to this emerging side of tennis.

Coaching techniques at this time were still undeveloped. The possibilities and the limitations of teaching players were less understood than they are today. Inevitably the success achieved by coaches was less marked.

A new era of tennis began with the end of World War II in 1945. Wartime experience in training young recruits in motor skills influenced tennis teaching. Players too were younger than ever and their minds were more malleable. Since then the introduction of Open tennis with its powerful incentive for successful competition has been a strong spur for players to perfect their technique.

However, most coaching concerns players who are just beginning. For them the most important thing is to learn not only how to make the various strokes but how to score and the general procedure of playing a game (see THE RULES AND THEIR INTERPRETATION).

Note: The instructions that follow are for right-handed players.

The easiest shot for a player new to the game is usually the forehand drive and for this reason coaches nearly always start here. They begin by demonstrating how to hold the racket with a 'shake-hands' grip – holding the racket out with the strings vertical, and shaking hands with the handle. The forefinger should be extended slightly – as though tucked around the trigger of a gun.

Below The Forehand Drive (Buster Mottram).
(1) Mottram awaits the ball in a facing-the-net ready position just behind the baseline. His left hand cradles the 'throat' of the racket, allowing for ease of grip changing.
(2) The preparation starts with the bodyweight on the back (right) foot. The extended left arm is an aid to balance and in turning the shoulders sideways. Notice that the racket face remains open (vertical to the ground) throughout.
(3) Mottram uses an Eastern grip and meets the ball opposite his front (left) knee. The weight has already moved onto his front foot. His eyes are on the ball. The racket face should lift slightly upwards as the ball is struck to impart a little topspin.
(4) The follow through therefore shows a rising finish. Note the perfect balance and the wrist firmness which has controlled the ball off a solid racket face.

A ball that is struck in front of the player will go up in the air. To send it over the net into the opponent's court it is necessary to play the ball from a sideways position – as in cricket or hockey or golf. This is the next basic to master and the coach will at this stage also emphasize the most important rule of all – that the player must keep his eye on the ball during the stroke.

Footwork cannot be disregarded. From the facing-the-net position which is necessary when awaiting the opponent's return, the player must learn how to move his feet to arrive in the sideways-hitting position. This movement and its coordination with the racket swing can most easily be mastered by dropping a ball in the appropriate spot with the outstretched 'free hand' and then combining the footwork and swing to send it over the net into the opposite court.

Many coaches who start beginners off in this way then develop the stroke by feeding simple balls to their pupils who, by easy progressive stages, build up their coordination with a moving ball. At the same time a sound pattern of footwork and racket work can be established.

A common fault at this stage is to swing the racket with an insufficiently firm wrist. A ball that meets the racket only an inch or two off centre will tend to twist the racket face. Only a firm wrist at impact can control this movement. In the forehand drive the racket should be used as an extension of the arm rather than as a separate portion hinged at the wrist. Thus in tennis the stroke is a swing *through* the ball, not a slap at it.

For this reason, power for the drive is best generated by the body not the wrist. Top-class players all have the ability to get their bodyweight moving forwards when driving the ball. The secret is in the pivoting from the hips, allowing the body weight to be tumbled forwards onto the front foot just before the drive is made.

The higher that players aim to advance in the game, the more precise and effective must be their methods. In tournament tennis the ball must be driven hard and accurately. This means that footwork must be fast and well-executed to allow players to position themselves correctly to the ball. It also means that spin on the ball assumes more importance than at lower levels of play.

Topspin brings the ball down into court and therefore allows the player a greater margin of error over the net and within the lines when hitting hard. Underspin does the reverse but is valuable for the extra touch and control it can give the player during the time the ball remains in contact with the strings. Underspin is therefore more useful with softer hit shots such as the dropshot and defensive lob.

To be most effective the basic forehand drive should therefore carry a small amount of topspin. This can be applied without difficulty if the racket is moving slightly upwards to the ball in the forward swing.

An oval-shaped swing facilitates this upward-moving forward swing and allows the entire stroke to be played with an easy rhythm.

In making the backswing the player should take the racket out of the ready position in a rising direction – the upper part of the oval – before bringing the racket down to the bottom of the backswing loop from which the upward-moving swing to the ball can be made.

Many players do not appreciate that the size of the backswing (not its shape) should vary according to the power required. Consider how you would vary underarm throwing of a ball for long and short distances. Similarly a powerful forehand drive from the baseline requires a bigger backswing than one played from much nearer the net.

Control over the ball comes during the time it remains in contact with the strings. This can be increased significantly if the player learns to swing through the ball into a full and firmly played follow-through.

Where should the ball be struck in relation to the body, and should one learn to play the ball 'early' or after it has reached the top of its bounce?

The impact position relative to the body depends on the grip being used. Players who hit the forehand drive using a Continental grip (in which the hand is on top of the handle) will need to take the ball more to the side than those who use the 'shake hands' grip. For the 'shake-hands' gripper a sound guide is to hit the ball when it is opposite the front knee – the left knee if the player is right-handed.

It is much easier to play the drives if the ball is struck when it is falling from the top of its bounce. Beginners should therefore play the ball in this way. As skill develops, an earlier ball can be taken with the stroke being played at the top of the ball's bounce. Driving the ball earlier than this, as it is rising, is difficult and should not be attempted until the footwork and racket work have been well grooved as habits. It is strictly the technique of accomplished and talented tournament players.

Many of the basics for sound forehand drive stroke production also apply to the backhand drive. Watching the ball carefully, playing the drive with a locked wrist and swinging *through* the ball into a full follow-through are all vital for the success of this stroke.

Where so many beginners find trouble with backhand play is in the lack of power they feel in hitting the ball on this side of the body.

It is important to ensure that you have a sound grip. The hand should be positioned on top of the handle and the thumb either extended across the back of the grip where it can act as a brace, or wrapped around it. A change of grip is therefore required from the forehand shake-hands grip and this change is approximately one quarter of a turn of the handle in a clockwise direction. The forefinger should be slightly spread as for the forehand grip. It is a good thing to get used to this grip and the ability to find it quickly by practising the change from the forehand grip. The best way is to make several 'shadow' swings at an imaginary ball, ensuring that the face of the racket is kept vertical throughout each of the two different strokes. Mastery of this grip change is an important first step in building up a sound backhand.

By far the most common error in backhand drive development is the failure of beginners to use their shoulders correctly. They tend to face the net while making the stroke, with the result that the body then restricts the backswing. The stroke then becomes a push or prod at the ball.

Once players learn to get the right foot well forward, allowing the shoulders to turn fully, they find they can produce the unrestricted wind-up for a sound forward swing. The feeling of power in this action is one of the first things that many coaches try to encourage as a means of developing pupils' confidence.

The backswing is best made with the left hand remaining in contact with the racket. This gives added control over the wind-up and also encourages the all important shoulder turn to clear the body out of the path of the racket. The left hand, which lightly supports the 'throat' of the racket in the ready position, should therefore

Below The Backhand Drive (Evonne Goolagong).
(1) An alert ready position is important. By 'cradling' the racket in the left hand, the grip change from the forehand stroke is made easier. The racket face is kept open to the ball.
(2) The full turn of the shoulders is vital in building up power. For this the right foot must be well forward. The left hand stays in contact with the racket to aid control until the forward swing begins.
(3) The bodyweight should be on the front (right) foot just before impact. Notice how firm Miss Goolagong's wrist and arm are during the hit. A common error is to drop the racket head.
(4) A perfectly balanced finish with the racket head still firmly controlled with a locked wrist. From here the return will be made to the original ready position.

Above Service (Virginia Wade).

(1) The sideways stance and ready position for the service stroke are well shown here. The front foot is a few inches behind the baseline and does not move until the ball has been struck.

(2) One of the excellent features of Miss Wade's service is the way she keeps the hitting face of the racket closed, i.e. towards her as her arms part and the wind-up begins.

(3) The service is a 'throwing' action, with the left arm 'placing' the ball into position above the head and slightly forwards, and the right arm throwing the head of the racket 'through' the ball.

(4) Racket head speed is built up by allowing the racket to drop down behind the head before it is whipped up-and-over the ball.

(5) The way that top players use their full height and reach is well shown here. Care in positioning the ball in the air and watching it are two vital points in good serving.

(6) Powerful serving combines the actions of the legs, shoulders, arm and wrist. A full shoulder action allows the racket to finish to the player's left side and also gives a kick start to the run-in for the first volley.

remain in this position until the forward swing begins. The left arm then assists the player's balance during the remainder of the stroke.

It is important to appreciate what is involved in the backhand drive footwork. To be able to get the bodyweight going forward into the stroke, the right foot should finish well forward. This allows the ball to be driven hard, with the racket moving slightly upwards as the ball is struck. However, many backhand returns have to be made when the player has to stretch across the court to reach the ball. In this situation the stroke should be played with the right foot well across and the return made with underspin for control.

Probably the best way to develop sound technique in the backhand drive is by stage-by-stage developments. The method of taking the racket back with the left hand, the forward swing, pivot, footwork and follow-through of the basic backhand drive can be more easily learned and coordinated by shadow strokes made without the distraction of a moving ball.

After a short session of 'shadow' swinging, the same stroke and footwork pattern can then be coordinated to the easiest possible moving ball – one dropped into correct position by the player. The technique of tossing the ball gently out of the left hand before returning the hand to its original position on the racket for the backswing is soon mastered.

'Shadow' swinging can be dispensed with when the correctly executed basic stroke pattern can be produced on this simple dropped ball. At this stage sound habits are forming. With regular practice they will grow stronger and reproduce themselves automatically as the opponent's return claims more and more of the player's attention.

The more deeply grooved a sound basic pattern of stroke-making becomes, the less likelihood there will be of the stroke falling apart under the pressure of matchplay. As long as the player is able to move quickly into position, a well-learned technique will not easily let him down.

The drive with the racket face fully open as the ball is struck, preferably with slight topspin, is the basic shot to master first. Later, the sliced backhand should also be added as an important variation.

A great deal of emphasis in modern coaching is attached to the development of the service stroke. This is because it is possible to go further in the game with a fine service than with any other single stroke. It is a confidence builder, and advanced players look upon their serving ability as a barometer of general performance. To serve well is to play well and the reverse is nearly always true. At the same time it is also recognized

that the advanced service, with its variations of speed and spin, is perhaps the hardest stroke of all to learn and certainly the most difficult one to teach.

Beginners, however, must first concern themselves with the necessity of putting the ball into court, for no play is possible until this has been mastered to a degree. The problem they all face is to coordinate the correct action of the racket arm with the flight of the ball that must also be correctly positioned with the other arm.

To master the difficulties pupils are usually taught to serve in easy stage-by-stage progressions — as with the other strokes. For example, although the best servers in world-class tennis use a Continental or 'chopper' grip, the beginner will find it easier to use the forehand 'shake-hands' grip when making the first attempts to serve. This grip allows the full face of the racket to be brought to the ball.

The advanced service swing, which is a 'throwing' action from a sideways stance, should also be modified for simplicity.

A sideways stance, however, should be taken up right from the start. The front (left) foot should point towards the right-hand net post and, to avoid footfaulting by treading on the line as the ball is struck, it should be placed a few inches behind the baseline. The back foot, shoulder width away from the front foot, should be comfortably placed so that a straight line drawn touching the heels would point towards the court the server is aiming for.

The action involved in serving a ball is both complicated and difficult to describe. Consequently coaches always advise their pupils to think of the service stroke as an ordinary overarm 'throwing' action. This simplifies the stroke for most, and serving becomes easier to understand when the player first learns to throw a ball well.

However, even when this has been achieved and the correct action can be visualized as throwing the head of the racket at the ball, it will still be found more effective to develop coordination and control over the ball when starting with a simplified action.

The easiest way to hit the ball into the correct service court is to place the ball about a foot above the head and slightly forward of it and hit it with a careful patting action. As soon as players find it possible to direct the ball with consistent accuracy, they should begin to form a small backswing throwing loop from which more power can be developed. This backswing should then be widened stage by stage within the player's control, until the full throwing action has been achieved. At the same time the ball must be positioned and struck higher up with each progression until the player is able to use full height and reach.

Once players have mastered the full service action and gained consistent control

Above The Forehand Volley (Stan Smith).
(1) Notice the preparation for this shot from the facing-the-net ready position. Smith's shoulders are already turning. The ball should be taken well forward on the forehand side.
(2) There has been little backswing. Low volleys are firm-wristed *pushes* through the ball, which is controlled with the aid of a little underspin. Higher volleys should be *punched* downwards.
(3) Notice how carefully Smith watches the ball and his perfect balance on his left foot. An important point is the way he has maintained the angle between the racket shaft and his forearm throughout the shot.

over the ball, it is time to consider the use of a more advanced grip and the development of speed and spin which can then be more easily achieved.

The Continental or 'chopper' grip is ideally suited for high-class serving, because it locates the wrist in a position where it can exert the maximum racket-head speed, from whiplash effect at the top of the throwing action. It also allows the strings to meet the ball at varying angles to impart different types of spin.

The slice service, in which (for right-handers) the racket strikes a glancing blow to the ball from left to right, is the easiest variation to learn after the basic flat-hit service stroke. Thereafter the topspin service, in which the strings brush upwards on the ball, is the most commonly used spin service in tournament play. If the server imagines the ball to have a clock face then the racket strings should brush across it from seven to one o'clock (see SPIN, PART 2).

Most players attempting to spin their services for the first time find the ball being deflected too far to their left. This is because they are failing to angle the entire racket swing. Not only must the shoulders be turned more fully in the backswing but the racket's path to the ball must travel towards the right-hand net post.

Spin is used in serving for two reasons. It gives swerve to the ball through the air and disconcerting reactions off the ground for the opponent; when thoroughly learned it provides the server with more control and a bigger safety margin.

Effective serving encourages attacking play in which volleying takes a leading part. Meeting the ball near the net before it bounces can hustle the opponent and create wider angles of return for winning shots. Volleying, however, needs a different technique from that of driving. Whereas the drives should be swings, the high volleys must be visualized as 'punches' and the low volleys as 'pushes' through the ball.

First attempts at volleying on either side are best carried out with the same grip that would be used for the drive. A common mistake at this stage is in taking a big backswing, nearly always resulting in the ball flying out over the baseline. The racket head must be kept higher above wrist level in volleying than in driving and the backswings kept short and firm-wristed. Many coaches get these points over to their pupils by comparing the forehand volley to the action of the hand in catching a shoulder-high ball. The hand is extended out to the side and well forward before meeting the ball.

Volleys that are played from below net level should be nursed back into court with slight underspin which aids the player's feel for the ball off the strings. It is important to bend from the knees when playing the low volley, at the same time keeping the back straight. To reach the ball when it is wide, the left foot should step across for the forehand volley and the right foot for the backhand volley. The higher volleys, however, should be punched down into court with considerable power, using a flat hit stroke produced with a stiff arm and firm wrist.

Many tournament players find that the speed of the game prevents them from changing from one volleying grip to the other during fast exchanges at the net. The one-grip method should not be attempted, however, until considerable skill has developed. This method can then conveniently be practised at the same time as the advanced service. The Continental grip is best for both serving and one-grip volleying.

The half-volley, which is a shot played just after the ball has bounced, is one of the most difficult to play with consistent control. For this reason it should be avoided

whenever possible. When the player is forced to play a half-volley, however, the main points to remember are to get well down to the ball, to keep the wrist firm, the stroke short, and, above all, to watch the ball with great care.

When players move into the correct volleying position, 8-10 ft (2·4-3·0 m) from the net, their opponents will defend with passing shots or lobs.

A lob is a lofted forehand or backhand return that aims to drive the volleyer back from the net position. When they are within reach lobs should be met with the overhead smash – the most spectacular shot in tennis. The smash should be thought of as a service stroke with a restricted wind-up. The vital point for players to remember in attempting the smash is that, the instant they see the lob go up, they must turn sideways and then move in that position to get under the ball. When the lob is an easy one it should be killed with power. Deep lobs are more difficult and the chances of a successful smash must be assessed against the greater ease of returning the ball after it has bounced. The backhand smash is the most difficult shot of all. It is played with the shoulders well round and a pronounced wrist flip. The fact that the ball is usually only reached by jumping makes this a shot for the expert.

Practice is essential for improvement. The development of sound basic shots, and the gradual elimination of unforced errors from them, is a far more effective way of playing than a hit-or-miss attitude which produces a few flashy winners.

The way that players perform depends on their mental attitudes. Deep concentration, which is most necessary for high-level play, can only be produced through continuous effort. Tennis is the conquest of frustration, needing an iron will at the highest level and considerable mental control even from the beginner's stage. The right state of mind, which is harder to master than stroke perfection, is a composite of a burning will to win, ice-cold control in the crisis, deep concentration and courage in adversity. It makes for a fascinating challenge at all levels.

Above The Backhand Volley (Lew Hoad).
(1) Hoad keeps the racket head well up as he moves forward and prepares for the shot. Like all good volleyers, he gets his feet into position whenever he has time to do so.
(2) His bodyweight is going into the shot. Eyes are on the ball and the right arm is braced. He is locking his wrist for the impact.
(3) He keeps his wrist locked right through the ball. Notice the sideways position of the shoulders and the perfect balance throughout this compact and solid shot.
Below The Smash (John Newcombe).
(1) This is a modified service stroke. The instant the lob goes up, turn into the sideways position. Move in that sideways position to reach the ball. Use the service grip.
(2) The preparation for the powerful 'throwing' action. The left hand is 'pointing' towards the falling ball. It is vital to watch it carefully. If the ball cannot be reached without jumping, the take-off is from the back (right) foot.
(3) The ball must be pulled down into court with a wristy 'up and over' racket action. Correct timing of this difficult stroke comes from practice and care in keeping the eyes on the ball.
(4) A full shoulder action will allow the racket to finish to the left side of the player. Balance is regained on the left foot. Pick the direction and hit hard, but never wildly.

Transforming Juniors to Seniors
John Barrett

There is a gap between promise and fulfilment that even some outstanding junior players never bridge. A bright career at the age of 18 often becomes a discarded memory by the early 20s with only a meagre pile of press cuttings and fading photographs as a reminder of modest and fleeting fame. Inevitably, in a highly competitive sport like tennis, the wastage of talent is great. Sometimes this is due to lack of ambition or waning interest in an individual. Often, however, it is caused by a lack of proper guidance at this most critical stage of a player's career when his personality is being moulded and all the worldly pressures associated with rebellious adolescence are upon him.

Only a handful of the world's tennis nations have ever had a properly planned development program for leading juniors, largely because the game is controlled by men who have no specialized knowledge in this area. Moreover, they are reluctant to vest control of junior development in the hands of experts because their own influence would be diminished.

Accordingly most of the successful developers of junior talent have been individual coaches or advisers, who have been able to build up a special rapport with their dedicated pupils. Pop Summers, who helped Fred Perry to steer a winning course, Eleanor 'Teach' Tennant, who produced Maureen Connolly, Arthur Roberts who guided Angela Mortimer, Tom Stowe, who moulded Don Budge and even Ion Țiriac who, as a father figure, watched over the development of the young Ilie Năstase, found the correct formula while national associations have mostly failed.

Quite apart from the talent of the player, the personality of the coach is central to successful development and these sensitive individuals are rare. The only country that has been prepared to give such a man the necessary wide-ranging authority is Australia. In the 1950s, when young Australian teams were being sent overseas to gain experience on the world's circuits, Harry Hopman was in the position of coach, manager, guide, philosopher and friend to some outstanding tennis talent. Those young Australians, who so often complained of their geographical isolation from the rest of the tennis world, were in fact lucky that success depended upon travelling around together as a team. For six months at a time, and then again at the end of the year as Davis Cup captain, Hopman organized their lives. The list reads like a catalogue of tennis immortals – Frank Sedgman, Ken McGregor, Mervyn Rose, Lew Hoad, Ken Rosewall, Rod Laver, Neale Fraser, Ashley Cooper, Roy Emerson, Fred Stolle, Mal Anderson, Owen Davidson, John Newcombe, Tony Roche – all were greatly influenced by Hopman during their years of development. 'Hop' was not always popular – but that was not part of his job. Although at the time the players outwardly hated the discipline and the early morning runs, the physical training, the hard practice sessions and the fines for those who stepped out of line, inwardly they recognized the need for such a system and they respected Hopman's complete dedication to success.

All young people respond to reasoned discipline. The coach's success will depend upon the degree of understanding he has of the individual needs of his pupils. No two players have exactly the same problems so their requirements will be different. Technically a player who is aiming high will have formed his game by the time he is passing out of the junior ranks. His technical advance thereafter will consist of modifying the shots he already has (refining his grip, shortening his swing as the pace at which his opponents hit the ball increases, meeting the ball earlier to accelerate his attack) and adding new ones. When he was 17 Lew Hoad hit his backhand mostly with slice. As his confidence, experience and strength grew he learned to hit over the early-taken ball with tremendous topspin, and developed a shot that was at times quite unplayable. Manuel Santana, in an early Davis Cup match in 1959, won the deciding rubber against Great Britain when he took 12 of the last 13 games against Mike Davies. His lobbing that day was uncannily accurate but carried no topspin. Seven years later when he won Wimbledon he had added to his repertoire two of the most telling shots

in tennis — topspin lobs on the forehand and backhand that were devastatingly effective. That is how a player advances.

Fitness, too, plays a vital role in the advance. So many players with abundant talent fail to make progress because they are either ignorant of the need for fitness training or unprepared to do the work. Hard training develops the mind as well as the body. A man who has developed the capacity to push himself to exhaustion, without the stimulus of competition, will be a much more difficult opponent to beat than the talented but soft player.

Running is a basic ingredient of any sort of fitness. The cardio-vascular and cardio-respiratory mechanisms (the circulation and oxygenation of the blood) can best be improved by a well-planned running program. This will include long-distance work, for stamina in periods of rest from competition; interval running, to improve recovery times; and speed work, before and during competitive periods, to improve court coverage. Skipping goes hand-in-hand with running to promote light, balanced movement on the court.

General fitness is most easily achieved through some form of circuit training in which the individual strives to improve upon his own past performance. The exercises should be simple, skill-less and require a minimum of apparatus. Specific exercises to improve performance in weak muscle groups will be a matter for each individual to discuss with his coach.

A typical day during a training period might look something like this:

    07.15   Get up, quick wash, dress in tracksuit
    07.30   Run one mile, perform repetitions of three simple exercises (e.g. press-
            ups, sit-ups, step-ups)
    08.00   Shower
    08.30   Breakfast (substantial)
10.00-12.30 Tennis practice
    13.00   Lunch (not too heavy)
15.00-16.30 Tennis practice
17.30-18.15 Three days a week – circuit training
            Two days a week – interval running
    19.30   Dinner (a good meal)
    22.15   Bed

Perhaps the greatest difficulty facing the coach is to plan a tournament program that gives the developing player the correct degree of competition. Even before he is out of

Above John Barrett with five of the nine original 'Barrett Boys', a group which he supervised for his own special training scheme, with LTA approval, 1965-8. Left to right, back row: David Lloyd, John Barrett, Keith Wooldridge; front row: John Clifton, Peter Curtis, Clay Iles

junior ranks a good player will be competing in under-21 and senior events. Until the moment comes when his growing reputation and list of successes gains him immediate entry to international tournaments it is difficult for him to get sufficient high-level competition to maintain his progress. Given that a player trains and practises properly, his improvements will depend entirely on the amount of matchplay he can organize against players better than himself, when the ball is hit a little earlier, a little harder and a little closer to the lines than he has been used to.

The same is true of his on-court practice. Unless he is put under some sort of pressure his technique can never be tested. This is why the two-against-one practice routine, widely used by all the leading international players, is so useful. Two intelligent feeders of the ball, of a similar standard to the player being trained, can sustain the sort of pressure that will make tremendous demands on his physical condition, his powers of concentration and his stroke technique – all in the space of 20-30 minutes.

Money is often a problem with developing players – too much is as bad as too little and the correct balance is hard to strike. Ideally the player should have enough money to sustain the necessities of life without frills and not enough to develop expensive tastes. Ideally again, only success should bring financial rewards and earnings of this sort should be wisely invested.

This, then, is the framework within which the young, dedicated player can best fulfil his potential. Ultimately, though, it is the attitude of the player himself which will determine his rate of progress. There is little magic involved in becoming a good tennis player. Those few who reach world class have been prepared to work a little harder than their rivals and, for the moment, deny themselves some of life's pleasures. The champions have something extra – a depth of character that drives them to dominate their opponents and a pride in performance that will not accept anything that is second-rate.

Below Australia retained the Davis Cup in 1965 by beating Spain 4-1 in Sydney. Left to right: Australians Tony Roche, John Newcombe, Fred Stolle, Roy Emerson and (non-playing) captain Harry Hopman; Spaniards (non-playing) captain Jaime Bartroli, Manuel Santana, Luis Arilla, Jaime Couder, Juan Gisbert

Training Top Internationals
Harry Hopman

Preparation for Davis Cup play changes as a team progresses to the final Challenge Round and, of course, changes with individual training habits and form at the time.

In the years when Australia dominated the Davis Cup competition (1950-67), years in which I was always advising and guiding our players in my capacity of non-playing captain — our teams from Australia and our main antagonists, the United States, prepared in different ways for Challenge Rounds. In the 1950s and 1960s Australian Challenge Rounds were played in the last week of December of the year of the competition and, although the Australian summer major tournament season had been in progress for at least two months, a player occasionally would be overweight and not at his peak playing form. It was easy for some to relax for too long at the seaside or around their homes, after a tough overseas campaign with tournaments and matches for five to seven months.

The Davis Cup Challenge Rounds in the United States came at the end of a five- to six months tour, which included top world tournaments as well as the early rounds of the Davis Cup. The basis for preparation always had to be sound health and rugged fitness. Occasionally in Australia we had to settle for something less than top fitness for one of our players; but that never happened in a Challenge Round in the United States, because there was little or no outside interference from officials, families or friends.

Before any team I captained left Australia I usually managed to gather some members in Melbourne for two weeks of physical toughening which involved a little of almost everything that can be performed in a well-equipped gymnasium, with emphasis on stomach, arm, back and leg work, and a little 'playing' with weights—often exaggerated in Press stories as weight training.

If weather prevented outside preparation we would use an electric running machine for both long-distance and sprint work, alternating jogging and short bursts of sprinting over approximately 150 yards (137m). If our training was out of doors (at the back of tennis courts or in grassed park lands) we would concentrate on agility work.

I stress that our players did very little weight training. A newcomer to a Davis Cup squad of six-eight players, from which our Davis Cup team of four would be selected, would sometimes work on weights, and sometimes a youngster of top potential would be put to work on weights to build up some physical need to progress.

When an Australian Davis Cup team was on tour, with winning back the Davis Cup as the main objective, we used every day in some way towards that goal. For instance, a practice session in the morning during the Wimbledon Championships was for all team members — not just for those still in the Championships; when weather prevented play and I considered that a 'team' request for a day at the movies and shopping would be relaxation, a run in Hyde Park came before the movies.

Practice sessions between Davis Cup engagements and major tournaments would include stroke practice under the sort of fast rallying pressure met in matchplay. Different ways of achieving this were: (a) one man rallying from the backcourt against two at the net; (b) one man at the net against two trying to pass him from the baseline; (c) two and two at the net for 15-20 minutes of rapid-fire volleying to sharpen reflexes. These practice sessions also included endurance and agility exercises; and, if facilities were available, some running with emphasis on sprints. Practice *sets,* singles and doubles, were also played. These were interrupted periodically for discussion of strokes and tactics.

In most years our leading contenders for Davis Cup singles positions prospered on different ways and hours of practice. This is very important and, I think, played such a tremendous part in Australia's great run of success that I will stress it with examples.

In 1959 Neale Fraser spent half his practice time seeking accuracy in hitting towards the sidelines with his backhand service returns; in placing his big left-handed service to get wider and still wider kick to the forehand and more slice to the backhand in the forehand or first court, and flat power to the forehand and wide slice to the backhand in the second or left court; and accuracy and disguise with his forehand lob. Rod Laver, on the other hand, worked mainly at groundstrokes to disguise the direction of his passing shots, and placed emphasis on hitting a wide, dipping cross-court forehand and a heavy and firm underslice with power from his down-the-line backhand.

In 1964, when Roy Emerson and Fred Stolle played the singles, as we campaigned to win back the Davis Cup lost the previous year, their preparation was totally different.

Roy was solid and very strong. Fred was slight, wiry and strong. I detail their training for ten days in August when we used that time and an Inter-Zone Final against Sweden, at Båstad, as training for the US Championship singles at Forest Hills, N.Y., and the Davis Cup Challenge Round to follow at Cleveland, Ohio. John Newcombe, Tony Roche and Owen Davidson, members of our Davis Cup Squad of that year, fitted into our training picture perfectly. Our opposition was Jan-Erik Lundqvist and Ulf Schmidt in singles and doubles, and our anticipation of a result of either 5-0 or 4-1 was enough reason to use the beautiful August weather at Båstad for basic training for later play.

In the mornings Emerson would serve and first-volley only against left-hander Davidson's strong forehand (Lundqvist and Schmidt were right-handed) for up to 75 minutes. Meanwhile Newcombe and Stolle (with Roche as the third man) would be working out in two-against-one play at the baseline and the net – as well as practising serving, service returning, serve-and-volleying – concentrating on accuracy in placement on all their shots. Stolle would be through for the morning by the time Emerson finished his serving and joined the others in some two-against-one practice for maybe 30 minutes.

The mid-afternoons would be spent in general all-round practice with some sets played, and again Emerson would play longer than Stolle. Sometimes this practice would be held in the early afternoon to get used to the sun's position – as it would be for the first singles match of each day – when serving and smashing against it.

Immediately after play we ran five or six miles along a track through trees near the shoreline. It passed through a number of cow paddocks with gate entrances. It was approximately three miles to the end of the track and we returned to the tennis club the same way. The most interesting feature of that daily run was that Emerson and Davidson quickly drew ahead, leaving Newcombe and Roche leading out from Stolle and Hopman. Yes, Fred managed to keep pace with me! I was 58 that August and Fred was two months off 26. 'Emmo' and 'Davo' hurdled each of the gates, and once they hurdled the last gate coming back as Fred and I were about to open it on the way out, about 400 yards from the turning point. By the time we arrived back Emerson and Davidson were doing exercises. Fred went immediately to enjoy the wonderful relaxation of a massage, while 'Emmo' happily continued training until the table and masseur were ready for him. I ran without a partner the last two days. Fred felt fine and was allowed to miss out. In their different ways, with their different styles of play, both were in great shape.

One month later in Cleveland, Ohio, they were no fitter, but their games were sharper. In preparation for the Challenge Round against Chuck McKinley and Dennis Ralston, our fellows played more tennis and ran fewer miles – and on many days none at all. The main difference in our play preparation was more time spent seeking accuracy in hitting close to the lines, better timing in taking the ball a little earlier than usual, and more speed in volley reflex movements when close in to the net. And then, a few days before the opening day when all were in confident form, a tapering off in practice and more time resting. The long-term preparation paid off, for Australia regained the Cup from the United States by 3 matches to 2.

Matchplay: Psychology and Tactics
A symposium edited by Roy McKelvie

A detailed questionnaire was sent to leading world players and to those past champions who in our opinion were considered great tacticians. The following answered: Lennart Bergelin (Sweden), Donald Budge (US), Jaroslav Drobný (GB), Cliff Drysdale (S. Africa), Jan Kodeš (Czechoslovakia), Jack Kramer (US), Ramanathan Krishnan (India), Rod Laver (Australia), Fred Perry (GB), Adrian Quist (Australia), Ted Schroeder (US), Frank Sedgman (Australia), Stan Smith (US), Mrs Margaret duPont (US), Miss Françoise Durr (France), Miss Evonne Goolagong (Australia), Mrs Ann Jones (GB), Miss Alice Marble (US), Miss Angela Mortimer (GB), Miss Dorothy Round (GB), Miss Virginia Wade (GB).

Tilden once said 'Today too much emphasis is laid on physical effort, quick result and snap judgment. In the increased rush of modern living the need for thoughtful, careful planning and preparation has been overlooked and sacrificed.' He was writing at a time when great players, among them Drobný, Kramer, Schroeder, Sedgman and Mrs duPont, all contributors to this compendium of matchplay, were at their peak or approaching it. What would Tilden have said had he been alive today? Those early postwar years were restful compared with today's haste, the hectic, almost frantic rush and bustle of modern international tennis.

Tilden and his contemporaries played their tennis in a more leisurely age. Tournaments were fewer, air travel was in its infancy and there was plenty of time to prepare mentally and physically for, say, a Davis Cup match or Wimbledon and Forest Hills. Sponsors were unknown. So was prize money, now reaching huge proportions. The game belonged to the middle classes; the players were ladies and gentlemen. Professionals were people who coached, not highly trained, highly paid gladiators.

Now the pattern and the social structure of the game have changed. The Smiths, Lavers, Rosewalls, Năstases and Mrs Courts of this world are professional performers and must be prepared to play on synthetic surfaces in the United States, often at night, one week, in South Africa on cement or ant-heap courts the next, and on grass in England the third. Changing climates, food, altitudes and conditions have to be accepted as the price to pay for success and the riches it brings. Nearly every week of the year there are tournaments and championships of major importance somewhere in the world. Tilden, and other great masters, would undoubtedly have thought that the game had gone mad, yet had he, and they, been born into this age they would certainly have adjusted themselves.

Despite all this no one can seriously claim that the game is played less skilfully, entertainingly or less fiercely competitively than at other times in its history. The accent in both men's and women's tennis may have moved from the groundstroke player to the serve-volleyer – a move Tilden deplored – but players like Năstase, Rosewall, Santana, Evert, Goolagong and Jones keep on cropping up to restore the balance between the baseline and the forecourt. Today's tennis brains work faster; tennis bodies have to accept greater strains. But the fundamentals of matchplay have not changed, just as the fighter pilots of World War II found that the fundamentals of aerial combat were the same as in World War I, though they had to be performed at vastly greater speeds.

Over 40 years ago René Lacoste of France, Tilden's equal as a tennis thinker and philosopher, wrote *Lacoste on Tennis* (1928); his chapter on 'Match Play' is as apposite today as it was then. Some of his points and illustrations are worth consideration. For instance he says 'It is not necessarily the player who wins the most points who wins the match. It is the player who wins the games enabling him to win at least one more set than his adversary.' And he warns 'No adversary plays better than one who is nearly beaten. Desperation can be a hardy ally.' Here are two illustrations which answer two of the following questions, 18 and 41: 'When Borotra beat me at Wimbledon in 1927 he noticed immediately that I couldn't pass him with my backhand. Instead of attacking that side which might have allowed me to tune up ["groove" is the modern

Above René Lacoste *(left)* with Jean Borotra *(right)*. Lacoste answered our question 18 (in 1928) by saying that in 1927 Borotra did not play to his weakness and risk 'grooving' his stroke, but kept his weak side for the kill.

word] he contented himself with holding serve up to 4-4. Then with four rapid returns to my backhand followed by four winning volleys he broke my serve' . . . 'During the third set of a match against Tilden, at St Cloud in 1927, I was taken by cramp. I changed tactics, hit harder and tried to place my returns from side to side without concerning myself with winning the set. I had to save energy. When it came to the fifth I was less fatigued and nervous than Tilden, and won.'

What follows is an attempt at finding the most common answers to the many problems that beset and perplex anyone involved in matchplay. The scene is set at Wimbledon where the surface is grass. But the answers can apply to any surface and any event wherever it may be played.

1. Since you started your competitive career, what changes have you noticed in (i) the game (ii) the equipment?

Smith: (a) more players hit topspin backhands; (b) the addition of the tie-break; (c) more good players, fewer easy first-round matches; (d) gradual decrease in grass-court tennis; (e) too much tennis and travel for top players; (f) more money and players too greedy (Goolagong makes a similar point); (g) more professionals and pressure; (h) more participant and spectator interest. Goolagong adds 'Tennis is becoming more businesslike and less enjoyable'. Krishnan: 'Open tennis has made competition tougher. Playing for big money has improved players' temperaments. Everyone looks more mature and players look after themselves better'. Laver claims there are more injuries. Kramer: 'The kids begin to play serve-volley too early and lose the chance of becoming all-court players and learning a defence'.

Most players mention the introduction of synthetic surfaces and improved footwear. But few think the rackets have improved: steel produces greater speed but wood is better for control. 'The good laminated racket remains the best implement' says Schroeder.

2. You are a potential winner of the Wimbledon singles – you're your own master. The draw has just been made. Do you study it closely? Does it affect you mentally?

The majority of players either look at the draw or study it carefully but mainly for individual reasons. Kramer is concerned with the whereabouts of dangerous outsiders; Laver with left-handers. Very few think it affects them mentally. Marble says 'I study the draw carefully, hoping it will not be too easy. I always appreciate a difficult draw rather than an easy one. But it does not affect me mentally because I know that if I cannot beat everyone I will not become a champion.' Those making a careful study of the draw: Bergelin, Drobný, Drysdale, Kodeš, Kramer, Sedgman, Durr, Jones, Marble, Mortimer ('But not in 1961 when I won Wimbledon because I didn't think I had a chance'), Round. Those scanning the draw with interest: Laver, Quist, duPont. Those disregarding the draw completely: Budge, Perry, Schroeder, Goolagong.

Kodeš ('A hard draw makes me relaxed, an easy one tight'), Bergelin ('I felt a tension') and Smith think it affects them mentally.

3. In your quarter you've got (i) a cannonball serve-and-volley expert (ii) a groundstroke player (e.g. Rosewall), (iii) an artist (e.g. Năstase, Santana). With these in mind, how do you approach the fortnight's competition and these particular hurdles?

There are two schools of thought: (a) those who view each type of opponent as a separate problem, represented by Sedgman, who says 'I think of each opponent separately and try to establish a mental picture of how to play each one. But I concentrate on only one at a time.' In the same school are Bergelin, Drobný, Drysdale, Quist, Smith, Durr, Goolagong, Round ('For a hard server I practise against a man'), Wade ('I practise against a player of the same style as my opponent'); (b) those who try to impose their own game on all types of opponents, among them Budge, Kramer, Laver and Perry

('The only ones that worried me were the big hitters and servers') and Schroeder, duPont, Jones and Mortimer ('In women's tennis the differences are not so marked').

4. After the draw, what is your daily routine? (i) sleeping (ii) eating (iii) physical training (iv) practice (v) social schedule?

Schroeder answers for the majority: 'The emphasis is on a normal routine with regularity the key, i.e. to bed, eating etc. always at the same time. This minimizes the effect of the building pressure as the championship draws near and also when it progresses.'

Kramer, Laver and Smith sleep eight to nine hours, eat a high-protein meal not less than two hours before playing, do no special training during the Championships but practise before their matches. For recreation Kramer walks, plays cards or goes to the movies.

Bergelin was the only player to do P.T. (before breakfast). The rest think players should be fit enough. Budge says 'I never knew when the draw was made so I just went on playing and practising'. Drysdale and Marble recommend nine hours' sleep. Most agree that social life should be kept to a minimum. Mortimer says 'P.T. and socializing did not enter my life'. Drobný says 'I hate parties'. Sedgman is against over-practising but, like most, is in favour of a high-protein diet. Perry, for the week before Wimbledon, led a spartan and eremite life.

5. Do you watch and scout your coming opponent's matches, or are you so familiar with everyone's play that you do not worry?

Opinion was divided. Budge: 'I always tried to be familiar with my opponents' games. I watched matches simply for enjoyment but never before I had to play one'. Kramer: 'It's always wise to watch good players just to pick up trends in their game'. Smith agrees. Those who watch forthcoming opponents: Bergelin, Drobný, Drysdale (rarely), Kodeš, Quist (if concerned), duPont and Round ('only unknown opponents'), Durr, Marble, Mortimer, Wade ('sometimes and then briefly'). Those who do not: Budge, Laver ('I know most of them backwards'), Perry, Schroeder, Sedgman, Goolagong, Jones ('I have seen them all during the year').

6. (i) You're the first match on court – what is your routine from the time you wake? (ii) You've the third or fourth match on court – how do you spend the waiting period?

Drobný, though he rises at 07.00 hours, earlier than any other player except Bergelin, and only eats a Continental breakfast, speaks for the majority: 'I have half an hour's practice at Queen's Club, reach Wimbledon at midday, have a light lunch, retire to the dressing-room and, perhaps, have a massage. If I'm one of the later matches I have a larger lunch at 1·30. I try to relax in the players' concourse.' All agree that lunch must be at least two hours before play. Most have a good breakfast around 09.00-09.30 hours. More than half have a short morning practice. Some stay in their hotels until as late as possible. Writing letters, reading or listening to the radio are the commonest forms of relaxing. 'The main thing is not to have a cluttered or frustrating morning' says Drysdale. An interesting sidelight comes from Kramer: 'I try not to watch tight matches before I play. It tears you emotionally.'

7. Does your pre-match routine become a superstition?

No: Budge, Drobný, Drysdale, Laver, Perry, Quist, Schroeder, Sedgman, Jones, Round; Smith and Goolagong say it is more of a discipline than a superstition.
Yes: Kodeš, Kramer ('especially if I'm winning'; a disturbance of his physical routine affects him mentally), Durr ('I feel guilty if I don't have any'), Mortimer. Marble admits 'I was extremely superstitious; the way I dressed, the routine of packing my tennis bag and about wearing my lucky tennis pin.'

8. How do the conditions of the day affect you? For instance, do you have several rackets with varying string tensions to use depending on whether it is

sunny and fast or damp and slippery? What other adjustments do you make?

Kramer says: 'No matter what the conditions, you must start with your favourite racket'. He also stresses the importance of having salt tablets available in case of cramp, especially on hot days. Though most say they dislike windy and/or damp conditions, few say it affects them seriously or that they make any adjustments but Smith admits 'Slippery courts make my movements tentative'. Budge says: 'I always kept six rackets, uniform in weight and tension, and played with them under all conditions'. Laver worries more about his handle grip being right than about string tension or weight. DuPont and Marble used heavy socks over their shoes in wet conditions; Bergelin spikes. All, except Bergelin, Durr and Perry (the last with three tight rackets and one slacker), had all their rackets strung to the same tension irrespective of the conditions.

9. How does the wind affect your play? What adjustments do you make (i) in your service (ii) in your groundstrokes (iii) in your volleys?

Nearly everyone agrees that in serving the toss must be lower than normal, while Budge and Smith stress a slower first serve and/or the use of spin. They also advise more margin for groundstrokes, while volleys with the wind need a shorter backswing. All agree that the ball must be watched more carefully. Schroeder answers (i) 'Serve bouncers with the wind; flat serves and slices against it. Take advantage of a cross wind to serve opponent out of court.' Kramer answers (ii) 'Shorten strokes with the wind; come to the net and lob more against it.' Marble answers (iii) 'I use a short punch volley with the wind; a longer backswing against it.'

Above Evonne Goolagong in 1971, when she defeated Margaret Court 6-4, 6-1, to win the Wimbledon Championship

10. If you have a favourite racket, how much does it mean to you?

The players are equally divided between those who have a favourite racket and those who do not. Quist, who says his favourite becomes an extension of his arm, quotes the case of Jack Crawford who won the 1933 French and Wimbledon titles and reached the final of the US Championships with the same square-top racket. Marble suggests that athletes are as superstitious as actors: 'We have a favourite racket even if 24 have been made from the same mould. It's all psychological and when we get to the point when we don't have a favourite then we've matured.' Kramer's favourite racket meant so much to him that he 'nursed' it and extended its life: 'I was a psycho. My game went down when I broke a string.'

11. Do you let your opponent go on court first?

Four answers:
Yes: Bergelin, Drobný ('Or at the same time'), Quist, Round ('For a visitor').
No: Perry, Schroeder, Mortimer ('I prefer to lead the way'), Wade ('Not usually').
Immaterial: Budge, Drysdale, Kodeš, Kramer, Laver, Sedgman, duPont ('Don't think about it. Just do what is convenient, appropriate or polite'), Goolagong, Jones.
Together: Marble ('Making small talk').

12. Do you prefer to spin yourself or not?

The majority consider that it is of no consequence who spins the racket. Budge: 'I couldn't care less'. Kramer prefers to spin but does not know why. Schroeder and Durr prefer not to spin; Marble thinks it is a matter of mutual agreement and points out that Mrs Helen Wills Moody always let her opponent spin. Perry says 'I always threw up the racket before reaching the umpire's chair and said "Call it". It made the crowd look at me.' Bergelin, Mortimer and Round preferred to spin.

13. (i) You've won the toss – what is your choice and why? (ii) If your opponent wins, what end do *you* choose and why?

The majority, including the women, choose to serve first for the obvious advantage of the chance of getting, and keeping, one game ahead. But Perry and Mortimer let the 'big servers' serve first, as they see the best chance of a break before the player is warmed up. Quist: 'If my opponent has a cannonball I prefer to let him serve into the wind, if there is any.' On a cold day Laver sometimes lets an opponent serve first. Smith often does too. He appears to think this may give him service at a vital point in a possible tie-break. Drysdale ('To put pressure on and have time to acclimatize') and Durr ('Because my shoulder isn't warm') prefer to receive, as does Jones if she feels nervous ('It gives me a chance to get rid of the tensions').

All, when given choice of end, take one into the sun or wind, with this qualification from Schroeder: 'If the wind is very strong and blowing straight down court I choose to return into the wind. This gives maximum advantage to my serve in the next game'.

14. What grip do you use for (i) forehand (ii) backhand (iii) service?

Thirteen of the 21 players use Eastern or modified Eastern forehands, Kramer being one of the few with a really true Eastern grip. Of the rest there are seven Continental forehands and Miss Durr whose grip is all her own invention.

Seventeen players use a Continental grip for the backhand. Bergelin uses an Eastern, Schroeder an Eastern with an eighth to a quarter turn (rotating the racket clockwise), Miss Durr has her own stroke and Drysdale is a two-hander. Seventeen players use the Continental grip for serving. Bergelin remains with the Eastern, Schroeder and duPont vary according to the type of serve, and Durr has a grip of her own.

15. If you are a grip changer, how do you hold the racket when waiting to receive service?

Most grip changers hold the racket with the forehand grip. As Kramer says, 'The forehand takes a much longer swing and it's best to be ready for it.'

16. If you are a double-handed player, how do you (i) use this weapon (ii) protect yourself from being over-stretched?

Drysdale, a double-handed player: '(i) Hit offensively on the return of serve – 75 per cent across court – and passing shots. (ii) Stand further back to take opponent's return of serve; always try to dictate play to avoid being run about too much. Two-handers require an extra step and good positioning.'

17. If you are playing a double-handed player, what are your thoughts and what is your mode of attack?

Below Vivian McGrath, the first great two-handed player

The Australian Vivian McGrath was the first of the world-class two-handed players; his old rival, Quist, says 'I learned from experience not to attack the single hand but to play his double-handed side until I could exploit the weakness of the single.' It is accepted that two-handed players have great strength on that side but are restricted in reach, vulnerable to angles and passing shots and are not usually strong volleyers. Sedgman advocates concentrating on the single side but is in a minority. Bergelin, Krishnan and Smith suggest hitting occasionally straight at the player; Kramer prefers to serve to the single side and volley wide: 'If you can't serve fast enough to avoid the double side serve at it and stay back. Double-handers have difficulty in following their returns to the net.'

18. Knowing that your opponent is much stronger on one side than the other, do you play to his weakness all the time and risk grooving his stroke or do you play to his strength, keeping his weak side for the kill?

Opinion is fairly evenly divided. Bergelin, Perry, Quist, Goolagong, Mortimer, Round and Wade prefer to attack the strong side to open up the weak. Budge, Kodeš, Krishnan, Sedgman, Smith, duPont and Durr attack weakness, with occasional switches to the strong side or 'down the middle to unbalance the opponent' as Sedgman put it. Laver does the same until he feels his opponent is too prepared for it. Drysdale uses both sides 'to keep him guessing'. Drobný plays to a pattern irrespective of his opponent, and another left-hander, Jones, suggests that 'some strokes will break down under continuous bombardment'. Kramer prefers to serve to strength, volley to weakness, but Schroeder tends to hit to strength on critical points 'as I have a better idea what the probable return will be. Against Frank Parker, I would attack his backhand as neither he, nor I, had any idea where his forehand would go.'

19. Do you make most passing shot winners across court or down the line?

The men are evenly divided: most of the women prefer to pass across court. 'Sixty-five per cent down the line, 35 per cent across court' says Drysdale. Kodeš and Laver hit them 50-50. 'Cross court on the backhand, down the line on the forehand' says Marble. Kramer: 'As I hit flat I hit them down the line'. Schroeder: 'There's no basic rule. A passing shot is a low-percentage one and must be played when the chance of a winner is highest. Everything else being equal the shot should go across court. There's a greater distance available. But wind, especially a cross-court wind, is an important factor.'

20. (i) In *your* repertoire of strokes, do you regard the lob as an offensive or defensive shot? (ii) In what situation do you lob and what kind of lob do you use?

Most of the men regard the lob as both offensive and defensive. More women regard it as an offensive shot against a net-rusher. But all agree that it is a shot to use against an opponent who crowds the net and most consider the top-spin lob, 'Kinsey loop' as Marble describes it, as the most effective. Kramer says 'Use it also to set up passing-shot openings, especially on crucial points. It is a potential confidence shaker, as a volleyer who misses a couple of smashes will generally start overplaying his volleys and even his approach shots. Continual lobbing can soften up a serve-volleyer.' . . . 'All players who have had good successes against Gonzalez have used the lob well.' Krishnan cites, as an example, a 1958 Wimbledon Centre Court men's doubles when he and Naresh Kumar put out the holders, Budge Patty and Gardnar Mulloy, by lobbing. Quist gives as a classic example the 1948 Australian Championships final: he and John Bromwich were down two sets to one, 5-2 and 40-15 on Sedgman's serve. As a last resort they hoisted a couple of lobs. Both were missed and Quist and Bromwich went on to win the title.

21. Do you prefer to smash on the full or on the bounce?

Only Quist and Sedgman prefer to smash on the bounce . . . 'because it is easier to time and size up the position'. But Budge, Kramer, Krishnan, Smith and Jones say they let skyscraper lobs bounce before smashing and several do the same if the sun is strongly in their eyes. Drysdale lets a short lob on a true court bounce and Marble also lets a lob bounce if she wishes to make a sharp angle.

22. (i) In your four-minute warm-up what are you trying to do? (ii) Are you watching your opponent's form or concentrating on your own?

Kramer reflects the majority opinion: 'Mainly I try to build up confidence by getting the feel of the ball and a sense of control. Always make sure to hit some overheads – good looseners – and plenty of serves. It is important to make sure you're ready to play at top speed and to win your opening serve.' DuPont: 'The warm-up is the time to do just that and get your eye on the ball and concentrate.' Very few players pay any attention to their opponents. 'The warm-up is totally different from the match' says Drysdale; Schroeder goes further: 'The warm-up is a waste of time and what my opponent does is no concern of mine.'

23. At what point, before or during the match, do you first start trying to out-think and outwit your opponent? Depending on his temperament and style of play what line of action might you take?

Most players, particularly the men, are less concerned with out-thinking or out-witting their opponents than with imposing their own game, or will, on them. Sedgman: 'From the start I try and exert my influence on the match and, if I'm winning, keep on going. I change my tactics at any point during the game if I'm losing.' Budge adds 'I never tried to outwit an opponent'. Only a few, among them Quist, Smith,

Above Fred Perry, Wimbledon Champion in 1935. Compare this photograph with the picture of Evonne Goolagong on page 142. Both clearly illustrate how some great players have perfect balance. Every part of the body is counterpoised against another and reacting with equal force.

Round and Wade, begin their thinking beforehand; Drysdale, Kramer, Schroeder, Durr and Mortimer enter a match with their normal style of play. As Schroeder says: 'My primary object is to hold serve during the early stages and not until 3-3 or 4-4 put on the pressure.' Durr and Wade think similarly. Laver agrees but intriguingly says 'I like to change tactics continually'.

24. (i) At the start, when serving, are you trying to make sure of getting your first serve in or do you immediately try to ace your opponent? (ii) If you find your first service is not going in, do you use more spin? How does your faulty serving affect your confidence?

Getting a deep first serve into court rather than an ace is, by far, the majority opinion. Only Sedgman, Goolagong and Wade occasionally go for aces. Schroeder: 'Use three-quarter speed serves. A good player is not going to be intimidated so there is no purpose in going for an ace from the outset.' DuPont stresses depth of serve rather than speed. Laver goes for speed but not an ace 'to keep my opponent away from the net'. The majority favour the use of spin and variation when the first serve is not working well. Smith: 'I try the kicker and if I get a lead of, say 40-love or 40-15 I hit a hard one. The serve will come eventually.' Marble adds 'Toss the ball higher and to the right'. Confidence appears to be unaffected.

25. How do you vary your service depending on (i) the conditions (ii) your opponent's game?

Schroeder, for the majority: 'Slice with a cross wind and on a wet court to keep the ball low. Hit a flat serve against a cross wind. Use American twist with the wind to get a high bounce. Don't use American twist into the wind. The ball sits up.' He adds 'It will soon become apparent which type of serves the opponent returns best. Play to his weakness but hit to his strength often enough to keep him honest.' Laver uses more slice on grass and serves mainly to the weaker side; duPont tosses the ball lower in a wind; Perry served low into the body of American opponents, avoiding the high-kicking American serve they were used to; Kramer likes to establish his serve-volley over his opponent's backhand but varies pace, length, direction to stop the returns becoming grooved.

26. What is your basic attitude on your own service to (i) slice returns (ii) drive returns?

Most men agree that sliced returns are easier to handle as they tend to float. 'Slice cannot penetrate' declares Sedgman. Kodeš and Smith say 'Serve kickers and get to the net quickly and close.' Drobný offers a variation: 'Stay back and go in on the second return.' Bergelin and Schroeder offer another: 'Serve deep and force opponent back far enough so that he must make his slice from low down.' Laver enjoys variety, adding 'I don't play my best in a groove'.

The women vary according to their styles of play. 'Stay back on slice, volley drive' says Jones. Marble declares 'Get to the net quickly against slice but against heavy drivers such as Mrs Moody or Miss Connolly serve deep down the middle.'

Schroeder: 'Against drive returns keep the ball low to make the opponent hit up, and vary serve.' Smith: 'Serve to corners or at opponent.'

27. What is your basic attitude on your own return of service playing against (i) flat services (ii) slice serves (iii) kickers?

Kramer, Perry and duPont speak for the majority with almost the same words: 'Block flat serves; stand in close and lift sliced serves'. Regarding kickers Perry says 'Take them waist high on the way up'. Kramer: 'Play close in. Normally a sliced or chipped return works best as it's difficult to drive a high kicker on the backhand.' DuPont thinks a very firm wrist is needed to bring the ball down. There are variations. Budge, being tall, stands inside the baseline for all serves, whereas Drobný and Kodeš, being shorter, stand back when receiving flat serves. Bergelin when receiving kickers, likes to run round his backhand.

28. Do you prefer playing a serve-volleyer or a baseliner?

The men prefer a baseliner when playing on grass at Wimbledon. The women, with three exceptions, prefer a serve-volleyer. Kramer: 'A good serve-volleyer is tougher to beat but a baseliner with a strong serve presents a problem as you cannot attack off his serve. With good groundstrokes he can get to the net. But a baseliner with a moderate serve is easy on grass. He has to keep trying to pass the volleyer and finally his groundstrokes will crumble.' Krishnan: 'A baseliner gives me more time to think, play my strokes and get a rhythm. A serve-volleyer keeps me in suspense.' Quist adds 'Only on rare occasions can a baseliner hurt your game.' Of the few dissentients (including Laver), Budge says 'A net rusher is easier because the points are shorter. A good baseliner makes you a little more patient in getting ready for the kill.'

29. If you like a target to shoot at, at the net, how do you react if your opponent stays back?

There are two schools of thought.

Bringing the opponent into the net with dropshots and angles is advocated by Bergelin, Perry, Smith and most of the women including Durr, Marble, Mortimer, Round and Wade. Drobný: 'I take the net. He who takes the net first wins in most cases.' Budge, Drysdale, Krishnan, Quist and duPont are among those who take a similar view.

Kramer, Schroeder and Sedgman go for depth of shot. 'Generally I don't hit so hard and become steadier' says Sedgman; Schroeder adds 'Keep the ball in play, choose the moment to go in and make him go for winners.'

30. If you are basically a serve/volleyer, how do you react if you are being successfully passed, or lobbed, or put under pressure for your first volley?

Above Rod Laver, unique in winning the Grand Slam twice (1962, 1969), serves mainly to the weaker side of his opponent (see question 25).

Kramer: 'Move around to break up your opponent's service-return rhythm. Use more spin on your first serve and stay back occasionally.' Most agree with this and stress the importance of concentrating on service: 'Serve deep and use spin' say Marble and duPont. 'Change pace and vary the attack' adds Krishnan. Smith, supported by Bergelin, takes a slightly different view: 'Get to the net faster and hit the first volley down the middle. Sometimes stay back and then go in on a short return. If being lobbed don't close quite so fast.' Laver, aware that he tends to rush his shots, forces himself to slow down and concentrate on watching the ball.

31. What steps do you take to break your opponent's service as soon as possible?

Smith puts it in its simplest terms: 'Run round second serves and hit hard forehands'. Kramer varies by hitting low returns, only becoming aggressive if the opposing serve is deep and the server quick onto the volley. Krishnan takes an early ball and aims at the server's feet. Quist moves forward or back and Budge stands in closer. All run round their backhands. Schroeder is philosophical: 'Make no determined efforts to break unless opportunity arises but apply increasing pressure as the set progresses by making the opponent work harder'. Wade agrees with this. Goolagong and Marble get to the net as quickly as possible. Drysdale, Sedgman and Mortimer let strong servers serve first, because they are possibly at their most vulnerable in the opening game of the match.

32. Having broken service, how do you ensure that you retain your own?

Concentration, getting first serves and volleys in deep and making the opponent go for winners is the general answer. Kodeš and Wade stress the importance of winning the first two points of each service game; Goolagong goes for the first point. Schroeder and Marble came up with similar answers; the former: 'Take fewer chances on your serve. Play the percentages.' Marble adds 'Take chances when ahead in a game, fewer when behind.'

33. You have a break in hand and you're serving for the set. Do you go for an all-out attack, or do you play safe?

The majority regard this as a moment not to take risks. Smith: 'Play relatively safe with first serve and volley. Take the net and make the opponent go for passing shots. Play basic, tough tennis. Nothing fancy.' Kramer adds 'Don't change tactics if you have been holding serve. Don't gamble on low volleys. Make sure that if you are going to lose the game your opponent must make four or more winning placements.'

The majority go along with these two; Schroeder calls it 'conservative but not safe play'. Sedgman, Round and Wade stress the importance of winning the first two points. Budge, Drysdale, Quist and duPont play their normal game; Drobný says 'You can't play safe on grass'. Laver advocates going for a second break as it brings added confidence, for he admits 'My serve can fall apart at any time'.

34. Having lost your service, how do you react?

Most agree it is best to go for an immediate break back. This can be achieved in various ways. Sedgman advocates 'Fast, low service returns'; Perry 'Go back to work'; Bergelin 'Try new variations'; Laver 'Hit a little harder as opponent is liable to play safe'; Marble 'Pitch in and get closer to the net'; Wade points out 'There are often two breaks in a row'. Goolagong and Mortimer say 'Don't worry' or 'Forget it'; Krishnan says with oriental philosophy 'Nothing is lost but I say something different to my opponent to surprise him'. This may border on gamesmanship.

35. Your opponent is serving for the set with a break in hand. How do you react?

Schroeder says 'Keep the ball in play while retaining some margin of error. Force opponent to hit as difficult a shot as possible. Make him hit winners but don't rely on his making errors. If opportunity arises go for a winner.' Smith adds 'Go for winners off the second serve and make opponent know you are going for everything'. Jones

Below Angela Mortimer in 1958, when she was runner-up at Wimbledon. She became the first British Wimbledon singles champion for 24 years in 1961.

and Mortimer stress the importance of making opponents win the points. Sedgman and Krishnan are prepared to take risks but not desperate ones.

36. The set looks like slipping away. How hard do you try (i) to recover (ii) to ensure that you will serve first in the next set?

The great majority considers that every attempt should be made to recover the set whatever the score. But Bergelin, Drysdale, Kodeš, Kramer and Durr stress the importance of saving energy if the set looks hopeless. Kramer goes further: 'It depends on which set. If you are a set up then you can let it go if it looks hopeless. But if the score is set-all you must try and recover.' No players, men or women, with one important exception, consider it of paramount importance to ensure serving first in the next set. Laver will strive to hold serve in a losing position to gain service in the next set.

37. How do you approach (or how would you have approached) the tie-break? Do you regard it as your friend or enemy?

The younger players are in favour of the tie-break; the older view it with some suspicion as 'an enemy of the game and fitness' as Perry and Round put it. Wade: 'I prefer the 12-point English system. It's fair. But it's too early at 6-6 as there's always an edgy patch between 4-4 and 7-7 before a set settles into a pattern. If the tie-break comes at 6-6 one spends half the set worrying about it.' Laver: 'I have had reasonable success with different systems but the 12-point is the only good one.' Goolagong, as do the majority, also prefers the British system: 'The 9-point tie-break doesn't give a player sufficient time to settle down'. On the other hand, Smith says 'The 9-pointer is a great friend when one is confident'. Kramer suggests it puts more emphasis on competitive ability than on stamina.

38. You have won the first set. How do you ensure that you maintain your concentration and command?

Smith sums up the majority opinion: 'Try to win the first game or two of the second set. Don't change tactics or try anything fancy.' Krishnan adds 'I tell myself I must win two more sets for the match'. Jones warns that 'In a three-set match this is the most important moment' and duPont, with whom Laver agrees, suggests 'Think about the ball. Try and keep your mind uncluttered.'

39. You have lost the first set (i) by your own failures – how do you try to remedy them? (ii) by your opponent's superior play – what counter-measures do you take?

(i) Budge: 'Either don't make the same mistakes or change tactics'. Nearly every player takes the same view. 'Steady down' says duPont. 'Concentrate on footwork' suggests Drobný. Drysdale advises 'Try different techniques such as standing further back to receive serve and staying back instead of going in to the net'. Smith puts it 'Dig in harder. Don't get afraid.' But Laver is unworried as he knows he is a slow starter.
(ii) The majority change pace and rhythm and try to stay with their opponent, waiting for the moment when there may be a break in concentration. 'I try to keep her on court as long as possible' says Jones. 'Slow down a bit' suggests Wade. 'Play a few soft, high shots' adds Marble. But Bergelin and Perry advise taking an earlier ball. Laver maintains pressure, confident that his opponent will not keep it up.

40. Is the result of the first set of major significance to you?

Yes: Drobný, Drysdale, Krishnan, Laver, Perry, Quist, Schroeder, duPont, Jones, Marble, Mortimer, Round.
DuPont: 'I want to be on top all the time'. Schroeder: 'Every set is important. Over a long tournament physical and mental fatigue become real factors.'
No: Kodeš ('I believe in the last point of the match'), Sedgman, Durr.
Indifferent: Bergelin, Budge, Kramer, Goolagong. But it becomes important to Smith 'only if I win it' and Kramer 'only if I played well but lost it'.

Above Lennart Bergelin in play against Art Larsen at Wimbledon in 1950

41. What importance do you attach to pacing your game, i.e. conserving your energy? How and when do you do it?

There is some variation of opinion. Budge, Perry, Quist ('depending on age'), Sedgman, Smith ('I may change my mind when older'), Goolagong, Jones and Wade regard pacing as unnecessary unless playing in great heat, as one should be fit enough anyway. Mortimer considers it unnecessary in the women's game. Kodeš and Krishnan preserve energy by choosing the right points to go all out on. Bergelin: 'If two sets up but heavily down in the third I slow down but keep my opponent running'. Drobný suggests 'Don't try too many aces or rush the net so much if leading in a set or on your own serve'. DuPont and Marble stress the importance of getting the first serve in and not rushing between points.

Both Kramer and Schroeder make a big point of not getting involved in long games on the opponent's serve early in the set. 'The key times are the later stages of a set and the match'. Laver is not worried about his stamina, which he claims is always good for five sets but still believes 'It's very important to pace yourself.'

42. If you know that you are fitter than your adversary, how do you use this to your advantage?

Most agree with Kramer: 'Try to extend the points. Lots of lobs, especially in the early games of a set. If I get off to a slow start I don't get that desperate feeling, knowing I should win on strength if necessary.' The lob is the shot most favoured by players to sap an opponent's energy, followed by the dropshot and rallying across court or up-and-down. Quist suggests high lobs and bustling play. Smith adds a neat touch: 'Smile more'. Only three players take a different view: Drysdale advocates 100 per cent pace; Mortimer a 6-0, 6-0 win if possible and Goolagong likes to win as quickly as possible.

43. At the changeover, describe your routine: (i) natural (ii) artificial – if forced into change by your opponent.

Kramer: 'In my day the changeover was to change courts, not to rest. I used the time to towel, mainly the racket handle. I don't believe in drinking unless it's a long match and then only warm tea and lots of sugar. A stalling opponent bothered me so I usually moved quickly to draw attention to him.' Schroeder: 'My routine is geared to my needs, not to influence my opponent. If I'm tired I take longer. If I have him in a spot I take longer to give him time to think about it. I am not influenced by anything my opponent does.' In answering (ii) there are variations of these themes. Bergelin and Krishnan behave as if nothing is happening whatever the situation. They say it makes opponents feel uncertain. Perry: 'Never do the same thing twice'; duPont: 'I disregard my opponent completely even to the extent of walking round the far end of the net'. Drobný: 'Hurry or slow down to suit yourself'. All agree that drinking must be kept to the minimum.

44. How does a doubtful umpire's decision affect you (i) when in your favour (ii) when against you? Do you get over this quickly or does it nag?

Budge: 'I never question a call. When I'm on court I'm a contestant not an official.' DuPont: 'The officials are there to call the match. I'm there to play it. Bad calls usually even up anyway.' Most are in favour of forgetting wrong calls, for and against, though Schroeder thinks it needs mental discipline. A few say it nags for a time and Drobný says 'I feel guilty. I get mad. It nags.' But no one suggests throwing a point. Kodeš and Smith have opposing views. Smith: 'In Davis Cup matches I accept all calls and get on with the game'. Kodeš: 'I get more affected by calls in Davis Cup matches abroad'.

45. In the final set do you always prefer to serve first? If not, why not?

The answer is 'Yes' in nearly every case. Kramer: 'The pressure seems to be less with the score even instead of coming up from behind, especially from 4-4 onwards'. Schroeder adds uncompromisingly 'Anyone who does not doesn't understand the game'.

46. You are serving in the final set at 4 games all and 30-40. What type of service do you use?

The large majority agree it is essential to get the first serve deep into court. To ensure this most advise the use of spin and/or three-quarter pace. The direction should be towards weakness or straight at the receiver. Laver (a left-hander) tries slicing into his opponent's body or wide. Schroeder: 'Not having a serve as strong as Budge, Kramer or Gonzalez, I hit a three-quarter pace slice or spin as deep as I can and slightly to my opponent's backhand. If he is left-handed I slice down the centre line to make him stretch as far as possible.'

47. At match point against you, how do you play the point (i) on your service (ii) on your opponent's?

(i) Nearly everyone agrees on the need for getting in the first serve, using spin if necessary. Only Budge (occasionally), Laver and Kodeš are prepared to go for aces. Kramer, Schroeder and Perry stress making the opponent go for the winner or, as others put it, play the point.

(ii) 'Play the point conservatively. I try and force my opponent to take the most difficult volley off my return. One cannot count on an error in a situation like this' says Schroeder, but Laver forces the issue.

Bergelin and Quist advocate moving in to receive serve. Jones likes to make a low return of serve, hoping for a passing-shot opening. Marble thinks the same way but uses a deep return or one that carries topspin and dips to the volleyer's toes.

Budge and Smith suggest a prayer.

Above Jack Kramer in 1947, when he won the Wimbledon singles

Centre Court Classics
Peter Wilson

The wonderful thing about Wimbledon is its continuity, coupled with its constant change. It is now almost 45 years since I saw my first Wimbledon final. The 12 matches chosen here seem to me to sum up the attraction – and the magic – which is Wimbledon.

Almost certainly the greatest women's singles final before World War II was in July 1919 between the holder, who did not have to play through the tournament in those days but remained aloof until the Challenge Round, and her 20-year-old challenger, who had never played on a grass court before this tournament. The champion was Mrs Lambert Chambers, an Englishwoman who had first won the Championship 16 years earlier in 1903 – and six times since; the challenger, a French girl, Suzanne Lenglen.

If ever there was a confrontation of two sporting generations this was it. Looking at the photographs of the two you can almost hear the creaking of Mrs Lambert Chambers' stays, the crackle of her (no doubt) starched petticoats, and feel the chafing of her shirt-sleeves buttoned at the wrists. Suzanne, on the other hand, had a one-piece dress with sleeves ending 'daringly' just *above* the elbow, her hemline only just *below* the knee. Some women spectators actually walked out during her matches, muttering 'shocking' or 'disgusting'!

Often sports' outstanding events become historic only in the memory. But people must have known this was going to be one of the great ones. In the Royal Box were King George V, Queen Mary and the Princess Royal. Lord Curzon and Admiral Beatty were there too. It was as though the 'Old Guard' had summoned up their biggest guns to defend entrenched position.

It was youth *v.* age with a vengeance. When Mrs Lambert Chambers, as Dorothea Douglass, had first won Wimbledon Suzanne had been a three-year-old!

And now let the old champion take up the story which she described as 'The Game of my Life' in *The LTA Book of the Game, 1957*:

> I could generally tell at the start of a match whether I was going to be at my best or not – I felt on top of the world that day. Then Suzanne went 4-1, and then she led 5-3; all this time we were having strenuous rallies and in the ninth game she came to set point – but by two dropshots running, when Suzanne was outside the baseline, I was able to save the situation . . .

Suzanne Lenglen

Those are the stark facts – it was not in the character of the Englishwoman to embroider them – but consider the 'nerve' necessary to play two consecutive dropshots with the set within a point of being lost on each of them.

Then it was Mrs Lambert Chambers' turn to have two set points at 6-5 and the French girl's turn to prove her courage by going all out for winners. Finally Suzanne took the first set 10-8 with, according to her opponent, 'a drop volley most wonderfully executed'.

With one of the players nearer 40 than 30, surely the spectators must have thought that such a long first act must have ended the drama. They did not know their Mrs Lambert Chambers. In her own words:

> Although years younger than I was, Suzanne seemed more tired than I, and that gave me great encouragement to go on fighting.

The second set was a real see-saw. The champion led 4-1, then according to one eyewitness tried to volley too much and was caught at 4-4. To continue in her own words:

> I hung on desperately and had now got my backhand working just as forcefully as my forehand, which was not always the case, and I ran out winner of the second set at 6-4.

We can picture the scene so well: the veteran Englishwoman dominating the court

Above Mrs Lambert Chambers
Colour plate Evonne Goolagong, 1971
Wimbledon Champion. Her next outstandingly
memorable match at Wimbledon was a 1972
semi-final against Chris Evert (see page 163).

like some great white galleon but harassed, always harassed, by the darting frigate,
Suzanne Lenglen.

At the end of that second set Mrs Lambert Chambers recorded:

Suzanne again seemed distressed and asked for some brandy. I must admit I was
beginning to feel I had had enough exercise for one day, and there was another set
to be played . . .

What a set it was to be. This time the French girl swept to a 4-1 lead, helped by some
net-cords which must have fallen with the shock of guillotine strokes on the champion.
But although 'I was getting terribly tired, footsore and weary; I had run many miles
and, as well as the physical, there was mental tiredness, which for me was perhaps
more upsetting', the Englishwoman still made it 4-4.

The 12th game was crucial. Mrs Lambert Chambers led 6-5 and 40-15 – two match
points. She takes up the tale again:

Suzanne in my bag of victories! Alas! it was not to be: that winning point had always
been a nightmare to me (whether I was playing the best or merely a rabbit). My arm
felt like cottonwool . . .

Suzanne was evidently also feeling the strain, because she came up to the net on a
short return – a thing she would never do normally. I lobbed her, but not quite deep
enough; she put her racket up and the ball touched the tip of the wood and hit the top
of the net, falling on my side! She told me afterwards she never saw the ball and if
ever there was a lucky shot it was that one.

Score now 40-30. Suzanne again came up to the net on a short return to my forehand. If I had been asked what shot I should like her to give me in order for me to
make the winning shot – it would have been this one! I had scored over and over
again in this match, as in many others, with a short cross-court dipping forehand,
which I now played, but unluckily for me (it was, I am sure, because it was match
point) the ball hit the top of the net and fell my side: why, oh why, could it not have
dropped the other side!

I do not remember anything about the rest of the match, but I must have won
another game because Suzanne won that set at 9-7 and the match 10-8, 4-6, 9-7.

There are the bare bones, modestly exposed by a modest sportswoman, but let us put
some flesh on them. That was the greatest number of games ever played in a Wimbledon women's singles final until Mrs Margaret Court beat Mrs Billie Jean King 14-12,
11-9 – one set fewer but two games more (see below).

During the 1919 match the champion's husband was watching play on an outside
court, unable to stand the strain. As for Curzon and Beatty, either the great Foreign
Secretary or the hero of Jutland claimed to have lost his collar stud in the excitement!
The two players were asked to go to the Royal Box but . . .

This was quite impossible as we were both laid out, utterly exhausted. I remember Suzanne's feet were bleeding. Their Majesties came again to Wimbledon and
sent for me and I had a long chat with them about the match. The King said, 'I don't
know how you were feeling but I felt *quite* ill'.

There was no doubt in Mrs Lambert Chambers' mind that Suzanne stood alone –
supreme. And even the next year the Englishwoman was still good enough to get to
the Challenge Round against her, which disproves any idea that she was merely a 'has-
been'.

In 1927 one of the wettest Championships was held; full seeding was introduced for
the first time and one of the men's semi-finals and the final must have been two of the
most dramatic encounters ever seen.

We are indebted to the late F. R. Burrow, a great Wimbledon referee, for the impressions of these two matches, contained in his book, *The Centre Court and Others*
published in 1937.

One man was the centre of attention in the 1927 Wimbledon – William Tatem Tilden II. 'Big Bill' Tilden had won Wimbledon in 1920 and 1921 but had not revisited Britain as the United States, whose brightest star he was, had held the Davis Cup until the end of 1926 and there was no (lawn-tennis) point in his coming in the days when the return trip, by sea, took something like two weeks.

But now the French, who won the men's singles at Wimbledon from 1924 to 1929 inclusive, had also captured the Cup and Tilden had to challenge them on their own continent.

Tilden was arguably – in his own mind probably unarguably – the greatest player who ever lived. His opponent in the semi-final was a small, neat, spring-heeled Frenchman, Henri Cochet, from Lyons. In F. R. Burrow's opinion, Cochet's reaching the final that year was the most astounding event that had happened in his time at Wimbledon – and Burrow was the assistant referee as far back as 1907.

Towering over his opponent, Tilden set out, almost literally, to blast him off the court. The American won the first set 6-2, the second 6-4, and reached 5-1 and 15-all in the third. Now let Burrow take over:

Above Henri Cochet and 'Big Bill' Tilden after their Wimbledon semi-final in 1927. Cochet went on to defeat Jean Borotra in the final, 4-6, 4-6, 6-3, 6-4, 7-5.
Colour plate 'Pancho' Gonzalez, who won Wimbledon's longest-ever singles match against Pasarell in 1969 (see page 160). He dominated the postwar professional game.

I heard that the match was nearly over and went up to the stand just to see the finish. I was away for quite a long time! In the seventh game (Cochet serving) Tilden hit three terrific drives to finish the match, but they were all out.

This didn't appear likely to stop him, however, as he had hardly been losing a point in any of his service games. But something suddenly went wrong with this powerful weapon. He lost his service game, to love!

Point after point went to Cochet, now in full cry: he actually won seventeen aces running, and in the five games which took him from 1-5 to 6-5 only lost two points altogether.

The spectators were almost too spellbound to applaud, but when the little Frenchman at last got the set at 7-5, he got such a round of cheers as is seldom heard. But people could not understand what had happened to Tilden, nor how he could possibly have gone suddenly all to pieces.

Hating a long match, and at the same time knowing how Cochet revelled in one, Tilden had timed its duration perfectly; but, just on the very point of fulfilment of the plan, the machinery broke down.

Tilden did not quit. In the fourth set he trailed 1-3 but levelled at 4-4. Again he led 3-2 in the final set but his body was tired, his mind battered, his spirit bruised. Cochet ran him up and down the court – much more tiring than from side to side – and the cannonball serves were now spattered with the misfires of double faults. Cochet won 2-6, 4-6, 7-5, 6-4, 6-3.

Witnesses of this epic say that even when Cochet was on the uttermost brink of defeat he still kept on moving in, taking an earlier and even earlier ball on the rise. It paid off in the nick of time.

Eleven years later Tilden wrote in *My Story* (1938):

I have heard many interesting, curious, quite inaccurate accounts of what happened. One ingenious explanation was that King Alfonso of Spain arrived at 5-1 in the third set and I decided to let him see some of the match . . . Ridiculous! I didn't even know he was there!

Another was that a group of Hindus hypnotized me. If they did I didn't know it, but they certainly did a swell job. Personally, I have no satisfactory explanation. All I know is my coordination cracked wide open and I couldn't put a ball in court.

I know that what Cochet did had nothing to do with it. He played the same tennis all the way through the match, naturally gaining in confidence as I faded, but in no way did he produce anything sensational to save the match.

Be that as it may, Cochet was in the final – against another of the then ubiquitous Frenchmen, Jean Borotra.

For the third match in succession Cochet lost the first two sets. But Borotra with his

Above Ellsworth Vines *(left)* chances his arm with his famous forehand, while Jack Crawford *(right),* as ever, has something up his sleeve on his backhand.

constant net assault and acrobatic volleys and smashes had taken so much out of himself that he had to let the next two go 3-6, 4-6. Then, apparently fully recovered, he raced to a 5-2 lead in the fifth. At 5-3 he had his first match point but hit a return of serve into the net. In the next game he had his second. He double-faulted. Then came an incident very rare in top-class singles. Both men were inside the service line at the same time. Borotra stood at match point for the third time. There was a lightning volleying duel. Cochet won it on the backhand – but was it a double hit? Borotra seemed to think so; as did a number of well-placed spectators.

Should it have been Borotra's title? The umpire ruled not. Three more times in that game only one point separated the 'Bounding Basque' from the title. Twice he volleyed out. Once Cochet saved himself with a drive which raised the chalk from a sideline. Borotra double-faulted again to lose the game – and the little man from Lyons swept through the next two to win 4-6, 4-6, 6-3, 6-4, 7-5.

Back to Tilden again, still brooding about that semi-final defeat:

> By an irony of fate, Cochet, with Brugnon [yet another Frenchman!] suffered almost a like fate against Hunter and me in the doubles final when they led two sets to love, 5-3, 40-15 on Cochet's service for the match, only to have us pull out the set and win in the fifth.

If a poll were taken about the best men's singles final at Wimbledon in the past 40 years the Jack Crawford-Ellsworth Vines match in 1933 would probably head it; certainly it would have to be included in the top six.

What a contrast the two men presented. Vines, from California, the defending champion, was 6 ft 2 in (1·88 m) tall and, apparently, about six inches wide! His 'trademark' was a flat, white, peaked cap. The year before, when beating Enrique Maier of Spain, 6-2, 6-3, 6-2, Crawford 6-2, 6-1, 6-3 and, in the final, 'Bunny' Austin 6-4, 6-2, 6-0, the lanky Californian probably produced the best quarter-, semi- and final ever achieved by one player.

Crawford, the Australian, some four years older than Vines and more heavily built, affected a square-topped racket and a heavy cricket shirt of which one sleeve always remained buttoned at the wrist although, when a match grew really tense, he would daringly roll up the one on his playing arm. He looked as though he had stepped from between the frames of the age-yellowed portraits of the giants of the past which hung in the clubhouse. At first it seemed as though Vines's power – at his peak he had a tremendously hard forehand drive and a very fast service – was going to sweep Crawford off the court once again. The American led 5-2 and, although Crawford rallied briefly, clinched the first set at 6-4.

The second was a classic example of what happens when the irresistible force meets the immovable object. Crawford, with the advantage of serving first, led 7-6, 8-7, 9-8, 10-9 (the tie-break had not yet been introduced!).

The obvious tactics were for Crawford to attack Vines's relatively weaker backhand. But obvious tactics were not going to win the title. So, like the lion tamer putting his head between the gaping fangs, every now and then Crawford would feed Vines a succession of high-bouncing, apparently suicidal, shots to his forehand.

But the American needed three or four rallies really to get the range for his broadsword forehand and, as soon as he got in the groove, Crawford would return to nagging away at his backhand with sliced shots which kept low.

In the 20th game of the second set Vines was not getting so many of his first services in. Crawford pounced. Finally a sweeping drive punctured the frailer shell of Vines's backhand and the set went to Crawford 11-9.

The third and fourth sets were comparatively unimportant. The Australian kept the pressure on against Vines, deflated by losing the marathon second, and took the third 6-2. Then he, in turn, had to relax and the defending champion hammered the ball home, as though by sheer speed to blast the racket out of his adversary's grasp, and took the fourth set, also 6-2.

So, as they squared up for the decisive set, each man had won 23 games and the match was still an even money bet.

As throughout the match, Crawford started with the advantage of serving first. His anticipation was so uncanny that it bordered on extrasensory perception. All the time he nagged and worried away at Vines's backhand – but he could not chain the lightning of those still searing services.

And then, leading 5-4, the Australian struck. Vines was at the net. But a lob just cleared his groping racket. One point to Crawford.

A return of service made the American's backhand crumple like brown paper. Two points to Crawford.

Vines gave his next service all he had left and surged up to the net. Crawford made perhaps the most memorable shot of this truly memorable match as he took the thunderbolt on the half volley, his back-hand return flashing across Vines's body to nick the left-hand sideline.

Three match points. Vines served. A fault. To their eternal shame some spectators applauded. The American, who, like his opponent, had behaved superbly throughout the match, bowed ironically.

He served again. Crawford struck it a blow of iron with his forehand and Vines's return dropped into the net.

In the competitors' stand there was a soft sigh and a pretty, fair-haired woman slid gently off her seat in a dead faint! It was Mrs Crawford, who had held on to see her husband become the champion and then surrendered to the strain.

Below The two Helens — Wills Moody and Jacobs (left) — rivals for years

The writer has seen more good women's finals than men's at Wimbledon. But none was more nerve-stretching and heart-clutching than the one in 1935 when for the third time the two Helens — Wills Moody and Jacobs — met in the Championship final. Both had been brought up in the same town in California. Both had gone to the same coach. They had been rivals for years.

In the 1929 Wimbledon final Miss Wills had won 6-1, 6-2; in 1932, now Mrs Moody, she had triumphed 6-3, 6-1 over 'the other Helen' — how that constantly repeated phrase must have galled the golden-skinned Californian with the Grecian profile and the lovely legs. But by 1935 the icy, somewhat aloof, almost daunting 'Helen I' was not quite as unbeatable as she had been a few years earlier. Suffering from a bad back, she had conceded victory to Helen Jacobs in the final of the 1933 US Championships.

Could Helen II, at last, bring off her dearest wish in sport? It did not seem impossible. Early in the season Mrs Moody had lost a set to Mary Hardwick and a match to Kay Stammers, and at Wimbledon an unknown Czech, Miss Cepková, had been a set up against her and within a point of leading 4-1 in the second. Yet the old ascendancy seemed to come back for the 1935 final on the Centre Court – this was Mrs Moody's seventh and she had won all but the first, and that was 11 years earlier.

Hitting as only she could – Mrs Moody's game was essentially 'old-fashioned' in that she achieved her unparalleled Wimbledon successes mostly from the back of the court – she stood in the middle of the baseline and kept Miss Jacobs racing to the corners in pursuit of a relentless stream of powerful full-length drives. When she reached 4-0 it looked as though this was going to be 'just another Moody final'. Then Miss Jacobs began to fight back. She was within a point of levelling at 4-4 but the 'Snow Queen' was still doing most of the attacking and, in the end, Miss Jacobs' valiant retrieving was in vain.

The second set was Miss Jacobs'. Her length improved; her favourite forehand chop became as dangerous as a scimitar. Mrs Moody tried to come to the net but she was never able to run up and down the court as well as she could cover it from side to side. Before long it was one set all, each won 6-3.

There was a falling-off at the start of the third. Fatigue pressed down on both women. Fiddle-string nerves were stretched ever more taut. Miss Jacobs was the first to recover. She hustled her older opponent from the net and with a particularly savage service knocked the racket from Mrs Moody's hand to gain a 4-2 lead, which she increased to 5-2. Mrs Moody, still apparently icily impervious, gnawed back one game. And then came the crunch.

At 5-3 Miss Jacobs had match point. There was a rally with rackets flashing like rapiers. The younger Helen was at the net. She looked impassable. But the great champion produced a great shot for a great occasion: a lob which sailed over with the infuriating elusiveness of thistledown.

That stroke won not only the point but the match for Mrs Moody. Miss Jacobs put two comparatively easy volleys out of court. Helen II never quit – that was not her nature – and actually served two clear aces when trailing 5-6. But the 'Snow Queen' never relaxed her grip once she had an opponent on the run. The vice tightened and finally Helen II was forced to hit out three times in succession. How evenly matched they were was proved by the fact that both won the same number of points – 107!

Wimbledon had a truly vintage year in 1953. Most of the matches described here were finals. But when Jaroslav Drobný, born a Czech, temporarily stateless, briefly holding Egyptian papers and finally naturalized British, met Budge Patty, born in Arkansas, brought up in California but essentially shaped by Europe, it was only the third round of the 1953 Championships. They were fated to meet on many occasions. It was never easy for winner or loser. Once (at Lyons) there was neither victor nor vanquished for, after they had played 100 games without finishing even the third set, the club officials announced that the match would then terminate!

Certainly it was not easy that June afternoon in 1953. The two men went onto court at about five p.m. Before they left it every other match on the other 15 courts had either been finished or suspended because of the hour. From the first it was clear that this was going to be a nip-and-tuck match. Drobný's greater weight of stroke gave him the first set at 8-6. Patty's mobility, slightly better passing shots and ability to return some of Drob's best services, gave him the second. But at what a cost, for the score was 18-16. The only set not to go to advantage games was the third. In this Drobný, obviously upset at having lost the marathon second set, briefly went to pieces and Patty won it 6-3.

Even so, as they started the fourth, they had already played 57 games – nearly the equivalent of five 7-5 sets. And it was clear that the battle still had long to run for Drobný got an early break to lead 3-1. Patty changed his tactics, exploiting the advice an old player once gave me: 'Don't forget there's plenty of room in the air'. Although Drobný's overhead was one of his most powerful strokes – the forehand volley was Patty's great strength – the Czech missed some smashes and suddenly, at 5-4, Patty was only one point from a four-set victory.

Drobný was at the net. Patty's passing shot flashed past him like an express train

Above Jaroslav Drobný
Below Budge Patty

through an abandoned station and dropped – out, by inches. Twice more in the next game Patty needed only one point to win. Each time Drobný's curving left-handed service saved him from the brink.

By the time Drobný had taken the fourth set at 8-6 both men were suffering from cramp and muscle strain. Patty sipped brandy. Drobný periodically looked up at the stands where Rita, his wife of less than two months, tried to give him smiling encouragement. Across the turf the shadows lengthened. The Centre Court was enveloped in an uncanny silence for, as the hour advanced, the others became deserted, ghost courts; the eerie stillness was punctuated only by the almost frantic applause as each hero, in turn, produced yet another coup.

At 6-5 it looked as though Patty had done it again. He had three more match points at this stage. Each time with his awkward-looking, but extremely effective, left-handed smash Drobný scraped the lobs down out of the air and made winners from them.

But, on one of these points, on the now dew-greasy court, the heavyset Czech slipped and slithered along the turf, nearly hitting the net with his racket which would, of course, have cost him the match.

Drobný had, by now, long changed his familiar dark glasses for clear lenses. The bulbs on the famous electric scoreboard began to shine like car headlights on a dark night and at 8-8 Drobný, most reasonably, protested against the light. The match had already lasted nearly 4¼ hours. The referee, Colonel John Legg, ordered play to continue. But at 10-10 he came to the umpire's chair and announced that only two more games would be played.

They were enough. Both men were 'out on their feet'. But somehow Drobný dredged up a superhuman effort and won eight points in a row, taking first Patty's service and then holding his own, to love.

There was a tremendous ovation when the umpire announced 'Game, set and match to Drobný, 8-6, 16-18, 3-6, 8-6, 12-10'. The 93 games had lasted 4 hours and 23 minutes. It was, up to that time, the longest singles match ever played at Wimbledon.

But both were finished as far as that year's Championships were concerned. Patty, of course was out. Drobný soon went out to the Dane, Kurt Nielsen, who became only the second unseeded man to reach the final. He achieved this again in 1955 when he was defeated by Trabert.

It would be hard to find a women's singles final that technically excelled that of 1953 when Maureen (Little Mo) Connolly beat her countrywoman, Doris Hart, 8-6, 7-5.

There was no doubt that Little Mo at 18 was the greatest teenager of all time. It did not look like being a great final. The two had met before, most recently in the last stage of the French championships when Miss Hart, trying to slow down the game, had been soundly beaten. This time the older girl, whom lawn tennis had rescued from the ravages of polio, decided to live dangerously and, if necessary to die boldly. Game after game both girls displayed a repertoire embracing almost every shot in the book. The power rested with Miss Connolly, as did the mobility, for the plucky Miss Hart was still fettered by one leg which, years before, had been distorted by her childhood illness. Miss Hart had the greater delicacy of touch, when it came to the dropshot or the stop volley. Her volleying, in general, was more polished than Little Mo's and her service more reliable. No one, however, has been able to swing the ball about so penetratingly from the baseline as Miss Connolly: when she took a lead of 5-3 against the service it looked as though she were going to retain the lawn-tennis world's top title, which she had won at her first attempt when only 17, quite easily.

Then nerves entered into it, as they always do in any great match. On her own service the teenager served two double faults and netted an easy volley.

Was experience going to trammel the power of youth? Both girls held their service for 6-6. It was still anyone's match. Then, quite suddenly, the thousands round the court could see why Little Mo was so good – and how good she was. It was as though an invisible pipeline extended from her racket to the lines bounding the court. She had

Below Maureen 'Little Mo' Connolly shakes hands with Doris Hart, after defeating her 8-6, 7-5, in the 1953 Wimbledon singles final.

played this way before at Boston, New York, Paris and Wimbledon; no one could stand up against it, so merciless was the accuracy, so unremitting the pressure.

Sure enough Miss Connolly took the first set 8-6 and led 3-1 in the second. She was now demonstrating that sergeant-major-like march from one side of the baseline to the other between points, and 'pecking' her head, in complete concentration, like a chicken following a trail of corn.

But Doris raised her game magnificently. Now it was Little Mo who was being swung, in wide arcs, by the lasso of her opponent's racket. Service and volley and placement – Miss Hart had them all.

And 5-5 was called. Despite her physical handicap it seemed that if Miss Hart could win a set from the defending champion she still had a very real chance. In the five matches she had taken to reach the final Miss Connolly had lost only 8 games; in the final she had already lost 11.

Then, as a crisis seemed again to be building up, Little Mo struck. The power was that of a lumberjack, the deft accuracy that of a Nottingham lacemaker. Once more there was no gainsaying the radiant youth. She held her own service and took Doris Hart's to love. A wonderful confrontation was over.

Afterwards the champion said, 'The best game I ever played in my life'. And Miss Hart agreed that *she* had probably played better than when she won the title in 1951.

How sad it was that Miss Hart, one of the supreme stylists of the game, was never to play in another Wimbledon singles final and that Little Mo, this vital, vibrant girl, after completing her hat-trick at Wimbledon the following year when still only 19, was ruled out of further competitive play by a horse-riding accident and was struck down by cancer when still in her 30s. But the two left an imperishable imprint on the memories of all who saw that great match in July 1953.

Almost certainly the best two players who never won the Wimbledon singles were Pancho Gonzalez and Ken Rosewall. Rosewall had his chances – he was the beaten finalist in 1954, 1956 and 1970 – but Gonzalez, because of the ban on professionals, entered only before he reached his peak and after he had passed it. Yet one match, in 1969, would have made Gonzalez a Wimbledon immortal if he had never played another there.

It was lateish on the opening day of the Championships when the 41-year-old Gonzalez and his 25-year-old opponent, Puerto Rican-born Charlie Pasarell walked onto the Centre Court. By the time 20 games had been played, without either man getting the essential two ahead, the bush telegraph that sweeps through Wimbledon had worked so well that the standing section was so closely packed that people almost had to clap up and down. Time after time – 11 times in all – Pasarell was at set point but, curiously enough, only once did he look like clinching this apparently vital marathon set. As was written at the time:

> Return parried near-ace, lob countered smash, passing shot blunted volley. But even the brilliance of the play could not lighten the ever-increasing gloom. The electric scoreboard was glowing so brilliantly that you expected someone to ask the operator to dip his headlights.

At last, leading 23-22, Pasarell, who had lost his 11th set point when Gonzalez, with unbelievable sangfroid, ignored a sizzling drive and watched it drop . . . inches out, on his 12th hoisted a lob. Gonzalez left this one too – he had to – and it landed perfectly by the baseline. And Pasarell had won a first set which equalled the longest one in a Wimbledon singles match (1962).

Everyone thought that the match would then be carried over until the next day. In fact Pasarell held his service and Gonzalez went to the umpire to appeal against the light. That official referred the question to the referee, Captain Mike Gibson, who ordered 'Play on'.

Gonzalez was visibly furious. Once he snarled, 'You can't see a ball'. Another time he slung his racket towards the umpire's chair and a ballboy had to skip out of the way.

Above Charlie Pasarell
Below Gonzalez summons his last reserves at 8 all in the final set (after 108 games). The final score in this record-breaking match was 22-24 (the scoreboard couldn't cope!), 1-6, 16-14, 6-3, 11-9 (112 games in all).

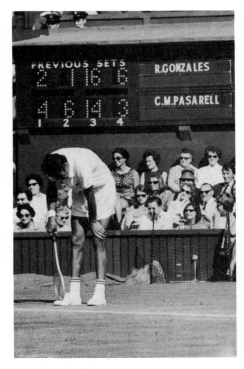

He scarcely tried to hit the ball properly, even when he could see it, and he lost the second set 6-1 in less than a quarter of an hour. The first had lasted nearly two hours!

Throughout the second set Gonzalez had conducted a running verbal battle with some of the crowd and, when he stormed off in the increasing gloom, some of them booed him. They were to regret that the next day. For although the two sets that had been completed had comprised 53 games there were still 59 to be played!

The third set began with both men fresh again the following day – if Gonzalez, at 41, could be fresh after what had gone before – and it lasted another 30 games before the old tiger won it 16-14. He fairly raced through the fourth, which he won 6-3.

But Pasarell, a past pupil of Pancho's, was no quitter. Suddenly, unexpectedly, he hit back. To quote again from what was written at the time:

With Pasarell leading 5-4, Gonzalez was beaten by a lob, stranded by a passing shot, and then put a forehand volley out. THREE MATCH POINTS.

Again Pasarell lobbed. It fell over the baseline. Like some primitive warrior invoking the power of his spear. Gonzalez gripped his steel racket even tighter, and crashed down a winning serve. One more match point to go – and Pasarell lobbed out.

Still not the end. At 6-5 Pasarell had three more match points. A blacksmith's smash, a gossamer stop volley and a winning service took care of these.

At 8-7 there was a seventh match point. After all this, was that 16-year age discrepancy added to the handicap of having to start again two sets to love down, going to prove too much?

No. Gonzalez won two points by leaving apparent winners through an almost radar-pinpointed perception of what shots were going to drop out.

In the 111th game it was the younger man who cracked. A double fault, a ragged volley out of court, a wonderful lob from Gonzalez and another weak volley meant Pasarell had dropped his service to love.

The old tiger sensed the kill, licked his chops, and went for blood.

After five hours and ten minutes Gonzalez had, for the first time, achieved an overall lead. And the veteran who had first played at Wimbledon 20 years earlier did not squander it. His service got him to 40-love.

Three match points. He needed only one, for poor Pasarell, as he had done so often when he wanted only one point to win, now that he was only one point from defeat, lobbed out.

Wimbledon's longest-ever singles – and one of the greatest triumphs ever seen there – was over. And those who the day before had jeered stayed now to cheer.

Below Margaret Court

With the possible exception of Maria Bueno, undoubtedly the two greatest women's singles champions at Wimbledon in the past decade were Mrs Margaret Court of Australia and Mrs Billie Jean King of the United States.

In 1970 Mrs Court and Mrs King met for the second time in the world's most important final in which one or the other, or both, had now appeared for eight successive years.

When she has all her stops out, with victory in her sights, Margaret Court, more than any woman player, resembles a battleship with a full complement of guns firing in unison. Without being a 'classical' strokemaker, 'Big Marge' makes some shots that no other woman in the world could make – because no other woman could even get to the ball.

But Mrs King is certainly one of the greatest competitors and, in a single, as adroit and nimble a volleyer as there can ever have been, sometimes seeming to twist like an eel as she volleys back the low returns which have bounced almost on her shoelaces.

The equation was complicated by increasing fatigue, which eventually washed over Mrs King in wave after sickening wave, leaving her at the end as pale as a bowl of junket and groaning as though she were in sheer physical agony – as, indeed, she probably was. And Mrs Court had her left ankle heavily bandaged (from a quarter-

Above Billie Jean King. A pass that hurt

final injury) and underneath the covering it was black and swollen, so the Australian must have wondered whether the pain-killing injections she had been given would last out the match.

In the epic first set there were four service breaks but, although Mrs King served at 5-4, 7-6 and 8-7, the compact little American never had a single set point. The more memorable strokes were made by Mrs Court – her passing shots seemed equally to stretch her opponent's body and the dimensions of the court – but for sheer resolution, in the face of that ever-mounting fatigue, you could not match Mrs King for bulldog determination.

The first set point came when Mrs King was trailing 11-12. Imagine the courage required to play a dropshot at such a point. But this is what Mrs King produced and went on to win the game from the net.

The first flickering signposts to defeat, however, had appeared. At 12-13 the tiredness which stretches the muscles until you can almost hear them creak, and blurs the reactions, figuratively jogged the bouncing Californian's elbow so that she volleyed out to give Mrs Court three more set points.

She needed only one. She unfurled a backhand passing shot down the line like a master swordsman tearing a blade from its scabbard.

This 14-12 set had lasted 1 hour and 27 minutes – well over the average for a complete women's match and, moreover, it was the longest played in a singles final – *men's as well as women's* – in the history of Wimbledon.

Mrs King was too good a tactician, too close a student of the game, not to know that if she got involved in many more of those searing, stretching rallies, those frantic dashes to the net and the even more frantic scrambles back, chasing the tormenting lobs, her strength just would not last. No one could successfully challenge Margaret Court to a purely physical confrontation. So the American turned the court into a minefield of dropshots. She did not have to run so much herself, and there was always the chance that the Australian's ankle might give out.

Margaret Court seemed to revel in the challenge. While Mrs King, groping and groaning, but refusing to give up, held on by the very gut of her racket, Mrs Court increased the pressure, pounding down that magnificent service, putting on the seal of inevitability with forehand volleys.

The 20th game. A netted forehand volley by the American and Mrs Court had two points for the match. (She had had one previously, at 7-6.) A smash, in which Mrs King seemed to extend her short stature like a telescope, and a forehand winner. Deuce.

A third match point. Billie Jean brought up the chalk from a sideline with a backhand pass. A fourth – and this time the American saved the match with a forehand pass.

But it could not last for ever. On the fifth point (the sixth match point in all), she was caught with the ball at her feet and netted a backhand and one of the truly great matches of all time was over. Its two hours and 26 minutes made it the longest-ever women's final and the aggregate of 46 games was two more than in the immortal Suzanne Lenglen-Mrs Lambert Chambers match played over 50 years earlier.

No wonder that afterwards Mrs King said, 'This was perhaps the toughest match I've played'. And Mrs Court commented, 'I feel tired and my ankle is aching. I didn't know how long the pain-killing injections would last, but I would have stayed there until I fell over'.

It was fitting that some ten weeks later the great Australian added the US title to the Australian, French and Wimbledon ones and so became only the second girl, after the incomparable Little Mo Connolly, to complete the Grand Slam.

A strain of almost savage irony has run through the Wimbledon career of Ken Rosewall – a career that reached the 20-year mark in 1971. Three times a Wimbledon finalist, his best chance to win the title would have been in the eleven years in which, having turned professional in 1957, he was ineligible to compete.

In a 1971 quarter-final his opponent was Cliff Richey, ranked no. 1 in the United States, seeded sixth at Wimbledon, just over 12 years his junior.

Above Ken Rosewall. 'I've got it coming to me.'
Below Cliff Richey. 'Anything you can do . . .'

From the start, Rosewall, dark face lined with wind and weather, seamed with memories of the frustrations of defeat and victories dearly bought around the world, set out with tantalizing dropshot and teasing lob to make the younger man run, and run, and run. (See colour plate, page 333.)

But the power of the American, concentrated on whipping forehand passing shots and big services on big points, had given him a lead of two sets to love and 4-2 in the third set, with Rosewall 0-30 down on his own service. It must be all over.

Then the veteran's racket, in the very nick of time, turned into the conjuror's wand. The stop volleys, the smashes – even more devastating coming from such an undistinguished frame – the service placements, all began to form patterns as impossible to handle as a cactus.

Perhaps Richey tried too hard. It is difficult not to when an 'old man' whom you have on the hook suddenly turns from fish to angler. In any case, trailing 4-5, the American was foot-faulted on his second service to become 0-30 down. Three set points – and Rosewall won the third.

At the start of the fourth set they had been playing for five minutes over two hours. It looked like Richey again. Rosewall's service had been broken and, like a butterfly with a broken wing, he fluttered behind at 6-7. Then he waved the magic wand again – this time over himself.

That miraculous return of service, particularly of course on the backhand, blunted Richey's most potent weapon or, even more shatteringly, turned it against him. And now it was two sets all.

To quote what was written immediately after the match:

At this point, while the two men were towelling themselves before the final crunch – it is right to pay tribute to the magnificently sporting way in which Richey played this match. In the past he has been seen in the role of a villain.

Now, at two sets all, he was still playing well and, more importantly, with courage. He had 14,000-and-one opponents to overcome – he was foot-faulted something like a dozen times and I should say the luck, in the form of net cords and dubious balls, was stacked against him.

But, even if the dice were loaded, he continued to throw them, in the shape of the white balls, on the green baize of the turf.

By the time the fifth set was properly under way there was an uncanny 'delayed action' sound coming from outside the Centre Court where thousands of frenzied fans, unable to get in, congregated underneath the electric scoreboard, applauding wildly as the points flashed up.

In the fifth set Rosewall led 5-4 – and lost four match points. He trailed 15-40 at 5-5. It was still a gambler's match. Finally, at 6-5, on his fifth match point, Ken slipped in a backhand, silent and deadly as the midnight assassin's knife and, seconds under four hours, he was the winner, while Richey – game, sporting, Cliff Richey – clambered over the net and said 'Congratulations, iron-man!'

Alas, that epic had sweated the sap out of Rosewall and, in the semi-final, he won just five games from John Newcombe, whom he had taken to five sets in the previous year's final.

It was a semi-final, this time of the women's singles in 1972, that was the next outstandingly memorable match. It concerned the new, young, unexpected champion of 1971, Evonne Goolagong and the precocious 17-year-old American, Chris Evert. It was their eagerly awaited first encounter and entirely lived up to anticipation.

Neither of the girls had had an easy passage to the last-but-one round. Miss Goolagong had had a very tough match, dropping a set, against the Russian Olga Morozova, and France's Françoise Durr had extended her to 8-6, 7-5. Miss Evert who, by a fluke of the draw, had met no one but fellow Americans, had dropped a set to Valerie Ziegenfuss, needed 28 games to beat Mary Ann Eisel and dropped another set to Patti Hogan in the quarter-finals.

But 'Little Miss Icicle' showed not the slightest signs of nerves as she shaped up to Miss Goolagong – perhaps the most popular girl player since the heyday of Christine Truman.

It was rather the difference in characters than the quality of much of the play that made this match unforgettable for, in the first set in particular, it was errors rather than winners that were decisive; and most of them came from the champion.

Every now and then Miss Evert would hit one of those tremendous two-handed passing shots. One marvels where such a slender frame finds such power; it must be as unbelievable as being stung by a primrose. But, for the most part, Miss Evert was content to let the champion beat herself; when the young American led 3-0 in the second set it looked as though her tactics were correct.

Then, almost it seemed in desperation, Evonne, who had won only three points in those three games, began to hit back. She won the next game and the fifth was one of the decisive ones. The tension had affected even the officials. One linesman corrected his call. Another was so inaudible that a rally continued for several strokes after he had called 'Out'.

Miss Goolagong made a fantastic shot – a cross-court backhand pass off a smash – and now she was very much in the match.

Miss Evert, who had seemed almost inhumanly cool and impregnable, suddenly began to show signs of human frailty. Evonne was positively glowing with confidence. She varied her length and pace and that almost coquettish, sliced half-court forehand shot was teasing the blonde teenager into unaccustomed errors. Suddenly the scales had tilted dramatically. Miss Goolagong had won the second set, taking six games in a row with the loss of only ten points.

But the struggle was by no means over – although the odds, unfairly in this instance, went against the American youngster as the crowd made it abundantly clear that their sympathies were with Evonne, even though she was the champion and the Centre Court fans normally support the underdog.

Many games went against the service but luck – a net-cord volley to lead 5-4, – the shot of the match – a low volley that looked like a conjuring trick, and increasing

Below Chrissie *(left)* 'I don't quite get it.' 'Well, take that!' Is Evonne *(centre)* too concerned with her opponent here? Her eye is certainly a long way off the ball, while *(right)* Stan's gaze devours it . . .

fatigue on Miss Evert's part were all conspiring to sweep the champion home. The young woman – less than four weeks away from her 21st birthday – was just too strong for the not fully developed schoolgirl.

In the tenth game the American was so tired that she could not consistently throw the ball up straight when serving. For once even the cuddly Evonne was ruthless, taking the final game to love with a backhand volley that sent the ball away dead as a severed head after the guillotine blade has descended. It had been a wonderful comeback by the champion.

Until 1972, only eight nations, Great Britain, New Zealand, Australia, the United States, France, Czechoslovakia, Peru and Spain, had produced the winner of the men's singles at Wimbledon. That summer there was a chance of a new country appearing on the roll of distinction, for against an American, Corporal Stan Smith of the US Army, there was pitted Ilie Năstase who, technically at least, also held a military rank, lieutenant in the Rumanian Army.

Almost at once both men hit their best form. Smith was wonderfully acrobatic for a man of 6 ft 4 in (1·93 m). Năstase scored with some of those typical elastic-wristed shots. Oddly enough Smith was missing the easy volleys. One of them cost him the vital 4-5 break in the first set and things looked desperate for the tall, blond American when he dropped his service, on a double fault, at the opening of the second set.

But the Rumanian's temperament is as fragile as some of his 'touch' shots. All at once a service call against him started him fretting and fuming. He changed his racket – once in the middle of a game – like a nervous gambler throwing away unwanted cards. The stork-like Smith took the second set in 25 minutes. Năstase was at his worst in this set, after having started it at his best. He went to 2-0 with passing shots and a topspin lob. Then there was a dubious baseline call against him. It rankled and festered in his mind.

Whenever the ball went into the net he glared at that inoffensive piece of equipment as though it had deliberately raised itself to trap his shot. He conversed with an Italian lawyer friend in the crowd. More racket trouble; more trouble with linesmen. He lost the third set in 24 minutes and it looked as though the match were over with the Rumanian having beaten himself.

Suddenly he settled down. His friend left the stands and Năstase accepted his choice of rackets. His return of service became so arrow-accurate that Smith's speed of delivery was a weapon turned against himself. As the pressure increased, Smith began to fumble the easy volleys again. An oblique passing shot stretched the American's 76 inches and the extension of his racket to the limit – and it was not enough. In exactly two hours the men were level at two sets all.

Everything hinged on the fifth game of the final set. There were no fewer than seven deuces in it. Three times Năstase, who had now conquered himself, looked like subduing Smith, too, when he was within a point of gaining the vital breakthrough.

But Smith had two superior strengths. One was purely physical, and it enabled him to cover much more of the court than his opponent could without tiring. The other was mental. No matter how fortune treated him he maintained an outward composure and an inner determination.

In the 48th game, after more than 2½ hours of relentless competition, much of it of the highest possible class, with Smith showing that he had much more than just a serve-and-volley, slam-bang game and Năstase displaying the touch of a fencing master, the Rumanian at last began to show signs of fatigue. He could not get his first service in. He was making unforced errors. Yet he managed to produce a winning volley to save one match point and then Smith lost a second with a poor return of service.

At 6-5 Năstase saved a third match point and the twang of his racket as he made the volley was echoed by the nerves of the crowd. But on the fourth the tension was too much and the Rumanian missed an easy backhand. Smith was the Champion, at the end of the greatest Wimbledon men's final since Jack Crawford's heroic victory over Ellsworth Vines in 1933.

Below . . . and Ilie perhaps doesn't see the point of it at all.

Great Players of All Time
Allison Danzig

An all-time ranking of lawn-tennis players is not as feasible as a rating of athletes in some of the other sports. In foot racing the clock furnishes a constant gauge; in jumping the tape measure is the immutable computer.

In lawn tennis the cold, ineluctable figures of time, distance, addition, percentages do not apply. The number of times the player won the Wimbledon, United States, French and Australian Championships can count heavily in his favour, but the player who competed in the years when there were no jet planes, nor aircraft of any kind, was not crossing the Atlantic or the Pacific nearly as often as does the international competitor today. The calibre of the competition in the period when the player was in his prime – the number of players of the first class who were his contemporaries – has to be taken into account in appraising his record. The type of court on which the player learned the game and developed his style and the problems he faced in adjusting to other surfaces also enter into consideration. The Wimbledon, United States and Australian Championships have been played from the beginning on grass and the Davis Cup Challenge Rounds too from 1900 to 1963, except from 1928 to 1933, and yet the vast majority of tournament players have virtually no experience on this fast surface until they are far enough advanced to qualify for those blue-ribbon events.

Nevertheless, regardless of the difficulties of an all-time ranking, of rating a player of the 1920s in comparison with a player of the 1960s and 1970s, there is almost complete unanimity among those who saw him in his prime that the greatest lawn-tennis player who ever lived was William T. Tilden II.

Those who reject this statement scornfully ask how a player in his prime almost half a century ago could possibly be rated as superior to Laver, Gonzalez, Rosewall, Smith, Ashe, Newcombe. They regard the game of today as so different from what it was in the 1920s, so much faster and more exacting and more aggressive, with improved rackets and balls, that Tilden and his contemporaries would be outclassed in current competition. So far as the rackets and balls are concerned, any benefit their improvement imparts to the player's ability would accrue to Tilden were he competing today, and so can be dismissed as irrelevant. At the root of the incredulity is the widespread belief that the game has changed so much in style, method, speed, vigour. Specifically, it is attributable to the 'Big Game' – the game of the big serve and volley, which is supposed to have come into vogue after World War II, when Jack Kramer and Ted Schroeder, under the captaincy of Walter L. Pate, went to Australia to challenge for the Davis Cup that had been lost in 1939.

It is true enough that Kramer and Schroeder and Gonzalez beat the Australians with the 'Big Game' and that the Americans were hoisted with their own petard in the 1950s and 1960s by the Australians. But the 'Big Game' was in tennis long before Kramer and Schroeder exploited it. Maurice McLoughlin and Richard Norris Williams II were its exponents before the US Championships, which both of them won, moved from New-port to Forest Hills in 1915. In 1914, in the Davis Cup Challenge Round at Forest Hills, McLoughlin defeated Norman Brookes of Australasia in a record-breaking first set, 17-15 (he also won the next two sets, 6-3, 6-3) and hardly once in that 32-game set did he fail to start for the net behind his high-powered service. Brookes, too, went in repeatedly when serving, though he placed greater reliance on his groundstrokes.

But in the years that Tilden ruled at Forest Hills, from 1920 up to 1926, the 'Big Game' was known and played, though not called that. Tilden had one of the biggest serves in history, clocked at 151 mph in 1933. Gerald Patterson, Ellsworth Vines, Frank Shields and John Doeg all had mighty services, and all went to the net behind them. Jean Borotra's was not quite as fast but he was forever rushing pell-mell for the net whether serving or returning serve. Wilmer Allison, who was to beat Fred Perry and Sidney Wood and win the championship in 1935, had the same itch to go in on his serve in the 1920s and 1930s. Henri Cochet, who ended Tilden's 6-year sway in 1926, was no big server but he camped in mid-court and the forecourt to bring the volley and half volley into play with his dreamy touch in winning four open French, two Wimbledon and one US titles.

Tilden was no net rusher and many had the mistaken idea that he volleyed badly and had no confidence in going to the net. This should have been dispelled by his superlative volleying in defeat against Cochet in 1926 and against René Lacoste in the 1927 US Championship final. In both matches he was impelled to seek the net because he had a weak knee and decided it would be subjected to less strain if he sought to win the point forthwith at the net, rather than engage in prolonged rallies in the back-court.

Tilden preferred to stay in the backcourt, despite the fact that he had one of the most fearful serves of all, because he loved to play tennis as a game of chess, to outmanoeuvre his opponent and exact the winning opening through tactical skill rather than overpower his opponent with a bludgeon serve and the volley adjunct. He preferred to stay back also because he had as strong a combination of forehand and backhand drives as any player this observer has seen in half a century, because he was a master of spin almost without equal, with a forehand chop that was the unkindest cut next to Wallace Johnson's, and a wicked backhand slice, and because he used the dropshot as adroitly as any of his contemporaries.

He also had one of the finest physiques for lawn tennis – tall, broad-shouldered, thin-shanked; was unsurpassed in footwork, though Fred Perry may have been a bit faster; was a master of tactics; loved the game and enjoyed playing before a gallery as much as any player that ever lived, and had great endurance despite the fact that he smoked incessantly off the court. His pronounced courage won the hearts of galleries in his defeats as he rarely did in victory. There was only one stroke of which it cannot be said he was the master – the overhead smash.

George (Pat) Hughes, one of the finest doubles players Britain has produced, who won the Wimbledon doubles and played Davis Cup doubles with Charles Tuckey, and who won recognition as one of the soundest writers on lawn tennis, scoffed at the idea of Tilden being outdated and outclassed by the game of the big serve and volley. Writing in *World Sport* of July, 1955, he said, 'Patterson played exactly the same game as is being played today, yet it was hopelessly inadequate against the great Tilden, who had the technique to pass the volleyer and to annihilate the baseliner . . . Against J. C. Parke, the lanky Yank produced a game never before seen at Wimbledon. Drives were mixed with chops and slices; no two shots were alike . . . Parke was outclassed . . .' In every all-time ranking (known to this writer) by authorities who saw Tilden in his prime, only two failed to put him ahead of all other players. One was the late A. Wallis Myers, one of the most distinguished English historians of lawn tennis, who bracketed Tilden and H. L. Doherty together at the top. The other was Jean Borotra, who put René Lacoste, his Davis Cup team mate, at no. 1 and Tilden at 2. Lacoste was his *bête noir* on the courts, terrifying Jean with the lobs that always trapped him as he rushed madly for the net. Myers's ranking was made in 1932, Borotra's in 1934.

Tilden was ranked first by Budge (in 1940), Riggs (1946), B. C. Wright (1946) and Allison (1958).

Late in 1969, after Rod Laver had scored his second Grand Slam, the international panel of tennis writers that picked the player of the year for the Martini & Rossi Gold Racket ranked the players of the world for all time. Their selections, in order, were Tilden, Budge, Laver, Gonzalez, Kramer, Perry, Cochet, Lacoste, Hoad and Vines. Receiving the next most votes, in order, were Rosewall, R. L. Doherty, Brookes, Sedgman and Johnston (tied), Willie Renshaw, Jack Crawford, and Baron Gottfried von Cramm, Pancho Segura, Tony Wilding, and Roy Emerson in a four-way tie. Those casting votes in the ranking were Lance Tingay, Rex Bellamy and David Gray of Britain, Philippe Chatrier and Judith Elian of France, Rino Tommasi of Italy, Jim Russell and George McGann of Australia, and Neil Amdur, Bud Collins, Allison Danzig, Will Grimsley, Murray Olderman, Ned Potter and Steve Snider of the United States. Tilden received seven first-place votes and 118 points (10 points for first place, nine for second, on down to one for tenth). Budge was first on two ballots and had 103 points,

Above William Tatem Tilden *(right)* and René Lacoste *(left),* two black belts of the tennis world

Laver was voted no. 1 by three and had 96 points. Kramer received the only other first-place vote.

Recently Harry Hopman, Australia's extremely successful Davis Cup captain, who now makes his home in Port Washington, Long Island, New York, was asked for his all-time ranking and obliged with the following list: Tilden, Budge, Perry, Laver, Cochet, Lacoste, Johnston, H. L. Doherty, Vines and, tied for tenth place, Gonzalez and Emerson.

The writer's own list is almost identical with Hopman's selection but not in the same order: Tilden, Cochet, Budge, Lacoste, Kramer, Perry, Johnston, Laver, Vines and tied for tenth, Gonzalez and Emerson. Until I had Harry's list I had Gonzalez alone at no. 10 and Rosewall was the one I worried most about getting in, in view of his remarkable performance at the age of 35 in 1970, when he won the US Open, got to the final at Wimbledon, losing to Newcombe in five sets, and was voted the player of the year. But Hopman's choice of Emerson got me thinking about what a wonderful athlete he had been for so many years – tireless, perpetual motion in carrying the attack to his opponent, never out of humour, never discouraged – he won the Australian Championship six times, the US, Wimbledon and French titles twice each, and he was runner-up to Laver in the Australian, French and US Championships in 1962, the year of Laver's Grand Slam, and he probably would have been at Wimbledon too had he not fallen and been injured. Also, there are few players with better Davis Cup records – 15 of 18 matches won in 9 Challenge Rounds, and only one of 12 lost in singles. So Emerson was bracketed with Gonzalez at no. 10.

Cochet is my choice for second-best player of all time because he had more natural ability than any other to become a world champion, and, with the touch of the artist, developed a game of such toughness, despite its seeming moderation and restraint, as to go past Tilden, Borotra, Lacoste, whose declining health was to lead to his early retirement, Perry, Austin and all others. Cochet, after administering, in 1926, Tilden's first defeat in the US Championship since 1919, beat him again in the 1927 Wimbledon semi-finals and in the Davis Cup Challenge Rounds of 1928, 1929 and 1930. The Wimbledon victory of 1927 came after he had been crushed by Tilden in the first two sets and trailed at 5-1 in the third – one of the most incredible pull-ups on record. In the quarter-finals he had beaten Frank Hunter after losing the first two sets, and Borotra, too, took the first two sets in the final. In 1928 Cochet, who had gained the deciding victory over Johnston in the 1927 challenge round, to win the Davis Cup for France for the first time, became the national hero when he scored three victories in the Challenge Round after Lacoste had lost to Tilden in the opening match. In 1929, with Lacoste retiring from cup play, Cochet more than ever was the toast of Paris.

Tilden in 1928 said of him: 'In these inspired moments of his, Cochet is the greatest of all Frenchmen and in my opinion possibly the greatest player who has ever lived'.

Budge is most often ranked second to Tilden and there are those who put him at the top. Tall, big of frame and powerful, he had an all-court game of great severity and without a weakness, and he had marked staying powers and the ideal temperament. He is particularly famed for his backhand, generally rated as superior to all others, but he could put on great pressure too with his forehand. He could be devastating from both sides and his return of service has hardly ever been excelled, confounding to both the volleyer and the baseliner. He was mighty of service and overhead and an excellent volleyer.

Tilden in 1940 said, 'I think Don Budge is the greatest tennis player of all time'. In the 1947 edition of *My Story,* he wrote 'For all-round consistency Donald Budge at the peak of his game was the finest of them all . . . No man to my knowledge ever equalled the high average of play that Budge produced over a period of fully six years – amateur and pro. I consider him the finest player 365 days a year that ever lived.'

Lacoste was the supreme baseline player with a control of the ball and a depth of stroke equalled by few. His game was the antithesis of Cochet's daring, imaginative attack in which the volley and half volley figured so prominently. No player was more calculating than Lacoste, who analysed each opponent's game for its weaknesses and strong points. Phlegmatic and inscrutable on the court, he concentrated on

Above Donald Budge, the greatest backhander of all time

attacking the vulnerable points and in keeping the ball going back with a length and direction that exerted inexorable pressure. He was a master of the lob with few equals.

Lacoste's performance against Tilden in the 1927 final of the US Championship was a classic demonstration of defence against one of the most murderous and varied on-slaughts Forest Hills has seen. For close on two hours the 34-year-old Tilden attacked with drive, chop and slice, with cannonball and twist serves, resorted to the volley as he rarely had before, brought all his cunning and courtcraft to bear and fought with a courage that never wavered and had the 14,000 in the stands cheering madly, yet he could not win a set. He led at 7-6 and 40-0 on his service in the first set, was ahead at 3-1 in the second set and led again in the third, 5-2 and had two more set points, but the match ended 11-9, 6-3, 11-9 in favour of the 23-year-old sphinx with the brooding eyes, who kept the ball going back with the inevitability of fate, unshakeable in control against pace and spin.

It was Lacoste's second successive victory in the US Championship, which he won in 1926 by beating Borotra in the final, and he was the first player from overseas to win the title twice. His victory over Tilden in the 1927 Challenge Round was the key match that won the Davis Cup for France for the first time. He won Wimbledon in 1925 and 1928 and the French title in 1925, 1927 and 1929. His failing health forced him to withdraw from the lists after 1929 at the age of 25, else he might have won many more honours.

Jack Kramer is selected for fifth place in the ranking by a hair over Fred Perry. Both were sterling competitors and splendid athletes, as well as superbly equipped in strokes. Perry had as fine a physique as anyone who ever played first-class tennis. No one was ever more fit, faster or surer of foot – or of himself. Kramer, a little taller, made full use of his height in a powerful service and overhead and he brought the volley into play without delay, going in on virtually every serve on fast surfaces and often on his return of service. He played the Big Game all the way, but he had groundstrokes, as well as a serve, to get him to the net. Perry was not in as much of a hurry to get to close quarters, but he did not lag. He did not have as big a serve as Kramer, Budge and Vines, but his running forehand, taking the ball early, was as good an approach shot as anyone ever needed to give him access to the net.

Johnston had the misfortune to be Tilden's contemporary, otherwise he might have won the US Championship seven times. He was the champion in 1915 and 1919, defeating McLoughlin and Tilden in the two finals. Five times he lost to Tilden in the final (1920, 1922-5), and to Dick Williams in 1916. A little man, Johnston lacked a big serve, but he had a mighty forehand drive, made with the Western grip and heavy topspin, and he is ranked as the greatest volleyer of his time next to Vincent Richards, and some put the two at the top for all time. In Davis Cup play Johnston had one of the best of all records: in eight Challenge Rounds he won 13 of 16 matches. Most of his cup matches were won by crushing margins. No player was ever more a favourite of American galleries than was 'Little Bill'.

When Rodney Laver scored his second Grand Slam in 1969, he was hailed as the greatest player the world had seen as the US trophy was presented to him at Forest Hills. He was not quite the superman in 1970 when he lost to Roger Taylor at Wimbledon and to Dennis Ralston in the US Open Championship, yielded up his US professional crown and met various other setbacks, though he collected the record sum of $201,453 in prize money for the year. Then he was off in meteoric fashion in 1971. In thirteen successive victories over top professionals in the so-called $210,000 winner-takes-all classic, he collected $160,000 in a little more than two months. Surely he was the greatest. Then the gloss rubbed off again. Tom Gorman beat him at Wimbledon after eliminating him at Queen's. He did not play in the US or French Open Championships, but he suffered defeat against Mark Cox in the Australian Championship and losses repeatedly against Marty Riessen, Roger Taylor, Tom Okker, Bill Bowrey and others, and Rosewall beat him in the WCT final for $50,000. Nevertheless he collected $292,717 for the year and was called the first lawn-tennis millionaire.

In 1972 Laver was not the world's all-time best player he had appeared to be in

Below Rod Laver, the greatest left-hander of all time, who won the Grand Slam twice

1969, but he still had strong credentials for recognition in a record that includes two Grand Slams, four Wimbledon Championships as amateur and professional, two US titles and repeated triumphs in the Longwood professional championships.

Vines at the peak of his form could probably have beaten any player that ever lived. His lightning-bolt service was regarded by some as the best of all. No one hit a forehand flatter or harder or kept the ball so close to the net. He was murderous overhead and a volleyer of the first rank. He looked slow in ambling about the court but he did not have to run much for the ball. He hit so hard and so close to the lines that few of his shots came back. They either won or were in the net or out of court for the most part. No one played a riskier game with the possible exception of Dick Williams. Wimbledon galleries were aghast at the fury of his attack as he beat Crawford in the semifinals and Bunny Austin in the final in 1932, allowing each only six games and sending service ace after service ace beyond their reach. Cochet was helpless against his speed too in the final at Forest Hills, though some said Cochet was sailing on a French liner later in the day and had no intention of being late. In 1933 Vines suffered repeated reverses, but his final at Wimbledon, losing to Crawford, was classed by some as the greatest of all time (see CENTRE COURT CLASSICS).

Gonzalez did not have the groundstrokes of Tilden, Budge, Perry, Kramer, but he had one of the best services of all. He had the heart of a gladiator, moved with the easy grace of a cat and operated with deadly efficiency in the forecourt. He got to the top with only two years of experience on grass, reigned in 1948 and 1949, though he did not win at Wimbledon, and then entered the professional ranks, which he dominated for five years until he went into semi-retirement in 1960. His endurance became legendary in his comebacks and his fame was never greater than when he defeated Charles Pasarell at Wimbledon in 1969 in the longest match ever played there, lasting 5 hours and 12 minutes and requiring 112 games, 22-24, 1-6, 16-14, 6-3, 11-9. Gonzalez was 41 years old and Pasarell 25 (see CENTRE COURT CLASSICS).

It is difficult to leave out Rosewall, with his magnificent groundstrokes, which would have won many more titles had his service been comparable to Hoad's, Gonzalez' or Laver's. It is difficult too, to omit Sedgman, one of the cleverest operators around the net lawn tennis has known, and Hoad, whose strength and spin of stroke and service could have made him supreme had he not been plagued with injuries, both as an amateur and a professional, and Borotra, a magnificent match player, one of the boldest attackers, of whom H. S. Scrivener wrote in the London *Morning Post* in 1930: 'Undoubtedly the finest match of the meeting [Wimbledon championships of that year] was the semi-final in which Tilden defeated Borotra . . . When both were playing for all they were worth I do not think I have ever seen finer tennis anywhere.'

How, too, can one omit H. L. Doherty, who won Wimbledon five years in succession and all of his twelve Davis Cup matches, as well as the United States title; his brother Reginald, who won Wimbledon four times in succession; Norman Brookes, with his court wizardry that was so great a challenge for so many years, even against Tilden in 1920; and Anthony Wilding, a magnificent figure who won Wimbledon four times?

Not having seen the Dohertys or Wilding or Brookes, until he was well past his prime in the 1920s, it is hardly possible for the present writer to compare them with Tilden, Budge, Kramer, Perry, Vines and others who followed. H. S. Scrivener's authoritative comment, which appeared in the *Morning Post* in 1930, seems pertinent:

The Dohertys in their palmiest days had not the precision combined with the power of Tilden and the few players like Borotra who are capable of standing up to him. They did not make the lightning thrusts and parries that Tilden and his peers have to make today for the simple reason that they did not have to. Their beautifully regular and severe, but actually less intensive game was good enough. Yet so naturally gifted were they that I think if there had been a few more like their great rival S. H. Smith knocking about in those days, they would have raised their game higher. I also think that, had they lived in these days, they would have quite possibly fought their way to the top, though the furious rate at which lawn tennis is played today might have proved too much for their not very robust constitutions.

Colour plate Chris Evert, the youngest player ever to represent the United States in the Wightman Cup and runner-up in the 1973 French women's singles

Colour plate Roy Emerson, twice Champion of Wimbledon, the US and France, six times Australian Champion, and an outstanding athlete

Ever since Suzanne Lenglen and Helen Wills met in their celebrated match at Cannes on the French Riviera in 1926, they have been rivals for the position at the top of the all-time women's lawn tennis rankings. Until that match Mlle Lenglen had reigned as the undisputed world champion from the time she defeated Mrs Dorothea Lambert Chambers, seven times winner of the title, in the 1919 Wimbledon challenge round, 10-8, 4-6, 9-7. The French queen of the courts defeated Miss Wills, 6-3, 8-6, at Cannes — the only time they ever met in a tournament singles match. So her supremacy remained unchallenged. But since then, as Miss Wills (later Mrs Frederick Moody) compiled record-breaking victories at Wimbledon and in the US Championship, more and more adherents have argued that she should be ranked ahead of Mlle Lenglen and all others. In 1926, they insist, she had not yet attained the full maturity of her game at the age of 19 and another meeting a few years later would have brought a different result. Mlle Lenglen's proponents counter with the argument that the Frenchwoman, just short of her 27th birthday in 1926, would have passed her zenith in a later meeting. They point out that, although she may not have won as many major championships as did Mrs Moody, she most often beat her opponents by utterly crushing margins in winning six Wimbledon and six French Championships, and that she would undoubtedly have added to her laurels had she not left the amateur ranks in 1926. Mrs Moody won eight Wimbledon, seven US and four French titles between 1923 and 1938. Because of ailments she was out of competition for a number of years.

Helen Wills and Suzanne Lenglen played entirely different styles of tennis. The American won with power and court tactics. No woman player hit a ball harder from both forehand and backhand and with such control. She had a deep, forcing service and was strong overhead and a skilled volleyer, but it was almost entirely from the baseline that she won her matches. The overpowering pace and length of her groundstrokes were irresistible. She was not fast or nimble of foot, and opponents who made any headway against her were usually those who had command of the dropshot and used changes of length to run her forward and back and abstained from driving exchanges. Mlle Lenglen had nothing like Miss Wills's power, though her forehand was severe. She had exceptional control of the ball and could place it with a precision unmatched, so concentrated on outmanoeuvring her opponent. She went to the net more often than Miss Wills and could volley like a man. Contrasting with Miss Wills, who was poised, unemotional and almost never changed expression, Mlle Lenglen was temperamental, and could become highly nervous and even burst into tears, though she was so far superior to her opponents that she rarely had cause for misgivings. In France and at Wimbledon she was treated like a queen, the greatest attraction in lawn tennis. In 1926 she kept Queen Mary waiting in the royal box at Wimbledon, in part through a misunderstanding as to the time her match was scheduled and failure of communication, and the reception she received was so unnerving that she became hysterical and withdrew from the tournament. That was the end of her reign and amateur career. She signed a professional contract late in 1926 with C. C. Pyle, the American promoter, to go on tour with Vincent Richards, Mary K. Browne and others. Thus it was that she and Helen Wills, who underwent surgery for appendicitis after the match at Cannes and was out of the French and Wimbledon Championships, never played each other again.

Mrs Kathleen (McKane) Godfree of England, a Wimbledon champion who played both Miss Wills and Mlle Lenglen, regarded the latter as the greatest of all women players. Mlle Lenglen has been at the top of most rankings over the years. In 1950 the Associated Press, in its rankings of the players of half a century, put Miss Wills ahead of Mlle Lenglen. Recently, Harry Hopman put Miss Wills first and Mlle Lenglen second in his all-time ranking. After them he ranked Maureen Connolly, Dorothea Lambert Chambers, Alice Marble, Helen Jacobs, Molla Mallory, Billie Jean King, Margaret Smith Court and, tied for tenth, Maria Bueno and Louise Brough.

The present writer brackets Mlle Lenglen and Miss Wills together at no. 1. How can anyone be put ahead of Mlle Lenglen after her 1925 performance at Wimbledon, when she lost only five games in as many matches, defeated the defending champion, Mrs

Godfree, in love sets in the semi-finals and gave up only 21 points in the final? And how can anyone be put ahead of Helen Wills, who had won seven US, five Wimbledon and four French Championship finals with the loss of a single set until she yielded the second set to Dorothy Round in the Wimbledon final of 1933, and who in 1928 won the Wimbledon and French Championships and her Wightman Cup matches without yielding more than three games in any set?

After Mlle Lenglen and Miss Wills I rank, in order, Maureen Connolly Brinker, Alice Marble, Helen Jacobs, Margaret Smith Court, Billie Jean King, Maria Bueno, Molla Mallory, and Louise Brough. Regretfully it is necessary to omit Dorothy Round, Margaret Osborne duPont, Kathleen McKane Godfree, Doris Hart, Lili de Alvarez, Althea Gibson, Pauline Betz Addie, May Sutton Bundy, Elizabeth Ryan, Sarah Palfrey Danzig, Dorothea Lambert Chambers, Hazel Hotchkiss Wightman, Mary K. Browne, Kay Stammers Menzies and Betty Nuthall.

Maureen Connolly won three Wimbledon and US Championships before she reached the age of 20 in 1954, and had not fate cruelly brought her tournament career to an end that year, when she was injured while horseriding, she might have broken all records. A little girl from San Diego, Calif., in 1951 she astonished Forest Hills galleries with the jolting speed of her groundstrokes, the most overpowering since Helen Wills's. The next year Wimbledon galleries marvelled at the ferocity with which she hit the ball. She won the Championship three years in a row at both Forest Hills and Wimbledon, and also the French and Australian titles in 1953 (the first Grand Slam by a woman), as well as all of her nine Wightman Cup matches, before she had developed a first-class service or mastered the volley to any great degree. She had won on the sheer weight of her drives, her great speed around the court, her remarkable concentration and determination and her sound tactical knowledge. In another two or three years, with the progress anticipated in her serving and volleying, she might well have become the most formidable player of them all. The tennis world mourned her passing in 1969.

Alice Marble played lawn tennis more like a man than any other woman of her time. She volleyed incessantly, going in on her service, and also took the ball on the rise off the ground. Few women mastered the overhead smash as she did or the American twist service. Trim of figure, she moved quickly and gracefully and, both in her appearance and her style of game, she was one of the most attractive women players of all time. She did not hit as hard or as deep as Helen Wills and Maureen Connolly and her control was not as consistent, in part because she hit boldly for winners, but her game at its peak was a delight to watch.

Helen Jacobs won the US Championship four years running, won the title at Wimbledon where she was runner-up five times (four times to Helen Wills), and was one of the very few people to defeat Miss Wills after the latter reached the top (in the 1933 Championship final at Forest Hills when Miss Wills defaulted with the score 3-0 against her in the third set). At Wimbledon in 1935 she led Miss Wills 5-2 in the final set and was within a stroke of victory but lost. Miss Jacobs had unsurpassed fighting qualities. She was one of the best women volleyers of them all, strong overhead, and had a backhand that stood like Gibraltar under the heaviest bombardment. She could master the forehand drive, but her chop, comparable to Elizabeth Ryan's, was one of the most feared in the game.

Margaret Smith Court, one of the strongest of women players, with a height and reach equalled by few champions, and unusually mobile for her size, plays lawn tennis in the manner of Alice Marble. Her game is all attack and she is a formidable figure at the net, with her ability as a volleyer and her decisiveness overhead.

Billie Jean King plays the same aggressive game as Mrs Court and is much quicker afoot than the great majority of women players. With her speed and agility she is exceptionally effective at the net. Few women have been her equal as a volleyer or in dispatching lobs. Off the ground she is forceful and maintains exemplary length on both her forehand and undercut backhand. Her fighting qualities too are exemplary. She is the first to win the women's Wimbledon title three years in succession since Maureen Connolly did so in the 1950s. She won her third US crown in 1972. In 1973

Above The great Suzanne Lenglen
Below The masterful Helen Wills Moody

she became the first player since World War II to win Wimbledon five times. She has won more prize money than any other woman athlete in history.

Maria Bueno was an artist of the racket comparable to Suzanne Lenglen. The lovely girl from Brazil played with a grace, skill, comprehension and versatility that made her one of the game's biggest attractions. Unfortunately, her career was cut short by a knee injury but she won Forest Hills four times and Wimbledon three times.

Mrs Molla Mallory won the US Championship seven times and was also the winner of the wartime 1917 tournament. She is especially famous for her victory over Mlle Lenglen in the second round of the 1921 Championship at Forest Hills, the Frenchwoman defaulting after losing the opening set and a few points in the second set. In 1926 Mrs Mallory, whose reign had been ended by Helen Wills in 1923, won back the crown by defeating Elizabeth Ryan in the final after trailing 0-4 in the third set. Norwegian by birth, Molla Bjurstedt came to the United States to establish herself as the champion in 1915 and remained at the top until Miss Wills defeated her in 1923, except in 1919, when Hazel Hotchkiss Wightman was the winner of the title. Mrs Mallory ruled through the might of her forehand drive, her great fighting qualities and her endurance. She had one of the weakest of serves, a backhand that was largely defensive and she almost never went to the net unless drawn up by a dropshot. But she could run for ever, never gave up and pummelled her forehand.

Louise Brough (later Mrs Clapp) was one of the ablest of women volleyers, had one of the best American twist services, and overspin drives on both forehand and backhand. Shy and almost apologetic in manner, she had no inhibitions on the lawn-tennis court and attacked with a severity that few opponents could resist. She won four Wimbledon Championships and was runner-up three times, and won the US crown once, losing five times in the final. She won all of her 12 Wightman Cup singles matches. Her doubles record is remarkable. She won the US Championship with Margaret Osborne duPont 12 times, they won at Wimbledon five times and she won ten Wightman Cup doubles matches, eight with Mrs duPont.

Above Louise Brough
Below Margaret Court

A summary of the all-time rankings by the present writer, Harry Hopman and Lance Tingay follows.

Allison Danzig	Harry Hopman	Lance Tingay
Men		
1. Tilden	1. Tilden	1. Tilden
2. Cochet	2. Budge	2. Budge
3. Budge	3. Perry	3. Laver
4. Lacoste	4. Laver	4. Gonzalez
5. Kramer	5. Cochet	5. Hoad
6. Perry	6. Lacoste	6. Perry
7. Johnston	7. Johnston	7. Cochet
8. Laver	8. H. L. Doherty	8. Wilding
9. Vines	9. Vines	9. H. L. Doherty
10. { Gonzalez / Emerson	10. { Gonzalez / Emerson	10. W. Renshaw
Women		
1. { Lenglen / Wills (Moody)	1. Wills (Moody)	1. Lenglen
	2. Lenglen	2. Wills (Moody)
3. Connolly	3. Connolly	3. Connolly
4. Marble	4. Lambert Chambers	4. Court
5. Jacobs	5. Marble	5. King
6. Court	6. Jacobs	6. duPont
7. King	7. Mallory	7. Mallory
8. Bueno	8. King	8. Betz
9. Mallory	9. Court	9. Marble
10. Brough	10. { Bueno / Brough	10. Lambert Chambers

Reporting the Championships

The Press
David Gray

When it was decided to hold a gentlemen's singles at Wimbledon in 1877, the donors of the first prize, a silver challenge cup, were the proprietors of *The Field* magazine. That gesture of encouragement symbolizes the closeness of the link that has existed between the most important of lawn-tennis tournaments and those who have communicated the news of its development to the public.

The Field was the game's first debating forum. It published all the early arguments about the shape of the game – the size of the court, the advantages of the cloth-covered ball, the legality of the volley, and the fierce controversy over service domination. It was, for example, in a letter to *The Field* (1885) that Henry Jones, a senior member of the All England Club, suggested the basis for the modern system of handicapping. For a new sport, competing for publicity with such established Victorian sports and pastimes as archery, shooting and croquet, lawn tennis was lucky in that its supporters could claim such a share of journalistic attention.

The first Championships were reported in detail but with a mere recital of scores:

> Mr Gore won three sets running of Mr Gillson, by six games to two, six to love, and six to three respectively. Mr Hankey won three sets to one of Mr Dalby, the first by six games to four, the second by six to two. The third set Mr Dalby won by six games to three, but Mr Hankey came to the front in the fourth set, winning by six games to two . . .

There was no attempt to dramatize the play until the second round. The first comment about an injured player at any Wimbledon Championship was a remark made about a thumb, which Julian Marshall, one of the game's first notable legislators, had damaged some weeks before the tournament: 'It is still very weak and interferes with his backhand strokes. He was obliged to be very careful all through not to knock the thumb, and hence he did not play quite up to his true form.' Of Spencer Gore, the first champion, *The Field* says: 'He displayed great activity, covering an enormous area of ground, and returning many balls which seemed impossible to reach. He also played extremely well with his head.'

In the 1880s and 1890s the reports of the Championships in *The Field* were markedly livelier than those in the daily newspapers. For instance, the *Daily Telegraph* (which later appointed as its correspondent, Arthur Wallis Myers, the game's most important critic and historian in the years between the world wars) dealt in the plainest and most cursory terms with the Wimbledon of 1889, Willie Renshaw's last and most exciting Championship. There was a good deal of public interest in the matches by then, but it was hardly reflected in the reports that appeared. By the turn of the century, however, there was a decided improvement in the way the daily newspapers reported the game. Sportswriting was becoming an art. Just as writing on cricket was becoming more lively, so the reporting of lawn tennis – an ideal sport for those who like to read about the conflict between personalities and strategies – followed the same pattern. The newspapers began to publish more tournament results. The American invasion – Holcombe Ward, W. J. Clothier ('who woke up for a big smash now and then') and May Sutton ('the healthiest young woman seen for some time on this side of the Atlantic') – was noted with enthusiasm. Heroes were created and characters cherished. In 1905 there is an affectionate obituary of H. S. Mahony, the champion in 1896, who died after falling from a bicycle in Ireland on the third day of the Championships, and any later critic of the game would have been pleased to have written the description of the notable British player, S. H. Smith, which occurs in the *Daily Telegraph*'s report of play at Wimbledon:

> For years his gloomy remorseless driving has held the crowds in sad attention. It is in better order than ever now. But it has been reinforced by a small collection of new shots, shots showing in their variety and courage a suspicion of brilliance and positive humanity. For the first time Smith has made a volley by preference.

Above Henry Jones, a senior member of the All England Club, who proposed that the first Championship at Wimbledon should be held

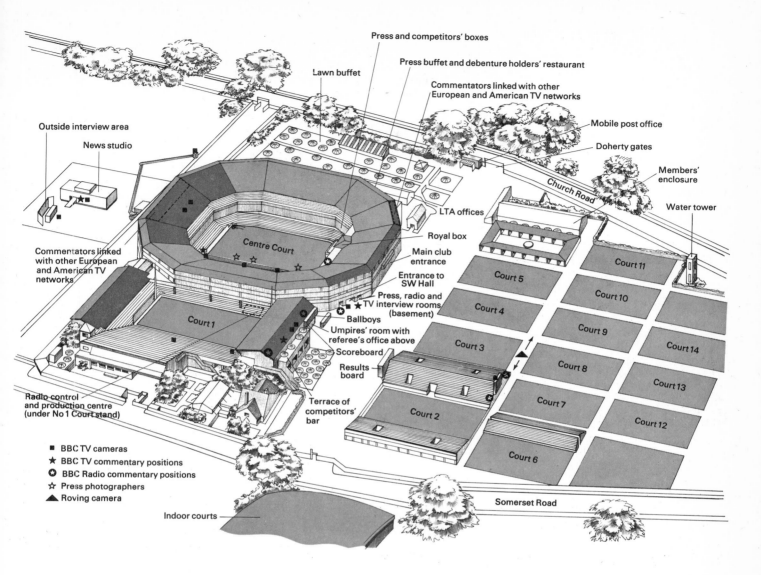

Press and competitors' boxes

Lawn buffet

Press buffet and debenture holders' restaurant

Commentators linked with other
European and American TV networks

Mobile post office

Doherty gates

Members'
enclosure

Water tower

Outside interview area

News studio

LTA offices

Royal box

Main club
entrance

Entrance to
SW Hall

Press, radio and
TV interview rooms
(basement)

Ballboys

Umpires' room with
referee's office above

Scoreboard

Results
board

Terrace of
competitors'
bar

Commentators linked
with other European
and American TV
networks

Centre Court

Church Road

Court 1

Court 5

Court 4

Court 3

Court 2

Court 6

Court 11

Court 10

Court 9

Court 8

Court 7

Court 14

Court 13

Court 12

Radio control
and production centre
(under No 1 Court stand)

- BBC TV cameras
★ BBC TV commentary positions
◎ BBC Radio commentary positions
☆ Press photographers
▲ Roving camera

Indoor courts

Somerset Road

Above The All England Lawn Tennis and
Croquet Club during the Wimbledon
Championships. The usual positions of radio
and television cameras and commentators are
indicated by the symbols in the key (positions
vary from year to year). The radio commentary
symbol just above and behind the referee's
office marks a lookout position covering all
the outside courts.

Compared with the staid commentaries of even ten years earlier, the change in
approach, style and quality of observation is remarkable. Crowds were flocking to
the Championships at Worple Road and newspapers, which devoted so much space to
cricket and racing, had suddenly woken up to the popularity of lawn tennis. It was a
time for enthusiasm. The prose becomes more passionate and more authoritative. A
golden age was beginning. The Davis Cup, the Dohertys, Anthony Wilding and Norman Brookes had arrived on the scene and fortunately the Edwardian newspapers
found writers with the skill and knowledge to describe the new excitements. Suddenly
lawn tennis was news.

Wallis Myers, the lawn-tennis editor of *The Field* and a frequent contributor to the
Daily Telegraph, was formally appointed lawn-tennis correspondent of that newspaper in 1908 and in his articles and his books he played a major part in popularizing
the game. H. S. Scrivener, a founder of the Lawn Tennis Association and the referee at
Wimbledon for some years, contributed to the *Morning Post,* and among others who
wrote about the game was Sir Basil Liddell Hart, who was lawn-tennis correspondent
of the *Manchester Guardian* before he concentrated on military history.

Wimbledon itself kept pace with this surge of interest. When the new ground was
built at Church Road to cater for the generation of spectators who wanted to see Lenglen, Tilden and the French Musketeers, no fewer than 150 places were provided for
journalists in the Centre Court. These are today mostly allocated to newspapers which

keep the same seat throughout the fortnight and often from year to year. Nearly 500 other press passes are issued daily to those who report on or assist in the task of covering the tournament. No other lawn-tennis event attracts so many journalists.

Applications for press tickets are received from almost every major country associated with the ILTF. Some foreign newspapers send lawn-tennis specialists from their head offices. Others ask their London representatives to report on the tournament for them. All requests for accreditation are scrutinized by the All England Club, which asks for advice from the Newspaper Publishers' Association and the Newspaper Society (the organizations that look after the interests of periodicals and Commonwealth and foreign newspapers) and from the Lawn Tennis Writers' Association, which was formed after World War II in Britain for those who specialize in reporting the game. Most of its members are British, but it does include some journalists from abroad.

In recent years there has been increasing cooperation between this association and the management committee at Wimbledon. Before the war and for some years afterwards relations between the Club and the press were distant, even to the point of frigidity. The formation of the LTWA and the Club's increased understanding of the importance of good public relations have ended most of the points of discontent and now the press facilities at Wimbledon are the envy of lawn-tennis journalists in other countries and of those who cover and organize other international sporting events.

The Wimbledon management committee and the LTWA meet during the winter to discuss problems and improvements and there are daily meetings between the two bodies during the Championships. The fruits of this liaison include considerable improvements in the accommodation for the press. Between 1966 and 1973 the space in the press writing rooms and restaurant was doubled and new rooms for television and interviewing were built. Keeping ahead of its rivals has always been a point of honour at Wimbledon. The French Federation has improved the writing facilities at the Stade Roland Garros, but they still do not compare with those at the All England Club, and at Forest Hills there is no separate writing room for journalists. The reporter must watch, write and telephone from a seat in the marquee which denies him a proper view of the court. At neither of those grounds is there a special press restaurant.

As Wimbledon is the annual meeting place of players and administrators, so it is also a reunion for those who specialize in reporting the game. British newspapers, with the most knowledgeable tennis public in the world to satisfy, employ more tennis specialists than their foreign counterparts. For them the tennis year is growing longer. Once it was merely a summer sport, with occasional winter interludes like the British Covered Court Championships and the annual visit of the professionals to Wembley. Now, the growth of winter indoor play, with tournaments like the Dewar Cup circuit in sports halls in provincial towns, added to increased public interest in tournaments abroad, has caused British newspapers to employ full-time tennis writers.

In many other countries, where there are fewer tournaments and the lawn-tennis public is smaller, the tennis reporter will also be responsible for another sport. Like the British writer, he will travel to Davis Cup matches and major international events, but, whereas the British public has been educated by regular lawn-tennis reports in the serious and most of the popular papers and by frequent radio and television commentaries, the reporter from abroad often finds himself writing for a comparatively small number of enthusiasts.

For the British, tennis is a national game. In many other countries, it is still a minority sport and its reporters have to write in the knowledge that they are communicating with a minority. Nowhere was this more noticeable than in the United States, where interest in tennis had expanded rapidly but without reaching the great mass of the public (although that state of affairs is changing as more and more matches are shown on national television networks there). For a number of years Allison Danzig of the *New York Times* and Al Laney of the *New York Herald Tribune* wrote with specialist knowledge about the American game, but when they retired in the 1960s almost the only specialist newspaper writer on lawn tennis – certainly the only one who travelled much further than Wimbledon – was Bud Collins of the *Boston Globe*.

Most American tennis writing – some of it bright, shrewd and interesting – came from football writers in the close season and columnists who paid only occasional visits to tournaments. As a result, lawn-tennis journalism in the United States often seems less organized than in Britain and some other European countries. Newspapers cover tournaments in their own areas, but they are reluctant to give more than brief agency reports about events in other parts of the country and abroad. The American tennis explosion has so far failed to have much effect on those who make the decision to fill columns with baseball news and long pre-season football commentaries.

Apart from newspapers, the tennis reader relies for information on a number of specialist magazines, published in different countries but often with large numbers of overseas subscribers. One feature of the expansion of the game which followed the introduction of open tennis in 1968 was a comparable expansion in magazine coverage. Big sponsors meant increased advertising and it became easier for tennis journals, which so often had a high mortality rate, to survive.

The Field remained a major influence until shortly before World War II, when Wallis Myers stopped writing for it and its editors began to devote less space to covering the tennis scene outside the Wimbledon fortnight. Other magazines such as *Pastime* also kept the Victorian reader in touch with what was happening on courts as scattered as Edgbaston, Liverpool, Moffat and Eastbourne; and soon *Lawn Tennis,* edited for some years by Scrivener, became the game's official journal, carrying advertisements which persuaded the holiday player of the delights of competing at Budleigh Salterton or Folkestone, reporting play in straight and unsensational detail, giving news of the decisions of the LTA and often carrying articles of great depth and authority on the general condition of the game.

Lawn Tennis – or *Lawn Tennis and Badminton* as it became with the incorporation of a badminton section, an attempt to attract additional subscribers from the winter game which lost a good deal of its point when the Badminton Association produced its own magazine – just failed to survive until the open-tennis boom made life easier for magazine publishers. It is also possible to argue that it had fallen too far behind the times. Its layout was dull and its pages were small. Its place as the official journal was taken by *British Lawn Tennis and Squash,* which then shortened its name and reverted to the historic title of *Lawn Tennis.* There was a certain irony in this development. *British Lawn Tennis,* edited by C. M. Jones, a prewar Davis Cup player, had begun publication as a magazine aimed at putting the players' viewpoint and was often severely critical of the policies of the LTA. For *British Lawn Tennis* to find itself in the position of being asked to put the official viewpoint (although still keeping the freedom to comment on LTA business) was a case of the political and sporting wheel turning full circle.

The new *Lawn Tennis,* however, was never allowed to keep a monopoly position. For a short time the supporters of the defunct *Lawn Tennis and Badminton* produced a magazine called *Tennis Pictorial Illustrated* and then this was merged into a new publication called *Tennis World,* which took up a vigorously independent position. Like the other new European tennis magazines – *Tennis Club* in Italy and *Inter Tenis* in Spain – which were to follow it, *Tennis World* was heavily influenced by the successful example of *World Tennis* – 'a magazine written by and for the players' – which Gladys Heldman, the wife of an oil executive and the daughter of a US Supreme Court Judge, founded in New York in 1952. This was the game's first modern magazine, aggressively informative and opinionated, full of large advertisements and good photographs, and Mrs Heldman used it to fight a series of battles for the improvement and expansion of the game. She demanded open tennis, more liberal and sensible attitudes by the USLTA and the ILTF and – in the fiercest of her campaigns – the establishment of an independent, self-governing women's federation with equality in prize money for women players. *World Tennis,* always written at white heat, could be wrongheaded but it was never dull and never short of ideas.

World Tennis did not have matters all its own way in the United States. Another bright magazine, *Tennis,* describing itself as 'the national magazine of the racquet

THE STRAIN MUST BE TERRIFIC! – TO REFRAIN FROM KICKING LINESMEN,

TO RESTRAIN TEARS – IN THE CASE OF A WOMAN – AT LOSING,

OR VIOLENCE IN THE CASE OF A MAN

TO KEEP FROM MURDERING SPECTATORS, "HIT HARDER"

TO REPRESS EXUBERANT SIGNS OF JOY AT WINNING, HOORAY!}

TO TRY AND SMILE IN DEFEAT.

W. K. HAZELDEN.

Above 'Self-Control in First Class Tennis', as it appeared to a *Daily Mirror* cartoonist in 1934
Below This photograph of Wimbledon in 1935 was taken on a 5 x 4-in (12.7 x 10.2-cm) glass negative.

sports', was founded in Chicago in 1964 and the USLTA produces *Tennis USA* to put the official viewpoint. In France *Tennis et Golf*, the source of so much information on the history and development of the European game, and *Smash*, edited by René Mathieu and his wife, Simone, the most famous clay-court competitor of her day, gave way to *Tennis de France*, founded in 1953 by Philippe Chatrier, a journalist and a player. He later used it, to rally French support for open tennis and for expansionist policies, with so much success that he and his supporters took control of the French Federation in 1969 and in 1972 he was elected to its presidency. *Tennis SA*, a smaller magazine of similar quality published in Johannesburg, also played an important part in arguing the case for big tournaments and high sponsorship.

The ambitious publications tended to be independent. In Italy the field had been dominated since World War II by the grandiose *Il Tennis Italiano* until Rino Tommasi, a journalist and boxing promoter, founded *Tennis Club* in Rome specifically to oppose the Italian Federation's refusal to accept open tennis. This was probably the most attractively designed magazine of the 1970s, although *Inter Tenis*, which began publication in Madrid in 1971 with Manuel Santana as a member of its editorial board, and the Japanese *Modern Tennis* challenged it closely.

Some small 'official' publications remain. Most European tennis federations support – or recognize – magazines like the Dutch *Lawn Tennis*, the Swedish *Tennis Tidningen* or *Tennis* in Denmark and Germany (where the official magazine in Düsseldorf has a more opulent rival in *Tennis Revue*, which deals with the social scene as well as commenting on play and personalities), but these are run for the most part on small budgets and are comparatively unambitious in the coverage of events outside their own countries. They provide national news. For international information their readers usually turn to the larger British and American magazines.

Photography
Arthur Cole

When four acres of grassland were rented in Worple Road, Wimbledon, in the summer of 1877, to stage the first Wimbledon tennis championships, the medium of photography had been born but at such an early stage it was limited: the operator (or 'artist', as he was called) chose his subject, judged his distances, and calculated his exposures rather as a portrait painter of the period mixed a delicate flesh tone of oils on his palette. Arresting action was not feasible at this time – even portraiture on an overcast day required the setting of one-second exposures or longer, combined with a large aperture which greatly restricted the depth of focus. The cameras were cumbersome and weighty, supported by a sturdy tripod. The image was recorded on 5 x 4 in (12·7 x 10·2 cm) glass plates coated with the sensitized emulsion layer. When the plate had been exposed, it was removed from the camera back inside a light-tight sheath, the latent image to await development. The photographer probably carried about twelve of these plates as a standard pack.

Above A battery of cameramen on the Centre Court, including *(left to right)* Michael Cole, Gerry Cranham (tallest) and Russ Adams (in the striped jacket)

Around the early 1900s Eastman Kodak USA greatly advanced the development of their cameras, lenses, and materials; 5 x 4-in cameras could now be loaded with faster films, enabling the sports photographer to capture action photographs by using higher shutter speeds and smaller apertures.

In 1907 the very first colour photographic image was recorded, as a transparency produced from the Lumière autochrome plate. This method was used for the following 28 years until, in 1935, the first commercially successful multi-layer colour film was produced, namely Kodachrome, in the form of 8-mm movie film.

In 1936 came Kodachrome colour slides in 35-mm for still cameras, and black-and-white films were sensitized to a comparatively high speed. The 35-mm camera was ideal for action work, having a fast wind-on lever action, and interchangeable lenses. The 35-mm film was compact, quick and easy to load. The 120, 220 and 620 films were also widely used at this time, with great success.

By the 1950s many very advanced cameras were available to both amateur and professional photographers. One of the most coveted was the German Leica, with a variety of high speeds and wide range of apertures. This precision instrument was reliable, the action was speedy, and the optics (Carl Zeiss) were the best money could buy. Various lenses were produced for this camera, including wide angle, standard, and telephoto (long-focus). Such reliability and versatility were in great demand.

The 1960s and '70s brought an almost unlimited range of photographic equipment and super accessories. Powerful telephoto lenses (400- and 500-mm) are used a great deal for tennis photography. For these long-focus lenses the highest shutter speed is necessary to ensure a sharp image to be recorded, and focusing is critical. The 300-mm is commonly used to arrest a service on the point of impact, which invariably makes for a powerful picture; 400-mm and 500-mm are suitable lengths for shooting downcourt. Perspectives distorted, and distances condensed, the camera is with the player on every stroke. A familiar sight at the Wimbledon final is the 'line up' of the photographers sitting tightly together in the front row, three Nikons hanging from each neck, scores of massive telephoto lenses lying on the rough green concrete wall, the photographers awaiting the arrival of the finalists, loading up their films, rummaging into bags, waving exposure meters, scrunching empty canisters and packets underfoot – that familiar litter!

Many years have passed since photography included the very posed portraits of players, immaculately attired and with an inevitably self-conscious facial expression. Nowadays, candid photography, made possible by the use of long-focus lenses, fast mechanisms, and a different outlook towards the subject matter, has given birth to a totally new approach to characteristics, idiosyncrasies, and expressions of tennis personalities.

Tennis enthusiasts, whether journalists, press photographers, or merely spectators, seek the more intimate angles of the sport that candid photography has made feasible.

The camera and its operator have been granted great freedom of expression. The camera can even gain access to the dressing-room of a losing Wimbledon finalist to record the natural expression of exhaustion – the weary head, apparently supported on its frame only by heavy towelling, the visible beads of sweat indicating the inner agitation of mind, the memory of that double fault, that sticky handgrip, those ten thousand eyes. The camera's mechanical development has been pursued only by the keen eye of the professional operator in his search to make an accurate record of every angle of an event with awareness and freedom.

The techniques of tennis photography are similar to those of most sports photography: the camera shutter has to be released at that critical moment when fractions of a second can capture or lose an expression or spectacular stance. Knowledge of the game is important in knowing when to shoot. For example, as a player's first service is usually more powerful than the second, this is the one to take; or focusing the camera on a certain part of the court (the baseline or up near the net) and waiting for the player to strike within that area ensures a good sharp picture. It is an asset for the photographer to know a little about individual players, for often knowing when *not* to take a picture rather than when to take one is important. For example, if Pancho Gonzalez is concentrating on a service at a critical stage and he is disturbed by a camera click he will amble towards the camera and growl, menacingly. But the tennis photographer has almost unlimited freedom: he can shoot at any time of the game, providing his camera is reasonably quiet (some $2\frac{1}{4}$-in cameras are noisy and best kept for studio work), unlike golf, where the photographer is forbidden to shoot before impact. Of course, a photographer covering a football match is virtually free to use the noisiest equipment he chooses, but only squatting behind or near the goal.

Spectators sitting behind the camera battery on the Wimbledon court are often amazed by the number of photographs taken during a single match. They evidently do not realize that the press photographer is constantly on the alert for a spectacular picture, an unusual angle, an expression, or the 'surprise picture', for example a broken racket. National newspaper readers want to see a player falling, jumping, laughing or crying. A classical action picture comes second to the sensational expression. Considering all these points, the professional cannot afford *not* to keep his camera constantly firing. When players complain about the noise of cameras, they should remember that they are earning their money by entertaining the spectators. The photographers are not present to be entertained. They are there to earn their money too. Modern 35-mm cameras are very quiet and players' complaints about 'clicks' should be ignored.

Whether or not the photographer uses black-and-white film or colour, or both, depends solely on his market. The press photographer who attends the game for a daily newspaper will, of course, use only black-and-white film. The photographer employed by a magazine will use both, as both may be required. A freelance photographer must decide for himself since only he knows his clients' needs. However, many photographers keep one camera loaded with colour film and another with black-and-white, both at the ready. The weather often determines the possibilities for colour photography. Although modern colour film enables the photographer to take pictures in adverse conditions, the results are not always pleasing, so on a very overcast day the faster black-and-white films are nearly always used.

Sometimes a photographer is lucky enough to be taking a normal action picture when an abnormal event occurs: an astonishing example is the photograph on the opposite page.

A shot that would have been historic but that nobody took was a photograph of Graebner threatening Năstase at the Royal Albert Hall, London, in 1972, on the occasion when Graebner, irritated by Năstase, jumped over the net, grabbed his opponent by the shirt, and, raising his racket in the air, threatened to crash it into his head. During this incident, there were fewer than half a dozen photographers in attendance, and although one or two took some expressive photos of both players, no one apparently took Graebner actually raising his racket. This was probably because the photo-

Below This fine action photo of P. Lotz is an example of a movement caught by chance.

graphers did not fully realize the severity of the incident and it happened so quickly that no one was ready! Prodigious sums of money – £1,000 in one case – were offered for the photograph that apparently did not exist.

For the Wimbledon Championships, applications are sent, well in advance, to the Newspapers Proprietors' Association (NPA), which considers all applications on merit. Press passes and badges are distributed to the leading national papers, photo agencies and tennis publications throughout the world. Unfortunately these facilities are often abused, and this hinders the professional. Press-badge holders have seats reserved for them on the Centre, Nos 1 and 2 courts only. There are no allocations on any of the remaining outside courts, which often makes the photographer's work very difficult: when an exciting match draws a big crowd on every side of the court, the photographer may find it impossible to reach any position from which he can shoot.

One month before Wimbledon, the writer's entire camera stock, including lenses, are checked for mechanical failure. Any camera or lens not performing satisfactorily is immediately serviced. Film stocks are checked.

For the photographer, the first day is as busy as any other in the fortnight. Every player on the outside courts must be photographed in action, and if possible portraits are also taken. Players losing in the first round must be taken on this first day. Action and portrait photos even of less well-known players are in great demand from tournament sponsors, and the players change their appearances so quickly (hair length, moustache grown one month and taken off the next, sideboards, etc.) that their files must be kept up-to-date.

For the first week the coverage is much the same as for the first day, photographing as many players as possible. Besides keeping a sharp lookout for seeded players eliminated in the early rounds, the photographers are busy with 'human interest' pictures of the spectators: the arrays of multi-coloured flowery hats, Christian Dior fashions, attendance of royalty and 'personalities' all help to make the Wimbledon fortnight unique.

By the beginning of the second week the photographers have probably taken about two thousand pictures, black-and-white and colour, the films have all been processed, the best contact prints have been selected, and finished prints made to show to prospective clients. The second week draws large crowds, which means that between matches the photographers concentrate on taking many 'general' pictures from many different levels and angles. This includes, for the writer, climbing to the top of the ivy-covered water tower, disturbing the pigeons on his ascent, for a view of all the outside courts. The veterans' event is also popular and offers interesting pictures. Readers like to remember the champions of yesteryear.

The day before the finals is a busy one. Apart from the routine work, there seems to be much around and within Wimbledon to photograph: the milling crowds, the hivelike area beneath the results board, the strawberries-and-cream eaters, the excited autograph hunters who block the stairway to the competitors' tea room, the long ticket queues, touts shifting along the railings, hands deep in pockets, fists clasping tickets and banknotes, the enthusiastic all-night pavement sleepers.

The finals are covered by as many photographers as possible, each carrying at least three cameras, loaded with black-and-white and colour films. Some operators will shoot from the sidelines, the others down court from the Royal Box end. Just before the presentations all cameras are loaded and climactic clicking begins. There is total disorganization at this time because the management does not plan an orderly photosession – the 'art' of photography becomes a battle for position and generally the heaviest and most persistent photographer wins. Photographers sometimes come out of this chaos without a single picture!

After the men's singles, the doubles finals and the presentations in the Royal Box are covered. Two photographers take the presentations from the court below, using long-focus lenses, the others from the press box beside the Royal Box.

By the end of the two weeks of Wimbledon about 12,000 photographs have been taken, and the negatives are filed for future reference.

Above A lucky shot – as Ilie Năstase (on an outside court at Wimbledon in 1971) was playing a forehand from the baseline, the head of the racket broke on impact and flew into the net. Năstase, still finishing the stroke, holds only the stem!

Radio
Max Robertson

Doing a modern running commentary on a good singles match is like playing it yourself but from both sides of the net. The constant effort of anticipating and giving as accurate a current description as possible, sustained over long periods of time at extremely fast speech speed, demands both mental and physical stamina. At the end of it the commentator feels the elation of the winner and very often the exhaustion of the loser.

Not only that but he knows the frustration of the ephemeral. For him no printed word that may be read and re-read with growing appreciation. A good metaphor must not be cheapened by repetition but is like a high-flying bird shot on the wing, plummeting never to fly again. Of course, there are recordings but they can never relive the 'live' and are seldom used save as rationed capsules of time to evoke the nostalgia of memory lane.

When in 1954 Drobný, in his third final, at last grasped the prize, the Centre Court experienced one of its great moments of catharsis. Rex Alston was commentating during the final set and, knowing what his co-commentator was feeling, after the applause had died down said 'and now let's ask Max Robertson to sum up'. The writer then had one of those rare spells when the artist knows that he is completely at one with what he is striving to do. He poured out his feelings for ten minutes and the words felt golden. But, alas, a program switch from Wimbledon to Lords had doomed them to oblivion, for they were not even recorded.

That was a moment lost for ever. Others can be salvaged. In a Centre Court match the Dutch player, Hans van Swol, a blond Goliath, was playing France's Robert Abdesselam, a diminutive David. In the final set the giant's game was crumbling when suddenly a squirrel darted onto the Centre Court. There was no broadcasting at that moment but the writer yelled to the engineers to start recording and did a commentary on the scene (since often used in 'look-back' programs and quizzes) while the squirrel ran rings round the ballboys. Finally one of them nabbed the artful dodger and, though bitten for his pains, managed to remove it from the court. This all lasted some three minutes. Revitalized by his rest, van Swol went on to win the match.

Below, left Max Robertson in 1952
Below, right John Snagge in 1942

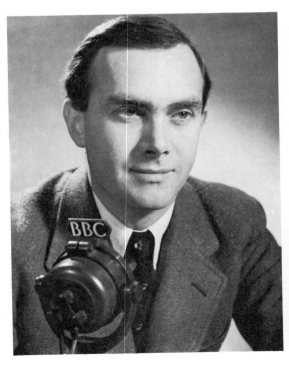

Above Gerald A. Cock, in charge of Programs in 1927, later the BBC's first Director of Television

The high-speed commentary, a kind of tennis shorthand that aims to allow the attuned listener to place the ball and 'see' the strokes, has evolved with the jet age and is totally unlike the leisurely approach of the early commentators of the late 1920s that matched the more expansive life style of the day. Nor can today's sophisticated production and engineering set-up, which ensures that the listener hears not only the commentary and expert comment, but also the umpire, the sounds of play, the general atmosphere (all blended to an artistic nicety that transports him to the courtside) be in any way likened to the experimental trappings that went with the early outside broadcasts or 'OBs'.

So back to the beginning and the word as it then was. The BBC, the first public service broadcasting system in the world, had begun its transmissions in November 1922, the first year of new Wimbledon. The flavour of the period is savoured in two excerpts from the first correspondence between the BBC and the All England Club.

On 18 February 1927 Gerald Cock (then in charge of Programs and later to be the BBC's first Director of Television – see TELEVISION) wrote to Cdr G. W. Hillyard,

> Dear Sir, I am taking this early opportunity of ascertaining how you and your associates would view the possibility of carrying out a broadcast running commentary of portions of some of the important championship matches to be held at Wimbledon next summer . . .

Cock received this reply, dated 19 February:

> Dear Sir, Cdr Hillyard, to whom your letter was addressed, resigned the secretaryship of this club in December 1924. I will place your letter before my Committee at their next meeting and advise you their decision in the matter.
>
> *signed* D. R. Larcombe.

On 6 April the Committee agreed but reserved a guillotine veto:

> In the event of any complaints or other inconvenience we are to be entitled to terminate this authority upon giving you twelve hours' notice in writing.

On the physical side, in a memo, Cock wrote:

> To get into the place at all we must build a platform alongside the camera stand, over a sunken passage leading to the Press and Members' stands . . . it is in a very good position for seeing the game and could be used both for Control Point and commentators, having about 4′ frontage and about 7′ depth.

The estimate for the Wimbledon fortnight including tickets, lines costs, building the platform, engineers' expenses and commentators' fees was £93 1s 0d, about one fiftieth of the cost today.

The first commentators were Captain H. B. T. (Teddy) Wakelam (chosen because he was used to umpiring tennis and as a Rugby commentator was known to be 'fluent on the microphone') and Col R. H. Brand (the Corporation's official host). A test was arranged for them on 29 May, after which they were engaged as follows: Capt Wakelam 29 June, 1 and 2 July; Col Brand 30 June, 2 July.

Writing of the new enterprise and the final Saturday, Cock said,

> I think it is essential to have two commentators . . . it is going to be a tiring job and, in order to prevent the commentators' voices from being heard by ticket holders in the seats close by, there will be very little ventilation in the hut.

The broadcasts were thought to be 'of real value' and next year (1928) there was something from Wimbledon on every day of the Championships. The following year's estimate included 'a special ventilator in the glass front' to ease the commentators' burden, and two windows in the gentlemen's dressing room that were overlooked by the commentary position had their glass frosted at BBC cost. In 1929 program time was allotted on a scale comparable with today, some 1½-2 hours daily.

In 1931 Wakelam's and Brand's commentaries went out on the London Regional

Above Seymour J. de Lotbinière, ('Lobby')
Head of Outside Broadcasts in 1936
Below Freddie Grisewood, Wimbledon
commentator in the late 1930s but better
known for his chairmanship of the BBC's
'Any Questions'

wavelength only, allowing more flexibility to get the finish of the matches. In 1932, after complaints from music-loving listeners that their programs were being broken into, Wimbledon tennis was switched back to the National wavelength, the London Regional being reserved for music.

By 1934 the already crowded commentary point was having further demands made on it by foreign broadcasting organizations, so a new reinforced concrete stand was built, and in 1935 not only were there foreign broadcasts (one to the United States by a Mr Tunis) but Major C. L. Cooper-Hunt had temporarily joined the commentary team and Britain's Dorothy Round (the reigning champion) and America's Elizabeth Ryan (winner of more Wimbledon titles – though no singles – than any other player) were also tried, only the former being officially approved.

In 1936 when Cock moved to Television, S. J. de Lotbinière ('Lobby') began a long and distinguished reign as Head of Outside Broadcasts, and for the first time, when a match had no home interest, there were Wimbledon broadcasts to Empire Service listeners only. All these extra broadcasts were putting more and more strain on the control position, so that in 1937 Major Larcombe hired (for £5) an old pay box to the BBC as a control point. This was situated in the Southwest Hall near the bottom of the commentary point stairs.

For a decade the main commentators had been Brand and Wakelam but now F. H. (Freddie) Grisewood (of later 'Any Questions' fame), Tommy Woodroofe ('The Fleet's Lit Up') and John Snagge (inveterate Boat Race commentator) were brought into the team and it was their radio commentary that was combined with the BBC's first-ever television OBs at Wimbledon that year. One *avant-garde* listener went so far as to suggest that commentators referred to women by their surnames only during rally commentary.

The end of many eras came in 1939 – Wimbledon commentary style being one. Grisewood, with a somewhat faster delivery, had emerged as the leading tennis voice in that fateful year, the year that the red-hot favourite, Baron Gottfried von Cramm, was forbidden by Hitler to compete in the Championships. Tennis talent played other roles for the next six years.

In 1946 Wimbledon, with its perennially magical organization, was quick to cast off the shrouds of its wartime chrysalis, and emerge again as the brilliant emerald butterfly the tennis world knows. Not to be outshone, the BBC planned a wide coverage; the commentary team included Freddie Grisewood, Raymond Glendenning (whose all-round sports-commentary performance had made him famous), Stewart McPherson (whose Canadian-type quickfire boxing and ice-hockey commentaries thrilled millions), Rex Alston and Max Robertson – all but the first being new to the Centre Court. Robertson had done most of his prewar broadcasting with the Australian Broadcasting Commission, which believed in fast commentary and led the world with its racing commentators.

This team was commentating not only for listeners in Britain but, through various overseas services, to countless listeners all over the world. Indeed the final of the men's singles, with Geoff Brown of Australia involved, was taken throughout by the Australian Broadcasting Commission. The European Service too, which as a result of its war work was still widely listened to, broadcast Wimbledon commentaries and reports in many languages.

From the 1946 trials a regular Wimbledon team of Freddie Grisewood (who moved wholly to television in 1950), Raymond Glendenning, Rex Alston and Max Robertson carried on for some years until first Alston (1963) dropped out, and then Glendenning (1965), the newcomers being Maurice Edelston (1963), a football international, and latterly Bill Threlfall (1969), who had been Navy Tennis Champion for several years.

Since World War II these commentators have had the help of expert summarizers to expound on tactics and strategy between odd games and sets. For a year or two, until he started his distinguished career as a television tennis commentator (1951), Dan Maskell filled this role. The next notable summarizer was Alf Chave (first heard in 1957), a pillar of Australian tennis in general and Queensland's in particular. His

Above Bert Kingdon

distinctive twangy voice and his pithy to-the-point comments soon made him a favourite with listeners. He had the great gift of knowing not only exactly what was needed to be said but of being able to fit it effortlessly to the particular pause in a match's rhythm. When he died suddenly in August 1970 tennis description lost one of its great voices and Wimbledon one of its characters.

Fred Perry, Britain's last and perhaps greatest men's champion, has been a regular summarizer for many years, and others who have often taken part are Tony Mottram, Britain's leading postwar player for a decade, Bea Walter, an international and Wightman Cup Captain, and latterly Bob Howe, that brilliant Australian two-fisted doubles player, whose tactical comments are always shrewd.

Just as commentary and summary have developed, so of course, have the production facilities and technique. For a few years in the early 1950s the writer was responsible for Wimbledon Radio broadcasting arrangements, but the man who, starting in 1957, has been for longest in command, under various Heads of Outside Broadcasts, and who has recommended and carried out most of the major postwar improvements is Bert Kingdon. The production of a Wimbledon OB is now quite an operation.

From the original single box on the Centre Court (which grew to three in the late 1930s) and the portable box that used to be erected on a corner of No. 1 Court for a few years just after the war (with the one 'pay-box' control point for both) there has developed a broadcasting complex. On the left of the Royal Box, BBC Sound Radio, having swallowed the TV commentary area in 1970 (after the TV position had been moved to the other end of the Court in 1968) has five commentary boxes to accommodate the demands of its own and many overseas broadcasting organizations. On No. 1 Court, at the back of the south end, there is a permanent box (first built at the western end of the back row in the early 1950s, then moved to near the centre and finally settled immediately to the left of the gangway).

Since about 1960 there has been 'the lookout', a position at the back of No. 1 Court overlooking all the outside courts and invaluable for the latest intelligence, which for years was ably supplied by Basil Curtis, once a County player. In 1972 Kingdon, with the All England Club's cooperation, arranged for a new double-barrelled commentary platform with two positions overlooking between them Courts 2, 3, 9, 10 and 11. There has also been since 1961 a special radio interview room to which the victims are led, alas last, shredded after the press and television have finished with them.

All these points, with their manifold microphones, headphones and telephones, are serviced and watched over in the permanent control point just off the Southwest Hall, first built in the late 1940s and extended in 1960 and again in 1965. The technical operation of setting up and dismantling this becomes annually more complex as new facilities are demanded and provided. Many skilled OB engineers have contributed their share to what has become one of radio's showpieces, but none more than Teddy Pearson, who reigned from 1958 to 1969.

It is here that Bert Kingdon, Geoff Dobson, Ken Pragnell (or others of the less regular producers) has his command seat like a submarine captain. The television sets showing the play on Centre and No. 1 Courts are his periscopes, the engineers monitoring the outgoing transmissions are his ASDIC and SONAR operators, at the flick of a switch he can call up any or all points under his control and, if necessary, he has immediate communication with his base at Broadcasting House. The producer directs the broadcast, deciding when to switch from court to court, from commentary to summary or to the lookout for results. He also monitors what is said and often suggests or corrects during a commentator's pause while the umpire calls the score.

If the control point is like a submerged submarine, the Centre Court from outside looks like a giant aircraft carrier with its flightdeck the arena; the players are the aircraft, the ballboys their handlers; the umpire is Commander (Air); the press photographers with their big lenses are the traversing anti-aircraft guns, the spectators the sensitive radar antennae; the Royal Box is the bridge and the broadcasters are the Signals, transmitting at high speed and doing their utmost to give the world an accurate split-second account of the engagement.

Television
Dan Maskell

In 1973 the Championships at Wimbledon provided more than 80 hours of viewing and, in their final stages, were seen and heard in some 15 countries with the commentary done 'live' by each country's own commentator. As in 1971-2, Australians, via satellite, saw and heard the play on the Centre Court as it happened. Televised tennis had indeed come a long way from the first showing of a tennis player on television, Miss Kay Stammers, Great Britain's Wightman Cup star, in the evening program 'Picture Page' on television's opening day 35 years earlier.

Television took its first feeble steps as a public service from a studio in Alexandra Palace in North London on 2 November 1936, but it was not until 5 May 1937 that Gerald Cock, the first Director of Television, wrote to Major Dudley Larcombe, the Secretary of the All England Club,

> to ask the Committee to be allowed to carry out experimental transmissions from the Centre Court during the forthcoming Wimbledon fortnight . . . we would be tackling unknown quantities – we do not know yet whether we could achieve a satisfactory link between Wimbledon and Alexandra Palace – the new apparatus has not yet been used over that distance.

That letter, written just seven days before the televising of the Coronation procession of King George VI, the first real outside broadcast, reveals the courage, confidence, faith and enthusiasm of those entrusted to fulfil the high hopes of this as yet little-known technology. Douglas Birkinshaw, Superintendent Engineer of TV, who was in charge of the camera position on the central plinth of the Hyde Park Corner archway during the Coronation procession, was responsible for the technical operation of the forthcoming Wimbledon. After a preliminary survey they had only four weeks to have everything ready for the first televising of Wimbledon, but they were thinking not only of the Championships but (according to a letter of 2 June) 'possibly the Davis Cup Inter-Zone Finals . . . and the Challenge Round on July 24th, 25th and 26th'!

All kinds of problems had to be resolved – 'it is hoped to use two cameras – each would require 700 feet of cable'; the restricted space for cameras, the power vans and the low-lying ground were discussed; a letter of 21 May refers to 'a 5-metre radio link which was *working in time* for the Coronation but only *just* working'. A letter dated 19 June, two days before the Championships were to begin, records . . .

> . . . cause of interference with signal for our mobile transmitter at Wimbledon – has been traced to Hornsey Central Hospital. Mr Homewood, secretary of the Hospital, has agreed 'so far as possible to suspend diathermy activities during times, we, the BBC, are transmitting.'

The following memo circulated through Alexandra Palace from the Director of TV on the same day about the announcement to be made from Alexandra Palace before switching over to Wimbledon:

> *Announcement for Wimbledon, Monday 21st June.* Ladies and Gentlemen. Everyone knows that The Lawn Tennis Championship Meeting is taking place at Wimbledon over the next two weeks, starting today. By the courtesy of the All England Lawn Tennis Club we've been able to make arrangements to televise matches in the Centre Court throughout the fortnight. For the first time anywhere in the world then television will bring into viewers' homes pictures of outstanding international events at the exact moment they are taking place *without* the aid of an intermediate link of special cable. Vision is, in fact, being transmitted by wireless from Wimbledon to Alexandra Palace and from Alexandra Palace to you, simultaneously, but of course on a different wavelength. It is a great experiment.
>
> 'At this moment ? is playing ? so over we go to Wimbledon to hear the match described by ? . *Signed* G. A. Cock.

Above, left Dan Maskell
Above, right Jack Kramer

Press reports the next day were enthusiastic; that in the *Daily Telegraph* was typical:

> Tennis history was made yesterday when the play from the Centre Court at Wimbledon was successfully televised for more than 25 minutes in the afternoon programme . . . Televiewers first saw the match in which H. W. Austin beat G. L. Rogers and could observe every movement of the players. Even the passage of the marks of the lawnmower over the grass were distinctly visible. There were also scenes of spectators in the stands and their faces could be seen clearly. The television pictures were accompanied by a commentary by Mr F. H. Grisewood.

Every day during that first week of the Championships viewers saw some play from the Centre Court, with a number of international competitors. The commentators were Freddie Grisewood, Captain H. B. T. Wakelam and Colonel R. H. Brand.

The general opinion was that tennis and television were a 'natural'; preparations were immediately finalized to televise the Davis Cup for the first time, the Inter-Zone Final between Germany and the United States, two weeks later. Television could hardly have had greater luck for its Davis Cup début, for rarely has there been a more exciting tie than the 3-2 victory of the United States.

The BBC and the All England Club were well satisfied with their joint efforts in 1937. On 22 January 1938 the Club Secretary, Major Larcombe, wrote to the Director of Television, Gerald Cock, 'The Committee is ready to grant facilities for TV free again, as this work in this field is still considered to be in the experimental stage – rather than on the plane of a fully-fledged industry.' Around this date 2,000 TV sets had been sold (as against over 8 million radio licences). Plans were well in hand for televising the 1938 Wimbledon.

A third camera was used and minor technical improvements were made. A newspaper noted: 'during the Ladies Doubles semi-final viewers saw the arrival of Her Majesty Queen Mary', another 'the arrival of TRH the Duke and Duchess of Kent'.

In a post-Wimbledon report Ian Orr-Ewing (now Lord Orr-Ewing) wrote on 10 July 1939: 'The best matches seemed to start about 5 o'clock in the evening – why not have in the future evening sessions, particularly on weekdays, and a camera on Court 1 to relieve dull matches on the Centre Court?' But World War II intervened.

The Championships resumed in 1946. Almost the first Press reports concerned with postwar sport on television appeared in mid-January. The *Daily Telegraph* (17 January) announced:

> Sports Events by TV.   BBC plans for an early start . . . Sporting and topical events will be the principal feature of the BBC programmes when the Alexandra Palace station resumes transmissions in May or June. Improved transmitting cameras developed during the war will give clearer and sharper pictures than before. Mr Maurice Gorham, the newly appointed Television Director . . . said . . . the RAF has handed back the sound transmitter and work is going ahead on the aerial and vision transmitter . . . The *reliable* range of the reconditioned station is estimated at 40-45 miles . . . [when it was opened the range was 25 miles].

The All England Club now had a new Secretary, Colonel Duncan Macaulay, an enthusiastic visionary, who, like his Committee, was eager to see the Championships restored to their former glory. S. J. de Lotbinière, Director of Outside Broadcasting,

Above Lee's cartoon in the *London Evening News* on the day of the first postwar Wightman Cup match carried the following caption: 'No, she's not quite up to her form today. She's rather Television Conscious.'

through Philip Dorté, TV Outside Broadcasts and Film Supervisor, showed equal enthusiasm; with Ian Orr-Ewing, TV Outside Broadcasts Manager, they met at the Club on 12 March. Once again the confidence, faith and cooperation of the late 1930s showed itself for they not only laid the foundations for televising the Championships but also considered televising the earlier Wightman Cup match on 14-15 June.

On the opening day, 14 June, the *London Evening News* carried an amusing and topical cartoon by Lee. Thirty-five minutes of play were televised from 3.00 p.m. in a program called 'The Eyes of the World'. Ian Orr-Ewing was back again presenting the program, Freddie Grisewood was commentating, and sharing this with him was Peter Dimmock, to whom, as a negotiator with sporting bodies, BBC television was to be heavily indebted.

Later that day and again the next, viewers saw the Americans carry on where they had left off in 1939, with a team immeasurably better than any produced by either country since the Wightman Cup began in 1923. A bonus for tennis fans, and indeed for all TV viewers, was the program presented by Peter Dimmock on the afternoon following the Wightman Cup. It carried a somewhat enigmatic title, 'Are Ladies Faster?' and was a pictorial story of the last 60 years of women's tennis, interspersing 'live' appearances with rare pieces of film lent by the National Film Library showing play in 1900 and the early 1920s. Among those taking part were Mrs Lambert Chambers, Mrs L. A. Godfree, and the well-known TV announcer Miss Jasmine Bligh, dressed in early tennis costume.

Despite bomb damage, the Championships began nine days later, hailed as a 'psychological lift for the nation to have Wimbledon — this great British institution — in action so soon after hostilities had ceased'. TV, however, did not start to cover the play until the middle Saturday, 29 June: Ian Orr-Ewing presented it with Freddie Grisewood and Peter Dimmock as his commentators. The second week saw Max Robertson, better-known for his outstanding commentaries on radio, helping out on TV between radio broadcasts. The presentation too was now being shared by Philip Dorté, Orr-Ewing, Keith Rogers and Peter Dimmock, the last-named covering the Finals on the last day, Saturday 6 July. On that day, at 6.20 p.m., interviews from Wimbledon were introduced for the first time: the two new champions, America's attractive, athletic groundstroke expert Miss Pauline Betz, and the very tall Frenchman Yvon Petra, were interviewed by Miss Alice Marble, the truly great champion of 1939. Mr Robert Carr, later to become British Home Secretary, assisted Freddie Grisewood with a 'test' commentary on the Thursday of the second week. His interest in the game was wide and varied; in later years he umpired finals on the Centre Court.

Breakdowns in transmission were surprisingly few considering all the difficulties but the *Daily Mirror* of 4 July headlined: 'The silent violinist on the Centre Court', explaining that

. . . during a men's doubles semi-final there was a five-second fade during which viewers saw a man playing a violin while the tennis commentary went on! The BBC explanation was that 'there was a temporary failure so viewers were switched to Alexandra Palace because, for technical reasons, an image had to be maintained on the screen' . . . During this match viewers saw Budge Patty fall into the crowd chasing a wide ball. His racket cut open the head of a middle-aged man who had to have hospital treatment.

Sport continued to get a fair share of general television, which by 1948 had an estimated 200,000 viewers. It was making an impact on those concerned with the development of sport and physical recreation in its widest sense; as instanced by Peter Dimmock writing in *Sporting Life*: 'This new science can play a large part in sport, and thanks to TV, viewers may become active fans of that particular sport from then on.' The truth of this was very apparent to the writer, who was travelling the country coaching, lecturing and demonstrating the game in an effort to rehabilitate it at educational establishments and clubs, many of which had had little opportunity for tennis during the war.

Above Billy Knight, British Davis Cup stalwart 1955-64 and Wimbledon commentator from 1967
Below Peter Dimmock

As the years raced by TV covered every day of Wimbledon and almost every hour of play. In 1949-51 Grisewood had with him as commentators C. M. (Jimmy) Jones (now Editor of *British Lawn Tennis and Squash*). In 1951 Grisewood and Jones were joined by Dan Maskell and Michael Henderson. Grisewood and Maskell continued in 1952-3; in 1954 they were joined by Dennis Coombe and in 1955 by Peter West. Jack Kramer appeared as a commentator for the first time in 1960, which was Grisewood's last year. In 1966 Kramer and West (Michael Henderson's last year was 1962) were joined, until her tragic death in 1969, by Maureen Connolly. Billy Knight, former British Hard Court champion and Davis Cup player, joined the team in 1967. As the audiences grew so did the televised events – Davis Cup ties, tournaments leading up to Wimbledon, the big professional events at Wembley and the Junior Championships.

On 6 June 1954 came Eurovision, a link-up of eight countries; in September 1955 commercial television started and the BBC no longer had a television monopoly. It competed with the BBC in televising Wimbledon from 1956 to 1963 when it was realized that this double coverage was not commercially viable. On 11 July 1962 came the first exchange of a live transatlantic program by satellite (Telstar). In 1964 the second BBC channel, BBC 2, was born. It was on this channel that colour TV made its public début in Britain in 1967, with tennis from Wimbledon. A. P. 'Slim' Wilkinson, the BBC's Executive Producer of the Championships for many years, wrote:

This outside broadcast was unique as it was the first regularly scheduled colour broadcast in Europe, and as such was the first really stringent test of our colour OB operation – you now know that it worked beautifully and provided an encouraging portent for the start of national colour transmissions that year.

Although 1967 marked the beginning of transmissions in colour from Wimbledon it was also the closing chapter in our monochrome coverage as the real lesson learned from the operation was that colour cameras would not work so satisfactorily at the Royal Box end of the Centre Court where we had always placed our cameras in the South Stand. Consequently, the following year the whole of our camera dispositions were moved to the north end, involving a great deal of rebuilding – for example, the commentary box had to be repositioned and all the Eurovision commentators had to be accommodated in a new complex at the rear of the North Stand. The expenditure and effort involved have been proved to be worthwhile and I believe that the colour transmissions from the Centre Court now are technically as good as can be provided, and certainly the equal of anything I've seen anywhere else in the world.

He also commented that fashions and the general environment of Wimbledon were increasingly used in the program presentation.

For the actual televising of the Championships, the Executive producer will confer with the Club, probably some months before they are due to take place. Dates, times of transmissions and facilities are confirmed; later an inspection is carried out with a planning engineer on the ground. Some cables, commentary boxes and other necessary equipment have now become installed as part of the permanent fixtures of the Club, but any changes to be made in camera positions or other vital components will be noted so that the various outside broadcast departments are informed in good time. A small hutted and tented 'village' adjacent to the Centre Court, which houses almost everything except the court-side cameras and commentary boxes, has recently grown up because of the complexity of colour television. It includes parked vehicles, each containing highly expensive equipment for a particular job and enough room for the experienced and efficient technicians. The nerve-centre is, in fact, a mobile control room. Other important features of the 'village' are the administrative huts where the Executive Producer and his team of producers forgather. The commentators also do their last-minute homework in the 'village' and relax there when away from the scene of action. The biggest tent is the canteen.

Eventually everything is linked up at the ground and the control room, and tests are carried out to make sure that the pictures and sound output are being picked up at

Above Bryan Cowgill
Below A. P. 'Slim' Wilkinson

a prearranged point and passed into the transmitter networks. The next task for the Executive Producer is to decide on the commentators for the fortnight. Some days before the opening day he will draw up an outside broadcasts script, mainly concerned with visual sequences, the appropriate opening and closing announcements and any changes that may have to be made.

Early on the first day all sorts of technicians are at work, including the Post Office engineers who work closely with their BBC counterparts. Well before zero hour pictures are fed into the nerve centre for a dress rehearsal.

In the control room is the producer and in front of him are the monitors showing the picture coming from each camera. On either side of him are his secretary and the engineer in charge of the technicians who operate and control the equipment. Additional monitors are situated above the camera monitor screens, one showing the picture being transmitted, the other coming in from the nearest transmitter (the radio check picture). In 1973 there were some 20 monitors under constant supervision.

At about 11.30 a.m. each day the Executive Producer has an informal meeting with his team, with the commentators present, to discuss the general plan of the day. Then everybody moves out to 'battle stations' and again everything is checked. The cameramen and commentators all wear headgear comprising earphones and microphone. The earphones are 'split', one bringing in the program sound and the other the producer's instructions. In order to avoid confusion when the producer is giving instructions each camera is numbered. On the producer's desk are two rows of buttons and two faders which enable him to change cameras instantaneously or mix slowly from the picture of one camera to that of another. The commentators each have one monitor screen showing the picture being transmitted.

A minute or so before going on the air, the producer is watching his radio check picture and listening to the announcer preparing to hand over to Wimbledon. Through his microphone he warns all his team: 'coming to us in a few seconds' and on the appropriate cue transmits his opening shot and captions and follows with something like 'On you, camera 1, slowly pan round the crowd; take it up, commentator; camera 2, watch for the players and warn me; camera 3 be ready to zoom into close-up as they get to the umpire's chair, and, commentator, identify as soon as possible.'

The commentator matches his commentary to the crowd shot and, as the players appear, identifies them. As one player spins the racket the producer transmits a picture showing both players and the umpire waiting for the decision of the winner of the toss. The producer then says something like 'Camera 1, take Brown back to the baseline (if the commentator is talking about Brown) and now, 2, give me his opponent'. As soon as the monitor shows the opponent the commentator matches his comments to him. The producer then instructs Camera 3 to give him a close-up of the scoreboard; the commentator then reminds the viewer that the contest between Brown and Jones is a first-round match and the dots show that Brown will serve first.

While the players practise, both in vision, the other commentator is brought in and named by the first. He comments on the way the match may go and the general pattern of the tactics and then cues the producer that he would like a picture of one man by saying something like 'and Brown's forehand drive, one of the best in the game . . .' And so the match goes on, the producer always in charge, suggesting to, and guiding, the commentators whenever necessary. When producer and commentators have worked together over a long time they easily follow each other – pictures guided by commentary and *vice versa*. Should the commentators have suggestions for the producer or need an immediate picture they can speak direct to him on a 'closed' line (the 'lazy mike').

The commentator's job is to enlighten the viewer and involve him. If he succeeds in doing this perhaps he is in a way, with the rest of the team, fulfilling the aim of the BBC from its earliest days, 'to inform, educate and entertain'. No country has contributed to the development of TV more than Britain and, among so many pioneers in the history of televised tennis, none more than Peter Dimmock, Bryan Cowgill, and 'Slim' Wilkinson.

PART 2

A

For biographical notes in this section we have drawn on published records and the works of many recognized tennis historians: we are also particularly indebted to Lance Tingay and John Barrett.

Space has perforce restricted our entries for individual players to those who have won the singles in the 'Big Four' Championships and others who, in our judgment, have been of sufficient stature in their time. We have included a few top-liners (not greats) of today, as well as some likely to be in the near future. We have excluded automatic mention of winners of the French Championships before they became open in 1925. This list clearly is not exhaustive and we regret not having space for hundreds more who have been fine performers.

The following abbreviations are used in this section:

ILTF GP	ILTF Grand Prix
ILTF GP (M)	ILTF Grand Prix Masters' Tournament
WCT	World Championship of Tennis
WCT (F)	World Championship of Tennis (Final)
r/u	runner-up
r/u*	runner-up in All-Comers' Final when there was a Challenge Round
s/f	semi-finalist
q/f	quarter-finalist
U21	under 21

Adamson, Miss Nelly see Mrs Nelly LANDRY

Advantage see SCORING

Afghanistan
Afghanistan has been an Associate Member of the ILTF since 1963. BR
GOVERNING BODY: Afghanistan LTA, c/o National Olympic Federation, Kabul

African Lawn Tennis Confederation
The African Lawn Tennis Confederation, consisting of 19 African countries, was formed during the third ALL-AFRICA GAMES held in Lagos, Nigeria, in January 1973.

Age Groups
Term used in Great Britain to describe the national invitation tournaments held for players under 16, under 14, and under 12 (on the 31 December preceding the event), each year at EASTBOURNE (since 1970). In the United States there are many age-group tournaments, ranging from those for boys and girls under 12 to men over 70 (see VETERANS), the qualifying date being the 1 October preceding the tournament. In other countries age groups vary: in France juniors are 17-18, *cadets* 15-16, *minimes* 13-14, *Benjamins* 11-12, *poussins* under 11, the qualifying date for age being the 31 December of the year of the tournament; in Belgium there are juniors (under 18), *scolaires* (under 16), *cadets* (under 14) and *minimes* (under 13). See also JUNIOR.

Akhurst, Miss Daphne [Mrs R. Cozens] (Australia)
Born Ashfield, N.S.W., 22 April 1903; died 9 Jan. 1933; Wimbledon women's singles q/f 1925, s/f 1928; women's doubles s/f 1928; mixed doubles r/u 1928; Australian women's singles won 1925-6, 1928-30; women's doubles won 1924-5, r/u 1926, won 1928-9; mixed doubles won 1924-5, r/u 1926; French women's singles q/f 1928. Her record of five Australian women's singles titles stood until surpassed by Nancye BOLTON in 1951 and by Margaret Smith COURT in 1964.

Albert Hall see ROYAL ALBERT HALL, LONDON

Alexander, Frederick B. (USA)
Born 14 Aug. 1880, died 1969; US men's singles q/f 1904, 1906, r/u* 1908; men's doubles r/u 1905-6, won 1907-10, r/u 1911, won 1917, r/u 1918, s/f 1919; mixed doubles r/u 1918; Australian men's singles and doubles won 1908. The first American to win the Australian singles. Davis Cup 1908.

Alexander, John G. (Australia)
Born Sydney, 4 July 1951; Wimbledon men's doubles s/f 1971; Australian men's doubles r/u 1970, 1973. Davis Cup 1968-9. WCT pro 1971-3. WCT 3rd Group A (F q/f) 1973.

Algeria
Algeria was admitted as an Associate Member of the ILTF in 1963 and became a Full Member in 1964. BR
GOVERNING BODY: Fédération Algérienne de Lawn Tennis, Route de Badjarah, Hussein-Dey, Algiers

All-Africa Games
The All-Africa Games, held like the OLYMPIC GAMES and PAN-AMERICAN GAMES every four years, include lawn tennis among their sports. The first All-Africa Games were held in Brazzaville in July 1965.

All-Africa Lawn Tennis Championships
The Amateur Championships of Africa, organized by a group of African nations and run on similar lines to the ASIAN AMATEUR CHAMPIONSHIPS and EUROPEAN AMATEUR CHAMPIONSHIPS, was held in December 1973.

All England Championships see WIMBLEDON and RECORDS SECTION, PART 3.

All England Lawn Tennis and Croquet Club
The All England Croquet Club, with four acres of land bordering the London and South Western Railway line near Worple Road, Wimbledon, was founded in 1869 and enlarged its scope with lawn tennis in 1875 (see THE BIRTH AND SPREAD OF LAWN TENNIS, PART 1), so successful a move that the club's name was changed to the All England Croquet and Lawn Tennis Club in 1877. In 1882 the name changed again, to its present title, the All England Lawn Tennis and Croquet Club. After World War I, it moved to its present quarters in Church Road, Wimbledon, where the Championships (see WIMBLEDON) have been held since 1922. The building of the new club was financed by the issue of debentures in 1919 and the sum of £73,000 raised by the All England Club. The Club has a membership of 375, excluding honorary members. In addition, about 90 temporary members are elected annually. Debenture holders have the privilege of two free reserved Centre Court seats for each day of the Championships in a special enclosure behind the Royal Box.

Today the club has 15 grass courts, including the famous Centre Court, and 10 hard courts, two of which are covered. A feature of the club's administration is the continual improvement of facilities (particularly for the

Championships) – many of them in response to suggestions by the public. DC

All England Married Couples Championship see THE GROWTH OF THE GAME (PART 1)

Alley American colloquial term for the area between the inner and outer SIDELINES

Allison, Wilmer Lawson (USA)
Born San Antonio, Texas, 8 Dec. 1902; Wimbledon men's singles r/u 1930, q/f 1936; men's doubles won 1929-30, r/u 1935, s/f 1936; US men's singles q/f 1929, s/f 1932, r/u 1934, won 1935; men's doubles s/f 1928, r/u 1930, won 1931, r/u 1932, 1934, won 1935, r/u 1936, s/f 1938; mixed doubles won 1930, r/u 1931, s/f 1936; Australian men's singles s/f 1933; men's doubles s/f 1933. Davis Cup 1929-33, 1935-6.

Alvarez, Miss Lili de [Comtesse de la Valdene] (Spain)
Born Rome, 9 May 1905. Wimbledon women's singles r/u 1926-8; French women's singles q/f 1927, s/f 1930-1, s/f 1936; mixed doubles r/u 1927.

Amateur see PLAYING STATUS

American Tennis Association
The governing body for Black American players, founded 1916. It first held singles championships for men and women in 1917 (the first winners were Tally Holmes and Lucy Slowe) and added competitions for doubles, juniors, and veterans (seniors) later. Former Wimbledon and US National champion Althea Gibson and former US National champion Arthur Ashe, Jr, were earlier ATA singles champions.

American Twist see SERVICE

Amritraj, Vijay (India)
Born Madras, 14 Dec. 1953; Wimbledon q/f 1973 (2 points from beating KODEŠ, the eventual winner; US men's singles q/f 1973 with dramatic 5-set win over LAVER, whom he had beaten two weeks earlier at Bretton Woods, N. H. Charming, respectful court manners have won him a host of admirers.

Anderson, James O. (Australia)
Born Enfield, N.S.W. 17 Sept. 1895, died 19 July 1960; Wimbledon men's singles s/f 1922, 1925; men's doubles won 1922; US men's singles s/f 1921, q/f 1922; men's doubles s/f 1923; Australian men's singles won 1922, 1924-5, r/u 1926; men's doubles won 1924, r/u 1925-6. Davis Cup for Australasia 1921-2, for Australia 1923, 1925. Outstanding in the Australian game of the early 1920s.

Anderson, Malcolm J. (Australia)
Born Rockhampton, Queensland, 5 Mar. 1935; Wimbledon men's singles q/f 1956, 1958; US

men's singles won 1957, r/u 1958; men's doubles s/f 1956, 1958; Australian men's singles q/f 1956, s/f 1957, r/u 1958, 1972; men's doubles s/f 1956, r/u 1957, s/f 1958,won 1973; mixed doubles s/f 1955, won 1957; French men's doubles won 1957. Davis Cup 1954, 1957-8, 1972- . Turned professional in 1959. Married Daphne Emerson, sister to Roy. WCT contract pro 1968-9.

Above Malcolm J. Anderson

Annie Soisbault Cup
Similar to the GALEA CUP for boys, the Coupe Annie Soisbault de Montaigu, named after the daughter of a President of the French LTA, is the European team competition for girls under 21. The team number is undefined; it can include a playing captain. The competition, decided by two singles and one double, began in 1965 in France, was staged at Deauville 1965-7 and subsequently at Le Touquet Tennis Club. The first winner (1965) was the Netherlands. DC

Anza Trophy see SOUTH AFRICA

Argentina
At the beginning of the 20th century, British immigrants, especially those working for the railroad companies, founded several lawn-tennis clubs. As the game spread it became necessary to create a governing body to regulate it. The Asociación Argentina de Tennis was founded on 2 September 1921.

Important international players have come from Argentina, in particular Enrique Morea, Jr, who in the period immediately after World War II was considered one of the best players in the world. The Mitre Cup, symbol of the most important annual team contest held in this part of the world, has been won many times by Argentinian teams. For many years the AAT has concentrated on promoting lawn tennis all over the country and on improving its quality. The unceasing efforts of its officials have kept Argentina at the top of South

American tennis. The first 50 years have also produced positive results in membership; the 20 clubs that founded the AAT had grown by 1972 to 12 affiliated federations, 241 tennis clubs, 16,000 registered players and approximately 250,000 unregistered players. Lawn tennis is second only to football in national popularity.

Every year the AAT organizes an Inter-club tournament. In 1972 677 teams took part (457 men's and 220 women's), with over 4,000 players. This tournament has been held since 1921, when 34 teams competed. The AAT sponsors other tournaments all over the country.

The most important event organized by the AAT is the Championship of the Republic, an open championship that forms part of the ILTF Grand Prix (Class B), in which most of the world's best players compete. In 1971 over 30,000 spectators attended.

Argentina has competed with success in the DAVIS CUP since 1926, and has taken part in the FEDERATION CUP since 1964.

Argentina has been a full member of the ILTF since 1923; one of its greatest administrators, E. Morea, Sr, was a member of the Committee of Management. BR
GOVERNING BODY: Asociación Argentina de Tennis, Avenida Presidente Julio A. Roca, 546-7° Piso, Buenos Aires

Above **Argentina**. Anna Maria Arias

Asbóth, József (Hungary)
Born Szombathely, Hungary, 18 Sept. 1927; Wimbledon men's singles s/f 1948; French men's singles won 1947; mixed doubles s/f 1947. Davis Cup 1938-9, 1948-9, 1952-5, 1957. Became pro 1958. Hungary's most successful player, at his best on clay courts and full of artistry.

Above József Asbóth

Ashe, Arthur Robert (USA)

Born Richmond, Va., 10 July 1943; Wimbledon men's singles s/f 1968-9; men's doubles r/u 1971; US men's singles s/f 1965, won 1968 (open and closed), s/f 1969, q/f 1970, s/f 1971, r/u 1972; men's doubles s/f 1966, r/u 1968; Australian men's singles r/u 1966-7, won 1970, r/u 1971; French men's singles q/f 1970; men's doubles r/u 1970, won 1971. Davis Cup 1963, 1968-. ILTF GP 2nd 1970. Joined WCT 1971. WCT 5th (s/f F) 1971; 6th (s/f F) May 1972; 2nd (won F) Nov. 1972; 2nd Group B (r/u F) 1973.

A player of mercurial brilliance, he has sometimes been erratic in the application of his skill. His outstanding feat was winning the first US Open Championship in 1968. He looked like repeating this performance in 1972, but failed in the last match to consolidate a lead of two sets to one and 4-2 in the fourth against the Rumanian Ilie Năstase. He was the winner of the longest singles ever played in the Davis Cup, when representing the US in the Challenge Round against West Germany at Cleveland, Ohio, in 1970. In the fifth rubber, when the tie was already decided, Ashe beat Christian Kuhnke 6-8, 10-12, 9-7, 13-11, 6-4, a total of 86 games. A Negro, Ashe's applications to compete in the South African Championships made him a central figure in the controversy over apartheid when the South African government refused to grant him a visa. He won 25 matches out of his 15 Davis Cup rubbers for the US, 1963, 1965-70. (See colour plate, page 85.)

Asian Championships

The International Lawn Tennis Championships of Asia are one of the eight ILTF OFFICIAL CHAMPIONSHIPS and are held at different centres in India. The first were held in December 1949 in Calcutta.

At the Annual Meeting of the ILTF in July 1971 it was decided that a new event, 'The Championships of Asia for Amateurs', should be played the following year with financial assistance from the ILTF. Thirteen countries, Hong Kong, India, Indonesia, Iran, Japan, Korea, Malaysia, Philippines, Singapore, Sri Lanka (Ceylon), Taiwan, Thailand and Viet Nam sent (men's) teams to Hong Kong, where the Championships were played in Kings Park, Kowloon on 20-26 February 1972. T. Sakai (Japan) won the singles and, with J. Kamiwazumi, the doubles. BR

Asian Games see REGIONAL GAMES

Association of Tennis Professionals

see THE POSTWAR PRO GAME, OPEN TENNIS (PART 1)

Atkinson, Miss Juliette P. (USA)

US women's singles won 1895, r/u 1896, won 1897-8, s/f 1901; women's doubles won 1894-8, 1901-2; mixed doubles won 1894-6. An early American stalwart of the women's game.

Above Arthur Ashe

Aussem, Miss Cilly (Germany)

Born Cologne, 4 Jan. 1909; Wimbledon women's singles q/f 1928, s/f 1930, won 1931, q/f 1934; French women's singles q/f 1927, s/f 1929-30, won 1931, q/f 1932, s/f 1934; women's doubles r/u 1931; mixed doubles won 1930. Germany's most successful woman player and the only one to win the Wimbledon singles.

Austin, Henry Wilfred [Bunny] (Gt Britain)

Born London, 20 Aug. 1906; Wimbledon men's singles s/f 1929, q/f 1931, r/u 1932, q/f 1933-5, s/f 1936-7, r/u 1938, q/f 1939; men's doubles s/f 1926-7; mixed doubles r/u 1934; US men's singles q/f 1929; mixed doubles r/u 1929; French men's singles q/f 1934, s/f 1935, q/f 1936, r/u 1937; men's doubles s/f 1931, 1936; mixed doubles r/u 1931. Davis Cup 1929-37, second singles player in the team that held the Cup, 1933-6.

Above Henry Wilfred ('Bunny') Austin

Australasia see AUSTRALIA

Australia

The first Australian lawn tennis championship tournament took place in Melbourne in 1880, followed by the State Championship held by the Sydney Lawn Tennis Club at the Sydney Cricket Ground in New South Wales in 1885. During this period, and probably until after World War I, many Australians considered tennis to be a social game, not to be compared as a sport with the more rugged team games.

The Lawn Tennis Association of Australasia was formed at a special meeting held in Sydney in 1904 and Mr W. H. Forrest was elected as the first President. Its formation came from a resolution passed by the New South Wales Lawn Tennis Association that representatives should be invited from each State of the Commonwealth of Australia and from New Zealand to discuss the formation of a National Association so that these two countries should become one tennis nation under the laws governing the International Tennis Contest. The first Australasian singles championship, played in Melbourne in 1905, was won by Rodney Heath; the great New Zealander, Anthony Wilding, won in 1906. Australasia was represented at the discussions concerning the formation of the ILTF on 26 October 1912, and was one of the founder members represented at its inaugural meeting in 1913.

Australia, as a tennis nation, has figured prominently on the international scene since 1907. Nineteen Australian men between 1907 (Norman E. Brookes) and 1971 (J. D. Newcombe) have won the Wimbledon singles title. Margaret Court has won the women's singles three times (1963, 1965, 1970) and Evonne Goolagong once (1971).

Australasia (Australia and New Zealand combined) first took part in the DAVIS CUP in 1905 and won it from the British Isles for the first time in 1907, when Norman Brookes and Anthony Wilding defeated the British Isles team of Arthur W. Gore and H. Roper Barrett 3-2 at Wimbledon. Australasia won it again in 1908, 1909, 1911, 1914, and 1919. Brookes and Wilding defeated the United States Team of T. C. Bundy and R. N. Williams and M. E. McLoughlin in 1914 just before the outbreak of World War I. History repeated itself at the Merion Cricket Club, Pa. (USA) in September 1939 when Australia defeated the United States on the eve of World War II.

In 1922, New Zealand wished to become a separate tennis nation and withdrew its affiliation from the LTA of Australasia. Its association was recognized by the ILTF as a National Association in 1923; however, the LTA of Australasia, with headquarters in Sydney, continued to function as the Australasian body until in June 1926 it moved to Melbourne and changed its name to 'The Lawn Tennis Association of Australia'.

That year Norman E. Brookes was elected President and held office until 1955. Known to his contemporaries as 'The Wizard', and of medium height with pale blue eyes and sallow complexion, Brookes (1877-1968) was not only President of the LTA but was the dominant figure in Australian tennis during those 29 years. Sir Norman (he was knighted in 1939) was present, with Lady Brookes, during play at the 1939 Davis Cup Challenge Round in Philadelphia when the Australian team of Crawford, Hopman, Bromwich and Quist, after losing the first two matches to Riggs and Parker respectively, came from behind to win. John Bromwich and Adrian Quist played in both singles and doubles, and Sir Norman Brookes accepted the Davis Cup on behalf of the LTA of Australia (as distinct from Australasia) for the first time.

In the postwar years Sir Norman and Dame Mabel (Lady Brookes was created DBE in 1955) continued to play a dominant role in Australian tennis. Both Sir Norman and Dame Mabel were dedicated to the interests of the game and, as a Davis Cup selector, Sir Norman wielded considerable influence, particularly in the choice of players to represent Australia in the Davis Cup. These two outstanding people gave tennis enormous prestige in Australia for almost thirty years and they will be remembered as long as the game is played.

Norman Brookes retired from the Davis Cup scene as a player after the US Davis Cup team of W. T. Tilden and W. M. Johnston in 1920 defeated the Australasian team of Brookes and Gerald Patterson 5-0 at Auckland, New Zealand. Australian tennis between 1920 and 1930 was taken over by Gerald Patterson, J. O. Anderson, J. B. Hawkes, P. O'Hara Wood and many other distinguished players. Gerald Patterson, a nephew of the famous opera singer Dame Nellie Melba, was a powerful

Above **Australia**. N. E. Brookes and A. F. Wilding *(far side)* defeated A. W. Gore and H. Roper Barrett in the 1907 Davis Cup.

figure with a tremendous service and overhead, a weird loop-the-loop backhand – which at best could be described as colourful– and a tremendous will to win. Patterson won at the old Wimbledon in 1919 and at the first new Wimbledon in 1922.

J. O. Anderson was the exact opposite to Patterson. Tall, lean, with a wonderful forehand drive and a firm but defensive backhand, 'J.O.' was the only Australian to beat the great American W. M. Johnston. This occurred in the opening match of the Davis Cup Challenge Round against the Unites States in New York in 1923, when he defeated Johnston in five sets. The Americans won the Challenge Round 4-1.

In late 1932, the distinguished American team of Ellsworth Vines, Wilmer Allison, John Van Ryn and Keith Gledhill toured Australia. The tall, rangy Vines, with his thunderbolt service, slow walk and powerful groundstrokes was a great draw and the superb doubles combination of Allison and Van Ryn made an impression on spectators in every State. The Americans played a series of matches against the Australians in Sydney, Melbourne and Adelaide. When the 17-year-old schoolboy wonder, Vivian McGrath, defeated Wilmer Allison in the first Australia v. United States contest in Sydney, the press gave tennis front-page coverage. And then McGrath's superb victory over the world champion, Ellsworth Vines, in the quarter-final of the Australian Championships in Melbourne, gave tennis a 'shot in the arm'. Keith Gledhill's net-rushing tactics upset McGrath in the semi-final and the singles title was won by Jack Crawford, whose passing shots were always a few feet away from Gledhill's racket.

Jack Crawford defeated Ellsworth Vines to become Wimbledon champion in 1933, one of the most popular prewar champions from the Australian point of view. Gerald Patterson had been the last previous Australian winner in 1922, and the Championship from 1923

until 1933 had been dominated by American and French players. Crawford played a major role in the Australian scene from 1928 to 1940. He was not only a great player with a beautiful style, but his long trousers and buttoned-down shirt, and his flat-topped racket, gave him an aura of old-world charm which made him popular wherever he played. His mannerisms of spinning his racket when receiving service and brushing his hand through his hair, gave the crowd a great deal of pleasure.

The writer played Crawford in two National singles finals; it was an unusual experience because the gallery played every shot with him. A missed ball from 'Craw' drew an 'oh' from the spectators. He was certainly one of the giants of Australian tennis. We were doubles partners for several years on Davis Cup tours and his charm and grace of manner endeared him to everyone. In 1933 he won the Australian, French and Wimbledon titles, losing the American to Fred Perry in five sets. He represented Australia in the Davis Cup nine times and was included in the winning 1939 team but did not play. His last great victory was against John Bromwich in the semi-final of the Australian singles championship at the White City, Sydney, in 1940, which he won in straight sets with a classic display of beautifully controlled shots which kept the younger man running all over the court. He continued playing in friendly matches until he retired.

Australia formed a new Davis Cup team in 1933, spearheaded by Jack Crawford with Vivian McGrath, Don Turnbull and Adrian Quist. From 1933 to 1935 the Australians travelled five to six weeks by sea to challenge unsuccessfully for the Cup in the European zone. This long travel period made it a difficult task. Therefore in 1936 it was decided to change tactics and enter in the American zone, which meant less travel – about three weeks by sea – and it assisted the Australians to play the Americans on grass courts. The Australians lost in 1937 and 1938 but finally broke through against the United States in Philadelphia in 1939 and returned home with the Davis Cup.

The game at home became an international

Above **Australia**. J. H. Crawford *(left)* and A. K. Quist won the 1935 Wimbledon doubles.

spectacle when four great teams visited Australia: first the French, in 1928, headed by Jean Borotra, with 'Toto' Brugnon and Christian Boussus; then the Japanese, Sato, Harada and Nunoi; the Americans Vines, Gledhill, Allison and Van Ryn in 1932; and finally in 1933-4 the British team, Pat Hughes (captain), Harold Lee and Frank Wilde, led by Fred Perry.

Perry had beaten Crawford to win the US title, and the Australia v. Great Britain matches played in the capital cities along the same lines as the 1932 matches against the United States proved great attractions, stimulating public interest and providing match-play for the Australians and British. The most exciting matches were the Perry-Crawford clashes: the wonderful rallies sustained by the artistry of Crawford and the lightning-fast Perry will never be forgotten by those who were privileged to see this beautiful tennis. The postwar champions, Sedgman, Hoad, Rosewall, Cooper, Laver, Emerson, with their sustained net attack, were outstanding in ability and skill, but it is doubtful whether the public enjoyed their net-rushing tactics (which, of course, were highly successful) as much as they did the rallies and groundstroke skill displayed in the Perry-Crawford matches.

In those days, the Test Matches, as they were called, were taken seriously by the players and public. An exciting and tense atmosphere was created by the press and radio; also a friendly rivalry existed at the time among the Australian, American and British players. Winning the Test series became very important. The Australian players gained the greatest benefit from crossing swords with champions from other countries.

Perhaps the greatest period for Australian tennis was in the postwar years. The Davis

Cup had been won in 1939; the public, sickened by World War II, were ready for the 1946 defence of the Davis Cup in Melbourne. Crowds filled the Kooyong Stadium to witness the US v. Australian Challenge Round and to see the eclipse of the Australians – Bromwich, Pails, Quist and Long – by Kramer, Schroeder, Parker and Mulloy. These four Americans with their superb attacking tennis notched a 5-0 victory. It was four years before Australia regained the Davis Cup with two newcomers to international tennis, Frank Sedgman and Ken McGregor, who with John Bromwich defeated Schroeder, Mulloy and Tom Brown at Forest Hills, N.Y., in 1950.

A great champion emerged in Frank Sedgman, who in 1951 became the first Australian to win the US National singles title in the 70 years of its history. Australian tennis spectators loved Frank because he represented what they considered to be a typical Australian: fresh-looking, a grim fighter and a good sportsman. Also a Wimbledon winner in 1952, he turned professional in January 1953 and, with his great doubles partner Ken McGregor, became associated with Jack Kramer's professional tennis group.

The likeable Kramer made a great impact on tennis in Australia. 'Jake' was almost part of the Australian scenery. He not only played as a professional in Australia but he offered such good financial conditions to Sedgman, McGregor, Hoad, Rosewall, Hartwig, Cooper and others to turn professional that he incurred the wrath of the Lawn Tennis Association of Australia, who considered that he was ruining tennis in Australia. Kramer was a realist and a first-class negotiator. He spent much time flying to and from Australia signing up players and trying without success to have an official talk with the Council of the LTA of Australia. Kramer gave the young Australians the chance, which they accepted, of earning money for playing tennis. His knowledge of the game is outstanding and history also records him as one of the greatest players of all time.

Australia was fortunate in having two remarkable 19-year-old youngsters in Lew Hoad and Ken Rosewall who had the skill to step into the breach caused by the loss to professional tennis of Sedgman and McGregor. Both players have written a chapter in Australian tennis history; their 1953 defence of the Davis Cup in Melbourne against the formidable challenge of Bill Talbert's US team of E. Victor Seixas and Anthony Trabert will be remembered for all time. Australia won 3-2 after trailing two matches to one after the second day's play. Press, radio and tennis experts were stunned when the untried Hoad and Hartwig were chosen as a doubles team at the last moment to replace the Australian, Wimbledon and French doubles champions, Hoad and Rosewall: the Davis Cup selectors, headed by Sir Norman Brookes, decided that Hartwig's form in practice warranted the replacement of Rosewall. The American pair, Trabert and

Seixas, won the doubles in straight sets. The local press severely castigated the selectors for their decision to change the pairing. Hoad had beaten Seixas in straight sets in the opening match on the first day. He would have to beat Trabert on the third day to level at two all. Australians who watched this battle witnessed one of the most bitterly fought matches ever played in the country. Hoad's youth, plus the fact that Trabert had beaten Rosewall, and the sensational last-minute change in the doubles team, had created an atmosphere loaded with tension and excitement. Hoad won the first two sets 13-11, 6-3, but Trabert, displaying

Above **Australia**. F. A. Sedgman, the first Australian to win the US Championships (1951)

magnificent courage, fought back to level at two sets all. After the first set, a slow drizzle of rain made the court slippery; later the atmosphere became heavy, making ball control difficult. Trabert was granted permission to wear spikes at 1-4 in the second set and later Hoad also called for spikes. It was the closeness of the contest and excitement rather than the outstanding quality of play that kept spectators on the edges of their seats. The fifth set was a game of services, with Trabert holding his serve fairly easily while Hoad was continually in difficulty with his, but always exploding with an ace to stay in the match. With the score at 6-5 to Hoad but with Trabert to serve, new balls were handed to the American. One could have heard a pin fall at this stage and a great roar from the crowd greeted Hoad's victory when he made three fine service returns to clinch the match and level the scores at two rubbers all. The final result was 13-11, 6-3, 2-6, 3-6, 7-5 to Hoad. It was a contest that could have been won by either player and the strain was so intense for both that several hours elapsed before they were in complete control of their emotions. Rosewall defeated Seixas in the final rubber in a five-set match which was an anti-climax after the gruelling Hoad/Trabert affair.

The Australian tennis public was so accustomed to watching Davis Cup Inter-Zone Finals and Challenge Rounds in Sydney, Melbourne, Adelaide and Brisbane when enthusiastic crowds came to see their countrymen ward off the formidable challenges from the Americans, Spaniards, Italians, Mexicans and Indians, that it came as a surprise to realize that tennis was in fact declining both as a spectator and participant sport during the 1950s and '60s. Sports-goods manufacturers, in conjunction with State associations, introduced tennis foundations in an effort to revive interest in the game. Private courts were being sold because of the rise in value of real estate. Confusion about the differences in professional and amateur status and general apathy were among the many reasons for the decline of interest. The public continued to support the Challenge Round contests (but not tournaments) because of the great international appeal of the Davis Cup. In December 1954, 25,568 people each day – the largest crowd ever to watch a Challenge Round – watched the United States team of E. Victor Seixas and Anthony Trabert defeat Lew Hoad, Ken Rosewall and Rex Hartwig three matches to two at the White City Courts in Sydney. So great was the public interest that £90,000 (A$180,000) was refunded to those who were unable to gain admission. It was a magnificent achievement by the Americans to defeat such a high-class Australian team, composed of the same players who had beaten them the previous year.

The story of Australian tennis would be incomplete without reference to John Bromwich, the writer's wonderful doubles partner. He was a superb touch player with his two-handed forehand drive and sweeping single-hander shots. Always poking out his tongue and pushing back his blond forelock, Bromwich looked a character: he was in the writer's opinion the greatest right-court doubles player of all time [while many thought Quist to be the greatest left-court player – Ed.]. His featherweight racket, strung loosely, struck the ball with a curious 'plop', sounding like a melon hitting the ground. Bromwich and Quist won the Australian doubles championship eight years running, 1938–50 [Quist winning it 10 times running, the first two with Don Turnbull, an all-time record for one of the Big Four Open Championships – Ed.]. Another two-handed player, Geoff Brown, with a thunder-bolt service and powerful two-handed drive, reached the 1946 Wimbledon final and played in the Davis Cup for Australia. Among other great players who have left an indelible print in Australia's history are Malcolm An-

derson, Ashley Cooper, Roy Emerson, Neale Fraser, Rod Laver, Dinny Pails, Tony Roche, Mervyn Rose, Bill Sidwell and Fred Stolle, who all played in Davis Cup matches, in Australia and overseas. Their names appear on the Roll of Honour boards in Australia, France, Great Britain and the United States.

One of the greatest singles finals ever played in Australia was the match between Rod Laver and Ken Rosewall in the 1970 Dunlop International Tournament, the first fully sponsored major championship held in Australia. At the White City, Sydney, in March 1970, both players with superb groundstroke control backed up by magnificent volleying and passing shots, battled game after game in hot weather for five long and bitterly contested sets. The match was finally won by Laver 6-3 in the fifth set. A great sense of rivalry was apparent in the sheer tenacity of play and the chasing of balls far beyond the reach of either player. The large crowd became so immersed in the efforts of both men that sometimes a silence developed before the thunderous burst of applause. Every game in the match turned into a battle. When an occasional easy shot was missed, the spectators were so stunned they remained silent. Reaching the net was the ultimate goal of both players, but because of the dazzling display of high-powered passing shots, it frequently became necessary for Rosewall, then Laver, to remain backcourt. Consequently the public was treated to many superb rallies before either man ventured to the net. The standard of play was so high that only a 'super' shot was good enough to win the point. When the final point in this tremendous match was missed by Rosewall, the huge crowd gave both players a standing

Below **Australia.** A. K. Quist *(left)* and J. E. Bromwich in the 1950 Australian Championships, the last year in their record-breaking sequence of eight wins in a row.

ovation lasting several minutes.

Women's tennis has a special place in the Australian story because of the dedicated efforts of those women councillors and former international players who devoted so much time and energy to the administration of the game and to efforts to lift the standard of women's tennis. Two such councillors were Floris Conway and Nell Hopman. They spearheaded a movement which resulted in the LTA of Australia's decision to send official women's teams overseas, and it was the drive and energy of Mrs Hopman which caused the first Federation Cup match in Australia to be staged in Melbourne in 1965. Having set herself the task, she succeeded in raising about A$30,000 (£15,000), which guaranteed the cost of bringing the challenging teams to Australia. This was not only a success story in itself but proved that women, playing in a team competition, could pack the Centre Court at Kooyong and that their tennis could be of a standard high enough to have great spectator appeal in Australia.

Perhaps because of the great distance separating Australia from Europe, the LTA of Australia and the State associations did not for many years consider it necessary to promote women's tennis and send teams overseas on a regular basis. However, a women's team consisting of Daphne Akhurst, Mrs Harper and Miss Boyd did travel overseas in 1925. They were joined by Miss St George and Mrs Utz and the fact that Daphne Akhurst reached the Wimbledon semi-final indicated that Australia could muster strength in women's tennis. Later, Joan Hartigan, travelling privately, also made her presence felt by reaching the Wimbledon semi-finals in 1934 and 1935.

It was unfortunate that Australia was unable to send women's teams overseas during the period when Nancye Wynne (Mrs Bolton) and Thelma Long were at their peak. Nancye Bol-

ton was a player almost in the same class as Margaret Court, who had won the Australian title 11 times by 1973. With her 1963, 1965 and 1970 Wimbledon victories and US triumphs, Margaret is regarded by experts as one of the best players in the history of women's tennis (see GREAT PLAYERS OF ALL TIME, PART 1).

Although teams did not tour overseas regularly, the LTA of Australia did invite many of the world's greatest women players to Australia: D. M. Bundy, Doris Hart, Louise Brough, Maureen Connolly, Shirley Fry, Althea Gibson (United States) as well as Dorothy Round, Angela Mortimer and Virginia Wade (Great Britain) have been to Australia; their presence and ability did much to stimulate interest in the women's game.

Australian women have won the FEDERATION CUP six times, 1964-5, 1968, 1970-1 and 1973, and players such as Margaret Court, Lesley Turner (Bowrey), Kerry Melville, Judy Tegart, Karen Krantzcke, Lesley Hunt and Evonne Goolagong have contributed so much to the game, that women's tennis in Australia is now achieving the international recognition that Floris Conway and Nell Hopman always believed would come, if the Australian girls could be continually exposed to the best international competition. Evonne Goolagong, a youngster from the wide open spaces who made good with the guidance and help of Vic Edwards, has provided one of the greatest 'rags to riches' stories the game has known, with her charming manners, pleasant smile and attitude towards the game, coupled with her remarkable Wimbledon victory over Margaret Court in 1971.

Australia has won the Davis Cup 22 times: six triumphs being Australasian victories and 16 Australian. For tennis enthusiasts the years between 1946 and 1967 will always represent not only the most exciting and colourful decades in Australian tennis history but proof that Australia, with Esca Stephens, Davis Cup selector and New South Wales LTA President, and many other outstanding administrators, had become expert in the staging of splendid Davis Cup Challenge Round spectacles.

Many reasons have been given for Australia's postwar success in Davis Cup tennis. It is interesting to examine some of them. First, as a group, sports-goods manufacturers have employed almost every Australian Davis Cup player during the past 30 years. By providing employment which allowed players to compete twelve months of the year, these manufacturers created a tennis system which was probably superior to that of any country in the world.

Within the framework of tennis administration, the State and National associations have provided first-class coaching. Coaches handle special squads of boys and girls in metropolitan and country areas. Money is made available by oil, tobacco and ice-cream companies, and the Rothmans National Foundation. Coaches are either directly or in-

Above **Australia.** The 1925 ladies' team *(l-r):* Miss Akhurst, Mrs Harper, Miss St George, Miss Boyd

directly involved with sports-goods manufacturers; they spot the promising youngsters, who in turn become associated with one of the sports-goods firms.

Always active have been a number of dedicated officials, such as Harry Hopman, whose name has been inseparably linked with the success of the Australian Davis Cup teams. He was unique in almost fanatical devotion to the game and also his sincere belief that physical fitness was absolutely essential (no one would disagree). He not only worked with Davis Cup players to prepare them for the Cup matches, but was also a student of human nature and probably understood the peculiarities of his young players as well as their parents. His success as a Davis Cup captain became known all over the world; he worked hard at his job and brought out the best in his team. He also spent much time helping youngsters to improve their game and his great liking for children gave him the right approach towards teenagers. There are many coaches in Australia, not of Hopman's stature, and it is their business to make money from coaching. However, they are a contributing factor in the improvement of young players. One of the better-known professionals is Victor A. Edwards, who gave Evonne Goolagong the opportunity to progress. A sensitive man although outwardly impassive, Vic Edwards plays every shot with Evonne and suffers when she misses the easy ones. Dinny Pails and Mervyn Rose, whose background in the international sphere has well equipped them to coach youngsters, are also doing a great deal for the game.

While associating Harry Hopman with Australian Davis Cup teams, we must not forget Cliff Sproule, a first-class administrator whose knowledge of the game is second to none. He became known as 'the Prince of

Referees'. He refereed 14 of the 16 Davis Cup Challenge Rounds played in Australia since World War II. He built up a reputation among local and overseas stars as the finest referee in the world. He was a Davis Cup player and Captain of Australia's 1936 team (Jack Crawford, Vivian McGrath and Adrian Quist) who lost the Challenge Round to Great Britain, having defeated the US team of Budge, Allison, Mako, Van Ryn, 3 matches to 2 at Germantown Cricket Club, Philadelphia, the first occasion in 20 years that Australia had beaten the United States. Another dedicated official who has done much for Australian tennis is Wayne Reid, the President of the LTA of Australia.

For special coaching of advanced youngsters, the six State associations conduct their own classes at the main stadia, usually on grass courts. From these groups, the best boys and girls attend more advanced coaching in national classes, usually conducted after the Australian Championships. Perhaps the most important move to engender a competitive spirit in young players was made in 1923 by Sir Richard Linton, when he donated the Linton Cup for junior interstate competition for boys. This trophy is synonymous with Australian tennis. Junior teams from the six States compete annually. Matches are played on Davis Cup lines but with two singles and one doubles match. Originally the qualifying age was under 21; it was later reduced to under 19. Probably every Davis Cup player since 1924 has been blooded in Linton Cup competition. The competition was so successful that South Australian businessman George Wilson presented the Wilson Cup for girls in 1931, and this event has achieved the same prestige and standing as the Linton Cup.

The Linton and Wilson Cup matches and the State and National Championships are always played on grass courts in the capital cities, Sydney, Melbourne, Adelaide, Brisbane, and recently Perth. However, while the major State and National titles are played on turf, about 95 per cent of tennis in Australia is played on some type of hard surface, such as clay, asphalt, red porous courts (En-tout-cas) and cement. A large majority of Australia's Davis Cup stars – Crawford, Hopman, Brom-

Below **Australia.** Evonne Goolagong, aged 16, with Vic Edwards

Above **Australia.** Lew Hoad *(left)* and Ken Rosewall at Wimbledon in 1952

wich, Pails, Sedgman, Hoad, Rosewall, Laver, Anderson, Emerson, and many others – learned their game on hard courts. The centre court area and a few specially prepared outside turf courts make an excellent playing surface at Kooyong (Melbourne), White City (Sydney), King's Park (Perth), War Memorial Drive (Adelaide) and Milton (Brisbane), but for accuracy of bound, the grass surface does not generally compare with that of a first-class hard court.

From an Australian viewpoint the Championships of New South Wales (Sydney) and Victoria (Melbourne) carry almost the same prestige as the National titles. This is probably because these two States have the largest populations and for many years dominated the tennis scene. During the last decade or so, Queensland – with its improved facilities at Milton (Brisbane) and the emergence of such great players as Rod Laver, Malcolm Anderson and Roy Emerson – has become a stronger force nationally. The atmosphere and surroundings at War Memorial Drive (Adelaide) and King's Park (Perth) create that comfortable and casual feeling of relaxation which many players enjoy while competing in major events. But another reason for the importance of the titles of New South Wales and Victoria is the fact that all leading competitors participate. A singles victory in the New South Wales or Victorian Championships also has a strong bearing on international representation and may affect selection for a Davis Cup team. However, the Australian Championships are the premier event and until the 1960s were accepted with those of Wimbledon, France and the United States as one of the 'Big Four' in world tennis.

The Lawn Tennis Association of Australia is a combination of the State associations of New South Wales, Victoria, Queensland, South Australia, Western Australia and Tasmania, each of which has two representatives. The Australian Capital Territory Association is affiliated direct to the New South Wales LTA. The President is elected by the Council of 12 delegates. Since the headquarters of the LTA of Australia are in Melbourne, each State generally appoints its two national representatives from local residents, to save the time and expense of councillors from other States journeying to Melbourne each month for meetings. For example, Perth, the capital of Western Australia, is over 2,000 miles from Melbourne. The delegates in Melbourne are generally instructed by their associations how to vote on important matters, but may handle more general matters of business as they arise.

Although the LTA of Australia has been responsible, with its constituent States, for the staging of Davis Cup Inter-Zone Finals and Challenge Rounds in the postwar years, it has no national tennis centre. Each State association has its own playing area: for instance, the New South Wales LTA owns the grounds and stands of the White City, Sydney; the LTA of Victoria owns those at Kooyong, Melbourne. The LTA of Australia is simply an association of associations; it controls all aspects of the game, national and international. Its Council arranges all international matches and sanctions, regulates and controls within the Commonwealth of Australia all international and interstate matches, as well as the Australian Championships and matches between individual States and other nations. For Records of the Australian Championships, see PART 3. AQ
GOVERNING BODY: The Lawn Tennis Association of Australia, 218 Jolimont Road, East Melbourne, Victoria 3002

Australian Grip see GRIPS

Austria

Austria was one of the Founder Members of the ILTF in 1913. The Association was expelled in 1919 after World War I, was readmitted in 1925, expelled during World War II and was readmitted as a Full Member

in 1947. It competed in the DAVIS CUP in 1905, 1924-5, 1927-34 and 1936-7. In 1938 Austria became part of the German Reich and ceased to compete as a separate nation. It returned to the DAVIS CUP in 1948 and has been a regular competitor since 1957. It has also taken part in the FEDERATION CUP and many European competitions. BR
GOVERNING BODY: Österreichischer Tennisverband, 1020 Vienna, Rustenschacherallee 1

Auteuil see FRANCE; also THE GROWTH OF THE GAME (PART 1)

Ayala, Luis (Chile)
Born Santiago, Chile, 18 Sept. 1932; Wimbledon men's singles q/f 1959-61; mixed doubles s/f 1957; US men's singles q/f 1957, 1959; mixed doubles s/f 1958; French men's singles r/u 1958, s/f 1959, r/u 1960; men's doubles s/f 1956; mixed doubles r/u 1955, won 1956, r/u 1957. Davis Cup 1952, 1955-7. Became pro in 1961.

Below **Luis Ayala**

B

Backcourt

The area of the court from the service line to the baseline and between the sidelines including the 'tramlines' in doubles. It is often called 'no man's land' because it is considered too far back for volleys and too far forward if playing defensively. See court dimensions under RULES (PART 1). JO

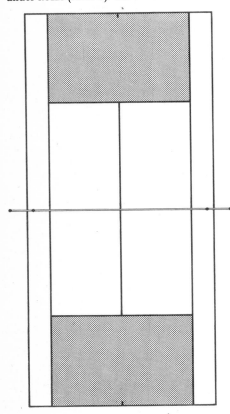

Above **Backcourt**

Backhand

For a right-handed player all strokes played from the left-hand side of the body, ideally with the right foot, shoulder, and, as the term implies, the back of the racket hand towards the net. JO

Backhand Grip see GRIPS

Backswing

The act of taking the racket back and behind the body to build up power and rhythm before striking the ball. JO

Baddeley, Herbert (Gt Britain)

Born 11 Jan. 1872; died 20 July 1931; Wimbledon men's singles s/f 1894-6; men's doubles s/f 1889-90, won 1891, r/u 1892, r/u* 1893, won 1894-6, r/u 1897. Twin brother of Wilfred.

Baddeley, Wilfred (Gt Britain)

Born 11 Jan. 1872; died 30 Jan. 1929; Wimbledon men's singles q/f 1890, won 1891-2, r/u 1893-4, won 1895, r/u 1896, s/f 1897; men's doubles s/f 1889-90, won 1891, r/u 1892, r/u* 1893, won 1894-6, r/u 1897. At the age of 19 years 5 months 23 days the youngest man to win the Wimbledon singles. A really great matchplayer.

Bahamas see COMMONWEALTH CARIBBEAN LTA

Baker, Miss Beverly see Mrs J. G. FLEITZ

Balkan Championships see RUMANIA

Ball, History of the

The real tennis ball was once stuffed with wool. King Louis XI of France decreed in 1480 that balls should be covered with good leather (usually sheepskin) and filled with good hair or wool stuffing, and that the filling should not be adulterated, as had often been the practice, by using the first thing that came to hand such as old rags or bran (see THE ORIGINS OF LAWN TENNIS, PART 1). In the early days the ball was struck with the hand and consequently a rigid specification for the ball was unnecessary.

M. de Garsault describes the manufacture of real tennis balls two hundred years ago in *Art du Paumier-Raquetier et de la Paume* (1767). The ball was formed from strips of woollen cloth packed tightly together and then bound round with string and hammered in a wooden cup to give it shape and compactness. Finally it was covered with white cloth. It was about 2 inches (5 cm) in diameter but de Garsault suggests that balls should be made in proportion to the court, small for a short court and larger for a long one. According to Julian Marshall, in *Annals of Tennis* (1878), early tennis balls were white so that they showed up well against the black walls of the court; he points out that in Spain, where the courts had white walls, the balls used were black.

In London tennis balls were made by the Ironmongers' Company as far back as the middle of the fifteenth century and very likely much earlier. It has been suggested that the balls might have been made of iron! A more likely explanation is that as the Ironmongers had their own tennis court and made their own balls, they found it profitable to make them for other London players. That the right was jealously guarded is shown by a petition to Edward IV praying the king to prohibit the import of 'tenys balles'.

The tightly packed balls of real tennis bounced well enough on hard stone floors but

Above **Wilfred Baddeley**

not on grass. It was for this very obvious reason that when Major Harry Gem formed the first lawn tennis club in Leamington in 1872 (see THE BIRTH AND SPREAD OF LAWN TENNIS, PART 1) he provided that the ball should be of 'india rubber or other substance answering the purpose, punctured or not as may be agreed upon or as circumstances require'. The circumference of the ball, Gem stipulated in his rules, was to be about 7½ in (19.05 cm) but with a latitude of half an inch (about 1 cm) either more or less. The weight was to be about 1½ oz (42.52 g) with a variation of ¼ oz (about 7 g) either way. The balls should be 'white or nearly so as they could be obtained' as they were then more visible in imperfect light than if they were red or any dark colour.

In the first edition of Major Walter Wingfield's rules (1874) there is no mention of the type of ball or its size or weight. When the Tennis Committee of the MCC published new rules of lawn tennis in May 1875 it was provided that the ball should be hollow and made of india-rubber. The size was to be exactly 2¼ in (5.71 cm) in diameter and the weight exactly 1½ oz (42.52 g). The balls might be covered with white cloth, it was added, for use in fine weather. This last suggestion followed a letter published in *The Field* on 5 December 1874 in which Mr J. M. Heathcote had stated that he found an advantage in covering the balls which he used with white flannel. Coloured balls, even parti-coloured balls, were also in use.

In the rules drawn up for the first Wimbledon championships (1877) the All England Club stipulated that balls were to be 2¼ – 2⅝ in (5.71 – 6.67 cm) in diameter and 1¼ – 1½ oz (35.44 – 42.52 g) in weight. Very little change has taken place since then. The cloth cover which had previously been sewn at the seam was cemented by Slazengers from 1924. Up until 1928 both seamed and stitched balls were available. Stitching was discontinued in 1928 when production went over entirely to the cement seam. In about 1931 the pressure inside the ball was increased. For current regulations see RULE 3 (PART 1). TT

Ballboys

Major championships and tournaments invariably recruit tennis-minded boys or girls to keep the playing area clear and ensure a constant supply of balls to the players. A full team for a championship match is six: two at each end, one on each side of the net. For their positions see illustration under UMPIRES AND LINE JUDGES. DC

Ball in Play

A ball is in play from the moment at which it is delivered in service until a point has been scored or a LET called. JO

Baranyi, Szabolcs (Hungary)

Born Nagyvarád, 31 Jan. 1944; European Amateur Championships won 1969; Hungarian National Championships won 1969. Davis Cup 1969-

Barazzutti, Corrado (Italy)

Born 19 Feb. 1953; won Orange Bowl and Roland Garros Junior Championship 1971, Bonfiglio Trophy 1972; ranked no. 2 in Italy.

Barbados

Lawn tennis has been played in Barbados for the last 70 years on private courts and in one or two clubs. The Barbados LTA was established in 1948. In the last 10 years there has been a change from grass to hard courts and a distinct increase in junior play. In 1972 there were 10 clubs with nearly 200 players.

Barbados as such does not compete in the Davis Cup Competition but it forms part of the COMMONWEALTH CARIBBEAN LTA, under whose aegis the various Caribbean territories continue to play in the Davis Cup Competition every year.

Barbados is an Associate Member of the ILTF. BR

GOVERNING BODY: Barbados Lawn Tennis Association, P.O. Box 615c, Bridgetown

Barger, Miss M. see Mrs Maud WALLACH

Barlow, H. S. (Gt Britain)

Born April 1860; Wimbledon men's singles r/u* 1889-90, q/f 1891-2, s/f 1893, q/f 1894-5; men's doubles s/f 1887, r/u* 1891, won 1892, r/u 1893, r/u* 1894, s/f 1895. A fine stroke-player but lacking match temperament.

Barrett, Herbert Roper (Gt Britain)

Born Upton, Essex, 24 Nov. 1873; Wimbledon men's singles s/f 1899, q/f 1900, s/f 1901, q/f 1902, r/u* 1908-9, r/u 1911, q/f 1912; men's doubles r/u* 1899, r/u 1900, r/u* 1901, s/f 1902, r/u* 1908, won 1909, r/u 1910, s/f 1911, won 1912-13, r/u 1914, s/f 1921-2. Davis Cup (British Isles) 1900, 1907, 1912-14, 1919. Non-

playing captain of Britain's winning Davis Cup team 1933-6.

Barthès, Pierre (France)

Born Béziers, 13 Dec. 1941; US men's doubles won 1970; Australian men's doubles s/f 1965; French men's singles q/f 1965. Davis Cup 1964-5. Became pro 1965. One of France's best players since World War II and one of the Handsome Eight in 1968. Left WCT 1970. ILTF GP 6th 1971.

Baseline

The line at each end of the court parallel to the net. See illustration and THE RULES AND THEIR INTERPRETATION (PART 1). JO

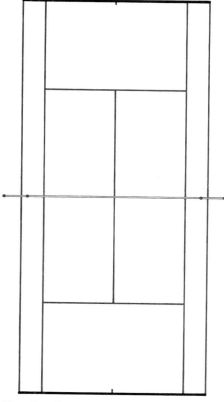

Above **Baseline**

Beckenham see KENT CHAMPIONSHIPS

Belgium

The Fédération Royale Belge de Lawn-Tennis was founded on 10 March 1902, under the name of the Ligue Belge de Lawn Tennis, with A. Solvay as President. The Ligue later took the name of Fédération Belge de Lawn-Tennis and was granted the 'Royal' in 1930.

The first Belgian championships were organized in 1895 and the first winner of the men's singles was Baron Robert de Rossius d'Humain. The championships have been held every year (except during both world wars). The list of champions includes many players well known in international tennis: Paul de Borman, Willy le Maire de Warzée, Jean

Washer, Philippe Washer, Jackie Brichant, Mme Paul de Borman, Mme Josane de Meulemeester-Sigart, Mlle Nelly Adamson, Mlle C. Mercelis.

Belgium was one of the founder members of the ILTF, being represented at the inaugural meeting on 1 March 1913 in Paris. One of the Belgian representatives, Mr P. de Borman, President of the FRBLT from 1924 to 1948, was President of the Committee of Management and of the ILTF itself three times. Pierre Geelhand de Merxem, a Vice-President of the FRBLT, was a member of the ILTF Committee of Management from 1962 to 1973. In 1958 the General Assembly of the ILTF met in Brussels.

Belgium has been represented in the DAVIS CUP since 1904, except during the two world wars. In 1904 the Belgian team of de Borman and W. le Maire de Warzée defeated the French (Decugis and Aymé) at Wimbledon by 3 matches to 2, and went on to be defeated in the Challenge Round 5-0 by the British Isles (Laurie and Reggie Doherty and F. L. Riseley). Between the world wars, the Belgian team (A. Lacroix, C. Naeyaert, L. de Borman and P. Geelhand de Merxem) played in the semi-finals of the European Zone. After World War II Belgium won the European Zone Finals in 1953 when the Belgium team was composed of Philippe Washer, J. Brichant and P. Geelhand de Merxem. The Inter-Zone Finals took place in Australia, where Belgium was defeated by the United States 4-1. In 1957 the Belgian team won the European Zone again but was eliminated by the United States, 3-2.

Belgium has participated in the KING'S CUP since its foundation (1936), in the GALEA CUP since its foundation (1950), and in the FEDERATION CUP since its foundation (1963) except for 1965 when it was held in Australia. Belgium has also taken part in the ANNIE SOISBAULT CUP since 1965, in the VALERIO CUP since 1971 and the Princess Sophia Cup since 1972. Besides these official meetings, Belgium plays friendly matches with its neighbours (the Netherlands, France, Luxembourg, Switzerland and Germany).

Belgium runs an annual National Championships for men, women and veterans. The men and the women are divided into seven groups, the veterans into four. The men's teams are composed of six players who play six singles and three doubles; the women and veterans have teams of four players who contest four singles and two doubles. In 1973, 1,252 teams (10,000 individuals) played in inter-club matches.

The FRBLT also organizes a Championship for juniors, reserved for boys and girls aged 9 to 17 (i.e. under 18 on 31 December of the year of the Championship). This is divided into four classes: *minimes, cadets, scolaires* and *juniors.*

Each year the FRBLT publishes an official classification of the players (men and women) who have obtained at least four results during the season. This is divided into three grades and enables clubs to compete with their equals

Belgian Championships Winners

Men's Singles	
1895	R. de Rossius d'Humain
1896	M. Nagelmaekers
1897	R. Rossius d'Humain
1898	P. de Borman
1899	P. de Borman
1900	P. de Borman
1901	W. le Maire de Warzée
1902	P. de Borman
1903	P. de Borman
1904	P. de Borman
1905	P. de Borman
1906	W. le Maire de Warzée
1907	W. le Maire de Warzée
1908	W. le Maire de Warzée
1909	W. le Maire de Warzée
1910	W. le Maire de Warzée
1911	P. de Borman
1912	P. de Borman
1913	G. Watson
1914	L. Trasenster
1915-18	*No Competition*
1919	A. Lammens
1920	J. Washer
1921	J. Washer
1922	J. Washer
1923	J. Washer
1924	J. Washer
1925	J. Washer
1926	J. Washer
1927	J. Washer
1928	A. Lacroix
1929	L. de Borman
1930	L. de Borman
1931	L. de Borman
1932	G. van Zuylen
1933	C. Naeyaert
1934	A. Lacroix
1935	A. Lacroix
1936	A. Lacroix
1937	C. Naeyaert
1938	P. Geelhand
1939	C. Naeyaert
1940	*No Competition*
1941	C. Naeyaert
1942	J. Van den Eynde
1943	J. Van den Eynde
1944	*No Competition*
1945	P. Washer
1946	P. Washer
1947	P. Washer
1948	P. Washer
1949	P. Washer
1950	J. Peten
1951	P. Washer
1952	P. Washer
1953	P. Washer
1954	P. Washer
1955	J. Brichant
1956	J. Brichant
1957	J. Brichant
1958	J. Brichant
1959	J. Brichant
1960	J. Brichant
1961	J. Brichant
1962	J. Brichant
1963	E. Drossard
1964	E. Drossard
1965	E. Drossard
1966	P. Hombergen
1967	P. Hombergen
1968	P. Hombergen
1969	P. Hombergen
1970	P. Hombergen
1971	P. Hombergen
1972	P. Hombergen
1973	B. Mignot

Women's Singles	
1897	Miss M. Habets
1898	Mrs P. Trasenster
1899	Mrs P. Comblen
1900	Mrs P. Trasenster
1901	Mrs P. Comblen
1902	Miss L. Gevers
1903	Miss J. Chazal
1904	Mrs P. Trasenster
1905	Miss M. Dufresnoy
1906	Miss M. Dufresnoy
1907	Miss M. Dufresnoy
1908	Miss M. Dufresnoy
1909	Mrs J. Chaudoir
1910	Miss M. Dufresnoy
1911	Mrs P. de Borman
1912	Mrs P. de Borman
1913	Miss J. Liebrechts
1914	Mrs P. de Borman
1915-18	*No Competition*
1919	Mrs P. de Borman
1920	Mrs P. de Borman
1921	Mrs E. Dupont
1922	Mrs P. de Borman
1923	Mrs R. Storms
1924	Mrs P. de Borman
1925	Mrs E. Guyot de Mishaegen
1926	Miss P. Alison
1927	Mrs R. Storms
1928	Miss J. Sigart
1929	Miss J. Sigart
1930	Mrs E. Dupont
1931	Miss J. Sigart
1932	Miss J. Sigart
1933	Miss N. Adamson
1934	Miss N. Adamson
1935	Miss N. Adamson
1936	Mrs J. De Meulemeester
1937	Miss M. de Borman
1938	Mrs G. de Bary
1939	Miss Y. Hoyaux
1940	*No Competition*
1941	Mrs G. de Bary
1942	Miss Y. Hoyaux
1943	Miss M. David
1944	*No Competition*
1945	Mrs J. Van Leer
1946	Mrs J. De Meulemeester
1947	Miss M. de Borman
1948	Miss M. de Borman
1949	Miss M. de Borman
1950	Mrs A. Van Cutzem
1951	Miss C. Mercelis
1952	Miss J. De Ridder
1953	Miss C. Mercelis
1954	Miss C. Mercelis
1955	Miss C. Mercelis
1956	Miss C. Mercelis
1957	Miss C. Mercelis
1958	Miss C. Mercelis
1959	Miss C. Mercelis
1960	Miss C. Mercelis
1961	Miss C. Mercelis
1962	Miss E. Bellens
1963	Miss C. Mercelis
1964	Miss C. Mercelis
1965	Mrs Kafin-Rotta
1966	Miss C. Mercelis
1967	Miss I. Loeys
1968	Miss I. Loeys
1969	Miss I. Loeys
1970	Miss M. Van Haver
1971	Miss M. Gurdal
1972	Miss M. Gurdal
1973	Miss M. Gurdal

at different levels. In 1973, 13,457 players (men and women) played competition matches; 5,723 men and 2,281 women were classified. In December 1973, the FRBLT had 281 affiliated clubs, representing nearly 40,000 players. AD

GOVERNING BODY: Fédération Royale Belge de Lawn-Tennis, 164 Avenue Louise, 1050 Brussels

Bergelin, Lennart (Sweden)

Born Alingsås, Sweden, 10 June 1925; Wimbledon men's singles q/f 1946, 1948, 1951; men's doubles s/f 1948; mixed doubles 1947; Australian men's singles q/f 1955; French men's singles q/f 1948, 1951; men's doubles won 1948, s/f 1949. Davis Cup 1946-51, 1953-5. A fine touch player, especially of half-court shots. Mentor of Björn BORG.

Bermuda see THE BIRTH AND SPREAD OF LAWN TENNIS (PART 1)

Bernard, Marcel (France)

Born Lille, France, 18 May 1914; US men's doubles s/f 1932; French men's singles s/f 1932, q/f 1933, 1935, s/f 1936, won 1946, s/f 1947, q/f 1948-9; men's doubles r/u 1932, won 1936, s/f 1937, won 1946, s/f 1947, 1949; mixed doubles won 1935-6. Davis Cup 1935-7, 1946-8, 1950, 1953, 1955-6. A left-hander and probably France's best player outside the ranks of the FOUR MUSKETEERS.

Betz, Miss Pauline M. [Mrs R. Addie] (USA)

Born Dayton, Ohio, 6 Aug. 1919; Wimbledon women's singles won 1946; women's doubles r/u 1946; mixed doubles s/f 1946; US women's singles r/u 1941, won 1942-4, 1946; women's doubles r/u 1942-5, s/f 1946; French women's

Colour plate Françoise Durr, the best French woman player in four decades, reached the Wimbledon semi-finals and the quarter-finals at Forest Hills in 1970.

Below Pauline M. Betz

singles r/u 1946; women's doubles r/u 1946; mixed doubles won 1946. Wightman Cup 1946. Turned professional 1947. A most agile and effective all-round player, as disciplined as a dancer, perhaps the best of the many outstanding American women who dominated the game after World War II. Her career in the game was cut short early in 1947 when, for no more than discussing the terms of a professional contract, the USLTA deprived her of her amateur status. She did not lose a set in winning the Wimbledon singles and her longest set was 6-4 in the final against her compatriot Louise BROUGH. See GREAT PLAYERS OF ALL TIME (PART 1).

Bingley, Miss Blanche
see Mrs G. W. HILLYARD

Bisque
As in golf, an extra handicap used rather like a joker at cards, occasionally given in a friendly game. The receiver of a bisque may take it at any time to gain an important point. The term derives from real tennis. JO

Bjurstedt, Miss M. see Mrs M. MALLORY

Bloomer, Miss Shirley see Mrs C. BRASHER

Bolivia
Lawn tennis was introduced into Bolivia in 1912 by British engineers employed on the railways and in mining in the mountains. There were courts at 10,000 ft (3,048 m) above sea level. The first four clubs were established between 1920 and 1930, including Sucre Tennis Club and the La Paz Club where the South American Championships have been played. There are now nearly 200 clay courts in Bolivia. In 1937 the national tennis association was founded in Catavi, the mining centre. It was admitted to the ILTF in 1949 as an Associate Member and became a Full Member in 1959. It is also affiliated to the South American Confederation. Bolivia took part in the DAVIS CUP in 1971. BR
GOVERNING BODY: Federación Boliviana de Lawn Tennis, Casilla No. 2790, La Paz

Bolivia Cup see SOUTH AMERICAN CHAMPIONSHIPS

Bolton, Mrs N. [Miss Nancye Wynne] (Australia)
Born Melbourne, 10 June 1917; Wimbledon women's singles q/f 1947; mixed doubles r/u 1947, 1951; US women's singles s/f 1947; women's doubles s/f 1938; mixed doubles s/f 1938; Australian women's singles r/u 1936, won 1937, s/f 1938, q/f 1939, won 1940, 1946-8, r/u 1949, s/f 1950, won 1951, s/f 1952; women's doubles won 1936-40, 1947-9, r/u

Colour plate Lew Hoad, Wimbledon champion 1956-7, came within one match of winning the Grand Slam in 1956 when he was defeated by Ken Rosewall in the final at Forest Hills.

1950, won 1951-2; mixed doubles r/u 1938, won 1940, 1946-8; French mixed doubles r/u 1938. A player of exceptional grace, fluency and power though, with small margin of error, liable to be beaten when her timing was less than perfect. Her career spanned World War II. Her example raised both the status and standards of the women's game in Australia.

Above **Nancye Bolton**

Bonfiglio Trophy see ITALY

Bonne Bell Cup
An annual international women's team competition between Australia and the United States. Like the WIGHTMAN CUP, it consists of five singles matches and two doubles. The first competition, held in Cleveland, Ohio, in July 1972, was won by Australia, 5-2.

Boothby, Miss Dora P. [Mrs A. Geen] (Gt Britain)
Wimbledon women's singles q/f 1905, s/f 1908, won 1909, r/u 1910-11; women's doubles won 1913, s/f 1922. She had the unenviable distinction (1911) of being the only Wimbledon singles finalist to lose 6-0, 6-0 (to Mrs Lambert Chambers).

Borg, Björn (Sweden)
Born 6 June 1956; Wimbledon men's singles q/f 1973; US men's singles q/f 1973. Only 16, he was ranked no. 1 in Sweden in 1972; still 16, seeded 6 at first senior Wimbledon (1973). Right-handed with two-handed backhand. Pro.

Borotra, Jean (France)
Born Arbonne, Basses-Pyrénées, France, 13 Aug. 1898; Wimbledon men's singles won 1924, r/u 1925, won 1926, r/u 1927, q/f 1928, r/u 1929, s/f 1930-1; men's doubles s/f 1923, won 1925, 1932-3, r/u 1934, s/f 1936, 1939; mixed doubles won 1925, s/f 1933; US men's

singles r/u 1926, q/f 1927; men's doubles s/f 1922; mixed doubles s/f 1922, 1925, won 1926, s/f 1927-8; Australian men's singles won 1928; men's doubles won 1928; mixed doubles won 1928; French men's singles won 1924, r/u 1925, s/f 1926, 1928, r/u 1929, s/f 1930, won 1931; men's doubles won 1924-5, s/f 1926, r/u 1927, won 1928-9, s/f 1930, 1932-3, won 1934, 1936, s/f 1937; mixed doubles won 1924, s/f 1925, r/u 1926, won 1927, s/f 1930, 1932, won 1934, s/f 1937. Davis Cup 1922, 1924-37 (including winning years 1927-32), 1947. One of the FOUR MUSKETEERS and the first outstanding apostle of the serve-volley technique. His backhand volley and backhand return of service were great strokes unique to him. His popularity with British crowds was enormous and his ability to sway their emotions theatrical in skill. The 'Bounding Basque' – a tribute to his acrobatic volleying feats – had only to don his beret to be cheered. His opponents found not only his playing skill but his personality hard to cope with. A striking example of physical fitness, he was still playing good-class veteran's lawn tennis at the age of 74 – and still following his service up to the net.

Below **Jean Borotra**, the 'Bounding Basque'

Bouman, Miss Kea [Mrs Tiedeman] (Netherlands)

Born 23 Nov. 1903; Wimbledon women's singles q/f 1926; US women's singles s/f 1927; mixed doubles s/f 1927; French women's singles s/f 1926, won 1927, s/f 1928; women's doubles won 1929; Netherlands women's singles won 1923-6. The finest Dutch woman player between the world wars.

Bounce (Bound)

The upward movement of the ball after it has landed on the ground. It can be greatly affected in direction and height by variety of SPIN imparted to it by different strokes and by the nature and condition of the court surface. JO

Bournemouth see BRITISH HARD COURT CHAMPIONSHIPS

Boussus, Christian (France)

Born Hyères, 5 March 1908; Wimbledon men's singles s/f 1928; men's doubles s/f 1932; Australian mixed doubles s/f 1928, won 1935; French men's singles q/f 1928, r/u 1931, q/f 1933, s/f 1934, q/f 1935, s/f 1936-7, q/f 1938; men's doubles r/u 1932, s/f 1936; mixed doubles r/u 1938. Davis Cup 1934-7, 1939. Left-handed.

Bowrey, William W. ['Tex'] (Australia)

Born Sydney, 25 Dec. 1943; Wimbledon men's doubles r/u 1966, s/f 1967; US men's singles q/f 1966; men's doubles r/u 1967; Australian men's singles q/f 1965-7, won 1968, q/f 1969; men's doubles s/f 1963-6, r/u 1967, s/f 1968; mixed doubles r/u 1966, s/f 1967-8. Davis Cup 1967. WCT pro 1968-71; retired 1972 to teach in Texas.

Bowrey, Mrs W. W. see Miss L. TURNER

Boyd, Miss Esna F. (Australia)

Wimbledon women's singles q/f 1925; women's doubles s/f 1928; Australian women's singles r/u 1922, 1924-6, won 1927, r/u 1928; women's doubles won 1922-3, r/u 1925, won 1926, r/u 1927, won 1928; mixed doubles won 1922, r/u 1924, won 1926-7, r/u 1928; French mixed doubles s/f 1928.

BP Cup

An international team competition, sponsored by BP, for men and women under 21, similar to the GALEA CUP but for teams of maximum three and held indoors in Britain. The first took place at TORQUAY in 1973 following a successful triangular tournament in 1972 which Great Britain won from France and Spain. Countries competing in 1973 were (men) Belgium, Czechoslovakia, France, Great Britain, Italy, Netherlands, Spain, the United States, (women) Czechoslovakia, France, Great Britain, Netherlands. Britain won the men's event; Czechoslovakia the women's. DC

BP International Tennis Fellowship

In June 1968, during the first open Wimbledon, the British Petroleum International Tennis Fellowship was launched with John Barrett, former British Davis Cup captain and player, as Director, and Rod Laver and Ken Rosewall as Professional Advisers. The chief object of the Fellowship is to encourage young players at all levels. In its first year Mark Cox, Gerald Battrick and Paul Hutchins received bonus payments totalling over £4,000; since then thousands of pounds in bonuses have been paid to other members as the Fellowship has grown in strength. Considerable financial help is available to the large and eager group of young boys and girls who compete in junior tournaments, and players under 21 can qualify for junior membership if they have won a singles event in any age group at a tournament recognized by the LTA. There are now over 800 junior members who receive help with their tennis problems from Laver and Rosewall; many have taken part in playing clinics conducted by these world-famous stars. Now BP subsidiaries have started similar Fellowships in Australia, South Africa and France. BP also sponsors tennis in NEW ZEALAND.

In 1972 BP began sponsoring the British Davis Cup squad and also supported a new venture, the formation of a junior Davis Cup squad for outstanding young players under 21. In August 1972 a British under-21 team, all members of the Fellowship, won the GALEA CUP for the first time. The Fellowship also presented BP Golden Shield awards to the man and woman under 21 voted Young Players of the Year in 1971 and 1972. The winners in both years were both Australians, John Alexander and Evonne Goolagong. As well as sponsoring these activities, the Fellowship publishes *World of Tennis*, an annual which includes information on international tennis, plus the results of every championship and tournament of note held in the previous season. The Fellowship's latest venture is the BP CUP. DC

Brandon Trophy see COMMONWEALTH CARIBBEAN LTA

Brasher, Mrs C. [Miss Shirley Bloomer] (Gt Britain)

Born Grimsby, 13 June 1934; Wimbledon women's singles q/f 1956, 1958; mixed doubles s/f 1958; US women's singles s/f 1956, q/f 1957; women's doubles s/f 1955; French women's singles q/f 1955-6, won 1957, r/u 1958; women's doubles r/u 1955, won 1957, s/f 1958-9; mixed doubles won 1958. Wightman Cup 1955-60. An unspectacular but resolute competitor, her performance on hard courts brought her world no. 3 rating in 1957.

Brazil

Brazil has been a Full Member of the ILTF since 1930. There are now 13 affiliated State Federations and 220 affiliated clubs. Every year each State Federation organizes an inter-club tournament for various age-groups, in addition to a State Individual Championship, and arranges training of young players. The Confederaçao organizes National Championships for all ages and categories (in 1973, 964 players took part), and arranges other international competitions for South American nations.

It first competed in the DAVIS CUP in 1932, taking part regularly since 1957, and has reached the Inter-Zone semi-finals four times. It has also competed in the FEDERATION CUP three times. Brazil's most famous player, Maria Bueno, won the Wimbledon Championships in 1959, 1960 and 1964. A postage stamp was issued in her honour. Another leading postwar player of international repute was Armando Vieira, several times Brazilian champion and Davis Cup stalwart. The American Robert Falkenburg, 1948 Wimbledon champion, who married a Brazilian, represented Brazil in the Davis Cup 1954-5.

Dr Paulo da Silva Costa of Brazil was President of the ILTF in 1966-7. BR

GOVERNING BODY: Confederaçao Brasileira de Tenis, Rua Anfilofio de Carvalho No. 29, Grupo 407/8-ZC-P. Centro, Rio de Janeiro

Bristol (U.K.)

The Bristol Lawn Tennis Club, at Redland Green, a fine residential suburb two miles from the city centre, was founded in 1912 and has been the venue of one of Britain's major tournaments, the West of England Championships, since 1920. War years apart, the event continued until 1968 when it became open and, heavily sponsored by the local tobacco firm of W. D. and H. O. WILLS & Company Ltd, was restyled the W.D. and H.O. Wills Open Tennis

Below Shirley (Bloomer) Brasher

Championships. Up to 1974 Wills made this its major tennis sponsorship of the season. To attract the world's best players, prize money was increased considerably and topped £20,000, one of the biggest amounts paid in Britain except at Wimbledon. In 1972 the men's champion, Bob Hewitt of South Africa, received £3,800 – his biggest prize at the time – and Billie Jean King of the United States, who won the women's singles, picked up £2,000, then Europe's richest prize for a woman's competition.

The Bristol event, played two weeks before Wimbledon, always attracts international stars who wish to gain experience on grass courts.

The names of many players who have gone on to win Wimbledon appear on the trophies, which, since 1946, have mainly been taken by players from overseas.

The Bristol Club has ten grass courts and seven hard, although not all are used for the tournament. Such is the demand for tickets that three courts, besides the Centre Court, are turned into show courts and have temporary stands built around them. Another court, facing the clubhouse, is used as a lawn for Wimbledon-style strawberries and cream, a feature which helps to attract 20,000 people to the ground for the tournament.

In 1971 Bristol broke the record for box-office receipts when, for the first time in Britain, a men-only WCT event was held for the 32 Dallas-based contract professionals. Rain ruined the tournament, however; five inches fell in one night alone and only 13 minutes' play was possible in three days. The tournament was never finished. For the 1972 tournament a plastic dome was installed which could be inflated over the whole of the Centre Court by means of hot air coming from two electric fans. It rose to a height of seven feet which at least enabled the groundsman to prepare the court even when it was raining outside.

Bristol made headlines in newspapers throughout the world in the summer of 1969 when the Great Britain v. South Africa DAVIS CUP tie was interrupted by anti-apartheid demonstrators hurling flour bombs onto the court. DC

British Caribbean LTA see COMMONWEALTH CARIBBEAN LTA

British Covered Court Championships
Although the QUEEN'S CLUB was for 70 years the traditional home of the British Covered Court Championships, it has become since the 1950s their graveyard. They declined rapidly, both in importance and in strength of entry, and became a liability to the LTA, even with sponsorship in the late 1960s.

The last British Covered Court Championships to be played at Queen's were in 1968 when, in that year only, they were part of the first DEWAR CUP circuit. Records reveal that they did not start there, for the first mention

British Covered Court Championships Winners

Men's Singles		Women's Singles	
1885	H. F. Lawford	1890	Miss L. Jacks
1886	E. L. Williams	1891	Miss M. Shackle
1887	E. W. Lewis	1892	Miss M. Shackle
1888	E. W. Lewis	1893	Miss M. Shackle
1889	E. W. Lewis	1894	Miss L. Austin
1890	E. W. Lewis	1895	Miss C. Cooper
1891	E. W. Lewis	1896	Miss L. Austin
1892	E. G. Meers	1897	Miss L. Austin
1893	H. S. Mahony	1898	Miss L. Austin
1894	H. S. Mahony	1899	Miss L. Austin
1895	E. W. Lewis	1900	Miss T. Lowther
1896	E. W. Lewis	1901	Mrs G. W. Hillyard
1897	W. V. Eaves	1902	Miss T. Lowther
1898	W. V. Eaves	1903	Miss T. Lowther
1899	W. V. Eaves	1904	Miss D. K. Douglass
1900	A. W. Gore	1905	Miss H. Lane
1901	H. L. Doherty	1906	Miss D. K. Douglass
1902	H. L. Doherty	1907	Miss G. Eastlake Smith
1903	H. L. Doherty	1908	Mrs Lambert Chambers
1904	H. L. Doherty	1909	Miss D. Boothby
1905	H. L. Doherty	1910	Mrs Lambert Chambers
1906	H. L. Doherty	1911	Mrs Lambert Chambers
1907	A. F. Wilding	1912	Miss E. D. Holman
1908	A. W. Gore	1913	Mrs Lambert Chambers
1909	M. J. G. Ritchie	1914	Miss E. D. Holman
1910	F. G. Lowe	1915-18	*No Competition*
1911	A. H. Gobert	1919	Mrs Lambert Chambers
1912	A. H. Gobert	1920	Miss E. Ryan
1913	P. M. Davson	1921	Miss E. D. Holman
1914	M. J. G. Ritchie	1922	Miss E. D. Holman
1915-18	*No Competition*	1923	Mrs R. C. Clayton
1919	P. M. Davson	1924	Mrs A. E. Beamish
1920	A. H. Gobert	1925	Miss J. Reid-Thomas
1921	A. H. Gobert	1926	Miss P. Saunders
1922	A. H. Gobert	1927	Miss E. Bennett
1923	J. D. P. Wheatley	1928	Mrs L. A. Godfree
1924	P. D. B. Spence	1929	Mrs L. R. C. Michell
1925	S. M. Jacob	1930	Miss J. C. Ridley
1926	J. Borotra	1931	Miss M. Heeley
1927	E. Higgs	1932	Miss M. C. Scriven
1928	J. Borotra	1933	Mrs M. R. King
1929	J. Borotra	1934	Mrs M. R. King
1930	J. Borotra	1935	Miss M. C. Scriven
1931	J. Borotra	1936	Miss A. Lizana
1932	J. Borotra	1937	Miss M. C. Scriven
1933	J. Borotra	1938	Miss M. C. Scriven
1934	H. W. Austin	1939-47	*No Competition*
1935	J. Borotra	1948	Miss G. C. Hoahing
1936	K. Schroeder	1949	Miss P. J. Curry
1937	H. W. Austin	1950	Miss J. Quertier
1938	J. Borotra	1951	Miss J. S. V. Partridge
1939-47	*No Competition*	1952	Miss A. Mortimer
1948	J. Borotra	1953	Miss A. Mortimer
1949	J. Borotra	1954	Miss A. Mortimer
1950	J. Drobný	1955	Miss J. A. Shilcock
1951	G. L. Paish	1956	Miss A. Buxton
1952	J. Drobný	1957	Miss J. A. Shilcock
1953	J. Drobný	1958	Miss J. A. Shilcock
1954	J. Drobný	1959	Miss A. Mortimer
1955	W. Skonecki	1960	Miss A. Mortimer
1956	A. Huber	1961	Miss A. Mortimer
1957	*No Competition*	1962	Miss A. S. Haydon
1958	M. G. Davies	1963	Miss D. M. Catt
1959	R. K. Wilson	1964	Mrs P. F. Jones
1960	W. A. Knight	1965	Mrs P. F. Jones
1961	J. A. Pickard	1966-7	*No Competition*
1962	R. K. Wilson	1968	Mrs B. M. Court
1963	R. K. Wilson	1969	Mrs P. F. Jones
1964	M. J. Sangster	1970	Mrs B. J. King
1965	R. K. Wilson	1971	Mrs B. J. King
1966-7	*No Competition*	1972-3	*No Competition*
1968	R. Hewitt		
1969	R. Laver		
1970	R. Laver		
1971	I. Năstase		
1972-3	*No Competition*		

of the Covered Court Championships shows that they were held at the old Hyde Park Court in 1885. But they were certainly staged at Queen's since just before the turn of the century although even then one historian writes of the entry 'fluctuating in size and quality'. The Dohertys were as invincible indoors as they were on the Wimbledon turf. Reggie never won the indoor singles title, but his brother Laurie held it for six years running and was unbeaten when he retired in 1906. The brothers were also covered-court doubles champions for seven years, but not in succession, for in 1904-5 Laurie partnered G. W. Hillyard.

In the 1911 championships an overseas player was successful for the first time: André Gobert (France) who won both singles and doubles without losing a set, and lost his service only twice in the entire singles competition. In 1912 Gobert had another remarkable championship, culminating in an outstanding final against the New Zealand holder

of the Wimbledon singles, Captain Anthony Wilding. Wilding had not lost a set on his way to the final; when he led Gobert by two sets to love, the outcome seemed assured. Gobert won the third and fourth sets with a brilliant serve-and-volley display and went on to lead 4-0 in the deciding set. Wilding managed to pull up to 4-4 but Gobert took the next two games to retain his title. A week later, he went to Stockholm and won the Olympic gold medal. Seven years of military training then interrupted his progress, but he returned to Queen's in 1920 and won the singles again.

In the 1930s another Frenchman, Jean Borotra, held pride of place at Queen's. He was also successful in the championships of 1948 and 1949, the first two competitions held after World War II; by 1949 he was 51.

Jaroslav Drobný followed Borotra as champion in 1950, and also won three years running, 1952-4. But the decline in stature of the championships was becoming evident and after the Austrian Alfred Huber had taken the title in

1956 the competition became a much more domestic affair. In 1957, and 1966-7, there were no competitions at all. In 1968 DEWAR revived the dying event and it was won by Bob Hewitt (South Africa). In 1966 there should have been a championship, for ROTHMANS had agreed to sponsor it but, as the date approached, they felt the entry did not warrant the expense and it was quietly dropped. After Dewar had experimented for one year the Championships regained some of their former prestige when W.D. & H.O. WILLS Ltd took them under its financial wing and incorporated them in its Embassy Championships at Wembley. Rod Laver won the singles in 1969 and 1970, and Ilie Năstase in 1971. On the last two occasions it was also an ILTF GRAND PRIX event. In 1972 there was no competition since WCT players had been barred and the sponsor withdrew support. DC

British Hard Court Championships

This major event, at the West Hants Club, Bournemouth, Hampshire, the most important in Britain apart from Wimbledon, made history in 1968 as the world's first open tournament. On April 22, John Clifton (Great Britain) served the first ball to Owen Davidson (Australia) in a first-round match which Davidson won in four sets. Ken Rosewall became the first winner of an open men's singles title by beating Rod Laver 3-6, 6-2, 6-0, 6-3 in the final; Virginia Wade won the women's singles by defeating Winnie Shaw 6-4, 6-1; and Christine Janes and her sister Nell Truman became the first winners of an open event when they took the women's doubles. The most exciting moments of this great week came early in the men's singles when Mark Cox became the first player to beat a contract professional in open competition by defeating Pancho Gonzalez 0-6, 6-2, 4-6, 6-3, 6-3 in the second round. Cox went on to beat another contract professional, Roy Emerson, on the following day.

The Championships began in 1924 (at Torquay, moving to Bournemouth in 1927); from the start the entries were of high quality. Randolph Lycett and Elizabeth Ryan were the first singles champions. Two of the famous French Musketeers also won the men's singles title: Jacques Brugnon (1926) and René Lacoste (1927). Fred Perry, Jaroslav Drobný and Billy Knight, three players of distinctly differing styles, all became champions in their turn. Perry, then at the height of his fame, set up a championship record by winning the men's singles five years running (1932-6). Drobný became the only other man to win the title more than three times, with four victories (1950-2 and 1957). In beating Geoff Brown 7-5, 6-0, 6-4 in the 1950 final Drobný's dropshot was described as 'the deadliest of all time'. Knight, unlike Perry and Drobný, did not win Wimbledon, but Bournemouth admirably suited his determined game. The British left-hander won the title three times (1958, 1963-4)

British Hard Court Championships Winners (Bournemouth)

Men's Singles		Women's Singles	
1924	R. Lycett	1924	Miss E. Ryan
1925	P. D. B. Spence	1925	Miss E. Ryan
1926	J. Brugnon	1926	Miss J. Fry
1927	R. Lacoste	1927	Miss B. Nuthall
1928	R. Lacoste	1928	Miss E. A. Goldsack
1929	H. W. Austin	1929	Miss E. L. Heine
1930	H. G. N. Lee	1930	Miss J. Fry
1931	C. Boussus	1931	Mrs R. Mathieu
1932	F. J. Perry	1932	Mrs R. Mathieu
1933	F. J. Perry	1933	Miss D. E. Round
1934	F. J. Perry	1934	Miss D. E. Round
1935	F. J. Perry	1935	Miss K. E. Stammers
1936	F. J. Perry	1936	Miss K. E. Stammers
1937	H. W. Austin	1937	Miss A. Lizana
1938	Kho Sin Kie	1938	Miss M. C. Scriven
1939	Kho Sin Kie	1939	Miss K. E. Stammers
1940-5	*No Competition*	1940-5	*No Competition*
1946	J. E. Harper	1946	Mrs. E. W. A. Bostock
1947	E. W. Sturgess	1947	Mrs N. Bolton
1948	E. W. Sturgess	1948	Mrs B. E. Hilton
1949	P. Masip	1949	Miss P. J. Curry
1950	J. Drobný	1950	Miss P. J. Curry
1951	J. Drobný	1951	Miss D. J. Hart
1952	J. Drobný	1952	Miss D. J. Hart
1953	E. Morea	1953	Miss D. J. Hart
1954	A. J. Mottram	1954	Miss D. J. Hart
1955	S. Davidson	1955	Miss A. Mortimer
1956	B. Patty	1956	Miss A. Mortimer
1957	J. Drobný	1957	Miss S. J. Bloomer
1958	W. A. Knight	1958	Miss S. J. Bloomer
1959	L. A. Gerrard	1959	Miss A. Mortimer
1960	M. G. Davies	1960	Miss C. C. Truman
1961	R. Emerson	1961	Miss A. Mortimer
1962	R. Laver	1962	Miss R. Schuurman
1963	W. A. Knight	1963	Mrs P. F. Jones
1964	W. A. Knight	1964	Mrs P. F. Jones
1965	J. E. Lundqvist	1965	Mrs P. F. Jones
1966	K. Fletcher	1966	Mrs P. F. Jones
1967	J. E. Lundqvist	1967	Miss S. V. Wade
1968	K. R. Rosewall	1968	Miss S. V. Wade
1969	J. Newcombe	1969	Mrs B. M. Court
1970	M. Cox	1970	Mrs B. M. Court
1971	G. Battrick	1971	Mrs B. M. Court
1972	R. A. Hewitt	1972	Miss E. F. Goolagong
1973	A. Panatta	1973	Miss S. V. Wade

and only lost the 1959 final after taking the first two sets from Lew Gerrard. After Knight had come from 2-5 down in the final set to beat Cliff Drysdale in the 1964 final Fred Stolle said 'They should roll up this Centre Court and give it to Billy'.

Since the event became open, Britain has had two successes in the men's singles, Mark Cox winning in 1970 and unseeded Gerald Battrick in 1971, and fiery Bob Hewitt became a popular champion in 1972 after being the beaten finalist in 1967, 1969 and 1970.

Adriano Panatta became the first Italian winner in 1973, when he gained a surprise victory from Ilie Năstase of Rumania.

Doris Hart set the record of four successive wins (1951-4). Ann Jones equalled this feat (1963-6), and Angela Mortimer (Mrs John Barrett) was champion in 1955-6, 1959 and 1961. Kay Stammers won in 1935-6 and 1939; Margaret Court, 1969-71. Mrs Court had, however, to make two unusual comebacks to win the title in 1969 and 1971. In 1969 she was 1-4 down in the final set to Winnie Shaw but then won five games running to take the title. In 1971 she again trailed 1-4, this time in the opening set to Evonne Goolagong, but played so well from this point that she won 7-5, 6-1. Virginia Wade has also won the title three times, 1967-8 and 1973.

Prize money at the first Open in 1968 totalled only £3,690 but increased to £8,650 in 1969. WILLS sponsored the event for these two years; ROTHMANS took over in 1970 and increased the prize money to £15,000, a figure equalled in 1971 and 1972. See also THE GROWTH OF THE GAME (PART 1). JO

British Isles

The British Isles, representing Great Britain and Ireland, played in the DAVIS CUP from 1900 to 1922. From 1923 GREAT BRITAIN and IRELAND challenged separately.

British Junior Championships

Three National junior championships, singles, and doubles, on hard courts, covered courts and grass courts, are held annually for boys and girls, who are under the age of 18 on 31 December of the previous year. The oldest event is the hard-court tournament, generally known as 'Junior Wimbledon'. This is now held at the All England Club and has been staged every year from 1908 except for 1914-18 and 1939-45. The first championships were played at Ventnor. Folkestone, Scarborough, Felixstowe, Windlesham, Surbiton, Weybridge and Beddington Park were also used as venues before Wimbledon became the official home in 1924. Ann (Haydon) Jones is the only Junior Wimbledon champion (1954-5) who has ever won Wimbledon. The junior covered court championships were first held during the winter of 1955-6 and have always been at the Queen's Club, London. The grass-court championships began in 1970 and are held at Devonshire Park, Eastbourne. JO

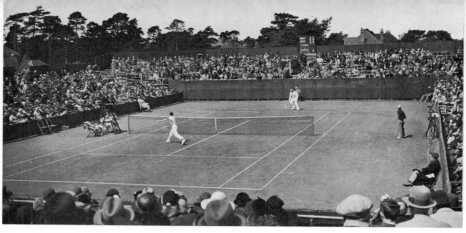

Above **British Hard Court Championships.**
Fred Perry *(near side)* v. Jack Crawford in 1937

Winners of the Junior Championships of Great Britain ('Junior Wimbledon')

Boys' Singles		Girls' Singles	
1908	C. G. Eames, Jr	1908	Miss L. E. Bull
1909	C. A. Caslon	1909	Miss E. M. Hirst
1910	P. W. James	1910	Miss V. Fison
1911	H. L. de Morpurgo	1911	Miss V. M. Speer
1912	V. Burr	1912	Miss V. M. Speer
1913	B. Martyr	1913	Miss G. B. Palmer
1914-18	*No Competition*	1914-18	*No Competition*
1919	C. H. Weinberg	1919	Miss D. Bouette
1920	C. H. Weinberg	1920	Miss J. W. Austin
1921	J. Weakley	1921	Miss J. W. Austin
1922	H. W. Austin	1922	Miss G. R. Sterry
1923	N. H. Latchford	1923	Miss B. Corbin
1924	J. S. Olliff	1924	Miss B. Nuthall
1925	J. S. Olliff	1925	Miss B. Nuthall
1926	E. R. Avory	1926	Miss B. Nuthall
1927	R. A. Court	1927	Miss N. Mackintosh
1928	F. H. D. Wilde	1928	Miss M. Heeley
1929	J. W. Nuthall	1929	Miss M. C. Scriven
1930	D. G. Freshwater	1930	Miss P. G. Brazier
1931	C. E. Hare	1931	Miss S. K. W. Hewitt
1932	H. D. B. Faber	1932	Miss J. R. Harman
1933	M. D. Deloford	1933	Miss E. N. S. Dickin
1934	R. E. Mulliken	1934	Miss D. Rowe
1935	H. T. Baxter	1935	Miss V. E. Scott
1936	H. T. Baxter	1936	Miss G. C. Hoahing
1937	G. L. Emmett	1937	Miss R. Thomas
1938	D. G. Snart	1938	Miss J. Nicoll
1939-45	*No Competition*	1939-45	*No Competition*
1946	A. G. Roberts	1946	Miss P. Rodgers
1947	A. G. Roberts	1947	Miss N. T. Seacy
1948	J. A. T. Horn	1948	Miss J. S. V. Partridge
1949	J. A. T. Horn	1949	Miss L. M. Cornell
1950	J. Prouse	1950	Miss L. M. Cornell
1951	R. K. Wilson	1951	Miss E. M. Watson
1952	W. A. Knight	1952	Miss V. A. Pitt
1953	W. A. Knight	1953	Miss V. A. Pitt
1954	G. E. Mudge	1954	Miss A. S. Haydon
1955	O. S. Prenn	1955	Miss A. S. Haydon
1956	J. I. Tattersall	1956	Miss C. C. Truman
1957	J. I. Tattersall	1957	Miss C. C. Truman
1958	H. M. Harvey	1958	Miss C. Webb
1959	J. Baker	1959	Miss R. A. Blakelock
1960	S. J. Matthews	1960	Miss R. A. Blakelock
1961	S. J. Matthews	1961	Miss F. E. Walton
1962	S. J. Matthews	1962	Miss J. C. French
1963	G. R. Stilwell	1963	Miss M. E. Greenwood
1964	G. Battrick	1964	Miss W. M. Shaw
1965	D. A. Lloyd	1965	Miss J. A. Congdon
1966	J. P. R. Williams	1966	Miss J. A. Congdon
1967	J. de Mendoza	1967	Miss D. Bridger
1968	A. F. C. Whittaker	1968	Miss D. P. Oakley
1969	M. W. Collins	1969	Miss V. A. Burton
1970	M. W. Collins	1970	Miss N. A. Dwyer
1971	C. Mottram	1971	Miss G. Coles
1972	C. Mottram	1972	Miss G. Coles
1973	J. Smith	1973	Miss S. Barker

British Under-21 Championships

This event for men and women, first held in 1962, has always been staged by the Northern Club, Manchester. The championships are normally played on grass courts but the tournament referee has the option of using any surface should the weather be bad and this has happened frequently; on occasions matches have been held on the covered courts at Stalybridge, Cheshire, 17 miles away. The championships are not restricted to British players, despite the title. Bill Bowrey (Australia) was the first winner of the men's singles in 1962, and another Australian, Wendy Gilchrist, won the women's singles in 1969. The tournament is considered ideal for those players too old for junior events but still climbing towards top-class senior standard. JO

Bromwich, John Edward (Australia)

Born Kogarah, N.S.W., 14 Nov. 1918; Wimbledon men's singles r/u 1948, s/f 1949; men's doubles s/f 1947, won 1948, 1950; mixed doubles won 1947-8, r/u 1949; US men's singles s/f 1938-9, 1947; men's doubles won 1939, 1949-50; mixed doubles r/u 1938, won 1947, r/u 1948, s/f 1950; Australian men's singles q/f 1936, r/u 1937-8, won 1939, s/f 1940, won 1946, r/u 1947-9, q/f 1950-1, s/f 1954; men's doubles r/u 1937, won 1938-40, 1946-50, r/u 1951, s/f 1954; mixed doubles won 1938, r/u 1939, 1947, 1949, 1954; French men's singles q/f 1950; men's doubles s/f 1950. Davis Cup 1937-9, 1946-7, 1949-50. Basically left-handed with a double-fisted forehand, with rare delicacy of touch. He used a very light racket loosely strung to exert exquisite ball control, always relying on placing more than pace. His doubles skill was tremendous,

as made evident by his long record of success, most notably in harness with QUIST. In doubles in the Davis Cup he was only once defeated in 21 rubbers. Wimbledon spectators were disappointed at his spectacular loss in the singles final of 1948 when after leading 5-2 in the fifth set and having three match balls he was beaten by FALKENBURG. He and BRUGNON both may be seen as the finest-ever doubles players.

Brookes, Norman Everard (Australia)

Born Melbourne, 14 Nov. 1877, died 1968; Wimbledon men's singles r/u 1905, won 1907, won 1914, r/u 1919; men's doubles r/u* 1905, won 1907, 1914, s/f 1919; US men's singles q/f 1919; men's doubles won 1919; Australian men's singles won 1911; men's doubles r/u 1911, won 1924. Davis Cup 1905, 1907-9, 1911-12, 1914, 1919-20. One of the great left-handers and the first of the great Australians. He was the first overseas player to win the men's singles at Wimbledon (1907) and in his Davis Cup career, playing for Australasia, 1905 to 1920, he took part in more live rubbers in the Challenge Round (19) than any other competitor. His total of eight Challenge Round doubles was also unique. He was knighted in 1939. See also AUSTRALIA.

Brough, Miss A. Louise [Mrs A. L. Clapp] (USA)

Born Oklahoma City, 11 Mar. 1923; Wimbledon women's singles r/u 1946, s/f 1947, won 1948-50, s/f 1951, r/u 1952, r/u 1954, won 1955, s/f 1956, q/f 1957; women's doubles won 1946, r/u 1947, won 1948-50, r/u 1951-2, won 1954, s/f 1956; mixed doubles won 1946-8, r/u 1949, won 1950, s/f 1951-2, r/u 1955; US women's singles r/u 1942-3, s/f 1944-5, q/f

1946, won 1947, r/u 1948, s/f 1949, s/f 1952-3, r/u 1954, q/f 1956, r/u 1957, q/f 1959; women's doubles won 1942-50, r/u 1952-4, won 1955-7; mixed doubles won 1942, s/f 1945, r/u 1946, won 1947-9; Australian women's singles and doubles won 1950; French women's doubles won 1946-7, won 1949, r/u 1950. Wightman Cup 1946-8, 1950, 1952-7 : 22 rubbers, won 22. A fine competitor and a notable all-round player, markedly effective on the volley. She was triple Wimbledon champion in 1950 and would have been in 1949 also had she not lost the final in the mixed. In the Wightman Cup she was invincible. Probably the best exponent of the serve-volley technique among women after Alice MARBLE, with a formidable kicking delivery. Her partnership with Margaret DUPONT was probably the most effective women's doubles pairing of all time. See GREAT PLAYERS OF ALL TIME (PART 1).

Brown, Geoffrey E. (Australia)

Born Murrurundi, N.S.W., 4 April 1924; Wimbledon men's singles r/u 1946, q/f 1947, q/f 1949; men's doubles r/u 1946, s/f 1947, 1949, r/u 1950; mixed doubles r/u 1946, 1950; US men's doubles s/f 1948; Australian men's singles s/f 1948-9, q/f 1952-3; men's doubles r/u 1949, s/f 1952-3. Davis Cup 1947-8. With a left-handed forehand, he possessed an explosive service and a tremendous two-handed punch on his right-hand side.

Brown, Tom P. (USA)

Born San Francisco, 26 Nov. 1922; Wimbledon men's singles s/f 1946, r/u 1947, q/f 1948; men's doubles won 1946, r/u 1948; mixed doubles won 1946, s/f 1947-8; US men's singles r/u 1946, q/f 1947, 1950, 1954; men's doubles s/f 1948; mixed doubles s/f 1944, won 1948; Australian men's singles s/f 1947; men's doubles s/f 1947; mixed doubles s/f 1947; French men's singles s/f 1946-7; men's doubles s/f 1946, r/u 1947; mixed doubles r/u 1946. Davis Cup 1950, 1953.

Browne, Miss Mary K. (USA)

Born 1897. Wimbledon women's doubles won 1926; mixed doubles r/u 1926; US women's singles won 1912-14, r/u 1921, s/f 1924, 1926; women's doubles won 1912-14, 1921, 1925, r/u 1926; mixed doubles won 1912-14, 1921; French women's singles r/u 1926; women's doubles s/f 1926. Wightman Cup 1925-6. Her career as a leading American woman player spanned World War I. She joined with Suzanne LENGLEN as a pro in 1926.

Brugnon, Jacques [Toto] (France)

Born Paris, 11 May 1895; Wimbledon men's singles s/f 1926, q/f 1927-8; men's doubles s/f 1925, won 1926, r/u 1927, won 1928, s/f 1930, r/u 1931, won 1932-3, r/u 1934, s/f 1936, 1939; mixed doubles s/f 1932; US men's singles q/f 1926-8; men's doubles s/f 1928; mixed doubles s/f 1927; Australian men's

Below, left **John Bromwich**

Below, right **Louise Brough**

doubles won 1928; mixed doubles s/f 1928; French men's singles r/u 1921, s/f 1924, q/f 1927-9; men's doubles won 1922, r/u 1925-6, won 1927-8, r/u 1929, won 1930, 1932, s/f 1933, won 1934, s/f 1936; mixed doubles won 1921-3, 1925-6. Davis Cup 1927-34. One of the FOUR MUSKETEERS and certainly one of the greatest-ever doubles players.

Budge, J. Donald (USA)

Born Calif., 13 June 1916; Wimbledon men's singles s/f 1935-6, won 1937-8; men's doubles s/f 1935, won 1937-8; mixed doubles r/u 1936, won 1937-8; US men's singles q/f 1935, r/u 1936, won 1937-8; men's doubles r/u 1935, won 1936, r/u 1937, won 1938; mixed doubles r/u 1936, won 1937-8; Australian men's singles won 1938; men's doubles s/f 1938; French men's singles won 1938; men's doubles r/u 1938. Davis Cup 1935-8. His rolled backhand changed the technique of the game, transforming what had always been a defensive stroke into an attacking one. Probably no player of any time had a better return of service. It is a matter for debate whether he or TILDEN was the greatest player before 1939 or, indeed, of all time. His fifth-set recovery against von CRAMM in their Davis Cup clash of 1937, coming from 1-4 to win 6-8, 5-7, 6-4, 6-2, 8-6, was a memorable display of superlative power strokes. He was the first to win the GRAND SLAM when he took the four major championships in 1938 and turned professional the same year. He made a striking professional début by beating both Ellsworth VINES and Fred PERRY at Madison Square Garden in 1939. See also THE POSTWAR PRO GAME and GREAT PLAYERS OF ALL TIME (PART 1).

Bueno, Miss Maria Esther (Brazil)

Born São Paulo, Brazil, 11 Oct. 1939; Wimbledon women's singles q/f 1958, won 1959-60, s/f 1962, q/f 1963, won 1964, r/u 1965-6, q/f 1968; women's doubles won 1958, 1960, s/f 1962, won 1963, s/f 1964, won 1965-6, r/u 1967; mixed doubles r/u 1959-60, s/f 1962, 1965, r/u 1967; US women's singles q/f 1958, won 1959, r/u 1960, s/f 1962, won 1963-4, s/f 1965, won 1966, s/f 1968; women's doubles r/u 1958-9, won 1960, 1962, r/u 1963, won 1966, 1968; Australian women's singles q/f 1960, r/u 1965; women's doubles won 1960, s/f 1965; mixed doubles s/f 1960; French women's singles s/f 1958, q/f 1959, s/f 1960, q/f 1961, r/u 1964, s/f 1965-6, q/f 1967-8; women's doubles won 1960, r/u 1961, s/f 1964, 1968; mixed doubles s/f 1958, won 1960, s/f 1964, r/u 1965. Probably the most graceful, majestic and fluent hitter of the ball of all time. Her impeccable timing enabled her to get vast pace for little muscular effort. Her service could be devastating in speed and length. But with little margin of error, the balance between success and failure was always delicately poised. She was unlucky with injuries and unlucky, too, to be at her peak in the same years as the more robust Margaret COURT,

against whom she lost more often than she won. She became a national heroine of Brazil. After her Wimbledon triumphs (1959-60) she was honoured by a statue in her native São Paulo and by a postage stamp. (See colour plate, page 86 and GREAT PLAYERS OF ALL TIME, PART 1.)

Above Maria Bueno

Bulgaria

The first lawn-tennis courts in Bulgaria were built in 1896 in Sofia and tennis gradually developed in the towns of Varna, Ruse, Plovdiv, and elsewhere. The first tennis club was founded in Bulgaria in 1911 and the national championships have been held regularly. However, tennis as a sport really developed in Bulgaria after World War II when more courts were constructed.

The Bulgarian Lawn Tennis Federation was affiliated to the ILTF in 1932, was expelled in 1946 and readmitted in 1951. It has been particularly active in the last ten years. Bulgaria has regularly participated in the DAVIS CUP since 1964, took part in the FEDERATION CUP in 1966 and 1968-9, has organized the University Games and the Balkan Championships, and in 1969 was given the honour of holding the second European Amateur Championships.

In 1972 there were nine clubs affiliated to the BLTF with over 2,000 registered members, but there are also many other amateurs playing the game. There are about 120 tennis courts in the country. BR
GOVERNING BODY: Bulgarian Lawn Tennis Federation, Boul. Tolboukhin 18, Sofia

Bundy, Miss Dorothy M. [Mrs Cheney] (USA)

Born Los Angeles, Calif. 1 Sept. 1916; Wimble-

don women's singles s/f 1946; women's doubles s/f 1946; mixed doubles r/u 1946; US women's singles q/f 1936, s/f 1937, q/f 1939, s/f 1944, q/f 1945; women's doubles s/f 1944-5; mixed doubles r/u 1944, s/f 1955; Australian women's singles won 1938; women's doubles r/u 1938; French women's singles s/f 1946; mixed doubles r/u 1946. Wightman Cup 1937-9. The first American to win the Australian women's singles. Daughter of May SUTTON.

Bungert, Wilhelm P. (W. Germany)

Born Mannheim, 1 April 1939; Wimbledon men's singles s/f 1963-4, r/u 1967 (unseeded); Australian men's singles q/f 1962; French men's doubles r/u 1962; South African men's singles won 1963. Davis Cup 1958-71. A player of great flair but lacking consistency.

Burma

Lawn tennis was introduced into Burma early in the 20th century and was played largely in British clubs. After independence the Burma Lawn Tennis Federation was founded in 1949 and affiliated to the ILTF in 1951. There are at present 200-300 affiliated clubs and several thousand players.

The Burma National Championships began in 1905 and are played regularly in Rangoon. Burma first entered a team in the DAVIS CUP in 1955. There are now coaching schemes for promising young players. BR
GOVERNING BODY: Burma Tennis Federation, Aungsan Stadium, Rangoon

Buttsworth, Mrs Coral [Miss C. McInnes] (Australia)

Australian women's singles won 1931-2, r/u 1933; women's doubles won 1932. Her career was confined to Australia.

Buxton, Miss Angela (Gt Britain)

Born Liverpool, 16 Aug. 1934; Wimbledon women's singles q/f 1955, r/u 1956; women's doubles won 1956; US women's doubles s/f 1955; French women's singles q/f 1954, s/f 1956; women's doubles s/f 1955, won 1956. Wightman Cup 1954-6. A good tactician of great determination.

Bye

A player who draws a bye goes through to the next round of a competition without playing a match. When the number of entries in a draw is not exactly 2, 4, 8, 16, 32, 64 or a higher power of 2, there must be byes in the first round to achieve the right number of players in the second. The number of byes is equal to the difference between the number of entries and the next higher power of two: for example, if there are 57 entries there will be 7 byes (64 minus 57). In an artificial draw byes can be used to ensure that SEEDED players or nations do not have to compete too early. In most draws byes are placed according to a set formula. See also DRAW. DC

C

Cahill, Miss Mabel E. (USA)
US women's singles won 1891-2; women's doubles won 1891-2; mixed doubles won 1892.

Cămărăşescu Cup SEE RUMANIA

Cambodia
Cambodia has been an Associate Member of the ILTF since 1963. BR
GOVERNING BODY: Fédération Cambodgienne de Tennis, 98 Vithei Dekcho Damdin, Phnom-Penh

Cameroon Republic
Although lawn tennis has been played in the Cameroons for many years the national association was founded only in 1966 and affiliated to the ILTF as an Associate Member in 1971. There are 20 clubs. The National Championships have been played at the capital, Yaoundé, since 1968. BR
GOVERNING BODY: Fédération Camerounaise de Lawn-Tennis, B.P. 1121, Yaoundé

Campbell, Oliver Samuel (USA)
Born 25 Feb. 1871; Wimbledon men's doubles s/f 1892; US men's singles s/f 1888, won 1890-2; men's doubles won 1888, r/u 1889, won 1891-2, r/u 1893. The youngest man to win the US singles championship: 19 years 6 months 9 days old when he won in 1890.

Canada
Not long after Canadian Confederation was proclaimed (1867) interest in the game of lawn tennis began to spread and develop. The Toronto Lawn Tennis Club was formed before what is believed to be Canada's first officially recorded tennis tournament, played in 1878 on the lawns of the Montreal Cricket Club. About that time a tournament at Toronto attracted players from other places in Ontario: Ottawa, Barrie, London, St Catherines, Peterborough and Brantford. In 1880 an outstanding player appeared on the Canadian tennis scene: J. F. Hellmuth, K.C., of the London, Ontario, Tennis Club. Hailed as Champion of Montreal, Hellmuth entered the US Tennis Championships at Staten Island, N.Y., reaching the final of the men's singles where he met O. E. Woodhouse of the West Middlesex (England) LTC, who defeated the Canadian 54-50 in points in a four-set final. Woodhouse was one of England's best players: that summer he had defeated both the Renshaw brothers in

singles at Wimbledon (see THE BIRTH AND SPREAD OF LAWN TENNIS and THE UNITED STATES STORY, PART 1).

Interest in tennis mushroomed throughout Canada during the years that followed. New clubs appeared at Victoria and Vancouver on the Pacific Coast, at Winnipeg, Manitoba, on the Prairies, at both Saint John and Fredericton in New Brunswick and on the Atlantic Coast at Halifax in Nova Scotia. Again, in 1887, the London, Ontario, TC produced an outstanding player: C. S. Hyman, who captured the men's singles title in 1887-9 in tournaments held in Toronto.

In 1890 the Canadian Lawn Tennis Association was formed, at meetings held at the Queen's Hotel, Toronto, on 1 and 2 July. C. S. Hyman was the first President. An official Canadian Championship tournament was staged in Toronto on 1 September 1890. E. E. Tanner of Buffalo, N.Y. won the men's singles. Meanwhile, also in 1890, the Province of Quebec LTA Inter-Club Series was organized in Montreal, and McGill University defeated Saint Antoine 4-2 to capture the league title. A Canadian women's singles championship event was included in the third annual championships of the CLTA, held in 1892 on the courts of the Toronto LTC. A Miss Osborne became the first woman champion of Canada, defeating a Mrs Smith 9-7, 7-9, 6-2, 8-6 in a *four-set* final. Maritime Provinces Champion Miss MacLaren of Saint John, N.B., also competed but lost in the semi-finals.

Canada entered world-wide competition for the first time in 1913 by filing a challenge for the DAVIS CUP. Surprisingly, it eliminated South Africa 3-1 and Belgium 4-0 to reach the final, losing to the United States 0-3 at Wimbledon. The United States went on to win the Challenge Round from the British Isles, the holders. The Canadian team, led by

Below **Canada.** The lawn tennis tournament in Toronto, 1881

R. B. Powell, included B. P. Schwengers, H. G. Mayes and Captain J. F. Foulkes. CLTA Past President Garnet H. Meldrum was the non-playing team captain. Canada continues to take part in major international competitions such as the Davis Cup and FEDERATION CUP.

Canada joined the ILTF in 1923. The present CLTA Representative in Europe is J. Trevor Spurgen of London, England. The International Lawn Tennis Club of Canada was formed in 1965 and was accepted the same year for membership in the body of INTERNATIONAL LAWN TENNIS CLUBS.

Canadian seniors (VETERANS) compete in many international competitions. They play the United States each year for the Gordon Trophy donated by Canadian industrialist G. Blair Gordon. They also compete for the Stevens Cup at Forest Hills, N.Y., and are eligible to contest the DUBLER CUP in Europe through membership of the VETERAN INTERNATIONAL TENNIS ASSOCIATION.

Since 1968 the annual National Championships in Toronto have been divided into two sections, open and closed. Leading up to these important National Championships are ten Provincial Championships scheduled for play from coast to coast (Vancouver to Montreal) during July and August.

Promotion of junior tennis in Canada has occupied the attention of the CLTA from as early as 1905, when individual events were arranged for National titles. In 1949 a full-scale Canadian Junior Championship meeting was organized by the CLTA. The tournament has now expanded to include both closed and open championships. The 21-event meeting annually attracts an entry of over 300 juniors from all over Canada and the United States. Rod Laver of Australia is a former winner of the Boys 18 Singles crown.

The 1967 Canadian Centennial Junior Tennis Championships were held in Ottawa, Ontario, on the courts of the Rideau Lawn Tennis Club, and attracted entries from 11 member nations of the ILTF: Australia, Barbados, Great Britain, Kenya, Norway, Tanzania, Thailand, Trinidad, Tobago, Uganda and the United States. Britain sent J. O. R. Williams of Wales, who won the Boys 18 Singles, and Corinne Molesworth. The United States sent Junior Wightman Cup team Peaches Bartkowicz, Patti Hogan, Vicki Rogers and Linda Tuero. Former Canadian Prime Minister the Rt Hon. Lester Bowles Pearson presided over the awarding of the Centennial Medals. More than 300 juniors competed.

Leading up to the National Junior Championship tournament, which is held at different venues, more than a score of both open and closed Provincial Junior Championships are held from coast to coast.

The Canadian Lawn Tennis Association directs the holding of all of these activities under the auspices of the Provincial Lawn Tennis Associations. Vast distances, as much as 3,000 miles in one instance, separate the ten autonomous Provincial LTAs. Each of these groups operates as a separate entity electing officers and committee chairmen annually. The Province of Quebec LTA was organized in 1899, although a group of tennis officials in the Montreal area had operated as an unofficial Quebec governing body as early as 1890 when the PQLTA Inter-Club Series started. The British Columbia LTA is unique in being a member group of the Pacific Northwest LTA, a sectional association of the United States LTA, as well as being a direct member of the Canadian LTA. The British Columbia LTA program is closely integrated with those in the US states of Oregon, Washington and California. The Ontario LTA was formed in Barrie in 1918. This is Canada's largest provincial association and comprises more than 100 tennis clubs with a total individual membership exceeding 7,000.

The many and varied activities of the Canadian LTA are supported by revenue from player registration fees, Federal Government grants and commercial sponsors. Every member of a member club of a Provincial LTA pays $1.35 to his or her club to assist in the promotion of both Provincial LTA and Canadian LTA activities: 75 cents goes to the CLTA and 60 cents is retained by the Provincial LTA. Canada has more than 300 tennis clubs and 21,000 registered players. The National Advisory Council on Fitness and Amateur Sports gives financial assistance for many CLTA activities, including support for both Davis Cup and Federation Cup teams. The grant from the Federal Government to send more than 100 juniors to the Canadian Junior Championships exceeds $27,000. ROTHMANS of Pall Mall Canada Ltd generously underwrites the holding of both the Canadian Open and the Canadian Closed Tennis Championships. Tournaments sponsored by Rothmans are also held in Vancouver, B.C., Montreal, P.Q. and Quebec City, P.Q. In 1972 Rothmans assisted Provincial LTAs with Inter-Sectional Team matches and sponsored the Canadian Inter-

Canadian Championships Winners

Men's Singles

1890	E. E. Tanner
1891	F. S. Mansfield
1892	F. H. Hovey
1893	H. E. Avery
1894	R. W. P. Matthews
1895	W. A. Larned
1896	R. D. Wrenn
1897	L. E. Ware
1898	L. E. Ware
1899	M. D. Whitman
1900	M. D. Whitman
1901	W. A. Larned
1902	B. C. Wright
1903	B. C. Wright
1904	B. C. Wright
1905	*No Competition*
1906	I. C. Wright
1907	J. F. Foulkes
1908	T. Y. Sherwell
1909	J. F. Foulkes
1910	J. F. Foulkes
1911	B. P. Schwengers
1912	B. P. Schwengers
1913	R. Baird
1914	T. M. Sherwell
1915-18	*No Competition*
1919	S. Kashio
1920	P. Bennett
1921	W. J. Bates
1922	F. Anderson
1923	W. L. Rennie
1924	G. M. Lott
1925	W. F. Crocker
1926	L. De Turenne
1927	J. A. Wright
1928	W. Allison
1929	J. A. Wright
1930	G. L. Rogers
1931	J. Wright
1932	F. Parker
1933	J. Murio
1934	M. Rainville
1935	E. Smith
1936	J. Tidball
1937	W. Senior
1938	F. Parker
1939	P. Morley Lewis
1940	D. McDiarmid
1941-45	*No Competition*
1946	P. Morley Lewis
1947	J. Evert
1948	W. Tully
1949	H. Rochon
1950	B. Macken
1951	T. Vincent
1952	R. Savitt
1953	M. G. Rose
1954	B. Bartzen
1955	R. Bedard
1956	N. Brown
1957	R. Bedard
1958	R. Bedard
1959	R. Garrido
1960	L. Legenstein
1961	W. Reed
1962	J. Couder
1963	W. Reed
1964	R. Emerson
1965	R. Holmberg
1966	A. Fox
1967	M. Santana
1968	R. Krishnan
1969	C. Richey
1970	R. Laver
1971	J. Newcombe
1972	I. Năstase
1973	T. Okker

Women's Singles

1919	Miss M. Zinderstein
1920	Mrs H. Bickle
1921	Mrs H. Bickle
1922	Mrs H. Bickle
1923	Miss F. Best
1924	Mrs H. Bickle
1925	Miss M. Leaming
1926	Miss M. Leaming
1927	Miss C. Swartz
1928	Miss M. Gladman
1929	Miss O. Wade
1930	Miss O. Wade
1931	Miss E. Cross
1932	Miss O. Wade
1933	Miss G. Wheeler
1934	Miss C. Deacon
1935	Miss M. Osborne
1936	Dr E. Bartosh
1937	Miss E. M. Dearman
1938	Mrs R. Bolte
1939	Miss E. Blackman
1940	Miss E. Young
1941-45	*No Competition*
1946	Mrs B. Lewis
1947	Miss G. Kelleher
1948	Miss P. Macken
1949	Mrs B. Lewis
1950	Miss B. Knapp
1951	Mrs L. Davidson
1952	Miss M. Ramirez
1953	Miss M. Ramirez
1954	Miss K. Fageros
1955	Mrs H. Sladek
1956	Miss J. Laird
1957	Mrs L. Brown
1958	Miss E. Dodge
1959	Mrs M. Martin
1960	Miss D. Floyd
1961	Miss A. Haydon
1962	Miss A. Barclay
1963	Miss A. Barclay
1964	Miss B. Senn
1965	Miss J. M. Heldman
1966	Miss R. Bentley
1967	Miss K. Harter
1968	Miss J. Bartkowicz
1969	Miss F. Urban
1970	Mrs B. M. Court
1971	Miss F. Durr
1972	Miss E. F. Goolagong
1973	Miss E. F. Goolagong

Provincial Tennis Team Championships at Ottawa at which every Canadian province was represented. PEPSI-COLA Canada Ltd has spent more than $100,000 during the past decade sponsoring junior tennis in Canada. Its annual grant exceeds $16,000.

Canada has an unusual sports support program, initiated by Federal Health Minister the Hon. John Munro, which is the lifeblood of the CLTA. The Sports Administrative Centre at Ottawa provides a salary for the CLTA Executive Director, office space, secretarial and clerical assistance and the use of all office facilities. The Executive Directors of more than 30 other national sports organizations are also housed in the Sports Administrative Centre.

R. N. Watt of Westmount, P.Q., has been the only Canadian so far to head the ILTF. He was President of the CLTA in 1937-45. His son, M. Laird Watt, C.A., of Hampstead, P.Q., was CLTA President, 1962-3. R. N. Watt and M. Laird Watt were US Father and Son Champions in 1933, 1934 and 1937.

A villain emerges in every history and Canadian tennis history is no exception. In 1913 an immigrant from Germany arrived in Ottawa and joined the Rideau Lawn Tennis Club. He was a wine salesman and went by the name of Ribben. An accomplished tennis player, he reached the semi-finals of the men's singles in the 1913 and 1914 Ottawa City Championships. When World War I was declared Ribben left suddenly for Germany with the Royal Canadian Mounted Police hot on his trail. After World War II and the Nuremberg Trials the first Nazi war criminal to hang was Ribben – German Foreign Minister Joachim von Ribbentrop. ECC

GOVERNING BODY: Canadian Lawn Tennis Association, Federal Government Sports Administration Centre, 333 River Road, Vanier City, Ontario K1L 8B9

Carter, Miss Mary see Mrs S. J. REITANO

Casals, Miss Rosemary (USA)

Born San Francisco, 16 Sept. 1948; Wimbledon women's singles s/f 1967, s/f 1969-70, s/f 1972, q/f 1973; women's doubles won 1967-8, 1970-1, 1973; mixed doubles won 1970, s/f 1971, won 1972; US women's singles s/f 1966, 1969, r/u 1970-1, q/f 1972-3; women's doubles r/u 1966, won 1967, r/u 1968, 1970, s/f 1972, r/u 1973; mixed doubles r/u 1967, 1972, s/f 1973; Australian women's singles s/f 1967, q/f 1968-9; mixed doubles s/f 1969; French women's singles q/f 1969-70; women's doubles r/u 1968, 1970; mixed doubles s/f 1968, 1970. Federation Cup 1967. Wightman Cup 1967. ILTF GP 3rd 1972. Became professional 1968.

Centre Court

All tennis venues have one main court at a championship or tournament which is often called the Centre Court – but the term is generally associated throughout the world

Above **Rosemary Casals**

with Wimbledon's famous Centre Court. It is a hallowed piece of turf, never used between Championships since the Davis Cup Challenge Round was last played there in 1936, with the one exception of the Professional Tournament played at Wimbledon in August 1967.

Wimbledon's Centre Court, part of the 'new' Wimbledon opened in 1922, has 10,681 seats and room for slightly fewer than 3,000 standing, almost double the crowd capacity on No. 1 court. For Centre Court classic matches see PART 1. DC

Centre Mark

A line 4 in (10·16 cm) long and 2 in (5·08 cm) wide drawn inside the court at right angles from the baseline at its centre point. The player serving does so first from the right side of the centre mark. After the point has been decided he serves from the left side and alternately for the rest of the game. Should he touch the ground at or beyond the centre the foot-fault judge should call a fault (see FOOT FAULT). JO

Centrope Cup see HUNGARY

Ceylon see SRI LANKA

Chair, Umpire's see UMPIRE'S CHAIR

Chambers, Mrs Dorothea Katherine Lambert [Miss D. K. Douglass] (Gt Britain)

Born Ealing, 3 Sept. 1878, died 1960; Wimbledon women's singles q/f 1900, s/f 1902, won 1903-4, r/u 1905, won 1906, r/u 1907, q/f 1908, won 1910-11, 1913-14, r/u 1919-20; women's doubles r/u 1913, s/f 1914; r/u 1919, 1920, s/f 1923-5; mixed doubles r/u 1919, s/f 1925; US women's singles q/f 1925; women's doubles

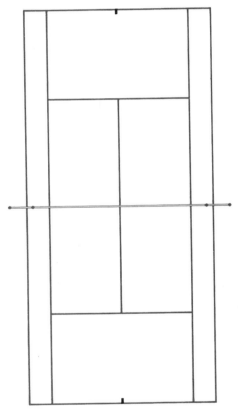

Above **Centre Mark**

s/f 1925. Wightman Cup 1925-6. Became coaching professional 1928. Probably the greatest woman player before 1914; her loss in the 1919 Wimbledon challenge round to Suzanne LENGLEN, after having two match balls, was one of the most famous encounters in the history of the game (see CENTRE COURT CLASSICS, PART 1). She played in the Wightman

Cup for Gt Britain in 1926, 23 years after her first Wimbledon singles title and when 47 years old. Despite the interval during World War I she won Wimbledon seven times, a record only equalled by William RENSHAW and beaten by Helen Wills MOODY. See GREAT PLAYERS OF ALL TIME (PART 1).

Championship of Europe see THE GROWTH OF THE GAME (PART 1)

Changing Ends
The players change ends after every odd game throughout a match (see RULE 26, PART 1). They must take not more than one minute to refresh themselves. JO

Changing Order of Service see RULE 33 (PART 1)

Chase in Real Tennis, see THE ORIGINS OF LAWN TENNIS (PART 1)

Chile
Of Chile's population of 9 million, 3 million live in Santiago, the capital and the lawn tennis centre. Tennis is also played in many other towns, in particular Valparaiso and Viña del Mar. The Federación de Lawn Tennis de Chile, which has been a Full Member of the ILTF since 1927, has 150 affiliated clubs with approximately 600 courts. There are about 10,000 players. Principal clubs are the French, the Israelite, the Spanish and the Catholic University Clubs of Santiago.

Tennis was first played in Chile in the 20th century and has developed to such an extent that its national tournaments and top players are well known throughout the world. Among players of international class have been the Harnecker brothers, Anita Lizana, who was so popular at Wimbledon, and Davis Cup players Luis Ayala, Patricio Rodriguez, Patricio Cornejo, Jaime Fillol and Jaime Pinto. The most promising young players are Belus Prajoux and Hans Gildermeister. The Chilean Federation is making a special effort to encourage young players and has several training schools.

Chile first took part in the DAVIS CUP in 1928 when its team travelled to Spain and lost 4 matches to 1. Since World War II it has done particularly well and in 1972 reached the American Zone Final after defeating the strong Brazilian team. It took part in the FEDERATION CUP in 1968. BR

GOVERNING BODY: Federación de Lawn Tennis de Chile, Casilla 1149, Santiago

Chile Cup see SOUTH AMERICAN CHAMPIONSHIPS

China
Up to 1938 the Chinese National Amateur Athletic Federation, with headquarters in Peking, was, as the body controlling tennis in China, affiliated to the ILTF. At the first ILTF meeting after World War II (1946), a new

Above **Mrs Dorothea Lambert Chambers** (1910)

organization, the All China Athletic Federation, in Peking (succeeded by the China Sports Federation of the People's Republic of China) was recognized as the successor to the previous association. In 1957 the China National Association (Formosa) applied for affiliation on the grounds that their association represented lawn tennis in all China. The application was refused. In 1970, however, it was agreed that the LTA of the Republic of China (TAIWAN) should be affiliated. As a result, claiming that there could not be 'two Chinas', the All China Sports Federation of the Peoples' Republic of China (Peking) withdrew. China's best player, who played at Wimbledon before World War II, was Kho Sin Kie. BR

Chop
Sometimes known as underspin, the reverse of topspin (see SPIN). The ball is struck from top to bottom so that the bottom of the ball rotates towards the line of flight. Chop increases wind resistance at the bottom of the ball but reduces it at the top. Depending on the court surface, atmospheric condition and the way the chop is applied, the ball may be made to keep low by skidding slightly, or stop short and 'sit up', even recoiling slightly if the chop is extreme. It is in the latter way that good DROPSHOTS are performed. JO

Chopper Grip see GRIPS

Church Cup
An American team competition for men, originally (1918-32) between teams from Boston, New York and Philadelphia. From 1946 (it was not held 1933-45) the teams represented New England, the Eastern and the Middle States; they were joined by the Middle Atlantic States in 1947. The first winner was New York, which defeated Philadelphia 6-3. The Cup was given by George Myers Church.

'Closed' Grips see GRIPS

'Closed' Tournament see OPEN

Clothes see FASHION, MEN'S CLOTHING

Clothier, William J. (USA)
Born Philadelphia, 27 Sept. 1881, died 1962; Wimbledon men's doubles s/f 1905; US men's singles q/f 1901, r/u* 1903, 1904, q/f 1905, won 1906, s/f 1908, r/u 1909, s/f 1912, q/f 1913, s/f 1914; men's doubles r/u 1907; mixed doubles r/u 1912. Davis Cup 1905, 1909.

Coaching see THE BASIC TEACHING OF TENNIS (PART 1)

Cochet, Henri (France)
Born Lyons, France, 14 Dec. 1901; Wimbledon men's singles s/f 1925-6, won 1927, r/u 1928, won 1929, q/f 1930, s/f 1933; men's doubles s/f 1925, won 1926, r/u 1927, won 1928, s/f 1930, r/u 1931; mixed doubles s/f 1930, s/f 1932; US men's singles s/f 1926, won 1928, r/u 1932; men's doubles s/f 1928, s/f 1932; mixed doubles s/f 1926, won 1927, s/f 1932; French men's singles won 1922, s/f 1924, q/f 1925, won 1926, s/f 1927, won 1928, s/f 1929, won 1930, 1932, r/u 1933; men's doubles r/u 1923-6, won 1927, r/u 1928-9, won 1930, 1932, s/f 1933; mixed doubles r/u 1923, 1925, won 1928-9, r/u 1930, s/f 1932. Davis Cup 1922-4, 1926-33 (in winning team 1927-32). One of the FOUR MUSKETEERS. A player of rare genius in that his ability to half-volley and always to take an exceptionally early ball enabled him to dispense with the normal demands of quick footwork. He looked lazy on the court, was unpredictable and sometimes had bad defeats. But his recuperative capacity was strong as exemplified by the most remarkable Wimbledon singles victory of all time in 1927 (see CENTRE COURT CLASSICS, PART 1). In the quarter-final he lost the first two sets to the American Frank Hunter, in the semi-final he lost the first two sets and recovered from 1-5 in the third to TILDEN and in the final he lost the first two sets and saved six match points against BOROTRA. He became a professional in 1933 but was reinstated as an amateur in 1945. See GREAT PLAYERS OF ALL TIME (PART 1).

Colombia
The Colombian Tennis Association controls the game of lawn tennis in Colombia through its affiliated leagues. The CTA was founded in 1930 and affiliated to the ILTF in 1934. It is also affiliated to the South American Federation, the Pan-American Federation and the local Olympic Committee.

Colombia has played in the DAVIS CUP since 1959 and in the FEDERATION CUP in 1972; their best players, in particular William Alvarez, Iván Molina, and Jairo Velasco, have taken part in tournaments overseas. Señorita Isabel Fernandez de Soto has been the outstanding woman in the last few years.

There are 40 tennis clubs with about 200 courts, practically all with clay surfaces.

Apart from the clubs, the development of the game on public courts is encouraged to give everyone in the country an opportunity to play. There are some 2,000 affiliated players, but the actual figure of those who play the game is much higher.

The National Sports Association gives assistance for coaching.

Many international players have had the pleasure of competing in the International Championships of Colombia, first played in Bogota, but recently in the city of Barranquilla. BR

GOVERNING BODY: Asociación Colombiana de Tennis, Apartado aéro 10.917, Calle 15, No. 13-18 Piso 4°, Interior 4, Bogota

Colombia Cup see SOUTH AMERICAN CHAMPIONSHIPS

Commercial Union Life Assurance Company

Insurance company and sponsor of the ILTF GRAND PRIX from 1 January 1972, succeeding PEPSI-COLA. Its announcement that it would contribute £100,000 a year for two years, including £20,000 for the annual Masters' Tournament, marked the first time that a British financial institution had entered into sports sponsorship on such a scale. A key figure in the negotiations was Mr Allan Heyman, Q.C., President of the ILTF in 1971-4. Commercial Union's interests fit the pattern of Grand Prix events for, like the competition, it is worldwide, but exists substantially in the United States, Canada, Australia, South Africa and Western Europe. The mainspring of Commercial Union's support of lawn tennis has been its Assistant General Manager, Geoff Mullis. DC

Commonwealth Caribbean LTA

Originally called the British Caribbean LTA, this association was formed by the LTAs of the Bahamas, BARBADOS, GUYANA, JAMAICA, St Lucia, St Vincent and TRINIDAD AND TOBAGO in 1947, changing its name to the Commonwealth Caribbean LTA in 1970. It provides a team for the DAVIS CUP and sponsors an annual Inter-Caribbean tournament, the Brandon Trophy. Some of the LTAs in the smaller territories are not separately affiliated to the ILTF. BR

Congo, Democratic Republic of see ZAIRE

Congo Republic

The LTA of the Congo Republic (capital Brazzaville) first affiliated to the ILTF in 1961. It reaffiliated as an Associate Member in 1973. BR

GOVERNING BODY: Fédération Congolaise de Lawn-Tennis, B.P. 2092, Brazzaville

Connolly, Miss Maureen ['Little Mo'; Mrs N. Brinker] (USA)

Born San Diego, Calif., 17 Sept. 1934, died 1969; Wimbledon women's singles won 1952-4; women's doubles r/u 1952-3; mixed doubles s/f 1954; US women's singles won 1951-3; women's doubles r/u 1952, s/f 1953; mixed doubles s/f 1952; Australian women's singles and doubles won 1953; mixed doubles r/u 1953; French women's singles won 1953-4; women's doubles r/u 1953; won 1954; mixed doubles r/u 1953, won 1954. Wightman Cup 1951-4. Certainly one of the all-time greats of the women's game and the first woman to win the GRAND SLAM (1953). She was only 16 when she won her first US championship and 17 when she won Wimbledon at her first attempt. She was still under 20 when her career came to an end after breaking her leg while riding. In 1953-4 she won the Wimbledon singles for the total loss of only 19 games in six matches. She was essentially a baseliner, driving with rare accuracy and power. Her backhand was over-whelmingly strong. She was naturally a left-hander who adapted to play from the other wing. See CENTRE COURT CLASSICS and GREAT PLAYERS OF ALL TIME (PART 1).

Connors, James Scott [Jimmy] (USA)

Born East St Louis, Ill. 2 Sept. 1952; Wimbledon men's singles q/f 1973; men's doubles won 1973; US men's singles q/f 1973; mixed doubles s/f 1973; r/u French men's doubles

Below **Maureen ('Little Mo') Connolly**

1973; won US Indoor Open and US Pro 1973. ILTF GP 7th 1972. Joined WCT 1972. Two-handed on right-hand side.

Continental Grip see GRIPS

Cooke, Mrs E. T. see Miss Sarah PALFREY

Cooper, Ashley John (Australia)

Born Melbourne, 15 Sept. 1936; Wimbledon men's singles r/u 1957, won 1958; men's doubles s/f 1956, r/u 1958, r/u 1973; mixed doubles s/f 1973; US men's singles q/f 1956, r/u 1957, won 1958; men's doubles s/f 1956, won 1957, s/f 1958; Australian men's singles q/f 1954-6, 1973; men's doubles s/f 1955-6, r/u 1957, won 1958; French men's singles s/f 1956-8; men's doubles r/u 1956, won 1957-8. Davis Cup 1957-8. Became a professional in 1959. A solid and persistent, if rather mechanical, player.

Cooper, Miss Charlotte see Mrs A. STERRY

Coupe For all competitions known as Coupe ——— see ——— CUP

Court Dimensions (current) see RULES 1 and 32 (PART 1); (in the past) see THE BIRTH AND SPREAD OF LAWN TENNIS (PART 1)

Court, Mrs Margaret [Miss M. Smith] (Australia)

Born Albury, N.S.W., 16 July 1942; Wimbledon women's singles q/f 1961, won 1963, r/u 1964, won 1965, s/f 1966, q/f 1968, s/f 1969, won 1970, r/u 1971, s/f 1973; women's doubles r/u 1961, s/f 1962, r/u 1963, won 1964, r/u 1966, won 1969, s/f 1970, r/u 1971; mixed doubles s/f 1961, won 1963, r/u 1964, won 1965-6, 1968, s/f 1969, r/u 1971; US women's

Above **Jimmy Connors**

singles s/f 1961, won 1962, r/u 1963, won 1965, q/f 1968, won 1969-70, s/f 1972, won 1973; women's doubles won 1963, r/u 1964, won 1968, r/u 1969, won 1970, r/u 1972; mixed doubles won 1961-5, won 1969-70, 1972; Australian women's singles won 1960-6; r/u 1968, won 1969-71, 1973; women's doubles r/u 1960, won 1961-3, r/u 1964, won 1965, r/u 1966, s/f 1968, won 1969-71, 1973; mixed doubles won 1963-5, s/f 1966, r/u 1968; French women's singles q/f 1961, won 1962, q/f 1963, won 1964, r/u 1965, s/f 1966, won 1969-70, 1973; women's doubles r/u 1962-3, won 1964-6, r/u 1969, s/f 1970, won 1973; mixed doubles s/f 1961, won 1963-5, won 1969, s/f 1970, r/u 1973. Federation Cup 1963-5, 1968-71. ILTF GP 6th 1972.

An athlete of rare power and Australia's greatest woman player. With her long reach she added a new dimension to women's volleying. In achievement her record surpasses by far that of any other player, man or woman. Uniquely she has won every title, singles, women's doubles and mixed doubles of every important championship. Between 1960 and the end of 1972 when she won the Australian singles for the 11th time she won 85 major titles. She was GRAND SLAM winner in 1970 and, with Ken FLETCHER, took the Grand Slam of mixed doubles in 1963. See colour plate, page 104, GREAT PLAYERS OF ALL TIME and CENTRE COURT CLASSICS (PART 1).

Court Surfaces see PART 1

Court Tennis see THE ORIGINS OF LAWN TENNIS (PART 1)

Covered Courts
Courts that have a roof to protect them from bad weather. They are usually situated inside buildings but some outdoor courts or 'air halls' have been converted by the use of inflatable plastic balloon-like coverings that can be taken down in warm weather. Covered courts are most frequently found in Scandinavia, where long winters prevent play outdoors for several months each year. JO

Cox, Mark (Gt Britain)
Born Leicester, 5 July 1943; Wimbledon men's doubles s/f 1966; US men's singles q/f 1966; Australian men's singles q/f 1967; mixed

doubles s/f 1963. Davis Cup 1967-9, 1973. At the world's first open tournament, the British Hard Court Championships at Bournemouth (April 1968), as an amateur he beat two of the world's leading professionals, GONZALEZ and EMERSON. WCT pro 1968-73. WCT 4th (F q/f) 1972; 4th Group B 1973.

Coyne, Miss T. see Mrs T. D. LONG

Cramm, Baron Gottfried von (Germany)
Born Germany, 7 July 1909; Wimbledon men's singles r/u 1935-7; men's doubles s/f 1933, s/f 1937; mixed doubles won 1933, s/f 1935; US men's singles r/u 1937; men's doubles won 1937; Australian men's singles s/f 1938; men's doubles r/u 1938; French men's singles won 1934, r/u 1935, won 1936; men's doubles won 1937. Davis Cup 1932-53. Noted for his purity

Above **Margaret Court**

of classic style and impeccable sportsmanship, he brought the German game to a peak in the late 1930s. Ironically he found his greatest fame as a loser rather than winner, his defeat by BUDGE in the Inter-Zone final of the Davis Cup in 1937, with Budge winning 6-8, 5-7, 6-4, 6-2, 8-6, from 2-5 in the fifth set, being held as one of the greatest matches ever. Then, too, he was three times singles finalist at Wimbledon, losing in 1935 and 1936 to PERRY and in 1937 to Budge. He fell foul of the Nazi regime in Germany and was imprisoned by the Gestapo in 1938. After World War II he won the German singles in 1949, aged 40.

Crawford, John Herbert (Australia)
Born Australia, 22 March 1908; Wimbledon men's singles s/f 1932, won 1933, r/u 1934, s/f 1935, q/f 1936-7; men's doubles won 1935; mixed doubles r/u 1928, won 1930; US men's

singles q/f 1928, r/u 1933; mixed doubles s/f 1928, 1933; Australian men's singles q/f 1927, s/f 1928, 1930, won 1931-3, r/u 1934, won 1935, r/u 1936, s/f 1937, 1939; men's doubles s/f 1927, won 1929-30, r/u 1931, won 1932, r/u 1933, s/f 1934, won 1935, r/u 1936, s/f 1938-9, 1949; mixed doubles s/f 1927, r/u 1929-30, won 1931-3, s/f 1938; French men's singles q/f 1928, won 1933, r/u 1934, s/f 1935; men's doubles s/f 1930, 1934, won 1935; mixed doubles won 1933, s/f 1934. Davis Cup 1928, 1930, 1932-7. The purity of his game was like a breath from the past in the 1930s and his classic ground strokes combined with his flat-topped racket and long-sleeved shirts which he seldom rolled up evoked an image of the game before 1914. His Wimbledon singles victory in the final over Ellsworth VINES in 1933 (see CENTRE COURT

Above **Gottfried von Cramm**

CLASSICS, PART 1) was acknowledged as one of the most perfect matches ever played. He was possibly the last of the great classic style players. See also AUSTRALIA.

Cross-Court
An adjective used to describe all strokes played diagonally, from the right-hand court to the opposing right-hand court or from the left-hand court to the opposing left-hand court. JO

Cuba
The Federación Amateur Cubana de Lawn Tennis has been a Full Member of the ILTF since 1928. It first took part in the DAVIS CUP in 1924. BR
GOVERNING BODY: Federación Amateur Cubana de Lawn Tennis, Hotel Habana Libre, Habana

Cyprus

The Cyprus LTA was founded in 1951 when Cyprus was a British colony and it was affiliated to the LTA of Great Britain. It became an Associate Member of the ILTF in 1972, reporting 10 affiliated clubs with about 500 players. It runs spring and autumn championships in Nicosia and a summer tournament at Troodos. BR

GOVERNING BODY: Cyprus Lawn Tennis Association, Egypt Avenue, Nicosia

Czechoslovakia

The roots of lawn tennis in Bohemia lie in ball games played by the knights of the Middle Ages. In the 15th and 16th centuries these games became so popular that they were played at the various feudal courts all over Bohemia. Special rooms (like the famous Ball-Game Room of Emperor Rudolf II at Prague Castle) were constructed for these games, and tennis in the 16th century is described in the accounts of the early Bohemian travellers Martin Kabátník and Krištof Harant of Polžice and Bezdružice. It appears that Czech commoners as well as feudal lords played these games in the Middle Ages.

Tennis courts were recorded in 480 places in Bohemia before 1888. They were constructed of various materials – macadam, concrete and layers of brick – and were usually situated in gardens. At Litomyšl Castle there were three courts, one with a wooden floor, one of brick, and one of concrete.

Lawn tennis has a considerable history in Bohemia. The first competition was held in 1879 in the grounds of Duke Kinski's castle at Choceň, with prize money, two years after the first Wimbledon Championship. It was apparently not only the first championship in Bohemia, but also the first in the Austro-Hungarian Empire, and thus in central Europe. A tennis championship was held in the same year at the Bon Repos Castle near Nové Benátky, in the district of Mladá Boleslav (on the first grass court in Bohemia) and the winner was rewarded by a barrel of Rhine wine. Zbraslav Castle was the venue for the first inter-town competition, between Zbraslav and Rakovník; a huge cucumber was the prize. The court of Count Loweter at Třebenice was a real curiosity – instead of sand, Czech garnets were used.

A Prague company in Paris, Goldšmíd Brothers, largely contributed to the spread of tennis by importing rackets and balls from 1880. Tennis became more and more popular and from 1890 it was played not only as a social game but also as a competitive sport. In 1890-3 a number of clubs without regular status were founded in Bohemia; nevertheless there was some sort of organization in Prague and also outside the capital, in Chrudim Choceň, Plzeň, Brandýs and Orlicí, Heřmanův Městec, Hluboká, Přelouč, Prostějov, Orlík,

Above **Czechoslovakia.** Tennis players in Bohemia in 1898

and other places. At that time the Czech Lawn Tennis Circle, the German Lawn Tennis Circle, the Nostic and Lobkowitz Circle at Štvanice, the Prague Club, the Skating Club at Letná, the Prague Regatta and Lawn Tennis Club at Zbrojnice had been formed. These clubs had their own sand courts.

In 1894 Mr J. Klenka translated the English rules and the first regular Czech Lawn Tennis Club (IČLTK Prague) was established in Bohemia. The Prague LTC and the German club, Prague DLTC, began in 1895 and tennis spread into Czech rural areas.

The first lawn-tennis courts in Slovakia were built in the park of the former Grasalkovič Palace in Bratislava (1880) and at Piešťany, thanks to the support of Dr Fodor. The first tennis clubs were established in Banská Bystrica, Komárno and Bratislava in 1899. The

Below **Czechoslovakia.** V. Černik, one of his country's great Davis Cup players

first championship to be played in Slovakia was held in 1908.

The Czech Lawn Tennis Association was founded in 1906 and Czech players were able to compete in international championships since Czech tennis was of a quite high standard at that time. The first player of significance was Zdena Hammer, who had to use the pseudonym Z. Marteau because college rules at the time did not allow the students to take part in sports. His doubles partner was K. Neumann (who used the pseudonym K. Marteau). The Žemla brothers used the pseudonyms Jánský and Rázný when they were doubles partners in the 'Extra-Ordinary' Olympic Games in Athens in 1906. Jánský won the third place and a bronze medal, being defeated by M. Germot (France) in the semi-final. The Žemla brothers won a bronze in doubles.

After recognition of the Czech Lawn Tennis Association by the ILTF in 1921, tennis really developed and grew in Bohemia. Earlier, many championships were held, not only in Prague but also in the provinces, in 1910 for example at Louny, Plzeň, Písek, Mladá Boleslav, Mariánske Lázně, and Karlovy Vary. A number of outstanding foreign players including Wilding, Ritchie, Paine, Frotzheim, and Kleinschroth took part. Tennis matches took place between Austria and Germany in 1903-4 and 1910, and Czech players composed more than half of the entire Austrian team. Tennis matches between Prague and Dresden, and Prague and Munich, were held in 1910. Czech tennis enjoyed a good reputation all over the world due to the tremendous success of Žemla, Just and Ardelt.

World War I brought tennis to a halt in 1914. However, friends of tennis and players gathered on 13 December 1918 to establish the Czechoslovak Tennis Association and to encourage the development of tennis in Czechoslovakia. L. Žemla, F. Buriánek, Josef and Karel Koželuh had great success at Pershing's Games in Paris in 1919; Srbková and Žemla came third in the mixed doubles at the Antwerp Olympic Games in 1920.

The popularity of tennis soon spread over the whole of the new republic of Czechoslovakia, and a number of excellent tennis players made their country famous internationally. Karel Koželuh, Jaroslav Drobný, Věra Suková-Pužejová and Jan Kodeš have been this small country's best-known representatives in the game.

The story of Karel Koželuh (1895-1950) begins like a fairy tale: Once upon a time, there were a poor father and mother and they had seven sons and one daughter. The father was a baker with not enough money to feed eight children. But they were all keen on sport. To help their parents, the children began to earn money by picking up tennis balls for players. Karel became the most famous. By the age of six he was earning his living as a ballboy. By the age of 12 he was teaching aristocrats how to play tennis. When he was 14 he became a coach at the Sports Club in Munich and a year later he was coaching at the Iphitos Tennis Club there. After a short time he was invited to the Professional Tournament at Wiesbaden (1911), where, despite his youth, he defeated all the best professionals, including Najuch, 6-2, 6-3. By now his fame was growing fast. He was also playing football, for Teplitzer FC and finally for Sparta Praha; he became a very fine ice-hockey player, shooting the decisive goal in the final match against Switzerland at Strba in the Tatra Mountains in 1924 when Czechoslovakia became European champions – a goal that was memorable because Koželuh played the shot lying down.

His greatest success in tennis was in the World Professional Championships at Deauville in 1923, where his rivals were such players as Burke, Ramillion, Najuch and de Plaa. Koželuh won the most important professional trophy, the Bristol Cup, three times, but achieved his most glorious moment in the United States, when W. T. Tilden himself was forced to say (in 1928) that the player able to defeat Karel Koželuh did not exist. At that time Koželuh was over 30. His fame as a professional brought him $100 per playing hour – a sum that no one had received before.

Jaroslav Drobný was not only an outstanding tennis player but also a great hockey player and it took a long time for him to decide for tennis. This 'magician of the tennis ball' could vary 'cannonballs' of service, forehand and smash with smooth, short volleys, lobs and dropshots. He took Czechoslovakia to victory in the Davis Cup European Zone Finals twice (1947-8) and reached the semi-final of the US Championships in 1947. In 1949 he reached the Wimbledon final for the first time and was beaten by Ted Schroeder. In 1952 he reached it again and was defeated by Frank Sedgman. In 1954 he was successful, winning the Wimbledon final from Ken Rosewall after a splendid match, 13-11, 4-6, 6-2, 9-7. He was near the top of the world ranking list for more than 20 years and won many European championships including the French twice and the Italian three times.

Věra Suková (née Pužejová, born 1931) began by playing basketball and moved to tennis quite late, at the age of 17 or 18, but after three years was Champion of Czechoslovakia, a title she held from April 1954 to 1960. She won the Championships of Hungary and Austria, and with Jiří Javorský won the French mixed doubles in 1957. Her greatest success was in 1962 when she reached the Wimbledon singles final and was beaten by Karen Susman 6-4, 6-4. She is now a state coach.

Jan Kodeš comes from a sporting family. His father took part in bicycle races and played tennis. His mother is a keen tennis player, still taking part in veteran competitions. One of his

Above **Czechoslovakia.** Věra Suková in 1962, when she was Wimbledon runner-up to Karen Susman

two elder sisters, Vlasta Vopičková, is a leading tennis player and has won the Czechoslovak women's singles (1969-70). Honza (Johnny) Kodeš played more football (soccer) as a boy than tennis and still likes to play as a centre forward in the Czechoslovak tennis players' team. He has been playing tennis since the age of 9 and has been National Champion at all levels of tennis, beginning with the under-14 age-group. He became Junior (under-18) Champion of Czechoslovakia in 1964 for the first time and was third at the junior tournaments in Paris and at Wimbledon. In 1965 and 1966 he contributed largely to Czechoslovakia's victories in the GALEA CUP. He became Champion of Czechoslovakia in 1966 and has been a player (see PLAYING STATUS) since 1968. He achieved his greatest successes in 1970 and 1971 when he won the French Championships and 1973, when he won Wimbledon and reached the final of the US Open Championships. Kodeš has a great fighting spirit and stubborn will, quick legs (to which playing football has certainly contributed), an excellent backhand and brilliant strategy.

Czechoslovakia played in the DAVIS CUP for the first time in 1921 and was defeated by Belgium 3-2 in the first round at Štvanice in Prague. The first great Czechoslovak success was achieved in 1924 when the team of Jan Koželuh, von Rohrer, Žemla and Macenauer reached the European Zone finals, having defeated New Zealand 4-0, Switzerland 4-1 and, in the semi-finals, Denmark 3-2. They were in turn beaten by the French team of Lacoste, Cochet and Brugnon. Between the world wars Czechoslovakia reached the finals of the European Zone in 1924, 1928, 1931, 1934, 1935 and 1937.

After World War II Czechoslovakia achieved its greatest Davis Cup success. In 1947 it won the European Zone, beating Sweden, Switzerland, New Zealand, France and Yugoslavia, and came through to the Inter-Zone finals where it was defeated by Australia

Below **Czechoslovakia.** Karel Koželuh *(extreme right)* with some members of his family

Czechoslovakia

4-1. In 1948 the situation repeated itself: Czechoslovakia, with Jaroslav Drobný and Vladimir Černik, eliminated Brazil, Belgium, Italy and Sweden to win the European Zone, and was narrowly defeated by Australia in the Inter-Zone finals, 3-2. In 1971, after 23 years, Czechoslovakia reached the Inter-Zone semi-finals again by beating Egypt, Portugal, the USSR and Spain, to be defeated by Brazil. The Czech team included Jan Kodeš, František Pála, Jan Kukal and Vladimír Zedník.

Czechoslovakia has also competed in the FEDERATION CUP (since 1963), the GALEA CUP and KING'S CUP, and won the Galea Cup in 1963, 1965, 1966, and 1970. It has done well in the King's Cup. Although Bohemia itself does not have any halls used exclusively for tennis, Czechoslovakia won the King's Cup in 1969 and was third in 1966, 1967, 1968 and 1971.

Above **Czechoslovakia.** Paddle tennis gives the youngest the chance to start.

The success of tennis in this country has been due to good organization, especially for young people. There are competitions for under-12, under-14 and under-18 age groups. These competitions provide young players with the necessary match experience. There is special instruction for children. School tennis clubs arrange training for 6-year-olds, who are allowed to play only with a small wooden racket, on small courts with low nets. This children's tennis, played with wooden paddles, provides the youngest ones with the chance to start. It requires little space and the cost of practising is negligible. Paddle tennis introduces children to a basic technique of strokes and they can enjoy it all year round. The light wooden paddle, smaller court (6 x 12 m or 20 x 40 ft) and lower net (80 cm or 2 ft 8 in) are easier for starting. Heavy rackets, high nets and normal court dimensions often overawe and discourage children. Children who acquire a good basic technique and liking for the game generally continue to play when older. Paddle tennis is a suitable supplement for physical education in schools. A schoolyard, gymnasium or just a convenient small space can be found in schools everywhere. Paddle tennis makes a sound contribution to lawn tennis and is the chief source of Czech tennis successes. AB

GOVERNING BODY: Czechoslovak Tennis Association, Praha 1, Na Porici 12

Czechoslovak International Championship Winners

Men's Singles

1894	K. Rademacher
1895	E. Pleschner (Gautsch)*
1896	E. Pleschner (Gautsch)*
1897	R. Kinzel (Walter)*
1898	A. Ryba (Novotný)*
1899	A. Ringhoffer
1900	F. Čistecký
1901	Z. Hammer (Marteau)*
1902	F. Čistecký
1903	Z. Žemla (Jánský)*
1904	F. Čistecký
1905	A. Ringhoffer
1906	L. Žemla (Rázný)*
1907	L. Žemla (Rázný)*
1908	A. G. K. Logie
1909	L. Žemla (Rázný)*
1910	L. Žemla (Rázný)*
1911	L. Žemla (Rázný)*
1912	L. Žemla (Rázný)*
1913	L. Žemla (Rázný)*
1914	L. Žemla (Rázný)*
1915-19	*No Competition*
1920	S. Žemla
1921	S. Žemla
1922	K. Ardelt
1923	S. Žemla
1924	K. Aeschlimann
1925	J. Koželuh
1926	J. Koželuh
1927	J. Koželuh
1928	J. Koželuh
1929	H. Cochet
1930	J. Maleček
1931	J. Sato
1932	M. de Morpurgo
1933	R. Menzel
1934	R. Menzel
1935	R. Menzel
1936	F. Perry
1937	R. Menzel
1938	D. Budge
1939	F. Cejnar
1940-44	*No Competition*
1945	J. Drobný
1946	J. Drobný
1947	J. Drobný
1948	J. Drobný
1949	J. Drobný
1950	J. Asboth
1951-55	*No Competition*
1956	D. Candy
1957	J. Javorský
1958	N. Pietrangeli
1959	J. Javorský
1960	J. Javorský
1961	I. Gulyás
1962	V. Skonecki
1963	K. N. Fletcher
1964	J. Javorský
1965	*No Competition*
1966	A. D. Roche
1967	*No Competition*
1968	M. Holeček
1969	I. Gulyás
1970	J. Kodeš
1971	J. Kodeš
1972	*No Competition*
1973	F. Pála

* pseudonym

Women's Singles

1895	Miss M. Cífková
1896	Miss M. Cífková
1897	Miss H. F. Gerard
1898	Miss M. Cífková
1899	Miss M. Cingrošová
1900	Mrs M. Petáková-Cingrošová
1901	Miss G. Wacker
1902	Miss E. Mattuch
1903	Miss E. Mattuch
1904	Miss H. Rosenbaum
1905	Miss M. Speed
1906	Miss E. Mattuch
1907	Mrs M. Neresheim
1908	Mrs O. Garricková-Masaryková
1909	Mrs O. Garricková-Masaryková
1910	Miss E. Mattuch
1911	Miss V. Bjurstedt
1912	*No Competition*
1913	Miss V. Schmidt
1914	Miss V. Schmidt
1915-19	*No Competition*
1920	Miss M. Lindová
1921	Miss E. Völker
1922	Miss M. Neppachová
1923	*No Competition*
1924	Miss H. Šindelářová
1925	Miss H. Šindelářová
1926	Miss A. Varady
1927	K. Řezníčková
1928	Miss E. Deutschová
1929	Miss M. Koželuhová
1930	Miss M. Deutschová
1931	Miss H. Krahwinkel
1932	Miss V. Hammerová
1933	Miss M. Deutschová
1934	Miss E. Ryan
1935	Miss E. L. H. Miller
1936	Miss E. Käppel
1937	Miss E. Käppel
1938	Miss E. L. H. Miller
1939	Miss H. Wheeler
1940-44	*No Competition*
1945	Miss H. Straubeová
1946	Miss M. Rurac
1947	Mrs S. Körmöczy
1948	Miss M. Erdödy
1949	Miss J. Jedrzejowska
1950	Mrs S. Körmöczy
1951-55	*No Competition*
1956	Miss P. Vollmer
1957	Miss V. Pužejová
1958	Miss V. Pužejová
1959	Miss V. Pužejová
1960	Miss V. Pužejová
1961	Miss J. Lehane
1962	Miss A. Dmitrieva
1963	Mrs V. Suková
1964	Mrs V. Suková
1965	*No Competition*
1966	Miss K. Melville
1967	*No Competition*
1968	Miss H. Gourlay
1969	Mrs V. Vopičková
1970	Mrs V. Vopičková
1971	Miss M. Neumannová
1972	*No Competition*
1973	Miss E. F. Goolagong

Colour caption Ann (Haydon) Jones, Wimbledon champion in 1969, twice runner-up at Forest Hills (1961 and 1967) and holder of the British Wightman Cup record

D

Dahomey

Dahomey has been an Associate Member of the ILTF since 1962. BR
GOVERNING BODY: Fédération Dahoméenne de Lawn-Tennis, École Urbaine de Foun-Foun, Porto-Novo

Dalton, Mrs D. E. see Miss J. A. M. TEGART

Danzig, Mrs J. see Miss Sarah PALFREY

Darmon, Pierre (France)

Born Tunis, 14 Jan. 1934; Wimbledon men's doubles r/u 1963; Australian men's singles q/f 1965; French men's singles q/f 1958, 1962, r/u 1963, s/f 1964, q/f 1967; men's doubles s/f 1959; mixed doubles s/f 1962. Davis Cup 1956-67.

David, Herman Francis (Gt Britain)

Born 26 June 1905; Davis Cup 1932; non-playing Davis Cup captain 1953-8. Chairman All England Club (1959-   ). His courage and foresight made him a leading protagonist in the move towards Open Tennis (see OPEN TENNIS, PART 1).

Davidson, Owen Keir (Australia)

Born Melbourne, 4 Oct. 1943; Wimbledon men's singles s/f 1966; men's doubles r/u 1966, s/f 1967; mixed doubles won 1967, s/f 1968, won 1971, 1973; US men's singles q/f 1966-7; men's doubles r/u 1967, 1972, won 1973; mixed doubles won 1966-7, s/f 1972, won 1973; Australian men's singles q/f 1962-5, q/f 1967; men's doubles s/f 1963-6, r/u 1967, won 1972; mixed doubles s/f 1964, r/u 1965, won 1967; French men's singles q/f 1967; mixed doubles s/f 1965, won 1967, r/u 1968. Pro 1967-70 with All England Club. WCT pro 1968-9; then taught in Texas.

Davidson, Sven (Sweden)

Born Borås, Sweden, 13 July 1928; Wimbledon men's singles q/f 1953, 1955, s/f 1957, q/f 1958; men's doubles won 1958; US men's singles q/f 1953, s/f 1957; mixed doubles s/f 1953; French men's singles q/f 1954, r/u 1955, 1956, won 1957; men's doubles s/f 1956. Davis Cup 1950-60. Possibly Sweden's finest player prior to BORG.

Colour plate In 1973 Billie Jean King won the Wimbledon singles for the fifth time (a post-war record). She also defeated Bobby Riggs (1939 Wimbledon Champion) at Houston (see FASHION).

Davis, Dwight Filley (USA)

Born St Louis, Mo., 5 July 1879, died 28 Nov. 1945; Wimbledon men's doubles r/u 1901; US singles r/u* 1898, 1899, q/f 1900; men's doubles won 1899-1901. The donor of the DAVIS CUP, he played in the Competition 1900, 1902. He was President of the USLTA in 1923, US Secretary of War 1925-9 and later Governor General of the Philippines. Left-handed.

Davis Cup

The Davis Cup, more properly the International Lawn Tennis Championship, had its origins in Anglo-American rivalry which dates from the cradle days of the game. As early as 1883 there was an international doubles at the All England Club, Wimbledon, when two American brothers, C. M. and J. S. Clark, unsuccessfully challenged the Renshaw twins, William and Ernest. The first official moves to promote the competition were made in 1897 when, following an invitation by Dr Dwight, president of the US Lawn Tennis Association, the Council of the British LTA approved a resolution 'that it is desirable in the interests of lawn tennis that a match be arranged between the United Kingdom and the United States'.

It was not until 1900 that what was to become one of the greatest of international sporting events began. By then the concept had widened; the opening paragraph of the original regulations read:

The Competition shall be called the International Lawn Tennis Championship and shall be open to any nation which has a recognized Lawn Tennis Association and for the purpose of these regulations, Australia with New Zealand, Austria, Belgium, the British Isles, British South Africa, Canada, France, Germany, Holland, India, Sweden and Norway, Switzerland and the United States of America shall be regarded as separate nations.

Below **Owen Davidson**

Dwight F. DAVIS of St Louis donated the trophy, a massive solid silver punchbowl lined with gold and valued at a thousand dollars. The only challengers in 1900 were the British Isles, with a team lacking the three best players, Reggie and Laurie Doherty and S. H. Smith. The pioneer British band was Arthur W. Gore, Ernest D. Black and H. Roper Barrett. They sailed on the S. S. *Campania*, arrived in New York on the first Saturday in August, the tie being scheduled for Longwood, near Boston, the following week.

They were not met and were at something of a loss to know what to do. They first visited the Niagara Falls and made their way to Boston from there, receiving a great welcome and being put up at the University Club. Roper Barrett afterwards recorded his impressions of the inaugural Davis Cup tie. He described the conditions as abominable. The grass was twice as long as the worst in England, the net sagged by as much as two or three inches and had to be adjusted every few games. The balls were terrible. He compared them, when served with American twist, to 'animated egg-plums', swerving wildly in the air before breaking by as much as four or five feet.

All this nonplussed the visitors and, adding to the difficulties, the tie was played in a heat wave with a temperature of 136°F. (57·8°C.) in the sun. Against a strong home side the British were routed. On the first day the American champion M. D. Whitman easily beat Gore, losing only six games. Dwight Davis, the trophy donor, was extended more by Black, who won the first set, the only one taken by Britain. On the second day Davis and Holcombe Ward beat Black and Roper Barrett in three ten-game sets. The tie petered out the following day when the weather broke with Davis leading Gore by one set and nine games all in the second. From a British viewpoint it was not a very happy start.

Below **Sven Davidson**

In 1901 the British challenge was withdrawn when it was found impossible to put forward the best possible side. The following year it was renewed, this time with high hopes of success for then both the Dohertys were available. Dr Joshua Pim came in as the third member, his original nomination, for some obscure reason of medical etiquette, being under the identity of Mr X. The tie was played at the Crescent Athletic Club, Bay Ridge, New York, on 6, 7 and 8 August.

The battle order differed from 1900, two singles being scheduled for the first day, the reverse singles for the second and the double on the last. For the United States Whitman was in the singles with W. A. Larned, the American title holder. Davis and Ward were still the doubles pair. The British nominations were surprising for Laurie Doherty, the reigning Wimbledon champion, did not get the top singles place; it was given to Reggie Doherty with Pim as the number two. Whitman drew first blood by beating Pim. Reggie Doherty levelled the score by beating Larned in a rubber unfinished on the first day and finished the following morning. Reggie survived a tough battle, for he dropped the first two sets, but, exhausted, was no match for Whitman in the afternoon. At the same time Pim lost to Larned and that was a 3-1 margin for America. There were 5,000 spectators on the first day, 6,000 on the second. On the third, even with the issue settled, 10,000 paid to see the doubles, the biggest crowd at a lawn tennis match up to that time. The victory of the Doherty brothers was, of course, a foregone conclusion.

In 1903, with Britain again the sole challenger, the Davis Cup changed hands for the first time. The venue was the Longwood Club in Boston. Larned was again in the American side but with newcomers, the brothers R. D. and G. L. Wrenn. For Britain there were the Doherty brothers supported by H. S. Mahony in what was strictly laid down as a reserve capacity. Just before the tie the British were at panic stations, Reggie Doherty having an injured arm. The British captain, W. H. Collins, moved boldly when he learned that if he substituted Mahony he would have to stick to his choice. He conceded a walk-over to Larned. Laurie Doherty had a three-set win over R. D. Wrenn to make it one rubber each on the Tuesday night. On the Wednesday it rained. Thursday was the same and by Friday Reggie Doherty was fit again, joining his brother to win the doubles. On the Saturday the last two singles were played side by side on adjacent courts. Laurie got home 7-5 in the fifth set against Larned and Reggie won 6-4 in the fifth against R. D. Wrenn. That was a 4-1 success to Britain, the only American rubber being the walk-over.

The scope of the Davis Cup immediately widened with the British victory. With Wimbledon the venue the financial strain for European nations was lessened. In 1904

Above **Davis Cup.** H. Ward and D. Davis (US) *(left)* beat the Dohertys (BI) in 1902 at New York.

challenges were made by Austria, Belgium and France, with Austria subsequently withdrawing. None was forthcoming from the United States since their best players were not available and finance was a problem. Belgium beat France narrowly in the play-off at Wimbledon but were outclassed in the title match. Indeed a winning margin was achieved after nine sets only and the British victory, with only a total of 17 games on the wrong side, stands as the most one-sided Challenge Round in the history of the competition.

Australasia (Australia and New Zealand) entered to make 1905 a memorable year. There were originally five challengers but Belgium withdrew, leaving semi-finals with America against France, Australasia against Austria. Both were played at the same time at the Queen's Club, London, the final being scheduled on the same courts two days later. Neither America nor Australia had difficulty in coming through for the first of many Davis Cup ties they were destined to oppose each other. The leading Australasians were Norman Brookes, who had made his mark at Wimbledon, and the New Zealander Tony Wilding, a Cambridge undergraduate destined to dominate the game. The Americans, Larned, Beals Wright, Holcombe Ward and William Clothier, all of whom were at one time or another US singles champions, astonished the British by the rigour of their training. They beat Australasia 5-0 but yielded by the same score in the Challenge Round to Britain. The Americans had played three Davis Cup ties in twelve days, all without the ten-minute rest after the third set.

The pattern was much the same in 1906, except that this time Austria and France withdrew to leave a straight play-off, Australasia against America, before the Challenge Round. They played at Newport, Monmouthshire, and America squeezed a narrow 3-2 victory only to be routed 5-0 by the might of the Doherty brothers and S. H. Smith.

After seven years and six competitions Britain had won the Davis Cup four times, the United States twice. The retirement of the Dohertys brought a change of fortune. Laurie had played 12 Davis Cup rubbers and lost none. Reggie had played eight and lost only one. Without them the British effort declined and when in 1907 Australasia and America were

again the only challengers there was nothing to stop the triumph of Brookes and Wilding. It removed the Challenge Round to the other side of the world.

In 1908 in Melbourne, in 1909 in Sydney and in 1911 in Christchurch (there was a blank year in 1910 with no challengers) Australasia kept the cup against the challenge of America. Only the British Isles intervened, travelling each year to the United States to be beaten. But in 1912 Britain, having beaten France at Folkestone, got a walk-over from the United States and was successful against Australasia in Melbourne. James Parke, a diligent Irish baseliner, and Charles Dixon were the main instruments of the British success that was made the easier by the absence of Wilding from the other side.

The British victory made for a bumper year in 1913 with a record seven challengers, Germany, Canada and South Africa coming in for the first time. The Americans made all the running. With the 'Californian Comet' Maurice McLoughlin loosing his cannonballs, supported by Norris Williams, they beat Australasia in New York, Germany at Nottingham and Canada at Wimbledon to qualify for the Challenge Round. McLoughlin was beaten, despite his tremendous serving, by Parke in the opening singles but achieved the winning lead for America when he beat Dixon in three sets on the third day.

Australasia, with Brookes and Wilding in full cry, roared through the preliminary rounds of 1914, beating Canada 5-0 in Chicago, Germany 5-0 in Pittsburg and the British Isles 3-0 in Boston. They took the cup by 3-2, with a winning lead at 3-1, against the United States at Forest Hills, by which time World War I was four days old.

The first 13 competitions for the Davis Cup had brought success five times to Britain, five times to Australasia and only three times to the United States. Nine nations in all had taken part. Its big days were still to come. Nevertheless it had proved a lusty infant.

The resumption in 1919 was no more than an echo of the prewar pattern. Britain, still including Ireland and known as the British Isles, emerged from four challengers with victories over South Africa and France to assault Australasia without success in Sydney. Germany had been expelled and did not play again until 1927. The United States did not take part that year.

In 1920 the United States began the long run

Above **Davis Cup.** J. C. Parke (BI) *(near)* defeated M. McLoughlin (US) in the 1913 Challenge Round.

of triumph that was still unrivalled when the Challenge Round system was brought to an end after the season of 1971. America beat France 3-0 at Eastbourne, the British Isles 5-0 at Wimbledon. It walked over the Netherlands and then went to Auckland to beat Australasia 5-0. 'Big Bill' Tilden and 'Little Bill' Johnston did it all between them, each playing five singles and three doubles without defeat.

It was the first of seven invincible years for Tilden and Johnston. From 1920 to 1926 rival nations assaulted the citadel of an American-dominated Davis Cup without success. The Challenge Rounds were at Forest Hills, New York, 1921 to 1923. Japan was beaten 5-0, Australasia 4-1 and, with New Zealand having taken on her own identity, Australia 4-1 again. At Philadelphia, 1924-1926, Australia was beaten 5-0, France 5-0 and France 4-1.

There were only three rubbers on the wrong side. Tilden with Vincent Richards yielded a double in 1922. Johnston lost the opening single to James Anderson in 1923. And in the last rubber of the tie against France (1926) Tilden suffered the first singles loss of his Davis Cup career. It was in four sets to René Lacoste, a dead rubber in any case but the writing was on the wall.

This American success was at the top of an expanding competition. The Netherlands entered in 1920. The following year brought challenges from Spain, Czechoslovakia, India, Denmark and Japan. Rumania and Italy competed for the first time in 1922. In 1923 there were Switzerland, Argentina, Hawaii and, reflecting its new independent status, Ireland. New Zealand, now distinct from Australia, played in 1924 as did Hungary, Cuba, China and Mexico. Sweden, Portugal and Poland were the newcomers of 1925.

The growth brought problems of congestion. In 1923 the system of zoning was started, with a division into American and European Zones and an Inter-Zone final as the qualifying tie for entry into the Challenge Round.

Significantly in 1923 the first Inter-Zone finalists were Australia (playing for the first time under that designation) and France. This was the emergence of France as a major lawn-tennis power and it never looked back. In 1923 it won the European Zone only to be beaten 4-1 by Australia at the Inter-Zone stage. In 1924 France was beaten 3-2 by Australia at

the Inter-Zone stage. The next year, by which time its success in Europe was taken for granted, France beat Australia and became the challenger. In 1926, when France's status as challenger was taken for granted, it yielded to America, 4-1. In 1927 France gained the reward of the trophy itself, ending the seven-year reign of the United States and initiating the six-year spell of invincibility which, more than any other factor, turned hard-court lawn tennis in Europe into a major sport.

The American supremacy, which was then broken, had been built on the exploits of Tilden and Johnston. Until his defeat by Lacoste in the last rubber of the Challenge Round in 1926, Tilden had gone through 16 straight Davis Cup singles rubbers without loss. His last Davis Cup rubber was in 1930 when his tally of 41 rubbers in all was marred by only seven losses. Out of 30 singles he won 25. Where he stands almost without a peer (rivalled only by Laurie Doherty, who was never beaten in the Davis Cup at all) is in his record in the Challenge Round, where he won 13 successive singles before tasting defeat. He

Below **Davis Cup.** Two of the Musketeers, Jacques Brugnon *(right)* and Jean Borotra (near side of net), playing Fred Perry *(right)* and Patrick Hughes

lost a live Challenge Round singles only twice, to Lacoste in 1927 and to Cochet in 1929.

The French success at Philadelphia in 1927 was excitingly brought about. Tilden and Johnston again defended in singles. Tilden was paired with Frank Hunter in the doubles and not long before they had beaten Cochet and Toto Brugnon in the Wimbledon final after surviving match points. France, bearing Wimbledon in mind, brought in Cochet as a singles player for the first time in the Challenge Round. He had won Wimbledon by beating Jean Borotra in the final and Tilden in a dramatic semi-final after trailing 2-6 4-6 1-5.

Borotra, on his Wimbledon showing, was the logical singles number two. He had lost to Cochet by the narrowest of margins, one of six match points turning on a debatable decision, and had earlier defeated Lacoste. But Lacoste's previous Challenge Round record demanded his inclusion. Borotra and Brugnon made the French doubles pairing.

France drew the first blood, Lacoste excelling himself by beating Johnston decisively. 'Little Bill' won no more than seven games. Personal problems had prevented his normal training. But Tilden, burning to avenge his Wimbledon defeat, thundered out a 3-sets-to-1 win over Cochet. The doubles went to America in the fifth set. That was a lead of 2 rubbers to 1 for the USA. But on the last day both French singles men were meteoric. Lacoste, shrewd and immaculate from the baseline, mastered Tilden and Cochet quelled Johnston, each for the loss of one set only. All French effort from the start had been towards wearing Tilden out. The strategy succeeded and it was a great and glorious day for France. A hard-court nation had won the Cup. The grip on it was not easily loosened.

The power of the FOUR MUSKETEERS as a team can hardly be over-estimated. Three, Cochet, Borotra and Lacoste, were singles players. Brugnon was a doubles specialist. The options open to the French were always wide, a choice of two out of three for the singles and virtually any one of three good doubles combinations, since Brugnon was equally able to play with any of his colleagues. Of the nine Challenge Rounds played by France only one of the six combinations possible among four men was not used, Cochet with Lacoste.

Between them the Four Musketeers played 164 Davis Cup rubbers for France and won 120. Lacoste, who retired from the game, fell out after 1928, having taken 40 out of 51 rubbers. Cochet, winner of 44 out of 58 rubbers, was certainly the most spectacular performer and three times in his career he struck the shot that decided the fate of the Cup, in 1927 when he beat Johnston, in 1929 when he beat George Lott, and in 1931 when he beat Fred Perry.

The entry in 1928 was a record 33, with 26 challengers in the European Zone. Among the last was Australia, absent from the competition for two years, destined to learn something of the difficulties confronting a grass-court nation in Europe. In Genoa, Australia was beaten 4-1 by Italy. Finland, making a début, had a unique experience, playing a tie at two venues. Against Yugoslavia it achieved a winning 3-0 lead in Zagreb but, because of rain, the last two singles were staged four days later in Belgrade. A bigger field entailed a greater disparity of class. The year 1928 was the first when a Davis Cup rubber was resolved by the humiliating score of 6-0, 6-0, 6-0, when George Lott for the United States routed P. Kong of China in Kansas City. Between that date and the end of 1973 there were to be 17 such occasions when the loser failed to break into the score.

The French dug themselves in on the hard courts at the Stade Roland Garros. For three years they defended successfully against the challenge of the United States, always getting a victory in the fourth rubber. In 1931 Great Britain was the challenger. A fourth rubber victory by Cochet against Perry settled this and in 1932 it was another American challenge that had to be turned back, again in the fourth rubber. But in 1933 the trophy changed hands and Great Britain took it.

The British Davis Cup results in the early postwar years had not been outstanding, except only for the unsuccessful Challenge Round effort against Australasia in 1919. In 1920 the United States won 5-0 at Wimbledon. Australasia triumphed 3-2 at Pittsburgh in 1921. In 1922 it was foiled by circumstance. The British began by beating Italy 4-0 at Roehampton. The side consisted of Kingscote, who was 34, Gordon Lowe, who was 38, and Frank Riseley, who was 44. Spain was the next opponent but, pleading that it would be impossible to send a team to America if it won, the LTA conceded a walk-over.

Above **Davis Cup.** Players in Budapest in 1938 *(left to right):* J. D. Budge (US), J. Asbóth and G. Dallos (Hungary), G. Mako (US)

That was the nadir of British fortunes. In 1923 there was a win over Belgium but a loss to Spain. In 1924 Belgium, Spain and South Africa were brought down and the loss was to France, the victors in 1925 and 1926 as well, on the last occasion in the final of the European Zone. Denmark was the winner against Britain in 1927 and Italy in 1928. In 1929 Bunny Austin played for the first time. This was a rise in standards and Britain again reached the European Zone final where the loss was 2-3 only against Germany. Australia was too good in 1930. In 1931 Fred Perry made his début. As with Brookes and Wilding for Australasia before 1914, as with Tilden and Johnston for America and as with the Four Musketeers for France, Perry and Austin made the Davis Cup a matter of national glory for their country and a personal triumph for themselves. The prize was almost gained in 1931. Against Monaco, Belgium, South Africa, Japan and Czechoslovakia the only concession was one rubber in all. In Paris in the Inter-Zone final the United States was beaten 3-2 on the outcome of the last two singles. But France was not yet ready for surrender and Cochet's defeat of Perry on the last day left the *status quo* undisturbed.

In 1932 France kept the Davis Cup with its fifth victory over the United States. Britain suffered a rebuff, losing to Germany in Berlin. The British led 2-1 but Gottfried von Cramm beat Austin and Daniel Prenn beat Perry after trailing 2-5 in the fifth set.

A year later Perry and Austin more than made amends. Early progress was one-sided against Spain, Finland, Italy and Czechoslovakia. Australia, the opposition in the European Zone final, did not prove dangerous. The Inter-Zone final against the USA was opened unexpectedly when Austin, despite his devastating loss in the Wimbledon final the year before to Ellsworth Vines, used the slow pace of the Stade Roland Garros to turn the tables, winning 6-1, 6-1, 6-4. At Wimbledon (1932) Austin had also won only six games.

The last rubber in this tie had a dramatic end. Britain already had a winning lead when

Perry faced Vines. For the American there was a double misfortune. First, when leading 2 sets to 1 and 3-2 in the fourth set, he hurt his ankle. Then in the fifth set, with the score at Perry 1-6, 6-0, 4-6, 7-5, 7-6, 40-15, match point, Vines fainted and had to be carried off court. So Britain won 4-1.

In the Challenge Round France did not yield the Davis Cup without a struggle. Cochet was still the key man of their team but for the second singles they took something of a gamble in naming the young André Merlin. Austin beat him in three sets in the opening rubber and Perry mastered Cochet in five sets to put Britain 2-0 in front. This lead was whittled away. Borotra and Brugnon had little difficulty in taking the doubles against Pat Hughes and Harry Lee, this being a deliberate tactical disposition of British reserve rather than front-line strength. Cochet then beat Austin in five sets to put the issue squarely between Perry and Merlin. As it happened young Merlin surpassed himself, won the first set and came within a point of taking the second, but Perry eventually beat him in the fourth set to give Great Britain its first success in the Davis Cup since 1912. The British reign lasted four years, as long as Perry remained an amateur. His Davis Cup record was superb, stressing what a magnificent match player he was. Of the 52 rubbers he played for Britain he won 45 and out of 38 singles he won 34.

By 1933 the entry had risen to 34 nations. The number was embarrassingly large for, with the Challenge Round in Europe it meant a crowded timetable to produce a challenging nation by late July. An effort was made to relieve the congestion in both 1933 and 1934 when a qualifying competition was introduced in the European Zone, the weaker nations being required to play the qualifying rounds in the latter half of the preceding season. The move, logical enough, was unpopular among the nations thus relegated. By 1934 the number of nations ever to have taken part was 41, a total not exceeded until after World War II.

The Philippines first played in 1926, Greece and Yugoslavia in 1927, Chile, Finland and Norway in 1928, Monaco and Egypt in 1929, Paraguay and Uruguay in 1931, Brazil in 1932. A now non-existent country made a fleeting appearance in 1934 in the qualifying competition for 1935. This was Estonia, which a quarter of a century later was to produce a player as good as Tomas Lejus. However, the Davis Cup loyalty of Lejus belonged not to Estonia but to the USSR.

The boiling cauldron of European politics before World War II had its effect on the Davis Cup. In 1936 challengers numbered 23. Austria had no national identity after 1937, Czechoslovakia after 1938. Both became part of Germany and the Davis Cup regulations had to be amended to give new national qualification for players concerned. Accordingly Roderick Menzel, after a notable lawn-tennis career for Czechoslovakia, found him-

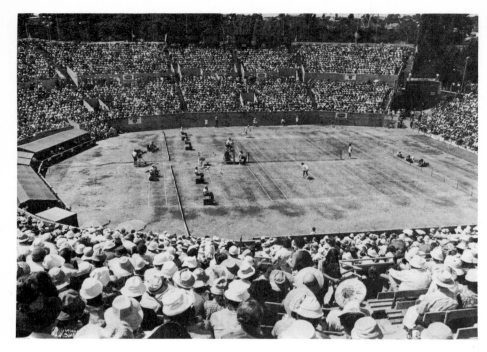

Above **Davis Cup.** Kooyong Stadium, Melbourne, in 1946, when Australia lost 0-5 to the United States in the first postwar Challenge Round

self in 1939 playing for Germany, a nation he had often tried to beat. The oddest quirk of fortune befell two Austrians, Baworowski and von Metaxa, a doubles partnership of long standing, when in 1939 Poland met Germany. They found themselves on the opposite sides of the net, von Metaxa playing for Germany and Baworowski for Poland!

The British grip on the Davis Cup was tightly maintained in Challenge Rounds at Wimbledon in both 1934 and 1935 when the US challenge was thrust back. In 1936 Australia beat the United States in the American Zone final and came through as challenger after a notable Inter-Zone tie against Germany on Wimbledon's No. 1 Court. Germany won one rubber only in this but it was memorable, with von Cramm beating Adrian Quist 4-6, 6-4, 4-6, 6-4, 11-9, after the loser had been denied three match balls and the winner nine. In the subsequent Challenge Round Britain led Australia 2-0 after the first day, but did not retain the Cup until the fifth rubber when Perry beat Jack Crawford in three sets.

Later in 1936 Perry, having won Wimbledon for the third year in succession and the US title for the third time, became a professional. It was the end of the road for Britain in the Davis Cup, for the gentle if immaculate skill of Austin was insufficient on its own. It was self-evident at the start of the 1937 season that the Davis Cup would change hands and that the United States would probably be the winners. The red-headed Californian Don Budge had already signalled his high promise.

As it happened the seemingly hopeless British defence began with spirit when Austin beat Frank Parker in the first rubber of the Challenge Round. But the superiority of American prowess was measured 4-1 and it was obvious that the key to the American victory was cut a week earlier when the the United States beat Germany 3-2 in the Inter-Zone final. The heart of this rugged contest was the singles on the third day when Budge beat von Cramm after a match of majestic qualities, one of the finest in the history of the game. Budge not only recovered the loss of the first two sets but from a deficit of 1-4 in the decider won 6-8, 5-7, 6-4, 6-2, 8-6.

The United States, winners again in 1937 after 10 unsuccessful years, beat Australia in the Challenge Round of 1938. The trophy went back to Australia in 1939 after an American lead of 2-0, the only Challenge Round to be salvaged from such a deficit. The Australian side was the same as the year before, Quist and the gentle craftsman John Bromwich. The Americans had lost Budge, a recruit late in 1938 to the professional ranks.

The impact of this striking recovery was largely lost since the tie spread over the outbreak of hostilities in Europe, as had happened between the same nations in 1914. But both Bromwich and Quist played the part of heroes after losing the first two singles to Bobby Riggs and Frank Parker respectively. The doubles was won at the expense of Jack Kramer and Jack Hunt. Quist then won narrowly against Riggs in the fifth set, leaving Bromwich to master Parker by the devastating score of 6-0, 6-3, 6-1. Accordingly the Davis Cup was maintained in Australian possession for another interregnum period – it was there during World War I also.

In the 1919 to 1939 period the major growth of the Davis Cup was reached when

European nations, France and Great Britain, held it. The growth after its resumption in 1946 was despite the joint dominance of the two grass-court nations outside Europe – Australia and the United States. So far as the trophy was concerned the years 1946 to 1959 became stereotyped. No nation other than Australia or the United States disputed the Challenge Round. Nonetheless the competition as a whole prospered as never before. Luxembourg, Pakistan, Turkey, Israel, the British West Indies, Ceylon (now Sri Lanka), Burma, Malaysia, Lebanon, Venezuela, Thailand, Korea, Iran and Colombia were all Davis Cup nations by 1959. Later newcomers were Indonesia, Ecuador, Morocco, USSR, Rhodesia, Bulgaria, Viet Nam, Peru (which had challenged only to withdraw in 1933 and 1934), Hong Kong and Bolivia. The last, an entrant in 1971, was the 65th nation to participate.

Various steps were taken to make the competition practicable. In 1952 an Eastern Zone was added. The same year seeding was introduced into the European Zone. A second attempt to cope with the congestion in the European Zone, where it was at its most acute, came in 1955 when nations with poor performance were put on a rota for non-acceptance for one year. This experiment lasted four years. In 1966 the European Zone, based on an entry of 32, was made as a straight draw with full seeding but divided into two sections, each section winner going through to an inter-zone semi-final stage against the winners of the American and Eastern Zones.

The United States regained the trophy in 1946 with ease, the simplicity of their success reflecting the maintenance of standards throughout the war years. The Americans won 5-0 against the Philippines and 5-0 against Mexico to win their zone. Then 5-0 against Sweden was followed by 5-0 against Australia. None of the subsequent three years, when they successfully defended against Australia, had them in danger and the Californian Ted Schroeder, who won Wimbledon at his first and only attempt in 1949, was their anchor man throughout.

The nearest Schroeder came to singles defeat in the Davis Cup in the four years of American triumph was 1947. In taking the United States to a winning lead he beat Dinny Pails by 6-3, 8-6, 4-6, 9-11, 10-8, the 71 games representing the longest live singles rubber, as measured in the number of games, ever played in the Challenge Round.

Four years' American dominance was followed by four years' Australian control, with Frank Sedgman near the peak of his power as an amateur. When he left off Lew Hoad and Ken Rosewall took over. But Australia was forced to a fifth-rubber effort, with Sedgman beating Vic Seixas in three sets, to keep the Cup in 1951, and there was a similar tense Challenge Round when Australia had its fourth postwar success in 1953. On this occasion Rosewall beat Seixas in the fifth rubber.

The United States regained the cup in 1954 in what was a two-man effort on both sides, Seixas and Tony Trabert winning the first three rubbers against Hoad and Rosewall. The Australians were equally emphatic the following year in challenging at Forest Hills, and 1956 and 1957 were their years also. It was during this period that Seixas, a doughty if unpolished performer, made himself the leading American Davis Cup stalwart, with a total of 55 rubbers of which 38 were wins.

In 1958, Ashley Cooper and Mal Anderson had taken over the leadership from Hoad and Rosewall, who had both turned professional. Australia submitted to Alex Olmedo and Barry MacKay when the United States, having led 3-1, won 3-2 in Brisbane. The total number of games played in this Challenge Round was 270, the highest on record, helped along by the 82 games in which Olmedo and Ham Richardson beat Anderson and Neale Fraser 10-12, 3-6, 16-14, 6-3, 7-5, this being the longest live rubber, singles or doubles, played at that stage.

Australia, now with Rod Laver in the team for the first time, regained the trophy in 1959 after a close affair at Forest Hills. It turned on the fifth rubber when Fraser beat MacKay in four sets. It was the 14th successive Challenge Round between Australia and the United States since 1946 and the 16th in succession. There was not much in the honours, nine victories to Australia, seven to the United States.

Both Australia and the United States, when challenging nations, competed in the American Zone. It was almost as if the European Zone had become the servants' hall in the mansion of the aristocrats, the highest honour obtainable being an invitation to walk upstairs for the Inter-Zone final. But below stairs there was a lot of keen and good lawn tennis. Between 1946 and 1959 only four European nations reached the Inter-Zone final, Italy, Sweden, Czechoslovakia and Belgium. The Italians did so six times in this period, and it was appropriate that this was the nation that first broke into the Australian-American Challenge Round preserve in 1960 with a victory over the United States. They did so in Perth and repeated the success the next year in Rome. But in neither Challenge Round against Italy, 1960 and 1961, was Australia put under any real pressure and a decline of Australian public interest in the Davis Cup, which had in earlier years been at fever pitch, may be dated from the Italian breakthrough.

If Nicola Pietrangeli and Orlando Sirola, the Italian players concerned, thrived but little in the Challenge Rounds, the overall Davis Cup record of Pietrangeli was outstanding. No man played more. His record was unique. Between 1954 and 1972 he played 164 rubbers, winning 119, in a total of 66 ties.

The extent of this achievement may be measured by those that follow, as recorded in 1973. Jacques Brichant, who played for Bel-

Above **Davis Cup.** M. del Bello *(right)*/G. Cucelli (Italy, *near side*) lost to E. V. Seixas *(left)*/M. A. Trabert (US) in the 1952 Inter-Zone final.

gium 1949 to 1965, played 121 rubbers, winning 71, in 42 ties. Manuel Santana played 119 rubbers, winning 91, in 46 ties for Spain.

The record of Great Britain in the quarter-century after 1946 was that of a good second-liner, the exploits of Perry and Austin vanishing into memories of the past. Tony Mottram and Geoff Paish did valiant work for a decade, usually performing to the peak of their capacity. To reach the semi-final of the European Zone became routine but not until 1958 (by which time Bobby Wilson and Billy Knight had taken over with Mike Davies pressing closely) was the actual final reached, when Italy was too strong in Milan. An outstanding year for Britain was 1963, when Mike Sangster was hurling service cannonballs about. A victory over Sweden made Great Britain the champions of Europe. The United States were then too strong in the Inter-Zone semi-final played at Bournemouth on hard courts.

The peak of British success was in 1969 with Mark Cox and Graham Stilwell. Switzerland and Ireland were beaten as a matter of routine. Germany was defeated in Birmingham, England, despite the loss of a double that was the longest in games in the history of the cup. Wilhelm Bungert and Christian Kuhnke beat Cox and Peter Curtis 10-8, 17-19, 13-11, 3-6, 6-2, a total of 95 games in all. South Africa was brought down at Bristol, that tie being the scene of anti-apartheid demonstrations. A win over Brazil at Wimbledon took Britain into the Inter-Zone final where, at Wimbledon again, Rumania reached the Challenge Round. The record for the longest rubber was broken in

August 1973 when in the American Zone final Stan Smith and Erik Van Dillen (USA) beat Jaime Fillol and Pat Cornejo (Chile) 7-9, 37-39, 8-6, 6-1, 6-3 – a total of 122 games. The match took place in Arkansas.

The challenger to Australia in 1962 was Mexico, carried there primarily by the electric brilliance of Rafael Osuna. The Mexicans' key success was against the United States in the semi-final of the American Zone. They proved more vital challengers than Italy but Australia was never in danger.

For the next two years, 1963 and 1964, the Challenge Round reverted to its old pattern. In the first of these years the United States broke the four-year sequence of Australian success, with Dennis Ralston and Chuck McKinley carrying the major responsibilities against John Newcombe and Roy Emerson. A fifth-rubber victory by McKinley over Newcombe turned the tie. McKinley and Ralston could not do as much when they defended the Cup at home against Emerson supported by Fred Stolle. Australia had revenge in 1964, again in a fifth-rubber climax with Emerson beating McKinley in four sets.

The Australians' success was measured in a four-year spell but their three home victories, all by 4-1, were against Spain, India and again Spain. In 1965 the United States did not survive a gruelling continental hard-court test on Spanish soil and their victors went on to beat India. In 1966 the United States again fell in the first of the Inter-Zone ties to Brazil, this allowing India to come through. In 1967 came the oddest defeat to the United States in all its lawn-tennis history. In the American Zone final it lost to Ecuador, in Ecuador, despite having Cliff Richey and Arthur Ashe. Australia beat Spain on the outcome of the first three rubbers for the loss of only 27 games, the most one-sided in the record since 1904.

Open lawn tennis began in 1968, but the Davis Cup remained restricted to amateurs under the discipline of national associations. Australia was immediately changed from top-line talent to second best, for Emerson, New-combe, Stolle and Tony Roche became professionals under contract. The peculiarities of lawn tennis politics meant that the United States was left with vastly stronger players.

The United States took the Davis Cup quite easily from Australia. In 1969, 1970 and 1971 Australia, which had not failed to be in the Challenge Round since 1937, was left struggling to survive. Australia was beaten by Mexico in 1969. In 1970, switching to the Eastern Zone, Australia lost to India, and in 1971 went out to Japan.

In the meantime the United States was able to dispose coolly of European opposition in the Challenge Round, by 5-0 against Rumania in 1969, by the same score against West Germany in 1970. Ironically the winning lead at 3-0 was achieved without the loss of a set but the final rubber, a dead one, in which Ashe beat Kuhnke, was resolved by 6-8, 10-12, 9-7, 13-11, 6-4. This was the longest singles in the Davis Cup.

At the annual meeting of the Davis Cup nations in 1971 it was agreed that the Challenge Round be abolished. Accordingly the American tie against Rumania in Cleveland in 1971 was the last Challenge Round to be played. Stan Smith and Frank Froehling were too good for Ilie Năstase and Ion Ţiriac. In the last rubber, when the issue was decided, Năstase beat Froehling 6-3, 6-1, 1-6, 6-4, and that lively, temperamental and brilliant Rumanian was the last player to hit a ball in a Challenge Round in lawn tennis. It was the 60th Challenge Round of the Davis Cup.

In the 60 times the Davis Cup had taken place, 1900-71, only four nations, the United States, Australia, Great Britain and France, won the trophy. This was out of 65 nations taking part. There were six victories for France, nine for Great Britain, 22 for Australia and 23 for the United States. The total number of ties played was 1,430.

The trophy donor, Dwight Davis, hoped that the event would contribute to the friendship of nations. International controversy intruded in the 1960s, provoked by opposition to South Africa's apartheid policy. In 1964 Poland withdrew rather than play against South Africa. Rumania did so in 1968. Both Poland and Czechoslovakia did so in 1969. The disruption provoked the suspension of South Africa as a competitor in 1970 and her entry was rejected in 1971.

In the first 60 years of competition six nations played more than 100 ties: USA 157, Great Britain 147, Italy 135, France 133, Australia 124, Sweden 102. For Records of the Davis Cup, see PART 3. See also colour plate, page 103. LT

Above **Davis Cup.** C. Kuhnke *(far left)*/W. Bungert (W. Germany) beat M. Cox *(near left)*/P. Curtis (GB) 10-8, 17-19, 13-11, 3-6, 6-2 in 1969.

Davis Cup Administration

What began as a challenge match between the United States and Great Britain in 1900 has since developed into a worldwide competition with teams from 54 countries in 1973. It is governed by an Annual Meeting held in London every July, at which the rules are made and changed, competing countries air their views and suggest ideas for improvements, discuss financial problems, approve accounts, and help those countries that need assistance.

Before 1973 the actual control of the competition was given to the Champion Nation of the previous year which appointed its own committee of management. In addition an honorary secretary of the Davis Cup Nations was elected every year at the Annual Meeting. One of the peculiarities of this appointment was that the delegates actually elected the honorary secretary for the Annual Meeting, but he remained from one meeting to the next to be responsible for the administration of this world event. He took action, answered questions, saw that accounts were kept and draws were made, published the rules and prepared for the next meeting. These duties were not listed although the present honorary secretary, Basil Reay, and his predecessor, Anthony Sabelli, the only honorary secretaries (both British) did the work for the last 50 years. At the Annual Meeting of Davis Cup nations in July 1973, it was decided that the competition should be supervised by a committee of management appointed by the Annual Meeting.

The Competition is open to all Full Members of the ILTF and one or two others specially elected. It is now organized in zones: the Eastern, the American (in two sections, North and South), and European Zones; the last is divided into European Zone A and European Zone B, the division made in the draw and not on any geographical principle. Each zone has a local committee chiefly concerned with finance and the committee makes the draw – with the one proviso that play in all zones must be completed by stipulated dates so that the four zonal winners can play to find the champion. Until 1971 the Champion Nation of one year did not play until the Challenge Round of the next year when it was challenged by the winning country of the Inter-Zone final. In 1971, however, it was agreed that this system gave the Champion Nation an unfair advantage in that it did not have to play until the end and then its team played on their own courts at a time which suited them, while in every other case there were elaborate regulations requiring a fair distribution of home and away matches. Now the four zonal winners play semi-finals, from which the two winning teams play in the final.

The nations pay subscriptions to a Central Fund when they enter, and when they win a round. In this way a modest reserve has been built up. The home nation in each tie also pays an agreed percentage of the receipts to the Special Travelling Expenses (STE) Fund, from which grants are made to countries that incur heavy expenses. The financial conditions are clearly laid down and are based on a democratic principle that the rich should help the poor. For example, if there is a good gate in a Davis Cup tie in Paris a fixed percentage is paid to the Fund; when there is a handful of spectators at another tie and practically no gate money, the travelling expenses of the visiting team are paid from the Fund. All accounts are carefully checked by the Secretary of the STE Committee and payments are made as far as the cash in hand will allow. Every country benefits and can therefore enter the Competition without undue worry about the cost.

Problems are usually settled amicably although there have been several difficult cases (see ADMINISTRATION OF THE WORLD GAME, PART 1). BR

Above **The Davis Cup**

Dayton Racquet Co. Inc.

The company was founded in Dayton, Ohio, in 1920 and moved to Arcanum in 1934. It began as an engineering company and turned to steel tennis rackets in the 1960s. Like other steel rackets, tried in the 1920s, they have steel strings. The Dayton Racquet Co. also manufactures rackets for badminton, paddle tennis and racquet ball (rackets) JB

HEAD OFFICE: 302 Albright Street, Arcanum, Ohio 45304, USA

Dead

Colloquial synonym for OUT OF PLAY. For a 'dead' tie (in team competitions) see RUBBER

Decugis, Max (France)

Born Paris, 21 Feb. 1882, died 1949; Wimbledon men's singles s/f 1911-12; men's doubles won 1911, r/u 1912; mixed doubles s/f 1919; French men's singles (closed) won 1903-4, 1907-9, 1912-14, r/u 1920, 1923, men's doubles won 1902-14, 1920; mixed doubles won 1904-6, 1908-9, 1914, 1920. Davis Cup 1904-5, 1912-14, 1919.

Denmark

The first Danish club that included tennis in its program was the Boldklub in Copenhagen, where football and cricket have also been played since before 1883. Tennis became an organized sport in Denmark in 1904 and was administered by the Dansk Boldspil Union, an association established to administer football and cricket. The same year this association became a member of the British Lawn Tennis Association as the ILTF did not then exist. The Danish LTA retains this membership – an honour to Denmark as it is the only country outside the Commonwealth to do so.

The first national tennis championships were played in 1904 but only for men's singles.

In March 1913 Erik Larsen represented the Dansk Boldspil Union at the inaugural meeting in Paris of the ILTF. Denmark, as a founder member, was awarded two votes.

On 3 April 1920 the Dansk Lawn-Tennis Forbund (Danish LTA) was founded as a subdivision of the Dansk Boldspil Union. In 1936 the LTA became an independent organization under the Danish Sports Association. By 1972 the Danish LTA had 184 member clubs with an individual membership of 30,000 and about 700 outdoor courts and 60 indoor courts.

In 1921 Denmark organized the World Championship indoor tournament with such success that this was offered to Denmark again the following year, but the invitation could not be accepted. In 1921 the World Championship women's singles was won by the Danish champion Elsebeth Brehm, who also won the women's doubles with Ebba Meyer.

Denmark has taken part in the DAVIS CUP almost every year since 1921, reaching the European Zone Final three times, losing to France in 1927, Sweden in 1950, and Belgium in 1953. Denmark has also competed in the FEDERATION CUP since 1963 and in the KING'S CUP since it began and has won the latter six times.

The best-known Danish international players are Einar Ulrich and his sons Torben and Jørgen, Kurt Nielsen, Jan Leschly and Hilde

Below **Max Decugis**

Sperling. Hilde Sperling was born in Germany but married a Dane in 1934; she played twice in the final of the Wimbledon women's singles, once in the women's doubles and won the mixed doubles (1933) with Gottfried von Cramm. She also reached the Wimbledon singles semi-finals four times and won the French singles 1935-7.

Einar Ulrich and his two sons have together played more than 200 Davis Cup matches – a world record; they have also won many major foreign titles. Einar Ulrich took part in administrative work on the national as well as the international level: he was for many years honorary secretary of the Danish LTA and at his death in 1969 he was its president and also a member of the Committee of Management of the ILTF. His many international connections provided Danish tennis with unique goodwill abroad.

Kurt Nielsen probably obtained the best results. Besides winning many international and national titles he was twice a Wimbledon finalist (1953 and 1955, both times unseeded) and unlucky not to win. Torben Ulrich, Jørgen Ulrich and Jan Leschly have won many national championships and also international titles.

Allan Heyman, a Danish subject living in England, who has represented Denmark since 1949 on the British Lawn Tennis Association, succeeded Einar Ulrich in 1969 as a member of the ILTF Committee of Management, and was nominated as its President in 1971. At that time the ILTF was in serious conflict with WORLD CHAMPIONSHIP TENNIS. It is a tribute to Allan Heyman's great skill as ILTF President that many problems, arising from the rapid development of professionalism in lawn tennis, were solved. See OPEN TENNIS (PART 1). BR

GOVERNING BODY: Dansk Lawn-Tennis Forbund, Vester Voldgade 11, 1552 Copenhagen V

Deuce see SCORING

Devonshire Park see EASTBOURNE

Dewar Cup

Until 1968 British tennis lacked a consolidated autumn-winter indoor season, spread over a number of successive weeks. The British Covered Court Championships at the Queen's Club had become a hit-and-miss affair: for a number of years they fluctuated between October and March and there was no competition in 1958, 1966 and 1967.

The Dewar Cup began in 1968, a highly successful competition sponsored by John Dewar and Sons Ltd, the whisky firm with its headquarters in Perth, Scotland. The Cup's formula was later to be expanded by WCT and ILTF in the ILTF GRAND PRIX. The idea from the beginning has been to take international-class tennis for both men and women to provincial towns and cities which rarely had the chance

Above **The Dewar Cup**

to see top stars in action. In 1968 Dewar Cup tournaments were staged at Stalybridge (Cheshire), Perth (Scotland), Aberavon (South Wales), and Torquay (Devon). The finals were split between the Queen's Club and Crystal Palace (both in London) and incorporated the British Covered Court Championships. The first Dewar Cup winners were Bob Hewitt (South Africa) and Margaret Court (Australia). Four of the finals were televised live. In 1969 the circuit was trimmed slightly by omitting the matches at Queen's. The winners were both British, Mark Cox and Virginia Wade.

The first major changes to the circuit came in 1970 when the Scottish 'leg' was moved from Perth, where it had outgrown the only available stadium, to Meadowbank, Edinburgh, which had been opened for the Commonwealth Games in the summer of the same year. That year too the finals were moved from Crystal Palace to the Royal Albert Hall, where they have been held since. The 1970 winners were a young Australian, John Alexander, then little-known, and the French no. 1, Françoise Durr. In 1971, Billingham, Teesside, replaced Stalybridge; there were British winners again, Gerald Battrick and Virginia Wade.

Perhaps 1972 brought the most significant change: the Grand Finals also became the last tournament in the COMMERCIAL UNION Grand Prix series for men. Thus, instead of the usual eight-points qualifiers going through to the Albert Hall final, the men's singles became an entry of 32 and the last week of the competition had to be split between Nottingham, where the fine University Sports Hall has two courts on which three rounds could be completed, and the ROYAL ALBERT HALL where the last eight competed. John Dewar increased the prize money and the cost of the promotion was increased to £25,000. Ilie Năstase (Rumania) won the £2,000 first prize for men, and Margaret Court won the women's singles (not one of the Grand Prix tournaments) for the second time.

The Dewar Cup has always attracted good crowds and every tournament final is a complete sell-out at the box-office. In 1970 yellow balls were used for the first time because they are easier to see under lights than white ones, and in that year too matches were played on Nygrass synthetic carpet. Since 1971, how-

ever, Uniturf has been used as the playing surface. Presentation has always been a feature of the Dewar Cup: since its inception, Scottish tradition has been kept up by the tournament finalists being piped onto court. DC

Dixon, Charles Percy (Gt Britain)
Born Grantham, Lincs., 7 Feb. 1873; died 29 April 1939; Wimbledon men's singles r/u* 1901, q/f 1908-9, r/u* 1911, q/f 1919; men's doubles s/f 1899, 1908, won 1912-13, r/u 1914; mixed doubles s/f 1909; Australian men's singles q/f 1913; men's doubles won 1912. Davis Cup (British Isles) 1909, 1911-13.

Dod, Miss Charlotte [Lottie] (Gt Britain)
Born Bebington, Cheshire, 24 Sept. 1871, died 1962; Wimbledon women's singles won 1887-8, 1891-3; Irish women's singles won 1887. An outstanding woman athlete of her age (she was the first woman to volley and smash), she has a unique place in lawn tennis history as the youngest-ever champion. She was 15 years 10 months old when she won Wimbledon for the first time in 1887 and was never beaten there. Her all-round sports ability extended to archery, ice skating, hockey and golf. She represented England at hockey in 1889-90 and was British Ladies Golf Champion in 1904.

Doeg, John Hope (USA)
Born Sonora Co., Mexico, 7 Dec. 1908; Wimbledon men's singles s/f 1930; men's doubles r/u 1930; US men's singles q/f 1928, s/f 1929, won 1930, s/f 1931; men's doubles s/f 1927, won 1929-30. Davis Cup 1930. A young protégé of TILDEN who did not fulfil his early promise to the high degree expected. Left-handed.

Below **H. L. ('Laurie') Doherty** *(seated)* **and R. F. ('Reggie') Doherty**

Above **Lottie Dod,** the youngest-ever champion

Doherty, Hugh Lawrence [Laurie] (Gt Britain)
Born London 8 Oct. 1876, died 11 Aug 1919; Wimbledon men's singles q/f 1897, r/u 1898, s/f 1900, won 1902-6; men's doubles s/f 1896, won 1897-1901, r/u 1902, won 1903-5, r/u 1906; US men's singles s/f 1902, won 1903; men's doubles won 1902-3. Davis Cup (British Isles) 1902-6. Brother of R. F. DOHERTY. Generally acknowledged as the finest exponent before 1914. He set the standard not only of playing skill but of sportsmanship and when he died he earned the honour, rare in those days for a sportsman, of a leader in *The Times*. His personality popularized lawn tennis as a spectator sport. He was the only overseas man between 1881 and 1925 to take the American singles title and his record in the Challenge Round of the Davis Cup – 12 rubbers won out of 12 played – was perfect. See GREAT PLAYERS OF ALL TIME (PART 1).

Doherty, Reginald Frank [Reggie] (Gt Britain)

Born London, 16 Oct. 1874, died 29 Dec. 1910; Wimbledon men's singles q/f 1895; won 1897-1900, r/u 1901; men's doubles r/u 1896, won 1897-1901, r/u 1902, won 1903-5, r/u 1906; US men's singles r/u 1902, q/f 1903; men's doubles won 1902-3; S. African men's singles won 1909. Davis Cup (British Isles) 1902-6. He yielded the laurels as best player in the world to his younger brother Laurie but contemporary critics declared that he was really the better player. He was unlucky in being plagued by indifferent health. Reggie and Laurie Doherty both rank as founding fathers of the game, and the south-west entrance to the All England Club commemorates them with 'The Doherty Gates'.

Double(s)

A contest between two pairs, divided into three categories: men's, women's and mixed doubles. The doubles court is 9 ft (2·97 m) wider than in singles, taking in the area of the 'tramlines' normally marked on both sides of a singles court. Service is alternated between the pairs with all four players serving in turn. Players receiving service must receive from the same court for the whole of a set. At the end of each set either pair may change its ORDER OF SERVICE or the court from which either partner receives service. Otherwise the same rules apply as in singles. JO

Double Fault

Two successive FAULTS from the same court delivered by the server, who thus loses the point. See RULES 6, 7, 8, 9 and 10 (PART 1). JO

Douglass, Miss Dorothea K.

see Mrs Lambert CHAMBERS

Down the Line

Opposite to CROSS COURT, strokes played from either hand parallel or nearly parallel to the sidelines. JO

Draw

The method by which a player's position in the tournament schedule is decided. Apart from certain 'seeded' players (see SEEDS), whose position in the draw is fixed in advance, the draw is normally produced by drawing players' names at random from a hat. A further complication used to occur in major international tournaments when 'nominated' players from any one country were kept in separate quarters of the draw. See BYE. DC

Dress see FASHION, MEN'S CLOTHING

Drive

The most widely used stroke in the game, played either on the forehand or backhand. The ball is struck hard, normally either flat or with top-spin, after it has bounced and usually from the back court or behind the baseline. JO

Drobný, Jaroslav ['Drob'] (Czechoslovakia)

Born Prague, 12 Oct. 1921; Wimbledon men's singles s/f 1946, q/f 1947, r/u 1949, s/f 1950, r/u 1952, s/f 1953, won 1954, q/f 1955; men's doubles s/f 1950, r/u 1951, s/f 1952; mixed doubles s/f 1948; US men's singles s/f 1947-8, q/f 1949; mixed doubles s/f 1947, 1949; Australian men's doubles r/u 1950; French men's singles r/u 1946, 1948, 1950, won 1951-2, s/f 1953; men's doubles s/f 1946, won 1948, r/u 1950, s/f 1951-3, 1956; mixed doubles s/f 1946, won 1948. Davis Cup 1946-8. An outstanding hard-court player, he precociously took BUDGE to five sets in Prague in 1938 when he was only 16. His prime success

Above **Jaroslav Drobný**
Below **Cliff Drysdale**

at Wimbledon, where he was the first left-handed men's singles champion since 1914, came after two disappointing failures as runner-up. This victory in 1954 was ecstatically popular although Drobný, a refugee from Czechoslovakia in 1948, was at that time technically Egyptian and only later (in 1959) adopted British nationality. See CENTRE COURT CLASSICS (PART 1).

Dropshot

A stroke, played on either forehand or backhand, in which the ball is hit gently and, almost invariably, with underspin (see SPIN) into the opposing forecourt as close to the net as possible. It is generally used when the opponent is retreating or is behind the baseline, so that it is difficult for him to reach the ball before it has bounced twice. JO

Drysdale, E. Clifford (S. Africa)

Born Nelsprint, Transvaal, 26 May 1941; Wimbledon men's singles s/f 1965-6, q/f 1969; US men's singles r/u 1965, q/f 1968; men's doubles s/f 1962, won 1972; Australian men's singles q/f 1971; French men's singles q/f 1964, s/f 1965-6, q/f 1967. Davis Cup 1964- . WCT 4th (F q/f) 1971, 4th (F q/f) May 1972, 5th (F s/f) Nov. 1972. One of the 'Handsome Eight'; WCT contract pro 1968-72. Basically right-handed with a two-handed backhand and an occasional two-handed forehand.

Dubler Cup

An international competition for men run by the VETERAN INTERNATIONAL TENNIS ASSOCIATION in much the same way as the Davis Cup. The competition began in 1958 when Italy won. The matches consist of four singles and one double; the early stages are played on a zonal basis. The cup is named after its donor, Mr Léon Dubler, president of the Veteran International Tennis Association. DC

Above **The Dubler Cup**

Dublin see IRISH OPEN CHAMPIONSHIPS

Dunlop Company Ltd

One of the largest sports-goods manufacturers in the world, with eight factories producing sports equipment in the United Kingdom, two each in Australia, New Zealand, South Africa and the United States, and one each in France,

Japan and West Germany. The company, until 1968 known as the Dunlop Rubber Company Ltd, was founded in 1889 by John Boyd Dunlop (1840-1921), a Scottish veterinary surgeon who invented the first practical pneumatic bicycle tyre. It began to produce golf balls in 1910 and later branched out into tennis equipment. In the 1920s it was first in the field with multi-ply tennis rackets which were much stronger than solid wood. Though it is a big sponsor of golf events Dunlop does not sponsor tennis tournaments, but it helps with the organization of many and also has a large number of leading players under contract. JB

Above **Margaret duPont**
Below **Françoise Durr**

HEAD OFFICE: Dunlop House, 25 Ryder Street, London, SW1, England

duPont, Mrs Margaret E. [Miss M. E. Osborne] (USA)

Born Joseph, Oreg., 4 March 1918; Wimbledon women's singles s/f 1946, won 1947, s/f 1948, r/u 1949-50, q/f 1951, 1954, 1958; women's doubles won 1946, r/u 1947, won 1948-50, r/u 1951, won 1954, r/u 1958; mixed doubles s/f 1946-9, 1951, r/u 1954, won 1962; US women's singles r/u 1944, q/f 1945-6, r/u 1947, won 1948-50, q/f 1953, 1956; women's doubles won 1941-50, r/u 1953-4, won 1955-7, s/f 1961-2; mixed doubles won 1943-6, s/f 1947, r/u 1948-9, won 1950, r/u 1954, won 1956, s/f 1957, won 1958-60; French women's singles won 1946, s/f 1947, won 1949, q/f 1950, s/f 1951; women's doubles won 1946-7, 1949, r/u 1950; mixed doubles s/f 1951. Wightman Cup 1946-50, 1954-5, 1957, 1962. Like her doubles partner Louise BROUGH, she was an outstanding exponent of the serve-and-volley technique. Their singles achievements ran in curious parallel, for whereas Mrs duPont won Wimbledon in 1947 only and Miss Brough took the title for the next three years, Miss Brough's Forest Hills victory in 1947 was followed by three years when Mrs duPont took the title. The 1949 Wimbledon final provided an outstanding clash between them, Miss Brough winning 10-8, 1-6, 10-8 after one of the finest title matches ever staged. Even more outstanding was the 1948 US final when Mrs duPont beat her doubles partner 4-6, 6-4, 15-13. She was invincible in the Wightman Cup in a run of 18 rubbers played between 1946 and 1957. SEE GREAT PLAYERS OF ALL TIME (PART 1). She is now Vice-President, Southwestern Tennis Association, for the El Paso area and writes a weekly newspaper column.

Durr, Miss Françoise (France)

Born Algiers, 25 Dec. 1942; Wimbledon women's singles q/f 1966, 1968, s/f 1970, q/f 1971, 1972; women's doubles r/u 1968, 1970, s/f 1971, r/u 1972-3; mixed doubles s/f 1966; US women's singles q/f 1965-6, s/f 1967, q/f 1970; women's doubles s/f 1966, 1968, 1970, r/u 1971, won 1972; mixed doubles r/u 1969, s/f 1970; Australian women's singles q/f 1965, 1967; women's doubles s/f 1969; mixed doubles s/f 1967; French women's singles q/f 1965-6, won 1967, s/f 1972-3; women's doubles r/u 1965, won 1967-71, r/u 1973; mixed doubles s/f 1965, won 1968, r/u 1969-70, won 1971, r/u 1972, won 1973. Federation Cup 1963-6, 1971-. ILTF GP 2nd 1971, 7th 1972.

Became professional 1968. Stylistically her success is the triumph of unorthodoxy, but she is the best French woman player in four decades. See also colour plate, page 205 and FRANCE.

Dutch Antilles see NETHERLANDS ANTILLES

E

Eastbourne, Sussex (UK)

Devonshire Park, Eastbourne, with 21 grass courts and six hard courts, is generally regarded as one of the five major lawn tennis venues in Britain. Tennis was first played there in 1870 and the South of England Grass Court Championships were started in 1881. Since then Eastbourne has also staged many British Davis Cup ties and several other ties in which both countries involved were foreign. It is also the present home of the top men's and women's groups in the INTER-COUNTY CHAMPIONSHIPS. Other events held at Devonshire Park include the Registered Professional Coaches' Championships (from 1912); the British Junior Grass Court Championships (from 1970); and the Junior National Invitation Championships for players under 12 (from 1972), under 14 (from 1970), and under 16 (from 1970). JO

Eastern Grass Court Championships (USA)

The Eastern Grass Court Championships, the official championships of the Eastern LTA, were first played at the Westchester Country Club (formerly the Westchester Biltmore Country Club), Rye, N.Y., in 1927. They remained there until 1946 when they were transferred to the Orange Lawn Tennis Club, South Orange, N.J., where they have been held for the last 27 years. The first titles were won by Julius Seligson, men's singles; Takeichi Harada of Japan and Jerome Lang, men's doubles; Molla Bjurstedt Mallory, women's singles, and Alice Francis and Edna Hauselt, women's doubles.

Robert L. Riggs won the men's singles title four times (1937-1940), William F. Talbert three times (1944, 1945, 1951). Other players who won the title twice were Clifford Sutter (1930, 1932); Frank A. Parker (1934, 1948); Ted Schroeder (1942, 1947); Lew Hoad, Australia (1953, 1954); Rod Laver, Australia (1960, 1970); Fred Stolle, Australia (1962, 1965). Other Eastern champions besides Riggs, Parker, Schroeder, Laver and Stolle who also were or became national singles champions include John Doeg, William T. Tilden, Fred J. Perry (Gt Britain), Donald Budge, Donald McNeill, Mal Anderson (Australia), Arthur Ashe, Stan Smith and Ilie Năstase (Rumania).

The Eastern men's doubles championship was won four times by Budge and Gene Mako, who also won the title with Gardnar Mulloy.

Winning three times were Mulloy and Talbert (Talbert also won with Francisco Segura and Mulloy with Mako). Jack Kramer and Schroeder won three times (Schroeder also won with Sidney B. Wood, Jr, and with Joseph P. Hunt). Another winner was Neale Fraser (Australia), who won three times, with his compatriots Rex Hartwig, Ken Rosewall and Ashley Cooper as his partners. Eastern doubles champions who also have won the US national doubles championship include Budge/Mako, Kramer/Schroeder, Mulloy/Talbert, Fraser/Cooper, Hoad/Rosewall, McGregor/Sedgman, Emerson/Stolle.

Louise Brough and Doris Hart won the women's singles four times. Alice Marble and Billie Jean King won three times. Other players who twice captured the title were Sarah Palfrey Cooke, Elsie Goldsack Pittman, Margaret Osborne duPont, Althea Gibson, Karen Hantze and Margaret Smith Court. Foreign players who have competed for the the title include Margaret Smith (Australia), Dorothy Round Little and Kay Stammers (Gt Britain), Sylvia J. Henrotin (France), Jadwiga Jedrzejowska (Poland) and Olgo Morozova (USSR).

Louise Brough and Margaret Osborne du-Pont won the women's doubles seven times; Margaret also won with Sarah Palfrey (then Mrs Cooke) and with Margaret Varner. Sarah Palfrey (then Mrs Fabyan) and Alice Marble won four doubles championships in a row (1937-1940), and Shirley Fry and Doris Hart won three straight (1951-1953). In 1943 Miss Hart, playing with Pauline Betz, had already won the title.

The first foreign team to capture the Eastern women's doubles was Freda James and Kay Stammers (Gt Britain) in 1934. Freda James had won the title the year before, playing with Elizabeth Ryan. Renee Schuurman and Sandra Reynolds of South Africa won in 1959. The English Virginia Wade and the Californian Rosemary Casals took the title in 1970. Miss Casals also won in 1966 and 1967 with Billie Jean King. A Russian pair won a women's championship in the United States for the first time when Olga Morozova and Marina Kroshina defeated Carol Caldwell Graebner and Patti Hogan (USA) in the 1972 Eastern Grass Court championship. FES

Eastern Grip see GRIPS

Ecuador

Until 1967 lawn tennis in Ecuador was controlled by the National Sporting Organization, but in 1967 the Asociación Ecuatoriana de Tennis was given autonomy and affiliated to the ILTF.

There are only 30 clubs and fewer than 100 courts in the country, but Ecuador has played in the DAVIS CUP regularly since 1961 and even won the American Zone in 1967 when they defeated the US team. In 1968 the Ecuador team won the South Section of the American Zone, defeating Chile. Every year the National Championships have entries from over 200 players. Ecuador first took part in the FEDERATION CUP in 1972.

With a population of fewer than six million, Ecuador has done well to produce Pancho Segura and other good players such as Miguel Olvera, Eduardo Zuleta, Pancho Guzman and Maria Eugenia Guzman.

Every ten years Ecuador organizes the SOUTH AMERICAN CHAMPIONSHIPS. BR
GOVERNING BODY: Asociación Ecuatoriana de Tennis, P.O. Box 1030, Guayaquil

Edgbaston see MIDLAND COUNTIES CHAMPIONSHIPS

Edinburgh see SCOTTISH CHAMPIONSHIPS

Egypt

Lawn tennis has been played in Egypt since the early part of the 20th century, particularly at the Gezireh LTC in Cairo, one of the leading clubs in Africa.

The Egyptian Lawn Tennis Association was established in 1923. In 1926 Egypt was admitted to full membership of the ILTF after long discussions by the Committee of Management of the ILTF, which had had separate applications from the Egyptian LTA and the Egyptian Union of Sports Societies.

During the early years lawn tennis was played chiefly in Cairo, Alexandria and the provincial capitals, but during the last 20 years more clubs have been established, more courts built and there has been emphasis on junior development.

Eastern Grass Court Championships Winners

Men's Singles		Women's Singles	
1927	J. Seligson	1927	Mrs M. Mallory
1928	J. Doeg	1928	Mrs M. S. Bundy
1929	W. T. Tilden	1929	Miss S. Palfrey
1930	C. Sutter	1930	Miss M. Gladman
1931	F. J. Perry	1931	Miss E. G. Pittman
1932	C. Sutter	1932	Miss E. G. Pittman
1933	S. B. Wood	1933	Miss D. Round
1934	F. A. Parker	1934	Miss K. Stammers
1935	B. M. Grant	1935	Miss A. S. Lamme
1936	J. D. Budge	1936	Miss S. J. Henrotin
1937	R. L. Riggs	1937	Miss J. Jedrzejowska
1938	R. L. Riggs	1938	Miss A. Marble
1939	R. L. Riggs	1939	Miss A. Marble
1940	R. L. Riggs	1940	Miss A. Marble
1941	F. L. Kovacs	1941	Miss P. Betz
1942	F. R. Schroeder	1942	Miss A. L. Brough
1943	F. Segura	1943	Miss M. Osborne
1944	W. F. Talbert	1944	Miss A. L. Brough
1945	W. F. Talbert	1945	Mrs S. P. Cooke
1946	W. D. McNeill	1946	Miss S. Fry
1947	F. R. Schroeder	1947	Miss M. Osborne
1948	F. A. Parker	1948	Miss A. L. Brough
1949	G. Mulloy	1949	Miss D. Hart
1950	H. Flam	1950	Miss D. Hart
1951	W. F. Talbert	1951	Miss P. C. Todd
1952	K. McGregor	1952	Miss D. Hart
1953	L. Hoad	1953	Miss D. Hart
1954	L. Hoad	1954	Miss A. L. Brough
1955	S. Giammalva	1955	Miss B. S. Davison
1956	H. Richardson	1956	Miss A. Gibson
1957	R. Savitt	1957	Miss M. A. Mitchell
1958	M. J. Anderson	1958	Miss A. Gibson
1959	A. Olmedo	1959	Miss R. Schuurman
1960	R. Laver	1960	Miss K. Hantze
1961	C. McKinley	1961	Miss K. Hantze
1962	F. Stolle	1962	Miss M. Smith
1963	E. Scott	1963	Miss M. Smith
1964	A. R. Ashe	1964	Miss B. J. Moffitt
1965	F. Stolle	1965	Miss B. J. Moffitt
1966	A. D. Roche	1966	Mrs D. F. Fales
1967	M. C. Riessen	1967	Mrs L. W. King
1968	C. Pasarell	1968	Miss M. A. Eisel
1969	S. R. Smith	1969	Miss P. Hogan
1970	R. Laver	1970	Miss K. A. Melville
1971	C. Graebner	1971	Miss C. Evert
1972	I. Năstase	1972	Miss O. Morozova
1973	C. Dibley	1973	Miss F. Bonicelli

Above **Roy Emerson**

European Amateur Championships

The European Amateur Championships were first held in 1969 in Turin. Teams from 12 nations – Austria, Belgium, Bulgaria, Czechoslovakia, Greece, Hungary, Italy, Norway, Poland, USSR, Spain and Switzerland – took part. Mrs V. Vopičková (Czechoslovakia) won the women's singles and S. Baranyi (Hungary) won the men's singles. These are one of the ILTF OFFICIAL CHAMPIONSHIPS.

European Indoor Championships see
KING'S CUP

Evert, Christine Marie (USA)

Born Ft Lauderdale, Fla., 21 Dec. 1954; Wimbledon women's singles s/f 1972, r/u 1973; US women's singles s/f 1971-3; women's doubles s/f 1973; mixed doubles s/f 1973; French women's singles r/u 1973; women's doubles s/f 1973. Wightman Cup 1971- ; at 16 years and 8 months (1971) the youngest player ever to represent the United States. Also the youngest semi-finalist in the US women's singles (1971). Two-handed on left-hand side. See colour plate page 171 and CENTRE COURT CLASSICS (PART 1).

Evert, Jeanne (USA)

Born Ft Lauderdale, Fla., 5 Oct. 1957; younger sister of Chris, who beat her sister's record as the youngest (15 years 10 months 10 days) US Wightman Cup player in 1973. Her talent for maintaining long rallies with accuracy brought her wins against Rosemary CASALS and Margaret COURT in 1972. Plays like her sister with two-fisted backhand and looks like a shorter, stockier version of her.

Below **Chris Evert**

Egypt has taken part in the DAVIS CUP since 1929.

Many local tournaments are held; the chief international events are the International Championships of Egypt played at the Gezireh Sporting Club, Cairo (where the stadium seats 7,000) during the first two weeks in March and the International Tournament at Alexandria played immediately afterwards. The Egyptian LTA also runs the Nations' Cup, an annual knock-out competition, held three days before the Cairo Championships. BR

GOVERNING BODY: The Egyptian Lawn Tennis Association, 13 Kasr el Nil, Cairo

'Elbow', the

Term applied to players who become extremely nervous at the crucial stage of a match, usually when they are in a winning position. It may be derived from a tendency to keep the elbow tucked in and not have a full swing. DC

Embassy Championships

see W.D. & H.O. WILLS

Emerson, Roy S. (Australia)

Born Blackbutt, Queensland, 3 Nov. 1936; Wimbledon men's singles s/f 1959, q/f 1960-1, 1963, won 1964-5, q/f 1966, 1970; men's doubles won 1959, 1961, s/f 1962-3, r/u 1964, 1967, s/f 1968-9, won 1971; mixed doubles s/f 1957; US men's singles q/f 1956, 1959, won 1961, r/u 1962, won 1964, q/f 1965, s/f 1966,

q/f 1967, 1969; men's doubles s/f 1956-7, won 1959-60, 1965-6, s/f 1969, r/u 1970; Australian men's singles q/f 1958-9, s/f 1960, won 1961, r/u 1962, won 1963-7, q/f 1971; men's doubles s/f 1956, r/u 1958, s/f 1959, r/u 1960-1, won 1962, r/u 1964-5, won 1966, s/f 1967, won 1969; mixed doubles r/u 1956; French men's singles q/f 1959, 1961, r/u 1962, won 1963, q/f 1964, s/f 1965, q/f 1966, won 1967, q/f 1968; men's doubles r/u 1959, won 1960-5, r/u 1967-9; mixed doubles r/u 1960, s/f 1961. Davis Cup 1959-67. Became professional in 1968, with National Tennis League; WCT contract professional 1971-2. WCT 3rd Group A (F q/f) 1973.

He ranks high among the nimble athletes of the game and, indeed, ran 100 yards in 10 seconds as a schoolboy. His mercurial speed about the court and strong forehand gave him the highest honours after years of effort when he played under the shadow of Australians of genius like ROSEWALL and HOAD. He was unlucky to be robbed by injury of his chance of winning the Wimbledon singles for the third successive year in 1966, when he started favourite. See colour plate, page 172, and GREAT PLAYERS OF ALL TIME (PART 1).

Equipment for Playing see THE
DEVELOPMENT OF PLAYING EQUIPMENT (PART 1)

Estonia

Estonia challenged separately in the DAVIS CUP in 1935. It now comes under the USSR.

F

Fabyan, Mrs S. P. see Miss Sarah PALFREY

Fairlie, Brian see NEW ZEALAND

Falkenburg, Robert (USA/Brazil)

Born Los Angeles, 29 Jan. 1926; Wimbledon men's singles q/f 1947, won 1948, q/f 1949; men's doubles won 1947, s/f 1948; US men's singles q/f 1944-5, s/f 1946, q/f 1947-8; men's doubles won 1944, s/f 1946; mixed doubles s/f 1944, r/u 1945, s/f 1948. Represented Brazil in the Davis Cup, 1954-5 (11 matches of which he won 3 singles and one double). Perhaps a lucky Wimbledon champion after being three match points down against BROMWICH, but he had a thunderous service and the gambler's capacity for a daring shot on important points.

Above **Robert Falkenburg**

Fashion

The men's doubles played at Leamington Spa in 1872 (see THE BIRTH AND SPREAD OF LAWN TENNIS, PART 1) is credited with being the first organized game of lawn tennis. The first women to play were the English and Irish. The circumstances of its birth automatically made nineteenth-century lawn tennis the prerogative of the leisured classes, for whom current etiquette in both behaviour and appearance was all important.

Without special rules or precedents the first women players wore what they would have chosen for a garden party: an elaborately flounced ground-length dress with ornamented sleeves, high neck and cinched waist, made from wool cloth or silk faille and worn with a comparably elaborate hat over a bustle, corset, petticoats and long drawers. Their first dress concession was to adopt flat, india-rubber-soled shoes, invariably black so they would not be seen to be soiled by the grass.

Above **Fashion.** This cartoon, which appeared in *Punch* on 10 October 1874, carried the caption: *'L'embarras des richesses. Young Robinson (mentally), "O would I were a ball that I might fly to - - - all!"*

A *Punch* cartoon dated 1874 shows a women's foursome wearing heavily cuffed and bustled outfits. Fashion plates depicting women players first appeared in the mid-1870s and by 1877 the *Queen* magazine was offering regular advice on 'Lawn Tennis Costume'. Coloured or striped flannel or serge were then considered the most suitable fabrics. Long protective aprons were borrowed from the earlier game of Badminton, some having two or four pockets to hold balls. 'Norfolk' jackets were thought appropriate over contrasting skirts. Panels of embroidered flowers were suggested as giving an 'outdoor' effect.

Everyday fashion of the mid-1870s called for three, even four, different fabrics to be combined in one costume. Fur trimmings were lavishly used and even recommended for tennis. Tennis costumes actually varied very little from party clothes until increasing movement about the courts made perspiration a problem. At that time it was unthinkable for a lady to be seen to perspire and with the beginning of tournament, or 'public', play (Dublin, 1879), a strong case for all-white dress was put forward.

All-white costumes designed specifically for 'good' players then followed in the early 1880s, though these still closely resembled the mood and silhouette of contemporary clothes. From its sporting associations in men's fashion the straw boater was considered more appropriate than the elaborate hats of earlier days. Women were first admitted to Wimbledon in 1884; the first photo on the next page shows the first lady champion Miss Maud Watson, wearing an all-white costume of that date.

By the end of the 1880s leisured ladies were playing lawn tennis in most European countries. Several royal families played regularly at the fashionable watering resorts. This is presumably why Continental tennis costumes (particularly the ornate hats and heavily trimmed 'leg o' mutton' sleeves worn by the German ladies) were more elaborate than any worn in Britain.

Lawn tennis was introduced to the United States by Miss Mary Ewing Outerbridge (1874), who had seen it played by British officers and their consorts in Bermuda. Understandably, therefore, the first American ladies who played chose similar costumes, though heavy felt hats were more favoured in New York than English straw boaters. Henceforth tennis clothing was generally similar in the two countries.

In Australia and New Zealand English-type costumes were also adopted, though dark-coloured skirts were in favour much later there than in Europe.

For the next fifteen years tennis costume settled for being generally an all-white version of everyday summer fashion. Miss Lottie Dod's short calf-length skirts and cricket cap were notable exceptions, accepted because she was only 15 at her first Wimbledon appearance (1887) and her tennis attire was virtually the same as her school uniform.

At the turn of the century England's leading player, Mrs Alfred Sterry, wrote, 'Nothing looks smarter and more in keeping with the game than a nice-hanging white skirt, about two inches off the ground, with white blouse, white collar and pale silk (neck) band . . .' (see photo on next page).

By then the bustle had disappeared but the hour-glass silhouette was still in vogue and even for tennis waists remained tightly laced into boned corsets. Coloured ribbon bands with brooch fastenings were superseding collars and women were being seen outdoors for the first time without hats. Some good players even tucked a flower into their waistbands. Mrs Lambert Chambers, however, who dominated Edwardian tennis, persisted with rather severe blouse-and-skirt outfits

Below **Fashion.** These fashion plates for tennis wear appeared in Budapest in 1897.

Above **Fashion.** (1) Miss Maud Watson, the first woman Wimbledon champion, in 1884. (2) Mrs Alfred Sterry, five times Wimbledon champion, in 1910. (3) Mrs Lambert Chambers, seven times Wimbledon winner. (4) Miss May Sutton in 1907. The first to roll up her sleeves, she won in 1905.

styled with function and 'good taste' foremost in mind (see third photo above).

In 1905 Miss May Sutton, the first Wimbledon champion from overseas (thus uninhibited by British etiquette) caused widespread indignation by rolling back her sleeves from her wrists because she was 'too hot'. This was the first instance of a woman player putting performance before etiquette and in so doing Miss Sutton set up the first significant milestone in the progress of tennis fashion.

For the next decade skirts stayed at ground length but flared from smooth hips and were worn over starched petticoats with crimped *broderie anglaise* frills at the ankles. Cotton *piqué* became a favourite for skirts. Cotton muslin blouses featured frilled *jabot* necklines, though some players still considered it more 'competent' to wear starched collars and cuffs with men's neckties and coloured Petersham 'schoolboy' belts.

Miss Elizabeth Ryan, all-time record holder of Wimbledon titles, recounts that at her first English appearances (1914) the ladies' dressing rooms customarily provided a rail above the fire on which players' corsets were hung to dry. 'It was not a pretty sight', recalls Miss Ryan, 'as many of them were blood-stained from the wounds they had inflicted.'

Corsets were still there in strength, but hats had all but disappeared from the courts when World War I put a four-year stop to most aspects of fashion.

The arrival of the French player, Suzanne Lenglen, at the reopening of Wimbledon (1919) was to influence all future fashion and, together with Miss Gussy Moran 30 years later, to establish the two most memorable milestones in its progress.

Lenglen appeared in a flimsy, one-piece cotton 'frock'. The skirt was pleated from the waist but it reached only to mid-calf. Moreover, it was worn without petticoats or corsets and its short sleeves showed her bare elbows. In contrast to the starched layers and general bulk of the other players' clothing the effect was staggering. She was described as 'shocking' and spoken of as 'indecent', but her all-conquering supremacy at the game coincided with the beginning of women's postwar 'liberation'. Her daring exactly matched the mood of the hour and in a short time she had an adoring following.

Lenglen came to Wimbledon for seven successive years. In 1920 she returned with a short hair style swathed in two yards of brightly coloured silk. The 'Lenglen Bandeau', as it was soon universally called, swept through all areas of fashion. Within two years little one-piece frocks of all types were inseparable from the name of Lenglen.

When Lenglen returned in 1923 she had changed her cotton frocks for the same style in white *toile-de-soie* designed by a Paris couturier, the first time silk dresses had been seen in tennis. With these she wore hip-length silk cardigans, always matching her bandeaux, and rarely appeared twice in the same colour scheme. Putting glamour and luxury into tennis she often wore shiny silk stockings and, for coming on court, a calf-length white 'steamer' coat with fur collar.

Lenglen's home was in Nice. The postwar home of the Russian ballet was in nearby Monte Carlo. All her life her thinking and training had been deeply influenced by the ballet. She was the first to equate the grace of tennis with the grace of dancing, the first to realize that flowing movements in her tennis dresses could accentuate her own flowing rhythms.

At the peak of her fame (1926) she used for her bandeaux the new shaded (*dégradé*) silk chiffons which had been introduced in a recent

Below **Fashion.** Suzanne Lenglen in 1925. Her dress influenced all future tennis fashion.

Above **Fashion.** Helen Wills in 1924. She ruled the Centre Court 1927-38 and never varied her attire.

Diaghilev production. With these she wound a matching length, 'Isadora-Duncan-style', around her neck. She fastened her bandeaux with a diamond arrow on her forehead and on most days pinned an admirer's flower corsage to her fur collar. Her philosophy was logical. In the introvert and essentially amateur society of tennis in the early 1920s she was the instinctive and totally professional star. As such her insistence on supremacy was uncompromising and her every match an appearance. She rejected corsets, etiquette, preconceived concepts of decency, etc., as obstacles to the performance she felt she owed to her spectators. With this thinking, coupled with unbounded technical skill, she gave lawn tennis an importance never previously known in sport and revolutionized the entire concept of women's dress.

After Lenglen's departure from Wimbledon (1926), Helen Wills automatically succeeded her as queen of the Centre Court (1927-38). Since childhood Miss Wills had worn a white sailor suit and white eyeshade for tennis. She never varied her appearance at Wimbledon and as all the women of the tennis world had been conditioned to seven years of copying Lenglen's Centre Court innovations, they quickly gave up their bandeaux for the Wills eyeshade.

The pagoda-like trouser-dress worn by Lili de Alvarez in 1929 must surely rank as one of the curiosities of tennis fashion. In that same year Billie Tapscott caused an echoing wave of criticism by being the first player even seen at Wimbledon without stockings.

In 1930 came necklines cut down to the waist at the back of Eileen Bennett's and Betty Nuthall's tennis dresses and in 1932 Helen Jacobs played the ladies' singles final in what are now called Bermuda-length shorts. These had broad navy stripes down the side seams and were worn with a monogrammed, short-sleeved shirt in fine knitted wool.

Miss Jacobs' long shorts, although still forbidden in official American matches the following year, were the unsuspecting forerunner of the later leg-show trend.

In the middle 1930s culotte skirts bridged the gap between ever-shortening hemlines and current concepts of modesty. In the late 1930s, Alice Marble introduced women to the serve-volley masculine game appropriately garbed in crew-neck cotton T-shirt, jaunty jockey cap and the shortest shorts seen at that time.

The only tennis seen in Europe during World War II was in exhibitions for the Red Cross. For these the writer made England's leading player, Kay Stammers Menzies, some romantic dresses in pastel moss crêpe. In wartime players were not handicapped by the established all-white convention and they agreed that anything likely to relieve the monotony of uniform would be welcome.

To Wimbledon's reopening (1946) the American stars came in abbreviated, pleated white culottes with baggy blouse tops featuring split shoulder-cap sleeves. Some conceded coloured belts to an otherwise bleak and unfeminine picture. By force of circumstance the British perpetuated the prewar fashions of 1939. Tennis had not been interrupted in the United States as in Europe, yet the new champion, Pauline Betz, said in 1946 that it was as difficult to buy tennis clothes in the United States as it was in Britain.

Of my own work and influence on tennis fashion (from 1947) I will say the following:

The first essential for any design influence to be effective is a ready source of supply of the commodity in question. I was fortunate that kind destiny and a faithful staff made possible uninterrupted production of my ideas from the beginning.

Below **Fashion.** Helen Jacobs *(right)* and Dorothy Round in 1934

Above **Fashion.** 'Gorgeous Gussy' shocked 1949 audiences with her lace-trimmed panties.

In the 1920s the Lenglen accent on 'spectacle' helped enormously to popularize tennis. From 1926 to 1946 enthusiasm for the game rode its own impetus and the fashion aspect became unimportant until television (1946) brought entirely new audiences, mostly ignorant of the sport's technical attractions.

I was brought up in Nice in the immediate aura of Lenglen and her triumphant reading of public taste. With such memories I saw that 1946 tennis styles would not attract the new TV public. Hence my first coloured trims for Joy Gannon (1947), Betty Hilton (1948) and my so-called 'sexy' outfit for Gussy Moran (1949).

In the 1960s tennis fashion fell on relatively lean days as it was then that the clothing industry first cast its eyes on tenniswear. Some commercial interests came out very strongly in favour of basic ready-to-wear

Below **Fashion.** Billie Jean King in 1962, wearing a typical outfit of the period

Above **Fashion.** 1972 Virginia Slims outfits. *Left to right* Brenda Kirk (S. Africa), Leta Liam (Indonesia), Virginia Wade (GB), Nell Truman (GB), Wendy Overton (US), Maria Nasuelli (Italy), Karen Krantzke (Australia), Ted Tinling, Pam Austen (US), Lany Kaligis (Indonesia), Evonne Goolagong (Australia), Ingrid Bentzer (Switzerland), Kerry Melville (Australia), Valerie Ziegenfuss (US), Kerry Harris (Australia); *seated* Pam Teeguarden (US), Jill Cooper (GB), Vicky Berner (Canada), Winnie Wooldridge (GB)

shirt-and-skirt styles and the young champions of that period, Billie Jean King and Margaret Smith Court, invariably appeared in conventionally pleated or kilt-type skirts with cotton-knit tops.

Throughout this period I preached that the future of tennis lay in spectator appeal and thus TV and commercial sponsorship. Fashion would obviously play an important part and I thought this philosophy already well proven by the worldwide sensation of Gussy Moran's outfit and the acknowledged popularity of many other of my ultra-feminine designs.

To me fashion in tennis is the most readily understandable line of communication between performer and spectator. To communicate tennis more attractively I determined on a policy of putting the successive seasonal trends of magazine fashion into my tennis designs and I follow this today more than ever.

Lately TV exposure of women's tennis across the world has effectively switched authoritative criticism of tennis fashion from Wimbledon to the much wider judgments of commercial acceptance. The success of the Virginia Slims women's circuit (from 1970) has proved beyond doubt that the spectators' favourable endorsement is now a designer's first responsibility to all concerned. The success of the alternative USLTA women's circuit was undoubtedly enhanced by the appealingly cute styles promoted by its bright star, Chris Evert.

Before us now (1973-4) lies a tennis world of colour. I believe British spectators will still prefer predominantly white tennis wear for

Above **Fashion.** Billie Jean King's dress, made for her Houston match with Riggs in 1973, was in mint green polyester knit, with sky-blue collar and a horizontal band in royal blue with rhinestones and green sequins.

some years to come but the eye-appeal and personal identity provided by colour has shown that a really valid, all-embracing tennis fashion plays an ever-growing part in the game's capacity to revitalize and adjust itself to the passage of time.

Spanning a hundred years of tennis fashion one single factor has remained constant: perspiration is still an unsightly and unresolved problem! Ted Tinling.

Postwar Highlight Innovations and Trendsetters Selected by Ted Tinling

First lace dress	Maria Weiss	1950
First nylon dress	Pat Ward	1950
First 'See-Thru' dresses	television	1950
First Orlon dress	Althea Gibson	1951
First polyester dresses	several players	1953
First paper dresses	Anthea Warwick Ilse Buding Sylvana Lazzarino	1957
Tennis Wigs	Shirley Bloomer Karol Fageros Pat Ward	1959

Joy Gannon	1947-8
Joan Curry	1948-50
Betty Hilton	1948
Barbara Schofield	1948-52
Gussy Moran	1949-50
Lorna Cornell	1950-2
Beverly Baker	1951-5
Maureen Connolly	1952-4
Lea Pericoli	1955-71
Yola Ramirez	1957-62
Rosie Reyes	1957-62
Shirley Bloomer	1957-65
Sandra Reynolds	1957-64
Renee Schuurman	1957-64
Maria Bueno	1958-67
Christine Truman	1958-70
Evonne Goolagong Virginia Wade Rosemary Casals Billie Jean King	1972-
Evonne Goolagong	1973-

Fault

A service that is not good for any of the reasons covered by RULES 6, 7, 8 and 9 (PART 1). See also DOUBLE FAULT, FOOTFAULT. JO

Federation Cup

The need for a worldwide team competition for women was finally filled in 1963 with the inauguration of the Federation Cup. After rejecting offers from various nations to donate a trophy for a 'Davis Cup for women', the ILTF decided to celebrate its 50th anniversary by giving the trophy and naming it after itself. A large, lovely silver flower bowl with turned-up handles, sitting on a silver and black wooden base, the Federation Cup has contributed much to the advancement of women's tennis during its first decade. There has been a steady increase in stature, with nearly 50 countries having challenged for the Cup. The greatest number of nations to compete in any one year is 31 (in South Africa, 1972). 30 took part in 1973.

In its first decade eight different countries were the scene of this annual competition, held at a single centre over a period of one week or less. It is drawn in the same way as an elimination tournament, with some nations seeded. Each round consists of two singles and one doubles match. The numbers one and two singles players each play their counterparts, followed by the double. The members of the doubles team may or may not play singles, making a minimum of two and maximum of four players from each country. Captains may be playing or non-playing; there have been

Above **Federation Cup**. Brenda Kirk *(right)* and Pat Pretorius clinch match point and the Cup for South Africa in Johannesburg in 1972.

many of both, as well as several men captains. Bill Kellogg was the captain of the first winning team from the United States.

All full member nations of the ILTF are eligible to compete for the Federation Cup, but only three have won it. The first nine years were dominated by Australia and the United States. Every time they played each other in the final round, only a close 2-1 score decided the winner. Whenever either of them played a different nation in the final round, it won 3-0 (without losing a match). Outstanding members of those winning teams were Margaret Smith Court, Lesley Turner, Judy Tegart Dalton, Kerry Melville, Karen Krantzke, Evonne Goolagong and Lesley Hunt (Australia); Darlene Hard, Billie Jean Moffitt King, Nancy Richey Gunter, Karen Hantze Susman, Carole Caldwell Graebner, Julie M. Heldman, Rosemary Casals and Peaches Bartkowicz (United States). Not until June 1972 did South Africa become the first nation other than Australia or the United States to break into the winning column, when their sixth-seeded team of Pat Walkden Pretorius, Brenda Kirk and Greta Delport successively disposed of Belgium, Brazil, France, the United States, and in the final round Great Britain, which had

defeated Australia. Playing on their home courts in Johannesburg before an unprecedented crowd of 7,000 wildly cheering spectators, the South African women succeeded in doing what some of their former supposedly superior representatives had been unable to do – win the Federation Cup.

Great Britain has been runner-up three times, West Germany twice; the Netherlands once. Ann Haydon Jones, Virginia Wade, Winnie Shaw and Joyce Williams sparked the challenging teams of England and Great Britain. West German stars were Helga Niessen Masthoff, Helga Schultz Hoesl and Edda Buding; the top Dutch players were Marijke Jansen Schaar, Astrid Suurbeek and Lidy Jansen-Venneboer. A few of the many other outstanding players to have taken part are the great Maria Bueno (Brazil); Françoise Durr, Janine Lieffrig, Gail Chanfreau and Rosie Darmon (France); Lea Pericoli and Sylvana Lazzarino (Italy); Kazuko Sawamatsu (Japan); Betty Stöve and Trudi Walhof (the Netherlands); Christine Truman Janes, Elizabeth Starkie and Deirdre Catt Keller (Gt Britain); Renee Schuurman, Annette Van Zyl du Plooy, Laura Rossouw, Margaret Hunt, Glenda Swan and Maryna Godwin Proctor (S. Africa); Jan Lehane and Robyn Ebbern (Australia); and Mary Ann Eisel, Patti Hogan, Susan Walsh and Kathy Harter (USA).

Although it is not mandatory to take part

every year, a few nations challenged all or most of the first ten years of play: Australia, United States, Great Britain, Italy, South Africa, France, West Germany, the Netherlands, Canada, Belgium, Switzerland and Czechoslovakia. These 12 countries, as well as Hungary, Denmark, Austria and Norway, sent teams to London in 1963 for the first Federation Cup matches, which celebrated not only the 50th anniversary of the ILTF but also the 75th anniversary of the British Lawn Tennis Association. The matches were scheduled for the grass courts of the Queen's Club but most of the play on three of the four days was indoors. Regulations permit a shift to any surface if the weather is bad. Heavy rain made all outdoor courts unplayable and the use of the club's indoor courts introduced many of the young competitors to wooden surfaces. The final between Australia and the United States was superb, thrilling the capacity indoor crowd. Margaret Smith completely dominated Darlene Hard in the first match, losing only three games. Billie Jean Moffitt evened the score by coming from behind to down Lesley Turner 5-7, 6-0, 6-3. The clinching doubles match might well have gone to Australia as they had only to hold serve one of three times for a straight sets victory. However, the revamped team of Hard/Moffitt, rather than the originally scheduled Hard/Carole Caldwell duo, fought and scrambled to an exciting 3-6,

13-11, 6-3 first-ever win of the Federation Cup. The United States did not win again until 1966.

Australia has the unique distinction of having won the Federation Cup twice in one year, with a completely different team each time. The 1970 competition was won by Judy Dalton and Karen Krantzke in Freiburg, Germany, in May. Then the 1971 matches actually took place in 1970, at the end of December, at Perth, Western Australia, where hometown heroine Margaret Court, another Perth girl Lesley Hunt, and the first aboriginal girl to represent her country in tennis, Evonne Goolagong, won the series, as their compatriots had done earlier in the year, without the loss of one match. Australia won again in 1973.

For detailed records see PART 3. MdP

Field Tennis (1767) see THE ORIGINS OF LAWN TENNIS (PART 1)

Fillol, Jaime (Chile)
Born 3 June 1946; Wimbledon men's doubles s/f 1972; US men's doubles s/f 1970; French men's doubles r/u 1972. Davis Cup 1970-

FILT (Fédération Internationale de Lawn-Tennis)
see INTERNATIONAL LAWN TENNIS FEDERATION

Finland
The LTA of Finland was founded in April 1911 with five lawn tennis clubs, two with covered courts. By 1972 there were 91 clubs with a membership of nearly 10,000. Outdoor courts numbered 250. There are now 65 covered courts.

The first official lawn tennis championships in Finland were played in Hangö (Hanko) in 1912 for the NORDIC CUP – an annual competition for Scandinavian players which is still held.

Finland affiliated to the ILTF in 1918, when the country was given independence. It was expelled in 1946 but readmitted in 1947, and in 1972 had the honour of staging the Annual Meeting of the ILTF.

Teams from Finland have competed in the DAVIS CUP since 1928, in the FEDERATION CUP since 1968 and in numerous international championships.

Every fourth year the SCANDINAVIAN CHAMPIONSHIPS (on covered courts) are played in Finland. BR
GOVERNING BODY: Suomen Tennisliitto, Box 25202, Helsinki 25

Fitzwilliam Club, Dublin, see IRELAND

Fleitz, Mrs J. G. [Miss Beverly Baker] (USA)
Born Providence, R.I., 13 Mar. 1930; Wimbledon women's singles s/f 1951, r/u 1955, q/f 1956; women's doubles s/f 1951, 1955, r/u 1959; US women's singles q/f 1948-9, s/f 1950, q/f 1954-5, s/f 1958; French women's singles

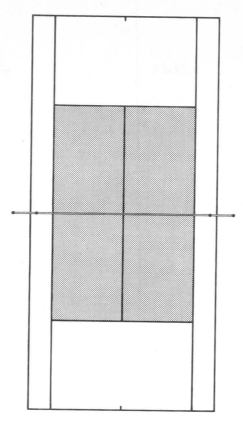

Above Forecourt

q/f 1951, s/f 1955; women's doubles won 1955. Wightman Cup 1949, 1956, 1959. Ambidextrous.

Fletcher, Kenneth N. (Australia/Hong Kong)
Born Queensland, 15 June 1940; Wimbledon men's singles q/f 1962, 1966-7; men's doubles s/f 1961, r/u 1964-5, won 1966, r/u 1967; mixed doubles won 1963, r/u 1964, won 1965-6, r/u 1967, won 1968, s/f 1969; US mixed doubles won 1963; Australian men's singles q/f 1960-1, r/u 1963, s/f 1964; men's doubles s/f 1960, 1962, r/u 1963-4; mixed doubles won 1963-4; French men's singles q/f 1963, 1966; men's doubles won 1964, r/u 1965, 1967; mixed doubles won 1963-5. Domiciled in Hong Kong since 1964.

Follow Through
Term describing the path of the racket after it has made contact with the ball. It precisely indicates the type of stroke that has been played.

Foot Fault
A faulty service caused by the server before impact either changing his position by walking or running or touching, with either foot, any area of the ground other than that behind the baseline and within the imaginary extension of the centre mark and sideline. See RULE 7 (PART 1). JO

Footwear
Special shoes, designed solely for the game, have been worn by tennis players since early days at Wimbledon. At the beginning they were comparatively primitive with a plain rubber sole and a one-piece canvas upper. Today's shoes are much improved with serrated or ribbed soles, reinforced rubber toecaps, strong canvas uppers, built-up soles with arched sponge insoles for greater comfort, and heels strengthened by nylon. Shoes with spikes, like track shoes, have occasionally been worn on damp grass courts to give players a better grip. This practice is generally discouraged by tournament officials. See also THE DEVELOPMENT OF PLAYING EQUIPMENT (PART 1). JO

Footwork
The action of the feet in moving into position to play a shot. Correct footwork is essential for proper balance and effective 'grooving' of strokes. See THE BASIC TEACHING OF TENNIS (PART 1). JO

Forecourt
The area of the court from the net to the service line and between the sidelines, taking in the 'tramlines' in doubles. JO

Forehand
A stroke played from the right-hand side. The reverse applies to a left-handed player. JO

Forehand Grip see GRIPS

Forest Hills see US CHAMPIONSHIPS and THE UNITED STATES STORY (PART 1)

Four Musketeers
Jean Borotra, Jacques Brugnon, Henri Cochet and René Lacoste, who were responsible for FRANCE's pre-eminence internationally in the 1920s. Between them they played 164 DAVIS CUP rubbers, winning 120. They won the Cup 1927-32. See also THE GROWTH OF THE GAME (PART 1).

France
The origins of lawn tennis in France are a little obscure. The first clubs were certainly founded by Englishmen but there is disagreement about which they were. Le Havre Athletic Club celebrated its centenary in 1972. It was founded by English graduates from Oxford and Cambridge and adopted (and still retains) the colours of those two great English universities, dark blue and light blue. But in 1872 they played association football and rugby football. It was not until the summer of 1884 that three grass courts were marked out on the football pitches. A few years later they were transformed to hard courts and increased to seven.

The Dinard Tennis Club in Brittany also claims to be the first. It was founded in 1878 by some Englishmen who spent seaside holidays there. The club grew rapidly and many champions took part in its annual tournament between 1920 and 1930, including Christian Boussus, Henri Cochet, Antoine Gentien, and the famous navigator Alain Gerbault.

A little later, two clubs in Paris, which subsequently became important, were founded: the Racing Club of France (1882) and the Stade Française (1883). Then the sports society of the Île de Puteaux was founded in 1885 and French lawn tennis really began.

The Île de Puteaux is on the Seine, near Paris, and tennis is still played there. It used to be more of a fashionable club where ladies chatted over tea than a sporting one, but champions also met there and the early French Championships were held there. The first were staged in 1891 and won by J. Briggs. The next year the title went to J. Schoepfer, known as a writer as Claude Anet. Then came the reign of André Vacherot, who won three years running but was unthroned in 1897 by P. Aymé. That year women were admitted: Mlle Masson was the first woman champion of France and won the title five times. Between 1880 and 1900 many clubs began in other places: the Lawn Tennis Club of Lille (1890), the Club de la Tête d'Or in Lyons (1894) and the Tennis Club of Paris (1895), the latter with covered courts, a great innovation which permitted play in winter.

The Tennis Club of Paris is still one of the largest clubs in the capital. It has nine outdoor courts and six indoor which adjoin the Pierre de Coubertin stadium where all the great covered-court events are contested. The Coubertin stadium was built in 1937 by the city of Paris and was inaugurated in February 1938 when France and Sweden met for the Challenge Round of the KING'S CUP in the presence of H.M. Gustaf V of Sweden. Demolished by a raid in World War II, it was rebuilt and now hosts all the great tennis events, basketball, volley ball, and other sports. It seats about 4,000.

In about 1900 Max Decugis, aged 18, showed himself to be a champion of international status. He is now in his 90s, lives on the Côte d'Azur and still takes a lively interest in tennis. He was the first Frenchman to play modern tennis. Serving and smashing with power, volleying well, he always played with ferocious energy and fought back to win from desperate situations; for example, he won against the famous New Zealander Anthony Wilding at Brussels after being down 2 sets to 0, 5 games to 0 and 0-40.

Four champions brightened French tennis in 1900-20. They were not the Musketeers. In France champions come in fours. This first four comprised Max Decugis, André Gobert, Maurice Germot and William Laurentz.

André Gobert was 1m 92 (6 ft 4 in) tall, very athletic, and possessed a splendid game. Unfortunately his nerves were not of the same high standard. The least thing could upset him completely. One day, in 1920, playing in doub-

Above **France.** André Gobert in 1912. He left tennis to concentrate on golf.

les on the Wimbledon Centre Court against Tilden and Johnston, he began to serve double faults. 'Watch out' said Laurentz. Gobert replied 'I can't serve with the King behind me.' In fact, King George V and Queen Mary had just come into the Royal Box. That was the end of Gobert. He left tennis for golf and became French champion in that sport too.

Maurice 'Fifi' Germot was small, thin, and always smiling. Supple, adroit, precise and with an excellent volley, he was a great doubles player. He was exactly the same age as Decugis, with whom he formed a partnership unbeatable in France. They were champions of France ten times between 1904 and 1920.

Below **France.** Simone Mathieu, French champion in 1938-9

Germot also won the title with Marcel Dupont and Gobert. In this first group of four Germot played the role that Brugnon took several years later in the Musketeers—that of the perfect partner.

William H. Laurentz was of Belgian origin but always played in France. Extremely quick and clever at the volley and with a game of brilliant and effective attack, he imposed himself for 15 years on the international scene. He was the unfortunate victim of an accident in 1912 when a service ball from Gobert ricocheted off his racket and hit him in the eye. He had to have an operation, but he was world champion at Saint-Cloud eight years later. He was selected for the Davis Cup five times.

In 1914, at the World Clay Court Championships held in the Stade Français at Saint-Cloud, the public were astonished by a little girl, with hair down her back held by a ribbon, who returned all the balls and defeated all her opponents, successively eliminating the English Mrs Satterthwaite (6-3, 8-6), the Belgian Mme de Borman (6-2, 6-3), the French Suzanne Amblard (6-2, 4-6, 6-3) and in the finals another Frenchwoman, Mme Golding (6-2, 6-1). She also won the women's doubles with the American Elizabeth Ryan and was only defeated in the mixed finals with Comte Salm by Miss Ryan and Decugis. She was called Suzanne Lenglen and was just 15. She was to dominate international women's tennis for seven years (1919-26).

An only child, she spent part of the year on the Côte d'Azur with her parents and at the age of 11 had been given a racket and her first lessons by her father. Quickly seeing his daughter's talent, he decided to concentrate on her and make her a champion, so he

Above **France.** Suzanne Lenglen and Helen Wills at their famous meeting in Cannes in 1926. Suzanne won 6-3, 8-6.

studied the game of the best players who came to the Riviera and proposed the best strokes of each one as a model for Suzanne, while letting her keep her own style. He made her skip and do dancing exercises, practise every day against a wall until her movements were perfect, and, to train her to place her shots precisely, he would put on the court a handkerchief which she had to hit.

At 13 or 14 she won an important tournament in Nice. Anthony Wilding chose her as his partner in the mixed doubles at Cannes which they won. In spring 1914 she was defeated in the final of the French Championships by Marguerite Broquedis, the great French woman champion of the period. But

two weeks later Mlle Lenglen won her first title of world champion.

During World War I Suzanne and her parents stayed at Nice. Suzanne took up the game again at Wimbledon in 1919 and reached the Challenge Round on 5 July quite easily, meeting the holder, the Englishwoman Mrs Lambert Chambers. It was a fantastic battle (see CENTRE COURT CLASSICS, PART 1). After saving two match balls in the third set almost by a miracle, Suzanne, at the end of her strength, finally triumphed 10-8, 4-6, 9-7. Her victory unleashed indescribable enthusiasm. She became the queen of Wimbledon and was adored there more than anywhere else. She kept her title until 1923. In 1924 she was ill with jaundice and could not take part in the Championships, but she returned in 1925 and won for the last time.

French Championships (Closed) Winners
Men's Singles

1891	J. Briggs
1892	J. Schopfer
1893	L. Riboulet
1894	A. Vacherot
1895	A. Vacherot
1896	A. Vacherot
1897	P. Aymé
1898	P. Aymé
1899	P. Aymé
1900	P. Aymé
1901	A. Vacherot
1902	M. Vacherot
1903	M. Decugis
1904	M. Decugis
1905	M. Germot
1906	M. Germot
1907	M. Decugis
1908	M. Decugis
1909	M. Decugis
1910	M. Germot
1911	A. H. Gobert
1912	M. Decugis
1913	M. Decugis
1914	M. Decugis
1915-19	*No Competition*
1920	A. H. Gobert
1921	J. Samazeuilh
1922	H. Cochet
1923	P. Blanchy
1924	J. Borotra

In 1925 entries were accepted from all countries (see PART 3 for detailed records)

Women's Singles

1897	Miss F. Masson
1898	Miss F. Masson
1899	Miss F. Masson
1900	Miss J. Prevost
1901	Mrs P. Girod
1902	Miss F. Masson
1903	Miss F. Masson
1904	Miss K. Gillou
1905	Miss K. Gillou
1906	Mrs. K. Fenwick
1907	Mrs C. De Kermel
1908	Mrs K. Fenwick
1909	Miss J. Mathey
1910	Miss J. Mathey
1911	Miss J. Mathey
1912	Miss J. Mathey
1913	Miss M. Broquedis
1914	Miss M. Broquedis
1915-19	*No Competition*
1920	Miss S. Lenglen
1921	Miss S. Lenglen
1922	Miss S. Lenglen
1923	Miss S. Lenglen
1924	Miss D. Vlasto

In 1925 entries were accepted from all countries (see PART 3 for detailed records)

In 1926 a new star rose in the United States: Helen Wills. Statuesque, impassive, her dominance expressed through the accuracy of her game, she embarked for Europe, arrived on the Côte d'Azur and entered for the tournament at Cannes. Suzanne was there. Naturally they met in the final on 16 February and it was the match of the century. It was marred by one incident. Suzanne had won the first set 6-3 and was leading 6-5 in the second. Match point. A straight stroke from Helen Wills seemed wide. There was a call, 'out'. The American was about to shake Suzanne's hand when the umpire corrected the call: it was not the linesman who had cried 'out' but a spectator. In fact the ball was good and the match continued. Suzanne, upset for a moment, lost the next points and the game, but she regained control of her nerves and the result was 6-3, 8-6. The same year she became a professional and made a tour of the United States. She was not seen for several years. In 1937 she founded a tennis school but her health caused her anxiety and she died of leukaemia in Paris on 4 July 1938.

In 1921 two totally unknown players, a Lyonnais and a Basque, met at the Racing Club of France in the final of the Criterium. Henri Cochet, the Lyonnais, defeated Jean Borotra, the Basque, in the fifth set. Those who saw that final realized that they had seen two future champions. In 1922 Cochet and Borotra made their Davis Cup débuts and defeated the Danish team. In 1923 the famous four, Cochet, Borotra, Lacoste and Brugnon, came together for the first time, and beat Ireland 4-1. It was the beginning of a remarkable period. Who called them the Musketeers? Nobody knows for sure, but probably a journalist.

Henri Cochet was born in Lyon where his father was secretary of the Tennis Club. Small, supple, calm, he had a marvellous sense of anticipation which allowed him always to foresee the stroke that his opponent was about to play, so that without apparent effort he was on the ball and finding a surprise return. He was one of the few to beat Tilden despite not having any specially powerful strokes. He had little or no service, a middling return, but a remarkable half-volley and volley, extraordinary reflexes, an iron will, a very good forehand and a definitive smash. His ball went quickly because he struck it very early, always advancing towards the net.

Jean Borotra was born at Arbonne, near Biarritz, on the Basque coast. His first sports were pelota and also bicycling. He used to bicycle to school 10 km to Bayonne and back twice a day, and later claimed that those 20 km every day gave him legs of steel. Tennis was not important to him until after World War I and he appeared for the first time in Paris in June 1921 when he played against Cochet in the Criterium final. This tall boy wearing a Basque beret, hurling himself at the net with each ball, produced a strong impression on the public. His bounding at the volley led to his English nickname, the 'Bounding Basque'. His life was a perpetual whirlwind. He threw himself into business and sport with equal success, travelling the world on business and playing tennis. In his 70s he has given up nothing, has hardly slowed down. He even played in the veterans' tournament in Wimbledon in 1972, 50 years after his first appearance at the All England Club.

Quite different from Borotra, Jean-René Lacoste is also a kind of phenomenon. He made his tennis début at the age of 15 when spending a holiday in England. Lacoste was really not talented at tennis. He held his racket in the middle of the handle, he was rather undeveloped physically, but he had a tenacious will and a great gift of observation. He trained methodically for hours and hours, alternating exercises and tennis, trying to imitate the champions whom he had seen play and carefully noting all his comments in a little notebook. He never gave up this habit and his notebooks, full of observations on all the champions he met during his career, became legendary. Even when offered a small fortune he would not part with them. Unfortunately he left tennis in 1929, worried about his health.

The fourth Musketeer, Jacques 'Toto' Brugnon, is the oldest of the team. He was a particularly great doubles player but also achieved fine results in singles, reaching the Wimbledon semi-finals in 1926. Modest, self-effacing,

Below **France.** The Four Musketeers. *Left to right* R. Lacoste, H. Cochet, P. Gillou (captain), J. Brugnon, J. Borotra

charming, he contributed much to French Davis Cup victories.

France first took part in the Davis Cup in 1904. Its team was composed of Decugis and Aymé, who were defeated 3-2 by Belgium. The next year Decugis and Germot were eliminated 5-0 by the US team. After a gap of five years, France entered again in 1912 and was defeated by the British Isles. In 1913 and 1914 it was beaten again by Germany and the British Isles. At last, in 1919, France achieved its first victory by defeating Belgium; it then lost to the British Isles. In 1920, with Gobert and Laurentz, it was dominated by the United States (3-0). In 1921, it was defeated by India; Brugnon appeared in the French team for the first time. In 1923 the era of the Musketeers began. Four years later, in September 1927 at Philadelphia, the French carried off the Davis Cup, at last.

Now that the Davis Cup was in Paris, it had to be defended. There was no stadium for tennis in the capital large enough to hold the public who wanted to see the Challenge Round. The city of Paris gave to the Fédération Française de Lawn-Tennis a site of about three hectares at the Auteuil gate, and two big Parisian clubs, the Stade Français and the Racing Club of France, were charged with building a stadium with a centre court surrounded by benches. It was called Roland Garros after a famous aviator who flew across the Mediterranean for the first time (from Saint-Raphaël to Bizerte on 23 September 1913) and who was killed in aerial combat in 1918. He had been a prominent member of the Stade Français athletics team.

The Stade Roland Garros was opened on 19 and 20 May 1928 with a tournament between French and British women. The benches of the centre court held 8,000. (They were enlarged later and now hold about 13,000.) There are nine clay and two hard courts. The French International Championships followed; then, in July, the first Davis Cup Challenge Round held in Paris, which France won against the United States. France held on to the Cup until 1933. That year, Jean Borotra, aged 35, refused to play in the singles. Lacoste, captain of the French team, chose André Merlin as the second singles player, Cochet being the no. 1. Merlin, in spite of his energy and determination, was defeated by Perry and Austin (Gt Britain) and France lost the Cup.

After six years of glory began a lean period for French tennis. Cochet turned professional. In 1934-9 the best French tennis players were Christian Boussus, Antoine Gentien, André Merlin, Marcel Bernard, Yvon Petra, Bernard Destremau, Henri Bolelli, Pierre Pellizza, Jean Lesueur, André Martin-Legeay.

On the women's side, one player dominated all the others: Simone Mathieu, Courageous, determined, a fighter, she possessed a solid back-court game. Her forehand was scorching and she never gave up. With her were Suzanne Devé-Desloges, Arlette Halff, Sylvia Henrotin, a remarkable volleyer, and, a bit later, Nelly Adamson Landry, French international champion in 1948.

After the loss of the Davis Cup in 1933 Borotra and Brugnon were the only Musketeers left in the team. They played in the double in 1934. That year with Boussus and Merlin in singles France crushed Austria, defeated Germany and then was eliminated by Australia at Roland Garros. Merlin was the hero of this meeting. He won his two singles, defeating Crawford and McGrath, while Boussus lost his in the fifth set. The double was also lost in the fifth set by Borotra and Brugnon to Crawford and Quist. In 1935 France met Australia again and was beaten 3-2.

In 1936 Destremau appeared in the French team. He won his two singles against China, then in the following round against the Netherlands he beat Hughan and even Timmer, who was one of the best European and world players at the time. In the third round France was beaten by Yugoslavia, although Destremau had seized a victory from the solid Punčec after a terrible battle, 9-7 in the fifth set. Borotra/Bernard took the doubles but the tough lefthander Pallada beat Boussus and Destremau, and Punčec beat Boussus.

In 1937, Petra was selected for the first time, with Bernard, Destremau and Borotra. France beat Norway but was eliminated 4-1 by Czechoslovakia in the next round. In 1938 France made a good showing. With Petra and Destremau in singles and Bolelli/Pellizza or Petra/Lesueur in doubles, France successively eliminated the Netherlands, Monaco and Italy, and qualified for the European Zone semi-

Above **France.** Bernard Destremau, ranked no 1 in France 1950-1

finals where it was beaten by Germany in Berlin. In 1939 Boussus returned to the French team with Destremau and Petra/Pellizza in the double. After beating China, France went down to Great Britain.

After World War II, in 1946, French tennis took a new and brilliant turn: Petra was Wimbledon Champion and Bernard French Champion. No Frenchman has won these since.

Marcel Bernard was without doubt the most gifted player in France after the Musketeers. Left-handed, relaxed, good at anticipation, he played inspired tennis. He came to the fore very early, collecting junior and *scolaire* titles and was classed in the first series (see ranking below) at the age of 16. In 1932 he triumphed over the Japanese champion Jiro Sato and reached the semi-finals of the French International Championships, where he was beaten by Cochet. In 1946 he achieved his greatest success when he carried off the Inter-

national title at Roland Garros from Drobný. In 1949 he renewed his victory over the Czech in the Davis Cup. In December 1968 he was elected President of the FFLT.

In 1946 the French Davis Cup team of Petra, Pellizza, Destremau and Bernard beat Great Britain, then Switzerland, at Lausanne. In the next round, at Roland Garros, France met Yugoslavia. Petra and Bernard won the first two singles and France appeared to be in a good position. But instead of playing in the double the two men on form, Petra and Bernard, the French captain put forward Pellizza and Destremau, who were beaten in five sets after a mediocre match; the next day, against all expectation, the two Yugoslavs took the two last singles. Petra worked like a demon against Punčec, saving many match points, and held the fourth set 9-7, but, exhausted, went down 0-6 in the last set.

In 1947 Destremau, Bernard, Pellizza, Borotra and Abdesselam played in turn India, Monaco and Czechoslovakia, which with Drobný and Cernik, won narrowly.

In 1948 Petra and Pellizza became professionals and France lost two trump cards. France was eliminated in the second round by Hungary. The only French victory was that of Bernard against József Asbóth, but in 1949, with Bernard, Abdesselam and Bolelli, France reached the European final, losing to Italy, 3-2, at Roland Garros.

In 1950 Paul Rémy, who had made his Davis Cup début the year before against Luxembourg, was again selected. His career was long and brilliant until he became a professional in 1958. In 1950 and 1951 France was quickly beaten by Denmark and Great Britain. In 1952 Destremau was 35 and Robert Haillet, 21, made his début. France was defeated by

Below **France.** Marcel Bernard, 1946 French champion in singles and doubles

Belgium. The following year Haillet beat von Cramm and France beat Germany. Rémy and Haillet were pillars of the French team for many years.

In 1956 Pierre Darmon made his first Davis cup appearance. Eleven years later he was still there. He was the strongest French player of the postwar generation. Supple and quick at the volley, intelligent, deft, subtle, he would have gone further if he had been able to concentrate on the game but he was always thinking of other things. In 1968 his wife and he each won the National singles title, an achievement new in French history. (M. and Mme Chanfreau did the same in 1970.) It was Darmon's last title. In 1969 he abandoned competitive tennis to devote his time to his business and his family.

France did not reach the European finals again until 1964. In 1957-8 the French team was beaten by Italy, then by Great Britain. Jean-Noël Grinda and Jean-Claude Ducos de la Haille Molinari were tried without much success. Darmon and Haillet remained the best. In 1963 a new doubles team, Beust/Contet, made its appearance. They were both small but fast volleyers and acquitted themselves well; but were still beaten by the Spanish at Barcelona.

For France 1964 was a better year. Barthès was chosen for the first time and France reached the final of the European Zone against Sweden at Båstad.

Pierre Barthès was built like an athlete, 1 m 82 (6 ft) tall, 85 kg (187 lb 6 oz). He would have been a good rugby footballer. Ranked nationally in the top twenty at 18, he made no immediate impact. An Australian tour in 1964-5 helped him to progress but his game remained very erratic. The professionals offered him a contract in 1966 which he accepted and won several brilliant victories. Becoming independent again in 1972, he was ranked no. 1 in France but his superiority over other French players was not confirmed.

From 1965 to 1973 France pursued her Davis Cup career with neither distinction nor premature defeat except for an unexpected loss to Yugoslavia in 1969 which ended the Beust/Contet partnership. Other names appeared in the French team: François Jauffret, Georges Goven, Patrick Proisy, Patrice Dominguez, Jean Baptiste Chanfreau. In 1971 and 1972 France lost to Spain. In 1973 it was beaten by the USSR in a semi-final of the European Zone.

The French International Championships, held at Roland Garros at the end of May and beginning of June, are considered to be the unofficial world championships on clay courts. They have been open to all comers since 1925 and were won that year by Lacoste. The Musketeers won until 1932 (Cochet). The reign of the foreigners began in 1933 when the Australian Jack Crawford won. During World War II (1941-5) the tournament was national and Destremau (twice) and Petra (three times) took the title. In 1946 it became international again; Bernard triumphed over Drobný in the final, the last Frenchman to win.

In 1950 Patty beat Drobný in a great final. Drobný won the title twice running (1951-2). In 1953 Rosewall, aged 18, became the youngest French champion. The athletic Tony Trabert won in 1954-5 and then Hoad (1956), who beat Sven Davidson, who had been defeated in the final in the previous year.

At last in 1957 Davidson, third-time finalist, took the title from Flam. In 1958 Mervyn Rose, the talented left-hander, won; then Nicola Pietrangeli, who won twice running (1959-60) and just missed a third consecutive victory when he was beaten in the final by Santana (1961). In 1962 came Laver's first victory after a series of terrible battles against Mulligan,

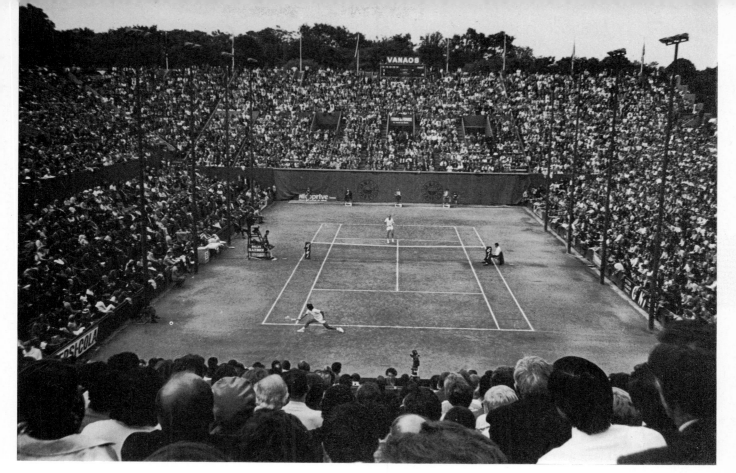

Above **France**. The 1972 French Championships at Stade Roland Garros. P. Proisy *(near side)* lost to A. Gimeno in the final 4-6, 6-3, 6-1, 6-1.

Fraser and Emerson (in the final), in which Emerson led by two sets to nil. That year also saw the first victory for Margaret Smith, who won again in 1964, 1969, 1970 and 1973. In 1963 Darmon defeated Santana, but was beaten in the final by Emerson. In 1964 Santana and Pietrangeli met in the final, a new success for the Spaniard who had beaten Darmon in the semi-finals after a tough five-set battle. Then there was a series of Australian victors: Stolle, Roche, Emerson, Rosewall, Laver. In 1966 Jauffret had a notable victory over Emerson. In 1967 came satisfaction for France: Françoise Durr won the women's singles, beating the Australian Lesley Turner to become the first French woman champion since Nelly Landry in 1948.

Françoise Durr is by a long way the best French woman player of recent years. In spite of a weak service and a very individual style, she has done very well internationally; she always fights with much energy but her nerves let her down at important moments so that she loses matches she ought to win. The second French woman player is the ex-Australian Gail Sherriff, Mme Chanfreau.

In 1968 the International Championships were Open and Rosewall triumphed 15 years after his first victory – he was 33 and the oldest winner after having been the youngest. Nancy Richey won the women's singles, Françoise Durr and Ann Jones the women's doubles.

In 1969 the French did not survive the third round. Goven was beaten by Okker and the title went to Laver over Rosewall. Françoise Durr was eliminated in the third round of the women's event by Mrs Bowrey. Margaret Court triumphed over Mrs Jones in the final.

In 1970 the WCT professionals did not take part in the International Championships. Kodeš took the title from Franulović. Goven beat Santana, then Jauffret, and qualified for the semi-finals where he lost to Kodeš in four sets. Jauffret, who defeated the Italian Panatta, was eliminated in the quarter-finals. On the women's side, Françoise Durr did not survive the quarter-finals. In 1971 Kodeš won again by beating Nastăse in the final. Only one Frenchman, Proisy, reached the quarter-finals where he lasted four sets to Kodeš. Jauffret, in the fifth round, had gone five sets against Kodeš. Evonne Goolagong had her first victory.

The year 1972 belonged to Proisy, who defeated in succession Mandarino, Gisbert, Fletcher, Kodeš and Orantes. He was beaten in the final by Gimeno, nine years after a Frenchman had last played in the final.

In 1951 the FFLT decided to start a championship closed to French players, which helped to establish rankings at the end of the year. The first National Championship was won by Bernard Destremau, who took it again in 1953. Paul Rémy and Robert Haillet inscribed their names on the rolls several times, but Pierre Darmon holds the record for victories – nine (between 1957 and 1968). Françoise Durr (4 times) and Gail Chanfreau (3 times) hold the women's record.

The National is held each year in a different town, at the beginning of October. Preference is given to southern towns because of the time of year: Marseilles, Cannes, Nice, Aix-en-Provence, Bordeaux. Qualifying rounds are played at Roland Garros; 16 men and 8 women at the most are qualified for the final phase. Certain players can be qualified *ex officio*. The National is open to players ranked in the first series and to players of the second series who have reached the singles quarter-finals of the Criterium of France and the semi-finals of the Criterium for women.

The French International Covered Court Championships have always attracted an important foreign entry. Founded after World War I, they were organized in turn by the Tennis Club of Paris and the Sporting Club. Jean Borotra, with his speed and volleying game, was naturally the 'king of the floor', carrying off the singles title 12 times between 1922 and 1947. His last victory, at the age of 49, was without doubt his greatest achievement. The championship was held at Lyon and among the foreigners were the Swedes Lennart Bergelin and Torsten Johansson, aged respectively 22 and 27. Borotra was the age of the two of them combined. Still bounding, more astonishing than ever, he triumphed over them and carried off the title once again. It was not until 22 years later, in 1969, that another Frenchman, Jean-Pierre Courcol, succeeded in being French Covered Court champion.

Team championships in France are contested each year by certain clubs classed in four divisions for men and three for women. In the first division, the teams of the Racing Club of France are largely dominant.

Among other official events are the Criterium of France on clay courts for men and women ranked in the second series, the Espérance de France for players ranked in the third series, and the Omnium for non-classified players, all staged at Roland Garros. The winners of the singles automatically go up to the next series. The Championships of Paris for teams are contested by more than 1,000 teams.

Another very classic tournament is the Marcel Porée Cup, founded in 1921 in memory of Marcel Porée, a member of the Racing Club de France who was killed in a car accident. It is held each September by the Racing Club at the Croix-Catelan. Jauffret has won it since 1969.

In the early days, tennis was directed in France by a Commission which formed part of the Union of French Athletic Sports Societies. In 1920 the Fédération Française de Lawn-Tennis was founded. Henry Wallet, president of the Commission, was its first president.

France took an active part in the creation of the ILTF. Henry Wallet and the Swiss Mr Barde organized the first meeting in Paris on 26 October 1912 to which seven nations came. At the inaugural assembly, held in Paris on 1 March 1913, 12 countries were present; France was represented by Messrs Gallay, Gillou, Muhr, Roy and Wallet. There have been four French presidents of the ILTF: Henry Wallet, Maurice Rances, Pierre Gillou and Jean Borotra.

Tennis really developed in France after World War I. At the beginning of the century there were 25 clubs, over 500 in 1920; 1,000 in 1938; 1,500 in 1950. Naturally the successes of Decugis, Gobert, Suzanne Lenglen and the Musketeers encouraged this progress. France has also created two international events for teams under 21, the GALEA CUP for boys and the ANNIE SOISBAULT CUP for girls, which have stimulated young players. It has taken part regularly in the FEDERATION CUP since 1963. In 1938 the FFLT had 19,290 licensed members; in 1950, 53,347; in 1951 56,896; in 1954 60,427. The numbers have increased every year except in 1956 with the independence of Morocco and Tunisia, and in 1960 when Algeria became independent. The 100,000 mark was passed in 1965 (105,882). The 200,000 mark was passed in 1972. There are 1,830 clubs and 5,500 courts, of which 500 are covered. Most of the courts are clay but the use of 'hard' courts, with a porous surface, is growing. They offer the advantages of winter play and rapid drying after rain. Courts of turf have been tried but the maintenance is too costly and they have been abandoned. One club, the International Club of Lys, on the outskirts of Paris, has two turf courts that Pierre Darmon commissioned when he was director of the club. The four Musketeers inaugurated these courts many years ago.

There are many more players than those officially licensed and who take part in tournaments; it is estimated that 600,000 French people play tennis.

Many hundreds of tennis schools have been created where *scolaires* are taught tennis free. These courses are given by teachers, monitors or professors. There were 370 professors and 233 monitors in 1972; the figures increase regularly each year.

In 1971 two new schemes for young people produced good results. A French championship for teams of *minimes* brought to Roland Garros 200 boys and girls of 12-14 representing nearly all the leagues. As an experiment the FFLT has selected a dozen boys among the best juniors, *cadets* and *minimes*, and has brought them to Nice, where they follow normal studies at the Lycée but also have an hour of tennis work every day and three hours of physical training a week. The experiment began in 1970 and seems to have been successful.

The FFLT is made up of regional leagues of which three are overseas. In most of them there is a technical regional counsellor who visits clubs to supervise the young players, to run collective courses, etc. At the head of this organization is the national technical adviser, at present Gil de Kermadec. He is answerable

Below **Neale Fraser**

to the Ministry for Youth and Sports and naturally to the FFLT.

The Management Committee elected by the General Assembly on 7 December 1968 agreed that amateurs should simply be called 'players' and could receive money. It also voted for open events. Its efforts for young players have greatly contributed to the development of tennis. A pool of sports journalists grants a certain sum to the FFLT, which dispenses it for the French teams.

The annual classification of French players necessitates enormous work from the end of October to the end of December. Over 4,000 players, of whom about 1,000 are women, figure in the official ranking, created by Commandant Émile Dève in 1914. Players are divided into three categories: first series, in which the number varies but there are rarely more than 20 men and 12 women; second series, in which men are graded by handicap of owe 15 or receive 15; third series from 15/2 to 30. At the end of each season players send their performance records to the FFLT. The ranking is prepared successively by regional commissioners, inter-regional and national; in the last resort the Federal Bureau accepts or modifies the commission's recommendations. ABe

GOVERNING BODY: Fédération Française de Lawn-Tennis, 15 rue de Téhéran, Paris 8

Above Shirley Fry

Fraser, Neale Andrew (Australia)

Born St Kilda, Melbourne, 3 Oct. 1933; Wimbledon men's singles q/f 1956, s/f 1957, r/u 1958, q/f 1959, won 1960, s/f 1962; men's doubles r/u 1955, s/f 1956, r/u 1957-8, won 1959, 1961, s/f 1962, 1972, r/u 1973; mixed doubles s/f 1955, r/u 1957, 1959, won 1962; US men's singles s/f 1956, 1958, won 1959-60; men's doubles s/f 1954, 1956, won 1957, s/f 1958, won 1959-60; mixed doubles won 1958-60; Australian men's singles s/f 1956, r/u 1957, s/f 1958, r/u 1959-60, s/f 1962; men's doubles r/u 1954, s/f 1955-6, won 1957-8, s/f 1959, r/u 1960, won 1962; mixed doubles s/f 1954, won 1956, s/f 1957; French men's singles q/f 1957-8, s/f 1959, q/f 1960, s/f 1962; men's doubles s/f 1957, won 1958, r/u 1959, won 1960, 1962. Davis Cup 1955-63. A dogged Australian left-hander who never gave up.

French Championships see FRANCE and RECORDS (PART 3)

Froitzheim, Otto see GERMANY, FEDERAL REPUBLIC OF

Fromholtz, Miss Dianne Lee (Australia)

Born 10 Aug. 1956; Australian women's singles q/f 1973; British Hard Court Championship s/f 1973. A left-hander with a good swinging service and fine backhand, who made an impressive first trip to Europe in 1973.

Fry, Miss Joan [Mrs T. A. Lakeman] (Gt Britain)

Born Horsham, Sussex, May 1906; Wimbledon women's singles r/u 1925 (to LENGLEN), s/f 1927; mixed doubles r/u 1929; US women's singles q/f 1925; women's doubles r/u 1927; French women's singles s/f 1926; women's doubles s/f 1926, 1928, 1930. Wightman Cup 1925-7, 1930.

Fry, Miss Shirley J. [Mrs K. Irvin] (USA)

Born Akron, Ohio, 30 June 1927; Wimbledon women's singles q/f 1948, 1950, r/u 1951, s/f 1952-3, q/f 1954, won 1956; women's doubles s/f 1949, r/u 1950, won 1951-3, r/u 1954, s/f 1956; mixed doubles r/u 1953, won 1956; US women's singles q/f 1944, 1950, r/u 1951, s/f 1952-4, q/f 1955, won 1956; women's doubles s/f 1945-8, r/u 1949-50, won 1951-4, r/u 1955-6; mixed doubles s/f 1950, r/u 1951, s/f 1952-3, r/u 1955, s/f 1956; French women's singles r/u 1948, q/f 1950, won 1951, r/u 1952, s/f 1953; women's doubles r/u 1948, won 1950-3; mixed doubles s/f 1948, 1950, r/u 1952, s/f 1953. Wightman Cup 1947-9, 1951-3, 1955-6. A fine all-round player who was inevitably dominated by the exceptionally high standards of her American contemporaries such as Margaret DUPONT, Louise BROUGH, Doris HART and Maureen CONNOLLY. Her Wimbledon doubles success with Miss Hart (1953) was remarkably achieved 6-0, 6-0 against Miss Connolly and Julie Sampson, losing only four games in the whole event.

Galea Cup

The Galea Cup Competition was started in 1950 by the French Madame Edmond de Galea in memory of her son Christian, to fill the gap between the junior and full DAVIS CUP levels of international team competition. The format is similar: two cross singles and one double, but rubbers are the best of three sets (instead of five) until the final stages. Although widely referred to as the 'European Under-21 team championship', entry is in fact worldwide; countries which have competed include Canada, Mexico and Iran.

The first competition was held in Deauville, France, when France, Italy, Belgium and Spain took part and Italy won. These four founder nations are still the mainstay of the event. Over the years more nations have entered: in 1972 the total was 25. Since 1952 the competition has been played on a zonal basis; the four zone winners contest the final stages in Vichy.

The Galea Cup has been the international starting point for many well-known European players, including Andrés Gimeno, Nikki Pietrangeli, Manuel Santana, Manuel Orantes and Pierre Darmon. See also POSTWAR DEVELOPMENT (PART 1). DC

Game see SCORING

Gauge of String see THE DEVELOPMENT OF PLAYING EQUIPMENT (PART 1)

Gem, Major Harry see LEAMINGTON LAWN TENNIS CLUB; THE BIRTH AND SPREAD OF LAWN TENNIS (PART 1)

Gemmell, R. H. (Australia)

A prominent Australian immediately after World War I, winning the men's singles in 1921 and the men's doubles in 1921, s/f 1926.

Germains Lawn Tennis see SPHAIRISTIKE

German Democratic Republic

The Lawn Tennis Association of the German Democratic Republic was founded in 1949. Today it has 28,750 members including 10,000 juniors in 368 clubs.

A system of championships exists for all age groups and both sexes. Of the tournaments, the Zinnowitz International Tournament is a well-known springboard for junior talent. Players of the Democratic Republic have won

German International Championships Winners

Men's Singles		Women's Singles	
1892	W. Bonne	1896	Miss M. Thomsen
1893	G. Winzer	1897	Mrs G. W. Hillyard
1894	G. Voss	1898	Miss E. Lane
1895	G. Voss	1899	Miss C. Cooper
1896	G. Voss	1900	Mrs G. W. Hillyard
1897	G. W. Hillyard	1901	Miss C. Lowther
1898	S. M. Mahony	1902	Miss M. Ross
1899	C. Hobart	1903	Miss V. Pinckney
1900	G. W. Hillyard	1904	Miss E. Lane
1901	M. Decugis	1905	Miss E. Lane
1902	M. Decugis	1906	Miss L. Berton
1903	M. J. G. Ritchie	1907	Miss M. von Madarasz
1904	M. J. G. Ritchie	1908	Miss M. von Madarasz
1905	M. J. G. Ritchie	1909	Miss A. Heimann
1906	M. J. G. Ritchie	1910	Miss M. Rieck
1907	O. Froitzheim	1911	Miss M. Rieck
1908	M. J. G. Ritchie	1912	Miss D. Koering
1909	O. Froitzheim	1913	Miss D. Koering
1910	O. Froitzheim	1914–19	*No Competition*
1911	O. Froitzheim	1920	Mrs J. Friedleben
1912	O. von Müller	1921	Mrs J. Friedleben
1913	H. Schomburgk	1922	Mrs J. Friedleben
1914–19	*No Competition*	1923	Mrs J. Friedleben
1920	O. Kreutzer	1924	Mrs J. Friedleben
1921	O. Froitzheim	1925	Mrs N. Neppach
1922	O. Froitzheim	1926	Mrs J. Friedleben
1923	H. Landmann	1927	Miss C. Aussem
1924	B. von Kehrling	1928	Miss D. Akhurst
1925	O. Froitzheim	1929	Mrs P. von Reznicek
1926	H. Moldenhauer	1930	Miss C. Aussem
1927	H. Moldenhauer	1931	Miss C. Aussem
1928	D. Prenn	1932	Miss L. Payot
1929	C. Boussus	1933	Miss H. Krahwinkel
1930	C. Boussus	1934	Mrs H. Sperling
1931	R. Menzel	1935	Mrs H. Sperling
1932	G. von Cramm	1936	Mrs H. Sperling
1933	G. von Cramm	1937	Mrs H. Sperling
1934	G. von Cramm	1938	Mrs H. Sperling
1935	G. von Cramm	1939	Mrs H. Sperling
1936	*No Competition*	1940–47	*No Competition*
1937	H. Henkel	1948	Miss U. Rosenow
1938	O. Szigeti	1949	Miss M. Weiss
1939	H. Henkel	1950	Miss D. Head
1940–47	*No Competition*	1951	Mrs N. Bolton
1948	G. von Cramm	1952	Miss D. Head
1949	G. von Cramm	1953	Mrs D. Knode
1950	J. Drobný	1954	Mrs A. J. Mottram
1951	L. Bergelin	1955	Miss B. Penrose
1952	E. W. Sturgess	1956	Mrs T. Long
1953	B. Patty	1957	Miss Y. Ramirez
1954	B. Patty	1958	Miss L. Coghlan
1955	A. Larsen	1959	Miss E. Buding
1956	L. Hoad	1960	Miss S. Reynolds
1957	M. G. Rose	1961	Miss S. Reynolds
1958	S. Davidson	1962	Mrs S. Price
1959	W. A. Knight	1963	Miss R. Schuurman
1960	N. Pietrangeli	1964	Miss M. Smith
1961	R. Laver	1965	Miss M. Smith
1962	R. Laver	1966	Miss M. Smith
1963	M. Mulligan	1967	Miss F. Durr
1964	W. Bungert	1968	Mrs A. du Plooy
1965	C. Drysdale	1969	Mrs J. A. M. Tegart
1966	F. Stolle	1970	Mrs H. Hösl
1967	R. Emerson	1971	Mrs B. J. King
1968	J. D. Newcombe	1972	Mrs H. Masthoff
1969	A. Roche	1973	Mrs H. Masthoff
1970	T. Okker		
1971	A. Gimeno		
1972	M. Orantes		
1973	E. Dibbs		

some international titles, but it should be noted that in the Democratic Republic lawn tennis is played solely under amateur rules. Everybody can afford to play tennis, as fees are nominal and special equipment is available at low prices.

LTA elections are held every second year at all levels. Every fourth year a General Conference decides on future development. A monthly magazine, with 3,000 subscribers, reflects LTA activities in all branches.

In 1964 the ILTF admitted the East German association as a Full Member.

The Democratic Republic has not yet played in the DAVIS CUP or in the FEDERATION CUP but they have competed regularly in the GALEA CUP. BR

GOVERNING BODY: Deutscher Tennis-Verband der DDR, 1055 Berlin, Storkower Strasse 118

Germany, Federal Republic of

The Deutscher Lawn Tennis Bund (DLTB) was founded on 19 May 1902 in Berlin, to preserve and further the interests of the game. It was particularly concerned with the organization of tournaments in Germany, the translation of the official rules and terms used in play and scoring into German, and ruling on doubtful or controversial questions of interpretation. Its foundation ushered in a steady, progressive development of tennis.

It is no longer possible to state with certainty when the first tennis court was built in Germany. What is known is that in 1877 the first courts of the English Club at Bad Homburg vor der Höhe had been marked out. Later the Spa management took them over. Germany's first court could have been that built at Baden-Baden, where the first German tennis club was founded in 1881. There were several families in Hamburg and Dresden in the 1880s with courts of their own, so it is not surprising that the first international tennis championship in Germany was held in Hamburg in 1892.

The development of tennis from a social game to a sport took a relatively long time in Germany. In Baden-Baden, Bad Homburg vor der Höhe and other spas in the 1890s, several excellent small tournaments were held in which the best British and American players took part, headed by Laurie Doherty. Supported by the devoted work of the various associations the DLTB grew steadily up to the outbreak of World War I. At its foundation the DLTB comprised 23 clubs with 2,000 members. Ten years later there were 150 clubs and 22,291 members. More tournaments were being played and city and spa authorities vied with one another in healthy competition.

In 1913 the DLTB was one of the founder members of the ILTF. Dr H. O. Behrens, nominated by the British representative, was unanimously elected chairman of the foundation assembly on 1 March in Paris. Dr W. Lürmann and Dr O. Nirrnheim represented the DLTB. Dr Behrens was elected to the Management Committee together with R. J. McNair (Gt Britain), Henry Wallet (France), Gordon Inglis (Australasia) and Paul de Borman (Belgium).

In 1911 the first covered-court tournament was held in Bremen. This was the first, and for a long time the only, covered court in Germany: it had a great influence on the development of German tennis – and not just the covered-court variety. The loss of the building in World War II was very sad.

World War I interrupted the development of tennis in Germany, but reconstruction had begun by 1919. There were 150 clubs affiliated to the Deutscher Tennis Bund (DTB). From 1920 on the number of clubs grew rapidly until in 1924 there were 351, with 42,000 memners. In 1927 Germany was accepted into the ILTF again (it had been expelled in 1919) and friendly contact with foreign associations was restored.

Inspired by this, the associations and clubs began to build new courts. Work proceeded steadily in Hamburg on the championship courts and soon there was a new covered court there. In nearly all the spas and resorts facilities for tennis were available and the famous tournaments at these places enjoyed steadily increasing popularity. In 1927 there were 75,000 members in 700 clubs, playing on 2,638 courts. Two years later, in 1929, there were 91,913 members in 920 clubs with 3,670 courts; by 1931 there were 98,668 members in 1,053 clubs and 4,100 courts. Tennis was well on the way to becoming a widely based sport. After 1933 German public sport was reorganized and alongside the DTB, which nominally remained in existence, a tennis 'department' was created by the government. The DTB continued to exist because of the international scope of tennis and DTB membership of the ILTF, but its functions were wholly taken over by the Department. Progress was interrupted by the outbreak of World War II.

In 1945 organized tennis had virtually ceased to exist. The formation of associations and clubs was forbidden. Many establishments had been destroyed or confiscated. There was no tennis equipment in a time of social distress. In spite of this attempts were made through personal and private initiative to get tennis started again and on 7 February 1947 the Nordwestdeutscher Tennisausschuss (NW German Tennis Board) was set up, on which the representatives of the separate *Länder* within the British Zone could meet. In Southern Germany the representatives met for the first time on 6 July 1947 in Würzburg and here a working party was formed for the three zones and Berlin which was to be embodied in the Tennisausschuss, founded on 10/11 January 1948 in Wiesbaden. In contrast to the old DTB, in which the clubs were the constituent members, the Tennisausschuss was a federation of the *Land* associations: this was the only

Above **Federal Republic of Germany.** Henner Henkel, French champion in 1937

arrangement possible at the time. The Board acted as a central liaison for the game and arranged matches. The first international meeting was between a German team and the Swedes, who subsequently made a return visit.

The Deutscher Tennis Bund was reconstituted on 5/6 February 1949 in Assmannshausen, and was the first postwar German sport association. Great difficulties had had to be overcome but the establishment of the DTB made things easier for other sports associations. The DTB was accepted back into the ILTF on 12 July 1950.

The Hamburg Tennis Club held the first postwar championship on 24-27 July 1947 at Rothenbaum. In the same year there were tournaments at Cologne, Frankfurt, Bremen, Heidelberg, and other places. Many courts had been commandeered and others had had

to be completely rebuilt. But the first postwar figures available (1948) record a membership of 71,677 and 537 clubs. In 1948 the first postwar junior championships were held in Cologne under the direction of Gottfried von Cramm. Before the war they had been held from 1924 in Frankfurt.

The membership of the DTB grew rapidly after a slight setback in 1950: by 1953 there were 108,935 members in 992 clubs with 3,132 outdoor courts and 16 indoor courts; by 1961 there were 200,847 members in 1,405 clubs, with 5,590 outdoor courts and 82 indoor courts; by 1971 there were 407,382 members of whom 94,581 were juniors, in 2,212 clubs with 8,512 outdoor courts and 367 indoor courts. More and more people were attracted to a sport that before the war had seemed to be the preserve of the well-to-do strata of society. At the same time, economic progress meant that more courts and better facilities could be offered.

From about 1948, the building of tennis courts and clubrooms was widely supported by state and municipal authorities. The clubs and associations of the DTB also made considerable sacrifices to improve their facilities. In recent years there has been an increase in the building of covered courts, a trend that is continuing.

After long years of preparation and planning the DTB training centre was inaugurated on 13 March 1970 at Hanover. Its aims are to encourage the best German players and develop young talent, and to build up a new Davis Cup team; it is hoped that its influence will extend to all levels and aspects of German tennis. The centre itself proves that sports buildings can be beautiful as well as practical: the hall, with covered courts, offices, refreshment rooms, etc., was designed to take up the minimum area of land. The roof is of rabbeted aluminium, supported on reinforced concrete beams spanning 37 m (121 ft). The courts are illuminated by spotlights which eliminate shadows better than conventional systems. After much deliberation a cork-lino covering on a resilient floor was decided upon, reproducing the characteristics of a normal tennis court.

The DTB's efforts to improve the quality of tennis and popularize it more widely are beginning to bear fruit, especially in the schools, where the game must be developed if tennis is to be rid of the odium of 'exclusiveness' that still clings to it in places. Since there is much to be said for getting the feel of the court, net, racket, etc. as early as possible, the DTB's aim in future is to concentrate on initiating youngsters.

Poll findings suggest that about 6.3 million citizens of the Bundesrepublik would like to make tennis their game if there were enough facilities. But many clubs have already limited their membership. Pressure of increased general interest, increase in leisure time, and tennis in schools will no doubt lead provincial and local authorities to pay more attention to the needs of the sport and to make sites available for the building or extension of courts.

Many great players have acted as examples and pacemakers in tennis. Otto Froitzheim (born 24 April 1884) was for 25 years at the top of German tennis. In 1912 he became world hard-courts champion in singles and doubles (with Oskar Kreuzer) and won the German International Tennis Championship singles at Hamburg seven times (1907, 1909-11, 1921-2, 1925) and the doubles four times. In 1907 he was European singles champion and the following year he won the silver medal at the Olympic Games in London. In 1914 he reached the Wimbledon men's singles final, losing to the world's best player, Norman Brookes. Otto Froitzheim beat the New Zealander Tony Wilding several times on Continental hard courts. He also defeated Ritchie, Decugis, Alonso, Hunter, Koželuh and von Kehrling, among others. He also achieved success in his professional career, proving that it was pos-

sible for a good sportsman to make his way in this sphere. After his activities in Berlin, Cologne and Wiesbaden he became government vice-president in Aachen. Froitzheim was also active in the administration of tennis as chairman of the Rot-Weiss LTC of Berlin and a committee member of the DTB. He died on 27 October 1962 after a long and severe illness.

Gottfried von Cramm was a successful Davis Cup and tournament player for Germany. He reached the men's singles finals at Wimbledon three times (1935-7) and also the 1937 finals at Forest Hills. In the course of his great career he defeated Allison, Roderich Menzel, Don Budge, Fred Perry, Jack Crawford, Jaroslav Drobný, and many other players of world rank. From 1932 to 1953 he was the top German player and represented his country 37 times in the Davis Cup. With Henner Henkel he reached the Inter-Zone final of the Davis Cup, and in 1932-9 he ranked consistently among the world's top players, taking the title six times at the Hamburg German International Tennis Championships. He won the men's doubles there with Budge Patty in 1956. Before World War II he was regarded as 'the best player in the world who never won Wimbledon'.

Gottfried von Cramm, a successful businessman, has always been active in the administration of the sport; today he is the president of the Rot-Weiss LTC and as an honorary member of the DTB he sits on its committee.

Another famous player, Dr Heinrich Kleinschroth, played for Germany in Davis Cup ties from 1913 until 1930 and captained the German team that won the European Zone in 1936. He competed in the major European and American tournaments over a long period and, over 80, is a familiar figure on the courts at Munich.

Henner Henkel (born 9 October 1915) was German Junior Champion in 1932 and 1933 and won many German championships in the following years. He soon became internationally known for his excellent volleying and had many successes in Germany too. A fine doubles player, he was von Cramm's partner several times in the Davis Cup. A chivalrous sportsman, he was killed in Russia in 1943 in World War II. Today the German Junior Championships of the DTB bear his name.

Wilhelm Bungert (born 1 April 1939) is one of the most successful players of the younger generation. He began in 1955 by winning the German Junior Championship and repeated his victory in 1957. In the succeeding years he won many international singles and doubles victories and with 43 Davis Cup matches (1958-71) to his credit he holds the German record for this competition. He has won many national championship titles and won the German International Championship in 1964. In the 1967 Wimbledon men's singles final (having been unseeded) he lost to Newcombe. GS
GOVERNING BODY: Deutscher Tennis Bund eV, 3 Hannover, Bonner Strasse 12A

Above Althea Gibson

Germot, Maurice ['Fifi'] see FRANCE

Ghana
Ghana has been an Associate Member of the ILTF since 1954, and is also a member of the AFRICAN LAWN TENNIS CONFEDERATION. BR
GOVERNING BODY: Ghana LTA, Sports Council of Ghana, P.O. Box 1272, Accra

Gibson, Miss Althea [Mrs W. Darbon] (USA)
Born Silver, S.C., 25 Aug. 1927; Wimbledon women's singles q/f 1956, won 1957-8; women's doubles won 1956-8; mixed doubles r/u 1957-8; US women's singles q/f 1953, r/u 1956, won 1957-8; women's doubles r/u 1957-8; mixed doubles s/f 1954, 1956, won 1957; French women's singles and doubles won 1956. Wightman Cup 1957-8. The first Negro to achieve outstanding success in lawn tennis. With her tall, muscular frame she brought the same vigorous athletic approach to the game later carried further by Margaret COURT, a big stride and long arms creating new dimensions in the effectiveness of women's volleying. Miss Gibson found lawn tennis fame rather late; she was almost 30 when she won her first Wimbledon singles. She became a professional in 1958, thereby cutting herself off from the major events.

Gimeno, Andrés (Spain)
Born Barcelona, 3 Aug 1937; Wimbledon men's singles s/f 1970; US men's doubles r/u 1968; Australian men's singles q/f 1959, r/u 1969; French men's singles q/f 1960, s/f 1968, q/f 1969, won 1972; men's doubles r/u 1960; mixed doubles s/f 1956. Davis Cup 1958-60. ILTF GP 5th 1972. Pro 1960; WCT 1971-2.

Gobert, André see FRANCE and OLYMPIC GAMES

Godfree, Leslie A. (Gt Britain)
Born Brighton, 27 April 1885; died 1972; Wimbledon men's doubles won 1923; s/f 1924; mixed doubles r/u 1924, won 1926, r/u 1927; French mixed doubles s/f 1926. Davis

Cup 1923-7 (11 doubles matches, winning 6, losing 5). Captain Davis Cup team 1925. President Umpires' Association. Unique in hitting the first ball on the new Wimbledon Centre Court in 1922.

Godfree, Mrs Leslie A. [Miss Kitty McKane] (Gt Britain)

Born London *c.* 1898; Wimbledon women's singles q/f 1919, r/u 1923, won 1924, s/f 1925, won 1926, q/f 1927; women's doubles s/f 1921, r/u 1922, s/f 1923, r/u 1924, 1926, s/f 1927, 1931, 1933-4; mixed doubles won 1926, r/u 1927, s/f 1933; US women's singles r/u 1925; women's doubles won 1923, 1927; mixed doubles r/u 1923, won 1925; French women's singles r/u 1925, q/f 1926; women's doubles r/u 1925-6; mixed doubles s/f 1926. Wightman Cup 1923-7, 1930, 1934. The outstanding British woman player of the early 1920s and also notable with her husband, Leslie GODFREE, as the only husband and wife to win the mixed doubles at Wimbledon (1926). She was the only player to beat Helen Wills MOODY at Wimbledon – when she won in 1924.

Gonzalez, Ricardo A. [Pancho] (USA)

Born Los Angeles, Calif. 9 May 1928; Wimbledon men's doubles won 1949; US men's singles won 1948-9, q/f 1968; men's doubles s/f 1949; mixed doubles s/f 1949; French men's singles s/f 1949, 1968; men's doubles won 1949. Davis Cup 1949. Became a professional in 1949. A candidate as the greatest player of all time, though the measure of his prowess was made difficult by his becoming a professional long before he had time to make his strongest mark in the traditional events of the game. He combined exceptionally strong hitting with delicacy of touch and, at his peak, had a cannonball service second to none. He dominated the court not only by his high skill but by the strength of a compelling personality. Practically every match he played became an outstanding occasion and he was 41 years old when he won a memorable 112-game record singles against PASARELL at Wimbledon in 1969 (see CENTRE COURT CLASSICS, PART 1). As a reverberating force in the game, which he dominated as a pro, he could only be compared with Tilden. WCT contract pro 1971-2. See colour plate, page 154, THE POSTWAR PRO GAME and GREAT PLAYERS OF ALL TIME (PART 1).

Goolagong, Miss Evonne F. (Australia)

Born Barellan, N.S.W., 31 July 1951; Wimbledon women's singles won 1971, r/u 1972, s/f 1973; women's doubles r/u 1971, s/f 1973; mixed doubles r/u 1972, s/f 1973; US women's singles r/u 1973; womens doubles s/f 1972-3; Australian women's singles q/f 1970, r/u 1971-3; women's doubles won 1971, s/f 1973; French women's singles won 1971, r/u 1972, s/f 1973; women's doubles s/f 1971; mixed

Right **Evonne Goolagong**

doubles won 1972: Federation Cup 1971-
ILTF GP 2nd 1972.

An outstandingly popular champion who
gratified and charmed all who watched her
achieve her great success as champion of
France and Wimbledon (1971). A naturally
gifted performer, her obvious enjoyment of
the game, whether in victory or defeat, was
infectious. Her game varies between apparent
carelessness and a wide variety of virtuoso
strokes. She is part Australian aboriginal by
race, being born to a humble family in a re-
mote part of New South Wales before being
discovered and taken into the home of the
coach Vic Edwards. See colour plate, page
153, AUSTRALIA and CENTRE COURT CLASSICS
(PART 1).

Gore, Arthur Wentworth (Gt Britain)
Born Lyndhurst, Hants., 2 Jan. 1868, died 1
Dec., 1928; Wimbledon men's singles q/f 1892,
s/f 1898, r/u 1899, r/u* 1900, won 1901, r/u
1902, q/f 1904, s/f 1905, r/u* 1906, 1907, won
1908-9, r/u 1910, 1912, q/f 1914; men's
doubles r/u* 1889, s/f 1892-3, 1898, r/u* 1899,
s/f 1900, r/u* 1904, 1908, won 1909, r/u 1910,
s/f 1911; mixed doubles s/f 1908; US men's
singles s/f 1900. Davis Cup 1900, 1907, 1912.
An outstanding baseliner who competed at
every Wimbledon from 1888 to 1927 – a
record span of 39 years!

Gore, Spencer W. (Gt Britain)
Born 10 May 1850, died 19 April 1906; Wimbledon men's singles won 1877, r/u 1878. The
very first champion, though he wrote scath-
ingly about the merits of lawn tennis as compared with real tennis or rackets (see THE
BIRTH AND SPREAD OF LAWN TENNIS, PART 1).

Gorman, Thomas Warner (USA)
Born Seattle, Wash., 19 Jan. 1946; Wimbledon men's singles s/f 1971; US men's singles
s/f 1972; men's doubles s/f 1973; French men's
singles s/f 1973; men's doubles r/u 1971, s/f
1972; Pacific SW Open s/f 1970, s/f 1972.
Davis Cup 1972. ILTF GP 7th 1971, 8th 1972.
Became professional 1969.

Goss, Miss Eleanor (USA)
Wimbledon women's singles q/f 1923; women's doubles s/f 1924; US women's singles
r/u 1918, s/f 1923-5, q/f 1926-7; women's doubles won 1918-20, r/u 1923-4, s/f 1925, 1927;
mixed doubles s/f 1923. Wightman Cup
1923-8.

Graebner, Clark Edward (USA)
Born Cleveland, Ohio, 4 Nov. 1943; Wimbledon men's singles s/f 1968, q/f 1969-70; men's
doubles s/f 1965-6, 1971; mixed doubles s/f
1972; US men's singles q/f 1966, r/u 1967, s/f
1968, q/f 1971; men's doubles s/f 1965, r/u
1966, s/f 1967-8; Australian men's singles q/f
1966; French men's doubles won 1966; mixed
doubles r/u 1966. Davis Cup 1965-8. ILTF GP
7th 1971. Became professional 1969.

Above **Green Shield.** 'Pancho' Gonzalez at the
1972 Green Shield Beckenham Tournament

Grand Slam
The winning of the four major championships
in one year (Wimbledon, the US, French and
Australian). It has so far been achieved in sin-
gles by only four players: Donald Budge
(1938), Rod Laver (1962 and 1969), Maureen
Connolly (1953) and Margaret Court (1970).
Frank Sedgman and Ken McGregor of Aus-
tralia are the only pair to have achieved the
Grand Slam in doubles (1951).

Grass Roots Scheme
Term applied in Britain to the launching and
development of the complete beginner. After
looking for financial backing for some ten
years, the Lawn Tennis Association (of Great
Britain), with the help of GREEN SHIELD, started
in 1970 a training scheme at grass-roots level
with a pilot project in northwest England. The
scheme was not intended to discover star
players overnight, but primarily to find and
develop raw beginners or those who had been
playing for less than a year. By 1972 all nine of
the LTA's regions were involved and the number of children receiving coaching exceeded
20,000.

The Grass Roots scheme is divided into two
stages. For the complete beginner, and juniors
with very little experience, there are courses
(for a small charge) of six lessons throughout
each summer. This instruction is given by an
LTA-certificated coach, on a county basis
with each county having a number of local
centres. The counties themselves come under
regions, usually five to a region. The scheme is
widely publicized in schools, colleges and
public libraries; children send application

forms to their local centre or county organizer.
Promising players can qualify for a course of
advanced coaching during the winter.

The second stage of the scheme depends
heavily on Green Shield's financial support.
Advanced coaching is important since it gives
more talented players the essential chance to
develop their game. Outstanding players can
hope to move up to national coaching and ultimately play for their country. DC

Grays of Cambridge Ltd
One of the leading manufacturers in Britain of
tennis rackets and balls and other sporting
equipment. The company was founded in
1855 in Cambridge by Henry John Gray, one
of five brothers, and originally specialized in
the sport of rackets. When lawn tennis became popular in the mid-1870s the company
began to produce equipment for the new game
and quickly flourished. Grays have taken over
several other sporting companies including L.
J. Nicholls, cricket specialists, in 1940 and
John WISDEN and Co Ltd, in August 1970.
HEAD OFFICE: Playfair Works, Benson
Street, Cambridge

Great Britain
As (with IRELAND) the BRITISH ISLES, a founder
member of the INTERNATIONAL LAWN TENNIS
FEDERATION. For history of tennis see articles
in PART 1. See also WIMBLEDON, BRITISH
COVERED COURT CHAMPIONSHIPS, BRITISH HARD
COURT CHAMPIONSHIPS, SCOTLAND, WALES,
LAWN TENNIS ASSOCIATIONS, etc.

Greece
Greece has been a Full Member of the ILTF
since 1925. It first took part in the DAVIS CUP
in 1927 and has been a regular competitor since

1963. It has also sent teams to the FEDERATION CUP since 1968 and staged that event in Athens in 1969. BR

GOVERNING BODY: Fédération Hellénique de Lawn Tennis, 8 rue Omirou (133), Athens

Green Shield Trading Stamp Company Ltd

One of Britain's largest sponsors of lawn tennis. In its first three years' involvement with the sport it donated £100,000 excluding promotional costs, a major share going to the GRASS ROOTS SCHEME which began in 1970. Since then Green Shield has also sponsored senior and junior events, and given financial support to Britain's WIGHTMAN CUP and FEDERATION CUP teams. It has also sponsored the Welsh Championships at NEWPORT, Monmouthshire, which were later renamed the Green Shield Welsh Open Championships, and a new tournament at Leicester, the Green Shield Midland Open Championships. Three new tournaments were added in 1971: the Northumberland Open at Newcastle, the Ilkley Open in Yorkshire and the Registered Coaches Professional Championship at EASTBOURNE, Sussex. In 1972 Green Shield sponsored the KENT GRASS COURT CHAMPIONSHIPS at Beckenham for the first time. Support was withdrawn from Leicester but other tournament sponsorship remained the same.

Green Shield now supports all the British national events for under-18s, including Junior Wimbledon and the British Junior Wightman Cup squad, the latter since 1972. DC

Gregory, Dr John Colin (Gt Britain)

Born Beverley, Yorks., 28 July 1903, died 10 Jan. 1959; Wimbledon men's singles q/f

1926, 1930; men's doubles r/u 1929, s/f 1930; mixed doubles s/f 1929; Australian men's singles won 1929; men's doubles s/f 1929; French men's singles q/f 1930; men's doubles s/f 1928-9; mixed doubles s/f 1930. Davis Cup 1926-30, 1952. A Yorkshire stalwart who at the age of 48 came to Britain's rescue in the Davis Cup in 1952 in Yugoslavia. With injury to his team he abandoned his role as non-playing captain to help win the doubles. He was chairman of the All England Club, 1955-9.

Grips

A sound and comfortable grip is essential to play lawn tennis well. There are two grips commonly used by the world's leading players, the Eastern (its first exponents came from the Eastern United States) and the Continental (first popular in Europe).

The most widely used grip for the forehand drive is the Eastern. For this grip the palm of the hand is parallel with the racket face, flat against the back of the handle. To obtain the grip, hold the racket at its throat in the left hand so that the edge of the frame is parallel to the ground with the cross strings perpendicular and the handle pointing straight at the stomach. Put the right hand flat against the gut and parallel to the racket face. Then draw the right hand backwards and down the racket handle until the hand is at the end of the handle. Then close the fingers and thumb round the handle as if shaking hands.

The Continental grip is similar to the Eastern except that the right hand moves approximately half an inch (just over one centimetre) to the left until the apex of the 'V' formed by the thumb and index finger is right over the left hand bevel of the handle. The

palm is now more on top of the handle and the racket face is slightly open.

The Western grip, now almost obsolete, was obtained by making an Eastern grip and then turning the hand half an inch to the right. It was developed by players who learned their tennis on high-bounding cement courts in California.

Some players – Fred Perry was a typical example – retain the same grip for all strokes, but most leading players change their grip for a backhand stroke.

There are only two standard grips for a backhand, either with the thumb placed straight up the back of the handle or diagonally across it; the rest of the hand falls naturally into position.

The standard grip for the service, volley and overhead shots is the Continental forehand grip, but many top players use an Eastern grip for both forehand and volley, though rarely for the service.

Some players use two hands on the racket for all shots except service and smash: the most notable modern exponent is Frew McMillan of South Africa. Others use two hands for either forehand or backhand; Chris Evert of the United States is a typical example.

Another grip, now almost extinct, is the old-fashioned Australian grip: the Western forehand is used and the racket is then turned over for backhand shots so that the same face of the racket strikes the ball.

An 'open' grip is one that tends to open the racket face skywards from the vertical, while a 'closed' grip tends to tilt the racket face towards the ground. Taking forehand drive grips as an example, the Eastern grip is neutral (i.e. the racket face is vertical), while the Con-

---

Grips. *Below* The Eastern forehand 'shake-hands' grip. The forefinger is spread slightly. Before the fingers close, the palm is parallel with the racket face.

Below The Continental 'chopper grip'. The forefinger is spread slightly. This grip is best for advanced serving.

Below The Eastern backhand drive grip. The forefinger is spread slightly and the thumb placed *across* the back of the handle.

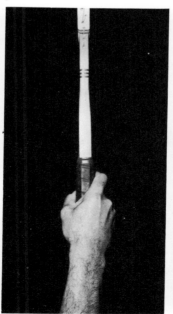

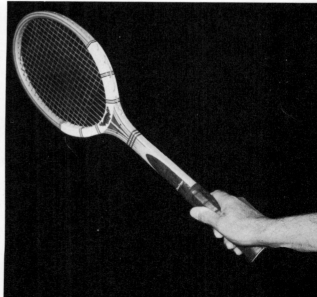

tinental grip is an 'open' grip and the Western grip is a 'closed' grip.

See also THE DEVELOPMENT OF TECHNIQUE AND STROKEPLAY, THE BASIC TEACHING OF TENNIS (PART 1). JO

Groundstroke

A stroke by which the ball is struck after it has bounced. Normally it refers to DRIVES. JO

Guatemala

Guatemala has been an Associate Member of the ILTF since 1960. BR
GOVERNING BODY: Federación Nacionale de Tenis, Apartado Postal 371, Cuidad de Guatemala

Gulyás, Istvan see HUNGARY

Gunter, Mrs K. S. see Miss Nancy RICHEY

Guyana

Lawn tennis has been played in Guyana (formerly British Guiana) since 1900 on the sugar estates and at the leading clubs. Inter-club tournaments and challenge matches with neighbouring countries developed and in 1935 a national association was formed. After World War II, with Trinidad and Jamaica, it formed the British Caribbean LTA (see COMMONWEALTH CARIBBEAN LTA). In 1972 Ivan Phillips, a leading player of the 1950s, gave a trophy for an annual women's competition. BR
GOVERNING BODY: Guyana Lawn Tennis Association, P.O. Box 88, Georgetown

Below **Ellen Hansell** *(right)* with three other early American players *(left to right),* Bertha Townsend (champion 1888-9), Margie Ballard and Louise Allerdice

H

Hackett, Harold Humphrey (USA)
Born 17 July 1878, died 20 Nov. 1937; US men's singles q/f 1906; men's doubles won 1907-10, r/u 1911. Davis Cup 1908-9, 1913.

Hadow, P. Frank (Gt Britain)
Born 24 Jan. 1855, died 29 June 1946; Wimbledon men's singles won 1878. Having won Wimbledon in the second year at his first and only attempt, while on leave from Ceylon (Sri Lanka), he never afterwards bothered to play the game, and never saw a first-class match again until he attended the 50th anniversary meeting in 1926. In beating S. W. GORE in the first Challenge Round, 7-5, 6-1, 9-7, he was the first player to play and win an advantage set at Wimbledon. He was also the only player who played at Wimbledon without losing a set.

Half Volley
A stroke, played immediately after the ball has bounced. Being more difficult than a groundstroke or volley to control it is usually employed when a player is not in a position to use either of these and is more often used in doubles than in singles. JO

Hampton Court see THE ORIGINS OF LAWN TENNIS (PART 1)

Handicapping
A table of handicaps, based on odds owed and received, is designed to help weaker players enjoy tournament competition. When two players who are handicapped to owe odds meet, the one who owes the smaller odds is put forward to scratch and then meets his opponent at the difference between the face value. Similarly, when two players receiving odds meet, the player receiving the smaller odds is put back to scratch and the match is played at face value between the two. No competitor is allowed, under LTA rules, to have a handicap of over owe 50 or more than receive 40, and no competitor can receive more than 30 from any opponent. However, when a player is prevented by this regulation from receiving his full handicap he gets the additional points to which he is entitled up to a limit of owe 50 by way of owed odds. For this purpose, two owed odds are regarded as the equivalent of one received point. See tables of received odds and owed odds on the following page. DC

'Handsome Eight'
see THE POSTWAR PRO GAME (PART 1), MEN'S CLOTHING, WORLD CHAMPIONSHIP TENNIS

Hansell, Miss Ellen [Mrs Allerdice] (USA)
The first US women's singles champion (1887).

Hantze, Miss Karen see Mrs J. R. SUSMAN

Hard, Miss Darlene R. (USA)
Born Los Angeles, Calif. 6 Jan. 1936; Wimbledon women's singles s/f 1955, r/u 1957, 1959, q/f 1960, 1962, s/f 1963; women's doubles s/f 1955, won 1957, 1959-60, s/f 1962, won 1963; mixed doubles s/f 1956, won 1957, 1959-60, r/u 1963; US women's singles s/f 1954, 1956, s/f 1957, r/u 1958, s/f 1959, won 1960-1, r/u 1962, q/f 1963; women's doubles s/f 1954, 1956, r/u 1957, won 1958-62, r/u 1963; mixed doubles s/f 1954, r/u 1956-7, 1961; Australian women's singles q/f 1962; women's doubles r/u 1962; mixed doubles r/u 1962; French women's singles q/f 1957, won 1960; women's doubles won 1955, r/u 1956, won 1957, 1960, r/u 1961; mixed doubles won 1955, r/u 1956, s/f 1960, won 1961. Federation Cup 1963. Wightman Cup 1957, 1959-60, 1962-3. Outstanding in her all-court play, most formidable in doubles.

Below **Darlene Hard**

Table of Received Odds

	1st Game	2nd Game	3rd Game	4th Game	5th Game	6th Game
1/6th of 15		15				
2/6th of 15		15		15		
3/6th of 15		15		15		15
4/6th of 15	15	15		15		15
5/6th of 15	15	15	15	15		15

Example A player receiving four-sixths of fifteen receives nothing in the third and fifth games, and fifteen in the first, second, fourth and sixth games, of a set.

Note The table is not carried beyond the sixth game, as in the next and every succeeding six games the odds recur in the same positions.

The above odds may be received in augmentation of other received odds. Fifteen is one point received at the beginning of every game of a set. Thirty is two points received at the beginning of every game of a set. Forty is three points received at the beginning of every game of a set.

Table of Owed Odds

	1st Game	2nd Game	3rd Game	4th Game	5th Game	6th Game
1/6th of 15					15	
2/6th of 15			15		15	
3/6th of 15	15		15		15	
4/6th of 15	15		15		15	15
5/6th of 15	15		15	15	15	15

Example A player owing two-sixths of fifteen would owe fifteen in the third and fifth games, and nothing in the first, second, fourth and sixth games, of a set.

Table of Odds to be Owed to Players whose Handicap on Difference is more than Receive 30

A player whose handicap is as stated at top of column shall receive 30 and in addition shall be owed the odds stated in such column opposite the handicap of his opponent.

Opponent	Rec. 40	Rec. 30·5	Rec. 30·4	Rec. 30·3	Rec. 30·2	Rec. 30·1
Owe 50	Owe 50	Owe 50	Owe 50	Owe 50	Owe 50	Owe 50
Owe 40·5	Owe 50	Owe 50	Owe 50	Owe 50	Owe 50	Owe 50
Owe 40·4	Owe 50	Owe 50	Owe 50	Owe 50	Owe 50	Owe 50
Owe 40·3	Owe 50	Owe 50	Owe 50	Owe 50	Owe 50	Owe 50
Owe 40·2	Owe 50	Owe 50	Owe 50	Owe 50	Owe 50	Owe 40·5
Owe 40·1	Owe 50	Owe 50	Owe 50	Owe 50	Owe 40·5	Owe 40·3
Owe 40	Owe 50	Owe 50	Owe 50	Owe 50	Owe 40·4	Owe 40·2
Owe 30·5	Owe 50	Owe 50	Owe 50	Owe 40·5	Owe 40·3	Owe 40·1
Owe 30·4	Owe 50	Owe 50	Owe 50	Owe 40·4	Owe 40·2	Owe 40
Owe 30·3	Owe 50	Owe 50	Owe 40·5	Owe 40·3	Owe 40·1	Owe 30·5
Owe 30·2	Owe 50	Owe 50	Owe 40·4	Owe 40·2	Owe 40	Owe 30·4
Owe 30·1	Owe 50	Owe 40·5	Owe 40·3	Owe 40·1	Owe 30·5	Owe 30·3
Owe 30	Owe 50	Owe 40·4	Owe 40·2	Owe 40	Owe 30·4	Owe 30·2
Owe 15·5	Owe 40·5	Owe 40·3	Owe 40·1	Owe 30·5	Owe 30·3	Owe 30·1
Owe 15·4	Owe 40·4	Owe 40·2	Owe 40	Owe 30·4	Owe 30·2	Owe 30
Owe 15·3	Owe 40·3	Owe 40·1	Owe 30·5	Owe 30·3	Owe 30·1	Owe 15·5
Owe 15·2	Owe 40·2	Owe 40	Owe 30·4	Owe 30·2	Owe 30	Owe 15·4
Owe 15·1	Owe 40·1	Owe 30·5	Owe 30·3	Owe 30·1	Owe 15·5	Owe 15·3
Owe 15	Owe 40	Owe 30·4	Owe 30·2	Owe 30	Owe 15·4	Owe 15·2
Owe ·5	Owe 30·5	Owe 30·3	Owe 30·1	Owe 15·5	Owe 15·3	Owe 15·1
Owe ·4	Owe 30·4	Owe 30·2	Owe 30	Owe 15·4	Owe 15·2	Owe 15
Owe ·3		Owe 30·1	Owe 15·5	Owe 15·3	Owe 15·1	Owe ·5
Owe ·2		Owe 30	Owe 15·4	Owe 15·2	Owe 15	Owe ·4
Owe ·1		Owe 15·5	Owe 15·3	Owe 15·1	Owe ·5	Owe ·3
Scratch		Owe 15·4	Owe 15·2	Owe 15	Owe ·4	Owe ·2
Receive ·1		Owe 15·2	Owe 15	Owe ·4	Owe ·2	
Receive ·2		Owe 15	Owe ·4	Owe ·2		
Receive ·3		Owe ·4	Owe ·2			
Receive ·4		Owe ·2				
Receive ·5						
Receive 15						

Handicapping. *Left and above* Tables of received odds and owed odds

Hart, Miss Doris J. (USA)

Born St Louis, Mo., 20 June 1925; Wimbledon women's singles q/f 1946, r/u 1947-8, s/f 1950, won 1951, q/f 1952, r/u 1953, s/f 1954-5; women's doubles r/u 1946, won 1947, r/u 1948, 1950, won 1951-3, r/u 1954; mixed doubles s/f 1947, r/u 1948, s/f 1950, won 1951-5; US women's singles q/f 1944, s/f 1945, r/u 1946, s/f 1947, q/f 1948, r/u 1949-50, s/f 1951, r/u 1952-3, won 1954-5; women's doubles r/u 1942-5, s/f 1946, r/u 1947-50, won 1951-4, r/u 1955; mixed doubles r/u 1945, s/f 1948, r/u 1950, won 1951-5; Australian women's singles won 1949, r/u 1950; women's doubles won 1950; mixed doubles won 1949-50; French women's singles q/f 1946, r/u 1947, s/f 1948, won 1950, r/u 1951, won 1952, r/u 1953; women's doubles r/u 1946-7, won 1948, 1950-3; mixed doubles r/u 1948, won 1951-3. Wightman Cup 1946-55. An unusually graceful player with rare fluency both of stroke and foorwork, she took up the game at the age of six as a remedial exercise for an illness that threatened to cripple her. In becoming triple champion at Wimbledon in 1951 she lost a set only in mixed doubles. Her first Wimbledon success, the women's doubles with Pat Todd in 1947 (they won from a third set deficit of 0-40, and three match balls against them) was spectacular. She became a coaching professional in 1955. See CENTRE COURT CLASSICS (PART 1).

Below Doris Hart

Harten Cup see SOUTH AMERICAN CHAMPIONSHIPS

Hartigan, Miss Joan Marcia (Australia)

Born Sydney, N.S.W., 6 June 1912; Wimbledon women's singles s/f 1934-5; Australian women's singles won 1933-4, 1936, s/f 1939, women's doubles r/u 1933; mixed doubles won 1934. The first Australian woman to make her mark on the international game.

Hartley, Canon John T. (Gt Britain)

Born 9 Jan. 1849, died 21 Aug. 1935; Wimbledon men's singles won 1879-80, r/u 1881; men's doubles won 1882. The only Wimbledon champion who was a beneficed clergyman. He was noted for his use of the lob. See illustration, page 348.

Hartwig, Rex Noel (Australia)

Born N.S.W., 2 Sept. 1929; Wimbledon men's singles q/f 1954; men's doubles r/u 1953, won 1954-5; US men's singles r/u 1954; men's doubles won 1953, s/f 1954; mixed doubles r/u 1953, s/f 1955; Australian men's singles r/u 1954, s/f 1955; men's doubles won 1954, s/f 1955; mixed doubles won 1953-4; French men's doubles s/f 1954; mixed doubles r/u 1954. Davis Cup 1953-5. Became pro 1955.

Hawaii

Hawaii competed in the DAVIS CUP in 1923. Its LTA now forms part of the USLTA.

Hawkes, John Bailey (Australia)

Born 7 June 1899; Wimbledon men's doubles r/u 1928; US men's doubles s/f 1923, r/u 1925, 1928; mixed doubles r/u 1923, won 1925, 1928; Australian men's singles s/f 1922, won 1926, r/u 1927; men's doubles won 1922, 1926-7, s/f 1928, r/u 1930; mixed doubles won 1922, 1926-7, r/u 1928; French men's singles s/f 1928; mixed doubles s/f 1928. Davis Cup (Australasia) 1921, (Australia) 1923, 1925. An Australian stalwart of the mid-1920s and notably the loser, after having match points, of the longest Australian men's singles final, against PATTERSON in 1927.

Hawton, Mrs Mary K. (Australia)

Wimbledon women's doubles r/u 1957, s/f 1958, s/f 1960; US women's singles q/f 1957; women's doubles s/f 1957-8, 1960; Australian women's singles s/f 1952-4, 1956, q/f 1958, s/f 1959, q/f 1960-1; women's doubles r/u 1951-3, won 1954-6, r/u 1957, won 1958, s/f 1959-60, r/u 1961; French women's doubles r/u 1958, s/f 1960.

Haydon, Miss A. S. see Mrs P. F. JONES

Haygarth, Mrs P. see Miss R. SCHUURMAN

Haymarket Tennis Court see THE ORIGINS OF LAWN TENNIS (PART 1)

Head, Miss Dorothy see Mrs D. P. KNODE

Heath, Rodney Wilfred (Australia)

Born Melbourne, Vic., 1887; Wimbledon men's singles q/f 1911; men's doubles r/u 1919; Australian men's singles won 1905, 1910; men's doubles won 1906, r/u 1910, won 1911. Davis Cup for Australasia 1911-12. Winner of the first Australian Championship.

Heine, Miss E. L. see Mrs E. L. H. MILLER

Helwig, Miss Helen R. [Mrs Pouch] (USA)

US women's singles won 1894, r/u 1895; women's doubles won 1894-5. A pioneer of the American women's game.

Henkel, Henner Ernst Otto (Germany)

Born Posen, 9 Oct. 1915; died Stalingrad 1943; Wimbledon men's singles q/f 1937, s/f 1938-9; men's doubles s/f 1937, r/u 1938; mixed doubles r/u 1938; US men's doubles won 1937; Australian men's doubles r/u 1938; French men's singles won 1937; men's doubles won 1937. Davis Cup 1935-9. With von CRAMM he made Germany a formidable Davis Cup force before World War II, when he was one of the German casualties at Stalingrad.

Hewitt, Robert A. J. (Australia/S. Africa)

Born Sydney, N.S.W., 12 Jan. 1940; Wimble-

Above **Bob Hewitt**

don men's singles q/f 1962, 1964, 1966; men's doubles s/f 1960, r/u 1961, won 1962, 1964, r/u 1965, won 1967, s/f 1968-70, won 1972; mixed doubles r/u 1963; US men's singles q/f 1967; men's doubles s/f 1971; Australian men's singles s/f 1960, 1962-3; men's doubles s/f 1960, r/u 1962, won 1963-4; mixed doubles won 1961; French men's doubles s/f 1961-4, r/u 1965, s/f 1968, won 1972; mixed doubles s/f 1959, 1961, 1968, won 1970, s/f 1972. Davis Cup (South Africa) 1965-9. Emigrated to South Africa 1964. Outstanding run of 39 doubles wins with MCMILLAN in 1967. ILTF GP 6th 1972.

Hillyard, Mrs G. W. [Miss Blanche Bingley] (Gt Britain)

Born Greenford, Middlesex, 3 Nov. 1863, died 1938; Wimbledon women's singles s/f 1884, r/u 1885, won 1886, r/u 1887-8, won 1889, r/u* 1891, r/u 1892-3, won 1894, won 1897, won 1899-1900, r/u 1901, s/f 1905, q/f 1906, s/f 1907, s/f 1912. A zealous pioneer of the women's game. She played in the first women's singles championship at Wimbledon in 1884 and reached the semi-final as late as 1912 when she was 48. Her husband, Commander George Hillyard, R.N., was secretary of the All England Club 1907-24.

H. M. King Gustaf V of Sweden Cup see KING'S CUP

Above **Blanche Hillyard**

Hoad, Lewis A. [Lew] (Australia)

Born Glebe, N.S.W., 23 Nov. 1934; Wimbledon men's singles q/f 1953-5, won 1956-7; men's doubles s/f 1952, won 1953, s/f 1954, won 1955-6, r/u 1957; mixed doubles s/f 1953-5; US men's singles q/f 1952, s/f 1953, q/f 1954, s/f 1955, r/u 1956; men's doubles s/f 1952, r/u 1954, won 1956; mixed doubles r/u

1952, s/f 1954-5, r/u 1956; Australian men's singles r/u 1955, won 1956, s/f 1957; men's doubles won 1953, r/u 1955, won 1956-7; mixed doubles r/u 1955; French men's singles q/f 1953, won 1956; men's doubles s/f 1952, won 1953, r/u 1954, 1956, s/f 1957; mixed doubles won 1954. Davis Cup 1952-6. A wrist of steel enabled him to play shots beyond the capacity of the normal individual and all experts agree that his standard of performance puts him among the all-time greats. His most majestic effort was his defeat of his compatriot Ashley COOPER in the Wimbledon final of 1957 when he played a power game of peerless quality. He came within one match of winning the 'Grand Slam' in 1956 when beaten by his partner Ken ROSEWALL in the final at Forest Hills. He became a professional in 1957 and set up a tennis ranch in 1968 in Spain. See colour plate, page 206, and GREAT PLAYERS OF ALL TIME (PART 1).

Hobart, Clarence (USA)
Wimbledon men's singles s/f 1890, 1898, q/f 1899; men's doubles r/u 1898-9; US men's singles r/u 1891, s/f 1893, q/f 1894, 1901, r/u* 1905, s/f 1907; men's doubles won 1890, 1893-4; mixed doubles won 1892-3, 1905.

Homans, Miss Helen (USA)
US women's singles r/u 1905, won 1906; women's doubles won 1905. Champion of America in a quiet year.

Hong Kong
Hong Kong has been an Associate Member of the ILTF since 1965. It has competed in the DAVIS CUP since 1970. BR
GOVERNING BODY: Hong Kong Lawn Tennis Association, 407-409 Gloucester Building, Hong Kong

Hopman, Harry C. (Australia)
Born Sydney, N.S.W., 12 Aug. 1906; Wimbledon mixed doubles r/u 1932, 1935, s/f 1946; US men's singles q/f 1938-9; men's doubles s/f 1934, 1938, 1950; mixed doubles s/f 1938, won 1939; Australian men's singles s/f 1929, r/u 1930-2, s/f 1936-7, q/f 1939; men's doubles won 1929-30, r/u 1931-2, s/f 1934-5, 1939, 1949; mixed doubles won 1930, 1936-7, 1939; French men's singles q/f 1930; men's doubles r/u 1930, 1948. Davis Cup 1928, 1930, 1932; playing captain 1938-9, non-playing captain 1950-9. Now president of the Port Washington Tennis Academy, Long Island, N.Y. Australian squash champion 1933-4, 1936. As a trainer his record is unrivalled. See AUSTRALIA; also TRAINING TOP INTERNATIONALS (PART 1).

Hopman, Mrs Nell (Australia)
Born Sydney, N.S.W., 19 March 1909; died 10 Jan. 1968; Wimbledon mixed doubles r/u 1935; US mixed doubles s/f 1938; Australian women's singles s/f 1935, 1938, r/u 1939, 1947, q/f 1954; women's doubles r/u 1935, 1937, s/f 1939, 1947, r/u 1955, s/f 1956; French

women's doubles won 1954; mixed doubles s/f 1938.

Hotchkiss, Miss Hazel V. see Mrs G. W. WIGHTMAN

Hour-Glass Court
The lawn tennis court, as it appeared in Major Wingfield's Rules for Sphairistiké in 1874, was the shape of an hour-glass; this shape was retained until 1877 when it was discarded by the first Wimbledon Championships rules committee. See THE BIRTH AND SPREAD OF LAWN TENNIS and THE RULES AND THEIR INTERPRETATION (PART 1).

Howe, Robert N. (Australia)
Born Sydney N.S.W., 3 Aug. 1925; Wimbledon men's doubles s/f 1956-7, 1962; mixed doubles s/f 1956, won 1958, r/u 1960-1; US men's doubles s/f 1958; mixed doubles r/u 1957; Australian men's singles q/f 1958, 1963; men's doubles r/u 1959, s/f 1960; mixed doubles won 1958, s/f 1959-60; French men's doubles r/u 1958, 1961; mixed doubles r/u 1956, s/f 1957, r/u 1958, won 1960, 1962, s/f 1963, 1967.

Howe Shield see NEW ZEALAND

Hoylake, Cheshire (UK)
This tournament, open (in the modern sense) since 1970, is held after Wimbledon in July; it is the only major event in Britain to be played on the courts of a public park, that of West Kirby, a few miles west of Liverpool.

The Rothmans Hoylake Open Championships, as it is now known since ROTHMANS began to sponsor it in 1970, has rapidly taken over from Manchester's Northern Club the title of 'Wimbledon of the North', although Mancunians strongly deny this. In 1972 part of the COMMERCIAL UNION women's Grand Prix was played there.

Although Hoylake has been in the LTA's calendar since 1949, it had its beginnings in a very small way before World War II as a purely local event. In 1948 John White, secretary of the Cheshire LTA and also of the tournament, persuaded the local authority to guarantee the event against loss, and in 1949 it raised its standards to include players at county level. It grew in stature, however, 10 years later when the committee obtained support from the *Liverpool Daily Post* which enabled it to attract players of international class.

Hoylake is also unique in Britain in that the tournament is played in the long summer evenings and so can attract as many as 20,000 people during the week. Because the venue is a public park, permanent buildings are negligible; for tournament week tents are used for dressing rooms, the press, etc. Profits over the years have steadily been ploughed back: stands have been bought and the courts considerably improved. In recent years the tournament has attracted such world-class players as John Newcombe, Tony Roche, Manuel Santana, Margaret Smith Court, Billie Jean King, Evonne Goolagong and Virginia Wade. DC

Hoylake Lawn Tennis Tournament Winners

Men's Singles		Women's Singles	
1949	W. Devine	1949	Mrs B. Dixon
1950	T. A. Cowdy	1950	Miss A. Layfield
1951	D. A. Samaai	1951	Miss A. Layfield
1952	K. H. Ip	1952	Miss R. Walsh
1953	G. D. Oakley	1953	Miss M. Harris
1954	G. D. Oakley	1954	Miss P. J. Curry
1955	G. D. Oakley	1955	Miss S. J. Bloomer
1956	J. F. O'Brien	1956	Miss S. J. Bloomer
1957	P. B. Franklin	1957	Miss M. R. O'Donnell
1958	I. Pimentel	1958	Miss M. R. O'Donnell
1959	R. Krishnan	1959	Miss S. M. Armstrong
1960	A. Gaertner	1960	Miss R. Schuurman
1961	J. Hillebrand	1961	Miss M. R. O'Donnell
1962	R. Becker	1962	Miss A. Mortimer
1963	R. Howe	1963	Mrs P. F. Jones
1964	J. Hillebrand / F. S. Stolle } divided	1964	Miss R. H. Bentley / Miss M. Schacht } divided
1965	M. J. Sangster	1965	Miss M. Smith
1966	M. J. Sangster	1966	Miss M. Smith
1967	J. D. Newcombe	1967	Miss V. Wade
1968	M. J. Sangster	1968	Mrs M. Court
1969	R. O. Ruffels	1969	Miss S. V. Wade
1970	J. D. Newcombe	1970	Miss E. Goolagong
1971	A. J. Pattison	1971	Mrs L. W. King
1972	D. Irvine / R. Keldie } divided	1972	Miss E. Goolagong / Miss B. Stöve } divided
1973	A. R. Giltinan	1973	Miss P. S. A. Hogan

Above **Hungary.** This set of tennis postage stamps was issued in 1965.

Hughes, George Patrick (Gt Britain)
Born Sutton Coldfield, 21 Dec. 1902; Wimbledon men's singles q/f 1931, 1933; men's doubles s/f 1931, r/u 1932, s/f 1935, won 1936, r/u 1937, s/f 1938; US mixed doubles s/f 1931; Australian men's doubles won 1934, r/u 1935; French men's singles s/f 1931, q/f 1934, 1937; men's doubles s/f 1931, won 1933, r/u 1936, s/f 1937; mixed doubles s/f 1934, 1936-7. Davis Cup 1929, 1931-6.

Hungary
'Ready—play' was heard for the first time in Hungary in 1881 on a private court belonging to the Liedemann family in Budapest. The first tennis club, the Budapest Lawn Tennis Egyesulet, was established in 1883 and the indoor game began in 1897 in an exhibition hall in Budapest. The first tournament was arranged at Balatonfüred, a little spa on Lake Balaton, and the championship was held in the same place in 1890. The first official Championship of Hungary, held in 1894, when men and women competed against one another in singles, was won by Miss Paulina Palffy.

The first book of rules in Hungarian was published in 1893 and the first international match was played in 1897 between Hungary and Austria. Each team included an Englishman: Hungary, Arthur Yolland, and Austria, H. W. Gendon. The first international interclub match was held in 1899, and the first international tournament in 1903 in Budapest was won by the later Olympic Champion, M. J. G. Ritchie of Great Britain.

The Hungarian Lawn Tennis Association was founded on 7 April 1907 with 15 member clubs. In that year Miss Margit Madarasz won the German Championship and Anthony F. Wilding of New Zealand took part in the Hungarian International Tournament in Budapest.

In May 1909 Mr A. Yolland was sent by the Hungarian LTA to the LTA of Great Britain to find out if it was possible to affiliate the Hungarian LTA, for at the time there was a dispute between the Hungarian and Austrian associations. Mr Yolland also proposed to the LTA of Great Britain that there should be an INTERNATIONAL LAWN TENNIS FEDERATION. Hungary became a member of the ILTF in 1913, its inaugural year.

In 1911 the first 'inter-countries' meeting was held in Budapest; the Hungarian team lost 11-14 to Austria. In 1912 Bela von Kehrling won his first Hungarian Championship; he held the title for 20 years. He was also the first Hungarian to play at Wimbledon, in 1924, when he reached the semi-finals of the men's doubles with the Italian Baron de Morpurgo. Von Kehrling was an excellent player who won the German singles and doubles titles.

In 1923 the first Covered Court Championship of Hungary was held, and in the same year a Team Championship with mixed doubles was established. In 1924 a Hungarian team first played in the DAVIS CUP in Copenhagen.

In 1926 the first tournament for juniors was held, and in 1927 a tennis stadium seating 2,500 was built in Budapest. The official Handbook of the Hungarian LTA was first printed in 1928. In the same year the Hungarian Davis Cup team reached the semi-finals of the European Zone.

By 1935, 134 clubs and 1,065 registered players were affiliated to the LTA. In 1937 the Central European Tennis Cup began. The Hungarian women's team won it in 1938 and 1940; the men's team in 1940. In 1938 Otto Szigeti won the German Championships in Hamburg.

After World War II tennis began again with an exhibition match on 9 June 1945 in Budapest, and in 1946 the LTA reaffiliated to the ILTF. Many international successes followed. József Asbóth won the French Championships in 1947 and reached the Wimbledon semi-finals in 1948. The Davis Cup team reached the semi-finals of the European Zone in 1949; the same year the stadium on the Margaret Island in Budapest, seating 5,200, was erected. Mrs Zsuzsi Körmöczy, one of the most famous players of the time, won the French Championship in Paris in 1958 and did very well at Wimbledon. Istvan Gulyás (born Budapest, 14 Oct. 1941) won the singles of the Championship of Hungary 15 times and the doubles 18 times. He was the runner-up in the French and German (closed) championships in 1966, and received the International Coubertin Fair Play Award and the Hungarian Fair Play Award in 1967. He played 51 Davis Cup rubbers for Hungary between 1958 and 1968.

The first modern covered court at the Dozsa club was built in 1959, then two other courts in 1960, and in 1967 the very modern hall at the Club VTSK. In 1970 a court was built in Miskolc.

Hungary began competing in the GALEA CUP in 1957, the FEDERATION CUP in 1963, the Centrope Cup in 1964, the ANNIE SOISBAULT CUP in 1965 and the KING'S CUP in 1969.

The Hungarian National Championships accept entries from every district and county. There are, all over the country, sports schools and tennis schools which ensure the development of the game. Coaches are officially trained at the School of Physical Education; among other excellent coaches Ferenc Schmidt is preeminent. In 1972 there were 202 clubs with 12,000 players affiliated to the Hungarian LTA. BR

GOVERNING BODY: Magyar Tenisz Szövetség, Rosenberg Hold utca 1, Budapest V

Hunt, Joseph R. (USA)

Born San Francisco, Calif., 17 Feb. 1919, died 2 Feb. 1944; US men's singles q/f 1937-8, s/f 1939-40, won 1943; men's doubles s/f 1937. Davis Cup 1939. A career of promise was checked by the onset of World War II. He was killed while training as a pilot in Florida.

Hunt, Lamar

see OPEN TENNIS (PART 1)

Hunter, Francis Townsend (USA)

Born New York, 28 June 1894; Wimbledon men's singles s/f 1921, r/u 1923, q/f 1927; men's doubles won 1924, won 1927, s/f 1928-9; mixed doubles won 1927, s/f 1928, won 1929; US men's singles q/f 1915, 1921, s/f 1923, s/f 1927, r/u 1928-9, q/f 1930; men's doubles s/f 1924, won 1927, s/f 1929-30; French men's singles q/f 1929; men's doubles s/f 1927, s/f 1929; mixed doubles r/u 1928-9. Davis Cup 1927-9.

ILTF see INTERNATIONAL LAWN TENNIS FEDERATION

ILTF Grand Prix

The Grand Prix series of tournaments was devised in 1968 by the ILTF in the hope that large prizes would give top-class players some inducement not to become contract professionals and thus lose their eligibility for the Davis Cup and their national tournaments (see OPEN TENNIS, PART 1). Several tournaments were selected for inclusion in the series. The tournaments had to pay the ILTF a small fee and contribute 10 per cent of their advertised prize money into a pool which was added to the sponsor's contribution, the pool then being distributed among the leading players, according to a points order of merit table (points being given according to results in each tournament) at the end of the year. In 1970 and 1971 the Grand Prix was sponsored by PEPSI-COLA INC. In 1972 sponsorship was taken over by the COMMERCIAL UNION ASSURANCE COMPANY, whose contribution has been £100,000 each year.

In the first year, 1970, the Grand Prix was for men only, and 20 tournaments in different countries were included. The American Davis Cup player, Cliff Richey, made a whirlwind start and by the penultimate event, the Embassy British Indoor Championships at Wembley, Richey was virtually the assured winner. He did, in fact, win the series by five points from Arthur Ashe and claimed the first prize of $25,000. The prize structure reached down to the 20th place.

In 1971 the series was extended to 31 tournaments and a women's Grand Prix of 18 events. Again the winners were American: Stan Smith with $25,000 and Billie Jean King with $10,000. The increased prize money in 1972, when the Grand Prix was sponsored by Commercial Union and stretched over 33 tournaments for men and 31 for women, enabled the winners, Ilie Năstase of Rumania and Mrs King, to pick up £21,000 and £9,000 respectively.

To achieve Grand Prix status, tournaments must fulfil certain minimum conditions, particularly regarding the number of players in the draw and the prize money offered. Tournaments are then assigned a certain classification, based mainly on the amount of prize money but also on prestige and location. A player receives more points for win-

ning a major championship (e.g. Wimbledon or Forest Hills) than for other tournaments, whose points are detailed according to their category. Davis Cup ties take on the mantle of tournaments in the sense that players are able to earn points. Players do not therefore lose their overall Grand Prix chances by representing their countries.

At the end of the Grand Prix the leading men (on points), the number varying, compete in a modified ROUND ROBIN tournament called the Masters', staged by the sponsors of the Grand Prix. The first was held in Tokyo in 1970 and won by Stan Smith. DC

ILTF Official Championships

The ILTF recognizes nine 'official lawn tennis championships': the Championships of Great Britain, Australia, France, Italy, South Africa and the United States held by the LTAs of those countries; and the Scandinavian, South American and Asian Championships. Other LTAs may apply to the ILTF to have their national championships officially recognized temporarily. The Official Championships are open to amateurs and players (see PLAYING STATUS) who are in good standing with their national LTA and the ILTF, provided that their LTA is affiliated to the ILTF; touring professionals who are in good standing with the LTA of the country in which the Championship is held, and the ILTF, may compete in those Official Championships that are open to all playing categories.

India

Indian lawn tennis is almost as old as the game in Britain. It was brought to India by the British in 1880. In 1885 the first regular tennis championships, the Punjab Tennis Championships, were held at Lahore Gymkhana, followed by the Bengal Championships, first held in Calcutta in 1887. Thereafter, at regular intervals, various tournaments were held in different places and the interest in playing started gaining momentum. But it was not until 1920 that the number of players in India was large enough to need an organization to control the game. Accordingly, on 21 March 1920, a meeting of what is now known as the All India Lawn Tennis Association was held in Lahore. At this meeting a constitution and by-laws on the lines of the constitution of the (British) Lawn Tennis Association were framed and two Honorary Secretaries were appointed. The first Annual General Meeting of the All India LTA was held at the Town Hall, Delhi, on 27 November 1920, the first President being Mr S. P. O'Donnell. It was at this meeting also that a decision to participate in the 1921 DAVIS CUP was taken. Thereafter, different provinces formed their own Provincial Associations and were affiliated to the parent organization. The Provincial Associations came to be known as State Associations when India gained independence in 1947. In 1972, 20 bodies, made up of 16 State Associations, the International Lawn

Tennis Club of India, and three Sports Control Boards, were affiliated to the All India LTA. Its affairs are conducted by an Executive Committee consisting of eight persons annually elected at the Annual General Meeting.

Each State Association, in its turn, has a number of clubs and educational institutions affiliated to it, the number in each state varying according to its size and circumstances. In the country as a whole there are approximately 1,800 clubs, with 6,000-7,000 courts, both grass and hard. Some of the clubs have excellent grass courts. Clubs such as Delhi Gymkhana, New Delhi and South Club, Calcutta, have 20-30 or more grass courts, besides gravel courts.

From the first championship, played in 1885 in Lahore Gymkhana, regional tournaments have been regularly held. In 1920 the All India LTA decided to hold championships at National level and the tournament which had been held at Allahabad since 1910 became the All India Championships, Allahabad being in the geographical centre of the country. In 1945 it was decided to have two tournaments at All-India level, one on grass (the National Lawn Tennis Championships of India) and the other on hard courts (the All India Hard Court Championships). These were first held in 1946-7 (the tennis season in India covers five months from October/November till the end of March).

India has had the honour of staging the International Championships of Asia since its inception on various surfaces.

Besides these tournaments, there are about 20 others held in different parts of the country. Some of these are regional ones and some intended for local players. However, all players are entitled to compete in any of them.

India played for the first time in the DAVIS CUP in 1921 when its team consisted of M. Sleem, S. M. Jacob, L. S. Deane, A. A. Fyzee and A. H. Fyzee. In its very first appearance India beat France 4-1 and reached the semifinals, where it lost to Japan. In 1922 India beat Rumania 5-0 but lost to Spain 1-4. Thereafter, except for a few years, India has regularly played in the Davis Cup. India has won the Eastern Zone Finals for several years and has reached the Inter-Zone Finals nine times. In 1962 it lost to Mexico 0-5, in 1963 to the United States 0-5, in 1965 to Spain 2-3. But in 1966 India achieved its best Davis Cup result when, in the Inter-Zone Finals, it beat Brazil 3-2 (Brazil having earlier defeated the United States 3-2). It eventually lost the Challenge Round against Australia 1-4. In 1968 India had further success: after winning the Eastern Zone Finals and beating West Germany in the Inter-Zone Semi-Finals, it lost to the United States in the Inter-Zone Finals in Puerto Rico.

India has looked after the Davis Cup Special Travelling Expenses Fund (Eastern Zone) for a number of years and has been host to the players of several Asian countries. India was also responsible for the establishment, through the

good offices of the ILTF, of the Amateur Championships of Asia, first held in Hong Kong in February 1972. The Honorary Secretary of the All India LTA, Mr R. K. Khanna, has been appointed by the ILTF as the Chairman of the Organizing Committee for the Amateur Championships of Asia.

In order to impart proper training and promote junior tennis, coaching centres have been established all over the country. These are supervised and controlled by coaches who are trained for a year or so at the National Institute of Sports. The All India LTA also organizes annual coaching camps where promising juniors, boys and girls, are assembled for a minimum period of two weeks. Besides playing tennis under competitive conditions at these camps, the juniors are given general physical training by the most senior coaches in the country. Immediately after the camps, the National Junior Championships are held. In addition, two events for Juniors under 18 and

Indian National Championships Winners

Men's Singles

1952-3	S. C. Misra
1953-4	R. Krishnan
1954-5	J. Arkinstall
1955-6	S. Davidson
1956-7	R. Krishnan
1957-8	U. Schmidt
1958-9	R. Krishnan
1959-60	R. Krishnan
1960-1	R. Krishnan
1961-2	R. Emerson
1962-3	R. Krishnan
1963-4	R. Krishnan
1964-5	R. Krishnan
1965-6	J. Mukerjea
1966-7	P. Lall
1967-8	P. Lall
1968-9	I. Năstase
1969-70	P. Lall
1970-1	J. Mukerjea
1971-2	G. Misra
1972-3	V. Amrithraj

Below **India.** Premjit Lall, one of India's great Davis Cup players, in 1972

under 14 are staged in every regional tournament.

From the beginning of the century, India has produced tennis players of note. Indian players have regularly competed at Wimbledon and in other international tournaments in different parts of the world. Ghaus Mohammad was the first Indian to reach the Wimbledon quarter-finals (1939); he played in the Queen's Club finals the same year. In 1954 Ramanathan Krishnan was the first Asian to win the Junior Invitation Wimbledon, beating Ashley Cooper of Australia. He was also the first Indian to reach the semi-finals at Wimbledon (which he did two years running, 1960-1). Krishnan, Premjit Lall and Jaidip Mukerjea were responsible for India's excellent Davis Cup record over several years in the 1960s. It was through the untiring efforts of these three players that India reached the Challenge Round in 1966. In 1959 Krishnan was the first Indian to be awarded the Seaboard Trophy in Pennsylvania as the best sportsman of the year.

The All India LTA was affiliated to the ILTF in 1925. It has been represented on the Committee of Management of the ILTF through its Honorary Secretary, Mr R. K. Khanna, since 1967. RKK

GOVERNING BODY: All India LTA, 7/3 Asaf Ali Road, New Delhi 1

Indonesia

The Indonesian LTA became a Full Member of the ILTF in 1967. Indonesia first competed in the DAVIS CUP in 1961 and has done so regularly since 1967. It first took part in the FEDERATION CUP in 1969. Two women, Lina Kaligis and the ambidextrous Lita Sugiarto-Liem, reached high international standard and earned Indonesia status as no. 8 seeds in the 1973 Federation Cup. Indonesia also competes in the Asian Games, Sri Lanka National Championships, the Malaysia National Championships, etc. BR

GOVERNING BODY: Indonesian Lawn Tennis Association, Depora, Senejan-Djakarta

Inter-County Championships ('Inter-County Week')

The Lawn Tennis Association (Great Britain) stages annual inter-county championships (including Scotland and Wales, divided into regions), on grass and hard courts. The two are completely different in concept.

The grass-court championships are held during one week in July at a number of different centres, a pattern set in 1925. They began in 1895 for men only: Gloucestershire won. The women's event was held for the first time in 1899 and the title went to Surrey. From the mid-1920s inter-county week on grass has been one of the highlights of the tennis calendar. Six counties play in each of seven groups of men and seven groups of women, and a two-up and two-down promotion and relegation system is operated. Group one men and group one women compete at Devonshire Park,

Eastbourne. Frinton, in Essex, is also a large enough centre to take a group of men and a group of women. The other ten venues vary.

The LTA makes small grants to each county taking part and to each centre that stages a group meeting. The 'week' was sponsored for the first time in 1973 by the PRUDENTIAL ASSURANCE COMPANY and became known as the Prudential County Cup Week.

The hard-court championships began in 1921 when Surrey won both men's and women's titles. It is played as an elimination competition on a basis of geographical grouping, with the semi-finals and finals held since 1965 at the West Hants Club, Bournemouth. The hard-court championships are contested in five stages, preliminary, intermediate, quarter-final, semi-final and final. The grass-court competition is completed in a week during the summer, but the hard-court championships are spread over almost a full year, for as soon as one final is over the preliminary stages of the following year's event start. After the quarter-finals are completed in April, there is a break during the grass-court season until the semi-finals and final are played at Bournemouth in September. A junior inter-county championship began in 1967 and is now sponsored by GREEN SHIELD. DC

International Lawn Tennis Championship see DAVIS CUP

International Lawn Tennis Clubs

The International LTC of Great Britain was founded in 1924 by A. Wallis Myers. Similar clubs now exist in France, the United States, the Netherlands, Czechoslovakia, Sweden, Belgium, Argentina, Denmark, South Africa, India, Australia, New Zealand, Italy and Canada. Their aim is to promote, by social union and matchplay, good fellowship and friendly rivalry among players of all nations. A Council of the International Clubs meets annually in London on the second Wednesday of Wimbledon. The club colours are silver-grey and pink. The different nations identify themselves by varying the thickness of the stripes (see illustration). JO

International Lawn Tennis Federation (ILTF or FILT)

The ILTF, the world governing body for tennis, was founded at a meeting held at the headquarters of the Union des Sociétés Françaises des Sports Athlétiques, 34 rue de Provence, Paris, on Saturday, 1 March 1913 with the following 13 countries represented: Australasia, Mr Gordon Inglis; Austria, Mr Zborzil; Belgium, Chevalier Paul de Borman; British Isles, Messrs R. J. McNair, H. H. Monckton, A. E. M. Taylor and B. Sabelli; Denmark, Mr E. Larsen; France, Messrs R. Gallay, P. Gillou, Allan H. Muhr, Pierre Roy and Henry Wallet; Germany, Messrs Behrens, Lürmann and Nirrnheim; Holland, Mr Feith; Russia, Mr E. Gambs; South Africa, Mr E. Raymond Clarke;

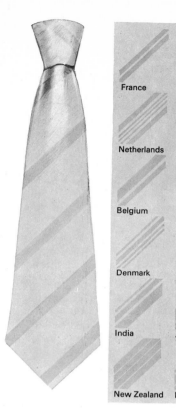

Above **International Lawn Tennis Clubs.** The club ties have pink stripes on a grey background, the number and width varying with the country as shown. The tie on the left is that of Great Britain.

Sweden, Mr Setterwall; Switzerland, Mr Charles Barde; United States, informally represented by Mr Sabelli, without a vote.

There are two types of members, Full Members with voting rights, and Associate Members, who are not yet regarded as qualified for Full Membership and do not have a vote.

There are now some 100 member nations. See ADMINISTRATION OF THE WORLD GAME (PART 1). **ADDRESS:** Barons Court, London W14 9EG, England

International Professional Championships see LONDON PROFESSIONAL INDOOR TENNIS CHAMPIONSHIPS

International Tennis Players Association see THE POSTWAR PRO GAME and OPEN TENNIS (PART 1)

Iran

The Iranian Tennis Federation was founded in 1937, although the game was played in clubs before then. In 1948 Iran was admitted to full membership of the ILTF. The country has entered a team in the DAVIS CUP, first in Asia and then in Europe, since 1959, and has also competed in the Shahenshah Cup, a team competition for Near Eastern countries. The Iranian women's team played in the FEDERATION CUP in 1972 in South Africa. The leading tournament is the Iranian International Championships, played in Teheran since 1966 under royal patronage, with many international entries. There are other local tournaments and leagues. All the major towns have courts and in Teheran there are three stadia, one seating 6,000 spectators. A 10,000-seat stadium is under construction.

In 1972 there were about 50 clubs with over 1,000 active players; the number is growing rapidly with the encouragement given to juniors. Outstanding players in Iran include G. Aftandilian, A. Tessai, and the Akbari brothers, who have done particularly well in recent years. BR

GOVERNING BODY: Iranian Tennis Federation, Sports Federations Joint Bureau, P.O. Box 11-1642, Teheran

Iraq

Lawn tennis was introduced into Iraq by foreign oil companies and the British forces camped in Habbaniya. It was later played by young Iraqis who studied in Europe and returned full of enthusiasm for the game. In the early 1930s tennis was played mostly in a few private clubs and there were no large tournaments.

In 1959 the Iraq Tennis Federation was founded and from then small tournaments were held for both beginners and advanced players. Some effort was made to encourage girls to play. With enthusiastic encouragement from the government a number of tennis courts were constructed in schools, colleges, clubs and public parks and at last the game became popular. In 1960 the Iraq Tennis Federation was elected an Associate Member of the ILTF. In 1963 an Iraqi team played against Syria and won by eight matches to one; in 1964 a team took part in the Shashenshah Cup in Iran.

In recent years coaches, encouraged by the Iraq Ministry of Youth, have been invited to visit Iraq to train young players. Since equipment is expensive an approach has been made to the government for a reduction in customs duty on equipment purchased from abroad. BR

GOVERNING BODY: Iraq Tennis Federation, P.O. Box 22, Baghdad

Ireland

Lawn tennis was introduced into Ireland shortly before 1877 and the Irish Lawn Tennis Association was established in Dublin in November 1908. In that year it affiliated with the LTA of Great Britain and was given the status of an English county. In 1877 the world-famous Fitzwilliam Club was founded in Dublin by ten men, Messrs Browne, Graves, Greene, Kennedy, J. Latouche, C. Latouche, Stopford, McMurdo, Wingfield and Guiness. To a very large degree the game in Ireland revolved about Fitzwilliam; the IRISH CHAMPIONSHIPS were staged there annually and attracted the world's best players of both sexes. These Championships have been running continu-

ously (except in 1922 and during the two world wars) since 1879 and Ireland is proud that in that year the *first-ever* women's singles championship was held, the winner being Miss May Langrishe.

In particular many Irish and British players competed in tournaments in both countries, becoming champions at Wimbledon and in Dublin. In 1912 in Melbourne Ireland's J. C. Parke contributed in no small degree to the British Isles' capture of the Davis Cup from Australia by beating both Norman Brookes and R. W. Heath in the singles.

In 1923, following political changes in Ireland, the Association decided to become an independent national body embracing the whole country and duly affiliated to the ILTF in 1925. This arrangement meant that all players from Northern Ireland and from the Republic of Ireland came under the Irish LTA and it enabled Ireland to enter in the DAVIS CUP with a strong team. From that date Ireland has taken part in 54 complete matches, losing 40 and winning 14. As a small nation Ireland has nothing to be ashamed of in this performance. Its women's team has competed in the FEDERATION CUP.

The Irish LTA functions for the whole of Ireland and by means of four Provincial Councils and a General Council assiduously works to implement its second rule, which reads 'the object of the Association shall be to control and advance the interests and standards of play in Ireland'. All the officers are honorary. City Leagues and Provincial Club Competitions are run all over the country by various bodies appointed for this purpose and Inter-Provincial Championships are staged annually for senior, intermediate and junior players. In addition, the General Council is responsible for all Davis Cup and international events. In 1972 the number of affiliated clubs was 225, representing some 20,000 players. BR

GOVERNING BODY: Irish LTA, 15 Cilleana, Raheny, Dublin 5

Irish Open Championships

This important event, first held in 1879, now staged annually in Dublin the week after Wimbledon, is the second oldest of all the major championships. The men's singles began two years after Wimbledon began but the Irish were the first to hold a women's singles, won by Miss May Langrishe. They also held a mixed doubles in their first year, whereas Wimbledon did not allow women to compete until 1884.

The Fitzwilliam Club, founded in 1877 in Dublin, has always administered the Championships but for 24 years the men's events were held in Fitzwilliam Square under the control of club officials. The women's singles and mixed doubles, however, were played on the club courts because the square was thought to be too public for the ladies. The first Irish champion, 'St Leger' Gould, Wimbledon runner-up in 1879, won from a field of 15 com-

Above **Ireland.** Miss May Langrishe, the first woman tennis champion, photographed in 1888

petitors and was given a prize valued at £20. He was to gain more notorious fame later for he was tried and convicted for murder.

The Championships quickly became established and Willie Renshaw, Herbert Lawford and Ernest Renshaw, all Wimbledon champions, each won the Irish title three times between 1880 and 1888. Ernest won again in 1892.

Willoughby Hamilton, in 1889, became the first Irish-born winner since Gould. Others who won the men's title in the early years were Joshua Pim, Wilfred Baddeley, Harold Mahony and Reggie and Laurie Doherty. Maud Watson, the first Wimbledon champion, Lottie Dod, Blanche Hillyard and 'Chattie' Cooper were prominent winners among the women. But two players, not quite so celebrated as some of their contemporaries, were Irish record holders: James Cecil Parke and Miss 'Molly' Martin. Parke won the men's title eight times including six successive wins from 1908 to 1913. Miss Martin was women's champion nine times between 1889 and 1903.

After World War I the Championships lost lustre and were not even held in 1922. Sidney Wood, Wimbledon champion in 1931, won the Irish title in 1932 but between the wars it was the women who attracted most attention with Elizabeth Ryan, four times champion, Jadwiga Jedrzejowska, Hilde Sperling, Anita Lizana, Helen Wills Moody and Alice Marble all winning the singles.

Since World War II the Championships have generally attracted seven or eight leading men and women with the remainder of the entry made up of home players.

But the advent of Open tennis in 1968 gave the tournament encouragement and, now sponsored by P. J. Carroll and Co. Ltd, a brewery firm, it has again become one of the most attractive events on the international calendar. Since then Tom Okker, Bob Hewitt (twice), Tony Roche, Cliff Drysdale and Mark Cox have won the men's title; Margaret Court (twice), Billie Jean King, Virginia Wade (twice) and Evonne Goolagong have won the women's.

The Championships were staged on grass until 1973 when they were transferred to hard courts because the Fitzwilliam Club moved to a new site. The new club has seven hard courts, four grass courts, an indoor court with seating for 3,000, squash courts and a fine clubhouse. JO

Israel

The Israel LTA has been a Full Member of the ILTF since 1950. It has competed in the DAVIS CUP regularly since 1957 and took part in the FEDERATION CUP in 1972. In 1973 there were 65 affiliated organizations and several thousand affiliated players, including many juniors. Each year the Israel LTA stages two international tournaments, a team competition for affiliated clubs, and junior championships. BR

GOVERNING BODY: Israel Lawn Tennis Association, P.O. Box 20073, Tel Aviv

Italy

Lawn tennis began in Italy in 1878 when an English Club was founded in Bordighera, a small seaside resort on the Italian Riviera. Twenty years later, when the author of the first tennis manual published in Italy, the Englishman Wilfred Baddeley, was asked how many courts there were, his answer was 'I think that, all added up, private and social, fine and poor, those (too few) with proper dimensions and the others (too many) whose dimensions are not respected, the great number of them in clay, cement, etc. and the very few in grass, I say, I think to be not far from the truth by giving a figure between five and six hundred. This is already something or at least the beginning of something. I wish to point out that, among these, more than six

Irish Championships Winners

Men's Singles

1879	V. 'St Leger' Gould	1967	K. Wooldridge
1880	W. Renshaw	1968	T. Okker
1881	W. Renshaw	1969	R. A. Hewitt
1882	W. Renshaw	1970	A. D. Roche
1883	E. Renshaw	1971	C. Drysdale
1884	H. F. Lawford	1972	R. A. Hewitt
1885	H. F. Lawford	1973	M. Cox
1886	H. F. Lawford		
1887	E. Renshaw		
1888	E. Renshaw		
1889	W. J. Hamilton		
1890	E. W. Lewis		
1891	E. W. Lewis		
1892	E. Renshaw		
1893	J. Pim		
1894	J. Pim		
1895	J. Pim		
1896	W. Baddeley		
1897	W. V. Eaves		
1898	H. S. Mahony		
1899	R. F. Doherty		
1900	R. F. Doherty		
1901	R. F. Doherty		
1902	H. L. Doherty		
1903	W. S. Drapes		
1904	J. C. Parke		
1905	J. C. Parke		
1906	F. S. Riseley		
1907	M. J. G. Ritchie		
1908	J. C. Parke		
1909	J. C. Parke		
1910	J. C. Parke		
1911	J. C. Parke		
1912	J. C. Parke		
1913	J. C. Parke		
1914	C. J. Tindell Green		
1915-18	No Competition		
1919	C. Campbell		
1920	V. Miley		
1921	C. Campbell		
1922	No Competition		
1923	G. M. Mackay		
1924	L. A. Meldon		
1925	C. F. Scroope		
1926	P. Landry		
1927	G. R. O. Crole-Rees		
1928	G. L. Rogers		
1929	J. S. Olliff		
1930	H. G. N. Lee		
1931	E. A. McGuire		
1932	S. B. Wood		
1933	D. N. Jones		
1934	C. E. Malfroy		
1935	A. C. Stedman		
1936	G. L. Rogers		
1937	G. L. Rogers		
1938	O. Anderson		
1939	M. D. Deloford		
1940-45	No Competition		
1946	D. Pails		
1947	A. J. Mottram		
1948	E. W. Sturgess		
1949	N. Cockburn		
1950	H. Weiss		
1951	A. Segal		
1952	N. Kumar		
1953	N. Kumar		
1954	H. Stewart		
1955	H. Stewart		
1956	B. Patty		
1957	A. J. Cooper		
1958	N. A. Fraser / M. G. Davies	divided	
1959	J. W. Frost		
1960	R. D. Ralston		
1961	W. Bond		
1962	R. Laver		
1963	R. K. Wilson		
1964	R. K. Wilson		
1965	A. D. Roche		
1966	J. Cromwell		

Women's Singles

1879	Miss M. Langrishe	1967	Miss A. Soady
1880	Miss D. Meldon	1968	Mrs B. M. Court
1881	No Competition	1969	Mrs L.W. King
1882	Miss H. Abercrombie	1970	Miss V. Wade
1883	Miss M. Langrishe	1971	Miss V. Wade
1884	Miss M. Watson	1972	Miss E. F. Goolagong
1885	Miss M. Watson	1973	Mrs B. M. Court
1886	Miss M. Langrishe		
1887	Miss L. Dod		
1888	Mrs G. W. Hillyard		
1889	Miss L. Martin		
1890	Miss L. Martin		
1891	Miss L. Martin		
1892	Miss L. Martin		
1893	Miss L. Stanuell		
1894	Mrs G. W. Hillyard		
1895	Miss C. Cooper		
1896	Miss L. Martin		
1897	Mrs G. W. Hillyard		
1898	Miss C. Cooper		
1899	Miss L. Martin		
1900	Miss L. Martin		
1901	Miss M. E. Robb		
1902	Miss L. Martin		
1903	Miss L. Martin		
1904	Miss W. A. Longhurst		
1905	Miss W. A. Longhurst		
1906	Miss W. A. Longhurst		
1907	Miss H. M. Garfit		
1908	Miss H. M. Garfit		
1909	Miss H. M. Garfit		
1910	Miss A. Holder		
1911	Mrs D. R. Barry		
1912	Mrs D. R. Larcombe		
1913	Mrs D. R. Barry		
1914	Miss I. Clarke		
1915-18	No Competition		
1919	Miss E. Ryan		
1920	Miss E. Ryan		
1921	Miss E. Ryan		
1922	No Competition		
1923	Miss E. Ryan		
1924	Miss H. Wallis		
1925	Miss E. F. Boyd		
1926	Miss H. Wallis		
1927	Mrs M. Watson		
1928	Mrs Blair White		
1929	Miss E. L. Heine		
1930	Miss H. Wallis		
1931	Mrs Blair White		
1932	Miss J. Jedrzejowska		
1933	Miss H. Wallis		
1934	Mrs H. Sperling		
1935	Miss S. G. Chuter		
1936	Miss A. Lizana		
1937	Miss T. R. Jarvis		
1938	Mrs F. S. Moody		
1939	Miss A. Marble		
1940-45	No Competition		
1946	Miss A. L. Brough		
1947	Mrs E. W. A. Bostock		
1948	Mrs S. Summers		
1949	Mrs T. D. Long		
1950	Mrs H. Weiss		
1951	Miss E. F. Lombard		
1952	Miss M. Connolly		
1953	Miss A. Mortimer		
1954	Miss M. Connolly		
1955	Mrs J. Fleitz		
1956	Miss S. J. Bloomer		
1957	Miss S. Reynolds		
1958	Mrs D. Knode		
1959	Miss R. Schuurman		
1960	Mrs D. Knode		
1961	Miss A. S. Haydon		
1962	Miss M. Schacht		
1963	Miss B. J. Moffitt		
1964	Miss M. E. Bueno		
1965	Miss M. E. Bueno		
1966	Miss M. Smith		

Above **Italy.** Nicola Pietrangeli, who played 164 Davis Cup rubbers for Italy between 1954 and 1972, winning 119, a record.

tenths are spread out in cities and "villas" of the north (specially around the Lakes), two tenths in the central areas, around Florence and Rome, and the last two tenths in the south. The game has made outstanding progress in the recent years thanks mainly to the Italian Association whose headquarters are in Rome.'

The earliest clubs were founded in 1890 in Rome and Turin, the latter with 40 members and its own tennis court. Tennis had already been played in Turin as early as 1880 by a group of enthusiasts who, without a proper court, used to play on a field roughly adapted for the purpose and kindly put at their disposal by a ball-game club, the Società del Giuoco del Pallone. Other clubs were soon founded in the most important towns: the Lawn Tennis Society of Genoa (1893); the Milan Tennis Club (1893), with five courts; the Lawn Tennis Club of Viareggio (1896); the Lawn Tennis Society of Premeno (1899); and

the Lawn Tennis Club of Arezzo (1899). These clubs and other short-lived ones were the founders of the Italian Lawn Tennis Association referred to by Baddeley, which was founded in Rome on 16 April 1894 and represented the first organized attempt to promote and develop the game in Italy.

Unfortunately, four years later, this association ceased to exist. The reason was perhaps that, since it was run by the leading players themselves, when they were forced to choose between the two roles they naturally chose to play. Although 12 years of official lethargy followed, enthusiasm and progress increased and competitions of all kinds were held in every important town. Finally the Tennis Club of Florence took the initiative in founding a much-needed National Association, in Florence, on 18 May 1910. A year later, it was transferred to Genoa, where the very competent Beppe Croce was called to formulate a new constitution. On 16 February 1913 this constitution was approved by the Association's General Assembly and its author was

appointed Chairman. Later in the year the Association affiliated to the ILTF.

The chairmanship of Beppe Croce remains one of the most important milestones in the development of the game in Italy. From a report he presented to the General Assembly in January 1929 at the end of his mandate, we know that in 1928 there were 94 affiliated clubs and about 7,000 members; there had been 50 major tournaments that year besides three championships; and there had been six Davis Cup matches and four friendly matches with Belgium, Czechoslovakia, Spain and Switzerland. During the next 23 years the number of affiliated clubs went up to 319 and club members to 18,394 (of which 5,048 were players); but the last 20 years (1951-71) show the greatest increase: today there are 1,358 affiliated clubs; 80,000 club members (of which 24,000 are players), and 3,081 tennis courts excluding the many private ones. Moreover, 594 tournaments were held during 1970, a number which went up to 744 in 1971.

The Italian Tennis Federation runs its own national tennis school for coaches and organizes special courses during the summer for children aged 10-15, to make the game known and to encourage its practice. These courses are held at special tennis centres called Centri Federali Estivi. There are an average of 10 courts per centre, besides a gymnasium and modern living quarters. Each course, run by the Federation's coaches, lasts two weeks and there are six sessions per season during the school holidays. The Federation's activity was particularly rewarded in 1971 when the Roland Garros Junior Tournament, for the best European juniors, was won by Corrado Barazzutti; the Bonfiglio Trophy (founded in 1962 in memory of a promising young player, Antonio Bonfiglio) for the world's top under-21 players, was won by Adriano Panatta; the Orange Bowl Trophy, for the best juniors of the world, was won by Corrado Barazzutti; and the KING'S CUP was won by the Italian team.

The first Italian International Championships (now the Italian Open) were held in Milan on 25 April 1930. In 1935 the event took place in Rome and then was suspended until 1949. In 1950 it began again in Rome, yet in 1951 it did not take place. However, from 1952 it has been regularly held and attended by the best players of the world. Today it is sponsored by an insurance company. Sponsorship is a very recent phenomenon in Italy. Publicity on the Centre Court was not authorized by the Italian National Olympic Committee (under whose jurisdiction comes the Italian Tennis Federation, like the governing bodies of most sports in Italy) until 1971, and until then Italian firms had been little interested in advertising through tennis.

Italy has taken part in the DAVIS CUP since 1922 and, except for 1936, 1946 and 1947, has never failed to compete. Its first great achievements came in 1928 and 1930 when, with

Uberto de Morpurgo, Giorgio de' Stefani and Placido Gaslini, Italy won the European Zone. But it was not until 1952 that Italy won its third, this time double achievement, the European Zone and the first Inter-Zone final, with Giovanni Cucelli, Marcello del Bello, Rolando del Bello and Fausto Gardini. The fourth and fifth victories came three years later with two successful results in the European Zone, one in 1955 with Fausto Gardini, Giuseppe Merlo, Nicola Pietrangeli and Orlando Sirola and the other in 1956 with Merlo, Pietrangeli and Sirola. In 1958, the result of 1952 was repeated when Italy won both the European Zone and the first Inter-Zone final with Merlo, Pietrangeli and Sirola: in 1959 the same team came first in the European Zone. Yet 1960 and 1961 were Italy's golden Davis Cup years: after winning the European Zone and the following Inter-Zone finals, the Italian team, this time composed of only Pietrangeli and Sirola, twice reached the Challenge Round against Australia, played in Sydney and Melbourne. Their opponents were, on both occasions, Roy Emerson, Rod Laver and Neale Fraser.

Uberto de Morpurgo and Giorgio de' Stefani were the first Italian players to appear in the world's top ten ranking. The former was number nine in 1928, number 10 in 1929 and number 8 in 1930. The latter was number 9 in

Below **Italy.** Rome, May 1972, the scene of the Italian Championships

Italian Championships Winners

Men's Singles		Women's Singles	
1930	W. T. Tilden	1930	Miss L. de Alvarez
1931	G. P. Huges	1931	Miss L. Valerio
1932	A. Merlin	1932	Miss I. Adamoff
1933	E. Sertorio	1933	Miss E. Ryan
1934	G. Palmieri	1934	Miss H. Jacobs
1935	W. Hines	1935	Mrs H. Sperling
1936-49	*No Competition*	1936-49	*No Competition*
1950	J. Drobný	1950	Mrs A. Bossi
1951	J. Drobný	1951	Miss D. Hart
1952	F. Sedgman	1952	Miss J. S. V. Partridge
1953	J. Drobný	1953	Miss D. Hart
1954	J. E. Patty	1954	Miss M. Connolly
1955	F. Gardini	1955	Miss P. Ward
1956	L. A. Hoad	1956	Miss A. Gibson
1957	N. Pietrangeli	1957	Miss S. Bloomer
1958	M. G. Rose	1958	Miss M. E. Bueno
1959	L. Ayala	1959	Miss C. C. Truman
1960	B. MacKay	1960	Mrs S. Körmöczy
1961	N. Pietrangeli	1961	Miss M. E. Bueno
1962	R. Laver	1962	Miss M. Smith
1963	M. F. Mulligan	1963	Miss M. Smith
1964	J. E. Lundqvist	1964	Miss M. Smith
1965	M. F. Mulligan	1965	Miss M. E. Bueno
1966	A. D. Roche	1966	Mrs P. F. Jones
1967	M. F. Mulligan	1967	Miss L. Turner
1968	T. Okker	1968	Mrs W. Bowrey
1969	J. Newcombe	1969	Miss J. D. Heldman
1970	I. Năstase	1970	Mrs L. W. King
1971	R. Laver	1971	Miss V. Wade
1972	M. Orantes	1972	Miss L. Tuero
1973	I. Năstase	1973	Miss E. Goolagong

Above **Italy**. Adriano Panatta

1934. They belong to the first great period of Italian tennis (1927-30); Italy owes to them the first two big victories in the European Zone of the Davis Cup in 1928 and 1930.

Giovanni Palmieri, the ball-boy who became a magnificent player, was at the age of 25 an occasional practice opponent of the members of his club when he was noticed by the Chairman of the Italian Tennis Federation, Minister Lessona. Two years later, in 1932, he was playing in the Davis Cup and was Italy's national champion five years running (1932-6).

Gianni Cucelli, the brilliant winner of the first Italian Davis Cup match after World War II (1949), held against France in Paris, was known as the 'lion' of the court and was the undisputed leader of Italian tennis in 1945-50.

Nicola Pietrangeli, the only child of a famous Italian sportsman and a Soviet mother, was born in Tunis. His father introduced him to the game and they used to play together for fun. Pietrangeli's first victory occurred in strange circumstances, when he visited his father in a prisoner-of-war camp and took part in a tournament organized by his father. His victory over his father was the first of a brilliant career. Today he holds 24 major titles and the Italian Gold Medal for Athletic Valour, awarded to him in 1965. He was ranked among the top ten of the world from 1956 to 1961 and again in 1964; his best position was number three in 1959-60. He has been French singles champion twice (1959-60); doubles champion once with Sirola (1959); singles champion of the Mediterranean Games against Manuel Santana (Spain) in 1965; he won the Italian Open twice (1957 and 1961), defeating Rod Laver (Australia); he has won many major international championships including those in Buenos Aires, Rio de Janeiro, Hamburg, Cairo, Båstad and Monte Carlo. He reached the semi-finals at Wimbledon in 1960. With 164 matches, he holds the world record for Davis Cup participation; he was four times architect of

Above **Helen Jacobs**

Italian victories in the European Zone and twice a participant in the Challenge Round. His most recent success was in the KING'S CUP, where he was the key figure in the first Italian victory, winning both the singles and the doubles with Adriano Panatta.

Adriano Panatta is showing signs of becoming Pietrangeli's successor and is at present the number one player of Italy. At the age of 20 he was a member of the Italian Davis Cup team and has already defeated the two best players in the world on hard courts: Ilie Năstase (Rumania) and Jan Kodeš (Czechoslovakia). He has also beaten Stan Smith (United States).

Italy has also competed regularly in the FEDERATION CUP since it began in 1963. LB
GOVERNING BODY: Federazione Italiana Tennis, 00100 Roma, Viale Tiziano 70

J

Jacobs, Miss Helen Hull (USA)

Born Globe, Ariz., 6 Aug. 1908; Wimbledon women's singles r/u 1929, q/f 1930, s/f 1931, r/u 1932, s/f 1933, r/u 1934-5, won 1936, q/f 1937, r/u 1938, q/f 1939; women's doubles r/u 1932, 1936, 1939; US women's singles s/f 1927, r/u 1928, s/f 1929, q/f 1931, won 1932-5; r/u 1936, s/f 1937, 1941; women's doubles s/f 1928-9, r/u 1931, won 1932, s/f 1933, won 1934-5, r/u 1936; mixed doubles r/u 1932, won 1934, s/f 1936-7; French women's singles r/u 1930, q/f 1931-2, s/f 1933, r/u 1934, s/f 1935, q/f 1937; women's doubles r/u 1934. Wightman Cup 1927-37, 1939. Her longstanding rivalry with her fellow American Helen Wills MOODY was a feature of the game between the world wars. It brought two notable disappointments to Miss Jacobs. In the 1933 US women's singles final she was leading 8-6, 3-6, 3-0 against Mrs Moody only to be denied the satisfaction of probable victory by her opponent's retirement on the plea of illness. Two years later she met Mrs Moody in the Wimbledon final and reached match point at 5-3 in the third set. Miss Jacobs missed an easy smash when the wind deflected the ball and Mrs Moody went on to win. Miss Jacobs was a fine exponent of the volley, favouring a chopped forehand as an approach shot. See CENTRE COURT CLASSICS and GREAT PLAYERS OF ALL TIME (PART 1).

Jamaica

The Jamaica LTA became an Associate Member of the ILTF in 1937, and a Full Member in 1963. It takes part in the DAVIS CUP as part of the COMMONWEALTH CARIBBEAN LTA. BR
GOVERNING BODY: Jamaica Lawn Tennis Association, 30 Millsborough Crescent, Kingston

Janes, Mrs Gerald [Miss Christine C. Truman] (Gt Britain)

Born Loughton, Essex, 16 Jan. 1941; Wimbledon women's singles s/f 1957, 1960, r/u 1961, s/f 1965; women's doubles r/u 1959; US women's singles q/f 1958, r/u 1959, s/f 1960, q/f 1961, 1963; women's doubles s/f 1958, 1963; mixed doubles s/f 1958; Australian women's singles s/f 1960; women's doubles won 1960; mixed doubles s/f 1960; French women's singles q/f 1958, won 1959, q/f 1961, s/f 1963, q/f 1964; women's doubles s/f 1959; mixed doubles s/f 1967. Wightman Cup 1957-63, 1967-9, 1971. An exemplary sportswoman, an uninhibited player with a naturally powerful forehand, she was held in affectionate esteem by the British public to a unique degree. In 1958, when she was 17, she had a spectacular win over Althea GIBSON in the Wightman Cup that was the key to the first

Below **Christine Truman Janes**

British success in that event since 1930. In her 1961 Wimbledon singles final against Angela MORTIMER, the first all-British final since 1914, she had what seemed a winning lead; the sadness of the crowd at her inability to sustain it, after a fall in which she twisted an ankle, was assuaged only by the fact that the winner was British too.

Japan

Tennis was formally introduced into Japan in 1880 by Mr George Adams Leland (1850-1924), an American who had been invited by the Japanese Government to be an instructor at the Training Institute for Physical Education Teachers, attached to the Tokyo Higher Normal School (now the Tokyo University of Education). Leland taught his students to play with rackets and balls he had brought from the United States. The new game was received with great interest, but since equipment had to be imported it was quite expensive. The Japanese players began to use toy rubber balls, without the flannel covering, in place of the conventional lawn tennis balls, and, finding these practical, the Higher Normal School in 1890 placed an order with the Mitatsuchi Rubber Company (now the Showa Rubber Company) to undertake the trial manufacture of this type of ball. This was the origin of Japan's unique soft-ball tennis.

Graduates of the Training Institute for Physical Education Teachers were employed at schools throughout Japan and it was not long before tennis, stimulated by the domestic manufacture of the balls, spread widely. The Tokyo Higher Normal School also arranged demonstrations of tennis for teachers and students of other schools, and its tennis team frequently toured Japan to play exhibition matches, thus contributing to the rapid spread of the game.

The first Japanese inter-varsity matches were played between teams of the Tokyo Higher Normal School and the Higher Commercial School (now Hitotsubashi University) in 1898, the former winning. This event stimulated other schools and universities to establish teams and inter-varsity matches were played among them.

Scoring in soft-ball tennis is similar to that of lawn tennis, except that instead of 15, 30, 40 and game, points are 1, 2, 3 and game, 3-3 being deuce. The game is usually played as doubles. The great difference in play from lawn tennis is that each doubles team consists of the rearguard, who always plays in the back court and serves, while his partner, the advance guard, always plays at the net. Matches are decided by one set; the team first winning five games wins the match. Good teamwork between the net player and his back-court partner is the key to a winning combination and is fascinating to watch.

The soft-ball tennis court is of the same dimensions as that used in lawn tennis, with the net poles standing 1.6 m (5 ft 3 in). Originally lawn-tennis rackets were used by soft-ball tennis players, but cheaper rackets made in Japan came into use. Their shape is slightly different from that of the conventional racket in that they are slightly flattened at the top. The standard size is fixed: the frame is 32 cm (12¾ in long), 22 cm (8¾ in) wide at its widest point; the handle 37 cm (14⅖ in) long; total length 69 cm (27⅕ in). The ball has a thin

Above **Japan.** The softball tennis championships in Tokyo, 1972

All Japan Championships Winners

Men's Singles

1922	M. Fukuda	1972	J. Kamiwazumi
1923	T. Harada	1973	J. Kamiwazumi
1924	T. Tawara		
1925	T. Tawara		
1926	Y. Ohta		
1927	T. Abe		
1928	G. Makino		
1929	T. Harada		
1930	J. Satoh		
1931	T. Kuwabara		
1932	R. Nunoi		
1933	H. Nishimura		
1934	J. Yamagishi		
1935	J. Yamagishi		
1936	J. Yamagishi		
1937	G. von Cramm		
1938	J. Yamagishi		
1939	F. Punčec		
1940	H. Kodera		
1942	T. Washimi		
1946	G. Fujikura		
1947	B. Nakano		
1948	B. Nakano		
1949	J. Kumamaru		
1950	J. Kumamaru		
1951	J. Kumamaru		
1952	J. Kumamaru		
1953	K. Kamo		
1954	A. Miyagi		
1955	A. Miyagi		
1956	K. Kamo		
1957	A. Miyagi		
1958	H. Richardson		
1959	B. MacKay		
1960	A. Miyagi		
1961	O. Ishiguro		
1962	U. Schmidt		
1963	O. Ishiguro		
1964	K. Watanabe		
1965	O. Ishiguro		
1966	I. Konishi		
1967	K. Watanabe		
1968	K. Watanabe		
1969	I. Watanabe		
1970	M. Mulligan		
1971	J. Kamiwazumi		

Women's Singles

1924	T. Kuroi	1972	K. Sawamatsu
1925	T. Kuroi	1973	H. Goto
1926	S. Hayama		
1927	T. Moriwaki		
1928	S. Toda		
1929	R. Takiguchi		
1930	T. Kobayashi		
1931	T. Kobayashi		
1932	K. Minami		
1933	M. Hayashi		
1934	M. Hayashi		
1935	T. Nakano		
1936	S. Toda		
1937	M. L. Horn		
1938	T. Kizen		
1939	J. Kamo		
1940	S. Sawada		
1942	M. Yamakawa		
1946	S. Kamo		
1947	S. Kamo		
1948	S. Kamo		
1949	S. Kamo		
1950	S. Kamo		
1951	S. Kamo		
1952	R. Miyagi		
1953	S. Kamo		
1954	R. Miyagi		
1955	S. Kamo		
1956	R. Miyagi		
1957	R. Miyagi		
1958	R. Miyagi		
1959	R. Miyagi		
1960	R. Miyagi		
1961	R. Miyagi		
1962	R. Miyagi		
1963	R. Miyagi		
1964	H. Schretz		
1965	K. Kuromatsu		
1966	Y. Obata		
1967	K. Sawamatsu		
1968	K. Sawamatsu		
1969	K. Sawamatsu		
1970	K. Sawamatsu		
1971	K. Hatanaka		

rubber covering without the flannel exterior. Its standard measurements and specifications are: diameter 66 mm ($2\frac{3}{5}$ in); weight 30.5 g ($1\frac{1}{10}$ oz); bounce: 65-80 cm ($25\frac{3}{5}$-$31\frac{1}{2}$ in) when dropped from a height of 150 cm (4 ft 11 in).

Before George Leland's formal introduction of tennis to Japan, some Christian missionaries living in the major ports of Yokohama and Kobe had played tennis privately. These missionaries, mainly American, British and Canadian, stimulated the development of Karuizawa, in the mountains and plateau just to the north of Tokyo, as a summer resort. From about 1886 they built summer cottages, a church and then tennis courts. About 150 of these foreign residents and a small number of Japanese who had studied in Europe or the United States enjoyed playing tennis. What is believed to be the first open tennis tournament in Japan was played at Karuizawa in 1902 or 1903.

In 1887, the two tennis courts in the compounds of the British Legation in Tokyo were made available for the use of an international group of tennis enthusiasts, including a number of Japanese, sponsored by Mr Hugh Frazer, the British Minister. The Japanese Government under Prime Minister Prince Hirobumi Ito was impressed by these efforts, and in 1890 the Ministry of Education gave a grant of grounds in the heart of Tokyo for tennis courts. This led to the foundation of the most active and distinguished international tennis club in Japan, what is now the Tokyo Lawn Tennis Club, formally established after the turn of the century. Its international character and stature is shown by the list of its past presidents, which includes 11 foreign ambassadors and a member of the Imperial Household.

Japan took part in the DAVIS CUP for the first time in 1921. The first Japanese team, of Ichiya Kumagai, Zenzo Shimizu and Seiichiro Kashio, eliminated India and Australia in victories which surprised world tennis fans and earned them the right to challenge the US team, the Cup holders. All three Japanese players had learned tennis while attending university; they had played the uniquely Japanese softball tennis, taking up lawn tennis only after they had served in overseas offices of their companies. Although Japan lost 0-5 to the US team in the Challenge Round, the Japanese players fought valiantly against the powerful US team of W. T. Tilden and W. M. Johnston.

In the early years the Japanese team entered mainly in the American Zone, but in 1930 it entered the European Zone, when T. Harada, Y. Ohta and T. Abe reached the zone finals, after defeating Hungary, India, Spain and Czechoslovakia, but lost 2-3 to the Italians Morpurgo and de' Stefani. In 1955 the Davis Cup Eastern Zone was established: Japan has

Colour plate Rod Laver, the only player in the history of the game to have won the Grand Slam twice and the greatest left-hander of all time

naturally competed in this zone since then.

In 1920 Zenzo Shimizu was the first Japanese to enter the All-England Championships at Wimbledon and reached the All-Comers' Final where he lost to W. T. Tilden of the United States (who went on to win the Championship), 4-6, 4-6, 11-13. In 1922 Shimizu reached the quarter-finals, losing to M. Alonso (Spain) 6-3, 5-7, 6-3, 4-6, 6-8.

In 1933 Jiro Sato (Japan) defeated Bunny Austin (Great Britain) in the quarter-finals but lost in the semi-finals to Jack Crawford (Australia), who went on to win the Championship. In the men's doubles, Sato and Nunoi reached the final, where they lost to J. Borotra and J. Brugnon (France). In 1934 Ryuki Miki (Japan), with Miss Dorothy Round (Great Britain), won the mixed doubles championship.

In OLYMPIC tennis competition, Ichiya Kumagai and Seiichiro Kashio represented Japan at the 1920 Games in Antwerp. Kumagai lost in the finals to Raymond (S. Africa) and received the silver medal. Teamed with Kashio, he won his second silver medal when they lost the men's doubles finals to Turnbull and Woosnam (Gt Britain). Japan has also competed in the FEDERATION CUP since 1964.

Tennis has become one of the most popular sports in Japan; the players range from teen-agers to adults in their 70s. There are about 300,000 lawn-tennis players and 1,500,000 soft-ball-tennis players. The 13,000 lawn-tennis courts and 9,000 soft-ball-tennis courts now available in Japan do not meet the needs of all who wish to play.

Their Imperial Highnesses the Crown Prince and Princess of Japan, enthusiastic tennis players of a fairly high standard, frequently participate in club tournaments. All Japanese tennis players are amateurs.

The Japan LTA was founded on 11 March 1925 and affiliated to the Japan Athletic Association on the same date. It affiliated to the ILTF on 24 March 1925. During World War II it was ousted from the ILTF and reinstated on 24 July 1950. YO

GOVERNING BODY: Japan Lawn Tennis Association, c/o Kishi Taiikukan, 1-1-1 Jinnan, Shibuya-ku, Tokyo

Jedrzejowska, Miss Jadwiga ['Jed']

Born Krakow, 15 Oct. 1912; Wimbledon women's singles q/f 1935, s/f 1936, r/u 1937, q/f 1938-9; mixed doubles s/f 1935, s/f 1937; US women's singles r/u 1937, q/f 1938; women's doubles r/u 1938; French women's singles, s/f 1937, r/u 1939; women's doubles s/f 1934, r/u 1936, won 1939, s/f 1947; mixed doubles r/u 1947.

Jessup, Mrs J. B. [Miss Marion Zinderstein] (USA)

Wimbledon women's singles q/f 1924; wo-

Colour plate Jan Kodeš, 1973 Wimbledon champion and twice runner-up in the US Open (1971, 1973). He was also French Open champion in 1970 and 1971.

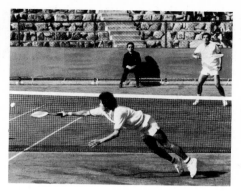

Above **Japan.** K. Hirai *(near side)* v. J. Kamiwazumi in the 1972 Championships

men's doubles s/f 1924; US women's singles r/u 1919-20, q/f 1924; women's doubles won 1918-20, 1922, r/u 1924, s/f 1925; mixed doubles won 1919. Wightman Cup 1924, 1926.

Jeu de Paume see THE ORIGINS OF LAWN TENNIS (PART 1)

Johnson, Wallace Ford (USA)

Born Merion, Pa., 13 July 1899; US men's singles q/f 1907, r/u 1912, s/f 1913, q/f 1914, 1916, s/f 1919-20, r/u 1921, q/f 1924-5; men's doubles s/f 1920, 1922-3; mixed doubles won 1907, 1909, 1911, s/f 1915, won 1920, s/f 1922-3. Davis Cup 1913.

Johnston, William M. (USA)

Born San Francisco, 2 Nov. 1894, died 1 May 1946; Wimbledon men's singles won 1923; men's doubles s/f 1920; US men's singles won 1915, r/u 1916, won 1919, r/u 1920, 1922-5, q/f 1926, s/f 1927; men's doubles won 1915-16, 1920, s/f 1921-2, 1924-6, r/u 1927. Unlucky always to be overshadowed by his great contemporary 'Big Bill' TILDEN. He was known as 'Little Bill'. He shared with Tilden the American Davis Cup triumphs 1920 to 1927 and was beaten only three times in 21 rubbers. He was ranked world number one in 1919 and only once less than second 1920 to 1925. See GREAT PLAYERS OF ALL TIME (PART 1).

Jones, Miss Marion (USA)

Wimbledon women's singles q/f 1900; US women's singles r/u 1898, won 1899, r/u* 1901, won 1902, r/u 1903; women's doubles won 1902; mixed doubles won 1901. The first American woman to play at Wimbledon.

Jones, Mrs P. F. [Miss Ann S. Haydon] (Gt Britain)

Born Birmingham, 17 Oct. 1938; Wimbledon women's singles s/f 1958, q/f 1959, s/f 1960; 1962-3, q/f 1964, s/f 1966, r/u 1967, s/f 1968, won 1969; women's doubles s/f 1963-4, 1966-7, r/u 1968; mixed doubles r/u 1962, s/f 1963, 1968, won 1969; US women's singles q/f 1957, s/f 1959, s/f 1960, r/u 1961, s/f 1963, q/f 1964-5, r/u 1967, s/f 1968; women's doubles s/f 1958-9, r/u 1960, s/f 1963,

1968; Australian women's singles and doubles s/f 1969; French women's singles s/f 1957, q/f 1958, won 1961, s/f 1962, r/u 1963, q/f 1965, won 1966, q/f 1967, r/u 1968-9; women's doubles s/f 1958, r/u 1960, s/f 1962, won 1963, s/f 1966, won 1968-9; mixed doubles r/u 1960, 1966-7. Federation Cup 1963-7, 1971. Possibly the most dogged and intelligent player among British women. A left-hander, she took seriously to lawn tennis after a notable career in table tennis, where she was five times finalist for a world championship. Her ultimate success as Wimbledon singles champion came when she was 30. In 12 Wightman Cup appearances 1957-70 she won 16 out of 31 rubbers, a British record. See colour plate, page 223.

Junior

As defined by the ILTF, a player who has not reached the age of 18 on the 31 December preceding the date of any match or competition in which he or she is entered. In the United States, 'Junior' refers only to boys of 18 and under. Girls of 18 and under are called 'Girls 18'. See also AGE GROUPS. DC

Junior Wimbledon see BRITISH JUNIOR CHAMPIONSHIPS

Below **Ann Jones**

Kent Lawn Tennis Championships Winners (Beckenham)

Men's Singles		Women's Singles	
1886	H. Chipp	1888	Miss Jacks
1887	F. A. Bowlby	1889	Miss M. Shackle
1888	E. G. Meers	1890	Miss Jacks
1889	H. S. Barlow	1891	Miss M. Shackle
1890	E. G. Meers	1892	Miss M. Shackle
1891	E. G. Meers	1893	Miss M. Shackle
1892	H. S. Barlow	1894	Miss Austin
1893	H. S. Barlow	1895	Miss Austin
1894	H. A. B. Chapman	1896	Miss Austin
1895	H. S. Barlow	1897	Miss Austin
1896	M. F. Goodbody	1898	Miss C. Cooper
1897	G. Greville	1899	Miss Austin
1898	W. V. Eaves	1900	Mrs Greville
1899	H. S. Mahony	1901	Miss D. K. Douglass
1900	A. W. Gore	1902	Miss D. K. Douglass
1901	H. L. Doherty	1903	Miss C. M. Wilson
1902	H. L. Doherty	1904	Miss D. K. Douglass
1903	H. L. Doherty	1905	Miss C. M. Wilson
1904	H. S. Mahony	1906	Miss D. K. Douglass
1905	N. E. Brookes	1907	Miss M. Sutton
1906	A. W. Gore	1908	Miss A. M. Morton
1907	A. F. Wilding	1909	Miss D. P. Boothby
1908	H. Roper Barrett	1910	Mrs D. Lambert Chambers
1909	H. Roper Barrett	1911	Mrs D. Lambert Chambers
1910	B. C. Wright	1912	Mrs R. J. McNair
1911	A. F. Wilding	1913	Mrs D. Lambert Chambers
1912	A. F. Wilding	1914	Mrs Hannam
1913	A. E. Beamish	1915-18	*No Competition*
1914	A. R. F. Kingscote	1919	Miss E. Ryan
1915-18	*No Competition*	1920	Mrs R. J. McNair / Miss E. Ryan *divided*
1919	A. R. F. Kingscote	1921	Miss E. Ryan
1920	A. R. F. Kingscote	1922	Miss K. McKane
1921	A. R. F. Kingscote	1923	Miss E. Ryan
1922	A. R. F. Kingscote	1924	Miss E. Ryan
1923	W. M. Johnston	1925	Miss E. Ryan
1924	A. R. F. Kingscote	1926	Miss L. de Alvarez
1925	R. Lycett	1927	Miss H. Wills
1926	G. R. O. Crole-Rees	1928	Miss E. Ryan
1927	D. M. Greig	1929	Mrs B. C. Covell
1928	C. H. Kingsley	1930	Miss J. Sandison
1929	H. G. N. Lee	1931	Miss P. Mudford
1930	H. W. Austin	1932	Miss M. Heeley
1931	J. C. Gregory	1933	Miss D. E. Round
1932	E. R. Avory	1934	Mrs M. King
1933	V. G. Kirby	1935	Miss D. E. Round
1934	H. W. Austin	1936	Miss A. Lizana
1935	J. Yamagishi	1937	Miss J. Jedrzejowska
1936	D. N. Jones	1938	Miss J. Jedrzejowska
1937	J. Yamagishi	1939	Miss A. Marble
1938	J. S. Olliff	1940-45	*No Competition*
1939	M. D. Deloford	1946	Miss V. S. Dace
1940-45	*No Competition*	1947	Mrs K. Menzies
1946	G. E. Brown	1948	Mrs H. Weiss
1947	O. W. Sidwell	1949	Mrs P. C. Todd
1948	F. Sedgman	1950	Miss G. Moran
1949	G. Mulloy	1951	Miss B. Rosenquest
1950	G. E. Brown	1952	Mrs H. Redick-Smith
1951	D. W. Candy	1953	Miss M. Connolly
1952	H. Richardson	1954	*Abandoned*
1953	G. Worthington	1955	Miss A. L. Brough
1954	*Abandoned*	1956	*Abandoned*
1955	T. Trabert	1957	Miss A. Gibson
1956	*Abandoned*	1958	Miss S. Reynolds
1957	M. Anderson	1959	Miss D. Hard
1958	N. Fraser	1960	Miss C. Mercelis
1959	A. Olmedo	1961	Miss M. Smith
1960	R. Mark	1962	Miss J. Lehane
1961	J. A. Douglas	1963	Miss M. Smith
1962	B. Phillips-More	1964	Miss M. Smith / Miss M. Bueno *divided*
1963	K. Fletcher	1965	Miss M. Smith
1964	J. D. Newcombe	1966	Miss K. Krantzcke
1965	J. D. Newcombe	1967	Mrs P. F. Jones
1966	J. D. Newcombe	1968	Mrs B. M. Court
1967	O. K. Davidson	1969	Miss D. Carter
1968	F. Stolle	1970	Miss P. Hogan
1969	O. Bengston	1971	Miss K. Melville
1970	C. Graebner	1972	Miss O. Morozova
1971	S. R. Smith	1973	Miss D. Fromholtz
1972	A. Metreveli		
1973	A. Metreveli		

Kehrling, B. von see HUNGARY

Kent Grass Court Championships (UK)
These championships, played on grass courts temporarily formed from the outfield of the Beckenham Cricket Club, date back to 1886 and have provided three landmarks in British tennis history, in 1926, 1958 and 1972.

In 1926 Senorita Lili de Alvarez of Spain beat Mrs Molla Mallory, Norwegian by birth but representing the United States, 6-4, 6-2 in the women's singles final, the first time that two foreign women had met in the final of a British tournament other than Wimbledon.

In 1958 the first two Russian players to compete in Britain, Anna Dmitrieva and Andrei Potanin, both 17, made their British début at Beckenham, taking part in both the junior and senior events. Three weeks later they were the first Russians to compete at Wimbledon when they played in the girls' and boys' singles respectively.

In 1972 Alex Metreveli won the men's singles and Olga Morozova the women's singles at Beckenham, the first time that two Russians had won both singles events at a British tournament.

An earlier Kent landmark was in 1905 when Norman Brookes (Australia), making his British début, became the first overseas winner of the men's singles by beating Arthur Wentworth Gore in the Challenge Round. This was a shock result as Gore was considered second only to Laurie Doherty in Britain, whereas Brookes, who later won Wimbledon twice, was unknown.

Lt-Col Algernon Kingscote set a record at Beckenham with six victories in the men's singles (1914, 1919-22 and 1924). Mrs Dorothea Lambert Chambers won the women's singles title seven times (as Miss Douglass in 1901, 1902, 1904 and 1906 and, after her marriage, in 1910, 1911, 1913). Elizabeth Ryan of California won the women's singles six times (1919, 1921, 1923-5, 1928) and also shared the title with Mrs Winifred McNair in 1920 when bad weather prevented the final from being played.

Since World War II Margaret Court has been the most successful woman at Beckenham, with four victories in 1961, 1963, 1965, 1968, and one division with Maria Bueno, in 1964. John Newcombe won the men's title three years running (1964-6). The championships are now sponsored by GREEN SHIELD.

Previous sponsors have been ROTHMANS and the public relations firm of West and Nally. JO

Kenya

The Kenya Lawn Tennis Association was formed in December 1922 at Nairobi, affiliated to the ILTF in 1934 as an Associate Member and was elected a Full Member in 1973. The main events are the Kenya National Championships, Inter-Club Leagues (founded 1923), Inter-Club Championships (founded 1924), Junior Championships (founded 1927) and an Inter-Schools Competition (founded 1951). Nairobi has a stadium with 1,000 seats and floodlighting. Since 1956 funds have been raised by an annual tournament levy to provide a well-based junior training scheme. Kenyan players have taken part at Wimbledon, in the All Africa Games and in the 1968 Olympic Games in Mexico. In 1972 the Association had 28 clubs in Nairobi and 11 in the provinces. BR
GOVERNING BODY: Kenya LTA, P.O. Box 43184, Nairobi

Kick Service see SERVICE

King, Mrs L. W. [Miss Billie Jean Moffitt] (USA)

Born Long Beach, Calif., 22 Nov. 1943; Wimbledon women's singles q/f 1962, r/u 1963, s/f 1964-5, won 1966-8, r/u 1969-70, s/f 1971, won 1972-3; women's doubles won 1961-2, r/u 1964, won 1965, 1967-8, 1970-3; mixed doubles r/u 1966, won 1967, s/f 1968, won 1971, s/f 1972, won 1973; US women's singles q/f 1964, r/u 1965, won 1967, r/u 1968, q/f 1969, won 1971-2; women's doubles r/u 1962, won 1964, r/u 1965-6, won 1967, 1969, r/u 1968, s/f 1972, r/u 1973; mixed doubles s/f 1960, 1963, won 1967, won 1971, s/f 1972, won 1973; Australian women's singles s/f 1965, won 1968, r/u 1969; women's doubles r/u 1965, s/f 1968, r/u 1969; mixed doubles won 1968; French women's singles q/f 1967, s/f 1968, q/f 1969-70, won 1972; women's doubles r/u 1968, 1970, won 1972; mixed doubles won 1967, r/u 1968, s/f 1969, won 1970. Federation Cup 1963-7; Wightman Cup 1961-7, 1970. ILTF GP 1st 1971-2.

Completely equipped in strokes and a very great match player, she took the women's game to new heights of professional expertise, making herself the leading apostle of the movement to bring women's earnings closer to those gained by men. In this she was outstandingly successful; in 1971 she was the first woman to win more than $100,000 in a year, much of it from the US (WT) women's professional circuit. In traditional events she came to a new peak of achievement in 1972 by winning the French, Wimbledon and US singles titles for the loss of only one set in all. An outstanding exponent of the serve-volley technique and specially notable for her skill with the low volley. She won her fifth Wimbledon title in 1973 (a postwar record). A devout exponent of Women's Lib, which she

Above **Billie Jean King**

underlined by defeating Bobby Riggs (1939 Wimbledon Champion) 6-4, 6-3, 6-3 in Houston in September 1973, in the most publicized match of all time. See colour plate, page 224, CENTRE COURT CLASSICS and GREAT PLAYERS OF ALL TIME (PART 1).

Kingscote, Algernon R. F. (Gt Britain)

Born India, 3 Dec. 1888; died 21 Dec. 1964; Wimbledon men's singles r/u* 1919, q/f 1921, q/f 1924; men's doubles r/u* 1920; Australian men's singles won 1919. A British Davis Cup stalwart in the post-World War I years, playing for the British Isles 1919-20 and 1922, and for Great Britain 1924.

King's Cup (H. M. King Gustaf V of Sweden Cup)

The King's Cup, donated in 1936 by HM King Gustaf V of Sweden for competition by international men's teams, was intended to be the indoor equivalent of the DAVIS CUP outdoors. However, since people play tennis on open courts throughout the world, but only a small percentage play indoors, the tournament can probably never attain the scope and status of the Davis Cup. Today 15-20 nations compete, all from Europe.

The tournament was at first played in the same way as the Davis Cup was originally played, the holder meeting the winner of the All-Comers in a Challenge Round. This system was abandoned after World War II and now all nations compete from the beginning, with the exception of the nation arranging the final stages (semi-finals, final and tie for third prize) which is automatically drawn to compete there. Since 1957 the tournament has been confined to November. It used to start in November and finish in January or February.

In the first rounds four singles matches (the best of three sets) are played. The doubles consist of the best of five sets unless the team captains agree on three. In the final round all ties are played with two singles and one double, all of the same length as the first rounds. The original trophy was won by Germany in 1939. After the war it could not be found and a new trophy was donated in 1952. The event is sponsored by Mr Marcus Wallenberg. SH

Kinsey, Howard O. (USA)

Born St Louis, Mo., 3 Dec. 1899, died 1966; Wimbledon men's singles r/u 1926; men's doubles won 1924 (with his brother Robert), r/u 1926; mixed doubles r/u 1926; US men's singles q/f 1924-5; men's doubles s/f 1921, won 1924, s/f 1925; mixed doubles r/u 1922; French men's doubles won 1926. Turned professional 1926.

Kiyomura, Miss Ann (USA)

Born 22 Aug. 1955; Ranked no. 1 U18 in 1973; US U18 Champion 1972 and winner of Wimbledon Junior Invitation.

Kleinschroth, H. see GERMANY, FEDERAL REPUBLIC OF

Knode, Mrs D. P. [Miss Dorothy Head] (USA)

Born Richmond, Calif., 4 July 1925; Wimbledon women's singles s/f 1953, q/f 1955, s/f 1957; US women's singles q/f 1946-7, s/f 1955, q/f 1956, s/f 1957, q/f 1958-9; women's doubles s/f 1944, 1949; mixed doubles s/f 1955; French women's singles s/f 1952-3, r/u 1955, 1957, q/f 1958; women's doubles r/u 1956; mixed doubles s/f 1957; Wightman Cup 1955-8, 1960.

King's Cup

1936	France
1937	France
1938	Germany
1939-51	*No Competition*
1952	Denmark
1953	Denmark
1954	Denmark
1955	Sweden
1956	Sweden
1957	Sweden
1958	Sweden
1959	Denmark
1960	Denmark
1961	Sweden
1962	Denmark
1963	Yugoslavia
1964	Great Britain
1965	Great Britain
1966	Great Britain
1967	Great Britain
1968	Sweden
1969	Czechoslovakia
1970	France
1971	Italy
1972	Spain
1973	Sweden

Kodeš, Jan (Czechoslovakia)

Born Prague, 1 March 1946; Wimbledon men's singles s/f 1972, won 1973; US men's singles r/u 1971, 1973; French men's singles won 1970-1, q/f 1972-3; men's doubles s/f 1972. Davis Cup 1968- . ILTF GP 8th 1970, 4th 1971-2. As a French Open Champion perhaps his most remarkable *tour de force* was in reaching the final of the US Open Championships at Forest Hills in 1971 as an unseeded player, after declaring that play on grass was a joke. The joke was on his opponents in 1973 when he won Wimbledon and reached the US final for the second time. See colour plate, page 274, and CZECHOSLOVAKIA.

Above Jan Kodeš

Korea

Korea has been a Full Member of the ILTF since 1949. It has taken part regularly in the DAVIS CUP since 1959. The relatively high standard of Korean women's play surprised the lawn tennis world when they appeared for the first time in international competition in the 1973 FEDERATION CUP. Miss J. S. Yang was good enough to beat ranking players of the United States. BR

GOVERNING BODY: Korean Lawn Tennis Association, Room 706, Sports Building, 19 Makyo-Dong, Chungku, Seoul

Körmöczy, Mrs Zsuzsi [Suzi] (Hungary)

Born Budapest, 25 Aug. 1924; Wimbledon women's singles q/f 1953, 1955, s/f 1958; French women's singles q/f 1947, s/f 1956, q/f 1957, won 1958, r/u 1959, s/f 1961.

Krahwinkel, Miss Hilde see Mrs H. SPERLING

Kramer, John Albert [Jack] (USA)

Born Las Vegas, Nev., 5 Aug. 1921; Wimbledon men's singles won 1947; men's doubles won 1946-7; US men's singles s/f 1940, q/f 1941, r/u 1943, won 1946-7; men's doubles won 1940-1, 1943, 1947; mixed doubles won 1941. Davis Cup 1939, 1946-7. The outstanding player of the immediate post-World War II period. He would almost certainly have won Wimbledon in 1946 but for a blistered hand, and his victory in 1947 for the loss of 37 games in seven matches was the most one-sided win of all time. Fluent, powerful and accurate, he created the concept of 'percentage' lawn tennis, the playing of a shot with the greatest chance of success. He was just as successful as a professional, which he became in 1947, and, later, as a promoter. A ruthless and intelligent performer on the court. See GREAT PLAYERS OF ALL TIME (PART 1).

Kramer Cup see THE POSTWAR PRO GAME (PART 1)

Kreutzer, Oskar see GERMANY, FEDERAL REPUBLIC OF

Above Jack Kramer

Krishnan, Ramanathan (India)

Born Madras, 11 April 1937; Wimbledon men's singles s/f 1960-1; French men's singles q/f 1962. Davis Cup 1953-8. Winner of the 1954 Wimbledon Junior event, he was a beautiful touch player reminiscent perhaps of COCHET in his mastery of the half-volley.

Kuwait

The Kuwait Tennis Association was founded in 1967 and affiliated to the ILTF as an Associate Member in 1971. It runs senior and junior tournaments. BR

GOVERNING BODY: Kuwait Tennis Association, Ahmad Al-Mehri Building, Fahad Al-Salem Street, P.O. Box 20496, Kuwait

L

Lacoste, Jean-René (France)

Born Paris, 2 July 1905; Wimbledon men's singles r/u 1924, won 1925, s/f 1927, won 1928; men's doubles s/f 1923, won 1925; US men's singles q/f 1924-5, won 1926-7; mixed doubles r/u 1926-7; French men's singles r/u 1924, won 1925, r/u 1926, won 1927, r/u 1928, won 1929; men's doubles r/u 1923, won 1924-5, s/f 1926, r/u 1927, won 1929; mixed doubles s/f 1927-9. Davis Cup 1923-8. One of the FOUR MUSKETEERS. He was the last great player in the men's game to act on the assumption that the perfect baseliner would beat the perfect volleyer. His groundstrokes were superlatively controlled. He was probably the most studious player of all time, for he kept notebooks in which he carefully recorded the strengths and weaknesses of his contemporaries. His theories were born out by his success on grass courts as well as hard but, among giants, he was the last of a line. See FRANCE and also GREAT PLAYERS OF ALL TIME (PART 1).

Lambert Chambers, Mrs D.
see CHAMBERS, Mrs D. Lambert

Lance, Miss Sylvia [Mrs Harper] (Australia)

Born Sydney, N.S.W., 19 Oct. 1895; Australian women's singles won 1924, s/f 1926, r/u 1927, 1930; women's doubles won 1923-5, s/f 1926, r/u 1927, 1929-30; mixed doubles won 1923, s/f 1926-8.

Landry, Mrs Nelly [Miss N. Adamson] (Belgium/France)

Born Tilbury, England, Dec. 1916 of Belgian parents; French by marriage. Wimbledon women's singles q/f 1948; French women's singles q/f 1936, r/u 1938, q/f 1946, won 1948, r/u 1949, q/f 1951, 1953, s/f 1954; women's doubles s/f 1936, r/u 1938, s/f 1950-1; mixed doubles s/f 1948, 1954. France's best woman player in the late 1940s. She became a professional in 1956. Left-handed.

Langrishe, Miss Mary Isabella 'May' (Ireland)

Died 1939. The first winner of a women's singles championship (Irish 1879, 1883, 1886); Wimbledon women's singles s/f 1891. See IRELAND and THE BIRTH AND SPREAD OF LAWN TENNIS (PART 1).

Lansdowne House see THE BIRTH AND
SPREAD OF LAWN TENNIS (PART 1)

Larcombe, Mrs Dudley R. [Miss Ethel W. Thomson] (Gt Britain)
Born London, 8 June 1879, died Aug 1965;
Wimbledon women's singles r/u* 1903, q/f
1905, won 1912, r/u 1914; women's doubles
s/f 1913, r/u 1914, 1919-20; mixed doubles r/u
1913, won 1914, s/f 1919-21).

Larned, William A. (USA)
Born 30 Dec. 1872, died 16 Dec. 1926;
Wimbledon men's singles q/f 1896, 1905;
men's doubles s/f 1905; US men's singles r/u*
1892, q/f 1893, r/u* 1894-6, s/f 1897, r/u 1900,
won 1901-2, r/u 1903, s/f 1904-5, won 1907-
11; men's doubles r/u 1907. Davis Cup 1902-3,
1905, 1908-9, 1911. He was 28 when he won
his first US singles in 1901 and the oldest ever
at 38 when he won for the seventh time in 1911.

Larsen, Arthur D. ['Art'] (USA)
Born San Leando, Calif., 6 April 1925; Wimbledon men's singles q/f 1950-1, 1953; men's
doubles s/f 1956; US men's singles q/f 1949,
won 1950, s/f 1951, q/f 1954; Australian men's
singles s/f 1951; men's doubles s/f 1951;
French men's singles q/f 1950, r/u 1954; men's
doubles s/f 1955. Davis Cup 1951-2, winning 4
out of 4 rubbers. A left-hander, he was one of
the finest touch players ever to develop in the
United States. He defied normal training
routine to an extraordinary degree. Sadly, his
career was cut short by severe head injuries
received in a motorcycle accident in 1957.

Laver, Rodney George (Australia)
Born Rockhampton, Queensland, 9 Aug. 1938;
Wimbledon men's singles r/u 1959-60, won
1961-2, 1968-9, q/f 1971; men's doubles r/u
1959, s/f 1960-2, 1968-9, won 1971; mixed
doubles won 1959-60; US men's singles q/f
1959, r/u 1960-1, won 1962, 1969; men's
doubles s/f 1959, r/u 1960, s/f 1969, r/u 1970,
1973; Australian men's singles won 1960, r/u
1961, won 1962, 1969; men's doubles won
1959-61, s/f 1962, won 1969; mixed doubles
r/u 1959; French men's singles s/f 1961, won
1962, r/u 1968, won 1969; men's doubles s/f
1959, won 1961, r/u 1968-9; mixed doubles r/u
1959, s/f 1960, won 1961. Davis Cup 1959-63.
ILTF GP 4th (M r/u) 1970. WCT contract pro
1971-2. WCT 1st (F r/u) 1971-May 1972, 2nd
Group A (F s/f) 1973.

Unique in the history of the game in being
the only player to win the Grand Slam twice. A
master performer in every facet of play, he
went through four successive Wimbledon
Championships without defeat, for after winning in 1961 and 1962 he was barred as a
professional until he came back to win again
at the first two open meetings of 1968 and
1969. Although it is a matter of debate whether
TILDEN, BUDGE or Laver should be hailed as the
greatest player of all time, Laver is indisput-
ably the best left-hander ever. In 1962 he won

Above **Rod Laver**

every major championship for which he
entered, those of Australia, Italy, France,
Wimbledon, Germany and the United States,
a feat surpassing anything done before. See
colour plate, page 273, and GREAT PLAYERS OF
ALL TIME (PART 1).

Lawford, Herbert F. (Gt Britain)
Born London 15 May 1851; died 20 April 1925;
Wimbledon men's singles s/f 1878, r/u 1880,
s/f 1881-2, r/u 1884-6, won 1887, r/u 1888,
s/f 1889; men's doubles won 1879. He was a
massive man, with a powerful baseline game.

Lawn Tennis Associations
The first governing body of lawn tennis was
the Marylebone Cricket Club, London, which,
in its capacity as the governing body for
rackets and real tennis, issued the first official
code of rules for lawn tennis in 1875 (see THE
BIRTH AND SPREAD OF LAWN TENNIS, PART 1).
From there jurisdiction passed to the All
England Croquet and Lawn Tennis Club
which, in 1877, drew up the rules for the first
Wimbledon Championships. The first truly
national association founded for lawn tennis,
the United States National Lawn Tennis
Association, which adopted the All England
Club's rules for its own championships, was
formed in 1881 (it dropped the 'National' in
1920). Its address is: 51 East 42nd Street (Suite
1008), New York, N.Y. 10017. The Lawn
Tennis Association (of Great Britain) was not
formed until 1888, when it took over the
administration of the game in Britain from the
All England Club. Its address is: Barons Court,
West Kensington, London W14 9EG. As the
game spread around the world, other nations

formed their own national associations; for the
addresses of these, see the entry on the
country concerned.

Lawn Tennis Foundation of Great Britain
Formed in 1961, this is the only full-time non-
profit-making organization in Britain to enter
the field of lawn tennis sponsorship. Its
Council of 18 members includes members of
the tennis trade (which no other organization
within the sport admits to its governing
bodies), representatives of the Lawn Tennis
Association, registered professional coaches,
physical education departments, the National
Playing Fields Association and the All England
Club. In its early days, it concentrated on providing coaching centres for beginners and
giving financial support, professional advice
and assistance to County Lawn Tennis Associations. Over 1,000 centres all over Britain were
opened between 1962 and 1970, when they
were handed over to the LTA's GRASS
ROOTS SCHEME. The Foundation now seeks to
develop lawn tennis in national youth-club
movements, including the Scout and Girl
Guide Associations, by clinics, demonstrations
and exhibitions. One of its largest projects is
the Nestlé Schools Tournament, now attracting
over 32,000 entries, most of them near beginner level. The Foundation is financed mainly
by contributions from its members in the
tennis trade. DC

Lawn Tennis Writers' Association see
THE PRESS (PART 1)

Leamington Lawn Tennis Club
Founded in Leamington, in Warwickshire,
England, in 1872 with Major Harry Gem as

President, the Leamington Lawn Tennis Club was the first-ever club, as far as is known, devoted exclusively to lawn tennis (see THE BIRTH AND SPREAD OF LAWN TENNIS (PART 1). The club no longer exists, but in June 1972 the Lawn Tennis Association marked the centenary of its founding by unveiling a plaque on the site where Gem lived. DC

Lebanon

Lawn Tennis has been played in Lebanon for over 50 years but the Lebanese Association, part of the Lebanese Lawn Tennis and Table Tennis Association, was established only in 1946 when it affiliated to the ILTF. It sends representatives to all meetings. There are few tennis clubs in Lebanon so that Beirut has been the venue for both the national championships (from 1946) and the international championships (from 1956), which attract a good foreign entry. Promising juniors are trained by the Association, which has several qualified coaches. Lebanon has played in the DAVIS CUP six times since 1957, as an 'Extra European' nation. BR
GOVERNING BODY: Fédération Libanaise de Lawn-Tennis, c/o M. Émile A. Yazbeck, Immeuble Assicurazioni Generali, Place de l'Étoile, B.P. 5798, Beirut

Left Court see illustration and THE RULES AND THEIR INTERPRETATION (PART 1)

Below **Left Court**

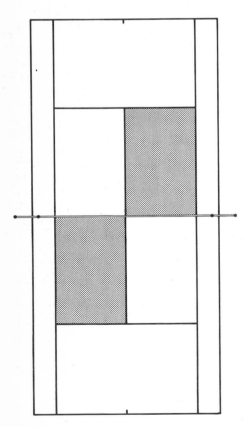

Lehane, Miss J. [Mrs C. O'Neill] (Australia)

Born Grenfell, N.S.W., 9 July 1941; Wimbledon women's singles q/f 1963; women's doubles s/f 1960, r/u 1961; US women's singles q/f 1960-1; women's doubles s/f 1960; Australian women's singles s/f 1959; r/u 1960-3, s/f 1964, s/f 1967, q/f 1971; mixed doubles won 1960-1, s/f 1963, r/u 1964; French women's singles q/f 1960, 1962-4; women's doubles s/f 1960-2; mixed doubles s/f 1961.

Lenglen, Miss Suzanne (France)

Born Paris, 24 May 1899, died 1938; Wimbledon women's singles won 1919-23, s/f 1924, won 1925; women's doubles won 1919-23; mixed doubles won 1920, 1922, s/f 1923, won 1925; French women's singles won 1920, 1925-6; women's doubles won 1920-3, 1925-6; mixed doubles won 1914, 1920-3, 1925-6. A legendary all-time great with an unparalleled record of invincibility. In eight years' play (1919-26) till she became a professional after her 'walk-out' from WIMBLEDON, she was only once beaten in singles, when, in the 1921 US Championships, sick, she retired after losing the first set to Molla MALLORY in her opening match. Her ball control was impeccable and she leaped about the court like a ballerina. In winning the 1925 Wimbledon she lost only five games; in winning the French title in 1926 she lost only four. Her incomparable skill and magnetic personality helped transform lawn tennis into a major spectator sport. In at least five major tournaments she won every singles round 6-0, 6-0. See FASHION, FRANCE; also CENTRE COURT CLASSICS and GREAT PLAYERS OF ALL TIME (PART 1).

Let

A let (derived from the old meaning of impediment, or obstruction or omission) is the replaying of a point when ordered by the umpire in his sole discretion, as a result of doubt, a disputed or reversed linesman's decision, or a rally being interrupted by any untoward happening that might affect the players. The whole point is replayed (including two services unless the doubt is over the second service).

Liberia

Tennis was introduced to Liberia at the beginning of the 20th century but it was not until 1961 that the country took part in its first international contest – during the Independence celebrations in Sierra Leone. The Association has been an Associate Member of the ILTF since 1966. BR
GOVERNING BODY: Liberia Tennis Association, National Sports and Athletic Commission, P.O. Box 502, Broad Street, Monrovia

Libya

Libya joined the ILTF as a Full Member in 1937 but was expelled during World War II. The

Association was refounded in 1966 and re-admitted as an Associate Member in 1968. BR
GOVERNING BODY: General Libyan Arab Tennis Federation, Baladiya Street, P.O. Box 879, Tripoli

Line Judges see UMPIRES AND LINE JUDGES

Linton Cup see AUSTRALIA

Little, Mrs Leigh see Miss Dorothy E. ROUND

Lizana, Miss Anita [Mrs R. T. Ellis] (Chile)

Born Santiago, Chile, 1915; Wimbledon women's singles q/f 1936-7; US women's singles won 1937. Famous for her dropshot, she was the first world-class player to come from Latin America.

Lob

A stroke by which the ball is played high into the air to land as near the baseline as possible. It is generally used as the answer to a SMASH but can be used with a lower trajectory as an attacking stroke – at its most devastating when played with topspin (see SPIN). JO

London Grass Court Championships (UK)

This event at the QUEEN'S CLUB is traditionally held the week before Wimbledon when interest in tennis is at its height. Many of the world's leading players enter because of the need for grass-court practice but it is often considered an artificial championship because many players refuse to make a supreme effort on the eve of Wimbledon and there are often 'shock' results.

Since the men's singles were first held at Queen's in 1890 only nine players have won both the London title and the Wimbledon Championship in the same year. Joshua Pim (1893), Harold Mahony (1896) and Tony Wilding (1910-12) achieved this feat before World War I but between the wars only Donald Budge (1937) managed it. Since 1945 Ted Schroeder (1949), Frank Sedgman (1952), Rod Laver (1962), Roy Emerson (1964-5) and John Newcombe (1967) have broken the spell but no man has done the double since open tennis began in 1968.

Probably the unluckiest winner was Gottfried von Cramm (Germany) in 1939. In the semi-final he trounced Bobby Riggs (United States) 6-1, 6-0 and then beat Ghaus Mohammad (India) 6-1, 6-3 in the final. The German would have been a warm favourite to win Wimbledon but Hitler refused to allow him to compete. Von Cramm was recalled to Germany and Riggs, whom he had beaten so decisively at Queen's, won Wimbledon.

Six women, Charlotte Cooper (1896, 1898), Ethel Larcombe (1912), Pauline Betz (1946), Louise Brough (1949, 1955), Ann Jones (1969) and Margaret Court (1970) have won the London title and Wimbledon in the same

Above **London Grass Court Championships.**
J. Bricka *(near left)*/M. Smith v. M. Bueno *(far left)*/
D. Hard (1962)

year but Mrs Court must be considered fortunate to have done so: in the 1970 final she was losing 2-6, 0-5, 0-15, to Britain's Winnie Shaw. Yet the Australian girl fought back so well that she won 2-6, 8-6, 6-2.

The youngest finalist in either singles event was Jean Forbes (S. Africa), now Mrs Cliff Drysdale, who was only 15 when she lost in 1955 to Miss Brough. Miss Forbes was too young to compete at Wimbledon that year but proved her worth by beating Darlene Hard, Heather Brewer and Dorothy Knode on her way to the London final.

Three men have won the singles four times: M. J. G. Ritchie, father of the present Queen's Club secretary (1902, 1904, 1906, 1909); Tony Wilding (1907, 1910-12); Roy Emerson (1963-6). Charlotte Cooper, later Mrs Sterry, had a record five victories in the women's singles (1896-8, 1900, 1902). Since 1970 the championships have been sponsored by ROTHMANS. The 1973 winners of the singles were Ilie Năstase and Olga Morozova. JO

London Professional Indoor Tennis Championships

This event, held 15 times between 1951 and 1967 at the Empire Pool, Wembley, is generally considered to have produced the finest lawn tennis seen in Britain before open tournaments began in 1968. It enabled the leading professionals, then barred from ILTF tournaments, to make an annual visit to London; many of the world's best players, including Pancho Gonzalez, Ken Rosewall, Rod Laver, Frank Sedgman, Lew Hoad, Tony Trabert and Pancho Segura, were regular competitors. Played on a fast, wood surface

in a stadium seating more than 8,000, this event, put on in the autumn, drew large crowds during the closing stages. Rosewall (1957 and 1960-3) created a record by winning the singles five times.

Laver won the singles for the last four years of the Championships (1964-7), and Gonzalez (1951, 1952 and 1956) won three times. Gonzalez also won the Wembley event in 1950. But in that year the tournament was named the International Professional Championships and the 'London' title was not included until 12 months later.

There was no contest during 1954 and 1955 but the Championships were revived in 1956; the singles final of that year produced perhaps the greatest match in the history of the tournament, when Gonzalez beat Sedgman 4-6, 11-9, 11-9, 9-7, in two hours 55 minutes and it was so enthralling that the BBC, due to televise the contest for just one hour, continued for another two until the match finally ended long past midnight.

For the next 11 years the standard of play was so high that it helped to bring in open tennis. Herman David, chairman of the All England Club, was so impressed by many of the finals that, long before the historic LTA Annual Meeting in 1967, he was openly saying that the professionals must be allowed to compete at Wimbledon.

Wembley had staged professional tennis 11 times before the inauguration of these Championships. The first event at the Empire Pool was held in 1934 and attracted Ellsworth Vines and Bill Tilden. Fred Perry made his professional début in Britain at Wembley in 1937 and Donald Budge did the same in May 1939. Five prewar events were followed by six more professional tournaments between 1947 and 1950 but it was not until the LTA gave official recognition in 1951 to the

London Championships that Wembley gained worldwide tennis renown.

The Championships stopped in 1967 because of the start of Open tennis but Wembley continued its tradition with the Jack Kramer Tournament of Champions in 1968, the W. D. & H. O. Wills Championships in 1969 and the Embassy Trophy in 1970 and 1971, each of which carried total prize money of £20,000 (the last three incorporated the BRITISH COVERED COURT CHAMPIONSHIPS). No event was held in 1972 because of the dispute between Lamar Hunt (WCT) and the ILTF which was settled too late for a tournament to be arranged. No event was held in 1973 either. JO

Long, Mrs T. D. [Miss Thelma Coyne] (Australia)

Born Sydney, N.S.W., 30 May 1918; Wimbledon women's singles q/f 1952; women's doubles s/f 1950, 1952, r/u 1957, s/f 1958; mixed doubles s/f 1949-50, r/u 1952, s/f 1957; US women's singles q/f 1952; women's doubles s/f 1938, 1952, 1958; mixed doubles r/u 1938, 1952; Australian women's singles s/f 1939, 1949, r/u 1951, won 1952, 1954, r/u 1955-6; women's doubles s/f 1935, won 1936-40, 1947-9, r/u 1950, won 1951-2, s/f 1954, won 1956, 1958, s/f 1959; mixed doubles s/f 1938, r/u 1948, won 1951-2, 1954-5; French women's singles q/f 1951; women's

Below **Thelma Long**

doubles s/f 1951, r/u 1958; mixed doubles r/u 1951, won 1956. One of the most effective women's doubles players produced by Australia; her career extended over two decades.

Lott, George M., Jr (USA)

Born Springfield, Ill., 16 Oct. 1906; Wimbledon men's singles q/f 1929-30, 1934; men's doubles s/f 1928-9, r/u 1930, won 1931, 1934; mixed doubles won 1931; US men's singles q/f 1924, s/f 1928, r/u 1931, q/f 1932; men's doubles s/f 1927, won 1928-30, s/f 1932, won 1933-4; mixed doubles won 1929, s/f 1930, won 1931, s/f 1932, r/u 1933, won 1934; French men's singles q/f 1931; men's doubles won 1931. Davis Cup 1928-31, 1933-4. Became pro 1934.

Love see SCORING

LTA see LAWN TENNIS ASSOCIATIONS

Lundqvist, Jan-Erik (Sweden)

Born Stockholm, 14 April 1937; French men's singles s/f 1961, 1964; men's doubles s/f 1960; US Indoor won 1965; Italian men's singles won 1964. Davis Cup 1961, 1963-4.

Lutz, Robert Charles (USA)

Born Lancaster, Pa., 29 Aug. 1947; Wimbledon men's singles q/f 1969; US men's doubles won 1968; Australian men's singles s/f 1971; men's doubles (Open and Amateur) won 1970, s/f 1971. Davis Cup 1968-70. WCT contract pro 1971-   . WCT 8th (F q/f) 1971, 7th (F q/f) May 1972, 7th (F r/u) Nov 1972.

Below Chuck McKinley

Luxembourg

Lawn tennis has been played in Luxembourg since the end of the 19th century. The Luxembourg LTA was founded in 1946 and affiliated to the ILTF the same year. It then had six clubs with about 150 members. Luxembourg has played in the DAVIS CUP regularly since 1947. It first took part in the FEDERATION CUP in 1972. There are a number of tournaments and an inter-club championship. In 1967 the ILTF held its Annual Meeting in Luxembourg and in 1971 the third European Amateur Championships were played there. In 1972 there were 23 clubs with 1,354 affiliated members.
BR
GOVERNING BODY: Fédération Luxembourgeoise de Tennis, Case Postale 2659, Luxembourg 1

Lycett, Randolph (Gt Britain)

Born Birmingham, 27 Aug. 1886; died 11 Feb. 1935; Wimbledon men's singles q/f 1920-1, r/u 1922; men's doubles r/u 1919, won 1921-3, s/f 1924, 1926-7; mixed doubles won 1919, r/u 1920, won 1921, r/u 1922, won 1923, s/f 1925; Australian men's doubles won 1905, 1911. Davis Cup (British Isles) 1921, (Gt Britain) 1923.

Below Frew McMillan

M

McAteer, Miss Myrtle (USA)

US women's singles won 1900, r/u 1901; women's doubles won 1899, r/u 1900, won 1901.

MacCall, George see OPEN TENNIS (PART 1)

McGrath, Vivian B. (Australia)

Born N.S.W., 17 Feb. 1916; Wimbledon men's singles q/f 1935, 1937; Australian men's singles s/f 1933-5, q/f 1936, won 1937, s/f 1939-40; men's doubles s/f 1934, won 1935, r/u 1936, s/f 1938-9; French men's singles q/f 1935; men's doubles r/u 1933-5. Davis Cup 1933-7. Two-handed on left-hand side; the first notable exponent of the double-fisted backhand stroke.

McGregor, Ken (Australia)

Born Adelaide, 2 June 1929; Wimbledon men's singles r/u 1951, q/f 1952; men's doubles won 1951-2; mixed doubles s/f 1951-2; US men's doubles s/f 1950, won 1951, r/u 1952; mixed doubles won 1950; Australian men's singles r/u 1950-1, won 1952; men's doubles s/f 1950, won 1951-2; French men's singles s/f 1951-2; men's doubles won 1951-2; mixed doubles s/f 1950-1. Davis Cup 1950-2. Notable as doubles partner of SEDGMAN with whom, in 1951, he won the Grand Slam of men's doubles championships. He was also a good Australian-rules footballer. Became professional 1953.

McKane, Miss K. see Mrs L. A. GODFREE

McKinley, Charles R. [Chuck] (USA)

Born St Louis, Mo., 5 Jan. 1941; Wimbledon men's singles r/u 1961, won 1963, s/f 1964; US men's singles q/f 1960, s/f 1962-4; men's doubles won 1961, r/u 1962, won 1963-4. Davis Cup 1960-5. An incredibly fast mover about the court, who retrieved 'impossibles'.

McLoughlin, Maurice Evans (USA)

Born Carson City, Nevada, 7 Jan. 1890, died 10 Dec. 1957; Wimbledon men's singles r/u 1913; US men's singles r/u* 1909, q/f 1910, r/u 1911, won 1912-13, r/u 1914-15, q/f 1919; men's doubles r/u 1909, won 1912-14, r/u 1915-16. Davis Cup 1909, 1911, 1913-14. Known as the 'Californian Comet', he was the first player to develop the cannonball service.

McMillan, Frew Donald (S. Africa)

Born Springs, 20 May 1942; Wimbledon men's

doubles won 1967, s/f 1968-70, won 1972; mixed doubles s/f 1966-7, 1970-1; US men's singles q/f 1972; men's doubles s/f 1971; mixed doubles s/f 1964, r/u 1970, s/f 1971; French men's doubles s/f 1968, 1971, won 1972, s/f 1973; mixed doubles won 1966, s/f 1967-8. Davis Cup 1965-9. WCT contract pro 1970-1. Had remarkable run of 39 doubles wins with HEWITT in 1967. Two-handed both sides, occasionally using a right-handed forehand.

McNeill, W. Donald (USA)
Born Chickasha, Okla., 30 April 1916; US men's singles q/f 1939, won 1940, s/f 1941, 1944, q/f 1946; men's doubles won 1944, r/u 1946; mixed doubles r/u 1944; French men's singles won 1939; men's doubles won 1939. The first American to win the French men's singles championship.

Madagascar
Madagascar was an Associate Member of the ILTF 1961-73. In 1965 it reported 18 clubs and several hundred players. BR
GOVERNING BODY: Fédération Malgache de Lawn-Tenis, B.P. 582, Tananarive

Madison Square Garden, New York
see POSTWAR DEVELOPMENT, THE UNITED STATES STORY (PART 1)

Mahony, Harold S. (Ireland)
Born Ireland, 13 Feb. 1867, died 28 June 1905; Wimbledon men's singles s/f 1891-2, r/u* 1893, won 1896, r/u 1897, r/u* 1898, s/f 1899, 1901-2; men's doubles s/f 1891, r/u* 1892, s/f 1897, r/u* 1903; US men's doubles r/u 1897. A lively Irishman with reputedly the worst forehand in the game; with a tremendous reach he volleyed to victory.

Mako, C. Gene (USA)
Born Budapest, Hungary, 24 Jan. 1916; Wimbledon men's doubles s/f 1935, won 1937-8; mixed doubles s/f 1937; US men's singles r/u 1938; men's doubles r/u 1935, won 1936, r/u 1937, won 1938; mixed doubles s/f 1935, won 1936; Australian men's doubles s/f 1938; mixed doubles s/f 1938; French men's doubles r/u 1938; mixed doubles s/f 1938. Davis Cup 1935-8. Became pro 1946.

Malawi
Lawn tennis was played in Malawi before 1903 when the first men's singles championship was held. Previously part of the LTA of RHODESIA, the Malawi LTA was established in 1954 and affiliated to the ILTF as an Associate Member in 1966. In 1972 there were eight clubs. The Malawi Championships have been played since 1954 at the Blantyre Sports Club and Limbe Country Club in alternate years. The outstanding players are Alfio Vatteroni and Phillip Coombes. BR
GOVERNING BODY: LTA of Malawi, P.O. Box 43, Blantyre

Malaysia
Tennis was introduced to Malaysia by the British before 1900 and the first players were mostly British or Europeans. The LTA of Malaya (for the peninsula as a whole and not the various political divisions) was formed in 1921. It became an Associate Member of the ILTF in 1937 and a Full Member in 1963. The name was changed to LTA of Malaysia in 1964 to include the other states of the new Federation of Malaysia. The game has developed quickly during the last 20 years. Today there are nearly 5,000 players and over 100 clubs and schools with more than 500 tennis courts.

The tournaments organized by the LTA of Malaysia include the Junior Inter-State Competition, Junior Championships, National Hard Court Championships, National Grass Court Championships, and Inter-State Competition. There is also an annual match between Malaysia and Singapore for men, women

Below **Donald McNeill**

and juniors. The Malaysian Open Championships began in 1921 with the men's singles. The six States' champions met at the Singapore Cricket Club to decide the Championship of Malaya for a cup presented by Mr L. E. Gaunt. The competition continued in this form, play taking place in the evenings only till 1925.

Malaysia takes part in the Asian Games and the SEAP Games (see REGIONAL GAMES), and has played in the DAVIS CUP since 1957.

The first open tournament (for amateurs from all countries) was held at the Selangor Club, Kuala Lumpur, in August 1926. Many international players have taken part in these Championships, including Neale Fraser, John Newcombe, Tony Roche, Colin Dibley (Australia), Ramanathan Krishnan, Premjit Lall (India), Felicismo Ampon (Philippines) and top-ranking players from other countries in Asia and from New Zealand.

Chin Kee Onn won the Malayan title in 1934, 1937 and 1939. Goon Kok Ying and Goon Lok Lem won the Malayan doubles in 1937 and

1939. The most outstanding woman player was Mrs Gladys Loke Chua, who won the Malayan singles title in 1955. The leading player for the past decade has been S. A. Azman. He has played in the Davis Cup, Asian and SEAP Games. He and Tan Song Kean, ranked no. 2, were sent to Australia for training and participation in the 1960/1 Australian Circuit.

The Davis Cup nations paid a great compliment to Malaysia in 1972 when they invited its Secretary, Mr Rajaratnam, to serve on a select committee to reorganize the Davis Cup competition. BR

GOVERNING BODY: The Lawn Tennis Association of Malaysia, No. 11, Jalan 6/18, Petaling Jaya, Selangor

Mallory, Mrs Molla B. [Miss M. Bjurstedt] (USA)

Born Norway, 1892, died 1959; Wimbledon women's singles s/f 1920, q/f 1921, r/u 1922, q/f 1923, s/f 1926; mixed doubles s/f 1923; US women's singles won 1915-16, 1918, s/f 1919, won 1920-22, r/u 1923-4, s/f 1925, won 1926, q/f 1927, s/f 1928-9; women's doubles won 1916-17, r/u 1918, s/f 1919, r/u 1922, s/f 1926; mixed doubles r/u 1915, s/f 1916, won 1917, r/u 1918, won 1922-3, r/u 1924, s/f 1925-6, 1928. Wightman Cup 1923-5, 1927-8. The greatest American woman player before the emergence of Helen Wills MOODY. She was the only player to beat Suzanne LENGLEN in singles after World War I (in the opening match of the 1921 US Championships). See GREAT PLAYERS OF ALL TIME (PART 1).

Manchester (UK) see NORTHERN LAWN TENNIS CHAMPIONSHIPS

Marble, Miss Alice (USA)

Born Plumes County, Calif., 28 Sept. 1913; Wimbledon women's singles s/f 1937-8, won 1939; women's doubles won 1938-9; mixed doubles won 1937-9; US women's singles q/f 1933, won 1936, q/f 1937, won 1938-40; women's doubles r/u 1932, s/f 1936, won 1937-40; mixed doubles won 1936, 1938-40. Wightman Cup 1933, 1937-9. Despite a physique by no means robust she took the women's game to a new dimension by adopting a serve-volley technique hitherto only played by men. Her example was the foundation of the high standard of the American women's game in the years immediately after World War II; it is certain that but for the war her achievement internationally would have been higher. See GREAT PLAYERS OF ALL TIME (PART 1).

Marcel Porée Cup see FRANCE

Mark, Robert (Australia)

Born Albury, N.S.W., 28 Nov. 1937; Wimbledon men's doubles r/u 1959, s/f 1960-1; mixed doubles s/f 1959-60; US men's singles q/f 1960, men's doubles s/f 1957, 1959, r/u 1960, s/f 1961; mixed doubles r/u 1959, won 1961; Australian men's singles s/f 1959, q/f 1960; men's doubles r/u 1958, won 1959-61; mixed doubles s/f 1957, won 1959, r/u 1960; French men's doubles s/f 1959, r/u 1961; S. African men's singles won 1962.

Martin, Billy (USA)

Born Chicago, Ill., 25 Dec. 1956. His precocious ability became widely noticed when he represented the United States in the 1973 BP Under-21 international matches at Torquay, England. Right-handed with two-handed backhand.

Marylebone Cricket Club

The first governing body for lawn tennis. See THE ORIGINS OF LAWN TENNIS, THE BIRTH AND SPREAD OF LAWN TENNIS, THE RULES AND THEIR INTERPRETATION, THE PRESS (PART 1); LAWN TENNIS ASSOCIATIONS

Maskell, Dan (Gt Britain)

Born 11 April 1908; British Professional Champion 16 times, 1928-36, 1938-9, 1946-50. First permanent Coach to All England Club, 1929-39, 1946-55; LTA Training Manager 1953-73. Well known BBC TV tennis commentator.

Masters' Tournament see ILTF GRAND PRIX

Match

A contest between two players in singles, or two pairs in doubles. It may be decided over one set or the best of three sets or the best of five sets. For major championships such as those at Wimbledon, Forest Hills and Paris, matches for men's singles and doubles are normally the best of five sets but at most tournaments they are the best of three. Today women never play more than the best of three. In 1970 the ILTF sanctioned the use of the TIE-BREAK to finish a set instead of the traditional advantage set. See RUBBER, SCORING. JO

Mathieu, Mrs René [Miss Simone Passemard] (France)

Born Neuilly-sur-Seine, 31 Jan. 1908; Wimbledon women's singles s/f 1930-2, q/f 1933, s/f 1934, q/f 1935, s/f 1936-7, q/f 1938-9; women's doubles won 1933-4, r/u 1935, won 1937, r/u 1938; mixed doubles s/f 1932, r/u 1937; US women's singles q/f 1938; women's doubles r/u 1938; French women's singles q/f 1925-6, r/u 1929, q/f 1930-1, r/u 1932-3, s/f 1934, r/u 1935-7, won 1938-9; women's doubles s/f 1929, r/u 1930, s/f 1931-2, won 1933-4, 1936-9; mixed doubles s/f 1935-6, won 1937-8. The best Frenchwoman of the 1930s, she had trenchant and patient driving skill.

Mauritius

The Mauritius Lawn Tennis Association, founded in 1910, first affiliated to the ILTF as a Full Member in 1936 but now an Associate Member, controls five clubs with about 50 courts. Two championships are played each year, on grass between May and July and on hard courts during September and October. Matches are also played with teams from Madagascar and Réunion. Mauritius has not yet sent players to any international competition, but the game is developing. BR

GOVERNING BODY: Mauritius Lawn Tennis Association, Rue Dr Ferrière, Port-Louis

MCC see MARYLEBONE CRICKET CLUB

Mediterranean Games see REGIONAL GAMES

Melville, Miss Kerry A. (Australia)

Born Sydney, N.S.W., 7 Aug. 1947; Wimbledon women's singles q/f 1971, 1973; women's doubles s/f 1966, 1969-70; US women's singles s/f 1966, q/f 1970, s/f 1971, r/u 1972, q/f 1973; women's doubles s/f 1970-1; Australian women's singles s/f 1966-7, 1969, r/u 1970, s/f 1973; women's doubles won 1968, s/f 1969, r/u 1970, 1973; French women's singles s/f 1967, q/f 1969; women's doubles s/f 1969. Federation Cup 1967-9. ILTF GP 5th 1972.

Men's Clothing

Since tennis began in the 1870s men's clothing, unlike women's, has seen comparatively few changes. From the earliest days the predominant colour was white and until World War II men generally played in white shirts with long white flannels, white socks and rubber-soled canvas shoes. But in 1946, when tennis was resumed in earnest after World War II, the top players all began to wear shorts and their example was quickly followed by club players. Today it is rare to see men competing in flannels, whatever their standard of play.

In 1968 coloured shirts first came into prominence when American promoter Dave Dixon introduced his professional group, known as the 'Handsome Eight', and insisted they all play in different colours for easier identification (see WORLD CHAMPIONSHIP TENNIS).

Since long hair has become popular among men several players have taken to wearing bandannas to keep their hair out of their eyes and for greater neatness of appearance. JO

Menzies, Mrs M. see Miss K. E. STAMMERS

Metreveli, Alexander (USSR)

Born Tbilisi, Georgia, 2 Nov. 1944; Wimbledon singles r/u 1973; mixed doubles r/u 1968, r/u 1970, s/f 1973; Australian men's singles s/f 1972, q/f 1973; men's doubles s/f 1972; French men's singles q/f 1966, s/f 1972; men's doubles s/f 1966; mixed doubles s/f 1971. Davis Cup 1963, 1967. WCT contract pro 1972-3. First player from the USSR to reach Wimbledon singles final (1973) and the first to reach mixed final (with Olga Morozova, 1968).

Mexico

Mexico first affiliated to the ILTF in 1928 as a Full Member. It has competed in the DAVIS CUP

Above **Men's Clothing.** This statuette, dated 1884, is thought to be of William Renshaw, triple Wimbledon champion by that date.

since 1924, reaching the Challenge Round in 1962, in which Rafael OSUNA and Antonio PALAFOX took part. It first played in the FEDERATION CUP in 1964. Its best-known women players have been Yola RAMIREZ and Rosa Maria Reyes (Mrs Pierre DARMON). BR
GOVERNING BODY: Federación Mexicana de Tenis A.C., Durango No. 225-304, Mexico 7

Midland Counties Lawn Tennis Championship (UK)

This event at Edgbaston, Birmingham, which began in 1899, was once one of the foremost tournaments in Britain.

One of the early giants was Sidney Smith of Stroud, Gloucestershire, whose forehand drive is still remembered as one of the greatest in

tennis history. Though he had one leg encased in an iron support he won the Midland title a record six times (1900-5) and was runner-up at Wimbledon in 1900. He rarely strayed from the baseline because of his bad leg but his flat, powerful forehand, known as the 'Smith Punch', was so accurate that he made his opponents do most of the running.

Stanley Doust, an Australian and later a respected lawn-tennis correspondent of the *Daily Mail*, was champion four times (1909, 1912-13 and 1919) before Bill Tilden became the first male Wimbledon winner also to capture the Midland title (1920). It was another 34 years before Jaroslav Drobný held both titles. Wimbledon champions Charlotte Cooper, Dora Boothby, Ethel Larcombe, Dorothy Round, Doris Hart and Angela Mortimer all appear on the Midland Championship roll but in the mid-1950s the tournament began to decline. From 1963 the *Birmingham Post and Mail* backed it for three years in an effort to revive its former glory. Roy Emerson won the men's singles that year when he beat Rafael Osuna (Mexico) 4-6, 6-3, 7-5 in a surprise reversal of form. Osuna led 4-1 in the third set and looked certain to win when rain halted play for 70 minutes. He could not regain the same flair when they resumed play and Emerson came storming back to win the title.

Two years later the Championships were notable for the performances of the then up-and-coming Virginia Wade. Miss Wade beat Lesley Turner (Mrs Bowrey) in the quarter-finals and Pat Walkden (Mrs Pretorius) in the semi-finals. Then, on her 20th birthday, she was beaten 6-3, 4-6, 7-5, by Margaret Smith (Mrs Court) in the final. To complete an eventful week, Miss Wade was selected for the Wightman Cup for the first time on the day of the semi-finals.

Since 1965 the championships have been reduced to a virtually local affair, though there was a determined but unsuccessful sponsored attempt to restore some distinction to them in 1970. JO

Miller, Mrs E. H. [Miss Esther L. Heine; 'Bobbie'] (S. Africa)

Born Estcourt, Natal, 5 Dec. 1910; Wimbledon women's singles q/f 1929; women's doubles r/u 1927, s/f 1938; mixed doubles s/f 1927; French women's singles s/f 1927, q/f 1929; women's doubles won 1927, r/u 1929; S. African women's singles won 1928 (aged 18), 1931-2, 1936-7.

Mitre Cup see SOUTH AMERICAN CHAMPIONSHIPS

Mixed Doubles

Matches played between pairs composed of both sexes are traditionally considered to be the social part of any tournament. More and more tournaments, however, leaning towards restricted entry events, have tended to discard the mixed doubles and it is always the

first event to be abandoned if the tournament runs into bad weather. At most major championships mixed doubles pairs enter as pairs and the draw takes place before the championships begin; sometimes the draw is left until the tournament is under way and players are more easily able to make plans. Partners do not necessarily have to be of the same nationality. DC

Mohammad, Ghaus see INDIA

Molesworth, Mrs B. H. (Australia)
Australian women's singles won 1922-3, r/u 1934; women's doubles s/f 1922, won 1930, won 1933-4, s/f 1935.

Monaco
The first lawn tennis tournament in Monaco was held in 1897 and has been played practically every year since then. On the trophies are such famous names as those of the DOHERTY brothers, A. F. WILDING, H. COCHET and W. T. TILDEN. In 1925 the Butler Trophy Competition was established for men's doubles teams. In 1927 the Condamine Tennis Club was formed and in 1928 the Monte Carlo Country Club was built, with 22 courts. The Lawn Tennis Association of Monaco was established in 1927 and was immediately elected a Full Member of the ILTF with voting rights. In relation to its small area Monaco has played a great part in the game of lawn tennis. A team from Monaco takes part regularly in the DAVIS CUP (in which it first competed in 1929) and the GALEA CUP and Monaco has organized a succession of open tournaments. The Annual General Meeting of the ILTF was held in Monaco in 1970. BR
GOVERNING BODY: Fédération Monégasque de Lawn Tennis, 14 Quai Antoine Ier, Monaco (Principauté)

Monte Carlo see MONACO; also THE GROWTH OF THE GAME (PART 1)

Moody, Mrs F. S. [Miss Helen Wills; Mrs Roark] (USA)
Born Berkeley, Calif., 6 Oct. 1905; Wimbledon women's singles r/u 1924, won 1927-30, 1932-3, 1935, 1938; women's doubles won 1924, 1927, 1930; mixed doubles s/f 1928, won 1929; US women's singles r/u 1922, won 1923-5, 1927-9, 1931, r/u 1933; women's doubles won 1922, 1924-5, 1928, r/u 1933; mixed doubles r/u 1922, won 1924, 1928; French women's singles won 1928-30, 1932; women's doubles won 1930, 1932; mixed doubles r/u 1928-9, 1932. Wightman Cup 1923-5, 1927-32, 1938. She was second only to Suzanne LENGLEN with her record of invincibility and certainly one of the great all-time players. She won the Wimbledon singles eight times (a record) in nine challenges and in 1927-32 did not lose a set in singles anywhere. She paraded her superb driving skill without sign of emotion and was known as 'Little Poker

Above **Helen Wills Moody** in 1935

Face'. Her footwork, curiously, was by no means athletic but her groundstrokes were so powerful and trenchantly employed that her comparative immobility was never a handicap. An estrangement with the American authorities made her a non-competitor in the US Championships after 1933. See CENTRE COURT CLASSICS and GREAT PLAYERS OF ALL TIME (both PART 1).

Moody & Co. Inc.

Moody & Co. is the largest wholesaler of tennis equipment in the United States, boasting that it carries everything for tennis except the surface of the court. The company has over 2,500 accounts throughout the United States, Virgin Islands and parts of South America. JB
HEAD OFFICE: Box 13, Milford, Conn. 06460, U.S.A.

Moon, E. F. (Australia)

Wimbledon mixed doubles s/f 1928; US mixed doubles r/u 1928; Australian men's singles s/f 1927, 1929, won 1930, q/f 1935-6; men's doubles r/u 1928-9, s/f 1930, won 1932, q/f 1933, s/f 1934; mixed doubles won 1929, 1934; French men's singles q/f 1930; men's doubles s/f 1930. Unbeaten in his one year, 1930, as one of Australia's Davis Cup team.

Moore, Miss Elisabeth Holmes (USA)

Died 22 Jan 1959, aged 82; US women's singles r/u* 1891, r/u 1892, won 1896, r/u 1897, won 1901, r/u 1902, won 1903, r/u 1904, won 1905; women's doubles won 1896, won 1903, s/f 1914; mixed doubles won 1902, won 1904. Notable for the length of her All-Comers'

final match against Marion JONES in the US meeting of 1901 when she won 4-6, 1-6, 9-7, 9-7, 6-3, – 58 games.

Morea, Enrique (Argentina)

Born Buenos Aires, 11 April 1924; Wimbledon mixed doubles r/u 1952-3, 1955, s/f 1961; US men's doubles s/f 1947; mixed doubles s/f 1953; French men's singles s/f 1953-4; men's doubles r/u 1946, s/f 1947, 1955; mixed doubles won 1950, s/f 1952-3. Davis Cup 1948, 1952, 1955.

Morocco

The Royal Moroccan LTA was founded in 1956 and affiliated to the ILTF in 1957. Since 1959 the International Championships of Morocco for a trophy given by King Hassan II have been played in Casablanca, with a good foreign and national entry. Morocco has played in the DAVIS CUP five times since 1964, and first took part in the FEDERATION CUP in 1966. In 1972 there were over 60 lawn tennis clubs, about half of them in Casablanca. In 1956 there were some 2,000 affiliated players; by 1972 the number had doubled as the main object of the Association is to popularize the game, particularly among young people. BR
GOVERNING BODY: Fédération Royale Marocaine de Lawn-Tennis, Maison des Sports, Parc de la Ligue Arabe, Casablanca

Morpurgo, Baron U. L. see ITALY; also THE GROWTH OF THE GAME (PART 1)

Mortimer, Miss Angela [Mrs John Barrett] (Gt Britain)

Born Plymouth, 21 April 1932; Wimbledon women's singles q/f 1953-4, 1956, r/u 1958,

q/f 1959-60, won 1961; women's doubles s/f 1953-4, won 1955, s/f 1956; US women's singles q/f 1952, s/f 1961; women's doubles s/f 1952, 1955, 1959; mixed doubles s/f 1953; Australian women's singles won 1958; women's doubles and mixed doubles r/u 1958; French women's singles won 1955, r/u 1956; women's doubles s/f 1955. Wightman Cup 1953, 1955-6, 1959-61. Her determined, steady play backed by unruffled patience made her (1961) the first British women's singles victor at Wimbledon for 24 years.

Morton, Miss A. M. (Gt Britain)

Wimbledon women's singles s/f 1901, r/u* 1902, q/f 1903, r/u* 1904, s/f 1905, r/u* 1908-09, q/f 1912; women's doubles won 1914.

Mottram, Anthony John (Gt Britain)

Born Coventry, 8 June 1920; Wimbledon men's singles q/f 1948; men's doubles r/u 1947; French men's doubles s/f 1948; mixed doubles s/f 1950-1. Davis Cup 1947-55. Became pro 1955. Britain's National Coach since 1970.

Mottram, Christopher [Buster] (Gt Britain)

Born Kingston, Surrey, 25 April 1955; son of A. J. MOTTRAM; youngest-ever winner of British Under-21 title at 16 (1971). Beat LAVER in 1973 Melia Trophy q/f in Madrid, 6-3, 5-7, 6-2.

'Mr G', the pseudonym of King Gustaf V of SWEDEN; see also THE GROWTH OF THE GAME (PART 1)

Below **Tony Mottram**

'**Mr X**', the pseudonym of Dr Joshua PIM; see also DAVIS CUP.

Mulligan, Martin F. (Australia/Italy)
Born Sydney, N.S.W., 18 Oct. 1940; Wimbledon men's singles r/u 1962 (unseeded); men's doubles s/f 1960; Australian men's singles q/f 1960, s/f 1964; men's doubles s/f 1960, r/u 1961; mixed doubles s/f 1960; French men's singles q/f 1959, 1961-2, 1970. Davis Cup (Italy) 1968- . Moved to Italy in 1964.

Mulloy, Gardnar (USA)
Born Miami, Fla., 22 Nov. 1914; Wimbledon men's singles s/f 1948, q/f 1950; men's doubles r/u 1948-9, s/f 1951, 1953-4, won 1957 (aged 43); mixed doubles r/u 1956; US men's singles s/f 1942, 1946, q/f 1947, 1949, s/f 1950, q/f 1951, r/u 1952, q/f 1953; men's doubles won 1942, 1945-6, s/f 1947, won 1948, r/u 1950, s/f 1951-2, r/u 1953, 1957, s/f 1961; mixed doubles r/u 1955, s/f 1956-8; Australian men's singles s/f 1947; French men's singles q/f 1952-4; men's doubles r/u 1951-2, s/f 1953-4. Davis Cup 1946, 1948-50, 1952-3, 1957.

Murray, R. Lindley (USA)
Born San Francisco, Calif., 3 Nov. 1893, died 1970; US men's singles s/f 1916, won 1917 (National Patriotic Tournament), won 1918, q/f 1919. Left-handed.

Musketeers, Four   see FOUR MUSKETEERS and FRANCE

Myers, A. Wallis   see THE PRESS (PART 1)

Below Ilie Năstase

N

Nahant, Mass. see THE BIRTH AND SPREAD OF LAWN TENNIS, THE UNITED STATES STORY (PART 1)

Năstase, Ilie (Rumania)
Born Bucharest, 19 July 1946; Wimbledon men's singles r/u 1972; men's doubles s/f 1970, won 1973; mixed doubles won 1970, s/f 1971, won 1972; US men's singles won 1972; men's doubles s/f 1972; mixed doubles s/f 1971, r/u 1972; French men's singles q/f 1970, r/u 1971, won 1973; men's doubles r/u 1966, s/f 1967-9, won 1970, r/u 1973; mixed doubles s/f 1970, 1972. Davis Cup 1968- . ILTF GP 2nd (M won) 1971, 1st (M won) 1972. See colour plate, page 292, and CENTRE COURT CLASSICS (PART 1).

National Junior Tennis League (USA)
see THE UNITED STATES STORY (PART 1)

National Public Parks Championships (USA)   see THE UNITED STATES STORY (PART 1)

National Tennis Educational Foundation (USA)   see THE UNITED STATES STORY (PART 1)

National Tennis League
see THE POSTWAR PRO GAME and OPEN TENNIS (PART 1)

Nations' Cup   see EGYPT

Navratilová, Martina (Czechoslovakia)
Born Prague, 18 Oct. 1956; French women's singles q/f 1973. Her aggressive skill was first made apparent outside Czechoslovakia in the 1972 Annie Soisbault Cup, and again in the 1973 BP Under-21 international matches at Torquay, England. Left-handed.

Neely, Miss Carrie B. (USA)
US women's singles r/u* 1903, r/u 1907, q/f 1908, 1914; women's doubles won 1903, 1905, 1907, r/u 1908; mixed doubles won 1898.

Nepal
The All Nepal Tennis Association affiliated to the ILTF as an Associate Member in 1971. In spite of the mountainous nature of the country, tennis is played in various towns in the south and is very popular in Kathmandu, where there are several clubs. Two official tournaments are held annually. BR
GOVERNING BODY: All Nepal Tennis Asso-

ciation, c/o National Sports Council, Bagh Durbar, Kathmandu

Nestlé Schools Tournament
The Nestlé Schools Tournament, sponsored by the Nestlé Company and organized by the LAWN TENNIS FOUNDATION OF GREAT BRITAIN, has been held annually since 1963. In 1973 it had over 32,000 entrants in England, Ireland, Scotland and Wales.

Net
The net, which stretches across the middle of the court, is suspended from a cord or metal cable which joins or passes over the top of two posts, situated on either side of the court, 3 ft (0·91 m) from the sidelines. These posts are 3 ft 6 in (1·07 m) high but the net slopes to 3 ft (0·91 m) at the centre where it is held taut by a strap not more than 2 in (5 cm) wide. There is also a 2-2½ in (5-6·3 cm)-wide tape band covering the cord or metal cable. See RULE 1 (THE RULES AND THEIR INTERPRETATION (PART 1). JO

Net Cord
A stroke, other than a service, where the ball touches the top of the net but continues to the far side of the court and lands within the bounds of the court. If a service ball touches the top of the net and lands correctly within the service court on the other side a LET is given and the ball is served again. JO

Netherlands
There were only 16 clubs in existence, two dating from 1882 and one from 1885, when 14 gentlemen met in Amsterdam on 5 June 1899 and decided to found the Netherlands LTA. These 16 clubs were distributed not only in the big cities of the west, but also in the less populous east and north. After the first 15 difficult years tennis spread all over the country so that by 1939, when the Association was granted the title 'Royal' and HRH Prince Bernhard of the Netherlands became patron, affiliated clubs numbered 350, with about 22,000 members. After 1950 the game's popularity increased: in 1973 there were 860 affiliated clubs with over 151,000 members. Today 200 new courts are built every year. More than 90 per cent are hard courts similar to En-tout-cas; the rest are of porous concrete.

From 1899 to 1918 the six people who held the position of honorary secretary/treasurer of the Netherlands LTA worked unaided, using their own homes as offices. One man held the position from 1918 to 1945, on a voluntary basis at first, later with a small salary, working from his home at The Hague. To prevent the Germans from tracing and rounding up young men to be sent to labour in Germany, the British Royal Air Force in March 1945 attacked the building in The Hague housing official census records. A number of bombs missed their target and destroyed several houses, including the Association's office. Since 1946 the office has been in Amsterdam, under the direction of an executive secretary with a staff of ten.

The Royal Netherlands LTA has been a Full Member of the ILTF since its foundation in 1913 and has competed in the DAVIS CUP since 1920. Including 1973 the Netherlands had played 76 Davis Cup ties, losing 47, winning 29. The best results were obtained between 1923 and 1930 when in the European Zone the Dutch team reached the quarter-finals three times, the semi-finals once, and the finals once (1925). Well-known interwar Dutch Davis Cup players were Jonkheer C. van Lennep, G. J. Scheurleer, F. A. Diemer Kool, H. Timmer, and after 1945 Hans van Swol, Ivo Rinkel, Huib Wilton, Jan Hajer and, of course, Tom Okker. The Netherlands have also competed in the FEDERATION CUP since 1963.

Official National Championships have been held every year since 1899, except in 1943 and 1944. Miss M. C. Rollin Couquerque, with 40,

and H. Timmer, with 23 national titles in singles and doubles, lead the list of national champions. Other well-known Dutch players in the past were Miss Kea Bouman, who won the French International Championships in 1927, Miss L. Everts, winner of 24 national titles, Mrs J. Roos, Mrs P. F. Van der Storm, Hans van Dalsum and Miss Betty Stöve, who won the women's doubles with Billie Jean King at Wimbledon in 1972.

The first official international tournament dates from 1908. The RNLTA organized International Championships from 1936 to 1957. Since 1962 the Hilversumse LTC, which had held an international tournament for many years, has organized the International Championships of the Netherlands. Winners include Mrs D. Knode, Miss Maria Bueno, Mrs Margaret Court, Miss Evonne Goolagong, Mlle Françoise Durr, G. de'Stefani, Henri Cochet, Eric Sturgess, Rod Laver, Roy Emerson, Cliff

Drysdale, John Newcombe and Tom Okker.

An important factor in the development of the game in the Netherlands is the national tennis league held on Saturdays and Sundays. Most people consider it to be the most important activity of the Association. In 1900 it began on Sundays with only 4 teams, which had increased to 120 by 1920 and nearly 500 by 1940. After World War II the league competition became very popular and spread to Saturdays as well, so that (1973) 2,530 teams took part in the Sunday league and 2,450 teams in the Saturday league. The league starts in the second half of April (the tennis season in the Netherlands begins on 1 April) and takes seven or eight weekends, usually ending on the first weekend in June. Nearly 30,000 players take part each weekend, women, men, girls and boys. Beginners as well as players at national level take part in it, with matches at home and abroad. This type of organization is unique.

After the league has ended the tournament season runs from mid-June to the end of September. More than 250 tournaments are organized by the Association, the *Distrikts* (counties) and the affiliated clubs. In June, July and August one or two tournaments attracting international entries are held every week, while there are not only tournaments for the better players but also for beginners, veterans, and juniors. Training for juniors starts with the clubs, the best being selected for training at district level. After about three or four years the most talented are brought together under the supervision of the Association's coaches. Special training camps as well as youth championships are organized for those under 12, under 14, under 16 and under 18. Although the general standard of play has greatly improved during the last 15 years, no more players of international standard – with the exception of Marijke Schaar, Betty Stöve and Tom Okker – have appeared. Only a few teams at the top of the tennis-league ladder are sponsored, as well as some of the international tournaments. Companies and individuals in the Netherlands have not yet become accustomed to tennis sponsorship. The Dutch Sports Federation supports training for all sports in the Netherlands, and the Leo van der Kar Foundation also helps promising young players by special training facilities. The Netherlands government contributes towards the training of coaches, publicity, and the Association's office expenses.   OJvdH

GOVERNING BODY: Koninklijke Nederlandse Lawn Tennis Bond, P.O. Box 5113, Amsterdam

Netherlands Antilles

The Netherlands Antilles LTA has been affiliated to the ILTF as an Associate Member since 1947. BR

GOVERNING BODY: Nederlands Antilliaanse Lawn Tennis Bond, P.O. Box 1941, Willemstad, Curaçao

Netherlands National Championships Winners

Men's Singles		Women's Singles	
1922	R. C. Nauta	1922	Miss L. Lhoest
1923	H. Timmer	1923	Miss K. Bouman
1924	M. van der Feen	1924	Miss K. Bouman
1925	C. van Lennep	1925	Miss K. Bouman
1926	C. van Lennep	1926	Miss K. Bouman
1927	H. Timmer	1927	Miss M. Rollin Couquerque
1928	H. Timmer	1928	Miss M. Rollin Couquerque
1929	H. Timmer	1929	Miss M. Rollin Couquerque
1930	H. Timmer	1930	Miss M. Rollin Couquerque
1931	J. van der Heide	1931	Miss E. Belzer
1932	H. Timmer	1932	Miss M. Rollin Couquerque
1933	H. Timmer	1933	Miss M. Rollin Couquerque
1934	H. Timmer	1934	Miss M. Rollin Couquerque
1935	H. Timmer	1935	Miss M. Rollin Couquerque
1936	T. Hughan	1936	Miss G. Terwindt
1937	T. Hughan	1937	Miss G. Terwindt
1938	A. C. van Swol	1938	Miss M. Rollin Couquerque
1939	T. Hughan	1939	Miss M. Rollin Couquerque
1940	A. C. van Swol	1940	Miss M. Rollin Couquerque
1941	A. C. van Swol	1941	Miss M. Rollin Couquerque
1942	T. Hughan	1942	Miss M. Rollin Couquerque
1943-44	*No Competition*	1943-44	*No Competition*
1945	I. Rinkel	1945	Mrs G. Blaisse-Terwindt
1946	H. Wilton	1946	Mrs G. Blaisse-Terwindt
1947	H. Wilton	1947	Miss M. Rollin Couquerque
1948	A. C. van Swol	1948	Mrs J. Roos-van der Wal
1949	A. C. van Swol	1949	Miss P. Hermsen
1950	T. Hughan	1950	Miss P. Hermsen
1951	H. Wilton	1951	Mrs J. Roos
1952	H. Wilton	1952	Mrs J. Roos
1953	J. A. Karamoy	1953	Miss F. ten Bosch
1954	J. van Dalsum	1954	Mrs J. Roos
1955	J. van Dalsum	1955	Mrs P. van den Storm
1956	J. A. Karamoy	1956	Mrs J. Roos
1957	J. van Dalsum	1957	Mrs Rouwenhorst
1958	W. Maris	1958	Mrs F. de Soet-ten Bosch
1959	J. A. Karamoy	1959	Mrs J. Vletter
1960	J. van Dalsum	1960	Miss M. Weurman
1961	P. van Eysden	1961	Mrs J. Baars-Wienese
1962	W. Maris	1962	Mrs E. de Jong
1963	J. Hajer	1963	Mrs J. Ridderhof-Seven
1964	T. Okker	1964	Miss T. Groenman
1965	T. Okker	1965	Miss T. Groenman
1966	T. Okker	1966	Miss T. Groenman
1967	T. Okker	1967	Miss A. Suurbeek
1968	T. Okker	1968	Mrs M. Schaar-Jansen
1969	N. Fleury	1969	Mrs M. Schaar-Jansen
1970	F. Hemmes	1970	Miss B. Stöve
1971	F. Hemmes	1971	Mrs M. Schaar-Jansen
1972	J. Hordijk	1972	Miss B. Stöve
1973	J. Hordijk	1973	Mrs M. Schaar-Jansen

Newcombe, John D. (Australia)

Born Sydney, N.S.W., 23 May 1944; Wimbledon men's singles won 1967, r/u 1969, won 1970-1; men's doubles s/f 1961, won 1965-6, 1968-9; US men's singles r/u 1966, won 1967, q/f 1968, s/f 1970, won 1973; men's doubles s/f 1966, won 1967, r/u 1972, won 1973; mixed doubles won 1964; Australian men's singles q/f 1962-4, s/f 1965-7, q/f 1969-70, q/f 1972, won 1973; men's doubles s/f 1962, r/u 1963, s/f 1964, won 1965, r/u 1966, won 1967, s/f 1969, won 1971, 1973; mixed doubles s/f 1963, r/u 1965, s/f 1966; French men's singles q/f 1965, 1969; men's doubles r/u 1964, s/f 1965-6, won 1967, 1969, 1973; mixed doubles r/u 1965, s/f 1969. Davis Cup 1963-7. ILTF GP 7th 1970. WCT 6th (F q/f) 1971, 8th (F q/f) May 1972, 1st (F q/f) Nov. 1972. WCT contract pro 1968-72.

A power player without frills, he was given weighty responsibility at the age of 19 in defence of the Davis Cup for Australia in 1963. Beaten in both his singles, by RALSTON and then by MCKINLEY in the decisive fifth rubber, it was not until four years later that he fulfilled his early promise. Then he became the last 'amateur' to win Wimbledon, in 1967. His fate in 1972 was curious when as Wimbledon Open Champion for the two preceding years he was thwarted in his title defence by the rejection of his entry as one of the banned WORLD CHAMPIONSHIP TENNIS contract professionals. With Tony ROCHE he dominated men's doubles. See colour plate, page 291.

Above John Newcombe

New England Merchants National Bank of Boston

SEE THE POSTWAR PRO GAME (PART 1)

Newport, Monmouthshire (UK)

Newport has been the home of the Welsh Championships since 1897. They were first staged (1886-95) by the Roath (Cardiff) and Penarth Lawn Tennis Clubs (see WALES); the first winner was E. de S. H. Browne. After a break in 1896, the Newport Athletic Club offered to stage the Championships. At first Newport was perhaps a strange venue for tennis, for the Athletic Club had been founded

Welsh Championships Winners (Newport)

Men's Singles

Year	Winner	Year	Winner
1886	E. de S. H. Browne	1973	R. Taylor
1887	E. de S. H. Browne		
1888	W. J. Hamilton		
1889	W. J. Hamilton		
1890	W. J. Hamilton		
1891	H. S. Barlow		
1892	H. S. Barlow		
1893	G. C. Ball-Greene		
1894	G. C. Ball-Greene		
1895	W. V. Eaves		
1896	*No Competition*		
1897	S. H. Smith		
1898	S. H. Smith		
1899	S. H. Smith		
1900	S. H. Smith		
1901	S. H. Smith		
1902	S. H. Smith		
1903	J. M. Boucher		
1904	S. H. Smith		
1905	S. H. Smith		
1906	S. H. Smith		
1907	J. M. Boucher		
1908	J. M. Boucher		
1909	J. M. Boucher		
1910	C. P. Dixon		
1911	C. P. Dixon		
1912	H. A. Kitson		
1913	C. P. Dixon		
1914	C. P. Dixon		
1915-19	*No Competition*		
1920	P. Freeman		
1921	M. J. G. Ritchie		
1922	M. Alonso		
1923	J. M. Boucher		
1924	G. R. O. Crole-Rees		
1925	J. M. Hillyard		
1926	H. C. Fisher		
1927	D. H. Williams		
1928	E. C. Peters		
1929	C. H. Kingsley		
1930	D. H. Williams		
1931	J. Sato		
1932	I. Tłoczynski		
1933	N. G. Farquharson		
1934	D. Prenn		
1935	H. W. Artens		
1936	A. C. Stedman / C. Malfroy } divided		
1937	A. C. Stedman		
1938	G. L. Rogers		
1939	C. Tănăsescu		
1940-45	*No Competition*		
1946	C. Spychała		
1947	C. Spychała		
1948	C. Spychała / D. H. Slack } divided		
1949	F. Ampon		
1950	K. H. Ip / I. Tłoczynski } divided		
1951	J. W. Cawthorn		
1952	N. Kumar		
1953	W. R. Seymour		
1954	*Abandoned*		
1955	O. G. Williams		
1956	A. Huber		
1957	J. Drobný		
1958	R. Becker		
1959	R. K. Wilson		
1960	A. R. Mills		
1961	A. F. Rawstone		
1962	M. J. Sangster		
1963	W. F. Jacques		
1964	R. A. J. Hewitt		
1965	R. Emerson		
1966	R. A. J. Hewitt		
1967	J. D. Newcombe		
1968	W. W. Bowrey		
1969	M. Cox		
1970	K. Rosewall		
1971	K. Rosewall		
1972	A. Pattison		

Women's Singles

Year	Winner	Year	Winner
1887	Miss M. Watson	1973	Miss J. Heldman
1888	Mrs G. W. Hillyard		
1889	Miss C. Pope		
1890	*No Competition*		
1891	Miss C. Pope		
1892	Miss M. Sweet-Escott		
1893	Miss M. Cochrane		
1894	Miss P. Jackson		
1895	Miss N. Corder		
1896	*No Competition*		
1897	Miss H. Ridding		
1898	Miss A. E. Parr		
1899	Miss M. A. Robb		
1900	Miss C. Hill		
1901	Miss W. A. Longhurst		
1902	Miss W. A. Longhurst		
1903	Miss C. M. Wilson		
1904	Miss C. M. Wilson		
1905	Miss M. Sutton		
1906	Miss M. Sutton		
1907	Miss M. Sutton		
1908	Miss M. Garfit		
1909	Miss M. Garfit		
1910	Miss H. Aitchinson		
1911	Miss D. Boothby		
1912	Mrs H. Hannam		
1913	Mrs H. Hannam		
1914	Mrs H. Hannam		
1915-19	*No Competition*		
1920	Mrs H. Hannam		
1921	Mrs M. Leisk		
1922	Mrs H. Hannam		
1923	Miss L. K. C. Raikes		
1924	Miss E. Ryan		
1925	Mrs P. C. Satterthwaite		
1926	Mrs J. Seel		
1927	Mrs P. C. Satterthwaite		
1928	Miss E. F. Rose		
1929	Miss E. F. Rose		
1930	Miss E. Hemmant		
1931	Miss E. Hemmant		
1932	Miss J. Jedrzejowska		
1933	Miss R. M. Hardwick		
1934	Mrs H. K. Sperling		
1935	Miss J. Jedrzejowska		
1936	Miss J. Jedrzejowska		
1937	Mrs R. Mathieu		
1938	Mrs R. Mathieu		
1939	Mrs R. Mathieu		
1940-45	*No Competition*		
1946	Miss G. Hoahing		
1947	Miss J. Curry		
1948	Miss J. Curry		
1949	Miss G. E. Woodgate		
1950	Miss B. Scofield		
1951	Miss A. Mortimer		
1952	Miss B. Penrose		
1953	Mrs W. Brewer / Miss S. Kamo } divided		
1954	Miss J. W. Middleton		
1955	Mrs J. Weiss		
1956	Miss A. Haydon		
1957	Miss A. Mortimer		
1958	Miss A. Mortimer		
1959	Miss A. Mortimer		
1960	Miss A. Mortimer		
1961	Miss A. Haydon		
1962	Miss A. Haydon		
1963	Miss C. Rosser		
1964	Miss M. E. Bueno		
1965	Miss A. Van Zyl		
1966	Miss M. E. Bueno		
1967	Miss J. A. M. Tegart		
1968	Miss K. Pigeon		
1969	Mrs M. S. Court		
1970	Miss E. Goolagong		
1971	Miss V. Wade		
1972	Miss K. Melville		

(1875) to provide facilities for Rugby football and cricket. Athletics soon followed and, for an extra half a guinea, members could take part in tennis and archery. In 1890 an indoor court was made available – one of the earliest in Britain. Since then badminton, bowls, hockey, netball and table tennis have been added; in 1972 part of the 15½ acres was leased to a separately-organized squash club. Thus Newport is a sports complex unequalled among private clubs in Britain and, with its dozen courts (grass and hard), extensive hall, social centre and car parks, is ideal for a major tournament.

The Championships have always attracted a strong international entry and only two Welshmen have ever won: Peter Freeman (1920) and D. H. Williams (1927). In 1956 Mike Davies (Britain's no. 1 at the time and now an executive with WCT) was almost the third when he lost to the Austrian Alfred Huber. The younger Davies readily agreed to play a five-set match in the final. He won the first two sets

Newport Casino Men's Invitational Tournament
Singles' Winners

1915	R. N. Williams
1916	I. Kumagai
1917-18	*No Competition*
1919	W. T. Tilden
1920	C. J. Griffin
1921	W. Washburn
1922	W. M. Johnston
1923	H. O. Kinsey
1924	W. M. Johnston
1925	W. M. Johnston
1926	W. T. Tilden
1927	W. T. Tilden
1928	G. Lott
1929	W. T. Tilden
1930	W. T. Tilden
1931	E. Vines
1932	E. Vines
1933	F. X. Shields
1934	W. Allison
1935	D. Budge
1936	R. Riggs
1937	D. Budge
1938	D. Budge
1939	E. T. Cooke
1940	D. McNeill
1941	D. McNeill
1942	W. Talbert
1943-5	*No Competition*
1946	G. Mulloy
1947	F. R. Schroeder
1948	W. Talbert
1949	R. Gonzalez
1950	F. R. Schroeder
1951	F. Sedgman
1952	F. Sedgman
1953	A. Trabert
1954	H. Richardson
1955	H. Richardson
1956	K. Rosewall
1957	M. Anderson
1958	A. Cooper
1959	N. A. Fraser
1960	N. A. Fraser
1961	R. Emerson
1962	R. Laver
1963	R. Osuna
1964	R. Emerson
1965	M. Santana
1966	F. Stolle
1967	J. Newcombe

easily and was going well in the third when, to the crowd's consternation, Huber collapsed on court. After ten minutes the match was re-started and Davies, having lost his winning momentum, went down to defeat.

Sponsorship came to Newport in 1963, first from the local paper, the *South Wales Argus*, followed in turn by W. D. and H. O. WILLS, BP and, since 1970, GREEN SHIELD. One popular feature of the tournament is that all players stay in members' homes. Many well-known supporters of lawn tennis have been associated with the tournament through the years but special mention must be made of Mr George Bell, chairman of the LTA in 1964 and President of the Welsh LTA since 1954, who became associated with the tournament in 1919, first as secretary, then as chairman. His service of well over 50 years is believed to be a world record for any tournament official; in that time he has never missed watching a day's play. DC

Newport, Rhode Island (USA)
The Newport Invitation tournament (men's singles and doubles) was started in 1915 to fill the void when the National Championships (see US CHAMPIONSHIPS) were moved to the West Side Tennis Club, Forest Hills, N.Y., after having been held at the Newport Casino, Newport, Rhode Island, since the US Championships began in 1881.

All the form and externals of the former national title events were evident at the first Newport Invitation meeting and it was reported that 'there was a new and delightful spirit of friendliness and comradery engendered and fostered by the popular committee chief (Craig Biddle), always noticeable'.

There were 50 contenders in the first tournament, including practically all the leading stars of the country. In the final, Richard Norris Williams II then the national champion, defeated Maurice E. McLoughlin, US champion in 1913 and 1914, 5-7, 6-4, 6-3, 6-3. The doubles were won by Clarence J. Griffin and William M. Johnston, who later won the national doubles three times. They defeated Williams and Watson Washburn 6-3, 6-4, 3-6, 6-2.

The first foreign player to win at Newport was Ichiya Kumagai (Japan), who defeated Johnston in the 1916 singles final. Other Newport winners in the early years included William T. Tilden II, Griffin, who defeated his partner Johnston in the 1920 final, Johnston and Howard Kinsey.

The great Australasian team of Gerald L. Patterson and Norman E. Brookes was the first foreign pair to win the Newport Invitation doubles. In 1919 they beat Wallace F. Johnson and Vincent Richards and also won the national title. Other early winners were Griffin and Johnston, Williams and Washburn, and Howard and Robert Kinsey, who were national doubles champions in 1924.

William F. Talbert won Newport in 1942, the year before the suspension of the tourna-

ment during the war years. He won again in 1948. Only five other players have won the title more than once during the last 25 years. They are Ted Schroeder, Frank Sedgman, Hamilton Richardson, Don McNeill and Neale Fraser. Foreign winners, besides Sedgman and Anderson, include the Australians Ken Rosewall, Rod Laver, Roy Emerson, Fred Stolle, John Newcombe (Australia), Rafael Osuna (Mexico) and Manuel Santana (Spain). During this period many formidable doubles teams won at Newport, among them Jack Kramer/Schroeder, Talbert/Gardnar Mulloy, Vic Seixas/Tony Trabert, McKinley/Dennis Ralston, Sedgman/Ken McGregor, who also won Wimbledon, Roy Emerson/Fred Stolle and Owen Davidson/Bowrey, Michael Davies/Bob Wilson, Antonio and Gustavo Palafox (Mexico), Clark Graebner/Marty Riessen. Neale Fraser won the Newport doubles three times with different partners, Rex Hartwig, Rosewall and Ashley Cooper, all Australians.

In 1966 the Newport Invitation was called the Hall of Fame tournament as the Hall of Fame enshrinement ceremonies were held at the same time.

The last Newport Invitation amateur tournament was played in 1967. After that it became a professional tournament in which variations of the VASSS (Van Alen Streamlined Scoring System) were used. In 1972 the Newport Casino became a venue on the women's Virginia Slims professional circuit. FES

New Zealand
In recent years the development of ever-faster intercontinental air travel has brought New Zealand well within the orbit of the world's leading players, who are now able to visit the South Pacific during New Zealand's main tournament season, which usually runs from the middle of December to the middle of February.

The first club, the Parnell Lawn Tennis Club in Auckland, N.I., was founded in 1872 although it began as a croquet club and tennis followed a little later. Over the years about 800 clubs have been formed and they provide the basis of the game today. Many of the courts are grass, for the splendid locally-grown grasses of chewings, fescue and browntop provide fine close-cut surfaces upon which play is never more pleasant. The many asphalt or bitumen courts provide satisfactory conditions for many months of the year. However, recently a new type of porous concrete court has been engineered locally called Quik-dry: this provides a fine true playing area with good drainage and fast drying. It is predicted that this type of surface, though somewhat expensive, will grow in favour as it requires little maintenance.

The New Zealand Lawn Tennis Association

Colour plate John Newcombe, US Open champion in 1973 in singles and doubles (with Owen Davidson). He was the last 'amateur' to win Wimbledon (1967) and was champion again 1970-1.

was formed in 1886. From 1904 to 1922 it was affiliated to the Lawn Tennis Association of Australasia but affiliated separately to the ILTF in 1923. During this period Australasia won the DAVIS CUP in 1907-9, 1911 (when the Challenge Round was played in Christchurch), 1914 and 1919. A nine-member Management Committee is elected at the annual meeting of the Council which in turn is a body representing the 21 district associations.

New Zealand has taken part in the Davis Cup since 1924 as a separate nation, and over the past decade has sent a team overseas in most years. Not included in a specific zone, it enters the European, North American or Western zones according to the circumstances at the time. Its best performance was in 1973, when New Zealand, with Brian Fairlie and Onny Parun, beat Austria 3-2 and then Yugoslavia 3-2. The improvement in doubles play was responsible for success in both cases. In the zone semi-final versus Rumania the New Zealand players failed to reproduce earlier form and lost 1-4.

The big national event of the year is the BP National Senior Championships held on a three-year cycle at Auckland, Christchurch and Wellington: these attract all the leading players as well as many overseas competitors. Another annual highlight is the Benson & Hedges Open at Auckland which features many of the world's leading players, in a week of concentrated day and night competition. This tournament has won world renown and the prize money in 1972 rose to $18,000. Other events include district representative matches for men for the Wilding Shield and a similar contest for women for the Nunneley Casket. Junior Boys compete for the Slazenger Shield and girls for the Howe Shield.

Most local tournaments are held during the main season, from October to April for grass- and somewhat longer for hard-court clubs. These tournaments are made possible by dint of much effort and a great deal of enthusiasm. Over the years local associations have created some very fine headquarters which are scattered throughout the country. The home of the Auckland Association, long known as 'The Little Wimbledon of the South Pacific', nestles in a huge city park; a dozen grass courts are flanked by three modern stands and many other facilities. At Whangarei in the north the Northland Association has recently spent $120,000 on a superb headquarters with 12 Quik-dry courts. At Central Park in Wellington there are nearly 20 courts, both grass and porous concrete, in a treelined setting. In Christchurch the foresight of a group in the 1920s has ensured for all time a vast area accommodating some 35 grass, hard and porous concrete courts with the centre two surrounded by spacious stands. Many other

Colour plate Ilie Năstase, US Open champion and Wimbledon runner-up in 1972, French champion in 1973. He also topped the ILTF/Commercial Union Grand Prix in 1972.

New Zealand Championships Winners

Men's Singles		Women's Singles	
1886	P. C. Fenwicke	1886	Miss M. Lance
1887	P. C. Fenwicke	1887	Miss E. Harman
1888	P. C. Fenwicke	1888	Miss E. Gordon
1889	M. Fenwicke	1889	Miss E. Gordon
1890	J. M. Marshall	1890	Miss J. Rees
1891	R. D. Harman	1891	Miss N. Douslin
1892	M. Fenwicke	1892	Miss J. Rees
1893	M. Fenwicke	1893	Miss M. F. Speirs
1894	J. R. Hooper	1894	Miss K. Hitchings
1895	H. A. Parker	1895	Miss K. M. Nunneley
1896	J. M. Marshall	1896	Miss K. M. Nunneley
1897	J. R. Hooper	1897	Miss K. M. Nunneley
1898	C. C. Cox	1898	Miss K. M. Nunneley
1899	J. R. Hooper	1899	Miss K. M. Nunneley
1900	A. W. Dunlop	1900	Miss K. M. Nunneley
1901	J. C. Peacock	1901	Miss K. M. Nunneley
1902	H. A. Parker	1902	Miss K. M. Nunneley
1903	H. A. Parker	1903	Miss K. M. Nunneley
1904	H. A. Parker	1904	Miss K. M. Nunneley
1905	H. A. Parker	1905	Miss K. M. Nunneley
1906	A. F. Wilding	1906	Miss K. M. Nunneley
1907	H. A. Parker	1907	Miss K. M. Nunneley
1908	A. F. Wilding	1908	Miss L. Powdrell
1909	A. F. Wilding	1909	Miss L. Powdrell
1910	J. C. Peacock	1910	Miss E. Travers
1911	G. Ollivier	1911	Miss P. A. Stewart
1912	R. N. K. Swanston	1912	Miss A. Gray
1913	A. G. Wallace	1913	Miss A. Gray
1914	G. Ollivier	1914	Miss A. Gray
1915-18	*No Competition*	1915-18	*No Competition*
1919	G. Ollivier	1919	Mrs S. C. Hodges
1920	W. T. Tilden	1920	Miss N. Curtis
1921	J. T. Laurentson	1921	Miss N. Curtis
1922	G. Ollivier	1922	Miss S. Lance
1923	A. W. Sims	1923	Miss M. Speirs
1924	G. Ollivier	1924	Mrs W. J. Melody
1925	G. Ollivier	1925	Miss M. Speirs
1926	E. D. Andrews	1926	Miss A. Howe
1927	G. Ollivier	1927	Miss M. Speirs
1928	E. L. Bartleet	1928	Miss M. Macfarlane
1929	C. Angas	1929	Miss D. Nicholls
1930	A. C. Stedman	1930	Mrs H. M. Dykes
1931	C. Angas	1931	Miss J. Hartigan
1932	E. D. Andrews	1932	Miss D. Nicholls
1933	C. E. Malfroy	1933	Miss L. Bickerton
1934	F. J. Perry	1934	Miss D. Nicholls
1935	V. B. McGrath	1935	Miss D. Nicholls
1936	D. C. Coombe	1936	Miss D. Nicholls
1937	A. D. Brown	1937	Miss M. Beverley
1938	N. V. Edwards	1938	Miss M. Hardcastle
1939	J. E. Bromwich	1939	Miss N. Wynne
1940-45	*No Competition*	1940-45	*No Competition*
1946	R. S. McKenzie	1946	Miss M. Beverley
1947	R. S. McKenzie	1947	Miss M. Beverley
1948	R. S. McKenzie	1948	Miss E. G. Attwood
1949	J. E. Robson	1949	Mrs J. J. McVay
1950	G. A. Worthington	1950	Miss M. Beverley
1951	R. S. McKenzie	1951	Miss J. F. Burke
1952	J. E. Robson	1952	Miss J. MacGibbon
1953	G. A. Worthington	1953	Miss J. F. Burke
1954	J. A. Barry	1954	Miss J. F. Burke
1955	J. A. Barry	1955	Miss J. F. Burke
1956	J. E. Robson	1956	Miss S. Cox
1957	M. G. Davies	1957	Miss R. Morrison
1958	R. N. Howe	1958	Miss S. Cox
1959	R. N. Howe	1959	Miss R. Morrison
1960	L. A. Gerrard	1960	Miss R. Morrison
1961	L. A. Gerrard	1961	Miss R. Morrison
1962	L. A. Gerrard	1962	Miss J. Davidson
1963	L. A. Gerrard	1963	Miss R. Morrison
1964	L. A. Gerrard	1964	Miss R. H. Bentley
1965	B. Phillips-Moore	1965	Mrs R. Davy
1966	K. Fletcher	1966	Miss K. Melville
1967	M. Cox	1967	Miss B. Vercoe
1968	B. Fairlie	1968	Miss M. Pryde
1969	B. Fairlie	1969	Miss B. Vercoe
1970	O. Parun	1970	Miss M. Pryde
1971	C. Dibley	1971	Miss E. Goolagong
1972	O. Parun	1972	Miss M. Schallau
1973	S. Ball	1973	Miss E. Goolagong

centres too possess facilities of which local people are justly proud.

Coaching activity has increased in the past few years and some 25 full-time or part-time coaches affiliated to the New Zealand Lawn Tennis Professional Coaches Association are playing a notable part in fostering the game and playing standards. One result has been that New Zealand has become a recognized annual entrant in the Australian Linton and Wilson Cups for juniors, held in one or other of the state capitals each January. New Zealand staged these top-rating events for the first time in 1973 at Wilding Park in Christchurch, and the Government issued commemorative postage stamps with a tennis player in action.

A wide range of business houses interested in tennis are happy to associate their name and products with the tennis scene in one way and another. On the national side BP (NZ) Limited is the oldest sponsor. Its link has continued since 1954 and has progressed from involvement in junior affairs to sponsorship of the New Zealand Lawn Tennis Championships since 1963.

In the 1971-2 season it extended its sponsorship by introducing a BP Tennis Grand Prix of $1,000 competed for in six of the major tournaments, finishing in the BP National Championships.

The Rothmans Sports Foundation supports coaching and its generous grant at national level enables the New Zealand LTA to distribute a subsidy to all affiliated Associations. Rothmans also subsidizes a promising National Development squad of 12 or so junior boys who receive special coaching. A group of girls has just been added.

Qantas Limited, official air carriers for the New Zealand LTA, also lends its support. Spalding Limited is engaged in a three-year sponsorship that includes adoption of its ball.

Four of New Zealand's leading players have gained international status: the great Anthony Wilding, Wimbledon champion 1910-13, and, to a lesser degree, Lew Gerrard, who won the British Hard Court Championships in 1959, Brian Fairlie, who won the 1973 Rothmans International Tournament at the Albert Hall, and reached the quarter-finals of the US men's singles in 1970, and Onny Parun, who reached the Wimbledon quarter-finals 1971-2 and the 1973 US quarter-finals. Jeff Simpson is also on the world tournament circuit; other up-and-coming players are Tony Parun, Ross McGhie and Russell Simpson. Marilyn Pryde is New Zealand's leading woman player and, with Judith Connor, has represented New Zealand in the FEDERATION CUP (in which New Zealand has competed since 1965).

New Zealand is generally regarded as a sports-loving nation. Tennis-club membership has risen from some 36,000 in 1964 to well over 50,000 today, reflecting the growing domestic interest in the game. It has adopted the slogan 'Tennis – the sport for a lifetime'. JDV

GOVERNING BODY: New Zealand Lawn Tennis Association, 3rd floor, Huddart Parker Building, Post Office Square, Wellington

Above **New Zealand.** Anthony Wilding in 1907

Nigeria

The Nigeria Lawn Tennis Association was founded in 1927, affiliated to the ILTF as an Associate Member in 1964 and as a Full Member in 1972. There are over 200 associated clubs with several thousand players. A number of Nigerian coaches have been trained in Britain. The most important event is the All Nigerian Open Championships, played at Lagos since 1927. A special effort is being made to help juniors and Nigeria plays a great part in the All Africa Games. In 1972 a team of Nigerians competed in British tournaments; several players have toured abroad sponsored by industrial concerns. BR

GOVERNING BODY: Nigeria LTA, c/o National Sports Council of Nigeria, National Stadium, Surulere

Nordic Cup

This competition, first held in 1920 (won by Denmark), is confined to the four Scandinavian countries, Denmark, Finland, Norway and Sweden. It was originally held as a knockout tournament but since 1953 has been staged on a round-robin basis. Each match, staged between 1 May and 15 September, consists of four singles and one double but, unlike the DAVIS CUP, the double is always played last. JO

Northern Lawn Tennis Championships (UK)

One of the oldest tennis clubs, the Northern Club, now in Didsbury, Manchester, began in the late 1870s. Records begin in 1881 when the club was at Old Trafford, but before then there was a Northern Lawn Tennis Association, and a tournament was first played under its banner on the Broughton Cricket Club ground in July 1880. At an entrance fee of one guinea it attracted 30 competitors to the men's singles, won by R. T. Richardson. A history of the club (published in 1936) describes the tournament as 'successful, though not pecuniarily, for we had little money, and had to obtain guarantees from a number of supporters to the amount of £5 each. The guarantors were called upon to pay nearly the full amount of their guarantees. The game was in its infancy, and there were not enough interested in the neighbourhood to make a big gallery.' Another cricket ground, at Kersal, was home for the tournament in 1881 and it moved to Liverpool in 1882.

The Northern Club as such took control of the tournament in 1884 but the event alternated between Manchester and Liverpool until the late 1920s, after the Club had left Old Trafford. Soon after the turn of the century, the Old Trafford district, once beautifully wooded parkland, was showing the first signs of becoming the vast industrial area that it is today, as traffic on the Manchester Ship Canal increased. By 1909 membership of the Club had fallen away alarmingly: 'Perhaps the most serious consequences of the changes which were taking place, was the ever increasing dirt. During the later years at Old Trafford, new balls became black after only a few games, and a collision with the stop-netting caused a well defined pattern of it to appear on one's clean flannels.' That same year the Club moved to Didsbury, which gradually became one of the finest playing arenas in Britain. Future development will leave it with 17 grass courts, three hard, three all-weather, one covered, six squash and a croquet lawn.

The honours board shows the strength of the tournament which, for some 40 years up to 1970, gave it its nickname of 'Wimbledon of the North'. Since then the event has declined in importance.

Below **Northern Lawn Tennis Championships.** Mrs A. Sterry *(left)* in Manchester in 1907.

The Club has always been public spirited in the development of the game: one of its officials, Captain J. C. Hobbs, presided at a meeting in London in 1888 which led to the formation of the Lawn Tennis Association. DC

Norton, B.I.C. (S. Africa)
Born Cape Province, 10 Oct. 1899; died 1957. Wimbledon men's singles r/u 1921, s/f 1923; US men's singles s/f 1923; men's doubles won 1923. His 1921 challenge to TILDEN has remained one of the most discussed matches in the history of the game (see SOUTH AFRICA).

Norway
Lawn tennis was first played at the Christiania (now Oslo) Football Club in 1881, where there was a grass court. Real progress was made when the Christiania Lawn Tennis Club (now the Oslo Tennis Club) was built in 1900 with five hard courts. It now has 12. The Norges Tennisforbund was founded in 1909 with five clubs and affiliated to the ILTF in 1931. By 1971 there were 94 clubs with 7,333 players. One of the clubs, Hammerfest Tennisklubb, is the northernmost in the world. In Oslo there are eight permanent covered courts and a number of 'air halls' (outdoor courts protected by inflated plastic covers).

The first Norwegian Championships were held in 1910. Norway's outstanding player was Miss Molla Bjurstedt, who won the Bronze Medal in the Olympic Games in Stockholm in 1912. In 1915 she won the first of 22 US titles; as Mrs Mallory she reached the final at Wimbledon in 1922, losing to Mlle Lenglen. Outstanding among the men was Johan Haanes, champion for 20 years until 1953.

Norway has played in the DAVIS CUP frequently since 1928, and has also competed in the FEDERATION CUP since 1963 and in the SCANDINAVIAN CHAMPIONSHIPS. In the KING'S CUP Norway has reached the final once (1937) and the semi-finals three times. BR
GOVERNING BODY: Norges Tennisforbund, Kirkegt. 8, Oslo 1

Nunneley Casket see NEW ZEALAND

Nuthall, Miss Betty [Mrs F. C. Shoemaker] (Gt Britain)
Born Surbiton, Surrey, 23 May 1911; Wimbledon women's singles q/f 1927, 1930-2; women's doubles s/f 1927, 1929, 1931, 1939; mixed doubles s/f 1931, 1933, 1939; US women's singles r/u 1927, q/f 1929, won 1930, s/f 1931, 1933; women's doubles r/u 1927, s/f 1929, won 1930-1, 1933, s/f 1934; mixed doubles won 1929, s/f 1930, won 1931, s/f 1934; French women's singles r/u 1931, s/f 1932-3; women's doubles s/f 1928, won 1931, r/u 1932; mixed doubles won 1931-2, r/u 1933, s/f 1934. Wightman Cup 1927-9, 1931-4, 1939. The British 'pin-up' girl between the world wars and the first overseas player (1930) to win the US women's singles title.

O

Odds see HANDICAPPING

O'Hara Wood, A. and P. see WOOD, O'Hara

Okker, Tom S. (Netherlands)
Born Amsterdam, 22 Feb. 1944; Wimbledon men's singles q/f 1968-9; men's doubles r/u 1969; mixed doubles s/f 1964; US men's singles r/u 1968, s/f 1971; Australian men's singles q/f 1970, s/f 1971; men's doubles r/u 1971, s/f 1973; French men's singles q/f 1967, s/f 1969; men's doubles s/f 1967, 1969, won 1973; mixed doubles s/f 1969. Davis Cup 1964- . WCT contract pro 1968-72. WCT 2nd (F s/f) 1971, 3rd (F q/f) May 1972, 3rd (F s/f) Nov. 1972.

Above Tom Okker

Olmedo, Alejandro [Alex] (USA)
Born Arequipa, Peru, 24 March 1936; Wimbledon men's singles won 1959; US men's singles q/f 1958, r/u 1959; men's doubles won 1958, r/u 1959; mixed doubles r/u 1958; Australian men's singles won 1959; men's doubles s/f 1959. Davis Cup 1958-9. The first Peruvian-born player to reach top rank. Became pro

1959, making an impressive début; one of the few to beat GONZALEZ.

Olympic Games
Lawn tennis was an Olympic sport seven times between 1896 and 1924, at Athens (1896), Paris (1900), St Louis (1904), London (1908), Stockholm (1912), Antwerp (1920) and Paris (1924).

By 1924, perhaps not unexpectedly, a serious dispute existed between the International Olympic Committee and the ILTF over the definition of amateurism (see OPEN TENNIS, PART 1) and lawn tennis ceased to be an Olympic sport although it was played as a demonstration sport at the 1968 Games in Mexico. But even when it was included, it never reached the high standard of other sports. Mr J. P. Boland, who won the men's gold medal in Athens in 1896, does not seem to have been successful in any other lawn-tennis event, and although subsequent winners were better known within the game, the Olympic competition never gained the interest of the sport's major tournaments. In 1908 Wimbledon staged an Olympic tournament on grass but it was an anti-climax after the Championships. At the Queen's Club, the Olympic covered-court event attracted only 11 competitors for the men's singles (three of whom scratched) and nine for the women's singles (two of whom withdrew).

Below Alex Olmedo

The highlight year for Olympic tennis appears to have been 1912. A. Wallis Myers wrote in *Twenty Years of Lawn Tennis* (1921) that no lawn-tennis matches in Sweden ever attracted so much attention as the Olympic competition: 'The Royal Family were daily spectators, the galleries and the columns of the newspapers were filled to overflowing. I cannot recall any contests on which native votaries, from the King downwards, concentrated so much interest or displayed such a feverish anxiety to see every ball served.' New Zealand's Tony Wilding, reigning Wimbledon Champion, was beaten in the semi-finals so his expected clash for the gold medal with the Frenchman André Gobert did not materialize. Gobert eventually won the tournament; the women's gold went to Mrs F. J. Hannam (Great Britain). Wallis Myers also describes an Olympic match at Antwerp (1920) between Gordon Lowe (Great Britain) and A. J. Zerlendi (Greece) which was played in three sections and divided by a night. The withdrawal of ballboys for a self-appointed lunch interval also helped to stretch the match to five and threequarter hours – an Olympic record – before Lowe won. This was the year, too, when spectators had the unusual experience of seeing Mlle Lenglen on the losing side – in the semi-final of the women's doubles in which the renowned Frenchwoman and Mlle D'Ayen opposed Mrs McNair and Miss K. McKane, who narrowly won after Mlle Lenglen, supporting a weaker partner, had made a desperate attempt to turn the tide. She was invincible in the singles, however, and also won the gold in the mixed doubles. But the years of American domination were approaching and it was no surprise when they swept the board at the Colombes Stadium in Paris (1924), including a gold medal for the brilliant Helen Wills who went on to win Wimbledon eight times between 1927 and 1938.

Over the years there have been forlorn attempts to bring back lawn tennis to the Olympic calendar. At the ILTF's Annual General Meeting in 1972 it was agreed that the International Olympic Committee's ruling on eligibility be formally recognized and that other amendments be made to ILTF rules on amateurism. See PLAYING STATUS; also OPEN TENNIS (PART 1). DC

Open

Term used since the early days of lawn tennis to indicate a tournament open to all comers of any nationality as opposed to 'closed' tournaments for nationals of the country concerned. Since 1968 'open' has taken on a new meaning to describe a tournament open to all categories of player (see PLAYING STATUS).

'Open' grip see GRIPS

Orange Bowl Championships

An international individual competition for under-18 boys and girls, held annually in Dec-

ember at Miami Beach, Fla., USA. The first winners (1947) were Lew McMasters and Joan Johnson.

Orange Lawn Tennis Club

see THE UNITED STATES STORY (PART 1)

Orantes, Manuel (Spain)

Born Granada, 6 Feb. 1949; Wimbledon men's singles s/f 1972; US men's singles q/f 1971; men's doubles s/f 1972; Australian men's singles q/f 1968; men's doubles s/f 1968; French men's singles s/f 1972; Orange Bowl won 1966 (first unseeded player to win in 17 years); Wimbledon Junior Invitation won 1967; Italian men's singles won 1972. ILTF GP 3rd 1972. Davis Cup 1967- . Left-handed.

Order of Play

An essential part of the tournament REFEREE's duties is to produce the daily order of play, which sets out, subject to bad weather, etc., the program of matches. Generally the day's 'order' is produced before close of play on the previous evening, so that players know roughly when they are expected at the ground, printers can bring programs up to date, and press, public and officials know when star players may be seen in action. DC

Order of Service

This is decided by TOSS and, in singles, remains constant throughout the match. In DOUBLES a pair may decide to change its order of service at the end of each set. See also RULES 5, 14, 33 (PART 1). JO

Osborne, Miss Margaret

see Mrs M. E. DUPONT

Osorio Cup see SOUTH AMERICAN CHAMPIONSHIPS

Osuna, Rafael H. (Mexico)

Born Mexico City, 15 Sept. 1938; Wimbledon men's singles q/f 1962, 1964-5; men's doubles won 1960, 1963, s/f 1964; US men's singles s/f 1961-2, won 1963, s/f 1964-5; men's doubles s/f 1960, r/u 1961, won 1962, r/u 1963; French men's doubles s/f 1965. Davis Cup 1958-68. The greatest Mexican player of all time, mercurially fleet of foot and a fine volleyer, he was killed in an aircrash near Monterrey, Mex. in June 1969.

Outerbridge, Mary Ewing

see THE BIRTH AND SPREAD OF LAWN TENNIS, THE UNITED STATES STORY (PART 1)

Out of Play (Dead)

A ball is said to be out of play or dead from the instant that a point is determined until the start of the next point.

Overarm Service see SERVICE

Overspin see SPIN

P

Pacific Coast Championships (USA)

The Pacific Coast Championships, men's singles and doubles, began in 1889. Until 1908 they were played at Del Monte in Northern California. From 1909 there were two Pacific Coast Sectional Championships in men's doubles, one played in Southern California and the other in Northern California. Since 1962 the Pacific Coast International Championships, men's doubles, have also carried the Northern California Sectional title.

The California Tennis Club in San Francisco was the scene of the tournament during its early years. From 1951 to 1971 it was held at the Berkeley (Calif.) Tennis Club. It was called the Pacific Coast International Championships since 1962 and from 1969 was held as an open championship.

Having directed the Pacific Coast International Championships since their beginning, in 1970 the Northern California Tennis Association contracted with an independent promoter, Barry MacKay, who together with the Redwood Bank put together what up to that time was the most successful Pacific Coast International tournament. The same sponsorship was in effect in 1971 when arrangements were made for the tournament to become part of both the ILTF and WCT Grand Prix circuits. Women's events in the PCI Open were dropped in 1971 when the WT women's professional circuit started, although an informal women's singles and doubles tournament was held in conjunction with the Open Championships. In 1972, the PCI, both men's and women's events, was moved to Albany, Calif. In 1973, under new commercial sponsorship, its name was dropped altogether, and a substitute event, the Fireman's Fund International Championships, were held in its place at Alamo, Calif.

Since the start of the Pacific Coast Championships many great players who were or became national grass-court champions have captured the Pacific Coast title. These include Maurice McLoughlin, Bill Johnston, who won the Pacific title ten times, Ellsworth Vines, Fred Perry, Donald Budge, Bob Riggs, Jack Kramer, Ted Schroeder, Art Larsen, Tony Trabert, Ashley Cooper, Rafael Osuna, Manuel Santana, Fred Stolle, Stan Smith, Arthur Ashe and Rod Laver. Women who captured the Pacific and also the National Grass Court Championships (since 1943) include Louise Brough, Margaret Osborne duPont, Pauline

Betz, Shirley Fry, Maureen Connolly, Althea Gibson, Darlene Hard, Maria Bueno and Margaret Court.

In the early days the men's doubles were dominated by the Hardy brothers, Sumner and Samuel, who won the Pacific doubles six times. Also winning six times were Clarence Griffin and Bill Johnston who were national doubles champions, too. Teams capturing both titles were Howard and Robert Kinsey, Wilmer Allison/John Van Ryn, Budge/Gene Mako, Kramer/Schroeder, Vic Seixas/Trabert, Osuna/Antonio Palafox and Bob Lutz/Stan Smith.

Women's Pacific Coast doubles champions who also won the grass-court championship include Brough/Osborne, Hard/Bueno, Rosemary Casals/Billie Jean King and Bueno/Margaret Court. FES

Pacific Southwest Championships (USA)

The Pacific Southwest Tennis Championships were started in 1927 by the Tennis Patrons' Association of Southern California. At the beginning the Patrons intended to conduct an annual tennis tournament, enlisting many national and international tennis players with the idea of making this an outstanding social and sporting event in Southern California. That this purpose was carried out most successfully is confirmed by a review of the famous players who competed in and won this tournament during the 45 years it has been held on the cement courts of the Los Angeles Tennis Club. Perry T. Jones, President of the Southern California Tennis Association from 1954 to his death on the eve of the 1970 tournament, was its efficient director for 38 years.

The championship got off to an auspicious start in 1927 with William T. Tilden II doing the 'hat trick' by winning the men's singles, the doubles with Francis T. Hunter and the mixed doubles with Molla B. Mallory.

Two players have won the men's singles four times, Frank Parker (1941-2, 1944-5) and Roy Emerson of Australia (1959, 1962, 1964 and 1967). Three-time champions were Fred Perry (1932-4), Donald Budge (1935-7), Jack Kramer (1943, 1946-7), Vic Seixas (1952, 1954, 1957) and Pancho Gonzalez, who after having won the title in 1949 did so again 20 years later as he regained the championship in 1969 and won for a third time in 1971.

Other foreign players in addition to Perry and Emerson to win the men's singles were Henri Cochet of France (1928) and the Australians Adrian Quist (1938), John Bromwich (1939), Ken Rosewall (1953), and Rod Laver (1968, 1970).

The Pacific Southwest doubles were won four times by Jack Kramer, twice with Ted Schroeder (1941, 1947), once with Charles Olewine (1942), and once with Parker (1943). Besides winning with Kramer, Parker won doubles titles with five other partners: Donald McNeill (1940), Robert Kimbell (1944), Pancho

Pacific Coast Championships Winners

Men's Singles

Year	Winner	Year	Winner
1889	W. H. Taylor	1970	A. R. Ashe
1890	W. H. Taylor	1971	R. Laver
1891	W. H. Taylor	1972	J. S. Connors
1892	W. H. Taylor	1973	*No Competition*
1893	T. A. Driscoll		
1894	Samuel Hardy		
1895	Samuel Hardy		
1896	Samuel Hardy		
1897	G. F. Whitney		
1898	Sumner Hardy		
1899	G. F. Whitney		
1900	G. F. Whitney		
1901	G. F. Whitney		
1902	L. R. Freeman		
1903	A. E. Bell		
1904	J. D. McGavin		
1905	G. J. Janes		
1906	M. H. Long		
1907	M. E. McLoughlin		
1908	M. H. Long		
1909	G. J. Janes		
1910	M. H. Long		
1911	M. E. McLoughlin		
1912	M. E. McLoughlin		
1913	W. Johnston		
1914	W. Johnston		
1915	H. L. Hahn		
1916	W. Johnston		
1917	W. Johnston		
1918	R. Roberts		
1919	W. Johnston		
1920	W. E. Davis		
1921	W. Johnston		
1922	W. Johnston		
1923	H. Kinsey		
1924	H. Kinsey		
1925	W. Johnston		
1926	W. Johnston		
1927	W. Johnston		
1928	C. Holman		
1929	R. Seller		
1930	G. M. Lott		
1931	H. E. Vines		
1932	F. J. Perry		
1933	K. Gledhill		
1934	F. J. Perry		
1935	J. D. Budge		
1936	J. D. Budge		
1937	J. D. Budge		
1938	H. C. Hopman		
1939	R. L. Riggs		
1940	R. L. Riggs		
1941	F. L. Kovacs		
1942	T. P. Brown		
1943	J. U. Jossi		
1944	E. Amark		
1945	T. P. Brown		
1946	J. A. Kramer		
1947	J. A. Kramer		
1948	F. R. Schroeder		
1949	F. R. Schroeder		
1950	A. D. Larsen		
1951	F. R. Schroeder		
1952	R. Savitt		
1953	T. Trabert		
1954	T. Trabert		
1955	T. Trabert		
1956	A. J. Cooper		
1957	S. Davidson		
1958	B. Patty		
1959	B. MacKay		
1960	B. MacKay		
1961	A. Palafox		
1962	J. E. Lundqvist		
1963	R. Osuna		
1964	M. Santana		
1965	M. Riessen		
1966	F. E. Stolle		
1967	C. Pasarell		
1968	S. R. Smith		
1969	S. R. Smith		

Women's Singles

Year	Winner	Year	Winner
1890	Miss Wilkinson	1970	Miss N. Richey
1891	Miss B. Crouch	1971	Miss M. Louie
1892	Miss Morgan	1972-3	*No Competition*
1893	Miss B. Crouch		
1894	Miss Hooper		
1895			
1896			
1897			
1898	Miss M. Jones		
1899	Miss V. Sutton		
1900	Miss M. Hall		
1901	Miss M. Sutton		
1902	Miss M. Sutton		
1903	Miss M. Sutton		
1904	Miss M. Sutton		
1905	Miss M. Sutton		
1906	Miss H. Hotchkiss		
1907	Miss F. Sutton		
1908	Miss M. Sutton		
1909	Miss F. Sutton		
1910	Miss M. Sutton		
1911	Miss M. Sutton		
1912	Miss F. Sutton		
1913	Miss S. Van Vliet		
1914	Mrs H. A. Niemeyer		
1915	Mrs H. H. Wightman		
1916	Miss H. Baker		
1917	Mrs H. H. Wightman		
1918	Miss A. Myers		
1919	Miss H. Baker		
1920	Miss H. Baker		
1921	Miss H. Baker		
1922	Miss H. N. Wills		
1923	Miss H. N. Wills		
1924	Miss C. Hosmer		
1925	Miss H. N. Wills		
1926	Miss H. H. Jacobs		
1927	Miss H. H. Jacobs		
1928	Miss E. Cross		
1929	Miss E. Burkhardt		
1930	Mrs H. W. Moody		
1931	Miss E. Cross		
1932	Miss A. Marble		
1933	Miss A. Marble		
1934	Miss K. Stammers		
1935	Miss E. Burkhardt		
1936	Miss M. Osborne		
1937	Miss A. Lizana		
1938	Mrs R. Mathieu		
1939	Mrs S. P. Fabyan		
1940	Miss V. Wolfenden		
1941	Miss M. E. Osborne		
1942	Miss M. E. Osborne		
1943	Miss A. L. Brough		
1944	Miss M. E. Osborne		
1945	Miss P. Betz		
1946	*No Competition*		
1947	Miss M. E. Osborne		
1948	Miss G. Moran		
1949	Miss D. Hart		
1950	Mrs P. C. Todd		
1951	Miss D. Head		
1952	Miss S. J. Fry		
1953	Miss M. Connolly		
1954	Miss V. W. Kovacs		
1955	Miss A. Mortimer		
1956	Miss S. Bloomer		
1957	Miss A. Gibson		
1958	Miss C. C. Truman		
1959	Mrs D. H. Knode		
1960	Miss D. R. Hard		
1961	Miss D. R. Hard		
1962	Miss D. R. Hard		
1963	Miss D. R. Hard		
1964	Miss J. A. M. Tegart		
1965	Miss J. A. M. Tegart		
1966	Miss M. Bueno		
1967	Miss F. Durr		
1968	Mrs B. M. Court		
1969	Mrs B. M. Court		

Segura (1945), Schroeder (1948) and Gonzalez (1949). Schroeder shared in two more doubles titles, one with Tony Trabert (1950), the other partnered by Budge Patty (1951).

The Australian 'whiz kids' Lew Hoad and Ken Rosewall captured the doubles three times (1953-4, 1956). Hoad also won with fellow Australian Rex Hartwig (1955). Another Australian, Roy Emerson, took the doubles five times, twice with two other Australians, Laver (1961-2) and Fred Stolle (1964-5) and once with Bob Hewitt, born in Sydney (N.S.W.) but representing South Africa since 1964 (1967).

Kea Bouman of Holland won the first Pacific Southwest women's singles in 1927. Only four other foreign players have ever won the singles. Three were from Britain: Betty Nuthall (1929), Dorothy Round (1933), Ann Haydon (1960). The other was from Brazil, Maria Bueno (1964, 1966). Altogether 27 players have won the women's singles of this important US tournament.

Beverly Baker Fleitz won the singles four times (1947, 1955, 1958-9). Of the winners 11 had been or became US national singles champions: Betty Nuthall, Alice Marble, Sarah Palfrey Cooke, Pauline Betz, Louise Brough, Maureen Connolly, Shirley Fry, Althea Gibson, Maria Bueno, Darlene Hard and Billie Jean King.

An unusual final occurred in the 1970 women's singles championship when there was a double default at 6-6, the second point of the tie-breaker for Rosemary Casals v. Mrs King. Both contestants walked off the court when the referee, Jack Kramer, refused their request to remove a lineswoman.

The Pacific Southwest women's doubles championship was won six times by Margaret Osborne and Louise Brough. Miss Brough also teamed with Midge Gladman Van Ryn for the seventh time. The doubles was won three times by all-foreign teams including Mrs B. C. Covell and Mrs Dorothy Shepherd-Barron, British Wightman Cup players (1929);

Mme Simone Mathieu of France and Margot Lumb of Britain (1938); and Françoise Durr of France and Ann Haydon Jones, Britain (1968).

Other foreign stars who teamed with US players to capture the Pacific Southwest women's doubles were Thelma Long, of Australia, who won with Shirley Fry (1952); Nell Hopman, of Australia, with Maureen Connolly (1953); Maria Bueno, Brazil, with Darlene Hard (1958, 1960, 1963), Ann Haydon with Miss Hard (1961) and Judy Tegart of Australia, with Carole Caldwell (1962). FES

Padder Tennis

Formulated in England in the late 1940s, but following closely a form of shipboard tennis played long before, padder tennis is a hybrid of table tennis and lawn tennis, played with a conventional tennis ball and wooden bats 15 in (38.1 cm) and 8 in (20.3 cm) wide. The dimensions of the court are exactly half those of a lawn tennis court, i.e. 39 x 18 ft (11.89 x 5.49 m) and there are no 'tramlines'. The net is 2 ft 6 in (0.76 m) high at the posts and 2 ft 3 in (0.69 m) at the centre. The rules are basically the same as those for lawn tennis.

Because it occupies only one quarter of the ground area of a lawn tennis court it can be played indoors or out of doors with inexpensive equipment and is a popular game with schools. It makes an excellent introduction to lawn tennis. For similar derivatives see Paddle Tennis (CZECHOSLOVAKIA) and also PLATFORM TENNIS. JB

Paddle Tennis see CZECHOSLOVAKIA

Pails, Dennis Robert ['Dinny'] (Australia)
Born Nottingham, England, 4 Nov. 1921; Wimbledon men's singles q/f 1946, s/f 1947;

Below Dinny Pails

Pacific Southwest Championships Winners

Men's Singles		Women's Singles	
1927	W. T. Tilden	1927	Miss K. Bouman
1928	H. Cochet	1928	Mrs M. S. Bundy
1929	J. H. Doeg	1929	Miss B. Nuthall
1930	H. E. Vines	1930	Miss E. Burkhardt
1931	H. E. Vines	1931	Mrs A. M. Harper
1932	F. J. Perry	1932	Mrs A. M. Harper
1933	F. J. Perry	1933	Miss D. Round
1934	F. J. Perry	1934	Mrs E. B. Arnold
1935	J. D. Budge	1935	Mrs E. B. Arnold
1936	J. D. Budge	1936	Miss G. Wheeler
1937	J. D. Budge	1937	Miss A. Marble
1938	A. Quist	1938	Miss D. M. Bundy
1939	J. E. Bromwich	1939	Miss A. Marble
1940	R. L. Riggs	1940	Miss D. M. Bundy
1941	F. A. Parker	1941	Mrs S. P. Cooke
1942	F. A. Parker	1942	Miss P. M. Betz
1943	J. A. Kramer	1943	Miss A. L. Brough
1944	F. A. Parker	1944	Miss P. M. Betz
1945	F. A. Parker	1945	Miss M. E. Osborne
1946	J. A. Kramer	1946	Miss P. M. Betz
1947	J. A. Kramer	1947	Miss B. J. Baker
1948	F. R. Schroeder	1948	Miss A. L. Brough
1949	R. A. Gonzalez	1949	Mrs H. P. Perez
1950	F. A. Sedgman	1950	Mrs H. P. Perez
1951	F. A. Sedgman	1951	Miss M. C. Connolly
1952	E. V. Seixas	1952	Miss M. C. Connolly
1953	K. R. Rosewall	1953	Miss D. Hart
1954	E. V. Seixas	1954	Miss A. L. Brough
1955	T. Trabert	1955	Mrs B. B. Fleitz
1956	H. Flam	1956	Miss A. Gibson
1957	E. V. Seixas	1957	Miss A. Gibson
1958	H. F. Richardson	1958	Mrs B. B. Fleitz
1959	R. S. Emerson	1959	Mrs B. B. Fleitz
1960	B. B. MacKay	1960	Miss A. S. Haydon
1961	J. A. Douglas	1961	Miss D. R. Hard
1962	R. S. Emerson	1962	Miss C. A. Caldwell
1963	A. Ashe	1963	Miss D. R. Hard
1964	R. S. Emerson	1964	Miss M. E. Bueno
1965	R. D. Ralston	1965	Mrs C. C. Graebner
1966	A. E. Fox	1966	Miss M. E. Bueno
1967	R. S. Emerson	1967	Mrs L. W. King
1968	R. G. Laver	1968	Miss R. Casals
1969	R. A. Gonzalez	1969	Mrs L. W. King
1970	R. G. Laver	1970	Miss S. Walsh
1971	R. A. Gonzalez	1971	*No winner* (King/Casals default)
1972	S. R. Smith	1972	Miss M. A. Redondo
1973	J. S. Connors	1973	Miss K. May

men's doubles r/u 1946, s/f 1947; Australian men's singles r/u 1946, won 1947. Davis Cup 1946-7. Distinguished as the number one men's singles seed for Wimbledon in 1946; his nerve failed after losing his way on the tube and keeping Queen Mary and the Centre Court crowd waiting for 20 minutes. Became pro 1947.

Pakistan

The All Pakistan Lawn Tennis Association was founded in 1947, the year when Pakistan came into being, and affiliated to the ILTF in 1949. Today there are about 100 associated clubs with over 1,000 players. The most important Championships staged by this Association are the National Tennis Championships held in Lahore since 1949. The other major championships, in addition to the Divisional Championships organized by this Association, are the KMC Championships, Karachi, the National Hard Court Championships, Karachi, and the M.A. Rahim Memorial Tennis Championships, Lahore.

The All Pakistan LTA has also started coaching schemes for promising players.

Pakistan has competed in the DAVIS CUP since 1948. Because of political troubles the Pakistani team has had some difficulty in recent years in doing so but it is confident that the game will develop. Its most famous tennis players have been Khawaja Iftikhar Ahmad, Haroon Rahim, Munir Pirzada and Munawar Iqbal. The leading player at present is Haroon Rahim, US Amateur Champion (1970), who has beaten many leading international players. He has also done well in doubles. BR
GOVERNING BODY: All Pakistan LTA, 428 Alfalah Building, Shahrah-E-Qaid-I-Azam, Lahore

Palafox, Antonio (Mexico)

Born Guadalaja, 28 April 1936; Wimbledon men's doubles won 1963, s/f 1964; US men's singles q/f 1965; men's doubles r/u 1961, won 1962, r/u 1963; mixed doubles r/u 1960; French men's doubles s/f 1960; mixed doubles s/f 1960. Davis Cup 1959-65. Turned professional 1966.

Palfrey, Miss Sarah [Mrs Fabyan, Mrs E. T. Cooke, Mrs J. Danzig] (USA)

Born Sharon, Mass. 18 Sept. 1912; Wimbledon women's singles q/f 1934, 1938, s/f 1939; women's doubles r/u 1930, 1936, won 1938-9; mixed doubles r/u 1936, 1938, s/f 1939; US women's singles q/f 1933, r/u 1934-5, s/f 1938, q/f 1939, won 1941, 1945; women's doubles won 1930, 1932, s/f 1933, won 1934-5, r/u 1936, won 1937-41, s/f 1945; mixed doubles won 1932, r/u 1933, won 1935, r/u 1936, won 1937, 1941; French women's doubles r/u 1934; mixed doubles won 1939. Wightman Cup 1930-9. A gifted volleyer and outstanding doubles player, she ranked US no. 4 in 1929, no. 1 in 1945. She renounced her amateur status in 1946.

Panamá

The Asociación de Tenis de Panamá was founded in 1964 and affiliated to the ILTF as an Associate Member in 1972 when it reported 7 affiliated clubs and about 800 players. BR
GOVERNING BODY: Asociación de Tenis de Panamá, Apartado 313, Zona 9-A, Republic of Panamá

Pan-American Games (Pan-American Championships)

Tennis was included in the Pan-American Games in Buenos Aires (1951), Mexico City (1955), Chicago (1959), São Paulo (1963) and Winnipeg (1967). It was then excluded. In these five Games, Mexico was the most successful country and Mexicans Gustavo Palafox and Yola Ramírez the outstanding players. Of the 26 medals amassed by Mexicans (10 gold, 10 silver and six bronze) Palafox won five gold and two bronze (1951, 1955, 1959) and Miss Ramírez won four gold, two silver and one bronze (1955, 1959, 1963). Their gold medals were all in doubles. Argentinians Maria Weiss and Enrique Morea gave the top performances in a single Games (1951), each winning the singles and doubles. Morea won a silver as well for second in the mixed doubles with Felisa Zappa, and Mrs Weiss a bronze for her third with Alejo Russell. Tomas Koch of Brazil (1967), Ronnie Barnes of Brazil (1963) and Rosie Reyes of Mexico (1959) also won both singles and doubles in one year.

Following Mexico in total medals were: the United States, which did not compete in 1951, 17 medals (five gold, three silver, nine bronze); Argentina 13 (four gold, seven silver, two bronze); Brazil 11 (five gold, two silver and four bronze); Chile three (one gold, one silver and one bronze); Ecuador three (one silver and two bronze); Canada two (one silver and one bronze). BC

Panatta, Adriano (Italy)

Born Rome, 9 July 1950; Italian National won 1970-2; French men's singles q/f 1972, s/f 1973; British Hard Court singles won 1973, beating Ilie NĂSTASE in the final. Davis Cup 1971- .

Paraguay

Paraguay was first affiliated to the ILTF as a Full Member in 1928, was expelled in 1949 and was later readmitted as an Associate Member. It first competed in the DAVIS CUP competition in 1931. BR
GOVERNING BODY: Asociación Paraguaya de Lawn Tennis, Casilla Correo 26, Asunción

Parke, James Cecil (Ireland)

Born Clones, Ireland, 26 July 1881, died 1942; Wimbledon men's singles s/f 1910, 1913, q/f 1914; men's doubles s/f 1910, r/u* 1911-13, 1920; mixed doubles r/u 1913, won 1914; Australian men's singles won 1912; men's doubles won 1912. Davis Cup (British Isles) 1908-9, 1912-14, 1920. His Davis Cup career

spanned World War I. A notable all-round games player, he played Rugby for Ireland.

Parker, E. F. (Australia)

Australian men's singles r/u 1909, won 1913; men's doubles won 1909, 1913. A good pre-World War I Australian overshadowed by Norman BROOKES.

Parker, Frank A. (USA)

Born Milwaukee, 31 Jan. 1916; Wimbledon men's singles s/f 1937, q/f 1949; men's doubles s/f 1948, won 1949; US men's singles q/f 1934, s/f 1936-7, q/f 1939-41, r/u 1942, q/f 1943, won 1944-5, q/f 1946, r/u 1947, q/f 1948, s/f 1949; men's doubles r/u 1933, s/f 1935-6, won 1943, s/f 1946-7, r/u 1948, s/f 1949; mixed doubles s/f 1934; French men's singles won 1948-9; men's doubles s/f 1948, won 1949. Davis Cup 1937, 1939, 1946, 1948. An American notable for his prowess on slow, hard courts. He ranked in the US top ten for 17 consecutive years 1933 to 1949, when he turned professional, and was head of the list in 1944 and 1945. He lacked powerful shots but was formidable with good ball control and accurate command of length and placement.

Parun, Onny see NEW ZEALAND

Pasarell, Charles Manuel (USA)

Born San Juan, Puerto Rico, 12 Feb. 1944; US men's singles q/f 1965; men's doubles s/f 1964, r/u 1965, s/f 1968; Australian men's doubles s/f 1971; French men's doubles r/u 1970. Davis Cup 1966-8. WCT contract pro 1971- . The loser of the longest-ever singles at Wimbledon (see CENTRE COURT CLASSICS, PART 1).

Below **Charlie Pasarell**

Patterson, Gerald L. (Australia)

Born Melbourne, 17 Dec. 1895, died 13 June 1967; Wimbledon men's singles won 1919, r/u 1920, won 1922; men's doubles s/f 1919, r/u 1922; mixed doubles won 1920; US men's singles s/f 1922, 1924; men's doubles won 1919, r/u 1922, 1924-5, 1928; Australian men's singles r/u 1914, 1922, 1925, won 1927; men's doubles won 1914, 1922, r/u 1924, won 1925-7, s/f 1928, r/u 1932. Davis Cup for Australasia 1919-20, 1922 and for Australia 1924-5, 1928. He was the first man to win the Wimbledon singles when the Challenge Round system was abolished in favour of 'playing through' in 1922. With a cannonball service and strong net attack he was the first Australian power player. He was non-playing Davis Cup captain in 1946.

Patty, J. Edward [Budge] (USA)

Born Arkansas, 11 Feb. 1924; Wimbledon men's singles s/f 1947, q/f 1948, won 1950, s/f 1954-5; men's doubles s/f 1946, 1949-52, 1954, won 1957; mixed doubles s/f 1946; US men's singles q/f 1951, 1953, 1957; men's doubles s/f 1951, r/u 1957; French men's singles q/f 1946, s/f 1948, r/u 1949, won 1950, q/f 1952, s/f 1954, q/f 1955; men's doubles s/f 1948-50, 1952-5; mixed doubles won 1946, s/f 1948. Davis Cup 1951. Famous for his forehand volley. A player of artistry with impeccable timing. A Europeanized American, who spent much of his life in Paris. See CENTRE COURT CLASSICS (PART 1).

Pelota see THE ORIGINS OF LAWN TENNIS (PART 1) and SPHAIRISTIKÉ.

Penrose, Miss Beryl [Mrs Collier] (Australia)

Born Sydney, N.S.W., 22 Dec. 1930; Wimbledon women's singles q/f 1955; mixed doubles s/f 1955; Australian women's singles q/f 1953, won 1955, s/f 1957; women's doubles r/u 1953, won 1954-5, r/u 1956; mixed doubles r/u 1954, won 1956; French women's singles q/f 1955; women's doubles s/f 1955; mixed doubles s/f 1952, 1955.

Pepsi-Cola (a division of Pepsico Inc.)

This American soft-drinks manufacturer sponsored the first two years of the ILTF GRAND PRIX (1970-1), its total commitment for each year being about $250,000. Cliff Richey (USA) was the first winner of the prize of $25,000. Stan Smith (USA) won the same sum in 1971. In 1971 Pepsi-Cola also sponsored the first women's Grand Prix: Billie Jean King won the $10,000 prize.

Pepsi-Cola initiated the Masters' Tournament, won by Smith in Tokyo (1970) and Ilie Năstase in Paris (1971). After this the company relinquished its Grand Prix sponsorship, which was promptly taken up by the COMMERCIAL UNION ASSURANCE COMPANY. Pepsi-Cola Canada Ltd is one of the main sponsors of tennis in CANADA. DC

Above **Gerald Patterson**

Perera, J. B. see THE BIRTH AND SPREAD OF LAWN TENNIS (PART 1) and SPHAIRISTIKÉ.

Perry, Frederick John (Gt Britain)

Born Stockport, Cheshire, 18 May 1909; Wimbledon men's singles s/f 1931, q/f 1932, won 1934-6; men's doubles s/f 1931, r/u 1932; mixed doubles s/f 1931, won 1935-6; US men's singles s/f 1931, won 1933-4, s/f 1935, won 1936; mixed doubles won 1932, s/f 1933-4; Australian men's singles won 1934, r/u 1935; men's doubles won 1934, r/u 1935; French men's singles q/f 1932-4, won 1935, r/u 1936; men's doubles s/f 1931-2, won 1933, s/f 1935-36; mixed doubles won 1932, r/u 1933. Davis Cup 1931-6. Possibly the greatest British man player of all time and certainly the best British match player. His running forehand was his most notable shot and, played with Continental grip, unique to him. He was the only man to play through and win the Wimbledon singles in three successive years. In the Davis Cup, where he was the main architect of the British success 1933 to 1936, he won 45 out of his 52 rubbers, an 86 percentage success unequalled by any who played 50 or more rubbers. He did not lose a set in any of his three Wimbledon singles finals and was the first man to be champion of Australia, France, Wimbledon and the United States, though not in the same year. Curiously his ability to play well on the big occasions was balanced by virtual ineptitude on the practice court. He became a pro in 1936 and had famous prewar clashes with VINES and BUDGE. See THE START OF THE PRO GAME and GREAT PLAYERS OF ALL TIME (PART 1).

Peru

Peru was affiliated to the ILTF as a Full Member in 1934 but agreed to become an Associate Member in 1972. It competed in the DAVIS CUP in 1968 and 1972. Its most famous player, OLMEDO, won Wimbledon in 1959. BR
GOVERNING BODY: Federación Peruana de Lawn Tennis, Casilla 2243, Lima

Petra, Yvon (France)

Born Cholon, Indo-China, 8 March 1916; Wimbledon men's singles won 1946, q/f 1947; mixed doubles r/u 1937; US mixed doubles r/u 1937; French men's singles q/f 1937, won 1943-5, s/f 1946, q/f 1947; men's doubles won 1938, 1942-4, r/u 1945, won 1946, s/f 1947; mixed doubles won 1937. Davis Cup 1937-9, 1946-7. Became pro 1948. A giant of a player, with a big serve and forehand; a fine opportunist.

Philadelphia Cricket Club

see THE BIRTH AND SPREAD OF LAWN TENNIS, THE UNITED STATES STORY (PART 1)

Philippines

The Philippine LTA has been a Full Member of the ILTF since 1936. Its team first competed in the DAVIS CUP in 1926 and has a very good record. Its best known players have been Felicismo Ampon and his doubles partner F. Deyro. The Philippine LTA staged the second Asian Championships for Amateurs in 1973. BR
GOVERNING BODY: Philippine Lawn Tennis Association, P.O. Box 4143, Manila

Pietrangeli, Nicola (Italy)

Born Tunis, 11 Sept. 1933; Wimbledon men's singles q/f 1955, s/f 1960; men's doubles r/u 1956, s/f 1957-9; Australian men's singles q/f 1957; French men's singles q/f 1956, won 1959-60, r/u 1961, q/f 1962-3, r/u 1964; men's doubles r/u 1955, s/f 1957-8, won 1959, s/f 1965; mixed doubles won 1958. Davis Cup 1954- . A player of superb touch, though never of consistency, he had a unique place in the annals of the game as the outstanding stalwart of the Davis Cup. Between 1954 and 1972 he played 164 Davis Cup rubbers for Italy, winning 119, this being 43 more than the rubbers played by the next on the list, Jacques Brichant of Belgium. His total was amassed in

Above **John Player & Sons Ltd.** Four of the company's 1936 cigarette cards, showing S. B. Wood, S. Fabyan, N. Adamson and H. Hopman

66 ties, including two in the Challenge Round against Australia in 1960 and 1961. An engaging artist of the game with fine timing bringing economy of effort. See also ITALY.

Pilić, Nicola (Yugoslavia)

Born Split, Yugoslavia, 27 Aug. 1939; Wimbledon men's singles s/f 1967; men's doubles r/u 1962; US men's singles q/f 1973; men's doubles s/f 1962, won 1970; French men's singles s/f 1967, r/u 1973. Davis Cup 1961-7. WCT contract pro 1968-72. WCT 7th (F q/f) Nov. 1972. Left-handed.

Pim, Dr Joshua (Ireland)

Born Ireland, 20 May 1869, died 15 April 1942; Wimbledon men's singles s/f 1890, r/u 1891-2, won 1893-4; men's doubles r/u 1890, 1891, r/u* 1892, won 1893. Davis Cup (British Isles) 1902. Nominated under pseudonym ('Mr X') for Davis Cup.

Platform Tennis

This originates from a game known as Paddle Tennis, played on the streets of New York with wooden 'paddles' and a sponge rubber ball. Fessenden Blanchard and James Cogswell are recognized as the inventors of Platform Tennis. In 1928 they built the first court in Scarsdale, N.Y., on a raised wooden platform

(to overcome the problems of snow in winter) surrounded by chickenwire netting 8 ft (2.44 m) high. Later the size of the enclosure was reduced to the present, with a court of 44 x 20 ft (13.41 x 6.10 m) and the netting 12 ft (3.66 m) high.

Before World War II the game had spread to tennis clubs and country clubs in New England and was governed by the 1934 Paddle Tennis Association which, in 1950, became the American Platform Tennis Association. There are now over 250 member clubs and the game is expanding at a rate exceeding 20 per cent per year.

The game follows the rules and scoring of lawn tennis except that only one service is allowed and the ball may be hit after it has bounced off the wire surround before it has bounced twice. JB

Player, John & Sons

John Player, one of Britain's largest tobacco companies, is a comparative newcomer to sponsorship in lawn tennis. It first became associated through the Nottingham tournament in 1970, introducing a major ROUND ROBIN there with prize money by 1973 of almost £30,000. DC
HEAD OFFICE: Nottingham NG7 5PY

Playing Status

After the ILTF ruling in 1968 (see OPEN TENNIS, PART 1) four categories of players emerged: (1) contract professionals, those contracting to a promoter and acknowledging only his jurisdiction; (2) registered (or authorized) players, who may play for prize money but acknowledge the authority of their national associations; (3) coaching professionals, who receive fees for giving instruction in the game; (4) amateurs, players who do not receive (after reaching their 16th birthday) directly or indirectly, pecuniary advantage by the playing, teaching, demonstrating or pursuit of the game.

Players who had lost their amateur status could be reinstated by their national associations if they returned to these requirements. It was left to individual countries to make their own playing definitions for the last three categories. This led to refined distinctions whereby, for example, apart from contract professionals, in the United States there are amateurs and professionals, in the United Kingdom players only, and in the USSR and eastern Europe amateurs only.

Poaching

A term that applies only in doubles when a player intercepts a shot that would naturally have gone to his partner. This ploy is most frequently used in mixed doubles when the man tries to shield a weak partner from excessive pressure. It is also used as a surprise weapon in top class doubles, particularly men's. JO

Point see SCORING

Poland

Tennis was first played in Poland towards the end of the 19th century in cities such as Warsaw, Lwów (Lvov), Poznań, Kraków and Łódź, and the first tennis publications appeared then, among them advertisements of equipment (1883) and handbooks (1896). The first tournaments were held in 1898.

The first international tournament, in which players from Vienna and Prague competed against the best players from Warsaw, Poznań and Lwów, was held in 1912 in Kraków. In the same period the best Polish players such as E. Kleinadel and the Kowalewsky brothers played successfully in tournaments in Berlin and Karlsbad.

When Poland recovered its independence in 1918 tennis spread all over the country. The Polski Związek Tenisowy (the Polish LTA) was founded in 1921 and affiliated to the ILTF in 1923. The same year the first Polish Championships were organized and a Polish team has taken part in the DAVIS CUP regularly since 1925.

From 1930 to 1939 Poland's top players were Ignacy Tloczynski and Jozef Hebda, who had many international successes. Just before World War II, Tloczynski was high on the European ranking list. Many international competitions and tournaments gave the Warsaw public a chance to see first-class world players such as Henri Cochet, Jean Borotra, Jacques Brugnon, 'Bunny' Austin, Fred Perry, Georgio de'Stefani and Baron Gottfried von Cramm. Jadwiga Jedrzejowska's successes abroad were the greatest achievements of Polish tennis. She beat top players including Helen Jacobs, Alice Marble, Simone Mathieu and Kay Stammers; she was the international champion of Poland, Hungary, Austria, Wales and Ireland, and won many other tournaments. Her greatest successes were reaching the singles finals at Wimbledon and Forest Hills in 1937.

In 1938 the Polish team won the Central European Cup, beating Czechoslovakia, Hungary, Yugoslavia, Italy and Rumania.

During World War II many tennis players lost their lives and during the German occupation of Poland sports were forbidden to Poles. At this time Jadwiga Jedrzejowska was invited to Sweden by King Gustaf V but she refused and remained in Poland.

After the war the Polish LTA's activities were renewed and in 1946 the Championships of Poland were held again. Some Polish players, such as Tloczynski, Cz. Spychala, E. Wittman and M. Stolarów, stayed in Britain where they had many successes. Wl. Skonecki was the best postwar Polish player, doing well among European players in many tournaments and contributing to Poland's defeat of Chile and Mexico in the Davis Cup. W. Gasiorek was Polish champion 12 times after 1959 and also had many international successes.

Poland takes part in the DAVIS CUP, the KING'S CUP; also the GALEA, ANNIE SOISBAULT,

Above **The Queen's Club** (1897). Note the lady bicycling on the running track.

VALERIO and Centrope Cups and competed in the FEDERATION CUP in 1966-9. BR
GOVERNING BODY: Polski Związek Tenisowy, 00-551 Warsaw, ul.Mokotowska 39m.6

Portugal

Lawn tennis has been played in Portugal since the end of the 19th century. The first international championships were played in Lisbon in 1902. The Federação Portuguesa de Lawn Tennis was established in 1925 and affiliated to the ILTF the same year. At present there are 41 associated clubs with 231 affiliated players. Many others play on public courts and in non-affiliated clubs. Portugal has competed in the DAVIS CUP since 1925 and took part in the FEDERATION CUP in 1968.

Leading players who have represented Portugal have included José De Verda, A. Casanovas, Eduardo Ricciardi, José Roquette, D. Avilez, A. Vaz Pinto and J. Lagos. BR
GOVERNING BODY: Federação Portuguesa de Lawn Tennis, Rua do Arco do Cego, 90-6° Esq., Lisbon 1

Below **Poland.** Jadwiga Jedrzejowska in 1937

Press

A piece of equipment used to keep the racket frame straight and prevent warping by applying equal pressure to the whole of both sides. It is generally used for a racket which has been tightly strung. Metal frames, of course, do not require them. DC

Press Coverage see THE PRESS (PART 1)

Price, Mrs L. E. G. [Miss Sandra Reynolds] (S. Africa)

Born Bloemfontein, 4 Mar. 1939; Wimbledon women's singles q/f 1957, s/f 1959, r/u 1960, s/f 1961; women's doubles s/f 1957, 1959, r/u 1960, 1962; US women's singles q/f 1959, 1962; women's doubles s/f 1962; Australian women's singles q/f 1959; women's doubles won 1959; mixed doubles won 1959; French women's singles s/f 1959-60, q/f 1962; women's doubles won 1959, s/f 1960, won 1961-2.

Prince's Club, Knightsbridge (London) see THE BIRTH AND SPREAD OF LAWN TENNIS (PART 1)

Princess Sophia Cup

An annual international team competition for girls under 19, organized on DAVIS CUP lines by the Royal Spanish Tennis Federation. It consists of four singles matches and one double and its Honorary Chairman is Princess Sophia of Spain. It was first held in Malaga in 1972 and won by Rumania.

Professional see PLAYING STATUS, also OPEN TENNIS (PART 1) etc.

Professional Tennis Association see THE START OF THE PRO GAME (PART 1)

Professional World Tournament see LONDON PROFESSIONAL INDOOR TENNIS CHAMPIONSHIPS

Prudential Assurance Company

This British insurance company started sponsoring tennis in 1973 by putting £7,500 into the LTA's INTER-COUNTY WEEK, which was renamed the Prudential County Cup. DC
HEAD OFFICE: Holborn Bars, London EC1

Pužejová, Miss V. see Mrs V. SUKOVÁ

Pyle, C. C. ('Cash and Carry') see THE START OF THE PRO GAME (PART 1)

Q

Queen's Club, The, London (UK)

A correspondent of *The Times* once wrote, 'As Lord's is to cricket, Queen's is to games played with racket and ball' and this is still true for the court-game player. The Club is situated on 13 acres of the 'Queen's field', at Barons Court, West London, purchased in 1887 for an Athletic Club when the old Prince's Rackets and Tennis Club (see THE BIRTH AND SPREAD OF LAWN TENNIS, PART 1) closed. At the beginning there were facilities for almost every kind of ball game: apart from the lawn-tennis courts marked out on the sports ground there were two real-tennis courts, two rackets courts (one converted in the 1920s to squash courts), two covered lawn-tennis courts, Eton fives courts and an asphalt skating rink. The large sports field, used for Oxford and Cambridge Rugby Association football and athletics, had a running track around it which was also popular for the new sport of bicycling. One landmark was the OLYMPIC covered-court event held there in 1908, although it attracted only 11 competitors for the men's singles and nine for the women's and several withdrew.

When the field sports and football left Queen's in the early 1920s because of lack of space for spectators the ground was increasingly given over to lawn tennis. There are now 15 grass, 13 hard and five covered courts. Queen's is the home of the LONDON GRASS COURT CHAMPIONSHIPS, held just before Wimbledon and therefore attracting a large international entry. The BRITISH COVERED COURTS CHAMPIONSHIPS, held there until 1968, were popular with the French: Jean Borotra's brilliant volleying game was ideally suited to the fast wooden floor and he won the singles 11 times between 1926 and 1949.

In World War II Queen's was hit by several bombs: the two latest covered courts, built in 1924 on the site of the old skating rink, were destroyed; so were two of the squash courts; one of the two real-tennis courts and the Eton fives courts were damaged. But it never closed. Today it is one of the largest tennis clubs in Britain, with nearly 2,000 members. Owned by the LTA since 1954, it has provided the training ground for those selected by the LTA for special courses, especially during the winter. It is also the recognized meeting place for players and officials from all over the world. Davis Cup and King's Cup matches have also been played there and in 1963 Queen's staged the first Federation Cup matches. MR

Quist, Adrian Karl (Australia)

Born Medindia, S. Australia, 4 Aug. 1913; Wimbledon men's singles q/f 1936; men's doubles won 1935, 1950; mixed doubles s/f 1935; US men's singles q/f 1933; men's doubles s/f 1933, won 1939; mixed doubles s/f 1938; Australian men's singles s/f 1934-5, won 1936, s/f 1938, r/u 1939, won 1940, q/f 1947, won 1948, q/f 1951; men's doubles r/u 1934, s/f 1935, won 1936-40, 1946-50, r/u 1951, s/f 1952-4; mixed doubles s/f 1935; French men's doubles r/u 1933, s/f 1934, won 1935, s/f 1950; mixed doubles r/u 1934, s/f 1955. Davis Cup 1933-9, 1946, 1948, his greatest year being 1936 when, in the final of the North American Zone, he beat ALLISON in the singles and, with CRAWFORD, beat BUDGE and MAKO in the doubles from two sets down, 4-6, 2-6, 6-4, 7-5, 6-4. One of Australia's finest players and specially noteworthy for his doubles skill, being regarded as one of the outstanding left-court players and placement smashers of all time. He had trenchant, heavy shots. His first Wimbledon doubles title, in 1935, he took with Crawford. Fifteen years later, 1950, he won with BROMWICH, the partner with whom he shared the last eight of his ten successive victories in the Australian Championships (an all-time record for a major championship) and one of the best tennis understandings there has ever been.

Below **Adrian Quist**

R

Racket, History of the

In Chaucer's *Troylus and Cryseyde* (1373-4) the line 'But canstow playen racket to and fro' indicates how ancient is the racket in ball games. But the use of the racket can almost certainly be dated centuries earlier (see THE ORIGINS OF LAWN TENNIS, PART 1).

The Italians are thought to have been the first to protect the hand with a glove when playing (real) tennis. Julian Marshall, in *Annals of Tennis* (1878), says that the glove not only protected the palm but also afforded a greater power of driving the ball and either in Italy or in France 'ingenious persons conceived the brilliant idea of stretching across the glove an elastic network of strings to which handles were soon added by an easy and natural step'. The racket, or *battoir*, consisted of little more than a strengthened glove with a short handle which soon developed into a wooden frame over which was stretched a parchment. From this it was found that the catgut fastened to the glove could be used to better effect if stretched or strung on a wooden frame. Play with the hand and play with the racket were accepted as alternative methods for many years until finally the racket, with improvements, ousted the hand. The racket seems to have been strung diagonally until the end of the 17th century.

M. de Garsault, in *Art du Paumier-Raquetier et de la Paume* (1767), described fully how rackets were made in the 18th century and illustrated his account with many fine engravings. Julian Marshall, writing in 1878, tells how the racket frame is shaped to give it that 'peculiar twist, or inclination', which is considered necessary in the head of a (real) tennis racket so that balls near to the floor may be easily returned. At that time the best rackets in England were imported from France, but the siege of Paris of 1870 made this difficult if not entirely impossible, especially as most of the seasoned wood from which the rackets were made was being burned as fuel. Julian Marshall points to another reason for the great demand for rackets which had lately sprung up: the use of (real) tennis rackets for the game of lawn tennis, he said, had doubtless overtaxed the supply.

When Major Harry Gem and his friends played the first organized games of lawn tennis in 1872 it seems almost certain that they used ordinary (real) tennis rackets. Special lawn-tennis rackets were not introduced until

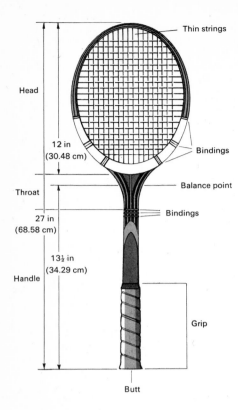

Head

12 in
(30.48 cm)

Thin strings

Bindings

Throat

Balance point

Bindings

27 in
(68.58 cm)

13½ in
(34.29 cm)

Handle

Grip

Butt

Above **Racket.** The parts and dimensions of a typical lawn tennis racket

1874 when Major Walter Wingfield started to market his 'Sphairistiké or Lawn Tennis'. His rackets had long handles and a slightly smaller head. Very soon, however, a great variety of specially designed lawn-tennis rackets were on the market. These were symmetrical but otherwise similar to the normal (real) tennis racket. Major Wingfield's rules placed no restriction on the size or shape of the racket and before long all kinds were produced with the intention, or so the advertisements said, of aiding the player. There were rackets with widely spaced strings and diagonally strung ones; ones with knotted gut and even one with a parchment centre. A racket with a curved handle (known as a 'bent' racket) was sold in the United States; its advantage, it was claimed, was that the head always pointed back towards the court to which the ball should be played. Other rackets had mercury in the hollow handle to transfer the weight, as a shot was played, from the handle to the head. There were even rackets with steel frames.

A famous English racket maker of the 1880s was Thos. J. Tate, whose rackets were so sought after by the leading players that he was able to charge 40 shillings, double the price of any other.

For the recent development of the lawn-tennis racket see THE DEVELOPMENT OF PLAYING EQUIPMENT, THE GROWTH OF THE GAME and POSTWAR DEVELOPMENT (all these in PART 1). TT

Rackets (the game) see THE ORIGINS OF LAWN TENNIS (PART 1)

Radio Coverage of Wimbledon see PART 1

Rally
The series of strokes between delivery of service and the conclusion of a point. JO

Ralston, R. Dennis (USA)
Born Bakersfield, Calif., 27 July 1942; Wimbledon men's singles s/f 1965, r/u 1966, q/f 1968; men's doubles won 1960, s/f 1965; mixed doubles r/u 1962, s/f 1963, 1964, r/u 1966; US men's singles s/f 1960, q/f 1963-5, 1968, 1970; men's doubles s/f 1960, won 1961, r/u 1962, won 1963-4, r/u 1966; mixed doubles s/f 1960, r/u 1961, s/f 1964, r/u 1969, s/f 1970; Australian men's singles s/f 1970; men's doubles s/f 1971; French men's doubles won 1966. Davis Cup 1960-6. Turned professional 1966. WCT contract pro 1968-71.

Ramirez, Miss Yola (Mexico)
Born Mexico City, 1 March 1935; Wimbledon women's singles q/f 1959, 1961; US women's singles q/f 1961; women's doubles r/u 1961; Australian women's singles s/f 1962; French women's singles r/u 1960-1; women's doubles r/u 1957, won 1958, r/u 1959; mixed doubles s/f 1958, won 1959.

Rankings
Lists are compiled by national LTAs once a year, grading their players on performances over the previous 12 months. Most countries concentrate on ranking their top ten men and ten women. In Britain official rankings began in 1956 when Mike Davies and Angela Mortimer topped the lists. Occasionally the number ranked changes. In the United States rankings are much more important. Men's rankings began as far back as 1885 and women's in 1913. Today Americans are ranked in every age category, from under-12 to over-70, singles and doubles: generally the top 50 players are ranked.

Various unofficial ranking lists of the world's best players exist. The first for the top ten players was issued in 1914 for men and 1925 for women. These were compiled by A. Wallis Myers, still respected as perhaps the greatest writer on lawn tennis (see THE PRESS, PART 1); since 1952 Lance Tingay, also of the *Daily Telegraph*, has issued his own unofficial world rankings. DC

Rawlings Sporting Goods Co.
Founded in 1898 as a retail store in St Louis with manufacturing facilities for baseball uniforms, football suits and hunting clothes, in 1907 it dropped out of retailing and formed a new company, the Rawlings Manufacturing Company. The new enterprise survived total destruction by fire in 1909 and expanded to produce sporting and athletic clothing and equipment that sold well in the United States in the 1930s and 1940s.

In 1953 Rawlings Sporting Goods Company and Rawlings Manufacturing Company became two distinct entities. Well established in the tennis field, which they had entered in 1916, they were acquired by A. G. Spalding & Bros in 1955. In 1963 Spalding sold Rawlings to a group of investors who continued to expand the sports business with emphasis on baseball and American football equipment. In November 1967 Rawlings became a subsidiary of the Automatic Sprinkler Corporation of America. Two years later it entered the fast-growing ice hockey clothing and equipment market. The next year it acquired the Medalist Golf Ball Company and sponsored its first professional tennis tournament, the $30,000 Pro Tennis Classic in St Louis and introduced three aluminium rackets bearing John Newcombe's name.

In 1973 Rawlings launched a publicity campaign, 'Rawlings the Big Name in Sports', to mark 75 years as a leader in the sporting goods industry. JB
HEAD OFFICE: 2300 Delmar Boulevard, St Louis, Mo., USA

Real Tennis see THE ORIGINS OF LAWN TENNIS (PART 1); also BALL and RACKET

Receiver the player who is receiving service. See TOSS. JO

Records
For the major championships and team competitions see PART 3; see also entries for individual events.

Redondo, Marita (USA)
Born San Diego, Calif., 19 Feb. 1956; she came into prominence in 1973 when she defeated Evonne Goolagong and took a set from Chris Evert, both in Akron, Ohio.

Referee
The official appointed by the tournament committee to control the event. He becomes, thereafter, an *ex-officio* member of the committee. Before the tournament he is consulted about seedings and at major events is present at the draw. During the tournament he decides any point of law which an umpire feels himself unable to settle, or which may be referred to him on appeal from the decision of an umpire. In all such cases the decision of the referee is final. He is also responsible for producing the daily ORDER OF PLAY and for ensuring that this is expeditiously carried out. This may involve quick-thinking juggling if bad weather, injury or matches of unusual length upset his calculations, which should take into account not only the entertainment of the public but also reasonable recovery periods for competitors who have two or three matches to play on the same day. DC

Regent Sports Corporation
This company, founded in 1946, produces

tennis rackets and tennis balls. It also makes balls for baseball and basketball. Its advisers include Don Budge and Alex Olmedo. JB
HEAD OFFICE: 45 Ranick Road, Hauppauge, Long Island, N.Y. 11787, USA

Regional Games

Tennis is one of the sports of various regional games run on the lines of the OLYMPIC GAMES. These include the ALL-AFRICA GAMES, the PAN-AMERICAN GAMES, the Asian Games, the Mediterranean Games, the South Pacific Games and the South East Asian Peninsula (SEAP) Games. All these are held every four years, except for the SEAP Games, held every two years.

Reitano, Mrs S. J. [Miss Mary Carter] (Australia)

Born Sydney, N.S.W., 29 Nov. 1934; Australian women's singles s/f 1954-5, won 1956, s/f 1958, won 1959, s/f 1960-2; women's doubles s/f 1953, 1955, r/u 1956, s/f 1957-8, r/u 1959, s/f 1960, won 1961, r/u 1962; mixed doubles r/u 1960-1; French women's singles q/f 1959; women's doubles s/f 1955, 1959; mixed doubles s/f 1955. A neat performer from Australia who improved her game by playing frequently in Europe.

Renshaw, James Ernest (Gt Britain)

Born Leamington, 3 Jan 1861, died 2 Sept. 1899; Wimbledon men's singles q/f 1880, r/u 1882-3, s/f 1884, r/u* 1885, q/f 1886, r/u* 1887, won 1888, r/u 1889, s/f 1891; men's doubles won 1880-1, 1884-6, 1888-9, r/u* 1891. The twin of William, with whom he ranks as the creator of modern lawn tennis. The 'Renshaw' smash was in the 1880s viewed with awe. Of the two brothers he had the greater delicacy of touch but he lost to William all the three Wimbledon title matches he played against him.

Renshaw, William Charles (Gt Britain)

Born Leamington, 3 Jan. 1861, died 12 Aug. 1904; Wimbledon men's singles won 1881-6, q/f 1888, won 1889, r/u 1890; men's doubles won 1880-1, 1884-6, 1888-9. With his seven Wimbledon singles titles and seven doubles championships (all with his twin, Ernest) he ranks as the doyen of champions. His skill and his personality turned the game into a spectator sport. See GREAT PLAYERS OF ALL TIME (PART 1).

Return

This usually means the stroke made by a player after receiving a service. It also applies to all counter-strokes during the course of a RALLY. JO

Reverse Twist Service see SERVICE and THE DEVELOPMENT OF TECHNIQUE AND STROKEPLAY (PART 1)

Reynolds, Miss S. see Mrs L. E. G. PRICE

Rhodesia

The Rhodesian Lawn Tennis Association held its first annual championships in 1897. At that time the Association was affiliated to the South African Lawn Tennis Union; in 1932 it seceded from the South African LTU and affiliated directly to the Lawn Tennis Association of Great Britain, to which it is still affiliated.

The history of Rhodesian tennis is very closely related to Rhodesia's history. The area of the Association's jurisdiction originally covered Rhodesia (then known as Southern Rhodesia); in 1933 its area was extended to include Zambia (then Northern Rhodesia) and Mozambique. In 1949 Mozambique withdrew, then on the creation of the Federation of Rhodesia and Nyasaland in 1953 Malawi (then

Below **William** *(left)* and **Ernest Renshaw**

Nyasaland) was brought in and the Association became the LTA of Rhodesia and Nyasaland. When the Federation dissolved in 1963, Zambia and Malawi withdrew their affiliation and the Association was again the Rhodesia LTA. In the last 50 years the number of affiliated players has risen from 2,000 to 4,288.

As a special concession Rhodesia was admitted to the DAVIS CUP in 1960 although not a full member of the ILTF. It has competed in this event five times since then. Rhodesia has played in the FEDERATION CUP since 1966, and has also played friendly matches against teams from Australia, Great Britain, Italy, the Netherlands, South Africa, Spain, the United States, France and West Germany. Rhodesian junior teams have also taken part in international tournaments in Miami, Fla.

The LTA stages each year National, Closed and Junior Championships and also Senior and Junior Inter-Provincial Tournaments in which the four provincial sub-associations compete. Rhodesian teams regularly take part in the Senior and Junior Inter-Provincial Tournaments in South Africa by invitation from the South African LTU. Two trophies for Rhodesia's annual Championships were donated by Cecil John Rhodes, the founder of Rhodesia.

Rhodesian players who have performed with distinction in many international events include Adrian Bey (in the last eight at Wimbledon twice), Donald Black (in the last 16 at Wimbledon once), Hank Irvine, Andrew Pattison and Mrs Pat (Walkden) Pretorius, a member of the South African team that won the Federation Cup in 1972. BR

GOVERNING BODY: Rhodesian LTA, P.O. Box 8219, Belmont, Bulawayo

Rice, Horace M. (Australia)
Born 1873; Australian men's singles won 1907, r/u 1910-11, 1915; men's doubles r/u 1907, won 1910, 1915; mixed doubles won 1923. Davis Cup (Australasia) 1913. He was champion of New South Wales in 1900, of Queensland in 1901. Left-handed.

Rice, Miss L. (Gt Britain)
Wimbledon women's singles r/u* 1889; won 1890. She became Wimbledon singles champion by winning only two matches, the entry in 1890 being four.

Richards, Vincent (USA)
Born Yonkers, N.Y., 20 March 1903, died 1959; Wimbledon men's singles q/f 1924: men's doubles won 1924, r/u 1926; mixed doubles s/f 1923, 1926; US men's singles s/f 1922, 1924-6; men's doubles won 1918, 1921-2, s/f 1924, won 1925-6; mixed doubles won 1919, s/f 1923, won 1924, r/u 1925; French men's singles s/f 1926; men's doubles won 1926. Davis Cup 1922-6. Turned professional 1926.

Below **Nancy Richey**

Richardson, Hamilton (USA)
Born Baton Rouge, La., 24 Aug. 1933; Wimbledon men's singles s/f 1956; men's doubles s/f 1951, 1965; US men's singles s/f 1952, 1954, q/f 1955-6, 1960, 1962; men's doubles s/f 1954, r/u 1956, s/f 1957, won 1958; Australian men's singles q/f 1953-4; men's doubles s/f 1952-3; mixed doubles r/u 1953; French men's singles s/f 1955; men's doubles s/f 1951, 1955. Davis Cup 1952-6, 1958, 1965.

Richey, George Clifford (USA)
Born San Angelo, Texas, 31 Dec. 1946; Wimbledon men's singles q/f 1971; US men's singles s/f 1970, 1972; Australian men's singles q/f 1967; French men's singles s/f 1970. Davis Cup 1966-7, 1970. WCT contract pro 1972- . ILTF GP 1st 1970, 5th 1971. See CENTRE COURT CLASSICS (PART 1) for an account of his 1971 Wimbledon quarter-final match with ROSEWALL.

Richey, Miss Nancy [Mrs K. S. Gunter] (USA)
Born San Angelo, Tex., 23 Aug. 1942; Wimbledon women's singles q/f 1964-6, s/f 1968, q/f 1969, 1971-2; women's doubles s/f 1965, won 1966, r/u 1967; US women's singles q/f 1960, 1963, s/f 1964-5, r/u 1966, s/f 1970; women's doubles s/f 1964, won 1965-6, s/f 1971; Australian women's singles r/u 1966, won 1967; women's doubles won 1966; French women's singles s/f 1965, r/u 1966, won 1968, s/f 1969; women's doubles s/f 1968, r/u 1969. Federation Cup 1964, 1968-9. Wightman Cup 1962-9. ILTF GP 4th 1972.

She was one of America's best hard-court players; the only one to win the US Clay Court singles six times (1963-8). She won the first Open Championship of France (1968) as an amateur. Like her brother Cliff RICHEY she was more resolute than stylish.

Riessen, Martin Clare ['Marty'] (USA)
Born Evanston, Ill., 4 Dec. 1941; Wimbledon

Below **Bobby Riggs**

men's singles q/f 1965; men's doubles s/f 1965-6, r/u 1969; mixed doubles r/u 1971; US men's singles q/f 1963, 1971; men's doubles s/f 1961, 1965-7, 1969, 1971, 1973; mixed doubles s/f 1963, won 1969-70, 1972, r/u 1973; Australian men's singles q/f 1971; men's doubles s/f 1969, r/u 1971; French men's doubles s/f 1969, won 1971; mixed doubles won 1969. Davis Cup 1961, 1963, 1965, 1967. WCT contract pro 1968-72. WCT 7th (F q/f) 1971, 5th (F s/f) May 1972, 5th (F q/f) Nov. 1972, 3rd Group B (F q/f) 1973.

Riggs, Robert Lorimer (USA)
Born Los Angeles, Calif., 25 Feb. 1918; Wimbledon men's singles won 1939; men's doubles won 1939; mixed doubles won 1939; US men's singles s/f 1937; won 1939, r/u 1940, won 1941; men's doubles s/f 1936, 1939; mixed doubles won 1940; French men's singles r/u 1939. Davis Cup 1938-9. A shrewd all-round player, he won all three events at his first and only challenge at Wimbledon. Not only that – he backed himself with a bookmaker to do so. But for World War II he would almost certainly have had fuller achievement. After the war he played as a professional but was best known for his 'bally-hoo' matches in 1973 with Margaret COURT (won 6-2, 6-1) and Billie Jean KING (lost 4-6, 3-6, 3-6).

Right Court see illustration and THE RULES AND THEIR INTERPRETATION (PART 1)

Below **Right Court**

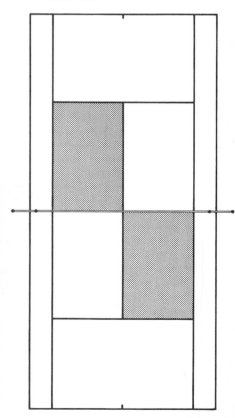

Riseley, Frank L. (Gt Britain)
Born Clifton, 6 July 1877; Wimbledon men's singles q/f 1896-7, r/u 1903-4, q/f 1905, r/u 1906; men's doubles r/u* 1900, won 1902, r/u 1903-5, won 1906. Davis Cup (British Isles) 1904, 1922.

Ritchie, M. J. G. (Gt Britain)
Born London, 18 Oct. 1870; died 28 Feb. 1955; Wimbledon men's singles q/f 1898, r/u* 1902-4, s/f 1905, q/f 1906, s/f 1907-8, r/u 1909, s/f 1919; men's doubles s/f 1889, r/u* 1903, s/f 1904, 1906-7, won 1908, 1910, r/u 1911, s/f 1919. Davis Cup (British Isles) 1908.

River Oaks (USA)
The first River Oaks invitation tournament was held by the River Oaks Country Club, Houston, Texas, on 6-13 April 1931 under the chairmanship of J. D. Norton. There was seating for 1,200 spectators, 900 in a covered grandstand and 300 in bleachers. The seating capacity was doubled in 1931. Ellsworth Vines, who was to win his first US National singles championship later in the year, won the first River Oaks singles tournament, defeating Bruce Barnes in the final in three straight sets. The first doubles title was captured by George Lott and Wilbur Coen. Lott also won the doubles in 1932 with Vines and in 1933 with Wilmer Allison.

For 40 years, during which the invitation tournament was held annually except in 1942-5, the Houston fixture attracted many of the country's leading players and more recently many outstanding players from abroad. The tournament was held as a WCT tournament only in 1973.

In 1932, Vines, then US National champion, was defeated by Martin Buxby. Another noteworthy achievement was that of Richard Savitt, former Wimbledon champion, when he won in 1954, by defeating Sven Davidson (Sweden), Gardnar Mulloy, Victor Seixas, 1953 Wimbledon champion and, in the final, Ham Richardson.

Brian (Bitsy) Grant is the only player to have won River Oaks four times, each time by defeating Allison in the final (1934-7). Allison was US champion when he bowed to Grant in 1936 for the third time.

Mulloy captured the River Oaks title three times (1946, 1952-3). Half a dozen other players won the singles twice. They include Frank Guernsey, Barry MacKay, Cliff Richey, Frank Parker and Rod Laver. The last two were also National champions. Other leading players who won at River Oaks and also at Forest Hills were Bob Riggs, Jack Kramer, Ted Schroeder, Art Larsen, Tony Trabert, Manuel Santana, Roy Emerson and John Newcombe.

Altogether, 11 Wimbledon champions have won River Oaks, an indication of the importance of this event, which was held in the early spring as part of the southern circuit. Winners of both tournaments have been Vines, Riggs, Kramer, Falkenberg, Schroeder, Savitt, Trab-ert, Laver, Emerson, Santana and Newcombe.

In recent years foreign players have more or less dominated the tournament. Besides Laver, others who have won the Houston event over the last ten years include Santana, Emerson, Newcombe, Marty Mulligan (ex-Australian now of Italy) and Zeljko Franulović (Yugoslavia).

River Oaks doubles champions include the following who also have won the US doubles: Don Budge/Gene Mako, William Talbert/Mulloy, Seixas/Trabert, Neale Fraser/Emerson, Fred Stolle/Emerson.

Women's events were held at River Oaks except for the war years, until 1960, then again in 1968 and 1969. The first women's National champion to win at River Oaks was Sarah Palfrey Fabyan in 1940. Two other players to have won both the invitation tournament and the national title were Maria Bueno of Brazil (1968) and Margaret Smith Court of Australia (1969). FES

Riviera see FRANCE; also THE GROWTH OF THE GAME (PART 1)

Roark, Mrs Helen Wills Moody
see Mrs F. S. MOODY

Robb, Miss Muriel E. (Gt Britain)
Wimbledon women's singles q/f 1899-1901, won 1902; Irish women's singles won 1901; Welsh women's singles won 1899; Scottish women's singles won 1901. The winner (1902) of the most unorthodox women's singles final at Wimbledon. In the challenge round against Mrs STERRY the score to Miss Robb was 4-6, 13-11, when rain held up play. The whole match was replayed the next day when Miss Robb won 7-5, 6-1, to give her claim to have won the longest (53 games) women's final.

Roche, Anthony Dalton (Australia)
Born Tarcutta, N.S.W., 17 May 1945; Wimbledon men's singles q/f 1966, r/u 1968, s/f 1969, q/f 1970; men's doubles won 1965, 1968-9; mixed doubles r/u 1965, 1969; US men's singles q/f 1964, r/u 1969-70; men's doubles s/f 1966, won 1967; Australian men's singles q/f 1964, s/f 1965, q/f 1966, s/f 1967, 1969, q/f 1970; men's doubles s/f 1964, won 1965, r/u 1966, won 1967, s/f 1969, won 1971; mixed doubles s/f 1965, won 1966, r/u 1967, s/f 1969; French men's singles r/u 1965, won 1966, r/u 1967, s/f 1969; men's doubles r/u 1964, s/f 1965-6, won 1967, 1969; mixed doubles s/f 1966. Davis Cup 1965-7. WCT

River Oaks Championships Winners

Men's Singles		Women's Singles	
1931	H. E. Vines	1932	Miss A. M. Reichert
1932	W. Allison	1933	Miss B. Miller
1933	F. A. Parker	1934	Miss J. Sharp
1934	B. M. Grant	1935	Miss J. Sharp
1935	B. M. Grant	1936	Miss E. Dean
1936	B. M. Grant	1937	Miss M. G. Van Ryn
1937	B. M. Grant	1938	Miss M. G. Van Ryn
1938	W. Sabin	1939	Miss M. M. Barnett
1939	F. Guernsey	1940	Miss S. P. Fabyan
1940	R. L. Riggs	1941	Miss D. M. Bundy
1941	F. L. Kovacs	1942-5	No Competition
1942-5	No Competition	1946	Miss V. W. Kovacs
1946	G. Mulloy	1947	Miss B. Krase
1947	J. A. Kramer	1948	Miss G. Moran
1948	F. A. Parker	1949	Miss V. W. Kovacs
1949	F. R. Schroeder	1950	Miss D. Head
1950	R. Falkenburg	1951	Miss G. Heldman
1951	A. Larsen	1952	Miss G. Heldman
1952	G. Mulloy	1953	Miss E. Norton
1953	G. Mulloy	1954	Miss E. Norton
1954	R. Savitt	1955	Miss E. Norton
1955	A. Trabert	1956	Miss P. Naud
1956	H. Richardson	1957	Miss P. Naud
1957	H. Flam	1958	Miss M. Bueno
1958	B. MacKay	1959	Miss M. Montgomery
1959	B. Bartzen	1960-7	No Competition
1960	B. MacKay	1968	Miss M. Bueno
1961	R. Laver	1969	Mrs B. M. Court
1962	R. Laver	1970-3	No Competition
1963	M. Santana		
1964	R. Emerson		
1965	R. Krishnan		
1966	M. Mulligan		
1967	J. D. Newcombe		
1968	C. Richey		
1969	Z. Franulović		
1970	C. Graebner		
1971	C. Richey		
1972	R. Laver		
1973	(WCT) K. Rosewall		

contract pro 1968-73. At the start of the 1970s an arm injury set back and may well have cut short what promised to be a great career. Left-handed.

Roosevelt, Miss Ellen C. (USA)

US women's singles and doubles won 1890; mixed doubles won 1893. Third in line of the pioneer US women's singles champions.

Roper Barrett, H. see H. Roper BARRETT

Rose, Mervyn G. (Australia)

Born Coffs Harbour, N.S.W., 23 Jan. 1930; Wimbledon men's singles s/f 1952-3, q/f 1954, 1957, s/f 1958; men's doubles r/u 1953, won 1954, s/f 1955, 1958; mixed doubles r/u 1951, won 1957; US men's singles s/f 1952; men's doubles r/u 1951, won 1952-3; mixed doubles r/u 1951, s/f 1952; Australian men's singles q/f 1950-1, s/f 1952, r/u 1953, won 1954, q/f 1955-6, s/f 1958; men's doubles s/f 1950-1, r/u 1952-3, won 1954, s/f 1955, r/u 1956, s/f 1958; French men's singles q/f 1951, 1954-5, s/f 1957, won 1958; men's doubles s/f 1951, r/u 1953, s/f 1954, r/u 1957; mixed doubles r/u 1951, s/f 1952, r/u 1953, s/f 1954. Davis Cup 1950-57. Turned professional in 1958. A fine touch player with an acute appreciation of tactics and an unorthodox approach to training. Left-handed.

Below **Mervyn Rose**

Above **Ken Rosewall**

Rosewall, Kenneth R. (Australia)

Born Sydney, N.S.W., 2 Nov. 1934; Wimbledon men's singles q/f 1953, r/u 1954, s/f 1955, r/u 1956, 1970, s/f 1971; men's doubles s/f 1952, won 1953, s/f 1954, r/u 1955, won 1956, r/u 1968; mixed doubles r/u 1954; US men's singles q/f 1952, s/f 1953-4, r/u 1955, won 1956, s/f 1968, q/f 1969, won 1970, s/f 1973; men's doubles s/f 1952, r/u 1954, won 1956, s/f 1970, r/u 1973; mixed doubles r/u 1954, won 1956; Australian men's singles q/f 1952, won 1953, s/f 1954, won 1955, r/u 1956, won 1971-2; men's doubles won 1953, r/u 1955, won 1956, r/u 1969, won 1972; French men's singles won 1953, 1968, r/u 1969; men's doubles s/f 1952, won 1953, r/u 1954, won 1968; mixed doubles s/f 1953. Davis Cup 1953-6. Turned professional 1957. WCT contract pro 1971-2. ILTF GP 3rd 1970. WCT 3rd (F won) 1971, 2nd (F won) May 1972, 1st Group B (F s/f) 1973. Generally held to be the finest groundstroke player of the post-World-War II era and especially notable for the quality of an impeccable backhand. He was one of the leaders of the game as an amateur (1952-6), as a pro (1956-68) and subsequently in the context of Open Tennis. Like GONZALEZ, he stands among the contenders as an all time 'great' despite never winning the Wimbledon singles. See colour plate, page 333 and CENTRE COURT CLASSICS (PART 1).

Rothmans of Pall Mall Ltd

Lawn-tennis sponsorship in Britain by Rothmans began in 1963 when the tobacco company supported the KENT CHAMPIONSHIPS. This was so successful that in 1964 Rothmans sponsored seven tournaments and doubled the the number in 1965. In December 1967 it embarked on a covered-court event, the Rothmans Invitation Tournament at Crystal Palace. More innovations followed in 1969, including support for the British Davis Cup squad during its most successful run for over 30 years when the team reached the Inter-Zone final.

Rothmans also took over from W.D. & H.O. Wills the sponsorship of the BRITISH HARD COURT CHAMPIONSHIPS at Bournemouth.

Rothman's largest venture is now the big Rothmans International Tournament held at the ROYAL ALBERT HALL since March 1970. In 1973, with over £20,000 in prize money and an entry of 32 for this event, now part of the WORLD CHAMPIONSHIP TENNIS circuit, it became necessary to play the preliminary matches at the new Deeside Leisure Centre in North Wales.

Rothmans now sponsors some dozen tournaments each season, including the prestigious pre-Wimbledon grass-court events at Surbiton, Eastbourne and the Queen's Club, and the post-Wimbledon tournament at Hoylake which in 1972 became a women's Grand Prix event. Rothmans also sponsors lawn tennis in CANADA and NEW ZEALAND. DC

Rough side of racket see TOSS

Round, Miss Dorothy E. [Mrs R. Little] (Gt Britain)

Born Dudley, Worcs., 13 July 1909; Wimbledon women's singles q/f 1931-2, r/u 1933, won 1934, q/f 1935-6, won 1937; women's doubles s/f 1931; mixed doubles won 1934-6; US women's singles s/f 1933; women's doubles r/u 1931, s/f 1933; mixed doubles s/f 1933; Australian women's singles won 1935; women's doubles s/f 1935; French women's doubles s/f 1930. Wightman Cup 1931-6. The second of two British women's singles champions at Wimbledon between the world wars, she had formidable power and accuracy of groundstrokes. At one time her refusal to play on Sunday brought some embarrassment to the French authorities. She was the first overseas challenger to win the Australian women's singles and dominated the British game 1933-7.

Round-Arm Service see SERVICE

Round Robin

Or 'American tournament', a tournament in which each competitor plays all the others on a league basis.

Above **Royal Albert Hall, London.** The 1970 Rothmans International Tournament

Royal Albert Hall, London

This world-famous concert hall, built in 1872, had for many years been used as a sports arena, staging major sports from world-championship boxing to five-a-side soccer, table tennis, six-day cycling and all-in wrestling, but it was not looked upon as a likely setting for international lawn tennis until 1969. The idea of using it for this purpose is credited to Gerald Williams, the LTA's promotion manager, who was searching for a large arena in central London as ROTHMANS wished to stage a major international tournament indoors and to attract Rod Laver, Ken Rosewall and many other WCT professionals. After other halls had been considered and rejected, it was discovered that by raising the floor of the Albert Hall by some ten feet (three metres) a large enough playing area could be constructed and covered with a synthetic surface. The seating in this grand circular build-

ing was first-class. More important, the players were available for an event in March 1970. No one knew how long it would take flooring contractors to build the foundations and lay the new wooden floor, put down the Nygrass carpet and erect the court surrounds, but by the time a few chosen players, including Christine (Truman) Janes and Jaroslav Drobný, had arrived for the 'rehearsal' demonstration matches, everything was amazingly shipshape. When the opening night of the tournament arrived (4 March 1970) indoor tennis at the Royal Albert Hall was an instant success. In the autumn of the same year the finals of the DEWAR CUP were also moved into the Albert Hall and have been staged there ever since.

Memorable occasions at the Albert Hall include the marathon match in that first tournament when Britain's Mark Cox was defeated by the American Marty Riessen (in the days before the tie-break!) 25-27, 8-6, 7-5 (Riessen went on to win the event) and the argument in the Rothmans Tournament of 1972 between Ilie Năstase and Clark Graebner.

Champagne suppers served in the boxes – a feature of a tennis night out at the Albert Hall – are invariably sold out long before a tournament starts. DC

Royal Tennis see THE ORIGINS OF LAWN TENNIS (PART 1)

Rubber

A term increasingly used for an individual singles or doubles match in a team competition, as opposed to 'tie' which is used for the whole match between the two teams. For example, a DAVIS CUP tie is settled by the best of five rubbers.

The term 'dead' is sometimes applied to a match (rubber) that remains to be played in the tie when one side already has a winning lead (i.e. in the Davis Cup when the score is already 3-0 or 3-1). DC

Rules of Lawn Tennis see THE RULES AND THEIR INTERPRETATION (PART 1)

Rumania

Lawn tennis was known and played in Rumania soon after it was patented by Major Walter Clopton Wingfield in Britain. It was introduced by young people who had studied abroad and by foreign diplomats and businessmen. Soon after the first courts were built, the first Rumanian Tennis Clubs were founded: the Raqueta (1898) in Bucharest and the Galatz Tennis Club (also 1898) in Galatz. Tennis spread quickly to towns all over the country and tennis clubs and inter-club matches were organized.

At the beginning of the 20th century two main clubs were founded in Bucharest, the Doherty Club (1906) and the Tennis Sports Club (1907). One of Rumanian tennis's pioneers, Mircea Iconomu, 85 in 1972, remembered his surprise when he returned from France, where he had studied and won a tennis competition at Montpelier, to find that Bucharest already possessed tennis courts. He played with the best players of those times, including a match in 1908 with Mişu Stern, the best player of the day in Bucharest, watched by over 50 spectators.

The organization of lawn tennis clubs encouraged the game itself as well as competitions, club and inter-club activities. More tournaments were held in 1909-10, among them inter-school tournaments, singles and doubles, and the Cămărăşescu Cup (which became known as the National Championships in 1948). The pupils of Saint Sava and Gheorghe Lazăr High Schools in Bucharest distinguished themselves in these. The first Cămărăşescu Cup competition was won by the Doherty Club team. The Rumanian Tennis Club (RTC) was founded in Bucharest on 8 May 1910 and became one of the most powerful in the country, contributing much to the development and quality of Rumanian tennis. Its players and teams won many tournaments.

Rumanian Championships Winners

Men's Singles		Women's Singles	
1911	M. Stern	1911	Miss M. Perieţeanu
1912	L. San Galli	1912	Miss S. Alexandrescu
1913	L. San Galli	1913	Miss S. Bărbulescu
1914	A. San Galli	1914	Miss S. Bărbulescu
1915	*No Competition*	1915	*No Competition*
1916	J. Rathingham	1916	Miss S. Bărbulescu
1917-19	*No Competition*	1917-19	*No Competition*
1920	A. San Galli	1920	Miss S. Bărbulescu
1921	A. San Galli	1921	Miss S. Bărbulescu
1922	I. Rossetti	1922	Miss M. Golescu
1923	G. Lupu	1923	Miss M. Golescu
1924	G. Lupu	1924	Miss M. Golescu
1925	G. Lupu	1925	Miss M. Golescu
1926	G. Poulieff	1926	Miss E. Stefănescu
1927	G. Poulieff	1927	Miss E. Stefănescu
1928	G. Lupu	1928	Miss E. Schlosser
1929	N. Mişu	1929	Miss M. Fullop
1930	C. Cantacuzino	1930	Miss L. Zissowitz
1931	G. Poulieff	1931	Miss E. Stefănescu
1932	G. Poulieff	1932	Miss L. Zissowitz
1933	A. Botez	1933	Miss L. Popper
1934	A. Botez	1934	Miss C. Somogy
1935	A. Schmidt	1935	Miss C. Somogy
1936	A. Schmidt	1936	Miss C. Somogy
1937	C. Caralulis	1937	Miss C. Somogy
1938	C. Tănăsescu	1938	Miss L. Popper
1939	C. Tănăsescu	1939	Miss M. Berescu
1940	C. Tănăsescu	1940	Miss M. Berescu
1941	C. Tănăsescu	1941	Miss M. Rurac
1942	C. Tănăsescu	1942	Miss M. Rurac
1943	C. Tănăsescu	1943	Miss M. Rurac
1944	C. Tănăsescu	1944	Miss M. Rurac
1945	C. Tănăsescu	1945	Miss M. Rurac
1946	C. Tănăsescu	1946	Miss M. Rurac
1947	G. Viziru	1947	Miss E. Stăncescu
1948	G. Viziru	1948	Miss E. Stăncescu
1949	T. Bădin	1949	Miss I. Todorovski
1950	G. Viziru	1950	Miss I. Todorovski
1951	G. Viziru	1951	Miss E. Stăncescu
1952	C. Caralulis	1952	Miss E. Stăncescu
1953	G. Viziru	1953	Miss E. Stăncescu
1954	G. Viziru	1954	Miss E. Stăncescu
1955	C. Zacopceanu	1955	Miss I. Ponova
1956	G. Viziru	1956	Miss E. Stăncescu
1957	G. Viziru	1957	Miss E. Roşianu
1958	G. Viziru	1958	Miss J. Namian
1959	I. Ţiriac	1959	Miss J. Namian
1960	I. Ţiriac	1960	Miss J. Namian
1961	I. Ţiriac	1961	Miss M. Ilina
1962	I. Ţiriac	1962	Miss J. Namian
1963	I. Ţiriac	1963	Miss J. Namian
1964	I. Ţiriac	1964	Miss J. Namian
1965	I. Ţiriac	1965	Miss I. Dibar
1966	I. Ţiriac	1966	Miss E. Dumitrescu
1967	I. Năstase	1967	Miss I. Dibar
1968	I. Năstase	1968	Miss I. Dibar
1969	I. Santei	1969	Miss I. Dibar
1970	P. Mărmureanu	1970	Miss A. Kun
1971	P. Mărmureanu	1971	Miss A. Kun
1972	M. Viorel	1972	Mrs I. Dibar-Gohn
1973	T. Ovici	1973	Miss V. Ruzici

The first National Championships were held on 30 May-10 June 1911; the first champion was Mişu Stern. A championship was organized in Iaşi in the same year. It included the first women's singles in Rumania, which was won by Jana Alexandrescu from Sinaia.

Steady tennis development was marked by the foundation in 1912 within the Rumanian Federation of Sporting Societies of the Lawn Tennis Committee, an official body which led and organized tennis activities all over the country. It issued a set of rules and graded the players in two categories. Meanwhile Rumanian players began to take part in international tournaments, including the Wimbledon Championships in which Mişu Stern competed in 1915.

World War I left its evil mark on the development of tennis in Rumania; the number of players and of competitions both decreased. But Mişu Nicolae, one of the best players of the period, won international tournaments in Monte Carlo, Cannes and Nice in 1919, and distinguished himself at Wimbledon, Hurlingham and Hendon as well as in the World Championships in Brussels. Along with the organization of internal competitions, Rumania developed international links, joining the ILTF as a Full Member in 1924. An important event in this sense was the staging of the first International Championships of Rumania in 1922. In 1920-2 Rumanian players took part in tournaments in Paris (Roland Garros) and at Wimbledon, the World Championships in Brussels, and the Olympic Games in Paris. In 1922 a Rumanian team competed for the first time in the DAVIS CUP and was defeated by the Indian team at Beckenham (England) 5-0. Internal activity was marked by national recognition of players from towns such as Arad, Cluj, Lugoj, Oradea, Petroşani, Galatzi, Tîrgul Mureş and Sibiu. Some international competitions organized in the border towns attracted players from Yugoslavia, Hungary and Austria. On 12 March 1929 the Federation of Tennis Societies was founded (its constitution is dated 13 February); it affiliated to the International Lawn Tennis Federation the same year.

In 1929 the Rumanian team took part for the first time in the Balkan Cup, competing with Yugoslav, Bulgarian, Greek and Turkish teams. The first University Tennis Competitions were held in 1930.

In the next few years Rumanian tennis made remarkable progress in growth, number of players and quality. In the 1930s a number of players of international class such as A. Botez, Gică Poulieff, G. Lupu, Magda Rurac, Arnulf Schmidt, Cristea Caralulis, and Constantin Tănăsescu distinguished themselves. Magda Rurac and Constantin Tănăsescu were recognized as being among the best players in Europe. During this time Rumanian teams continued to take part in the Davis Cup and Balkan Cup and more players competed in various international tournaments.

The social and political changes that occurred in Rumania after 23 August 1944 encouraged the development of tennis. The state gave support to all sports, including tennis, by establishing new grounds, and by providing equipment and trainers, all free of charge, for young people. Rumania was readmitted to the ILTF in 1947 as a Full Member.

While the well-known players Tănăsescu (nine times national champion) and Magda Rurac (eight times national champion) continued to be active, young and gifted players like the brothers Gheorghe and Marin Viziru made their mark. Their efforts have been successfully followed by Ion Ţiriac and Ilie Năstase, the two greatest Rumanian players, whose excellent performances have been achieved in international tournaments all over the world. Keenness and talent played a great part in Rumania's winning through to the Challenge Round of the Davis Cup in 1969 and 1971. In 1972 the Rumanian team reached the Final against the United States, after defeating Switzerland 5-0, Iran 5-0, Italy 4-1, the USSR 3-2 and Australia 4-1. The Final, held in Bucharest at the S.C. Progresul on 13-15 October, and won 3-2 by the United States, was watched by about 7,000 spectators each day. It was the first Final staged in Europe for 35 years.

Rumania first played in the FEDERATION CUP in 1973, reaching the semi-finals.

Rumania's crowning achievements include Ilie Năstase's reaching the final at the French Championships (1971) and, with Ion Ţiriac, winning the men's doubles at Roland Garros (1970), winning the Italian Championships (1970) and, with Casals, winning the Wimbledon mixed doubles (1970). His victories over great players such as Rod Laver, John Newcombe, Roy Emerson, Stan Smith, Arthur Ashe, Roger Taylor, Tony Roche, Nicola Pilić, Tom Okker, Zelko Franulović and Jan Kodeš combined to place Năstase sixth in the 1970 world open rankings and justified his being considered the best European player. In 1972 he reached the Wimbledon final and won at Forest Hills.

Today Rumanian tennis enjoys unprecedented growth, in numbers of courts, tennis sections and clubs affiliated to the Rumanian Lawn Tennis Federation, and numbers of players. More and more competitions are held: senior, junior and children's national championships, a national team championship, and the established tournaments organized by the district committees such as the Transylvanian Championship in Cluj, the Dr Petru Groza Cup in Oradea, the Mureşul Cup in Tîrgu Mures, the Peace Cup in Arad, and the Danube Cup in Galatz. Many other competitions such as the international championships of Rumania for juniors and young people are held too. Rumanian teams take part in the Davis Cup, GALEA CUP, ANNIE SOISBAULT CUP, VALERIO CUP, PRINCESS SOPHIA CUP, and the annual Balkan Championships. The last, a continuation of the Balkan Cup, are organized in turn by Bulgaria, Yugoslavia, Greece, Rumania and Turkey: the Rumanian men's team has won it six times, the women's three times. AL

GOVERNING BODY: Federatia Romana de Tenis, Vasile Conta 16, Bucharest

Ryan, Miss Elizabeth (USA)

Born Los Angeles, Calif., 5 Feb. 1892; Wimbledon women's singles q/f 1912, r/u* 1914, s/f 1919, r/u* 1920, r/u 1921, q/f 1922, s/f 1923, q/f 1924, s/f 1927-8, r/u 1930; women's doubles won 1914, 1919-23, 1925-7, s/f 1928-9, won 1930, r/u 1932, won 1933-4; mixed doubles won 1919, r/u 1920, won 1921, r/u 1922, won 1923, r/u 1925, s/f 1926, won 1927-8, s/f 1929, won 1930, 1932; US women's singles q/f 1925, r/u 1926, q/f 1934; women's doubles r/u 1925, won 1926, r/u 1933, s/f 1934; mixed doubles s/f 1925, won 1926, 1933, r/u 1934; French women's singles q/f 1926, 1930-1; women's doubles s/f 1926, won 1930, r/u 1931, won 1932-4; mixed doubles s/f 1930, 1933, r/u 1934. Wightman Cup 1926. Possibly the most assiduous tournament competitor of all time, this Californian came first to Great Britain in 1912 and after World War I played mostly in Britain and Europe. She rarely missed a week of tournament play but at the top level she had her greatest success in doubles. She won more Wimbledon titles than any other player. In 19 playing years (1912-34) she won at least 659 tournament events including the last women's championship of Imperial Russia (1914). She was a strong volleyer, her approach always a heavily chopped forehand.

Below Elizabeth Ryan

St Lucia and St Vincent see COMMONWEALTH CARIBBEAN LTA

Sangster, Michael J. (Gt Britain)

Born Torquay, Devon, 11 Sept. 1940; Wimbledon men's singles s/f 1961; US men's singles s/f 1961, q/f 1964; men's doubles r/u 1964; Australian men's singles q/f 1961, 1964; mixed doubles r/u 1964; French men's singles s/f 1963; men's doubles s/f 1963. Davis Cup 1960-8. Had (early 1960s) a very big service.

San Marino

San Marino has been an Associate Member of the ILTF since 1950. BR

GOVERNING BODY: Federazione Sammarinese Tennis, 47031 Republic of San Marino

Santana, Manuel (Spain)

Born Madrid, 10 May 1938; Wimbledon men's singles q/f 1962, s/f 1963, won 1966; men's doubles s/f 1963; US men's singles won 1965, s/f 1966; French men's singles q/f 1960, won 1961, s/f 1962-3, won 1964; men's doubles won 1963, s/f 1964. Davis Cup 1958-68. Outstandingly the finest Spanish player of all time. His style and touch were all his own, characterized by a heavy topspin from both backhand and forehand that was productive of angled passing shots normally regarded as impossible. His artistic virtuosity combined with a happy temperament and a tendency only to find inspiration after losing the first two sets made him supremely popular. His skill twice took Spain to the Challenge Round of the Davis Cup (1965 and 1967) against Australia, although with insufficient support the trophy remained elusive.

Sato, Jiri see JAPAN

Savitt, Richard (USA)

Born Bayonne, N.J., 4 March 1927; Wimbledon men's singles won 1951, q/f 1952; men's doubles s/f 1951; US men's singles s/f 1950-1, q/f 1952, 1956, 1958; Australian men's singles won 1951, s/f 1952; men's doubles s/f 1951-2; French men's singles q/f 1951-2; men's doubles r/u 1951-2. Davis Cup 1951. Formidable for his rolled backhand.

Scandinavian Championships

In 1936 the Swedish Lawn Tennis Association celebrated its 30th anniversary and decided to stage an international tournament in Stock-

Scandinavian Championships

holm. The venue was the covered courts of the B-Hall in Stockholm, where H. M. King Gustaf V played regularly with his club members (the hall was built in the early 1920s and was destroyed by fire in the late 1940s). The event attracted a number of prominent European players, such as the Frenchmen Borotra, Feret and Lesueur, the German woman champion Horn and the famous Hilde Sperling, at that time a Danish citizen. The men's singles was won by Karl Schröder.

The ILTF recognized the 1936 tournament as an 'official championship' and confirmed and extended the decision for the future at its Annual General Meeting the same year. Since then it has been played as the only official championship indoors. The events played are men's and women's singles and doubles. The mixed doubles ceased in 1970.

The four Scandinavian countries, Denmark, Finland, Norway and Sweden, agreed in 1936 to stage the Championships every year, the venue circulating between the four capitals concerned, Copenhagen, Helsinki, Oslo and Stockholm. For various reasons the order has been changed at times but generally each country stages the tournament every fourth year. It is usually held at the end of January or beginning of February.

In 1967 qualifying competitions were introduced, mostly in order to give young people an opportunity to play several matches in a few days and also to concentrate the actual tournament into a shorter period of time. This arrangement has worked out well: many young Scandinavians travel to the venue to play the qualifying matches, staged as round robins in some four or five groups. The organizing nation contributes a certain amount of money to the expenses of the winners of each qualifying group.

The Championships have been held every year since 1936 with the exception of 1940-7. Many prominent players have taken part, for a number of years the Scandinavians dominating the men's events and the British the women's.

With the introduction of open tournaments (1968-9) the increased expenses involved caused great difficulties for the organizers. Without sponsorship it has proved impossible to invite leading players of sufficient calibre to maintain the tournament's standard as the official world covered-court event. SH

THE LAWN TENNIS ASSOCIATION SCORING SHEET
EVENT: _____ MATCH { JONES v SMITH
UMPIRE: P. Brown
Important: Please sign your name here.
COURT No.: _____

SET No.: 1 — SET WON BY JONES — GAMES 6-3
SET No.: 2 — SET WON BY JONES — (Set 3 is on the back of this sheet) GAMES 6-1
MATCH WON BY JONES — SCORE 6-3 6-1
CHALLENGE HOUSE · 618 MITCHAM ROAD · Slazenger · CROYDON · SURREY

Above **Scoresheet.** Dots are recommended by the British Umpires' Association for recording the points won but strokes may be used. Double faults are marked by an X and set or match points by a ring round the dot.

Scandinavian Covered Court Championships Winners

Men's Singles

1936	K. Schröder
1937	A. Jacobsen
1938	F. Punčec
1939	H. Bolelli
1940-47	*No Competition*
1948	B. Fornstedt
1949	K. Nielsen
1950	S. Davidson
1951	T. Johansson
1952	K. Nielsen
1953	K. Nielsen
1954	S. Davidson
1955	K. Nielsen
1956	B. Patty
1957	S. Davidson
1958	K. Nielsen
1959	S. Davidson
1960	J. E. Lundqvist
1961	U. Schmidt
1962	U. Schmidt
1963	J. E. Lundqvist
1964	J. Ulrich
1965	R. Taylor
1966	R. K. Wilson
1967	J. E. Lundqvist
1968	J. Leschly
1969	O. Bengtson
1970	J. E. Lundqvist
1971	J. Hrebec
1972	J. Leschly
1973	B. Borg

Women's Singles

1936	Mrs H. Sperling
1937	Mrs H. Sperling
1938	Miss R. M. Hardwick
1939	Mrs H. Sperling
1940-47	*No Competition*
1948	Mrs N. Landry
1949	Mrs H. Sperling
1950	Mrs H. Sperling
1951	Miss B. Sandén
1952	Miss J. Quertier
1953	Miss A. Mortimer
1954	Miss A. Mortimer
1955	Miss A. Mortimer
1956	Miss A. Mortimer
1957	Miss J. A. Shilcock
1958	Miss E. Vollmer
1959	Miss A. Mortimer
1960	Miss A. S. Haydon
1961	Miss A. Mortimer
1962	Miss A. S. Haydon
1963	Miss A. S. Haydon
1964	Miss C. C. Truman
1965	Miss E. Starkie
1966	Mrs P. F. Jones
1967	Miss H. Niessen
1968	Miss S. V. Wade
1969	Miss C. Sandberg
1970	Miss J. Williams
1971	Miss C. Sandberg
1972	Miss W. Shaw
1973	Mrs I. Bentzer

Scarborough Lawn Tennis Club (UK)

Scarborough was Yorkshire's main lawn tennis centre from the early 1920s until 1968, when plans to convert it into a sports centre were approved.

Several Davis Cup matches have been played there and it was for a long time the home of the Yorkshire and the North of England Championships. Soaring maintenance costs, however, brought financial difficulties and major events ceased to be staged there, although the Yorkshire Championships returned for one year in 1971 before finding a new home in Hull. Scarborough LTC had 19 first-class grass courts. In the new complex it is planned to have five grass courts, five hard and one floodlit tarmac. DC

Schroeder, Frederick R. [Ted] (USA)

Born Newark, N.J., 20 July 1921; Wimbledon men's singles won 1949; men's doubles r/u 1949; US men's singles q/f 1940, s/f 1941, won 1942, r/u 1949; men's doubles won 1940-1, s/f 1946, won 1947; mixed doubles won 1942. Davis Cup 1946-51. A Wimbledon champion at his first and only attempt, despite being match point down in his quarter-final against SEDGMAN. A great match player and scrambler, known for his Popeye corn-cob pipe.

Schuurman, Miss Renee
[Mrs P. Haygarth] (S. Africa)

Born Durban, 26 Oct. 1939; Wimbledon women's singles q/f 1960, s/f 1961, q/f 1962-3; women's doubles s/f 1957, 1959, r/u 1960, 1962; US women's doubles s/f 1962; Australian women's singles r/u 1959; women's doubles won 1959; mixed doubles r/u 1959; French women's singles q/f 1960, s/f 1962; women's doubles won 1959, s/f 1960, won 1961-3.

Scoresheet

The scoresheet is used by the umpire to record the progress of the match (see illustration).

Scoring

The ten major terms used in normal scoring are: love, 15, 30, 40, deuce, advantage server, advantage receiver, game, set and match. (For the origins of these terms see THE ORIGINS OF LAWN TENNIS, PART 1.)

A game begins at 'love-all' (0-0). A player's first point scores 15; on winning his second point he advances to 30; on winning a third point he reaches 40. If he gains a fourth point he wins the game unless his opponent has also won three points. At three points all (40-40) or *deuce*, if the next point is won by the player serving, the score is strictly called *advantage server*; if won by the player receiving, it is called *advantage receiver*. Normally though, advantage is called by name to the player holding it, e.g. 'Advantage Smith'. If the player holding the advantage wins the next point as well he wins the game. If he loses it the score reverts to deuce. There is no limit to the number of deuces and advantages in a game.

A player who first wins six games wins a *set*. If the score in games has reached 5-5 in what is known as an *advantage set*, one player must gain a two-game lead before winning the set. (For the tie-break system and the 'professional set' see below.)

A *match* is generally the best of three sets. In major championships men play the best of five sets in both singles and doubles. Except in the early days (see THE BIRTH AND SPREAD OF LAWN TENNIS, PART 1, and SCOTTISH CHAMPIONSHIPS) women have usually played the best of three sets.

When lawn tennis began there was no universal method of scoring. Players invented their own systems. The vast majority copied rackets scoring, with a game (in lawn tennis a set) of 15 points up, a point only being scored if the rally was won by the server. If won by the receiver he then became server. By 1876 the All England Croquet Club (today the All England Lawn Tennis and Croquet Club; see THE BIRTH AND SPREAD OF LAWN TENNIS, PART 1) was using the clock system: 15 for the first point (a quarter past the hour), 30 for the second (half past the hour), 45 – later changed to 40 – for the third (three quarters past the hour); the fourth point (back to the figure 12) indicated game. No one is sure why the third

point changed from 45 to 40 but it may simply have been because it is easier to say or to hear correctly.

The modern system was used at the first Wimbledon in 1877 (except that there were no advantage sets until 1878) and remained constant until the introduction of the TIE-BREAK at the Philadelphia Open Championships in February 1970. It was then unofficially used, but the same year the USLTA gained ILTF recognition for a nine-point tie-break at Forest Hills. Wimbledon followed with a 12-point tie-break in 1971. This, too, was officially recognized.

Since World War II two other types of scoring have been used on occasions but they have never been given the official blessing of the ILTF.

Before open tennis was introduced in 1968, the professionals, often pressed for time and because of television schedule commitments, resorted to playing one-set matches in which the winner was the first player to win 10 games, or, if the score reached 9-9, the first to gain a two-game advantage.

In the mid-1960s James Van Alen introduced the VAN ALEN STREAMLINED SCORING SYSTEM (VASSS) which he claimed would do much to shorten matches and make tennis depend more on skill than stamina.

See also HANDICAPPING. JO

Above **Ted Schroeder**

Scotland

According to the Scottish LTA's *Fifty years of Lawn Tennis in Scotland* (1927), Scottish lawn tennis began in Edinburgh, in the summer of 1875, on the Grange Cricket Ground. Three years later (1878) the first Scottish Championships were held (men's singles and doubles). Women's singles began in 1886 but mixed

doubles were not introduced until 1904 and women's doubles had to wait until 1909. At first, the Championships were controlled by the clubs that donated the cups. The men's singles cup belonged to St Andrew's Club, the women's singles and one of the men's doubles cups to the Dyvours Club, and the other doubles cup to the Edinburgh University Club. In 1894 some players felt that this was unsatisfactory and formed the Scottish Lawn Tennis Association so that it could buy the cups and control the tournaments. The first Championships held under its auspices took place in 1895 at Moffat (Dumfriesshire), where they remained until they moved to Bridge of Allan (Stirlingshire) in 1908.

Today the Scottish LTA has nine affiliated District Associations: the North of Scotland, North East, Midland Counties, Central District, East of Scotland, Border Counties, West of Scotland, South West and Ayrshire Associations. The Scottish LTA, under its national coach, runs numerous training courses at clubs, schools and colleges throughout the country. For the Lawn Tennis Association's INTER-COUNTY CHAMPIONSHIPS, Scotland enters four teams in each of the men's and women's competitions. They represent not individual Scottish counties but North, South, East and West of Scotland. There are about 200 clubs affiliated to the nine Districts. Playing members of these clubs now total just under 9,000, with another 9,000 for junior membership.

Apart from the prewar exploits of Ian Collins, the best of Scottish tennis has probably been seen during the last few years when John Clifton, Harry Matheson, Joyce Williams and Winnie Shaw (Mrs Wooldridge) defeated English invaders. Clifton made the British Davis Cup team, and both Mrs Williams and Mrs Wooldridge have made many Wightman Cup appearances and have frequently been among Britain's top four women players. DC

GOVERNING BODY: Scottish Lawn Tennis Association; Hon. Secretary, Mr D. Manson, 1 Royal Terrace, Edinburgh EH7 5AD

Below **Scotland.** Miss L. H. Paterson (singles champion 1894-6) at Dyvours in 1892

Scottish Championships Winners

Men's Singles

1878	J. Patten MacDougall	1965	J. G. Clifton
1879	L. M. Balfour-Melville	1966	J. G. Clifton
1880	J. Patten	1967	G. B. Primrose
1881	J. G. Horn	1968	J. G. Clifton
1882	J. G. Horn	1969	J. G. Clifton
1883	J. G. Horn	1970	R. O. Ruffels
1884	R. A. Gamble	1971	J. G. Clifton
1885	P. B. Lyon	1972	D. A. Lloyd / H. L. Roulston divided
1886	P. B. Lyon		
1887	H. Grove		
1888	P. B. Lyon	1973	J. Royappa
1889	E. de S. H. Browne		
1890	E. de S. H. Browne		
1891	E. de S. H. Browne		
1892	A. W. Gore		
1893	A. W. Gore		
1894	R. M. Watson		
1895	R. F. Doherty		
1896	R. F. Doherty		
1897	R. F. Doherty		
1898	H. L. Doherty		
1899	E. D. Black		
1900	C. R. D. Pritchett		
1901	W. V. Eaves		
1902	F. L. Riseley		
1903	F. W. Payn		
1904	A. F. Wilding		
1905	A. M. Mackay		
1906	A. M. Mackay		
1907	A. M. Mackay		
1908	R. B. Powell		
1909	T. M. Mavrogordato		
1910	R. B. Powell		
1911	A. W. Dunlop		
1912	J. C. Parke		
1913	H. M. Rice		
1914	J. F. Stokes		
1915-18	No Competition		
1919	C. Branfoot		
1920	C. R. Blackbeard		
1921	G. M. Elliott		
1922	P. D. B. Spence		
1923	P. D. B. Spence		
1924	C. H. Kingsley		
1925	A. Blair		
1926	I. G. Collins		
1927	I. G. Collins		
1928	I. G. Collins		
1929	J. C. Gregory		
1930	J. C. Gregory / J. H. Crawford divided		
1931	V. G. Kirby		
1932	E. R. Avory		
1933	D. MacPhail		
1934	C. L. Burwell		
1935	R. Murray		
1936	D. MacPhail		
1937	H. Billington		
1938	M. D. Deloford		
1939	D. MacPhail		
1940-45	No Competition		
1946	D. MacPhail		
1947	T. A. Slawek		
1948	G. Eros		
1949	N. G. Cockburn		
1950	A. K. Quist / T. A. Slawek divided		
1951	E. W. Sturgess		
1952	I. Ayre		
1953	W. A. Knight		
1954	R. K. Wilson		
1955	J. A. Pickard		
1956	C. V. Baxter		
1957	R. D. Bennett		
1958	C. V. Baxter		
1959	C. V. Baxter		
1960	J. R. Maguire		
1961	J. M. Gracie		
1962	J. T. Wood		
1963	H. S. Matheson		
1964	J. T. Wood		

Women's Singles

1886	Miss M. Boulton	1965	Mrs G. M. Williams
1887	Miss Butler	1966	Miss W. M. Shaw
1888	Miss Butler	1967	Mrs G. M. Williams
1889	Miss Butler	1968	Mrs G. M. Williams
1890	Miss H. Jackson	1969	Miss M. J. Love
1891	Miss H. Jackson	1970	Mrs G. M. Williams
1892	Miss H. Jackson	1971	Mrs G. M. Williams
1893	Miss J. M. Corder	1972	Mrs G. M. Williams / Miss C. A. Molesworth divided
1894	Miss L. H. Paterson		
1895	Miss L. H. Paterson		
1896	Miss L. H. Paterson	1973	Miss J. P. Cooper
1897	Miss M. Hunter		
1898	Mrs O'Neill		
1899	Miss C. Cooper		
1900	Miss M. Hunter		
1901	Miss M. E. Robb		
1902	Miss A. M. M. Ferguson		
1903	Miss M. T. Crawford		
1904	Miss W. A. Longhurst		
1905	Mrs C. White		
1906	Miss A. M. M. Ferguson		
1907	Miss A. M. M. Ferguson		
1908	Miss H. M. Garfit		
1909	Miss H. M. Garfit		
1910	Mrs D. R. Larcombe		
1911	Mrs D. R. Larcombe		
1912	Mrs D. R. Larcombe		
1913	Mrs R. Welsh		
1914	Mrs R. Welsh		
1915-18	No Competition		
1919	Miss M. M. Fergus		
1920	Miss M. Thom		
1921	Mrs R. Welsh		
1922	Mrs R. Welsh		
1923	Mrs R. Welsh		
1924	Miss M. Thom		
1925	Miss M. Thom		
1926	Miss M. Thom		
1927	Miss R. Watson		
1928	Miss J. C. Ridley		
1929	Miss J. C. Ridley		
1930	Miss W. A. Mason		
1931	Miss G. R. Sterry		
1932	Mrs A. Robertson		
1933	Miss W. A. Mason		
1934	Miss J. Hartigan		
1935	Miss A. Lizana		
1936	Miss A. Lizana		
1937	Miss A. Lizana		
1938	Miss R. M. Hardwick		
1939	Mrs E. M. Grant		
1940-45	No Competition		
1946	Mrs R. T. Ellis		
1947	Mrs J. B. Fulton		
1948	Miss J. Gannon		
1949	Miss G. Hoahing		
1950	Miss J. W. K. Stork		
1951	Mrs H. M. Proudfoot		
1952	Miss B. Bartlett		
1953	Miss S. J. Bloomer		
1954	Miss J. M. Petchell		
1955	Miss E. M. Watson		
1956	Miss C. C. Truman		
1957	Miss R. H. Bentley		
1958	Miss E. A. Walker		
1959	Miss N. T. Seacy		
1960	Miss J. S. Barclay		
1961	Miss R. A. Blakelock / Miss F. V. M. MacLennan divided		
1962	Miss J. S. Barclay		
1963	Miss J. S. Barclay		
1964	Mrs G. M. Williams		

Scottish Lawn Tennis Championships

The Scottish Championships, instituted in 1878, have been held at no fewer than 17 separate venues, the first being the Grange Cricket Ground, Edinburgh, and with the exception of one visit to Whitecraigs in 1958 the most recent (since 1947) Craiglockhart, Edinburgh. The Scottish Championships, only one year younger than Wimbledon, hold a place of high esteem in the British calendar. For their first six years (1878-83) they were contested on two covered courts. These, placed end-to-end, with wooden flooring and lit only by side windows, were contained in a building at the Grange Cricket Ground, Raeburn Place, Edinburgh, affectionately known as the 'Tin Temple'. In those early days, native talent generally prevailed: the first Scottish champion was J. Patten MacDougall, Registrar-General for Scotland. This was probably fitting, for the game had been introduced in the mid-1870s by a small group of legal dignitaries taking early morning exercise at the old Grindlay Street Drill Hall before repairing to their chambers. In those early days, too, Wimbledon champions visited Scotland. Those whose names appear on the honours board include the Doherty brothers, A. W. Gore and A. F. Wilding, also a comparative 'modern', Jack Crawford, the elegant Australian. The period 1895-1907, when the championships were at Moffat (Dumfriesshire), was a golden era and one about which such noted historians as A. Wallis Myers, R. Wood Hawks and W. Cairns all wrote enthusiastically. The winners of those years included the two Dohertys, Captain Wilding, Mrs Charlotte Sterry and Miss M. E. Robb, all world (Wimbledon) champions.

The next vintage period probably started about 1926 with the advent of a superb doubles exponent, Ian Collins. In 1925, however, a frustrated tennis writer lamented: 'There was the usual almost complete lack of advertising, reflected in the attendance.' The personalities of the late 1920s changed all that and crowds of 5,000 watched the finals at the end of the decade when Collins, Dr John Gregory and Joan Ridley won the titles. Collins became a Scottish idol: he won the singles title three times and never lost a Davis Cup double in six rubbers with Dr Gregory. He not only defeated Henri Cochet in the 1932 Wimbledon Championship but also won a cricket cap against Australia and an Oxford golf Blue. (He missed a soccer Blue after breaking his leg steeplechasing.) He was followed into the Davis Cup team by Don MacPhail, whose four Scottish titles spanned 14 years (1933-46). MacPhail was an outstanding player until the war interrupted his career.

More recently, John Clifton, the protégé of a superb coach, Ignacy Tłoczynski, won his first title when only 19 and is the present record holder with five championships (1965-6, 1968-9, 1971).

The first women's championship took place

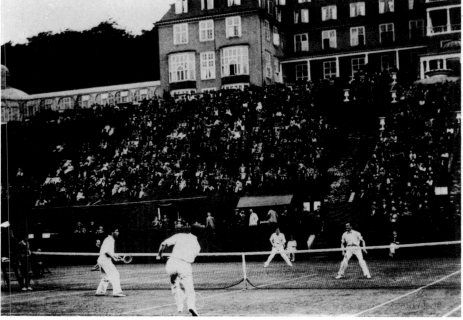

Scottish Championships. *Top* R. M. Watson *(left)* and E. B. Fuller, doubles champions 1891, with the 'Tin Temple' in the background. *Above* A pre-war men's doubles final at Peebles

in 1886. Seven ladies from four families competed and the final, won by Miss M. Boulton, was over five sets. Winnie Mason, of Glasgow, who had the biggest forehand shot in British women's tennis, won the title in 1930 and 1933, and her daughter, Winnie Shaw (Mrs Wooldridge) won in 1966.

The Chilean Anita Lizana was always a great favourite with Scottish crowds. She was champion four times, in 1935-7 and, as Mrs Ronald Ellis, having married a Scot, again in 1946. Joyce Barclay (Mrs Williams), a talented youngster from Dundee, who became Scottish senior champion when only 15, won the singles title nine times and shared it once in the 13 years between 1960 and 1972, a tremendous record of consistency. DC

Scriven, Miss Margaret Croft [Mrs F. H. Vivian] (Gt Britain)
Born Leeds, 17 Aug. 1912; Wimbledon women's singles q/f 1931, 1933-4, 1937; women's doubles s/f 1934; US mixed doubles s/f 1933; French women's singles won 1933-4, s/f 1935, q/f 1937; women's doubles s/f 1933, won 1935; mixed doubles s/f 1931, 1934. Wightman Cup 1933-4, 1938. A lefthander, awkward in style, she had patient success on hard courts on the merits of a punishing forehand. She won the British junior championship (1929) without having had a lesson.

Seamco Sporting Goods
Now a division of Dart Industries Inc., the original company was established in 1877 as the Seamless Rubber Company. Since the 1920s it has made all types of inflated balls and recently produced an alloy-framed tennis racket. Its consultant is Ken Rosewall. JB
HEAD OFFICE: New Haven, Conn., USA

SEAP Games see REGIONAL GAMES

Sears, Miss Eleonora Randolph (USA)
Born 1881; US women's singles r/u* 1911, r/u 1912, q/f 1915, r/u* 1916, s/f 1917, q/f 1918; women's doubles won 1911, s/f 1912, won 1915-17; mixed doubles r/u 1912, won 1916, s/f 1917.

Sears, Miss Evelyn (USA)
US women's singles won 1907, r/u 1908, s/f 1916; women's doubles won 1908.

Sears, Richard Dudley (USA)
Born Boston. Mass., 26 Oct. 1861, died 18 April 1943; Wimbledon men's doubles s/f 1884; US men's singles won 1881-7; men's doubles won 1882-7. The first US champion, when he was 19.

Sears Cup
An American team competition for women, their counterpart of the CHURCH CUP. It began in 1927 when New England defeated the Eastern States 5-2, and has been played every year since then with either three or four teams taking part. The Cup was named after Eleonora SEARS.

Sedgman, Frank A. (Australia)
Born Mont Albert, Victoria, 29 Oct. 1927; Wimbledon men's singles q/f 1949, r/u 1950, q/f 1951, won 1952; men's doubles won 1948, 1951-2; mixed doubles r/u 1948, s/f 1950, won 1951-2; US men's singles q/f 1949, won 1951-2; men's doubles won 1950-1, r/u 1952; mixed doubles s/f 1948, r/u 1950, won 1951-2; Australian men's singles won 1949-50, s/f 1951, r/u 1952; men's doubles r/u 1947-8, s/f 1949-50, won 1951-2; mixed doubles won 1949-50; French men's singles s/f 1951, r/u 1952; men's doubles r/u 1948, won 1951-2; mixed doubles r/u 1948, won 1951-2. Davis Cup 1949-52.

A beautiful mover and uncanny in anticipation, he was outstanding in the forecourt and possessed of a brilliant forehand. He was equally formidable in doubles and he and his compatriot MCGREGOR won all the four major championships in 1951. As triple champion at Wimbledon in 1952 he was the last man to bring off the feat. He never lost a double in the Davis Cup. He became a professional in 1953 and his match at Wembley against GONZALEZ in 1956, which Gonzalez won 4-6, 11-9, 11-9, 9-7, was reckoned among the best ever played. He was the first Australian to win the US singles title. See AUSTRALIA.

Seeding
The placing in the draw by various formulae of leading players, so that they cannot meet each other before the later rounds. In ILTF tournaments the seeding is restricted in numbers as follows:

Two may be seeded with not less than eight entries; four may be seeded with not less than

16 entries; six may be seeded with not less than 24 entries; eight may be seeded with 32 or more entries.

Modified seeding was used at Wimbledon for the first time in 1924. Complete seeding of both men's and women's singles was instituted in 1927, and the following year all five events were seeded. DC

Segura, Francisco ['Pancho'] (Ecuador)

Born Guayaquil, 20 June 1921; Wimbledon men's doubles s/f 1946; US men's singles q/f 1946-7; men's doubles s/f 1947; French men's doubles r/u 1946. Became pro 1947. He had a double-fisted forehand of rare accuracy and power and his enthusiastic fighting qualities made him one of the most popular men in the professional ranks in the 1950s.

Seixas, Elias Victor (USA)

Born Philadelphia, 30 Aug. 1923; Wimbledon men's singles s/f 1950, q/f 1952, won 1953, q/f 1954, s/f 1956, q/f 1957; men's doubles r/u 1952, s/f 1953, r/u 1954, s/f 1955; mixed doubles won 1953-6; US men's singles r/u 1951, 1953, won 1954, s/f 1955-6, q/f 1957-8; men's doubles won 1952, s/f 1953, won 1954, r/u 1956, s/f 1957; mixed doubles won 1953-5, s/f 1956-7; Australian men's singles s/f 1953, q/f 1954-5; men's doubles s/f 1953-4, won 1955; French men's singles q/f 1950, r/u 1953, q/f 1954-5; men's doubles s/f 1950, 1953, won 1954-5; mixed doubles won 1953. Davis Cup 1951-7. His rather rough style was compensated by a rugged match temperament. With 55 rubbers he played more Davis Cup than any other American. He was one of the first great exploiters of the attacking topspin lob.

Senegal

Senegal has been an Associate Member of the ILTF since 1961. BR
GOVERNING BODY: Fédération Sénégalaise de Lawn-Tennis, B.P. 510, Dakar

Seniors in the United States term used for VETERANS

Server the player whose turn it is to serve. See ORDER OF SERVICE, TOSS.

Service

There are three effective service actions used today: the flat service, the slice service and the topspin service. They are described here as if both server and receiver were right-handed.

The flat service, being hit with little or no spin, has the fastest forward motion and tends to come off the surface extremely quickly after landing. The ball is thrown straight up and hit with an open-faced racket with the follow through down the left side of the body. A player possessing a 'big' flat service is often referred to as serving 'cannonballs'.

The slice service imparts sidespin to the ball, making it break sharply to the right of the

receiver when it hits the ground and usually keeping it low. The ball is thrown slightly to the right of the body and in front of the head. Then the racket is brought slightly down and across the ball to finish on the left-hand side of the body, thus imparting sidespin.

The topspin service is opposite to the slice in that it makes the ball break towards the opponent's left and bound quite high. The follow through finishes on the left side of the body, as in the slice. The ball is thrown a little further to the left than in the flat service. The body turns and bends under the ball and the racket strikes the ball a glancing blow in an upwards and outwards direction.

When this action is exaggerated it becomes a kick service (or American twist). The racket action then tends to take the racket to the right-hand side of the body.

Other service actions, rarely used today, include the overarm, round-arm and under-arm deliveries, and the reverse twist.

The overarm and round-arm actions are similar to those of a bowler at cricket. The overarm is brought straight up and over and the round-arm is round the body and slightly above the shoulder which makes the ball go towards an opponent's forehand.

In the underarm service the ball is thrown in front of the body about waist high and hit upwards over the net. Top- or sidespin can also be imparted by moving the racket sharply up and over or to the left or right of the ball just before and during impact. See also THE DEVELOPMENT OF TECHNIQUE AND STROKEPLAY (PART 1). JO

Service Court see SERVICE LINE

Service Grips see GRIPS

Service Line

There are two service lines, one on either side of the court, 21 ft (6·40 m) from the net and parallel to it. They, together with the centre line, net and inner sideline, circumscribe the service court – the area in which a service from the opposite end must land to be good (see SERVICE). See illustration and Rule 1 (THE RULES AND THEIR INTERPRETATION, PART 1). JO

Serving Out of Turn see RULES (PART 1)

Set see SCORING

Shahenshah Cup see IRAN

Shakespeare, Tennis in, see THE ORIGINS OF LAWN TENNIS (PART 1)

'Shamateurs'

A term applied to players in the era of pre-Open tennis (before April 1968) who took 'under-the-counter' payments to compensate for the small prizes for playing in tournaments – a practice strictly forbidden by the amateur code. See PLAYING STATUS. DC

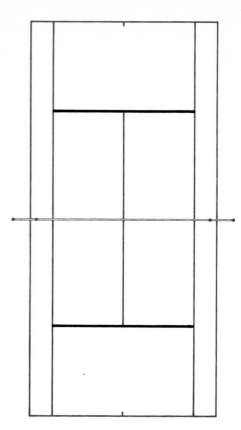

Above **Service Line**

Shepherd-Barron, Mrs Dorothy C. [Miss D. C. Shepherd] (Gt Britain)

Born Beighton, Norfolk, 24 Nov. 1897; died 1953; Wimbledon women's singles q/f 1921, 1924; women's doubles s/f 1921, 1924, r/u 1929, won 1931; mixed doubles r/u 1923-4, 1934; US women's singles q/f 1931; women's doubles r/u 1929, s/f 1931; mixed doubles s/f 1929, 1931; French women's doubles s/f 1926; mixed doubles r/u 1931; Wightman Cup 1924, 1926, 1929, 1931; non-playing captain 1951.

Shoes see FOOTWEAR

Sideline

There are four sidelines on a lawn-tennis court, two inner and two outer. They are 78 ft (23·77 m) long and are bisected by the net which is at right angles to them. In singles the ball must land on or between the inner sidelines and the baseline, but in doubles the ball is good if it lands on or between the outer sidelines and the baseline. The inner and outer sidelines are commonly known as the 'tramlines'; the 'alley' is the area between them. See RULES 1 and 32 (THE RULES AND THEIR INTERPRETATION, PART 1). JO

Singapore

Singapore has been an Associate Member of the ILTF since 1966, when the country became independent. A team regularly takes

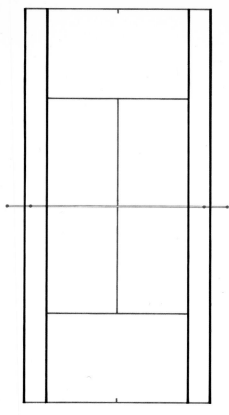

Above **Sideline**

part in the lawn-tennis events of the SEAP Games which were held in Singapore in 1973. There are very many excellent courts on the island. BR

GOVERNING BODY: Singapore Lawn Tennis Association, 13A Yen San Building, 268 Orchard Road, Singapore

Single(s)

A match between two players. The singles court is bounded by baseline and inner SIDE-LINES. JO

Slazengers Ltd

The first company to produce tennis equipment on a large scale, was founded in 1877 by three brothers, Albert, Horatio and Ralph Slazenger, who had been in the rainwear business in Manchester, England. Its foundation year coincided with the first Wimbledon Championships and, as the popularity of lawn tennis and many other sports began to grow, the company flourished. By the mid-1890s it had become very substantial. It quickly became noted for good-quality tennis balls and rackets; in 1902 came its most celebrated achievement, providing balls and equipment at Wimbledon, which it has continued to do ever since.

In 1964 Slazengers began to produce sports clothing under the Panther emblem. Today it has factories producing many types of sports equipment and clothing in Australia, Canada,

France, New Zealand and South Africa as well as Britain, and a marketing company in the United States. In Britain it spends tens of thousands of pounds a year maintaining a special department which provides a complete service to tournaments. It hires out tennis equipment to most British championships and retains the services of many leading players. JB

HEAD OFFICE: Challenge House, Mitcham Road, Croydon, Surrey, England

Slice

A stroke imparting a mixture of under- and sideSPIN, in which the ball rotates from top to bottom but also sideways. Generally the ball will fly through the air with a flatter trajectory and keep low on bouncing. JO

Slice Service see SERVICE

Slocum, Henry Warner, Jr (USA)

Born 28 May 1862; US men's singles q/f 1886, r/u 1887, won 1888-9, r/u 1890; men's doubles r/u 1885, 1887, won 1889. The second US singles champion.

Slow-Balling (Soft-Balling)

As the term implies, the ball is hit softly, or with much SPIN, so that it moves and bounces comparatively slowly and with a higher trajectory than normal. It is resorted to as a variant of tactics, especially against an opponent who likes to play a hardhitting or pressurizing game. The soft, slow ball gives him no pace from which to countergenerate his own and often disturbs his quicker playing rhythm. DC

Smash

The most aggressive stroke in lawn tennis. Similar to service action in that the ball is struck well above the head, it is used as the counter to the lob and generally hit as hard as possible, though smashes are often just as effective when not hit at full power but well angled away from the defending opponent. JO

Smith, Miss Margaret see Mrs B. M. COURT

Smith, Sidney H. (Gt Britain)

Born Stroud, Glos., 3 Feb. 1872; Wimbledon men's singles s/f 1897, q/f 1898, r/u* 1899, r/u 1900, q/f 1901, s/f 1902-4, r/u* 1905, s/f 1906; men's doubles r/u* 1897-8, 1900, s/f 1901, won 1902, r/u 1903-5, won 1906. Davis Cup (British Isles) 1905-6.

Smith, Stanley Roger (USA)

Born Pasadena, Calif., 19 Dec. 1946; Wimbledon men's singles r/u 1971, won 1972; men's doubles r/u 1972; US Open men's singles q/f 1970, won 1971, q/f 1972, s/f 1973; men's doubles won 1968, r/u 1971, s/f 1972; mixed doubles r/u 1967; Australian men's doubles won 1970; French men's singles q/f 1971-2; men's doubles r/u 1971. Davis Cup 1968- . ILTF GP 5th (M won) 1970, 1st (M r/u) 1971,

Above **Stan Smith**

2nd (M r/u) 1972, WCT 1st Group A (F won) 1973.

By American standards a relatively slow developer, he was 24 when he had his first outstanding success as US singles champion in 1971. A painstaking performer without frills, his orthodox power play owed as much to determination as to flair, all of which made him a match winner of rare capacity. In 1972 he took part in two notable achievements, in winning the Wimbledon final against the Rumanian Ilie NĂSTASE after the best title match seen there in four decades and in winning the Davis Cup for the United States in unusually demanding circumstances in Bucharest. Despite hostile crowds, controversial line decisions and strange behaviour by both opponents, Năstase and Ion Ţiriac, Smith, with only the assistance of Erik Van Dillen in the doubles, retained the cup for the United States. This last was a sporting achievement of considerable magnitude. See colour plate, page 336, DAVIS CUP and CENTRE COURT CLASSICS (PART 1).

Smooth side of racket see TOSS

Soft-Ball Tennis

A game derived from lawn tennis, using a rubber ball, developed in JAPAN in the 1890s. It is not to be confused with softball, a variation of baseball in which a larger, softer ball is used, or with 'soft-balling', sometimes used as a synonym for SLOW-BALLING.

South African Championships Winners

Men's Singles	
1891	L. A. Richardson
1892	L. A. Richardson
1893	W. L. Edwards
1894	L. Giddy
1895	L. Giddy
1896	L. Giddy
1897	L. Giddy
1898	L. Giddy
1899	L. G. Heard
1900-02	*No Competition*
1903	R. W. G. Clarke
1904	P. W. Sherwell
1905	H. A. Kitson
1906	J. Richardson
1907	Dr A. Rowan
1908	H. A. Kitson
1909	R. F. Doherty
1910	A. F. Wilding
1911	H. A. Kitson
1912	G. H. Dodd
1913	H. A. Kitson
1914	C. L. Winslow
1915-19	*No Competition*
1920	B. I. C. Norton
1921	L. Raymond
1922	L. Raymond
1923	L. Raymond
1924	L. Raymond
1925	I. J. Richardson
1926	J. Condon
1927	G. Eaglestone
1928	G. Eaglestone
1929	C. J. J. Robbins
1930	L. Raymond
1931	L. Raymond
1932	M. Bertram
1933	C. J. J. Robbins
1934	N. G. Farquharson
1935	N. G. Farquharson
1936	N. G. Farquharson
1937	J. Palada
1938	N. G. Farquharson
1939	E. W. Sturgess
1940	E. W. Sturgess
1941-5	*No Competition*
1946	E. W. Sturgess
1947	E. Fannin
1948	E. W. Sturgess
1949	E. W. Sturgess
1950	E. W. Sturgess
1951	E. W. Sturgess
1952	E. W. Sturgess
1953	E. W. Sturgess
1954	E. W. Sturgess
1955	W. R. Seymour
1956	I. C. Vermaak
1957	E. W. Sturgess
1958	U. Schmidt
1959	G. L. Forbes
1960	E. Buchholz
1961	G. L. Forbes
1962	R. Mark
1963	W. P. Bungert
1964	A. A. Segal
1965	E. C. Drysdale
1966	R. Emerson
1967	M. Santana
1968	T. S. Okker
1969	R. Laver
1970	R. Laver
1971	K. Rosewall
1972	C. Richey
1973	J. S. Connors

Women's Singles	
1891	Miss H. Grant
1892	Miss H. Grant
1893	Miss H. Grant
1894	Miss H. Grant
1895	Miss R. Biddulph
1896	Mrs H. Green
1897	Miss N. Hickman
1898	Miss N. Hickman
1899	Miss N. Hickman
1900-02	*No Competition*
1903	Miss F. Kuys
1904	Mrs H. A. Kirby
1905	Mrs H. A. Kirby
1906	Mrs H. A. Kirby
1907	Mrs H. A. Kirby
1908	Miss B. Kelly
1909	Mrs G. Washington
1910	Mrs H. A. Kirby
1911	Mrs G. Washington
1912	Mrs H. A. Kirby
1913	Miss M. Coles
1914	Miss O. Mathias
1915-19	*No Competition*
1920	Mrs C. L. Winslow
1921	Miss N. Edwards
1922	Mrs T. McJannett
1923	Mrs C. K. Pitt
1924	Mrs I. E. Peacock
1925	Mrs I. E. Peacock
1926	Mrs I. E. Peacock
1927	Mrs T. McJannett
1928	Miss E. L. Heine
1929	Mrs T. McJannett
1930	Miss R. Tapscott
1931	Miss E. L. Heine
1932	Mrs E. L. H. Miller
1933	Mrs C. J. J. Robbins
1934	Mrs C. J. J. Robbins
1935	Mrs A. Allister
1936	Mrs E. L. H. Miller
1937	Mrs E. L. H. Miller
1938	Mrs C. J. J. Robbins
1939	Mrs O. Craze
1940	Mrs O. Craze
1941-5	*No Competition*
1946	Mrs M. Muller
1947	Mrs M. Muller
1948	Mrs S. P. Summers
1949	Mrs S. P. Summers
1950	Miss S. J. Fry
1951	Mrs S. P. Summers
1952	Miss D. J. Hart
1953	Mrs H. Redick-Smith
1954	Mrs H. Redick-Smith
1955	Mrs H. Redick-Smith
1956	Miss D. Kilian
1957	Mrs H. Brewer
1958	Miss B. Carr
1959	Miss S. Reynolds
1960	Mrs V. Vukovich
1961	Miss S. Reynolds
1962	Mrs A. A. Segal
1963	Miss A. Van Zyl
1964	Miss D. Hard
1965	Miss C. C. Truman
1966	Mrs L. W. King
1967	Mrs L. W. King
1968	Mrs B. M. Court
1969	Mrs L. W. King
1970	Mrs B. M. Court
1971	Mrs B. M. Court
1972	Miss E. Goolagong
1973	Miss C. Evert

Somalia

The Somali Amateur Tennis Association was founded in 1969 and affiliated to the ILTF as an Associate Member in 1972 when it reported 10 affiliated clubs and about 500 players. BR
GOVERNING BODY: Somali Amateur Tennis Association, P.O. Box 523, Mogadishu

South Africa

Most sports were introduced to South Africa by British settlers or members of British military garrisons. Soon after lawn tennis began in England in the 1870s an Englishman, L. Nevill, and a few other fellow countrymen launched the game in Natal. The date of their enterprise is not known but it is safe to assume that when the first Wimbledon Championships were held in 1877 lawn tennis was beginning to spread over the vast distances of South Africa. The earliest recorded events took place in 1881. One was the first tournament, held in Durban, Natal, and the other the public appearance in Johannesburg of E. L. Williams, then a schoolboy. Williams won the country's first distinction overseas in 1884 when he and an Englishman, E. Lewis, reached the final of the men's doubles at Wimbledon and were defeated by the famous Renshaw brothers.

In 1882 two clubs were formed, the Berea Lawn Tennis Club in Durban and the Port Elizabeth Lawn Tennis Club. Within a short time Eastern Province, Western Province, Transvaal, the Orange Free State and Griqualand West all had excellent exponents of the game but in the early years Port Elizabeth (Eastern Province) became the major centre of South African Tennis.

In 1891 the Port Elizabeth LTC assumed the functions of a governing body of the game and

Below **South Africa.** Ian Vermaak in 1959

Above **South Africa**. Eric Sturgess

instituted annual national championships, controlled from 1903 by the South African Lawn Tennis Union, formed that year. As a mark of respect to the Port Elizabeth LTC for its endeavours in advancing the game its courts were chosen for the first official national championships in 1903. Thereafter the venue for the tournament varied between Johannesburg, Cape Town, Durban, Port Elizabeth, East London, Bloemfontein, Kimberley and Pretoria, until in 1931 it was established permanently at Ellis Park, Johannesburg. By this time the administration of tennis had developed into a series of steps leading from elementary stages right up to international status. A player joins a club which is affiliated to a provincial association, which in turn is affiliated to the national body (SALTU), itself affiliated to the ILTF. South Africa joined the ILTF in 1913 as one of its 12 foundation members.

The original provinces which came under the control of the SALTU were the seven associations of Eastern Province, Border, Transvaal, Western Province, Natal, Griqualand West and Orange Free State. Later Transvaal and Western Province were divided into new areas which embraced Northern, Eastern and Western, and Boland in the Cape. Today there are just over 1,000 clubs affiliated to the national body with a total membership of 39,000 senior players and about 36,000 juniors. No estimate is possible of the number of private clubs in existence or of the number of those who play merely for recreation. In the populous Transvaal the number of private courts is relatively very high.

Since 1968 the non-white body, the South African National Lawn Tennis Union, with 14 provincial associations and an estimated membership of 15,000, has been affiliated to the South African Lawn Tennis Union as a federal member with full voting powers on a national level. On a provincial level the two unions are connected by liaison committees.

Tennis can be played out of doors in all parts of South Africa all year round. Most courts have an all-weather surface which is not unduly affected by rain. A typical surface consists of an ash and stone foundation surmounted by cement with a thin plastic top painted green or red. There are a few, mostly private, grass courts, no grass-court tournaments, no courts of En-tout-cas and no indoor courts.

Coaching is available in all centres. Each provincial association has a part-time coach. Private coaches are kept busy all over the country for in the past 15 years tennis has grown in popularity to an unprecedented degree. Part of the boom is due to the sudden interest taken by Afrikaans-speaking people who number some 60 per cent of the white population; since 1967 tennis has been part of the curriculum of Afrikaans schools. Success in the DAVIS CUP, increase in newspaper and radio publicity, the advent of sponsorship and the modernization of the national championships have all helped to stimulate the popularity of tennis.

South Africa has always been a keen participant in international competitions. The first team event in which the country was represented was the 1908 OLYMPIC GAMES in London. In the Games at Stockholm in 1912 Charlie Winslow won the singles and Winslow and H. A. Kitson the doubles. Before tennis was excluded from the Games Louis Raymond won the singles at Antwerp in 1920.

When South Africa entered the Davis Cup in 1913 it was one of eight nations in the contest. Mainly for financial reasons its appearance in the competition was irregular until 1927. From then until 1959 it entered every second year. From 1959 onwards it has competed annually. Because of controversy over the South African government's apartheid policy, its entry was refused in 1970, 1971 and 1972.

The first Davis Cup match played in South Africa took place in Durban in July 1967 when Brazil was beaten 5-0. In the same year the country rose to its highest pinnacle in the competition by reaching the Inter-Zone final, one stage before the Challenge Round. The tie, played in Johannesburg, was lost to Spain 2-3.

To keep close contact with world tennis, South Africa invited a succession of teams to visit the country, starting in the summer of 1908-9 with G. W. Hillyard's team from Britain. This was the first time Springbok colours were awarded. Another early team was led by A. Wallis Myers. All the visitors were from Britain until 1928, the year of the first women's team from Australia, which was followed by representatives of widely varied nations. A French team was led by Jean Borotra and others came from Yugoslavia, Czechoslovakia, Australia, the United States and Germany. There was also a combined team of different nationalities and a team from the International LT Club of Great Britain. Sometimes they engaged in test matches.

Another international venture which quickly raised an early response from South Africa was the FEDERATION CUP. South Africa has competed each year since its inception in 1963 and won the cup for the first time in 1972 when the competition was held in Johannesburg.

For a period, from 1952 to 1968, South Africa and Australia competed irregularly for the Anza Trophy, presented by the Australia-New Zealand Association in Cape Town. Of the six matches played South Africa won four, Australia one and one was drawn. Lack of enthusiasm and the attraction of more lucrative events led to the contest's disappearance. Since 1959 the country's top junior male players have taken part in the annual ORANGE BOWL and SUNSHINE CUP competitions in Miami, Fla.

At home the major tournaments are the South African National Championships held at Ellis Park in Johannesburg over Easter until 1973 when the month was changed to November – they became 'open' in 1969 – and the five events which make up the Sugar Circuit. Ellis Park consists of 22 courts with a centre court normally holding 6,000-7,000 spectators. Invitations to overseas players are a feature of the Circuit, which started in 1962 and embraces provincial championships at Bloemfontein (Orange Free State), Port Elizabeth (Eastern Province), East London (Border), Cape Town (Western Province) and Durban (Natal). A recent innovation was a tournament played in Johannesburg during November and confined to top-class professionals.

South Africans have not yet won a singles title at Wimbledon nor the French nor US Championships, but only weird and controversial behaviour denied Brian Norton the distinction at Wimbledon in 1921. In the Challenge Round against W. T. Tilden he led by two sets to love and lost 5-7 in the fifth set after holding two match points. Tilden had been ill and left a nursing home in Paris to accept the challenge of Norton, a close friend. Wallis Myers wrote of the match, 'Norton knew his condition and by a misguided sympathy – for he owed something to the traditions of Wimbledon – ostentatiously "threw" the third and fourth sets after winning the first two easily . . . it was an unprecedented occurrence at Wimbledon.'

The country's most accomplished player Eric Sturgess, who spent his best years for tennis on war service, reached the final of the US Championships in 1948 and lost to Pancho Gonzalez. Ian Vermaak was runner-up for the French title in 1959. Another singles finalist was Sandra Reynolds (Mrs Price), who lost to Maria Bueno at Wimbledon in 1960.

Sturgess, who had a slim figure with a moderate service but superb control of his groundstrokes, possessed a dedication and application to hard work unequalled by his countrymen. He reached the Wimbledon singles semifinals twice and won the mixed doubles twice, with his compatriot Mrs Sheila Summers in 1949 and Louise Brough (United States) in 1950. He was South African singles champion 11 times (first at the age of 18) and altogether won 22 national titles. Since he was playing at a time when financial rewards and other numerous modern perks for tennis were unknown, his opportunities for going abroad were limited.

A memorable singles feat was accomplished by Norman Farquharson (four times national champion) when on the Centre Court at Wimbledon in the first round of 1937 he defeated the defending champion Fred Perry. It is in doubles, however, that South Africans have attained their highest honours. As far back as 1928 P. D. B. Spence won the mixed doubles at Wimbledon with Elizabeth Ryan (United States) and twice, in 1967 and 1972, the former Australian Bob Hewitt, who settled in South Africa, and Frew McMillan became the men's doubles champions. In 1972 Cliff Drysdale won the US title in partnership with Roger Taylor (Gt Britain).

South African women's tennis was never stronger than when it was represented by Sandra Price (née Reynolds) and Renee Schuurman (Mrs Haygarth) in the 1960s. They won the French doubles three times – Miss Schuurman gained a fourth victory in partnership

Above **South Africa.** Sandra Price in 1960

with Mrs Ann Jones (Great Britain) – and were runners-up twice at Wimbledon. They won titles in several countries.

One of South Africa's finest women players was Bobbie Heine, later Mrs Miller, who became national singles champion for the first of five times at the age of 18. A tall, attractive player, she made her first visit overseas at the age of 17 and, with Mrs Irene Peacock, a settler from England, won the French doubles and reached the final at Wimbledon. At 19 she won the British Hard Court singles championship and many other minor titles. Her successor as a youthful prodigy was Annette Van Zyl (Mrs du Plooy) who at 17 years and seven months became the youngest player to win the South African National singles championship.

The latest women players to distinguish themselves were Mrs Pat Pretorius (formerly Miss Walkden of Rhodesia) and Brenda Kirk, who carried South Africa to victory in the 1972 Federation Cup. Miss Kirk won all her matches, both singles (as no. 2) and doubles. LD

GOVERNING BODY: The South African Lawn Tennis Union, P.O. Box 2211, Johannesburg

South American Championships

The South American Championships, organized by the South American Tennis Confederation (founded 1948) to which all ten South American LTAs belong, consist of the Mitre Cup for men (first winner, in 1921, Argentina), the Osorio Cup for women (first winner, in 1957, Chile), the Bolivia Cup for Boys 18 (first winner, in 1953, Brazil), the Colombia Cup for Girls 18 (first winner, in 1965, Argentina), the Harten Cup for Boys 15 (first winner, in 1963, Brazil) and the Chile Cup for Girls 15 (first winner, in 1965, Chile). All these competitions are run on DAVIS CUP lines.

South of England Grass Court Championships SEE EASTBOURNE

South Pacific Games SEE REGIONAL GAMES

Spain

Neither the origins nor the precise dates of the beginnings of lawn tennis in Spain are known. The oldest documented fact is that the Asociación de Lawn Tennis de Barcelona was founded in 1903 and was affiliated to the Lawn Tennis Association (of Great Britain). International contests organized by the Lawn Tennis Club of Barcelona were held first from 1903 to 1908. The Asociación de Lawn Tennis de España was founded in 1909, with Don Jorge Satrústegui as its first chairman. It was an early member of the ILTF in 1913. It changed its name in 1935 to Federación Española de Tenis and in 1956 adopted its present name, Real Federación Española de Tenis. It receives state aid through the Delegación Nacional de Deportes (National Sports Association), which encourages the steady development of the game.

Lawn tennis in Spain is organized in 11 regional federations which come under the Spanish Federation: Andalusia, Aragon, Asturias, Balearic Islands, Canary Islands, Catalonia, Centre, Old Castile, Galicia, Levant and Vasco-Navarre. The number of affiliated players is steadily increasing, in spite of the fact that in Spain players must acquire licences to take part in competitions. Affiliated players numbered 7,000 in 1969, 13,000 in 1970 and 20,000 in 1971. There are about 275,000 members (including the 20,000 affiliated players) of about 300 affiliated clubs throughout the country. A licence is not required for club membership. There are 1,100 affiliated courts, headed by the Catalonia Federation with 426 courts and 8,332 affiliated players.

All top-grade clubs run tennis schools for children and juniors. Such schools are placed under the leadership of competent coaches and trainers. The most outstanding boys and girls are selected for the Escuela Superior de Tenis de la Federación Española in Barcelona, where they undergo a strict régime of physical culture and training. The pupils of the Escuela Superior number about 20 players. They are periodically supervised by Lew Hoad, engaged

Above **Spain**. Manuel Orantes *(left)* and Manuel Santana

by the Spanish Federation as a technical adviser. They are carefully observed by competent specialists and their future potential is studied.

The considerable growth of lawn tennis in Spain during the last decade has been mainly due to the achievements of Manuel Santana in the Davis Cup, and international championships such as those at Roland Garros (where he was champion in 1961 and 1964), Forest Hills (1965) and Wimbledon (1966).

Spain took part in the DAVIS CUP for the first time in 1921. By 1972 it had taken part 36 times, winning 51 and losing 36 in a total of 87 ties. Santana holds the Spanish record for contesting 85 singles, of which he won 69 and lost only 16; Gisbert played 42 matches and Couder 26. Spain reached the Challenge Round twice, in 1965 and 1967, losing to Australia in Sydney and Brisbane, 4–1, on both occasions. Spain was an Inter-Zone finalist three times, winning against India (1965) and South Africa (1967) and losing to the United States (1968) in Cleveland. The Spanish team has won the GALEA CUP five times (1956-8, 1968 and 1969). Spain also competes in the FEDERATION CUP, VALERIO CUP, ANNIE SOISBAULT CUP and PRINCESS SOPHIA CUP.

The most important national contest is the Campeonato de España, held from 1910 on, and won by Santana eight times, Masip seven times and Couder four times. The most outstanding women champions were Pilar Barril (nine times) and Maria Josefa Riba (seven times). During the season important international competitions are held in Spain, the oldest being those staged in Barcelona and San Sebastián. Others take place in Madrid, Vigo, Bilbao, Santander and Oviedo. Several matches for the ILTF GRAND PRIX take place every year in Barcelona and Madrid. The Commercial

Spanish Championships Winners
Men's Singles

1910	L. Uhagón
1911	L. Uhagón
1912	J. Alonso
1913	V. Marín
1914	J. M. Sagnier
1915	M. Alonso
1916	M. Gomar
1917	M. Gomar
1918	M. Gomar
1919	M. Alonso
1920	M. Alonso
1921	F. K. Peak
1922	*No Competition*
1923	E. Flaquer
1924	E. Flaquer
1925	R. Morales
1926	F. Sindreu
1927	E. Flaquer
1928	F. Sindreu
1929	E. Maier
1930	E. Maier
1931	E. Maier
1932	E. Maier
1933	E. Maier
1934	E. Maier
1935	E. Maier
1936	P. Masip
1937-39	*No Competition*
1940	J. M. Blanc
1941	J. M. Blanc
1942	L. Carles
1943	P. Castellá
1944	P. Castellá
1945	P. Masip
1946	P. Masip
1947	P. Masip
1948	P. Masip
1949	P. Masip
1950	P. Masip
1951	E. Martínez
1952	F. Olózaga
1953	C. Ferrer
1954	E. Martínez
1955	J. M. Couder
1956	J. M. Couder
1957	A. Gimeno
1958	M. Santana
1959	A. Gimeno
1960	M. Santana
1961	M. Santana
1962	M. Santana
1963	M. Santana
1964	M. Santana
1965	J. M. Couder
1966	J. M. Couder
1967	M. Orantes
1968	M. Santana
1969	M. Santana
1970	M. Orantes
1971	M. Orantes
1972	A. Gimeno
1973	J. Higueras

Women's Singles

1925	Miss C. Liencres
1926	Miss B. Dutton
1927	Miss R. Torras
1928	Miss B. Dutton
1929	Miss L. Alvarez
1930	Miss M. Lerena
1931	Miss B. Dutton
1932	Miss B. Dutton
1933	Miss B. Dutton
1934	Miss J. Chávarri
1935	Miss J. Chávarri
1936	Miss J. Chávarri
1937-39	*No Competition*
1940	Miss L. Alvarez
1941	Miss J. Chávarri
1942	Miss I. Maier
1943	Miss J. Chávarri
1944	Miss M. J. Riba
1945	Miss J. Chávarri
1946	Miss M. J. Riba
1947	Miss M. J. Riba
1948	Miss M. J. Riba
1949	Miss M. J. Riba
1950	Miss M. J. Riba
1951	Miss M. Solsona
1952	Miss P. Barril
1953	Miss M. J. Riba
1954	Miss P. Barril
1955	Miss P. Barril
1956	Miss P. Barril
1957	Miss M. Terán
1958	Miss P. Barril
1959	Miss A. Guri
1960	Miss P. Barril
1961	Miss P. Barril
1962	Miss P. Barril
1963	Miss P. Barril
1964	Miss C. Hernández-Coronado
1965	Miss A. M. Estalella
1966	Miss A. M. Estalella
1967	Miss C. Hernández-Coronado
1968	Miss A. M. Estalella
1969	Miss A. M. Estalella
1970	Miss C. Hernández-Coronado
1971	Miss C. Hernández-Coronado
1972	Miss C. Hernández-Coronado
1973	Miss C. Perea

Union Masters' Tournament was held in the new Palau Blaugrana in Barcelona in December 1972.

Spain's greatest postwar players have been Manuel Santana, Andres Gimeno and Manuel Orantes. GPdO
GOVERNING BODY: Real Federación Española de Tenis, Avda Generalisimo Franco 618, 3°D, Barcelona 15

Spalding
A.G. Spalding & Brother was founded in 1876 by a famous baseball player, Albert Goodwill Spalding (1850-1915) and his brother James (the name was changed in 1878 to A. G. Spalding & Brothers) and was a pioneer in the development of tennis in the United States. It introduced the famous 'Slocum Tennis Racket' (called after the second US singles champion) in 1888, made of white ash with a leather handle and strung with the finest gut available. Today, as well as other equipment, Spalding offers four outstanding top-grade rackets.
HEAD OFFICE: Meadow Street, Chicopee, Mass. 01014, USA

Sperling, Mrs S. [Miss Hilde Krahwinkel] (Germany/Denmark)
Born Essen, 26 March 1908; originally German but Danish by marriage. Wimbledon women's singles r/u 1931, q/f 1932, s/f 1933, 1935, r/u 1936, q/f 1937, s/f 1938-9; women's doubles r/u 1935; mixed doubles r/u 1930, won 1933, s/f 1935-6; French women's singles s/f 1931-2, won 1935-7; women's doubles r/u 1935. Her capacity to run and to retrieve made her a fearsome opponent.

Sphairistiké
The name given by Major Walter Clopton Wingfield, M.V.O., to his game of lawn tennis (see THE BIRTH AND SPREAD OF LAWN TENNIS, PART 1) comes from the name of the ancient Greek ball game known as *Sphairisis*. In the preface to the instructions of his revised rules (a second edition) of November 1874, Major Wingfield quotes Pliny as evidence of the existence of *Sphairisteria*, courts on which the ball game was played. He also claimed that statues were erected by the Athenians to Ariston of Carystius, who was a noted player.

Sphairistiké is but one of the early formulated games of lawn tennis. Correspondence in the *Field* (1874) discussed rival claims. Two were Pelota, the game played by Major Harry Gem and J. B. Perera (Rules of 1870 in the Birmingham Public Library) and Germains Tennis, devised by J. H. Hale of Germains, Chesham, Bucks, and sold by John WISDEN & Co. at five gns a set (Rules published 1874).

Spin
Pure CHOP is imparting spin vertically downwards to the ball. Pure cut is imparting spin horizontally or nearly so under the ball. Slice is imparting spin to the side of the ball. Two

Above **Sphairistiké**. The label from a box containing Major Wingfield's game

or all three of these may be combined in infinite degree. Chop and cut, depending on the court surface and atmospheric conditions, can impart either skid or a low bound or stop or 'break' or a 'sit-up' bound, the latter being a way that DROPSHOTS are played. Topspin is imparting spin by brushing the racket strings up and over the top of the ball. JO

Below **Spin**. The top two are for the forehand drive, the bottom two for service; all as seen by a right-handed player.

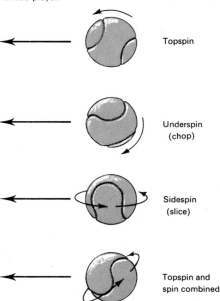

Topspin

Underspin (chop)

Sidespin (slice)

Topspin and spin combined

Sponsorship
The earliest form of tennis sponsorship was provision of free equipment by sports-goods companies in return for mention of their names in tournament programs and on court. For example, Slazenger's name appears on the umpire's chair at Wimbledon, and always has done, in return for the adoption of its equipment and balls for the Championships.

Today sponsorship provides the largest source of income for the game and most of the prize money, amounting to well over £2 million, comes directly from sponsors. Sponsorship does not end with the provision of prize money; the total expenditure by sponsors on behalf of tennis must be about £4 million.

The approach to sponsorship varies from country to country, the most important area being the United States, where most of the prize money is available. This is without doubt linked closely with television. Companies were quick to realize that an important section of the population of both sexes could be exposed to their products or services at a relatively reasonable cost. Where a sponsor puts up all the prize money or a large proportion the tournament takes the sponsor's name into its title. However, in the United States, this does not generally apply: the tournament organizers arrange for several sponsors who receive advertising exposure in relation to their contributions. The main exception to this is the VIRGINIA SLIMS women's circuit: many (but not all) of these tournaments are sponsored by Philip Morris Inc. (the parent company of Virginia Slims) and take the name of the cigarette into their titles; others take the name of their own main sponsor. Virginia Slims provides a service to all the tournaments in the circuit but the actual running of the tournament is left to the local organizers.

At Forest Hills there are so far no sponsors but Millers High Life Beer (also part of the Philip Morris Group) buys most of the television time during the tournament and this enables the West Side Tennis Club to collect a large fee from the television companies. It also receives an income from concessions granted to erect stands within the grounds – a feature of US tennis not seen to any great extent in Europe.

Because of the ban on any form of tobacco advertising on television in the United States (although this does not prevent a tobacco company from being involved in sponsorship) there has been a remarkable move towards banks and other service companies sponsoring tournaments. It is now estimated that over 50 per cent of US tournaments are sponsored by banks.

In Australia sponsorship has in the past been relatively modest, with sports-goods companies, mainly DUNLOP, predominating, and Australia has not kept up with the rest of the world in terms of prize money. In 1972 a company called Tennis Camps of Australia was set up to organize tournaments and find sponsors. As a result the 1973 prize money was increased considerably.

In Europe, Britain has by far the largest number of major tournaments. All except Wimbledon are sponsored. The main sponsors are tobacco companies, ROTHMANS having the lion's share. This is no doubt due to the ban of tobacco advertising on television which has released a considerable amount of money for other advertising. In Britain one sponsor per tournament is normal and so the sponsor takes a much greater part in the organization of the tournament than anywhere else in the world. In some cases the whole organization is in the sponsor's hands. It is becoming increasingly popular for sponsors to be involved in junior development, a very worthwhile trend; in Britain GREEN SHIELD plays a most important role here. As in the United States, there has recently been increased interest in sponsorship from the service industries, banks, insurance companies, etc.

Canada follows the British pattern closely. ROTHMANS again is the main sponsor and takes a major part in the organization of the Canadian Championships.

Tennis in Spain has been fortunate in having an individual benefactor of the game, the Conde de Godo, who, through his various companies, has contributed not only to the major tournaments but also to minor ones and to junior development. Madrid has had the patronage of the Melia Hotel Group. In many parts of the world hotels contribute to tournaments in kind if not in cash.

France is probably the most inventive country as far as sponsorship is concerned. In 1972

the French Championships had as their main sponsor Vanaos, manufacturers of sun-tan oil. However, as in most European countries, the sponsors take no part in the running of the tournament. The ground and the centre court have a multiplicity of signs which often change as the tournament progresses, indicating that the sponsors pay for advertising by the day.

Except for West Germany, where there is little sponsorship, the pattern in the rest of Europe is the same as in France. Italy's Championships were sponsored in 1972, mainly by Ausonia, an insurance company. Austria's main sponsor is Head, a sports-goods company, Switzerland's the Palace Gstaad, a hotel. In each case there are many other sponsors. Sweden is blessed with a great tennis benefactor, Marcus Wallenberg, whose banking, insurance and industrial companies all sponsor tournaments.

South Africa also follows the European pattern. The sponsor of the Championships is the South African Brewery, while the well-known Sugar Circuit is backed by the South African Sugar Association.

In every country there is competition by soft-drinks manufacturers to provide cooling drinks for the players. Pepsi-Cola and Coca-Cola are the main ones; they have both contributed to tournaments for many years.

There is also series sponsorship, headed by the ILTF GRAND PRIX, which is sponsored by COMMERCIAL UNION. Similar smaller competitions are the DEWAR CUP in Britain sponsored by John Dewar & Sons Ltd and the Rothmans Mediterranean Spring Circuit.

In many countries the DAVIS CUP, FEDERATION CUP and WIGHTMAN CUP teams are sponsored. In some cases payments are made to the players; in others tournament expenses are covered. British Petroleum sponsors juniors in many countries through the BP INTERNATIONAL TENNIS FELLOWSHIP.

Individual players have always been sponsored by the sports-good companies DUNLOP, SLAZENGER, WILSON, SPALDING, Head, and others, which offer services and equipment in exchange for exclusive use of their products. In this area of sponsorship clothing is offered by the firms of Fred Perry Sportswear, Lacoste, Ted Tinling and others, in return for the players' use of their gear. GM

Squash Rackets see THE ORIGINS OF LAWN TENNIS (PART 1)

Sri Lanka

Lawn tennis was first introduced to Sri Lanka (Ceylon) by British coffee planters. The winner of the Wimbledon Championship of 1878 was P. F. Hadow, an old Harrovian and coffee planter on leave from Ceylon. Hadow returned to Ceylon after his Wimbledon victory and never again played the game seriously. The first recorded public tennis tournament was held in Ceylon in 1886 when E. de Fonblanque

won the Championship Singles. He won the title ten times, a record which still remains unbroken, although Oscar Pinto, the greatest Sinhalese player, came close to it when he captured the title seven times in the 1920s and 1930s. The first Sinhalese to take part in the Ceylon Championships was Fred de Saram in 1909. The first Sinhalese to win the Championship Singles was E. R. de Saram in 1919.

The Ceylon Lawn Tennis Association was formed in 1915. His Excellency Sir Robert Chalmers, the British Governor at the time, was elected its first President. The Secretary was Stanley H. Dyer. The first Sinhalese Secretary of the LTA was Lionel Fonseka, elected in 1921. He continued to hold that office with distinction until he was elected President in 1954.

Ceylon first played in the DAVIS CUP in 1957 in the European Zone and thereafter in the Eastern Zone every year, reaching the Zone Final in 1958. It also participated in the ASIAN GAMES held at Bangkok and at Tokyo, and won a bronze medal in the doubles. In 1950 Ceylon was given the privilege of staging the Asian Championships, in which many foreign stars took part including Frank Sedgman, Tony Mottram and Doris Hart. In 1954 Ceylon was again host to the Asian Championships in which Jaroslav Drobný, Althea Gibson, Billy Knight and F. Ampon competed.

In 1972 the Ceylon LTA was re-named the Sri Lanka LTA. BR
GOVERNING BODY: Sri Lanka Lawn Tennis Association, P.O. Box 1177, 106 York Street, Colombo 1

Stade Roland Garros see FRANCE; for Records of the French Championships see PART 3

Stammers, Miss Kay E.
[Mrs M. Menzies] (Gt Britain)
Born St Albans, Herts., 3 April 1914; Wimbledon women's singles q/f 1935-6, 1938, r/u 1939; q/f 1946-7; women's doubles won 1935-6, s/f 1939, 1946-7; US women's singles q/f 1934, s/f 1935-6, q/f 1937-8, s/f 1939; women's doubles s/f 1935-8, r/u 1939; mixed doubles r/u 1935; French women's singles q/f 1934; women's doubles won 1935. Wightman Cup 1935-9, 1946-8; non-playing captain 1959-60. One of Britain's most attractive and fluent players. Left-handed.

Staten Island Cricket and Baseball Club
see THE BIRTH AND SPREAD OF LAWN TENNIS; also THE UNITED STATES STORY (PART 1)

Sterry, Mrs Alfred [Miss Charlotte Cooper] (Gt Britain)
Born Ealing, 1871, died 1966; Wimbledon women's singles s/f 1893, q/f 1894, won 1895-6, r/u 1897, won 1898, r/u 1899-1900, won 1901, r/u 1902, 1904, won 1908, r/u* 1912, q/f 1913; women's doubles r/u 1913, s/f 1914. A noted stalwart of the early game. Her

daughter, Gwen Sterry, became a British Wightman Cup player (1927).

Stevens Cup
The Stevens Cup, awarded to the winner of an international world senior (veterans') team competition for men over 45, was donated in 1961 by Richard Stevens in honour of his father Richard Stevens, Sr, who was ranked in the first US ten for eight years and was Treasurer of the USLTA for 18 years. The first tie was played in 1964, when the United States won from India at the Newport Casino, 5-0. By 1972 there were 16 participating nations from five continents, and the competitors included former national champions, Wimbledon champions and Davis Cup players.

'Sticky' abbreviation for SPHAIRISTIKÉ; see also THE BIRTH AND SPREAD OF LAWN TENNIS (PART 1)

Stoefen, Lester Rollo (USA)
Born Des Moines, Iowa, 30 March 1911; died 10 Feb. 1970; Wimbledon men's singles q/f 1933-4; men's doubles won 1934; US men's singles q/f 1932, s/f 1933, q/f 1934; men's doubles won 1933-4; mixed doubles r/u 1934. Davis Cup 1934.

Stolle, Frederick S. (Australia)
Born Hornsby, N.S.W., 8 Oct. 1938; Wimbledon men's singles r/u 1963-5; men's doubles r/u 1961, won 1962, 1964, r/u 1968, 1970; mixed doubles won 1961, s/f 1962-3, won 1964, s/f 1965-6, 1968, won 1969; US men's singles r/u 1964, won 1966, q/f 1969, 1972; men's doubles won 1965-6, s/f 1970; mixed doubles won 1962, 1965; Australian men's singles s/f 1961, q/f 1962, s/f 1963, r/u 1964-5, s/f 1966, q/f 1969; men's doubles s/f 1961, r/u 1962, won 1963-4, r/u 1965, won 1966, r/u 1969; mixed doubles won 1962, r/u 1963, s/f 1965; French men's singles won 1965, q/f 1966, 1969; men's doubles s/f 1961-4, won 1965, 1968; mixed doubles r/u 1962-4. Davis Cup 1964-6. Turned professional in 1967. A tall, able Australian, notable for what he just missed achieving. Like von CRAMM, he was losing singles finalist at Wimbledon three years running (1963-5), yielding in the first year to MCKINLEY and in the next two to his compatriot EMERSON. His doubles skill brought him most success. WCT contract pro 1970-2.

Stop Netting
The netting or wire fence at each end of the court, designed to prevent the ball from going well beyond the confines of the court and thus delaying play. For first-class play the court area should be 120 x 60 ft (36·6 x 18·3 m). JO

Stöve, Miss Betty (Netherlands)
Born Rotterdam, 24 June 1945; Wimbledon women's doubles won 1972, r/u 1973; US women's doubles won 1972; Australian women's doubles s/f 1967; French women's

doubles won 1972, r/u 1973. Federation Cup 1969-

Stroke
The action of hitting the ball and the result thereof. For the different strokes see DROP-SHOT, LOB, SERVICE, SPIN, VOLLEY, etc.

Sturgess, Eric W. (S. Africa)
Born Johannesburg, 10 May 1920; Wimbledon men's singles s/f 1949, q/f 1950, s/f 1951, q/f 1952; men's doubles s/f 1949-50, r/u 1951-2; mixed doubles won 1949-50, s/f 1951; US men's singles r/u 1948; mixed doubles won 1949; Australian men's singles s/f 1950; men's doubles r/u 1950; mixed doubles r/u 1950; French men's singles r/u 1947, s/f 1948-50, r/u 1951, s/f 1952; men's doubles won 1947, s/f 1948, r/u 1949-50, s/f 1951; mixed doubles won 1947, 1949, r/u 1952. Davis Cup 1947-51. A most graceful player, winner of his national singles a record 11 times.

Sudan
Lawn tennis has been played in the Sudan for nearly 70 years, mainly in clubs in Khartoum and various provincial centres, but the Sudan LTA was not officially established until 1956. The Sudan Government was most cooperative and several new courts were constructed. In the same year the first Sudan Open Competition was held.

Below **Fred Stolle**

The Sudan was elected an Associate Member of the ILTF in 1956 and was accepted as a Full Member with voting rights in July 1964. At present there are 12 clubs in the Khartoum area and ten well-established clubs in the provinces. Recently a junior training centre has been established with four hard and four grass courts and professional coaching. The Sudan LTA holds five open tournaments, four junior competitions and one national championship.

Players from the Sudan have competed in ILTF Championships. BR
GOVERNING BODY: Sudan Lawn Tennis Association, P.O. Box 1553, Khartoum

'Sudden Death'
Term first used for the last game in a non-advantage set (see SCORING); since 1970 the term has also been applied to the shorter, nine-point, TIE-BREAK.

Sugar Circuit see SOUTH AFRICA

Suková, Mrs Vera [Miss Pužejová] (Czechoslovakia)
Born Uherské Hradiště, 1931. Wimbledon women's singles q/f 1961, r/u 1962; mixed doubles s/f 1960-1; US women's singles q/f 1962; French women's singles s/f 1957, q/f 1959-60, s/f 1963, q/f 1964; women's doubles s/f 1956-57.

Sunshine Cup
An international team competition for under-18 boys, run on Davis Cup lines and held each

January at Miami Beach, Fla., USA. The first winner, in 1959, was Brazil.

Surinam

Lawn tennis is slowly developing in Surinam, where there are few clubs but many private courts. The Surinaamse Tennis Bond has annual matches with teams from neighbouring countries and has recently sent promising young players to the Netherlands and the United States with tennis scholarships so that a stronger national team can be built up. Surinam has been affiliated to the ILTF as an Associate Member since 1968. BR
GOVERNING BODY: Surinaamse Tennis Bond, P.O. Box 1834, Paramaribo

Susman, Mrs J. R. [Miss Karen Hantze] (USA)

Born San Diego, Calif., 11 Dec. 1942; Wimbledon women's singles q/f 1960-1, won 1962; women's doubles s/f 1960, won 1961-2, r/u 1964; US women's singles q/f 1959, 1964; women's doubles r/u 1962, won 1964, r/u 1965; French women's singles q/f 1964. Federation Cup 1964; Wightman Cup 1960-2, 1965. An aggressive player and one of the three Wimbledon champions coached by Eleanor Tennant (the others were Alice MARBLE and Maureen CONNOLLY). Her habit of carefully conserving energy between rallies brought accusations of 'gamesmanship'.

Sutton, Miss May [Mrs T. C. Bundy] (USA)

Born Plymouth, England, 25 Sept. 1887; Wimbledon women's singles won 1905, r/u 1906, won 1907, q/f 1929; US women's singles won 1904, at the age of 16, the youngest ever to do so; s/f 1921-2; women's doubles s/f 1922, r/u 1925, s/f 1928. Wightman Cup 1925. She was the first overseas player to win at Wimbledon (1905) at the age of 17. Her daughter was Dorothy BUNDY.

Sweden

In 1879 the Swedish Crown Prince (later HM Gustaf V) introduced lawn tennis from England to Särö, a small seaside resort on the Swedish west coast near Gothenburg, where he spent some weeks almost every summer. Two years later the first proper tennis court was built at Tullgarn, the private country castle of the Crown Prince. The first covered court was built in Stockholm in 1896. During the 19th century eight clubs were founded and in the first decade of the 20th another 17.

The need for a national organization became apparent in 1906 and the Svenska Tennisförbundet (Swedish LTA) was founded, mainly to represent the game abroad and to make sure that national championships were arranged. The LTA suffered for years from lack of funds and the major clubs had to make generous contributions to cover its expenses. Sweden affiliated to the ILTF in 1913.

The number of clubs steadily increased to

Above **Karen Susman**

over 160 by the beginning of World War II. In the mid-1950s the number reached 400; today the Swedish LTA has over 800 member clubs with more than 60,000 players. About 200,000 people play tennis fairly regularly.

Mrs Sigrid Fick in 1923 became the first Swedish player to win a foreign championship, the German covered-court women's singles. She was followed by Curt Östberg in 1930 when he became German covered-court champion and by Östberg and Schröder in 1934 when they won the German covered-court men's doubles. Two years later Schröder became the British indoor champion, defeating, among others, Borotra and Bunny Austin; he also won the American men's and mixed doubles. Schröder defended his title as British champion in 1937 but lost the final to Austin.

During the postwar period from 1946 to the early 1960s Lennart Bergelin, Torsten Johansson, Sven Davidson, Ulf Schmidt and Jan-Erik Lundqvist won a great number of

international championships all over the world. The most remarkable victories were those of Davidson in Paris (1957) on hard court, and of Davidson and Schmidt at Wimbledon (1958) in the men's doubles, the only Swedish win at Wimbledon. Lundqvist became Italian hard-court champion in 1964.

Sweden first competed in the DAVIS CUP in 1925, winning against Switzerland and then losing to the Netherlands. Since then Sweden has taken part every year except in 1931 and 1932, reaching the European Zone final 11 times and the Inter-Zone final six times. The most memorable Inter-Zone tie was in 1950, when Bergelin, playing barefoot, beat the two prominent Australians Sedgman and Bromwich on the slippery lawn of the Westchester Country Club outside New York. Since 1964 Sweden has also competed several times in the FEDERATION CUP.

In 1936 HM King Gustaf donated the KING'S CUP, intended to be the covered-court equivalent to the Davis Cup. Although it never achieved the status of the Davis Cup, it has

Swedish National Outdoor Championships Winners

Men's Singles		Women's Singles	
1902	W. Boström	1916	Miss L. Strömberg von Essen
1903	P. Qvarnström	1917	Miss A. Nisser
1904	G. Setterwall	1918	*No Competition*
1905	*No Competition*	1919	Miss S. Fick
1906	H. Leffler	1920	*No Competition*
1907	H. Carling	1921	Miss L. Strömberg von Essen
1908	G. Setterwall	1922	Miss V. Bendz
1909	W. Boström	1923	Miss S. Fick
1910	F. Möller	1924	Miss S. Fick
1911	C. Wennergren	1925	Miss S. Fick
1912	*No Competition*	1926	Miss S. Fick
1913	C. Wennergren	1927	Miss S. Fick
1914	C. Wennergren	1928	Miss S. Fick
1915	C. Wennergren	1929	Miss S. Fick
1916	C. O. Nylén	1930	Miss S. Fick
1917	A. Lindqvist	1931	Miss S. Fick
1918	*No Competition*	1932	Miss S. Fick
1919	S. Malmström	1933	Miss G. Roberg
1920	*Abandoned*	1934	Miss S. Wennerholm
1921	A. Lindqvist	1935	Miss G. Roberg
1922	A. Lindqvist	1936	Miss K. Forsell
1923	A. Thorén	1937	Miss G. Roberg
1924	S. Malmström	1938	Miss B. Gullbrandsson
1925	C. Wennergren	1939	Miss B. Gullbrandsson
1926	C. Wennergren	1940	Miss L. Hals
1927	C. Östberg	1941	Miss M. Lagerborg
1928	C. Östberg	1942	Miss M. Lagerborg
1929	S. Malmström	1943	Miss M. Lagerborg
1930	C. Östberg	1944	B. Gullbrandsson
1931	H. Ramberg	1945	Miss A. Björk
1932	C. Östberg	1946	Miss M. Lagerborg
1933	H. Ramberg	1947	Miss L. Hals-Klöfsten
1934	C. Östberg	1948	Miss B. Gullbrandsson
1935	K. Schröder	1949	Miss B. Gullbrandsson
1936	S. Karlborg	1950	Mrs B. Gullbrandsson-Sandén
1937	S. Nyström	1951	Mrs B. Gullbrandsson-Sandén
1938	K. Schröder	1952	Mrs B. Gullbrandsson-Sandén
1939	K. Schröder	1953	Mrs B. Gullbrandsson-Sandén
1940	N. Rohlsson	1954	Mrs B. Gullbrandsson-Sandén
1941	K. Schröder	1955	Mrs B. Gullbrandsson-Sandén
1942	N. Rohlsson	1956	Miss S. Gustafsson
1943	S. Mårtensson	1957	Miss S. Gustafsson
1944	T. Johansson	1958	Mrs B. Gullbrandsson-Sandén
1945	L. Bergelin	1959	Miss G. Rosin
1946	S. Bramstång	1960	Miss G. Rosin
1947	L. Bergelin	1961	Miss G. Rosin
1948	L. Bergelin	1962	Miss K. Frendelius
1949	T. Johansson	1963	Miss U. Sandulf
1950	L. Bergelin	1964	Miss C. Sandberg
1951	L. Bergelin	1965	Miss C. Sandberg
1952	L. Bergelin	1966	Miss C. Sandberg
1953	S. Davidson	1967	Miss C. Sandberg
1954	S. Stockenberg	1968	Miss C. Sandberg
1955	S. Davidson	1969	Miss C. Sandberg
1956	S. Davidson	1970	Miss C. Sandberg
1957	S. Davidson	1971	Miss I. Bentzer
1958	S. Davidson	1972	Miss C. Sandberg
1959	U. Schmidt	1973	Miss I. Larsson
1960	S. Davidson		
1961	J. E. Lundqvist		
1962	J. E. Lundqvist		
1963	J. E. Lundqvist		
1964	J. E. Lundqvist		
1965	J. E. Lundqvist		
1966	J. E. Lundqvist		
1967	L. Ölander		
1968	O. Bengtson		
1969	H. Zahr		
1970	H. Zahr		
1971	T. Svensson		
1972	B. Borg		
1973	B. Borg		

attracted much interest among the 15-20 nations that take part every year.

At Båstad, a small seaside resort on the west coast, summer tournaments have been held for a long time, in fact from the end of the 19th century. In 1948 they became the International Swedish Hard Court Championships. Most Wimbledon winners since World War II have competed there. National events are held simultaneously and the tournament at Båstad is nowadays by far the biggest in the country. In 1970 no fewer than 1,300 matches were played by 700 players from 25 nations. HM Gustaf V took part in 1930 and in 15 subsequent years. At the age of 84 he played two three-set matches on the same day, 61 games altogether! The success of the Båstad tournament, both nationally and internationally, depended, especially in the beginning, very much on his great interest. In fact, the development and popularity of lawn tennis in Sweden are mainly due to the personal contribution of King Gustaf V, who was for decades its symbol, and Marcus Wallenberg, whose outstanding interest and most generous support at all times has been of inestimable value.

Borgholm, Falkenberg, Saltsjöbaden, Varberg, Ystad, and several other places in Sweden run well-known tournaments every summer in which Scandinavian and sometimes players from other countries compete. The summer program contains some 60 tournaments all over the country.

The LTA is made up of 23 county associations, covering the whole country. The clubs (approximately 800) must all belong to a county association; no club is affiliated to the LTA direct. The clubs' annual affiliation fee depends on the number of individual registered players. The LTA largely depends on contributions from the State; these have been increased to keep pace with inflation. SH

GOVERNING BODY: Svenska Tennisförbundet, Lidingövägen 75, S 115 37 Stockholm

Below **Sweden.** Sigrid Fick, Swedish Outdoor champion ten times (1923-32)

Above **Switzerland**. Lolette Payot, winner of the French Championships in 1945

Switzerland

Switzerland was one of the Founder Members of the ILTF in 1913 and has been a Full Member ever since. It first competed in the DAVIS CUP in 1923 and has taken part in the FEDERATION CUP since 1963, except for 1965, 1970 and 1971. An outstanding player was Charles Aeschliman, who achieved 50 Davis Cup rubbers between 1923 and 1934. Its best-known woman player, Lolette Payot (Mrs Dodille) reached the Wimbledon quarter-finals three times (1931, 1933-4). The outstanding Swiss administrator was Charles Barde, who represented Switzerland at the first ILTF meeting in 1913. He gave nearly 60 years of international service to the game and was President of the ILTF several times.

In 1973 there were 465 affiliated organizations and 62,000 affiliated players. Many tournaments are held each year, the Swiss Championships being staged at Gstaad. A training scheme for juniors is organized at regional centres. BR

GOVERNING BODY: Association Suisse de Tennis, Laubeggstrasse 70, 3006 Berne

Syria

Until the Syrian Lawn Tennis Federation was established in 1953 lawn tennis was played in a number of clubs but not organized on a national basis. Syria affiliated to the ILTF in 1970 as an Associate Member. Today there are 27 clubs with possibly 1,000 players. The National Championships have been played in Damascus and Aleppo since 1953 and new coaching schemes for promising young players are now in operation. It is hoped that before long Syria will compete in the Davis Cup. BR

GOVERNING BODY: Syrian Tennis Federation, P.O. Box 4142, Damascus

Swedish Indoor Championships Winners

Men's Singles

1898	P. Qvarnström
1899	P. Qvarnström
1900	G. Setterwall
1901	G. Setterwall
1902	G. Setterwall
1903	P. Qvarnström
1904	G. Setterwall
1905	W. Boström
1906	G. Setterwall
1907	G. Setterwall
1908	G. Setterwall
1909	W. Boström
1910	G. Setterwall
1911	G. Setterwall
1912	G. Setterwall
1913	T. Grönfors
1914	T. Grönfors
1915	T. Grönfors
1916	C. O. Nylén
1917	O. Andersson
1918	N. Åhlund
1919	H. Müller
1920	M. Wallenberg
1921	T. Åkerholm
1922	A. Thorén
1923	J. Söderström
1924	H. Müller
1925	H. Müller
1926	M. Wallenberg
1927	C. Östberg
1928	S. Malmström
1929	S. Malmström
1930	C. Östberg
1931	C. Östberg
1932	C. Östberg
1933	C. Östberg
1934	C. Östberg
1935	S. Nyström
1936	*No Competition*
1937	S. Karlborg
1938	N. Rohlsson
1939	*No Competition*
1940	E. Thorén
1941	N. Rohlsson
1942	K. Schröder
1943	T. Johansson
1944	T. Johansson
1945	N. Rohlsson
1946	L. Bergelin
1947	L. Bergelin
1948	L. Bergelin
1949	*No Competition*
1950	S. Davidson
1951	T. Johansson
1952	T. Johansson
1953	S. Davidson
1954	S. Davidson
1955	L. Bergelin
1956	S. Davidson
1957	U. Schmidt
1958	S. Davidson
1959	U. Schmidt
1960	U. Schmidt
1961	U. Schmidt
1962	U. Schmidt
1963	J. E. Lundqvist
1964	J. E. Lundqvist
1965	J. E. Lundqvist
1966	J. E. Lundqvist
1967	J. E. Lundqvist
1968	O. Bengtson
1969	O. Bengtson
1970	H. Nerell
1971	O. Bengtson
1972	H. Zahr
1973	T. Svensson

Women's Singles

1913	Miss S. Fick
1914	Miss S. Fick
1915	Miss S. Fick
1916	Miss L. Strömberg von Essen
1917	Miss L. Strömberg von Essen
1918	Miss M. Cederschiöld
1919	Miss S. Fick
1920	Miss S. Fick
1921	Miss L. Strömberg von Essen
1922	Miss L. Strömberg von Essen
1923	Miss L. Strömberg von Essen
1924	Miss S. Fick
1925	Miss S. Fick
1926	Miss S. Fick
1927	Miss S. Fick
1928	Miss S. Fick
1929	Miss S. Fick
1930	Miss S. Fick
1931	Miss E. Aquilon
1932	Miss S. Fick
1933	Miss E. Aquilon
1934	Miss E. Aquilon
1935	Miss G. Roberg
1936	*No Competition*
1937	Miss E. Aquilon
1938	Miss M. Lagerborg
1939	*No Competition*
1940	Miss I. Schröder
1941	L. Hals
1942	Miss M. Lagerborg
1943	Miss L. Hals
1944	Miss B. Gullbrandsson
1945	Miss M. Lagerborg
1946	Miss M. Lagerborg
1947	Miss B. Gullbrandsson
1948	Miss A. Björk
1949	*No Competition*
1950	Miss M. Lagerborg
1951	Mrs B. Gullbrandsson-Sandén
1952	A. Björk
1953	M. Lagerborg
1954	Miss A. Björk
1955	Miss S. Gustafsson
1956	Miss S. Gustafsson
1957	Miss A. Björk
1958	Mrs B. Gullbrandsson-Sandén
1959	Miss U. Hultkrantz
1960	Miss G. Rosin
1961	Miss K. Frendelius
1962	Miss G. Rosin
1963	Miss G. Rosin
1964	Miss G. Rosin
1965	Miss C. Sandberg
1966	Miss C. Sandberg
1967	Miss K. Fredelius-Bartholdson
1968	Miss C. Sandberg
1969	Miss C. Sandberg
1970	Miss C. Sandberg
1971	Miss C. Sandberg
1972	Miss C. Sandberg
1973	Mrs I. Bentzer

T

Taiwan

In 1927, when Taiwan was under Japanese control, a governing body for lawn tennis was founded. The early records of the game have been lost but after World War II, when the Republic of China was established there with its capital at Taipei, lawn tennis was played at a number of clubs; in 1970 the Republic of China Association was affiliated to the ILTF as an Associate Member. It so happened that the Chinese People's Republic on the mainland was already affiliated. Thus there were two Chinas, separate countries with separate governments, affiliated to the ILTF, a situation which soon proved unacceptable and the mainland association withdrew in 1971 (see CHINA).

By 1972 in Taiwan there were 16 clubs and about 3,000 affiliated players. Taiwan played in the DAVIS CUP in 1972 and its women's team took part in the FEDERATION CUP in South Africa in 1972. BR
GOVERNING BODY: The Republic of China Tennis Association, 83 Chung Hwa Road, Taipei, Taiwan

Talbert, William F. (USA)

Born Cincinnati, Ohio, 4 Sept. 1918; US men's singles q/f 1942, s/f 1943, r/u 1944-5, q/f 1946, s/f 1949, q/f 1950; men's doubles won 1942, 1945-6, 1948, r/u 1950, s/f 1951-2, r/u 1953, s/f 1954; mixed doubles won 1943-6, s/f 1947, r/u 1948-9, s/f 1951-2; French men's singles s/f 1950; men's doubles won 1950; mixed doubles r/u 1950. Davis Cup 1946, 1948-54; captain 1953-7.

Tanner, Leonard Roscoe (USA)

Born Chattanooga, Tenn., 15 Oct. 1951; US Amateur Indoor won 1971; US singles q/f 1972; r/u Pacific SW and Pacific Coast 1972. Davis Cup 1971-2. Became a professional 1972. Left-handed.

Tanzania

Tanzania has been an Associate Member of the ILTF since 1967 when it reported 30 clubs with about 200 courts and several hundred players. BR
GOVERNING BODY: Tanzania Lawn Tennis Association, P.O. Box 1750, Dar es Salaam

Taylor, Roger (Gt Britain)

Born Sheffield, 14 Oct. 1941; Wimbledon men's singles s/f 1967, 1970, s/f 1973; US

men's singles q/f 1964; men's doubles s/f 1963, won 1972; mixed doubles s/f 1970; Australian men's singles s/f 1970; mixed doubles r/u 1962, s/f 1969. Davis Cup 1964-7. WCT contract pro 1968-72. WCT 4th Group B (F q/f) 1973. Left-handed.

Below Roger Taylor

Tegart, Miss Judy A. M. [Mrs D. E. Dalton] (Australia)

Born Melbourne, 12 Dec. 1937; Wimbledon women's singles q/f 1967, r/u 1968, q/f 1969, s/f 1971; women's doubles s/f 1963, r/u 1966, s/f 1967-8, won 1969, s/f 1970; mixed doubles r/u 1965, 1969, s/f 1970-1; US women's singles q/f 1968, 1971; women's doubles won 1970-1; mixed doubles r/u 1963-5, 1970, s/f 1971; Australian women's singles q/f 1962, 1964-7, s/f 1968, q/f 1970; women's doubles s/f 1961-3, won 1964, s/f 1966, won 1967, r/u 1968, won 1969-70; mixed doubles s/f 1965, won 1966, r/u 1967; French women's doubles won 1966, s/f 1967, 1970, 1972; mixed doubles s/f 1962-3, 1966. Federation Cup 1965-7, 1969-70. ILTF GP 4th 1971.

Tennis Elbow

A term describing a pain centred over the lower end of the humerus. It is caused by inflammation of the tendon brought on by strains and jars sustained in playing tennis and other court games. The term is also loosely applied to several varieties of arm injuries induced by similar activities. DC

Terry, Miss Aline M. (USA)

US women's singles won 1893, r/u 1894; women's doubles won 1893.

Thailand

Thailand was first affiliated to the ILTF as an Associate Member in 1952, became a Full Member in 1962 but agreed to be an Associate Member again in 1971. It competed in the DAVIS CUP 1958-61. BR

GOVERNING BODY: The Lawn Tennis Association of Thailand, c/o Sports Organization of Thailand, National Stadium, Bangkok

Thomson, Miss Ethel W.

see Mrs D. R. LARCOMBE

Three-Handed Tennis

A form of practice in which one player, wishing to sharpen his reflexes, is faced by two opponents. As soon as one ball is 'dead' another is hit towards the single player. JO

Tie see RUBBER

Tie-Break

There are two tie-break systems recognized by the ILTF, designed to eliminate marathon sets and introduced when a set score has reached either 6-6 or 8-8.

The 9-point method ('sudden death'), invented by James H. Van Alen of Newport (who was responsible for VASSS) unofficially introduced at the Philadelphia Open Championships in 1970 and favoured by the USLTA, is generally introduced when the score reaches 6-6 and is quicker than the 12-point method described below. In the 9-point tie-break, in singles, Player A serves twice, Player B then serves twice, Player A serves twice again and Player B then has three services. Players change ends after four points. The first player to win five points wins the set 7-6. In doubles the first three players serve two points each; the fourth serves three points. Each player must serve from the same end from which he served during the set. There are variations in

Above **William Tatem Tilden**

the final point (see THE RULES AND THEIR INTERPRETATION, PART 1).

The method used at Wimbledon (first in 1971) is the 12-point tie-break. After the score has reached 8-8, one more game is played, the first player to win seven points taking the set at 9-8. In singles, the player whose turn it is to serve in this last game has one service from the right court, his opponent then has two services, starting from the left court, and from then on each player serves twice in turn from alternate courts until one has won seven points. Players change ends after each series of six points but if the points total is tied at 6-6 the game continues until one player has a two-point lead. The same system applies in doubles except that the first player has one service but thereafter each player has two services in turn in the prescribed rotation.

At Wimbledon the tie-break is not used in the final set of any match. JO

Tilden, William Tatem (USA)

Born Philadelphia, 10 Feb. 1893, died 5 June 1953; Wimbledon men's singles won 1920-1, s/f 1927-9, won 1930; men's doubles s/f 1920, won 1927, s/f 1928-9; US men's singles r/u 1918-19, won 1920-5, q/f 1926, r/u 1927, won 1929, s/f 1930; men's doubles won 1918, r/u 1919, s/f 1920, won 1921-3, r/u 1926, won 1927, s/f 1929-30; mixed doubles r/u 1911, s/f 1912, won 1913-14, r/u 1916-17, 1919, won 1922-3, r/u 1924, s/f 1925-6; French men's singles r/u 1927, s/f 1929, won 1930; men's doubles s/f 1927, 1929; mixed doubles r/u 1927, won 1930. Davis Cup 1920-30. One of the immortals. He had everything, including a cannonball service. His finest achievement was perhaps less in winning Wimbledon at the age of 37 in 1930, less in being invincible in the US championships for six consecutive years than in taking 13 successive singles in the Challenge Round of the Davis Cup be-

tween 1920 and 1926. Not only his skill but his personality was commanding. He was as intellectual as he was athletic and wrote both plays and books. His loss in the final of the US Championships in 1919 led him to spend the winter remodelling his backhand and with the new stroke he came back to become champion. In 1922 he had part of a finger removed but none the less changed his grip successfully. He became professional in 1931 and was still playing good-class lawn tennis up to his death in 1953. See CENTRE COURT CLASSICS and GREAT PLAYERS OF ALL TIME (PART 1).

Ţiriac, Ion (Rumania)

Born Rumania, 9 May 1939; Wimbledon men's doubles s/f 1970; French men's singles q/f 1968; men's doubles r/u 1966, s/f 1967-9, won 1970; mixed doubles r/u 1967. Davis Cup 1959- . Eight times national champion and mentor of NĂSTASE.

Todd, Mrs P. C.
[Miss Patricia Canning] (USA)

Born San Francisco, Calif., 22 July 1922; Wimbledon women's singles q/f 1947, s/f 1948-50, 1952; women's doubles s/f 1946, won 1947, r/u 1948-9, s/f 1952; mixed doubles s/f 1948, r/u 1950, s/f 1952; US women's singles q/f 1945, s/f 1946, q/f 1947, s/f 1948, q/f 1949-50; women's doubles r/u 1946-8, s/f 1949-50, r/u 1951, s/f 1957; mixed doubles s/f 1947, 1949-51, 1957; French women's singles won 1947, s/f 1948, r/u 1950; women's doubles s/f 1946, r/u 1947, won 1948, s/f 1950; mixed doubles s/f 1946, won 1948, r/u 1950. Wightman Cup 1947-51. A player of statuesque grace, she suffered from being the contemporary of Louise BROUGH, Margaret DUPONT and Doris HART.

Below **Pat Todd**

Togoland

The Fédération Togolaise de Lawn-Tennis was founded in 1961 and became an Associate Member of the ILTF in 1965, when it reported six clubs with 128 players. BR
GOVERNING BODY: Fédération Togolaise de Lawn-Tennis, Lome

Topspin see SPIN

Torquay, Devon (UK)

This resort has staged the Palace Hotel tournament at the Palace Hotel since 1936 when the men's singles was won by Harry Lee and the women's by the Chilean Anita Lizana, who defeated Dorothy Round in an exciting final. The opening of the two covered courts at the hotel in that year coincided with the last occasion on which Britain won the Davis Cup. To mark their official opening, the trophy was put on view, and the steady stream of people who came to see it paid one shilling a time. The money raised was donated to a local charity.

The Palace Hotel tournament, begun with the encouragement of DUNLOP, at first attracted only 16 men and 14 women. After World War II it grew rapidly with the inauguration of popular handicap events. Between 1968 and 1972 the tournament was part of the DEWAR CUP circuit. Many top international players have appeared on these courts. Traditionally the tournament has always been controlled by the current Wimbledon referee, who often has to contend with a round-the-clock schedule. Recently the Palace Hotel has also been the training ground, under the guidance of the resident professional, Arthur Roberts, of a stream of top-class players, including former Wimbledon champion, Angela Mortimer (Mrs J. Barrett) and Davis Cup stalwart Mike Sangster, Joan Curry and Corinne Molesworth, who have both played in the Wightman Cup, and Arthur Roberts's son Paddy, who later became a British international. DC

Toss (1)

At the start of a match, the players 'toss' (usually by spinning a racket to fall 'rough' or 'smooth'). The winner may choose or require his opponent to choose: (a) the right to be server or receiver, in which case the other player chooses the side; or (b) the side, in which case the other player chooses the right to be server or receiver. DC

Toss (2) Australian synonym for LOB

Townsend, Miss Bertha [Mrs Toulmin] (USA)

The second American woman champion, winning the US women's singles 1888-9.

Trabert, Marion Anthony (USA)

Born Cincinnati, Ohio, 16 Aug. 1930; Wimbledon men's singles s/f 1954, won 1955; men's doubles s/f 1950, r/u 1954, s/f 1955; US men's

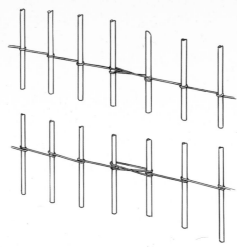

Above **Toss.** The trebling of a racket, showing *(top)* the 'rough' side, with strings crossing at the back, and *(below)* the 'smooth' side.

singles q/f 1951, won 1953, q/f 1954, won 1955; men's doubles s/f 1950-1, 1953, won 1954; Australian men's singles s/f 1955; men's doubles s/f 1954, won 1955; French men's singles won 1954-5; men's doubles won 1950, 1954-5. Davis Cup 1951-5. A remarkably dominant champion in his successful years. He won his Wimbledon singles and both his US singles titles without losing a set, his power centred on a trenchant backhand. He was more solid than spectacular but always effective. Became pro 1955.

Tramlines old-fashioned term for SIDELINES

Trinidad and Tobago

In 1911 the Tranquility Square Lawn Tennis Club in Trinidad called a meeting of clubs to see if a Lawn Tennis Association could be formed, but there was not sufficient support: in its annual report in 1914, the Club Secretary stated that 'owing to the lack of interest shown by members in the Lawn Tennis Association it was decided to let the matter drop'.

In 1921 the tennis clubs attached to the oil companies in the southern part of Trinidad formed a Southern Lawn Tennis Association, but it was not until 1948 that the clubs in the north of the island followed suit and the LTA of Trinidad and Tobago was established and affiliated to the (British) LTA. In the same

Below **Tony Trabert**

year, it became an Associate Member of the ILTF and a Full Member in 1966. It is also a member of the COMMONWEALTH CARIBBEAN LTA. BR
GOVERNING BODY: Lawn Tennis Association of Trinidad and Tobago, Red House, Lands & Surveys Dept., Port of Spain, Trinidad

Truman, Miss C. see Mrs G. JANES

Tunis

Tunis was admitted to the ILTF as a Full Member in 1935, having been an Associate Member. Expelled during World War II, it was readmitted in 1958. BR
GOVERNING BODY: Fédération Tunisienne de Lawn-Tennis, 65 Avenue de la Liberté, Tunis

Turkey

The Turkish Lawn Tennis Association was founded in 1923 as part of the Turkish Sports and Games Federation. In that year it affiliated to the ILTF and in 1945 established itself as an independent governing body for lawn tennis. Today it has six affiliated clubs with about 500 players and in recent years boys and girls have been coached at training schools run by the LTA in Ankara and Istanbul. The main event in Turkey is the Istanbul International Tennis Championship, played since 1946 in Ankara. Turkey has competed regularly in the DAVIS CUP since 1948. Outstanding Turkish players are Suat Subay, Fehmi Kizil, Nazmi Bari and Remzi Aydin. BR
GOVERNING BODY: Turkiye Tenis Federasyonu, Ulus Is Hani, Ankara

Turnbull, D. P. see AUSTRALIA

Turner, Miss Lesley R.
[Mrs W. W. Bowrey] (Australia)

Born N.S.W., 16 Aug. 1942; Wimbledon women's singles q/f 1962, s/f 1964, q/f 1965, 1967-9; women's doubles s/f 1961, won 1964, s/f 1967-8; mixed doubles won 1961, s/f 1962-3, won 1964, s/f 1965; US women's singles q/f 1961, s/f 1967; women's doubles won 1961, r/u 1964; mixed doubles r/u 1962; Australian women's singles q/f 1959, 1962, s/f 1963, r/u 1964, 1967, s/f 1968; women's doubles s/f 1962, r/u 1963, won 1964-5, r/u 1966, won 1967, r/u 1968; mixed doubles won 1962, r/u 1963, s/f 1965, won 1967, s/f 1968; French women's singles r/u 1962, won 1963, s/f 1964, won 1965, r/u 1967, q/f 1971; women's doubles s/f 1961-2, won 1964-5, s/f 1967, 1971; mixed doubles r/u 1962-4. Federation Cup 1963-5, 1967. One of Australia's most competent women players, though overshadowed by the greatness of her contemporary Margaret COURT.

Twist see SERVICE

Two-Handed Grip see GRIPS

U

Uganda

The Uganda LTA was formed in 1947 and the first major tournament was held that year. At first Council members were Europeans and Asians, but later they were joined by Africans. Many Africans started playing the game from the early 1950s: a prominent African player at that time was Prince George Mwanda. The Association has 12 clubs. The major tournament is the Uganda Open Championships, held in February as part of the East African Circuit. The Lugogo Stadium has seven tennis courts with a centre court seating 5,000. The main aim of the Association is to encourage juniors, in particular Uganda nationals, and to play in the Davis Cup. An open junior tournament is held in August every year including the Peter Hogg Junior Competition between Uganda, Tanzania and Kenya, played on Davis Cup lines. BR

GOVERNING BODY: Uganda LTA, P.O. Box 2107, Kampala

Umpires and Line Judges

A full complement of court officials for important events such as the finals of a major championship is 13: an umpire, a net-cord judge, a foot-fault judge and ten line judges.

It is the duty of the baseline, centreline, sideline and service-line judges to decide whether the ball is in or out of court; the net-cord judge decides whether services have touched the top of the net (see LET); and the foot-fault judge decides whether services have been correctly delivered (see FAULT).

The umpire is in overall authority. He introduces the players, keeps the score, ensures that the balls are changed at the right time and that the match is played according to the rules. He may make a line decision on appeal from one of the judges who may have been unsighted. A player may appeal to the umpire against a linesman's decision but may only appeal to the referee (through the umpire) on a point of law – not on a question of fact. See REFEREEING AND UMPIRING (PART 1). JO

Umpire's Chair

A central high chair from which the umpire has control of the match, placed beside a net-post, ideally with the sun behind it. It has also become the convenient place for the players to keep their accoutrements and refresh themselves for the statutory one minute at the changeover.

At the first Wimbledon in 1877 a chair was placed on a table to give the umpire a raised position. DC

Under-Arm Service see SERVICE

Underspin see CHOP, SPIN

United Arab Republic see EGYPT

Uruguay

Tennis was brought to Uruguay by the British. The Montevideo Tennis Club was founded in 1889 and by 1895 the number of players had increased considerably. The climate of Uruguay, which allows play outdoors all year, helped to make the game attractive. The Asociación Uruguaya de Lawn Tennis (the Uruguayan LTA) was established in 1915 when tournaments of all types were regularly scheduled. It developed a fine group of players, such as E. Stanham and R. Cat (1920-30) and C. Ponce de Leon and S. Harreguy (1930-40) and first competed in the DAVIS CUP in 1931. In 1935 Sir Eugene Millington Drake, head of the British Diplomatic Mission in Uruguay and a tennis lover, became President of the Uruguayan LTA. He stimulated development by building at his own cost a stadium at the Carrasco Lawn Tennis Club, contracting English professionals to come to teach in Montevideo and organizing international tournaments.

Since 1960 great interest has been taken in teaching young players through organized professional coaching. At present more than half the competitors in official tournaments are under 20, and more and more young people are being attracted to the sport. There are three tennis schools which provide official coaching for groups of young players. Two of these belong to clubs, while the third

Below **Umpires and Line Judges.** The positions for the 13 officials and six ball-boys. The one foot-fault judge changes ends every two games with the server; the two ballboys at the net run across the court.

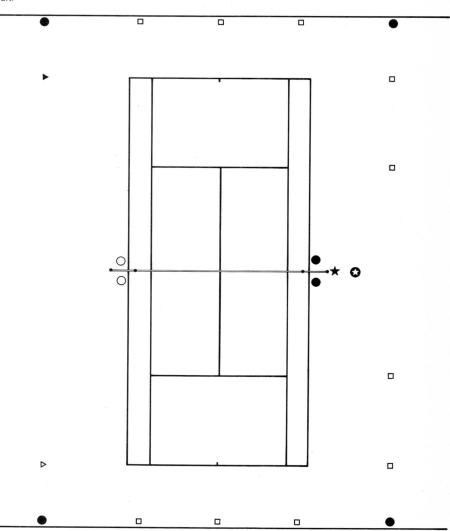

is the official training school of the LTA; to this only outstanding players are invited.

The Uruguayan women's team competed in the FEDERATION CUP in South Africa in 1972 and included the most promising young player, Miss Fiora Bonicelli.

In 1972 there were 18 clubs affiliated to the Asociación Uruguaya de Lawn Tennis, with 89 courts, and also 12 non-affiliated clubs with 30 courts. The Asociación has about 2,800 affiliated players. Over 500 players competed in tournaments and championships in 1971. In addition to regular club members, there are 5,000-7,000 occasional players. Uruguay has taken part in the Davis Cup since 1970 and in the FEDERATION CUP in 1972.

Max Mainzer, a very active tennis official in Uruguay, is at present a member of the ILTF Committee of Management. BR
GOVERNING BODY: Asociación Uruguaya de Lawn Tennis, Calle Pablo de Maria 1063, Montevideo

USA

For history of tennis see THE UNITED STATES STORY (PART 1). See also US CHAMPIONSHIPS, EASTERN GRASS COURT CHAMPIONSHIPS, PACIFIC COAST CHAMPIONSHIPS, and other articles on individual organizations, tournaments, etc.

USLTA see THE UNITED STATES STORY (PART 1); LAWN TENNIS ASSOCIATIONS

US Championships (Forest Hills)

The first Championship in the United States for men's singles and doubles was held on the grass courts of the Newport Casino, Newport, Rhode Island, 31 August – 3 September, 1881 (see NEWPORT). There were 26 players in the singles draw with two defaults. Richard D. Sears won the singles without losing a set. C. M. Clark and F. W. Taylor won the doubles.

The USLTA Championships, singles and doubles, were held at the Newport Casino without interruption for 34 years (1881-1914). The challenge-round system in the singles was inaugurated in 1884 but was abolished in 1912. From 1915 to 1920 (with the exception of 1917 when only patriotic tournaments were sanctioned by the USLTA, because of the participation of the United States in World War I), the West Side Tennis Club, Forest Hills, N.Y. staged the Championships and from 1921 to 1923 they were held at the Germantown Cricket Club, Philadelphia, Pa. In 1924, after the completion of the West Side Tennis Club stadium, the Championships returned to Forest Hills, and since then have been held there.

The USLTA Women's Singles Championship began in 1887. It was held by the Chestnut Hill Lawn Tennis Club on the grass courts of the Philadelphia Cricket Club from 1887 to 1891, and from 1892 to 1920 it was run by the Philadelphia Cricket Club. Since 1921 the Championship has been held at the West Side Tennis Club, Forest Hills. Originally the women's doubles and mixed doubles were played with the Women's Singles Championship. In 1921 the mixed doubles and in 1935 the women's doubles were transferred and made a part of the national doubles program.

In 1942, for the first time, all five major grass-court championships (men's singles and doubles, women's singles and doubles and mixed doubles) were included in the championships played at Forest Hills. This arrangement continued until 1945. From 1946 until 1967 the men's and women's doubles were played at the Longwood Cricket Club, Chestnut Hill, Mass., and the men's and women's singles and mixed doubles at Forest Hills.

Since the advent of the Open Championships in 1968 all five events have been played at Forest Hills. The USLTA amateur grass court championships (5 events) were held at the Longwood Cricket Club in 1968 and 1969. Since then the men's amateur championships have been played at the Meadow Club, Southampton, N.Y., and the women's amateur championships at the Wilmington Country Club, Wilmington, Delaware.

Sears won the US title seven years in succession (1881-7), a record that has never been equalled. Two other players also won the championship seven times. William T. Tilden II, won six times in a row (1920-5) and again in 1929. William A. Larned won five successive years (1907-11) and in 1901 and 1902. Foreign winners have included two from Great Britain, two from France, ten from Australia, one each from Mexico, Spain and Rumania. In winning at Forest Hills in 1962 and 1969 Rod Laver became the only player to win the grand slam twice.

The USLTA men's doubles championship began in 1881 and was held in conjunction with the singles. From 1890 to 1906 doubles tournaments were held in the East and the West, and the sectional winners then met for the right to play the standing-out champions in the Challenge Round. In 1918 the doubles championship was an elimination tournament, but the next year the plan of qualifying sectional winners was restored, although for the one year only. Since 1920 there has been no Challenge Round.

The first doubles champions were C. M. Clark and F. W. Taylor. Among the teams that won more than twice were Richard D. Sears/James Dwight, Holcombe Ward/Dwight F. Davis, Holcombe Ward/Beals C. Wright, Harold H. Hackett/Fred B. Alexander, Maurice E. McLoughlin/Thomas C. Bundy, William T. Tilden II/Vincent Richards, Jack Kramer/Ted Schroeder, Gardnar Mulloy/William F. Talbert, Charles McKinley/Dennis Ralston. A number of players were successful with different partners. These included George Lott, Jr, whose partners were John Hennessey, John H. Doeg (twice) and Lester Stoefen (twice); John Bromwich of Australia, who teamed with fellow Australians, Adrian K. Quist, Bill Sidwell and Frank Sedgman; Roy Emerson whose fellow Australian partners were Neale Fraser (twice) and Fred Stolle (twice). Stolle also won a third time with Ken Rosewall as partner.

The first foreign winners were the famous English Doherty brothers, Reggie and Laurie, who won the Wimbledon doubles eight times. In 1902 and 1903 they won the US doubles, having come to challenge the United States for the DAVIS CUP. The Dohertys defeated the US team of Ward and Davis in the Championships in 1902 and in the 1902 Challenge Round doubles, and the Wrenn brothers, Robert D. and George L., in the 1903 Davis Cup match. Another team of brothers, Robert and Howard Kinsey of California, won the US doubles championship in 1924. The first team of brothers to capture the national doubles title was Carr B. Neel and Samuel R. Neel (1896).

One of the foreign teams, Frank Sedgman and Ken McGregor of Australia, completed the only grand slam in doubles when they won the US title in 1951 after having won the Australian, French and Wimbledon doubles that year.

The first women's singles champion was Ellen Hansell in 1887. Molla Bjurstedt Mallory won the Championship eight times and Helen Wills seven times. Margaret Smith Court has won the amateur title four times and won the Open Championship three times. The women's singles winners include five from foreign countries: two from Great Britain, Betty Nuthall (1930) and Virginia Wade (1968 Open); one each from Australia, Margaret Smith Court (1962, 1965, 1968, 1969 – Open and Amateur – 1970, and 1973), Brazil, Marie E. Bueno (1959, 1963, 1964, 1966) and Chile, Anita Lizana (1937).

The USLTA women's doubles championship, which began in 1890 with Ellen Roosevelt and Grace W. Roosevelt as the winners, has had a number of outstanding teams through the years. The most successful by far was the team of Louise Brough and Margaret Osborne duPont, who won 12 championships (1942-50 and 1955-7). Margaret also won in 1941 with Sarah Palfrey Fabyan Cooke. Sarah also won the title eight other years, four with Alice Marble, three with Helen Jacobs and one with Betty Nuthall of Britain. One of the leading doubles players of the early days was US singles champion Juliette P. Atkinson. She won the doubles seven times, twice with Helen R. Helwig and twice with her sister Kathleen, once each with Myrtle McAteer, Marion Jones and Elisabeth H. Moore.

Hazel Hotchkiss Wightman won the title

Colour plate Ken Rosewall, seen here in his famous match with Cliff Richey in 1971 (see pages 162-3), is one of the greatest players never to have won Wimbledon.
Overleaf **Wimbledon.** The Centre Court, June 1973. I. Năstase (serving) and J. Connors (near side of net) beat J. Fassbender (left) and K. Meiler 6-4, 9-8, 6-3 in a semi-final and went on to beat J. R. Cooper and N. A. Fraser in the final, 3-6, 6-3, 6-4, 8-9, 6-1.

six times between 1909 and 1928, twice each with Edith Rotch, Eleonora Sears and Helen Wills. Later Doris Hart and Shirley Fry captured the doubles title four successive years (1951-4) and Darlene Hard won it five times, four with different partners. Another six-times champion, with different partners, was Margaret Smith Court. Maria Bueno (Brazil) also held the title five times, twice each with Miss Hard and Mrs Court and once with Nancy Richey Gunter. For championship records see PART 3. FES

US Clay Court Championships

The Clay Court Championships of the USLTA were established in 1910, largely through the efforts of Dr Philip B. Hawk and other Western experts. The first took place on the courts of the Omaha (Nebraska) Field Club with more than 100 entries. Among the competitors were Melville Long (San Francisco), Fred Anderson and Walter Merrill Hall (New York), Walter Hayes (Chicago), and Dr Hawk, president of the newly-formed Clay Court Association. Melville Long won.

The first clay-court doubles title was captured by Fred Anderson and Walter Hayes, who was to succeed Long as singles champion in 1911. In 1912 May Sutton of California won the first women's clay-court singles title.

Many leading players have won the men's and the women's clay-court titles. Among them several have also won the national grass-court championship: William T. Tilden II who won the clay title in six successive years; Frank Parker who won it five times and Robert L. Riggs, three times. The US Clay Court Championships for men have been held every year except in 1928, and became an open event in 1971 when the first foreign player to win the men's singles, Zeljko Franulović of Yugoslavia, repeated his 1969 victory. Manuel Orantes won in 1973.

Some of the many top US men's doubles teams who have won the Clay Court as well as the Grass Court Championships include Robert Kinsey/Howard Kinsey, Ellsworth Vines/Keith Gledhill, Donald Budge/Gene Mako, Jack Kramer/Ted Schroeder, Bill Talbert/Gardnar Mulloy, Vic Seixas/Tony Trabert, Chuck McKinley/Dennis Ralston, and Bob Lutz/Stan Smith. Prominent winners in the early years were George Church/Dean Mathey, Charles Garland/Samuel Hardy, and in more recent times, Clark Graebner (six times) and Marty Riessen.

The US Clay Court meeting was also held at the Omaha Field Club in two other years, 1911 and 1913. Down through the years some 16 clubs have been host to the men's Championships. Between 1935 and 1965 the Championships were held 26 times at the River Forest (Ill.) Tennis Club. The Woodstock

Colour plate Stan Smith, Wimbledon champion in 1972 (see page 165 for an account of his match against Năstase). He won the US Open in 1971, and his first World Championship of Tennis Final in 1973.

Country Club in Indianapolis, Ind., first held the clay-court event in 1922 and again in 1923 and 1929. Then after 40 years the Woodstock club once more was the venue for the Championships in 1969 and it had been held there since.

Other clubs which have been the scene of this tournament include the Pittsburgh Athletic Association, Cincinnati Tennis Club, Lakewood (Ohio) Tennis Club, Triple A Club, St Louis, Detroit Tennis Club, Rockhill Tennis Club, Kansas City, Mo., University Club, Memphis, Tenn., Chicago Town and Tennis Club, Salt Lake (Utah) Tennis Club, Atlanta (Ga.) Lawn Tennis Association and Town Club of Milwaukee.

The women's Clay-Court Championship began in 1912. It was not always held in conjunction with the men's tournament. There were a number of years when the women's

US Clay Court Championships Winners

Men's Singles

1910	M. H. Long	1945	W. F. Talbert
1911	W. T. Hayes	1946	F. A. Parker
1912	R. Norris Williams	1947	F. A. Parker
1913	J. R. Strachan	1948	R. A. Gonzalez
1914	C. J. Griffin	1949	R. A. Gonzalez
1915	R. Norris Williams	1950	H. Flam
1916	W. E. Davis	1951	M. A. Trabert
1917	S. Hardy	1952	A. Larsen
1918	W. T. Tilden	1953	E. V. Seixas
1919	W. Johnston	1954	B. Bartzen
1920	R. Roberts	1955	M. A. Trabert
1921	W. T. Hayes	1956	H. Flam
1922	W. T. Tilden	1957	E. V. Seixas
1923	W. T. Tilden	1958	B. Bartzen
1924	W. T. Tilden	1959	B. Bartzen
1925	W. T. Tilden	1960	B. Mackay
1926	W. T. Tilden	1961	B. Bartzen
1927	W. T. Tilden	1962	C. R. McKinley
1928	No Competition	1963	C. R. McKinley
1929	E. Pare	1964	D. Ralston
1930	B. M. Grant	1965	D. Ralston
1931	H. E. Vines	1966	C. Richey
1932	G. M. Lott	1967	A. Ashe
1933	F. A. Parker	1968	C. Graebner
1934	B. M. Grant	1969	Z. Franulović
1935	B. M. Grant	1970	C. Richey
1936	R. L. Riggs	1971	Z. Franulović
1937	R. L. Riggs	1972	R. A. Hewitt
1938	R. L. Riggs	1973	M. Orantes
1939	F. A. Parker		
1940	D. McNeill		
1941	F. A. Parker		
1942	S. Greenberg		
1943	S. Greenberg		
1944	F. Segura		

Women's Singles

1912	Miss M. Sutton	1945	Mrs S. P. Cooke
1913	No Competition	1946	Miss B. Krase
1914	Miss Mary K. Browne	1947	Mrs M. A. Prentiss
1915	Miss M. Bjurstedt	1948	Mrs M. Rurac
1916	Miss M. Bjurstedt	1949	Mrs M. Rurac
1917	Miss R. Sanders	1950	Miss D. Hart
1918	Miss C. R. Neely	1951	Miss D. Head
1919	Miss C. Gould	1952	Miss A. Kanter
1920	Miss M. Zinderstein	1953	Miss M. Connolly
1921	Mrs B. E. Cole	1954	Miss M. Connolly
1922	Mrs L. M. Bickle	1955	Miss D. H. Knode
1923	Miss M. MacDonald	1956	Miss S. J. Fry
1924-39	No Competition	1957	Miss A. Gibson
1940	Miss A. Marble	1958	Mrs D. H. Knode
1941	Miss P. M. Betz	1959	Miss S. M. Moore
1942	No Competition	1960	Mrs D. H. Knode
1943	Miss P. M. Betz	1961	Miss E. Buding
1944	Miss D. M. Bundy	1962	Miss D. Floyd
		1963	Miss N. Richey
		1964	Miss N. Richey
		1965	Miss N. Richey
		1966	Miss N. Richey
		1967	Miss N. Richey
		1968	Miss N. Richey
		1969	Mrs G. S. Chanfreau
		1970	Miss L. Tuero
		1971	Mrs B. J. King
		1972	Miss C. Evert
		1973	Miss C. Evert

US Hard Court Championships Winners

Men's Singles

1948	F. R. Schroeder
1949	F. R. Schroeder
1950	A. Larsen
1951	F. R. Schroeder
1952	A. Larsen
1953	T. Trabert
1954	G. J. Shea
1955	H. Flam
1956	A. Olmedo
1957	T. P. Brown
1958	T. P. Brown
1959	R. Krishnan
1960	W. Reed
1961	A. E. Fox
1962	R. Osuna
1963	A. Ashe
1964	D. Ralston
1965	D. Ralston
1966	S. R. Smith
1967	S. R. Smith
1968	S. R. Smith
1969	C. Graebner
1970	No Competition
1971	R. Lutz
1972-3	No Competition

Women's Singles

1948	Miss G. Moran
1949	Miss D. Hart
1950	Mrs P. C. Todd
1951	Mrs P. C. Todd
1952	Mrs M. A. Prentiss
1953	Miss A. Kanter
1954	Mrs B. B. Fleitz
1955	Miss M. Arnold
1956	Mrs N. C. Kiner
1957	Mrs B. B. Fleitz
1958	Mrs B. B. Fleitz
1959	Miss S. Reynolds
1960	Miss K. D. Chabot
1961	Miss N. Richey
1962	Miss C. Hanks
1963	Miss D. Hard
1964	Miss K. Harter
1965	Miss R. Casals
1966	Mrs L.W. King
1967	Miss J. Bartkowicz
1968	Miss M. Godwin
1969	Miss E. Pande
1970-3	No Competition

US Indoor Championships Winners

Men's Singles

1898	L. Ware
1899	*No Competition*
1900	J. A. Allen
1901	H. Ward
1902	J. P. Paret
1903	W. C. Grant
1904	W. C. Grant
1905	E. B. Dewhurst
1906	W. C. Grant
1907	T. R. Pell
1908	W. C. Grant
1909	T. R. Pell
1910	G. F. Touchard
1911	T. R. Pell
1912	W. C. Grant
1913	G. F. Touchard
1914	G. F. Touchard
1915	G. F. Touchard
1916	R. L. Murray
1917	S. H. Voshell
1918	S. H. Voshell
1919	V. Richards
1920	W. T. Tilden
1921	F. T. Anderson
1922	F. T. Hunter
1923	V. Richards
1924	V. Richards
1925	J. Borotra
1926	J. R. Lacoste
1927	J. Borotra
1928	W. Aydelotte
1929	J. Borotra
1930	F. T. Hunter
1931	J. Borotra
1932	G. S. Mangin
1933	G. S. Mangin
1934	L. R. Stoefen
1935	G. S. Mangin
1936	G. S. Mangin
1937	F. A. Parker
1938	D. McNeill
1939	W. Sabin
1940	R. L. Riggs
1941	F. L. Kovacs
1942-45	*No Competition*
1946	F. Segura
1947	J. A. Kramer
1948	W. F. Talbert
1949	R. A. Gonzalez
1950	D. McNeill
1951	W. F. Talbert
1952	R. Savitt
1953	A. D. Larsen
1954	S. Davidson
1955	T. Trabert
1956	U. Schmidt
1957	K. Nielson
1958	R. Savitt
1959	A. Olmedo
1960	B. McKay
1961	R. Savitt
1962	C. McKinley
1963	R. D. Ralston
1964	C. R. McKinley
1965	J. E. Lundqvist
1966	C. Pasarell
1967	C. Pasarell
1968	C. Richey
1969	S. R. Smith
1970	I. Năstase
1971	C. Graebner
1972	S. R. Smith
1973	J. S. Connors

Women's Singles

1907	Miss E. H. Moore
1908	Miss M. Wagner
1909	Miss M. Wagner
1910	Mrs F. G. Schmitz
1911	Miss M. Wagner
1912	*No Competition*
1913	Miss M. Wagner
1914	Miss M. Wagner
1915	Miss M. Bjurstedt
1916	Miss M. Bjurstedt
1917	Miss M. Wagner
1918	Miss M. Bjurstedt
1919	Mrs H. H. Wightman
1920	Miss H. Pollak
1921	Mrs M. B. Mallory
1922	Mrs M. B. Mallory
1923	Mrs B. E. Cole
1924	Mrs M. Z. Jessup
1925	Mrs M. Z. Jessup
1926	Miss E. Ryan
1927	Mrs H. H. Wightman
1928	Miss E. Sigourney
1929	Miss M. Blake
1930	Miss M. Palfrey
1931	Miss M. Sachs
1932	Miss M. Morrill
1933	Miss D. Chase
1934	Miss N. Taubele
1935	Miss J. Sharp
1936	Mrs M. G. Van Ryn
1937	Mrs S. Henrotin
1938	Miss V. Hollinger
1939	Miss P. M. Betz
1940	Mrs S. P. Fabyan
1941	Miss P. M. Betz
1942	Mrs P. C. Todd
1943	Miss P. M. Betz
1944	Miss K. Winthrop
1945	Mrs H. P. Rihbany
1946	Mrs H. P. Rihbany
1947	Miss P. M. Betz
1948	Mrs P. C. Todd
1949	Miss G. Moran
1950	Miss N. Chaffee
1951	Miss N. Chaffee
1952	Mrs N. C. Kiner
1953	Mrs T. Long
1954	Mrs D. W. Levine
1955	Miss K. Hubbell
1956	Miss L. Felix
1957	Mrs D. W. Levine
1958	Miss N. O'Connell
1959	Miss L. Felix
1960	Miss C. Wright
1961	Miss J. Hopps
1962	Miss C. Wright
1963	Miss C. Hanks
1964	Miss M. A. Eisel
1965	Miss N. Richey
1966	Mrs L. W. King
1967	Mrs L. W. King
1968	Mrs L. W. King
1969	Mrs M. A. E. Curtis
1970	Mrs M. A. E. Curtis
1971	Mrs L. W. King
1972	*No Competition*
1973	Miss E. Goolagong

tournament was not held, namely in 1913, from 1924 to 1939 inclusive, and in 1942. Some years the women's events were held separately from the men's, as in 1921-3 when the women's championships were held at the Park Club in Buffalo, N.Y.

Nancy Richey won the singles six times in a row (1963-8). Dorothy Head Knode took the title four times and two-time champions have been Pauline Betz, Magda Rurac, Maureen Connolly and Chris Evert.

A number of players besides Miss Connolly have won both the US Clay Court and Grass Court Championships. They include Mary Browne, Molla Bjurstedt, Alice Marble, Pauline Betz, Sarah Palfrey Cooke, Doris Hart, Shirley Fry and Althea Gibson.

The women's doubles began in 1914, but were not always held, the longest lapse being 1924-39. Other vacant years were 1915, 1916, 1921, 1942, 1948 and 1949. Few teams have won the title more than once. Pauline Betz and Doris Hart won it twice and Miss Hart also won with Shirley Fry and with Maureen Connolly. Other two-time champions were the Australians, Karen Krantzcke and Kerry Melville, and Carole Caldwell Graebner and Nancy Richey. Miss Richey also won with Valerie Ziegenfuss. Darlene Hard captured the doubles with four different partners, Althea Gibson, Billie Jean Moffitt, Susan Behlmar and Maria Bueno. FES

US Indoor Championships

The USLTA Indoor Championships began in 1898 at the Winter Lawn Tennis Club, Bray's Hall, Newton Center, Mass. There were 30 entries in the men's singles, which was won by Leonard Ware, who defeated Holcombe Ward, 7-5, 7-5, 6-1. It was not held in 1899, but in 1900 the Seventh Regiment Tennis Club, New York, N.Y., began its long record as the holder of the championship (1900-63). No tournaments were held in 1942-45. In 1941 the event was held at the Coliseum, Oklahoma City, Okla. Since 1964 the indoor men's championship has been held at the Wicomico Youth and Civic Center, Salisbury, Maryland. Eight players have won it more than twice. Wylie Grant won five times (1903-4, 1906, 1908, 1912); Gustave Touchard four times (1910, 1913-15); Jean Borotra, France, four times (1925, 1927, 1929, 1931); Gregory Mangin four times (1932-33, 1935-6). Three-times winners were Theodore Pell (1907, 1909, 1911); Vincent Richards (1919, 1923-4); Richard Savitt (1952, 1958, 1961); Stan Smith (1969-70 (closed), 1972).

The USLTA men's indoor championship began in 1900 at the Seventh Regiment Tennis Club. Calhoun Cragin and J. Paret were the first winners. Outstanding early players were Wylie Grant, who won the title six times, three times with Robert LeRoy, once with Theodore Pell and twice with Carleton Shafer; Harold Hackett and Frederick Alexander. Together Hackett and Alexander won the title three times while Alexander won twice with Theodore Pell and once with William Rosenbaum. In later years Bill Talbert captured the doubles title five times, three with Donald McNeill (1949, 1950, 1951), once with Budge Patty (1952) and once with Tony Trabert (1954).

Among foreign players who won the indoor doubles were Jean Borotra, who won four times, with A. W. Asthalter (1925), Jacques Brugnon (1927), Christian Boussus (1931), and Marcel Bernard (1948); also Andrés Gimeno/Manuel Santana (1960), Santana/José Luis Arilla (1964), Tomaz Koch/Tom Okker (1968), and Juan Gisbert/Manuel Orantes (1971).

The women's indoor singles began in 1907 and the doubles in 1908. These were held with the men's events at the Seventh Regiment Tennis Club, New York. When the men's championship was not held in the war years, 1942-5, the women's indoor tournament was held at the Longwood Covered Courts, Chestnut Hill, Mass., and continued there until 1966. In 1967 the championship was transferred to the Winchester (Mass.) Tennis Center, where it was held until 1972. That year a women's amateur indoor championship was held at East Providence, Rhode Island. The first singles winner was Elisabeth Moore. Early champions include Marie Wagner who won the indoor title six times (1908-9, 1911, 1913-14, 1917) and Molla Bjurstedt Mallory who won five times (1915-16, 1918, 1921-2). Pauline Betz captured four championships (1939, 1941, 1943, 1947) as did Billie Jean King (1966-8, 1971).

The women's indoor doubles championship began in 1908 when Mrs Helen Helwig Pouch and Elisabeth Moore won. Mrs Hazel Hotchkiss Wightman won the doubles ten times – four times with Marion Zinderstein Jessup (1919, 1921, 1924, 1927), five times with Sarah Palfrey (1928-31, 1933), and once with Pauline Betz (1943). The doubles title was captured five times by Katharine Hubbell and her partners – Ruth Jeffery (1955), Lois Felix (1956, 1959), Janet Hopps (1961), Mary Ann Eisel (1964). In addition to winning with Katherine Hubbell, Mary Ann Eisel also won four other times, three times with Carol Hanks Aucamp (1963, 1965, 1967), and with Valerie Ziegenfuss (1969).

Marjorie Gladman Buck shared four doubles titles. Her partners were Gertrude Moran (1949), Nancy Chaffee (1950, 1951), Ruth Jeffery (1960). FES

US Juniors see THE UNITED STATES STORY (PART 1)

US Professional Championships see THE POSTWAR PRO GAME (PART 1)

USPTA, the United States Professional Tennis Association (it dropped 'Lawn' from its name in 1970), see THE UNITED STATES STORY (PART 1)

Above **US Indoor Championships.** The Wicomico Youth and Civic Center, Salisbury, Maryland

US Girls' 18 Championships
Singles

1918	Miss K. Porter
1919	Miss K. Gardner
1920	Miss L. Dixon
1921	Miss H. N.Wills* **
1922	Miss H. N.Wills* **
1923	Miss H. Hooker
1924	Miss H. Jacobs* **
1925	Miss H. Jacobs* **
1926	Miss L. McFarland
1927	Miss M. Gladman
1928	Miss S. Palfrey**
1929	Miss S. Palfrey**
1930	Miss S. Palfrey**
1931	Miss R. Bishop
1932	Miss H. Fulton
1933	Miss B. Miller
1934	Miss H. Pedersen
1935	Miss P. Henry
1936	Miss M. E. Osborne* **
1937	Miss B. Winslow
1938	Miss H. I. Bernhard
1939	Miss H. I. Bernhard
1940	Miss A. L. Brough* **
1941	Miss A. L. Brough* **
1942	Miss D. Hart* **
1943	Miss D. Hart* **
1944	Miss S. J. Fry* **
1945	Miss S. J. Fry* **
1946	Miss H. Pastall
1947	Miss N. Chaffee
1948	Miss B. J. Baker
1949	Miss M. Connolly* **
1950	Miss M. Connolly* **
1951	Miss A. Kanter
1952	Miss J. A. Sampson
1953	Miss M. A. Ellenberger
1954	Miss B. N. Breit
1955	Miss B. N. Breit
1956	Miss M. Arnold
1957	Miss K. J. Hantze*
1958	Miss S. A. Moore
1959	Miss K. J. Hantze*
1960	Miss K. J. Hantze*
1961	Miss V. Palmer
1962	Miss V. Palmer
1963	Miss J. Heldman
1964	Miss M. A. Eisel
1965	Miss J. Bartkowicz
1966	Miss J. Bartkowicz
1967	Miss J. Bartkowicz
1968	Miss K. Pigeon
1969	Miss S. Walsh
1970	Miss S. Walsh
1971	Miss C. Evert
1972	Miss A. Kiyomura
1973	Miss C. Fleming

* later won Wimbledon;
** later won US Championships

US Junior Championships
Singles

1916	H. A. Throckmorton
1917	C. S. Garland
1918	H. L. Taylor
1919	V. Richards
1920	V. Richards
1921	V. Richards
1922	A. W. Jones
1923	G. M. Lott
1924	G. M. Lott
1925	C. M. Holman
1926	J. Doeg*
1927	F. X. Shields
1928	F. X. Shields
1929	K. Gledhill
1930	W. Hines
1931	J. Lynch
1932	F. A. Parker**
1933	D. Budge* **
1934	C. G. Mako
1935	R. L. Riggs* **
1936	J. Heldman
1937	J. R. Hunt*
1938	D. Freeman
1939	F. R. Schroeder* **
1940	R. D. Carrothers
1941	J. E. Patty*
1942	J. E. Patty*
1943	R. Falkenburg*
1944	R. Falkenburg*
1945	H. Flam
1946	H. Flam
1947	H. Behrens
1948	G. A. Bogley
1949	G. A. Bogley
1950	H. Richardson
1951	T. Rogers
1952	J. Frost
1953	J. Lesch
1954	G. Moss
1955	E. Reyes
1956	R. Laver* **
1957	A. Roberts
1958	E. Buchholz
1959	D. Ralston
1960	W. Lenoir
1961	C. Pasarell
1962	M. Belkin
1963	C. Richey
1964	S. R. Smith* **
1965	R. Lutz
1966	S. Avoyer
1967	J. Borowiak
1968	R. McKinley
1969	E. Van Dillen
1970	B. Gottfried
1971	R. Ramirez
1972	P. DuPre
1973	W. Martin

US Professional Championship Winners

1927	V. Richards
1928	V. Richards
1929	K. Koželuh
1930	V. Richards
1931	W. T. Tilden
1932	K. Koželuh
1933	V. Richards
1934	H. Nusslein
1935	W. T. Tilden
1936	J. Whalen
1937	K. Koželuh
1938	F. Perry
1939	E. Vines
1940	D. Budge
1941	F. Perry
1942	D. Budge
1943	B. Barnes
1944	*No Competition*
1945	W. Van Horn
1946	R. Riggs
1947	R. Riggs
1948	J. A. Kramer
1949	R. Riggs
1950	P. Segura
1951	P. Segura
1952	P. Segura
1953	R. A. Gonzalez
1954	R. A. Gonzalez
1955	R. A. Gonzalez
1956	R. A. Gonzalez
1957	R. A. Gonzalez
1958	R. A. Gonzalez
1959	R. A. Gonzalez
1960	A. Olmedo
1961	R. A. Gonzalez
1962	B. Buchholz
1963	K. Rosewall
1964	R. Laver
1965	K. Rosewall
1966	R. Laver
1967	R. Laver
1968	R. Laver
1969	R. Laver
1970	A. Roche
1971	K. Rosewall
1972	R. Lutz
1973	J. S. Connors

Above **USSR**. Olga Morozova in 1972

USSR

Tennis has been played in Russia for over 90 years and was mentioned by Tolstoy. Imperial Russia was a Founder Member of the ILTF. The last Russian Championships were held in St Petersburg (now Leningrad) in 1914 (see THE GROWTH OF THE GAME, PART 1).

After the Revolution, the game remained alive. The Lawn Tennis Federation of the USSR was founded in 1922 and affiliated to the ILTF in 1956; since then a dramatic improvement has been made in the development and standard of play. Today there are some 960 tennis clubs in the USSR with more than 50,000 active players.

The USSR Championships have been held in different cities since 1924; the first Champions were A. Stoliarov of Moscow (men's singles) and T. Sukhodolskaya of Leningrad (women's singles). The Moscow International Tournament has been held since 1957; players from many countries have taken part.

Boys and girls from the age of 8 or 9 are taught in special sports schools and outstanding young players are later given special training in technique and tactics by experienced coaches. Physical fitness is considered to be of outstanding importance.

The USSR has competed in the DAVIS CUP every year since 1962 and has done well in the European Zone. A women's team competed in the FEDERATION CUP in 1968.

Players from the USSR who have taken part in international tournaments with outstanding success are A. Metreveli (Tbilisi), Wimbledon runner-up 1973, T. Lejus (Tallin), S. Likhachev (Baku), V. Korotkov (Moscow), T. Kakulia (Tbilisi), A. Volkov (Moscow); women include O. Morozova (Moscow), Wimbledon quarter-finalist 1973, A. Dmitrieva (Moscow), G. Baksheeva (Kiev), M. Kroshina (Alma-Ata), Z. Iansone (Riga) and E. Biriukova (Baku).

There was great excitement in the 1970 Wimbledon Championships when Alex Metreveli and Olga Morozova nearly won the mixed doubles final – they lost the third set to Ilie Năstase and Rosemary Casals by the narrowest possible margin. BR
GOVERNING BODY: Lawn Tennis Federation of the USSR, Moscow 69, Skatertnyi pereulok 4

V

Valerio Cup

A relatively new European team championship for boys of under 18, for a trophy donated in memory of Vasco Valerio, a former Italian Davis Cup captain who died in 1969. Run in much the same way as the GALEA CUP, the competition is divided into four zones, with the finals in Lesa, Italy. Sweden won the first competition in 1970. DC

Van Alen Streamlined Scoring System
see VASSS

Van Dillen, Erik Jacobus (USA)

Born San Mateo, Calif., 21 Feb. 1951; US Hard Court men's doubles and Amateur men's doubles won 1969; US Open men's doubles r/u 1971, s/f 1972. Davis Cup 1971- . Became independent pro 1970. Played key minor role in famous US Davis Cup Final win (1972) *v* Rumania when, with SMITH, he won doubles against NĂSTASE and ȚIRIAC.

Van Ryn, John William (USA)

Born Newport News, Va., 30 June 1906; Wimbledon men's singles q/f 1931; men's doubles won 1929-31, s/f 1932, r/u 1935, s/f 1936; US men's singles q/f 1929-31, 1936-7; men's doubles s/f 1928, r/u 1930, won 1931, r/u 1932, 1934, won 1935, r/u 1936, s/f 1937-8, 1945; mixed doubles s/f 1935; Australian men's doubles s/f 1933; French men's singles q/f 1931; men's doubles won 1931. Davis Cup 1929-36.

VASSS

The Van Alen Streamlined Scoring System was the invention of an American millionaire, Mr James Van Alen, of Newport, Rhode Island. It was designed to shorten matches and make program planning easier for referees and television producers who have difficulties when games overrun their allotted time.

VASSS replaces what, to some, is confusing scoring terminology (love, 15, 30, 40, deuce) with a simple points system (the score increases by one for each point won). As in table tennis, the service changes from player A to player B every five points (when the score totals 5, 10, 15, etc.); the five-point sequence is called a 'hand'. The official set is fixed at 31 points, but if time is at a premium 21 points may be used. At 30-30 a nine-point tie-break comes into operation to decide the winner.

The VASSS 'No-Ad' method is closer to the traditional lawn tennis scoring but the advantage point is eliminated in the game and the advantage game in the set. The first player to win four points – scored 1, 2, 3, 4 (not 15, 30, 40) – wins the game and the first to win six games wins the set. If the score is level at five games all (5-5), the nine-point tie-break decides the 11th game and the set at 6-5.

VASSS can easily be used in handicap events. As Van Alen stated in an outline to his method in 1968, 'If A can beat B 31-22, that is no contest, but let A give B nine points start, and you have a match'. See also SCORING. DC

Venezuela

Lawn tennis has been played in Venezuela for many years, but the National Federation was not established until 1927, when the lawn-tennis championships also began at the Altamira Tennis Club, Caracas. Venezuela affiliated to the ILTF in 1957 and has played in the DAVIS CUP many times since then. The Federación Venezolana has 11 affiliated state associations with some 600 players. There are coaching schemes for juniors. Venezuelan players, in particular Iyo Pimentel and Eduardo Alvarez, have played on European and American circuits. BR
GOVERNING BODY: Federación Venezolana de Tennis, Altamira Tennis Club, Chacao, Edo. Miranda, Caracas

Vermaak, I. C. see SOUTH AFRICA

Veteran International Tennis Association (VITA)

The Veteran International Tennis Association was founded in 1956 as the international governing body for veterans (seniors) and is recognized by the ILTF. In 1973 it had 20 member countries in Europe and over 15 member countries in the rest of the world. Its official team competition the DUBLER CUP, began in 1958 as a result of the initiative of Dr Alessandro Loewy, long president of VITA. VITA also started its International Championship of Europe in 1958; the first winner of the singles was Francesco Garnero (Italy).

Veterans

Clubs for veterans (called seniors in the United States) exist in many countries. Membership is open to amateur players over a certain age (which varies from country to country). The objects of the clubs are to encourage the playing of lawn tennis for the love of the game, to encourage veterans to continue playing and to promote and support the inclusion of veterans' events at open tournaments.

In the United States neither men seniors (45 years and over) nor women seniors (40 years and over) have a separate club but come under the responsibility and control of the senior men's committee and the senior women's committee of the USLTA. There are separate subcommittees for senior men's subdivisions in the over-50, 55, 60, 65 and 70 classes. Membership of the USLTA is necessary for any individual to enter and play in any sanctioned tournament. The first National USLTA Senior Championship was held at Forest Hills in 1918. There are now between 150 and 200 senior tournaments in the United States including four national championships on grass, clay, hard courts and indoors.

The Veterans' Lawn Tennis Club of Great Britain was founded in December 1958. Its aim, as expressed in the rules, is to play the game of lawn tennis in the spirit in which it was first played, 'for the love and enjoyment of the game'. The Club now has over 200 members, mostly in Great Britain. Its colours are two narrow gold stripes on a dark green ground. These colours are said to represent the ever-green spirit of the veterans against the 'sear and yellow' of coming old age. The Club plays a number of international matches, in particular an annual match against Norway, alternating in London and Oslo. Club matches are played against, among others, the All England Club, the Queen's Club, the Navy, and the Hurlingham Club, where the Veterans also have their headquarters. The Veterans' Lawn Tennis Club of Great Britain became affiliated to the LTA (of Great Britain) in 1973.

Viet Nam

Tennis has been played in Viet Nam for about 50 years but the Viet Nam Lawn Tennis Federation was not established until 1947 when the country gained independence. It affiliated to the ILTF as a Full Member in 1955. There are 30 clubs with perhaps 1,000 members. National Championships have been played in Saigon since 1950 and Viet Nam has regularly competed in the DAVIS CUP since 1964.

In spite of a quarter of a century of war, lawn tennis has been kept alive. BR
GOVERNING BODY: Fédération de Lawn-Tennis du Viet-Nam, 135 Hai Ba Trung St, Saigon

Vilas, Guillermo (Argentina)

Born 17 Aug. 1952; he first brought himself into international prominence by his standard of play in the 1972 French Championships when he reached the last 16 at his first attempt; this was confirmed by his victories in the Davis Cup *v.* South Africa in 1973. Left-handed.

Vines, H. Ellsworth (USA)

Born Los Angeles, Calif., 29 Sept. 1911; Wimbledon men's singles won 1932, r/u 1933; US men's singles won 1931-2; men's doubles won 1932, s/f 1933: mixed doubles r/u 1932, won 1933; Australian men's doubles won 1933; mixed doubles r/u 1933. Davis Cup 1932-3. His finest year was certainly 1932. By general consensus his form that season was assessed as the most authoritative and punishing ever seen. It was based on a lightning forehand drive and a cannonball service. In winning the Wimbledon final against AUSTIN in 1932 the

Above **Virginia Slims.** An appropriate slogan for the women's circuit. *(Right)* Virginia Wade.

final point, an ace by Vines, was so fast that Austin afterwards confessed he did not know on which side the ball flew by him. He became

Below **Ellsworth Vines**

a professional in 1933 and after five years turned to golf, becoming one of America's leading exponents of that game. See CENTRE COURT CLASSICS and GREAT PLAYERS OF ALL TIME (PART 1).

Virginia Slims

The Virginia Slims circuit for women, carrying the brand name of an American tobacco company, Philip Morris Inc., began in August 1970 when Gladys Heldman, publisher and editor of the American magazine *World Tennis,* was asked to organize a tournament for eight women in Houston, Texas, in direct conflict with the traditional PACIFIC SOUTHWEST CHAMPIONSHIPS in Los Angeles. Virginia Slims agreed to put up a large share of the $7,500 prize money (see THE WOMEN'S PRO GAME, PART 1). In 1971 Mrs Heldman helped to organize a substantial prize-money circuit for women where no women's tournaments had existed before. The money was provided mainly by Virginia Slims with assistance from local sponsors. As a result, Billie Jean King made a record $117,000. In 1972 the Slims circuit ran from January to May and July to October, with nearly 60 women competing and at least six won more than $50,000. The final 1972 tournament at Boca Raton, Fla., offered a first prize of $25,000. DC

VITA see VETERAN INTERNATIONAL TENNIS FEDERATION

Volley

A stroke in which the ball is hit before it has bounced. It is generally played in the forecourt. There are several types of volley – high, low, stop (or drop), lob and drive. JO

Von Cramm, Baron Gottfried see CRAMM, von

W

Wade, Miss Sarah Virginia (Gt Britain)

Born Bournemouth, 10 July 1945; Wimbledon
women's singles q/f 1967, 1972-3; women's
doubles s/f 1966-7, r/u 1970, s/f 1972; US
women's singles q/f 1966, won 1968, s/f 1969-
70, q/f 1972-3; women's doubles s/f 1965-6,
1968, r/u 1969-70, 1972, won 1973; Australian women's singles won 1972, q/f 1973;
women's doubles won 1973; French women's
singles q/f 1970, q/f 1972; women's doubles
won 1973; mixed doubles s/f 1969, 1972;
Italian women's singles won 1971. Wightman
Cup 1965- . Federation Cup 1967- ; captain 1973. ILTF GP 5th 1971, 8th 1972. Very
gifted but quite unpredictable. Her game,
particularly her service (see THE BASIC TEACH-
ING OF TENNIS, PART 1) is potentially as good
as any woman's today.

Wales

Lawn tennis had early connections with Nantclwyd Hall, near Ruthin, North Wales, where
in December 1873 Major W. C. Wingfield, who
devised and patented a kit for lawn tennis (see
THE BIRTH AND SPREAD OF LAWN TENNIS, PART
1), dedicated his book of rules 'to the party
assembled at Nantclwyd Hall, the seat of the
Naylor-Leyland family'. The first record of
organized tennis in Wales appears to be in a
report of the Newport Athletic Club mention-
ing the establishment of the tennis section in
1879 and the construction of an indoor court
in 1890 for the sum of £2,000. By the mid-
1880s a number of clubs were established in
Wales. The Penarth Lawn Tennis Club held
its first Championships in 1885, and about
this time the Roath and Cardiff (presumably
the Cyncoed) Lawn Tennis Clubs were formed,
the former later changing its name to the
Cardiff Racquet and Lawn Tennis Club and
also its ground from the Roath area of Cardiff
to its present home in the grounds of Cardiff
Castle in the city centre.

Lawn tennis is administered in Wales by
the Welsh Lawn Tennis Association. Its membership is made up of the North Wales LTA
(formed in 1925), the Mid Wales LTA (formed
in 1961) and about 100 clubs, seven tournament committees and 47 schools. About 4,000
people over 18 play tennis in Wales and Monmouthshire and junior membership of schools
and clubs amounts to about 3,000. Unfortunately the Welsh LTA's records were lost during World War II so it is neither possible to
state the circumstances leading up to its for-

mation nor the exact date, but it certainly
existed in 1888, for in that year the present
Challenge Bowl, awarded annually to the Club
winning the Inter-Club League Competition,
was presented to the Cardiff Racquet and
Lawn Tennis Club. They were then playing in
a knock-out competition which continued as
such until 1903, after which it changed in form
and became the present League Competition.
It was only in 1927 that the first women's team
event started. Begun on elimination lines it became the present Ladies' League Competition.

The Welsh Championships apparently began in 1886. In the early years they seem to
have been mainly held at the Penarth Club or
the Roath LTC, Cardiff. From 1897 their home
was apparently the Newport Athletic Club.

The next tournament to emerge was the
Whitsun Tournament organized by the Dinas

Below **Virginia Wade**

Powis LTC in 1908. It was open to members of
clubs in South Wales. Its success prompted
the Club to create the Glamorganshire Championships in 1911, with a women's singles
event introduced in 1914. From 1915 to 1919
and from 1940 to 1945 there were no championships meetings. The Dinas Powis Club
was unable to stage the tournament from 1965
onwards and, from then on the Cardiff LTC
ran it until 1972, when it was discontinued for
lack of funds.

In 1922 the Llanelli Lawn Tennis Club inaugurated the County of Carmarthenshire
Championships which are held in the first
week of August and now incorporate 18
events, many of which are for juniors. In 1925
a Ladies' International Match between Wales
and Australia was held at Llanelli. Since 1926
Llanelli has been the venue for the Wales and
England Ladies' International Matches. Earlier
(1906), Newport (Mon.) was the venue for the

Davis Cup final between the United States and Australia, the former winning by three rubbers to two.

Two other tournaments, the North Wales Championships, at Criccieth, and the Welsh Covered Courts Championships, at the Craigside Hydro, Llandudno, have not been held for a number of years.

The staging of the International Men's Matches between Wales and England has been the exclusive right of the Newport Athletic Club Tennis Section. The first of these matches, referred to as 'Semi-International', took place in 1924. The first International Mixed Match between Wales and Ireland was played at Eirias Park, Colwyn Bay, North Wales in 1949. Ireland won by 11 rubbers to nil and continued to win until 1958. The first International Mixed Match against Scotland was held in 1953 at Glasgow. Scotland won by five rubbers to three. The International Match series between Wales, Ireland and Scotland began in 1962. The first match was played at Elm Park Golf and Sports Club, Dublin, in August 1962 when Wales was beaten by both Ireland and Scotland by six rubbers to two.

Welsh teams have also supported the British Inter-County Championships for many years and, indeed, they were held in Wales in 1933-34 and 1937. The clubs concerned were Tenby, Cardiff, Pwllheli, Criccieth and Vale of Clwyd.

The Welsh LTA has always endeavoured to develop its coaching, but its activities have been hampered by financial problems. But recently a number of donations and grants, for example from GREEN SHIELD, and DEWAR (one leg of the Dewar Cup has been held at the Afan Lido, Port Talbot, since 1968) have made it possible to extend the summer and winter coaching programs. The Association appointed its first full-time National Coach and Development Officer in 1971. The Association has for several years entered boys' and girls' teams in the Junior Inter-County Competition. For the first time in 1972 a Junior International Match was staged between Wales and Ireland at the Llanelli Club. Two outstanding Welsh juniors, both from Bridgend, have won Junior Wimbledon: Gerald Battrick (1964) and J. P. R. Williams (1966), who has since become perhaps the greatest Rugby Union fullback that Wales has ever produced.

In 1923 the Welsh LTA organized its first Junior Championships. The first three tournaments were held in the Cardiff area but in 1926 the event was transferred to the Penarth LTC, where, except in 1940-6, all subsequent tournaments were held.

Probably the best Welsh player ever, until he turned to professional administration with WCT, was Mike Davies, runner-up in the Wimbledon men's doubles in 1960, the last year of his successful Davis Cup career for Great Britain (37 rubbers). KME

GOVERNING BODY: Welsh Lawn Tennis Association; Hon. Secretary, The Chimes, Heol-y-bryn, Barry, Glamorgan

Above **Wales**. The scene at Newport (Mon.) during the 1972 Welsh Championships. The winner that year was A. Pattison *(left)*. K. Melville won the women's singles.

Wallach, Mrs Maud [Miss M. Barger] (USA)

Born 1871, died 2 April 1954. US women's singles won 1908, r/u 1909, q/f 1916; women's doubles r/u 1912; mixed doubles s/f 1908.

Ward, Holcombe (USA)

Born New York, 23 Nov. 1878, died 23 Jan. 1967; Wimbledon men's doubles r/u 1901, s/f 1905; US men's singles q/f 1897-9, won 1904, r/u 1905; men's doubles r/u 1898, won 1899-1901, r/u 1902, won 1904-6. Davis Cup 1900, 1902, 1905-6. A member of the American side in the first Davis Cup tie of 1900, partnering the Cup's donor Dwight DAVIS.

Watson, Miss Maud (Gt Britain)

Born 1863, died 1934; Wimbledon women's singles won 1884-5, r/u 1886; Irish women's singles won 1884-5; Welsh women's singles won 1887. The first woman champion at Wimbledon. See FASHION.

WCT see WORLD CHAMPIONSHIP TENNIS

Welsh Championships see NEWPORT, Monmouthshire

Wembley see LONDON PROFESSIONAL INDOOR TENNIS CHAMPIONSHIPS; also POSTWAR DEVELOPMENT (PART 1)

Westacott, Mrs V. (Australia)

Australian women's singles s/f 1935, r/u 1937, won 1939; women's doubles won 1933-4, s/f 1935, r/u 1937, 1939; mixed doubles r/u 1931, 1934, s/f 1935. Notable in Australia immediately before World War II.

West of England Championships see BRISTOL

West Side Club, New York, see US CHAMPIONSHIPS; see also THE UNITED STATES STORY (PART 1)

Whitman, Malcolm D. (USA)

Born 15 March 1877, died 28 Dec. 1932; US men's singles q/f 1896-7, won 1898-1900, r/u* 1902. Davis Cup 1900, 1902. The top singles player in the American side of the first Davis Cup tie of 1900.

Wightman, Mrs G. W. [Miss Hazel V. Hotchkiss] (USA)

Born Healdsburg, Calif., 20 Dec. 1886; Wimbledon women's doubles won 1924; US women's singles won 1909-11, r/u 1915, won 1919, q/f 1928; women's doubles won 1909-11, 1915, r/u 1923, won 1924, 1928; mixed doubles won 1909-11, 1915, 1918, 1920, r/u 1926-7. She won innumerable US titles and her career as a top player spanned World War I. She founded the WIGHTMAN CUP contest, and played 1923-4, 1927, 1929, 1931, continuing as non-playing captain till her final retirement. Olympic gold medallist 1924. She was still coaching youngsters in 1973.

Wightman Cup

The coveted Wightman Cup, a tall, elaborately decorated silver vase, 24 in (61 cm) high, with ornamental engraving, has been the symbol of world supremacy in women's tennis since 1923. When Mrs Hazel Hotchkiss Wightman first offered the handsome trophy for international competition, she did not intend her name to be used on it, and indeed, it is inscribed the 'Women's Lawn Tennis Team Championship between Great Britain and the United States'. However, it soon became known as the Wightman Cup as a tribute to this great American tennis champion and sportswoman.

Mrs Wightman's original idea was to include teams from all over the world. Participation by a French team was especially desirable, because of the excitement created by Suzanne Lenglen's outstanding accomplishments soon after World War I. Having closely followed the success of the men's DAVIS CUP competition, Mrs Wightman wished to start a similar competition for women. In 1920 she purchased the cup and presented it to the USLTA. However, other nations were not as enthusiastic about the idea as Mrs Wightman was, probably because of the financial difficulties of assembling competent teams, until 1923 when Great Britain decided to send a challenge team to the United States.

The articles of agreement between the national associations of the two countries involved were officially adopted in 1926 and amended in 1947. They are somewhat sketchy and incomplete, ending with section (j): 'In all cases not provided for in these regulations, or by mutual agreement, the Davis Cup regulations shall apply'.

Section (d) states that 'the form of match and the number of the players each team shall consist of, shall be determined from time to time by mutual agreement'. However, since its inception, the Wightman Cup competition has consisted of seven matches – five singles and two doubles. Because there are three singles players and two doubles pairs, who may take part in both events, the teams may consist of a minimum of four players, a maximum of seven. With seven, outstanding doubles teams have the opportunity to play, even though those players are not included in the singles encounters, and doubles superiority has decided more than one series. The captains may be playing or non-playing. The numbers one and two singles players cross-play. Each number three singles player plays only the other. The numbers one and two doubles teams each play only their counterparts. With the doubles being played as the last match daily, the order of singles play each day is determined by draw, made 24 hours before the starting time. Sometimes the order is altered, by mutual consent of the captains and referee, if such alteration will eliminate players on either side having to take part in two successive matches.

The annual matches are played alternately in Great Britain and the United States. Wimbledon has always been the scene of the British series, but in the United States the teams have met at seven different locations.

Wimbledon is always a two-day venue. On the first day there are two singles matches, involving the first two singles players, followed by a doubles match. On the second day the number three singles is usually the first match, followed by the first and second singles played in reverse order, then a doubles match. In the United States the same two-day venue was followed until 1965, when it was mutually agreed to spread the matches over three days in an effort to bring in more revenue. In 1967 the paid attendance over the three days was over 16,000, an all-time record, so the experiment proved successful and has been continued ever since.

In 1957, for the first time in tennis history, the Wightman Cup matches were played on other than grass courts. Fast-drying green composition courts were used, and were followed in later years by clay courts, cement, and a synthetic carpet court. Moving the series around proved worthwhile financially and stimulated spectator interest. Attendance at Wimbledon has always been good. In addition to the regular fans, many schools send hundreds of young girls to see their tennis idols fight to uphold the honour of their respective countries.

The team's captions sit on either side of the umpire's chair during the progress of the matches, to advise and encourage their players. Before the date of the matches, it is the responsibility of the captains to bring their team members up to a peak for the competition and to attend to important details, such as scheduling practice during the same time of day as the matches themselves are played so that the temperature and light will be similar, and arranging simple, easy work-outs in the week leading up to the matches, so that the players are not unnecessarily tired. From 1923 to 1931 Mrs Wightman was the playing captain of the American team. Then for 18 years she officiated as non-playing captain before relinquishing her post.

Nearly 3,000 spectators were at the West Side Tennis Club, Forest Hills, New York, Stadium courts, 11 August 1923, to watch the first international team match for women. The observance of Friday, 10 August, as a day of mourning for President Harding, carried the opening matches over until Saturday, one day later, and they concluded on Monday, since there was no play on Sundays. The 15 August 1923 issue of *American Lawn Tennis* magazine, published and edited by S. Wallis Merrihew, reported:

A team of visiting ladies, four in number, crossed the Atlantic and tried conclusions with a team selected from the top American players. The invaders – consisting of Kathleen McKane, by many regarded as the second player in Europe; Mrs A. E. Beamish, Mrs R. C. Clayton and Mrs B. C. Covell – made a formidable team. The defending team consisted of Mrs Wightman; Mrs Molla Bjurstedt Mallory, the American champion; Helen Wills, [the American champion-to-be]; and Eleanor Goss. In the first match on the Stadium, Miss Wills won the toss and elected to serve. The first ball was a 'let', the second a service ace; and an advance to the net and subsequent volley, followed by a fine passing drive, earned the first game for the Californian girl. Miss McKane's service game was a long deuce affair, with Miss Wills having advantage three times before winning the game. Miss Wills won her service again in another deuce game and got to 3-0. At 4-1 Miss McKane was broken through, but Miss Wills dropped her service next and then got home at 6-2. It seemed scarcely believable that the young girl was not only playing magnificent tennis but clearly outhitting, outguessing and outgaming her formidable opponent. When Miss McKane captured Miss Will's service in the second set, volleying well and decisively smashing her opponent's lob, the expected swinging of the pendulum in the opposite direction seemed to have occurred. At 2-0 there appeared to be confirmation of the change, Miss Wills netting a smash of a short lob. The play of Miss McKane improved and she got to 4-1, wresting Miss Will's service from her. Miss Wills rallied and won her opponent's delivery, but Miss McKane retaliated and went to 5-2 and 40-15 on her own service. Here was the place for Miss Wills to crack, if ever; and small blame if she had yielded. But she stiffened her game and started a rush that sent the gallery almost into a delirium of joy. Twice Miss McKane came to the net and volleyed just over the sidelines, with the set in her grasp. A hard drive to Miss McKane's backhand caused her to drive out, and Miss Wills was 3-5. The win of her service followed – 4-5. Sheer hard hitting carried Miss Wills to 40-0 in the tenth game and the next point made it 5-all. Instead of hesitating, Miss Wills pushed on, with Miss McKane's resistance crumbling, and won the set 7-5.

In the same issue of *American Lawn Tennis*, the foremost British tennis writer of the time, A. Wallis Myers, had this to say:

I think, psychologically, the American women were stronger than the English. The home players had more iron, both in their bodies and in their souls. They were all out to justify reputations which in the eyes of many of their countrymen had been fairly roughly handled in Europe. There is nothing like a little wounded pride (and I do not mean conceit) to stiffen the will. On the other hand, if you ask me to speak the truth, I think the visiting women, with the exception of Mrs Beamish, were disposed, before they came into court, to underestimate the severity of their task. Possibly their captain shared this optimism and made unwise preliminary plans accordingly. Maybe our ladies did not come to America only for the purpose of confirming their European supremacy over the American ladies; they came to strengthen the bands of friendship between the two countries, to

Above **Wightman Cup.** Mrs Hazel Wightman with the 1949 Wightman Cup team. *Left to right:* Margaret duPont, Doris Hart, Beverly Baker, captain 'Midge' Buck, Mrs Wightman (with the coveted cup), Pat Todd, Gertrude Moran, Shirley Fry and Louise Brough. The US team's victory by 7-0 that year was its fourth postwar win; it held the Cup until 1958.

inaugurate a friendly contest which cannot fail to stimulate the woman's game not only in our two countries, but all over the world. The game is always greater than the prize; international goodwill is greater than either. If women's international matches are to assume the same importance and encourage the same friendly rivalry as men's matches they will demand the same scientific organization, the same careful training, the same expert judgment of conditions abroad and of players' form in their own country as men's contests . . . I saw Mrs Wightman play for the first time . . . There is no strategist quite her equal in Europe today. Her volleying errors in her doubles match were errors only of fatigue, never

of position. Her low volleying was as delightful to watch as it must have been as disconcerting to play against. Her lobs and lob-volleys were wonderful in their delicacy and judgment. She cannot expect to cover court as quickly as she formerly did, but what she loses in activity she gains in tactical skill. She is one of the few players (Doherty, Brookes, Mrs Larcombe and Mlle Lenglen are others) who seem to attract the ball to the racket.

Unexpectedly, then, the United States had won this memorable first encounter with the loss of only two sets.

However, Great Britain turned the tables in the second contest, played at Wimbledon, 18-19 June 1924, winning 6-1. The only match the United States won was the doubles in which Helen Wills was Mrs Wightman's partner. Miss Wills lost both of her singles, one to Miss McKane (see Mrs L. GODFREE) and the other to Mrs Covell, her only singles losses in Wightman Cup play in nine different teams.

Five of the first eight series, which were divided four each, were decided by victory in the doubles matches (as was the case in many succeeding series). The outstanding doubles player of those early days was Elizabeth Ryan, twelve times winner of the Wimbledon women's doubles from 1919 to 1934. In 1926, with Mary K. Browne, she won the doubles that clinched the Wightman Cup tie, 4-3. However, it was the superiority of the British women in doubles play that accounted for many of their victories. During the first ten years of play the British won 13 of the 20 doubles matches played. Mrs Kathleen McKane Godfree, Mrs Lambert Chambers, Mrs H. Watson, Phyllis Mudford, Peggy Saunders Michell and Mrs Shepherd-Barron were some of the early British stars. In 1927 Betty Nuthall, Britain's youngest successful player, who had just cut off her curls, won her first international match, a third singles encounter against another newcomer, Helen Jacobs. Both were identified with the Wightman Cup for many years.

New stars of the second decade of play included Dorothy Round, Eileen Bennett Whittingstall, Peggy Scriven, Mary Heeley, Freda James and Kay Stammers for England; Sarah Palfrey, Alice Marble and Mrs Ethel Burkhardt Arnold for the United States. Miss Marble was a great player but her Wightman Cup experience was shortened by illness in 1934.

At one stretch the United States won the Wightman Cup 21 consecutive times (1931-1957). When the competition was resumed in 1946, following a six-year lapse due to World War II, the American women were formidable. They had been able to keep active during the war years, while the British women had had no opportunity to play. Pauline Betz, Margaret Osborne, Louise Brough, Doris Hart and Pat Todd, making their first trip abroad and captained by Mrs Wightman, won all seven matches without the loss of a set. The procession of successes did not, however, dampen the enthusiasm of players on either side of the Atlantic.

The leading British players who strove so valiantly to break the American hold included Mrs Kay Stammers Menzies, Mrs Jean Nicoll Bostock, Mrs Betty Hilton, Jean Quertier, Joy Gannon, Joan Curry, Mrs Jean Walker-Smith, Angela Mortimer, Pat Ward, Shirley Bloomer, Christine Truman and Ann Haydon, but the American contingent was further strengthened in 1951 by the first appearances of Maureen Connolly and Shirley Fry.

One of Britain's all-time favourites, Christine Truman, was the heroine of the 1958 series, winning all three of her matches and almost single-handedly regaining the Wightman Cup for England. Her biggest triumph was over the reigning Wimbledon and United States champion, Althea Gibson.

The 1961 victory of the youngest American team ever to take the courts against a roster of British champions, was one of the greatest upsets in the history of the Wightman Cup. Teenagers Karen Hantze, Billie Jean Moffitt and Justina Bricka, backed up by veteran Margaret Osborne duPont and Margaret Varner, won it 6-1. One of the doubles matches made history by being the only match ever to be won by default.

Great Britain's seventh win was scored in 1968, four matches to three, with Virginia Wade starring in the singles, and the Truman sisters, Christine and Nell, triumphing in the seventh and deciding match. Winnie Shaw was the other member of that winning team. Shirley Bloomer Brasher, Deirdre Catt and Elizabeth Starkie also starred for Britain during the 1960s, while the United States made use of the talents of Darlene Hard, Nancy Richey, Carole Caldwell, Mary Ann Eisel and Rosemary Casals.

Former contract pros were allowed to compete for the first time in 1970 and this brought back Ann Haydon Jones and Billie Jean Moffitt King. The following two years were highlighted by yet another outstanding United States teenager, Chris Evert, who set her teams on the way to two unexpected victories.

Wightman Cup. *Top* Winnie Shaw and Virginia Wade (GB) in the 1970 Wightman Cup at Wimbledon *Above* Peaches Bartkowicz in the 1969 event at Cleveland, Ohio

Over the years there have been numerous efforts to open up the Wightman Cup competition, but this private friendly battle between the women of Great Britain and the United States continues unchanged with a charm and interest all its own. For detailed records see PART 3. MdP

Wilding, Anthony F. (New Zealand)

Born Christchurch, 31 Oct. 1883, died France, 9 May 1915; Wimbledon men's singles q/f 1905, s/f 1906, q/f 1908, won 1910-13, r/u 1914; men's doubles s/f 1906, won 1907-8, 1910, r/u 1911, won 1914; mixed doubles r/u 1914; Australian men's singles won 1906, 1909; men's doubles won 1906, r/u 1908-9. Davis Cup for Australasia 1905-9, 1914. The greatest New Zealand player of all time learned his lawn tennis at Cambridge and was idolized as an outstanding sportsman during the course of his four successive Wimbledon singles victories. He was killed in action at Neuve Chapelle at the age of 31. See GREAT PLAYERS OF ALL TIME (PART 1) and also NEW ZEALAND.

Wilding Shield see NEW ZEALAND

Williams, Richard Norris (USA)

Born Geneva, Switzerland, 29 Jan. 1891, died 1968; Wimbledon men's singles q/f 1920, s/f 1924; men's doubles won 1920, r/u 1924; US men's singles q/f 1912, r/u 1913, won 1914, s/f 1915, won 1916, s/f 1917, 1919, q/f 1922-3, s/f 1925, q/f 1926, 1929; men's doubles r/u 1921, 1923, won 1925-6, r/u 1927; mixed doubles won 1912. Davis Cup 1913-14, 1921, 1923, 1925-6. One of the top US players of the early 1920s. His Davis Cup career spanned World War I and he was five times a member of the victorious Challenge Round team.

Wills, Miss Helen see Mrs F. S. MOODY

Wills, W. D. & H. O., Ltd.

This tobacco company sponsored a major British grass tournament at Bristol each June, generally two weeks before Wimbledon. Until 1973 one of the LTA's major sponsors, Wills became involved on a very small scale in the late 1950s when it assisted several small tournaments throughout Britain. It was almost ten years later that it became associated with more important events; in 1965-6 it sponsored the Scottish Hard Court Championships, and in 1967 the West of England Championships at Bristol, the company's home town. In 1969 it established the Wills Open Championships at Bristol, paying big prize money to attract the world's best players. In 1971 this tournament was a WCT event. Although it was stopped by rain it established record advance booking receipts for the Bristol Club.

Wills sponsored the world's first Open championships: the British Hard Court Championships at BOURNEMOUTH (1968). The company also sponsored the Embassy Indoor Championships, with prize money of £20,000 each year, at the Empire Pool, Wembley, from 1969 (in that year known as the Wills Indoor Championships) but stopped in 1972 after the dispute between the ILTF and contract professionals. It ceased sponsorship altogether in September 1973. DC

Wilson Cup see AUSTRALIA

Wilson Sporting Goods Co. Inc.

This leading American manufacturer of sporting goods was founded in 1914 when the Wilson Meat Packing Co. took over the Ashland Manufacturing Co. of Chicago which consisted of a single store and modest warehouse. Tennis equipment was included for the first time in the 1916 catalogue and has been a major line ever since. In 1924 the company introduced the pressurized tennis ball can, by which time its sale of rackets and balls were rising sharply. The firm changed its name to Wilson Sporting Goods Co. in 1930 when it had become a national concern with eight major distribution points and seven factories. The present tennis boom was anticipated by the management in the early 1960s when a new factory in northern New York State was opened. Set in the heart of the forests which supply the wood used to make rackets, it is the largest factory in the United States devoted exclusively to tennis. In 1962 Wilson opened a factory in Irvine, Ayrshire, making a definite impact on the British market. JO

Above **Wimbledon.** The scene at the very first Championships (1877) at Worple Road

Wimbledon

Although no longer formally regarded as 'the world championship on grass' by the ILTF, there has never been any doubt that Wimbledon is the most important, popular and glamorous of the game's annual tournaments.

The first notable lawn-tennis competition was held at Worple Road in the London suburb of Wimbledon in 1877. The rules of lawn tennis were designed for this tournament (see HISTORY OF THE RULES in THE RULES AND THEIR INTERPRETATION, PART 1).

The All England Club, founded for croquet in 1869 (see THE BIRTH AND SPREAD OF LAWN TENNIS, PART 1), improved its financial position in 1875 by admitting lawn-tennis players. For the first championship two years later, the prize was a silver cup valued at 25 guineas, given by J. H. Walsh, the editor of *The Field,* and a committee was appointed to draw up a set of rules which would end the confusions which had arisen about the scoring and the size of the net and the court. The committee consisted of Henry Jones, who had been largely responsible for the club's adoption of lawn tennis, Julian Marshall, a well-known real-tennis player, and C. G. Heathcote, whose brother, J. M. Heathcote, made the first lawn tennis ball by covering a rubber ball with white flannel. Some modifications were made in later years, but their basic formula stood the test of time and play. (See THE DEVELOPMENT OF PLAYING EQUIPMENT, PART 1 and BALL, HISTORY OF THE).

The early years were full of technical and strategic experiments. Spencer Gore, watched

Wimbledon Referees

1877-1886	H. Jones
1887-1889	S. A. E. Hickson
1890-1906	B. C. Evelegh
1907-1914	H. S. Scrivener
1919-1936	F. R. Burrow
1937-1939	H. Price
1946-1950	Capt. A. K. Trower
1951-1962	Col. W. J. Legg, O.B.E.
1963-	Capt. M. B. Gibson

by 200 spectators, won the title in the first year by the strength of his volleying, and W. Marshall, his opponent in the final, missed his chance in the third set by serving four double faults. Afterwards there was some controversy about the way matches had been dominated by service – servers won 376 games out of 601 – and some critics wanted to ban the 'overhand' service. They were for the most part supporters of real tennis and they argued that the new game should be an exercise in the art of rallying.

The following year the entry increased from 22 to 34, the net was lowered, and the service court reduced by 4 feet. Volleying was difficult, the rallies were 'interminable and not very interesting' and Gore, suffering from a sprained wrist, tried vainly to command the net. P. F. Hadow, like Gore a rackets player from Harrow, lobbed him to defeat in straight sets (the first being the first advantage set in The Championships) and returned to Ceylon. Hadow's place as champion was taken by another steady rallier, the Rev. J. T. Hartley, a Yorkshire vicar, who reached the semi-finals, returned to his parish to preach on the Sunday and came back to win the title.

In 1880 – when the entry was 60, the highest until after 1900 – he retained it by beating

Above **Wimbledon.** The Rev J. T. Hartley *(left),* Yorkshire, won the title for the second time in 1880, from H. F. Lawford. The previous year he had defeated V. 'St Leger' Gould.

the formidable H. F. Lawford, one of the great, enthusiastic and determined groundstroke players. But that was the end of his reign. The days of the 'safety-first' tennis were over. For Hartley and his rivals, certainty of return had been the most important factor. Now, however, the Renshaw twins, William and Ernest, superb athletes who had developed a remarkable armoury of aggressive shots on asphalt courts, began their attack.

The experienced O. E. Woodhouse beat them both on their first appearance, but for eight of the next nine years they ruled Wimbledon. Up to then it had been dominated by real-tennis and rackets players, who cut the ball heavily, and the rallies were long because it was difficult to kill the soft ball of that time by driving. The Renshaws, Ernest graceful and casual, Willie less stylish but hungrier for points, took short cuts to victory. The Renshaw volley and the Renshaw smash, perfected by hours of practice together, were the most discussed, admired and successful strokes in lawn tennis. Negative rallying was dead and the crowds flocked to Wimbledon to see the players who had buried it.

Willie Renshaw, winning by 6-0, 6-2, 6-1, took the title from Hartley in 1881 and held it until 1887, when he was unable to defend it because of an injured arm. Lawford, achieving his great ambition at last, interrupted the Renshaw supremacy by defeating Ernest in the All-Comers' Final. Ernest took his revenge the following year (the first time the Bagnell-Wild system – the present system – was used for the draw) and Willie won the title for a seventh time in 1889 before losing to W. J. Hamilton, an Irish player nicknamed 'The Ghost', in 1890.

That was the end of the reign of the Renshaws. Besides their singles victories, they had won the doubles championship (an event introduced at Oxford in 1879 and moved to Wimbledon in 1884) seven times between 1880 and 1889. The Baddeley twins, Wilfred, champion in 1891-2 and 1895, and Herbert, inherited their titles but not their hold on public affection and there were Irish victories for Joshua Pim (1893-4) and H. S. Mahony (1896).

Fortunately for Wimbledon, the Dohertys, as Wallis Myers remarked, 'burst into national fame at almost a moment's notice' and filled the stands at Worple Road again. There were three brothers: W. V., said to have been a brilliant player, who was president of the Oxford University Lawn Tennis Club but gave up

serious play to enter the church; R. F. ('Reggie'), born in 1874, and H. L. ('Laurie'), two years his junior. They played first at Wimbledon in 1896 and by then the tournament was no longer reserved for the British. The first Americans had entered and the rest of the world followed: by 1905 the entry was 71 and the countries represented included the United States, Australia, Belgium, Denmark, New Zealand, Sweden and South Africa. Anthony Wilding, another of Wimbledon's Edwardian heroes, Norman Brookes, and the US Davis Cup team were among the competitors.

The Dohertys ruled this increasingly international world for ten years. Reggie took the title from Mahony in 1897 and held it until 1901 when the tenacious Arthur Gore, making the 13th of his 40 appearances at the Championships between 1888 and 1927, defeated him. Laurie then took command in 1902-6. They also won the doubles eight times. In 1919 the full number of 128 entries for the men's singles was reached. In 1923, 133 were accepted in the draw but in 1925 it was decided to start a qualifying competition.

British supremacy never seemed assured again until Fred Perry appeared on the scene in the 1930s. In 1905 the left-handed Brookes from Melbourne reached the Challenge Round and May Sutton from California became the first overseas winner of the women's title. Two years later Brookes returned to carry off the men's title and he came back again in 1914, at the age of 36, to beat Wilding, who had been champion since 1910. Gore, steady from the baseline and possessing remarkable stamina and determination, won twice more in the post-Doherty years, but the Golden Age of British success at Wimbledon was over.

A. R. F. Kingscote reached the All-Comers' Final in 1919, the first postwar Championship meeting, but took only six games from Gerald Patterson, who went on to beat Brookes and become Wimbledon's second Australian champion. Thereafter in the 1920s the British were lucky if they had a semi-finalist in the men's singles. In 1922, the year of the move from the old ground at Worple Road to Church Road, the Challenge Round was abolished and holders played through. Two years later a form of seeding was used and in 1927 complete seeding was introduced. William Tilden became the first American man to win in 1920 and from 1924 to 1929 the brilliant French Musketeers, Jean Borotra, René Lacoste, Henri Cochet and, in doubles, Jacques Brugnon, dominated the tournament.

Their reign was followed by another period of American ascendancy. Tilden regained the title by beating Wilmer Allison in 1930, which must have compensated him for his defeat by Cochet in 1927 in Wimbledon's most dramatic semi-final (see CENTRE COURT CLASSICS, PART 1).

Sidney Wood, a 19-year-old American, was given a walk-over by the injured Frank Shields in the 1931 final, and in 1932 Ellsworth Vines, one of the fastest servers in the history of the game, became Wimbledon's fourth American champion by beating H. W. ('Bunny') Austin, 6-4, 6-2, 6-0. Jack Crawford, a stylish Australian, beat Vines in a classic final in 1933 and then for three years Fred Perry, hawk-eyed, confident and aggressive, regained the title for Britain. When he turned professional, Donald Budge, the first player to win all four of the major singles titles in a year, captured it and then, in 1939, Bobby Riggs, an astute American, won without losing a set.

After World War II Yvon Petra gained a surprising victory for France in 1946 and then the Americans – Jack Kramer, the master of the disciplined service-and-volley game, Bob Falkenberg, Ted Schroeder, Budge Patty and Dick Savitt – ruled until Frank Sedgman gained Australia's first postwar success (1952). Vic Seixas (1953) and Tony Trabert (1955) gained further successes for the United States and Jaroslav Drobný, an exiled Czech, won a popular victory at his third final in 1954.

His last victim then was the young Ken Rosewall and all the time there were signs of Australia's increasing power. Between 1956, the year of Lew Hoad's first title and 1962, when Rod Laver won for the second time, only Alex Olmedo, a Peruvian who lived in California, interrupted their sovereignty by winning in 1959. When Hoad, Rosewall and Laver

Above **Wimbledon.** No 2 Court at the new Wimbledon at Church Road in 1923. S. M. Jacobs (India) v. V. Richards (US)

turned professional, Ashley Cooper (1958), Neale Fraser (1960), Roy Emerson (1964-5) and John Newcombe (1967) kept them in command. Chuck McKinley (1963) was the only American champion in the decade and Manuel Santana (1966) the only European. With the introduction of open tennis in 1968, Laver regained the title and retained it in 1969. In 1970 Rosewall, in his third final, after a record interval of years, only to fall to Newcombe, who held on to win a five-set match against Stan Smith in 1971. The dispute between the ILTF and WCT prevented him from defending his title and Smith inherited it for the United States.

In 1973 Smith, in his turn, was prevented from playing. He supported the boycott of the Championships by ATP and, with more than 70 of the best players missing, Jan Kodeš (Czechoslovakia), who had not hitherto been regarded as a notable grass-court player, took the title from Alex Metreveli, the first player from the USSR to reach the final.

In all this time women's tennis had been increasing in public appeal. Wimbledon was the home of the women's game. Its great stars could command a larger share of public attention there than at other major championships where the subtleties of clever rallying were appreciated less. In the early years a group of formidable players gained sequences of victories. Maud Watson won the first ladies' championship in 1884, Blanche Bingley (Mrs Hillyard) conquered for the first time in 1886 and was still capable of reaching the semi-finals in 1912, and Lottie Dod won the title at the age of 15 years and 10 months in 1887; she retired after her fifth victory in 1893. Charlotte Cooper (Mrs Sterry) won the title

five times between 1895 and 1908 and Dorothea Douglass (Mrs Lambert Chambers) succeeded no fewer than seven times between 1903 and 1914. But the most dramatic final was towards the end of her career. In 1919 she held two match points against the young Suzanne Lenglen before losing 8-10, 6-4, 7-9 (see CENTRE COURT CLASSICS, PART 1). Miss Lenglen remained undefeated at Wimbledon although she yielded her title to the British player Kitty McKane (Mrs Godfree) when she was too ill to defend it. She regained it in 1925 but retired from the Championships the following year after a famous dispute with the referee and the management committee when her idea that her stature as a player entitled her to special treatment stretched the elasticity of the administration too far in its Jubilee year.

Mrs Godfree again stepped in to win, but a new era of American domination was beginning. Helen Wills (Mrs Moody) gained the first of her eight successes in 1927. The next British champion was Dorothy Round, Mrs Moody's victim in 1933. She beat Helen Jacobs in 1934 and Jadwiga Jędrzejowska in 1937. Then the Americans took command again. Alice Marble, Pauline Betz, Margaret Osborne, Louise Brough, Doris Hart, Maureen Connolly, Shirley Fry, Althea Gibson – the royal line seemed unending. When Maria Bueno (Brazil) won in 1959 she ended a sequence of American successes which had lasted since 1938.

In the next decade there were two British winners, Angela Mortimer (1961) and Ann Jones (1969) but it was notable for the emergence of the Australians. Margaret Smith (Mrs Court) became their first woman Wimbledon champion in 1963, and thereafter fought fierce duels against, first, Miss Bueno, who took her title in 1964 and then was forced to give it back to her the following year, and then Billie Jean Moffitt (Mrs King), one of the great Californians, whom she beat in 1963 and 1970.

Mrs King's record has been remarkable. She has played in every final from 1966 to 1973, except 1971 when she lost in the semi-finals to Evonne Goolagong, who went on to beat Mrs Court in Wimbledon's first all-Australian women's final. She was unbeaten from 1966 to 1969, when Mrs Jones defeated her in the final, and she came back to win again in 1972 and 1973.

The Championships last for two weeks at Wimbledon. In the other 50 weeks of the year the All England Club, which stages the tournament on its ground at Church Road, functions as an ordinary tennis club, while its committee and its staff plan for the next Championships. As Norah Gordon Cleather, who served the club for 25 years, remarked in her book, *Wimbledon Story* (1947), 'Even while the Championships of one year were in progress and competitors were battling on the courts, suggestions and ideas for improvements and innovations for the following meeting were already being discussed behind the scenes.'

Letters from the public and points raised in the press and by all the other groups who work at Wimbledon during the fortnight are scrutinized and considered and it is a combination of thoroughness, enterprise, desire for improvement and respect for tradition which has made Wimbledon not only the most popular and best organized of the game's great championships but also a considerable commercial undertaking.

The profits from Wimbledon subsidize the work of the Lawn Tennis Association, which includes coaching schemes, loans to clubs and financing overseas tours, and meet the costs of the club and the tournament. Its popularity can be judged from the fact that, apart from the profit taken from the tournament (a sum which reached £100,000 in several postwar years), other large amounts, ranging from £50,000 in 1930 to £110,000 in 1973, were returned to those who were unsuccessful in the ballot for tickets. That is a considerable advance on the profit of £500 taken by the club from their first Championships at the old Worple Road site in 1877.

Wimbledon's period of expansion dates from the move from Worple Road, where the ground was sold for £4,000 in 1923, and the opening of the Church Road ground, with its (not quite finished) new Centre Court with some 7,000 seats and standing room for about 3,000 spectators, in 1922. At Worple Road there had been 500 Centre Court seats and room for another 7,000 spectators in the ground; the 'new' Wimbledon – a bold and risky conception at that time – was built with the conviction that lawn tennis would become an important spectator sport.

At first there were fears that the new Centre Court (which was not in the centre of the ground but which took the name of the old principal central court at Worple Road) would never be filled. The pessimists were quickly confounded. For more than half a century the

Above **Wimbledon**. The scene in 1953, looking from the clubhouse towards No 2 Court

chief problem of the organizers of the Championships has been that of supplying enough places to meet the demand for seats, of trying to accommodate more and more people in the ground. The Centre Court now holds just under 14,000. On the first Friday of 1973 the ground held a record 32,445 people.

Many of those who pay at the gate on the day, but others have bought their tickets months in advance. Wimbledon's machinery for issuing tickets has been developed by years of experiment. Priority goes to the debenture holders (2,100 debentures of various types were issued in 1919 with a duration of 25 years, which was extended by World War II, and since then there have been other issues for shorter periods), to members, LTA Councillors and those who receive complimentary tickets.

The Royal Box contains 80 seats; the management committee box 20; there are allocations for overseas officials and national associations, for countries, clubs and schools, and a number of seats are reserved for daily sale to reward those enthusiastic enough to queue before the remaining places are put into the ballot. Draws for Centre Court tickets used to be held at specified intervals between February and April, but now only one ballot is held in February and books of tickets have been reduced in size from three to two (one day in each week).

As early as 1924 it had become necessary to curtail the number of tickets sold to individual applicants and over the years there has been some controversy over the way tickets are

allocated. In 1938, for example, the LTA suggested that more books of tickets should be made available to members of the British clubs and fewer to the general public, but the All England Club, with 12 delegates to the LTA's seven on the Championships Committee, opposed this. As Lt-Col Duncan Macaulay, who was its secretary from 1946 to 1963 and who played a major part in the revival and prosperity of the postwar Wimbledon, remarked: 'We felt that it was the man in the street who made the Championships and that we should never make Wimbledon a closed shop.'

Wimbledon's attitude to radio, television

Below **Wimbledon**. The Championship trophy for the men's singles

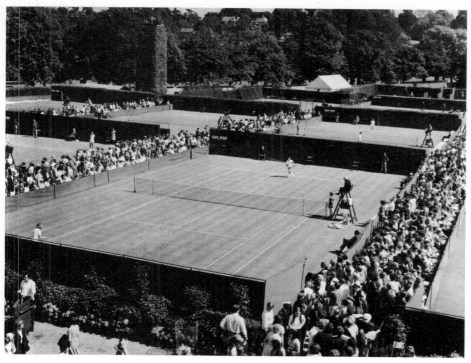

Above **Wimbledon.** The outside courts, with the ivy-covered water tower (left)

and the press in the years after the war sprang from the same feeling (see REPORTING THE CHAMPIONSHIPS, PART 1). Radio commentaries from Wimbledon had begun in 1927 and ten years later the first matches were televised (the Championships Committee encouraged television at a time when many other sporting bodies were fearful of its consequences and the resulting publicity did much to help the game to break out of its traditionally middle-class framework); and now about 500 journalists, photographers and messengers, many of them from abroad, attend the Championships every day. Considerable rebuilding has been necessary to accommodate the increasing numbers of those who report the tournament to the rest of the world and in recent years the Championships Committee, working through its Building and Press subcommittees, two important units in a committee structure which supervises all aspects of the organization of Wimbledon, has doubled the size of the press writing rooms and the press restaurant and built new interview rooms for press, radio and television under the men's dressing rooms.

This last improvement was the major work put in hand for the 1973 Championships and it was a further change in the physical shape of what is almost a small town during the fortnight of the tournament. Besides the various restaurants, bars and buffets run for officials, competitors and the public by the Town and County Catering Co. Ltd, a subsidiary of J. Lyons, and the special enclosures for county representatives and debenture holders, the

Church Road ground also contains a post office, a bank, first-aid rooms staffed by the St John Ambulance Brigade, information desks run by the Women's Royal Voluntary Service, and a photograph and bookstall.

There are 17 acres of ground for car parking, supervised by the Automobile Association and controlled by All England Motor Park, a subsidiary of the All England Ground Company, the owners of the land and buildings at Wimbledon (again a partnership between the All England Club and the LTA). And for the period of the Championships, the club's permanent office, maintenance and ground staff

Below **Wimbledon.** The Championship trophy for the women's singles

is supplemented by a large corps of temporary workers.

After play and in the mornings before the tournament resumes the ground is cleaned by a group of volunteer students, who live in tents during the Championships. Other students are enrolled by Town and County to assist with the catering. Stewarding arrangements are in the hands of the Championships Honorary Stewards' Association, many of them former officers, who supervise the seating ushers, always members of the armed forces on leave. There are program sellers, police, a contingent of the London Fire Brigade, commissionaires from the Ex-Servicemen's Associations, and ballboys, once from the Shaftesbury Homes and Dr Barnardo's Homes, but now from local schools and trained by the club. Wimbledon even has its own emergency water supply. The water tower is a distinctive landmark.

Supplying passes for those who keep the machinery of the Championships working, together with the differentiation between tickets for the various days of play – each day has a different colour and the colours are changed each year to prevent fraud – is a considerable task. Miss Cleather calculated that she had to deal with no fewer than 537 varieties of tickets ('I thought of them as a whirling snowstorm of pink, blue, yellow, mauve and green') and Wimbledon's recent estimate was that the figure has probably increased since then.

Once the tickets have been distributed Wimbledon is able to turn its attention to the players who will appear in the tournament. Entries have to be submitted by the beginning of June and they are scrutinized by the management committee, with the assistance of the Referee. A first list of acceptances is published two weeks before the start of the Championships and this is amended to deal with withdrawals and other changes. The Seeding Committee, another subcommittee of the main Championships Committee, announces its list of the placed players on the Tuesday before the tournament and the following day the draw is made at the All England Lawn Tennis and Croquet Club.

Both seedings and acceptances are based on recent form and those who enter are asked to give full information about their playing records to the committee. Those who are not accepted directly may be invited to play in the Qualifying Competition, held now at the Bank of England ground at Roehampton in the week before the Championships. There ten men and eight women can earn the right to compete in the singles and four places are reserved for qualifiers in the doubles. Often as many as 300 players have taken part in the qualifying tournament.

Up to 1968, the first year of open tennis, there were Northern and Southern qualifying competitions, but these were amalgamated because of the relative weakness of the Northern

Above **Wimbledon, 1949.** *Left to right:* Ted Schroeder (the Champion), Lt-Col Duncan Macauley, Secretary of the All England Club, HRH the Duchess of Kent, President of the All England Club, Viscount Templewood, President of the LTA, Sir Louis Greig, Chairman of the All England Club.

event. Both Hurlingham and the Roehampton Club have housed the Southern competition and Northern qualifying matches were played at such centres as Manchester, Chapel Allerton and Sutton Coldfield.

Some of those who fail to qualify join the 180 members of the Umpires' Association in officiating at the Championships. Wimbledon's umpires act in an honorary capacity, receiving meals and subsistence allowances for their work. The members of the Association – whose symbol is a lynx, embodying sharpness of the eye – have passed tests of knowledge of the rules and competence in controlling matches.

Senior umpires work in the Referee's office, allocating matches to their members, and assisting him generally with the program. The Referee, in consultation with the management committee, controls the playing side of the tournament. He is the arbiter in moments of dispute; he arranges the order of play and the use of courts, taking into account public appeal and fairness to competitors. Some of Wimbledon's referees have been notable figures in the game: H. S. Scrivener, F. R. Burrow, Hamilton Price, Duncan Macaulay, A. K. Trower and Col W. J. Legg, succeeded in 1963 by his son-in-law, Captain M. B. Gibson, who has also refereed at the US Championships at Forest Hills and at the South African Championships in Johannesburg.

The Referee and his staff begin work three weeks before the start of the Championships and their work ends when the last trophy has been presented. For the organizers of the Championships the post-mortems begin and normal serenity returns to the All England Club. After every Wimbledon Championships 1,200 dozen tennis balls are offered for sale, all made by Slazengers, who have supplied the Championships with balls and equipment since 1902, when the Slazenger ball replaced the Ayres ball, at the direct request of the players in 1901. These go first to clubs and then to the general public.

The Centre Court and Number One court are re-sown and other courts are returfed. For most of the year the courts are used by members and other events played at Wimbledon include WIGHTMAN CUP and DAVIS CUP matches – always on Court One (except for the Challenge Round played on the Centre Court when Britain held the trophy from 1934 to 1937) – the Junior Championships ('Junior Wimbledon'), the Services' Championships, the London Parks and Clubs Competition, and various school events. For Championship records see PART 3. For Press, radio, television and photographic coverage see PART 1. See also colour plate, page 334-5. DG

Wimbledon Professional Tournament
The Centre Court at Wimbledon has been the setting for only one purely professional tournament, played in August 1967, the year before Open tennis came into being. Eight contract professionals competed for a total of £12,500. Rod Laver won the £3,000 first prize, beating Ken Rosewall (£2,000) 6-2, 6-2, 12-10. Andrés Gimeno (£1,300) defeated Lew Hoad (£1,000) 6-3, 6-3 in the play-off for the third place. DC

Wingfield, Major Walter Clopton
see SPHAIRISTIKÉ, THE RULES AND THEIR INTERPRETATION (PART 1), and THE BIRTH AND SPREAD OF LAWN TENNIS (PART 1)

Wisden, John, and Company Ltd

This sporting-goods company was founded on 25 May 1850 by John Wisden, leading cricketer. A Sussex fast bowler with a career total of 2,707 wickets between 1848 and 1859, he opened his business in Leicester Square, London, and combined it with a tobacco shop. The sports side, which included tennis rackets and balls, prospered but Wisden is better known as the founder of the *Wisden Cricketer's Almanack* (first produced 1864). The company was taken over by GRAYS of Cambridge in August 1970. JO

Women's International Lawn Tennis Federation see OPEN TENNIS (PART 1)

Wood, Arthur O'Hara (Australia)

A Melbourne doctor who won the Australian men's singles and was r/u in doubles 1914.

Wood, Patrick O'Hara (Australia)

Wimbledon men's singles q/f 1919, 1922; men's doubles won 1919, r/u 1922; mixed doubles won 1922; US men's doubles r/u 1922, 1924; Australian men's singles won 1920, 1923, s/f 1925, q/f 1926, 1929; men's doubles won 1919-20, 1923, r/u 1924, won 1925, r/u 1926-7; mixed doubles s/f 1926. He played 23 singles and doubles matches for Austral(as)ia in the Davis Cup 1922, 1924, winning 9 singles and 8 doubles. Brother of A. O'Hara Wood.

Below Wimbledon. The famous pony roller (in 1938). It stands in the corner of the Centre Court and is still used, but with five men instead of the pony.

Wood, Sidney B. (USA)

Born Black Rock, Conn., 1 Nov. 1911; Wimbledon men's singles won 1931, q/f 1932, s/f 1934, q/f 1935; men's doubles s/f 1931; US men's singles s/f 1930, q/f 1932, s/f 1934, r/u 1935, s/f 1938, q/f 1945; men's doubles s/f 1931, 1944-5; French mixed doubles r/u 1932. Davis Cup 1931, 1934. At 19 years 8 months the second youngest men's singles champion (to W. BADDELEY) of Wimbledon and the only one to receive a walk-over in the final.

Woodhouse, O. E.

see THE BIRTH AND SPREAD OF LAWN TENNIS and THE UNITED STATES STORY (PART 1)

World Championship Tennis, Inc. (WCT)

WCT was founded in 1967 by Dave Dixon, the Texan oil millionaire Lamar Hunt, and Hunt's nephew Al Hill, Jr, who signed up eight leading players, Tony Roche and John Newcombe (Australia), Dennis Ralston and Butch Buchholz (United States), Cliff Drysdale (South Africa), Nikki Pilić (Yugoslavia), Pierre Barthès (France) and Roger Taylor (Great Britain). They started their professional playing careers in January 1968 in Sydney, Australia, as the 'Handsome Eight', wearing coloured shirts and using VASSS scoring. Early in 1968 Hunt and Hill bought out Dixon's interest and gave executive control to Bob Briner, the man who had formerly done the detailed work. Reorganization continued under Michael Davies, a former British Davis Cup player who had been one of the professionals signed by Jack Kramer in the early

1960s. See THE POSTWAR PRO GAME and OPEN TENNIS (PART 1).

In 1971 the 'World Championship of Tennis' was launched, a $1,000,000 points-linked circuit of 20 tournaments from which the eight leaders at the year's end played a final tournament for a record first prize of $50,000.

Hunt's concept of 'a professional game that is at once a financial and artistic success' was brilliantly realized. But friction with the ILTF over non-appearance of WCT players at traditional events and over WCT demands for corporation fees led to an ILTF ban on all WCT men from 1 January 1972. However, its own 32-man circuit flourished and by April a peace was agreed which resulted in WCT participation in the last major championship of 1972 – the US Open Championships.

To service growing worldwide requests for WCT tournaments, the 1973 circuit was split into two groups, one in Europe and the other in the United States. Each 32-man group played 11 tournaments, all of which took place between 1 January and early May, as part of the settlement with the ILTF, the top four of each group playing off in the Dallas Final. For results of the Finals see RECORDS (PART 3).

In 1974 three groups were created, involving 84 players competing in a total of 25 qualifying tournaments. JB

World Circuit

A name often used for the international calendar of major tournaments, deliberately dovetailed so that top-class players can compete and attract money gates (and sponsorship) all the year round. The annual order of the tournaments, and indeed the tournaments themselves, have changed from time to time to suit the circumstances of the day, particularly as a result of the 1972 agreement between the ILTF and WCT (see OPEN TENNIS and ADMINISTRATION OF THE WORLD GAME, PART 1). The four constants have remained the big four Championships of Australia (at the New Year), France (at the end of May), Wimbledon (at the end of June) and Forest Hills (at the beginning of September). MR

World Cup see THE POSTWAR PRO GAME (PART 1)

World Rankings see RANKINGS

World's Covered Court Championships, World's Grass Court Championships, World's Hard Court Championships, see THE GROWTH OF THE GAME (PART 1)

World Team Tennis

An indoor league competition between 16 American cities due to start a three-month season in May 1974, WTT is the brainchild of Dennis Murphy, who was instrumental in establishing the successful leagues in ice hockey (WHA) and basketball (ABA).

The WTT program calls for each team to play 44 matches (half at home and half away). Each match consists of a women's single, a men's single and a mixed double, all played on the 'no-ad' scoring system with tie-breaks at 5-5 in any set. The whole package will run for 2½ hours and will fit easily into short television slots.

This new concept of tennis had been bitterly opposed from the outset by the Association of Tennis Professionals (ATP), whose members are not permitted to receive guarantees in any form, and by the ILTF, whose European circuit, coinciding in time with the proposed WTT schedule, would be completely ruined by a wholesale signing of leading players to the cities of WTT.

In the 20 rounds of 'The Draft' 311 players were selected – from Chris Evert and Rod Laver in round one to Lenny Schoss and Fiorella Bonicelli in the final round. The success or failure of WTT will depend largely on the quality of the players it is able to sign to its reportedly lucrative contracts. The threat of official disciplinary action that would ban WTT players from any ILTF events, including the Davis Cup and Federation Cup, has made players think deeply about their ambitions. While a past champion like Fred Stolle might welcome the opportunity to extend his playing life and earning period, someone like young Björn Borg would hesitate to jeopardize the chance of winning one of the major championships.

By the end of 1973 WTT had been able to announce the signings of John Newcombe, Billie Jean King, Margaret Court, Evonne Goolagong, Owen Davidson, Clark Graebner, Linda Tuero and John Alexander; many more leading professionals, men and women, were thinking seriously of signing, including Jimmy Connors, Rosewall and Năstase. JB

Wrenn, Robert D. (USA)
Born 20 Sept. 1873; US men's singles s/f 1892, won 1893-4, r/u 1895, won 1896-7, q/f 1900; men's doubles won 1895, r/u 1896. Davis Cup 1903. The top-ranking US player in four out of the five years 1893 to 1897. A left-hander, he was only 19 (the third youngest) when he won his first US title in 1893.

Wright, Beals C. (USA)
Born Boston, Mass., 19 Dec. 1879, died 1961; Wimbledon men's singles r/u* 1910; men's doubles s/f 1905, r/u* 1907; US men's singles r/u* 1901, q/f 1904, won 1905, r/u 1906, 1908, r/u* 1910-11; men's doubles r/u 1901, won 1904-6, r/u 1908, 1918; mixed doubles s/f 1908; Davis Cup 1905, 1907-8, 1911. The first American to reach the final of the All Comers' men's singles at Wimbledon (1910). Left-handed.

W T T see WORLD TEAM TENNIS

Wynne, Miss Nancye see Mrs N. BOLTON

Y

Yugoslavia
Yugoslavia has been a Full Member of the ILTF since 1923. It first took part in the DAVIS CUP in 1927, also played in 1928-39, 1946-8, and has been a regular competitor since 1957. In 1939 Yugoslavia won the European Zone and has reached the European Zone Finals several times. Yugoslav teams have also taken part in the FEDERATION CUP and with some success in various European competitions, in particular the KING'S CUP.

Many famous players in prewar and postwar years competed in the leading championships and tournaments, among them Punčec, Jovanović, Kukuljević and Pilić. In 1962 Jovanović and Pilić reached the final of the Wimbledon men's doubles, losing to Hewitt and Stolle. Pilić has been a Wimbledon semi-finalist (1967) and runner up (1973) in the French singles. BR
GOVERNING BODY: Tenis Savez Yugoslavije, Terazije 35, Belgrade

Yugoslavian Championships Winners
Men's Singles

Year	Winner	Year	Winner
1920	N. Antolković	1961	B. Jovanović
1921-23	No Competition	1962	N. Pilić
1924	N. Antolković	1963	N. Pilić
1925	N. Antolković	1964	N. Pilić
1926	I. Balaš	1965	B. Jovanović
1927	A. Popović	1966	N. Pilić
1928	K. Friedrich	1967	N. Pilić
1929	F. Schäffer	1968	N. Špear
1930	F. Schäffer	1969	Z. Franulović
1931	F. Schäffer	1970	Z. Franulović
1932	F. Kukuljević	1971	Z. Franulović
1933	F. Punčec	1972	N. Špear
1934	F. Punčec	1973	N. Špear
1935	F. Punčec		
1936	F. Punčec		
1937	F. Punčec		
1938	F. Punčec		
1939	F. Punčec		
1940-45	No Competition		
1946	D. Mitić		
1947	D. Mitić		
1948	D. Mitić		
1949	D. Mitić		
1950	D. Mitić		
1951	M. Branović		
1952	J. Palada		
1953	V. Petrović		
1954	V. Petrović		
1955	J. Palada		
1956	I. Plećević		
1957	K. Keretić		
1958	K. Keretić		
1959	I. Panajotović		
1960	I. Plećević		

Z

Zaire
Zaire, formerly the Democratic Republic of The Congo, has been an Associate Member of the ILTF since 1971. BR
GOVERNING BODY: Fédération de Tennis du Zaire, B.P. 2596, Kinshasa

Zinderstein, Miss Marion
see Mrs M. JESSUP

Zinnowitz International Tournament
see GERMAN DEMOCRATIC REPUBLIC

Right Wimbledon. 1972. *Left to right:* Stan Smith (the Champion), Herman David, Chairman of the All England Club, Sir Carl Aarvold, President of the LTA, Major David Mills, Secretary of the All England Club, HRH the Duke of Kent, President of the All England Club. To meet the challenge of the fast-accelerating commercialism of the world game, the All England Club announced an unprecedented new prize structure for the 1974 Championships, the men's singles winner receiving £10,000, the women's £7,000; the total prize money being £97,100.

Women's Singles

Year	Winner	Year	Winner
1920	Miss J. Christaling	1961	Miss M. Djukić
1921-23	No Competition	1962	Miss M. Djukić
1924	Miss M. Würth	1963	Miss M. Djukić
1925	Miss M. Peleš	1964	Miss J. Genčić
1926	Miss M. Würth	1965	Miss T. Kokeza
1927	Miss J. Schweickhardt	1966	Miss I. Škulj
1928	Miss V. Gostiša	1967	Miss A. Pipan
1929	Miss V. Bokor	1968	Miss I. Škulj
1930	Miss V. Gostiša	1969	Miss I. Škulj
1931	Miss V. Gostiša	1970	Miss M. Jaušovec
1932	Miss V. Gostiša	1971	Miss M. Jaušovec
1933	Miss V. Gostiša	1972	Miss M. Jaušovec
1934	Miss H. Kovač	1973	Miss M. Jaušovec
1935	Miss H. Kovač		
1936	Miss H. Kovač		
1937	Miss H. Kovač		
1938	Miss A. Florjan		
1939	Miss H. Kovač		
1940-45	No Competition		
1946	Miss M. Crnadak		
1947	Miss M. Crnadak		
1948	Miss M. Crnadak		
1949	Miss M. Crnadak		
1950	Miss M. Crnadak		
1951	Miss M. Crnadak		
1952	Miss M. Crnadak		
1953	Miss M. Crnadak		
1954	Miss D. Lazlo		
1955	Miss M. Crnadak		
1956	Miss M. Crnadak		
1957	Miss B. Martinec		
1958	Miss J. Genčić		
1959	Miss M. Djukić		
1960	Miss T. Kokeza		

Wimbledon Championships

Men's Singles

Semi-Finals

1877
S. W. Gore C. G. Heathcote 6-2, 6-5, 6-2
W. C. Marshall a bye

1878
L. Erskine H. F. Lawford 6-3, 6-1, 6-3
P. F. Hadow a bye

1879
J. T. Hartley C. F. Parr 2-6, 6-0, 6-1, 6-1
V. 'St Leger' Gould a bye

1880
O. E. Woodhouse G. Montgomerie 6-4, 2-6, 6-3, 5-6, 6-1
H. F. Lawford M. Butterworth 6-2, 6-3, 6-3

1881
W. Renshaw H. F. Lawford 1-6, 6-3, 6-2, 5-6, 6-3
R. T. Richardson a bye

1882
E. Renshaw H. F. Lawford 6-4, 4-6, 6-2, 3-6, 6-0
R. T. Richardson F. Benson 6-1, 6-2, 6-1

1883
D. Stewart W. C. Taylor 6-0, 6-1, 6-3
E. Renshaw a bye

1884
C. W. Grinstead E. Renshaw 2-6, 6-4, 6-2, 6-2
H. F. Lawford H. Chipp 7-5, 6-4, 6-4

1885
E. Renshaw E. de S. H. Browne 6-4, 8-6, 2-6, 5-7, 6-4
H. F. Lawford J. Dwight 6-2, 6-2, 6-3

1886
H. F. Lawford T. R. Garvey 6-3, 6-2, 6-0
E. W. Lewis H. W. W. Wilberforce 3-6, 6-2, 1-6, 6-1, 6-3

1887
H. F. Lawford H. Grove 4-6, 6-3, 7-5, 7-5
E. Renshaw a bye C. Lacey Sweet retired

1888
E. Renshaw W. J. Hamilton 7-5, 7-5, 5-7, 6-3
E. W. Lewis W. C. Taylor 9-7, 6-4, 6-4

1889
H. S. Barlow W. J. Hamilton 3-6, 6-3, 2-6, 6-3, 6-3
W. Renshaw H. F. Lawford 7-5, 5-7, 6-3, 6-2

1890
W. J. Hamilton J. Pim 0-6, 6-4, 6-4, 6-2
H. S. Barlow E. W. Lewis 7-5, 6-4, 4-6, 7-5

1891
W. Baddeley E. Renshaw 6-0, 6-1, 6-1
J. Pim H. S. Mahony 6-4, 6-0, 6-2

1892
E. W. Lewis H. A. B. Chapman 2-6, 6-3, 6-1, 6-2
J. Pim H. S. Mahony 6-1, 12-10, 2-6, 6-2

1893
J. Pim H. S. Barlow 9-7, 6-2, 6-3
H. S. Mahony A. Palmer 3-6, 6-3, 6-3, 6-1

1894
W. Baddeley a bye T. Chaytor retired
E. W. Lewis H. Baddeley 2-6, 7-5, 6-3, 1-6, 7-5

1895
W. Baddeley a bye H. Baddeley retired
W. V. Eaves E. G. Meers 6-3, 7-9, 9-11, 6-4, 6-1

1896
H. S. Mahony H. A. Nisbet 6-4, 2-6, 8-6, 4-6, 6-3
W. V. Eaves H. Baddeley 6-4, 6-3, 6-4

1897
W. V. Eaves S. H. Smith 6-2, 5-7, 1-6, 6-2, 6-1
R. F. Doherty W. Baddeley 6-3, 6-0, 6-3

Finals

1877
S. W. Gore W. C. Marshall 6-1, 6-2, 6-4

1878
P. F. Hadow L. Erskine 6-4, 6-4, 6-4
Challenge Round
P. F. Hadow (C) S. W. Gore (H) 7-5, 6-1, 9-7

1879
J. T. Hartley V. 'St Leger' Gould 6-2, 6-4, 6-2
Challenge Round
J. T. Hartley (C) a bye P. F. Hadow (H) retired

1880
H. F. Lawford O. E. Woodhouse 7-5, 6-4, 6-0
Challenge Round
J. T. Hartley (H) H. F. Lawford (C) 6-0, 6-2, 2-6, 6-3

1881
W. Renshaw R. T. Richardson 6-4, 6-2, 6-3
Challenge Round
W. Renshaw (C) J. T. Hartley (H) 6-0, 6-2, 6-1

1882
E. Renshaw R. T. Richardson 7-5, 6-2, 2-6, 6-3
Challenge Round
W. Renshaw (H) E. Renshaw (C) 6-1, 2-6, 4-6, 6-2, 6-2

1883
E. Renshaw D. Stewart 0-6, 6-3, 6-0, 6-2
Challenge Round
W. Renshaw (H) E. Renshaw (C) 2-6, 6-3, 6-3, 4-6, 6-3

1884
H. F. Lawford C. W. Grinstead 7-5, 2-6, 6-2, 9-7
Challenge Round
W. Renshaw (H) H. F. Lawford (C) 6-0, 6-4, 9-7

1885
H. F. Lawford E. Renshaw 5-7, 6-1, 0-6, 6-2, 6-4
Challenge Round
W. Renshaw (H) H. F. Lawford (C) 7-5, 6-2, 4-6, 7-5

1886
H. F. Lawford E. W. Lewis 6-2, 3-6, 2-6, 4-6, 6-4
Challenge Round
W. Renshaw (H) H. F. Lawford (C) 6-0, 5-7, 6-3, 6-4

1887
H. F. Lawford E. Renshaw 1-6, 6-3, 3-6, 6-4, 6-4
Challenge Round
H. F. Lawford (C) a bye W. Renshaw (H) retired

1888
E. Renshaw E. W. Lewis 7-9, 6-1, 8-6, 6-4
Challenge Round
E. Renshaw (C) H. F. Lawford (H) 6-3, 7-5, 6-0

1889
W. Renshaw H. S. Barlow 3-6, 5-7, 8-6, 10-8, 8-6
Challenge Round
W. Renshaw (C) E. Renshaw (H) 6-4, 6-1, 3-6, 6-0

1890
W. J. Hamilton H. S. Barlow 2-6, 6-4, 6-4, 4-6, 7-5
Challenge Round
W. J. Hamilton (C) W. Renshaw (H) 6-8, 6-2, 3-6, 6-1, 6-1

1891
W. Baddeley J. Pim 6-4, 1-6, 7-5, 6-0
Challenge Round
W. Baddeley (C) a bye W. J. Hamilton (H) retired

1892
J. Pim E. W. Lewis 2-6, 5-7, 9-7, 6-3, 6-2
Challenge Round
W. Baddeley (H) J. Pim (C) 4-6, 6-3, 6-3, 6-2

1893
J. Pim H. S. Mahony 9-7, 6-3, 6-0
Challenge Round
J. Pim (C) W. Baddeley (H) 3-6, 6-1, 6-3, 6-2

1894
W. Baddeley E. W. Lewis 6-0, 6-1, 6-0
Challenge Round
J. Pim (H) W. Baddeley (C) 10-8, 6-2, 8-6

1895
W. Baddeley W. V. Eaves 4-6, 2-6, 8-6, 6-2, 6-3
Challenge Round
W. Baddeley (C) a bye J. Pim (H) retired

1896
H. S. Mahony W. V. Eaves 6-2, 6-2, 11-9
Challenge Round
H. S. Mahony (C) W. Baddeley (H) 6-2, 6-8, 5-7, 8-6, 6-3

1897
R. F. Doherty W. V. Eaves 6-3, 7-5, 2-0 retired
Challenge Round
R. F. Doherty (C) H. S. Mahony (H) 6-4, 6-4, 6-3

Men's Doubles

Finals

1879 *Founded by Oxford University*
L. R. Erskine/H. F. Lawford
F. Durant/G. E. Tabor

1880
W. Renshaw/E. Renshaw
O. E. Woodhouse/C. J. Cole

1881
W. Renshaw/E. Renshaw
W. J. Down/H. Vaughan

1882
J. T. Hartley/R. T. Richardson
J. G. Horn/C. B. Russell

1883
C. W. Grinstead/C. E. Welldon
C. B. Russell/R. T. Milford

1884 *Transferred from Oxford to Wimbledon*
W. Renshaw/E. Renshaw
E. W. Lewis/E. L. Williams 6-3, 3-6, 6-1, 1-6, 6-4

1885
W. Renshaw/E. Renshaw
C. E. Farrar/A. J. Stanley 6-3, 6-3, 10-8

1886 *Challenge Round Introduced*
C. E. Farrar/A. J. Stanley
H. W. W. Wilberforce/P. B. Lyon 7-5, 6-3, 6-1
Challenge Round
W. Renshaw/E. Renshaw (H)
C. E. Farrar/A. J. Stanley (C) 6-3, 6-3, 4-6, 7-5

1887
H. W. W. Wilberforce/P. B. Lyon
J. H. Crispe/E. Barratt Smith 7-5, 6-3, 6-2
Challenge Round
H. W. W. Wilberforce/P. B. Lyon (C) a bye
W. Renshaw/E. Renshaw (H) retired

1888
W. Renshaw/E. Renshaw
E. G. Meers/A. G. Ziffo 6-3, 6-2, 6-2
Challenge Round
W. Renshaw/E. Renshaw (C)
H. W. W. Wilberforce/P. B. Lyon (H) 2-6, 1-6, 6-3, 6-4, 6-3

1889
E. W. Lewis/G. W. Hillyard
G. R. Mewburn/A. W. Gore 6-2, 6-1, 6-3
Challenge Round
W. Renshaw/E. Renshaw (H)
E. W. Lewis/G. W. Hillyard (C) 6-4, 6-4, 3-6, 0-6, 6-1

1890
J. Pim/F. O. Stoker
E. W. Lewis/G. W. Hillyard 6-0, 7-5, 6-4
Challenge Round
J. Pim/F. O. Stoker (C) a bye
W. Renshaw/E. Renshaw (H) retired

1891
W. Baddeley/H. Baddeley
E. Renshaw/H. S. Barlow 4-6, 6-4, 7-5, 0-6, 6-2
Challenge Round
W. Baddeley/H. Baddeley (C)
J. Pim/F. O. Stoker (H) 6-1, 6-3, 1-6, 6-2

1892
E. W. Lewis/H. S. Barlow
J. Pim/H. S. Mahony 8-10, 6-3, 5-7, 11-9, 6-1
Challenge Round
E. W. Lewis/H. S. Barlow (C)
W. Baddeley/H. Baddeley (H) 4-6, 6-2, 8-6, 6-4

1893
J. Pim/F. O. Stoker
W. Baddeley/H. Baddeley 6-2, 4-6, 6-3, 5-7, 6-2
Challenge Round
J. Pim/F. O. Stoker (C)
E. W. Lewis/H. S. Barlow (H) 4-6, 6-3, 6-1, 2-6, 6-0

1894
W. Baddeley/H. Baddeley
H. S. Barlow/C. H. Martin 5-7, 7-5, 4-6, 6-3, 8-6
Challenge Round
W. Baddeley/H. Baddeley (C) a bye
J. Pim/F. O. Stoker (H) retired

1895
E. W. Lewis/W. V. Eaves
C. F. Simond/W. G. Bailey 6-4, 6-4, 6-3
Challenge Round
W. Baddeley/H. Baddeley (H)
E. W. Lewis/W. V. Eaves (C) 8-6, 5-7, 6-4, 6-3

1896
R. F. Doherty/H. A. Nisbet
E. R. Allen/C. G. Allen 3-6, 7-5, 6-4, 6-1
Challenge Round
W. Baddeley/H. Baddeley (H)
R. F. Doherty/H. A. Nisbet (C) 1-6, 3-6, 6-4, 6-2, 6-1

1897
R. F. Doherty/H. L. Doherty
C. G. L. Cazalet/S. H. Smith 6-2, 7-5, 2-6, 6-2
Challenge Round
R. F. Doherty/H. L. Doherty (C)
W. Baddeley/H. Baddeley (H) 6-4, 4-6, 8-6, 6-4

Winners in **bold type; (H)**/(H) holder; **(C)**/(C) challenger; w.o. walk-over

Men's Singles

Men's Doubles

Semi-Finals	Finals	Finals
1898	**1898**	**1898**
H. L. Doherty C. Hobart 6-1, 6-4, 6-3	**H. L. Doherty** H. S. Mahony 6-1, 6-2, 4-6, 2-6, 14-12	**H. A. Nisbet/C. Hobart**
H. S. Mahony A. W. Gore 6-2, 3-6, 4-6, 6-2, 6-4	*Challenge Round*	G. W. Hillyard/S. H. Smith 2-6, 6-2, 6-2, 6-3
	R. F. Doherty (H) H. L. Doherty (C) 6-3, 6-3, 2-6, 5-7, 6-1	**R. F. Doherty/H. L. Doherty (H)**
		H. A. Nisbet/C. Hobart (C) 6-4, 6-4, 6-2
1899	**1899**	**1899**
A. W. Gore H. S. Mahony 6-3, 4-6, 3-6, 7-5, 6-1	**A. W. Gore** S. H. Smith 3-6, 6-2, 6-1, 6-4	**H. A. Nisbet/C. Hobart**
S. H. Smith H. Roper Barrett 2-6, 10-8, 4-6, 8-6, 8-6	*Challenge Round*	A. W. Gore/H. Roper Barrett 6-4, 6-1, 8-6
	R. F. Doherty (H) A. W. Gore (C) 1-6, 4-6, 6-2, 6-3, 6-3	**R. F. Doherty/H. L. Doherty (H)**
		H. A. Nisbet/C. Hobart (C) 7-5, 6-0, 6-2
1900	**1900**	**1900**
A. W. Gore H. L. Doherty 4-6, 8-6, 8-6, 6-1	**S. H. Smith** A. W. Gore 6-4, 4-6, 6-2, 6-1	**H. Roper Barrett/H. A. Nisbet**
S. H. Smith H. A. Nisbet 6-0, 6-1, 6-1	*Challenge Round*	S. H. Smith/F. L. Riseley 6-2, 2-6, 6-8, 8-6, 6-2
	R. F. Doherty (H) S. H. Smith (C) 6-8, 6-3, 6-1, 6-2	**R. F. Doherty/H. L. Doherty (H)**
		H. Roper Barrett/H. A. Nisbet (C) 9-7, 7-5, 4-6, 3-6, 6-3
1901	**1901**	**1901**
C. P. Dixon H. S. Mahony 6-3, 6-4, 11-9	**A. W. Gore** C. P. Dixon 6-4, 6-0, 6-3	**D. F. Davis/H. Ward**
A. W. Gore H. Roper Barrett 8-6, 6-1, 7-5	*Challenge Round*	H. Roper Barrett/G. M. Simond 7-5, 6-4, 6-4
	A. W. Gore (C) R. F. Doherty (H) 4-6, 7-5, 6-4, 6-4	**R. F. Doherty/H. L. Doherty (H)**
		D. F. Davis/H. Ward (C) 4-6, 6-2, 6-3, 9-7
1902	**1902**	**1902**
M. J. G. Ritchie S. H. Smith 6-4, 4-6, 6-4, 6-4	**H. L. Doherty** M. J. G. Ritchie 8-6, 6-3, 7-5	**S. H. Smith/F. L. Riseley**
H. L. Doherty H. S. Mahony 4-6, 4-6, 8-6, 2-0 retired	*Challenge Round*	G. W. Hillyard/C. H. L. Cazalet 7-5, 2-6, 6-8, 6-3, 6-1
	H. L. Doherty (C) A. W. Gore (H) 6-4, 6-3, 3-6, 6-0	*Challenge Round*
		S. H. Smith/F. L. Riseley (C)
		R. F. Doherty/H. L. Doherty (H) 4-6, 8-6, 6-3, 4-6, 11-9
1903	**1903**	**1903**
F. L. Riseley S. H. Smith 7-5, 6-3, 7-9, 1-6, 9-7	**F. L. Riseley** M. J. G. Ritchie 1-6, 6-3, 8-6, 13-11	**R. F. Doherty/H. L. Doherty**
M. J. G. Ritchie G. A. Caridia 6-1, 6-0, 4-6, 6-1	*Challenge Round*	H. S. Mahony/M. J. G. Ritchie 8-6, 6-2, 6-2
	H. L. Doherty (H) F. L. Riseley (C) 7-5, 6-3, 6-0	**R. F. Doherty/H. L. Doherty (C)**
		S. H. Smith/F. L. Riseley (H) 6-4, 6-4, 6-4
1904	**1904**	**1904**
F. L. Riseley S. H. Smith 7-5, 5-7, 8-6, 5-7, retired	**F. L. Riseley** M. J. G. Ritchie 6-0, 6-1, 6-2	**S. H. Smith/F. L. Riseley**
M. J. G. Ritchie P. de Borman 6-3, 6-1, 6-1	*Challenge Round*	A. W. Gore/G. A. Caridia 6-3, 6-4, 6-3
	H. L. Doherty (H) F. L. Riseley (C) 6-1, 7-5, 8-6	**R. F. Doherty/H. L. Doherty (H)**
		S. H. Smith/F. L. Riseley (C) 6-1, 6-2, 6-4
1905	**1905**	**1905**
N. E. Brookes A. W. Gore 6-3, 9-7, 6-2	**N. E. Brookes** S. H. Smith 1-6, 6-4, 6-1, 1-6, 7-5	**S. H. Smith/F. L. Riseley**
S. H. Smith M. J. G. Ritchie 6-0, 3-6, 6-4, 4-6, 6-1	*Challenge Round*	N. E. Brookes/A. W. Dunlop 6-2, 1-6, 6-2, 6-3
	H. L. Doherty (H) N. E. Brookes (C) 8-6, 6-2, 6-4	*Challenge Round*
		R. F. Doherty/H. L. Doherty (H)
		S. H. Smith/F. L. Riseley (C) 6-2, 6-4, 6-8, 6-3
1906	**1906**	**1906**
A. W. Gore A. F. Wilding 9-7, 6-1, 8-6	**F. L. Riseley** A. W. Gore 6-3, 6-3, 6-4	**S. H. Smith/F. L. Riseley**
F. L. Riseley S. H. Smith 8-6, 2-6, 6-2, 6-4	*Challenge Round*	C. H. L. Cazalet/G. M. Simond 6-2, 6-2, 5-7, 6-4
	H. L. Doherty (H) F. L. Riseley (C) 6-4, 4-6, 6-2, 6-3	*Challenge Round*
		S. H. Smith/F. L. Riseley (C)
		R. F. Doherty/H. L. Doherty (H) 6-8, 6-4, 5-7, 6-3, 6-3
1907	**1907**	**1907**
A. W. Gore W. V. Eaves 9-7, 7-5, 6-2	**N. E. Brookes** A. W. Gore 6-4, 6-4, 6-2	**N. E. Brookes/A. F. Wilding**
N. E. Brookes M. J. G. Ritchie 6-0, 6-1, 6-4	*Challenge Round*	B. C. Wright/K. Behr 6-4, 6-4, 6-2
	N. E. Brookes (C) a bye H. L. Doherty (H) retired	**N. E. Brookes/A. F. Wilding (C)** a bye
		S. H. Smith/F. L. Riseley (H) retired
1908	**1908**	**1908**
A. W. Gore R. B. Powell 10-8, 6-4, 6-2	**A. W. Gore** H. Roper Barrett 6-3, 6-2, 4-6, 3-6, 6-4	**A. F. Wilding/M. J. G. Ritchie**
H. Roper Barrett M. J. G. Ritchie 6-3, 6-1, 3-6, 6-1	*Challenge Round*	A. W. Gore/H. Roper Barrett 6-1, 6-2, 1-6, 1-6, 9-7
	A. W. Gore (C) a bye N. E. Brookes (H) retired	*Challenge Round*
		A. F. Wilding/M. J. G. Ritchie (C) a bye
		N. E. Brookes/A. F. Wilding (H) retired
1909	**1909**	**1909**
M. J. G. Ritchie T. M. Mavrogordato 3-6, 6-3, 6-3, 6-2	**M. J. G. Ritchie** H. Roper Barrett 6-2, 6-3, 4-6, 6-4	**A. W. Gore/H. Roper Barrett**
H. Roper Barrett F. W. Rahe 6-4, 6-2, 6-8, 7-5	*Challenge Round*	S. N. Doust/H. A. Parker 6-2, 6-1, 6-4
	A. W. Gore (H) M. J. G. Ritchie (C) 6-8, 1-6, 6-2, 6-2, 6-2	**A. W. Gore/H. Roper Barrett (C)** a bye
		M. J. G. Ritchie/A. F. Wilding (H) retired
1910	**1910**	**1910**
A. F. Wilding J. C. Parke 7-5, 6-1, 6-2	**A. F. Wilding** B. C. Wright 4-6, 4-6, 6-3, 6-2, 6-3	**A. F. Wilding/M. J. G. Ritchie**
B. C. Wright A. H. Lowe 6-3, 3-6, 6-4, 6-3	*Challenge Round*	K. Powell/R. B. Powell 9-7, 6-0, 6-4
	A. F. Wilding (C) A. W. Gore (H) 6-4, 7-5, 4-6, 6-2	*Challenge Round*
		A. F. Wilding/M. J. G. Ritchie (C)
		A. W. Gore/H. Roper Barrett (H) 6-1, 6-1, 6-2
1911	**1911**	**1911**
C. P. Dixon M. Decugis 6-2, 5-7, 6-2, 6-3	**H. Roper Barrett** C. P. Dixon 5-7, 4-6, 6-4, 6-3, 6-1	**A. H. Gobert/M. Decugis**
H. Roper Barrett F. G. Lowe 6-2, 6-3, 6-2	*Challenge Round*	J. C. Parke/S. Hardy 6-2, 6-1, 6-2
	A. F. Wilding (H) H. Roper Barrett (C) 6-4, 4-6, 2-6, 6-2, retired	**A. H. Gobert/M. Decugis (C)**
		M. J. G. Ritchie/A. F. Wilding (H) 9-7, 5-7, 6-3, 2-6, 6-2
1912	**1912**	**1912**
A. H. Gobert M. Decugis 6-3, 6-3, 1-6, 4-6, 6-4	**A. W. Gore** A. H. Gobert 9-7, 2-6, 7-5, 6-1	**H. Roper Barrett/C. P. Dixon**
A. W. Gore A. E. Beamish 6-2, 0-6, 11-9, 6-4	*Challenge Round*	J. C. Parke/A. E. Beamish 6-8, 6-4, 3-6, 6-3, 6-4
	A. F. Wilding (H) A. W. Gore (C) 6-4, 6-4, 4-6, 6-4	*Challenge Round*
		H. Roper Barrett/C. P. Dixon (C)
		A. H. Gobert/M. Decugis (H) 3-6, 6-3, 6-4, 7-5
1913	**1913**	**1913**
M. E. McLoughlin J. C. Parke 6-4, 7-5, 6-4	**M. E. McLoughlin** S. N. Doust 6-3, 6-4, 7-5	**F. W. Rahe/H. Kleinschroth**
S. N. Doust O. Kreuzer 6-3, 6-2, 6-3	*Challenge Round*	J. C. Parke/A. E. Beamish 6-3, 6-2, 6-4
	A. F. Wilding (H) M. E. McLoughlin (C) 8-6, 6-3, 10-8	*Challenge Round*
		H. Roper Barrett/C. P. Dixon (H)
		F. W. Rahe/H. Kleinschroth (C) 6-2, 6-4, 4-6, 6-2
1914	**1914**	**1914**
O. Froitzheim T. M. Mavrogordato 6-3, 6-2, 7-5	**N. E. Brookes** O. Froitzheim 6-2, 6-1, 5-7, 4-6, 8-6	**N. E. Brookes/A. F. Wilding**
N. E. Brookes A. E. Beamish 6-0, 6-3, 6-2	*Challenge Round*	F. G. Lowe/A. H. Lowe 6-2, 8-6, 6-1
	N. E. Brookes (C) A. F. Wilding (H) 6-4, 6-4, 7-5	*Challenge Round*
		N. E. Brookes/A. F. Wilding (C)
		H. Roper Barrett/C. P. Dixon (H) 6-1, 6-1, 5-7, 8-6
1915-18 *No Competition*	**1915-18** *No Competition*	**1915-18** *No Competition*
1919	**1919**	**1919**
G. L. Patterson M. J. G. Ritchie 6-1, 7-5, 1-6, 6-3	**G. L. Patterson** A. R. F. Kingscote 6-2, 6-1, 6-3	**R. V. Thomas/P. O'Hara Wood**
A. R. F. Kingscote C. S. Garland 6-1, 6-4, 2-6, 5-7, 6-4	*Challenge Round*	R. Lycett/R. W. Heath 6-4, 6-2, 4-6, 6-2
	G. L. Patterson (C) N. E. Brookes (H) 6-3, 7-5, 6-2	*Challenge Round* w.o.

Winners in **bold type**; **(H)**/(H) holder; **(C)**/(C) challenger; w.o. walk-over

Wimbledon Championships

Men's Singles

Semi-Finals

1920
Z. Shimizu T. M. Mavrogordato 3-6, 6-4, 6-0, 6-2
W. T. Tilden C. S. Garland 6-4, 8-6, 6-2

1921
M. Alonso Z. Shimizu 3-6, 7-5, 3-6, 6-4, 8-6
B. I. C. Norton F. T. Hunter 6-0, 6-3, 5-7, 5-7, 6-2

1922
R. Lycett J. B. Gilbert 8-6, 9-7, 6-3
G. L. Patterson J. O. Anderson 6-1, 3-6, 7-9, 6-1, 6-3
1923
W. M. Johnston B. I. C. Norton 6-4, 6-2, 6-4
F. T. Hunter F. G. Lowe 6-3, 7-5, 6-4
1924
R. Lacoste R. N. Williams 6-1, 3-6, 6-2, 6-3
J. Borotra L. Raymond 6-2, 6-4, 7-5
1925
J. Borotra H. Cochet 5-7, 8-6, 6-4, 6-1
R. Lacoste J. O. Anderson 6-4, 7-5, 6-1
1926
H. O. Kinsey J. Brugnon 6-4, 4-6, 6-3, 3-6, 9-7
J. Borotra H. Cochet 2-6, 7-5, 2-6, 6-3, 7-5
1927†
H. Cochet(4) W. T. Tilden(2) 2-6, 4-6, 7-5, 6-4, 6-3
J. Borotra(3) R. Lacoste(1) 6-4, 6-3, 1-6, 1-6, 6-2
1928
H. Cochet(1) C. Boussus 11-9, 3-6, 6-2, 6-3
R. Lacoste(2) W. T. Tilden(3) 2-6, 6-4, 2-6, 6-4, 6-3
1929
H. Cochet(1) W. T. Tilden(3) 6-4, 6-1, 10-8, 5-7, 6-1
J. Borotra(2) H. W. Austin 6-1, 10-8, 5-7, 6-1
1930
W. L. Allison J. H. Doeg(4) 6-3, 4-6, 8-6, 3-6, 7-5
W. T. Tilden(2) J. Borotra(3) 0-6, 6-4, 4-6, 6-0, 7-5
1931
S. B. Wood(7) F. J. Perry(5) 4-6, 6-2, 6-4, 6-2
F. X. Shields(3) J. Borotra(1) 7-5, 6-4, 6-4
1932
H. E. Vines(2) J. H. Crawford(8) 6-2, 6-1, 6-3
H. W. Austin(6) J. Sato 7-5, 6-2, 6-1
1933
H. E. Vines(1) H. Cochet(3) 6-2, 8-6, 3-6, 6-1
J. H. Crawford(2) J. Sato 6-3, 6-4, 2-6, 6-4
1934
J. H. Crawford(1) F. X. Shields(5) 2-6, 4-6, 6-4, 6-3, 6-4
F. J. Perry(2) S. B. Wood(7) 6-3, 3-6, 7-5, 5-7, 6-3
1935
F. J. Perry(1) J. H. Crawford(3) 6-2, 3-6, 6-4, 6-4
G. von Cramm(2) J. D. Budge 4-6, 6-4, 6-3, 6-2
1936
F. J. Perry(1) J. D. Budge(5) 5-7, 6-4, 6-3, 6-4
G. von Cramm(2) H. W. Austin(7) 8-6, 6-3, 2-6, 6-3
1937
G. von Cramm(2) H. W. Austin(3) 8-6, 6-3, 12-14, 6-1
J. D. Budge(1) F. A. Parker(8) 2-6, 6-4, 6-4, 6-1
1938
H. W. Austin(2) H. Henkel(4) 6-2, 6-4, 6-0
J. D. Budge(1) F. Punčec(5) 6-2, 6-1, 6-4
1939
E. T. Cooke(6) H. Henkel(5) 6-3, 4-6, 6-4, 6-4
R. L. Riggs(2) F. Punčec(4) 6-2, 6-3, 6-4
1940-45 *No Competition*
1946
Y. Petra(5) T. Brown 4-6, 4-6, 6-3, 7-5, 8-6
G. E. Brown(3) J. Drobný 6-4, 7-5, 6-2
1947
T. Brown J. E. Patty 6-3, 6-3, 6-3
J. A. Kramer(1) D. Pails(4) 6-1, 3-6, 6-1, 6-0
1948
J. E. Bromwich(2) J. Asbóth 6-3, 14-12, 6-2
R. Falkenburg G. Mulloy(3) 6-4, 6-4, 8-6
1949
J. Drobný(6) J. E. Bromwich(5) 6-1, 6-3, 6-2
F. R. Schroeder(1) E. W. Sturgess(7) 3-6, 7-5, 5-7, 6-1, 6-2
1950
F. A. Sedgman(1) J. Drobný 3-6, 3-6, 6-3, 7-5, 6-2
J. E. Patty(5) E. V. Seixas(12) 6-3, 5-7, 6-2, 7-5
1951
R. Savitt(6) H. Flam(5) 1-6, 15-13, 6-3, 6-2
K. McGregor(7) E. W. Sturgess(8) 6-4, 3-6, 6-3, 7-5
1952
F. A. Sedgman(1) M. G. Rose(8) 6-4, 6-4, 7-5
J. Drobný(2) H. Flam(6) 6-2, 6-4, 0-6, 8-10, 6-4
1953
E. V. Seixas(2) M. G. Rose(8) 6-4, 10-12, 9-11, 6-4, 6-3
K. Nielsen J. Drobný(4) 6-4, 6-3, 6-2
1954
J. Drobný(11) J. E. Patty(7) 6-2, 6-4, 4-6, 9-7
K. R. Rosewall(3) M. A. Trabert(1) 3-6, 6-3, 4-6, 6-1, 6-1
1955
K. Nielsen K. R. Rosewall(2) 11-9, 6-2, 2-6, 6-4
M. A. Trabert(1) J. E. Patty(7) 8-6, 6-2, 6-2
1956
L. A. Hoad(1) H. Richardson(6) 6-4, 6-2, 6-4
K. R. Rosewall(2) E. V. Seixas(8) 6-3, 3-6, 6-8, 6-3, 7-5
1957
A. J. Cooper(2) N. A. Fraser(5) 1-6, 14-12, 6-3, 8-6
L. A. Hoad(1) S. Davidson(4) 6-4, 6-4, 7-5
1958
N. A Fraser(4) K. Nielsen(6) 6-4, 6-4, 17-19, 6-4
A. J. Cooper(1) M. G. Rose(3) 7-9, 6-2, 6-2, 6-3

Finals

1920
W. T. Tilden Z. Shimizu 6-4, 6-4, 13-11
Challenge Round
W. T. Tilden (C) G. L. Patterson (H) 2-6, 6-3, 6-2, 6-4

1921
B. I. C. Norton M. Alonso 5-7, 4-6, 7-5, 6-3, 6-3
Challenge Round
W. T. Tilden (H) B. I. C. Norton (C) 4-6, 2-6, 6-1, 6-0, 7-5

1922*
G. L. Patterson R. Lycett 6-3, 6-4, 6-2

1923
W. M. Johnston F. T. Hunter 6-0, 6-3, 6-1

1924
J. Borotra R. Lacoste 6-1, 3-6, 6-1, 3-6, 6-4

1925
R. Lacoste J. Borotra 6-3, 6-3, 4-6, 8-6

1926
J. Borotra H. O. Kinsey 8-6, 6-1, 6-3

1927†
H. Cochet(4) J. Borotra(3) 4-6, 4-6, 6-3, 6-4, 7-5

1928
R. Lacoste(2) H. Cochet(1) 6-1, 4-6, 6-4, 6-2

1929
H. Cochet(1) J. Borotra(2) 6-4, 6-3, 6-4

1930
W. T. Tilden(2) W. L. Allison 6-3, 9-7, 6-4

1931
S. B. Wood(7) w.o. F. X. Shields(3) scratched

1932
H. E. Vines(2) H. W. Austin(6) 6-4, 6-2, 6-0

1933
J. H. Crawford(2) H. E. Vines(1) 4-6, 11-9, 6-2, 2-6, 6-4

1934
F. J. Perry(2) J. H. Crawford(1) 6-3, 6-0, 7-5

1935
F. J. Perry(1) G. von Cramm(2) 6-2, 6-4, 6-4

1936
F. J. Perry(1) G. von Cramm(2) 6-1, 6-1, 6-0

1937
J. D. Budge(1) G. von Cramm(2) 6-3, 6-4, 6-2

1938
J. D. Budge(1) H. W. Austin(2) 6-1, 6-0, 6-3

1939
R. L. Riggs(2) E. T. Cooke(6) 2-6, 8-6, 3-6, 6-3, 6-2

1940-45 *No Competition*
1946
Y. Petra(5) G. E. Brown(3) 6-2, 6-4, 7-9, 5-7, 6-4

1947
J. A. Kramer(1) T. Brown(3) 6-1, 6-3, 6-2

1948
R. Falkenburg(7) J. E. Bromwich(2) 7-5, 0-6, 6-2, 3-6, 7-5

1949
F. R. Schroeder(1) J. Drobný(6) 3-6, 6-0, 6-3, 4-6, 6-4

1950
J. E. Patty(5) F. A. Sedgman(1) 6-1, 8-10, 6-2, 6-3

1951
R. Savitt(6) K. McGregor(7) 6-4, 6-4, 6-4

1952
F. A. Sedgman(1) J. Drobný(2) 4-6, 6-2, 6-3, 6-2

1953
E. V. Seixas(1) K. Nielsen 9-7, 6-3, 6-4

1954
J. Drobný(11) K. R. Rosewall(3) 13-11, 4-6, 6-2, 9-7

1955
M. A. Trabert(1) K. Nielsen 6-3, 7-5, 6-1

1956
L. A. Hoad(1) K. R. Rosewall(2) 6-2, 4-6, 7-5, 6-4

1957
L. A. Hoad(1) A. J. Cooper(2) 6-2, 6-1, 6-2

1958
A. J. Cooper(1) N. A. Fraser(4) 3-6, 6-3, 6-4, 13-11

Men's Doubles

Finals

1920
R. N. Williams/C. S. Garland
A. R. F. Kingscote/J. C. Parke 4-6, 6-4, 7-5, 6-2
Challenge Round
R. N. Williams/C. S. Garland (C) a bye
R. V. Thomas/P. O'Hara Wood retired
1921
R. Lycett/M. Woosnam
F. G. Lowe/A. H. Lowe 6-3, 6-0, 7-5
Challenge Round
R. Lycett/M. Woosnam (C) a bye
R. N. Williams/C. S. Garland (H) retired
1922*
J. O. Anderson/R. Lycett
G. L. Patterson/P. O'Hara Wood 3-6, 7-9, 6-4, 6-3, 11-9
1923
R. Lycett/L. A. Godfree
Count de Gomar/E. Flaquer 6-3, 6-4, 3-6, 6-3
1924
V. Richards/F. T. Hunter
R. N. Williams/W. M. Washburn 6-3, 3-6, 8-10, 8-6, 6-3
1925
R. Lacoste/J. Borotra
J. Hennessey/R. Casey 6-4, 11-9, 4-6, 1-6, 6-3
1926
H. Cochet/J. Brugnon
V. Richards/H. O. Kinsey 7-5, 4-6, 6-3, 6-2
1927
F. T. Hunter/W. T. Tilden
J. Brugnon/H. Cochet 1-6, 4-6, 8-6, 6-3, 6-4
1928
H. Cochet/J. Brugnon
G. L. Patterson/J. B. Hawkes 13-11, 6-4, 6-4
1929
W. L. Allison/J. Van Ryn
J. C. Gregory/I. G. Collins 6-4, 5-7, 6-3, 10-12, 6-4
1930
W. L. Allison/J. Van Ryn
J. H. Doeg/G. M. Lott 6-3, 6-3, 6-2
1931
G. M. Lott/J. Van Ryn
H. Cochet/J. Brugnon 6-2, 10-8, 9-11, 3-6, 6-3
1932
J. Borotra/J. Brugnon
G. P. Hughes/F. J. Perry 6-0, 4-6, 3-6, 7-5, 7-5
1933
J. Borotra/J. Brugnon
R. Nunoi/J. Sato 4-6, 6-3, 6-3, 7-3
1934
G. M. Lott/L. R. Stoefen
J. Borotra/J. Brugnon 6-2, 6-3, 6-4
1935
J. H. Crawford/A. K. Quist
W. L. Allison/J. Van Ryn 6-3, 5-7, 6-2, 5-7, 7-5
1936
G. P. Hughes/C. R. D. Tuckey
C. E. Hare/F. H. D. Wilde 6-4, 3-6, 7-9, 6-1, 6-4
1937
J. D. Budge/C. G. Mako
G. P. Hughes/C. R. D. Tuckey 6-0, 6-4, 6-8, 6-1
1938
J. D. Budge/C. G. Mako
H. Henkel/G. von Metaxa 6-4, 3-6, 6-3, 8-6
1939
E. T. Cooke/R. L. Riggs
C. E. Hare/F. H. D. Wilde 6-3, 3-6, 6-3, 9-7
1940-45 *No Competition*
1946
T. Brown/J. A. Kramer
G. E. Brown/D. Pails 6-4, 6-4, 6-2
1947
R. Falkenburg/J. A. Kramer
A. J. Mottram/O. W. Sidwell 8-6, 6-3, 6-3
1948
J. E. Bromwich/F. A. Sedgman
T. Brown/G. Mulloy 5-7, 7-5, 7-5, 9-7
1949
R. P. Gonzalez/F. A. Parker
G. Mulloy/F. R. Schroeder 6-4, 6-4, 6-2
1950
J. E. Bromwich/A. K. Quist
G. E. Brown/O. W. Sidwell 7-5, 3-6, 6-3, 3-6, 6-2
1951
K. McGregor/F. A. Sedgman
J. Drobný/E. W. Sturgess 3-6, 6-2, 6-3, 3-6, 6-3
1952
K. McGregor/F. A. Sedgman
E. V. Seixas/E. W. Sturgess 6-3, 7-5, 6-4
1953
L. A. Hoad/K. R. Rosewall
R. N. Hartwig/M. G. Rose 6-4, 7-5, 4-6, 7-5
1954
R. N. Hartwig/M. G. Rose
E. V. Seixas/M. A. Trabert 6-4, 6-4, 3-6, 6-4
1955
R. N. Hartwig/L. A. Hoad
N. A. Fraser/K. R. Rosewall 7-5, 6-4, 6-3
1956
L. A. Hoad/K. R. Rosewall
N. Pietrangeli/O. Sirola 7-5, 6-2, 6-1
1957
G. Mulloy/J. E. Patty
N. A. Fraser/L. A. Hoad 8-10, 6-4, 6-4, 6-4
1958
S. Davidson/U. Schmidt
A. J. Cooper/N. A. Fraser 6-4, 6-4, 8-6

Men's Singles

Men's Doubles

Semi-Finals

1959
R. G. Laver B. MacKay[3] 11-13, 11-9, 10-8, 7-9, 6-3
A. Olmedo[1] R. Emerson[8] 6-4, 6-0, 6-4
1960
R. G. Laver[3] N. Pietrangeli[5] 4-6, 6-3, 8-10, 6-2, 6-4
N. A. Fraser[1] R. Krishnan[7] 6-3, 6-2, 6-2
1961
R. G. Laver[2] R. Krishnan[7] 6-2, 8-6, 6-2
C. R. McKinley[8] M. J. Sangster 6-4, 6-4, 8-6
1962
R. G. Laver[1] N. A. Fraser[3] 10-8, 6-1, 7-5
M. F. Mulligan J. G. Fraser 6-3, 6-2, 6-2
1963
C. R. McKinley[4] W. P. Bungert 6-2, 6-4, 8-6
F. S. Stolle M. Santana[2] 8-6, 6-1, 7-5
1964
R. S. Emerson[1] W. P. Bungert 6-3, 15-13, 6-0
F. S. Stolle[6] C. R. McKinley[2] 4-6, 10-8, 9-7, 6-4
1965
R. S. Emerson[1] R. D. Ralston[7] 6-1, 6-2, 7-9, 6-1
F. S. Stolle[2] E. C. Drysdale 6-3, 6-4, 7-5
1966
M. Santana[4] O. K. Davidson 6-2, 4-6, 9-7, 3-6, 7-5
R. D. Ralston[6] E. C. Drysdale[7] 6-8, 8-6, 3-6, 7-5, 6-3
1967
W. P. Bungert R. Taylor 6-4, 6-8, 2-6, 6-4, 6-4
J. D. Newcombe[3] N. Pilić 9-7, 4-6, 6-3, 6-4
1968 *Open Championships began*
R. G. Laver[1]* A. R. Ashe[13] 7-5, 6-2, 6-4
A. D. Roche[15]* C. E. Graebner 9-7, 8-10, 6-4, 8-6
1969
R. G. Laver[1]* A. R. Ashe[5] 2-6, 6-2, 9-7, 6-0
J. D. Newcombe[6]* A. D. Roche[2]* 3-6, 6-1, 14-12, 6-4
1970
K. R. Rosewall[5]* R. Taylor[16]* 6-3, 4-6, 6-3, 6-3
J. D. Newcombe[2]* A. Gimeno[14]* 6-3, 8-6, 6-0
1971
S. R. Smith[4] T. W. Gorman 6-3, 8-6, 6-2
J. D. Newcombe[2]* K. R. Rosewall[3]* 6-1, 6-1, 6-3
1972
S. R. Smith[1] J. Kodeš[5] 3-6, 6-4, 6-1, 7-5
I. Năstase[2] M. Orantes[3] 6-3, 6-4, 6-4
1973
A. Metreveli[4] A. Mayer 6-3, 3-6, 6-3, 6-4
J. Kodeš[2] R. Taylor[3]* 8-9, 9-7, 5-7, 6-4, 7-5

Finals

1959
A. Olmedo[1] R. G. Laver 6-4, 6-3, 6-4
1960
N. A. Fraser[1] R. G. Laver[3] 6-4, 3-6, 9-7, 7-5
1961
R. G. Laver[2] C. R. McKinley[8] 6-3, 6-1, 6-4
1962
R. G. Laver[1] M. F. Mulligan 6-2, 6-2, 6-1
1963
C. R. McKinley[1] F. S. Stolle 9-7, 6-1, 6-4
1964
R. S. Emerson[1] F. S. Stolle[6] 6-4, 12-10, 4-6, 6-3
1965
R. S. Emerson[1] F. S. Stolle[2] 6-2, 6-4, 6-4
1966
M. Santana[4] R. D. Ralston[6] 6-4, 11-9, 6-4
1967
J. D. Newcombe[1] W. P. Bungert 6-3, 6-1, 6-1
1968 *Open Championships began*
R. G. Laver[1]* A. D. Roche[15]* 6-3, 6-4, 6-2
1969
R. G. Laver[1]* J. D. Newcombe[6]* 6-4, 5-7, 6-4, 6-4
1970
J. D. Newcombe[2]* K. R. Rosewall[5]* 5-7, 6-3, 6-2, 3-6, 6-1
1971
J. D. Newcombe[2]* S. R. Smith[4] 6-3, 5-7, 2-6, 6-4, 6-4
1972
S. R. Smith[1] I. Năstase[2] 4-6, 6-3, 6-3, 4-6, 7-5
1973
J. Kodeš[2] A. Metreveli[4] 6-1, 9-8, 6-3

Finals

1959
R. Emerson/N. A. Fraser
R. G. Laver/R. Mark 8-6, 6-3, 14-16, 9-7
1960
R. H. Osuna/R. D. Ralston
M. G. Davis/R. K. Wilson 7-5, 6-3, 10-8
1961
R. Emerson/N. A. Fraser
R. A. J. Hewitt/F. S. Stolle 6-4, 6-8, 6-4, 6-8, 8-6
1962
R. A. J. Hewitt/F. S. Stolle
B. Jovanović/N. Pilić 6-2, 5-7, 6-2, 6-4
1963
R. H. Osuna/A. Palafox
J. C. Barclay/P. Darmon 4-6, 6-2, 6-2, 6-2
1964
R. A. J. Hewitt/F. S. Stolle
R. Emerson/K. N. Fletcher 7-5, 11-9, 6-4
1965
J. D. Newcombe/A. D. Roche
K. N. Fletcher/R. A. J. Hewitt 7-5, 6-3, 6-4
1966
K. N. Fletcher/J. D. Newcombe
W. W. Bowrey/O. K. Davidson 6-3, 6-4, 3-6, 6-3
1967
R. A. J. Hewitt/F. D. McMillan
R. Emerson/K. N. Fletcher 6-2, 6-3, 6-4
1968 *Open Championships began*
J. D. Newcombe/A. D. Roche
K. R. Rosewall/F. S. Stolle 3-6, 8-6, 5-7, 14-12, 6-3
1969
J. D. Newcombe/A. D. Roche
T. S. Okker/M. C. Riessen 7-5, 11-9, 6-3
1970
J. D. Newcombe/A. D. Roche
K. R. Rosewall/F. S. Stolle 10-8, 6-3, 6-1
1971
R. S. Emerson/R. G. Laver
A. R. Ashe/R. D. Ralston 4-6, 9-7, 6-8, 6-4, 6-4
1972
R. A. J. Hewitt/F. D. McMillan
S. R. Smith/E. J. Van Dillen 6-2, 6-2, 9-7
1973
J. S. Connors/I. Năstase
J. R. Cooper/N. A. Fraser 3-6, 6-3, 6-4, 8-9, 6-1

Wimbledon Championships

Women's Singles

Semi-Finals	Finals
1884	**1884**
Miss M. Watson Miss Bingley 3-6, 6-4, 6-2	**Miss M. Watson** Miss L. Watson 6-8, 6-3, 6-3
Miss L. Watson Miss Leslie 6-4, 6-1	
1885	**1885**
Miss. B. Bingley Miss Guerney 6-1, 6-2	**Miss M. Watson** Miss B. Bingley 6-1, 7-5
Miss M. Watson Miss E. F. Hudson 6-0, 6-1	
1886	**1886** *Challenge Round Introduced*
Miss A. Tabor Miss M. Shackle 6-4, 7-5	**Miss B. Bingley** Miss A. Tabor 6-2, 6-0
Miss B. Bingley Miss L. Watson 6-3, 8-6	*Challenge Round*
	Miss B. Bingley (C) Miss M. Watson (H) 6-3, 6-3
1887	**1887**
Miss L. Dod Miss B. James 6-1, 6-1	**Miss L. Dod** Mrs C. J. Cole 6-2, 6-3
Mrs C. J. Cole Miss J. Shackle 6-4, 6-1	*Challenge Round*
	Miss L. Dod (C) Miss B. Bingley (H) 6-2, 6-0
1888	**1888**
Miss Howes Miss Patterson 6-4, 6-2	**Mrs G. W. Hillyard** Miss Howes 6-1, 6-2
Mrs G. W. Hillyard a bye Miss Phillimore retired	*Challenge Round*
	Miss L. Dod (H) Mrs G. W. Hillyard (C) 6-3, 6-3
1889	**1889**
Miss L. Rice Miss Jacks 6-2, 6-0	**Mrs G. W. Hillyard** Miss L. Rice 4-6, 8-6, 6-4
Mrs G. W. Hillyard Miss B. Steedman 8-6, 6-1	*Challenge Round*
	Mrs G. W. Hillyard (C) a bye Miss L. Dod (H) retired
1890	**1890**
Miss Jacks Mrs C. J. Cole 6-4, 7-5	**Miss L. Rice** Miss Jacks 6-4, 6-1
Miss L. Rice Miss M. Steedman 7-5, 6-2	*Challenge Round*
	Miss L. Rice (C) a bye Mrs G. W. Hillyard (H) retired
1891	**1891**
Miss L. Dod Miss B. Steedman 6-3, 6-1	**Miss L. Dod** Mrs G. W. Hillyard 6-2, 6-1
Mrs G. W. Hillyard Miss M. Langrishe 6-4, 6-1	*Challenge Round*
	Miss L. Dod (C) a bye Miss L. Rice (H) retired
1892	**1892**
Miss M. Shackle Miss B. Steedman 6-4, 6-3	**Mrs G. W. Hillyard** Miss M. Shackle 6-1, 6-4
Mrs G. W. Hillyard Miss Martin 1-6, 6-3, 9-7	*Challenge Round*
	Miss L. Dod (H) Mrs G. W. Hillyard (C) 6-1, 6-1
1893	**1893**
Miss M. Shackle Miss L. Austin 6-1, 6-2	**Mrs G. W. Hillyard** Miss M. Shackle 6-3, 6-2
Mrs G. W. Hillyard Miss C. Cooper 6-3, 6-1	*Challenge Round*
	Miss L. Dod (H) Mrs G. W. Hillyard (C) 6-8, 6-1, 6-4
1894	**1894**
Mrs G. W. Hillyard Miss Bryan 6-1, 6-1	**Mrs G. W. Hillyard** Miss L. Austin 6-1, 6-1
Miss L. Austin Miss S. Robins 6-1, 6-1	*Challenge Round*
	Mrs G. W. Hillyard (C) a bye Miss L. Dod (H) retired
1895	**1895**
Miss Jackson Mrs Pickering 6-4, 3-6, 8-6	**Miss C. Cooper** Miss Jackson 7-5, 8-6
Miss C. Cooper Mrs Draffen 6-2, 6-8, 6-1	*Challenge Round*
	Miss C. Cooper (C) a bye Mrs G. W. Hillyard (H) retired
1896	**1896**
Miss L. Austin a bye Mrs Horncastle retired	**Mrs Pickering** Miss L. Austin 4-6, 6-3, 6-3
Mrs Pickering Mrs Draffen 6-3, 7-5	*Challenge Round*
	Miss C. Cooper (H) Mrs Pickering (C) 6-2, 6-3
1897	**1897**
Mrs G. W. Hillyard a bye Mrs Horncastle retired	**Mrs G. W. Hillyard** Mrs Pickering 6-2, 7-5
Mrs Pickering Miss R. Dyas 6-4, 4-6, 6-1	*Challenge Round*
	Mrs G. W. Hillyard (C) Miss C. Cooper (H) 5-7, 7-5, 6-2
1898	**1898**
Miss Martin a bye Miss Legh retired	**Miss C. Cooper** Miss Martin 6-4, 6-4
Miss C. Cooper Miss L. Austin 6-4, 6-1	*Challenge Round*
	Miss C. Cooper (C) a bye Mrs G. W. Hillyard (H) retired
1899	**1899**
Mrs R. Durlacher Miss B. Steedman 6-4, 6-2	**Mrs G. W. Hillyard** Mrs. R. Durlacher 7-5, 6-8, 6-1
Mrs G. W. Hillyard Miss B. Tulloch 6-2, 3-6, 6-2	*Challenge Round*
	Mrs G. W. Hillyard (C) Miss C. Cooper (H) 6-2, 6-3
1900	**1900**
Miss C. Cooper Mrs G. Greville 6-1, 6-2	**Miss C. Cooper** Miss Martin 8-6, 5-7, 6-1
Miss Martin Mrs Evered 6-0, 6-2	*Challenge Round*
	Mrs G. W. Hillyard (H) Miss C. Cooper (C) 4-6, 6-4, 6-4
1901	**1901**
Miss Martin Miss A. M. Morton 7-5, 6-2	**Mrs A. Sterry** Miss Martin 6-3, 6-4
Mrs A. Sterry Miss Adams 6-1, 6-1	*Challenge Round*
	Mrs A. Sterry (C) Mrs G. W. Hillyard (H) 6-2, 6-2
1902	**1902**
Miss M. E. Robb Miss D. K. Douglass 6-4, 2-6, 9-7	**Miss M. E. Robb** Miss A. M. Morton 6-2, 6-4
Miss A. M. Morton Mrs G. Greville 7-5, 6-4	*Challenge Round*
	Miss M. E. Robb (C) Mrs A. Sterry (H) 7-5, 6-1*
1903	**1903**
Miss D. K. Douglass Miss T. Lowther 6-4, 6-3	**Miss D. K. Douglass** Miss E. W. Thomson 4-6, 6-4, 6-2
Miss E. W. Thomson Miss A. N. G. Greene 6-3, 6-1	*Challenge Round*
	Miss D. K. Douglass (C) a bye Miss M. E. Robb (H) retired
1904	**1904**
Mrs A. Sterry Miss A. N. G. Greene 6-2, 6-1	**Mrs A. Sterry** Miss A. M. Morton 6-3, 6-3
Miss A. M. Morton Miss C. M. Wilson 3-6, 6-4, 8-6	*Challenge Round*
	Miss D. K. Douglass (H) Mrs A. Sterry (C) 6-0, 6-3
1905	**1905**
Miss M. G. Sutton Miss A. M. Morton 6-4, 6-0	**Miss M. G. Sutton** Miss C. M. Wilson 6-3, 8-6
Miss C. M. Wilson Mrs G. W. Hillyard 7-5, 9-11, 6-2	*Challenge Round*
	Miss M. G. Sutton (C) Miss D. K. Douglass (H) 6-3, 6-4
1906	**1906**
Miss D. K. Douglass Miss B. Tulloch 6-2, 6-2	**Miss D. K. Douglass** Mrs A. Sterry 6-2, 6-2
Mrs A. Sterry Miss T. Lowther 4-6, 8-6, 6-4	*Challenge Round*
	Miss D. K. Douglass (C) Miss M. G. Sutton (H) 6-3, 9-7
1907	**1907**
Miss M. G. Sutton Miss L. Bosworth 6-2, 6-2	**Miss M. G. Sutton** Miss C. M. Wilson 6-4, 6-2
Miss C. M. Wilson Mrs G. W. Hillyard 6-3, 6-2	*Challenge Round*
	Miss M. G. Sutton (C) Mrs Lambert Chambers (H) 6-1, 6-4
1908	**1908**
Mrs A. Sterry Miss D. P. Boothby 6-2, 6-4	**Mrs A. Sterry** Miss A. M. Morton 6-4, 6-4
Miss A. M. Morton Mrs Lamplough 6-3, 6-4	*Challenge Round*
	Mrs A. Sterry (C) a bye Miss M. G. Sutton (H) retired
1909	**1909**
Miss A. M. Morton Mrs H. Edgington 6-0, 6-2	**Miss D. P. Boothby** Miss A. M. Morton 6-4, 4-6, 8-6
Miss D. P. Boothby Miss H. M. Garfit 6-2, 6-1	*Challenge Round*
	Miss D. P. Boothby (C) a bye Mrs A. Sterry (H) retired
1910	**1910**
Miss E. G. Johnson Mrs Lamplough 1-6, 6-0, 6-3	**Mrs Lambert Chambers** Miss E. G. Johnson 6-4, 6-2
Mrs Lambert Chambers Mrs R. J. McNair 6-1, 6-0	*Challenge Round*
	Mrs Lambert Chambers (C) Miss D. P. Boothby (H) 6-2, 6-2

360   Winners in **bold type**; **(H)**/(H) holder; **(C)**/(C) challenger; w.o. walk-over; *(1902) match replayed after overnight score of 4-6, 13-11

Women's Singles

Semi-Finals

1911
Mrs Hannam   Miss H. Aitchison   6-3, 6-8, 7-5
Miss D. P. Boothby   Mrs Parton   6-3, 6-4

1912
Mrs A. Sterry   Miss E. D. Holman   6-3, 4-6, 7-5
Mrs D. R. Larcombe   Mrs G. W. Hillyard   6-1, 6-0

1913
Mrs R. J. McNair   Miss E. D. Holman   2-6, 6-2, 7-5
Mrs Lambert Chambers   Miss H. Aitchison   6-2, 6-3

1914
Mrs D. R. Larcombe   Mrs H. Edgington   6-4, 6-3
Miss E. Ryan   Miss H. Aitchison   6-4, 6-3

1915-18   *No Competition*
1919
Mrs P. Satterthwaite   Mrs A. E. Beamish   6-4, 10-8
Miss S. Lenglen   Miss E. Ryan   6-4, 7-5

1920
Miss E. Ryan   Mrs Parton   6-4, 6-3
Mrs Lambert Chambers   Mrs M. Mallory   6-0, 6-3

1921
Mrs P. Satterthwaite   Mrs R. C. Clayton   8-6, 6-2
Miss E. Ryan   Mrs I. E. Peacock   8-6, 6-4

1922
Miss S. Lenglen   Mrs I. E. Peacock   6-4, 6-1
Mrs M. Mallory   Mrs A. E. Beamish   6-2, 6-2
1923
Miss S. Lenglen   Mrs A. E. Beamish   6-0, 6-0
Miss K. McKane   Miss E. Ryan   1-6, 6-2, 6-4
1924
Miss H. Wills   Mrs P. Satterthwaite   6-2, 6-1
Miss K. McKane   a bye   Miss S. Lenglen   retired
1925
Miss S. Lenglen   Miss K. McKane   6-0, 6-0
Miss J. Fry   Mrs Billout   6-2, 4-6, 6-3
1926
Miss L. de Alvarez   Mrs M. Mallory   6-2, 6-2
Mrs L. A. Godfree   Miss D. Vlasto   6-4, 6-0
1927†
Miss L. de Alvarez[2]   Miss E. Ryan[5]   2-6, 6-0, 6-4
Miss H. Wills[1]   Miss J. Fry   6-3, 6-1
1928
Miss H. Wills[1]   Miss E. Ryan[4]   6-1, 6-1
Miss L. de Alvarez[2]   Miss D. Akhurst   6-3, 6-0
1929
Miss H. Wills[1]   Miss E. A. Goldsack   6-2, 6-0
Miss H. H. Jacobs[8]   Miss J. C. Ridley   6-2, 6-2
1930
Mrs F. S. Moody[1]   Mrs R. Mathieu[5]   6-3, 6-2
Miss E. Ryan[3]   Miss C. Aussem[6]   6-3, 0-6, 4-4 retired
1931
Miss C. Aussem[1]   Mrs R. Mathieu[3]   6-0, 2-6, 6-3
Miss H. Krawinkel[4]   Miss H. H. Jacobs[5]   10-8, 0-6, 6-4
1932
Mrs F. S. Moody[1]   Miss M. Heeley   6-2, 6-0
Miss H. H. Jacobs[5]   Mrs R. Mathieu[3]   7-5, 6-1
1933
Miss D. E. Round[2]   Miss H. H. Jacobs[5]   4-6, 6-4, 6-2
Mrs F. S. Moody[1]   Miss H. Krawinkel[6]   6-4, 6-3
1934
Miss D. E. Round[2]   Mrs R. Mathieu[8]   6-4, 5-7, 6-2
Miss H. H. Jacobs[5]   Miss J. Hartigan   6-2, 6-2
1935
Mrs F. S. Moody[4]   Miss J. Hartigan[8]   6-3, 6-3
Miss H. H. Jacobs[3]   Mrs S. Sperling[2]   6-3, 6-0
1936
Miss H. H. Jacobs[1]   Miss J. Jedrzejowska[7]   6-4, 6-2
Mrs S. Sperling[5]   Mrs R. Mathieu[6]   6-3, 6-2
1937
Miss J. Jedrzejowska[4]   Miss A. Marble[5]   8-6, 6-2
Miss D. E. Round[7]   Mrs R. Mathieu[6]   6-4, 6-0
1938
Miss H. H. Jacobs   Miss A. Marble[2]   6-4, 6-4
Mrs F. S. Moody[1]   Mrs S. Sperling[4]   12-10, 6-4
1939
Miss K. E. Stammers[6]   Mrs S. P. Fabyan[8]   7-5, 2-6, 6-3
Miss A. Marble[1]   Mrs S. Sperling[3]   6-0, 6-0
1940-45 *No Competition*
1946
Miss P. M. Betz[1]   Miss D. Bundy[5]   6-2, 6-3
Miss A. L. Brough[3]   Miss M. E. Osborne[2]   8-6, 7-5
1947
Miss D. J. Hart[3]   Miss A. L. Brough[2]   2-6, 8-6, 6-4
Miss M. E. Osborne[1]   Mrs S. P. Summers[7]   6-1, 6-2
1948
Miss D. J. Hart[4]   Mrs W. duPont[1]   6-4, 2-6, 6-3
Miss A. L. Brough[2]   Mrs P. C. Todd[3]   6-3, 7-5
1949
Miss A. L. Brough[1]   Mrs P. C. Todd[3]   6-3, 6-0
Mrs W. duPont[2]   Mrs H. P. Rihbany   6-2, 6-2
1950
Miss A. L. Brough[1]   Miss D. J. Hart[3]   6-4, 6-3
Mrs W. duPont[2]   Mrs P. C. Todd[5]   8-6, 4-6, 8-6
1951
Miss D. J. Hart[3]   Miss B. Baker[5]   6-3, 6-1
Miss S. J. Fry[4]   Miss A. L. Brough[1]   6-4, 6-2
1952
Miss M. Connolly[2]   Miss S. J. Fry[3]   6-4, 6-3
Miss A. L. Brough[4]   Mrs P. C. Todd[5]   6-3, 3-6, 6-1

Finals

1911
Miss D. P. Boothby   Mrs Hannam   6-2, 7-5
Challenge Round
Mrs Lambert Chambers (H)   Miss D. P. Boothby (C)   6-0, 6-0
1912
Mrs D. R. Larcombe   Mrs A. Sterry   6-3, 6-1
Challenge Round
Mrs D. R. Larcombe (C) a bye Mrs Lambert Chambers (H) retired
1913
Mrs Lambert Chambers   Mrs R. J. McNair   6-0, 6-4
Challenge Round
Mrs Lambert Chambers (C) a bye Mrs D. R. Larcombe (H) retired
1914
Mrs D. R. Larcombe   Miss E. Ryan   6-3, 6-2
Challenge Round
Mrs Lambert Chambers (H)   Mrs D. R. Larcombe (C)   7-5, 6-4
1915-18   *No Competition*
1919
Miss S. Lenglen   Mrs P. Satterthwaite   6-1, 6-1
Challenge Round
Miss S. Lenglen (C) Mrs Lambert Chambers (H) 10-8, 4-6, 9-7
1920
Mrs Lambert Chambers   Miss E. Ryan   6-2, 6-1
Challenge Round
Miss S. Lenglen (H)   Mrs Lambert Chambers (C)   6-3, 6-0
1921
Miss E. Ryan   Mrs P. Satterthwaite   6-1, 6-0
Challenge Round
Miss S. Lenglen (H)   Miss E. Ryan (C)   6-2, 6-0
1922   *Challenge Round Abolished*
Miss S. Lenglen   Mrs M. Mallory   6-2, 6-0

1923
Miss S. Lenglen   Miss K. McKane   6-2, 6-2

1924
Miss K. McKane   Miss H. Wills   4-6, 6-4, 6-4

1925
Miss S. Lenglen   Miss J. Fry   6-2, 6-0

1926
Mrs L. A. Godfree   Miss L. de Alvarez   6-2, 4-6, 6-3

1927†
Miss H. Wills[1]   Miss L. de Alvarez[4]   6-2, 6-4

1928
Miss H. Wills[1]   Miss L. de Alvarez[2]   6-2, 6-3

1929
Miss H. Wills[1]   Miss H. H. Jacobs[5]   6-1, 6-2

1930
Mrs F. S. Moody[1]   Miss E. Ryan[8]   6-2, 6-2

1931
Miss C. Aussem[1]   Miss H. Krawinkel[4]   6-2, 7-5

1932
Mrs F. S. Moody[1]   Miss H. H. Jacobs[5]   6-3, 6-1

1933
Mrs F. S. Moody[1]   Miss D. E. Round[2]   6-4, 6-8, 6-3

1934
Miss D. E. Round[2]   Miss H. H. Jacobs[1]   6-2, 5-7, 6-3

1935
Mrs F. S. Moody[4]   Miss H. H. Jacobs[3]   6-3, 3-6, 7-5

1936
Miss H. H. Jacobs[2]   Mrs S. Sperling[5]   6-2, 4-6, 7-5

1937
Miss D. E. Round[7]   Miss J. Jedrzejowska[4]   6-2, 2-6, 7-5

1938
Mrs F. S. Moody[1]   Miss H. H. Jacobs   6-4, 6-0

1939
Miss A. Marble[1]   Miss K. E. Stammers[6]   6-2, 6-0

1940-45   *No Competition*
1946
Miss P. M. Betz[1]   Miss A. L. Brough[3]   6-2, 6-4

1947
Miss M. E. Osborne[1]   Miss D. J. Hart[3]   6-2, 6-4

1948
Miss A. L. Brough[2]   Miss D. J. Hart[4]   6-3, 8-6

1949
Miss A. L. Brough[1]   Mrs W. duPont[2]   10-8, 1-6, 10-8

1950
Miss A. L. Brough[1]   Mrs W. duPont[2]   6-1, 3-6, 6-1

1951
Miss D. J. Hart[3]   Miss S. J. Fry[4]   6-1, 6-0

1952
Miss M. Connolly[2]   Miss A. L. Brough[4]   7-5, 6-3

Women's Doubles

Finals

1913   *Full Championship event began*
Mrs R. J. McNair/Miss D. P. Boothby
Mrs A. Sterry/Mrs Lambert Chambers   4-6, 2-4 retired
1914
Miss E. Ryan/Miss A. M. Morton
Mrs D. R. Larcombe/Mrs Hannam   6-1, 6-3
1915-18   *No Competition*
1919
Miss S. Lenglen/Miss E. Ryan
Mrs Lambert Chambers/Mrs D. R. Larcombe   4-6, 7-5, 6-3
1920
Miss S. Lenglen/Miss E. Ryan
Mrs Lambert Chambers/Mrs D. R. Larcombe   6-4, 6-0
1921
Miss S. Lenglen/Miss E. Ryan
Mrs A. E. Beamish/Mrs I. E. Peacock   6-1, 6-2
1922
Miss S. Lenglen/Miss E. Ryan
Mrs A. D. Stocks/Miss K. McKane   6-0, 6-4
1923
Miss S. Lenglen/Miss E. Ryan
Miss J. Austin/Miss E. L. Colyer   6-3, 6-1
1924
Mrs G. W. Wightman/Miss H. Wills
Mrs B. C. Covell/Miss K. McKane   6-4, 6-4
1925
Miss S. Lenglen/Miss E. Ryan
Mrs A. V. Bridge/Mrs C. G. McIlquham   6-2, 6-2
1926
Miss E. Ryan/Miss M. K. Browne
Mrs L. A. Godfree/Miss E. L. Colyer   6-1, 6-1
1927
Miss H. Wills/Miss E. Ryan
Miss E. L. Heine/Mrs I. E. Peacock   6-3, 6-2
1928
Mrs Holcroft-Watson/Miss P. Saunders
Miss E. H. Harvey/Miss E. B. Bennett   6-2, 6-3
1929
Mrs Holcroft-Watson/Mrs L. R. C. Michell
Mrs B. C. Covell/Mrs D. C. Shepherd-Barron   6-4, 8-6
1930
Mrs F. S. Moody/Miss E. Ryan
Miss E. Cross/Miss S. Palfrey   6-2, 9-7
1931
Mrs D. C. Shepherd-Barron/Miss P. E. Mudford
Miss D. Metaxa/Miss J. Sigart   3-6, 6-3, 6-4
1932
Miss D. Metaxa/Miss J. Sigart
Miss E. Ryan/Miss H. H. Jacobs   6-4, 6-3
1933
Mrs R. Mathieu/Miss E. Ryan
Miss F. James/Miss A. M. Yorke   6-2, 9-11, 6-4
1934
Mrs R. Mathieu/Miss E. Ryan
Mrs D. Andrus/Mrs S. Henrotin   6-3, 6-3
1935
Miss F. James/Miss K. E. Stammers
Mrs R. Mathieu/Mrs S. Sperling   6-1, 6-4
1936
Miss F. James/Miss K. E. Stammers
Mrs S. P. Fabyan/Miss H. H. Jacobs   6-2, 6-1
1937
Mrs R. Mathieu/Miss A. M. Yorke
Mrs M. R. King/Mrs J. B. Pittman   6-3, 6-3
1938
Mrs S. P. Fabyan/Miss A. Marble
Mrs R. Mathieu/Miss A. M. Yorke   6-2, 6-3
1939
Mrs S. P. Fabyan/Miss A. Marble
Miss H. H. Jacobs/Miss A. M. Yorke   6-1, 6-0
1940-45   *No Competition*
1946
Miss A. L. Brough/Miss M. E. Osborne
Miss P. M. Betz/Miss D. J. Hart   6-3, 2-6, 6-3
1947
Miss D. J. Hart/Mrs P. C. Todd
Miss A. L. Brough/Miss M. E. Osborne   3-6, 6-4, 7-5
1948
Miss A. L. Brough/Mrs W. duPont
Miss D. J. Hart/Mrs P. C. Todd   6-3, 3-6, 6-3
1949
Miss A. L. Brough/Mrs W. duPont
Miss G. Moran/Mrs P. C. Todd   8-6, 7-5
1950
Miss A. L. Brough/Mrs W. duPont
Miss S. J. Fry/Miss D. J. Hart   6-4, 5-7, 6-1
1951
Miss S. J. Fry/Miss D. J. Hart
Miss A. L. Brough/Mrs W. duPont   6-3, 13-11
1952
Miss S. J. Fry/Miss D. J. Hart
Miss A. L. Brough/Miss M. Connolly   8-6, 6-3

Winners in **bold type**; **(H)**/(H) holder; **(C)**/(C) challenger; † full seeding (indicated by numbers in brackets) introduced 1927

Wimbledon Championships

Women's Singles

Semi-Finals

1953
Miss D. J. Hart[2]   Mrs D. P. Knode[4]   6-2, 6-2
Miss M. Connolly[1]   Miss S. J. Fry[3]   6-1, 6-1
1954
Miss A. L. Brough[4]   Miss D. J. Hart[2]   2-6, 6-3, 6-3
Miss M. Connolly[1]   Mrs C. Pratt[8]   6-1, 6-1
1955
Mrs J. G. Fleitz[3]   Miss D. J. Hart[2]   6-3, 6-0
Miss A. L. Brough[2]   Miss D. R. Hard[6]   6-3, 8-6
1956
Miss A. Buxton[6]   Miss P. E. Ward   6-1, 6-4
Miss S. J. Fry[5]   Miss A. L. Brough[1]   6-4, 4-6, 6-3
1957
Miss D. R. Hard[5]   Mrs D. P. Knode[4]   6-2, 6-3
Miss A. Gibson[1]   Miss C. C. Truman   6-1, 6-1
1958
Miss A. Mortimer   Mrs Z. Körmöczy[6]   6-0, 6-1
Miss A. Gibson[1]   Miss A. S. Haydon   6-2, 6-0
1959
Miss D. R. Hard[4]   Miss S. Reynolds[5]   6-4, 6-4
Miss M. E. Bueno[6]   Miss S. M. Moore[7]   6-2, 6-4
1960
Miss M. E. Bueno[1]   Miss C. C. Truman[3]   6-0, 5-7, 6-1
Miss S. Reynolds[8]   Miss A. S. Haydon[4]   6-3, 2-6, 6-4
1961
Miss C. C. Truman[6]   Miss R. Schuurman   6-4, 6-4
Miss A. Mortimer[7]   Miss S. Reynolds[1]   11-9, 6-3
1962
Mrs J. R. Susman[8]   Miss A. S. Haydon[5]   8-6, 6-1
Mrs V. Suková   Miss M. E. Bueno[3]   6-4, 6-3
1963
Miss M. Smith[1]   Miss D. R. Hard[4]   6-3, 6-3
Miss B. J. Moffitt   Mrs P. F. Jones[3]   6-4, 6-4
1964
Miss M. Smith[1]   Miss B. J. Moffitt[3]   6-3, 6-4
Miss M. E. Bueno[2]   Miss L. R. Turner[4]   3-6, 6-4, 6-4
1965
Miss M. E. Bueno[1]   Miss B. J. Moffitt[5]   6-4, 5-7, 6-3
Miss M. Smith[2]   Miss C. C. Truman   6-4, 6-0
1966
Mrs L. W. King[4]   Miss M. Smith[1]   6-3, 6-3
Miss M. E. Bueno[2]   Mrs P. F. Jones[1]   6-3, 9-11, 7-5
1967
Mrs L. W. King[1]   Miss K. M. Harter   6-0, 6-3
Mrs P. F. Jones[2]   Miss R. Casals   2-6, 6-3, 7-5
1968   *Open Championships began*
Mrs L. W. King[1]*   Mrs P. F. Jones[4]*   4-6, 7-5, 6-2
Miss J. A. M. Tegart[7]   Miss N. Richey   6-3, 6-1
1969
Mrs P. F. Jones[4]*   Mrs B. M. Court[1]   10-12, 6-3, 6-2
Mrs L. W. King[2]*   Miss R. Casals   6-1, 6-0
1970
Mrs B. M. Court[1]   Miss R. Casals[5]   6-4, 6-1
Mrs L. W. King[2]   Miss F. Durr   6-3, 7-5
1971
Mrs B. M. Court[1]   Mrs D. E. Dalton   4-6, 6-1, 6-0
Miss E. F. Goolagong[3]   Mrs L. W. King[2]   6-4, 6-4
1972
Miss E. F. Goolagong[1]   Miss C. Evert[4]   4-6, 6-3, 6-4
Mrs L. W. King[2]   Miss R. Casals[6]   6-2, 6-4
1973
Mrs L. W. King[2]*   Miss E. F. Goolagong[3]   6-3, 5-7, 6-3
Miss C. Evert[4]   Mrs. B. M. Court[1]   6-1, 1-6, 6-1

Finals

1953
Miss M. Connolly[1]   Miss D. J. Hart[2]   8-6, 7-5
1954
Miss M. Connolly[1]   Miss A. L. Brough[4]   6-2, 7-5
1955
Miss A. L. Brough[2]   Mrs J. G. Fleitz[3]   7-5, 8-6
1956
Miss S. J. Fry[5]   Miss A. Buxton[6]   6-3, 6-1
1957
Miss A. Gibson[1]   Miss D. R. Hard[5]   6-3, 6-2
1958
Miss A. Gibson[1]   Miss A. Mortimer   8-6, 6-2
1959
Miss M. E. Bueno[6]   Miss D. R. Hard[4]   6-4, 6-3
1960
Miss M. E. Bueno[1]   Miss S. Reynolds[8]   8-6, 6-0
1961
Miss A. Mortimer[7]   Miss C. C. Truman[6]   4-6, 6-4, 7-5
1962
Mrs J. R. Susman[8]   Mrs V. Suková   6-4, 6-4
1963
Miss M. Smith[1]   Miss B. J. Moffitt   6-3, 6-4
1964
Miss M. E. Bueno[2]   Miss M. Smith[1]   6-4, 7-9, 6-3
1965
Miss M. Smith[2]   Miss M. E. Bueno[1]   6-4, 7-5
1966
Mrs L. W. King[4]   Miss M. E. Bueno[2]   6-3, 3-6, 6-1
1967
Mrs L. W. King[1]   Mrs P. F. Jones[3]   6-3, 6-4
1968   *Open Championships began*
Mrs L. W. King[1]*   Miss J. A. M. Tegart[7]   9-7, 7-5
1969
Mrs P. F. Jones[4]*   Mrs L. W. King[2]*   3-6, 6-3, 6-2
1970
Mrs B. M. Court[1]   Mrs L. W. King[2]   14-12, 11-9
1971
Miss E. F. Goolagong[3]   Mrs B. M. Court[1]   6-4, 6-1
1972
Mrs L. W. King[2]   Miss E. F. Goolagong[1]   6-3, 6-3
1973
Mrs L. W. King[2]   Miss C. Evert[4]   6-0, 7-5

Women's Doubles

Finals

1953
Miss S. J. Fry/Miss D. J. Hart
Miss M. Connolly/Miss J. Sampson   6-0, 6-0
1954
Miss A. L. Brough/Mrs W. duPont
Miss S. J. Fry/Miss D. J. Hart   4-6, 9-7, 6-3
1955
Miss A. Mortimer/Miss J. A. Shilcock
Miss S. J. Bloomer/Miss P. E. Ward   7-5, 6-1
1956
Miss A. Buxton/Miss A. Gibson
Miss F. Muller/Miss D. G. Seeney   6-1, 8-6
1957
Miss A. Gibson/Miss D. R. Hard
Mrs K. Hawton/Mrs T. D. Long   6-1, 6-2
1958
Miss M. E. Bueno/Miss A. Gibson
Mrs W. duPont/Miss M. Varner   6-3, 7-5
1959
Miss J. Arth/Miss D. R. Hard
Mrs J. G. Fleitz/Miss C. C. Truman   2-6, 6-2, 6-3
1960
Miss M. E. Bueno/Miss D. R. Hard
Miss S. Reynolds/Miss R. Schuurman   6-4, 6-0
1961
Miss K. Hantze/Miss B. J. Moffitt
Miss J. Lehane/Miss M. Smith   6-3, 6-4
1962
Miss B. J. Moffitt/Mrs J. R. Susman
Mrs L. E. G. Price/Miss R. Schuurman   5-7, 6-3, 7-5
1963
Miss M. E. Bueno/Miss D. R. Hard
Miss R. A. Ebbern/Miss M. Smith   8-6, 9-7
1964
Miss M. Smith/Miss L. R. Turner
Miss B. J. Moffitt/Mrs J. R. Susman   7-5, 6-2
1965
Miss M. E. Bueno/Miss B. J. Moffitt
Miss F. Durr/Miss J. Lieffrig   6-2, 7-5
1966
Miss M. E. Bueno/Miss N. Richey
Miss M. Smith/Miss J. A. M. Tegart   6-3, 4-6, 6-4
1967
Miss R. Casals/Mrs L. W. King
Miss M. E. Bueno/Miss N. Richey   9-11, 6-4, 6-2
1968   *Open Championships began*
Miss R. Casals/Mrs L. W. King
Miss F. Durr/Mrs P. F. Jones   3-6, 6-4, 7-5
1969
Mrs B. M. Court/Miss J. A. M. Tegart
Miss P. S. A. Hogan/Miss M. Michel   9-7, 6-2
1970
Miss R. Casals/Mrs L. W. King
Miss F. Durr/Miss S. V. Wade   6-2, 6-3
1971
Miss R. Casals/Mrs L. W. King
Mrs B. M. Court/Miss E. F. Goolagong   6-3, 6-2
1972
Mrs L. W. King/Miss B. F. Stöve
Mrs D. E. Dalton/Miss F. Durr   6-2, 4-6, 6-3
1973
Miss R. Casals/Mrs L. W. King
Miss F. Durr/Miss B. F. Stöve   6-1, 4-6, 7-5

Mixed Doubles

Finals

1913 *Full Championship event began*
H. Crisp/Mrs C. O. Tuckey
J. C. Parke/Mrs D. R. Larcombe   3-6, 5-3   retired
1914
J. C. Parke/Mrs D. R. Larcombe
A. F. Wilding/Miss M. Broquedis   4-6, 6-4, 6-2
1915-18 *No Competition*
1919
R. Lycett/Miss E. Ryan
A. D. Prebble/Mrs Lambert Chambers   6-0, 6-0
1920
G. L. Patterson/Miss S. Lenglen
R. Lycett/Miss E. Ryan   7-5, 6-3
1921
R. Lycett/Miss E. Ryan
M. Woosnam/Miss P. L. Howkins   6-3, 6-1
1922
P. O'Hara Wood/Miss S. Lenglen
R. Lycett/Miss E. Ryan   6-4, 6-3
1923
R. Lycett/Miss E. Ryan
L. S. Deane/Mrs D. C. Shepherd-Barron   6-4, 7-5
1924
J. B. Gilbert/Miss K. McKane
L. A. Godfree/Mrs D. C. Shepherd-Barron   6-3, 3-6, 6-3
1925
J. Borotra/Miss S. Lenglen
H. L. de Morpurgo/Miss E. Ryan   6-3, 6-3
1926
L. A. Godfree/Mrs L. A. Godfree
H. O. Kinsey/Miss M. K. Browne   6-3, 6-4
1927
F. T. Hunter/Miss E. Ryan
L. A. Godfree/Mrs L. A. Godfree   8-6, 6-0
1928
P. D. B. Spence/Miss E. Ryan
J. H. Crawford/Miss D. Akhurst   7-5, 6-4
1929
F. T. Hunter/Miss H. Wills
I. G. Collins/Miss J. Fry   6-1, 6-4
1930
J. H. Crawford/Miss E. Ryan
D. Prenn/Miss H. Krahwinkel   6-1, 6-3
1931
G. M. Lott/Mrs L. A. Harper
I. G. Collins/Miss J. C. Ridley   6-3, 1-6, 6-1
1932
E. Maier/Miss E. Ryan
H. C. Hopman/Miss J. Sigart   7-5, 6-2
1933
G. von Cramm/Miss H. Krahwinkel
N. G. Farquharson/Miss M. Heeley   7-5, 8-6
1934
R. Miki/Miss D. E. Round
H. W. Austin/Mrs D. C. Shepherd-Barron   3-6, 6-4, 6-0
1935
F. J. Perry/Miss D. E. Round
H. C. Hopman/Mrs H. C. Hopman   7-5, 4-6, 6-2
1936
F. J. Perry/Miss D. E. Round
J. D. Budge/Mrs S. P. Fabyan   7-9, 7-5, 6-4
1937
J. D. Budge/Miss A. Marble
Y. Petra/Mrs R. Mathieu   6-4, 6-1
1938
J. D. Budge/Miss A. Marble
H. Henkel/Mrs S. P. Fabyan   6-1, 6-4
1939
R. L. Riggs/Miss A. Marble
F. H. D. Wilde/Miss N. B. Brown   9-7, 6-1
1940-45 *No Competition*
1946
T. Brown/Miss A. L. Brough
G. E. Brown/Miss D. Bundy   6-4, 6-4
1947
J. E. Bromwich/Miss A. L. Brough
C. F. Long/Mrs N. M. Bolton   1-6, 6-4, 6-2
1948
J. E. Bromwich/Miss A. L. Brough
F. A. Sedgman/Miss D. J. Hart   6-2, 3-6, 6-3
1949
E. W. Sturgess/Mrs S. P. Summers
J. E. Bromwich/Miss A. L. Brough   9-7, 9-11, 7-5
1950
E. W. Sturgess/Miss A. L. Brough
G. E. Brown/Mrs P. C. Todd   11-9, 1-6, 6-4
1951
F. A. Sedgman/Miss D. J. Hart
M. G. Rose/Mrs N. M. Bolton   7-5, 6-2
1952
F. A. Sedgman/Miss D. J. Hart
E. Morea/Mrs T. D. Long   4-6, 6-3, 6-4
1953
E. V. Seixas/Miss D. J. Hart
E. Morea/Miss S. J. Fry   9-7, 7-5
1954
E. V. Seixas/Miss D. J. Hart
K. R. Rosewall/Mrs W. duPont   5-7, 6-4, 6-3
1955
E. V. Seixas/Miss D. J. Hart
E. Morea/Miss A. L. Brough   8-6, 2-6, 6-3
1956
E. V. Seixas/Miss S. J. Fry
G. Mulloy/Miss A. Gibson   2-6, 6-2, 7-5
1957
M. G. Rose/Miss D. R. Hard
N. A. Fraser/Miss A. Gibson   6-4, 7-5

Finals

1958
R. N. Howe/Miss L. Coghlan
K. Nielsen/Miss A. Gibson   6-3, 13-11
1959
R. G. Laver/Miss D. R. Hard
N. A. Fraser/Miss M. E. Bueno   6-4, 6-3
1960
R. G. Laver/Miss D. R. Hard
R. N. Howe/Miss M. E. Bueno   13-11, 3-6, 8-6
1961
F. S. Stolle/Miss L. R. Turner
R. N. Howe/Miss E. Buding   11-9, 6-2
1962
N. A. Fraser/Mrs W. duPont
R. D. Ralston/Miss A. S. Haydon   2-6, 6-3, 13-11
1963
K. N. Fletcher/Miss M. Smith
R. A. J. Hewitt/Miss D. R. Hard   11-9, 6-4
1964
F. S. Stolle/Miss L. R. Turner
K. N. Fletcher/Miss M. Smith   6-4, 6-4
1965
K. N. Fletcher/Miss M. Smith
A. D. Roche/Miss J. A. M. Tegart   12-10, 6-3
1966
K. N. Fletcher/Miss M. Smith
R. D. Ralston/Mrs L. W. King   4-6, 6-3, 6-3
1967
O. K. Davidson/Mrs L. W. King
K. N. Fletcher/Miss M. E. Bueno   7-5, 6-2
1968 *Open Championships began*
K. N. Fletcher/Mrs B. M. Court
A. Metreveli/Miss O. Morozova   6-1, 14-12
1969
F. S. Stolle/Mrs P. F. Jones
A. D. Roche/Miss J. A. M. Tegart   6-2, 6-3
1970
I. Năstase/Miss R. Casals
A. Metreveli/Miss O. Morozova   6-3, 4-6, 9-7
1971
O. K. Davidson/Mrs L. W. King
M. C. Riessen/Mrs B. M. Court   3-6, 6-2, 15-13
1972
I. Năstase/Miss R. Casals
K. G. Warwick/Miss E. F. Goolagong   6-4, 6-4
1973
O. K. Davidson/Mrs L. W. King
R. Ramirez/Miss J. S. Newberry   6-3, 6-2

United States Championships

Men's Singles

Semi-Finals

1881 *Played in Newport, R.I.*
R. D. Sears Gray 6-3, 6-0
W. E. Glyn Shaw 6-2, 6-2
1882
R. D. Sears a bye
C. M. Clark Gray 6-3, 6-2
1883
R. D. Sears F. Keene 6-0, 6-0
J. Dwight R. F. Conover 6-4, 6-3
1884
H. A. Taylor W. P. Knapp 6-2, 2-6, 6-1
W. V. S. Thorne C. M. Clarke 2-6, 6-2, 6-3
1885
W. P. Knapp J. S. Clark 6-4, 6-3
G. M. Brinley W. V. R. Berry 3-6, 9-7, 6-1
1886
H. A. Taylor J. S. Clark 6-5, 6-2, 6-3
R. L. Beeckman C. A. Chase 6-4, 6-0, 6-2
1887
H. W. Slocum J. S. Clark 6-8, 6-4, 6-3, 6-3
H. A. Taylor W. L. Thacher 6-3, 6-1, 6-1
1888
H. W. Slocum O. S. Campbell 6-2, 6-3, 6-4
H. A. Taylor P. S. Sears 5-7, 6-4, 6-2, 6-2
1889
Q. A. Shaw W. P. Knapp 4-6, 6-1, 6-4, 6-4
O. S. Campbell E. G. Meers 5-7, 6-1, 5-7, 6-4, 6-2
1890
W. P. Knapp C. Hobart 10-8, 7-5, 6-2
O. S. Campbell R. P. Huntingdon 3-6, 6-2, 5-7, 6-2, 6-1
1891
C. Hobart V. G. Hall 6-2, 6-4, 6-2
F. H. Hovey M. D. Smith 6-4, 6-2, 3-6, 1-6, 6-4
1892
F. H. Hovey R. D. Wrenn 6-4, 7-5, 6-3
W. A. Larned E. L. Hall 2-6, 6-0, 6-4, 1-6, 8-6
1893
R. D. Wrenn S. T. Chase 8-6, 6-1, 6-2
F. H. Hovey C. Hobart 7-5, 6-0, 6-3
1894
M. F. Goodbody J. B. Read 3-6, 6-0, 6-0, 6-1
W. A. Larned M. G. Chace 6-4, 6-2, 8-6
1895
W. A. Larned R. S. Howland 7-5, 8-6, 6-1
F. H. Hovey C. B. Neel 6-4, 6-4, 6-4
1896
W. A. Larned E. P. Fischer 6-1, 6-2, 6-1
R. D. Wrenn C. B. Neel 2-6, 14-12, 4-6, 6-4, 6-1
1897
H. A. Nisbet W. A. Larned 3-6, 2-6, 9-7, 6-4, 6-4
W. V. Eaves L. E. Ware 6-0, 6-2, 6-4
1898
D. F. Davis W. S. Bond 6-1, 11-13, 6-4, 6-3
M. D. Whitman L. E. Ware 6-2, 6-0, 6-2
1899
J. P. Paret L. E. Ware 7-5, 6-2, 6-4
D. F. Davis K. Collins 6-4, 6-1, 8-6
1900
W. A. Larned B. C. Wright 11-9. 8-6, 1-6, 6-3
G. L. Wrenn A. W. Gore 9-7, 1-6, 0-6, 6-2, 6-2
1901
W. A. Larned L. E. Ware 6-3, 6-2, 6-2
B. C. Wright R. D. Little 7-5, 2-6, 6-1, 6-2
1902
R. F. Doherty H. L. Doherty w.o.
M. D. Whitman R. P. Huntington 10-8, 4-6, 6-1, 6-2
1903
H. L. Doherty R. H. Carleton 6-2, 6-0, 6-0
W. J. Clothier E. P. Larned 6-3, 6-1, 6-2
1904
W. J. Clothier W. A. Larned 6-4, 3-6, 2-6, 6-2, 6-3
H. Ward E. W. Leonard 6-3, 6-4, 6-4
1905
C. Hobart K. Collins 4-6, 6-4, 7-9, 6-4, 6-4
B. C. Wright W. A. Larned 4-6, 6-3, 6-2, 6-2
1906
K. H. Behr R. D. Little 2-6, 6-2, 6-8, 11-9, 6-4
W. J. Clothier J. D. E. Jones 6-3, 6-3, 6-3
1907
W. A. Larned C. Hobart 6-2, 6-2, 6-1
R. LeRoy I. Mollenhauer 4-6, 6-4, 1-6, 8-6, 6-0
1908
F. B. Alexander W. J. Clothier 7-5, 7-5, 6-3
B. C. Wright N. Emerson 6-2, 6-4, 5-7, 6-3
1909
W. J. Clothier T. C. Bundy 6-3, 6-3, 6-8, 7-5
M. E. McLoughlin G. F. Touchard 6-3, 4-6, 7-5, 6-2

Finals

1881 *Played in Newport, R.I.*
R. D. Sears W. E. Glyn 6-0, 6-3, 6-2
1882
R. D. Sears C. M. Clark 6-1, 6-4, 6-0
1883
R. D. Sears J. Dwight 6-2, 6-0, 9-7
1884 *Challenge Round began*
H. A. Taylor W. V. S. Thorne 6-4, 4-6, 6-1, 6-4
Challenge Round
R. D. Sears (H) H. A. Taylor (C) 6-0, 1-6, 6-0, 6-2
1885
G. M. Brinley W. P. Knapp 6-3, 6-3, 3-6, 6-4
Challenge Round
R. D. Sears (H) G. M. Brinley (C) 6-3, 4-6, 6-0, 6-3
1886
R. L. Beeckman H. A. Taylor 2-6, 6-3, 6-4, 6-2
Challenge Round
R. D. Sears (H) R. L. Beeckman (C) 4-6, 6-1, 6-3, 6-4
1887
H. W. Slocum H. A. Taylor 12-10, 7-5, 6-4
Challenge Round
R. D. Sears (H) H. W. Slocum (C) 6-1, 6-3, 6-2
1888
H. W. Slocum H. A. Taylor 6-4, 6-1, 6-0
Challenge Round w.o.
1889
Q. A. Shaw O. S. Campbell 1-6, 6-4, 6-3, 6-4
Challenge Round
H. W. Slocum (H) Q. A. Shaw (C) 6-3, 6-1, 4-6, 6-2
1890
O. S. Campbell W. P. Knapp 8-6, 0-6, 6-2, 6-3
Challenge Round
O. S. Campbell (C) H. W. Slocum (H) 6-2, 4-6, 6-3, 6-1
1891
C. Hobart F. H. Hovey 6-4, 3-6, 6-4, 6-8, 6-0
Challenge Round
O. S. Campbell (H) C. Hobart (C) 2-6, 7-5, 7-9, 6-1, 6-2
1892
F. H. Hovey W. A. Larned 6-0, 6-2, 7-5
Challenge Round
O. S. Campbell (H) F. H. Hovey (C) 7-5, 3-6, 6-3, 7-5
1893
R. D. Wrenn F. H. Hovey 6-4, 3-6, 6-4, 6-4
Challenge Round w.o.
1894
M. F. Goodbody W. A. Larned 4-6, 6-1, 3-6, 7-5, 6-2
Challenge Round
R. D. Wrenn (H) M. F. Goodbody (C) 6-8, 6-1, 6-4, 6-4
1895
F. H. Hovey W. A. Larned 6-1, 9-7, 6-4
Challenge Round
F. H. Hovey (C) R. D. Wrenn (H) 6-3, 6-2, 6-4
1896
R. D. Wrenn W. A. Larned 4-6, 3-6, 6-4, 6-4, 6-3
Challenge Round
R. D. Wrenn (C) F. H. Hovey (H) 7-5, 3-6, 6-0, 1-6, 6-1
1897
W. V. Eaves H. A. Nisbet 7-5, 6-3, 6-2
Challenge Round
R. D. Wrenn (H) W. V. Eaves (C) 4-6, 8-6, 6-3, 2-6, 6-2
1898
M. D. Whitman D. F. Davis 3-6, 6-2, 6-2, 6-1
Challenge Round w.o.
1899
J. P. Paret D. F. Davis 7-5, 8-10, 6-3, 2-6, 6-3
Challenge Round
M. D. Whitman (H) J. P. Paret (C) 6-1, 6-2, 3-6, 7-5
1900
W. A. Larned G. L. Wrenn 6-3, 6-2, 6-2
Challenge Round
M. D. Whitman (H) W. A. Larned (C) 6-4, 1-6, 6-2, 6-2
1901
W. A. Larned B. C. Wright 6-2, 6-8, 6-4, 6-4
Challenge Round w.o.
1902
R. F. Doherty M. D. Whitman 6-1, 3-6, 6-3, 6-0
Challenge Round
W. A. Larned (H) R. F. Doherty (C) 4-6, 6-2, 6-4, 8-6
1903
H. L. Doherty W. J. Clothier 6-3, 6-2, 6-3
Challenge Round
H. L. Doherty (C) W. A. Larned (H) 6-0, 6-3, 10-8
1904
H. Ward W. J. Clothier 10-8, 6-4, 9-7
Challenge Round w.o.
1905
B. C. Wright C. Hobart 6-4, 6-1, 6-3
Challenge Round
B. C. Wright (C) H. Ward (H) 6-1, 6-2, 11-9
1906
W. J. Clothier K. Behr 6-2, 6-4, 6-2
Challenge Round
W. J. Clothier (C) B. C. Wright (H) 6-3, 6-0, 6-4
1907
W. A. Larned R. LeRoy 6-2, 6-2, 6-4
Challenge Round w.o.
1908
B. C. Wright F. B. Alexander 6-3, 6-3, 6-3
Challenge Round
W. A. Larned (H) B. C. Wright (C) 6-1, 6-2, 8-6
1909
W. J. Clothier M. E. McLoughlin 7-5, 6-4, 9-11, 6-3
Challenge Round
W. A. Larned (H) W. J. Clothier (C) 6-1, 6-2, 5-7, 1-6, 6-1

Men's Doubles

Finals

1881 *Played in Newport, R.I.*
C. M. Clark/F. W. Taylor
A. Van Rensselaer/A. E. Newbold 6-5, 6-4, 6-5
1882
R. D. Sears/J. Dwight
W. Nightingale/G. M. Smith
1883
R. D. Sears/J. Dwight
A. Van Rensselaer/A. E. Newbold
1884
R. D. Sears/J. Dwight
A. Van Rensselaer/W. V. R. Berry
1885
R. D. Sears/J. S. Clark
H. W. Slocum/W. P. Knapp 6-3, 6-0, 6-2
1886
R. D. Sears/J. Dwight
H. A. Taylor/G. M. Brinley
1887
R. D. Sears/J. Dwight
H. A. Taylor/H. W. Slocum
1888
O. S. Campbell/V. G. Hall
C. Hobart/E. P. MacMullen
1889
H. W. Slocum/H. A. Taylor
V. G. Hall/O. S. Campbell
1890
V. G. Hall/C. Hobart
J. W. Carver/J. A. Ryerson
1891
O. S. Campbell/R. P. Huntington
V. G. Hall/C. Hobart
1892
O. S. Campbell/R. P. Huntington
V. G. Hall/E. L. Hall
1893
C. Hobart/F. H. Hovey
O. S. Campbell/R. P. Huntington
1894
C. Hobart/F. H. Hovey
C. B. Neel/S. R. Neel
1895
M. G. Chace/R. D. Wrenn
J. Howland/A. E. Foote
1896
C. B. Neel/S. R. Neel
R. D. Wrenn/M. G. Chace
1897
L. E. Ware/G. P. Sheldon
H. S. Mahony/H. A. Nisbet 11-13, 6-2, 9-7, 1-6, 6-1
1898
L. E. Ware/G. P. Sheldon
H. Ward/D. F. Davis 1-6, 7-5, 6-4, 4-6, 7-5
1899
H. Ward/D. F. Davis
L. E. Ware/G. P. Sheldon 6-4, 6-4, 6-3
1900
H. Ward/D. F. Davis
F. B. Alexander/R. D. Little 6-4, 9-7, 12-10
1901
H. Ward/D. F. Davis
I. E. Ware/B. C. Wright 6-3, 9-7, 6-1
1902
R. F. Doherty/H. L. Doherty
H. Ward/D. F. Davis 11-9, 12-10, 6-4
1903
R. F. Doherty/H. L. Doherty
K. Collins/L. H. Waidner 7-5, 6-3, 6-3
1904
H. Ward/B. C. Wright
K. Collins/R. D. Little
1905
H. Ward/B. C. Wright
F. B. Alexander/H. H. Hackett 6-3, 6-1, 6-2
1906
H. Ward/B. C. Wright
F. B. Alexander/H. H. Hackett 6-3, 3-6, 6-3, 6-3
1907
H. H. Hackett/F. B. Alexander
W. A. Larned/W. J. Clothier 6-3, 6-1, 6-4
1908
H. H. Hackett/F. B. Alexander
R. D. Little/B. C. Wright 6-1, 7-5, 6-2
1909
H. H. Hackett/F. B. Alexander
G. J. James/M. E. McLoughlin 6-4, 6-1, 6-0

Men's Singles

Men's Doubles

Semi-Finals

1910
B. C. Wright   E. H. Whitney   4-6, 7-5, 4-6, 6-2, 7-5
T. C. Bundy   F. C. Colston   6-8, 6-1, 6-3, 6-3

1911
M. E. McLoughlin   G. F. Touchard   6-2, 6-4, 6-3
B. C. Wright   T. C. Bundy   6-4, 6-3, 6-1

1912
M. E. McLoughlin   W. J. Clothier   8-6, 6-2, 3-6, 6-4
W. F. Johnson   K. Behr   4-6, 6-0, 6-3, 6-2

1913
M. E. McLoughlin   W. F. Johnson   6-0, 7-5, 6-1
R. N. Williams   N. W. Niles   6-4, 7-5, 3-6, 6-1

1914
R. N. Williams   E. F. Fottrell   6-4, 6-3, 6-2
M. E. McLoughlin   W. J. Clothier   6-4, 6-4, 6-3

1915
W. M. Johnston   R. N. Williams   5-7, 6-4, 5-7, 6-2, 6-2
M. E. McLoughlin   T. R. Pell   6-2, 6-0, 7-5

1916
R. N. Williams   C. J. Griffin   6-3, 6-3, 6-3
W. M. Johnston   R. L. Murray   6-2, 6-3, 6-1

1917 *National Patriotic Tournament*
R. L. Murray   J. R. Strachan   4-6, 6-3, 6-3, 6-1
N. W. Niles   R. N. Williams   6-2, 4-6, 6-4, 6-3

1918
R. L. Murray   S. H. Voshell   6-4, 6-3, 8-6
W. T. Tilden   I. Kumagai   6-2, 6-2, 6-0

1919
W. M. Johnston   W. F. Johnson   2-6, 6-1, 6-3, 6-3
W. T. Tilden   R. N. Williams   6-1, 7-5, 6-3

1920
W. T. Tilden   W. F. Johnson   14-12, 6-4, 6-4
W. M. Johnston   G. C. Caner   6-3, 4-6, 8-6, 6-4

1921
W. T. Tilden   W. E. Davis   10-8, 6-2, 6-1
W. F. Johnson   J. O. Anderson   6-4, 3-6, 8-6, 6-3

1922
W. T. Tilden   G. L. Patterson   4-6, 6-4, 6-3, 6-1
W. M. Johnston   V. Richards   8-6, 6-2, 6-1

1923
W. T. Tilden   B. I. C. Norton   6-3, 7-5, 6-2
W. M. Johnston   F. T. Hunter   6-4, 6-2, 7-5

1924
W. T. Tilden   V. Richards   4-6, 6-2, 8-6, 6-4
W. M. Johnston   G. L. Patterson   6-2, 6-0, 6-0

1925
W. T. Tilden   V. Richards   6-8, 6-4, 6-4, 6-1
W. M. Johnston   R. N. Williams   7-5, 6-3, 6-2

1926
R. Lacoste   H. Cochet   2-6, 4-6, 6-4, 6-4, 6-3
J. Borotra   V. Richards   3-6, 6-4, 4-6, 8-6, 6-2

1927
R. Lacoste   W. M. Johnston   6-2, 2-6, 6-4, 6-1
W. T. Tilden   F. T. Hunter   14-12, 6-1, 4-6, 9-7

1928
H. Cochet   F. X. Shields   6-2, 8-6, 6-4
F. T. Hunter   G. M. Lott   6-8, 6-4, 6-3, 6-4

1929
W. T. Tilden   J. H. Doeg   4-6, 6-2, 2-6, 6-4, 6-3
F. T. Hunter   F. Mercur   6-4, 6-8, 6-4, 6-3

1930
J. H. Doeg   W. T. Tilden   10-8, 6-3, 3-6, 12-10
F. X. Shields   S. B. Wood   6-2, 6-3, 4-6, 6-3

1931
H. E. Vines   F. J. Perry   4-6, 3-6, 6-4, 6-4, 6-3
G. M. Lott   J. H. Doeg   7-5, 6-3, 6-0

1932
H. E. Vines   C. S. Sutter   4-6, 8-10, 12-10, 10-8, 6-1
H. Cochet   W. L. Allison   1-6, 10-12, 4-6, 6-3, 7-5

1933
F. J. Perry   L. R. Stoefen   6-3, 6-2, 6-2
J. H. Crawford   F. X. Shields   7-5, 6-4, 6-3

1934
F. J. Perry   V. G. Kirby   6-2, 2-6, 6-4, 6-2
W. L. Allison   S. B. Wood   8-6, 6-2, 6-3

1935
W. L. Allison   F. J. Perry   7-5, 6-3, 6-3
S. B. Wood   B. M. Grant   6-2, 4-6, 12-10, 6-2

1936
F. J. Perry   B. M. Grant   6-4, 3-6, 7-5, 6-2
J. D. Budge   F. A. Parker   6-4, 6-3, 6-3

1937
J. D. Budge   F. A. Parker   6-2, 6-1, 6-3
G. von Cramm   R. L. Riggs   0-6, 8-6, 6-8, 6-3, 6-2

1938
J. D. Budge   S. B. Wood   6-3, 6-3, 6-3
C. G. Mako   J. E. Bromwich   6-3, 7-5, 6-4

1939
R. L. Riggs   J. R. Hunt   6-1, 6-2, 6-4, 6-1
S. W. Van Horn   J. E. Bromwich   2-6, 4-6, 6-2, 6-4, 8-6

1940
W. D. McNeill   J. A. Kramer   6-1, 5-7, 6-4, 6-3
R. L. Riggs   J. R. Hunt   4-6, 6-3, 5-7, 6-3, 6-4

1941
R. L. Riggs   F. R. Schroeder   6-4, 6-4, 1-6, 9-11, 7-5
F. Kovacs   W. D. McNeill   6-4, 6-2, 10-8

1942
F. R. Schroeder   G. Mulloy   9-7, 6-3, 6-4
F. A. Parker   F. Segura   6-1, 6-1, 2-6, 6-2

1943
J. R. Hunt   W. Talbert   3-6, 6-4, 6-2, 6-4
J. A. Kramer   F. Segura   2-6, 6-4, 7-5, 6-3

1944
F. A. Parker   W. D. McNeill   6-4, 3-6, 6-2, 6-2
W. F. Talbert   F. Segura   3-6, 6-3, 6-0, 6-8, 6-3

Finals

1910
T. C. Bundy   B. C. Wright   6-8, 6-3, 6-3, 10-8
Challenge Round
W. A. Larned (H)   T. C. Bundy (C)   6-1, 5-7, 6-0, 6-8, 6-4

1911
M. E. McLoughlin   B. C. Wright   6-4, 4-6, 7-5, 6-3
Challenge Round
W. A. Larned (H)   M. E. McLoughlin (C)   6-4, 6-4, 6-2

1912 *Challenge Round Abolished*
M. E. McLoughlin   W. F. Johnson   3-6, 2-6, 6-2, 6-4, 6-2

1913
M. E. McLoughlin   R. N. Williams   6-4, 5-7, 6-3, 6-1

1914
R. N. Williams   M. E. McLoughlin   6-3, 8-6, 10-8

1915 *Transferred from Newport to Forest Hills*
W. M. Johnston   M. E. McLoughlin   1-6, 6-0, 7-5, 10-8

1916
R. N. Williams   W. M. Johnston   4-6, 6-4, 0-6, 6-2, 6-4

1917 *National Patriotic Tournament*
R. L. Murray   N. W. Niles   5-7, 8-6, 6-3, 6-3

1918
R. L. Murray   W. T. Tilden   6-3, 6-1, 7-5

1919
W. M. Johnston   W. T. Tilden   6-4, 6-4, 6-3

1920
W. T. Tilden   W. M. Johnston   6-1, 1-6, 7-5, 5-7, 6-3

1921 *Transferred to Philadelphia, Pa.*
W. T. Tilden   W. F. Johnson   6-1, 6-3, 6-1

1922
W. T. Tilden   W. M. Johnston   4-6, 3-6, 6-2, 6-3, 6-4

1923
W. T. Tilden   W. M. Johnston   6-4, 6-1, 6-4

1924 *Transferred to Forest Hills, N.Y.*
W. T. Tilden   W. M. Johnston   6-1, 9-7, 6-2

1925
W. T. Tilden   W. M. Johnston   4-6, 11-9, 6-3, 4-6, 6-3

1926
R. Lacoste   J. Borotra   6-4, 6-0, 6-4

1927
R. Lacoste   W. T. Tilden   11-9, 6-3, 11-9

1928
H. Cochet   F. T. Hunter   4-6, 6-4, 3-6, 7-5, 6-3

1929
W. T. Tilden   F. T. Hunter   3-6, 6-3, 4-6, 6-2, 6-4

1930
J. H. Doeg   F. X. Shields   10-8, 1-6, 6-4, 16-14

1931
H. E. Vines   G. M. Lott   7-9, 6-3, 9-7, 7-5

1932
H. E. Vines   H. Cochet   6-4, 6-4, 6-4

1933
F. J. Perry   J. H. Crawford   6-3, 11-13, 4-6, 6-0, 6-1

1934
F. J. Perry   W. L. Allison   6-4, 6-3, 3-6, 1-6, 8-6

1935
W. L. Allison   S. B. Wood   6-2, 6-2, 6-3

1936
F. J. Perry   J. D. Budge   2-6, 6-2, 8-6, 1-6, 10-8

1937
J. D. Budge   G. von Cramm   6-1, 7-9, 6-1, 3-6, 6-1

1938
J. D. Budge   C. G. Mako   6-3, 6-8, 6-2, 6-1

1939
R. L. Riggs   S. W. Van Horn   6-4, 6-2, 6-4

1940
W. D. McNeill   R. L. Riggs   8-6, 6-8, 6-3, 7-5

1941
R. L. Riggs   F. Kovacs   5-7, 6-1, 6-3, 6-3

1942
F. R. Schroeder   F. A. Parker   8-6, 7-5, 3-6, 4-6, 6-2

1943
J. R. Hunt   J. A. Kramer   6-3, 6-8, 10-8, 6-0

1944
F. A. Parker   W. F. Talbert   6-4, 3-6, 6-3, 6-3

Finals

1910
H. H. Hackett/F. B. Alexander
T. C. Bundy/T. W. Hendrick   6-1, 8-6, 6-3

1911
R. D. Little/G. F. Touchard
H. H. Hackett/F. B. Alexander   7-5, 13-15, 6-2, 6-4

1912
T. C. Bundy/M. E. McLoughlin
R. D. Little/G. F. Touchard   3-6, 6-2, 6-1, 7-5

1913
T. C. Bundy/M. E. McLoughlin
J. R. Strachan/C. J. Griffin   6-4, 7-5, 6-1

1914
T. C. Bundy/M. E. McLoughlin
G. M. Church/D. Mathey   6-4, 6-2, 6-4

1915 *Transferred from Newport to Forest Hills*
W. M. Johnston/C. J. Griffin
M. E. McLoughlin/T. C. Bundy   6-2, 3-6, 4-6, 6-3, 6-3

1916
W. M. Johnston/C. J. Griffin
M. E. McLoughlin/W. Dawson   6-4, 6-3, 5-7, 6-3

1917 *National Patriotic Tournament*
F. B. Alexander/H. A. Throckmorton
H. C. Johnson/I. C. Wright   11-9, 6-4, 6-4

1918
W. T. Tilden/V. Richards
F. B. Alexander/B. C. Wright   6-3, 6-4, 3-6, 2-6, 6-2

1919 *Transferred to Chestnut Hill, Mass.*
N. E. Brookes/G. L. Patterson
W. T. Tilden/V. Richards   8-6, 6-3, 4-6, 4-6, 6-2

1920
W. M. Johnston/C. J. Griffin
W. F. Davis/R. E. Roberts   6-2, 6-2, 6-3

1921
W. T. Tilden/V. Richards
R. N. Williams/W. M. Washburn   13-11, 12-10, 6-1

1922
W. T. Tilden/V. Richards
G. L. Patterson/P. O'Hara Wood   4-6, 6-1, 6-3, 6-4

1923
W. T. Tilden/B. I. C. Norton
R. N. Williams/W. M. Washburn   3-6, 6-2, 6-3, 5-7, 6-2

1924
R. G. Kinsey/H. O. Kinsey
G. L. Patterson/P. O'Hara Wood   7-5, 5-7, 7-9, 6-3, 6-4

1925
R. N. Williams/V. Richards
G. L. Patterson/J. B. Hawkes   6-2, 8-10, 6-4, 11-9

1926
R. N. Williams/V. Richards
W. T. Tilden/A. H. Chapin   6-4, 6-8, 11-9, 6-3

1927
W. T. Tilden/F. T. Hunter
R. N. Williams/W. M. Johnston   10-8, 6-3, 6-3

1928
G. M. Lott/J. F. Hennessey
G. L. Patterson/J. B. Hawkes   6-2, 6-1, 6-2

1929
G. M. Lott/J. H. Doeg
B. Bell/L. N. White   10-8, 16-14, 6-1

1930
G. M. Lott/J. H. Doeg
J. Van Ryn/W. L. Allison   8-6, 6-3, 4-6, 13-15, 6-4

1931
W. L. Allison/J. Van Ryn
G. S. Mangin/B. Bell   6-4, 8-6, 6-3

1932
H. E. Vines/K. Gledhill
W. L. Allison/J. Van Ryn   6-4, 6-3, 6-2

1933
G. M. Lott/L. R. Stoefen
F. X. Shields/F. A. Parker   11-13, 9-7, 9-7, 6-3

1934 *Transferred to Philadelphia, Pa.*
G. M. Lott/L. R. Stoefen
W. L. Allison/J. Van Ryn   6-4, 9-7, 3-6, 6-4

1935 *Transferred to Chestnut Hill, Mass.*
W. L. Allison/J. Van Ryn
J. D. Budge/C. G. Mako   6-4, 6-2, 3-6, 2-6, 6-1

1936
J. D. Budge/C. G. Mako
W. L. Allison/J. Van Ryn   6-4, 6-2, 6-4

1937
G. von Cramm/H. Henkel
J. D. Budge/C. G. Mako   6-4, 7-5, 6-4

1938
J. D. Budge/C. G. Mako
A. K. Quist/J. E. Bromwich   6-3, 6-2, 6-1

1939
A. K. Quist/J. E. Bromwich
J. H. Crawford/H. C. Hopman   8-6, 6-1, 6-4

1940
J. A. Kramer/F. R. Schroeder
G. Mulloy/H. J. Prussoff

1941
J. A. Kramer/F. R. Schroeder
W. Sabin/G. Mulloy

1942 *Transferred to Forest Hills, N.Y.*
G. Mulloy/W. F. Talbert
F. R. Schroeder/S. B. Wood

1943
J. A. Kramer/F. A. Parker
W. F. Talbert/D. Freeman

1944
W. D. McNeill/R. Falkenburg
W. F. Talbert/F. Segura   7-5, 6-4, 3-6, 6-1

Winners in **bold type**; (H)/(H) holder; (C)/(C) challenger; w.o. walk-over

United States Championships

Men's Singles

Semi-Finals

1945
F. A. Parker E. T. Cooke 6-1, 8-6, 7-5
W. F. Talbert F. Segura 7-5, 6-3, 6-4
1946
J. A. Kramer R. Falkenburg 6-0, 6-4, 6-4
T. Brown G. Mulloy 6-4, 6-2, 6-4
1947
J. A. Kramer J. Drobný 3-6, 6-3, 6-0, 6-1
F. A. Parker J. E. Bromwich 6-3, 4-6, 6-3, 6-8, 8-6
1948
R. A. Gonzalez J. Drobný 8-10, 11-9, 6-0, 6-3
E. W. Sturgess H. Flam 9-7, 6-3, 6-2
1949
R. A. Gonzalez F. A. Parker 3-6, 9-7, 6-3, 6-2
F. R. Schroeder W. F. Talbert 2-6, 6-4, 4-6, 6-4, 6-4
1950
A. Larsen R. Savitt 6-2, 10-8, 7-9, 6-2
H. Flam G. Mulloy 2-6, 6-2, 9-11, 6-1, 6-3
1951
F. A. Sedgman A. Larsen 6-1, 6-2, 6-0
E. V. Seixas R. Savitt 6-0, 3-6, 6-3, 6-2
1952
F. A. Sedgman M. G. Rose 6-3, 6-3, 6-4
G. Mulloy H. Richardson 10-8, 6-0, 8-6
1953
M. A. Trabert K. R. Rosewall 7-5, 6-3, 6-3
E. V. Seixas L. A. Hoad 7-5, 6-4, 6-4
1954
E. V. Seixas H. Richardson 6-3, 12-14, 8-6, 6-2
R. N. Hartwig K. R. Rosewall 6-4, 6-3, 6-4
1955
M. A. Trabert L. A. Hoad 6-4, 6-2, 6-1
K. R. Rosewall E. V. Seixas 6-4, 6-4, 7-5
1956
K. R. Rosewall E. V. Seixas 6-0, 6-3
L. A. Hoad N. A. Fraser 15-13, 6-2, 6-4
1957
M. J. Anderson S. Davidson 5-7, 6-2, 4-6, 6-3, 6-4
A. J. Cooper H. Flam 6-1, 7-5, 6-4
1958
A. J. Cooper N. A. Fraser 8-6, 8-6, 6-1
M. J. Anderson U. Schmidt 6-4, 7-5, 6-2
1959
N. A. Fraser B. Bartzen 6-3, 6-2, 6-2
A. Olmedo R. Holmberg 15-13, 6-4, 3-6, 6-1
1960
N. A. Fraser R. D. Ralston 11-9, 6-3, 6-2
R. G. Laver E. Buchholz 4-6, 5-7, 6-4, 6-2, 7-5
1961
R. S. Emerson R. H. Osuna 6-3, 6-2, 3-6, 5-7, 9-7
R. G. Laver M. J. Sangster 13-11, 7-5, 6-4
1962
R. G. Laver R. H. Osuna 6-1, 6-3, 6-4
R. S. Emerson C. R. McKinley 4-6, 6-4, 6-3, 6-2
1963
R. H. Osuna C. R. McKinley 6-4, 6-4, 10-8
F. R. Froehling R. Barnes 6-3, 6-1, 6-4
1964
R. S. Emerson C. R. McKinley 7-5, 11-9, 6-4
F. S. Stolle R. H. Osuna 3-6, 8-6, 6-3
1965
M. Santana A. R. Ashe 2-6, 6-4, 6-2, 6-4
E. C. Drysdale R. H. Osuna 6-3, 4-6, 6-4, 6-1
1966
F. S. Stolle R. S. Emerson 6-4, 6-1, 6-1
J. D. Newcombe M. Santana 6-3, 6-4, 6-8, 8-6
1967
J. D. Newcombe E. L. Scott 6-4, 6-3, 6-3
C. E. Graebner J. Leschly 3-6, 3-6, 7-5, 6-4, 7-5
1968 *Open Championships began*
A. R. Ashe C. E. Graebner 3-6, 8-6, 7-5, 6-2
T. S. Okker K. R. Rosewall 8-6, 6-4, 6-8, 6-1
1969
R. G. Laver A. R. Ashe 8-6, 6-3, 14-12
A. D. Roche J. D. Newcombe 3-6, 6-4, 4-6, 6-3, 8-6
1970
K. R. Rosewall J. D. Newcombe 6-3, 6-4, 6-3
A. D. Roche C. Richey 6-2, 7-6, 6-1
1971
J. Kodeš A. R. Ashe 7-6, 3-6, 4-6, 6-3, 6-4
S. R. Smith T. S. Okker 7-6, 6-3, 3-6, 2-6, 6-3
1972
A. R. Ashe C. Richey 6-1, 6-4, 7-6
I. Năstase T. Gorman 4-6, 7-6, 6-2, 6-1
1973
J. D. Newcombe K. R. Rosewall 6-4, 7-6, 6-3
J. Kodeš S. R. Smith 7-5, 6-7, 1-6, 6-1, 7-5

Finals

1945
F. A. Parker W. F. Talbert 14-12, 6-1, 6-2
1946
J. A. Kramer T. Brown 9-7, 6-3, 6-0
1947
J. A. Kramer F. A. Parker 4-6, 2-6, 6-1, 6-0, 6-3
1948
R. A. Gonzalez E. W. Sturgess 6-2, 6-3, 14-12
1949
R. A. Gonzalez F. R. Schroeder 16-18, 2-6, 6-1, 6-2, 6-4
1950
A. Larsen H. Flam 6-3, 4-6, 5-7, 6-4, 6-3
1951
F. A. Sedgman E. V. Seixas 6-4, 6-1, 6-1
1952
F. A. Sedgman G. Mulloy 6-1, 6-2, 6-3
1953
M. A. Trabert E. V. Seixas 6-3, 6-2, 6-3
1954
E. V. Seixas R. N. Hartwig 3-6, 6-2, 6-4, 6-4
1955
M. A. Trabert K. R. Rosewall 9-7, 6-3, 6-3
1956
K. R. Rosewall L. A. Hoad 4-6, 6-2, 6-3, 6-3
1957
M. J. Anderson A. J. Cooper 10-8, 7-5, 6-4
1958
A. J. Cooper M. J. Anderson 6-2, 3-6, 4-6, 10-8, 8-6
1959
N. A. Fraser A. Olmedo 6-3, 5-7, 6-2, 6-4
1960
N. A. Fraser R. G. Laver 6-4, 6-4, 10-8
1961
R. S. Emerson R. G. Laver 7-5, 6-3, 6-2
1962
R. G. Laver R. S. Emerson 6-2, 6-4, 5-7, 6-4
1963
R. H. Osuna F. R. Froehling 7-5, 6-4, 6-2
1964
R. S. Emerson F. S. Stolle 6-4, 6-1, 6-4
1965
M. Santana E. C. Drysdale 6-2, 7-9, 7-5, 6-1
1966
F. S. Stolle J. D. Newcombe 4-6, 12-10, 6-3, 6-4
1967
J. D. Newcombe C. E. Graebner 6-4, 6-4, 8-6
1968 *Open Championships began*
A. R. Ashe T. S. Okker 14-12, 5-7, 6-3, 3-6, 6-3
1969
R. G. Laver A. D. Roche 7-9, 6-1, 6-3, 6-2
1970
K. R. Rosewall A. D. Roche 2-6, 6-4, 7-6, 6-3
1971
S. R. Smith J. Kodeš 3-6, 6-3, 6-2, 7-6
1972
I. Năstase A. R. Ashe 3-6, 6-3, 6-7, 6-4, 6-3
1973
J. D. Newcombe J. Kodeš 6-4, 1-6, 4-6, 6-2, 6-3

Men's Doubles

Finals

1945
G. Mulloy/W. F. Talbert
R. Falkenburg/J. Tuero 12-10, 8-10, 12-10, 6-2
1946 *Transferred to Chestnut Hill, Mass.*
G. Mulloy/W. F. Talbert
W. D. McNeill/F. Guernsey 3-6, 6-4, 2-6, 6-3, 20-18
1947
J. A. Kramer/F. R. Schroeder
W. F. Talbert/O. W. Sidwell 6-4, 7-5, 6-3
1948
G. Mulloy/W. F. Talbert
F. A. Parker/F. R. Schroeder 1-6, 9-7, 6-3, 3-6, 9-7
1949
O. W. Sidwell/J. E. Bromwich
F. A. Sedgman/G. Worthington 6-4, 6-0, 6-1
1950
J. E. Bromwich/F. A. Sedgman
G. Mulloy/W. F. Talbert 7-5, 8-6, 3-6, 6-1
1951
K. McGregor/F. A. Sedgman
D. W. Candy/M. G. Rose 10-8, 6-4, 4-6, 7-5
1952
M. G. Rose/E. V. Seixas
K. McGregor/F. A. Sedgman 3-6, 10-8, 10-8, 6-8, 8-6
1953
M. G. Rose/R. N. Hartwig
G. Mulloy/W. F. Talbert 6-4, 4-6, 6-2, 6-4
1954
E. V. Seixas/M. A. Trabert
L. A. Hoad/K. R. Rosewall 3-6, 6-4, 8-6, 6-3
1955
K. Kamo/A. Miyagi
G. Moss/W. Quillian 6-2, 6-3, 3-6, 1-6, 6-4
1956
L. A. Hoad/K. R. Rosewall
H. Richardson/E. V. Seixas 6-2, 6-2, 3-6, 6-4
1957
A. J. Cooper/N. A. Fraser
G. Mulloy/J. E. Patty 4-6, 6-3, 9-7, 6-3
1958
H. Richardson/A. Olmedo
S. Giammalva/B. MacKay 6-4, 3-6, 6-3, 6-4
1959
R. S. Emerson/N. A. Fraser
A. Olmedo/E. Buchholz 3-6, 6-3, 5-7, 6-4, 7-5
1960
R. S. Emerson/N. A. Fraser
R. G. Laver/R. Mark 9-7, 6-2, 6-4
1961
C. R. McKinley/R. D. Ralston
R. H. Osuna/A. Palafox 6-3, 6-4, 2-6, 13-11
1962
R. H. Osuna/A. Palafox
C. R. McKinley/R. D. Ralston 6-4, 10-12, 1-6, 9-7, 6-3
1963
C. R. McKinley/R. D. Ralston
R. H. Osuna/A. Palafox 9-7, 4-6, 5-7, 6-3, 11-9
1964
C. R. McKinley/R. D. Ralston
M. J. Sangster/G. Stilwell 6-3, 6-2, 6-4
1965
R. S. Emerson/F. S. Stolle
F. R. Froehling/C. M. Pasarell 6-4, 10-12, 7-5, 6-3
1966
R. S. Emerson/F. S. Stolle
R. D. Ralston/C. E. Graebner 6-4, 6-4, 6-4
1967
J. D. Newcombe/A. D. Roche
O. K. Davidson/W. W. Bowrey 6-8, 9-7, 6-3, 6-3
1968 *Open Championships began at Forest Hills, N.Y.*
R. C. Lutz/S. R. Smith
A. R. Ashe/A. Gimeno 11-9, 6-1, 7-5
1969
K. R. Rosewall/F. S. Stolle
C. M. Pasarell/R. D. Ralston 2-6, 7-5, 13-11, 6-3
1970
P. Barthès/N. Pilić
R. S. Emerson/R. G. Laver 6-3, 7-6, 4-6, 7-6
1971
J. D. Newcombe/R. Taylor
S. R. Smith/E. Van Dillen 6-7, 6-3, 7-6, 4-6, 5-3 tie-break
1972
C. Drysdale/R. Taylor
O. K. Davidson/J. D. Newcombe 6-4, 7-6, 6-3
1973
O. K. Davidson/J. D. Newcombe
R. G. Laver/K. R. Rosewall 7-5, 2-6, 7-5, 7-5

Women's Singles

Women's Doubles

Semi-Finals	Finals	Finals

1887
Miss N. F. Hansell
Miss L. Knight

1887 *Played in Philadelphia, Pa.*
Miss E. Hansell Miss L. Knight 6-1, 6-0

1888
Miss B. B. Townsend
Miss M. Wright

1888
Miss B. B. Townsend Miss M. Wright 6-2, 6-2
Challenge Round
Miss B. B. Townsend (C) Miss E. Hansell (H) default

1889
Miss L. D. Voorhees

1889
Challenge Round
Miss B. B. Townsend (H) Miss L. D. Voorhees (C)
7-5, 6-2

1890 *Played in Philadelphia, Pa.*
Miss E. C. Roosevelt/Miss G. W. Roosevelt

1890
Miss E. C. Roosevelt
Miss G. W. Roosevelt

1890
Miss E. C. Roosevelt Miss G. Roosevelt 6-3, 6-1
Challenge Round
Miss E. C. Roosevelt (C) Miss B. B. Townsend (H)

1891
Miss M. E. Cahill
Miss E. H. Moore

1891
Miss M. E. Cahill Miss E. H. Moore 6-5, 6-3, 6-4, 4-6, 6-2
Challenge Round
Miss M. E. Cahill (C) Miss E. C. Roosevelt (H)

1891
Miss M. E. Cahill/Mrs W. F. Morgan

1892
Miss E. H. Moore

1892
Challenge Round
Miss M. E. Cahill (H) Miss E. H. Moore (C)

1892
Miss M. E. Cahill/Miss A. M. McKinley

1893
Miss A. M. Terry
Miss A. M. Schultz

1893
Miss A. M. Terry Miss A. M. Schultz
Challenge Round
Miss A. M. Terry (C) Miss M. E. Cahill (H) default

1893
Miss A. M. Terry/Miss H. Butler

1894
Miss H. R. Helwig

1894
Challenge Round
Miss H. R. Helwig (C) Miss A. M. Terry (H)
7-5, 3-6, 6-0, 3-6, 6-3

1894
Miss H. R. Helwig/Miss J. P. Atkinson

1895
Miss J. P. Atkinson

1895
Challenge Round
Miss J. P. Atkinson (C) Miss H. R. Helwig (H)
6-4, 6-2, 6-1

1895
Miss H. R. Helwig/Miss J. P. Atkinson

1896
Miss E. H. Moore
Miss Wistar

1896
Miss E. H. Moore Miss Wistar
Challenge Round
Miss E. H. Moore (C) Miss J. P. Atkinson (H)
6-4, 4-6, 6-3, 6-2

1896
Miss E. H. Moore/Miss J. P. Atkinson

1897
Miss J. P. Atkinson

1897
Challenge Round
Miss J. P. Atkinson (C) Miss E. H. Moore (H)
6-3, 6-3, 4-6, 3-6, 6-3

1897
Miss J. P. Atkinson/Miss K. Atkinson

1898
Miss M. Jones

1898
Challenge Round
Miss J. P. Atkinson (H) Miss M. Jones (C)
6-3, 5-7, 6-4, 2-6, 7-5

1898
Miss J. P. Atkinson/Miss K. Atkinson

1899
Miss M. Jones
Miss M. Banks

1899
Miss M. Jones Miss M. Banks
Challenge Round
Miss M. Jones (C) Miss J. P. Atkinson (H) default

1899
Miss J. W. Craven/Miss M. McAteer

1900
Miss M. McAteer Miss Banks 6-4, 7-3
Miss E. Parker Miss Morriss 6-0, 6-2

1900
Miss M. McAteer Miss E. Parker 6-2, 6-2, 6-0
Challenge Round
Miss M. McAteer (C) Miss M. Jones (H) default

1900
Miss E. Parker/Miss H. Champlin
Miss M. McAteer/Miss M. Weimer 9-7, 6-2, 6-2

1901
Miss E. H. Moore Miss J. P. Atkinson
Miss M. Jones

1901
Miss E. H. Moore Miss M. Jones 4-6, 1-6, 9-7, 9-7, 6-3
Challenge Round
Miss E. H. Moore (C) Miss M. McAteer (H)
6-4, 3-6, 7-5, 2-6, 6-2

1901
Miss J. P. Atkinson/Miss M. McAteer

1902
Miss M. Jones

1902
Challenge Round
Miss M. Jones (C) Miss E. H. Moore (H) 6-1, 1-0 retired

1902
Miss J. P. Atkinson/Miss M. Jones

1903
Miss E. H. Moore
Miss C. B. Neely

1903
Miss E. H. Moore Miss C. B. Neely
Challenge Round
Miss E. H. Moore (C) Miss M. Jones (H) 7-5, 8-6

1903
Miss E. H. Moore/Miss C. B. Neely

1904
Miss M. G. Sutton

1904
Challenge Round
Miss M. G. Sutton (C) Miss E. H. Moore (H) 6-1, 6-2

1904
Miss M. G. Sutton/Miss M. Hall

1905
Miss E. H. Moore
Miss H. Homans

1905
Miss E. H. Moore Miss H. Homans 6-4, 5-7, 6-1
Challenge Round
Miss E. H. Moore (C) Miss M. G. Sutton (H) default

1905
Miss H. Homans/Miss C. B. Neely

1906
Miss H. Homans
Mrs M. Barger-Wallach

1906
Miss H. Homans Mrs M. Barger-Wallach
Challenge Round
Miss H. Homans (C) Miss E. H. Moore (H) default

1906
Mrs L. S. Coe/Mrs D. S. Platt

1907
Miss Evelyn Sears Mrs G. L. Chapman 6-2, 6-1
Miss C. B. Neely Mrs W. H. Pouch 8-6, 7-5

1907
Miss Evelyn Sears Miss C. B. Neely 6-3, 6-2
Challenge Round
Miss Evelyn Sears (C) Miss H. Homans (H) default

1907
Miss M. Weimer/Miss C. B. Neely
Miss E. Wildey/Miss N. Wildey 6-1, 2-6, 6-4

1908
Mrs M. Barger-Wallach Miss E. Rotch 6-2, 6-4
Miss M. Wagner Miss M. Johnson 7-5, 6-2

1908
Mrs M. Barger-Wallach Miss M. Wagner 4-6, 6-1, 6-3
Challenge Round
Mrs M. Barger-Wallach (C) Miss Evelyn Sears (H)
6-2, 1-6, 6-3

1908
Miss Evelyn Sears/Miss M. Curtis
Miss C. B. Neely/Miss M. Steever 6-3, 5-7, 9-7

1909
Miss H. V. Hotchkiss
Mrs M. Barger-Wallach

1909
Challenge Round
Miss H. V. Hotchkiss (C) Mrs M. Barger-Wallach (H)
6-0, 6-1

1909
Miss H. V. Hotchkiss/Miss E. E. Rotch

1910
Miss L. Hamond

1910
Challenge Round
Miss H. V. Hotchkiss (H) Miss L. Hamond (C) 6-4, 6-2

1910
Miss H. V. Hotchkiss/Miss E. E. Rotch

1911
Miss Eleonora Sears Miss G. Warren 6-1, 6-3
Miss F. Sutton Miss A. Browning 6-3, 6-2

1911
Miss F. Sutton Miss Eleonora Sears 6-2, 6-1
Challenge Round
Miss H. V. Hotchkiss (H) Miss F. Sutton (C)
8-10, 6-1, 9-7

1911
Miss H. V. Hotchkiss/Miss Eleonora Sears
Miss F. Sutton/Miss D. Green 6-4, 4-6, 6-2

1912
Miss M. K. Browne Miss A. Browning 6-4, 3-6, 9-7
Miss Eleonora Sears Miss M. Merrick 5-7, 6-0, 6-2

1912
Miss M. K. Browne Miss Eleonora Sears 6-4, 6-2
Challenge Round
Miss M. K. Browne (C) Miss H. V. Hotchkiss (H)
default

1912
Miss D. Green/Miss M. K. Browne
Mrs M. Barger-Wallach/Mrs F. Schmitz 6-2, 5-7, 6-0

1913
Miss E. Wildey Mrs H. J. D. Paul 6-1, 6-2
Miss D. Green Mrs R. H. Williams 7-5, 6-3

1913
Miss D. Green Miss E. Wildey 6-3, 6-4
Challenge Round
Miss M. K. Browne (H) Miss D. Green (C) 6-2, 7-5

1913
Miss M. K. Browne/Mrs R. H. Williams
Miss E. Wildey/Miss D. Green 12-10, 2-6, 6-3

Winners in **bold type**; **(H)**/(H) holder; **(C)**/(C) challenger; w.o. walk-over

United States Championships

Women's Singles

Semi-Finals

1914
Miss C. Cassel Miss I. Pendleton 6-2, 6-1
Miss M. Wagner Mrs E. Raymond 6-4, 6-4

1915
Miss M. Bjurstedt Miss M. Guthrie 3-6, 6-2, 6-2
Mrs G. W. Wightman Miss E. M. Fox 6-1, 6-4

1916
Miss Eleonora Sears Miss S. White 6-2, 6-3
Mrs E. Raymond Miss Evelyn Sears 6-2, 6-1

1917 *National Patriotic Tournament*
Miss M. Bjurstedt Mrs G. Harvey 4-6, 6-0, 6-0
Miss M. Vanderhoef Miss Eleonora Sears 8-6, 6-3
1918
Miss H. Pollack Miss C. Cassel 6-3, 6-0
Miss E. E. Goss Miss H. Ledoux 6-3, 6-4

1919
Mrs G. W. Wightman Mrs G. Harvey 6-2, 6-2
Miss M. Zinderstein Miss M. Bjurstedt 4-6, 6-1, 6-2
1920
Mrs M. Mallory
Miss M. Zinderstein
1921 *Transferred to Forest Hills, N.Y.*
Mrs M. Mallory Mrs M. Bundy 8-6, 6-2
Miss M. K. Browne Mrs Hitchins 6-3, 6-0
1922
Mrs M. Mallory Miss Bancroft 6-0, 6-4
Miss H. Wills Mrs M. Bundy 6-4, 6-3
1923
Miss H. Wills Miss E. E. Goss 6-4, 6-0
Mrs M. Mallory Mrs R. C. Clayton 6-4, 6-2
1924
Miss H. Wills Miss M. K. Browne 6-4, 4-6, 6-3
Mrs M. Mallory Miss E. E. Goss 6-3, 6-4
1925
Miss H. Wills Miss E. E. Goss 3-6, 6-0, 6-2
Miss K. McKane Mrs M. Mallory 4-6, 7-5, 8-6
1926
Mrs M. Mallory Miss M. Bayard 6-3, 6-3
Miss E. Ryan Miss M. K. Browne 6-1, 6-3
1927
Miss H. Wills Miss H. H. Jacobs 6-0, 6-2
Miss B. Nuthall Mrs H. Chapin 6-1, 4-6, 6-3
1928
Miss H. Wills Miss E. Cross 6-0, 6-1
Miss H. H. Jacobs Mrs M. Mallory 6-2, 7-5
1929
Miss H. Wills Mrs M. Mallory 6-0, 6-0
Mrs P. Watson Miss H. H. Jacobs 6-1, 4-6, 6-4
1930
Miss B. Nuthall Miss M. Morrill 6-8, 6-4, 6-2
Mrs L. A. Harper Baroness Levi 6-2, 6-3
1931
Mrs F. S. Moody Miss P. E. Mudford 6-2, 6-4
Mrs E. F. Whittingstall Miss B. Nuthall 6-2, 3-6, 6-4
1932
Miss H. H. Jacobs Mrs J. B. Pittman 6-2, 6-3
Miss C. A. Babcock Miss J. C. Ridley 4-6, 7-5, 6-3
1933
Miss H. H. Jacobs Miss D. E. Round 6-4, 5-7, 6-2
Mrs F. S. Moody Miss B. Nuthall 2-6, 6-3, 6-2
1934
Miss H. H. Jacobs Miss C. A. Babcock 7-5, 6-0
Miss S. Palfrey Mrs D. Andrus 6-3, 6-4
1935
Miss H. H. Jacobs Mrs M. R. King 6-4, 6-3
Mrs S. P. Fabyan Miss K. E. Stammers 9-7, 7-5
1936
Miss A. Marble Miss H. Pedersen 6-1, 6-1
Miss H. H. Jacobs Miss K. E. Stammers 6-4, 6-3
1937
Miss A. Lizana Miss D. M. Bundy 6-2, 6-3
Miss J. Jedrzejowska Miss H. H. Jacobs 6-4, 6-4
1938
Miss A. Marble Mrs S. P. Fabyan 5-7, 7-5, 7-5
Miss N. Wynne Miss D. M. Bundy 5-7, 6-4, 8-6
1939
Miss A. Marble Miss V. Wolfenden 6-0, 6-1
Miss H. H. Jacobs Miss K. E. Stammers 7-5, 6-0
1940
Miss A. Marble
Miss H. H. Jacobs
1941
Mrs E. T. Cooke
Miss P. M. Betz
1942
Miss P. M. Betz
Miss A. L. Brough
1943
Miss P. M. Betz
Miss A. L. Brough
1944
Miss P. M. Betz Miss A. L. Brough 6-2, 6-3
Miss M. E. Osborne Miss D. M. Bundy 4-6, 6-4, 6-0
1945
Mrs E. T. Cooke Miss A. L. Brough 6-3, 6-4
Miss P. M. Betz Miss D. J. Hart 6-3, 6-2
1946
Miss P. M. Betz Mrs P. C. Todd 6-2, 6-3
Miss D. J. Hart Mrs D. Arnold Prentiss 6-3, 6-2
1947
Miss A. L. Brough Mrs N. Bolton 2-6, 6-4, 7-5
Miss M. E. Osborne Miss D. J. Hart 7-5, 7-5

Finals

1914
Miss M. Wagner Miss C. Cassel 6-1, 7-5
Challenge Round
Miss M. K. Browne(H) Miss M. Wagner(C) 6-2, 1-6, 6-1
1915
Miss M. Bjurstedt Mrs G. W. Wightman 4-6, 6-2, 6-0
Challenge Round
Miss M. Bjurstedt(C) Miss M. K. Browne(H) default
1916
Mrs E. Raymond Miss Eleonora Sears 6-3, 6-4
Challenge Round
Miss M. Bjurstedt(H) Mrs E. Raymond(C) 6-0, 6-1
1917 *National Patriotic Tournament*
Miss M. Bjurstedt Miss M. Vanderhoef 4-6, 6-0, 6-2
1918
Miss E. E. Goss Miss H. Pollack 6-2, 7-5
Challenge Round
Miss M. Bjurstedt(H) Miss E. E. Goss(C) 6-4, 6-3
1919 *Challenge Round abolished*
Mrs G. W. Wightman Miss M. Zinderstein 6-1, 6-2
1920
Mrs M. Mallory Miss M. Zinderstein 6-3, 6-1
1921 *Transferred to Forest Hills, N.Y.*
Mrs M. Mallory Miss M. K. Browne 4-6, 6-4, 6-2
1922
Mrs M. Mallory Miss H. Wills 6-3, 6-1
1923
Miss H. Wills Mrs M. Mallory 6-2, 6-1
1924
Miss H. Wills Mrs M. Mallory 6-1, 6-2
1925
Miss H. Wills Miss K. McKane 3-6, 6-0, 6-2
1926
Mrs M. Mallory Miss E. Ryan 4-6, 6-4, 9-7
1927
Miss H. Wills Miss B. Nuthall 6-1, 6-4
1928
Miss H. Wills Miss H. H. Jacobs 6-2, 6-1
1929
Miss H. Wills Mrs P. Watson 6-4, 6-2
1930
Miss B. Nuthall Mrs L. A. Harper 6-4, 6-1
1931
Mrs F. S. Moody Mrs E. F. Whittingstall 6-4, 6-1
1932
Miss H. H. Jacobs Miss C. A. Babcock 6-2, 6-2
1933
Miss H. H. Jacobs Mrs F. S. Moody 8-6, 3-6, 3-0 retired
1934
Miss H. H. Jacobs Miss S. Palfrey 6-1, 6-4
1935
Miss H. H. Jacobs Mrs S. P. Fabyan 6-1, 6-4
1936
Miss A. Marble Miss H. H. Jacobs 4-6, 6-3, 6-2
1937
Miss A. Lizana Miss J. Jedrzejowska 6-4, 6-2
1938
Miss A. Marble Miss N. Wynne 6-0, 6-3
1939
Miss A. Marble Miss H. H. Jacobs 6-0, 8-10, 6-4
1940
Miss A. Marble Miss H. H. Jacobs 6-2, 6-3
1941
Mrs E. T. Cooke Miss P. M. Betz 6-1, 6-4
1942
Miss P. M. Betz Miss A. L. Brough 4-6, 6-1, 6-4
1943
Miss P. M. Betz Miss A. L. Brough 6-3, 5-7, 6-3
1944
Miss P. M. Betz Miss M. E. Osborne 6-3, 8-6
1945
Mrs E. T. Cooke Miss P. M. Betz 3-6, 8-6, 6-4
1946
Miss P. M. Betz Miss D. J. Hart 11-9, 6-3
1947
Miss A. L. Brough Miss M. E. Osborne 8-6, 4-6, 6-1

Women's Doubles

Finals

1914
Miss M. K. Browne/Mrs R. H. Williams
Mrs E. Raymond/Miss E. Wildey 8-6, 6-2
1915
Mrs G. W. Wightman/Miss Eleonora Sears
Mrs M. McLean/Mrs G. L. Chapman 10-8, 6-2

1916
Miss M. Bjurstedt/Miss Eleonora Sears
Miss E. Wildey/Mrs E. Raymond 4-6, 6-2, 10-8

1917 *National Patriotic Tournament*
Miss M. Bjurstedt/Miss Eleonora Sears
Mrs R. LeRoy/Miss P. Walsh 6-2, 6-4
1918
Miss M. Zinderstein/Miss E. Goss
Miss M. Bjurstedt/Mrs J. Rogge 7-5, 8-6
1919
Miss M. Zinderstein/Miss E. Goss

1920
Miss M. Zinderstein/Miss E. Goss

1921 *Transferred to Forest Hills, N.Y.*
Miss M. K. Browne/Mrs L. Williams

1922
Mrs J. B. Jessup/Miss H. Wills
Mrs M. Mallory/Miss Sigourney 6-4, 7-9, 6-3
1923
Miss K. McKane/Mrs B. C. Covell
Mrs G. W. Wightman/Miss E. Goss 2-6, 6-2, 6-1
1924
Mrs G. W. Wightman/Miss H. Wills
Miss E. Goss/Mrs J. B. Jessup 6-4, 6-3
1925
Miss M. K. Browne/Miss H. Wills
Mrs M. Bundy/Miss E. Ryan 6-4, 6-3
1926
Miss E. Ryan/Miss E. Goss
Miss M. K. Browne/Mrs A. H. Chapin 3-6, 6-4, 12-10
1927
Mrs L. A. Godfree/Miss E. H. Harvey
Miss J. Fry/Miss B. Nuthall 6-1, 4-6. 6-4
1928
Mrs G. W. Wightman/Miss H. Wills
Miss E. Cross/Mrs L. A. Harper 6-2, 6-2
1929
Mrs P. Watson/Mrs L. R. C. Michell
Mrs B. C. Covell/Mrs D. C. Shepherd-Barron 2-6, 6-3, 6-4
1930
Miss B. Nuthall/Miss S. Palfrey
Miss E. Cross/Mrs L. A. Harper 3-6, 6-3, 7-5
1931
Miss B. Nuthall/Mrs E. F. Whittingstall
Miss D. E. Round/Miss H. H. Jacobs 6-2, 6-4
1932
Miss H. H. Jacobs/Miss S. Palfrey
Mrs Painter/Miss A. Marble 8-6, 6-1
1933
Miss B. Nuthall/Miss F. James a bye
Mrs F. S. Moody/Miss E. Ryan retired
1934
Miss H. H. Jacobs/Miss S. Palfrey
Miss C. A. Babcock/Mrs D. Andrus 4-6, 6-3, 6-4
1935 *Transferred to Chestnut Hill, Mass.*
Miss H. H. Jacobs/Mrs S. P. Fabyan
Miss C. A. Babcock/Mrs D. Andrus 6-4, 6-2
1936
Mrs J. Van Ryn/Miss C. A. Babcock
Miss H. H. Jacobs/Mrs S. P. Fabyan 9-7, 2-6, 6-4
1937
Mrs S. P. Fabyan/Miss A. Marble
Miss C. A. Babcock/Mrs J. Van Ryn 7-5, 6-4
1938
Mrs S. P. Fabyan/Miss A. Marble
Mrs R. Mathieu/Miss J. Jedrzejowska 6-8, 6-4, 6-3
1939
Mrs S. P. Fabyan/Miss A. Marble
Miss K. E. Stammers/Mrs S. H. Hammersley 6-4, 8-6
1940
Mrs S. P. Fabyan/Miss A. Marble

1941
Mrs E. T. Cooke/Miss M. E. Osborne

1942 *Transferred to Forest Hills, N.Y.*
Miss A. L. Brough/Miss M. E. Osborne

1943
Miss A. L. Brough/Miss M. E. Osborne

1944
Miss A. L. Brough/Miss M. E. Osborne
Miss P. M. Betz/Miss D. J. Hart 4-6, 6-4, 6-3
1945
Miss A. L. Brough/Miss M. E. Osborne
Miss P. M. Betz/Miss D. J. Hart 6-4, 6-4
1946 *Transferred to Chestnut Hill, Mass.*
Miss A. L. Brough/Miss M. E. Osborne
Mrs D. Arnold Prentiss/Mrs P. C. Todd 6-2, 6-0
1947
Miss A. L. Brough/Miss M. E. Osborne
Miss D. J. Hart/Mrs P. C. Todd 5-7, 6-3, 7-5

Winners in **bold type**; **(H)**/(H) holder; **(C)**/(C) challenger; w.o. walk-over

Women's Singles

Semi-Finals

1948
Mrs W. duPont Miss G. Moran 10-8, 6-4
Miss A. L. Brough Mrs P. C. Todd 6-3, 6-3
1949
Mrs W. duPont Mrs B. E. Hilton 6-2, 6-3
Miss D. J. Hart Miss A. L. Brough 7-5, 6-1
1950
Mrs W. duPont Miss N. Chaffee 6-1, 1-6, 6-0
Miss D. J. Hart Miss B. Baker 6-4, 6-1
1951
Miss M. Connolly Miss D. J. Hart 6-4, 6-4
Miss S. J. Fry Mrs J. Walker-Smith 2-6, 6-2, 6-1
1952
Miss M. Connolly Miss S. J. Fry 4-6, 6-4, 6-1
Miss D. J. Hart Miss A. L. Brough 9-7, 8-6
1953
Miss M. Connolly Miss S. J. Fry 6-1, 6-1
Miss D. J. Hart Miss A. L. Brough 6-2, 6-4
1954
Miss D. J. Hart Miss S. J. Fry 6-2, 6-0
Miss A. L. Brough Miss D. R. Hard 6-2, 6-3
1955
Miss D. J. Hart Mrs D. P. Knode 6-1, 6-1
Miss P. E. Ward Miss B. Breit 6-1, 6-2
1956
Miss S. J. Fry Miss S. J. Bloomer 6-4, 6-4
Miss A. Gibson Mrs B. Pratt 6-1, 10-8
1957
Miss A. Gibson Mrs D. P. Knode 6-2, 6-2
Miss A. L. Brough Miss D. R. Hard 6-2, 6-4
1958
Miss A. Gibson Mrs J. G. Fleitz 6-4, 6-2
Miss D. R. Hard Miss J. Arth 7-5, 6-2
1959
Miss M. E. Bueno Miss D. R. Hard 6-1, 6-4
Miss C. C. Truman Miss A. S. Haydon 6-2, 6-3
1960
Miss D. R. Hard Miss D. Floyd 6-1, 7-5
Miss M. E. Bueno Miss C. C. Truman 6-3, 9-7
1961
Miss D. R. Hard Miss M. Smith 6-4, 3-6, 6-3
Miss A. S. Haydon Miss A. Mortimer 6-4, 6-2
1962
Miss M. Smith Miss M. E. Bueno 6-8, 6-3, 6-4
Miss D. R. Hard Miss V. Palmer 6-2, 6-3
1963
Miss M. E. Bueno Mrs P. F. Jones 1-6, 6-2, 9-7
Miss M. Smith Miss D. Catt 6-2, 6-0
1964
Miss M. E. Bueno Miss C. Hanks 6-4, 6-2
Mrs C. E. Graebner Miss N. Richey 2-6, 9-7, 6-4
1965
Miss M. Smith Miss N. Richey 6-2, 6-2
Miss B. J. Moffitt Miss M. E. Bueno 6-2, 6-3
1966
Miss M. E. Bueno Miss R. Casals 6-2, 10-12, 6-3
Miss N. Richey Miss K. Melville 6-3, 6-2
1967
Mrs L. W. King Miss F. Durr 6-2, 6-4
Mrs P. F. Jones Miss L. R. Turner 6-2, 6-4
1968 *Open Championships began*
Mrs L. W. King Miss M. E. Bueno 3-6, 6-4, 6-2
Miss S. V. Wade Mrs P. F. Jones 7-5, 6-1
1969
Mrs B. M. Court Miss S. V. Wade 7-5, 6-0
Miss N. Richey Miss R. Casals 7-5, 6-3
1970
Mrs B. M. Court Miss N. Richey 6-1, 6-3
Miss R. Casals Miss S. V. Wade 6-2, 6-7, 6-2
1971
Mrs L. W. King Miss C. Evert 6-3, 6-2
Miss R. Casals Miss K. Melville 6-4, 6-3
1972
Mrs L. W. King Mrs B. M. Court 6-4, 6-4
Miss K. Melville Miss C. Evert 6-4, 6-2
1973
Miss E. F. Goolagong Miss H. Masthoff 6-1, 4-6, 6-4
Mrs B. M. Court Miss C. Evert 7-5, 2-6, 6-2

Finals

1948
Mrs W. duPont Miss A. L. Brough 4-6, 6-4, 15-13
1949
Mrs W. duPont Miss D. J. Hart 6-4, 6-1
1950
Mrs W. duPont Miss D. J. Hart 6-3, 6-3
1951
Miss M. Connolly Miss S. J. Fry 6-3, 1-6, 6-4
1952
Miss M. Connolly Miss D. J. Hart 6-3, 7-5
1953
Miss M. Connolly Miss D. J. Hart 6-2, 6-4
1954
Miss D. J. Hart Miss A. L. Brough 6-8, 6-1, 8-6
1955
Miss D. J. Hart Miss P. E. Ward 6-4, 6-2
1956
Miss S. J. Fry Miss A. Gibson 6-3, 6-4
1957
Miss A. Gibson Miss A. L. Brough 6-3, 6-2
1958
Miss A. Gibson Miss D. R. Hard 3-6, 6-1, 6-2
1959
Miss M. Bueno Miss C. C. Truman 6-1, 6-4
1960
Miss D. R. Hard Miss M. E. Bueno 6-4, 10-12, 6-4
1961
Miss D. R. Hard Miss A. S. Haydon 6-3, 6-4
1962
Miss M. Smith Miss D. R. Hard 9-7, 6-4
1963
Miss M. E. Bueno Miss M. Smith 7-5, 6-4
1964
Miss M. E. Bueno Mrs C. E. Graebner 6-1, 6-0
1965
Miss M. Smith Miss B. J. Moffitt 8-6, 7-5
1966
Miss M. E. Bueno Miss N. Richey 6-3, 6-1
1967
Mrs L. W. King Mrs P. F. Jones 11-9, 6-4
1968 *Open Championships began*
Miss S. V. Wade Mrs L. W. King 6-4, 6-2
1969
Mrs B. M. Court Miss N. Richey 6-2, 6-2
1970
Mrs B. M. Court Miss R. Casals 6-2, 2-6, 6-1
1971
Mrs L. W. King Miss R. Casals 6-4, 7-6
1972
Mrs L. W. King Miss K. Melville 6-3, 7-5
1973
Mrs B. M. Court Miss E. F. Goolagong 7-6, 5-7, 6-2

Women's Doubles

Finals

1948
Miss A. L. Brough/Mrs W. duPont
Miss D. J. Hart/Mrs P. C. Todd 6-4, 8-10, 6-1
1949
Miss A. L. Brough/Mrs W. duPont
Miss D. J. Hart/Miss S. J. Fry 6-4, 8-6
1950
Miss A. L. Brough/Mrs W. duPont
Miss D. J. Hart/Miss S. J. Fry 6-2, 6-2
1951
Miss S. J. Fry/Miss D. J. Hart
Mrs P. C. Todd/Miss N. Chaffee 6-4, 6-2
1952
Miss S. J. Fry/Miss D. J. Hart
Miss A. L. Brough/Miss M. Connolly 10-8, 6-4
1953
Miss S. J. Fry/Miss D. J. Hart
Mrs W. duPont/Miss A. L. Brough 6-3, 7-9, 9-7
1954
Miss S. J. Fry/Miss D. J. Hart
Mrs W. duPont/Miss A. L. Brough 6-4, 6-4
1955
Miss A. L. Brough/Mrs W. duPont
Miss D. J. Hart/Miss S. J. Fry 6-3, 1-6, 6-3
1956
Miss A. L. Brough/Mrs W. duPont
Miss S. J. Fry/Mrs B. Pratt 6-3, 6-0
1957
Miss A. L. Brough/Mrs W. duPont
Miss A. Gibson/Miss D. R. Hard 6-2, 7-5
1958
Miss J. Arth/Miss D. R. Hard
Miss A. Gibson/Miss M. E. Bueno 2-6, 6-3, 6-4
1959
Miss J. Arth/Miss D. R. Hard
Miss M. E. Bueno/Miss S. H. Moore 6-2, 6-3
1960
Miss M. E. Bueno/Miss D. R. Hard
Miss A. S. Haydon/Miss D. Catt 6-1, 6-1
1961
Miss D. R. Hard/Miss L. R. Turner
Miss E. Buding/Miss Y. Ramirez 6-4, 5-7, 6-0
1962
Miss M. E. Bueno/Miss D. R. Hard
Miss B. J. Moffitt/Mrs J. R. Susman 4-6, 6-3, 6-2
1963
Miss R. A. Ebbern/Miss M. Smith
Miss D. R. Hard/Miss M. E. Bueno 4-6, 10-8, 6-3
1964
Miss B. J. Moffitt/Mrs J. R. Susman
Miss M. Smith/Miss L. R. Turner 3-6, 6-2, 6-4
1965
Mrs C. E. Graebner/Miss N. Richey
Miss B. J. Moffitt/Mrs J. R. Susman 6-4, 6-4
1966
Miss M. E. Bueno/Miss N. Richey
Mrs L. W. King/Miss R. Casals 6-3, 6-4
1967
Miss R. Casals/Mrs L. W. King
Miss M. A. Eisel/Mrs D. Fales 4-6, 6-3, 6-4
1968 *Open Championships began at Forest Hills, N.Y.*
Miss M. E. Bueno/Mrs B. M. Court
Miss R. Casals/Mrs L. W. King 4-6, 9-7, 8-6
1969
Miss F. Durr/Miss D. R. Hard
Mrs B. M. Court/Miss S. V. Wade 0-6, 6-3, 6-4
1970
Mrs B. M. Court/Mrs R. D. Dalton
Miss R. Casals/Miss S. V. Wade 6-4, 6-3
1971
Miss R. Casals/Mrs R. D. Dalton
Mrs G. Chanfreau/Miss F. Durr 6-3, 6-3
1972
Miss F. Durr/Miss B. Stöve
Mrs B. M. Court/Miss S. V. Wade 6-3, 1-6, 6-3
1973
Mrs B. M. Court/Miss S. V. Wade
Mrs L. W. King/ Miss R. Casals 3-6, 6-3, 7-5

United States Championships

Mixed Doubles

1892 *Played in Philadelphia, Pa.*
C. Hobart/Miss M. E. Cahill
1893
C. Hobart/Miss E. C. Roosevelt
1894
E. P. Fischer/Miss J. P. Atkinson
1895
E. P. Fischer/Miss J. P. Atkinson
1896
E. P. Fischer/Miss J. P. Atkinson
1897
D. L. Magruder/Miss L. Henson
1898
E. P. Fischer/Miss C. B. Neely
1899
A. L. Hoskins/Miss E. J. Rastall
1900
A. Codman/Miss M. J. Hunnewell
G. Atkinson/Miss Shaw 11-9, 6-3, 6-1
1901
R. D. Little/Miss M. Jones
1902
W. C. Grant/Miss E. H. Moore
1903
H. F. Allen/Miss H. Chapman
1904
W. C. Grant/Miss E. H. Moore
1905
C. Hobart/Mrs C. Hobart
1906
E. B. Dewhurst/Miss S. Coffin
1907
W. F. Johnson/Miss M. Sayres
1908
N. W. Niles/Miss E. E. Rotch
R. D. Little/Miss L. Hammond 6-4, 4-6, 6-4
1909
W. F. Johnson/Miss H. V. Hotchkiss
1910
J. R. Carpenter/Miss H. V. Hotchkiss
1911
W. F. Johnson/Miss H. V. Hotchkiss
H. M. Tilden/Miss E. Wildey 6-4, 6-4
1912
R. N. Williams/Miss M. K. Browne
W. J. Clothier/Miss Eleonora Sears 6-4, 2-6, 11-9
1913
W. T. Tilden/Miss M. K. Browne
C. S. Rogers/Miss D. Green 7-5, 7-5
1914
W. T. Tilden/Miss M. K. Browne
J. R. Rowland/Miss M. Myers 6-1, 6-4
1915
H. C. Johnson/Mrs G. W. Wightman
I. C. Wright/Miss M. Bjurstedt 6-0, 6-1
1916
W. E. Davis/Miss Eleonora Sears
W. T. Tilden/Miss F. A. Ballin 6-4, 7-5
1917 *National Patriotic Tournament*
I. C. Wright/Miss M. Bjurstedt
W. T. Tilden/Miss F. A. Ballin 10-12, 6-1, 6-3
1918
I. C. Wright/Mrs G. W. Wightman
F. B. Alexander/Miss M. Bjurstedt 6-2, 6-4
1919
V. Richards/Miss M. Zinderstein
W. T. Tilden/Miss F. A. Ballin
1920
W. F. Johnson/Mrs G. W. Wightman
1921 *Transferred to Chestnut Hill, Mass.*
W. M. Johnston/Miss M. K. Browne
1922
W. T. Tilden/Mrs M. Mallory
H. O. Kinsey/Miss H. Wills 6-4, 6-3
1923
W. T. Tilden/Mrs M. Mallory
J. B. Hawkes/Miss K. McKane 6-3, 2-6, 10-8
1924
V. Richards/Miss H. Wills
W. T. Tilden/Mrs M. Mallory 6-8, 7-5, 6-0
1925
J. B. Hawkes/Miss K. McKane
V. Richards/Miss E. H. Harvey 6-2, 6-4
1926
J. Borotra/Miss E. Ryan
R. Lacoste/Mrs G. W. Wightman 6-4, 7-5
1927
H. Cochet/Miss E. Bennett
R. Lacoste/Mrs G. W. Wightman 2-6, 6-0, 6-2
1928
J. B. Hawkes/Miss H. Wills
E. F. Moon/Miss E. Cross 6-1, 6-3
1929
G. M. Lott/Miss B. Nuthall
H. W. Austin/Mrs B. C. Covell 6-3, 6-3
1930
W. L. Allison/Miss E. Cross
F. X. Shields/Miss M. Morrill 6-4, 6-4
1931
G. M. Lott/Miss B. Nuthall
W. L. Allison/Mrs L. A. Harper 6-3, 6-3
1932
F. J. Perry/Miss S. Palfrey
H. E. Vines/Miss H. H. Jacobs 6-3, 7-5
1933
H. E. Vines/Miss E. Ryan
G. M. Lott/Miss S. Palfrey 11-9, 6-1

1934 *Transferred to Philadelphia, Pa.*
G. M. Lott/Miss H. H. Jacobs
L. R. Stoefen/Miss E. Ryan 4-6, 13-11, 6-2
1935 *Transferred to Chestnut Hill, Mass.*
E. Maier/Mrs S. P. Fabyan
R. Menzel/Miss K. E. Stammers 6-3, 3-6, 6-4
1936
C. G. Mako/Miss A. Marble
J. D. Budge/Mrs S. P. Fabyan 6-3, 6-2
1937
J. D. Budge/Mrs S. P. Fabyan
Y. Petra/Mrs S. Henrotin 6-2, 8-10, 6-0
1938
J. D. Budge/Miss A. Marble
J. E. Bromwich/Miss T. Coyne 6-1, 6-2
1939
H. C. Hopman/Miss A. Marble
1940
R. L. Riggs/Miss A. Marble
1941
J. A. Kramer/Mrs E. T. Cooke
1942 *Transferred to Forest Hills, N.Y.*
F. R. Schroeder/Miss A. L. Brough
1943
W. F. Talbert/Miss M. E. Osborne
1944
W. F. Talbert/Miss M. E. Osborne
W. D. McNeill/Miss D. M. Bundy 6-2, 6-3
1945
W. F. Talbert/Miss M. E. Osborne
R. Falkenburg/Miss D. J. Hart 6-4, 6-4
1946
W. F. Talbert/Miss M. E. Osborne
R. Kimball/Miss A. L. Brough 6-3, 6-4
1947
J. E. Bromwich/Miss A. L. Brough
F. Segura/Miss G. Moran 6-3, 6-1
1948
T. Brown/Miss A. L. Brough
W. F. Talbert/Mrs W. duPont 6-4, 6-4
1949
E. W. Sturgess/Miss A. L. Brough
W. F. Talbert/Mrs W. duPont 4-6, 6-3, 7-5
1950
K. McGregor/Mrs W. duPont
F. A. Sedgman/Miss D. J. Hart 6-4, 3-6, 6-3
1951
F. A. Sedgman/Miss D. J. Hart
M. G. Rose/Miss S. J. Fry 6-3, 6-2
1952
F. A. Sedgman/Miss D. J. Hart
L. A. Hoad/Mrs T. D. Long 6-3, 7-5
1953
E. V. Seixas/Miss D. J. Hart
R. N. Hartwig/Miss J. A. Sampson 6-2, 4-6, 6-4
1954
E. V. Seixas/Miss D. J. Hart
K. R. Rosewall/Mrs W. duPont 4-6, 6-1, 6-1
1955
E. V. Seixas/Miss D. J. Hart
G. Mulloy/Miss S. J. Fry 7-5, 5-7, 6-2
1956
K. R. Rosewall/Mrs W. duPont
L. A. Hoad/Miss D. R. Hard 9-7, 6-1
1957
K. Nielsen/Miss A. Gibson
R. N. Howe/Miss D. R. Hard 6-3, 9-7
1958
N. A. Fraser/Mrs W. duPont
A. Olmedo/Miss M. E. Bueno 6-4, 3-6, 9-7
1959
N. A. Fraser/Mrs W. duPont
R. Mark/Miss J. Hopps 7-5, 13-15, 6-2
1960
N. A. Fraser/Mrs W. duPont
A. Palafox/Miss M. E. Bueno 6-3, 6-2
1961
R. Mark/Miss M. Smith
R. D. Ralston/Miss D. R. Hard w.o.
1962
F. S. Stolle/Miss M. Smith
F. R. Froehling/Miss L. R. Turner 7-5, 6-2
1963
K. N. Fletcher/Miss M. Smith
E. Rubinoff/Miss J. A. M. Tegart 3-6, 8-6, 6-2
1964
J. D. Newcombe/Miss M. Smith
E. Rubinoff/Miss J. A. M. Tegart 10-8, 4-6, 6-3
1965
F. S. Stolle/Miss M. Smith
F. R. Froehling/Miss J. A. M. Tegart 6-2, 6-2
1966
O. K. Davidson/Mrs D. Fales
E. Rubinoff/Miss C. Aucamp 6-3, 6-1
1967
O. K. Davidson/Mrs L. W. King
S. R. Smith/Miss R. Casals
1968 *Open Championships began*
No Competition
1969
M. C. Riessen/Mrs B. M. Court
R. D. Ralston/Miss F. Durr 7-5, 6-3
1970
M. C. Riessen/Mrs B. M. Court
F. D. McMillan/Mrs R. D. Dalton 6-4, 6-4
1971
O. K. Davidson/Mrs L. W. King
R. Maud/Miss B. Stöve 6-3, 7-5

1972
M. C. Riessen/Mrs B. M. Court
I. Năstase/Miss R. Casals 6-3, 7-5
1973
O. K. Davidson/Miss L. W. King
M. C. Riessen/Mrs B. M. Court 6-4, 3-6, 7-5

Men's Singles

Semi-Finals

1905
R. W. Heath
A. H. Curtis
1906
A. F. Wilding
H. A. Parker
1907
H. M. Rice
H. A. Parker
1908
F. B. Alexander
A. W. Dunlop
1909
A. F. Wilding
E. F. Parker
1910
R. W. Heath
H. M. Rice
1911
N. E. Brookes
H. M. Rice
1912
J. C. Parke
A. E. Beamish
1913
E. F. Parker
H. A. Parker
1914
A. O'Hara Wood   R. C. Wertheim   6-3, 6-0, 2-6, 6-4
G. L. Patterson   R. Heath
1915
F. G. Lowe
H. M. Rice
1916-18   *No Competition*
1919
A. R. F. Kingscote

1920
P. O'Hara Wood

1921
R. H. Gemmell

1922
G. L. Patterson   J. B. Hawkes   8-6, 4-6, 7-5, 3-6, 10-8
J. O. Anderson   N. Peach   1-6, 6-2, 6-2, 6-4
1923
P. O'Hara Wood

1924
J. O. Anderson   G. M. Hone   6-2, 6-3, 6-2
R. E. Schlesinger   F. Kalms   7-5, 8-6, 6-0
1925
J. O. Anderson   P. O'Hara Wood   6-2, 6-3, 6-3
G. L. Patterson   R. E. Schlesinger   6-4, 4-6, 6-4, 6-4
1926
J. B. Hawkes   J. O. Anderson   6-8, 7-5, 6-3, 6-4
J. Willard   R. E. Schlesinger   3-6, 6-3, 6-0, 6-4
1927
J. B. Hawkes   J. Willard   6-0, 4-6, 6-2, 6-1
G. L. Patterson   E. F. Moon   6-3, 6-3, 9-7
1928
J. Borotra   J. H. Crawford   4-6, 6-3, 1-6, 7-5, 6-4
R. O. Cummings   R. E. Schlesinger   6-1, 2-6, 6-4, 8-6
1929
R. E. Schlesinger   H. C. Hopman   6-2, 6-1, 0-6, 6-2
J. C. Gregory   E. F. Moon   6-1, 7-5, 6-2
1930
E. F. Moon   J. H. Crawford   7-5, 6-4, 4-6, 6-3
H. C. Hopman   J. Willard   6-4, 6-2, 6-0
1931
J. H. Crawford   D. P. Turnbull
H. C. Hopman   R. O. Cummings
1932
J. H. Crawford   C. Sproule   6-4, 2-6, 6-2, 6-1
H. C. Hopman   J. Sato   0-6, 6-2, 6-3, 4-6, 6-4
1933
J. H. Crawford   W. L. Allison   6-3, 3-6, 3-6, 6-0, 6-3
K. Gledhill   V. B. McGrath   6-4, 6-1, 6-1
1934
F. J. Perry   V. B. McGrath   2-6, 5-7, 6-4, 6-4, 6-1
J. H. Crawford   A. K. Quist   6-4, 6-2, 6-2
1935
F. J. Perry   V. B. McGrath   6-2, 6-3, 6-1
J. H. Crawford   A. K. Quist   6-1, 1-6, 6-2, 3-6, 6-3
1936
J. H. Crawford   A. A. Kay   6-2, 9-7, 6-2
A. K. Quist   H. C. Hopman   4-6, 6-2, 10-8, 6-3
1937
J. E. Bromwich   J. H. Crawford   6-1, 7-9, 6-4, 8-6
V. B. McGrath   H. C. Hopman   6-4, 6-1, 7-5
1938
J. D. Budge   A. K. Quist   6-4, 6-2, 8-6
J. E. Bromwich   G. von Cramm   6-3, 7-5, 6-1
1939
J. E. Bromwich   V. B. McGrath   6-0, 6-3, 6-4
A. K. Quist   J. H. Crawford   6-1, 7-5, 6-4
1940
A. K. Quist   V. B. McGrath
J. H. Crawford   J. E. Bromwich
1941-45   *No Competition*
1946
J. E. Bromwich
D. Pails
1947
D. Pails   T. Brown   6-4, 6-2, 6-1
J. E. Bromwich   G. Mulloy   6-2, 6-4, 1-6, 6-4

Finals

1905
R. W. Heath   A. H. Curtis
1906
A. F. Wilding   H. A. Parker
1907
H. M. Rice   H. A. Parker
1908
F. B. Alexander   A. W. Dunlop
1909
A. F. Wilding   E. F. Parker
1910
R. W. Heath   H. M. Rice
1911
N. E. Brookes   H. M. Rice
1912
J. C. Parke   A. E. Beamish   3-6, 6-2, 1-6, 6-1, 7-5
1913
E. F. Parker   H. A. Parker
1914
A. O'Hara Wood   G. L. Patterson   6-4, 6-3, 5-7, 6-1
1915
F. G. Lowe   H. M. Rice
1916-18   *No Competition*
1919
A. R. F. Kingscote   E. O. Pockley   6-4, 6-0, 6-3
1920
P. O'Hara Wood

1921
R. H. Gemmell

1922
J. O. Anderson   G. L. Patterson   6-0, 3-6, 3-6, 6-3, 6-2
1923
P. O'Hara Wood

1924
J. O. Anderson   R. E. Schlesinger   6-3, 6-4, 3-6, 5-7, 6-3
1925
J. O. Anderson   G. L. Patterson   11-9, 2-6, 6-2, 6-3
1926
J. B. Hawkes   J. Willard   6-1, 6-3, 6-1
1927
G. L. Patterson   J. B. Hawkes   3-6, 6-4, 3-6, 18-16, 6-3
1928
J. Borotra   R. O. Cummings   6-4, 6-1, 4-6, 5-7, 6-3
1929
J. C. Gregory   R. E. Schlesinger   6-2, 6-2, 5-7, 7-5
1930
E. F. Moon   H. C. Hopman   6-3, 6-1, 6-3
1931
J. H. Crawford   H. C. Hopman   6-4, 6-2, 2-6, 6-1
1932
J. H. Crawford   H. C. Hopman   4-6, 6-3, 3-6, 6-3, 6-1
1933
J. H. Crawford   K. Gledhill   2-6, 7-5, 6-3, 6-2
1934
F. J. Perry   J. H. Crawford   6-3, 7-5, 6-1
1935
J. H. Crawford   F. J. Perry   2-6, 6-4, 6-4, 6-4
1936
A. K. Quist   J. H. Crawford   6-2, 6-3, 4-6, 3-6, 9-7
1937
V. B. McGrath   J. E. Bromwich   6-3, 1-6, 6-0, 2-6, 6-1
1938
J. D. Budge   J. E. Bromwich   6-4, 6-2, 6-1
1939
J. E. Bromwich   A. K. Quist   6-4, 6-1, 6-3
1940
A. K. Quist   J. H. Crawford
1941-45   *No Competition*
1946
J. E. Bromwich   D. Pails   5-7, 6-3, 7-5, 3-6, 6-2
1947
D. Pails   J. E. Bromwich   4-6, 6-4, 3-6, 7-5, 8-6

Men's Doubles

Finals

1905
T. Tachell/R. Lycett
E. T. Barnard/B. Spence
1906
A. F. Wilding/R. W. Heath
H. A. Parker/C. C. Cox
1907
H. A. Parker/W. A. Gregg
H. M. Rice/G. W. Wright
1908
F. B. Alexander/A. W. Dunlop
A. F. Wilding/G. G. Sharp
1909
E. F. Parker/J. P. Keane
A. F. Wilding/L. Crooks
1910
H. M. Rice/A. Campbell
R. W. Heath/J. L. O'Dea
1911
R. W. Heath/R. Lycett
N. E. Brookes/J. J. Addison
1912
J. C. Parke/C. P. Dixon
A. E. Beamish/F. G. Lowe
1913
E. F. Parker/A. H. Hedemann

1914
A. Campbell/G. L. Patterson
R. Heath/A. O'Hara Wood   7-5, 3-6, 6-3, 6-3
1915
H. M. Rice/C. V. Todd

1916-18   *No Competition*
1919
P. O'Hara Wood/R. V. Thomas

1920
P. O'Hara Wood/R. V. Thomas

1921
R. H. Gemmell/S. H. Eaton

1922
G. L. Patterson/J. B. Hawkes
J. O. Anderson/N. Peach   8-10, 6-0, 6-0, 7-5
1923
P. O'Hara Wood/C. B. St John

1924
N. E. Brookes/J. O. Anderson
G. L. Patterson/P. O'Hara Wood   6-2, 6-4, 6-3
1925
G. L. Patterson/P. O'Hara Wood
J. O. Anderson/F. Kalms   6-4, 8-6, 7-5
1926
G. L. Patterson/J. B. Hawkes
J. O. Anderson/P. O'Hara Wood   6-1, 6-4, 6-2
1927
G. L. Patterson/J. B. Hawkes
P. O'Hara Wood/I. McInnes   8-6, 6-2, 6-1
1928
J. Borotra/J. Brugnon
J. Willard/E. F. Moon   6-2, 4-6, 6-4, 6-4
1929
J. H. Crawford/H. C. Hopman
R. O. Cummings/E. F. Moon   6-1, 6-8, 4-6, 6-1, 6-3
1930
J. H. Crawford/H. C. Hopman
J. B. Hawkes/Fitchett   8-6, 6-1, 2-6, 6-3
1931
C. Donohoe/R. Dunlop
J. H. Crawford/H. C. Hopman   8-6, 6-2, 5-7, 7-9, 6-4
1932
J. H. Crawford/E. F. Moon
H. C. Hopman/G. L. Patterson   12-10, 6-3, 4-6, 6-4
1933
H. E. Vines/K. Gledhill
J. H. Crawford/E. F. Moon   6-4, 10-8, 6-2
1934
F. J. Perry/G. P. Hughes
A. K. Quist/D. P. Turnbull   6-8, 6-3, 6-4, 3-6, 6-3
1935
J. H. Crawford/V. B. McGrath
F. J. Perry/G. P. Hughes   6-4, 8-6, 6-2
1936
A. K. Quist/D. P. Turnbull
J. H. Crawford/V. B. McGrath   6-8, 6-2, 6-1, 3-6, 6-2
1937
A. K. Quist/D. P. Turnbull
J. E. Bromwich/J. E. Harper   6-2, 9-7, 1-6, 6-8, 6-4
1938
A. K. Quist/J. E. Bromwich
G. von Cramm/H. Henkel   7-5, 6-4, 6-0
1939
A. K. Quist/J. E. Bromwich
D. P. Turnbull/C. F. Long   6-4, 7-5, 6-2
1940
A. K. Quist/J. E. Bromwich

1941-45   *No Competition*
1946
A. K. Quist/J. E. Bromwich

1947
A. K. Quist/J. E. Bromwich
F. A. Sedgman/G. Worthington   6-1, 6-3, 6-1

Australian Championships

Men's Singles

Semi-Finals

1948
A. K. Quist O. W. Sidwell 6-1, 6-2, 1-6, 6-3
J. E. Bromwich G. E. Brown 3-6, 2-6, 6-4, 6-4, 7-5
1949
F. A. Sedgman O. W. Sidwell 6-3, 6-3, 6-2
J. E. Bromwich G. E. Brown 1-6, 6-3, 6-3, 6-3
1950
F. A. Sedgman E. W. Sturgess 6-2, 6-3, 6-8, 4-6, 6-4
K. McGregor O. W. Sidwell 7-5, 9-7, 6-3
1951
R. Savitt F. A. Sedgman 2-6, 7-5, 1-6, 6-3, 6-4
K. McGregor A. Larsen 11-9, 6-2, 5-7, 6-1
1952
K. McGregor R. Savitt 6-4, 6-4, 3-6, 6-4
F. A. Sedgman M. G. Rose 6-2, 6-4, 6-4
1953
K. R. Rosewall E. V. Seixas 6-3, 2-6, 7-5, 6-4
M. G. Rose I. Ayre 4-6, 4-6, 6-1, 6-4, 6-4
1954
M. G. Rose K. R. Rosewall 6-2, 6-3, 3-6, 1-6, 7-5
R. N. Hartwig J. E. Bromwich 8-6, 6-4, 9-7
1955
K. R. Rosewall M. A. Trabert 8-6, 6-3, 6-3
L. A. Hoad R. N. Hartwig 6-1, 6-4, 6-4
1956
L. A. Hoad N. A. Fraser 6-3, 6-2, 6-0
K. R. Rosewall H. Flam 6-4, 6-0, 6-2
1957
A. J. Cooper M. J. Anderson 6-4, 9-7, 6-4
N. A. Fraser L. A. Hoad 7-5, 3-6, 6-1, 6-4
1958
A. J. Cooper N. A. Fraser 6-2, 3-6, 10-8, 6-3
M. J. Anderson M. G. Rose 6-2, 5-7, 6-4, 19-17
1959
A. Olmedo B. MacKay 3-6, 8-6, 6-1, 3-6, 6-3
N. A. Fraser R. Mark 6-4, 6-4, 6-3
1960
R. G. Laver R. S. Emerson 4-6, 6-1, 9-7, 3-6, 7-5
N. A. Fraser R. A. J. Hewitt 8-6, 6-4, 11-9
1961
R. S. Emerson F. S. Stolle 8-6, 6-2, 7-5
R. G. Laver B. Phillips-Moore 6-2, 6-2, 6-4
1962
R. G. Laver R. A. J. Hewitt 6-4, 7-5
R. S. Emerson N. A. Fraser 6-4, 6-3, 6-1
1963
R. S. Emerson R. A. J. Hewitt 8-6, 6-4, 3-6, 9-7
K. N. Fletcher F. S. Stolle 6-3, 6-4, 7-5
1964
R. S. Emerson M. F. Mulligan 6-2, 9-7, 6-4
F. S. Stolle K. N. Fletcher 6-4, 3-6, 6-3, 3-6, 6-3
1965
R. S. Emerson J. D. Newcombe 7-5, 6-4, 6-1
F. S. Stolle A. D. Roche 6-4, 8-6, 9-7
1966
R. S. Emerson J. D. Newcombe 4-6, 6-2, 6-1, 6-2
A. R. Ashe F. S. Stolle 6-4, 1-6, 6-3, 10-8
1967
R. S. Emerson A. D. Roche 6-3, 4-6, 15-13, 13-15, 6-2
A. R. Ashe J. D. Newcombe 12-10, 20-22, 6-3, 6-2
1968
W. W. Bowrey B. Phillips-Moore 10-8, 6-4, 6-4
J. M. Gisbert R. O. Ruffels 10-8, 3-6, 6-2, 6-3
1969 *Open Championships began*
R. G. Laver A. D. Roche 7-5, 22-20, 9-11, 1-6, 6-3
A. Gimeno R. O. Ruffels 6-2, 11-9, 6-2
1970
A. R. Ashe R. D. Ralston 6-3, 8-10, 6-3, 2-1 (forfeit)
R. D. Crealy R. Taylor 6-3, 9-11, 8-6, 3-6, 8-6
1971
K. R. Rosewall T. S. Okker 6-2, 7-5, 6-4
A. R. Ashe R. C. Lutz 6-4, 6-4, 7-6
1972
K. R. Rosewall A. Stone 7-6, 6-1, 3-6, 6-2
M. J. Anderson A. Metreveli 7-6, 6-2, 7-6
1973
O. Parun K. Meiler 2-6, 6-3, 7-5, 6-1
J. D. Newcombe P. Proisy 7-6, 6-4, 6-2

Finals

1948
A. K. Quist J. E. Bromwich 6-4, 3-6, 6-3, 2-6, 6-3
1949
F. A. Sedgman J. E. Bromwich 6-3, 6-3, 6-2
1950
F. A. Sedgman K. McGregor 6-3, 6-4, 4-6, 6-1
1951
R. Savitt K. McGregor 6-3, 2-6, 6-3, 6-1
1952
K. McGregor F. A. Sedgman 7-5, 12-10, 2-6, 6-2
1953
K. R. Rosewall M. G. Rose 6-0, 6-3, 6-4
1954
M. G. Rose R. N. Hartwig 6-2, 0-6, 6-4, 6-2
1955
K. R. Rosewall L. A. Hoad 9-7, 6-4, 6-4
1956
L. A. Hoad K. R. Rosewall 6-4, 3-6, 6-4, 7-5
1957
A. J. Cooper N. A. Fraser 6-3, 9-11, 6-4, 6-2
1958
A. J. Cooper M. J. Anderson 7-5, 6-3, 6-4
1959
A. Olmedo N. A. Fraser 6-1, 6-2, 3-6, 6-3
1960
R. G. Laver N. A. Fraser 5-7, 3-6, 6-3, 8-6, 8-6
1961
R. S. Emerson R. G. Laver 1-6, 6-3, 7-5, 6-4
1962
R. G. Laver R. S. Emerson 8-6, 0-6, 6-4, 6-4
1963
R. S. Emerson K. N. Fletcher 6-3, 6-3, 6-1
1964
R. S. Emerson F. S. Stolle 6-3, 6-4, 6-2
1965
R. S. Emerson F. S. Stolle 7-9, 2-6, 6-4, 7-5, 6-1
1966
R. S. Emerson A. R. Ashe 6-4, 6-8, 6-2, 6-3
1967
R. S. Emerson A. R. Ashe 6-4, 6-1, 6-4
1968
W. W. Bowrey J. M. Gisbert 7-5, 2-6, 9-7, 6-4
1969 *Open Championships began*
R. G. Laver A. Gimeno 6-3, 6-4, 7-5
1970
A. R. Ashe R. D. Crealy 6-4, 9-7, 6-2
1971
K. R. Rosewall A. R. Ashe 6-1, 7-5, 6-3
1972
K. R. Rosewall M. J. Anderson 7-6, 6-3, 7-5
1973
J. D. Newcombe O. Parun 6-3, 6-7, 7-5, 6-1

Men's Doubles

Finals

1948
A. K. Quist/J. E. Bromwich
F. A. Sedgman/C. F. Long 1-6, 6-8, 9-7, 6-3, 8-6
1949
A. K. Quist/J. E. Bromwich
G. E. Brown/O. W. Sidwell 1-6, 7-5, 6-2, 6-3
1950
A. K. Quist/J. E. Bromwich
E. W. Sturgess/J. Drobný 6-3, 5-7, 4-6, 6-3, 8-6
1951
F. A. Sedgman/K. McGregor
J. E. Bromwich/A. K. Quist 11-9, 2-6, 6-3, 4-6, 6-3
1952
F. A. Sedgman/K. McGregor
M. G. Rose/D. Candy 6-4, 7-5, 6-3
1953
L. A. Hoad/K. R. Rosewall
D. Candy/M. G. Rose 9-11, 6-4, 10-8, 6-4
1954
R. N. Hartwig/M. G. Rose
N. A. Fraser/C. Wilderspin 6-3, 6-4, 6-2
1955
E. V. Seixas/M. A. Trabert
L. A. Hoad/K. R. Rosewall 6-4, 6-2, 2-6, 3-6, 6-1
1956
L. A. Hoad/K. R. Rosewall
M. G. Rose/D. Candy 10-8, 13-11, 6-4
1957
L. A. Hoad/N. A. Fraser
A. J. Cooper/M. J. Anderson 6-3, 8-6, 6-1
1958
A. J. Cooper/N. A. Fraser
R. S. Emerson/R. Mark 7-5, 6-8, 3-6, 6-3, 7-5
1959
R. G. Laver/R. Mark
D. Candy/R. N. Howe 9-7, 6-4, 6-2
1960
R. G. Laver/R. Mark
R. S. Emerson/N. A. Fraser 1-6, 6-2, 6-4, 6-4
1961
R. G. Laver/R. Mark
R. S. Emerson/M. F. Mulligan 6-3, 7-5, 3-6, 9-11, 6-2
1962
R. S. Emerson/N. A. Fraser
R. A. J. Hewitt/F. S. Stolle 4-6, 4-6, 6-1, 6-4, 11-9
1963
R. A. J. Hewitt/F. S. Stolle
K. N. Fletcher/J. D. Newcombe 6-2, 3-6, 6-3, 3-6, 6-3
1964
R. A. J. Hewitt/F. S. Stolle
R. S. Emerson/K. N. Fletcher 6-4, 7-5, 3-6, 4-6, 14-12
1965
J. D. Newcombe/A. D. Roche
R. S. Emerson/F. S. Stolle 3-6, 4-6, 13-11, 6-3, 6-4
1966
R. S. Emerson/F. S. Stolle
J. D. Newcombe/A. D. Roche 7-9, 6-3, 6-8, 14-12, 12-10
1967
J. D. Newcombe/A. D. Roche
O. K. Davidson/W. W. Bowrey 3-6, 6-3, 7-5, 6-8, 8-6
1968
R. D. Crealy/A. Stone
T. Addison/R. Keldie 10-8, 6-4, 6-3
1969 *Open Championships began*
R. S. Emerson/R. G. Laver
K. R. Rosewall/F. S. Stolle 6-4, 6-4
1970
R. C. Lutz/S. R. Smith
J. Alexander/P. Dent 8-6, 6-3, 6-4
1971
J. D. Newcombe/A. D. Roche
M. C. Riessen/T. S. Okker 6-2, 7-6
1972
K. R. Rosewall/O. K. Davidson
G. Masters/R. Case 3-6, 7-6, 6-2
1973
J. D. Newcombe/M. J. Anderson
J. Alexander/P. Dent 6-3, 6-4, 7-6

Women's Singles

Women's Doubles

Semi-Finals

1922
Mrs M. Molesworth Mrs H. S. Utz 6-2, 6-3
Miss E. F. Boyd Miss S. Lance 6-4, 10-8
1923
 Mrs M. Molesworth

1924
 Miss S. Lance
 Miss E. F. Boyd
1925
 Miss D. Akhurst
 Miss E. F. Boyd
1926
Miss D. Akhurst Miss M. Cox 6-1, 6-3
Miss E. F. Boyd Mrs S. Harper 6-4, 3-6, 6-3
1927
Miss E. F. Boyd Miss L. M. Bickerton 6-3, 6-1
Mrs S. Harper Mrs Turner 6-2, 6-0
1928
Miss D. Akhurst Mrs P. O'Hara Wood 6-2, 7-5
Miss E. F. Boyd Miss L. M. Bickerton 6-2, 6-3
1929
 Miss D. Akhurst
 Miss L. M. Bickerton
1930
Miss D. Akhurst Miss E. Hood 6-0, 6-2
Mrs S. Harper Miss L. M. Bickerton 6-3, 8-6
1931
 Mrs C. Buttsworth
 Mrs J. H. Crawford
1932
 Mrs C. Buttsworth
Miss K. Le Messurier Mrs J. H. Crawford
1933
 Miss J. Hartigan
 Mrs C. Buttsworth
1934
 Miss J. Hartigan
 Mrs M. Molesworth
1935
Miss D. E. Round Mrs V. Westacott 6-4, 6-2
Miss N. M. Lyle Mrs H. C. Hopman 6-1, 7-5
1936
 Miss J. Hartigan
 Miss N. Wynne
1937
 Miss N. Wynne
 Mrs V. Westacott
1938
Miss D. M. Bundy Mrs H. C. Hopman 6-2, 6-3
Miss D. Stevenson Miss N. Wynne 6-3, 6-3
1939
Mrs H. C. Hopman Miss T. Coyne 6-3, 6-4
Mrs V. Westacott Miss J. Hartigan 6-2, 6-3
1940
 Mrs N. Bolton

1941-45 *No Competition*
1946
 Mrs N. Bolton
 Miss J. Fitch
1947
Mrs N. Bolton Miss L. P. Jones 6-2, 6-1
Mrs H. C. Hopman Mrs T. D. Long 6-4, 6-1
1948
 Mrs N. Bolton
 Miss M. Toomey
1949
Miss D. J. Hart Mrs A. B. Baker 6-3, 6-1
Mrs N. Bolton Mrs T. D. Long 6-4, 6-2
1950
Miss A. L. Brough Miss J. Fitch 6-4, 6-4
Miss D. J. Hart Mrs N. Bolton 6-2, 6-3
1951
 Mrs N. Bolton
 Mrs T. D. Long
1952
Mrs T. D. Long Mrs M. K. Hawton 6-0, 7-5
Miss H. Angwin Mrs N. Bolton 4-6, 6-4, 6-4
1953
Miss M. Connolly Mrs M. K. Hawton 6-2, 6-1
Miss J. Sampson Mrs D. Fogarty 3-6, 6-4, 6-4
1954
Mrs T. D. Long Miss M. Carter 6-2, 6-3
Miss J. Staley Mrs M. K. Hawton 6-1, 6-1
1955
Miss B. Penrose Miss J. Staley 6-4, 8-6
Mrs T. D. Long Miss M. Carter 6-2, 6-1
1956
Miss M. Carter Miss D. Seeney 6-3, 7-5
Mrs T. D. Long Mrs M. K. Hawton 0-6, 6-3, 9-7
1957
Miss S. J. Fry Miss B. Penrose 6-3, 6-4
Miss A. Gibson Miss L. Coghlan 7-5, 6-3
1958
Miss A. Mortimer Miss B. Holstein 6-2, 6-0
Miss L. Coghlan Miss M. Carter 6-1, 6-1
1959
Mrs M. Reitano Miss J. Lehane 6-3, 6-0
Miss R. Schuurman Mrs M. K. Hawton 6-3, 6-0
1960
Miss M. Smith Mrs M. Reitano 7-5, 2-6, 7-5
Miss J. Lehane Miss C. C. Truman 7-5, 3-6, 7-5
1961
Miss M. Smith Miss R. A. Ebbern 6-2, 6-0
Miss J. Lehane Mrs M. Reitano 6-3, 4-6, 6-1

Finals

1922
Mrs M. Molesworth Miss E. F. Boyd 6-3, 10-8
1923
 Mrs M. Molesworth

1924
Miss S. Lance Miss E. F. Boyd 6-3, 3-6, 6-4
1925
Miss D. Akhurst Miss E. F. Boyd 1-6, 8-6, 6-4
1926
Miss D. Akhurst Miss E. F. Boyd 6-1, 6-3
1927
Miss E. F. Boyd Mrs S. Harper 5-7, 6-1, 6-2
1928
Miss D. Akhurst Miss E. F. Boyd 7-5, 6-2
1929
Miss D. Akhurst Miss L. M. Bickerton 6-1, 5-7, 6-2
1930
Miss D. Akhurst Mrs S. Harper 10-8, 2-6, 7-5
1931
Mrs C. Buttsworth Mrs J. H. Crawford 1-6, 6-3, 6-4
1932
Mrs C. Buttsworth Miss K. Le Messurier 9-7, 6-4
1933
Miss J. Hartigan Mrs C. Buttsworth 6-4, 6-3
1934
Miss J. Hartigan Mrs M. Molesworth 6-1, 6-4
1935
Miss D. E. Round Miss N. M. Lyle 1-6, 6-1, 6-3
1936
Miss J. Hartigan Miss N. Wynne 6-4, 6-4
1937
Miss N. Wynne Mrs V. Westacott 6-3, 5-7, 6-4
1938
Miss D. M. Bundy Miss D. Stevenson 6-3, 6-2
1939
Mrs V. Westacott Mrs H. C. Hopman 6-1, 6-2
1940
 Mrs N. Bolton

1941-45 *No Competition*
1946
Mrs N. Bolton Miss J. Fitch 6-4, 6-4
1947
Mrs N. Bolton Mrs H. C. Hopman 6-3, 6-2
1948
Mrs N. Bolton Miss M. Toomey 6-3, 6-1
1949
Miss D. J. Hart Mrs N. Bolton 6-3, 6-4
1950
Miss A. L. Brough Miss D. J. Hart 6-4, 3-6, 6-4
1951
Mrs N. Bolton Mrs T. D. Long 6-1, 7-5
1952
Mrs T. D. Long Miss H. Angwin 6-2, 6-3
1953
Miss M. Connolly Miss J. Sampson 6-3, 6-2
1954
Mrs T. D. Long Miss J. Staley 6-3, 6-4
1955
Miss B. Penrose Mrs T. D. Long 6-4, 6-3
1956
Miss M. Carter Mrs T. D. Long 3-6, 6-2, 9-7
1957
Miss S. J. Fry Miss A. Gibson 6-3, 6-4
1958
Miss A. Mortimer Miss L. Coghlan 6-3, 6-4
1959
Mrs M. Reitano Miss R. Schuurman 6-2, 6-3
1960
Miss M. Smith Miss J. Lehane 7-5, 6-2
1961
Miss M. Smith Miss J. Lehane 6-1, 6-4

Finals

1922
Miss E. F. Boyd/Miss M. Mountain
Mrs H. S. Utz/Miss St George 1-6, 6-4, 7-5
1923
 Miss E. F. Boyd/Miss S. Lance

1924
Miss D. Akhurst/Miss S. Lance
Mrs P. O'Hara Wood/Miss K. Le Messurier 7-5, 6-2
1925
Mrs S. Harper/Miss D. Akhurst
Miss E. F. Boyd/Miss K. Le Messurier 6-4, 6-3
1926
Mrs P. O'Hara Wood/Miss E. F. Boyd
Miss D. Akhurst/Miss M. Cox 6-3, 6-8, 8-6
1927
Mrs P. O'Hara Wood/Miss L. M. Bickerton
Mrs S. Harper/Miss E. F. Boyd 6-3, 6-3
1928
Miss D. Akhurst/Miss E. F. Boyd
Miss K. Le Messurier/Miss D. Weston 6-3, 6-1
1929
Miss D. Akhurst/Miss L. M. Bickerton
Mrs P. O'Hara Wood/Mrs S. Harper 6-2, 3-6, 6-2
1930
Mrs M. Molesworth/Miss E. Hood
Mrs S. Harper/Miss M. Cox 6-3, 0-6, 7-5
1931
Mrs D. A. Cozens/Miss L. M. Bickerton
Mrs H. S. Utz/Miss N. Lloyd 6-0, 6-4
1932
Mrs C. Buttsworth/Mrs J. H. Crawford
Miss K. Le Messurier/Miss D. Weston 6-2, 6-2
1933
Mrs M. Molesworth/Mrs V. Westacott
Mrs J. Van Ryn/Miss J. Hartigan 6-3, 6-3
1934
 Mrs M. Molesworth/Mrs V. Westacott

1935
Miss E. Dearman/Miss N. M. Lyle
Mrs H. C. Hopman/Miss L. M. Bickerton 6-3, 6-4
1936
Miss T. Coyne/Miss N. Wynne
Miss M. Blick/Miss K. Woodward 6-2, 6-4
1937
Miss T. Coyne/Miss N. Wynne
Mrs H. C. Hopman/Mrs V. Westacott 6-2, 6-2
1938
Miss T. Coyne/Miss N. Wynne
Miss D. M. Bundy/Miss D. E. Workman 9-7, 6-4
1939
Miss T. Coyne/Miss N. Wynne
Mrs V. Westacott/Miss M. Hardcastle 7-5, 6-4
1940
 Miss T. Coyne/Miss N. Wynne

1941-45 *No Competition*
1946
 Miss M. Bevis/Miss J. Fitch

1947
Mrs N. Bolton/Mrs T. D. Long
Miss J. Fitch/Miss M. Bevis 6-3, 6-3
1948
Mrs N. Bolton/Mrs T. D. Long
Miss M. Bevis/Miss N. Jones 6-3, 6-3
1949
Mrs N. Bolton/Mrs T. D. Long
Miss D. Toomey/Miss M. Toomey 6-0, 6-1
1950
Miss D. J. Hart/Miss A. L. Brough
Mrs N. Bolton/Mrs T. D. Long 6-2, 2-6, 6-3
1951
Mrs N. Bolton/Mrs T. D. Long
Mrs M. K. Hawton/Miss J. Fitch 6-2, 6-1
1952
Mrs N. Bolton/Mrs T. D. Long
Mrs R. Baker/Mrs M. K. Hawton 6-1, 6-1
1953
Miss M. Connolly/Miss J. Sampson
Mrs M. K. Hawton/Miss B. Penrose 6-4, 6-2
1954
Mrs M. K. Hawton/Miss B. Penrose
Mrs H. Redick-Smith/Mrs J. Wipplinger 6-3, 8-6
1955
Mrs M. K. Hawton/Miss B. Penrose
Mrs H. C. Hopman/Mrs A. R. Thiele 7-5, 6-1
1956
Mrs M. K. Hawton/Mrs T. D. Long
Miss B. Penrose/Miss M. Carter 6-2, 5-7, 9-7
1957
Miss S. J. Fry/Miss A. Gibson
Mrs M. K. Hawton/Miss F. Muller 6-2, 6-1
1958
Mrs T. D. Long/Mrs M. K. Hawton
Miss A. Mortimer/Miss L. Coghlan 7-5, 6-8, 6-2
1959
Miss S. Reynolds/Miss R. Schuurman
Mrs M. K. Hawton/Miss L. Coghlan 7-5, 6-4
1960
Miss M. E. Bueno/Miss C. C. Truman
Miss M. Smith/Miss L. Robinson 6-2, 5-7, 6-2
1961
Mrs M. Reitano/Miss M. Smith
Mrs M. K. Hawton/Miss J. Lehane 6-4, 3-6, 7-5

Australian Championships

Women's Singles

Semi-Finals

1962
Miss M. Smith Miss Y. Ramirez 6-2, 6-1
Miss J. Lehane Mrs M. Reitano 6-2, 2-6, 6-4
1963
Miss M. Smith Miss R. A. Ebbern 6-1, 6-3
Miss J. Lehane Miss L. R. Turner 5-7, 6-3, 6-2
1964
Miss M. Smith Miss J. Lehane 6-4, 6-2
Miss L. R. Turner Miss R. A. Ebbern 6-3, 6-1
1965
Miss M. Smith Miss B. J. Moffitt 6-1, 8-6
Miss M. E. Bueno Miss A. Van Zyl 6-2, 6-3
1966
Miss M. Smith Mrs C. E. Graebner 6-2, 6-4
Miss N. Richey Miss K. Melville 6-2, 8-6
1967
Miss N. Richey Miss K. Melville 6-4, 6-1
Miss L. R. Turner Miss R. Casals 4-6, 6-1, 6-4
1968
Mrs L. W. King Miss J. A. M. Tegart 4-6, 6-1, 6-1
Mrs B. M. Court Miss L. R. Turner 6-3, 6-2
1969 *Open Championships began*
Mrs B. M. Court Miss K. Melville 3-6, 6-2, 7-5
Mrs L. W. King Mrs P. F. Jones 4-6, 6-2, 6-3
1970
Mrs B. M. Court Miss K. Krantzcke 6-1, 6-3
Miss K. Melville Miss W. M. Shaw 8-6, 6-4
1971
Mrs B. M. Court Miss L. Hunt 6-0, 6-3
Miss E. F. Goolagong Miss W. M. Shaw 7-6, 6-1
1972
Miss E. F. Goolagong Miss H. Gourlay 6-2, 7-5
Miss S. V. Wade Miss K. Harris 7-6, 2-6, 6-0
1973
Mrs B. M. Court Miss K. Melville 6-1, 6-0
Miss E. F. Goolagong Miss K. Sawamatsu 6-4, 6-3

Finals

1962
Miss M. Smith Miss J. Lehane 6-0, 6-2
1963
Miss M. Smith Miss J. Lehane 6-2, 6-2
1964
Miss M. Smith Miss L. R. Turner 6-3, 6-2
1965
Miss M. Smith Miss M. E. Bueno 5-7, 6-4, 5-2 retired
1966
Miss M. Smith Miss N. Richey default
1967
Miss N. Richey Miss L. R. Turner 6-1, 6-4
1968
Mrs L. W. King Mrs B. M. Court 6-1, 6-2
1969 *Open Championships began*
Mrs B. M. Court Mrs L. W. King 6-4, 6-1
1970
Mrs B. M. Court Miss K. Melville 6-1, 6-3
1971
Mrs B. M. Court Miss E. F. Goolagong 2-6, 7-6, 7-5
1972
Miss S. V. Wade Miss E. F. Goolagong 6-4, 6-4
1973
Mrs B. M. Court Miss E. F. Goolagong 6-4, 7-5

Women's Doubles

Finals

1962
Miss R. A. Ebbern/Miss M. Smith
Miss D. R. Hard/Mrs M. Reitano 6-4, 6-4
1963
Miss R. A. Ebbern/Miss M. Smith
Miss J. Lehane/Miss L. R. Turner 6-1, 6-3
1964
Miss J. A. M. Tegart/Miss L. R. Turner
Miss M. Smith/Miss R. A. Ebbern 6-4, 6-4
1965
Miss M. Smith/Miss L. R. Turner
Miss B. J. Moffitt/Miss R. A. Ebbern 1-6, 6-2, 6-3
1966
Mrs C. E. Graebner/Miss N. Richey
Miss M. Smith/Miss L. Turner 6-4, 7-5
1967
Miss J. A. M. Tegart/Miss L. R. Turner
Miss E. Terras/Miss L. Robinson 6-0, 6-2
1968
Miss K. Krantzcke/Miss K. Melville
Miss L. R. Turner/Miss J. A. M. Tegart 6-4, 3-6, 6-2
1969 *Open Championships began*
Mrs B. M. Court/Miss J. A. M. Tegart
Mrs L. W. King/Miss R. Casals 6-4, 6-4
1970
Mrs J. Dalton/Mrs B. M. Court
Miss K. Melville/Miss K. Krantzcke 6-3, 6-1
1971
Mrs B. M. Court/Miss E. F. Goolagong
Miss L. Hunt/Miss J. Emerson 6-0, 6-0
1972
Miss K. Harris/Miss H. Gourlay
Miss P. Coleman/Miss K. Krantzcke 6-0, 6-4
1973
Mrs B. M. Court/Miss S. V. Wade
Miss K. Melville/Miss K. Harris 6-4, 6-4

Australian Championships

Mixed Doubles

Finals

1922
J. B. Hawkes/Miss E. F. Boyd
H. S. Utz/Mrs H. S. Utz 6-1, 6-1
1923
H. M. Rice/Miss S. Lance
1924
J. Willard/Miss D. Akhurst
G. M. Hone/Miss E. F. Boyd 6-3, 6-4
1925
J. Willard/Miss D. Akhurst
R. E. Schlesinger/Mrs S. Harper 6-4, 6-4
1926
J. B. Hawkes/Miss E. F. Boyd
J. Willard/Miss D. Akhurst 6-2, 6-4
1927
J. B. Hawkes/Miss E. F. Boyd
J. Willard/Miss Y. Anthony 6-1, 6-3
1928
J. Borotra/Miss D. Akhurst a bye
J. B. Hawkes/Miss E. F. Boyd retired
1929
E. F. Moon/Miss D. Akhurst
J. H. Crawford/Miss M. Cox 6-0, 7-5
1930
H. C. Hopman/Miss N. Hall
J. H. Crawford/Miss M. Cox 11-9, 3-6, 6-3
1931
J. H. Crawford/Mrs J. H. Crawford
A. Willard/Mrs V. Westacott
1932
J. H. Crawford/Mrs J. H. Crawford
J. Sato/Mrs P. O'Hara Wood 6-8, 8-6, 6-3
1933
J. H. Crawford/Mrs J. H. Crawford
H. E. Vines/Mrs J. Van Ryn 3-6, 7-5, 13-11
1934
E. F. Moon/Miss J. Hartigan
R. Dunlop/Mrs V. Westacott 6-3, 6-4
1935
C. Boussus/Miss L. M. Bickerton
V. G. Kirby/Mrs Bond 1-6, 6-3, 6-3

1936
H. C. Hopman/Mrs H. C. Hopman
A. A. Kay/Miss M. Blick 6-2, 6-0
1937
H. C. Hopman/Mrs H. C. Hopman
D. P. Turnbull/Miss D. Stevenson 3-6, 6-3, 6-2
1938
J. E. Bromwich/Miss J. Wilson
C. F. Long/Miss N. Wynne 6-3, 6-2
1939
H. C. Hopman/Mrs H. C. Hopman
J. E. Bromwich/Miss M. Wilson 6-8, 6-2, 6-3
1940
C. F. Long/Miss N. Wynne
1941-45 *No Competition*
1946
C. F. Long/Mrs N. Bolton
1947
C. F. Long/Mrs N. Bolton
J. E. Bromwich/Miss J. Fitch 6-3, 6-3
1948
C. F. Long/Mrs N. Bolton
O. W. Sidwell/Mrs T. C. Long 7-5, 4-6, 8-6
1949
F. A. Sedgman/Miss D. J. Hart
J. E. Bromwich/Miss J. Fitch 6-1, 5-7, 12-10
1950
F. A. Sedgman/Miss D. J. Hart
E. W. Sturgess/Miss J. Fitch 8-6, 6-4
1951
G. Worthington/Mrs T. C. Long
J. May/Miss C. Proctor 6-4, 3-6, 6-2
1952
G. Worthington/Mrs T. C. Long
T. Warhurst/Mrs A. R. Thiele 9-7, 7-5
1953
R. N. Hartwig/Miss J. Sampson
H. Richardson/Miss M. Connolly 6-4, 6-3
1954
R. N. Hartwig/Mrs T. C. Long
J. E. Bromwich/Miss B. Penrose 4-6, 6-1, 6-2

1955
G. Worthington/Mrs T. C. Long
L. A. Hoad/Miss J. Staley 6-2, 6-1
1956
N. A. Fraser/Miss B. Penrose
R. S. Emerson/Mrs M. K. Hawton 6-2, 6-4
1957
M. J. Anderson/Miss F. Muller
W. A. Knight/Miss J. Langley 7-5, 3-6, 6-1
1958
R. N. Howe/Mrs M. K. Hawton
P. Newman/Miss A. Mortimer 9-11, 6-1, 6-2
1959
R. Mark/Miss S. Reynolds
R. G. Laver/Miss R. Schuurman 4-6, 13-11, 6-2
1960
T. T. Fancutt/Miss J. Lehane
R. Mark/Mrs M. Reitano 6-2, 7-5
1961
R. A. J. Hewitt/Miss J. Lehane
J. Pearce/Mrs M. Reitano 9-7, 6-2
1962
F. S. Stolle/Miss L. R. Turner
R. Taylor/Miss D. R. Hard 6-3, 9-7
1963
K. N. Fletcher/Miss M. Smith
F. S. Stolle/Miss L. R. Turner 7-5, 5-7, 6-4
1964
K. N. Fletcher/Miss M. Smith
M. J. Sangster/Miss J. Lehane 6-3, 6-2
1965
J. D. Newcombe/Miss M. Smith
O. K. Davidson/Miss R. A. Ebbern
1966
A. D. Roche/Miss J. A. M. Tegart
W. W. Bowrey/Miss R. A. Ebbern 6-1, 6-3
1967
O. K. Davidson/Miss L. R. Turner
A. D. Roche/Miss J. A. M. Tegart 9-7, 6-4
1968
R. D. Crealy/Mrs L. W. King
A. Stone/Mrs B. M. Court w.o.
1969-73 *No Competition*

Men's Singles

Men's Doubles

Semi-Finals

1925 *Entries were first accepted from all countries †*
J. Borotra J. Washer 6-2, 6-1, 6-3
R. Lacoste S. M. Jacob 6-2, 6-1, 3-6, 6-4
1926
R. Lacoste J. Borotra 8-6, 3-6, 6-2, 6-4
H. Cochet V. Richards 6-1, 6-4, 6-4
1927
W. T. Tilden H. Cochet 9-7, 6-3, 6-2
R. Lacoste P. D. B. Spence 6-1, 6-3, 6-2
1928
H. Cochet J. Borotra 6-3, 2-6, 7-5, 6-4
R. Lacoste J. B. Hawkes 6-2, 6-4, 6-4
1929
R. Lacoste W. T. Tilden 6-1, 6-0, 5-7, 6-3
J. Borotra H. Cochet 6-3, 5-7, 7-5, 5-7, 6-4
1930
W. T. Tilden J. Borotra 2-6, 6-2, 6-4, 4-6, 6-3
H. Cochet H. L. de Morpurgo 7-5, 6-1, 6-2
1931
C. Boussus G. P. Hughes 6-1, 4-6, 6-2, 6-3
J. Borotra J. Sato 10-8, 2-6, 5-7, 6-1, 6-2
1932
G. de Stefani R. Menzel 6-3, 2-6, 7-5, 6-4
H. Cochet M. Bernard 6-1, 6-0, 6-4
1933
J. H. Crawford J. Sato 6-0, 6-2, 6-2
H. Cochet H. G. N. Lee 9-11, 6-3, 6-3, 6-3
1934
J. H. Crawford C. Boussus 6-3, 2-6, 7-5, 6-4
G. von Cramm G. de Stefani 3-6, 6-4, 6-1, 3-6, 6-2
1935
F. J. Perry J. H. Crawford 6-3, 8-6, 6-3
G. von Cramm H. W. Austin 6-2, 5-7, 6-1, 5-7, 6-0
1936
G. von Cramm M. Bernard 7-5, 6-1, 6-1
F. J. Perry C. Boussus 6-4, 7-5, 5-7, 6-2
1937
H. Henkel B. Destremau 6-1, 6-4, 6-3
H. W. Austin C. Boussus 7-5, 6-2, 1-6, 6-3
1938
R. Menzel F. Punĉec 6-4, 6-4, 6-4
J. D. Budge J. Pallada 6-2, 6-3, 6-3
1939
R. L. Riggs O. Szigeti 6-3, 6-0, 6-4
W. D. McNeill E. T. Cooke
1940-45 *No Open Competition*

1946
M. Bernard Y. Petra 5-7, 6-2, 6-3, 5-7, 6-2
J. Drobný T. Brown 7-5, 3-6, 6-4, 5-7, 6-2
1947
J. Asbóth T. Brown 6-2, 6-2, 6-1
E. W. Sturgess M. Bernard 3-6, 2-6, 6-3, 8-6, 6-3
1948
F. A. Parker E. W. Sturgess 6-2, 6-2, 6-1
J. Drobný J. E. Patty 2-6, 6-3, 4-6, 6-4, 6-3
1949
F. A. Parker E. W. Sturgess 6-2, 6-1, 6-4
J. E. Patty R. A. Gonzalez 6-4, 6-3, 3-6, 6-3
1950
J. E. Patty W. F. Talbert 2-6, 6-4, 4-6, 6-4, 13-11
J. Drobný E. W. Sturgess 6-4, 7-5, 3-6, 12-10
1951
J. Drobný F. A. Sedgman 6-0, 6-3, 6-1
E. W. Sturgess K. McGregor 10-8, 7-9, 8-6, 5-7, 9-7
1952
J. Drobný K. McGregor 6-3, 6-0, 4-6, 6-3
F. A. Sedgman E. W. Sturgess 7-5, 6-2, 8-6
1953
K. R. Rosewall E. Morea 2-6, 6-2, 6-4, 0-6, 6-2
E. V. Seixas J. Drobný 6-3, 6-2, 3-6, 6-3
1954
M. A. Trabert J. E. Patty 6-1, 7-5, 6-4
A. Larsen E. Morea 6-4, 6-3, 6-4
1955
M. A. Trabert H. Richardson 6-1, 2-2 retired
S. Davidson G. Merlo 6-3, 6-3, 6-2
1956
L. A. Hoad G. Merlo 6-4, 7-5, 6-4
S. Davidson A. J. Cooper 6-2, 9-7, 5-7, 6-3
1957
S. Davidson A. J. Cooper 6-4, 2-6, 2-6, 6-2, 6-3
H. Flam M. G. Rose 4-6, 6-4, 4-6, 6-2, 7-5
1958
M. G. Rose J. Brichant 10-8, 6-1, 6-3
L. Ayala A. J. Cooper 9-11, 4-6, 6-4, 6-2, 7-5
1959
N. Pietrangeli N. A. Fraser 7-5, 6-3, 7-5
I. C. Vermaak L. Ayala 6-2, 6-1, 6-4
1960
N. Pietrangeli R. Haillet 6-4, 7-5, 7-5
L. Ayala O. Sirola 6-4, 6-0, 6-2
1961
M. Santana R. G. Laver 3-6, 6-2, 4-6, 6-4, 6-0
N. Pietrangeli J. E. Lundqvist 6-4, 6-4, 6-4
1962
R. G. Laver N. A. Fraser 3-6, 6-3, 6-2, 3-6, 7-5
R. S. Emerson M. Santana 6-4, 3-6, 6-1, 2-6, 6-3

Finals

1925 *Entries were first accepted from all countries †*
R. Lacoste J. Borotra 7-5, 6-1, 6-4
1926
H. Cochet R. Lacoste 6-2, 6-4, 6-3
1927
R. Lacoste W. T. Tilden 6-4, 4-6, 5-7, 6-3, 11-9
1928
H. Cochet R. Lacoste 5-7, 6-3, 6-1, 6-3
1929
R. Lacoste J. Borotra 6-3, 2-6, 6-0, 2-6, 8-6
1930
H. Cochet W. T. Tilden 3-6, 8-6, 6-3, 6-1
1931
J. Borotra C. Boussus 2-6, 6-4, 7-5, 6-4
1932
H. Cochet G. de Stefani 6-0, 6-4, 4-6, 6-3
1933
J. H. Crawford H. Cochet 8-6, 6-1, 6-3
1934
G. von Cramm J. H. Crawford 6-4, 7-9, 3-6, 7-5, 6-3
1935
F. J. Perry G. von Cramm 6-3, 3-6, 6-1, 6-3
1936
G. von Cramm F. J. Perry 6-0, 2-6, 6-2, 2-6, 6-0
1937
H. Henkel H. W. Austin 6-1, 6-4, 6-3
1938
J. D. Budge R. Menzel 6-3, 6-2, 6-4
1939
W. D. McNeill R. L. Riggs 7-5, 6-0, 6-3
1940 *No Competition*
1941 *Tournoi de France (closed)*
B. Destremau
1942 *Tournoi de France (closed)*
B. Destremau
1943 *Tournoi de France (closed)*
Y. Petra
1944 *Tournoi de France (closed)*
Y. Petra
1945 *Tournoi de France (closed)*
Y. Petra B. Destremau 7-5, 6-4, 6-2
1946
M. Bernard J. Drobný 3-6, 2-6, 6-1, 6-4, 6-3
1947
J. Asbóth E. W. Sturgess 8-6, 7-5, 6-4
1948
F. A. Parker J. Drobný 6-4, 7-5, 5-7, 8-6
1949
F. A. Parker J. E. Patty 6-3, 1-6, 6-1, 6-4
1950
J. E. Patty J. Drobný 6-1, 6-2, 3-6, 5-7, 7-5
1951
J. Drobný E. W. Sturgess 6-3, 6-3, 6-3
1952
J. Drobný F. A. Sedgman 6-2, 6-0, 3-6, 6-4
1953
K. R. Rosewall E. V. Seixas 6-3, 6-4, 1-6, 6-2
1954
M. A. Trabert A. Larsen 6-4, 7-5, 6-1
1955
M. A. Trabert S. Davidson 2-6, 6-1, 6-4, 6-2
1956
L. A. Hoad S. Davidson 6-4, 8-6, 6-3
1957
S. Davidson H. Flam 6-3, 6-4, 6-4
1958
M. G. Rose L. Ayala 6-3, 6-4, 6-4
1959
N. Pietrangeli I. C. Vermaak 3-6, 6-3, 6-4, 6-1
1960
N. Pietrangeli L. Ayala 3-6, 6-3, 6-4, 4-6, 6-3
1961
M. Santana N. Pietrangeli 4-6, 6-1, 3-6, 6-0, 6-2
1962
R. G. Laver R. S. Emerson 3-6, 2-6, 6-3, 9-7, 6-2

Finals

1925 *Entries were first accepted from all countries*
R. Lacoste/J. Borotra
H. Cochet/J. Brugnon 7-5, 4-6, 6-3, 2-6, 6-3
1926
V. Richards/H. O. Kinsey
H. Cochet/J. Brugnon 6-4, 6-1, 4-6, 6-4
1927
H. Cochet/J. Brugnon
J. Borotra/R. Lacoste 2-6, 6-2, 6-0, 1-6, 6-4
1928
J. Borotra/J. Brugnon
H. Cochet/R. de Buzelet 6-4, 3-6, 6-2, 3-6, 6-4
1929
R. Lacoste/J. Borotra
H. Cochet/J. Brugnon 6-3, 3-6, 6-3, 3-6, 8-6
1930
H. Cochet/J. Brugnon
H. C. Hopman/J. Willard 6-3, 9-7, 6-3
1931
G. M. Lott/J. Van Ryn
V. G. Kirby/N. G. Farquharson 6-4, 6-3, 6-4
1932
H. Cochet/J. Brugnon
C. Boussus/M. Bernard 6-4, 3-6, 7-5, 6-3
1933
G. P. Hughes/F. J. Perry
A. K. Quist/V. B. McGrath 6-2, 6-4, 2-6, 7-5
1934
J. Borotra/J. Brugnon
J. H. Crawford/V. B. McGrath 11-9, 6-3, 2-6, 4-6, 9-7
1935
J. H. Crawford/A. K. Quist
V. B. McGrath/D. P. Turnbull 6-1, 6-4, 6-2
1936
J. Borotra/M. Bernard
C. R. D. Tuckey/G. P. Hughes 6-2, 3-6, 9-7, 6-1
1937
G. von Cramm/H. Henkel
N. G. Farquharson/V. G. Kirby 6-4, 7-5, 3-6, 6-1
1938
B. Destremau/Y. Petra
J. D. Budge/C. G. Mako 3-6, 6-3, 9-7, 6-1
1939
W. D. McNeill/C. Harris
1940 *No Competition*
1941 *Tournoi de France (closed)*
B. Destremau/C. Boussus
1942 *Tournoi de France (closed)*
B. Destremau/Y. Petra
1943 *Tournoi de France (closed)*
M. Bernard/Y. Petra
1944 *Tournoi de France (closed)*
M. Bernard/Y. Petra
1945 *Tournoi de France (closed)*
H. Cochet/P. Pellizza
Y. Petra/B. Destremau 2-6, 6-4, 8-6, 3-6, 6-0
1946
M. Bernard/Y. Petra
E. Morea/F. Segura 7-5, 6-3, 0-6, 1-6, 10-8
1947
E. Fannin/E. W. Sturgess
T. Brown/O. W. Sidwell 6-4, 4-6, 6-4, 6-3
1948
L. Bergelin/J. Drobný
H. C. Hopman/F. A. Sedgman 8-6, 6-1, 12-10
1949
R. A. Gonzalez/F. A. Parker
E. Fannin/E. W. Sturgess 6-3, 8-6, 5-7, 6-3
1950
W. F. Talbert/M. A. Trabert
J. Drobny/E. W. Sturgess 6-2, 1-6, 10-8, 6-2
1951
K. McGregor/F. A. Sedgman
G. Mulloy/R. Savitt 6-2, 2-6, 9-7, 7-5
1952
K. McGregor/F. A. Sedgman
G. Mulloy/R. Savitt 6-3, 6-4, 6-4
1953
L. A. Hoad/K. R. Rosewall
M. G. Rose/C. Wilderspin 6-2, 6-1, 6-1
1954
E. V. Seixas/M. A. Trabert
L. A. Hoad/K. R. Rosewall 6-4, 6-2, 6-1
1955
E. V. Seixas/M. A. Trabert
N. Pietrangeli/O. Sirola 6-1, 4-6, 6-2, 6-4
1956
D. W. Candy/R. M. Perry
A. J. Cooper/L. A. Hoad 7-5, 6-3, 6-3
1957
M. J. Anderson/A. J. Cooper
D. W. Candy/M. G. Rose 6-3, 6-0, 6-3
1958
A. J. Cooper/A. J. Fraser
R. N. Howe/A. Segal 3-6, 8-6, 6-3, 7-5
1959
O. Sirola/N. Pietrangeli
R. S. Emerson/N. A. Fraser 6-3, 6-2, 14-12
1960
R. S. Emerson/N. A. Fraser
J. Arilla/A. Gimeno 6-2, 8-10, 7-5, 6-4
1961
R. S. Emerson/N. A. Fraser
R. N. Howe/R. Mark 3-6, 6-1, 6-1, 6-4
1962
R. S. Emerson/N. A. Fraser
W. P. Bungert/C. Kuhnke 6-3, 6-4, 7-5

Winners in **bold type;** † winners of the (closed) French Championships before 1925 will be found on page 245; w.o. walk-over

French Championships

Men's Singles

Semi-Finals

1963
R. S. Emerson M. J. Sangster 8-6, 6-3, 6-4
P. Darmon M. Santana 6-3, 4-6, 2-6, 9-7, 6-2
1964
M. Santana P. Darmon 8-6, 6-4, 3-6, 2-6, 6-4
N. Pietrangeli J. E. Lundqvist 4-6, 6-3, 6-4, 6-4
1965
F. S. Stolle E. C. Drysdale 6-8, 6-4, 6-1, 4-6, 6-4
A. D. Roche R. S. Emerson 6-1, 6-4, 3-6, 6-0
1966
A. D. Roche F. Jauffret 6-3, 6-4, 6-4
I. Gulyás E. C. Drysdale 6-4, 2-6, 7-9, 6-2, 6-3
1967
R. S. Emerson I. Gulyás 6-3, 6-4, 6-2
A. D. Roche N. Pilić 3-6, 6-3, 6-4, 2-6, 6-4
1968 *Open Championships began*
K. R. Rosewall A. Gimeno 3-6, 6-3, 7-5, 3-6, 6-3
R. G. Laver R. A. Gonzalez 6-3, 6-3, 6-1
1969
R. G. Laver T. S. Okker 4-6, 6-0, 6-2, 6-4
K. R. Rosewall A. D. Roche 7-5, 6-2, 6-2
1970
J. Kodeš G. Goven 2-6, 6-2, 5-7, 6-2, 6-3
Z. Franulović C. Richey 6-4, 4-6, 4-6, 7-5, 7-5
1971
J. Kodeš Z. Franulović 6-4, 6-2, 7-5
I. Năstase F. R. Froehling 6-0, 2-6, 6-4, 6-3
1972
P. Proisy M. Orantes 6-3, 7-5, 6-2
A. Gimeno A. Metreveli 4-6, 6-3, 6-1, 2-6, 6-3
1973
N. Pilić A. Panatta 6-4, 6-3, 6-2
I. Năstase T. Gorman 6-3, 6-4, 6-1

Finals

1963
R. S. Emerson P. Darmon 3-6, 6-1, 6-4, 6-4
1964
M. Santana N. Pietrangeli 6-3, 6-1, 4-6, 7-5
1965
F. S. Stolle A. D. Roche 3-6, 6-0, 6-2, 6-3
1966
A. D. Roche I. Gulyás 6-1, 6-4, 7-5
†1967
R. S. Emerson A. D. Roche 6-1, 6-4, 2-6, 6-2
1968 *Open Championships began*
K. R. Rosewall R. G. Laver 6-3, 6-1, 2-6, 6-2
1969
R. G. Laver K. R. Rosewall 6-4, 6-3, 6-4
1970
J. Kodeš Z. Franulović 6-2, 6-4, 6-0
1971
J. Kodeš I. Năstase 8-6, 6-2, 2-6, 7-5
1972
A. Gimeno P. Proisy 4-6, 6-3, 6-1, 6-1
1973
I. Năstase N. Pilić 6-3, 6-3, 6-0

Men's Doubles

Finals

1963
R. S. Emerson/M. Santana
G. L. Forbes/A. Segal 6-2, 6-4, 6-4
1964
R. S. Emerson/K. N. Fletcher
J. D. Newcombe/A. D. Roche 7-5, 6-3, 3-6, 7-5
1965
R. S. Emerson/F. S. Stolle
K. N. Fletcher/R. A. J. Hewitt 6-8, 6-3, 8-6, 6-2
1966
C. E. Graebner/R. D. Ralston
I. Năstase/I. Tiriac 6-3, 6-3, 6-0
1967
J. D. Newcombe/A. D. Roche
R. S. Emerson/K. N. Fletcher 6-3, 9-7, 12-10
1968 *Open Championships began*
K. R. Rosewall/F. S. Stolle
R. G. Laver/R. S. Emerson 6-3, 6-4, 6-3
1969
J. D. Newcombe/A. D. Roche
R. S. Emerson/R. G. Laver 4-6, 6-1, 3-6, 6-4, 6-4
1970
I. Năstase/I. Tiriac
A. R. Ashe/C. M. Pasarell 6-2, 6-4, 6-3
1971
A. R. Ashe/M. C. Riessen
T. Gorman/S. R. Smith 6-8, 4-6, 6-3, 6-4, 11-9
1972
R. A. J. Hewitt/F. D. McMillan
P. Cornejo/J. Fillol 6-3, 8-6, 3-6, 6-1
1973
J. D. Newcombe/T. S. Okker
J. Connors/I. Năstase 6-1, 3-6, 6-3, 5-7, 6-4

Women's Singles

Semi-Finals

1925 *Entries were first accepted from all countries* †
Miss S. Lenglen Miss Contostavlos 6-2, 6-0
Miss K. McKane Miss D. Vlasto 6-2, 6-2
1926
Miss S. Lenglen Miss J. Fry 6-2, 6-1
Miss M. K. Browne Miss K. Bouman 8-6, 6-2
1927
Miss K. Bouman Miss E. L. Heine 5-7, 6-4, 6-3
Mrs Peacock Miss E. Bennett 5-7, 6-1, 9-7
1928
Miss H. Wills Miss C. Hardie 6-1, 6-1
Miss E. Bennett Miss K. Bouman 6-2, 8-6
1929
Mrs R. Mathieu Miss C. Aussem 8-6, 2-6, 6-2
Miss H. Wills Miss E. Bennett 6-2, 7-5
1930
Miss H. H. Jacobs Miss L. de Alvarez 6-1, 6-0
Mrs F. S. Moody Miss C. Aussem 6-2, 6-1
1931
Miss B. Nuthall Miss H. Krahwinkel 6-1, 6-2
Miss C. Aussem Miss L. de Alvarez 6-0, 7-5
1932
Mrs R. Mathieu Miss B. Nuthall 6-2, 6-4
Mrs F. S. Moody Miss H. Krahwinkel 6-3, 10-8
1933
Mrs R. Mathieu Miss H. H. Jacobs 8-6, 6-3
Miss M. C. Scriven Miss B. Nuthall 6-2, 4-6, 6-3
1934
Miss M. C. Scriven Miss C. Aussem 7-5, 6-3
Miss H. H. Jacobs Mrs R. Mathieu 6-2, 6-2
1935
Mrs H. Sperling Miss H. H. Jacobs 7-5, 6-3
Mrs R. Mathieu Miss M. C. Scriven 8-6, 6-1
1936
Mrs R. Mathieu Miss M. Horn 6-4, 6-4
Mrs H. Sperling Countess de la Valdène 6-2, 6-1
1937
Mrs R. Mathieu Miss J. Jedrzejowska 7-5, 7-5
Mrs H. Sperling Countess de la Valdène 6-1, 6-1
1938
Mrs N. Landry Miss M. Rollin-Couquerque 6-2, 6-4
Mrs R. Mathieu Mrs A. Halff 6-1, 6-1
1939
Mrs R. Mathieu
Miss J. Jedrzejowska
1940-45 *No Open Competition*

Finals

1925 *Entries were first accepted from all countries* †
Miss S. Lenglen Miss K. McKane 6-1, 6-2
1926
Miss S. Lenglen Miss M. K. Browne 6-1, 6-0
1927
Miss K. Bouman Mrs Peacock 6-2, 6-4
1928
Miss H. Wills Miss E. Bennett 6-1, 6-2
1929
Miss H. Wills Mrs R. Mathieu 6-3, 6-4
1930
Mrs F. S. Moody Miss H. H. Jacobs 6-2, 6-1
1931
Miss C. Aussem Miss B. Nuthall 8-6, 6-1
1932
Mrs F. S. Moody Mrs R. Mathieu 7-5, 6-1
1933
Miss M. C. Scriven Mrs R. Mathieu 6-2, 4-6, 6-4
1934
Miss M. C. Scriven Miss H. H. Jacobs 7-5, 4-6, 6-1
1935
Mrs H. Sperling Mrs R. Mathieu 6-2, 6-1
1936
Mrs H. Sperling Mrs R. Mathieu 6-3, 6-4
1937
Mrs H. Sperling Mrs R. Mathieu 6-2, 6-4
1938
Mrs R. Mathieu Mrs N. Landry 6-0, 6-3
1939
Mrs R. Mathieu Miss J. Jedrzejowska 6-3, 8-6
1940 *No Competition*
1941 *Tournoi de France (closed)*
Miss A. Weiwers
1942 *Tournoi de France (closed)*
Miss A. Weiwers
1943 *Tournoi de France (closed)*
Mrs N. Lafargue
1944 *Tournoi de France (closed)*
Miss R. Veber
1945 *Tournoi de France (closed)*
Miss L. D. Payot Mrs N. Lafargue 6-3, 6-4

Women's Doubles

Finals

1925 *Entries were first accepted from all countries*
Miss S. Lenglen/Miss D. Vlasto
Miss K. McKane/Miss E. Colyer 6-1, 9-11, 6-2
1926
Miss S. Lenglen/Miss D. Vlasto
Mrs L. A. Godfree/Miss E. Colyer 6-1, 6-1
1927
Mrs I. E. Peacock/Miss E. L. Heine
Mrs P. Watson/Miss P. Saunders 6-2, 6-1
1928
Mrs P. Watson/Miss E. Bennett
Miss S. Dévé/Mrs Lafaurie 6-0, 6-2
1929
Miss L. de Alvarez/Miss K. Bouman
Miss E. L. Heine/Mrs Neave 7-5, 6-3
1930
Mrs F. S. Moody/Miss E. Ryan
Mrs R. Mathieu/Miss S. Barbier 6-3, 6-1
1931
Mrs E. F. Whittingstall/Miss B. Nuthall
Miss E. Ryan/Miss C. Aussem 9-7, 6-2
1932
Mrs F. S. Moody/Miss E. Ryan
Mrs E. F. Whittingstall/Miss B. Nuthall 6-1, 6-3
1933
Mrs R. Mathieu/Miss E. Ryan
Mrs S. Henrotin/Miss C. Rosambert 6-1, 6-3
1934
Mrs R. Mathieu/Miss E. Ryan
Miss H. H. Jacobs/Miss S. Palfrey 3-6, 6-4, 6-2
1935
Miss M. C. Scriven/Miss K. E. Stammers
Miss Adamoff/Mrs H. Sperling 6-4, 6-0
1936
Mrs R. Mathieu/Miss A. M. Yorke
Miss S. Noel/Miss J. Jedrzejowska 2-6, 6-4, 6-4
1937
Mrs R. Mathieu/Miss A. M. Yorke
Mrs D. Andrus/Mrs S. Henrotin 3-6, 6-2, 6-2
1938
Mrs R. Mathieu/Miss A. M. Yorke
Mrs A. Halff/Mrs N. Landry 6-3, 6-3
1939
Mrs R. Mathieu/Miss J. Jedrzejowska
1940 *No Competition*
1941 *Tournoi de France (closed)*
Miss A. Weiwers/Miss St Omer Roy
1942 *Tournoi de France (closed)*
Miss A. Weiwers/Miss St Omer Roy
1943 *Tournoi de France (closed)*
Miss A. Weiwers/Miss St Omer Roy
1944 *Tournoi de France (closed)*
Mrs Grosbois/Mrs Manescau
1945 *Tournoi de France (closed)*
Mrs N. Lafargue/Mrs P. Fritz
Mrs R. Mathieu/Miss Brunnarius 6-3, 6-1

Winners in **bold type;** † winners of the (closed) French Championships before 1925 will be found on page 245; w.o. walk-over

Women's Singles

Women's Doubles

Semi-Finals

1946
Miss M. E. Osborne Miss A. L. Brough 7-5, 6-3
Miss P. M. Betz Miss D. Bundy 6-3, 6-4
1947
Mrs P. C. Todd Miss M. E. Osborne 2-6, 6-3, 6-4
Miss D. J. Hart Miss A. L. Brough 6-2, 7-5
1948
Mrs N. Landry Mrs P. C. Todd w.o.
Miss S. J. Fry Miss D. J. Hart 6-3, 4-6, 11-9
1949
Mrs W. duPont Mrs S. P. Summers 6-3, 6-3
Mrs N. Adamson Mrs A. Bossi 6-3, 6-0
1950
Miss D. J. Hart Miss A. L. Brough 6-2, 6-3
Mrs P. C. Todd Miss B. Scofield 6-2, 6-3
1951
Miss S. J. Fry Mrs W. duPont 6-2, 9-7
Miss D. J. Hart Mrs J. J. Walker-Smith 6-2, 6-1
1952
Miss D. J. Hart Miss D. Head 6-2, 8-6
Miss S. J. Fry Mrs H. Redick-Smith 7-5, 6-4
1953
Miss M. Connolly Mrs D. P. Knode 6-3, 6-3
Miss D. J. Hart Miss S. J. Fry 8-6, 6-4
1954
Miss M. Connolly Miss S. Lazzarino 6-0, 6-1
Mrs G. Bucaille Mrs N. Adamson 6-2, 6-4
1955
Miss A. Mortimer Mrs H. Brewer 6-1, 6-1
Mrs D. P. Knode Mrs J. G. Fleitz 6-2, 6-3
1956
Miss A. Gibson Miss A. Buxton 2-6, 6-0, 6-4
Miss A. Mortimer Mrs Z. Körmöczy 6-4, 6-3
1957
Miss S. J. Bloomer Miss V. Pužejová 6-4, 2-6, 6-4
Mrs D. P. Knode Miss A. S. Haydon 6-4, 10-8
1958
Mrs Z. Körmöczy Mrs A. Segal 6-1, 6-0
Miss S. J. Bloomer Miss M. E. Bueno 2-6, 6-1, 6-2
1959
Miss C. C. Truman Miss S. Reynolds 4-6, 8-6, 6-2
Mrs Z. Körmöczy Miss R. M. Reyes 6-3, 6-0
1960
Miss D. R. Hard Miss M. E. Bueno 6-3, 6-2
Miss Y. Ramirez Miss S. Reynolds 8-10, 6-3, 6-3
1961
Miss A. S. Haydon Mrs Z. Körmöczy 3-6, 6-1, 6-3
Miss Y. Ramirez Miss E. Buding 6-4, 4-6, 6-3
1962
Miss M. Smith Miss R. Schuurman 8-6, 6-3
Miss L. R. Turner Miss A. S. Haydon 6-4, 5-7, 6-3
1963
Miss L. R. Turner Miss C. C. Truman 11-9, 6-2
Mrs P. F. Jones Mrs V. Suková 6-0, 6-1
1964
Miss M. Smith Miss H. Schultze 6-3, 4-6, 6-2
Miss M. E. Bueno Miss L. R. Turner 3-6, 6-2, 6-0
1965
Miss L. R. Turner Miss M. E. Bueno 2-6, 6-4, 8-6
Miss M. Smith Miss N. Richey 7-5, 6-4
1966
Mrs P. F. Jones Miss M. E. Bueno 4-6, 8-6, 6-2
Miss N. Richey Miss M. Smith 6-1, 6-3
1967
Miss F. Durr Miss K. Melville 8-6, 6-3
Miss L. R. Turner Miss A. M. Van Zyl 6-1, 6-4
1968 *Open Championships began*
Miss N. Richey Mrs ! W. King 2-6, 6-3, 6-4
Mrs P. F. Jones Mrs A. M. du Plooy 7-5, 6-3
1969
Mrs B. M. Court Miss N. Richey 6-3, 4-6, 7-5
Mrs P. F. Jones Miss L. Bowrey 6-1, 6-2
1970
Miss H. Niessen Miss K. Krantzcke 6-3, 6-1
Mrs B. M. Court Mrs J. M. Heldman 6-0, 6-2
1971
Miss E. F. Goolagong Mrs M. Schaar 6-4, 6-1
Miss H. Gourlay Mrs K. Gunter 6-2, 6-3
1972
Mrs L. W. King Mrs H. Masthoff 6-4, 6-4
Miss E. F. Goolagong Miss F. Durr 9-7, 6-4
1973
Miss C. Evert Miss F. Durr 6-1, 6-0
Mrs B. M. Court Miss E. F. Goolagong 6-3, 7-6

Finals

1946
Miss M. E. Osborne Miss P. M. Betz 1-6, 8-6, 7-5
1947
Mrs P. C. Todd Miss D. J. Hart 6-3, 3-6, 6-4
1948
Mrs N. Landry Miss S. J. Fry 6-2, 0-6, 6-0
1949
Mrs W. duPont Mrs N. Adamson 7-5, 6-2
1950
Miss D. J. Hart Mrs P. C. Todd 6-4, 4-6, 6-2
1951
Miss S. J. Fry Miss D. J. Hart 6-3, 3-6, 6-3
1952
Miss D. J. Hart Miss S. J. Fry 6-4, 6-4
1953
Miss M. Connolly Miss D. J. Hart 6-2, 6-4
1954
Miss M. Connolly Mrs G. Bucaille 6-4, 6-1
1955
Miss A. Mortimer Mrs D. P. Knode 2-6, 7-5, 10-8
1956
Miss A. Gibson Miss A. Mortimer 6-0, 12-10
1957
Miss S. J. Bloomer Mrs D. P. Knode 6-1, 6-3
1958
Mrs Z. Körmöczy Miss S. J. Bloomer 6-4, 1-6, 6-2
1959
Miss C. C. Truman Mrs Z. Körmöczy 6-4, 7-5
1960
Miss D. R. Hard Miss Y. Ramirez 6-3, 6-4
1961
Miss A. S. Haydon Miss Y. Ramirez 6-2, 6-1
1962
Miss M. Smith Miss L. R. Turner 6-3, 3-6, 7-5
1963
Miss L. R. Turner Mrs P. F. Jones 2-6, 6-3, 7-5
1964
Miss M. Smith Miss M. E. Bueno 5-7, 6-1, 6-2
1965
Miss L. R. Turner Miss M. Smith 6-3, 6-4
1966
Mrs P. F. Jones Miss N. Richey 6-3, 6-1
1967
Miss F. Durr Miss L. R. Turner 4-6, 6-3, 6-4
1968 *Open Championships began*
Miss N. Richey Mrs P. F. Jones 5-7, 6-4, 6-1
1969
Mrs B. M. Court Mrs P. F. Jones 6-1, 4-6, 6-3
1970
Mrs B. M. Court Miss H. Niessen 6-2, 6-4
1971
Miss E. F. Goolagong Miss H. Gourlay 6-3, 7-5
1972
Mrs L. W. King Miss E. F. Goolagong 6-3, 6-3
1973
Mrs B. M. Court Miss C. Evert 6-7, 7-6, 6-4

Finals

1946
Miss A. L. Brough/Miss M. E. Osborne
Miss P. M. Betz/Miss D. J. Hart 6-4, 0-6, 6-1
1947
Miss A. L. Brough/Miss M. E. Osborne
Miss D. J. Hart/Mrs P. C. Todd 7-5, 6-2
1948
Miss D. J. Hart/Mrs P. C. Todd
Miss S. J. Fry/Mrs M. A. Prentiss 6-4, 6-2
1949
Miss A. L. Brough/Mrs W. duPont
Mrs B. E. Hilton/Miss J. Gannon 7-5, 6-1
1950
Miss D. J. Hart/Miss S. J. Fry
Mrs W. duPont/Miss A. L. Brough 1-6, 7-5, 6-2
1951
Miss D. J. Hart/Miss S. J. Fry
Mrs B. Bartlett/Miss B. Scofield 10-8, 6-3
1952
Miss D. J. Hart/Miss S. J. Fry
Mrs H. Redick-Smith/Mrs J. Wipplinger 7-5, 6-1
1953
Miss D. J. Hart/Miss S. J. Fry
Miss M. Connolly/Miss J. Sampson 6-4, 6-3
1954
Miss M. Connolly/Mrs H. C. Hopman
Mrs M. Galtier/Miss S. Schmitt 7-5, 4-6, 6-0
1955
Mrs J. G. Fleitz/Miss D. R. Hard
Miss S. J. Bloomer/Miss P. E. Ward 7-5, 6-8, 13-11
1956
Miss A. Gibson/Miss A. Buxton
Mrs D. P. Knode/Miss D. R. Hard 6-8, 8-6, 6-1
1957
Miss D. R. Hard/Miss S. J. Bloomer
Miss Y. Ramirez/Miss R. M. Reyes 7-5, 4-6, 7-5
1958
Miss Y. Ramirez/Miss R. M. Reyes
Mrs M. K. Hawton/Mrs T. D. Long 6-4, 7-5
1959
Miss S. Reynolds/Miss R. Schuurman
Miss Y. Ramirez/Miss R. M. Reyes 2-6, 6-0, 6-1
1960
Miss M. E. Bueno/Miss D. R. Hard
Mrs R. Hales/Miss A. S. Haydon 6-2, 7-5
1961
Miss S. Reynolds/Miss R. Schuurman
Miss M. E. Bueno/Miss D. R. Hard scratched
1962
Mrs S. Price/Miss R. Schuurman
Miss M. Smith/Miss J. Bricka 6-4, 6-4
1963
Mrs P. F. Jones/Miss R. Schuurman
Miss M. Smith/Miss R. A. Ebbern 7-5, 6-4
1964
Miss L. R. Turner/Miss M. Smith
Miss N. Baylon/Miss H. Schultze 6-3, 6-0
1965
Miss L. R. Turner/Miss M. Smith
Miss F. Durr/Miss J. Lieffrig 6-3, 6-1
1966
Miss M. Smith/Miss J. A. M. Tegart
Miss J. Blackman/Miss Toyne 4-6, 6-1, 6-1
1967
Miss F. Durr/Miss G. Sherriff
Miss A. M. Van Zyl/Miss P. Walkden 6-2, 6-2
1968 *Open Championships began*
Miss F. Durr/Mrs P. F. Jones
Mrs L. W. King/Miss R. Casals 7-5, 4-6, 6-4
1969
Miss F. Durr/Mrs P. F. Jones
Mrs B. M. Court/Miss N. Richey 6-0, 4-6, 7-5
1970
Mrs G. Chanfreau/Miss F. Durr
Miss R. Casals/Mrs L. W. King 6-3, 1-6, 6-3
1971
Mrs G. Chanfreau/Miss F. Durr
Miss H. Gourlay/Miss K. Harris 6-4, 6-1
1972
Mrs L. W. King/Miss B. Stöve
Miss W. Shaw/Miss N. Truman 6-1, 6-2
1973
Mrs B. M. Court/Miss S. V. Wade
Miss B. Stöve/Miss F. Durr 6-2, 6-3

French Championships

Mixed Doubles

Finals

1925 *Entries were first accepted from all countries*
J. Brugnon/Miss S. Lenglen
H. Cochet/Miss D. Vlasto   6-2, 6-2
1926
J. Brugnon/Miss S. Lenglen
J. Borotra/Mrs Le Besnerais   6-4, 6-3
1927
J. Borotra/Mrs M. Bordes
W. T. Tilden/Miss L. de Alvarez   6-4, 2-6, 6-2
1928
H. Cochet/Miss E. Bennett
F. T. Hunter/Miss H. Wills   3-6, 6-3, 6-3
1929
H. Cochet/Miss E. Bennett
F. T. Hunter/Miss H. Wills   6-3, 6-2
1930
W. T. Tilden/Miss C. Aussem
H. Cochet/Mrs F. Whittingstall   6-4, 6-4
1931
P. D. B. Spence/Miss B. Nuthall
H. W. Austin/Mrs D. C. Shepherd-Barron   6-3, 5-7, 6-3
1932
F. J. Perry/Miss B. Nuthall
S. B. Wood/Mrs F. S. Moody   6-4, 6-2
1933
J. H. Crawford/Miss M. C. Scriven
F. J. Perry/Miss B. Nuthall   6-2, 6-3
1934
J. Borotra/Miss C. Rosambert
A. K. Quist/Miss E. Ryan   6-2, 6-4
1935
M. Bernard/Miss L. D. Payot
A. M. Legeay/Mrs S. Henrotin   4-6, 6-2, 6-4
1936
M. Bernard/Miss A. M. Yorke
A. M. Legeay/Mrs S. Henrotin   7-5, 6-8, 6-3
1937
Y. Petra/Mrs R. Mathieu
R. Journu/Miss M. Horn   7-5, 7-5
1938
D. Mitić/Mrs R. Mathieu
C. Boussus/Miss N. Wynne   2-6, 6-3, 6-4
1939
E. T. Cooke/Mrs S. P. Fabyan
1940 *No Competition*
1941 *Tournoi de France (closed)*
R. Abdesselam/Miss A. Weiwers
1942 *Tournoi de France (closed)*
H. Pellizza/Mrs N. Lafargue

1943 *Tournoi de France (closed)*
H. Pellizza/Mrs N. Lafargue
1944 *Tournoi de France (closed)*
A. Gentien/Miss S. Pannetier
1945 *Tournoi de France (closed)*
A. Jacquemet/Mrs L. D. Payot
1946
J. E. Patty/Miss P. M. Betz
T. Brown/Miss D. Bundy   7-5, 9-7
1947
E. W. Sturgess/Mrs S. P. Summers
C. Caralulis/Miss J. Jedrzejowska   6-0, 6-0
1948
J. Drobný/Mrs P. C. Todd
F. A. Sedgman/Miss D. J. Hart   6-3, 3-6, 6-3
1949
E. W. Sturgess/Mrs S. P. Summers
G. D. Oakley/Miss J. Quertier   6-1, 6-1
1950
E. Morea/Miss B. Scofield   w.o.
W. F. Talbert/Mrs P. C. Todd   retired
1951
F. A. Sedgman/Miss D. J. Hart
M. G. Rose/Mrs T. D. Long   7-5, 6-2
1952
F. A. Sedgman/Miss D. J. Hart
E. W. Sturgess/Miss S. J. Fry   6-8, 6-3, 6-3
1953
E. V. Seixas/Miss D. J. Hart
M. G. Rose/Miss M. Connolly   4-6, 6-4, 6-0
1954
L. A. Hoad/Miss M. Connolly
R. N. Hartwig/Mrs J. Patorni   6-4, 6-3
1955
G. L. Forbes/Miss D. R. Hard
L. Ayala/Miss J. Staley   5-7, 6-1, 6-2
1956
L. Ayala/Mrs T. D. Long
R. N. Howe/Miss D. R. Hard   4-6, 6-4, 6-1
1957
J. Javorsky/Miss V. Pužejová
L. Ayala/Miss E. Buding   6-3, 6-4
1958
N. Pietrangeli/Miss S. J. Bloomer
R. N. Howe/Miss L. Coghlan   9-7, 6-8, 6-2
1959
W. A. Knight/Miss Y. Ramirez
R. G. Laver/Miss R. Schuurman   6-4, 6-4

1960
R. N. Howe/Miss M. E. Bueno
R. S. Emerson/Miss A. S. Haydon   1-6, 6-1, 6-2
1961
R. G. Laver/Miss D. R. Hard
J. Javorsky/Miss V. Pužejová   6-0, 2-6, 6-3
1962
R. N. Howe/Miss R. Schuurman
F. S. Stolle/Miss L. R. Turner   3-6, 6-4, 6-4
1963
K. N. Fletcher/Miss M. Smith
F. S. Stolle/Miss L. R. Turner   6-1, 6-2
1964
K. N. Fletcher/Miss M. Smith
F. S. Stolle/Miss L. R. Turner   6-3, 6-4
1965
K. N. Fletcher/Miss M. Smith
J. D. Newcombe/Miss M. E. Bueno   6-4, 6-4
1966
F. D. McMillan/Miss A. M. Van Zyl
C. E. Graebner/Mrs P. F. Jones   1-6, 6-3, 6-2
1967
O. K. Davidson/Mrs L. W. King
I. Ţiriac/Mrs P. F. Jones   6-3, 6-1
1968 *Open Championships began*
J.-C. Barclay/Miss F. Durr
O. K. Davidson/Mrs L. W. King   6-1, 6-4
1969
M. C. Riessen/Mrs B. M. Court
J.-C. Barclay/Miss F. Durr   7-5, 6-4
1970
R. A. J. Hewitt/Mrs L. W. King
J.-C. Barclay/Miss F. Durr   3-6, 6-3, 6-2
1971
J.-C. Barclay/Miss F. Durr
T. Lejus/Miss W. Shaw   6-2, 6-4
1972
K. Warwick/Miss E. F. Goolagong
J.-C. Barclay/Miss F. Durr   6-2, 6-4
1973
J.-C. Barclay/Miss F. Durr
P. Dominguez/Miss B. Stöve   6-1, 6-4

ILTF Grand Prix

Men

1970   *Sponsored by Pepsi Co*

	Points	Prize Money
1. C. Richey	60	$25,000
2. A. R. Ashe	55	$17,000
3. K. R. Rosewall	53	$15,000
4. R. G. Laver	51	$12,000
5. S. R. Smith	47	$10,500
6. Z. Franulović	35	$9,500
7. J. D. Newcombe	35	$8,500
8. J. Kodeš	33	$7,500

Masters' Tournament

Held in Tokyo, December 1970 and
played as a round robin

	Wins
1. S. R. Smith	4*
2. R. G. Laver	4
3. K. R. Rosewall	3*
4. A. R. Ashe	3
5. Z. Franulović	1
6. J. Kodeš	0

1971   *Sponsored by Pepsi Co*

	Points	Prize Money
1. S. R. Smith	187	$25,000
2. I. Năstase	172	$17,000
3. Z. Franulović	129	$15,000
4. J. Kodeš	124	$12,000
5. C. Richey	98	$10,500
6. P. Barthès	82	$9,500
7. C. E. Graebner	79	$8,500
8. T. W. Gorman	69	$7,500

Masters' Tournament

Held in Paris, December 1971 and
played as a round robin

	Wins
1. I. Năstase	6
2. S. R. Smith	4
3. C. Richey	3*
4. P. Barthès	3*
5. J. Kodeš	3*
6. Z. Franulović	1
7. C. E. Graebner	1

1972   *Sponsored by Commercial Union*

	Points	Prize Money
1. I. Năstase	659	£21,000
2. S. R. Smith	587	£14,700
3. M. Orantes	468	£10,500
4. J. Kodeš	332	£8,400
5. A. Gimeno	319	£6,720
6. R. A. J. Hewitt	263	£5,460
7. J. S. Connors	251	£5,040
8. T. W. Gorman	227	£4,620

Masters' Tournament

Held in Barcelona, December 1972 and played as two round
robins, the finalists of each taking part in a final stage of semi-
finals and final

Semi-Finals
I. Năstase J. S. Connors
6-2, 6-3, 6-2
S. R. Smith T. W. Gorman
6-7, 7-6, 5-7, 4-5 retired

Final
I. Năstase S. R. Smith
6-3, 6-2, 3-6, 2-6, 6-3

Women

1971   *Sponsored by Pepsi Co*

	Points	Prize Money
1. Mrs L. W. King	181	$10,000
2. Miss F. Durr	119	$7,500
3. Miss H. F. Gourlay	83	$6,500
4. Mrs D. E. Dalton	70	$5,250
5. Miss S. V. Wade	69	$4,000
6. Miss W. M. Shaw	51	$3,500
7. Mrs J. B. Chanfreau	49	$3,000
8. Miss L. E. Hunt	43	$2,500

1972   *Sponsored by Commercial Union*

	Points	Prize Money
1. Mrs L. W. King	719	£9,000
2. Miss E. F. Goolagong	400	£6,000
3. Miss R. Casals	316	£4,500
4. Mrs K. S. Gunter	316	£3,600
5. Miss K. A. Melville	250	£3,000
6. Mrs B. M. Court	234	£2,600
7. Miss F. Durr	224	£2,200
8. Miss S. V. Wade	183	£1,800

ILTF Grand Prix

Men

Masters' Tournament

Held in Boston, Mass., December 1973 and played as two round robins, the finalists of each taking part in a final stage of semi-finals and final

Semi-Finals
T. S. Okker J. D. Newcombe
3-6, 7-5, 3-5 retired
I. Năstase J. S. Connors
6-3, 7-5

Final
I. Năstase T. S. Okker
6-3, 7-5, 4-6, 6-3

Women

WCT

January – November 1971
Final Positions – Singles

	Tournaments played	(won)	Matches won	lost	WCT points
1. R. G. Laver	10	(4)	54	14	87·25
2. T. S. Okker	20	(2)	52	17	75
3. K. R. Rosewall	18	(4)	51	14	74
4. C. Drysdale	20	(1)	52	18	69·25
5. A. R. Ashe	20	(1)	43	18	68·25
6. J. D. Newcombe	12	(4)	36	8	60
7. M. C. Riessen	20	(1)	41	19	55
8. R. C. Lutz	20	(1)	31	19	41

Play Off, November 1971
Houston and Dallas, Texas
Semi-Finals
K. R. Rosewall T. S. Okker
6-3, 6-3, 6-1
R. G. Laver A. R. Ashe
6-3, 1-6, 6-3, 6-3

Final
K. R. Rosewall R. G. Laver
6-4, 1-6, 7-6, 7-6

Prize Money
$50,000 Winner
$20,000 Runner-Up
$ 8,000 Semi-Finalists
$ 3,500 Quarter-Finalists

January – May 1972
Final Positions – Singles

	Tournaments played	(won)	Matches won	lost	WCT points
1. R. G. Laver	20	(8)	65	12	113
2. K. R. Rosewall	19	(4)	62	15	94
3. T. S. Okker	20	(2)	49	18	70
4. C. Drysdale	20		47	20	64
5. M. C. Riessen	20	(1)	43	19	58
6. A. R. Ashe	20	(1)	37	19	53
7. R. C. Lutz	20	(1)	36	20	45
8. J. D. Newcombe	13	(2)	27	11	39

Play Off, May 1972
Dallas, Texas
Semi-Finals
R. G. Laver M. C. Riessen
4-6, 4-6, 6-1, 6-2, 6-0
K. R. Rosewall A. R. Ashe
6-4, 6-2, 7-6

Play Off for Third Place
A. R. Ashe M. C. Riessen 6-3, 6-1

Final
K. R. Rosewall R. G. Laver
4-6, 6-0, 6-3, 6-7, 7-6

Prize Money
$50,000 Winner
$20,000 Runner-Up
$10,000 Third Place
$ 6,000 Fourth Place
$ 3,500 Quarter-Finalists

May – November 1972
Final Positions – Singles

	Tournaments played	(won)	Matches won	lost	WCT points
1. J. D. Newcombe	11	(5)	38	6	67
2. A. R. Ashe	12	(3)	31	9	51
3. T. S. Okker	12		31	12	41
4. M. Cox	12	(1)	23	11	34
5. M. C. Riessen	12		24	12	31
5. C. Drysdale	12		22	12	31
7. N. Pilić	11		19	10	28
7. R. G. Lutz	12	(1)	18	11	28

Play Off, November 1972
Rome, Italy
Semi-Finals
R. C. Lutz C. Drysdale
6-4, 6-4
A. R. Ashe T. S. Okker
6-7, 6-3, 6-3

Play Off for Third Place
T. S. Okker C. Drysdale 6-3, 7-5

Final
A. R. Ashe R. C. Lutz
6-2, 3-6, 6-3, 3-6, 7-6

Prize Money
$25,000 Winner
$10,000 Runner-Up
$ 5,000 Third Place
$ 3,000 Fourth Place
$ 1,750 Quarter-Finalists

January – May 1973
Final Positions – Singles

Group A	Tournaments played	(won)	Matches won	lost	WCT points
1. S. R. Smith	11	(6)	41	5	75
2. R. G. Laver	10	(3)	37	7	63
3. J. Alexander	11		22	11	28
3. R. Emerson	10		20	9	28

Group B					
1. K. R. Rosewall	11	(3)	34	8	53
2. A. R. Ashe	11	(1)	26	10	41
3. M. C. Riessen	11	(1)	26	10	35
4. M. Cox	11	(1)	23	10	34
4. R. Taylor	11	(1)	21	10	34

Play Off, May 1973
Dallas, Texas
Semi-Finals
S. R. Smith R. G. Laver
4-6, 6-4, 7-6, 7-5
A. R. Ashe K. R. Rosewall
6-4, 6-2, 5-7, 1-6, 6-2

Play Off for Third Place
K. R. Rosewall R. G. Laver 6-3, 6-2

Final
S. R. Smith A. R. Ashe
6-3, 6-3, 4-6, 6-4

Prize Money
$50,000 Winner
$20,000 Runner-Up
$10,000 Third Place
$ 6,000 Fourth Place
$ 3,500 Quarter-Finalists

Records of All Time in the 'Big Four' Championships Davis, Federation and Wightman Cups

Record	Player	Year
Wimbledon Championships		
Youngest Winner	*C. Dod, aged 15 years 10 months	1887
	W. Baddeley, aged 19 years, 5 months, 23 days	1891
Oldest Winner	*A. W. Gore, aged 41. He was also the oldest finalist (1912) at 44	1909
	W. T. Tilden was the oldest player to win the title after World War I (1930) at 37	
Highest Number of Wins	W. Renshaw, seven times (before Challenge Round was abolished)	1881-6, 1889
	H. L. Doherty, five times	1902-6
	R. F. Doherty, four times	1897-1900
	A. F. Wilding, four times	1910-13
	R. Laver, four times (after Challenge Round was abolished)	1961-2, 1968-9
	H. Wills Moody, eight times	1927-30, 1932-3, 1935, 1938
	D. Lambert Chambers, seven times	1903-4, 1906, 1910-11, 1913-14
	B. Hillyard, six times	1886, 1889, 1894, 1897, 1899-1900
	S. Lenglen, six times	1919-23, 1925
Shortest Final	*20 games: F. Perry beat G. von Cramm (suffering from a pulled muscle) 6-1, 6-1, 6-0	1936
	*12 games: D. Lambert Chambers beat D. Boothby 6-0, 6-0	1911
Longest Final	58 games: J. Drobný beat K. Rosewall 13-11, 4-6, 6-2, 9-7	1954
	46 games: M. Court beat B. J. King 14-12, 11-9	1970
	53 games (when match replayed): M. E. Robb beat A. M. Sterry 4-6, 13-11; rain held up play; match replayed next day 7-5, 6-1	1902
Longest Singles Match	*112 games: R. A. Gonzalez beat C. Pasarell 22-24, 1-6, 16-14, 6-3, 11-9, in the first round	1969
	54 games: A. Weiwers beat O. Anderson 8-10, 14-12, 6-4, in the second round	1948
Longest Doubles Match	98 games: G. Scott/M. Pilić beat C. Richey/T. Ulrich 19-21, 12-10, 6-4, 4-6, 9-7, in the first round	1966
	48 games: P. Brazier/C. Wheatcroft beat M. Nonweiller/B. Soames 11-9, 5-7, 9-7, in the first round	1933
US Championships		
Youngest Winner	M. Sutton, aged 16 years, 9 months	1904
	M. Connolly, aged 16 years 11 months, 19 days	1951
	O. S. Campbell, aged 19 years, 6 months, 9 days	1890
Oldest Winner	W. T. Tilden, aged 36	1929
Highest Number of Wins	R. Sears, seven times	1881-7
	W. Larned, seven times	1901-2, 1907-11
	W. T. Tilden, seven times	1920-5, 1929
	M. Mallory, seven times	1915-16, 1918, 1920-2, 1926
	H. W. Moody seven times	1923-5, 1927-9, 1931
Shortest Final	23 games:	
	R. Sears beat W. Glyn 6-0, 6-3, 6-2	1881
	R. Sears beat C. Clark 6-1, 6-4, 6-0	1882
	H. Slocum beat H. Taylor 6-4, 6-1, 6-0	1888
	W. T. Tilden beat W. Johnston 6-1, 6-3, 6-1	1921
	13 games:	
	E. Hansell beat L. Knight 6-1, 6-0	1887
	H. Hotchkiss beat L. Barger-Wallach 6-0, 6-1	1909
	M. Mallory beat E. Raymond 6-0, 6-1	1916
	M. Bueno beat C. Graebner 6-1, 6-0	1964
Longest Final	*67 games:	
	R. A. Gonzalez beat F. E. Schroeder 16-18, 2-6, 6-1, 6-2, 6-4	1949
	*51 games: J. Atkinson beat M. Jones 6-3, 5-7, 6-4, 2-6, 7-5	1898
	*Longest three-set final: 48 games: M. duPont beat A. L. Brough 4-6, 6-4, 15-13	1948
Longest Singles Match	*100 games: F. Robbins beat D. Dell 22-20, 9-7, 6-8, 8-10, 6-4, in the first round	1969
Longest Doubles Match	*105 games: L. Loyo-Mayo/M. Lara beat M. Santana/L. Garcia 10-12, 24-22, 11-9, 3-6, 6-2, in the third round	1966
	C. Drysdale/R. Moore beat R. Emerson/R. Barnes 29-31, 8-6, 3-6, 8-6, 6-2, in a quarter-final	1967

* overall record in 'Big Four' Championships

Record	Player	Year
Australian Championships		
Youngest Winner	K. Rosewall, aged 18 years 2 months	1953
	M. Smith, aged 17 years 6 months	1960
Oldest Winner	K. Rosewall, aged 37 years 2 months	1972
Highest Number of Wins	R. Emerson, six times	1961, 1963-7
	*M. Court, eleven times	1960-6, 1969-71, 1973
Longest Singles Match	93 games: D. Ralston beat J. Newcombe 19-17, 20-18, 4-6, 6-3, in a quarter-final	1970
Longest Doubles Match	94 games: M. Senior/P. Avery beat W. Jacques/C. Mason 4-6, 18-16, 7-9, 17-15, 2-0 retired, in the first round	1968
French Championships		
Youngest Winner	K. Rosewall, aged 18 years 7 months	1953
	C. Truman, aged 18 years 5 months	1959
Oldest Winner	M. Bernard, aged 35	1946
Highest Number of Wins	M. Decugis, eight times ('closed' championships)	1903-4, 1907-9, 1912-14
	S. Lenglen, six times (four when championships were 'closed')	1920-3, 1925-6
Davis Cup		
Highest Number of Wins (country)	United States, 24 times	1900-72†
Highest Number of Consecutive Wins	United States, seven times	1920-6
Highest Number of Challenge Rounds (individual)	W. T. Tilden (US), 28 Challenge Round rubbers, winning 21	1920-30
	N. Brookes (Australasia), 22 Challenge Round rubbers, winning 15	1907-20
	H. Cochet (France), 20 Challenge Round rubbers, winning 14	1926-33
	H. L. Doherty (British Isles), 12 Challenge Round rubbers, winning all 12	1902-6
	H. W. Austin (Gt Britain), 12 Challenge Round rubbers, winning 8	1931-7
Highest Number of All Rounds (Individual)	N. Pietrangeli (Italy), 164 rubbers, winning 119	1954-72
	J. Brichant (Belgium), 121 rubbers	1949-65
	M. Santana (Spain), 117 rubbers	1958-70
Longest Singles Rubber	86 games: A. R. Ashe (US) beat C. Kuhnke (West Germany) 6-8, 10-12, 9-7, 13-11, 6-4, in the Challenge Round	1970
Longest Doubles Rubber	123 games: S. R. Smith/E. Van Dillen (USA) beat J. Fillol/P. Cornejo (Chile) 7-9, 37-39, 8-6, 6-1, 6-3 in the American Zone Final; the record doubles set of 76 games took 3 hours 45 min	1973
Federation Cup		
Highest Number of Wins (country)	Australia, six times	1963-73†
Wightman Cup		
Highest Number of Wins (country)	United States, 38 times	1923-73†
Highest Number of Consecutive Wins	United States, 21 times	1931-57
Highest Number of Matches (individual)	A. Jones (Gt Britain), 12 matches; 32 rubbers	1957-70
	H. H. Jacobs (US), 12 matches; 30 rubbers	1923-38
	H. Wills Moody (US), 10 matches; 30 rubbers	1923-38
Highest Number of Wins (individual)	A. L. Brough (US), 10 matches, winning all 22 rubbers, 12 singles and 10 doubles	1946-57
Longest Singles Match	46 games: B. J. King (US) beat C. Truman (Gt Britain) 6-4, 19-17	1963
Longest Doubles Match	40 games: H. H. Wightman/E. Goss (US) beat B. Covell/K. McKane (Gt Britain) 10-8, 5-7, 6-4	1923

* overall record in 'Big Four' Championships; † these years represent the period spanned by the first and the last and not necessarily a continuous sequence

Davis Cup

Final Rounds (to challenge)	Challenge Round Team Results	Challenge Round Winners
	1900 *Singles* **M. D. Whitman (US)** A. W. Gore (BI) 6-1, 6-3, 6-2 **D. F. Davis (US)** E. D. Black (BI) 4-6, 6-2, 6-4, 6-4 **M. D. Whitman (US)** E. D. Black (BI) not played **D. F. Davis (US)** A. W. Gore (BI) 9-7, 9-9 abandoned *Doubles* **H. Ward/D. F. Davis (US)** E. D. Black/H. Roper Barrett (BI) 6-4, 6-4, 6-4	**1900** (2)† **United States** British Isles 3-0 Boston, Mass., U.S.A.
	1901 *No Competition*	**1901** *No Competition*
	1902 *Singles* **R. F. Doherty (BI)** W. A. Larned (US) 2-6, 3-6, 6-3, 6-4, 6-4 **M. D. Whitman (US)** J. Pim (BI) 6-1, 6-1, 1-6, 6-0 **W. A. Larned (US)** J. Pim (BI) 6-3, 6-2, 6-3 **M. D. Whitman (US)** R. F. Doherty (BI) 6-1, 7-5, 6-4 *Doubles* **R. F. Doherty/H. L. Doherty (BI)** H. Ward/D. F. Davis (US) 3-6, 10-8, 6-3, 6-4	**1902** (2)† **United States (H)** British Isles (C) 3-2 Brooklyn, N.Y., U.S.A.
	1903 *Singles* **H. L. Doherty (BI)** R. D. Wrenn (US) 6-0, 6-3, 6-4 **W. A. Larned (US)** R. F. Doherty (BI) default **H. L. Doherty (BI)** W. A. Larned (US) 6-3, 6-8, 6-0, 2-6, 7-5 **R. F. Doherty (BI)** R. D. Wrenn (US) 6-4, 3-6, 6-3, 6-8, 6-4 *Doubles* **R. F. Doherty/H. L. Doherty (BI)** R. D. Wrenn/G. L. Wrenn (US) 7-5, 9-7, 2-6, 6-3	**1903** (2)† **British Isles (C)** United States (H) 4-1 Boston, Mass., U.S.A.
1904 **Belgium** France 3-2	**1904** *Singles* **H. L. Doherty (BI)** P. de Borman (B) 6-4, 6-1, 6-1 **F. L. Riseley (BI)** W. Lemaire (B) 6-1, 6-4, 6-2 **H. L. Doherty (BI)** W. Lemaire (B) default **F. L. Riseley (BI)** P. de Borman (B) 4-6, 6-2, 8-6, 7-5 *Doubles* **R. F. Doherty/H. L. Doherty (BI)** P. de Borman/W. Lemaire (B) 6-0, 6-1, 6-3	**1904** (4)† **British Isles (H)** Belgium (C) 5-0 Wimbledon, England
1905 **United States** Australasia 5-0	**1905** *Singles* **H. L. Doherty (BI)** H. Ward (US) 7-9, 4-6, 6-1, 6-2, 6-0 **S. H. Smith (BI)** W. A. Larned (US) 6-4, 6-4, 5-7, 6-4 **S. H. Smith (BI)** W. J. Clothier (US) 4-6, 6-1, 6-4, 6-3 **H. L. Doherty (BI)** W. A. Larned (US) 6-4, 2-6, 6-8, 6-4, 6-2 *Doubles* **R. F. Doherty/H. L. Doherty (BI)** H. Ward/B. C. Wright (US) 8-10, 6-2, 6-2, 4-6, 8-6	**1905** (6)† **British Isles (H)** United States (C) 5-0 Wimbledon, England
1906 **United States** Australasia 3-2	**1906** *Singles* **S. H. Smith (BI)** R. D. Little (US) 6-4, 6-4, 6-1 **H. L. Doherty (BI)** H. Ward (US) 6-2, 8-6, 6-3 **S. H. Smith (BI)** H. Ward (US) 6-1, 6-0, 6-4 **H. L. Doherty (BI)** R. D. Little (US) 3-6, 6-3, 6-8, 6-1, 6-3 *Doubles* **R. F. Doherty/H. L. Doherty (BI)** H. Ward/R. D. Little (US) 3-6, 11-9, 9-7, 6-1	**1906** (5)† **British Isles (H)** United States (C) 5-0 Wimbledon, England
1907 **Australasia** United States 3-2	**1907** *Singles* **N. E. Brookes (A)** A. W. Gore (BI) 7-5, 6-1, 7-5 **A. F. Wilding (A)** H. Roper Barrett (BI) 1-6, 6-4, 6-3, 7-5 **N. E. Brookes (A)** H. Roper Barrett (BI) 6-2, 6-0, 6-3 **A. W. Gore (BI)** A. F. Wilding (A) 3-6, 6-3, 7-5, 6-2 *Doubles* **A. W. Gore/H. Roper Barrett (BI)** N. E. Brookes/A. F. Wilding (A) 3-6, 4-6, 7-5, 6-2, 13-11	**1907** (5)† **Australasia (C)** British Isles (H) 3-2 Wimbledon, England
1908 **United States** British Isles 4-1	**1908** *Singles* **N. E. Brookes (A)** F. B. Alexander (US) 5-7, 9-7, 6-2, 4-6, 6-3 **B. C. Wright (US)** A. F. Wilding (A) 3-6, 7-5, 6-3, 6-1 **A. F. Wilding (A)** F. B. Alexander (US) 6-3, 6-4, 6-1 **B. C. Wright (US)** N. E. Brookes (A) 0-6, 3-6, 7-5, 6-2, 12-10 *Doubles* **N. E. Brookes/A. F. Wilding (A)** B. C. Wright/F. B. Alexander (US) 6-4, 6-2, 5-7, 1-6, 6-4	**1908** (3)† **Australasia (H)** United States (C) 3-2 Melbourne, Australia
1909 **United States** British Isles 5-0	**1909** *Singles* **N. E. Brookes (A)** M. E. McLoughlin (US) 6-2, 6-2, 6-4 **A. F. Wilding (A)** M. H. Long (US) 6-2, 7-5, 6-1 **N. E. Brookes (A)** M. H. Long (US) 6-4, 7-5, 8-6 **A. F. Wilding (A)** M. E. McLoughlin (US) 3-6, 8-6, 6-2, 6-3 *Doubles* **N. E. Brookes/A. F. Wilding (A)** M. E. McLoughlin/M. H. Long (US) 12-10, 9-7, 6-3	**1909** (3)† **Australasia (H)** United States (C) 5-0 Sydney, Australia
1910 *No Competition* **1911** **United States** British Isles 4-1	**1910** *No Competition* **1911** *Singles* **N. E. Brookes (A)** B. C. Wright (US) 6-4, 2-6, 6-3, 6-3 **R. W. Heath (A)** W. A. Larned (US) 2-6, 6-1, 7-5, 6-2 **N. E. Brookes (A)** M. E. McLoughlin (US) 6-4, 3-6, 4-6, 6-3, 6-4 **R. W. Heath (A)** B. C. Wright (US) default *Doubles* **N. E. Brookes/A. W. Dunlop (A)** B. C. Wright/M. E. McLoughlin (US) 6-4, 5-7, 7-5, 6-4	**1910** *No Competition* **1911** (4)† **Australasia (H)** United States (C) 5-0 Christchurch, New Zealand
1912 **British Isles** France 4-1	**1912** *Singles* **J. C. Parke (BI)** N. E. Brookes (A) 8-6, 6-3, 5-7, 6-2 **C. P. Dixon (BI)** R. W. Heath (A) 5-7, 6-4, 6-4, 6-4 **J. C. Parke (BI)** R. W. Heath (A) 6-2, 6-4, 6-4 **N. E. Brookes (A)** C. P. Dixon (BI) 6-2, 6-4, 6-4 *Doubles* **N. E. Brookes/A. W. Dunlop (A)** J. C. Parke/A. E. Beamish (BI) 6-4, 6-1, 7-5	**1912** (3)† **British Isles (C)** Australia (H) 3-2 Melbourne, Australia
1913 **United States** Canada 3-0	**1913** *Singles* **J. C. Parke (BI)** M. E. McLoughlin (US) 8-10, 7-5, 6-4, 1-6, 7-5 **R. N. Williams (US)** C. P. Dixon (BI) 8-6, 3-6, 6-2, 1-6, 7-5 **M. E. McLoughlin (US)** C. P. Dixon (BI) 8-6, 6-3, 6-2 **J. C. Parke (BI)** R. N. Williams (US) 6-2, 5-7, 5-7, 6-4, 6-2 *Doubles* **H. H. Hackett/M. E. McLoughlin (US)** H. Roper Barrett/C. P. Dixon (BI) 5-7, 6-1, 2-6, 7-5, 6-4	**1913** (8)† **United States (C)** British Isles (H) 3-2 Wimbledon, England
1914 **Australasia** British Isles 3-0	**1914** *Singles* **N. E. Brookes (A)** R. N. Williams (US) 6-1, 6-2, 8-10, 6-3 **M. E. McLoughlin (US)** A. F. Wilding (A) 6-2, 6-3, 2-6, 6-2 **A. F. Wilding (A)** R. N. Williams (US) 7-5, 6-2, 6-3 **M. E. McLoughlin (US)** N. E. Brookes (A) 17-15, 6-3, 6-3 *Doubles* **N. E. Brookes/A. F. Wilding (A)** M. E. McLoughlin/T. C. Bundy (US) 6-3, 8-6, 9-7	**1914** (7)† **Australasia (C)** United States (H) 3-2 Forest Hills, N.Y., U.S.A.
1915-18 *No Competition*	**1915-18** *No Competition*	**1915-18** *No Competition*

Final Rounds (to challenge)	Challenge Round Team Results	Challenge Round Winners

1919
British Isles France 3-2

1919 *Singles*
G. L. Patterson (A) A. H. Lowe (BI) 6-4, 6-3, 2-6, 6-3
A. R. F. Kingscote (BI) J. O. Anderson (A) 7-5, 6-2, 6-4
G. L. Patterson (A) A. R. F. Kingscote (BI) 6-4, 6-4, 8-6
J. O. Anderson (A) A. H. Lowe (BI) 6-4, 5-7, 6-3, 4-6, 12-10
Doubles
N. E. Brookes/G. L. Patterson (A)
A. R. F. Kingscote/A. E. Beamish (BI) 6-0, 6-0, 6-2

1919 (5)†
Australasia (H)
British Isles (C) 4-1
Sydney, Australia

1920
United States British Isles 5-0

1920 *Singles*
W. T. Tilden (US) N. E. Brookes (A) 10-8, 6-4, 1-6, 6-4
W. M. Johnston (US) G. L. Patterson (A) 6-3, 6-1, 6-1
W. T. Tilden (US) G. L. Patterson (A) 5-7, 6-2, 6-3, 6-3
W. M. Johnston (US) N. E. Brookes (A) 5-7, 7-5, 6-3, 6-3
Doubles
W. T. Tilden/W. M. Johnston (US)
N. E. Brookes/G. L. Patterson (A) 4-6, 6-4, 6-0, 6-4

1920 (6)†
United States (C)
Australasia (H) 5-0
Auckland, New Zealand

1921
Japan Australasia 4-1

1921 *Singles*
W. T. Tilden (US) Z. Shimizu (J) 5-7, 4-6, 7-5, 6-2, 6-1
W. M. Johnston (US) I. Kumagai (J) 6-2, 6-4, 6-2
W. T. Tilden (US) I. Kumagai (J) 9-7, 6-4, 6-1
W. M. Johnston (US) Z. Shimizu (J) 6-3, 5-7, 6-2, 6-4
Doubles
R. N. Williams/W. M. Washburn (US)
Z. Shimizu/I. Kumagai (J) 6-2, 7-5, 4-6, 7-5

1921 (11)†
United States (H)
Japan (C) 5-0
Forest Hills, N.Y., U.S.A.

1922
Australasia Spain 4-1

1922 *Singles*
W. T. Tilden (US) G. L. Patterson (A) 7-5, 10-8, 6-0
W. M. Johnston (US) J. O. Anderson (A) 6-1, 6-2, 6-3
W. M. Johnston (US) G. L. Patterson (A) 6-2, 6-2, 6-1
W. T. Tilden (US) J. O. Anderson (A) 6-4, 5-7, 3-6, 6-4, 6-2
Doubles
G. L. Patterson/P. O'Hara Wood (A)
W. T. Tilden/V. Richards (US) 6-4, 6-0, 6-3

1922 (11)†
United States (H)
Australasia (C) 4-1
Forest Hills, N.Y., U.S.A.

Inter-Zone Results

1923 *Zone Finals*
European Zone **France** Spain
American Zone **Australia** Japan
Inter-Zone Finals
Australia France 4-1

1923 *Singles*
J. O. Anderson (A) W. M. Johnston (US) 4-6, 6-2, 2-6, 7-5, 6-2
W. T. Tilden (US) J. B. Hawkes (A) 6-0, 6-2, 6-1
W. M. Johnston (US) J. B. Hawkes (A) 6-0, 6-2, 6-1
W. T. Tilden (US) J. O. Anderson (A) 6-2, 6-3, 1-6, 7-5
Doubles
W. T. Tilden/R. N. Williams (US)
J. O. Anderson/J. B. Hawkes (A) 17-15, 11-13, 2-6, 6-3, 6-2

1923 (17)†
United States (H)
Australia (C) 4-1
Forest Hills, N.Y., U.S.A.

1924 *Zone Finals*
European Zone
France Czechoslovakia
American Zone **Australia** Japan
Inter-Zone Finals
Australia France 3-2

1924 *Singles*
W. T. Tilden (US) G. L. Patterson (A) 6-4, 6-2, 6-2
V. Richards (US) P. O'Hara Wood (A) 6-3, 6-2, 6-4
W. T. Tilden (US) P. O'Hara Wood (A) 6-2, 6-1, 6-1
V. Richards (US) G. L. Patterson (A) 6-3, 7-5, 6-4
Doubles
W. T. Tilden/W. M. Johnston (US)
G. L. Patterson/P. O'Hara Wood (A) 5-7, 6-3, 6-4, 6-1

1924 (22)†
United States (H)
Australia (C) 5-0
Philadelphia, Pa., U.S.A.

1925 *Zone Finals*
European Zone
France Netherlands
American Zone
Australia Japan
Inter-Zone Finals
France Australia 3-1

1925 *Singles*
W. T. Tilden (US) J. Borotra (F) 4-6, 6-0, 2-6, 9-7, 6-4
W. M. Johnston (US) R. Lacoste (F) 6-1, 6-1, 6-8, 6-3
W. T. Tilden (US) R. Lacoste (F) 3-6, 10-12, 8-6, 7-5, 6-2
W. M. Johnston (US) J. Borotra (F) 6-1, 6-4, 6-0
Doubles
V. Richards/R. N. Williams (US)
R. Lacoste/J. Borotra (F) 6-4, 6-4, 6-3

1925 (23)†
United States (H)
France (C) 5-0
Philadelphia, Pa., U.S.A.

1926 *Zone Finals*
European Zone
France Great Britain
American Zone **Japan** Cuba
Inter-Zone Finals
France Japan 3-2

1926 *Singles*
W. M. Johnston (US) R. Lacoste (F) 6-0, 6-4, 0-6, 6-0
W. T. Tilden (US) J. Borotra (F) 6-2, 6-3, 6-3
W. M. Johnston (US) J. Borotra (F) 8-6, 6-4, 9-7
R. Lacoste (F) W. T. Tilden (US) 4-6, 6-4, 8-6, 8-6
Doubles
R. N. Williams/V. Richards (US)
H. Cochet/J. Brugnon (F) 6-4, 6-4, 6-2

1926 (24)†
United States (H)
France (C) 4-1
Philadelphia, Pa., U.S.A.

1927 *Zone Finals*
European Zone **France** Denmark
American Zone **Japan** Canada
Inter-Zone Finals
France Japan 3-0

1927 *Singles*
R. Lacoste (F) W. M. Johnston (US) 6-3, 6-2, 6-2
W. T. Tilden (US) H. Cochet (F) 6-4, 2-6, 6-2, 8-6
R. Lacoste (F) W. T. Tilden (US) 6-4, 4-6, 6-3, 6-3
H. Cochet (F) W. M. Johnston (US) 6-4, 4-6, 6-2, 6-4
Doubles
W. T. Tilden/F. T. Hunter (US)
J. Borotra/J. Brugnon (F) 3-6, 6-3, 6-3, 4-6, 6-0

1927 (26)†
France (C)
United States (H) 3-2
Philadelphia, Pa., U.S.A.

1928 *Zone Finals*
European Zone
Italy Czechoslovakia
American Zone
United States Japan
Inter-Zone Finals
United States Italy 4-1

1928 *Singles*
W. T. Tilden (US) R. Lacoste (F) 1-6, 6-4, 6-4, 2-6, 6-3
H. Cochet (F) J. F. Hennessey (US) 5-7, 9-7, 6-3, 6-0
H. Cochet (F) W. T. Tilden (US) 9-7, 8-6, 6-4
R. Lacoste (F) J. F. Hennessey (US) 4-6, 6-1, 7-5, 6-3
Doubles
H. Cochet/J. Borotra (F)
W. T. Tilden/F. T. Hunter (US) 6-4, 6-8, 7-5, 4-6, 6-2

1928 (33)†
France (H)
United States (C) 4-1
Auteuil, Paris, France

1929 *Zone Finals*
European Zone
Germany Great Britain
American Zone
United States Cuba
Inter-Zone Finals
United States Germany 5-0

1929 *Singles*
H. Cochet (F) W. T. Tilden (US) 6-3, 6-1, 6-2
J. Borotra (F) G. M. Lott (US) 6-1, 3-6, 6-4, 7-5
W. T. Tilden (US) J. Borotra (F) 4-6, 6-1, 6-4, 7-5
H. Cochet (F) G. M. Lott (US) 6-1, 3-6, 6-0, 6-3
Doubles
J. Van Ryn/W. L. Allison (US)
H. Cochet/J. Borotra (F) 6-1, 8-6, 6-4

1929 (30)†
France (H)
United States (C) 3-2
Auteuil, Paris, France

1930 *Zone Finals*
European Zone **Italy** Japan
American Zone
United States Mexico
Inter-Zone Finals
United States Italy 4-1

1930 *Singles*
W. T. Tilden (US) J. Borotra (F) 2-6, 7-5, 6-4, 7-5
H. Cochet (F) G. M. Lott (US) 6-4, 6-2, 6-2
J. Borotra (F) G. M. Lott (US) 5-7, 6-3, 2-6, 6-2, 8-6
H. Cochet (F) W. T. Tilden (US) 4-6, 6-3, 6-1, 7-5
Doubles
H. Cochet/J. Brugnon (F)
W. L. Allison/J. Van Ryn (US) 6-3, 7-5, 1-6, 6-2

1930 (29)†
France (H)
United States (C) 4-1
Auteuil, Paris, France

1931 *Zone Finals*
European Zone
Great Britain Czechoslovakia
American Zone
United States Argentina
Inter-Zone Finals
Great Britain United States 3-2

1931 *Singles*
H. Cochet (F) H. W. Austin (GB) 3-6, 11-9, 6-2, 6-4
F. J. Perry (GB) J. Borotra (F) 4-6, 10-8, 6-0, 4-6, 6-4
H. W. Austin (GB) J. Borotra (F) 7-5, 6-3, 3-6, 7-5
H. Cochet (F) F. J. Perry (GB) 6-4, 1-6, 9-7, 6-3
Doubles
H. Cochet/J. Brugnon (F)
G. P. Hughes/C. H. Kingsley (GB) 6-1, 5-7, 6-3, 8-6

1931 (31)†
France (H)
Great Britain (C) 3-2
Auteuil, Paris, France

Winners in **bold type**; **(H)**/(H) holder; **(C)**/(C) challenger; † total number of nations competing, including the holder in years with a Challenge Round

Davis Cup

Inter-Zone Results	Challenge Round Team Results	Challenge Round Winners

1932 *Zone Finals*
European Zone **Germany** Italy
American Zone
United States Brazil
Inter-Zone Finals
United States Germany 3-2

1932 *Singles*
J. Borotra (F) H. E. Vines (US) 6-4, 6-2, 3-6, 6-4
H. Cochet (F) W. L. Allison (US) 5-7, 7-5, 7-5, 6-2
J. Borotra (F) W. L. Allison (US) 1-6, 3-6, 6-4, 6-2, 7-5
H. E. Vines (US) H. Cochet (F) 4-6, 0-6, 7-5, 8-6, 6-2
Doubles
W. L. Allison/J. Van Ryn (US)
H. Cochet/J. Brugnon (F) 6-3, 11-13, 7-5, 4-6, 6-4

1932 (31)†
France (H)
United States (C) 3-2
Auteuil, Paris, France

1933 *Zone Finals*
European Zone
Great Britain Australia
American Zone
United States Argentina
Inter-Zone Finals
Great Britain United States 4-1

1933 *Singles*
H. W. Austin (GB) A. Merlin (F) 6-3, 6-4, 6-0
F. J. Perry (GB) H. Cochet (F) 8-10, 6-4, 8-6, 3-6, 6-1
H. Cochet (F) H. W. Austin (GB) 5-7, 6-4, 4-6, 6-4, 6-4
F. J. Perry (GB) A. Merlin (F) 4-6, 8-6, 6-2, 7-5
Doubles
J. Borotra/J. Brugnon (F)
G. P. Hughes/H. G. N. Lee (GB) 6-3, 8-6, 6-2

1933 (34)†
Great Britain (C)
France (H) 3-2
Auteuil, Paris, France

1934 *Zone Finals*
European Zone
Australia Czechoslovakia
American Zone
United States Mexico
Inter-Zone Finals
United States Australia 3-2

1934 *Singles*
H. W. Austin (GB) F. X. Shields (US) 6-4, 6-4, 6-1
F. J. Perry (GB) S. B. Wood (US) 6-1, 4-6, 5-7, 6-0, 6-3
F. J. Perry (GB) F. X. Shields (US) 6-4, 4-6, 6-2, 15-13
H. W. Austin (GB) S. B. Wood (US) 6-4, 6-0, 6-8, 6-3
Doubles
G. M. Lott/L. R. Stoefen (US)
G. P. Hughes/H. G. N. Lee (GB) 7-5, 6-0, 4-6, 9-7

1934 (29)†
Great Britain (H)
United States (C) 4-1
Wimbledon, England

1935 *Zone Finals*
European Zone
Germany Czechoslovakia
American Zone
United States Mexico
Inter-Zone Finals
United States Germany 4-1

1935 *Singles*
H. W. Austin (GB) W. L. Allison (US) 6-2, 2-6, 4-6, 6-3, 7-5
F. J. Perry (GB) J. D. Budge (US) 6-0, 6-8, 6-3, 6-4
H. W. Austin (GB) J. D. Budge (US) 6-2, 6-4, 6-8, 7-5
F. J. Perry (GB) W. L. Allison (US) 4-6, 6-4, 7-5, 6-3
Doubles
G. P. Hughes/C. R. D. Tuckey (GB)
W. L. Allison/J. Van Ryn (US) 6-2, 1-6, 6-8, 6-3, 6-3

1935 (31)†
Great Britain (H)
United States (C) 5-0
Wimbledon, England

1936 *Zone Finals*
European Zone
Germany Yugoslavia
American Zone
Australia United States
Inter-Zone Finals
Australia Germany 4-1

1936 *Singles*
H. W. Austin (GB) J. H. Crawford (A) 4-6, 6-3, 6-1, 6-1
F. J. Perry (GB) A. K. Quist (A) 6-1, 4-6, 7-5, 6-2
A. K. Quist (A) H. W. Austin (GB) 6-4, 3-6, 7-5, 6-2
F. J. Perry (GB) J. H. Crawford (A) 6-2, 6-3, 6-3
Doubles
J. H. Crawford/A. K. Quist (A)
G. P. Hughes/C. R. D. Tuckey (GB) 6-4, 2-6, 7-5, 10-8

1936 (24)†
Great Britain (H)
Australia (C) 3-2
Wimbledon, England

1937 *Zone Finals*
European Zone
Germany Czechoslovakia
American Zone
United States Australia
Inter-Zone Finals
United States Germany 3-2

1937 *Singles*
H. W. Austin (GB) F. A. Parker (US) 6-3, 6-2, 7-5
J. D. Budge (US) C. E. Hare (GB) 15-13, 6-1, 6-2
F. A. Parker (US) C. E. Hare (GB) 6-2, 6-4, 6-2
J. D. Budge (US) H. W. Austin (GB) 8-6, 3-6, 6-4, 6-3
Doubles
J. D. Budge/C. G. Mako (US)
C. R. D. Tuckey/F. H. D. Wilde (GB) 6-3, 7-5, 7-9, 12-10

1937 (25)†
United States (C)
Great Britain (H) 4-1
Wimbledon, England

1938 *Zone Finals*
European Zone
Germany Yugoslavia
American Zone **Australia** Japan
Inter-Zone Finals
Australia Germany 3-2

1938 *Singles*
R. L. Riggs (US) A. K. Quist (A) 4-6, 6-0, 8-6, 6-1
J. D. Budge (US) J. E. Bromwich (A) 6-2, 6-3, 4-6, 7-5
J. D. Budge (US) A. K. Quist (A) 8-6, 6-1, 6-2
J. E. Bromwich (A) R. L. Riggs (US) 6-4, 4-6, 6-0, 6-2
Doubles
A. K. Quist/J. E. Bromwich (A)
J. D. Budge/C. G. Mako (US) 0-6, 6-3, 6-4, 6-2

1938 (26)†
United States (H)
Australia (C) 3-2
Philadelphia, Pa., U.S.A.

1939 *Zone Finals*
European Zone
Yugoslavia Germany
American Zone **Australia** Cuba
Inter-Zone Finals
Australia Yugoslavia 4-1

1939 *Singles*
R. L. Riggs (US) J. E. Bromwich (A) 6-4, 6-0, 7-5
F. A. Parker (US) A. K. Quist (A) 6-3, 2-6, 6-4, 1-6, 7-5
A. K. Quist (A) R. L. Riggs (US) 6-1, 6-3, 3-6, 3-6, 6-4
J. E. Bromwich (A) F. A. Parker (US) 6-0, 6-3, 6-1
Doubles
A. K. Quist/J. E. Bromwich (A)
J. A. Kramer/J. R. Hunt (US) 5-7, 6-2, 7-5, 6-2

1939 (27)†
Australia (C)
United States (H) 3-2
Philadelphia, Pa., U.S.A.

1940-45 No Competition

1940-45 No Competition

1940-45 No Competition

1946 *Zone Finals*
European Zone
Sweden Yugoslavia
American Zone
United States Mexico
Inter-Zone Finals
United States Sweden 5-0

1946 *Singles*
F. R. Schroeder (US) J. E. Bromwich (A) 3-6, 6-1, 6-2, 0-6, 6-3
J. A. Kramer (US) D. Pails (A) 8-6, 6-2, 9-7
J. A. Kramer (US) J. E. Bromwich (A) 8-6, 6-4, 6-4
G. Mulloy (US) D. Pails (A) 6-3, 6-3, 6-4
Doubles
J. A. Kramer/F. R. Schroeder (US)
J. E. Bromwich/A. K. Quist (A) 6-2, 7-5, 6-4

1946 (21)†
United States (C)
Australia (H) 5-0
Melbourne, Australia

1947 *Zone Finals*
European Zone
Czechoslovakia Yugoslavia
American Zone **Australia** Canada
Inter-Zone Finals
Australia Czechoslovakia 4-1

1947 *Singles*
J. A. Kramer (US) D. Pails (A) 6-2, 6-1, 6-2
F. R. Schroeder (US) J. E. Bromwich (A) 6-4, 5-7, 6-3, 6-3
F. R. Schroeder (US) D. Pails (A) 6-3, 8-6, 4-6, 9-11, 10-8
J. A. Kramer (US) J. E. Bromwich (A) 6-3, 6-2, 6-2
Doubles
J. E. Bromwich/C. F. Long (A)
J. A. Kramer/F. R. Schroeder (US) 6-4, 2-6, 6-2, 6-4

1947 (23)†
United States (H)
Australia (C) 4-1
Forest Hills, N.Y., U.S.A.

1948 *Zone Finals*
European Zone
Czechoslovakia Sweden
American Zone **Australia** Mexico
Inter-Zone Finals
Australia Czechoslovakia 3-2

1948 *Singles*
F. A. Parker (US) O. W. Sidwell (A) 6-4, 6-4, 6-4
F. R. Schroeder (US) O. W. Sidwell (A) 6-2, 6-1, 6-1
F. A. Parker (US) A. K. Quist (A) 6-2, 6-2, 6-3
F. R. Schroeder (US) A. K. Quist (A) 6-3, 4-6, 6-0, 6-0
Doubles
W. F. Talbert/G. Mulloy (US)
O. W. Sidwell/C. F. Long (A) 8-6, 9-7, 2-6, 7-5

1948 (30)†
United States (H)
Australia (C) 5-0
Forest Hills, N.Y., U.S.A.

1949 *Zone-Finals*
European Zone **Italy** France
American Zone **Australia** Mexico
Inter-Zone Finals
Australia Italy 5-0

1949 *Singles*
F. R. Schroeder (US) O. W. Sidwell (A) 6-1, 5-7, 4-6, 6-2, 6-3
R. A. Gonzalez (US) F. A. Sedgman (A) 8-6, 6-4, 9-7
F. R. Schroeder (US) F. A. Sedgman (A) 6-4, 6-3, 6-3
R. A. Gonzalez (US) O. W. Sidwell (A) 6-1, 6-3, 6-3
Doubles
O. W. Sidwell/J. E. Bromwich (A)
W. F. Talbert/G. Mulloy (US) 3-6, 4-6, 10-8, 9-7, 9-7

1949 (29)†
United States (H)
Australia (C) 4-1
Forest Hills, N.Y., U.S.A.

1950 *Zone Finals*
European Zone **Sweden** Denmark
American Zone **Australia** Mexico
Inter-Zone Finals
Australia Sweden 3-2

1950 *Singles*
F. A. Sedgman (A) T. P. Brown (US) 6-0, 8-6, 9-7
K. McGregor (A) F. R. Schroeder (US) 13-11, 6-3, 6-4
F. A. Sedgman (A) F. R. Schroeder (US) 6-2, 6-2, 6-2
T. P. Brown (US) K. McGregor (A) 9-11, 8-10, 11-9, 6-1, 6-4
Doubles
F. A. Sedgman/J. E. Bromwich (A)
F. R. Schroeder/G. Mulloy (US) 4-6, 6-4, 6-2, 4-6, 6-4

1950 (27)†
Australia (C)
United States (H) 4-1
Forest Hills, N.Y., U.S.A.

Inter-Zone Results

1951 *Zone Finals*
European Zone
Sweden West Germany
American Zone
United States Canada
Inter-Zone Finals
United States Sweden 5-0

1952 *Zone Finals*
European Zone **Italy** Belgium
American Zone
United States Canada
Eastern Zone **India** a bye
Inter-Zone Finals
Italy India 3-2
United States Italy 5-0

1953 *Zone Finals*
European Zone **Belgium** Denmark
American Zone
United States Canada
Eastern Zone **India** a bye
Inter-Zone Finals
Belgium India 5-0
United States Belgium 4-1

1954 *Zone Finals*
European Zone **Sweden** France
American Zone
United States Mexico
Eastern Zone *No Competition*
Inter-Zone Finals
United States Sweden 5-0

1955 *Zone Finals*
European Zone **Italy** Sweden
American Zone **Australia** Canada
Eastern Zone **Japan** Philippines
Inter-Zone Finals
Australia Japan 4-0
Australia Italy 5-0

1956 *Zone Finals*
European Zone **Italy** Sweden
American Zone
United States Mexico
Eastern Zone **India** a bye
Inter-Zone Finals
United States Italy 4-1
United States India 4-1

1957 *Zone Finals*
European Zone **Belgium** Italy
American Zone
United States Brazil
Eastern Zone **Philippines** Japan
Inter-Zone Finals
United States Philippines 5-0
United States Belgium 3-2

1958 *Zone Finals*
European Zone **Italy** Great Britain
American Zone
United States Argentina
Asian Zone **Philippines** Ceylon
Inter-Zone Finals
Italy Philippines 5-0
United States Italy 5-0

1959 *Zone Finals*
European Zone **Italy** Spain
American Zone **Australia** Cuba
Eastern Zone **India** Philippines
Inter-Zone Finals
Australia Italy 4-1
Australia India 4-1

1960 *Zone Finals*
European Zone **Italy** Sweden
American Zone
United States Venezuela
Asian Zone **Philippines** India
Inter-Zone Finals
United States Philippines 5-0
Italy United States 3-2

1961 *Zone Finals*
European Zone **Italy** Sweden
American Zone
United States Mexico
Asian Zone **India** Japan
Inter-Zone Finals
United States India 3-2
Italy United States 4-1

1962 *Zone Finals*
European Zone **Sweden** Italy
American Zone **Mexico** Yugoslavia
Asian Zone **India** Philippines
Inter-Zone Finals
Mexico Sweden 3-2
Mexico India 5-0

1963 *Zone Finals*
European Zone
Great Britain Sweden
American Zone
United States Venezuela
Asian Zone **India** Japan
Inter-Zone Finals
United States Great Britain 5-0
United States India 5-0

Challenge Round Team Results

1951 *Singles*
E. V. Seixas (US) M. G. Rose (A) 6-3, 6-4, 9-7
F. A. Sedgman (A) F. R. Schroeder (US) 6-4, 6-3, 4-6, 6-4
F. R. Schroeder (US) M. G. Rose (A) 6-4, 13-11, 7-5
F. A. Sedgman (A) E. V. Seixas (US) 6-4, 6-2, 6-2
Doubles
K. McGregor/F. A. Sedgman (A)
F. R. Schroeder/M. A. Trabert (US) 6-2, 9-7, 6-3

1952 *Singles*
F. A. Sedgman (A) E. V. Seixas (US) 6-3, 6-4, 6-3
K. McGregor (A) M. A. Trabert (US) 11-9, 6-4, 6-1
F. A. Sedgman (A) M. A. Trabert (US) 7-5, 6-4, 10-8
E. V. Seixas (US) K. McGregor (A) 6-3, 8-6, 6-8, 6-3
Doubles
K. McGregor/F. A. Sedgman (A)
E. V. Seixas/M. A. Trabert (US) 6-3, 6-4, 1-6, 6-3

1953 *Singles*
L. A. Hoad (A) E. V. Seixas (US) 6-4, 6-2, 6-3
M. A. Trabert (US) K. R. Rosewall (A) 6-3, 6-4, 6-4
L. A. Hoad (A) M. A. Trabert (US) 13-11, 6-3, 2-6, 3-6, 7-5
K. R. Rosewall (A) E. V. Seixas (US) 6-2, 2-6, 6-3, 6-4
Doubles
E. V. Seixas/M. A. Trabert (US)
R. N. Hartwig/L. A. Hoad (A) 6-2, 6-4, 6-4

1954 *Singles*
M. A. Trabert (US) L. A. Hoad (A) 6-4, 2-6, 12-10, 6-3
E. V. Seixas (US) K. R. Rosewall (A) 8-6, 6-8, 6-4, 6-3
K. R. Rosewall (A) M. A. Trabert (US) 9-7, 7-5, 6-3
R. N. Hartwig (A) E. V. Seixas (US) 4-6, 6-3, 6-2, 6-3
Doubles
E. V. Seixas/M. A. Trabert (US)
L. A. Hoad/K. R. Rosewall (A) 6-2, 4-6, 6-2, 10-8

1955 *Singles*
K. R. Rosewall (A) E. V. Seixas (US) 6-3, 10-8, 4-6, 6-2
L. A. Hoad (A) M. A. Trabert (US) 4-6, 6-3, 6-3, 8-6
L. A. Hoad (A) E. V. Seixas (US) 7-9, 6-1, 6-4, 6-4
K. R. Rosewall (A) H. Richardson (US) 6-4, 3-6, 6-1, 6-4
Doubles
L. A. Hoad/R. N. Hartwig (A)
M. A. Trabert/E. V. Seixas (US) 12-14, 6-4, 6-3, 3-6, 7-5

1956 *Singles*
L. A. Hoad (A) H. Flam (US) 6-2, 6-3, 6-3
K. R. Rosewall (A) E. V. Seixas (US) 6-1, 6-4, 4-6, 6-1
K. R. Rosewall (A) S. Giammalva (US) 4-6, 6-1, 8-6, 7-5
L. A. Hoad (A) E. V. Seixas (US) 6-2, 7-5, 6-3
Doubles
L. A. Hoad/K. R. Rosewall (A)
S. Giammalva/E. V. Seixas (US) 1-6, 6-1, 7-5, 6-4

1957 *Singles*
M. J. Anderson (A) B. MacKay (US) 6-3, 7-5, 3-6, 7-9, 6-3
A. J. Cooper (A) E. V. Seixas (US) 3-6, 7-5, 6-1, 1-6, 6-3
E. V. Seixas (US) M. J. Anderson (A) 3-6, 4-6, 6-3, 0-6, 13-11
B. MacKay (US) A. J. Cooper (A) 6-4, 1-6, 4-6, 6-4, 6-3
Doubles
M. J. Anderson/M. G. Rose (A)
B. MacKay/E. V. Seixas (US) 6-4, 6-4, 8-6

1958 *Singles*
A. Olmedo (US) M. J. Anderson (A) 8-6, 2-6, 9-7, 8-6
A. J. Cooper (A) B. MacKay (US) 4-6, 6-3, 6-2, 6-4
A. Olmedo (US) A. J. Cooper (A) 6-3, 4-6, 6-4, 8-6
M. J. Anderson (A) B. MacKay (US) 7-5, 13-11, 11-9
Doubles
A. Olmedo/H. Richardson (US)
M. J. Anderson/N. A. Fraser (A) 10-12, 3-6, 16-14, 6-3, 7-5

1959 *Singles*
N. A. Fraser (A) A. Olmedo (US) 8-6, 6-8, 6-4, 8-6
B. MacKay (US) R. G. Laver (A) 7-5, 6-4, 6-1
A. Olmedo (US) R. G. Laver (A) 9-7, 4-6, 10-8, 12-10
N. A. Fraser (A) B. MacKay (US) 8-6, 3-6, 6-2, 6-4
Doubles
N. A. Fraser/R. S. Emerson (A)
A. Olmedo/E. Buchholz (US) 7-5, 7-5, 6-4

1960 *Singles*
N. A. Fraser (A) O. Sirola (I) 4-6, 6-3, 6-3, 6-3
R. G. Laver (A) N. Pietrangeli (I) 8-6, 6-4, 6-3
R. G. Laver (A) O. Sirola (I) 9-7, 6-2, 6-3
N. Pietrangeli (I) N. A. Fraser (A) 11-9, 6-3, 1-6, 6-2
Doubles
N. A. Fraser/R. S. Emerson (A)
N. Pietrangeli/O. Sirola (I) 10-8, 5-7, 6-2, 6-4

1961 *Singles*
R. S. Emerson (A) N. Pietrangeli (I) 8-6, 6-4, 6-0
R. G. Laver (A) O. Sirola (I) 6-1, 6-4, 6-3
R. G. Laver (A) N. Pietrangeli (I) 6-3, 3-6, 4-6, 6-3, 8-6
R. S. Emerson (A) O. Sirola (I) 6-3, 6-3, 4-6, 6-2
Doubles
N. A. Fraser/R. S. Emerson (A)
N. Pietrangeli/O. Sirola (I) 6-2, 6-3, 6-4

1962 *Singles*
R. G. Laver (A) R. H. Osuna (M) 6-2, 6-1, 7-5
N. A. Fraser (A) A. Palafox (M) 7-9, 6-3, 6-4, 11-9
N. A. Fraser (A) R. H. Osuna (M) 3-6, 11-9, 6-1, 3-6, 6-4
R. G. Laver (A) A. Palafox (M) 6-1, 4-6, 6-4, 8-6
Doubles
R. S. Emerson/R. G. Laver (A)
R. H. Osuna/A. Palafox (M) 7-5, 6-2, 6-4

1963 *Singles*
R. D. Ralston (US) J. D. Newcombe (A) 6-4, 6-1, 3-6, 4-6, 7-5
R. S. Emerson (A) C. R. McKinley (US) 6-3, 3-6, 7-5, 7-5
R. S. Emerson (A) R. D. Ralston (US) 6-2, 6-3, 3-6, 6-2
C. R. McKinley (US) J. D. Newcombe (A) 10-12, 6-2, 9-7, 6-2
Doubles
C. R. McKinley/R. D. Ralston (US)
R. S. Emerson/N. A. Fraser (A) 6-3, 4-6, 11-9, 11-9

Challenge Round Winners

1951 (27)†
Australia (H)
United States (C) 3-2
Sydney, Australia

1952 (30)†
Australia (H)
United States (C) 4-1
Adelaide, Australia

1953 (32)†
Australia (H)
United States (C) 3-2
Melbourne, Australia

1954 (31)†
United States (C)
Australia (H) 3-2
Sydney, Australia

1955 (35)†
Australia (C)
United States (H) 5-0
Forest Hills, N.Y., U.S.A.

1956 (33)†
Australia (H)
United States (C) 5-0
Adelaide, Australia

1957 (37)†
Australia (H)
United States (C) 3-2
Melbourne, Australia

1958 (37)†
United States (C)
Australia (H) 3-2
Brisbane, Australia

1959 (43)†
Australia (C)
United States (H) 3-2
Forest Hills, N.Y., U.S.A.

1960 (41)†
Australia (H)
Italy (C) 4-1
Sydney, Australia

1961 (43)†
Australia (H)
Italy (C) 5-0
Melbourne, Australia

1962 (42)†
Australia (H)
Mexico (C) 5-0
Brisbane, Australia

1963 (49)†
United States (C)
Australia (H) 3-2
Adelaide, Australia

Winners in **bold type**; **(H)**/(H) holder; **(C)**/(C) challenger; † total number of nations competing, including the holder in years with a Challenge Round

385

Davis Cup

Inter-Zone Results

1964 *Zone Finals*
European Zone **Sweden** France
American Zone **Australia** Chile
Asian Zone **Philippines** India
Inter-Zone Finals
Sweden Philippines 5-0
Australia Sweden 5-0

1965 *Zone Finals*
European Zone **Spain** South Africa
American Zone
United States Mexico
Eastern Zone **India** Japan
Inter-Zone Finals
Spain United States 4-1
Spain India 3-2

1966 *Zone Finals*
European Zone A **Brazil** France
European Zone B
West Germany South Africa
American Zone
United States Mexico
Eastern Zone **India** Japan
Inter-Zone Semi-Finals
Brazil United States 3-2
India West Germany 3-2
Inter-Zone Finals
India Brazil 3-2

1967 *Zone Finals*
European Zone A **Spain** USSR
European Zone B
South Africa Brazil
American Zone
Ecuador United States
Eastern Zone **India** Japan
Inter-Zone Semi-Finals
Spain Ecuador 5-0
South Africa India 5-0
Inter-Zone Finals
Spain South Africa 3-2

1968 *Zone Finals*
European Zone A
West Germany South Africa
European Zone B **Spain** Italy
American Zone
United States Ecuador
Eastern Zone **India** Japan
Inter-Zone Semi-Finals
United States Spain 4-1
India West Germany 3-2
Inter-Zone Finals
United States India 4-1

1969 *Zone Finals*
European Zone A
Great Britain South Africa
European Zone B **Rumania** USSR
American Zone **Brazil** Mexico
Eastern Zone **India** Japan
Inter-Zone Semi-Finals
Great Britain Brazil 3-2
Rumania India 4-0
Inter-Zone Finals
Rumania Great Britain 3-2

1970 *Zone Finals*
European Zone A **Spain** Yugoslavia
European Zone B
West Germany USSR
American Zone **Brazil** Canada
Eastern Zone **India** Australia
Inter-Zone Semi-Finals
Spain Brazil 4-1
West Germany India 5-0
Inter-Zone Finals
West Germany Spain 4-1

1971 *Zone Finals*
European Zone A
Czechoslovakia Spain
European Zone B
Rumania West Germany
American Zone **Brazil** Mexico
Eastern Zone **India** Japan
Inter-Zone Semi-Finals
Brazil Czechoslovakia 4-1
Rumania India 4-1
Inter-Zone Finals
Rumania Brazil 3-2

1972 *Zone Finals*
European Zone A **Rumania** USSR
European Zone B
Spain Czechoslovakia
American Zone
United States Chile
Eastern Zone **Australia** India
Inter-Zone Semi-Finals
Rumania Australia 4-1
United States Spain 3-2

1973 *Zone Finals*
European Zone A **Rumania** USSR
European Zone B **Czechoslovakia**
Italy
American Zone
United States Chile
Eastern Zone
Australia India
Inter-Zone Semi-Finals
United States Rumania 4-1
Australia Czechoslovakia 4-1

Challenge Round Team Results

1964 *Singles*
C. R. McKinley (US) F. S. Stolle (A) 6-1, 9-7, 4-6, 6-2
R. S. Emerson (A) R. D. Ralston (US) 6-3, 6-4, 6-2
F. S. Stolle (A) R. D. Ralston (US) 7-5, 6-3, 3-6, 9-11, 6-4
R. S. Emerson (A) C. R. McKinley (US) 3-6, 6-2, 6-4, 6-4
Doubles
C. R. McKinley/R. D. Ralston (US)
R. S. Emerson/F. S. Stolle (A) 6-4, 4-6, 4-6, 6-3, 6-4

1965 *Singles*
F. S. Stolle (A) M. Santana (S) 10-12, 3-6, 6-1, 6-4, 7-5
R. S. Emerson (A) J. M. Gisbert (S) 6-3, 6-2, 6-2
M. Santana (S) R. S. Emerson (A) 2-6, 6-3, 6-4, 15-13
F. S. Stolle (A) J. M. Gisbert (S) 6-2, 6-4, 8-6
Doubles
J. D. Newcombe/A. D. Roche (A)
J. L. Arilla/M. Santana (S) 6-3, 4-6, 7-5, 6-2

1966 *Singles*
F. S. Stolle (A) R. Krishnan (I) 6-3, 6-2, 6-4
R. S. Emerson (A) J. Mukerjea (I) 7-5, 6-4, 6-2
R. S. Emerson (A) R. Krishnan (I) 6-0, 6-2, 10-8
F. S. Stolle (A) J. Mukerjea (I) 7-5, 6-8, 6-3, 5-7, 6-3
Doubles
R. Krishnan/J. Mukerjea (I)
J. D. Newcombe/A. D. Roche (A) 4-6, 7-5, 6-4, 6-4

1967 *Singles*
R. S. Emerson (A) M. Santana (S) 6-4, 6-1, 6-1
J. D. Newcombe (A) M. Orantes (S) 6-3, 6-3, 6-2
M. Santana (S) J. D. Newcombe (A) 7-5, 6-4, 6-2
R. S. Emerson (A) M. Orantes (S) 6-1, 6-1, 2-6, 6-4
Doubles
R. S. Emerson/J. D. Newcombe (A)
M. Orantes/M. Santana (S) 6-4, 6-4, 6-4

1968 *Singles*
C. E. Graebner (US) W. W. Bowrey (A) 8-10, 6-4, 8-6, 3-6, 6-1
A. R. Ashe (US) R. O. Ruffels (A) 6-8, 7-5, 6-3, 6-3
C. E. Graebner (US) R. O. Ruffels (A) 3-6, 8-6, 2-6, 6-3, 6-1
W. W. Bowrey (A) A. R. Ashe (US) 2-6, 6-3, 11-9, 8-6
Doubles
R. C. Lutz/S. R. Smith (US)
J. Alexander/R. O. Ruffels (A) 6-4, 6-4, 6-2

1969 *Singles*
A. R. Ashe (US) I. Năstase (R) 6-2, 15-13, 7-5
S. R. Smith (US) I. Ţiriac (R) 6-8, 6-3, 5-7, 6-4, 6-4
S. R. Smith (US) I. Năstase (R) 4-6, 4-6, 6-4, 6-1, 11-9
A. R. Ashe (US) I. Ţiriac (R) 6-3, 8-6, 3-6, 4-0, default
Doubles
R. C. Lutz/S. R. Smith (US)
I. Năstase/I. Ţiriac (R) 8-6, 6-1, 11-9

1970 *Singles*
A. R. Ashe (US) W. P. Bungert (WG) 6-2, 10-8, 6-2
C. Richey (US) C. Kuhnke (WG) 6-3, 6-4, 6-2
C. Richey (US) W. P. Bungert (WG) 6-4, 6-4, 7-5
A. R. Ashe (US) C. Kuhnke (WG) 6-8, 10-12, 9-7, 13-11, 6-4
Doubles
R. C. Lutz/S. R. Smith (US)
W. P. Bungert/C. Kuhnke (WG) 6-3, 7-5, 6-4

1971 *Singles*
S. R. Smith (US) I. Năstase (R) 7-5, 6-3, 6-1
F. R. Froehling (US) I. Ţiriac (R) 3-6, 1-6, 6-1, 6-3, 8-6
S. R. Smith (US) I. Ţiriac (R) 8-6, 6-3, 6-0
I. Năstase (R) F. R. Froehling (US) 6-3, 6-1, 4-6, 6-4
Doubles
I. Năstase/I. Ţiriac (R)
S. R. Smith/E. Van Dillen (US) 7-5, 6-4, 8-6

Finals Team Results
Challenge Round Abolished

1972 *Singles*
S. R. Smith (US) I. Năstase (R) 11-9, 6-2, 6-3
I. Ţiriac (R) T. Gorman (US) 4-6, 2-6, 6-4, 6-3, 6-2
S. R. Smith (US) I. Ţiriac (R) 4-6, 6-2, 6-4, 2-6, 6-0
I. Năstase (R) T. Gorman (US) 6-1, 6-2, 5-7, 10-8
Doubles
S. R. Smith/E. Van Dillen (US)
I. Năstase/I. Ţiriac (R) 6-2, 6-0, 6-3

1973 *Singles*
J. D. Newcombe (A) S. R. Smith (US) 6-1, 3-6, 6-3, 3-6, 6-4
R. G. Laver (A) T. W. Gorman (US) 8-10, 8-6, 6-8, 6-3, 6-1
J. D. Newcombe (A) T. W. Gorman (US) 6-2, 6-1, 6-3
R. G. Laver (A) S. R. Smith (US) 6-3, 6-4, 3-6, 6-2
Doubles
J. D. Newcombe/R. G. Laver (A) S. R. Smith/E. Van Dillen (US) 6-1, 6-2, 6-4

Challenge Round Winners

1964 (50)†
Australia (H)
United States (H) 3-2
Cleveland Heights, Ohio,
U.S.A.

1965 (47)†
Australia (H)
Spain (C) 4-1
Sydney, Australia

1966 (47)†
Australia (H)
India (C) 4-1
Melbourne, Australia

1967 (49)†
Australia (H)
Spain (C) 4-1
Brisbane, Australia

1968 (50)†
United States (C)
Australia (H) 4-1
Adelaide, Australia

1969 (52)†
United States (H)
Rumania (C) 5-0
Cleveland Heights, Ohio,
U.S.A.

1970 (53)†
United States (H)
West Germany (C) 5-0
Cleveland Heights, Ohio,
U.S.A.

1971 (51)†
United States (H)
Rumania (C) 3-2
Charlotte, N.C., U.S.A.

Finals Winners
Challenge Round Abolished

1972 (55)†
United States
Rumania 3-2
Bucharest, Rumania

1973 (53)†
Australia
United States 5-0
Cleveland Heights, Ohio,
U.S.A.

Quarter- and Semi-Finals	Finals Team Results	Winners

1963 *Quarter-Finals*
Australia Hungary 3-0
South Africa France 3-0
Great Britain Austria 3-0
United States Netherlands 3-0
Semi-Finals
Australia South Africa 3-0
United States Great Britain 3-0

1963 *Singles*
Miss M. Smith (A) Miss D. R. Hard (US) 6-3, 6-0
Miss B. J. Moffitt (US) Miss L. R. Turner (A) 5-7, 6-0, 6-3
Doubles
Miss D. R. Hard/Miss B. J. Moffitt (US)
Miss M. Smith/Miss L. R. Turner (A) 3-6, 13-11, 6-3

1963 (16)†
United States
Australia 2-1
Queens Club, London,
England

1964 *Quarter-Finals*
Australia Canada 3-0
France Germany 2-1
Great Britain South Africa 2-1
United States Argentina 3-0
Semi-Finals
Australia France 3-0
United States Great Britain 3-0

1964 *Singles*
Miss M. Smith (A) Miss B. J. Moffitt (US) 6-2, 6-3
Miss L. R. Turner (A) Miss N. Richey (US) 7-5, 6-1
Doubles
Miss B. J. Moffitt/Mrs J. R. Susman (US)
Miss M. Smith/Miss L. R. Turner (A) 4-6, 7-5, 6-1

1964 (20)†
Australia
United States 2-1
Philadelphia, Pa., U.S.A.

1965 *Quarter-Finals*
Great Britain South Africa 2-1
United States Italy 3-0
Australia New Zealand 3-0
France Brazil 2-1
Semi-Finals
United States Great Britain 3-0
Australia France 3-0

1965 *Singles*
Miss L. R. Turner (A) Mrs C. E. Graebner (US) 6-3, 2-6, 6-3
Miss M. Smith (A) Miss B. J. Moffitt (US) 6-4, 8-6
Doubles
Miss B. J. Moffitt/Mrs C. E. Graebner (US)
Miss M. Smith/Miss J. A. M. Tegart (A) 7-5, 4-6, 6-4

1965 (11)†
Australia
United States 2-1
Melbourne, Australia

1966 *Quarter-Finals*
United States France 2-1
Great Britain Czechoslovakia 3-0
West Germany Italy 2-1
Australia Netherlands 2-1
Semi-Finals
United States Great Britain 2-1
West Germany Australia 2-1

1966 *Singles*
Miss J. M. Heldman (US) Miss H. Niessen (WG) 4-6, 7-5, 6-1
Mrs L. W. King (US) Miss E. Buding (WG) 6-3, 3-6, 6-1
Doubles
Mrs C. E. Graebner/Mrs L. W. King (US)
Miss H. Schultze/Miss E. Buding (WG) 6-4, 6-2

1966 (20)†
United States
West Germany 3-0
Turin, Italy

1967 *Quarter-Finals*
Australia France 2-1
Great Britain Italy 2-1
West Germany Canada 3-0
United States South Africa 3-0
Semi-Finals
Great Britain Australia 3-0
United States West Germany 3-0

1967 *Singles*
Miss R. Casals (US) Miss S. V. Wade (GB) 9-7, 8-6
Mrs L. W. King (US) Mrs P. F. Jones (GB) 6-3, 6-4
Doubles match abandoned at set-all

1967 (17)†
United States
Great Britain 2-0
Berlin, West Germany

1968 *Quarter-Finals*
Australia South Africa 2-1
Great Britain USSR 3-0
Netherlands Bulgaria 3-0
United States France 2-1
Semi-Finals
Australia Great Britain 3-0
Netherlands United States 2-1

1968 *Singles*
Miss K. Melville (A) Miss M. Jansen (N) 4-6, 7-5, 6-3
Mrs B. M. Court (A) Miss A. Suurbeek (N) 6-1, 6-3
Doubles
Mrs B. M. Court/Miss K. Melville (A)
Miss A. Suurbeek/Miss L. Venneboer (N) 6-3, 6-8, 7-5

1968 (23)†
Australia
Netherlands 3-0
Paris, France

1969 *Quarter-Finals*
United States Italy 3-0
Netherlands Czechoslovakia 2-1
Great Britain West Germany 2-1
Australia France 3-0
Semi-Finals
United States Netherlands 3-0
Australia Great Britain 3-0

1969 *Singles*
Miss N. Richey (US) Miss K. Melville (A) 6-4, 6-3
Mrs B. M. Court (A) Miss J. M. Heldman (US) 6-1, 8-6
Doubles
Miss P. Bartkowicz/Miss N. Richey (US)
Mrs B. M. Court/Mrs J. A. M. Tegart (A) 6-4, 6-4

1969 (20)†
United States
Australia 2-1
Athens, Greece

1970 *Quarter-Finals*
United States South Africa 3-0
West Germany France 3-0
Great Britain Netherlands 2-1
Australia Sweden 3-0
Semi-Finals
West Germany United States 2-1
Australia Great Britain 3-0

1970 *Singles*
Miss K. Krantzcke (A) Mrs H. Hoesl (WG) 6-2, 6-3
Mrs D. E. Dalton (A) Miss H. Niessen (WG) 4-6, 6-3, 6-3
Doubles
Miss K. Krantzcke/Mrs D. E. Dalton (A)
Mrs H. Hoesl/Miss H. Niessen (WG) 6-2, 7-5

1970 (22)†
Australia
West Germany 3-0
Freiburg-im-Breisgau,
West Germany

1971 *Quarter-Finals*
Australia w.o.
France Netherlands 2-1
United States South Africa 2-1
Great Britain New Zealand 3-0
Semi-Finals
Australia France 3-0
Great Britain United States 3-0

1971 *Singles*
Mrs B. M. Court (A) Mrs P. F. Jones (GB) 6-8, 6-3, 6-2
Miss E. F. Goolagong (A) Miss S. V. Wade (GB) 6-4, 6-1
Doubles
Mrs B. M. Court/Miss L. Hunt (A)
Miss S. V. Wade/Miss W. M. Shaw (GB) 6-4, 6-4

1971 (14)†
Australia
Great Britain 3-0
Perth, Australia

1972 *Quarter-Finals*
Australia Italy 3-0
South Africa France 2-1
United States Netherlands 3-0
Great Britain West Germany 2-1
Semi-Finals
Great Britain Australia 2-1
South Africa United States 2-1

1972 *Singles*
Miss S. V. Wade (GB) Mrs P. Pretorius (SA) 6-3, 6-2
Miss B. Kirk (SA) Miss W. M. Shaw (GB) 4-6, 7-5, 6-0
Doubles
Miss B. Kirk/Mrs P. Pretorius (SA)
Miss S. V. Wade/Mrs J. Williams (GB) 6-1, 7-5

1972 (31)†
South Africa
Great Britain 2-1
Johannesburg, South Africa

1973 *Quarter-Finals*
Rumania Great Britain 2-1
Australia Indonesia 3-0
West Germany United States 3-0
South Africa Netherlands 3-0
Semi-Finals
Australia West Germany 3-0
South Africa Rumania 2-1

1973 *Singles*
Miss E. F. Goolagong (A) Mrs P. Pretorius (SA) 6-0, 6-2
Miss P. Coleman (A) Miss B. Kirk (SA) 10-8, 6-0
Doubles
Miss E. F. Goolagong/Miss J. Young (A)
Mrs P. Pretorius/Miss B. Kirk (SA) 6-1, 6-2

1973 (29)†
Australia
South Africa 3-0
Bad Homburg, West Germany

Winners in **bold type**; † total number of nations competing; w.o. walk-over

Wightman Cup

1923 *Singles*
Miss H. Wills (US) Miss K. McKane (GB) 6-2, 7-5
Miss H. Wills (US) Mrs R. C. Clayton (GB) 6-2, 6-3
Mrs M. Mallory (US) Mrs R. C. Clayton (GB) 6-1, 8-6
Mrs M. Mallory (US) Miss K. McKane (GB) 6-2, 6-3
Miss E. E. Goss (US) Mrs A. E. Beamish (GB) 6-2, 0-6, 7-5
Doubles
Mrs G. W. Wightman/Miss E. E. Goss (US)
Miss K. McKane/Mrs B. C. Covell (GB) 10-8, 5-7, 6-4
Mrs M. Mallory/Miss H. Wills (US)
Mrs A. E. Beamish/Mrs R. C. Clayton (GB) 6-3, 6-2

1923
United States
Great Britain 7-0
Forest Hills, N.Y.

1924 *Singles*
Miss K. McKane (GB) Mrs M. Mallory (US) 6-3, 6-3
Miss K. McKane (GB) Miss H. Wills (US) 6-2, 6-2
Mrs B. C. Covell (GB) Miss H. Wills (US) 6-2, 6-4
Mrs B. C. Covell (GB) Mrs M. Mallory (US) 6-2, 5-7, 6-3
Mrs A. E. Beamish (GB) Miss E. E. Goss (US) 6-1, 8-10, 6-3
Doubles
Mrs G. W. Wightman/Miss H. Wills (US)
Miss K. McKane/Miss E. Colyer (GB) 2-6, 6-2, 6-4
Mrs B. C. Covell/Mrs D. C. Shepherd-Barron (GB)
Mrs J. B. Jessup/Miss E. E. Goss (US) 6-2, 6-2

1924
Great Britain
United States 6-1
Wimbledon

1925 *Singles*
Miss K. McKane (GB) Mrs M. Mallory (US) 6-4, 5-7, 6-0
Miss H. Wills (US) Miss K. McKane (GB) 6-1, 1-6, 9-7
Miss H. Wills (US) Miss J. Fry (GB) 6-0, 7-5
Mrs M. Mallory (US) Miss J. Fry (GB) 6-3, 6-0
Mrs Lambert Chambers (GB) Miss E. E. Goss (US) 7-5, 3-6, 6-1
Doubles
Mrs Lambert Chambers/Miss E. H. Harvey (GB)
Mrs M. Mallory/Mrs T. C. Bundy (US) 10-8, 6-1
Miss K. McKane/Miss E. Colyer (GB)
Miss H. Wills/Miss M. K. Browne (US) 6-0, 6-3

1925
Great Britain
United States 4-3
Forest Hills, N.Y.

1926 *Singles*
Miss E. Ryan (US) Miss J. Fry (GB) 6-1, 6-3
Mrs L. A. Godfree (GB) Miss E. Ryan (US) 6-1, 5-7, 6-4
Miss J. Fry (GB) Miss M. K. Browne (US) 3-6, 6-0, 6-4
Mrs L. A. Godfree (GB) Miss M. K. Browne (US) 6-1, 7-5
Mrs J. B. Jessup (US) Mrs D. C. Shepherd-Barron (GB)
6-1, 5-7, 6-4
Doubles
Mrs J. B. Jessup/Miss E. E. Goss (US)
Mrs Lambert Chambers/Mrs D. C. Shepherd-Barron (GB) 6-4, 6-2
Miss M. K. Browne/Miss E. Ryan (US)
Mrs L. A. Godfree/Miss E. Colyer (GB) 3-6, 6-2, 6-4

1926
United States
Great Britain 4-3
Wimbledon

1927 *Singles*
Miss H. Wills (US) Miss J. Fry (GB) 6-2, 6-0
Miss H. Wills (US) Mrs L. A. Godfree (GB) 6-1, 6-1
Mrs M. Mallory (US) Mrs L. A. Godfree (GB) 6-4, 6-2
Mrs M. Mallory (US) Miss J. Fry (GB) 6-2, 11-9
Miss B. M. Nuthall (GB) Miss H. H. Jacobs (US) 6-3, 2-6, 6-1
Doubles
Mrs G. W. Wightman/Miss H. Wills (US)
Mrs L. A. Godfree/Miss E. H. Harvey (GB) 6-4, 4-6, 6-3
Mrs J. Hill/Miss G. R. Sterry (GB)
Mrs A. H. Chapin/Miss E. E. Goss (US) 5-7, 7-5, 7-5

1927
United States
Great Britain 5-2
Forest Hills, N.Y.

1928 *Singles*
Miss H. Wills (US) Miss E. Bennett (GB) 6-3, 6-2
Miss E. Bennett (GB) Mrs M. Mallory (US) 6-1, 6-3
Miss H. Wills (US) Mrs H. Watson (GB) 6-1, 6-2
Mrs H. Watson (GB) Mrs M. Mallory (US) 2-6, 6-1, 6-2
Miss H. H. Jacobs (US) Miss B. M. Nuthall (GB) 6-3, 6-1
Doubles
Miss E. H. Harvey/Miss P. Saunders (GB)
Miss E. E. Goss/Miss H. H. Jacobs (US) 6-4, 6-1
Mrs H. Watson/Miss E. Bennett (GB)
Miss H. Wills/Miss P. Anderson (US) 6-2, 6-1

1928
Great Britain
United States 4-3
Wimbledon

1929 *Singles*
Miss H. Wills (US) Mrs H. Watson (GB) 6-1, 6-4
Miss H. Wills (US) Miss B. M. Nuthall (GB) 8-6, 8-6
Miss H. H. Jacobs (US) Miss B. M. Nuthall (GB) 7-5, 8-6
Mrs H. Watson (GB) Miss H. H. Jacobs (US) 6-3, 6-2
Miss E. Cross (US) Mrs L. R. C. Michell (GB) 6-3, 3-6, 6-3
Doubles
Mrs L. R. C. Michell/Mrs H. Watson (GB)
Miss H. Wills/Miss E. Cross (US) 6-4, 6-1
Mrs B. C. Covell/Mrs D. C. Shepherd-Barron (GB)
Mrs G. W. Wightman/Miss H. H. Jacobs (US) 6-2, 6-1

1929
United States
Great Britain 4-3
Forest Hills, N.Y.

1930 *Singles*
Mrs H. Watson (GB) Miss H. H. Jacobs (US) 2-6, 6-2, 6-4
Mrs F. S. Moody (US) Mrs H. Watson (GB) 7-5, 6-1
Mrs F. S. Moody (US) Miss J. Fry (GB) 6-1, 6-1
Miss H. H. Jacobs (US) Miss J. Fry (GB) 6-0, 6-3
Miss P. E. Mudford (GB) Miss S. Palfrey (US) 6-0, 6-2
Doubles
Miss E. H. Harvey/Miss J. Fry (GB)
Miss E. Cross/Miss S. Palfrey (US) 2-6, 6-2, 6-4
Mrs L. A. Godfree/Mrs H. Watson (GB)
Mrs F. S. Moody/Miss H. H. Jacobs (US) 7-5, 1-6, 6-4

1930
Great Britain
United States 4-3
Wimbledon

1931 *Singles*
Mrs F. S. Moody (US) Miss P. E. Mudford (GB) 6-1, 6-4
Mrs F. S. Moody (US) Miss B. M. Nuthall (GB) 6-4, 6-2
Miss H. H. Jacobs (US) Miss B. M. Nuthall (GB) 8-6, 6-4
Miss H. H. Jacobs (US) Miss P. E. Mudford (GB) 6-4, 6-2
Mrs L. A. Harper (US) Miss D. E. Round (GB) 6-3, 4-6, 9-7
Doubles
Mrs E. F. Whittingstall/Miss B. M. Nuthall (GB)
Mrs F. S. Moody/Mrs L. A. Harper (US) 8-6, 5-7, 6-3
Mrs D. C. Shepherd-Barron/Miss P. E. Mudford (GB)
Mrs G. W. Wightman/Miss S. Palfrey (US) 6-4, 10-8

1931
United States
Great Britain 5-2
Forest Hills, N.Y.

1932 *Singles*
Mrs F. S. Moody (US) Mrs E. F. Whittingstall (GB) 6-2, 6-4
Mrs F. S. Moody (US) Miss D. E. Round (GB) 6-2, 6-3
Miss H. H. Jacobs (US) Miss D. E. Round (GB) 6-4, 6-3
Mrs E. F. Whittingstall (GB) Miss H. H. Jacobs (US) 6-4, 2-6, 6-1
Mrs M. R. King (GB) Mrs L. A. Harper (US) 3-6, 6-3, 6-1
Doubles
Miss B. M. Nuthall/Mrs E. F. Whittingstall (GB)
Mrs F. S. Moody/Miss S. Palfrey (US) 6-3, 1-6, 10-8
Mrs L. A. Harper/Miss H. H. Jacobs (US)
Mrs L. R. C. Michell/Miss D. E. Round (GB) 6-4, 6-1

1932
United States
Great Britain 4-3
Wimbledon

Team Results	Winners

1933 *Singles*
Miss H. H. Jacobs (US) Miss D. E. Round (GB) 6-4, 6-2
Miss H. H. Jacobs (US) Miss M. C. Scriven (GB) 5-7, 6-2, 7-5
Miss S. Palfrey (US) Miss M. C. Scriven (GB) 6-3, 6-1
Miss D. E. Round (GB) Miss S. Palfrey (US) 6-4, 10-8
Miss B. M. Nuthall (GB) Miss C. A. Babcock (US) 1-6, 6-1, 6-3
Doubles
Miss H. H. Jacobs/Miss S. Palfrey (US)
Miss D. E. Round/Miss M. Heeley (GB) 6-4, 6-2
Miss B. M. Nuthall/Miss F. James (GB)
Miss A. Marble/Mrs J. Van Ryn (US) 7-5, 6-2

1933
United States
Great Britain 4-3
Forest Hills, N.Y.

1934 *Singles*
Miss H. H. Jacobs (US) Miss M. C. Scriven (GB) 6-1, 6-1
Miss H. H. Jacobs (US) Miss D. E. Round (GB) 6-4, 6-4
Miss S. Palfrey (US) Miss D. E. Round (GB) 6-3, 3-6, 8-6
Miss S. Palfrey (US) Miss M. C. Scriven (GB) 4-6, 6-2, 8-6
Miss B. M. Nuthall (GB) Miss C. A. Babcock (US) 5-7, 6-3, 6-4
Doubles
Miss H. H. Jacobs/Miss S. Palfrey (US)
Mrs L. A. Godfree/Miss B. M. Nuthall (GB) 5-7, 6-3, 6-2
Miss N. M. Lyle/Miss E. M. Dearman (GB)
Miss C. A. Babcock/Miss J. Cruickshank (US) 7-5, 7-5

1934
United States
Great Britain 5-2
Wimbledon

1935 *Singles*
Miss K. E. Stammers (GB) Miss H. H. Jacobs (US) 5-7, 6-1, 9-7
Miss H. H. Jacobs (US) Miss D. E. Round (GB) 6-3, 6-3
Miss D. E. Round (GB) Mrs A. M. Arnold (US) 6-0, 6-3
Mrs A. M. Arnold (US) Miss K. E. Stammers (GB) 6-2, 1-6, 6-3
Mrs S. P. Fabyan (US) Mrs M. R. King (GB) 6-0, 6-3
Doubles
Miss H. H. Jacobs/Mrs S. P. Fabyan (US)
Miss F. James/Miss K. E. Stammers (GB) 6-3, 6-2
Miss N. M. Lyle/Miss E. M. Dearman (GB)
Miss C. A. Babcock/Mrs D. Andrus (US) 3-6, 6-4, 6-1

1935
United States
Great Britain 4-3
Forest Hills, N.Y.

1936 *Singles*
Miss K. E. Stammers (GB) Miss H. H. Jacobs (US) 12-10, 6-1
Miss D. E. Round (GB) Miss H. H. Jacobs (US) 6-3, 6-3
Miss D. E. Round (GB) Mrs S. P. Fabyan (US) 6-3, 6-4
Mrs S. P. Fabyan (US) Miss K. E. Stammers (GB) 6-3, 6-4
Miss C. A. Babcock (US) Miss R. M. Hardwick (GB) 6-4, 4-6, 6-2
Doubles
Miss H. H. Jacobs/Mrs S. P. Fabyan (US)
Miss K. E. Stammers/Miss F. James (GB) 1-6, 6-3, 7-5
Mrs J. Van Ryn/Miss C. A. Babcock (US)
Miss N. M. Lyle/Miss E. M. Dearman (GB) 6-2, 1-6, 6-3

1936
United States
Great Britain 4-3
Wimbledon

1937 *Singles*
Miss A. Marble (US) Miss R. M. Hardwick (GB) 4-6, 6-2, 6-4
Miss A. Marble (US) Miss K. E. Stammers (GB) 6-3, 6-1
Miss H. H. Jacobs (US) Miss K. E. Stammers (GB) 6-1, 4-6, 6-4
Miss H. H. Jacobs (US) Miss R. M. Hardwick (GB) 2-6, 6-4, 6-2
Mrs S. P. Fabyan (US) Miss M. E. Lumb (GB) 6-3, 6-1
Doubles
Mrs S. P. Fabyan/Miss A. Marble (US)
Miss E. M. Dearman/Miss J. Ingram (GB) 6-3, 6-2
Miss K. E. Stammers/Miss F. James (GB)
Mrs J. Van Ryn/Miss D. M. Bundy (US) 6-3, 10-8

1937
United States
Great Britain 6-1
Forest Hills, N.Y.

1938 *Singles*
Miss K. E. Stammers (GB) Miss A. Marble (US) 3-6, 7-5, 6-3
Miss A. Marble (US) Miss M. C. Scriven (GB) 6-3, 3-6, 6-0
Mrs F. S. Moody (US) Miss M. C. Scriven (GB) 6-0, 7-5
Mrs F. S. Moody (US) Miss K. E. Stammers (GB) 6-2, 3-6, 6-3
Mrs S. P. Fabyan (US) Miss M. E. Lumb (GB) 5-7, 6-2, 6-3
Doubles
Mrs S. P. Fabyan/Miss A. Marble (US)
Miss F. James/Miss M. E. Lumb (GB) 6-4, 6-2
Miss E. M. Dearman/Miss J. Ingram (GB)
Mrs F. S. Moody/Miss D. M. Bundy (US) 6-2, 7-5

1938
United States
Great Britain 5-2
Wimbledon

1939 *Singles*
Miss A. Marble (US) Miss R. M. Hardwick (GB) 6-3, 6-4
Miss A. Marble (US) Miss K. E. Stammers (GB) 3-6, 6-3, 6-4
Miss H. H. Jacobs (US) Miss R. M. Hardwick (GB) 6-2, 6-2
Miss K. E. Stammers (GB) Miss H. H. Jacobs (US) 6-2, 1-6, 6-3
Miss V. E. Scott (GB) Mrs S. P. Fabyan (US) 6-3, 6-4
Doubles
Miss D. M. Bundy/Mrs A. M. Arnold (US)
Miss B. M. Nuthall/Miss N. B. Brown (GB) 6-3, 6-1
Mrs S. P. Fabyan/Miss A. Marble (US)
Mrs S. H. Hammersley/Miss K. E. Stammers (GB) 7-5, 6-2

1939
United States
Great Britain 5-2
Forest Hills, N.Y.

1940-45 *No Competition*

1940-45 *No Competition*

1946 *Singles*
Miss P. M. Betz (US) Mrs E. W. A. Bostock (GB) 6-2, 6-4
Miss P. M. Betz (US) Mrs M. Menzies (GB) 6-4, 6-4
Miss M. E. Osborne (US) Mrs E. W. A. Bostock (GB) 6-1, 6-4
Miss M. E. Osborne (US) Mrs M. Menzies (GB) 6-3, 6-2
Miss A. L. Brough (US) Miss P. J. Curry (GB) 8-6, 6-3
Doubles
Miss A. L. Brough/Miss M. E. Osborne (US)
Mrs E. W. A. Bostock/Mrs W. C. J. Halford (GB) 6-2, 6-1
Miss P. M. Betz/Miss D. J. Hart (US)
Mrs N. Passingham/Miss W. M. Lincoln (GB) 6-1, 6-3

1946
United States
Great Britain 7-0
Wimbledon

1947 *Singles*
Miss M. E. Osborne (US) Mrs E. W. A. Bostock (GB) 6-4, 2-6, 6-2
Miss M. E. Osborne (US) Mrs M. Menzies (GB) 7-5, 6-2
Miss A. L. Brough (US) Mrs M. Menzies (GB) 6-4, 6-2
Miss A. L. Brough (US) Mrs E. W. A. Bostock (GB) 6-4, 6-4
Miss D. J. Hart (US) Mrs B. E. Hilton (GB) 4-6, 6-3, 7-5
Doubles
Mrs P. C. Todd/Miss D. J. Hart (US)
Miss J. Gannon/Miss J. Quertier (GB) 6-1, 6-2
Miss A. L. Brough/Miss M. E. Osborne (US)
Mrs E. W. A. Bostock/Mrs B. E. Hilton (GB) 6-1, 6-4

1947
United States
Great Britain 7-0
Forest Hills, N.Y.

1948 *Singles*
Miss A. L. Brough (US) Mrs E. W. A. Bostock (GB) 6-2, 4-6, 7-5
Miss A. L. Brough (US) Mrs B. E. Hilton (GB) 6-1, 6-1
Mrs W. duPont (US) Mrs E. W. A. Bostock (GB) 6-4, 8-6
Mrs W. duPont (US) Mrs B. E. Hilton (GB) 6-3, 6-4
Miss D. J. Hart (US) Miss J. Gannon (GB) 6-1, 6-4
Doubles
Miss A. L. Brough/Mrs W. duPont (US)
Mrs M. Menzies/Mrs B. E. Hilton (GB) 6-2, 6-2
Mrs E. W. A. Bostock/Mrs N. W. Blair (GB)
Mrs P. C. Todd/Miss D. J. Hart (US) 6-3, 6-4

1948
United States
Great Britain 6-1
Wimbledon

Winners in **bold type**

Wightman Cup

Team Results	Winners

1949 *Singles*
Mrs W. duPont (US) Mrs B. E. Hilton (GB) 6-1, 6-3
Mrs W. duPont (US) Mrs J. J. Walker-Smith (GB) 6-4, 6-2
Miss D. J. Hart (US) Mrs J. J. Walker-Smith (GB) 6-3, 6-1
Miss D. J. Hart (US) Mrs B. E. Hilton (GB) 6-1, 6-3
Miss B. J. Baker (US) Miss J. Quertier (GB) 6-4, 7-5
Doubles
Miss D. J. Hart/Miss S. J. Fry (US)
Mrs N. W. Blair/Miss J. Quertier (GB) 6-1, 6-2
Mrs P. C. Todd/Miss G. A. Moran (US)
Mrs B. E. Hilton/Miss K. L. A. Tuckey (GB) 6-4, 8-6

1949
United States
Great Britain 7-0
Haverford, Pa.

1950 *Singles*
Miss A. L. Brough (US) Mrs J. J. Walker-Smith (GB) 6-0, 6-0
Miss A. L. Brough (US) Mrs B. E. Hilton (GB) 2-6, 6-2, 7-5
Mrs W. duPont (US) Mrs B. E. Hilton (GB) 6-3, 6-4
Mrs W. duPont (US) Mrs J. J. Walker-Smith (GB) 6-3, 6-2
Miss D. J. Hart (US) Miss P. J. Curry (GB) 6-2, 6-4
Doubles
Mrs P. C. Todd/Miss D. J. Hart (US)
Mrs J. J. Walker-Smith/Miss J. Quertier (GB) 6-2, 6-3
Miss A. L. Brough/Mrs W. duPont (US)
Mrs B. E. Hilton/Miss K. L. A. Tuckey (GB) 6-2, 6-0

1950
United States
Great Britain 7-0
Wimbledon

1951 *Singles*
Miss D. J. Hart (US) Miss J. Quertier (GB) 6-4, 6-4
Miss D. J. Hart (US) Mrs J. J. Walker-Smith (GB) 6-4, 2-6, 7-5
Miss S. J. Fry (US) Mrs J. J. Walker-Smith (GB) 6-1, 6-4
Miss J. Quertier (GB) Miss S. J. Fry (US) 6-3, 8-6
Miss M. C. Connolly (US) Miss K. L. A. Tuckey (GB) 6-1, 6-3
Doubles
Mrs P. C. Todd/Miss N. A. Chaffee (US)
Mrs A. J. Mottram/Miss P. E. Ward (GB) 7-5, 6-3
Miss D. J. Hart/Miss S. J. Fry (US)
Miss J. Quertier/Miss K. L. A. Tuckey (GB) 6-3, 6-3

1951
United States
Great Britain 6-1
Chestnut Hills, Mass.

1952 *Singles*
Miss D. J. Hart (US) Mrs I. Rinkel (GB) 6-3, 6-3
Miss D. J. Hart (US) Mrs J. J. Walker-Smith (GB) 7-5, 6-2
Miss M. C. Connolly (US) Mrs J. J. Walker-Smith (GB)
3-6, 6-1, 7-5
Miss M. C. Connolly (US) Mrs I. Rinkel (GB) 9-7, 6-2
Miss S. J. Fry (US) Miss J. S. V. Partridge (GB) 6-0, 8-6
Doubles
Miss D. J. Hart/Miss S. J. Fry (US)
Mrs I. Rinkel/Miss H. M. Fletcher (GB) 8-6, 6-4
Miss A. L. Brough/Miss M. C. Connolly (US)
Mrs A. J. Mottram/Miss P. E. Ward (GB) 6-0, 6-3

1952
United States
Great Britain 7-0
Wimbledon

1953 *Singles*
Miss M. C. Connolly (US) Miss A. Mortimer (GB) 6-1, 6-1
Miss M. C. Connolly (US) Miss H. M. Fletcher (GB) 6-1, 6-1
Miss D. J. Hart (US) Miss H. M. Fletcher (GB) 6-4, 7-5
Miss D. J. Hart (US) Miss A. Mortimer (GB) 6-1, 6-1
Miss S. J. Fry (US) Mrs I. Rinkel (GB) 6-2, 6-4
Doubles
Miss D. J. Hart/Miss S. J. Fry (US)
Mrs I. Rinkel/Miss H. M. Fletcher (GB) 6-2, 6-1
Miss A. L. Brough/Miss M. C. Connolly (US)
Miss A. Mortimer/Miss J. A. Shilcock (GB) 6-2, 6-3

1953
United States
Great Britain 7-0
Rye, N.Y.

1954 *Singles*
Miss M. C. Connolly (US) Miss H. M. Fletcher (GB) 6-1, 6-3
Miss M. C. Connolly (US) Miss J. A. Shilcock (GB) 6-2, 6-2
Miss D. J. Hart (US) Miss J. A. Shilcock (GB) 6-4, 6-1
Miss D. J. Hart (US) Miss H. M. Fletcher (GB) 6-1, 6-8, 6-2
Miss A. L. Brough (US) Miss A. Buxton (GB) 8-6, 6-2
Doubles
Miss A. L. Brough/Mrs W. duPont (US)
Miss A. Buxton/Miss P. A. Hird (GB) 2-6, 6-4, 7-5
Miss S. J. Fry/Miss D. J. Hart (US)
Miss H. M. Fletcher/Miss J. A. Shilcock (GB) unplayed

1954
United States
Great Britain 6-0
Wimbledon

1955 *Singles*
Miss A. L. Brough (US) Miss S. J. Bloomer (GB) 6-2, 6-4
Miss A. L. Brough (US) Miss A. Mortimer (GB) 6-0, 6-2
Miss A. Mortimer (GB) Miss D. J. Hart (US) 6-4, 1-6, 7-5
Miss D. J. Hart (US) Miss S. J. Bloomer (GB) 7-5, 6-3
Mrs D. P. Knode (US) Miss A. Buxton (GB) 6-3, 6-3
Doubles
Miss A. L. Brough/Mrs W. duPont (US)
Miss S. J. Bloomer/Miss P. E. Ward (GB) 6-3, 6-3
Miss D. J. Hart/Miss S. J. Fry (US)
Miss A. Buxton/Miss A. Mortimer (GB) 3-6, 6-2, 7-5

1955
United States
Great Britain 6-1
Rye, N.Y.

1956 *Singles*
Miss A. L. Brough (US) Miss A. Mortimer (GB) 3-6, 6-4, 7-5
Miss A. L. Brough (US) Miss A. Buxton (GB) 3-6, 6-3, 6-4
Miss S. J. Fry (US) Miss A. Buxton (GB) 6-2, 6-8, 7-5
Miss A. Mortimer (GB) Miss S. J. Fry (US) 6-4, 6-3
Miss S. J. Bloomer (GB) Mrs D. P. Knode (US) 6-4, 6-4
Doubles
Mrs J. G. Fleitz/Mrs D. P. Knode (US)
Miss S. J. Bloomer/Miss P. E. Ward (GB) 6-1, 6-4
Miss A. L. Brough/Miss S. J. Fry (US)
Miss A. Mortimer/Miss A. Buxton (GB) 6-2, 6-2

1956
United States
Great Britain 5-2
Wimbledon

1957 *Singles*
Miss A. Gibson (US) Miss S. J. Bloomer (GB) 6-4, 4-6, 6-2
Miss A. Gibson (US) Miss C. C. Truman (GB) 6-4, 6-2
Mrs D. P. Knode (US) Miss C. C. Truman (GB) 6-2, 11-9
Mrs D. P. Knode (US) Miss S. J. Bloomer (GB) 5-7, 6-1, 6-4
Miss A. S. Haydon (GB) Miss D. R. Hard (US) 6-3, 3-6, 6-4
Doubles
Miss A. Gibson/Miss D. R. Hard (US)
Miss S. J. Bloomer/Miss S. M. Armstrong (GB) 6-3, 6-4
Miss A. L. Brough/Mrs W. du Pont (US)
Miss A. S. Haydon/Miss J. A. Shilcock (GB) 6-4, 6-1

1957
United States
Great Britain 6-1
Sewickley, Pa.

1958 *Singles*
Miss A. Gibson (US) Miss S. J. Bloomer (GB) 6-3, 6-4
Mrs D. P. Knode (US) Miss S. J. Bloomer (GB) 6-4, 6-2
Miss C. C. Truman (GB) Mrs D. P. Knode (US) 6-4, 6-4
Miss C. C. Truman (GB) Miss A. Gibson (US) 2-6, 6-3, 6-4
Miss A. S. Haydon (GB) Miss M. Arnold (US) 6-3, 5-7, 6-3
Doubles
Miss S. J. Bloomer/Miss C. C. Truman (GB)
Mrs D. P. Knode/Miss K. K. Fageros (US) 6-2, 6-3
Miss A. Gibson/Miss J. S. Hopps (US)
Miss J. A. Shilcock/Miss P. E. Ward (GB) 6-4, 3-6, 6-3

1958
Great Britain
United States 4-3
Wimbledon

Team Results	Winners

1959 *Singles*
Mrs J. G. Fleitz (US) Miss A. Mortimer (GB) 6-2, 6-1
Mrs J. G. Fleitz (US) Miss C. C. Truman (GB) 6-4, 6-4
Miss C. C. Truman (GB) Miss D. R. Hard (US) 6-4, 2-6, 6-3
Miss D. R. Hard (US) Miss A. Mortimer (GB) 6-3, 6-8, 6-4
Miss A. S. Haydon (GB) Miss S. M. Moore (US) 6-1, 6-1
Doubles
Miss D. R. Hard/Miss J. Arth (US)
Mrs C. W. Brasher/Miss C. C. Truman (GB) 9-7, 9-7
Miss A. Mortimer/Miss A. S. Haydon (GB)
Miss J. S. Hopps/Miss S. M. Moore (US) 6-2, 6-4

1959
United States
Great Britain 4-3
Sewickley, Pa.

1960 *Singles*
Miss A. S. Haydon (GB) Miss K. Hantze (US) 2-6, 11-9, 6-1
Miss D. R. Hard (US) Miss A. S. Haydon (GB) 5-7, 6-2, 6-1
Miss D. R. Hard (US) Miss C. C. Truman (GB) 4-6, 6-3, 6-4
Miss C. C. Truman (GB) Miss K. Hantze (US) 7-5, 6-3
Miss A. Mortimer (GB) Miss J. S. Hopps (US) 6-8, 6-4, 6-1
Doubles
Miss K. Hantze/Miss D. R. Hard (US)
Miss A. S. Haydon/Miss A. Mortimer (GB) 6-0, 6-0
Mrs C. W. Brasher/Miss C. C. Truman (GB)
Miss J. S. Hopps/Mrs D. P. Knode (US) 6-4, 9-7

1960
Great Britain
United States 4-3
Wimbledon

1961 *Singles*
Miss K. Hantze (US) Miss C. C. Truman (GB) 7-9, 6-1, 6-1
Miss K. Hantze (US) Miss A. S. Haydon (GB) 6-1, 6-4
Miss B. J. Moffitt (US) Miss A. S. Haydon (GB) 6-4, 6-4
Miss C. C. Truman (GB) Miss B. J. Moffitt (US) 6-3, 6-2
Miss J. Bricka (US) Miss A. Mortimer (GB) 10-8, 4-6, 6-3
Doubles
Miss K. Hantze/Miss B. J. Moffitt (US)
Miss C. C. Truman/Miss D. M. Catt (GB) 7-5, 6-2
Mrs W. duPont/Miss M. Varner (US)
Miss A. S. Haydon/Miss A. Mortimer (GB) default

1961
United States
Great Britain 6-1
Chicago, Ill.

1962 *Singles*
Miss D. R. Hard (US) Miss A. S. Haydon (GB) 6-3, 6-8, 6-4
Miss D. R. Hard (US) Miss C. C. Truman (GB) 6-2, 6-2
Mrs J. R. Susman (US) Miss C. C. Truman (GB) 6-4, 7-5
Miss A. S. Haydon (GB) Mrs J. R. Susman (US) 10-8, 7-5
Miss D. M. Catt (GB) Miss N. Richey (US) 6-1, 7-5
Doubles
Mrs W. duPont/Miss M. Varner (US)
Miss D. M. Catt/Miss D. E. Starkie (GB) 6-2, 3-6, 6-2
Miss C. C. Truman/Miss A. S. Haydon (GB)
Miss D. R. Hard/Miss B. J. Moffitt (US) 6-4, 6-3

1962
United States
Great Britain 4-3
Wimbledon

1963 *Singles*
Mrs P. F. Jones (GB) Miss D. R. Hard (US) 6-1, 0-6, 8-6
Miss D. R. Hard (US) Miss C. C. Truman (GB) 6-3, 6-0
Miss B. J. Moffitt (US) Miss C. C. Truman (GB) 6-4, 19-17
Miss B. J. Moffitt (US) Mrs P. F. Jones (GB) 6-4, 4-6, 6-3
Miss N. Richey (US) Miss D. M. Catt (GB) 14-12, 6-3
Doubles
Miss D. R. Hard/Miss B. J. Moffitt (US)
Mrs P. F. Jones/Miss C. C. Truman (GB) 4-6, 7-5, 6-2
Miss N. Richey/Mrs H. G. Fales (US)
Miss D. M. Catt/Miss D. E. Starkie (GB) 6-4, 6-8, 6-2

1963
United States
Great Britain 6-1
Cleveland, Ohio

1964 *Singles*
Miss N. Richey (US) Miss D. M. Catt (GB) 4-6, 6-4, 7-5
Miss N. Richey (US) Mrs P. F. Jones (GB) 7-5, 11-9
Miss B. J. Moffitt (US) Mrs P. F. Jones (GB) 4-6, 6-2, 6-3
Miss B. J. Moffitt (US) Miss D. M. Catt (GB) 6-3, 4-6, 6-3
Miss C. A. Caldwell (US) Miss D. E. Starkie (GB) 6-4, 1-6, 6-3
Doubles
Mrs P. F. Jones/Miss D. M. Catt (GB)
Miss B. J. Moffitt/Miss C. A. Caldwell (US) 6-2, 4-6, 6-0
Miss A. Mortimer/Miss D. E. Starkie (GB)
Miss N. Richey/Mrs H. G. Fales (US) 2-6, 6-3, 6-4

1964
United States
Great Britain 5-2
Wimbledon

1965 *Singles*
Mrs P. F. Jones (GB) Miss B. J. Moffitt (US) 6-2, 6-4
Miss B. J. Moffitt (US) Miss D. E. Starkie (GB) 6-3, 6-2
Miss N. Richey (US) Miss D. E. Starkie (GB) 6-1, 6-0
Mrs P. F. Jones (GB) Miss N. Richey (US) 6-4, 9-7
Mrs C. E. Graebner (US) Miss S. V. Wade (GB) 3-6, 10-8, 6-4
Doubles
Mrs C. E. Graebner/Miss N. Richey (US)
Miss D. E. Starkie/Miss F. E. Truman (GB) 6-1, 6-0
Miss B. J. Moffitt/Mrs J. R. Susman (US)
Mrs P. F. Jones/Miss S. V. Wade (GB) 6-3, 8-6

1965
United States
Great Britain 5-2
Cleveland, Ohio

1966 *Singles*
Mrs P. F. Jones (GB) Miss N. Richey (US) 2-6, 6-4, 6-3
Miss N. Richey (US) Miss S. V. Wade (GB) 2-6, 6-2, 7-5
Mrs L. W. King (US) Miss S. V. Wade (GB) 6-2, 6-3
Mrs L. W. King (US) Mrs P. F. Jones (GB) 5-7, 6-2, 6-3
Miss W. M. Shaw (GB) Miss M. A. Eisel (US) 6-3, 6-3
Doubles
Mrs P. F. Jones/Miss S. V. Wade (GB)
Mrs L. W. King/Miss J. T. Albert (US) 7-5, 6-2
Miss N. Richey/Miss M. A. Eisel (US)
Miss D. E. Starkie/Miss R. H. Bentley (GB) 6-1, 6-2

1966
United States
Great Britain 4-3
Wimbledon

1967 *Singles*
Mrs L. W. King (US) Miss S. V. Wade (GB) 6-3, 6-2
Mrs L. W. King (US) Mrs P. F. Jones (GB) 6-1, 6-2
Miss N. Richey (US) Mrs P. F. Jones (GB) 6-2, 6-2
Miss N. Richey (US) Miss S. V. Wade (GB) 3-6, 8-6, 6-2
Miss C. C. Truman (GB) Miss R. Casals (US) 3-6, 7-5, 6-1
Doubles
Mrs L. W. King/Miss R. Casals (US)
Mrs P. F. Jones/Miss S. V. Wade (GB) 10-8, 6-4
Mrs C. E. Graebner/Miss M. A. Eisel (US)
Miss W. M. Shaw/Mrs G. M. Williams (GB) 8-6, 12-10

1967
United States
Great Britain 6-1
Cleveland, Ohio

1968 *Singles*
Miss S. V. Wade (GB) Miss M. A. Eisel (US) 6-0, 6-1
Miss S. V. Wade (GB) Miss N. Richey (US) 6-4, 2-6, 6-3
Miss N. Richey (US) Mrs G. T. Janes (GB) 6-1, 8-6
Miss M. A. Eisel (US) Mrs G. T. Janes (GB) 6-4, 6-3
Miss P. Bartkowicz (US) Miss W. M. Shaw (GB) 7-5, 3-6, 6-4
Doubles
Miss S. V. Wade/Miss W. M. Shaw (GB)
Miss N. Richey/Miss M. A. Eisel (US) 5-7, 6-4, 6-3
Mrs G. T. Janes/Miss F. E. Truman (GB)
Miss S. De Fina/Miss K. M. Harter (US) 6-3, 2-6, 6-3

1968
Great Britain
United States 4-3
Wimbledon

Winners in **bold type**

Wightman Cup

1969 *Singles*
Miss J. M. Heldman (US) Miss S. V. Wade (GB) 3-6, 6-1, 8-6
Miss N. Richey (US) Miss W. M. Shaw (GB) 8-6, 6-2
Miss P. Bartkowicz (US) Mrs G. T. Janes (GB) 8-6, 6-0
Miss S. V. Wade (GB) Miss N. Richey (US) 6-3, 2-6, 6-4
Miss J. M. Heldman (US) Miss W. M. Shaw (GB) 6-3, 6-4
Doubles
Mrs G. T. Janes/Miss F. E. Truman (GB)
Mrs P. W. Curtis/Miss V. Ziegenfuss (US) 6-1, 3-6, 6-4
Miss J. M. Heldman/Miss P. Bartkowicz (US)
Miss W. M. Shaw/Miss S. V. Wade (GB) 6-4, 6-2

1970 *Singles*
Mrs L. W. King (US) Miss S. V. Wade (GB) 8-6, 6-4
Mrs P. F. Jones (GB) Miss N. Richey (US) 6-2, 6-3
Miss S. V. Wade (GB) Miss N. Richey (US) 6-3, 6-2
Mrs L. W. King (US) Mrs P. F. Jones (GB) 6-4, 6-2
Miss J. M. Heldman (US) Mrs G. M. Williams (GB) 6-3, 6-2
Doubles
Mrs P. F. Jones/Mrs G. M. Williams (GB)
Mrs P. W. Curtis/Miss J. M. Heldman (US) 6-3, 6-2
Mrs L. W. King/Miss P. Bartkowicz (US)
Miss S. V. Wade/Miss W. M. Shaw (GB) 7-5, 3-6, 6-2

1971 *Singles*
Miss C. Evert (US) Miss W. M. Shaw (GB) 6-0, 6-4
Miss S. V. Wade (GB) Miss J. M. Heldman (US) 7-5, 7-5
Miss V. Ziegenfuss (US) Miss W. M. Shaw (GB) 6-4, 4-6, 6-3
Miss C. Evert (US) Miss S. V. Wade (GB) 6-1, 6-1
Mrs G. M. Williams (GB) Miss K. Pigeon (US) 7-5, 3-6, 6-4
Doubles
Miss V. Ziegenfuss/Miss M. A. Eisel (US)
Mrs G. T. Janes/Miss F. E. Truman (GB) 6-1, 6-4
Miss S. V. Wade/Mrs G. M. Williams (GB)
Miss C. Evert/Miss C. E. Graebner (US) 10-8, 4-6, 6-1

1972 *Singles*
Mrs J. Williams (GB) Miss W. Overton (US) 6-3, 3-6, 6-3
Miss C. Evert (US) Miss S. V. Wade (GB) 6-4, 6-4
Miss C. Evert (US) Mrs J. Williams (GB) 6-2, 6-3
Miss S. V. Wade (GB) Miss W. Overton (US) 8-6, 7-5
Miss P. Hogan (US) Miss C. Molesworth (GB) 6-8, 6-4, 6-2
Doubles
Miss C. Evert/Miss P. Hogan (US)
Miss F. E. Truman/Miss W. M. Shaw (GB) 7-5, 6-4
Miss W. Overton/Miss V. Ziegenfuss (US)
Miss S. V. Wade/Mrs J. Williams (GB) 6-3, 6-3

1973 *Singles*
Miss C. Evert (US) Miss S. V. Wade (GB) 6-4, 6-2
Miss P. Hogan (US) Miss V. Burton (GB) 6-4, 6-3
Miss C. Evert (US) Miss V. Burton (GB) 6-3, 6-0
Miss S. V. Wade (GB) Miss P. Hogan (US) 6-2, 6-2
Miss L. Tuero (US) Miss G. Coles (GB) 7-5, 6-2
Doubles
Miss S. V. Wade/Miss G. Coles (GB)
Miss C. Evert/Miss L. Redondo (US) 6-3, 2-6, 6-4
Miss J. Evert/Miss P. Hogan (US)
Miss L. Beaven/Miss L. J. Charles (GB) 6-2, 4-6, 8-6

1969
United States
Great Britain 5-2
Cleveland, Ohio

1970
United States
Great Britain 4-3
Wimbledon

1971
United States
Great Britain 4-3
Cleveland, Ohio

1972
United States
Great Britain 5-2
Wimbledon

1973
United States
Great Britain 5-2
Boston, Mass.